Praise for *Team of Rivals*

Winner of the Lincoln Prize
Winner of The New-York Historical Society Book Prize
Winner of the Barondess/Lincoln Award
Winner of the Bostonian Society's 2006 Bostonian History Award
Finalist for the National Book Critics Circle Award for biography
Finalist for the Los Angeles Times Book Prize in biography

"An elegant, incisive study of Lincoln and leading members of his cabinet that will appeal to experts as well as to those whose knowledge of Lincoln is an amalgam of high school history and popular mythology. . . . Goodwin has brilliantly described how Lincoln forged a team that preserved a nation and freed America from the curse of slavery."
—James M. McPherson, *The New York Times Book Review*

"A brilliantly conceived and well-written tour de force of a historical narrative. . . . Goodwin's contribution is refreshingly unique. . . . Goodwin's emotive prose elevates this tome from mere popular history to literary achievement."
—Douglas Brinkley, *The Boston Globe*

"A sweeping, riveting account. . . . Put simply, Goodwin's story of Lincoln's great, troubled, triumphant life is a star-spangled, high-stepping, hat-waving, bugle-blowing winner."
—*Daily News* (New York)

"Goodwin finds her Lincoln hiding in plain view. He is Lincoln the politician, but one whose political shrewdness ends up being indistinguishable from wisdom. She has written a wonderful book. There is a man in it."
—Garry Wills, *American Scholar*

"Probe[s] the 16th president's personal and public lives with insight, engaging narrative and careful research. . . . When it comes to political complexity and intrigue, Goodwin excels. . . . Riveting political history."
—*Chicago Tribune*

"*Team of Rivals* is one of the most compulsively readable books of history for a general audience to come along in a long time. An engagingly intimate look at Lincoln's private life and public actions, the book convincingly brings to life this man who may have been the most extraordinary individual in American history."
—*The Sunday Oregonian*

"This immense, finely honed book is no dull administrative or bureaucratic history; rather, it is a story of personalities—a messianic drama. . . . Portraits are drawn in spacious detail and with great skill. . . . Goodwin's narrative powers are great."

—*The Washington Post Book World*

"Captivating. . . . Immensely readable. . . . Goodwin . . . is a master storyteller."

—*The Christian Science Monitor*

"Magnificent. . . . Vastly readable. . . . Brilliantly told."

—*The Atlanta Journal-Constitution*

"This is a serious biography that ranges across an immense territory. . . . Goodwin has probed a vast trove of contemporary sources. . . . Her account of the 1860 Republican convention is spellbinding."

—*The New York Observer*

"*Team of Rivals* is well-executed popular history from one of the masters of the genre."

—*The New York Sun*

"Goodwin's gripping narrative propels the reader. . . . Offers fresh perspectives, astute analysis, and sensitive portrayals of her four main characters and a host of lesser ones. *Team of Rivals* is a masterful work of history."

—*The Providence Journal*

"Fascinating. . . . *Team of Rivals* makes us long for men of such integrity, goodness and insight."

—*The Commercial Appeal* (Memphis)

"Splendid . . . *Team of Rivals* tells of a day when men were true leaders."

—*U.S. News & World Report*

"If you think you know all there is to know about Abraham Lincoln, spend some time in the mid-1800s with Doris Kearns Goodwin in her new book, *Team of Rivals*. This masterful and extremely entertaining work shines light on the 16th president's astounding grasp of the subtleties of politics and his mastery of the presidency during the Civil War, adding even more luster to the Lincoln image."

—*The Courier-Journal* (Louisville, Kentucky)

"Goodwin's fine book makes an important contribution to our national understanding of this crucial era."

—*National Review*

"Restores Lincoln to his proper time and place. . . . Goodwin reveals something about Lincoln that's too often neglected: his remarkable capacity for empathy, affection and manipulation. These qualities informed his most critical political decisions."

—*Austin American-Statesman*

"A sweeping survey of Lincoln and his Cabinet that contributes a great deal to our understanding of Lincoln's character and political dexterity. . . . A master storyteller, Goodwin uses the intertwined lives of Lincoln and his key cabinet members . . . to weave a compelling narrative of wartime Washington."

—*American Heritage*

"Meticulous. . . . Goodwin vividly evokes Lincoln's struggles to avoid war, his resolve to fight hard once war became inevitable, and his unflagging effort to hold fast the fragile union."

—*St. Petersburg Times*

"A window into the political life and times of the late 19th century. . . . The book [has] an immediacy and freshness much like the intimacy of Ken Burns' documentary on the Civil War."

—*Chicago Sun-Times*

"Excellent. . . . Lincoln is brought to life beautifully in *Team of Rivals*. . . . Clarifies and preserves Lincoln's legacy with rare skill."

—*The Seattle Times*

"A wonderful book. . . . Goodwin has written a history that is also a good yarn. . . . This book ennobles politics, at least as practiced by Abraham Lincoln. Our democracy could use some ennobling these days."

—*The Sunday Star-Ledger* (Newark, N.J.)

"There is something for just about every reader in this book: the story of Union politics during the Civil War; an insight into how people lived in the 19th century; and riveting prose that will keep you reading."

—*The Roanoke Times*

"Doris Kearns Goodwin has written an enormous book possessed of a friendly grandeur and, against all odds, a considerable freshness."

—*The Atlantic Monthly*

"An intriguing contribution. . . . One of the few books on the Civil War period that presents a rounded portrait of Mary Todd Lincoln."

—*Richmond Times Dispatch*

"Original in conception and brilliant in execution. . . . This is history at full flood, an absorbing narrative. . . . In *Team of Rivals*, the political genius of Abraham Lincoln meets the historical genius of Doris Kearns Goodwin."

—*The Globe and Mail* (Toronto)

"Goodwin illuminates all aspects of the life of Lincoln with a dignity that befits one of the greatest Americans."
—*Pittsburgh Tribune-Review*

"A wonderful book that shows Lincoln clearly by broadening the focus to include his Cabinet. Perhaps just in time to make us envious, Goodwin gives us a portrait of effective democratic government in bad times, led by a political genius. . . . She has written a history that is also a good yarn. . . . This book ennobles politics, at least as practiced by Abraham Lincoln."
—Newhouse News Service

"*Team of Rivals* is fascinating, artfully constructed, beautifully written. It is as fresh as if this were the first book on Abraham Lincoln ever published."
—David Herbert Donald, author of *Lincoln*

"In this majestic work, Lincoln emerges both as a master politician and transcendent moral figure. Goodwin shows Lincoln's White House as it really was: a place of moral courage and triumph, but also intrigue and tragedy. The story of the president and his brilliant, fractious cabinet has never been so beautifully told."
—Michael Bishop, Executive Director, Abraham Lincoln Bicentennial Commission

"What an achievement! It is brilliant in its execution, compassionate in its presentation, and informative in every sense."
—Frank J. Williams, Chairman, The Lincoln Forum

"The book is splendid—I felt like I was at every cabinet meeting, every crisis conference, every hand-wringing visit to the telegraph office, watching Seward relax, Chase puff up, and Lincoln grow into the genius Goodwin asserts in the title. It's a triumph."
—Harold Holzer, author of *Lincoln at Cooper Union* and *The Lincoln-Douglas Debates*

"Nowhere is there a better understanding or more lyrical portrayal of those who served as Lincoln's top advisors. . . . Goodwin provides us with a comparative perspective producing new and compelling insights into Lincoln's personal and public life. Goodwin beautifully captures the infighting, the gossip and the high-stakes politics of the Lincoln presidency. . . . Any reader of this book will enthusiastically agree that Lincoln's political genius laid the foundation for Union victory, emancipation and ultimately the Thirteenth Amendment."
—Thomas F. Schwartz, Illinois State Historian

TEAM OF

DORIS KEARNS
GOODWIN

Simon & Schuster Paperbacks

RIVALS

THE POLITICAL GENIUS

of

ABRAHAM LINCOLN

New York   London   Toronto   Sydney   New Delhi

SIMON & SCHUSTER PAPERBACKS
A Division of Simon & Schuster, Inc.
1230 Avenue of the Americas
New York, NY 10020

This Simon & Schuster trade paperback edition November 2012

SIMON & SCHUSTER PAPERBACKS and colophon are registered
trademarks of Simon & Schuster, Inc.

For information about special discounts for bulk purchases,
please contact Simon & Schuster Special Sales at
1-866-506-1949 or business@simonandschuster.com.

The Simon & Schuster Speakers Bureau can bring authors to
your live event. For more information or to book an event,
contact the Simon & Schuster Speakers Bureau at
1-866-248-3049 or visit our website at www.simonspeakers.com.

Maps © 2005 Jeffrey L. Ward

Book design by Ellen R. Sasahara

Manufactured in the United States of America

10   9   8   7   6   5   4   3   2   1

The Library of Congress has cataloged the hardcover edition as follows:
Goodwin, Doris Kearns.
Team of rivals : the political genius of Abraham Lincoln / Doris Kearns Goodwin.
p.   cm.
Includes bibliographical references and index.
1. Lincoln, Abraham, 1809–1865. 2. Political leadership—United States—
Case studies. 3. Genius—Case studies. 4. Lincoln, Abraham, 1809–1865—Friends
and associates. 5. Presidents—United States—Biography. 6. United States—
Politics and government, 1861–1865. I. Title.
E457.45.G66 2005   973.7092—dc22   [B]   2005044615

ISBN: 978-0-684-82490-1
ISBN: 978-1-4516-8809-2 (pbk)
ISBN: 978-1-4165-4983-3 (ebook)

For Richard N. Goodwin,
my husband of thirty years

"The conduct of the republican party in this nomination is a remarkable indication of small intellect, growing smaller. They pass over . . . statesmen and able men, and they take up a fourth rate lecturer, who cannot speak good grammar."

—The *New York Herald* (May 19, 1860), commenting on Abraham Lincoln's nomination for president at the Republican National Convention

"Why, if the old Greeks had had this man, what trilogies of plays—what epics—would have been made out of him! How the rhapsodes would have recited him! How quickly that quaint tall form would have enter'd into the region where men vitalize gods, and gods divinify men! But Lincoln, his times, his death—great as any, any age— belong altogether to our own."

—Walt Whitman, "Death of Abraham Lincoln," 1879

"The greatness of Napoleon, Caesar or Washington is only moonlight by the sun of Lincoln. His example is universal and will last thousands of years. . . . He was bigger than his country—bigger than all the Presidents together . . . and as a great character he will live as long as the world lives."

—Leo Tolstoy, *The World,* New York, 1909

CONTENTS

MAPS AND DIAGRAMS

———

INTRODUCTION

I N 1876, the celebrated orator Frederick Douglass dedicated a monument in Washington, D.C., erected by black Americans to honor Abraham Lincoln. The former slave told his audience that "there is little necessity on this occasion to speak at length and critically of this great and good man, and of his high mission in the world. That ground has been fully occupied. . . . The whole field of fact and fancy has been gleaned and garnered. Any man can say things that are true of Abraham Lincoln, but no man can say anything that is new of Abraham Lincoln."

Speaking only eleven years after Lincoln's death, Douglass was too close to assess the fascination that this plain and complex, shrewd and transparent, tender and iron-willed leader would hold for generations of Americans. In the nearly two hundred years since his birth, countless historians and writers have uncovered new documents, provided fresh insights, and developed an ever-deepening understanding of our sixteenth president.

In my own effort to illuminate the character and career of Abraham Lincoln, I have coupled the account of his life with the stories of the remarkable men who were his rivals for the 1860 Republican presidential nomination—New York senator William H. Seward, Ohio governor Salmon P. Chase, and Missouri's distinguished elder statesman Edward Bates.

Taken together, the lives of these four men give us a picture of the path taken by ambitious young men in the North who came of age in the early decades of the nineteenth century. All four studied law, became distinguished orators, entered politics, and opposed the spread of slavery. Their upward climb was one followed by many thousands who left the small towns of their birth to seek opportunity and adventure in the rapidly growing cities of a dynamic, expanding America.

Just as a hologram is created through the interference of light from separate sources, so the lives and impressions of those who companioned Lincoln give us a clearer and more dimensional picture of the president himself. Lincoln's barren childhood, his lack of schooling, his relationships with male friends, his complicated marriage, the nature of his ambition, and his ruminations about death can be analyzed more clearly when he is placed side by side with his three contemporaries.

When Lincoln won the nomination, each of his celebrated rivals believed the wrong man had been chosen. Ralph Waldo Emerson recalled his first reception of the news that the "comparatively unknown name of Lincoln" had been selected: "we heard the result coldly and sadly. It seemed too rash, on a purely local reputation, to build so grave a trust in such anxious times."

Lincoln seemed to have come from nowhere—a backwoods lawyer who had served one undistinguished term in the House of Representatives and had lost two consecutive contests for the U. S. Senate. Contemporaries and historians alike have attributed his surprising nomination to chance— the fact that he came from the battleground state of Illinois and stood in the center of his party. The comparative perspective suggests a different interpretation. When viewed against the failed efforts of his rivals, it is clear that Lincoln won the nomination because he was shrewdest and can- niest of them all. More accustomed to relying upon himself to shape events, he took the greatest control of the process leading up to the nomi- nation, displaying a fierce ambition, an exceptional political acumen, and a wide range of emotional strengths, forged in the crucible of personal hard- ship, that took his unsuspecting rivals by surprise.

That Lincoln, after winning the presidency, made the unprecedented decision to incorporate his eminent rivals into his political family, the cab- inet, was evidence of a profound self-confidence and a first indication of what would prove to others a most unexpected greatness. Seward became secretary of state, Chase secretary of the treasury, and Bates attorney gen- eral. The remaining top posts Lincoln offered to three former Democrats whose stories also inhabit these pages—Gideon Welles, Lincoln's "Nep- tune," was made secretary of the navy, Montgomery Blair became post- master general, and Edwin M. Stanton, Lincoln's "Mars," eventually became secretary of war. Every member of this administration was better known, better educated, and more experienced in public life than Lincoln. Their presence in the cabinet might have threatened to eclipse the obscure prairie lawyer from Springfield.

It soon became clear, however, that Abraham Lincoln would emerge the undisputed captain of this most unusual cabinet, truly a team of rivals. The powerful competitors who had originally disdained Lincoln became colleagues who helped him steer the country through its darkest days. Seward was the first to appreciate Lincoln's remarkable talents, quickly realizing the futility of his plan to relegate the president to a figurehead role. In the months that followed, Seward would become Lincoln's closest friend and advisor in the administration. Though Bates initially viewed Lincoln as a well-meaning but incompetent administrator, he eventually concluded that the president was an unmatched leader, "very near being a perfect man." Edwin Stanton, who had treated Lincoln with contempt at their initial acquaintance, developed a great respect for the commander in chief and was unable to control his tears for weeks after the president's death. Even Chase, whose restless ambition for the presidency was never realized, at last acknowledged that Lincoln had outmaneuvered him.

This, then, is a story of Lincoln's political genius revealed through his extraordinary array of personal qualities that enabled him to form friendships with men who had previously opposed him; to repair injured feelings that, left untended, might have escalated into permanent hostility; to assume responsibility for the failures of subordinates; to share credit with ease; and to learn from mistakes. He possessed an acute understanding of the sources of power inherent in the presidency, an unparalleled ability to keep his governing coalition intact, a tough-minded appreciation of the need to protect his presidential prerogatives, and a masterful sense of timing. His success in dealing with the strong egos of the men in his cabinet suggests that in the hands of a truly great politician the qualities we generally associate with decency and morality—kindness, sensitivity, compassion, honesty, and empathy—can also be impressive political resources.

Before I began this book, aware of the sorrowful aspect of his features and the sadness attributed to him by his contemporaries, I had assumed that Lincoln suffered from chronic depression. Yet, with the exception of two despondent episodes in his early life that are described in this story, there is no evidence that he was immobilized by depression. On the contrary, even during the worst days of the war, he retained his ability to function at a very high level.

To be sure, he had a melancholy temperament, most likely imprinted on him from birth. But melancholy differs from depression. It is not an illness; it does not proceed from a specific cause; it is an aspect of one's nature. It has been recognized by artists and writers for centuries as a potential source of creativity and achievement.

Moreover, Lincoln possessed an uncanny understanding of his shifting moods, a profound self-awareness that enabled him to find constructive ways to alleviate sadness and stress. Indeed, when he is compared with his colleagues, it is clear that he possessed the most even-tempered disposition of them all. Time and again, he was the one who dispelled his colleagues' anxiety and sustained their spirits with his gift for storytelling and his life-affirming sense of humor. When resentment and contention threatened to destroy his administration, he refused to be provoked by petty grievances, to submit to jealousy, or to brood over perceived slights. Through the appalling pressures he faced day after day, he retained an unflagging faith in his country's cause.

The comparative approach has also yielded an interesting cast of female characters to provide perspective on the Lincolns' marriage. The fiercely idealistic Frances Seward served as her husband's social conscience. The beautiful Kate Chase made her father's quest for the presidency the ruling passion of her life, while the devoted Julia Bates created a blissful home that gradually enticed her husband away from public ambitions. Like Frances Seward, Mary Lincoln displayed a striking intelligence; like Kate Chase, she possessed what was then considered an unladylike interest in politics. Mary's detractors have suggested that if she had created a more tranquil domestic life for her family, Lincoln might have been satisfied to remain in Springfield. Yet the idea that he could have been a contented homebody, like Edward Bates, contradicts everything we know of the powerful ambition that drove him from his earliest days.

By widening the lens to include Lincoln's colleagues and their families, my story benefited from a treasure trove of primary sources that have not generally been used in Lincoln biographies. The correspondence of the Seward family contains nearly five thousand letters, including an eight-hundred-page diary that Seward's daughter Fanny kept from her fifteenth year until two weeks before her death at the age of twenty-one. In addition to the voluminous journals in which Salmon Chase recorded the events of four decades, he wrote thousands of personal letters. A revealing section of his daughter Kate's diary also survives, along with dozens of letters from her husband, William Sprague. The unpublished section of the diary that Bates began in 1846 provides a more intimate glimpse of the man than the published diary that starts in 1859. Letters to his wife, Julia, during his years in Congress expose the warmth beneath his stolid exterior. Stanton's emotional letters to his family and his sister's unpublished memoir reveal the devotion and idealism that connected the passionate, hard-driving war secretary to his president. The correspondence of Montgomery Blair's sister, Elizabeth Blair Lee, and her husband, Captain Samuel Phillips Lee, leaves a memorable picture of daily life in wartime Washington. The diary of Gideon Welles, of course, has long been recognized for its penetrating insights into the workings of the Lincoln administration.

Through these fresh sources, we see Lincoln liberated from his familiar frock coat and stovepipe hat. We see him late at night relaxing at Seward's house, his long legs stretched before a blazing fire, talking of many things besides the war. We hear his curious and infectious humor in the punch lines of his favorite stories and sit in on clamorous cabinet discussions regarding emancipation and Reconstruction. We feel the enervating tension in the telegraph office as Lincoln clasps Stanton's hand, awaiting bulletins from the battlefield. We follow him to the front on a dozen occasions and observe the invigorating impact of his sympathetic, kindly presence on the morale of the troops. In all these varied encounters, Lincoln's vibrant personality shines through. In the mirrors of his colleagues, he comes to life.

As a young man, Lincoln worried that the "field of glory" had been harvested by the founding fathers, that nothing had been left for his generation but modest ambitions. In the 1850s, however, the wheel of history turned. The rising intensity of the slavery issue and the threatening dissolution of the nation itself provided Lincoln and his colleagues with an opportunity to save and improve the democracy established by Washington, Jefferson, and Adams, creating what Lincoln later called "a new birth of freedom." Without the march of events that led to the Civil War, Lincoln still would have been a good man, but most likely would never have been publicly recognized as a great man. It was history that gave him the opportunity to manifest his greatness, providing the stage that allowed him to shape and transform our national life.

For better than thirty years, as a working historian, I have written on leaders I knew, such as Lyndon Johnson, and interviewed intimates of the Kennedy family and many who knew Franklin Roosevelt, a leader perhaps as indispensable in his way as was Lincoln to the social and political direction of the country. After living with the subject of Abraham Lincoln for a decade, however, reading what he himself wrote and what hundreds of others have written about him, following the arc of his ambition, and assessing the inevitable mixture of human foibles and strengths that made up his temperament, after watching him deal with the terrible deprivations of his childhood, the deaths of his children, and the horror that engulfed the entire nation, I find that after nearly two centuries, the uniquely American story of Abraham Lincoln has unequalled power to captivate the imagination and to inspire emotion.

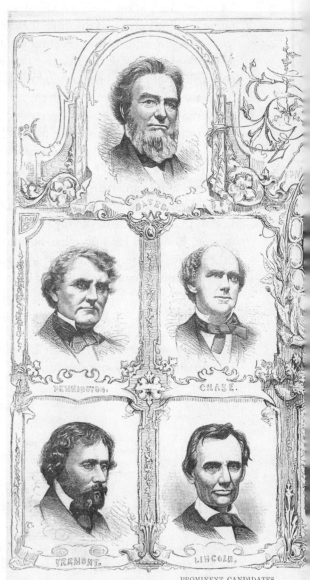

PROMINENT CANDIDATES

PART I

THE RIVALS

FOR THE REPUBLICAN PRESIDENTIAL NOMINATION AT CHICAGO.—[From Photographs by Brady.]

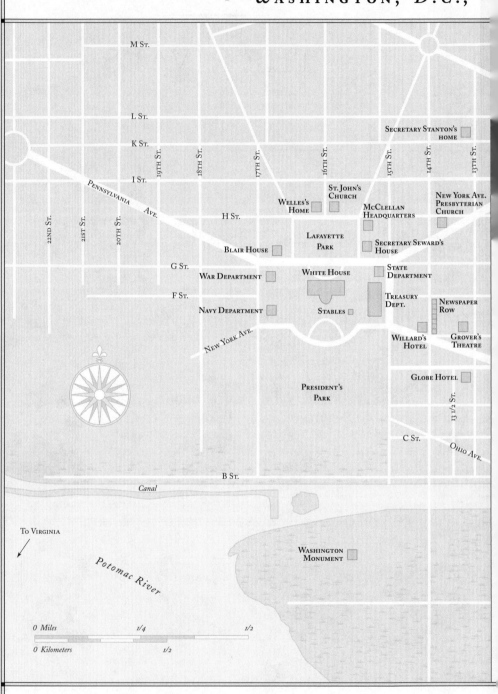

M St.

L St.

K St.

SECRETARY STANTON'S HOME

19TH ST. 18TH ST. 17TH ST. 16TH ST. 15TH ST. 14TH ST. 13TH ST.

I St.

PENNSYLVANIA AVE.

ST. JOHN'S CHURCH

WELLES'S HOME

NEW YORK AVE. PRESBYTERIAN CHURCH

McCLELLAN HEADQUARTERS

H St.

22ND ST. 21ST ST. 20TH ST.

LAFAYETTE PARK

SECRETARY SEWARD'S HOUSE

BLAIR HOUSE

G St.

WAR DEPARTMENT

WHITE HOUSE

STATE DEPARTMENT

F St.

TREASURY DEPT.

NEWSPAPER ROW

NAVY DEPARTMENT

STABLES

NEW YORK AVE.

WILLARD'S HOTEL

GROVER'S THEATRE

GLOBE HOTEL

13 1/2 ST.

PRESIDENT'S PARK

C St.

OHIO AVE.

B St.

Canal

TO VIRGINIA

WASHINGTON MONUMENT

Potomac River

0 Miles   1/4   1/2

0 Kilometers   1/2

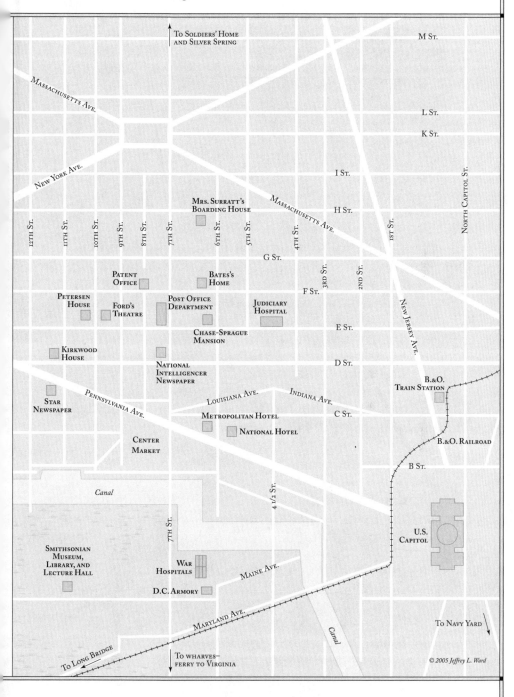

To Soldiers' Home
and Silver Spring

M St.

Massachusetts Ave.

New York Ave.

L St.

K St.

I St.

Mrs. Surratt's
Boarding House

Massachusetts Ave.

H St.

12TH St.

11TH St.

10TH St.

9TH St.

8TH St.

7TH St.

6TH St.

5TH St.

4TH St.

3RD St.

2ND St.

1ST St.

North Capitol St.

G St.

Patent
Office

Bates's
Home

F St.

Petersen
House

Ford's
Theatre

Post Office
Department

Judiciary
Hospital

E St.

New Jersey Ave.

Chase-Sprague
Mansion

Kirkwood
House

National
Intelligencer
Newspaper

D St.

B.&O.
Train Station

Star
Newspaper

Pennsylvania Ave.

Louisiana Ave.

Indiana Ave.

C St.

B.&O. Railroad

Metropolitan Hotel

National Hotel

Center
Market

B St.

Canal

4 1/2 St.

7TH St.

U.S.
Capitol

Smithsonian
Museum,
Library, and
Lecture Hall

War
Hospitals

Maine Ave.

D.C. Armory

Maryland Ave.

To Navy Yard

Canal

© 2005 Jeffrey L. Ward

To Long Bridge

To wharves—
ferry to Virginia

CHAPTER I

FOUR MEN WAITING

O N May 18, 1860, the day when the Republican Party would nominate its candidate for president, Abraham Lincoln was up early. As he climbed the stairs to his plainly furnished law office on the south side of the public square in Springfield, Illinois, breakfast was being served at the 130-room Chenery House on Fourth Street. Fresh butter, flour, lard, and eggs were being put out for sale at the City Grocery Store on North Sixth Street. And in the morning newspaper, the proprietors at Smith, Wickersham & Company had announced the arrival of a large spring stock of silks, calicos, ginghams, and linens, along with a new supply of the latest styles of hosiery and gloves.

The Republicans had chosen to meet in Chicago. A new convention hall called the "Wigwam" had been constructed for the occasion. The first ballot was not due to be called until 10 a.m. and Lincoln, although patient by nature, was visibly "nervous, fidgety, and intensely excited." With an outside chance to secure the Republican nomination for the highest office of the land, he was unable to focus on his work. Even under ordinary circumstances many would have found concentration difficult in the untidy office Lincoln shared with his younger partner, William Herndon. Two worktables, piled high with papers and correspondence, formed a T in the center of the room. Additional documents and letters spilled out from the drawers and pigeonholes of an outmoded secretary in the corner. When he needed a particular piece of correspondence, Lincoln had to rifle through disorderly stacks of paper, rummaging, as a last resort, in the lining of his old plug hat, where he often put stray letters or notes.

Restlessly descending to the street, he passed the state capitol building, set back from the road, and the open lot where he played handball with his friends, and climbed a short set of stairs to the office of the *Illinois State Journal*, the local Republican newspaper. The editorial room on the second floor, with a central large wood-burning stove, was a gathering place for the exchange of news and gossip.

He wandered over to the telegraph office on the north side of the square to see if any new dispatches had come in. There were few outward signs that this was a day of special moment and expectation in the history of Springfield, scant record of any celebration or festivity planned should Lincoln, long their fellow townsman, actually secure the nomination. That he had garnered the support of the Illinois delegation at the state convention at Decatur earlier that month was widely understood to be a "complimentary" gesture. Yet if there were no firm plans to celebrate his dark horse bid, Lincoln knew well the ardor of his staunch circle of friends already at work on his behalf on the floor of the Wigwam.

The hands of the town clock on the steeple of the Baptist church on Adams Street must have seemed not to move. When Lincoln learned that his longtime friend James Conkling had returned unexpectedly from the convention the previous evening, he walked over to Conkling's office above Chatterton's jewelry store. Told that his friend was expected within the hour, he returned to his own quarters, intending to come back as soon as Conkling arrived.

Lincoln's shock of black hair, brown furrowed face, and deep-set eyes made him look older than his fifty-one years. He was a familiar figure to almost everyone in Springfield, as was his singular way of walking, which gave the impression that his long, gaunt frame needed oiling. He plodded forward in an awkward manner, hands hanging at his sides or folded behind his back. His step had no spring, his partner William Herndon recalled. He lifted his whole foot at once rather than lifting from the toes and then thrust the whole foot down on the ground rather than landing on his heel. "His legs," another observer noted, "seemed to drag from the knees down, like those of a laborer going home after a hard day's work."

His features, even supporters conceded, were not such "as belong to a handsome man." In repose, his face was "so overspread with sadness," the reporter Horace White noted, that it seemed as if "Shakespeare's melancholy Jacques had been translated from the forest of Arden to the capital of Illinois." Yet, when Lincoln began to speak, White observed, "this expression of sorrow dropped from him instantly. His face lighted up with a winning smile, and where I had a moment before seen only leaden sorrow I now beheld keen intelligence, genuine kindness of heart, and the promise of true friendship." If his appearance seemed somewhat odd, what captivated admirers, another contemporary observed, was "his winning manner, his ready good humor, and his unaffected kindness and gentleness."

Five minutes in his presence, and "you cease to think that he is either homely or awkward."

Springfield had been Lincoln's home for nearly a quarter of a century. He had arrived in the young city to practice law at twenty-eight years old, riding into town, his great friend Joshua Speed recalled, "on a borrowed horse, with no earthly property save a pair of saddle-bags containing a few clothes." The city had grown rapidly, particularly after 1839, when it became the capital of Illinois. By 1860, Springfield boasted nearly ten thousand residents, though its business district, designed to accommodate the expanding population that arrived in town when the legislature was in session, housed thousands more. Ten hotels radiated from the public square where the capitol building stood. In addition, there were multiple saloons and restaurants, seven newspapers, three billiard halls, dozens of retail stores, three military armories, and two railroad depots.

Here in Springfield, in the Edwards mansion on the hill, Lincoln had courted and married "the belle of the town," young Mary Todd, who had come to live with her married sister, Elizabeth, wife of Ninian Edwards, the well-to-do son of the former governor of Illinois. Raised in a prominent Lexington, Kentucky, family, Mary had received an education far superior to most girls her age. For four years she had studied languages and literature in an exclusive boarding school and then spent two additional years in what was considered graduate study. The story is told of Lincoln's first meeting with Mary at a festive party. Captivated by her lively manner, intelligent face, clear blue eyes, and dimpled smile, Lincoln reportedly said, "I want to dance with you in the worst way." And, Mary laughingly told her cousin later that night, "he certainly did." In Springfield, all their children were born, and one was buried. In that spring of 1860, Mary was forty-two, Robert sixteen, William nine, and Thomas seven. Edward, the second son, had died at the age of three.

Their home, described at the time as a modest "two-story frame house, having a wide hall running through the centre, with parlors on both sides," stood close to the street and boasted few trees and no garden. "The adornments were few, but chastely appropriate," one contemporary observer noted. In the center hall stood "the customary little table with a white marble top," on which were arranged flowers, a silver-plated ice-water pitcher, and family photographs. Along the walls were positioned some chairs and a sofa. "Everything," a journalist observed, "tended to represent the home of a man who has battled hard with the fortunes of life, and whose hard experience had taught him to enjoy whatever of success belongs to him, rather in solid substance than in showy display."

During his years in Springfield, Lincoln had forged an unusually loyal circle of friends. They had worked with him in the state legislature, helped him in his campaigns for Congress and the Senate, and now, at this very moment, were guiding his efforts at the Chicago convention, "moving heaven & Earth," they assured him, in an attempt to secure him the nomination. These steadfast companions included David Davis, the Circuit Court judge for the Eighth District, whose three-hundred-pound body was matched by "a big brain and a big heart"; Norman Judd, an attorney for the railroads and chairman of the Illinois Republican state central committee; Leonard Swett, a lawyer from Bloomington who believed he knew Lincoln "as intimately as I have ever known any man in my life"; and Stephen Logan, Lincoln's law partner for three years in the early forties.

Many of these friendships had been forged during the shared experience of the "circuit," the eight weeks each spring and fall when Lincoln and his fellow lawyers journeyed together throughout the state. They shared rooms and sometimes beds in dusty village inns and taverns, spending long evenings gathered together around a blazing fire. The economics of the legal profession in sparsely populated Illinois were such that lawyers had to move about the state in the company of the circuit judge, trying thousands of small cases in order to make a living. The arrival of the traveling bar brought life and vitality to the county seats, fellow rider Henry Whitney recalled. Villagers congregated on the courthouse steps. When the court sessions were complete, everyone would gather in the local tavern from dusk to dawn, sharing drinks, stories, and good cheer.

In these convivial settings, Lincoln was invariably the center of attention. No one could equal his never-ending stream of stories nor his ability to reproduce them with such contagious mirth. As his winding tales became more famous, crowds of villagers awaited his arrival at every stop for the chance to hear a master storyteller. Everywhere he went, he won devoted followers, friendships that later emboldened his quest for office. Political life in these years, the historian Robert Wiebe has observed, "broke down into clusters of men who were bound together by mutual trust." And no political circle was more loyally bound than the band of compatriots working for Lincoln in Chicago.

The prospects for his candidacy had taken wing in 1858 after his brilliant campaign against the formidable Democratic leader, Stephen Douglas, in a dramatic senate race in Illinois that had attracted national attention. Though Douglas had won a narrow victory, Lincoln managed to unite the disparate elements of his state's fledgling Republican Party—that curious amalgamation of former Whigs, antislavery Democrats, nativists, foreigners, radicals, and conservatives. In the mid-1850s, the Republican

Party had come together in state after state in the North with the common goal of preventing the spread of slavery to the territories. "Of *strange, discordant*, and even, *hostile* elements," Lincoln proudly claimed, "we gathered from the four winds, and *formed* and fought the battle through." The story of Lincoln's rise to power was inextricably linked to the increasing intensity of the antislavery cause. Public feeling on the slavery issue had become so flammable that Lincoln's seven debates with Douglas were carried in newspapers across the land, proving the prairie lawyer from Springfield more than a match for the most likely Democratic nominee for the presidency.

Furthermore, in an age when speech-making prowess was central to political success, when the spoken word filled the air "from sun-up til sundown," Lincoln's stirring oratory had earned the admiration of a far-flung audience who had either heard him speak or read his speeches in the paper. As his reputation grew, the invitations to speak multiplied. In the year before the convention, he had appeared before tens of thousands of people in Ohio, Iowa, Indiana, Wisconsin, Kentucky, New York, and New England. The pinnacle of his success was reached at Cooper Union in New York, where, on the evening of February 27, 1860, before a zealous crowd of more than fifteen hundred people, Lincoln delivered what the *New York Tribune* called "one of the happiest and most convincing political arguments ever made in this City" in defense of Republican principles and the need to confine slavery to the places where it already existed. "The vast assemblage frequently rang with cheers and shouts of applause, which were prolonged and intensified at the close. No man ever before made such an impression on his first appeal to a New-York audience."

Lincoln's success in the East bolstered his supporters at home. On May 10, the fired-up Republican state convention at Decatur nominated him for president, labeling him "the Rail Candidate for President" after two fence rails he had supposedly split in his youth were ceremoniously carried into the hall. The following week, the powerful Chicago *Press and Tribune* formally endorsed Lincoln, arguing that his moderate politics represented the thinking of most people, that he would come into the contest "with no clogs, no embarrassment," an "honest man" who represented all the "fundamentals of Republicanism," with "due respect for the rights of the South."

Still, Lincoln clearly understood that he was "new in the field," that outside of Illinois he was not "the first choice of a very great many." His only political experience on the national level consisted of two failed Senate races and a single term in Congress that had come to an end nearly a dozen years earlier. By contrast, the three other contenders for the nomination were household names in Republican circles. William Henry Seward had been a celebrated senator from New York for more than a decade and governor of his state for two terms before he went to Washington. Ohio's Salmon P. Chase, too, had been both senator and governor, and had played a central role in the formation of the national Republican Party. Edward Bates was a widely respected elder statesman, a delegate to the convention that had framed the Missouri Constitution, and a former congressman whose opinions on national matters were still widely sought.

Recognizing that Seward held a commanding lead at the start, followed by Chase and Bates, Lincoln's strategy was to give offense to no one. He wanted to leave the delegates "in a mood to come to us, if they shall be compelled to give up their first love." This was clearly understood by Lincoln's team in Chicago and by all the delegates whom Judge Davis had commandeered to join the fight. "We are laboring to make you the second choice of all the Delegations we can, where we can't make you first choice," Scott County delegate Nathan Knapp told Lincoln when he first arrived in Chicago. "Keep a good nerve," Knapp advised, "be not surprised at any result—but I tell you that your chances are not the worst . . . brace your nerves for any result." Knapp's message was followed by one from Davis himself on the second day of the convention. "Am very hopeful," he warned Lincoln, but "dont be Excited."

The warnings were unnecessary—Lincoln was, above all, a realist who fully understood that he faced an uphill climb against his better-known rivals. Anxious to get a clearer picture of the situation, he headed back to Conkling's office, hoping that his old friend had returned. This time he was not disappointed. As Conkling later told the story, Lincoln stretched himself upon an old settee that stood by the front window, "his head on a cushion and his feet over the end," while Conkling related all he had seen and heard in the previous two days before leaving the Wigwam. Conkling told Lincoln that Seward was in trouble, that he had enemies not only in other states but at home in New York. If Seward was not nominated on the first ballot, Conkling predicted, Lincoln would be the nominee.

Lincoln replied that "he hardly thought this could be possible and that in case Mr. Seward was not nominated on the first ballot, it was his judgment that Mr. Chase of Ohio or Mr. Bates of Missouri would be the nominee." Conkling disagreed, citing reasons why each of those two candidates would have difficulty securing the nomination. Assessing the situation with his characteristic clearheadedness, Lincoln could not fail to perceive some truth in what his friend was saying; yet having tasted so many disappointments, he saw no benefit in letting his hopes run wild.

"Well, Conkling," he said slowly, pulling his long frame up from the settee, "I believe I will go back to my office and practice law."

• • •

WHILE LINCOLN STRUGGLED to sustain his hopes against the likelihood of failure, William Henry Seward was in the best of spirits. He had left Washington three days earlier to repair to his hometown of Auburn, New York, situated in the Finger Lakes Region of the most populous state of the Union, to share the anticipated Republican nomination in the company of family and friends.

Nearly sixty years old, with the vitality and appearance of a man half his age, Seward typically rose at 6 a.m. when first light slanted into the bedroom window of his twenty-room country home. Rising early allowed him time to complete his morning constitutional through his beloved garden before the breakfast bell was rung. Situated on better than five acres of land, the Seward mansion was surrounded by manicured lawns, elaborate gardens, and walking paths that wound beneath elms, mountain ash, evergreens, and fruit trees. Decades earlier, Seward had supervised the planting of every one of these trees, which now numbered in the hundreds. He had spent thousands of hours fertilizing and cultivating his flowering shrubs. With what he called "a lover's interest," he inspected them daily. His horticultural passion was in sharp contrast to Lincoln's lack of interest in planting trees or growing flowers at his Springfield home. Having spent his childhood laboring long hours on his father's struggling farm, Lincoln found little that was romantic or recreational about tilling the soil.

When Seward "came in to the table," his son Frederick recalled, "he would announce that the hyacinths were in bloom, or that the bluebirds had come, or whatever other change the morning had brought." After breakfast, he typically retired to his book-lined study to enjoy the precious hours of uninterrupted work before his doors opened to the outer world. The chair on which he sat was the same one he had used in the Governor's Mansion in Albany, designed specially for him so that everything he needed could be right at hand. It was, he joked, his "complete office," equipped not only with a writing arm that swiveled back and forth but also with a candleholder and secret drawers to keep his inkwells, pens, treasured snuff box, and the ashes of the half-dozen or more cigars he smoked every day. "He usually lighted a cigar when he sat down to write," Fred recalled, "slowly consuming it as his pen ran rapidly over the page, and lighted a fresh one when that was exhausted."

Midmorning of the day of the nomination, a large cannon was hauled from the Auburn Armory into the park. "The cannoneers were stationed at their posts," the local paper reported, "the fire lighted, the ammunition ready, and all waiting for the signal, to make the city and county echo to the joyful news" that was expected to unleash the most spectacular public celebration the city had ever known. People began gathering in front of Seward's house. As the hours passed, the crowds grew denser, spilling over into all the main streets of Auburn. The revelers were drawn from their homes in anticipation of the grand occasion and by the lovely spring weather, welcome after the severe, snowy winters Auburn endured that often isolated the small towns and cities of the region for days at a time. Visitors had come by horse and carriage from the surrounding villages, from Seneca Falls and Waterloo to the west, from Skaneateles to the east, from Weedsport to the north. Local restaurants had stocked up with food. Banners were being prepared, flags were set to be raised, and in the basement of the chief hotel, hundreds of bottles of champagne stood ready to be uncorked.

A festive air pervaded Auburn, for the vigorous senator was admired by almost everyone in the region, not only for his political courage, unquestioned integrity, and impressive intellect but even more for his good nature and his genial disposition. A natural politician, Seward was genuinely interested in people, curious about their families and the smallest details of their lives, anxious to help with their problems. As a public man he possessed unusual resilience, enabling him to accept criticism with good-humored serenity.

Even the Democratic paper, the *New York Herald*, conceded that probably fewer than a hundred of Auburn's ten thousand residents would vote against Seward if he received the nomination. "He is beloved by all classes of people, irrespective of partisan predilections," the *Herald* observed. "No philanthropic or benevolent movement is suggested without receiving his liberal and thoughtful assistance. . . . As a landlord he is kind and lenient; as an advisor he is frank and reliable; as a citizen he is enterprising and patriotic; as a champion of what he considers to be right he is dauntless and intrepid."

Seward customarily greeted personal friends at the door and was fond of walking them through his tree-lined garden to his white summerhouse. Though he stood only five feet six inches tall, with a slender frame that young Henry Adams likened to that of a scarecrow, he was nonetheless, Adams marveled, a commanding figure, an outsize personality, a "most glorious original" against whom larger men seemed smaller. People were drawn to this vital figure with the large, hawklike nose, bushy eyebrows, enormous ears; his hair, once bright red, had faded now to the color of straw. His step, in contrast to Lincoln's slow and laborious manner of walking, had a "school-boy elasticity" as he moved from his garden to his house and back again with what one reporter described as a "slashing swagger."

Every room of his palatial home contained associations from earlier days, mementos of previous triumphs. The slim Sheraton desk in the hallway had belonged to a member of the First Constitutional Congress in 1789. The fireplace in the parlor had been crafted by the young carpenter Brigham Young, later prophet of the Mormon Church. The large Thomas Cole painting in the drawing room depicting *Portage Falls* had been presented to Seward in commemoration of his early efforts to extend the canal system in New York State. Every inch of wall space was filled with curios and family portraits executed by the most famous artists of the day—Thomas Sully, Chester Harding, Henry Inman. Even the ivy that grew along the pathways and up the garden trellises had an anecdotal legacy, having been cultivated at Sir Walter Scott's home in Scotland and presented to Seward by Washington Irving.

As he perused the stack of telegrams and newspaper articles arriving from Chicago for the past week, Seward had every reason to be confident. Both Republican and Democratic papers agreed that "the honor in question was [to be] awarded by common expectation to the distinguished Senator from the State of New York, who, more than any other, was held to be the representative man of his party, and who, by his commanding talents and eminent public services, has so largely contributed to the development of its principles." The local Democratic paper, the Albany *Atlas and Argus*, was forced to concede: "No press has opposed more consistently and more unreservedly than ours the political principles of Mr. Seward. . . . But we have recognised the genius and the leadership of the man."

So certain was Seward of receiving the nomination that the weekend before the convention opened he had already composed a first draft of the valedictory speech he expected to make to the Senate, assuming that he would resign his position as soon as the decision in Chicago was made. Taking leave of his Senate colleagues, with whom he had labored through the tumultuous fifties, he had returned to Auburn, the place, he once said, he loved and admired more than any other—more than Albany, where he had served four years in the state senate and two terms as governor as a member of the Whig Party; more than the U.S. Senate chamber, where he had represented the leading state of the Union for nearly twelve years; more than any city in any of the four continents in which he had traveled extensively.

Auburn was the only place, he claimed, where he was left "free to act in an individual and not in a representative and public character," the only place where he felt "content to live, and content, when life's fitful fever shall be over, to die." Auburn was a prosperous community in the 1860s, with six schoolhouses, thirteen churches, seven banks, eleven newspapers, a woolen mill, a candle factory, a state prison, a fine hotel, and more than two hundred stores. Living on the northern shore of Owasco Lake, seventy-eight miles east of Rochester, the citizens took pride in the orderly layout of its streets, adorned by handsome rows of maples, elms, poplars, and sycamores.

Seward had arrived in Auburn as a graduate of Union College in Schenectady, New York. Having completed his degree with highest honors and finished his training for the bar, he had come to practice law with Judge Elijah Miller, the leading citizen of Cayuga County. It was in Judge Miller's country house that Seward had courted and married Frances Miller, the judge's intelligent, well-educated daughter. Frances was a tall, slender, comely woman, with large black eyes, an elegant neck, and a passionate commitment to women's rights and the antislavery cause. She was Seward's intellectual equal, a devoted wife and mother, a calming presence in his stormy life. In this same house, where he and Frances had lived since their marriage, five children were born—Augustus, a graduate of West Point who was now serving in the military; Frederick, who had embarked on a career in journalism and served as his father's private secretary in Washington; Will Junior, who was just starting out in business; and Fanny, a serious-minded girl on the threshold of womanhood, who loved poetry, read widely, kept a daily journal, and hoped someday to be a writer. A second daughter, Cornelia, had died in 1837 at four months.

Seward had been slow to take up the Republican banner, finding it difficult to abandon his beloved Whig Party. His national prominence ensured that he became the new party's chief spokesman the moment he joined its ranks. Seward, Henry Adams wrote, "would inspire a cow with statesmanship if she understood our language." The young Republican leader Carl Schurz later recalled that he and his friends idealized Seward and considered him the "leader of the political anti-slavery movement. From him we received the battle-cry in the turmoil of the contest, for he was one of those spirits who sometimes will go ahead of public opinion instead of tamely following its footprints."

In a time when words, communicated directly and then repeated in newspapers, were the primary means of communication between a political leader and the public, Seward's ability to "compress into a single sentence, a single word, the whole issue of a controversy" would irrevocably, and often dangerously, create a political identity. Over the years, his ringing phrases, calling upon a "higher law" than the Constitution that commanded men to freedom, or the assertion that the collision between the North and South was "an irrepressible conflict," became, as the young Schurz noted, "the inscriptions on our banners, the pass-words of our combatants." But those same phrases had also alarmed Republican moderates, especially in the West. It was rhetoric, more than substance, that had stamped Seward as a radical—for his actual positions in 1860 were not far from the center of the Republican Party.

Whenever Seward delivered a major speech in the Senate, the galleries were full, for audiences were invariably transfixed not only by the power of his arguments but by his exuberant personality and, not least, the striking peculiarity of his appearance. Forgoing the simpler style of men's clothing that prevailed in the 1850s, Seward preferred pantaloons and a long-tailed frock coat, the tip of a handkerchief poking out its back pocket. This jaunty touch figured in his oratorical style, which included dramatic pauses for him to dip into his snuff box and blow his enormous nose into the outsize yellow silk handkerchief that matched his yellow pantaloons. Such flamboyance and celebrity almost lent an aura of inevitability to his nomination.

If Seward remained serene as the hours passed to afternoon, secure in the belief that he was about to realize the goal toward which he had bent his formidable powers for so many years, the chief reason for his tranquillity lay in the knowledge that his campaign at the convention was in the hands of the most powerful political boss in the country: Thurlow Weed. Dictator of New York State for nearly half a century, the handsome, white-haired Weed was Seward's closest friend and ally. "Men might love and respect [him], might hate and despise him," Weed's biographer Glyndon Van Deusen wrote, "but no one who took any interest in the politics and government of the country could ignore him." Over the years, it was Weed who managed every one of Seward's successful campaigns—for the state senate, the governorship, and the senatorship of New York—guarding his career at every step along the way "as a hen does its chicks."

They made an exceptional team. Seward was more visionary, more idealistic, better equipped to arouse the emotions of a crowd; Weed was more practical, more realistic, more skilled in winning elections and getting things done. While Seward conceived party platforms and articulated broad principles, Weed built the party organization, dispensed patronage, rewarded loyalists, punished defectors, developed poll lists, and carried voters to the polls, spreading the influence of the boss over the entire state. So closely did people identify the two men that they spoke of Seward-Weed as a single political person: "Seward is Weed and Weed is Seward."

Thurlow Weed certainly understood that Seward would face a host of problems at the convention. There were many delegates who considered the New Yorker too radical; others disdained him as an opportunist, shifting ground to strengthen his own ambition. Furthermore, complaints of corruption had surfaced in the Weed-controlled legislature. And the very fact that Seward had been the most conspicuous Northern politician for nearly a decade inevitably created jealousy among many of his colleagues. Despite these problems, Seward nonetheless appeared to be the overwhelming choice of Republican voters and politicians.

Moreover, since Weed believed the opposition lacked the power to consolidate its strength, he was convinced that Seward would eventually emerge the victor. Members of the vital New York State delegation confirmed Weed's assessment. On May 16, the day the convention opened, the former Whig editor, now a Republican, James Watson Webb assured Seward that there was "no *cause* for doubting. It is only a question of time. . . . And I tell you, and stake my judgment upon it entirely, that nothing has, or can occur . . . to shake my convictions in regard to the result." The next day, Congressman Eldridge Spaulding telegraphed Seward: "Your friends are firm and confident that you will be nominated after a few ballots." And on the morning of the 18th, just before the balloting was set to begin, William Evarts, chairman of the New York delegation, sent an optimistic message: "All right. Everything indicates your nomination today sure." The dream that had powered Seward and Weed for three decades seemed within reach at last.

• • •

WHILE FRIENDS AND SUPPORTERS gathered about Seward on the morning of the 18th, Ohio's governor, Salmon Chase, awaited the balloting results in characteristic solitude. History records no visitors that day to the majestic Gothic mansion bristling with towers, turrets, and chimneys at the corner of State and Sixth Streets in Columbus, Ohio, where the handsome fifty-two-year-old widower lived with his two daughters, nineteen-year-old Kate and her half sister, eleven-year-old Nettie.

There are no reports of crowds gathering spontaneously in the streets as the hours passed, though preparations had been made for a great celebration that evening should Ohio's favorite son receive the nomination he passionately believed he had a right to expect. Brass bands stood at the ready. Fireworks had been purchased, and a dray procured to drag an enormous cannon to the statehouse, where its thunder might roll over the city once the hoped-for results were revealed. Until that announcement, the citizens of Columbus apparently went about their business, in keeping with the reserved, even austere, demeanor of their governor.

Chase stood over six feet in height. His wide shoulders, massive chest, and dignified bearing all contributed to Carl Schurz's assessment that Chase "looked as you would wish a statesman to look." One reporter observed that "he is one of the finest specimens of a perfect man that we have ever seen; a large, well formed head, set upon a frame of herculean proportions," with "an eye of unrivaled splendor and brilliancy." Yet where Lincoln's features became more warm and compelling as one drew near him, the closer one studied Chase's good-looking face, the more one noticed the unattractive droop of the lid of his right eye, creating "an arresting duality, as if two men, rather than one, looked out upon the world."

Fully aware of the positive first impression he created, Chase dressed with meticulous care. In contrast to Seward or Lincoln, who were known to greet visitors clad in slippers with their shirttails hanging out, the dignified Chase was rarely seen without a waistcoat. Nor was he willing to wear his glasses in public, though he was so nearsighted that he would often pass friends on the street without displaying the slightest recognition.

An intensely religious man of unbending routine, Chase likely began that day, as he began every day, gathering his two daughters and all the members of his household staff around him for a solemn reading of Scripture. The morning meal done, he and his elder daughter, Kate, would repair to the library to read and discuss the morning papers, searching together for signs that people across the country regarded Chase as highly as he regarded himself—signs that would bolster their hope for the Republican nomination.

During his years as governor, he kept to a rigid schedule, setting out at the same time each morning for the three-block walk to the statehouse, which was usually his only exercise of the day. Never late for appointments, he had no patience with the sin of tardiness, which robbed precious minutes of life from the person who was kept waiting. On those evenings when he had no public functions to attend, he would sequester himself in his library at home to answer letters, consult the statute books, memorize lines of poetry, study a foreign language, or practice the jokes that, however hard he tried, he could never gracefully deliver.

On the rare nights when he indulged in a game of backgammon or chess with Kate, he would invariably return to work at his fastidiously arranged drop-leaf desk, where everything was always in its "proper place" with not a single pen or piece of paper out of order. There he would sit for hours, long after every window on his street was dark, recording his thoughts in the introspective diary he had kept since he was twenty years old. Then, as the candle began to sink, he would turn to his Bible to close the day as it had begun, with prayer.

Unlike Seward's Auburn estate, which he and Frances had furnished over the decades with objects that marked different stages of their lives, Chase had filled his palatial house with exquisite carpets, carved parlor chairs, elegant mirrors, and rich draperies that important people of his time *ought* to display to prove their eminence to the world at large. He had moved frequently during his life, and this Columbus dwelling was the first home he had really tried to make his own. Yet everything was chosen for effect: even the dogs, it was said, seemed "designed and posed."

Columbus was a bustling capital city in 1860, with a population of just under twenty thousand and a reputation for gracious living and hospitable entertainment. The city's early settlers had hailed largely from New England, Pennsylvania, and Virginia, but in recent decades German and Irish immigrants had moved in, along with a thousand free blacks who lived primarily in the Long Street district near the Irish settlement. It was a time of steady growth and prosperity. Spacious blocks with wide shade trees were laid out in the heart of the city, where, the writer William Dean Howells recalled, beautiful young women, dressed in great hoopskirts, floated by "as silken balloons walking in the streets." Fashionable districts developed along High and State Streets, and a new Capitol, nearly as big as the United States Capitol, opened its doors in January 1857. Built in Greek Revival style, with tall Doric columns defining each of the entrances and a large cupola on top, the magnificent structure, which housed the governor's office as well as the legislative chambers, was proclaimed to be "the greatest State capitol building" in the country.

Unlike Seward, who frequently attended theater, loved reading novels, and found nothing more agreeable than an evening of cards, fine cigars, and a bottle of port, Chase neither drank nor smoked. He considered both theater and novels a foolish waste of time and recoiled from all games of chance, believing that they unwholesomely excited the mind. Nor was he likely to regale his friends with intricate stories told for pure fun, as did Lincoln. As one contemporary noted, "he seldom told a story without spoiling it." Even those who knew him well, except perhaps his beloved Kate, rarely recalled his laughing aloud.

Kate Chase, beautiful and ambitious, filled the emotional void in her father's heart created by the almost incomprehensible loss of three wives, all having died at a young age, including Kate's mother when Kate was five years old. Left on his own, Chase had molded and shaped his brilliant daughter, watching over her growth and cultivation with a boundless ardor. When she was seven, he sent her to an expensive boarding school in Gramercy Park, New York, where she remained for ten years, studying Latin, French, history, and the classics, in addition to elocution, deportment, and the social graces. "In a few years you will necessarily go into society," he had told her when she was thirteen. "I desire that you may be qualified to ornament any society in our own country or elsewhere into which I may have occasion to take you. It is for this reason that I care more for your improvement in your studies, the cultivation of your manners, and the establishment of your moral & religious principles, than for anything else."

After Kate graduated from boarding school and returned to Columbus, she blossomed as Ohio's first lady. Her father's ambitions and dreams became the ruling passions of her life. She gradually made herself absolutely essential to him, helping with his correspondence, editing his speeches, discussing political strategy, entertaining his friends and colleagues. While other girls her age focused on the social calendar of balls and soirées, she concentrated all her energies on furthering her father's political career. "She did everything in her power," her biographers suggest, "to fill the gaps in his life so that he would not in his loneliness seek another Mrs. Chase." She sat beside him at lyceum lectures and political debates. She presided over his dinners and receptions. She became his surrogate wife.

Though Chase treated his sweet, unassuming younger daughter, Janette (Nettie), with warmth and affection, his love for Kate was powerfully intertwined with his desire for political advancement. He had cultivated her in his own image, and she possessed an ease of conversation far more relaxed than his own. Now he could depend on her to assist him every step along the way as, day after day, year after year, he moved steadily toward his goal of becoming president. From the moment when the high office appeared possible to Chase, with his stunning election in 1855 as the first Republican governor of a major state, it had become the consuming passion of both father and daughter that he reach the White House—a passion that would endure even after the Civil War was over. Seward was no less ambitious, but he was far more at ease with diverse people, and more capable of discarding the burdens of office at the end of the day.

Yet if Chase was somewhat priggish and more self-righteous than Seward, he was more inflexibly attached to his guiding principles, which, for more than a quarter of a century, had encompassed an unflagging commitment to the cause of the black man. Whereas the more accommodating Seward could have been a successful politician in almost any age, Chase functioned best in an era when dramatic moral issues prevailed. The slavery debate of the antebellum period allowed Chase to argue his antislavery principles in biblical terms of right and wrong. Chase was actually more radical than Seward on the slavery issue, but because his speeches were not studded with memorable turns of phrase, his positions were not as notorious in the country at large, and, therefore, not as damaging in more moderate circles.

"There may have been abler statesmen than Chase, and there certainly were more agreeable companions," his biographer Albert Hart has asserted, "but none of them contributed so much to the stock of American political ideas as he." In his study of the origins of the Republican Party, William Gienapp underscores this judgment. "In the long run," he concludes, referring both to Chase's intellectual leadership of the antislavery movement and to his organizational abilities, "no individual made a more significant contribution to the formation of the Republican party than did Chase."

And no individual felt he *deserved* the presidency as a natural result of his past contributions more than Chase himself. Writing to his longtime friend the abolitionist Gamaliel Bailey, he claimed: "A very large body of the people—embracing not a few who would hardly vote for any man other than myself as a Republican nominee—seem to desire that I shall be a candidate in 1860. No effort of mine, and so far as I know none of my immediate personal friends has produced this feeling. It seems to be of spontaneous growth."

A vivid testimony to the power of the governor's wishful thinking is provided by Carl Schurz, Seward's avid supporter, who was invited to stay with Chase while lecturing in Ohio in March 1860. "I arrived early in the morning," Schurz recalled in his memoirs, "and was, to my great surprise, received at the uncomfortable hour by the Governor himself, and taken to the breakfast room." Kate entered, greeted him, "and then let herself down upon her chair with the graceful lightness of a bird that, folding its wings, perches upon the branch of a tree. . . . She had something imperial in the pose of the head, and all her movements possessed an exquisite natural charm. No wonder that she came to be admired as a great beauty and broke many hearts."

The conversation, in which "Miss Kate took a lively and remarkably intelligent part, soon turned upon politics," as Chase revealed to Schurz with surprising candor his "ardent desire to be President of the United States." Aware that Schurz would be a delegate at the convention, Chase sounded him on his own candidacy. "It would have given me a moment of sincerest happiness could I have answered that question with a note of encouragement, for nothing could have appeared to me more legitimate than the high ambition of that man," Schurz recalled. Chagrined, he nonetheless felt compelled to give an honest judgment, predicting that if the delegates were willing to nominate "an advanced anti-slavery man," they would take Seward before Chase.

Chase was taken aback, "as if he had heard something unexpected." A look of sadness came over his face. Quickly he regained control and proceeded to deliver a powerful brief demonstrating why he, rather than Seward, deserved to be considered the true leader of the antislavery forces. Schurz remained unconvinced, but he listened politely, certain that he had never before met a public man with such a serious case of "presidential fever," to the extent of "honestly believing that he owed it to the country and that the country owed it to him that he should be President." For his part, Chase remained hopeful that by his own unwavering self-confidence he had cast a spell on Schurz. The following day, Chase told his friend Robert Hosea about the visit, suggesting that in the hours they spent together Schurz had seemed to alter his opinion of Chase's chance at winning, making it "desirable to have him brought in contact with our best men." Despite Chase's best efforts Schurz remained loyal to Seward.

In the weeks before the convention, the Chase candidacy received almost daily encouragement in the *Ohio State Journal*, the Republican newspaper in Columbus. "No man in the country is more worthy, no one is more competent," the *Journal* declared. By "steady devotion to the principles of popular freedom, through a long political career," he "has won the confidence and attachment of the people in regions far beyond the State."

Certain that his cause would ultimately triumph, Chase refused to engage in the practical methods by which nominations are won. He had virtually no campaign. He had not conciliated his many enemies in Ohio itself, and as a result, he alone among the candidates would not come to the convention with the united support of his own state. Remaining in his Columbus mansion with Kate by his side, he preferred to make inroads by reminding his supporters in dozens of letters that he was the best man for the job. Listening only to what he wanted to hear, discounting troubling signs, Chase believed that "if the most cherished wishes of the people could prevail," he would be the nominee.

"Now is the time," one supporter told him. "You will ride triumphantly on the topmost wave." On the eve of the convention, he remained buoyant. "There is reason to hope," he told James Briggs, a lawyer from Cleveland—reason to hope that he and Kate would soon take their place as the president and first lady of the United States.

• • •

JUDGE EDWARD BATES awaited news from the convention at Grape Hill, his large country estate four miles from the city of St. Louis. Julia Coalter, his wife of thirty-seven years, was by his side. She was an attractive, sturdy woman who had borne him seventeen children, eight of whom survived to adulthood. Their extended family of six sons, two daughters, and nearly a dozen grandchildren remained unusually close. As the children married and raised families of their own, they continued to consider Grape Hill their primary home.

The judge's orderly life was steeped in solid rituals based on the seasons, the land, and his beloved family. He bathed in cold water every morning. A supper bell called him to eat every night. In the first week of April, he "substituted cotton for wollen socks, and a single breasted satin waistcoat for a double-breasted velvet." In July and August, he would monitor the progress of his potatoes, cabbage, squash, beets, and sweet corn. In the fall he would harvest his grape arbors. On New Year's Day, the Bates family followed an old country custom whereby the women remained home all day greeting visitors, while the men rode together from one house or farm to the next, paying calls on friends.

At sixty-six, Bates was among the oldest and best-loved citizens of St. Louis. In 1814, when he first ventured to the thriving city, it was a small fur trading village with a scattering of primitive cabins and a single ramshackle church. Four decades later, St. Louis boasted a population of 160,000 residents, and its infrastructure had boomed to include multiple churches, an extensive private and public educational system, numerous hospitals, and a variety of cultural facilities. The ever-increasing prosperity of the city, writes a historian of St. Louis, "led to the building of massive, ornate private homes equipped with libraries, ballrooms, conservatories, European paintings and sculpture."

Over the years, Bates had held a variety of respected offices—delegate to the convention that had drafted the first constitution of the state, member of the state legislature, representative to the U.S. congress, and judge of the St. Louis Land Court. His ambitions for political success, however, had been gradually displaced by love for his wife and large family. Though he had been asked repeatedly during the previous twenty years since his withdrawal from public life to run or once again accept high government posts, he consistently declined the offers.

Described by the portrait artist Alban Jasper Conant as "the quaintest looking character that walked the streets," Bates still wore "the old-fashioned Quaker clothes that had never varied in cut since he left his Virginia birthplace as a youth of twenty." He stood five feet seven inches tall, with a strong chin, heavy brows, thick hair that remained black until the end of his life, and a full white beard. In later years, Lincoln noted the striking contrast between Bates's black hair and white beard and teasingly suggested it was because Bates talked more than he thought, using "his chin more than his head." Julia Bates was also plain in her dress, "unaffected by the crinolines and other extravagances of the day, preferring a clinging skirt, a deep-pointed fichu called a Van Dyck, and a close-fitting little bonnet."

"How happy is my lot!" Bates recorded in his diary in the 1850s. "Blessed with a wife & children who spontaneously do all they can to make me comfortable, anticipating my wishes, even in the little matter of personal convenience, as if their happiness wholly depended on mine. O! it is a pleasure to work for such a family, to enjoy with them the blessings that God so freely gives." He found his legal work rewarding and intellectually stimulating, reveled in his position as an elder in the Presbyterian Church, and loved nothing more than to while away the long winter nights in his treasured library.

In contrast to Seward, whose restless energy found insufficient outlet in the bosom of his family, and to Chase, plagued all his days by unattained ambition, Bates experienced a passionate joy in the present, content to call himself "a very domestic, home, man." He had come briefly to national attention in 1847, when he delivered a spellbinding speech at the great River and Harbor Convention in Chicago, organized to protest President Polk's veto of a Whig-sponsored bill to provide federal appropriations for the internal improvement of rivers and harbors, especially needed in the fast-growing West. For a short time after the convention, newspapers across the country heralded Bates as a leading prospect for high political office, but he refused to take the bait. Thus, as the 1860 election neared, he assumed that, like his youth and early manhood, his old ambitions for political office had long since passed him by.

In this assumption, he was mistaken. Thirteen months before the Chicago convention, at a dinner hosted by Missouri congressman Frank Blair, Bates was approached to run for president by a formidable political group spearheaded by Frank's father, Francis Preston Blair, Sr. At sixty-six, the elder Blair had been a powerful player in Washington for decades. A Democrat most of his life, he had arrived in Washington from Kentucky during Andrew Jackson's first presidential term to publish the Democratic organ, the *Globe* newspaper. Blair soon became one of Jackson's most trusted advisers, a member of the famous "kitchen cabinet." Meetings were often held in the "Blair House," the stately brick mansion opposite the White House where Blair lived with his wife and four children. (Still known as the Blair House, the elegant dwelling is now owned by the government, serving as the president's official guesthouse.) To the lonely Jackson, whose wife had recently died, the Blairs became a surrogate family. The three Blair boys—James, Montgomery, and Frank Junior—had the run of the

White House, while Elizabeth, the only girl, actually lived in the family quarters for months at a time and Jackson doted on her as if she were his own child. Indeed, decades later, when Jackson neared death, he called Elizabeth to his home in Tennessee and gave her his wife's wedding ring, which he had worn on his watch chain from the day of her death.

Blair Senior had broken with the Democrats after the Mexican War over the extension of slavery into the territories. Although born and bred in the South, and still a slaveowner himself, he had become convinced that slavery must not be extended beyond where it already existed. He was one of the first important political figures to call for the founding of the Republican Party. At a Christmas dinner on his country estate in Silver Spring, Maryland, in 1855, he instigated plans for the first Republican Convention in Philadelphia that following summer.

Over the years, Blair's Silver Spring estate, just across the District of Columbia boundary, had become a natural gathering place for politicians and journalists. The house was situated amid hundreds of rolling acres surrounded by orchards, brooks, even a series of grottoes. From the "Big Gate" at the entrance, the carriage roadway passed through a forest of pine and poplar, opening to reveal a long driveway winding between two rows of chestnut trees and over a rustic bridge to the main house. In the years ahead, the Blairs' Silver Spring estate would become one of Lincoln's favorite places to relax.

The group that Blair convened included his two accomplished sons, Montgomery and Frank; an Indiana congressman, Schuyler Colfax, who would later become vice president under Ulysses Grant; and Charles Gibson, one of Bates's oldest friends in Missouri. Montgomery Blair, tall, thin, and scholarly, had graduated from West Point before studying law and moving to Missouri. In the 1850s he had returned to Washington to be closer to his parents. He took up residence in his family's city mansion on Pennsylvania Avenue. In the nation's capital, Monty Blair developed a successful legal practice and achieved national fame when he represented the slave Dred Scott in his bid for freedom.

Monty's charismatic younger brother Frank, recently elected to Congress, was a natural politician. Strikingly good-looking, with reddish-brown hair, a long red mustache, high cheekbones, and bright gray eyes, Frank was the one on whom the Blair family's burning ambitions rested. Both his father and older brother harbored dreams that Frank would one day become president. But in 1860, Frank was only in his thirties, and in the meantime, the Blair family turned its powerful gaze on Edward Bates.

The Blairs had settled on the widely respected judge, a longtime Whig and former slaveholder who had emancipated his slaves and become a

Free-Soiler, as the ideal candidate for a conservative national ticket opposed to both the radical abolitionists in the North and the proslavery fanatics in the South. Though he had never officially joined the Republican Party, Bates held fast to the cardinal principle of Republicanism: that slavery must be restricted to the states where it already existed, and that it must be prevented from expanding into the territories.

As a man of the West and a peacemaker by nature, Bates was just the person, Blair Senior believed, to unite old-line Whigs, antislavery Democrats, and liberal nativists in a victorious fight against the Southern Democratic slaveocracy. The fact that Bates had receded from the political scene for decades was an advantage, leaving him untainted by the contentious battles of the fifties. He alone, his supporters believed, could quell the threats of secession and civil war and return the nation to peace, progress, and prosperity.

Unsurprisingly, Bates was initially reluctant to allow his name to be put forward as a candidate for president. "I feel, tho' in perfect bodily health, an indolence and indecision not common with me," he conceded in July 1859. "The cause, I fear, is the mixing up of my name in Politics. . . . A large section of the Republican party, who think that Mr. Seward's nomination would ensure defeat, are anxious to take me up, thinking that I could carry the Whigs and Americans generally. . . . I must try to resist the temptation, and not allow my thoughts to be drawn off from the common channels of business and domestic cares. Ambition is a passion, at once strong and insidious, and is very apt to cheet a man out of his happiness and his true respectability of character."

Gradually, however, as letters and newspaper editorials advocating his candidacy crowded in upon him, a desire for the highest office in the land took command of his nature. The office to which he heard the call was not, as he had once disdained, "a mere seat in Congress as a subaltern member," but the presidency of the United States. Six months after the would-be kingmakers had approached him, Frank Blair, Jr., noted approvingly that "the mania has bitten old Bates very seriously," and predicted he would "play out more boldly for it than he has heretofore done."

By the dawn of the new year, 1860, thoughts of the White House monopolized the entries Bates penned in his diary, crowding out his previous observations on the phases of the moon and the state of his garden. "My nomination for the Presidency, which at first struck me with mere wonder, has become familiar, and now I begin to think my prospects very fair," he recorded on January 9, 1860. "Circumstances seem to be remarkably concurrent in my favor, and there is now great probability that the Opposition of all classes will unite upon me: And that will be equivalent to election. . . .

Can it be reserved for me to defeat and put down that corrupt and dangerous party [the Democratic Party]? Truly, if I can do my country that much
good, I will rejoice in the belief that I have not lived in vain."

In the weeks that followed, his days were increasingly taken up with
politics. Though he did not enjoy formal dinner parties, preferring intimate suppers with his family and a few close friends, Bates now spent more
time than ever before entertaining political friends, educators, and newspaper editors. Although still tending to his garden, he immersed himself in
periodicals on politics, economics, and public affairs. He felt he should
prepare himself intellectually for the task of presidential leadership by
reading historical accounts of Europe's most powerful monarchs, as well as
theoretical works on government. He sought guidance for his role as chief
executive in Carlyle's *Frederick the Great* and Adam Smith's *Wealth of
Nations*. Evenings once devoted to family were now committed to public
speeches and correspondence with supporters. Politics had fastened a
powerful hold upon him, disrupting his previous existence.

The chance for his nomination depended, as was true for Chase and Lincoln as well, on Seward's failure to achieve a first ballot victory at the convention. "I have many strong assurances that I stand second," Bates
confided in his diary, "first in the Northwest and in some states in New
England, second in New York, Pa." To be sure, there were pockets of opposition, particularly among the more passionate Republicans, who argued
that the party must nominate one of its own, and among the German-
Americans, who recalled that Bates had endorsed Millard Fillmore when he
ran for president on the anti-immigrant American Party four years earlier.
As the convention approached, however, his supporters were increasingly
optimistic.

"There is no question," the *New York Tribune* predicted, "as there has
been none for these three months past, that [Bates] will have more votes in
the Convention than any other candidate presented by those who think it
wiser to nominate a man of moderate and conservative antecedents." As
the delegates gathered in Chicago, Francis Blair, Sr., prophesied that Bates
would triumph in Chicago.

Though Bates acknowledged he had never officially joined the Republican Party, he understood that many Republicans, including "some of the
most moderate and patriotic" men, believed that his nomination "would
tend to soften the tone of the Republican party, without any abandonment
of its principles," thus winning "the friendship and support of many, especially in the border States." His chances of success looked good. How
strangely it had all turned out, for surely he understood that he had followed an unusual public path, a path that had curved swiftly upward when

he was young, then leveled off, even sloped downward for many years. But now, as he positioned himself to reenter politics, he sighted what appeared to be a relatively clear trail all the way to the very top.

•   •   •

ON THAT MORNING OF MAY 18, 1860, Bates's chief objective was simply to stop Seward on the first ballot. Chase, too, had his eye on the frontrunner, while Seward worried about Chase. Bates had become convinced that the convention would turn to him as the only real moderate. Neither Seward nor Chase nor Bates seriously considered Lincoln an obstacle to their great ambition.

Lincoln was not a complete unknown to his rivals. By 1860, his path had crossed with each of them in different ways. Seward had met Lincoln twelve years before at a political meeting. The two shared lodging that night, and Seward encouraged Lincoln to clarify and intensify his moderate position on slavery. Lincoln had met Bates briefly, and had sat in the audience in 1847 when Bates delivered his mesmerizing speech at the River and Harbor Convention. Chase had campaigned for Lincoln and the Republicans in Illinois in 1858, though the two men had never met.

There was little to lead one to suppose that Abraham Lincoln, nervously rambling the streets of Springfield that May morning, who scarcely had a national reputation, certainly nothing to equal any of the other three, who had served but a single term in Congress, twice lost bids for the Senate, and had no administrative experience whatsoever, would become the greatest historical figure of the nineteenth century.

CHAPTER 2

THE "LONGING TO RISE"

A BRAHAM LINCOLN, William Henry Seward, Salmon Chase, and Edward Bates were members of a restless generation of Americans, destined to leave behind the eighteenth-century world of their fathers. Bates, the oldest, was born when George Washington was still president; Seward and Chase during Jefferson's administration; Lincoln shortly before James Madison took over. Thousands of miles separate their birthplaces in Virginia, New York, New Hampshire, and Kentucky. Nonetheless, social and economic forces shaped their paths with marked similarities. Despite striking differences in station, talent, and temperament, all four aspirants for the Republican nomination left home, journeyed west, studied law, dedicated themselves to public service, joined the Whig Party, developed a reputation for oratorical eloquence, and became staunch opponents of the spread of slavery.

It was a country for young men. "We find ourselves," the twenty-eight-year-old Lincoln told the Young Men's Lyceum of Springfield, "in the peaceful possession, of the fairest portion of the earth, as regards extent of territory, fertility of soil, and salubrity of climate." The founding fathers had crafted a government more favorable to liberty "than any of which the history of former times tells us." Now it was up to their children to preserve and expand the great experiment.

The years following the Revolution fostered the belief that the only barriers to success were discipline and the extent of one's talents. "When both the privileges and the disqualifications of class have been abolished and men have shattered the bonds which once held them immobile," marveled the French visitor Alexis de Tocqueville, "the idea of progress comes naturally into each man's mind; the desire to rise swells in every heart at once, and all men want to quit their former social position. Ambition becomes a universal feeling."

The same observation that horrified Mrs. Frances Trollope on a visit to

America, that "any man's son may become the equal of any other man's son," propelled thousands of young men to break away from the small towns and limited opportunities their fathers had known. These ambitious youngsters ventured forth to test their luck in new careers as merchants, manufacturers, teachers, and lawyers. In the process, hundreds of new towns and cities were born, and with the rapid expansion of roads, bridges, and canals, a modern market economy emerged. Vast new lands and possibilities were opened when the Louisiana Purchase doubled the extent of America's territorial holdings overnight.

The newly liberated Americans crossed the Appalachian Mountains, which had separated the original colonies from the unsettled West. "Americans are always moving on," wrote Stephen Vincent Benét. "The stream uncrossed, the promise still untried/The metal sleeping in the mountainside." In the South, pioneers moved through the Gulf States toward the Mississippi River, extending cotton cultivation and slavery as they went. In the North, the movement west from New England and the mid-Atlantic brought settlers who created a patchwork of family farms and planted the seeds of thriving cities.

Bates traveled farthest, eight hundred miles from his home state of Virginia across Kentucky, Indiana, and Illinois to the young city of St. Louis in the newly established territory of Missouri. Chase made the arduous journey from New Hampshire to Cincinnati, Ohio, a burgeoning city recently carved from a forest rich with wild game. Seward left his family in eastern New York for the growing city of Auburn in the western part of the state. Lincoln traveled from Kentucky to Indiana, and then on to Illinois, where he would become a flatboatman, merchant, surveyor, and postmaster before studying law.

"Every American is eaten up with longing to rise," Tocqueville wrote. These four men, and thousands more, were not searching for a mythical pot of gold at the edge of the western rainbow, but for a place where their dreams and efforts would carve them a place in a fast-changing society.

• • •

OF THE CONTENDERS, William Henry Seward enjoyed the most privileged childhood. Blessed with a sanguine temperament that seemingly left him free from inner turmoil, he launched himself into every endeavor with unbounded vitality—whether competing for honors in school, playing cards with his classmates, imbibing good food and wine, or absorbing the pleasures of travel.

Henry Seward, as he would be called, was born on May 16, 1801. The fourth of six children, he grew up in the hill country of Orange County,

New York, in the village of Florida, about twenty-five miles from West Point. His father, Samuel Seward, had accumulated "a considerable fortune" through his various employments as physician, magistrate, judge, merchant, land speculator, and member of the New York state legislature. His mother, Mary Jennings Seward, was renowned in the community for her warmth, good sense, and kindly manner.

Affectionate and outgoing, with red hair and intelligent blue eyes, Henry was singled out among his brothers for a college education, "then regarded, by every family," he later wrote, "as a privilege so high and so costly that not more than one son could expect it." His "destined preferment," as he called it, led him at the age of nine to a preparatory academy in the village of Goshen, and then back to his own town when a new academy opened its doors. His day of study began, he recalled, "at five in the morning, and closed at nine at night." The regime imposed by the schoolmaster was rigorous. When young Henry faltered in his translations of Caesar or failed to decipher lines of Virgil's poetry, he was relegated to a seat on the floor "with the classic in one hand and the dictionary in the other." Although sometimes the pressure was "more than [he] could bear," he persisted, knowing that his father would never accept failure.

After the isolated hours consumed by books, Henry delighted in the sociability of winter evenings, when, he recalled, "the visit of a neighbor brought out the apples, nuts, and cider, and I was indulged with a respite from study, and listened to conversation, which generally turned upon politics or religion!" His pleasure in these social gatherings left Seward with a lifelong memory and appetite. Years later, when he established his own home, he filled evenings with a continuous flow of guests, always providing abundant food, drink, and conversation.

The Sewards, like other well-to-do families in the area, owned slaves. As a small child, Henry spent much of his time in the slave quarters, comprised of the kitchen and the garret above it. Basking in the warmth of the fireplace and the aroma of the turkeys and chickens roasting on the spit, he savored the "loquacious" and "affectionate" company of the garret's residents. They provided a welcome respite from the "severe decorum" of his parents' parlor on the other side of the house. As he grew older, however, he found it difficult to accept the diminished status of these slave friends, whose lives were so different from his own.

Although his father, an exception in the village, permitted his slaves to join his own children in the local schoolhouse, Henry puzzled over why "no other black children went there." More disturbing still, he discovered that one of his companions, a slave child his own age who belonged to a neighboring family, was regularly whipped. After one severe beating, the boy ran away. "He was pursued and brought back," Seward recalled, and was forced to wear "an iron yoke around his neck, which exposed him to contempt and ridicule," until he finally "found means to break the collar, and fled forever." Seward later would credit this early unease and personal awareness of the slaves' plight for his resolve to fight against slavery.

The youthful Seward was not alone in his budding dislike for slavery. In the years after the Revolutionary War, the state legislatures in eleven Northern states passed abolition laws. Some states banned slavery outright within their boundaries; others provided for a system of gradual emancipation, decreeing that all slaves born after a certain date would be granted freedom when they attained adulthood. The slaves Seward knew as a child belonged to this transitional generation. By 1827, slavery would be fully eradicated in New York. While Northern legislatures were eliminating the institution, however, slavery had become increasingly important to the economic life of the cotton-growing South.

At fifteen, Seward enrolled in upstate New York's prestigious Union College. His first sight of the steamboat that carried him up the Hudson was one he would never forget. Invented only a decade earlier, the steamboat seemed to him "a magnificent palace . . . a prodigy of power." His first glimpse of Albany, then a rural village with a population of twelve thousand, thrilled him—"so vast, so splendid, so imposing." Throughout his life, Seward retained an awe of the new technologies and inventions that fostered the industrial development of his rapidly expanding country.

At Union, Seward's open, affable nature made him dozens of friends. Upon his arrival, he later confessed, "I cherished in my secret thoughts aspirations to become . . . the valedictorian of my class." When he realized that his competitors for the honor seemed isolated from the social life of the school, he wondered if the prize was worth the cost. His ambitions were revitalized, however, when the president of Union announced that the Phi Beta Kappa Society "had determined to establish a fourth branch at Union College," with membership conferred on the top scholars at the end of junior year. There were then only three active branches of Phi Beta Kappa—at Harvard, Yale, and Dartmouth. To gain admission, Seward realized, would place him in the company of "all the eminent philosophers, scholars, and statesmen of the country."

He made a pact with his roommate whereby the two "rose at three o'clock in the morning, cooked and spread our own meals, washed our own dishes, and spent the whole time which we could save from prayers and recitations, and the table, in severe study, in which we unreservedly

and constantly aided each other." Years later, his jovial self-confidence intact, Seward wrote: "Need I say that we entered the great society without
encountering the deadly blackball?"

Seward began his senior year in good spirits. Without sacrificing his
popularity with classmates, he was poised to graduate as valedictorian. But
his prideful character temporarily derailed him. Strapped by the stingy al-
lowance his father provided, he had fallen into debt with various creditors
in Schenectady. The bills, mostly to tailors, were not large, but his father's
refusal to pay spurred a rash decision to leave college for good, so that he
might work to support himself. "I could not submit to the shame of credit
impaired," he later wrote. Without notifying his parents, he accompanied
a classmate to Georgia, where he found a good job teaching school. When
his father discovered Henry's whereabouts, he "implored [him] to return,"
mingling promises of additional funds with threats that he would pursue
the trustees of the school "with the utmost rigor of the law . . . if they
should continue to harbor the delinquent."

If his father's threats increased his determination to stay, a letter from
his mother, revealing "a broken heart," prompted Seward's return to New
York. The following fall, after working off his debt that summer, he resumed his studies at Union. "Matters prosper in my favor," he wrote to a
friend in January 1820, "and I have so far been inferior to none in my own
opinion." He was back on track to become valedictorian, and his election
as graduation speaker seemed likely. If denied the honor, he told his friend,
"his soul would disdain to sit in the hearing of some, and listen to some
whom he considers beneath even his notice." His goals were realized. He
graduated first in his class and was unanimously elected by classmates and
faculty to be Union College's commencement orator in June 1820.

From his honored place at Union College, Seward glided smoothly into
the profession of law. In an era when "reading the law" under the guidance
of an established attorney was the principal means of becoming a lawyer,
he walked directly from his graduation ceremony to the law office of a distinguished Goshen lawyer, and then "was received as a student" in the
New York City office of John Anthon, author of a widely known book on
the legal practice. Not only did Seward have two eminent mentors, he also
gained access to the "New York Forum," a society of ambitious law students who held mock trials and prosecutions to hone their professional
skills before public audiences.

Accustomed to winning the highest honors, Seward was initially chagrined to discover that his legal arguments failed to bring the loudest applause. His confidence as a writer faltered until a fellow law student, whose
orations "always carried away the audience," insisted that the problem was

not Henry's compositions, which were, in fact, far superior to his own, but his husky voice, which a congenital inflammation in the throat rendered "incapable of free intonation." To prove this point, Seward's friend offered to exchange compositions, letting Seward read one of his while he read one of Seward's. Seward recalled that he read his friend's address "as well as I could, but it did not take at all. He followed me with my speech, and I think Broadway overheard the clamorous applause which arose on that occasion in Washington Hall."

During his stay in New York, Seward formed an intimate friendship with a bookish young man, David Berdan, who had graduated from Union the year after him. Seward believed that Berdan possessed "a genius of the highest order." He had read more extensively than anyone Seward knew and excelled as a scholar in the classics. "The domains of History, Eloquence, Poetry, Fiction & Song," Seward marveled, "were all subservient to his command." Berdan had entered into the study of law at the same office as Seward, but soon discovered that his vocation lay in writing, not law.

Together, the two young men attended the theater, read poetry, discussed books, and chased after women. Convinced that Berdan would become a celebrated writer, Seward stood in awe of his friend's talent and dedication. All such grand expectations and prospects were crushed when Berdan, still in his twenties, was "seized with a bleeding at the lungs" while sojourning in Europe. He continued traveling, but when his tuberculosis worsened, he booked his passage home, in "the hope that he might die in his native land." The illness took his life before the ship reached New York. His body was buried at sea. Seward was devastated, later telling his wife that he had loved Berdan as "never again" could he "love in this world."

Such intimate male attachments, as Seward's with Berdan, or, as we shall see, Lincoln's with Joshua Speed and Chase's with Edwin Stanton, were "a common feature of the social landscape" in nineteenth-century America, the historian E. Anthony Rotundo points out. The family-focused and community-centered life led by most men in the colonial era was transformed at the dawn of the new century into an individual and career-oriented existence. As the young men of Seward and Lincoln's generation left the familiarity of their small communities and traveled to seek employment in fast-growing, anonymous cities or in distant territories, they often felt unbearably lonely. In the absence of parents and siblings, they turned to one another for support, sharing thoughts and emotions so completely that their intimate friendships developed the qualities of passionate romances.

After passing the bar examination, Seward explored the western part of the state, seeking the perfect law office from which to launch an illustrious career. He found what he wanted in Auburn when Judge Elijah Miller offered him a junior partnership in his thriving firm. Seward quickly assumed responsibility for most of the legal work passing through the office, earning the senior partner's trust and respect. The fifty-two-year-old judge was a widower who shared with his daughters—Lazette and Frances—the grandest residence in Auburn. It seemed to follow naturally that, less than two years later, Seward should woo and win Miller's twenty-year-old daughter, the beautiful, sensitive Frances. The judge insisted, as a condition of consent to the marriage, that the young couple join his household, which included his mother and unmarried sister.

Thus, at twenty-three, Seward found himself the tenant of the elegant country mansion where he and Frances would live for the rest of their lives. With a brilliant marriage and excellent prospects in his chosen profession, he could look ahead with confidence. To the end of his long life, he gazed optimistically to the future, believing that he and his countrymen were steadily advancing along a road toward increased knowledge, achievement, prosperity, and moral development.

• • •

SALMON PORTLAND CHASE, in contrast to the ever buoyant Seward, possessed a restless soul incapable of finding satisfaction in his considerable achievements. He was forever brooding on a station in life not yet reached, recording at each turning point in his life his regret at not capitalizing on the opportunities given to him.

He was born in the rolling hills of Cornish, New Hampshire, in 1808, the eighth of eleven children. His ancestors had lived in the surrounding country for three generations, becoming pillars of the community. Chase would remember that "the neighboring folk used to say" of the substantial Chase homestead that "in that yellow house more brains were born than in any other house in New England." Three of his father's brothers attended Dartmouth College. One became a distinguished lawyer, another a U.S. senator, and the third an Episcopalian bishop.

Salmon's father, Ithamar Chase, was a successful farmer, a justice of the peace, and a representative from his district to the New Hampshire council. He was "a good man," Chase recalled, a kind father and a loving husband to his young wife, Janette Ralston. He governed his large family without a single "angry word or violent e[x]clamation from his lips." Chase long remembered a day when he was playing a game of ninepins with his friends. His father interrupted, saying he needed his son's help in the field.

The boy hesitated. "Won't you come and help your father?" That was all that needed to be said. "Only a look. . . . All my reluctance vanished and I went with a right good will. He ruled by kind words & kind looks."

Young Salmon, like Seward, demonstrated an unusual intellectual precocity. His father singled him out to receive a better education "than that given to his other children." The boy thrived in the atmosphere of high expectations. "I was . . . ambitious to be at the head of my class," he recalled. During the summer months, his elder sister, Abigail, a schoolteacher in Cornish, kept him hard at work studying Latin grammar. If he failed to grasp his lessons, he would retreat to the garden and stay there by himself until he could successfully read the designated passages. At Sunday school, he strove to memorize more Bible verses than anyone else in his class, "once repeating accurately almost an entire gospel, in a single recitation." Eager to display his capacity, Chase would boast to adults that he enjoyed studying volumes of ancient history and perusing the plays of Shakespeare "for the entertainment they afforded."

While he was considered "quite a prodigy" in his written work, Chase was uneasy reciting in public. In contrast to Lincoln, who loved nothing better than to entertain his childhood friends and fellow students with stories, sermons, or passages from books, the self-conscious Chase was terrified to speak before fellow students, having "little notion of what I had to do or of the way to do it." With his "hands dangling and head down," he looked as awkward as he felt.

From his very early days, Chase showed signs of the fierce, ingrained rectitude that would both fortify his battle against slavery and incur the enmity of many among his fellows. Baptized Episcopalian in a pious family, where the Lord's day of rest was strictly kept, the young boy needed only one Sunday scolding for "sliding down hill with some boys on the dry pine leaves" to know that he would never "transgress that way again." Nor did he argue when his mother forbade association with boys who used profane language: he himself found it shocking that anyone would swear. Another indelible childhood memory made him abhor intemperance. He had stumbled upon the dead body of a drunken man in the street, his "face forward" in a pool of water "not deep enough to reach his ears," but sufficient, in his extreme state of intoxication, to drown him. The parish priest had delivered sermons on "the evils of intemperance," but, as Chase observed, "what sermon could rival in eloquence that awful spectacle of the dead drunkard—helplessly perishing where the slightest remnant of sense or strength would have sufficed to save."

When Chase was seven years old, his father made a bold business move. The War of 1812 had put a halt to glass imports from Europe, creating a pressing demand for new supplies. Sensing opportunity, Ithamar Chase liquidated his assets in Cornish to invest in a glass factory in the village of Keene. His wife had inherited some property there, including a fourteen-room tavern house. Chase moved his family into one section of the tavern and opened the rest to the public. While a curious and loquacious child like the young Lincoln might have enjoyed the convivial entertainments of a tavern, the reticent Salmon found the move from his country estate in Cornish unsettling. And for his father, the relocation proved calamitous. With the end of the war, tariff duties on foreign goods were reduced and glass imports saturated the market. The glass factory failed, sending him into bankruptcy.

The Chase family was unable to recover. Business failure led to humiliation in the community and, eventually, to loss of the family home. Ithamar Chase succumbed to a fatal stroke at the age of fifty-three, when Salmon was nine. "He lingered some days," Chase recalled. "He could not speak to us, and we stood mute and sobbing. Soon all was over. We had no father . . . the light was gone out from our home."

Left with heavy debts and meager resources, Janette Chase was forced to assume the burden of housing, educating, and providing for her numerous children on her own. Only by moving into cheap lodgings, and scrimping "almost to suffering," was she able to let Salmon, her brightest and most promising child, continue his studies at the local academy, fulfilling her promise to his "ever lamented and deceased father." When she could no longer make ends meet, she was forced to parcel her children out among relatives. Salmon was sent to study under the tutelage of his father's brother, the Episcopal bishop Philander Chase, who presided over a boys' school in Worthington in the newly formed state of Ohio. In addition to his work as an educator, Philander Chase was responsible for a sizable parish, and owned a farm that provided food and dairy products for the student body. Young Chase, in return for milking cows and driving them to pasture, building fires, and hauling wood, would be given room and board, and a classical and religious education.

In 1819, at the age of twelve, the boy traveled westward, first by wagon through Vermont and New York, then by steamboat across Lake Erie to Cleveland, a tiny lakeside settlement of a few hundred residents. There Salmon was stranded until a group of travelers passed through en route to Worthington. In the company of strangers, the child made his way on foot and horseback through a hundred miles of virgin forest to reach his uncle's home.

The bishop was an imposing figure, brilliant, ambitious, and hardworking. His faith, Chase observed, "was not passive but active. If any thing was to be done he felt that he must do it; and that, if he put forth all his energy, he might safely & cheerfully leave the event to Divine Providence." Certainty gave him an unbending zeal. He was "often very harsh & severe," recalled Chase, and "among us boys he was almost and sometimes, indeed, quite tyrannical." The most insignificant deviation from the daily regimen of prayer and study was met with a fearful combination of physical flogging and biblical precept.

"My memories of Worthington on the whole are not pleasant," Chase said of the time he spent with his domineering uncle. "There were some pleasant rambles—some pleasant incidents—some pleasant associates: but the disagreeable largely predominated. I used to count the days and wish I could get home or go somewhere else and get a living by work." One incident long remained in Chase's memory. As punishment for some infraction of the daily rules, he was ordered to bring in a large stack of wood before daybreak. He completed the task but complained to a fellow student that his uncle was "a darned old tyrant." Upon hearing these words, the bishop allowed no one to speak to the boy and forbade him to speak until he confessed and apologized. Days later, Chase finally recanted, and the sentence was revoked. "Even now," Chase said, telling the story decades later, "I almost wish I had not."

When the bishop was made president of Cincinnati College, Chase accompanied his uncle to Cincinnati. At thirteen, he was enrolled as a freshman at the college. The course of study was not difficult, leaving boys time to indulge in "a good deal of mischief & fun." Salmon Chase was not among them. "I had little or nothing to do with these sports," he recalled. "I had the chores to do at home, & when I had time I gave it to reading." Even Chase's sympathetic biographer Robert Warden observed that his "life might have been happier" had he "studied less and had more fun!" These early years witnessed the development of the rigid, self-denying habits that, throughout his life, prevented Chase from fully enjoying the companionship of others.

When Chase turned fifteen, his uncle left for England to secure funding for the new theological seminary that would become Kenyon College. At last, Chase was allowed to return to his mother's home in Keene, New Hampshire, where he planned to teach while preparing for admittance to Dartmouth College. His first position lasted only weeks, however. Employing the harsh methods of his uncle rather than the gentle precepts of his father, he administered corporal punishment to discipline his students. When irate parents complained, he was dismissed.

When Chase made his application to Dartmouth, he found that his schooling in Ohio, though filled with misery, had prepared him to enter as a third-year student. At Dartmouth, for the first time, he seemed to relax. Though he graduated with distinction and a Phi Beta Kappa key, he began to enjoy the camaraderie of college life, forging two lifelong friendships with Charles Cleveland, an intellectual classmate who would become a classics professor, and Hamilton Smith, who would become a well-to-do businessman.

No sooner had he completed his studies than he berated himself for squandering the opportunity: "Especially do I regret that I spent so much of my time in reading novels and other light works," he told a younger student. "They may impart a little brilliancy to the imagination but at length, like an intoxicating draught, they enfeeble and deaden the powers of thought and action." With dramatic flair, the teenage Chase then added: "My life seems to me to have been wasted." While Seward joyfully devoured the works of Dickens and Scott, Chase found no room for fiction in his Spartan intellectual life. After finishing the new novel by Edward Bulwer-Lytton, the author of *The Last Days of Pompeii*, he conceded that "the author is doubtless a gifted being—but he has prostituted God's noblest gifts to the vilest purposes."

The years after his graduation found nineteen-year-old Chase in Washington, D.C., where he eventually established a successful school for boys that attracted the sons of the cabinet members in the administration of John Quincy Adams, as well as the son of Senator Henry Clay. Once again, instead of taking pleasure in his position, he felt his talents went unappreciated. There were distinct classes of society in Washington, Chase told Hamilton Smith. The first, to which he aspired, included the high government officials; the second, to which he was relegated, included teachers and physicians; and the third mechanics and artisans. There was, of course, a still lower class comprised of slaves and laborers. The problem with teaching, he observed, was that any "drunken, miserable dog who could thre'd the mazes of the Alphabet" could set himself up as a teacher, bringing the "profession of teachers into utter contempt." Chase was tormented by the lowly figure he cut in the glittering whirl of Washington life. "I have always thought," he confessed, "that Providence intended me as the instrument of effecting something more than falls to the lot of all men to achieve."

Though this thirst to excel and to distinguish himself had been instilled in Chase early on by his parents, and painfully reinforced by the years with Philander Chase, such sleepless ambition was inflamed by the dynamic American society in the 1820s. Visitors from Europe, the historian Joyce Appleby writes, "saw the novelty of a society directed almost entirely by the ambitious dreams that had been unleashed after the Revolution in the heated imagination of thousands of people, most of them poor and young."

Casting about for a career befitting the high estimation in which he held his own talents, Chase wrote to an older brother in 1825 for advice about the different professions. He was contemplating the study of law, perhaps inspired by his acquaintance with Attorney General William Wirt, the father of two of his pupils. Wirt was among the most distinguished figures in Washington, a respected lawyer as well as a literary scholar. He had served as U.S. Attorney General under President James Monroe and had been kept in office by John Quincy Adams. His popular biography of the patriot and lawyer Patrick Henry had made a small name for him in American letters.

A warmhearted, generous man, Wirt welcomed his sons' teenage instructor into his family circle, inviting the lonely Chase to the small dinner parties, private dances, and luxurious levees attended by Washington's elite. At the Wirt household, filled with music and lively conversation, Chase found a respite from the constant pressure he felt to read and study in order to stay ahead of his students. More than three decades later, in the midst of the Civil War, Chase could still summon up vivid details of the "many happy hours" he spent with the Wirt family. "Among women Mrs. [Elizabeth] Wirt had few equals," he recalled. Particularly stamped in his memory was an evening in the garden when Elizabeth Wirt stood beside him, "under the clusters of the multiflora which clambered all over the garden portico of the house and pointed out . . . the stars."

Though supportive and eager to mentor the ambitious and talented young man, the Wirts delicately acknowledged—or so Chase felt—the social gulf that divided Chase from their family. Any attempt on the young teacher's part to move beyond friendship with any one of their four beautiful daughters was, he thought, discouraged. Since he was surrounded by the tantalizing fruits of professional success and social eminence in the Wirt family's parlor, it is no wonder that a career in law beckoned. His brother Alexander warned him that of all the professions, law entailed the most strenuous course of preparation: success required mastery of "thousands of volumes" from "centuries long past," including works of science, the arts, and both ancient and contemporary history. "In fine, you must become a universal scholar." Despite the fact that this description was not an accurate portrait of the course most law students of the day embarked upon, typically, Chase took it to heart, imposing a severe discipline upon himself to rise before daybreak to begin his monumental task of study. Insecurity and ambition combined, as ever, to fuel his efforts. "Day and night must be witness to the assiduity of my labours," he vowed in his diary;

"knowledge may yet be gained and golden reputation. . . . Future scenes of triumph may yet be mine."

Wirt allowed Salmon to read law in his office and offered encouragement. *"You* will be a distinguished writer," he assured Chase. "I am *sure* of it—You have all the sensibility, talent and enthusiasm essential to success in that walk." The young man wrote breathlessly to Wirt in return, "God [prospering] my exertions, I will imitate your example." As part of his self-designed course of preparation, Chase diligently took notes in the galleries of the House and Senate, practiced his elocution by becoming a member of Washington's Blackstone debating club, and read tirelessly while continuing his duties as a full-time teacher. After hearing the great Daniel Webster speak before the Supreme Court, "his voice deep and sonorous; and his sentiments high and often sublime," he promised himself that if "any degree of industry would enable me to reach his height, how day and night should testify of my toils."

Neither his opportunities nor his impressive discipline yielded Chase much in the way of satisfaction. Rather than savoring his progress, he excoriated himself for not achieving enough. "I feel humbled and mortified," he wrote in his diary, as the year 1829 drew to a close, "by the conviction that the Creator has gifted me with intelligence almost in vain. I am almost twenty two and have as yet attained but the threshold of knowledge. . . . The night has seldom found me much advanced beyond the station I occupied in the morning. . . . I almost despair of ever making any figure in the world." Fear of failure, perhaps intensified by the conviction that his father's failure had precipitated his death and the devastation of his family, would operate throughout Chase's life as a catalyst to his powerful ambition. Even as he scourged himself, he continued to believe that there was still hope, that if he could "once more resolve to struggle earnestly for the prize of well-doing," he would succeed.

As Seward had done, Chase compressed into two years the three-year course of study typically followed by college-educated law students. When the twenty-two-year-old presented himself for examination at the bar in Washington, D.C., in 1829, the presiding judge expressed a wish that Chase "study another year" before attempting to pass. "Please," Chase begged, "I have made all my arrangements to go to the Western country & practice law." The judge, who knew Chase by reputation and was aware of his connection with the distinguished William Wirt, relented and ordered that Chase be sworn in at the bar. Chase had decided to abandon Washington's crowded professional terrain for the open vista and fresh opportunities afforded by the growing state of Ohio.

"I would rather be *first* in Cincinnati than first in Baltimore, twenty years hence," Chase immodestly confessed to Charles Cleveland. "As I have ever been first at school and college . . . I shall strive to be first wherever I may be." Cincinnati had become a booming city in 1830, one of the West's largest. Less than two decades earlier, when the state was founded, much of Ohio "was covered by the primeval forest." Chase knew the prospects for a young lawyer would be good in the rapidly developing region, but could not help feeling, as he had upon his arrival in Washington, like "a stranger and an adventurer."

Despite past achievements, Chase suffered from crippling episodes of shyness, exacerbated by his shame over a minor speech defect that lent an unusual tone to his voice. "I wish I was as sure of your *elocution* as I am of everything else," William Wirt cautioned. "Your voice is a little nasal as well as guttural, and your articulation stiff, laborious and thick. . . . I would not mention these things if they were incurable—but they are not, as Demosthenes has proved—and it is only necessary for you to know the fact, to provide the remedy." In addition to the humiliation he felt over his speaking voice, Salmon Chase was tormented by his own name. He fervently wished to change its "awkward, *fishy*" sound to something more elegant. "How wd. this name do (Spencer de Cheyce or Spencer Payne Cheyce)," he inquired of Cleveland. "Perhaps you will laugh at this but I assure you I have suffered no little inconvenience."

Bent on a meteoric rise in this new city, Chase redoubled his resolve to work. "I made this resolution today," he wrote in his diary soon after settling in. "I will try to excel in all things." Pondering the goals he had set for his new life in the West, Chase wrote: "I was fully aware that I must pass thro' a long period of probation. . . . That many obstacles were to be overcome, many difficulties to be surmounted ere I could hope to reach the steep where Fame's proud temple shines," complete with "deserved honor, eminent usefulness and a 'crown of glory.' "

Nonetheless, he had made a good beginning. After struggling for several years to secure enough legal business to support himself, he developed a lucrative practice, representing various business interests and serving as counsel for several large Cincinnati banks. At the same time, following Benjamin Franklin's advice for continual self-improvement, he founded a popular lecture series in Cincinnati, joined a temperance society, undertook the massive project of collecting Ohio's scattered statutes into three published volumes, tried his hand at poetry, and wrote numerous articles for publication in various magazines. To maintain these multiple pursuits, he would often arise at 4 a.m. and occasionally allowed himself to work on Sundays, though he berated himself whenever he did so.

The more successful Chase became, the more his pious family fretted over his relentless desire for earthly success and distinction. "I confess I almost tremble for you," his elder sister Abigail wrote him when he was twenty-four years old, "as I observe your desire to distinguish yourself and apparent devotedness to those pursuits whose interests terminate in this life." If his sister hoped that a warm family life would replace his ambition with love, her hopes were brutally crushed by the fates that brought him to love and lose three young wives.

His first, Catherine "Kitty" Garniss—a warm, outgoing, attractive young woman whom he loved passionately—died in 1835 from complications of childbirth after eighteen months of marriage. She was only twenty-three. Her death was "so overwhelming, so unexpected," he told his friend Cleveland, that he could barely function. "I wish you could have known her," he wrote. "She was universally beloved by her acquaintances. . . . She was gifted with unusual intellectual power. . . . And now I feel a loneliness the more dreadful, from the intimacy of the connexion which has been severed."

His grief was compounded by guilt, for he was away on business in Philadelphia when Kitty died, having been assured by her doctor that she would recover. "Oh how I accused myself of folly and wickedness in leaving her when yet sick," he confided in his diary, "how I mourned that the prospect of a little addition to my reputation . . . should have tempted me away."

Chase arrived home to find his front door wreathed in black crepe, a customary sign "that death was within." There "in our nuptial chamber, in her coffin, lay my sweet wife," Chase wrote, "little changed in features—but oh! the look of life was gone. . . . Nothing was left but clay." For months afterward, he berated himself, believing that "the dreadful calamity might have been averted, had I been at home to watch over her & care for her." Learning that the doctors had bled her so profusely that she lost consciousness shortly before she died, he delved into textbooks on medicine and midwifery that persuaded him that, had she been treated differently, she need not have died.

Worst of all, Chase feared that Kitty had died without affirming her faith. He had not pushed her firmly enough toward God. "Oh if I had not contented myself with a few conversations on the subject of religion," he lamented in his diary, "if I had incessantly followed her with kind & earnest persuasion . . . she might have been before her death enrolled among the professed followers of the Lamb. But I procrastinated and now she is gone."

His young wife's death shadowed all the days of his life. He was haunted by the vision that when he himself reached "the bar of God," he would meet her "as an accusing spirit," blaming him for her damnation. His guilt rekindled his religious commitment, producing a "second conversion," a renewed determination never to let his fierce ambition supersede his religious duties.

The child upon whom all his affections then centered, named Catherine in honor of her dead mother, lived only five years. Her death in 1840 during an epidemic of scarlet fever devastated Chase. Losing one's only child, he told Charles Cleveland, was "one of the heaviest calamities which human experience can know." Little Catherine, he said, had "lent wings to many delightful moments . . . I fondly looked forward to the time when her increasing attainments and strength would fit her at once for the superintendence of my household & to be my own counsellor and friend." Asking for his friend's prayers, he concluded with the thought that "no language can describe the desolation of my heart."

Eventually, Chase fell in love and married again. The young woman, Eliza Ann Smith, had been a good friend of his first wife. Eliza was only twenty when she gave birth to a daughter, Kate, named in memory of both his first wife and his first daughter. For a few short years, Chase found happiness in a warm marriage sustained by a deep religious bond. It would not last, for after the birth and death of a second daughter, Eliza was diagnosed with tuberculosis, which took her life at the age of twenty-five. "I feel as if my heart was broken," Chase admitted to Cleveland after he placed Eliza's body in the tomb. "I write weeping. I cannot restrain my tears. . . . I have no wife, my little Kate has no mother, and we are desolate."

The following year, Chase married Sarah Belle Ludlow, whose well-to-do father was a leader in Cincinnati society. Belle gave birth to two daughters, Nettie and Zoe. Zoe died at twelve months; two years later, her mother followed her into the grave. Though Chase was only forty-four years old, he would never marry again. "What a vale of misery this world is," he lamented some years later when his favorite sister, Hannah, suffered a fatal heart attack at the dining room table. "To me it has been emphatically so. Death has pursued me incessantly ever since I was twenty-five. . . . Sometimes I feel as if I could give up—as if I *must* give up. And then after all I rise & press on."

• • •

LIKE SALMON CHASE, Edward Bates left the East Coast as a young man, intending, he said, "to go West and grow up with the country." The youngest of twelve children, he was born on a plantation called Belmont, not far from Richmond, Virginia. His father, Thomas Fleming Bates, was a member of the landed gentry with an honored position in his community. Educated in England, the elder Bates was a planter and merchant who owned dozens of slaves and counted Thomas Jefferson and James Madison among his friends. His mother, Caroline Woodson Bates, was of old Virginia stock.

These aristocratic Southerners, recalled Bates's old friend Charles Gibson, were "as distinctly a class as any of the nobility of Western Europe." Modeled on an ideal of English manorial life, they placed greater value on family, hospitality, land, and honor than on commercial success or monetary wealth. Writing nostalgically of this antebellum period, Bates's grandson Onward Bates claimed that life after the Civil War never approached the "enjoyable living" of those leisurely days, when "the visitor to one of these homesteads was sure of a genial welcome from white and black," when "the negroes adopted the names and held all things in common with their masters, including their virtues and their manners."

Life for the Bates family was comfortable and secure until the Revolutionary War, when Thomas Bates, a practicing Quaker, set aside his pacifist principles to take up arms against the British. He and his family were proud of his service in the Continental Army. The flintlock musket he carried was handed down to the next generations with the silver-plated inscription: "Thomas F. Bates, whig of the revolution, fought for liberty and independence with this gun. His descendants keep it to defend what he helped to win." His decision to join the military, however, cost him dearly. Upon returning home, he was ostracized from the Quaker meetinghouse and never recovered from the debts incurred by the family estate while he was away fighting. Though he still owned extensive property, he struggled thenceforth to meet the needs of his seven sons and five daughters.

Like Seward and Chase, young Edward revealed an early aptitude for study. Though schools in Goochland County were few, Edward was taught to read and write by his father and, by the age of eight, showed a talent for poetry. Edward was only eleven when his father's death brought an abrupt end to family life at Belmont. Left in straitened circumstances, his mother, like Chase's, sent the children to live with various relatives. Edward spent two years with his older brother Fleming Bates, in Northumberland, Virginia, before settling into the home of a scholarly cousin, Benjamin Bates, in Hanover, Maryland. There, under his cousin's tutelage, he acquired a solid foundation in the fields of mathematics, history, botany, and astronomy. Still, he missed the bustle and companionship of his numerous siblings, and pined for his family's Belmont estate. At fourteen, he entered Charlotte Hall, a private academy in Maryland where he studied literature and the classics in preparation for enrollment at Princeton.

He never did attend Princeton. It is said that he sustained an injury that forced him to end his studies at Charlotte Hall. Returning to Belmont, he enlisted in the Virginia militia during the War of 1812, armed with his father's old flintlock musket. In 1814, at the age of twenty-one, he joined the flood of settlers into Missouri Territory, lured by the vast potential west of the Appalachian Mountains, lately opened by the Louisiana Purchase. Over the next three decades, the population of this western region would explode at three times the rate of the original thirteen states. From his home in Virginia, Bates set out alone on the arduous journey that would take him across Kentucky, Illinois, and Indiana to the Missouri Territory, "too young to think much of the perils which he might encounter," he later mused, "the West being then the scene of many Indian outrages."

Young Bates could not have chosen a better moment to move westward. President Jefferson had appointed Bates's older brother Frederick secretary of the new Missouri Territory. When Edward arrived in the frontier outpost of St. Louis, Missouri was seven years away from statehood. Bates saw no buildings or homes along the riverbank, only battered canoes and flatboats chafing at their moorings. Some 2,500 villagers dwelt predominantly in primitive cabins or single-story wooden houses. When he walked down Third Street to the Market, he recalled, "all was in commotion: a stranger had come from the States! He was 'feted' and followed by young and old, the girls looking at him as one of his own town lasses, in Virginia, would have regarded an elk or a buffalo!"

With help from his brother, Bates secured a position reading law with Rufus Easton, a distinguished frontier lawyer who had served as a territorial judge and delegate to Congress. "After years of family and personal insecurity," Bates's biographer Marvin Cain writes, "he at last had a stable situation through which he could achieve the ambition that burned brightly in him." Mentored by his older brother Frederick, the lawyer Easton, and a close circle of St. Louis colleagues, Bates, too, passed his bar examination after two years of study and instantly plunged into practice. Lawyers were in high demand on the rapidly settling frontier.

The economic and professional prospects were so promising in St. Louis that the Bates brothers determined to bring the rest of their family there. Edward returned to Virginia to sell his father's estate, auction off any family slaves he would not transport to Missouri, and arrange to escort his mother and his older sister Margaret on the long overland journey. "The slaves sold pretty well," he boasted to Frederick, "a young woman at $537 and a boy child 5 years old at $290!" As for the land, he expected to realize about $20,000, which would allow the family to relocate west "quite full-handed."

Edward's attempts to settle family affairs in Virginia dragged on, complicated by the death of his brother Tarleton, a fervent Jeffersonian, killed in a duel with a Federalist. "I am ashamed to say I am still in Goochland," he wrote Frederick in June 1818, nearly a year after he had left St. Louis; it is "my misfortune rather than my fault for I am the greatest sufferer by the delay." Finally, with his female relatives ensconced in a carriage and more than twenty slaves following on horseback and on foot, the little party set forth on an exasperating, difficult expedition. "In those days," one of Bates's friends later recalled, "there were no boats on the Western rivers, and no roads in the country." To cross the wilds of Illinois and Indiana, a guide was necessary. The slow pace caused Bates to worry that Frederick would think him "a lazy or squandering fellow." He explained that if accompanied only by his family, he could have reached St. Louis "in a tenth part of the time & with 1/4 of the trouble and expense—the slaves have been the greatest objects of my embarrassment." The journey did have benefits, he reported: "Mother & Sister are more active, more healthy & more cheerful than when they started. They bear the fatigues of hot dry traveling surprisingly." And once they reached St. Louis, Bates assured his brother, he would "make up in comfort & satisfaction for the great suspense and anxiety I must have occasioned you."

As he again settled into the practice of law in St. Louis, the twenty-five-year-old Bates fully appreciated the advantages gained by his older brother's prominence in the community. In a fulsome letter, he expressed fervent gratitude to his "friend and benefactor," realizing that Fred's "public reputation" as well as his "private wealth & influence" would greatly enhance his own standing. His brother also introduced him to the leading figures of St. Louis—including the famed explorer William Clark, now governor of the Missouri Territory; Thomas Hart Benton, editor of the *Missouri Enquirer*; and David Barton, speaker of the territorial legislature and the guiding hand behind Missouri's drive for statehood. Before long, he found himself in a partnership with Joshua Barton, the younger brother of David Barton. Together, the two well-connected young men began to build a lucrative practice representing the interests of influential businessmen and landholders.

• • •

ABRAHAM LINCOLN faced obstacles unimaginable to the other candidates for the Republican nomination. In sharp contrast to the comfortable lifestyle the Seward family enjoyed, and the secure early childhoods of Chase and Bates before their fathers died, Lincoln's road to success was longer, more tortuous, and far less likely.

Born on February 12, 1809, in a log cabin on an isolated farm in the slave state of Kentucky, Abraham had an older sister, Sarah, who died in childbirth when he was nineteen, and a younger brother who died in infancy. His father, Thomas, had never learned to read and, according to Lincoln, never did "more in the way of writing than to bunglingly sign his own name." As a six-year-old boy, young Thomas had watched when a Shawnee raiding party murdered his father. This violent death, Lincoln later suggested, coupled with the "very narrow circumstances" of his mother, left Thomas "a wandering laboring boy," growing up "litterally without education." He was working as a rough carpenter and hired hand when he married Nancy Hanks, a quiet, intelligent young woman of uncertain ancestry.

In the years following Abraham's birth, the Lincolns moved from one dirt farm to another in Kentucky, Indiana, and Illinois. On each of these farms, Thomas cleared only enough land for his family's use. Lack of ambition joined with insufficient access to a market for surplus goods to trap Thomas in relentless poverty.

In later life, Lincoln neither romanticized nor sentimentalized the difficult circumstances of his childhood. When asked in 1860 by his campaign biographer, John Locke Scripps, to share the details of his early days, he hesitated. "Why Scripps, it is a great piece of folly to attempt to make anything out of my early life. It can all be condensed into a single sentence . . . you will find in Gray's Elegy: 'The short and simple annals of the poor.' "

The traces of Nancy Hanks in history are few and fragmentary. A childhood friend and neighbor of Lincoln's, Nathaniel Grigsby, reported that Mrs. Lincoln "was a woman Know(n) for the Extraordinary Strength of her mind among the family and all who knew her: she was superior to her husband in Every way. She was a brilliant woman." Nancy's first cousin Dennis Hanks, a childhood friend of Abraham's, recalled that Mrs. Lincoln "read the good Bible to [Abe]—taught him to read and to spell—taught him sweetness & benevolence as well." She was described as "beyond all doubt an intellectual woman"; said to possess "Remarkable" perception; to be "very smart" and "naturally Strong minded."

Much later, Lincoln, alluding to the possibility that his mother had come from distinguished stock, told his friend William Herndon: "All that I am or hope ever to be I get from my mother, God bless her."

In the early autumn of 1818, when Abraham was nine, Nancy Lincoln contracted what was known as "milk sickness"—a fatal ailment whose victims suffered dizziness, nausea, and an irregular heartbeat before slipping into a coma. The disease first struck Thomas and Elizabeth Sparrow, Nancy Lincoln's aunt and uncle, who had joined the Lincolns in Indiana the previous winter. The Sparrows had parented Nancy since she was a child and served as grandparents to young Lincoln. The deadly illness took the lives of the Sparrows in rapid succession, and then, before a fortnight had passed, Lincoln's mother became gravely ill. "I am going away from you, Abraham," she reportedly told her young son shortly before she died, "and I shall not return."

In an era when men were fortunate to reach forty-five, and a staggering number of women died in childbirth, the death of a parent was common-place. Of the four rivals, Seward alone kept parents into his adulthood. Chase was only eight when he lost his father. Bates was eleven. Both of their lives, like Lincoln's, were molded by loss.

The impact of the loss depended upon each man's temperament and the unique circumstances of his family. The death of Chase's father forced young Salmon to exchange the warm support of a comfortable home for the rigid boarding school of a domineering uncle, a man who bestowed or withdrew approval and affection on the basis of performance. An insatiable need for acknowledgment and the trappings of success thenceforth marked Chase's personality. Carl Schurz perceived this aspect of Chase's temperament when he commented that, despite all the high honors Chase eventually achieved, he was never satisfied. "He restlessly looked beyond for the will-of-the-wisp, which deceitfully danced before his gaze."

For Edward Bates, whose family of twelve was scattered by his father's death, the loss seems to have engendered a lifelong urge to protect and provide for his own family circle in ways his father never could. To his wife and eight surviving children, he dedicated his best energies, even at the cost of political ambition, for his happiness depended on his ability to give joy and comfort to his family.

While the early death of a parent had a transforming impact on each of these men, the loss of Lincoln's mother had a uniquely shattering impact on his family's tenuous stability. In the months following her death, his father journeyed from Indiana to Kentucky to bring back a new wife, aban-doning his two children to a place Lincoln later described as "a wild re-gion," where "the panther's scream, filled the night with fear and bears preyed on the swine." While Thomas was away, Lincoln's twelve-year-old sister, Sarah, did the cooking and tried to care for both her brother and her mother's cousin Dennis Hanks. Sarah Lincoln was much like her brother, a "quick minded woman" with a "good humored laugh" who could put anyone at ease. But the lonely months of living without adult supervision must have been difficult. When Sarah Bush Johnston, Lincoln's new stepmother, returned with Thomas, she found the abandoned children liv-ing like animals, "wild—ragged and dirty." Only after they were soaped, washed, and dressed did they seem to her "more human."

Within a decade, Lincoln would suffer another shattering loss when his sister Sarah died giving birth. A relative recalled that when Lincoln was told of her death, he "sat down on a log and hid his face in his hands while the tears rolled down through his long bony fingers. Those present turned away in pity and left him to his grief." He had lost the two women he had loved. "From then on," a neighbor said, "he was alone in the world you might say."

Years later, Lincoln wrote a letter of condolence to Fanny McCullough, a young girl who had lost her father in the Civil War. "It is with deep grief that I learn of the death of your kind and brave Father; and, especially, that it is affecting your young heart beyond what is common in such cases. In this sad world of ours, sorrow comes to all; and, to the young, it comes with bitterest agony, because it takes them unawares. The older have learned to ever expect it."

Lincoln's early intimacy with tragic loss reinforced a melancholy temperament. Yet his familiarity with pain and personal disappointment imbued him with a strength and understanding of human frailty unavailable to a man of Seward's buoyant disposition. Moreover, Lincoln, unlike the brooding Chase, possessed a life-affirming humor and a profound resilience that lightened his despair and fortified his will.

Even as a child, Lincoln dreamed heroic dreams. From the outset he was cognizant of a destiny far beyond that of his unlettered father and hardscrabble childhood. "He was different from those around him," the historian Douglas Wilson writes. "He knew he was unusually gifted and had great potential." To the eyes of his schoolmates, Lincoln was "clearly exceptional," Lincoln biographer David Donald observes, "and he carried away from his brief schooling the self-confidence of a man who has never met his intellectual equal." His mind and ambition, his childhood friend Nathaniel Grigsby recalled, "soared above us. He naturally assumed the leadership of the boys. He read & thoroughly read his books whilst we played. Hence he was above us and became our guide and leader."

If Lincoln's developing self-confidence was fostered initially by his mother's love and approval, it was later sustained by his stepmother, who came to love him as if he were her own child. Early on, Sarah Bush Lincoln recognized that Abraham was "a Boy of uncommon natural Talents." Though uneducated herself, she did all she could to encourage him to read, learn, and grow. "His mind & mine—what little I had seemed to run together—move in the same channel," she later said. "Abe never gave me a cross word or look and never refused in fact, or Even in appearance, to do any thing I requested him. I never gave him a cross word in all my life. He was Kind to Every body and Every thing and always accommodate[d] others if he could—would do so willingly if he could." Young Lincoln's self-assurance was enhanced by his physical size and strength, qualities that were valued highly on the frontier. "He was a strong, athletic boy," one friend related, "good-natured, and ready to out-run, out-jump and out-wrestle or out-lift anybody in the neighborhood."

In their early years, each of his rivals shared a similar awareness of unusual talents, but Lincoln faced much longer odds to realize his ambitions. His voyage would require a Herculean feat of self-creation. Perhaps the best evidence of his exceptional nature, as well as the genesis of his great gift for storytelling, is manifest in the eagerness with which, even at six or seven, he listened to the stories the adults exchanged as they sat by his father's fireplace at night. Knob Creek farm, where Lincoln lived from the age of two until seven, stood along the old Cumberland Trail that stretched from Nashville to Louisville. Caravans of pioneers passed by each day heading toward the Northwest—farmers, peddlers, preachers, each with a tale to tell.

Night after night, Thomas Lincoln would swap tales with visitors and neighbors while his young son sat transfixed in the corner. In these sociable settings, Thomas was in his element. A born storyteller, he possessed a quick wit, a talent for mimicry, and an uncanny memory for exceptional stories. These qualities would prove his greatest bequest to his son. Young Abe listened so intently to these stories, crafted from experiences of everyday life, that the words became embedded in his memory. Nothing was more upsetting to him, he recalled decades later, nothing made him angrier, than his inability to comprehend everything that was told.

After listening to adults chatter through the evening, he would spend, he said, "no small part of the night walking up and down, and trying to make out what was the exact meaning of some of their, to me, dark sayings." Unable to sleep, he would reformulate the conversations until, as he recalled, "I had put it in language plain enough, as I thought, for any boy I knew to comprehend." The following day, having translated the stories into words and ideas that his friends could grasp, he would climb onto the tree stump or log that served as an impromptu stage and mesmerize his own circle of young listeners. He had discovered the pride and pleasure an attentive audience could bestow. This great storytelling talent and oratorical skill would eventually constitute his stock-in-trade throughout both his legal and political careers. The passion for rendering experience into powerful language remained with Lincoln throughout his life.

The only schools in rural Kentucky and Indiana were subscription schools, requiring families to pay a tuition. Even when frontier families could afford the expense, their children did not always receive much education. "No qualification was ever required of a teacher," Lincoln recalled, "beyond *'readin, writin, and cipherin,'* to the Rule of Three. If a straggler supposed to understand latin, happened to sojourn in the neighborhood, he was looked upon as a wizzard." Allowed to attend school only "by littles" between stints of farmwork, "the aggregate of all his schooling," Lincoln admitted years later, "did not amount to one year." He had never even set foot "inside of a college or academy building" until he acquired his license to practice law. What he had in the way of education, he lamented, he had to pick up on his own.

Books became his academy, his college. The printed word united his mind with the great minds of generations past. Relatives and neighbors recalled that he scoured the countryside for books and read every volume "he could lay his hands on." At a time when ownership of books remained "a luxury for those Americans living outside the purview of the middle class," gaining access to reading material proved difficult. When Lincoln obtained copies of the King James Bible, John Bunyan's *Pilgrim's Progress, Aesop's Fables*, and William Scott's *Lessons in Elocution*, he could not contain his excitement. Holding *Pilgrim's Progress* in his hands, "his eyes sparkled, and that day he could not eat, and that night he could not sleep."

When printing was first invented, Lincoln would later write, "the great mass of men . . . were utterly unconscious, that their *conditions,* or their *minds* were capable of improvement." To liberate "the mind from this false and under estimate of itself, is the great task which printing came into the world to perform." He was, of course, also speaking of himself, of the transforming liberation of a young boy unlocking the miraculous mysteries of language, discovering a world of possibilities in the small log cabin on the frontier that he later called "as unpoetical as any spot of the earth."

"There is no Frigate like a Book," wrote Emily Dickinson, "to take us Lands away." Though the young Lincoln never left the frontier, would never leave America, he traveled with Byron's *Childe Harold* to Spain and Portugal, the Middle East and Italy; accompanied Robert Burns to Edinburgh; and followed the English kings into battle with Shakespeare. As he explored the wonders of literature and the history of the country, the young Lincoln, already conscious of his own power, developed ambitions far beyond the expectations of his family and neighbors. It was through literature that he was able to transcend his surroundings.

He read and reread the Bible and *Aesop's Fables* so many times that years later he could recite whole passages and entire stories from memory. Through Scott's *Lessons in Elocution*, he first encountered selections from Shakespeare's plays, inspiring a love for the great dramatist's writings long before he ever saw a play. He borrowed a volume of the *Revised Statutes of*

Indiana from the local constable, a work that contained the Declaration of Independence, the Constitution, and the Northwest Ordinance of 1787—documents that would become foundation stones of his philosophical and political thought.

Everywhere he went, Lincoln carried a book with him. He thumbed through page after page while his horse rested at the end of a long row of planting. Whenever he could escape work, he would lie with his head against a tree and read. Though he acquired only a handful of volumes, they were seminal works of the English language. Reading the Bible and Shakespeare over and over implanted rhythms and poetry that would come to fruition in those works of his maturity that made Abraham Lincoln our only poet-president. With remarkable energy and tenacity he quarried the thoughts and ideas that he wanted to remember. "When he came across a passage that Struck him," his stepmother recalled, "he would write it down on boards if he had no paper," and "when the board would get too black he would shave it off with a drawing knife and go on again." Then once he obtained paper, he would rewrite it and keep it in a scrapbook so that it could be memorized. Words thus became precious to him, never, as with Seward, to be lightly or indiscriminately used.

The volumes to feed Lincoln's intellectual hunger did not come cheaply. The story is often recounted of the time he borrowed Parson Weems's *Life of George Washington* from Josiah Crawford, a well-to-do farmer who lived sixteen miles away. Thrilled by this celebrated account of the first president's life, he took the book to his loft at night, where, by the light of a tallow candle, or if tallow was scarce, by a grease lamp made from hickory bark gathered in the woods, he read as long as he could stay awake, placing the book on a makeshift shelf between the cabin logs so he could retrieve it at daybreak. During a severe rainstorm one night, the book was badly soiled and the covers warped. Lincoln went to Crawford's house, explained what had happened, and offered to work off the value of the book. Crawford calculated the value of two full days' work pulling corn, which Lincoln considered an unfair reimbursement. Nevertheless, he straightway set to work and kept on until "there was not a corn blade left on a stalk." Then, having paid his debt, Lincoln wrote poems and songs lampooning "Josiah blowing his bugle"—Crawford's large nose. Thus Crawford, in return for loaning Lincoln a book and then exorbitantly penalizing him, won a permanent, if unflattering, place in American history.

A lucid, inquisitive, and extraordinarily dogged mind was Lincoln's native endowment. Already he possessed a vivid sensibility for the beauty of the English language. Often reading aloud, he was attracted to the sound of language along with its meaning—its music and rhythms. He found this in poetry, and to the end of his life would recite poems, often lengthy passages, from memory. He seemed especially drawn to poetry that spoke of our doomed mortality and the transience of earthly achievements. For clearly Lincoln, this acolyte of pure reason and remorseless logic, was also a romantic. All three of Lincoln's rivals shared his early love of books, but none had as difficult a task securing them or finding the leisure to read. In the household of his classically educated father, Seward had only to pick a book from well-stocked shelves, while both local academies he attended and Union College maintained substantial collections of books on history, logic, rhetoric, philosophy, chemistry, grammar, and geography. Chase, likewise, had access to libraries, at his uncle's boys' school in Worthington and at Dartmouth College. And while books were not plentiful where Bates grew up, he had the luxury of his scholarly relative's home, where he could peruse at will an extensive collection.

The distance between the educational advantages Lincoln's rivals enjoyed and the hardships he endured was rendered even greater by the cultural resistance Lincoln faced once his penchant for reading became known. In the pioneer world of rural Kentucky and Indiana, where physical labor was essential for survival and mental exertion was rarely considered a legitimate form of work, Lincoln's book hunger was regarded as odd and indolent. Nor would his community understand the thoughts and emotions stirred by his reading; there were few to talk to about the most important and deeply experienced activities of his mind.

While Lincoln's stepmother took "particular Care not to disturb him—would let him read on and on till [he] quit of his own accord," his father needed help with the tiresome chores of felling trees, digging up stumps, splitting rails, plowing, weeding, and planting. When he found his son in the field reading a book or, worse still, distracting fellow workers with tales or passages from one of his books, he would angrily halt the activity so work could continue. The boy's endeavors to better himself often incurred the resentment of his father, who occasionally destroyed his books and may have physically abused him.

Lincoln's relationship with his father grew strained, particularly when his last chance for schooling was foreclosed by his father's decision to hire him out. He labored for various neighbors butchering hogs, digging wells, and clearing land in order to satisfy a debt the family had incurred. Such conflict between father and son was played out in thousands of homes as the "self-made" men in Lincoln's generation sought to pursue ambitions beyond the cramped lives of their fathers.

The same "longing to rise" that carried Seward away from the Hudson

Valley brought Chase to the infant state of Ohio, and sent Bates to the Missouri Territory propelled Lincoln from Indiana to New Salem, Illinois. At twenty-two, he departed his family home with all his meager possessions bundled on his shoulder. New Salem was a budding town, with twenty-five families, three general stores, a tavern, a blacksmith shop, a cooper shop, and a tannery. Working simply to "keep body and soul together" as a flatboatman, clerk, merchant, postmaster, and surveyor, he engaged in a systematic regimen of self-improvement. He mastered the principles of English grammar at night when the store was closed. He carried Shakespeare's plays and books of poetry when he walked along the streets. Seated in the local post office, he devoured newspapers. He studied geometry and trigonometry while learning the art of surveying. And then, at the age of twenty-five, he decided to study law.

In a time when young men were apprenticed to practicing lawyers while they read the law, Lincoln, by his own account, "studied with nobody." Borrowing law books from a friend, he set about on his own to gain the requisite knowledge and skills. He buried himself in the dog-eared pages of Blackstone's *Commentaries;* he unearthed the thoughts in Chitty's *Pleadings;* he analyzed precepts in Greenleaf's *Evidence* and Story's *Equity Jurisprudence.* After a long day at one of his various jobs, he would read far into the night. A steadfast purpose sustained him.

Few of his colleagues experienced so solitary or steep a climb to professional proficiency. The years Seward and Chase spent in college eased the transition into legal study by exposing them to history, classical languages, and scientific reasoning. What is more, Lincoln had no outlet for discourse, no mentor such as Seward found in the distinguished author of *The Practice.* Nor did Lincoln have the social advantages Chase enjoyed by reading law with the celebrated William Wirt or the connections Bates derived from Rufus Easton.

What Lincoln lacked in preparation and guidance, he made up for with his daunting concentration, phenomenal memory, acute reasoning faculties, and interpretive penetration. Though untutored in the sciences and the classics, he was able to read and reread his books until he understood them fully. "Get the books, and read and study them," he told a law student seeking advice in 1855. It did not matter, he continued, whether the reading be done in a small town or a large city, by oneself or in the company of others. "The *books,* and your *capacity* for understanding them, are just the same in all places. . . . Always bear in mind that your own resolution to succeed, is more important than any other one thing."

•   •   •

I am Anne Rutledge who sleep beneath these weeds,
Beloved in life of Abraham Lincoln,
Wedded to him, not through union,
But through separation.
Bloom forever, O Republic,
From the dust of my bosom!
    —Edgar Lee Masters, *Spoon River Anthology*

At New Salem, Lincoln would take his law books into the woods and stretch out on a "wooded knoll" to read. On these forays he was likely accompanied by Ann Rutledge, whose father owned Rutledge's Tavern, where Lincoln boarded from time to time.

Ann Rutledge was, to our knowledge, Lincoln's first and perhaps most passionate love. Years after her death, he reportedly divulged his feelings for her to an old friend, Isaac Cogdal. When Cogdal asked whether he had been in love, Lincoln replied, "it is true—true indeed . . . she was a handsome girl—would have made a good loving wife . . . I did honestly—& truly love the girl & think often—often of her now."

Not a single piece of correspondence has been uncovered to document the particulars of their relationship. It must be pieced together from the recollections of neighbors and friends in the small, closely knit community of New Salem. Ann was a few years younger than Lincoln, had "Eyes blue large, & Expressive," auburn hair, and a beautiful face. "She was beloved by Every body." Her intellect was said to be "quick—Sharp—deep & philosophic as well as brilliant." New Salem resident William Greene believed "she was a woman worthy of Lincoln's love." What began as a friendship between Ann and Abraham turned at some point into romance. They shared an understanding, according to friends, that they would marry after Ann completed her studies at the Female Academy at Jacksonville.

Ann was only twenty-two in the summer of 1835. While New Salem sweltered through one of the hottest summers in the history of the state, a deadly fever, possibly typhoid, spread through the town. Ann, as well as several of Lincoln's friends, perished in the epidemic. After Ann's death, Abraham seemed *"indifferent,* to transpiring Events," one neighbor recalled, "had but Little to say, but would take his gun and wander off in the woods by him self." Elizabeth Abell, a New Salem neighbor who had become a surrogate mother to Lincoln, claimed she had "never seen a man mourn for a companion more than he did." His melancholy deepened on dark and gloomy days, for he could never "be reconcile[d]," he said, "to have the snow—rains and storms to beat on her grave." Acquaintances feared he had become "temporarily deranged," and that unless he pulled himself together, "reason would desert her throne."

Lincoln himself admitted that he ran "off the track" a little after Ann's death. He had now lost the three women to whom he was closest—his mother, his sister, and Ann. Reflecting on a visit to his childhood home in Indiana some years later, he wrote a mournful poem.

> *I hear the loved survivors tell*
> *How naught from death could save,*
> *Till every sound appears a knell,*
> *And every spot a grave.*

He "was not crazy," maintained Elizabeth Abell. He was simply very sad. "Only people who are capable of loving strongly," Leo Tolstoy wrote, "can also suffer great sorrow; but this same necessity of loving serves to counteract their grief and heal them."

Had Lincoln, like Chase, lived in a large city when Ann died, he might have concealed his grief behind closed doors. In the small community of New Salem, there was no place to hide—except perhaps the woods toward which he gravitated. Moreover, as he brooded over Ann's death, he could find no consolation in the prospect of a reunion in the hereafter. When his New Salem friend and neighbor Mrs. Samuel Hill asked him whether he believed in a future realm, he answered no. "I'm afraid there isn't," he replied sorrowfully. "It isn't a pleasant thing to think that when we die that is the last of us." Though later statements make reference to an omnipotent God or supreme power, there is no mention in any published document, the historian Robert Bruce observes—except in one ambiguous letter to his dying father—of any "faith in life after death." To the end of his life, he was haunted by the finality of death and the evanescence of earthly accomplishments.

Lincoln's inability to take refuge in the concept of a Christian heaven sets him apart from Chase and Bates. While Chase admitted that his "heart was broken" when he buried his second wife, Eliza Smith, he was convinced that "all is not dark. The cloud is fringed with light." Unlike his first wife, Kitty, Eliza had died "trusting in Jesus." He could therefore picture her in heaven, waiting for him to join her in eternal companionship.

Sharing the faith that gave solace to Chase, Bates was certain when his nine-year-old daughter, Edwa, died that she had been called by God "to a higher world & to higher enjoyment." In the child's last hours, he related, she "talked with calmness, and apparently without alarm, of her approaching death. She did not fear to die, still the only reason she gave for not wishing to die, was that she would rather stay with her mother."

Seward shared Lincoln's doubt that any posthumous reunion beckoned. When his wife and precious twenty-one-year-old daughter, Fanny, died within sixteen months of each other, he was devastated. "I ought to be able to rejoice that [Fanny] was withdrawn from me to be reunited with [her mother] the pure and blessed spirit that formed her own," he told a friend. "But, unfortunately I am not spiritual enough to find support in these reflections."

If Lincoln, like Seward, confronted the loss of loved ones without prospect of finding them in the afterlife to assuage the loss, one begins to comprehend the weight of his sorrow when Ann died. Nonetheless, he completed his study of law and received his law license and the offer to become a partner with John Stuart, the friend whose law books he had borrowed.

* * *

In April 1837, twenty months after Ann Rutledge's death, Lincoln left New Salem for Springfield, Illinois, then a community of about fifteen hundred people. There he planned to embark upon what he termed his "experiment" in law. With no place to stay and no money to buy provisions, he wandered into the general store in the town square. He asked the young proprietor, Joshua Speed, how much it would cost to buy "the furniture for a single bed. The mattress, blankets, sheets, coverlid, and pillow." Speed estimated the cost at seventeen dollars, which Lincoln agreed was "perhaps cheap enough," though he lacked the funds to cover that amount. He asked if Speed might advance him credit until Christmastime, when, if his venture with law worked out, he would pay in full. "If I fail in this," added Lincoln abjectly, "I do not know that I can ever pay you."

Speed surveyed the tall, discomfited figure before him. "I never saw a sadder face," he recalled thinking at the time. Though the two men had never met, Speed had heard Lincoln speak a year earlier and came away deeply impressed. Decades later, he could still recite Lincoln's concluding words. Turning to Lincoln, Speed said: "You seem to be so much pained at contracting so small a debt, I think I can suggest a plan by which you can avoid the debt and at the same time attain your end. I have a large room with a double bed upstairs, which you are very welcome to share with me." Lincoln reacted quickly to Speed's unexpected offer. Racing upstairs to deposit his bags in the loft, he came clattering down again, his face entirely transformed. "Beaming with pleasure he exclaimed, 'Well, Speed, I am moved!' "

Five years younger than Lincoln, the handsome, blue-eyed Speed had been raised in a gracious mansion on his family's prosperous plantation, cultivated by more than seventy slaves. He had received an excellent education in the best Kentucky schools and at St. Joseph's College at Bardstown. While he could have remained at home, enjoying a life of ease, he determined to make his way west with the tide of his restless generation. Arriving in Springfield when he was twenty-one, he had invested in real estate and become the proprietor of the town's general store.

Lincoln and Speed shared the same room for nearly four years, sleeping in the same double bed. Over time, the two young men developed a close relationship, talking nightly of their hopes and their prospects, their mutual love of poetry and politics, their anxieties about women. They attended political meetings and forums together, went to dances and parties, relaxed with long rides in the countryside.

Emerging from a childhood and young adulthood marked by isolation and loneliness, Lincoln discovered in Joshua Speed a companion with whom he could share his inner life. They had similar dispositions, both possessing an ambitious impulse to improve themselves and rise in the world. No longer a boy but not yet an established adult, Lincoln ended years of emotional deprivation and intellectual solitude by building his first and deepest friendship with Speed. Openly acknowledging the strength of this attachment, the two pledged themselves to a lifelong bond of friendship. Those who knew Lincoln well pointed to Speed as his "most intimate friend," the only person to whom he ever disclosed his secret thoughts. "You know my desire to befriend you is everlasting," Lincoln assured Speed, "that I will never cease, while I know how to do any thing."

Some have suggested that there may have been a sexual relationship between Lincoln and Speed. Their intimacy, however, like the relationship between Seward and Berdan and, as we shall see, between Chase and Stanton, is more an index to an era when close male friendships, accompanied by open expressions of affection and passion, were familiar and socially acceptable. Nor can sharing a bed be considered evidence of an erotic involvement. It was common practice in an era when private quarters were a rare luxury, when males regularly slept in the same bed as children and continued to do so in academies, boardinghouses, and overcrowded hotels. The room above Speed's store functioned as a sort of dormitory, with two other young men living there part of the time as well as Lincoln and Speed. The attorneys of the Eighth Circuit in Illinois where Lincoln would travel regularly shared beds—with the exception of Judge David Davis, whose immense girth left no room for a companion. As the historian Donald Yacovone writes in his study of the fiercely expressed love and devotion among several abolitionist leaders in the same era, the "preoccupation with elemental sex" reveals more about later centuries "than about the nineteenth."

If it is hard to delineate the exact nature of Lincoln's relationship with Speed, it is clear that this intimate friendship came at a critical juncture in his young life, as he struggled to define himself in a new city, away from home and family. Here in Springfield he would carry forward the twin careers that would occupy most of his life: law and politics. His accomplishments in escaping the confines of his barren, death-battered childhood and his relentless self-education required luck, a stunning audacity, and a breadth of intelligence that was only beginning to reveal itself.

CHAPTER 3

THE LURE OF POLITICS

IN THE ONLY COUNTRY founded on the principle that men should and could govern themselves, where self-government dominated every level of human association from the smallest village to the nation's capital, it was natural that politics should be a consuming, almost universal concern.

"Scarcely have you descended on the soil of America," wrote Alexis de Tocqueville in the year Lincoln was serving his first term in the state legislature, "when you find yourself in the midst of a sort of tumult; a confused clamor is raised on all sides; a thousand voices come to your ear at the same time, each of them expressing some social needs. Around you everything moves: here, the people of one neighborhood have gathered to learn if a church ought to be built; there, they are working on the choice of a representative; farther on, the deputies of a district are going to town in all haste in order to decide about some local improvements; in another place, the farmers of a village abandon their furrows to go discuss the plan of a road or a school."

"Citizens assemble with the sole goal of declaring that they disapprove of the course of government," Tocqueville wrote. "To meddle in the government of society and to speak about it is the greatest business and, so to speak, the only pleasure that an American knows. . . . An American does not know how to converse, but he discusses; he does not discourse, but he holds forth. He always speaks to you as to an assembly."

In an illustration from Noah Webster's *Elementary Spelling Book*, widely read in Lincoln's generation, a man strikes a heroic pose as he stands on a wooden barrel, speaking to a crowd of enthralled listeners. Behind him the Stars and Stripes wave proudly, while a poster bearing the image of the national eagle connotes the bravery and patriotism of the orator. "Who can wonder," Ralph Waldo Emerson asked, at the lure of politics, "for our ambitious young men, when the highest bribes of society are at the feet of the successful orator? He has his audience at his devotion. All other fames must hush before his."

For many ambitious young men in the nineteenth century, politics proved the chosen arena for advancement. Politics attracted Bates in Missouri, Seward in upstate New York, Lincoln in Illinois, and Chase in Ohio.

•   •   •

THE OLDEST OF THE FOUR, Edward Bates was the first drawn into politics during the 1820 crusade for Missouri's statehood. As the petition was debated in the U.S. Congress, an argument arose as to whether the constitutional protection for slavery in the original states applied to the newly acquired territories. An antislavery representative from New York introduced an amendment requiring Missouri first to agree to emancipate all children of slaves on their twenty-first birthday. The so-called "lawyer faction," including Edward Bates, vehemently opposed an antislavery restriction as the price of admission to the Union. Bates argued that it violated the Constitution by imposing a qualification on a state beyond providing "a republican form of government," as guaranteed by the Constitution.

To Northerners who hoped containment in the South would lead inevitably to the end of slavery, its introduction into the new territories aroused fear that it would now infiltrate the West and, thereby, the nation's future. For Southerners invested in slave labor, Northern opposition to Missouri's admission as a slave state posed a serious threat to their way of life. At the height of the struggle, Southern leaders declared their intent to secede from the Union; many Northerners seemed willing to let them go. "This momentous question," Jefferson wrote at the time, "like a fire bell in the night, awakened and filled me with terror. I considered it at once as the knell of the Union."

The Senate ultimately stripped the bill of the antislavery amendment, bringing Missouri into the Union as a slave state under the famous Missouri Compromise of 1820. Fashioned by Kentucky senator Henry Clay, who earned the nickname the *"Great Pacificator,"* the Compromise simultaneously admitted Maine as a free state and prohibited slavery in all the remaining Louisiana Purchase territory north of the latitude 36°30'. That line ran across the southern border of Missouri, making Missouri itself an exception to the new division.

Later that spring, Bates campaigned successfully for a place among the forty-one delegates chosen to write the new state's constitution. Though younger than most of the delegates, he "emerged as one of the principal authors of the constitution." When the time came to select candidates for state offices, the "lawyer faction" received the lion's share. David Barton and Thomas Benton were sent to Washington as Missouri's first senators, and Edward Bates became the state's first attorney general; his partner, Joshua Barton, became the first secretary of state. Two years later, Bates won a seat in the Missouri House, and two years after that, Frederick Bates was elected governor of the state.

This inner circle did not remain united for long, for tensions developed between Senators Barton and Benton. Barton's followers were primarily merchants and landowners, while Benton gradually aligned himself with the agrarian disciples of Jacksonian democracy. A tragic duel made the split irrevocable. In the course of his legal practice, Bates's partner, Joshua Barton, found proof of corruption in the office of Benton's friend and ally, Missouri's land surveyor-general, William Rector. Rector challenged Barton to a duel in which Barton was killed. Bates was devastated by the loss of his friend. He and David Barton went public with Joshua Barton's indictment implicating Benton as well as Rector. They demanded an investigation from U.S. Attorney General William Wirt, Chase's mentor and friend. The investigation sustained most of the charges and resulted in President Monroe's dismissal of Rector. The affair came to an end, but the rift between Barton and Benton never healed.

Proponents of Barton, including Bates, eventually coalesced into the Whig Party, while the Bentonites became Democrats. The Whigs favored public support for internal improvements designed to foster business in a new market economy. Their progressive agenda included protective tariffs, and a national banking system to develop and strengthen the resources of the country. The Democrats, with their base of power in the agrarian South, resisted these measures, appealing instead to the interests of the common man against the bankers, the lawyers, and the merchants.

Despite his immersion in the whirlpool of Missouri politics, an event occurred in 1823 that altered Bates's life and forever shifted his focus—he fell in love with and married Julia Coalter. Thereafter, home and family domesticity eclipsed politics as the signal pleasure of his life. His first child, named Joshua Barton Bates in honor of his slain partner, was born in 1824. Over the next twenty-five years, sixteen more children were born.

When Julia was young, family friend John Darby recalled, she was "a most beautiful woman." She came from a distinguished South Carolina family that settled in Missouri when she was a child. Her father was a wealthy man, having invested successfully in land. The husband of one of her sisters became governor of South Carolina. Another sister was married to the chancellor of the state of Missouri. A third sister married Hamilton Rowan Gamble, who served as a justice on Missouri's supreme court and wrote a dissenting opinion in the *Dred Scott* case. Despite these connections, Julia had little interest in politics. Her attentions were fully focused on her family. Her surviving letters, unlike those of Frances Seward, said nothing about the issues of the day, concentrating instead on her children's activities, their eating habits, their games, their broken bones. Her entire being, Darby observed, "was calculated to impart happiness around the domestic circle."

She succeeded in this beyond ordinary measure, providing Edward with what their friends uniformly described as an ideal home life. The enticements of public office gradually diminished in his contented eyes. When he sought and won a seat in the U.S. Congress in 1826, three years after his marriage, his pleasure in the victory was dimmed by the necessity of leaving home and hearth. Even short absences from Julia proved painful for him. "I have never found it so difficult to keep up my spirits," he confessed to her at one point when she had gone to visit friends for several days. "Indeed, ever since you left me, I have felt a painful consciousness of being alone. At court I can do well enough, but when I come home, to bed or board, I feel so utterly solitary, that I can enjoy neither eating nor sleeping. I mention these things not because it is either proper or becoming to feel them, but because they are novel to me. I never before had such a restless, dissatisfied, indefinable feeling; and never wish to have it again."

Disquiet returned a hundredfold when he departed on the lonely journey to take up his congressional seat in Washington, leaving his pregnant wife and small son at home. Writing from various taverns and boardinghouses along the way, he confessed that he was in "something of a melancholy and melting mood." There was a "magic" in her loveliness, which left him "like a schoolboy lover" in the absence of his "dear Julia." Now, after only a few weeks away, he was moved to cry, "a plague upon the vanity of petty ambition! Were I great enough to sway the destinies of the nation, the meed of ambition might be worth the sacrifice which it requires; but a mere seat in Congress as a subaltern member, is a contemptible price for the happiness which we enjoy with each other. It was always your opinion, & now I feel it to be true."

His spirits revived somewhat when he settled into a comfortable Washington boardinghouse and took his seat in Congress alongside David Crockett, James Polk, and Henry Clay. Though Bates seldom went out to parties, preferring to spend his nights reading and writing to his wife, he was thrilled, he told Julia, to spend a private evening with Henry Clay. "That man grows upon me more and more, every time I see him," he wrote. "There is an intuitive perception about him, that seems to see & understand at a glance, and a winning fascination in his manners that will suffer none to be his enemies who associate with him."

The main issues that confronted Bates during his congressional term concerned the disposition of western lands, internal improvements, and the tariff. On each of these issues, Senators Benton and Barton were antagonists. Benton had introduced a bill under which the federal government would make its lands available to settlers at a price so low that it was almost free. Cheap land, he argued, would bridle the rampant speculation that profited the few over the many. Barton countered with the claim that such cheap land would depress the entire Western economy. Bates sided with Barton, voting against the popular bill.

During the dispute over public lands, Bates published a pamphlet denouncing Benton that so angered "Old Bullion," as he was known, that the two men did not speak for nearly a quarter of a century. "My piece is burning into his reputation," Bates told Julia, "like aquafortis upon iron—the mark can never be effaced." Beyond his open quarrel with Benton, Bates got along well with his colleagues. His natural warmth and easy manner created respect and affection. Night sessions he found particularly amusing and intriguing, despite the "roaring disorder" of people "hawking, coughing, thumping with their canes & kicking about spit boxes." The hall, suffused with candlelight from members' desks, and from the massive chandelier suspended from the domed ceiling, "exhibit[ed] a most magnificent appearance."

Nonetheless, these few moments of pleasure could not compensate for missing the birth of his first daughter, Nancy. "As yet I only know that *she is*," he lamented, "I long to know *how* she is—*what* she is—who she is like . . . whether she has black eyes or gray—a long nose or a pug—a wide mouth or a narrow one—and above all, whether she has a pretty foot," for without a pretty foot, like her mother's, he predicted, she could never make "a *fine* woman."

"Oh! How I long to see & press you to my bosom," he told Julia, "if it were but for a moment. Sometimes, I almost realize the vision—I see you with such vivid and impassioned precision, that the very form developing is in my eye." In letter after letter, the physical immediacy of their relationship becomes clear. Responding to Julia's admission of her own downcast spirits, he wrote: "O, that I could kiss the tear from that cheek whose cheerful brightness is my sunshine."

Still, public life enticed him, and at the behest of his friends and supporters, Bates agreed to run for a second term. Despite his great personal popularity, he lost his bid for reelection in the wake of the great Jacksonian landslide that gave Benton and the Democrats complete control of Missouri politics. During the last days of his term, the usually soft-spoken Bates got into a heated argument with Congressman George McDuffie of South Carolina on the floor of the House. McDuffie ridiculed him personally, and Bates impulsively challenged the South Carolinian to a duel. Fortunately, McDuffie declined, agreeing to apologize for his offensive language. Years later, reflecting on the Southern "Code" of dueling, Bates's friend Charles Gibson maintained that as wicked as the code was, the vulgar public behavior following the demise of the practice was worse still. "The code preserved a dignity, justice and decorum that have since been lost," he argued, "to the great detriment of the professions, the public and the government. The present generation will think me barbarous but I believe that some lives lost in protecting the tone of the bar and the press, on which the Republic itself so largely depends, are well spent."

As the thirty-six-year-old Bates packed up his documents and books to return home, he assured Julia that he was genuinely relieved to have lost. While he loved his friends "as much as any man," he wrote, "for happiness I look alone to the bosom of my own family." Not a day passed, he happily reported, that he did not "divide and subdivide" his time by making plans for their future. He meant first of all "to take & maintain a station in the front rank" of his profession, so that he could provide for his family all the "various little comforts & amusements we have often talked over & wished we possessed."

Months and years slipped by, and Bates remained true to his word. Though he served two terms in the state legislature, where he was regarded as "the ablest and most eloquent member of that body," he decided in 1835 to devote his full attention to his flourishing law practice, rather than run for reelection. Throughout the prime of his life, therefore, Bates found his chief gratification in home and family.

His charming diary, faithfully recorded for more than three decades, provides a vivid testament to his domestic preoccupations. While ruminations upon ambition, success, and power are ubiquitous in Chase's introspective diary, Bates focused on the details of everyday life, the comings and goings of his children, the progress of his garden, and the social events in his beloved St. Louis. His interest in history, he once observed, lay less in the usual records of wars and dynasties than in the more neglected areas of domestic laws, morals, and social manners.

The smallest details of his children's lives fascinated him. When Ben, his fourteenth child, was born, he noted the "curious fact" that the child had a birthmark on the right side of his belly resembling a frog. Attempting to explain "one of the Mysteries in which God has shrouded nature," he recalled that a few weeks before the child was born, while his wife lay on the bed reading, she was unpleasantly startled by the sudden appearance of a tree frog. At the time, "she was lying on her left side, with her right hand resting on her body above the hip," Bates noted, "and in the corresponding part of the child's body is the distinct mark of the frog."

Faith in the powers of God irradiates the pages of his diary. His son Julian, a "bad stammerer from his childhood"—the family had begun to fear that "he was incurable"—miraculously began one day to speak without the slightest hesitation. "A new faculty," Bates recorded, "is given to one who seemed to have been cut off from one of the chief blessings of humanity." In return for this restoration to speech, Bates hoped that his son would eventually "qualify himself to preach the Gospel," for he had "never seen in any youth a more devoted piety." Sadly, the "miracle" did not last long; within six months Julian was stuttering again.

On rare occasions when his wife left to visit relatives, Bates mourned her absence from the home where she was both "Mistress & Queen." He reminded himself that he must not "begrudge her the short respite" from the innumerable tasks of caring for a large family. Giving birth to seventeen children in thirty-two years, Julia was pregnant throughout nearly all her childbearing years. Savoring the warmth of his family circle, Bates felt the loss of each child who grew up and moved away. "This day," he noted in 1851, "my son Barton, with his family—wife and one child—moved into his new house. . . . He has lived with us ever since his marriage in March 1849. This is a serious diminution of our household, being worried that, as our children are fast growing up, & will soon scatter about, in search of their own futures, we may soon expect to have but a little family in a large house."

The diaries Bates kept also reveal a deep commitment to his home city of St. Louis. Every year, on April 29, he marked the anniversary of his first arrival in the town. As the years passed, he witnessed "mighty changes in population, locomotion, commerce and the arts," which made St. Louis the jewel of the great Mississippi Valley and would, he predicted, eventually make it "the ruling city of the continent." His entries proudly record the first gas illumination of the streets, the transmission of the first telegraph between St. Louis and the eastern cities, and the first day that a railroad train moved west of the Mississippi.

Bates witnessed a great fire in 1849 that reduced the commercial section of the city to rubble and endured a cholera epidemic that same year that killed more than a hundred each day, hearses rolling through the muddy streets from morning till night. In one week alone, he recorded, the total deaths numbered nearly a thousand. His own family pulled through "in perfect health," in part, he believed, because they rejected the general opinion of avoiding fruits and vegetables. He agonized over the medical ignorance about the origin of the disease or its remedy. "No two of them agree with each other, and no one agrees with himself two weeks at a time." As the epidemic worsened, scores of families left the city in fear of contagion, but Bates refused to do so. To a friend who had offered sanctuary on his plantation outside of the city, he explained: "I am one of the oldest of the American inhabitants, have a good share of public respect & confidence, and consequently, some influence with the people. I hold it to be a sacred duty, that admits of no compromise, to stand my ground and be ready to do & to bear my part. . . . I should be ashamed to leave St. Louis under existing circumstances. . . . It would be an abandonment of a known duty."

Beyond commentary on his family and his city, Bates filled the pages of his diary with observations of the changing seasons, the progress of his flowers, and the phases of the moon. He celebrated the first crocus each year, his elm trees shedding seed, oaks in full tassel, tulips in their prime. So vivid are his descriptions of his garden that the reader can almost hear the rustling leaves of fall, or "the frogs . . . croaking, in full chorus" that filled the spring nights. With an acute eye he observed that plants change color with age. Meticulously noting variation and difference, he never felt that he was repeating the same patterns of activity year after year. He was a contented man.

However, he never fully abandoned his interest in politics. His passion for the development of the West led him to a major role in the River and Harbor Convention called in the late 1840s to protest President Polk's veto of the Whig-sponsored internal improvements bill. The assembly is said to have been "the largest Convention ever gathered in the United States prior to the Civil War." More than 5,000 accredited delegates and countless other spectators joined Chicago's 16,000 inhabitants, filling every conceivable room in every hotel, boardinghouse, and private dwelling. Desperate visitors to the overcrowded city even sought places to sleep aboard boats in Chicago's harbor.

Former and future governors, congressmen, and senators were there, including Tom Corwin from Ohio, Thurlow Weed and *New York Tribune* editor Horace Greeley from New York, and Schuyler Colfax of Indiana, who was chosen to serve as secretary of the convention. New York was also represented by Democrat David Dudley Field, designated to present Polk's arguments against federal appropriations for internal improvements in the states. Also in attendance, Greeley wrote, was "Hon. Abraham Lincoln, a tall specimen of an Illinoian, just elected to Congress from the only Whig District in the State." It was Lincoln's first mention in a paper of national repute.

"No one who saw [Lincoln] can forget his personal appearance at that time," one delegate recalled years later. "Tall, angular and awkward, he had on a short-waisted, thin swallow-tail coat, a short vest of same material, thin pantaloons, scarcely coming down to his ankles, a straw hat and a pair of brogans with woolen socks."

On the first day, Edward Bates was chosen president of the convention, much to his "deep astonishment," given the presence of so many eminent delegates. "If notice had been given me of any intention to nominate me for the presidency of the Convention, I should have shrunk from it with dread & repressed the attempt," Bates confided to his diary. He was apprehensive that party politics would render the convention unsuccessful and that he would then bear the brunt of responsibility for its failure. Yet so skillfully and impartially did he conduct the proceedings and so eloquently did he make the case for internal improvements and development of the inland waterways that he "leaped at one bound into national prominence." On a much smaller scale, Lincoln impressed the audience with his clever rebuttal of the arguments against public support for internal improvements advanced by Democrat Field.

At the close of the convention, Bates delivered the final speech. No complete record of this speech was made, for once Bates began speaking, the reporters, Weed confessed, were "too intent and absorbed as listeners, to think of Reporting." "No account that can now be given will do it justice," Horace Greeley wrote in the *New York Tribune* the following week. In clear, compelling language, Bates described the country poised at a dangerous crossroad "between sectional disruption and unbounded prosperity." He called on the various regions of the nation to speak in "voices of moderation and compromise, for only by statesmanlike concession could problems of slavery and territorial acquisition be solved so the nation could move on to material greatness." While he was speaking, Weed reported, "he was interrupted continually by cheer upon cheer; and at its close, the air rung with shout after shout, from the thousands in attendance." Overwhelmed by the reaction, Bates considered the speech "the crowning act" of his life, received as he "never knew a speech received before."

"The immense assembly," Bates noted in his diary, "seemed absolutely mesmerized—their bodies and hearts & minds subjected to my will, and answering to my every thought & sentiment with the speed and exactness of electricity. And when I ceased to speak there was one loud, long and spontaneous burst of sympathy & joyous gratification, the like of which I never expect to witness again."

Bates acknowledged when he returned home that his vanity had been "flattered," his "pride of character stimulated in a manner & a degree far beyond what I thought could ever reach me in this life-long retirement to which I have withdrawn." The experience was "more full of public honor & private gratification than any passage of my life . . . those three days at Chicago have given me a fairer representation & a higher standing in the nation, than I could have hoped to attain by years of labor & anxiety in either house of Congress."

With that single speech, Bates had become a prominent national figure, his name heralded in papers across the country as a leading prospect for high public office once the Whigs were returned to power. "The nation cannot afford to be deprived of so much integrity, talent, and patriotism," Weed concluded at the end of a long, flattering piece calling on Bates to reenter political life.

While Bates initially basked in such acclaim, within weeks of the convention's close, he convinced himself he no longer craved what he later called "the glittering bauble" of political success. Declining Weed's appeal that he return to public life, he wrote the editor a pensive letter. Once, he revealed to Weed, he had entertained such "noble aspirations" to make his mind "the mind of other men." But these desires were now gone, his "habits formed and stiffened to the standard of professional and domestic life." Consequently, there was "no office in the gift of prince or people" that he would accept. His refusal, he explained, was "the natural result" of his social position, his domestic relations, and his responsibilities to his large family.

• • •

SEWARD WAS NEXT to enter public life, realizing after several uninspired years of practicing law that he "had no ambition for its honors." Though resigned to his profession "with so much cheerfulness that [his] disinclination was never suspected," he found himself perusing newspapers and magazines at every free moment, while scrutinizing his law books only when he needed them for a case. He was discovering, he said, that "politics was the important and engrossing business of the country."

Fate provided an introduction to Thurlow Weed, the man who would secure his entry into the political world and facilitate his rise to prominence. Seward was on an excursion to Niagara Falls with Frances, her father, and his parents when the wheel of their stagecoach broke off, throwing the passengers into a swampy ravine. A tall, powerfully built man with deep-set blue eyes appeared and helped everyone to safety. He introduced himself as Thurlow Weed, editor of a Rochester newspaper, which "he printed chiefly with his own hand." That encounter sparked a friendship that would shape the destinies of both men.

Four years Seward's senior, Thurlow Weed could see at a glance that his new acquaintance was an educated young man belonging to the best society. Weed himself had grown up in poverty, his father frequently imprisoned for debt, his family forced to move from one upstate location to another. Apprenticed in a blacksmith's shop at eight years old, with only a few years of formal schooling behind him, he had fought to educate himself. He had walked miles to borrow books, studying history and devouring newspapers by firelight. A classic example of a self-made man, he no sooner identified an obstacle to his progress than he worked with discipline to counteract it. Concerned that he lacked a native facility for remembering names and appointments, and believing that "a politician who sees a man once should remember him forever," Weed consciously trained his memory. He spent fifteen minutes every night telling his wife, Catherine, everything that had happened to him that day, everyone he had met, the exact words spoken. The nightly mnemonics worked, for Weed soon became known as a man with a phenomenal recall. Gifted with abundant energy, shrewd intelligence, and a warm personality, he managed to carve out a brilliant career as printer, editor, writer, publisher, and, eventually, as powerful political boss, familiarly known as "the Dictator."

Weed undoubtedly sensed in the younger Seward an instinct for power and a fascination with politics that matched his own. In an era when political parties were in flux, Weed and Seward gravitated toward the proponents of a new infrastructure for the country, by deepening waterways and creating a new network of roads and rails. Such measures, Seward believed, along with a national banking system and protective tariffs, would enable the nation to "strengthen its foundations, increase its numbers, develop its resources, and extend its dominion." Eventually, those in favor of "the American system," as it came to be called, coalesced behind Henry Clay's Whig Party.

Weed's star rose rapidly in New York when, with Seward's help, he launched the *Albany Evening Journal,* first published in March 1830. The influential *Journal,* which eventually became the party organ for the Whigs (and later, for the Republicans), gave Weed a powerful base from which he would brilliantly shape public opinion for nearly four decades. Through his newspapers, Weed engineered Seward's first chance for political office. In September 1830, Seward secured the nomination for a seat in the state senate from the seventh district. That November, with Weed managing every step of the campaign, Seward won a historic victory as the youngest member to enter the New York Senate. He was twenty-nine.

Albany had nearly doubled in size since Seward had first seen it, but it was still a small town of 24,000 inhabitants. Originally settled by the Dutch, the state's capital boasted a stately array of brick mansions that belonged to wealthy merchant princes. The year before Seward's arrival, ground had been broken for the country's "first steam-powered railroad." This sixteen-mile track connecting Albany with Schenectady was "the first link in an eventual nationwide web of tracks."

The legislature consisted of 32 senators and 128 representatives, most of whom boarded in either the Eagle Tavern on South Market Street or around the corner on State Street, at Bemont's Hotel. Such close quarters, while congenial to politicians, were ill suited to families—especially those, like Seward's, with small children. Consequently, Seward decided to attend the four-month winter session alone.

"Weed is very much with me, and I enjoy his warmth of feeling," Seward confided to Frances after he had settled into Bemont's, describing his friend as "one of the greatest politicians of the age . . . the magician whose wand controls and directs" the party. Despite Weed's eminence, Seward proudly noted, he "sits down, stretches one of his long legs out to rest on my coal-box, I cross my own, and, puffing the smoke of our cigars into each other's faces, we talk of everything, and everybody, except politics." They enjoyed a mutual love of the theater and a passion for the novels of Charles Dickens and Walter Scott. Their shared ambition, for each other and their country, became a common bond that would keep their friendship alive until the end of their days.

Seward's gregarious nature was in perfect harmony with the clublike atmosphere of the boardinghouses, where colleagues took their daily meals together and spent evenings in one another's quarters gathered by the fire. "My room is a thoroughfare," he told Frances. Early in the session, he befriended an older colleague, Albert Haller Tracy, a senator from Buffalo who had served three terms in the U.S. Congress and had once been touted as a candidate for vice president. In recent years, however, a series of debilitating illnesses had stalled Tracy's political ambitions and "crushed all his aspirings." In Seward, perhaps, he found a young man who could fulfill the dreams he had once held dear. "I believe Henry tells him everything that passes in his mind," Frances Seward wrote to her sister, Lazette. "He and Henry appear equally in love with each other."

"It shames my manhood that I am so attached to you," Tracy confessed to Seward after several days' absence from Albany. "It is a foolish fondness from which no good can come." His friendship with another colleague, Tracy explained, was "just right, it fills my heart exactly, but yours crowds it producing a kind of girlish impatience which one can neither dispose of nor comfortably endure . . . every day and almost every hour since [leaving] I have suffered a womanish longing to see you. But all this is too ridiculous for the subject matter of a letter between two grave Senators, and I'll leave unsaid three fourths of what I have been dreaming on since I left Albany."

Seward at first reciprocated Tracy's feelings, professing a "rapturous joy" in discovering that his friend shared the "feelings which I had become half ashamed for their effeminacy to confess I possessed." In time, however, Tracy's intensity began to wear on the relationship. When Seward did not immediately respond to one of his letters, Tracy penned a petulant note. "My feelings confined in narrow channels have outstripped yours which naturally are more diffused—I was foolish enough to make an almost exclusive attachment the measure for one which is . . . divided with many."

Tracy's ardor would fuel an intense rivalry with Thurlow Weed. "Weed has never been to see us since Tracy came," Frances told her sister during a visit to Albany. "I am sorry for this although I can hardly account for it." Confronted with the need to choose, Seward turned to Weed, not Tracy, for vital collaboration. Although Tracy continued a cordial association with Seward, he harbored a smoldering resentment over Seward's increasing closeness to Weed. "Love—cruel tyrant as he is," Tracy reminded Seward, "has made reciprocity both the bond and aliment of our most hallowed affections." Absent that reciprocity, Tracy warned, it would be impossible to sustain the glorious friendship that they had once enjoyed.

A strange turn in Tracy's affections likely resulted from his mounting sense of distance from Seward. He transferred his unrequited love from Henry to Frances, who also was feeling distant from her husband. Though still deeply in love after ten years of marriage, Frances worried that her husband's passion for politics and worldly achievement surpassed his love for his family. She mourned "losing my influence over a heart I once thought so entirely my own," increasingly apprehensive that she and her husband were "differently constituted."

In 1832, Seward convinced Frances to accompany him to Albany for the legislative session that ran from January to March. Their quarters on the first floor of Bemont's Hotel were just below those taken by Tracy and his wife, Harriet. The two couples would often spend evenings or week-ends together, and Tracy often tagged along with Henry and Frances when his wife was on one of her frequent trips to their home in Buffalo. He joined them on walks, shopping trips, and excursions with the children. "He is a singular being," Frances confided to Lazette. "He certainly knows more than any man I ever was acquainted with." His conversation, she marveled, "reminds me of a book of synonyms. He hardly ever makes use of the same words to express ideas that have a shade of difference."

Capitalizing on Frances's hunger for companionship, Tracy insinuated himself into the private emotional world she once shared only with her husband. He spoke with her freely about his quarrels with his wife. He in-vited her into his sitting room to read poetry and study French. They talked about their battles with ill health. "I believe at present he could con-vince me that a chameleon was blue, green or black just as he should choose," Frances admitted to Lazette. Following one extended absence, Frances announced unabashedly that she was "very glad to see him as I love him very much." Though there is no indication that Frances and Tracy ever shared a physical relationship, they had entered into something that was considered, in the subtle realm of Victorian social mores, almost as shameful and inappropriate—a private emotional intimacy.

The following summer, Seward left his wife and family in Auburn to accompany his father on a three-month voyage to Europe. While his aging father's need for companionship provided a rationale for the sojourn, Sew-ard relished the opportunity to see foreign lands and observe new cultures. Father and son traveled extensively through England, Ireland, Holland, Switzerland, Italy, and France. "What a romance was this journey that I was making!" Seward recalled years later. Everywhere he went, however, his thoughts returned to America and his faith in his country's unique future.

"It is not until one visits old, oppressed, suffering Europe, that he can appreciate his own government," he observed, "that he realizes the fearful responsibility of the American people to the nations of the whole earth, to carry successfully through the experiment . . . that men are capable of self-government." He hungrily sought out American newspapers in library reading rooms, noting with regret ubiquitous reports of "malicious political warfare."

While Lincoln, Chase, and Bates would never visit the Old World, Seward, at the age of thirty-two, mingled comfortably with members of Parliament and received invitations to elegant receptions and dinner parties throughout Europe. In France, Seward spent a long weekend visiting with the Revolutionary War hero General Lafayette at his home, La Grange.

In Seward's absence, Frances corresponded frequently with Tracy. When Judge Miller noticed a letter in an unknown hand awaiting Frances on the mantelpiece, he demanded to see it. Frances did not know what to do, she explained to her sister. "I handed it to him and he very deliberately commenced breaking the seal for the purpose of reading it. My first impulse was to jump up and snatch the letter from his hand, which I did and then apologized by saying I would prefer reading it myself first. He appeared very much astonished that I should be so unreasonable."

As Tracy's letters multiplied, the deeply religious Frances began to contemplate the perilous shift in their friendship. Mortified in front of Henry, now returned from Europe, she proffered the letters, asking him to determine if Tracy was endeavoring to break their marital peace. At first Seward refused to read them, unwilling to impute such dishonorable intentions to Tracy. When a further letter arrived that caused Frances to collapse in tears, believing herself dishonored in both Tracy's and her husband's eyes, Seward resolved to confront him.

The next time the two men met in Albany, however, Seward made no mention of the delicate situation. Nor did he bring it up in the following months, for his attention was increasingly consumed by politics. Four years in the state senate had proved Seward an eloquent voice for reform. He had denounced imprisonment for debt, urged separate prisons for men and women, and pushed for internal improvements, all the while maintaining friendly relations on both sides of the aisle. It was time, Weed believed, to push his protégé toward higher office.

At the September 1834 convention in Utica, New York, Weed convinced members of the newly organized Whig Party that the young, energetic Seward would wage the best campaign for governor against the heavily favored Democrats. Seward was thrilled. Needing all the support he could gather, he did not want to risk alienating the influential Albert Tracy. Promises he had made to his wife could wait.

Brimming with high expectations in his upstart race, Seward eagerly embraced the Whig platform that promised to deliver for the nation something of the progress he had achieved for himself. Despite Weed's caution that he faced an uphill battle, his native optimism would not be dampened. The campaign, complete with slogans and songs, was a lively affair. To counter charges that the boyish, red-haired Seward was too young for high office, the Whigs offered a gallery of historical figures who had achieved greatness in their youth, including Charlemagne, Napoleon, Lafayette, Mozart, Newton, and, of course, Whig leader Henry Clay himself. Seward anticipated victory until the final votes were tallied over a three-day period in November 1834.

Defeat shook the usually buoyant Seward to the core. He began to reevaluate his present life, his marriage, and his future. Obliged to return to Albany that December for the final session of the state senate, where he was a lame duck, he fell into an uncharacteristic state of melancholy. Unable to sleep, Seward feared that his consuming ambition, which had kept him away from his wife and children for months, had jeopardized his marriage.

"What a demon is this ambition," he lamented from Albany, baring his soul in a long, emotional letter to his wife. Ambition had led him to stray, he now realized, "in thought, purpose, communion and sympathy from the only being who purely loves me." He confessed that he had thought her love only "an incident" among his many passions, when, in truth, it was "the chief good" of his life. This realization, he feared, had come too late "to win back" her love: "I banished you from my heart. I made it so desolate, so destitute of sympathy for you, of everything which you ought to have found there, that you could no longer dwell in it, and when the wretched T. [Tracy] took advantage of my madness and offered sympathies, and feelings and love such as I [never did], and your expelled heart was half won by his falsehoods. . . . God be praised for the escape of both of us from that fearful peril. . . . Loved, injured and angel spirit, receive this homage of my first return to reason and truth—say to me that understanding my own feelings, yours are not crushed."

Failing to receive an immediate reply from Frances, Seward tossed in his bed. He felt cold, clammy, and feverish. For the first time, the possibility occurred to him that his wife might have fallen out of love, and he was horrified. "I am growing womanish in fears," he admitted in a second heartfelt letter. "Tell me in your own dear way that I am loved and cherished in your heart as I used to be when I better deserved so happy a lot."

Finally, Seward received the answer he longed to hear. "You reproach yourself dear Henry with too much severity," Frances wrote. "Never in those times when I have wept the most bitterly over the decay of my young dreams . . . have I thought you otherwise than good and kind. . . . When I realized most forcibly that 'love is the whole history of woman and but an episode in the life of man' . . . even then I imputed it not to you as a fault but reproached myself for wishing to exact a return for affections which I felt were too intense." She assured him that "the love of another" could never bring her "consolation"—God had kept her "in the right path."

By return mail Seward pledged that he desired nothing but to return home, to share the family duties and read by the fireside on the long winter nights, "to live for you and for our dear boys," to be "a partner in your thoughts and cares and feelings." With Frances to support him, Seward promised to renew his Episcopal faith and attempt to find his way to God. He was "count[ing] with eagerness," he concluded, "the hours which intervene between this period and the time when that life will commence."

As Seward took leave of the many friends he had made in his four years in Albany, he decided against confronting Tracy. The day before his scheduled departure, however, a curious letter from his old friend provoked an immediate response. The letter opened with halcyon recollections of the early days of their acquaintance, when Tracy still possessed "golden dreams, of a devoted, peculiar friendship. How much I suffered," he wrote, "when I was first awakened to the perception that these were only dreams. . . . For this you are no way responsible. You loved me as much as you could . . . but it was less far less than I hoped." He explained that "this pain, this disappointment is my excuse for the capriciousness, and too frequent unkindness which I have displayed towards you."

In an emotional reply, Seward explained that Tracy misunderstood completely the nature of the "alienation" that had befallen them. "Availing yourself of the relation existing between us," Seward charged, "you did with or without premeditated purpose what as a man of honor you ought not to have done—pursued a course of conduct which but for the virtue and firmness of the being dearest to me" would have destroyed his entire family. Seward related his initial reluctance to read the letters Frances had surrendered to him; and his conclusion, after reading them, that Tracy "had failed to do me the injury you recklessly contemplated."

"Thenceforth Tracy," he wrote, "you lost that magic influence you once possessed over me. . . . You still have my respect as a man of eminent talents and of much virtue but you can never again be the friend of my secret thoughts. I part without anger, but without affection." Even at this heavy moment, Seward remained the consummate politician, unwilling to burn his bridges completely.

If Seward believed the crisis with Frances had forever muted the voice of his public ambitions with a contented domesticity, he was mistaken. No sooner had he returned to Auburn than he admitted to a friend: "It is seldom that persons who enjoy intervals of public life are happy in their periods of seclusion." Within days, he was writing to Weed, pleading with his old friend and mentor to "keep me informed upon political matters, and take care that I do not so far get absorbed in professional occupation, that you will cease to care for me as a politician."

In the summer of 1835, seeking distraction from the tedium of his legal practice, the thirty-four-year-old Seward organized a family expedition to the South. He and Frances occupied the backseat of a horse-drawn carriage, while their five-year-old son, Fred, sat up front with the coachman, former slave William Johnson. Their elder son, Gus, remained at home with his grandfather. Seward, as always, was thrilled by the journey. "When I travel," he explained, "I banish care and thought and reflection." Over a three-month period, the little party traveled through Pennsylvania and Virginia, stopping at the nation's capital on their way back. While their letters home extolled the warmth and generous hospitality extended to them by Southerners all along their route, their firsthand encounter with the consequences of slavery profoundly affected their attitudes toward the South.

At the time of their journey, three decades of immigration, commercial enterprise, and industrial production had invigorated Northern society, creating thriving cities and towns. The historian Kenneth Stampp well describes how the North of this period "teemed with bustling, restless men and women who believed passionately in 'progress' and equated it with growth and change; the air was filled with the excitement of intellectual ferment and with the schemes of entrepreneurs; and the land was honeycombed with societies aiming at nothing less than the total reform of mankind."

Yet, crossing into Virginia, the Sewards entered a world virtually unchanged since 1800. "We no longer passed frequent farm-houses, taverns, and shops," Henry wrote as the family carriage wound its way through Virginia's Allegheny Mountains, "but our rough road conducted us . . . [past] low log-huts, the habitations of slaves." They rarely encountered other travelers, finding instead "a waste, broken tract of land, with here and there an old, decaying habitation." Seward lamented: "How deeply the curse of slavery is set upon this venerated and storied region of the old dominion. Of all the countries I have seen France only whose energies have for forty years been expended in war and whose population has been more decimated by the sword is as much decayed as Virginia."

The poverty, neglect, and stagnation Seward surveyed seemed to pervade both the landscape and its inhabitants. Slavery trapped a large portion of the Southern population, preventing upward mobility. Illiteracy rates were high, access to education difficult. While a small planter aristocracy grew rich from holdings in land and slaves, the static Southern economy did not support the creation of a sizable middle class.

While Seward focused on the economic and political depredations of slavery, Frances responded to the human plight of the enslaved men, women, and children she encountered along the journey. "We are told that we see slavery here in its mildest form," she wrote her sister. But "disguise thyself as thou wilt, still, slavery, thou art a bitter draught." She could not stop thinking of the "wrongs of this injured race."

One day Frances stopped the carriage to converse with an old blind slave woman, who was at work "turning the ponderous wheel of a machine" in a yard. The work was hard, but she had to do something, she explained, "and this is all I can do now, I am so old." When Frances asked about her family, she revealed that her husband and all her children had been sold long ago to different owners and she had never heard from any of them again. This sad encounter left a lasting impression on Frances. She recorded the interview in detail, and later read it out loud to family and friends in Auburn.

A few days afterward, the Sewards came across a group of slave children chained together on the road outside of Richmond. Henry described the sorrowful scene: "Ten naked little boys, between six and twelve years old, tied together, two and two, by their wrists, were all fastened to a long rope, and followed by a tall, gaunt white man, who, with his long lash, whipped up the sad and weary little procession, drove it to the horse-trough to drink, and thence to a shed, where they lay down on the ground and sobbed and moaned themselves to sleep." The children had been purchased from different plantations that day and were on their way to be auctioned off at Richmond.

Frances could not endure to continue the journey. "Sick of slavery and the South," she wrote in her diary; "the evil effects constantly coming before me and marring everything." She begged her husband to cancel the rest of their tour, and he complied. Instead of continuing south to Richmond, they "turned their horses' heads northward and homeward." For decades afterward, indelible images of Southern poverty and the misery of enslaved blacks would strengthen Seward's hostility to slavery and mold Frances's powerful social conscience.

• • •

WHEN SEWARD RETURNED to Auburn, a lucrative opportunity beckoned. The Holland Land Company, which held more than three hundred thousand acres of undeveloped land in western New York, was searching for a manager to parcel the land and negotiate contracts and deeds with prospective settlers. The company offered Seward a multiyear contract with an annual salary of $5,000 plus a share in the profits. Though accepting the position meant he would reside for months at a time in Chautauqua County, more than a hundred miles from his family and home in Auburn, Seward did not hesitate.

He took a leave from his law firm and rented a five-bedroom house in Westfield, "more beautiful than you can have an idea," hopeful that his wife and family would join him during the summer months. In the meantime, he invited Weed's seventeen-year-old daughter, Harriet, to keep Frances company in Auburn, and to help with the two boys and their new baby girl, Cornelia, born in August 1836.

Seward soon found the land-developing business more engaging than law. The six young clerks he hired quickly became a surrogate domestic circle, though he assured Frances in his nightly letters that he missed her and his children terribly. Once more he reiterated how he yearned for the day when they would read aloud to each other by the fire. He had just finished and enjoyed three of Scott's Waverley novels, but "there are a thousand things in them, as in Shakespeare, that one may enjoy more and much longer if one has somebody to converse with while dwelling upon them." His children pined for him and the vibrant life his presence brought to the household. More than a half century later, his son Fred "so vividly remembered" one particular evening when his father read aloud from the works of Scott and Burns that he realized "it must have been a rare event."

Life in Westfield, meanwhile, settled into a pleasant routine. So long as Seward kept intact the image of his happy home in Auburn, he could fully immerse himself in new adventure elsewhere. His serenity was shattered when his little girl contracted smallpox and died in January 1837. Returning home for three weeks, he begged Frances, who had plunged into depression, to come back with him to Westfield. She refused to leave her two boys and "did not think it would be quite right to take them both from their Grandpa."

Back in Westfield, Seward wrote anxiously to Frances that the "lightness that was in all my heart when I thought of you and your sanctuary, and those who surrounded you there, was the main constituent of my cheerfulness." But now "I imagine you sitting alone, drooping, desponding, and unhappy; and, when I think of you in this condition, I cannot resist the sorrow that swells within me. If I could be with you, to lure you away to more active pursuits, to varied study, or more cheerful thoughts, I might save you for yourself, for your children, for myself."

The following summer, Frances was finally persuaded to join him in Westfield. In an exultant letter to Weed, Seward expressed his contentment. "Well, I am here for once, enjoying the reality of dreams," he wrote. "I read much, I ride some, and stroll more along the lake-shore. My wife and children are enjoying a measure of health which enables them to participate in these pleasures." He lacked but one thing to complete his happiness: "If you were here," he told Weed, "we would enjoy pleasures that would have seduced Cicero and his philosophic friends from Tusculum."

While Frances enjoyed her summer, she was unable to share her husband's great contentment. Returning to Auburn in September, she told Harriet Weed she had "found Westfield a very pleasant little village . . . but it was not my *home* and you can very well understand that I am more happy to be here—There is a sort of satisfaction, melancholy it is, in being once more in the room where my darling babe lived and died—in looking over her little wardrobe—in talking with those who missed and loved her."

By the fall of 1837, an economic slump had spread westward to Chautauqua County. This "panic" of 1837 brought widespread misery in its wake—bankrupt businesses, high unemployment, a run on banks, plummeting real estate values, escalating poverty. "I am almost in despair," Seward wrote home. "I have to dismiss three clerks; they all seem near to me as children, and are almost as helpless."

Once again, fortune smiled upon Seward in uncanny fashion. Because Democrats were blamed for the depression, the shrinking economy enlarged his party's political prospects. In the elections that fall, the Whigs swept the state. "There is such a buzz of 'glorious Whig victories' ringing in my ears," Seward wrote Weed, "that I hardly have time to think." Replying from Albany, where he was back in control, Weed was jubilant. "I have been two days endeavoring to snatch a moment for communion with you, to whom my heart always turns in joy or grief. . . . It is a great triumph—an overwhelming revolution. May that Providence which has given us deliverance, give us also wisdom to turn our power into healthful channels."

In the months that followed, Seward and Weed worked together to broaden the Whig Party beyond its base of merchants, industrialists, and prosperous farmers. Hoping to appeal to the masses of workingmen, who had generally voted Democratic since Andrew Jackson's day, Weed raised money for a new partisan weekly. Horace Greeley was chosen editor for the fledgling journal. The slight, rumpled-looking, nearsighted young Greeley occupied a garret in New York where he had edited a small magazine called *The New Yorker.* The new partisan weekly became an instant success, eventually evolving into the powerful *New York Tribune.* For nearly a quarter of a century, Weed, Seward, and Greeley collaborated to build support first for the Whigs and, later on, for the Republicans. For much of that time, the three were like brothers. If they often quarreled among themselves, they presented a united front to the world.

In the summer of 1838, Weed believed the time was right for Seward's second bid to become governor. At the Whig convention that September, "the Dictator" was everywhere, persuading one delegate after another that Seward was the strongest possible choice to top the ticket. To bolster his case, he distributed statistics from the 1834 gubernatorial race showing that, despite the Whigs' loss, Seward had claimed more votes than all the other Whig candidates. Weed's magic worked: his protégé received the nomination on the fourth ballot. "Well, Seward, we are again embarked upon a 'sea of difficulties,' and must go earnestly to work." In fact, most of the work was left to Weed, since it was thought improper in those days for candidates to stump on their own. And Weed did his job well. When the votes were counted, the thirty-seven-year-old Seward was the overwhelming victor.

Seward was thrilled to be back in the thick of things. "God bless Thurlow Weed!" he exulted. "I owe this result to him." Within a week of the election, however, Seward's nerve began to fail. "It is a fearful post I have coveted," he confided to his mentor. "I shudder at my own temerity, and have lost confidence in my ability to manage my own private affairs." Frances, pregnant with their third son, Will, had suffered weeks of illness and was nervous about the move to Albany. Confessing that he did not "know how to keep a house alone," he wondered if he could instead take up rooms at the Eagle Tavern.

Weed arrived in Auburn and immediately took charge. He secured a mansion with a full-time staff for the governor to rent, and convinced Frances to join her husband. The yellow brick house, Seward's son Fred recalled, "was in all respects well adapted for an official residence." Set on four acres, it contained a suite of parlors, a ballroom, a spacious dining room, and a library in one wing, with a suite of family rooms in another. While Seward combed through books on history and philosophy, preparing what proved to be a brilliant inaugural message to the legislature, Weed stocked the residence with wine and food, chose Seward's inaugural outfit, and met with hundreds of office seekers, eventually selecting every member of the governor's cabinet. Seward believed "it was [his] duty to receive, not make a cabinet."

During the transition period, Seward's impulsive remarks often aggravated the ever-cautious Weed. "Your letter admonishes me to a habit of caution that I cannot conveniently adopt," Seward replied. "I love to write what I think and feel as it comes up." Nonetheless, Seward generally deferred to Weed, recognizing a superior strategic prudence and experience. "I had no idea that dictators were such amiable creatures," he told Weed, no doubt provoking the approval of his proud mentor. "There were never two men in politics who worked together or understood each other better," Weed wrote years later in his memoir. "Neither controlled the other. . . . One did not always lead, and the other follow. They were friends, in the best, the rarest, and highest sense."

In later years, Seward told the story of a carriage ride he took from Albany shortly after his election. He had struck up a lively conversation with the coachman, who eventually asked him who he was. When Seward replied that he was governor of New York, the coachman laughed in disbelief. Seward said they had only to consult the proprietor of the next tavern along the road to confirm the truth. When they reached the tavern, Seward went in and asked, "Am I the Governor of the State of New York or not?" The man did not hesitate. "No, certainly not!" "Who is, then?" queried Seward. "Why . . . Thurlow Weed!" the man replied.

The youthful governor's inaugural address on New Year's Day, 1839, laid out an ambitious agenda: a vast expansion of the public school system (including better schools for the black population), the promotion of canals and railways, the creation of a more humane system for the treatment of the insane, and the abolition of imprisonment for debt. His vision of an ever-expanding economy, built on free labor, widespread public education, and technological progress, offered a categorical rejection of the economic and cultural malaise he had witnessed on his Southern trip in 1835.

"Our race is ordained to reach, on this continent, a higher standard of social perfection than it has ever yet attained; and that hence will proceed the spirit which shall renovate the world," he proclaimed to the New York legislature in the year of his election. If the energy, ingenuity, and ambitions of Northern free labor were "sustained by a wise and magnanimous policy on our part," Seward promised, "our state, within twenty years, will have no desert places—her commercial ascendancy will fear no rivalry, and a hundred cities will enable her to renew the boast of ancient Crete."

Looking once more to broaden the appeal of the Whig Party, Seward advocated measures to attract the Irish and German Catholic immigrants who formed the backbone of the state Democratic Party. He called on his fellow Americans to welcome them with "all the sympathy which their misfortunes at home, their condition as strangers here, and their devotion to liberty, ought to excite." He argued that America owed all the benefits of citizenship to these new arrivals, who helped power the engine of

Northern expansion. In particular, he proposed to reform the school system, where the virulently anti-Catholic curriculum frightened immigrants away, dooming vast numbers to illiteracy, poverty, and vice. To get these children off the streets and provide them with opportunities to advance, Seward hoped to divert some part of the public school funds to support parochial schools where children could receive instruction from members of their own faith.

Seward's school proposal provoked a violent reaction among nativist Protestants. They accused him of plotting "to overthrow republican institutions" by undoing the separation of church and state. Handbills charged that Seward was "in league with the Pope" and schemed to throw Protestant children into the hands of priests. In the end, the legislature passed a compromise plan that simply expanded the public school system. But the nativists, whose strength would grow dramatically in the decades ahead, never forgave Seward. Indeed, their opposition would eventually prove a fatal stumbling block to Seward's hopes for the presidential nomination in 1860.

If Seward's progressive policies on education and immigration made him an influential and controversial figure in New York State, his defiant stand against slavery in the "Virginia Case" brought him into national prominence in the late 1830s and early 1840s. In September 1839, a vessel sailing from Norfolk, Virginia, to New York was found to have carried a fugitive slave. The slave was returned to his master in Virginia in compliance with Article IV, Section 2, of the U.S. Constitution that persons held to service or labor in one state escaping into another should be delivered up to the owner. When Virginia also demanded the arrest and surrender of three free black seamen who had allegedly conspired to hide the slave on the vessel, the New York governor refused.

In a statement that brought condemnation throughout the South, Seward argued that the seamen were charged with a crime that New York State did not recognize: people were not property, and therefore no crime had been committed. On the contrary, "the universal sentiment of civilized nations" considered helping a slave escape from bondage "not only innocent, but humane and praiseworthy."

As controversy over the fate of the three sailors was prolonged, the Commonwealth of Virginia enacted a series of retaliatory measures to damage the commerce of New York, calling upon other Southern states to pass resolutions denouncing Seward and the state of New York for "intermeddling" with their time-honored "domestic institutions." Democratic periodicals in the North warned that the governor's stance would compromise highly profitable New York trade connections with Virginia and other slave states. Seward was branded "a bigoted New England fanatic." This only emboldened Seward's resolve to press the issue. He spurred the Whig-dominated state legislature to pass a series of antislavery laws affirming the rights of black citizens against seizure by Southern agents, guaranteeing a trial by jury for any person so apprehended, and prohibiting New York police officers and jails from involvement in the apprehension of fugitive slaves.

Such divisive incidents—the "new irritation" foreseen by Jefferson in 1820—widened the schism between North and South. Though few slaves actually escaped to the North each year—an estimated one or two hundred out of the millions held in bondage—the issue exacerbated rancor on both sides. In the North, William Lloyd Garrison's newspaper, the *Liberator,* called for immediate emancipation and racial equality, denouncing slavery as sinful and inhumane, advocating "all actions, even in defiance of the Constitution," to bring an end to *"The Empire of Satan."* Such scathing criticisms moved Southern leaders to equally fierce defenses. They proclaimed slavery a "positive good" rather than a mere necessity, of immense benefit to whites and blacks alike. As discord between North and South escalated, many Northerners turned against the abolitionists. Fear that the movement would destroy the Union incited attacks on abolitionist printers in the North and West. Presses were burned, editors threatened with death should their campaign persist.

In 1840, Seward was reelected governor, but by a significantly smaller margin. His dwindling support was blamed on the parochial school controversy, the protracted fight with Virginia, and a waning enthusiasm for social reform. Horace Greeley editorialized that Seward would "henceforth be honored more for the three thousand votes he has lost, considering the causes, than for all he has received in his life." Nonetheless, Seward decided not to run a third time: "All that can now be worthy of my ambition," he explained to a friend, "is to leave the State better for my having been here, and to entitle myself to a favorable judgment in its history."

Throughout the dispute with the state of Virginia, and every other controversy that threatened Seward's highly successful tenure, Weed had proved a staunch ally and friend, answering critics in the legislature, publishing editorials in the *Albany Evening Journal,* ever sustaining Seward's spirits. "What am I to deserve such friendship and affection?" Seward asked him in 1842 as his second term drew to its close. "Without your aid how hopeless would have been my prospect of reaching the elevation from which I am descending. How could I have sustained myself there . . . how could I have secured the joyous reflections of this hour, what would have been my prospect of future life, but for the confidence I so undenyingly reposed on your affection?"

Returning to Auburn, Seward resumed his law practice, concentrating now on lucrative patent cases. He found that his fight with Virginia had endeared him to antislavery men throughout the North. Members of the new Liberty Party bandied about his name in their search for a presidential candidate in 1844. Organized in 1840, the Liberty Party was born of frustration with the failure of either major party to deal head-on with slavery. The abrogation of slavery was their primary goal. Though flattered by the attention, Seward could not yet conceive of leaving the Whig Party.

Meanwhile, he continued to speak out on behalf of black citizens. In March 1846, a terrifying massacre took place in Seward's hometown. A twenty-three-year-old black man named William Freeman, recently released from prison after serving five years for a crime it was later determined he did not commit, entered the home of John Van Nest, a wealthy farmer and friend of Seward's. Armed with two knives, he killed Van Nest, his pregnant wife, their small child, and Mrs. Van Nest's mother. When he was caught within hours, Freeman immediately confessed. He exhibited no remorse and laughed uncontrollably as he spoke. The sheriff hauled him away, barely reaching the jail ahead of an enraged mob intent upon lynching him. "I trust in the mercy of God that I shall never again be a witness to such an outburst of the spirit of vengeance as I saw while they were carrying the murderer past our door," Frances Seward told her husband, who was in Albany at the time. "Fortunately, the law triumphed."

Frances recognized at once an "incomprehensible" aspect to the entire affair, and she was correct. Investigation revealed a history of insanity in Freeman's family. Moreover, Freeman had suffered a series of floggings in jail that had left him deaf and deranged. When the trial opened, no lawyer was willing to take Freeman's case. The citizens of Auburn had threatened violence against any member of the bar who dared to defend the cold-blooded murderer. When the court asked, "Will anyone defend this man?" a "death-like stillness pervaded the crowded room," until Seward rose, his voice strong with emotion, and said, "May it please the court, *I shall remain counsel for the prisoner until his death!*"

Seward's friends and family, including Thurlow Weed and Judge Miller, roundly criticized Seward for his decision. Only Frances stood proudly by her husband during the outburst that followed, assuring her sister that "he will do what is right. He will not close his eyes and know that a great wrong is perpetrated." To her son Gus she noted that "there are few men in America who would have sacrificed so much for the cause of humanity—he has his reward in a quiet conscience and a peaceful mind." Though

her house and children were her entire world, she never flinched when retaliation against Seward's decision threatened her family. She remained
steadfast throughout. Then in her early forties, she was a handsome
woman, despite the hard, drawn look imparted by ill health. Over the years
she had grown intellectually with her husband, sharing his passion for
reading, his reformer's spirit, and his deep hatred of slavery. Defying her
father and her neighbors, she sat in the courtroom each day, her quiet
bearing lending strength to her husband.

Seward spent weeks investigating the case, interviewing Freeman's family, and summoning five doctors who testified to the prisoner's extreme
state of mental illness. In his summation, he pleaded with the jury not to be
influenced by the color of the accused man's skin. "He is still your brother,
and mine. . . . Hold him then to be a man." Seward continued, "I am not
the prisoner's lawyer . . . I am the lawyer for society, for mankind, shocked
beyond the power of expression, at the scene I have witnessed here of trying a maniac as a malefactor." He argued that Freeman's conduct was "unexplainable on any principle of *sanity*," and begged the jury not to seek the
death sentence. Commit him to an asylum for the term of his natural life,
Seward urged: "there is not a *white* man or *white* woman who would not
have been dismissed long since from the perils of such a prosecution."

There was never any doubt that the local jury would return a guilty verdict. "In due time, gentlemen of the jury," Seward concluded, "when I shall
have paid the debt of nature, my remains will rest here in your midst, with
those of my kindred and neighbors. It is very possible they may be unhonored, neglected, spurned! But, perhaps years hence, when the passion
and excitement which now agitate this community shall have passed away,
some wandering stranger, some lone exile, some Indian, some negro, may
erect over them a humble stone, and thereon this epitaph, 'He was Faithful!' " More than a century afterward, visitors to Seward's grave at the Fort
Hill Cemetery in Auburn would find those very words engraved on his
tombstone.

While Seward endured the hostility of his hometown, his defense of
Freeman became famous throughout the country. His stirring summation
was printed in dozens of newspapers and reprinted in pamphlet form for
still wider distribution. Salmon Chase, himself a leading proponent of the
black man's cause, conceded to his abolitionist friend Lewis Tappan that he
esteemed Seward as "one of the very first public men of our country. Who
but himself would have done what he did for that poor wretch Freeman?"
His willingness to represent Freeman, Chase continued, "considering his
own personal position & the circumstances, was magnanimous in the
highest degree."

So in the mid-1840s, as Seward settled back into private life in Auburn, his optimism about the future remained intact. He had established a national reputation based upon principle and a vision of national progress. He trusted that when his progressive principles once more gained favor with the masses, he would return to public life.

• • •

ABRAHAM LINCOLN, like Seward and Bates, was drawn to politics in his early years. At the age of twenty-three, after only six months in New Salem, Illinois, he decided to run for the state legislature from Sangamon County. While it must have seemed next to impossible that a new settler who had just arrived in town with no family connections and little formal education could compete for office, his belief in himself and awareness of his superior intellectual abilities proved to be powerful motivators. Both his ambition and his uncertainty are manifest in the March 1832 statement formally announcing his candidacy on an essentially Whig platform that called for internal improvements, public education, and laws against usury: "Every man is said to have his peculiar ambition," he wrote. "I have no other so great as that of being truly esteemed of my fellow men, by rendering myself worthy of their esteem. How far I shall succeed in gratifying this ambition, is yet to be developed."

Lincoln already possessed the lifelong dream he would restate many times in the years that followed—the desire to prove himself worthy, to be held in great regard, to win the veneration and respect of his fellow citizens. "I am young and unknown to many of you," he continued. "I was born and have ever remained in the most humble walks of life. I have no wealthy or popular relations to recommend me. My case is thrown exclusively upon the independent voters of this county, and if elected they will have conferred a favor upon me, for which I shall be unremitting in my labors to compensate. But if the good people in their wisdom shall see fit to keep me in the background, I have been too familiar with disappointments to be very much chagrined." At the same time he made it clear that this try would not be his last, telling voters that only after being defeated "some 5 or 6 times" would he feel disgraced and "never to try it again."

His campaign was interrupted when he joined the militia to fight against the Sac and Fox Indians in what became known as the Black Hawk War. Mustered out after three months, he returned home shortly before the election. Not surprisingly, when the votes were tallied, the little-known Lincoln had lost the election. Despite his defeat, he took pride that in his own small town of New Salem, where he "made friends everywhere he went," he had received 277 of the 300 votes cast. This astonishing level of support was attributed to his good nature and the remarkable gift for telling stories that had made him a favorite of the men who gathered each night in the general store to share opinions and gossip. "This was the only time," Lincoln later asserted, that he "was ever beaten on a direct vote of the people." Two years later, he ran for the seat a second time. By then he had widened his set of acquaintances beyond New Salem and won easily, capturing the first of four successive terms in the state legislature. Until he joined the new Republican Party, Lincoln would remain a steadfast Whig—as were Seward, Bates, and, for a brief moment, Chase.

Lincoln's four successful campaigns for the legislature were conducted across a sparsely populated frontier county the size of Rhode Island. Young Lincoln was "always the centre of the circle where ever he was," wrote Robert Wilson, a political colleague. "His Stories . . . were fresh and Sparkling. never tinctured with malevolence." Though his face, in repose, revealed nothing "marked or Striking," when animated by a story, "Several wrinkles would diverge from the inner corners of his eyes, and extend down and diagonally across his nose, his eyes would Sparkle, all terminating in an unrestrained Laugh in which every one present willing or unwilling were compelled to take part." This rapid illumination of Lincoln's features in conversation would be observed by countless others throughout his entire life, drawing many into his orbit.

During the campaigns, candidates journeyed on horseback across "entirely unoccupied" prairies, speaking at country stores and small villages. "The Speaking would begin in the forenoon," Wilson recalled, "the candidates Speaking alternately until all who could Speak had his turn, generally consuming the whole afternoon." Nor were the contests limited to speeches on public issues. At Mr. Kyle's store, west of Springfield, a group of Democrats made a wager. " 'See here Lincoln, if you can throw this Cannon ball further than we Can, We'll vote for you.' Lincoln picked up the large Cannon ball—felt it—swung it around—and around and said, 'Well, boys if thats all I have to do I'll get your votes.' " He then proceeded to swing the cannonball "four or Six feet further than any one Could throw it."

When he moved to Springfield in 1837, Lincoln began to attract the circle of friends and admirers who would play a decisive role in his political ascent. While he worked during the day to build his law practice, evenings would find him in the center of Springfield's young men, gathered around a fire in Speed's store to read newspapers, gossip, and engage in philosophical debates. "They came there," Speed recalled, "because they were sure to find Lincoln," who never failed to entertain with his remarkable stories.

"It was a sort of social club," Speed observed. Whigs and Democrats alike gathered to discuss the events of the day. Among the members of this "club" were three future U.S. senators: Stephen Douglas, who would become Lincoln's principal rival; Edward Baker, who would introduce him at his first inaugural and become one of the first casualties of the Civil War; and Orville Browning, who would assist his fight for the presidential nomination.

Throughout his eight years in the state legislature, Lincoln proved an extraordinarily shrewd grassroots politician, working to enlist voter support in the precincts for his party's candidates. While Seward could concentrate on giving voice to the party platform, relying on Weed to build poll lists and carry voters to the polls, Lincoln engaged in every aspect of the political process, from the most visionary to the most mundane. His experience taught him what every party boss has understood through the ages: the practical machinery of the party organization—the distribution of ballots, the checklists, the rounding up of voters—was as crucial as the broad ideology laid out in the platform. The same intimate involvement in campaign organization that he displayed in these early years would characterize all of Lincoln's future campaigns.

His 1840 campaign plan divided the party organization into three levels of command. The county captain was "to procure from the poll-books a separate list for each Precinct" of everyone who had previously voted the Whig slate. The list would then be divided by each precinct captain "into Sections of ten who reside most convenient to each other." The captain of each section would then be responsible to "see each man of his Section face to face, and procure his pledge . . . [to] vote as early on the day as possible."

That same year, Lincoln and four Whig colleagues, including Joshua Speed, published a circular directed at the presidential campaign of William Henry Harrison. "Our intention is to organize the whole State, so that every Whig can be brought to the polls." To this end, the publication outlined a plan whereby each county would be divided into small districts, each responsible for making "a perfect list" of all their voters, designating which names were likely from past behavior to vote with the Whigs and which were doubtful. Committees in each district would then "keep a *constant watch* on the *doubtful voters*, and from time to time have them *talked to* by those *in whom they have the most confidence*." These committees were to submit monthly progress reports to the central state committee, ensuring an accurate survey of voters in each county before election day. Party workers could then be dispatched to round up the right voters and get them to the polls to support the Whig Party. In setting forth his campaign plan, as meticulously structured as any modern effort to "get out the vote," Lincoln did not neglect the necessity of fund-raising, asking each county to send *"fifty or one hundred dollars"* to subscribe to a newspaper "devoted exclusively to the *great cause* in which we are engaged."

· · ·

LINCOLN LIKENED his politics to an "old womans dance"—"Short & Sweet." He stood for three simple ideas: a national bank, a protective tariff, and a system for internal improvements. A state legislator could do little to promote a national bank or raise tariffs, but internal improvements, which then usually meant the improvement of roads, rivers, harbors, and railways, were largely a local matter. Many Whigs, Seward and Bates among them, spoke of improving waterways, but Lincoln had actually worked on a flatboat to bring meat and grain down the Mississippi to New Orleans; he had a flatboatman's knowledge of the hazards posed by debris and logs while navigating the Sangamon River. Nor would he ever forget the thrill of receiving his first dollar for transporting two gentlemen on his flatboat from the riverbank to their steamer, which was anchored "in the middle of the river." The experience of earning two half dollars in a single day made the world seem "wider and fairer," giving him confidence in the future.

Lincoln knew firsthand the deprivations, the marginal livelihood of the subsistence farmer unable to bring produce to market without dependable roads. He had been paid the meager wages of the hired hand. Primitive roads, clogged waterways, lack of rail connections, inadequate schools—such were not merely issues to Lincoln, but hurdles he had worked all his life to overcome in order to earn an ampler share of freedom. These "improvements" to the infrastructure would enable thousands of farming families to emerge from the kind of poverty in which the Lincoln family had been trapped, and would permit new cities and towns to flourish.

Lincoln's dedication to internal improvements and economic development was given strength, nourishment, and power, so the historian Gabor Boritt persuasively argues, by his passionate commitment "to the ideal that all men should receive a full, good, and ever increasing reward for their labors so they might have the opportunity to rise in life." Economic development provided the basis, Lincoln said much later, that would allow every American "an unfettered start, and a fair chance, in the race of life." To Lincoln's mind, the fundamental test of a democracy was its capacity to "elevate the condition of men, to lift artificial weights from all shoulders, to clear the paths of laudable pursuit for all." A real democracy would be a meritocracy where those born in the lower ranks could rise as far as their natural talents and discipline might take them.

Young Lincoln's great ambition in the 1830s, he told Joshua Speed, was to be the "DeWitt Clinton of Illinois." The pioneering New York governor had opened opportunities for all New Yorkers and left a permanent imprint on his state when he persuaded the legislature to support the Erie Canal project. In the Illinois legislature, Lincoln hoped to leave a similar imprint by way of an ambitious program of internal improvements.

During these same years, the young state legislator made his first public statement on slavery. The rise of abolitionism in the North and the actions of governors, such as Seward, who refused to fully respect fugitive slave provisions in the Constitution, led legislatures in both South and North to pass resolutions that censured abolitionism and confirmed the constitutional right to slavery. In conservative Illinois, populated by many citizens of Southern birth, the general assembly fell in line. By the lopsided vote of 77–6, the assembly resolved that "we highly disapprove of the formation of abolition societies," hold "sacred" the "right of property in slaves," and believe that "the General Government cannot abolish slavery in the District of Columbia, against the consent of the citizens."

Lincoln was among the six dissenting voices. With one other colleague who had also voted against the resolution, he issued a formal protest. This protest did not endorse abolitionism, for Lincoln believed then, as later, that the Constitution did not give Congress the power to interfere with slavery in the states where it was already established. Instead, resisting the tide of public opinion in Illinois, Lincoln proclaimed that "the institution of slavery is founded on both injustice and bad policy," and affirmed the constitutional power of Congress to abolish slavery in areas under federal control, such as the District of Columbia, though he recommended "that that power ought not to be exercised unless at the request of the people of said District."

Lincoln always believed, he later said, that "if slavery is not wrong, nothing is wrong," and he could not remember when he did not "so think, and feel." Though he was born in the slave state of Kentucky, his parents had been antislavery. Their opposition had led them to change religious congregations, and eventually, they had moved to the free state of Indiana "partly on account of slavery." Decades later, in his short autobiography written for the 1860 presidential campaign, Lincoln would describe his protest in the Illinois legislature as one that "briefly defined his position on the slavery question; and so far as it goes, it was then the same that it is now."

In these early years, however, Lincoln paid the slavery issue less atten-tion than Seward or Chase, believing that so long as slavery could be re-stricted to places where it already existed, it would gradually become extinct. He did not share Chase's professional and personal aversion to slaveowners and did not hesitate to take whatever clients came his way. In the course of his practice, Lincoln defended both slaveowners and fugitive slaves. While he hated to see fugitive slaves hunted down, he publicly crit-icized the governor of Maine when he, like Seward, refused to give up two men who had aided a fugitive slave from Georgia. For Lincoln, the consti-tutional requirements for the return of fugitive slaves could not be evaded.

Lincoln's dreams of becoming the DeWitt Clinton of Illinois collapsed when a sustained recession hit the state in 1837. Public sentiment turned against the costly and still-unfinished internal improvements system. For months, Lincoln fervently defended the system against the rising tide of criticism, likening the abandonment of the canal to "stopping a skiff in the middle of a river—if it was not going up, it *would* go down." Although his arguments fell on deaf ears, he refused to give ground, abiding by his father's old maxim: "If you make a bad bargain, *hug* it the tighter." His unwillingness to abandon the policies he had championed became self-destructive stubbornness. By 1840, the fourth year of recession, the mood in the legislature was set against continuing these projects. With funds no longer forthcoming, the improvements system collapsed. The state bank was forced to liquidate. Land values fell precipitously, and new pioneers were deterred from emigrating to Illinois.

As a vocal proponent of the system that had aggravated the state's fiscal catastrophe, Lincoln received a significant share of the blame. Though he managed to win a fourth term in 1840, he polled the least number of votes among the victorious candidates, his poorest showing since his first elec-tion. Belief in himself and his progressive agenda shaken, he resolved to re-tire from the legislature after his term was completed.

• • •

THIS FAILURE of Lincoln's political ambition coincided with a series of crises in his personal life. Despite his humor, intellectual passion, and ora-torical eloquence, he had always been awkward and self-conscious in the presence of women. "He was not very fond of girls," his stepmother re-membered. His gangly appearance and uncouth behavior did little to rec-ommend him to the ladies. "He would burst into a ball," recalled a friend, "with his big heavy Conestoga boots on, and exclaim aloud—'Oh—boys, how clean those girls look.' " This was undoubtedly not the compliment the girls were looking for. Lincoln's friend Henry Whitney provides a comic recollection of leaving Lincoln alone with some women at a social gathering and returning to discover him "as demoralized and ill at ease as a bashful country boy. He would put his arms behind him, and bring them to the front again, as if trying to hide them, and he tried apparently but in vain to get his long legs out of sight." His female friendships were confined mostly to older, safely married women.

Never at ease talking with women, Lincoln found writing to them equally awkward, "a business which I do not understand." In Stephen Vincent Benét's epic poem *John Brown's Body*, Lincoln expresses his difficulties with the fairer sex.

> . . . *when the genius of the water moves,*
> *And that's the woman's genius, I'm at sea*
> *In every sense and meaning of the word,*
> *With nothing but old patience for my chart,*
> *And patience doesn't always please a woman.*

His awkwardness did not imply a lack of sexual desire. "Lincoln had terribly strong passions for women—could scarcely keep his hands off them," said his law partner, William Herndon, who added that his "honor and a strong will . . . enabled him to put out the fires of his terrible passion." Judge David Davis, Lincoln's companion on the circuit, agreed with this assessment, noting that "his Conscience Kept him from seduction—this saved many—many a woman." Before his marriage Lincoln enjoyed close relations with young women and almost certainly found outlets for his sexual urges among the prostitutes who were readily available on the frontier.

A year after Ann Rutledge's death, Lincoln courted Mary Owens, the sister of his friend Mrs. Elizabeth Abell. Mary Owens was said to be "handsome," with dark blue eyes and "much vivacity." Well educated, she hailed from a comfortably affluent family in Kentucky and was noted as "a good conversationalist and a splendid reader."

Lincoln had met Miss Owens several years earlier when she visited her sister for a month in New Salem. In the aftermath of Ann Rutledge's death, Elizabeth Abell told Lincoln she thought the young pair would make a good match and proposed going to Kentucky to bring her sister back. Lincoln was "confoundedly well pleased" with the idea. He remembered that she was likable, smart, and a good companion, although somewhat "oversize."

When the twenty-eight-year-old Mary Owens returned to Illinois, however, a disturbing transformation had taken place. "She now appeared," he later wrote, with perhaps some exaggeration, "a fair match for Falstaff," with a "want of teeth, weather-beaten appearance," and a size unattainable in "less than thirtyfive or forty years." He tried in vain to persuade himself "that the mind was much more to be valued than the person." He attempted "to imagine she was handsome, which, but for her unfortunate corpulency, was actually true." He conjured up ways he "might procrastinate the evil day" when he had to make good on his promise of marriage, but finally felt honor-bound to keep his word.

His proposal, written on May 7, 1837, may well be one of the most curiously unappealing ever penned. "This thing of living in Springfield is rather a dull business after all," he observed of the dismal life she might share. "I am afraid you would not be satisfied. There is a great deal of flourishing about in carriages here, which it would be your doom to see without shareing in it. You would have to be poor without the means of hiding your poverty. Do you believe you could bear that patiently? . . . What I have said I will most positively abide by, provided you wish it. My opinion is that you had better not do it. You have not been accustomed to hardship, and it may be more severe than you now immagine. Yours, &c.— Lincoln."

Not surprisingly, Mary Owens turned him down. Her rejection prompted Lincoln to write a humorous, self-deprecating letter to his friend Eliza Browning, Orville Browning's wife. He acknowledged that he was "mortified almost beyond endurance" to think that "she whom I had taught myself to believe no body else would have, had actually rejected me with all my fancied greatness; and to cap the whole, I then, for the first time, began to suspect that I was really a little in love with her." He resolved "never again to think of marrying; and for this reason; I can never be satisfied with any one who would be block-head enough to have me."

Despite his disclaimer, eighteen months later, the thirty-one-year-old Lincoln became engaged to the lively and intelligent Mary Todd. The Edwards mansion on the hill, where Mary had come to stay with her sister, Elizabeth, was the center of Springfield society. Lincoln was among the many young men who gathered in the Edwards parlor, where the girls, dressed in the latest fashion, shared food, drink, and merry conversation.

To their friends and relatives, Mary and Abe seemed "the exact reverse" of each other—"physically, temperamentally, emotionally." She was short and voluptuous, her ample bosom accentuated by stays; he was uncommonly tall and cadaverous. While Mary possessed an open, passionate, and impulsive nature, "her face an index to every passing emotion," he was, even Mary admitted, a self-controlled man. What "he felt most deeply," Mary observed, "he expressed, the least." She was in her element at social gatherings, "the very creature of excitement." Vivacious and talkative, she was capable of making "a Bishop forget his prayers." While Lincoln's good nature made him "a welcome guest everywhere," one Springfield woman recalled, "he rarely danced," much preferring a position amid the men he could entertain effortlessly with his amusing stories.

For all their differences, the couple had much in common. Lincoln had always been attracted to intelligent women, and Mary was a woman of intellectual gifts who had earned "the highest marks" in school and taken home "the biggest prizes." Endowed with an excellent memory, a quick wit, and a voracious appetite for learning, she shared Lincoln's love for discussing books and poetry. Like Lincoln, she could recite substantial passages of poetry from memory, and they shared a love of Robert Burns. Indeed, four years after Lincoln's death, Mary journeyed to the poet's birthplace in Scotland, where, recalling one of her favorite poems about a lost love, she "sighed over poor 'Highland Mary's' grave."

Also, like Lincoln, she was fascinated by politics, having grown up in a political household. Among her happiest childhood memories were the sparkling dinner parties at her elegant brick house in Lexington, hosted by her father, Robert Todd, a Whig loyalist who had served in both the Kentucky House and Senate. At these sumptuous feasts, Lincoln's idol Henry Clay was a frequent guest, along with members of Congress, cabinet members, governors, and foreign ministers. Mesmerized by their discussions, Mary became, her sisters recalled, "a violent little Whig," convinced that she was "destined to be the wife of some future President."

Undoubtedly, Mary told Lincoln of her many personal contacts with Clay, including how she once proudly rode her new pony to the statesman's house. And she shared with him a vital interest in the political struggles of the day. "I suppose like the rest of us *Whigs*," she wrote a close friend in 1840, "you have been rejoicing in the recent election of Gen [William Henry] Harrison, a cause that has excited such deep interest in the nation and one of such vital importance to our prosperity—This fall I became quite a *politician*, rather an unladylike profession, yet at such a *crisis*, whose heart could remain untouched while the energies of all were called in question?" Lincoln was deeply engaged at the same time in "the *great cause*" of electing the "Old hero."

Beyond their love of poetry and politics, Mary and Abraham had both lost their mothers at an early age. Mary was only six when her thirty-one-year-old mother, Eliza Parker Todd, died giving birth to her seventh child. Eliza's death, unlike the death of Nancy Hanks, did not disrupt the physical stability of the household. The Todd slaves continued to cook the meals, care for the children, fetch the wood, bank the fires, and drive the carriages as they had always done. If Lincoln was fortunate in his father's choice of a second wife, however, Mary's loss was aggravated by her father's remarriage. Elizabeth Humphreys, a severe stepmother with cold blue eyes, gave birth to nine additional children, openly preferring her brood of Todds to the original clan. From the moment her stepmother moved in, Mary later recalled, her childhood turned "desolate." Henceforth, she lamented, her only real home was the boarding school to which she was exiled at the age of fourteen.

This estrangement, combined with a family history of mental instability and a tendency toward severe migraines, produced in Mary what one friend described as "an emotional temperament much like an April day, sunning all over with laughter one moment, the next crying as though her heart would break." She could be affectionate, generous, and optimistic one day; vengeful, depressed, and irritable the next. In the colloquial language of her friends, she was "either in the garret or cellar." In either mood, she needed attention, something the self-contained Lincoln was not always able to provide.

As their courtship proceeded, the very qualities that had first attracted the couple to each other may have become sources of conflict. Initially drawn to Mary by her ability to command any gathering with her intense energy, Lincoln may well have determined that this reflected a tiresome and compulsive need. Mary may have come to define Lincoln's patience and objectivity as aloofness and inconsiderateness. We know only that at some point in the winter of 1840–41, as they approached marriage, a break occurred in their relationship.

While the inner lives of men and women living long ago are never easy to recover, the difficulty is compounded here by the absence of intimate letters between Mary and Abraham. Seward, Chase, and Bates disclosed their deepest feelings in their diaries and letters, but not a single letter survives from the days of the Lincolns' courtship, and only a precious few remain from the years of their marriage. While the emotional lives of Lincoln's rivals still seem alive to us more than a century and a half after their deaths, the truth about Lincoln's courtship is harder to recapture. Inevitably, in the vacuum created by the absence of documents, gossip and speculation flourish.

Mary may have precipitated the break, influenced by the objections of her sister, Elizabeth, and her brother-in-law, Ninian Edwards, who believed she was marrying beneath her. Elizabeth warned Mary that she did not think that "Mr. L. & [she] were Suitable to Each other." The couple considered that Mary and Abraham's "natures, mind—Education—raising

&c were So different they Could not live happy as husband & wife." Mary had other suitors, including Edwin Webb, a well-to-do widower; Stephen Douglas, the up-and-coming Democratic politician; and, as Mary wrote her friend, Mercy Ann Levering, "an agreeable lawyer & grandson of *Patrick Henry—what an honor!*" Still, she insisted, "I love him not, & my hand will never be given, where my heart is not." With several good men to choose from, Mary may have decided she needed time to think through her family's pointed reservations about Lincoln.

Far more likely, Lincoln's own misgivings prompted a retreat from this second engagement. Though physically attracted to Mary, he seemed to question the strength of his love for her as he approached a final commitment. Joshua Speed recalled that "in the winter of 40 & 41," Lincoln "was very unhappy about his engagement to [Mary]—Not being entirely satisfied that his *heart* was going with his hand." Speed's choice of the same phrase that Mary used suggests that it must have been a common expression to indicate an embrace of marriage without the proper romantic feelings. "How much [Lincoln] suffered," Speed recalled, "none Know so well as myself—He disclosed his whole heart to me."

Recent scholarship has suggested that Lincoln's change of heart was influenced by his affection for Ninian Edwards's cousin Matilda Edwards, who had come to spend the winter in Springfield. "A lovelier girl I never saw," Mary herself conceded upon first meeting Matilda. Orville Browning traced Lincoln's "aberration of mind" to the predicament in which he found himself: "engaged to Miss Todd, and in love with Miss Edwards, and his conscience troubled him dreadfully for the supposed injustice he had done, and the supposed violation of his word." While there is no evidence that Lincoln ever made his feelings known to Matilda, Browning's observation is supported by an acquaintance's letter describing the complicated situation. Though Lincoln was committed to Mary, Springfield resident Jane Bell observed, he could "never bear to leave Miss Edward's side in company." He thought her so perfect that if "he had it in his power he would not have one feature in her face altered." His indiscreet behavior drew criticism from his friends, Bell claimed, who "thought he was acting very wrong and very imprudently and told him so and he went crazy on the strength of it."

Possibly, Lincoln's infatuation with Matilda was merely a distraction from the anxiety surrounding his impending marriage to Mary. According to Elizabeth Edwards, Lincoln was apprehensive about "his ability and Capacity to please and support a wife," and doubtful about the institution of marriage itself. He likely feared that a wife and family would undermine his concentration and purpose. He would be responsible for the life and happiness of a woman accustomed to wealth and luxury; he would be unable to read late into the nights, pursuing new knowledge and the mastery of law and politics.

His fear that marriage might hinder his career was a common one. The uncertainties of establishing a legal practice in the new-market economy of the mid-nineteenth century caused many young lawyers to delay wedlock, driving up the marriage age. The Harvard law professor Joseph Story is famously quoted as saying that the law "is a jealous mistress, and requires a long and constant courtship." What applied to the law applied still more to politics. For Lincoln, struggling to establish himself in both, marriage must have presented pitfalls for his enormous ambitions.

Lincoln drafted a letter to Mary ending the engagement. He asked Speed to deliver it, but Speed refused, warning that he should talk to her instead, for "once put your words in writing and they Stand as a living & eternal Monument against you." Lincoln did go to see Mary and, according to Speed, told her that he did not love her. As soon as she began to weep, he lost his nerve. "To tell you the truth Speed, it was too much for me. I found the tears trickling down my own cheeks. I caught her in my arms and kissed her." The engagement was temporarily renewed, and Lincoln was forced into another meeting to sever the engagement. This second confrontation left him devastated—both because he had hurt Mary and because he had long held his "ability to keep [his] resolves when they are made . . . as the only, or at least the chief, gem of [his] character."

• • •

DURING THIS GRIM WINTER, sorrows came to Lincoln "not single spies/But in battalions." Joshua Speed announced his intention to return in a few months' time to his family's plantation in Louisville, Kentucky. Speed's father had died, and he felt responsible for his grieving mother. On January 1, 1841, he sold his interest in the general store where he had lived and worked for seven years. Speed's departure would bring an end to the pleasant evenings around the fireplace, where the young men of Springfield had gathered to discuss politics. More discouraging for Lincoln, Speed's departure meant the loss of the one friend to whom he had opened his heart in free and easy communion. "I shall be verry lonesome without you," Lincoln told Speed. "How miserably things seem to be arranged in this world. If we have no friends, we have no pleasure; and if we have them, we are sure to lose them, and be doubly pained by the loss."

The awkward dissolution of his engagement to Mary and the anticipated loss of his best friend combined with the collapse of the internal improvement projects and the consequent damage to his reputation to induce a state of mourning that deepened for weeks. He stopped attending the legislature and withdrew from the lively social life he had enjoyed. His friends worried that he was suicidal. According to Speed, "Lincoln went Crazy—had to remove razors from his room—take away all Knives and other such dangerous things—&c—it was terrible." He was "delirious to the extent of not knowing what he was doing," Orville Browning recalled, and for a period of time was incapable of talking coherently. "Poor L!" James Conkling wrote to his future wife, Mercy Ann Levering; "he is reduced and emaciated in appearance and seems scarcely to possess strength enough to speak above a whisper. His case at present is truly deplorable."

In Lincoln's time, this combination of symptoms—feelings of hopelessness and listlessness, thoughts of death and suicide—was called hypochondriasis ("the hypo") or "the vapours." Its source was thought to be in the hypochondria, that portion of the abdomen which was then considered the seat of emotions, containing the liver, gallbladder, and spleen. Treatment for the liver and digestive system was recommended.

"I have, within the last few days, been making a most discreditable exhibition of myself in the way of hypochondriaism," Lincoln confessed to his law partner and friend John Stuart on January 20, 1841. Desperately, he sought a post office job for Dr. Anson Henry, who would leave Springfield if the job did not materialize. His presence, Lincoln told Stuart, was "necessary to my existence."

Three days later, Lincoln wrote Stuart again. "I am now the most miserable man living. If what I feel were equally distributed to the whole human family, there would not be one cheerful face on the earth. Whether I shall ever be better I can not tell; I awfully forebode I shall not. To remain as I am is impossible; I must die or be better, it appears to me."

Hoping medical treatment might assuage his sorrow, Lincoln consulted not only Dr. Henry but Dr. Daniel Drake at the medical college in Cincinnati; Drake was perhaps the most eminent medical scientist in the West. Lincoln described his condition at length in a letter and asked for counsel. The doctor wisely replied that he could not offer a diagnosis for Lincoln "without a personal interview."

Throughout the nadir of Lincoln's depression, Speed stayed at his friend's side. In a conversation both men would remember as long as they lived, Speed warned Lincoln that if he did not rally, he would most certainly die. Lincoln replied that he was more than willing to die, but that he had "done nothing to make any human being remember that he had lived, and that to connect his name with the events transpiring in his day and generation and so impress himself upon them as to link his name with something that would redound to the interest of his fellow man was what he desired to live for."

Even in this moment of despair, the strength of Lincoln's desire to engrave his name in history carried him forward. Like the ancient Greeks, Lincoln seemed to believe that "ideas of a person's worth are tied to the way others, both contemporaries and future generations, perceive him." Unable to find comfort in the idea of a literal afterlife in heaven, he found consolation in the conviction that in the memories of others, some part of us remains alive. "To see memory as the essence of life came naturally to Lincoln," Robert Bruce observes, for he was a man who "seemed to live most intensely through the process of thought, the expression of thought, and the exchange of thought with others." Indeed, in a poem inspired by a visit to his childhood home, Lincoln emphasized the centrality of memory, which he described as "thou midway world/'Twixt Earth and paradise."

Fueled by his resilience, conviction, and strength of will, Lincoln gradually recovered from his depression. He understood, he told Speed later, that in times of anxiety it is critical to "avoid being *idle*," that *"business and conversation of friends"* were necessary to give the mind "rest from that *intensity* of thought, which will some times wear the sweetest idea threadbare and turn it to the bitterness of death." He returned to his law practice and his duties in the legislature, resuming his work on behalf of the Whig Party. That summer of 1841, he remedied the absence of good conversation and intimate friendship with a monthlong visit to Speed in Kentucky. The following February, he delivered an eloquent address to a temperance society in Springfield. This speech not only revealed a man in full command of his powers; it illustrated Lincoln's masterful approach to leadership: he counseled temperance advocates that if they continued to denounce the dram seller and the drinker in "thundering tones of anathema and denunciation," nothing would be accomplished. Far better to employ the approach of "erring man to an erring brother," guided by the old adage that a "drop of honey catches more flies than a gallon of gall."

Mental health, contemporary psychiatrists tell us, consists of the ability to adapt to the inevitable stresses and misfortunes of life. It does not mean freedom from anxiety and depression, but only the ability to cope with these afflictions in a healthy way. "An outstanding feature of successful adaptation," writes George Vaillant, "is that it leaves the way open for future growth." Of course, Abraham Lincoln's capacity for growth would prove enormous.

In the same month that he delivered his temperance address, Lincoln reported to Speed that he was "quite clear of the hypo" and "even better than I was along in the fall." So long as he remained unsure of his feelings, however, he kept himself apart from Mary. During the long months of their separation, Mary missed him tremendously. In a letter to a friend she lamented that she had been "much alone of late," having not seen Lincoln "in the gay world for months."

She whimsically considered taking up Lyman Trumbull—a former beau of her friend Mercy Ann—a Democrat who was then serving as secretary of state for Illinois. "I feel much disposed in your absence, to lay in my *claims*, as he is talented & agreeable & sometimes *countenances* me," she told Mercy Ann. But in fact, she had no serious desire to take up with someone else, so long as Lincoln remained a possibility. Her patience paid off. During the summer of 1842, after the couple had gone nearly eighteen months without personal contact, mutual friends conspired to bring Mary and Abraham back together.

This time around, thanks in part to the wise counsel Lincoln had provided Speed regarding his friend's tortured love affair with a young woman he had met in Kentucky, Lincoln recognized in his own forebodings "the worst sort of nonsense." Learning that Speed was plagued with doubts following his betrothal to Fanny Henning, Lincoln labored to convince him that he truly loved the young woman. The problem, he told Speed, was simply an unrealistic expectation of what love was supposed to be like. Speaking of himself as well, Lincoln rhapsodized: "It is the peculiar misfortune of both you and me, to dream dreams of Elysium far exceeding all that any thing earthly can realize." Indeed, Lincoln mused, had he understood his own muddled courtship as well as he understood Speed's, he might have "sailed through clear."

His doubts about marriage beginning to fade, he searched for final reassurance from his newly married friend. " 'Are you now, in *feeling* as well as in *judgement*, glad you are married as you are?' From any body but me, this would be an impudent question not to be tolerated; but I know you will pardon it in me. Please answer it quickly as I feel impatient to know." Assured that his closest friend had survived the ordeal of marriage and was, in fact, very happy, Lincoln summoned the courage to renew his commitment to Mary.

On the evening of November 4, 1842, before a small group of friends and relatives in the parlor of the Edwards mansion, Abraham Lincoln and Mary Todd were married. "Nothing new here," Lincoln wrote a friend a week later, "except my marrying, which to me, is a matter of profound wonder." Three days short of nine months after the marriage, a son,

Robert Todd, was born to the Lincolns, to be followed three years later by a second son, Edward.

· · ·

LOOKING BACK to the winter of Lincoln's discontent, there is little doubt that he suffered what would later be called an incapacitating depression. While biographers have rightly looked to the twin losses of Mary Todd and Joshua Speed to explain Lincoln's descent into depression, less attention has been paid to the blow he must have suffered with the seeming disintegration of the political dreams that had sustained him for so many years. Manifestations of despair after Ann Rutledge's death had been awful to endure, but this episode was compounded by the shadow of a damaged reputation and diminished hope for the future.

Conscious of his superior powers and the extraordinary reach of his mind and sensibilities, Lincoln had feared from his earliest days that these qualities would never find fulfillment or bring him recognition among his fellows. Periodically, when the distance between his lofty ambition and the reality of his circumstances seemed unbridgeable, he was engulfed by tremendous sadness. If he rarely spoke of his inner feelings, he often expressed emotions through the poetry he admired. Gray's "Elegy," which Lincoln quoted in his small autobiography to explain his attitude toward his childhood poverty, asserts that "Full many a flower is born to blush unseen/And waste its sweetness on the desert air." The poet laments a dead young villager of immense but untapped talent. "Here rests his head upon the lap of earth/A youth to fortune and to fame unknown/Fair Science frowned not on his humble birth/And Melancholy marked him for her own." Lincoln's life had been a continuing struggle to escape such a destiny. In that troubling winter of 1841, he must have felt, at least for the moment, that his long struggle had been fruitless.

Some students of Lincoln have suggested that he suffered from chronic depression. One confusion in making this designation is the interchangeable use of the terms "sadness," "melancholy," and "depression." To be sure, Lincoln was a melancholy man. "His melancholy dript from him as he walked," said his law partner, William Herndon, an observation echoed by dozens of others. "No element of Mr. Lincoln's character was so marked, obvious and ingrained as his mysterious and profound melancholy," recalled Henry Whitney. "This melancholy was stamped on him while in the period of his gestation. It was part of his nature and could no more be shaken off than he could part with his brains."

At times Lincoln's melancholy signaled a withdrawal to the solitude of thought. As a child, he would retreat from others to read. In later life, he would work a problem through in private—whether a proof of Euclidean geometry or the meaning of the Declaration of Independence. Only when he had resolved the problems and issues in his own mind did he display the results of his private meditations. It is little wonder that others saw these withdrawals as evidence of melancholy. Furthermore, the very contours of Lincoln's face in repose lent him a sorrowful aspect. One observer remarked that "his face was about the saddest I ever looked upon." Another contemporary described his face as "slightly wrinkled about the brows, but not from trouble. It was intense, constant thought that planted the wrinkles there."

Unlike depression, melancholy does not have a specific cause. It is an aspect of temperament, perhaps genetically based. One may emerge from the hypo, as Lincoln did, but melancholy is an indelible part of one's nature. Lincoln understood this: "a tendency to melancholly," he told Joshua's sister, Mary, "is a misfortune not a fault."

"Melancholy," writes the modern novelist Thomas Pynchon, "is a far richer and more complex ailment than simple depression. There is a generous amplitude of possibility, chances for productive behavior, even what may be identified as a sense of humor." And, as everyone connected with Lincoln testified, he was an extraordinarily funny man. "When he first came among us," wrote a Springfield friend, "his wit & humor boiled over." When he told his humorous stories, Henry Whitney marveled, "he emerged from his cave of gloom and came back, like one awakened from sleep, to the world in which he lived, again." His storytelling, Speed believed, was "necessary to his very existence—Most men who have been great students such as he was in their hours of idleness have taken to the bottle, to cards or dice—He had no fondness for any of these—Hence he sought relaxation in anecdotes." Lincoln himself recognized that humor was an essential aspect of his temperament. He laughed, he explained, so he did not weep. He saw laughter as the "joyous, universal evergreen of life." His stories were intended "to whistle off sadness."

Modern psychiatry regards humor as probably the most mature and healthy means of adapting to melancholy. "Humor, like hope, permits one to focus upon and to bear what is too terrible to be borne," writes George Valliant. "Humor can be marvelously therapeutic," adds another observer. "It can deflate without destroying; it can instruct while it entertains; it saves us from our pretensions; and it provides an outlet for feeling that expressed another way would be corrosive."

The melancholy stamped on Lincoln's nature derived in large part from an acute sensitivity to the pains and injustices he perceived in the world. He was uncommonly tenderhearted. He once stopped and tracked back half a mile to rescue a pig caught in a mire—not because he loved the pig, recollected a friend, "just to take a pain out of his own mind." When his schoolmates tortured turtles by placing hot coals on their backs to see them wriggle, he told them "it was wrong." He refused to hunt animals, which ran counter to frontier mores. After he had broken with Mary, he wrote that the only thing that kept him from happiness was "the never-absent idea" that he had caused Mary to suffer.

Lincoln's abhorrence of hurting another was born of more than simple compassion. He possessed extraordinary empathy—the gift or curse of putting himself in the place of another, to experience what they were feeling, to understand their motives and desires. The philosopher Adam Smith described this faculty: "By the imagination we place ourselves in his situation . . . we enter as it were into his body and become in some measure him." This capacity Smith saw as "the source of our fellow-feeling for the misery of others . . . by changing places in fancy with the sufferer . . . we come either to conceive or to be affected by what he feels." In a world environed by cruelty and injustice, Lincoln's remarkable empathy was inevitably a source of pain. His sensibilities were not only acute, they were raw. "With his wealth of sympathy, his conscience, and his unflinching sense of justice, he was predestined to sorrow," observed Helen Nicolay, whose father would become Lincoln's private secretary.

Though Lincoln's empathy was at the root of his melancholy, it would prove an enormous asset to his political career. "His crowning gift of political diagnosis," suggested Nicolay, "was due to his sympathy . . . which gave him the power to forecast with uncanny accuracy what his opponents were likely to do." She described how, after listening to his colleagues talk at a Whig Party caucus, Lincoln would cast off his shawl, rise from his chair, and say: "From your talk, I gather the Democrats will do so and so . . . I should do so and so to checkmate them." He proceeded to outline all "the moves for days ahead; making them all so plain that his listeners wondered why they had not seen it that way themselves." Such capacity to intuit the inward feelings and intentions of others would be manifest throughout his career.

• • •

LINCOLN'S FEARS that marriage might hinder his ambitions proved unfounded. He and Mary eventually settled in a comfortable frame house at the corner of Eighth and Jackson, within easy walking distance of his law office. For the first time, he enjoyed the security and warmth of a family circle, without neglecting his devotion to reading, studying, traveling on the legal circuit, and cultivating politics. While the marriage was tumultuous at times, it provided Lincoln with a protected harbor from which he could come and go as he pleased while he continued his lifelong quest to become an educated person.

The adjustment to married life was harder for Mary than for her husband. Raised in a Southern mansion attended by slaves, she had never had to cook a meal, scrub the floor, chop wood, or pump water from the well. Nor, while living with her sister in the finest house in Springfield, had she ever worried about money, or hesitated before inviting friends for dinner parties and receptions. Now she was confronted with the innumerable chores of running a household when the money Lincoln earned barely covered living expenses. Though Lincoln helped with the marketing and the dishes and insisted, even in the leanest years of his practice, that she hire a maid to help with the children, most household tasks fell on Mary's shoulders.

Certainly such "hardships" were not shared by the wives of Lincoln's later rivals. When Julia Coalter married Edward Bates, her husband had upward of twenty slaves to nurse the children, clean the house, plant the vegetables, cook the meals, and drive the carriages. After Bates emancipated his slaves in the 1850s, several remained with the family as freedmen and women, while additional servants were found among the Irish and German immigrants in St. Louis. For Frances Seward, there was never a time when she was left alone to handle household chores. When she and Seward agreed to live in her father's Auburn estate, she inherited the faithful servants who had worked in the big house for decades. As governor, Seward was supplied with an experienced staff of household servants; while in Washington, he maintained a live-in staff to accommodate and entertain the endless stream of guests at dinner parties and receptions. When Frances suffered from migraine headaches, she could take to her bed without worrying that the domestic work would be left undone.

It was not simply Mary's relative poverty that made her early married life difficult. Both she and Lincoln had essentially detached themselves from their previous lives, cutting themselves off from parents and relatives and thereby creating a domestic lifestyle closer to the "nuclear family" of a later age than the extended family still common in the mid-nineteenth century. When Lincoln was away, Mary was left alone to deal with her terror of thunderstorms, her worries over the children's illnesses, and her spells of depression. Too proud to let her Springfield sisters know the difficulties she faced in these early years—particularly after the disapproval they had voiced over her choice of husband—Mary struggled stoically and proudly on her own.

Once again, her isolation stands in stark contrast to the familial support enjoyed by Frances Seward and Julia Bates. Frances could depend on the companionship not only of her widowed father but of three generations of women living in the same household—her favorite aunt, Cornelia; her sister and closest friend, Lazette, who spent months at a time in the Auburn house; and her beloved daughter, Fanny. Likewise, Julia Bates was surrounded by her children, several of whom continued to live with the family even after they married; and by her parents; her sisters; her brothers; and her husband's mother, all of whom lived nearby.

If Mary's solitary life with her husband brought hardship, the birth of two sons within the first forty months of their marriage brought great happiness. Both boys were high-spirited, intelligent, and dearly loved by their parents. In later years, Mary proudly noted that Lincoln was "the kindest—most tender and loving husband & father in the world. . . . Said to me always when I asked him for any thing—You know what you want—go and get it. He never asked me if it was necessary."

He was, by all accounts, a gentle and indulgent father who regularly took the boys on walks around the neighborhood, played with them in the house, and brought them to his office while he worked. While Herndon believed that Lincoln was too indulgent, that the children "litterally ran over him," leaving him "powerless to withstand their importunities," Lincoln maintained that children should be allowed to grow up without a battery of rules and restrictions. "It is my pleasure that my children are free—happy and unrestrained by paternal tyrrany," Mary recalled his saying. "Love is the chain whereby to lock a child to its parent."

• • •

WHEN, AT LAST, Illinois began to emerge from recession, Lincoln's hopes for a future in politics revived. "Now if you should hear any one say that Lincoln don't want to go to Congress," he wrote a friend three months after his marriage, "tell him . . . he is mistaken." His objective was the Seventh Congressional District—including Sangamon County— where the Whigs had a majority in a state that was otherwise solidly Democratic.

Lincoln's first goal was to win the endorsement of the Sangamon County Convention, which would appoint delegates to the congressional district nominating convention. The convention system had just been adopted by the Whigs to unify party members in the general election. "That 'union is strength' is a truth that has been known, illustrated and declared, in various ways and forms in all ages of the world," said Lincoln in support of the new system, pointing out that "he whose wisdom surpasses that of all philosophers, has declared that 'a house divided against itself cannot stand.' " Much later, of course, he would famously widen the application of this same biblical phrase beyond Sangamon County Whigs to the nation as a whole.

Lincoln's adversary in his home county was Edward Baker, a close friend after whom he named his second-born son. Despite a vigorous campaign, Lincoln fell short by a narrow margin. "We had a meeting of the whigs of the county here on last monday to appoint delegates to a district convention," Lincoln reported to Speed, "and Baker beat me & got the delegation instructed to go for him." Having been chosen a delegate himself, Lincoln ruefully remarked, "I shall be 'fixed' a good deal like a fellow who is made groomsman to the man what has cut him out, and is marrying his own dear 'gal.' "

Though bound not to oppose Baker in his own county, Lincoln still harbored a lingering hope that he might be nominated by another county, explaining to a friend in neighboring Menard County that his defeat in Sangamon was partially explained by his marriage into the Todd/Edwards clan. "It would astonish if not amuse, the older citizens of your County who twelve years ago knew me a strange[r], friendless, uneducated, penniless boy, working on a flat boat . . . to learn that I have been put down here as the candidate of pride, wealth, and arristocratic family distinction."

At the district convention in Pekin, the nomination went neither to Lincoln nor to Baker but to another young lawyer, John Hardin. At this convention, Lincoln successfully introduced a resolution that Baker would be the next candidate for the U.S. Congress, hoping to establish the idea of rotating terms that would later redound to his benefit. Baker was duly elected two years later, but when his term came to an end, Hardin wanted to return to Congress and was unwilling to yield to Lincoln.

Lincoln left nothing to chance in the contest that followed, seeking to prevent Whig papers from supporting Hardin, pressuring friends to influence neutrals in his favor. He asked friends to share the names of those who were against him. He sent letters to influential Whigs in every precinct. He planned "a quiet trip" through several counties, though he warned his friends, "Dont speak of this, or let it relax any of your vigilance."

His message remained the same throughout the campaign. Hardin and Baker had already served their terms in Congress, and now it was his turn. "That Hardin is talented, energetic, usually generous and magnanimous," he wrote a supporter, "I have, before this, affirmed to you, and do not now deny. You know that my only argument is that 'turn about is fair play.' " He wrote a long letter to Hardin, recalling the old understanding, but insisting that if he were "not, (in services done the party, and in capacity to serve in future) near enough your equal, when added to the fact of your having had a turn, to entitle me to the nomination, I scorn it on any and all other grounds."

Thoroughly outmaneuvered, Hardin withdrew from the contest. Lincoln was nominated, then easily elected to Congress, where the stage had already been set for the debate over the extension of slavery that would dominate the decade to come.

• • •

SALMON CHASE TRAVELED a different road to power than his three rivals. For many years he stayed clear of elective politics. "I am not a politician," he told a friend. "I feel disgusted with party strife and am greatly chagrined on seeing the means to which both parties resort to gain their ends."

The train of events that led Chase into the political world began in 1836, when James G. Birney, an Ohio abolitionist, began publishing the antislavery weekly *Philanthropist,* in Cincinnati. The paper's publication created consternation among Cincinnati's leading merchants and bankers, most of whom had substantial ties to the Southern plantation market. Adjacent to Kentucky, the state of Ohio depended on trade relations with its slaveholding neighbor to sustain a thriving economy. Birney himself had been a wealthy slaveowner in Kentucky before becoming an abolitionist. As soon as distribution of the *Philanthropist* commenced, a group of white community leaders, including many of the merchants Chase represented, attempted to close Birney down. When peaceful pressure failed, the group turned to violence.

On a hot summer night in July 1836, an organized mob broke into the shop where the abolitionist weekly was printed, dismantled the press, and tore up the edition that was about to be circulated. Refusing to be driven out, Birney continued to publish. Two weeks later, the mob returned. This time they succeeded in tearing apart the entire office. They threw tables and other equipment from the second-story window and then, to the cheers of the crowd, shoved out the printing press. While the mayor gazed on approvingly and the police were conspicuously absent, the press was hauled through the streets to the river. After it sank, the crowd began to shout for action against Birney himself, calling for the publisher to be tarred and feathered.

Though Chase had yet to take a public stand on the issue of abolition, he was appalled by the violence. Hearing of the mob's intention to raid the Franklin House where Birney was thought to reside, he raced to the hotel to warn the publisher. As the mob surged forward, Chase braced his arms against the door frame, blocking the hotel's entrance with his body. Six feet two, with broad shoulders, a massive chest, and a determined set to his jaw, Chase gave the rioters pause. The crowd demanded to know who he was. "Salmon P. Chase," the young lawyer replied. "You will pay for your actions," a frustrated member of the mob told him. "I [can] be found at any time," Chase said. "His voice and commanding presence caught the mood of the mob at just the right time," his biographer observes. The hour was late and the mob backed off.

The dramatic encounter had a profound effect on Chase. He became a hero in the antislavery community and began to see his future in a different way. In the years that followed, he became a leader in the effort to protect antislavery activists and their organizations. "No man of his time," the historian Albert Hart argues, "had a stronger conception of the moral issues" involved in the antislavery movement; "none showed greater courage and resolution." His passionate awakening to the antislavery cause was not surprising, given his receptiveness to religious arguments in favor of emancipation and equality. As time went by, however, Chase could not separate his own ambition from the cause he championed. The most calculating decisions designed to forward his political career were justified by advancement of the cause. His personal defeats would be regarded as setbacks for freedom itself. "By dedicating himself to moral activism," the historian Stephen Mazlish argues, "Chase could join his passion for personal advancement to the demands of his religious convictions. . . . 'Fame's proud temple' could be his and he need feel no guilt in its pursuit."

In 1837, a year after he had faced down the anti-Birney mob, Chase once more lent his support to the abolitionist publisher. He undertook the defense of a light-skinned young slave named Matilda, brought to Ohio on a business trip by a Missouri planter who was both her master and her natural father. While in Ohio, encountering black men and women in a free society, she begged her father to grant her liberty. When he refused, she took matters into her own hand, seeking refuge in Cincinnati's black community until her father returned to Missouri. She eventually secured employment in Birney's house, where she remained until she was discovered by a slave catcher and brought before a judge to be remanded to Missouri under the Fugitive Slave Law enacted by Congress in 1793 to enforce the constitutional provision requiring that slaves escaping from one state to another "be delivered up" to their original owners.

Perhaps Chase could have argued successfully that Matilda was not a fugitive from Missouri, since she had been brought into Ohio by her father. Rather, he chose to make a fundamental assault on the applicability of the Fugitive Slave Law to the free state of Ohio. He argued that as soon as Matilda stepped into Ohio, she acquired the legal right to freedom guaranteed by the Northwest Ordinance of 1787, which forbade the introduction of slavery into the vast Northwest Territory later occupied by the states of Ohio, Indiana, Illinois, and Michigan. To many opponents of slavery in later years, including Abraham Lincoln, the Ordinance of 1787 became, like the Declaration of Independence, a sacred document expressing the intent of the founding fathers to confine slavery within the boundaries of the existing states, prohibiting forever its future spread.

"Every settler within the territory, by the very act of settlement, became a party to this compact," Chase argued, "forever entitled to the benefit of its provisions." These provisions, he maintained, "are the birthright of the people of Ohio. It is their glorious distinction, that the genuine principles of American liberty are imbedded, as it were, in their very soil, and mingled with their very atmosphere. . . . Wherever [slavery] exists at all, it exists only in virtue of positive law . . . [and] can have no existence beyond the territorial limits of the state which sanctions it." The right to hold a person in bondage "vanishes when the master and the slave meet together" in a place, like Ohio, "where positive law interdicts slavery."

The conservative judge, as expected, ruled against Chase. The next day, Matilda was forcibly removed to the South and returned to slavery. The philosophical and legal arguments Chase had advanced, however, were considered so important by the antislavery community that they were printed in pamphlet form and distributed throughout the nation.

Publication of his arguments in the *Matilda* case brought Chase immediate acclaim in Northern intellectual circles. By anchoring his arguments firmly in history and law, he opened an antislavery approach that differed from the tactics of the allies of Garrison, who eschewed political organization, dismissed the founding fathers, and considered the Constitution "a covenant with death, an agreement with hell," because it condoned slavery. Where the Garrisonians called for a moral crusade to awaken the sleeping conscience of the nation, Chase targeted a political audience, hopeful that abolition could be achieved through politics, government, and the courts.

The time had come, Chase decided, to try for public office. Though he had not been active in party politics, he sought a nomination from the Whig Party to the state senate. To his disappointment, he was rebuffed as an abolitionist. Three years later, he tried again, seeking the Whig nomination for the Cincinnati City Council. Although he succeeded in gaining office, he was defeated for reelection after a single term, largely due to his position on temperance, which had led him to unpopular votes denying liquor licenses to city establishments.

Surveying the political landscape, Chase was unable to see a future for himself as either a Democrat or a Whig. Both parties, he wrote, submitted to the South upon the *"vital* question of slavery." Consequently, in 1841, he joined the fledgling Liberty Party, which was struggling to establish a solid base of support. The previous year, James Birney, since moved to New York to head the American Anti-Slavery Society, had gained the party's nomination for president. Unknown beyond abolitionist circles, Birney garnered only 7,000 votes.

Through the 1840s, Chase sought to guide the Liberty Party to a more moderate image so that it could gain wider appeal. Working closely with Gamaliel Bailey, Birney's astute successor at the *Philanthropist*, Chase persuaded the Ohio Liberty Party to adopt a resolution that explicitly renounced any intention "to interfere with slavery in the states where it exists." Concurring with Lincoln, Bates, and a number of progressive Whigs, they pledged to focus only on those areas where slavery was present "without constitutional warrant"—in the District of Columbia, on the high seas, in the new territories. At the same time, Chase encouraged his fellow party members to consider reaching outside their ranks to find a presidential candidate who could command a larger vote than the radical Birney, who, as Chase said, "has seen so little of public service."

In an 1842 letter to Joshua Giddings, the abolitionist congressman from Ohio's Western Reserve, Chase suggested that if John Quincy Adams or William Henry Seward "would accept the nomination, great additional strength might be gained for the party." He had no idea whether either man would accept, but ranked Governor Seward, "for his age," as "one of the first statesmen in the country," while former president Adams was "perhaps, the very first."

Though he had never met Seward, Chase opened an intriguing correspondence with the governor, in which they freely debated the role of third parties. Seward expressed his belief that "there can be only two permanent parties." In his view, the Democratic Party, with its strong base in the South, would always be the party of slavery, while the Whig Party would champion the antislavery banner, "more or less," depending "on the advancement of the public mind and the intentness with which it can be fixed on the question of Slavery." Seward conceded that while he was disheartened by the Whig Party's current "lukewarmness on the Subject of Slavery," he had no choice but to stay with the party he loved, and to hope for a more advanced position in the future. "To abandon a party and friends to whom I owe so much, whose confidence I do in some degree possess," he wrote, "would be criminal, and not more criminal than unwise."

Chase saw the situation differently. Though originally *"educated in the Whig school,"* with Whiggish views of the tariff, banking, and government, he had never considered party loyalty among his defining characteristics. Nor had he experienced the camaraderie of fellow party loyalists that Seward enjoyed when he and his colleagues boarded together in Albany during the lengthy legislative sessions. For Chase, the decision to leave the Whigs for the Liberty Party was not the momentous separation that it would have been for Seward.

Chase clearly understood that so long as the Liberty Party remained a "one idea" party, it would never attract majority support. Risking the displeasure of his abolitionist friends, who wanted no diminution of their principles, he envisioned a gradual movement of the Liberty Party toward one of the major parties. His efforts revealed a practical side to his principled stance, but old acquaintances in Ohio were troubled by his decision to set his sights on the more powerful Democratic Party, where he had a greater chance of statewide success than with the Whigs.

In his bid to cultivate Democratic leaders, Chase shifted his positions on the tariff and the banking system to align himself with the Democrats, though he insisted that the economic policies of either party were insignificant compared to the issue of slavery. For the moment, since neither major party would take a resolute stand on slavery, he remained with the Liberty Party, attending conventions, drawing up resolutions, and searching for candidates.

In the years that followed, in part because the free city of Cincinnati was a natural destination for runaways crossing the Ohio River from the slave state of Kentucky, a number of fugitive slave cases ended up in the Cincinnati courts. Chase volunteered his services in many such cases. The eloquent power of his arguments soon earned him the honorary title "Attorney General for the Negro." In the famous case that inspired Harriet Beecher Stowe's good-hearted John Van Trompe in *Uncle Tom's Cabin*, Chase represented John Van Zandt, an old farmer who had moved from Kentucky to Ohio so that he might live in a free state.

On an April night in 1842, Van Zandt was returning from the Cincinnati market to his home twenty miles north. On the road, he encountered a group of slaves who had crossed the river from Kentucky. "Moved by sympathy," Chase would argue, the farmer "undertook to convey them in his wagon to Lebanon or Springfield." En route, two slave catchers accosted the wagon. They captured the slaves and returned them to their Kentucky owner, receiving a $450 bounty for their efforts.

The owner then brought suit against Van Zandt for "harboring and concealing" the slaves, in violation of the 1793 Fugitive Slave Act. Chase "very willingly" agreed to represent the elderly farmer, who faced substantial penalties if found guilty. Chase's defense of Van Zandt transcended the particulars of the *Matilda* case, directly challenging the constitutionality of the Fugitive Slave Law. That law, he maintained, deprived fugitives of life and liberty without due process of law. "Under the constitution," he declared, "all the inhabitants of the United States are, without exception, persons,—persons, it may be, not free, persons, held to service . . . but still, persons," and therefore possessed of every right guaranteed under the Constitution and Declaration of Independence.

"What is a slave?" he asked. "A slave is a person held, as property, by legalized force, against natural right. . . . The very moment a slave passes beyond the jurisdiction of the state, in which he is held as such, he ceases to be a slave; not because any law or regulation of the state which he enters confers freedom upon him, but because he *continues* to be a man and *leaves behind* him the law of force, which made him a slave." Chase depicted slavery as "a creature of state law" and not a national institution. He argued that any slave state created after 1787, the year the Northwest Ordinance became law, existed in violation of the Constitution and the wishes of the founding fathers.

As most observers expected, the Cincinnati court refused to accept Chase's argument. Van Zandt was found guilty. As Chase left the courtroom, according to Harriet Beecher Stowe, then a Cincinnati resident, one of the judges reflected on the unpopularity of professed abolitionists: "There goes a young man who has *ruined* himself to-day."

Far from ruining his prospects, the *Van Zandt* case added considerable luster to Chase's national reputation. Appealing the decision to the U.S. Supreme Court, Chase enlisted Seward's help as co-counsel. The case moved slowly through the docket, affording the two men time to craft their written arguments. Chase presented the constitutional arguments, while Seward dealt with the technical ones. Though the Southern-dominated court wasted little time in affirming the lower court's ruling, the constitutional arguments Chase outlined became pillars of antislavery party doctrine.

Chase acknowledged that "poor old Van Zandt" was never able to recover from the loss and the damages inflicted upon him. Still, he believed that "even though my poor old client be sacrificed, the great cause of humanity will be a gainer." He had his 108-page argument reprinted in pamphlet form for wide distribution, and was delighted with the positive response it provoked. Antislavery activist Charles Sumner wrote from Massachusetts that "the question under the Ordinance of 1787 was novel" and might well "rally a *political* movement." President John Quincy

Adams's son, Charles Francis, extolled Chase, as did New Hampshire's Senator John Hale. Nothing gave him more satisfaction, than the praise he received from Seward, who expressed fervent hope that the "chaste and beautiful eloquence" of Chase's brief would be forever "preserved for the benefit of the cause of Freedom and for [Chase's] own fame." The fact that the case brought a personal and intellectual contact with Seward, Chase told abolitionist Lewis Tappan, proved "one of the gratifications, and one of the greatest too," of all his efforts.

Politicians were not alone in recognizing Chase's commitment. In gratitude for public service "in behalf of the oppressed" and his "eloquent advocacy of the rights of man," the black pastor of the Baker Street Church collected donations from his parishioners. In an emotional ceremony on May 6, 1845, attended by a large black congregation, Chase was honored with a beautifully engraved sterling silver pitcher. Presenting the gift on behalf of "the Colored People of Cincinnati," the Reverend A. J. Gordon told the enthusiastic gathering that "whenever the friendless objects of slaveholding cupidity" struggled to find freedom, they found in Chase "a firm, zealous and devoted friend." He assured Chase that his deeds on behalf of fugitive slaves and the black race would be "engraven on the tablets of our hearts . . . as long as memory retains her seat." Reverend Gordon avowed that when Chase was finally "called from [his] earthly labors," he would be ushered into paradise by God Himself, with the words "Well done thou good and faithful servant, enter into the joys of thy Lord. For inasmuch as you did it unto the least of these my brethren, you did it unto me!"

Chase was profoundly moved by the ceremony. Accepting the engraved pitcher, which he treasured the rest of his life, he pledged to continue his fight for freedom until "the colored man and white man are equal before the law." In his own state of Ohio, he lamented, various legal provisions known as the Black Laws excluded free blacks from public schools, the witness box, and the voting booth. These exclusions, he asserted (two years before Seward would make a similar argument), were clear infringements of the Constitution. "True Democracy makes no enquiry about the color of the skin, or the place of nativity," he ardently claimed. "Wherever it sees a man, it recognizes a being endowed by his Creator with original inalienable rights."

Laws denying black children public school education, while simultaneously requiring that their parents pay school taxes, were reprehensible, he argued. More unjust, blacks were banned from the witness box in all cases where either party was white. This exclusion exposed the black population "to every species of violence and outrage" from whites who felt secure from punishment so long as they committed their crimes only in the presence of black witnesses. "Every law on the statute book so wrong and mean that it cannot be executed, or felt, if executed, to be oppressive and unjust," averred Chase, "tends to the overthrow of all law, by separating in the minds of the people, the idea of law from the idea of right. . . .

"For myself," Chase concluded, "I am ready to renew my pledge—and I will venture to speak also in behalf of my co-workers,—that we go straight on, without faltering or wavering, until every vestige of oppression shall be erased from the statute book:—until the sun in all his journey from the utmost eastern horizon, through the mid-heaven, till he sinks beyond the western mountains into his ocean bed, shall not behold, in all our broad and glorious land, the foot print of a single slave." A tremendous round of applause was followed by an emotional rendition of the hymn "America." With a benediction, the exercises were brought to a close.

•   •   •

CHASE, UNLIKE SEWARD and Lincoln, did not make friends easily. A contemporary reporter observed that he knew "little of human nature," and that while "profoundly versed in man, he was profoundly ignorant of men." His abstractedness often lent an air of preoccupation, aggravated by his extreme nearsightedness. Both prevented him from gauging the reactions of others. Furthermore, his natural reserve, piety, temperance, and lack of humor made for uneasy relationships. Even his stately proportions and fastidious dress worked against social intimacy.

Despite his difficulty in making friends and instilling personal loyalties, Chase did form one significant relationship during the decade of the forties. His bond with Edwin M. Stanton would have important consequences during the Civil War, when the two men would serve together in Lincoln's cabinet. Six years younger than Chase, Stanton was a brilliant young lawyer from Steubenville, Ohio. He had been active in Democratic politics from his earliest days. A short, stout man, with thick brows and intense black eyes hidden behind steel-rimmed glasses, Stanton had grown up in a Quaker family dedicated to abolition. He later told the story that "when he was a boy his father had—like the father of Hannibal against Rome—made him swear eternal hostility to slavery."

When Chase and Stanton first met in Columbus in the early 1840s, each was dealing with appalling personal loss, for death had pursued Stanton much as it had pursued Chase. In the five-year span from 1841 to 1846, Stanton had lost his only daughter, Lucy; his young wife, Mary; and his only brother, Darwin. Confronting a similar reign of grief at almost the same time, Chase found in Stanton a solace and friendship more intense than if they had met at a different juncture in their lives.

In the summer of 1846, Stanton spent several days with Chase at his Cincinnati home. The wide-ranging conversations they enjoyed left a lasting impression on Stanton. "Since our pleasant intercourse together last summer," Stanton wrote Chase, "no living person has been oftener in my mind;—waking or sleeping,—for, more than once, I have dreamed of being with you. The strength of my regard and affection for you, I can, thus, tell more freely than were we face to face."

More than sorrow bound Chase and Stanton together. At the time of their acquaintance in the mid-1840s, both men were trying to find a footing in quick-shifting political currents. Chase had already taken his stand with the Liberty Party. Stanton, though intrigued by the newly formed party, remained a loyal Democrat. Over the course of many hours, in conversation and then by letter, they debated the merits of the new Liberty Party. Responding to Chase's worry about the narrowness of the party's platform, Stanton cited examples of single ideas that had achieved great triumphs: most notably, "Taxation & Representation," the slogan that guided the American Revolution. "I go for one idea in party," he wrote, "and in friendship my one idea is strong & sincere love for you." With Chase, Stanton felt free to criticize the Democratic Party, which had gravely disappointed him in a recent election when its candidate for governor came out in favor of the discriminatory Black Laws.

Chase tried to involve Stanton in the *Van Zandt* appeal, but Stanton declined, fearing he had neither the "physical nor intellectual strength sufficient to engage in the cause. Events of the past summer have broken my spirits, crushed my hopes, and without energy or purpose in life, I feel indifferent to the present, careless of the future." Chase apparently did not reply to this letter. "Many weeks have gone by," Stanton wrote in January 1847, "but your voice reaches me no more. Why is it? The question arises, as I move slowly & disappointed from the post office each day."

The correspondence picked up again in the spring, when Chase sent Stanton his argument in the *Van Zandt* case. "Rejoicing, as I do, to call you friend," Stanton wrote after reading through the lengthy document, "it gives me pleasure to acknowledge its intellectual merit." Rather than discuss it in writing, he hoped that he and Chase could soon meet and "spend two or three days" together. "I want to hear from you," Stanton concluded, "and so may as well confess it at once & throw myself upon your mercy."

They finally met in Cincinnati in July, but the visit was too abbreviated to satisfy Stanton. The desire for his friend's company had been lodged in his heart for so long, Stanton explained to Chase upon returning home to Steubenville, that the visit, while enjoyable, had left him ungratified. In the months that followed, however, they saw each other on a number of occasions and opened their hearts in correspondence. After receiving a particularly affectionate letter from Chase, Stanton fervently replied that it "filled my heart with joy; to be loved by you, and be told that you value my love is a gratification beyond my power to express." He went on to downplay reports Chase had heard that he had developed a "magnetic attraction" for a new woman. "I wish it were so," he admitted. "To love, and to be loved, is a necessary condition of my happiness . . . I have met with no one that exercises upon me the least attraction beyond the general qualities of the sex."

In the meantime, his friendship with Chase, and his memories of their time together, sustained him. "Allow me my dear friend again this evening to enter your study—you know I like it better than the parlor even without fire—but the fire is blazing there—let me take you by the hand throw my arm around you, say I love you, & bid you farewell."

As their friendship grew, Chase urged Stanton to involve himself more deeply in the struggle against slavery. He promised Stanton, who remained a Democrat, that he would join his campaign should he run for governor. But Stanton, who was now supporting his brother's family as well as his own, did not feel he could make the financial sacrifice. "How much I regret that your voice is not to be heard," a disappointed Chase wrote. "We have but a short life to live here my dear friend. But let us make it long by noble deeds. You have great gifts of God, energy, enthusiasm, talent, utterance. And now a great cause demands you."

Stanton's inability to commit himself more fully to the antislavery crusade cast a shadow on his relationship with Chase. When Stanton failed to attend a Democratic convention in Columbus where antislavery issues were on the agenda, Chase chastised him for placing personal interests above political duties. "Why—why are you not here?" Chase lamented. "If I had foreseen you would not attend the Convention, I am certain I should not have left home." Stanton's reply expressed hurt at the censure in Chase's letter, explaining that it was not merely private concerns that kept him away but a collision of obligations. "The practice of law," he conceded, "furnishes employment for all my time and faculties. . . . Such to be sure is not the condition that dreams of early love pictured for my manhood—but in the field of life some as sentinels must perform the lonely round while others enjoy the social festivity of the camp."

For Stanton, more than for Chase, the importance of the friendship exceeded political events and even personal ambition. "While public honors affords gratification," Stanton wrote, "such friendship as yours is to me of inestimable value." With sadness, he conceded that he was "well aware that public duties, the increasing pressure of private affairs as age advances, domestic vicissitudes and the inclination of the heart must cool the fervor of friendship among men." Still, he hoped that he and Chase might someday stand side by side in the struggle against slavery.

So as 1847 drew to a close, the four men who would contend for the 1860 presidential nomination were deeply and actively involved in the political, social, and economic issues that would define the growing nation. Each embraced a different position along the spectrum of growing opposition to slavery. Yet while Seward, Chase, and Bates had each developed a national renown, few beyond Illinois knew of the raw-boned young congressman coming to the nation's capital for the first time in his life.

CHAPTER 4

"PLUNDER & CONQUEST"

W ASHINGTON WAS A CITY in progress when the Lincolns arrived at the wooden railroad station in December 1847 for the opening of the congressional session. The cornerstone of the Washington Monument would not be laid until the following summer. Cobblestoned Pennsylvania Avenue was one of only two paved streets. Not yet fitted with its familiar high dome, the Capitol stood on a hill that boasted "a full view of the cities of Washington, Georgetown, and Alexandria, and the varied and forest-clad hills in Maryland and Virginia." In the backs of most houses, recalled one of Lincoln's colleagues, "stood pig-styes, cow-sheds, and pens for the gangs of unyoked geese. During the day the animals and fowls roamed at will in lordly insolence, singly or in herds and flocks, through the streets and over the fields."

Nevertheless, with forty thousand inhabitants (including several thousand slaves), the capital was a metropolis compared to little Springfield. It was filled with the landmarks and memorials of the history that so captivated the Lincolns. Some of the most illustrious personages of the age still walked the halls of Congress—John Quincy Adams tirelessly battling on behalf of antislavery petitions; the eloquent Daniel Webster, whose words, Lincoln believed, would outlive the age; John Calhoun, the acknowledged spokesman for the South, who had already led one effort at rebellion. These titans who had shaped the history of the past decades were joined by those who would play leading roles in the great drama to unfold— Jefferson Davis and Alexander Stephens, future president and vice president of the Confederacy; Stephen Douglas, Lincoln's great rival; and Robert Barnwell Rhett, agitator of rebellion.

The Lincolns took up residence in Mrs. Spriggs's Boarding House on Capitol Hill, on the site of the present Library of Congress. Soon a favorite among his fellow boarders, Lincoln was always ready with a story or anecdote to entertain, persuade, or defuse argument. Samuel Busey, a young doctor who took his meals at the boardinghouse, recalled that whenever Lincoln was about to tell a story, "he would lay down his knife and fork, place his elbows upon the table, rest his face between his hands, and begin with the words 'that reminds me,' and proceed. Everybody prepared for the explosions sure to follow."

For recreation, Lincoln took up bowling with his fellow boarders. Though a clumsy bowler, according to Dr. Busey, Lincoln "played the game with great zest and spirit" and "accepted success and defeat with like good nature and humor." When word spread "that he was in the alley there would assemble numbers of people to witness the fun which was anticipated by those who knew of his fund of anecdotes and jokes." As ever, his quick wit and droll geniality provided a source of "merriment" for everyone around him.

While Lincoln attended meetings and congressional sessions, Mary was largely confined to the single room she shared with her husband and two small children—Robert, now five, and Eddie, two, whose often boisterous antics and excited running through the corridors did not endear Mary to her fellow boarders. None of the other congressmen in their boardinghouse were accompanied by wives. Indeed, most of the legislators in the city had left their families behind. Without female friends, Mary was compelled to spend most of the day alone with the children. Furthermore, the mores of the day forbade her to attend social gatherings and parties without her continually occupied husband. After a few months, by mutual consent, Mary and the children left Washington. Unable to return to their Springfield home, which was rented out for the congressional term, she took the children to her father's elegant house in Lexington, Kentucky, beginning what would be the longest continuous separation from her husband in their twenty-three-year marriage.

• • •

EIGHTEEN MONTHS before Abraham Lincoln arrived in Washington, history had taken an irrevocable turn when Democratic president James Polk ordered American troops to occupy disputed territory between the borders of the United States and Mexico. Relations between Mexico and the United States had been strained for decades as quarrels over boundary lines simmered. Announcing that Mexico had fired upon American soldiers on American soil, Polk called on Congress not to declare war but to recognize that a state of war already existed.

The onset of war with Mexico aroused the patriotic spirit of the American people, who regarded the war as "a romantic venture in a distant and exotic land." The Congress called for 50,000 men, but within weeks, 300,000 volunteers had poured into recruiting centers. Lincoln's former rival, John Hardin, was "the first to enlist" in Illinois. He would be elected colonel of his regiment and would die a hero's death at the Battle of Buena Vista. Edward Baker, still retaining his seat in Congress, would raise a regiment and, "with drums rolling and fifes shrilling," would lead his troops "through flag-bedecked streets crowded with cheering thousands, amid the weeping farewells of women, the encouraging God-speeds of men."

From the start, many leading Whigs questioned both the constitutionality and the justice of the war. "It is a fact," Lincoln would later say, "that the United States Army, in marching to the Rio Grande, marched into a peaceful Mexican settlement, and frightened the inhabitants away from their homes and their growing crops." By the time Lincoln took his congressional oath, the combat had come to an end. The peace treaty had only to be signed, on terms spectacularly advantageous for the victorious United States. At this point, Lincoln conceded, it would have been easier to remain silent about the questionable origins of the war. The Democrats, however, would "not let the whigs be *silent*." When Congress reconvened, they immediately introduced resolutions blaming the war on Mexican aggression, thereby demanding that Congress endorse "the original justice of the war on the part of the President."

On December 13, less than two weeks after his arrival in Washington, Lincoln wrote his law partner, William Herndon: "As you are all so anxious for me to distinguish myself, I have concluded to do so, before long." Nine days later, he introduced a resolution calling on President Polk to inform the House "whether the particular spot of soil on which the blood of our *citizens* was so shed" belonged to Mexico or to the United States. He challenged the president to present evidence that "Mexico herself became the aggressor by invading *our soil* in hostile array."

The president, not surprisingly, did not respond to the unknown freshman congressman whose hasty reach for distinction earned him only the derisive nickname "spotty Lincoln." A few weeks later, Lincoln voted with his Whig brethren on a resolution introduced by Massachusetts congressman George Ashmun, which stated that the war had been "unnecessarily and unconstitutionally" initiated by the president.

The following week, on January 12, 1848, Lincoln defended his spot resolutions and his vote on the Ashmun resolution in a major speech. He claimed that he would happily reverse his vote if the president could prove that first blood was shed on American soil; but since he *"can* not, or *will* not do this," he suspected that the entire matter was, "from beginning to end, the sheerest deception." Having provoked both countries into war, Lincoln charged, the president had hoped "to escape scrutiny, by fixing the public gaze upon the exceeding brightness of military glory . . . that serpent's eye, that charms to destroy." He went on to liken the president's war message to "the half insane mumbling of a fever-dream." Perhaps re-calling the turtles tormented with hot coals by his boyhood friends, Lin-coln employed the bizarre simile of the president's confused mind "running hither and thither, like some tortured creature, on a burning sur-face, finding no position, on which it can settle down, and be at ease."

This maiden effort was not the tone of reasoned debate that later char-acterized Lincoln's public statements. Nor did it obey his oft-expressed be-lief that a leader should endeavor to transform, yet heed, public opinion. Compelling as Lincoln's criticisms might have been, they fell flat at a time when the majority of Americans were delighted with the outcome of the war. The Democratic *Illinois State Register* charged that Lincoln had dis-graced his district with his "treasonable assault upon President Polk," claimed that "henceforth" he would be known as "Benedict Arnold," and predicted that he would enjoy only a single term. Lincoln sought to clarify his position, arguing that although he had challenged the instigation of the war, he had never voted against supplies for the soldiers. To accept Polk's position without question, he claimed, was to "allow the President to in-vade a neighboring nation . . . *whenever he may choose to say* he deems it nec-essary."

Even the loyal Herndon feared that Lincoln's antiwar stance would de-stroy his political future. "I saw that Lincoln would ruin himself," Hern-don later explained. "I wrote to him on the subject again and again." Herndon was right to worry, for as it turned out, Lincoln's quest for dis-tinction had managed only to infuriate the Democrats, worry fainthearted Whigs, and lose support in Illinois, where the war was extremely popular. A prominent Chicago politician, Justin Butterfield, asked if he was against the Mexican War, replied: "no, I opposed one War [the War of 1812]. That was enough for me. I am now perpetually in favor of war, pestilence and famine." In the years ahead, Lincoln would write frequent letters de-fending his position. If he had hoped for reelection to Congress, however, despite the unofficial agreement with his colleagues that he would serve only one term, his prospects rapidly evaporated in the fever of war. Indeed, when Stephen Logan, the Whig nominee to replace him, was defeated, his loss was blamed on Lincoln.

As Seward understood better than Lincoln, Manifest Destiny was in the air. "Our population," Seward predicted, "is destined to roll its resistless waves to the icy barriers of the north, and to encounter Oriental civiliza-tion on the shores of the Pacific." Though he wasn't in favor of the war,

Seward's political astuteness told him it was a mistake to argue against it. He warned that he did "not expect to see the Whig party successful in overthrowing an Administration carrying on a war in which the Whig party and its statesmen are found apologizing for our national adversaries."

Back in Ohio, Salmon Chase told the abolitionist Gerrit Smith that he "would not have engaged in" the war, but in public he muted his opposition. For Chase was caught in a political dilemma. On the one hand, his antislavery allies in the Liberty Party were strongly against the war. If he wanted a seat in the U.S. Senate, however, he would need the support of Ohio Democrats, a task that would not be made easier by assaulting a Democratic president.

Of the four future presidential rivals, only Edward Bates matched the vehemence of Lincoln's opposition. He charged Polk with "gross & palpable lying," arguing that the true object of the war was "plunder & conquest." Bates said he was ashamed of his Whig brethren who voted for the war, "actuated by a narrow & groveling policy, and a selfish fear of injuring their own popularity, & injuriously affecting the coming Presidential election." To Bates, the war was part of a conspiracy to extend the reach of slavery—a belief he shared with many other Whigs, though not with Lincoln, who argued it was simply "a war of conquest brought into existence to catch votes."

Whether or not it was begun to extend slavery, the war brought the issue of slavery expansion to the forefront. While the early battles were still raging, a little-known congressman from Pennsylvania, David Wilmot, had penned a historic amendment to a war appropriations bill providing that "neither slavery nor involuntary servitude shall ever exist in any part of said territory" acquired from Mexico—lands that would eventually comprise California, Nevada, Utah, Arizona, and New Mexico. This Wilmot Proviso was repeatedly passed in the House and repeatedly blocked in the Southern-dominated Senate. Its status became a battleground in the conflict between North and South. The issue of slavery in the territories would become *the* defining issue in the years that followed.

Seward, Chase, and Lincoln all favored the ban on slavery from entering the territories acquired from Mexico. Even before the Wilmot Proviso had been introduced, Lincoln positioned himself against the expansion of slavery, a position he would hold for the rest of his career, arguing that while the Constitution protected slavery in the states where it already existed, "we should never knowingly lend ourselves directly or indirectly, to prevent that slavery from dying a natural death—to find new places for it to live in, when it can no longer exist in the old."

In Missouri, Bates also supported the Wilmot Proviso, though for different reasons. Bates considered the problem of extending slavery into these new lands a practical rather than a moral question. If Southerners brought their slaves into the West in large numbers, he feared that migration of free whites would come to a halt, thereby precluding growth and progress in the region. More important, he worried that the agitation over the slavery issue, which he blamed equally on Northern abolitionists and Southern extremists, would pull the country apart.

Bates had reason to fear so. South Carolina's John Calhoun led the vocal opposition to the Proviso, denouncing it as an unconstitutional act that would deny Southerners the right to move freely "with their property" into commonly held American territory. Moreover, if slavery were banned from the new territories, free states would join the Union and skew the balance of power. The South, already losing ground in the House of Representatives to the more populous North, would lose its historic strength in the Senate as well. Southern interests would be subject to the dictates of an increasingly hostile North. This was a future the South would never accept. "The madmen of the North and North West," editorialized the *Richmond Enquirer,* "have, we fear, cast the die, and numbered the days of this glorious Union." Thus the debate over the war became a conflict over slavery and a threat to the Union itself.

•   •   •

DURING THIS PERIOD of great political stress and turmoil, Lincoln came to sorely miss the companionship of his wife and the presence of his children. The couple's correspondence from this time gives us nearly all the direct evidence we have of their relationship. Almost all other information must be gleaned from outside observers, some of whom regarded Mary with extreme hostility or believed that she was unworthy of her husband.

"When you were here," Lincoln wrote Mary on April 16, 1848, "I thought you hindered me some in attending to business; but now, having nothing but business—no variety—it has grown exceedingly tasteless to me . . . I hate to stay in this old room by myself." He recounted with pride that he had gone shopping for the children, and told her how he enjoyed her letters. He was pleased to hear that, for the first springtime since he had known her, she had been "free from head-ache." Then he added teasingly, "I am afraid you will get so well, and fat, and young, as to be wanting to marry again."

"My dear Husband," Mary answered, writing on a Saturday night after the children were asleep. "How much, I wish instead of writing, *we* were together this evening, I feel very sad away from you." She described the children and their doings, and coyly needled that Mr. Webb, who had un-successfully sought her hand in their Springfield days, was coming to Shelbyville, Kentucky. "I must go down about that time & carry on quite a flirtation, you know *we*, always had a *penchant* that way." In closing, she re-assured him: "Do not fear the children, have forgotten you. . . . Even E(ddy's) eyes brighten at the mention of your name—My love to all."

Lincoln quickly responded: "The leading matter in your letter, is your wish to return to this side of the Mountains. Will you be a *good girl* in all things, if I consent?" Most likely, he was referring here to the problems Mary had experienced with the other boarders, and her unhappiness about the amount of work he had to do. Assuming that she had already affirma-tively answered his question, he continued: "Then come along, and that as *soon* as possible. Having got the idea in my head, I shall be impatient till I see you." These letters are replete with gossip about their acquaintances in Washington and Springfield, detailed news of the children, some mention of Lincoln's political activities, gentle teasing, and expressions of longing, both for companionship and, by implication, for intimacy. In the fall of 1848, Mary and the children returned to Washington.

In June of that year, Lincoln joined his fellow Whigs in Philadelphia, where they nominated Mexican War hero General Zachary Taylor for president, hoping that military glory could work its magic once more, as it had for George Washington, Andrew Jackson, and William Henry Harri-son. "I am in favor of Gen: Taylor," Lincoln wrote, "because I am satisfied we can elect him . . . and that we can not elect any other whig." He ex-plained to Herndon that the nomination of Taylor would strike the Dem-ocrats "on the blind side. It turns the war thunder against them. The war is now to them, the gallows of Haman, which they built for us, and on which they are doomed to be hanged themselves."

Seward was not happy with his party's choice of Taylor, a slaveholder with no political affiliation. Even worse was the selection of his rival New Yorker Millard Fillmore for vice president. Nor did he like the party's gauzy platform, which avoided any discussion of important national issues, including the divisive Wilmot Proviso. He said that he would "very will-ingly" throw his support "in favor of a different candidate if it could be seen that it would hasten the triumph of Universal Freedom." Thurlow Weed, desiring above all to win, insisted that Taylor was fundamentally a nationalist who would protect Northern interests better than the Demo-cratic candidate, Lewis Cass of Michigan. Cass was considered a "dough-face"—a Northern man with Southern principles. Moreover, the Democratic platform explicitly opposed Wilmot's attempt to introduce the slavery issue into congressional deliberations. Finally, Seward, like

Lincoln and Bates, supported Taylor, in the hope that his candidacy would allow the minority Whigs to attract Northern Democrats and independent voters, and thereby widen their base.

Chase, once again, pursued a different strategy. With the question of slavery in the territories at the forefront of national politics, he believed the time had come for a broad Northern party that would unite Liberty men with antislavery Democrats and "conscience" Whigs. He joined together with others, including Charles Sumner of Massachusetts, to convene an antislavery party convention in Buffalo, in August 1848. Ten thousand men answered the call. The spirited gathering elected Chase president of the convention and placed him in charge of drafting a platform for the new party, the Free Soil Party.

During the deliberations, a Buffalo delegate wrote to Bates asking if his name could be entered as a candidate for the vice presidency. That Bates would even be considered illustrates the fluidity of parties at this juncture, for even though he opposed slavery's expansion, he himself remained a slaveowner, his belief in the inferiority of the black race reflecting his Southern upbringing. In contrast to Seward and Chase, he supported Northern codes that prevented blacks from voting, sitting on juries, or holding office. When one of his female slaves escaped to Canada, he had been incredulous. "Poor foolish thing," he wrote in his diary. "She will never be as well off as she was in our house." She had left behind three daughters, whom he promptly sold, "determined at once to be no longer plagued with them."

Not surprisingly, Bates declined the Free Soil nomination. While he endorsed the party's "true doctrine" that "Congress ought never to establish slavery where they did not find it," he did not believe that this sole principle could sustain a national party. Even if offered the chance to be president, he claimed, he would never agree to "join a sectional, geographical party."

After several days of deliberation, the Buffalo convention nominated former president Martin Van Buren for president and Charles Francis Adams for vice president. Following the motto suggested by Chase of "Free Soil, Free Speech, Free Labor and Free Men," the party pledged to "prohibit slavery extension" to the territories, setting in motion a hard-fought three-way contest.

In September 1848, with Congress in recess, Lincoln made his first foray into presidential politics, campaigning for Zachary Taylor throughout the Northeast. Arriving uninvited in Worcester, Massachusetts, he was happy to oblige the chairman of a Whig gathering who found himself without a speaker. Reporting on Lincoln's impromptu speech, the Boston

Daily Advertiser observed that the tall congressman had "an intellectual face, showing a searching mind, and a cool judgment," and that he carried "the audience with him in his able arguments and brilliant illustrations." When he finished, "the audience gave three enthusiastic cheers for Illinois, and three more for the eloquent Whig member from that State."

During this campaign swing, at a great Whig rally at the Tremont Temple in Boston, Seward and Lincoln met for the first time. Lincoln later acknowledged that his meeting with Seward that night "had probably made a stronger impression on his memory than it had on Governor Seward's."

Both men were seated on the same platform in the spacious hall that served Boston as a religious and a secular meeting place. Seward, as the star attraction, spoke first, monopolizing most of the evening. Whereas most Whig speakers concentrated on internal improvements, the tariff, and public lands, Seward focused on slavery. He defended Taylor as a good man, trustworthy to support the Whigs' determination to prevent slavery from expanding into those territories acquired by the Mexican War, though he hoped "the time will come, and that not far distant, when the citizens of the whole country, as well as Massachusetts, will select for their leader a freeman of the north, in preference to a slaveholder." Gaining momentum, Seward predicted the "time will soon arrive when further demonstrations will be made against the institution of slavery," eventually moving public conscience to liberate all the nation's slaves.

The hour was late when Lincoln was introduced, but he captivated his audience with what the *Boston Courier* described as "a most forcible and convincing speech," which scored a series of capital "hits" against both Democrat Cass and Free-Soiler Van Buren, whom he nicknamed the "artful dodger" of Kinderhook, referring to his frequent shifts of party and position. He concluded "amidst repeated rounds of deafening applause." Recalling Lincoln's "rambling, story-telling" speech more than two decades later, Seward agreed that it put "the audience in good humor," but he pointedly noted that it avoided "any extended discussion of the slavery question."

The next night, Seward and Lincoln shared the same room in a Worcester hotel. "We spent the greater part of the night talking," Seward remembered years later, "I insisting that the time had come for sharp definition of opinion and boldness of utterance." Listening with "a thoughtful air," Lincoln said: "I reckon you are right. We have got to deal with this slavery question, and got to give much more attention to it hereafter than we have been doing." While Lincoln had consistently voted for the Wilmot Proviso, he had not delivered a single speech on the issue of slavery or initiated anything to promote the issue. As the conversation drew to a close and the two men went to sleep side by side, they must have presented a comical image—the one nearly half a foot longer and a decade younger; Seward's disorderly mass of straw-colored hair on the pillow beside Lincoln's wiry shock of black hair.

Years later, as president, Lincoln recalled his trip to Massachusetts. "I went with hay seed in my hair to learn deportment in the most cultivated State in the Union." He recalled in vivid detail a dinner at the governor's house—"a superb dinner; by far the finest I ever saw in my life. And the great men who were there, too! Why, I can tell you just how they were arranged at table," whereupon he proceeded to do just that.

The Whigs triumphed at the polls that November, bringing Zachary Taylor to the White House. It was to be the last national victory for the Whigs, who, four years later, divided on the slavery issue, would win only four states. To Chase's delight, Free-Soiler Martin Van Buren polled more than 10 percent of the vote among the Northern electorate—enough to prove that antislavery had become a force in national politics. Indeed, in several Northern states, including New York, the votes for Van Buren that otherwise might have gone to the Democrats spelled victory for the Whigs.

When Lincoln returned to Congress for the rump session, influenced, perhaps, by his encounter with Seward, he drafted a proposal for the gradual emancipation of slaves in the nation's capital, pending approval by the District's voters. Similar proposals had been attempted before, but Lincoln now added several elements. He included provisions to compensate owners for the full value of the slaves with government funds and to allow government officials from slaveholding states to bring their servants while on government business. Finally, to mitigate the fears of Southern slaveholders in surrounding states, he added a provision requiring District authorities "to provide active and efficient means to arrest, and deliver up to their owners, all fugitive slaves escaping into said District." It was this last provision that prompted abolitionist Wendell Phillips to castigate him as "that slave hound from Illinois."

Through long and careful conversations with dozens of fellow Whigs, Lincoln thought he had devised a reasonable compromise that could gain the support of both moderates in the South and the strong antislavery wing in the North. Yet, once the proposal was distributed, Lincoln found that his support had evaporated. Increasingly bitter divisiveness had eclipsed any possibility of compromise. Zealous antislavery men objected to both the fugitive slave provision and the idea of compensating owners in any way, while Southerners argued that abolishing slavery in the District would open the door to abolishing slavery in the country at large. Disappointed but realistic in his appraisal of the situation, Lincoln never introduced his bill. "Finding that I was abandoned by my former backers and having little personal influence," he said, "I *dropped* the matter knowing it was useless to prosecute the business at that time."

His congressional term ending in March 1849, Lincoln campaigned vigorously for a presidential appointment as Commissioner of the Land Office—the highest office that would go to Illinois. On the strength of his services to the Taylor campaign, he believed he deserved the position. As commissioner, he would be responsible for deciding how to distribute all the public lands in the state. The office was awarded to another. It was just as well that Abraham Lincoln was not appointed. His strengths were those of the public leader, not the bureaucratic manager. "If I have one vice," he later quipped, "and I can call it nothing else,—it is not to be able to say no!" He then smiled and added: "Thank God for not making me a woman, but if He had, I suppose He would have made me just as ugly as He did, and no one would ever have tempted me."

Before he returned to Springfield, the former flatboatman applied to patent a method of lifting boats over shoals and bars by means of inflatable "buoyant chambers." Unfortunately, no analogous device existed to refloat a political career run aground. His securely Whig congressional district had turned Democratic, a shift many Whigs blamed on Lincoln's criticisms of the war. He was out of office, with little immediate prospect of return. Assessing his brief congressional tenure, there was little to celebrate. His term, John Nicolay wrote, "added practically nothing to his reputation." He had been a diligent congressman, making nearly all the roll calls and serving his party faithfully, but his efforts to distinguish himself—to make a mark—had failed.

All these disappointments notwithstanding, Lincoln had forged relationships and impressed men who would contribute significantly to his future success, including Caleb Smith of Indiana and Joshua Giddings of Ohio, Westerners whose political careers were similar to his.

Born in Boston, Caleb Smith had migrated west as a young man, ending up in Indiana, where he read law, was admitted to the bar, and entered politics as a Whig. He was a "handsome, trimly-built man," with a "smooth oval face." Despite a lisp, his power on the stump was celebrated far and wide. It was said that he could make you "feel the blood tingling through your veins to your finger ends and all the way up your spine." Indeed, one contemporary observer considered Smith a more compelling public speaker than Lincoln. Later, at the 1860 Republican Convention, Smith would help swing the Indiana delegation to Lincoln, a move that would lay the foundation for Lincoln's presidential nomination.

Joshua Giddings had faced obstacles as formidable as Lincoln. He had left his family and small farming community in Ashtabula County, Ohio, to study law in the town of Canfield, Ohio. His decision stunned his friends and neighbors. "He had lived with them from childhood, and toiled with them in the fields," his son-in-law, George Julian, observed. "He had never enjoyed the means of obtaining even a common-school education, and they regarded his course as the effect of a vain desire to defeat the designs of Providence, according to which they believed that people born in humble life should be content with their lot." Fourteen years older than Lincoln, Giddings was first elected to Congress in 1838. Reelected continuously after that, he threw himself at once into John Quincy Adams's valiant struggle over the right of Congress to receive antislavery petitions. While Giddings was decidedly more militant on the slavery issue than Lincoln, the two became close friends. Boarding together at Mrs. Spriggs's house in Carroll Row on Capitol Hill, they shared hundreds of meals, conversations, and stories. So much did Giddings like and respect Lincoln that seven years later, in 1855, when Lincoln ran for the Senate, Giddings proclaimed that he "would walk clear to Illinois" to help elect him.

Among Lincoln's Whig colleagues was Alexander Stephens of Georgia, later vice president of the Confederate states. Transfixed by Stephens's eloquent speaking style, Lincoln wrote a friend that "a little slim, pale-faced, consumptive man . . . has just concluded the very best speech, of an hour's length, I ever heard. My old, withered, dry eyes, are full of tears yet." (Lincoln was not yet forty.) Many years later, the classically educated Stephens recalled: "Mr. Lincoln was careful as to his manners, awkward in his speech, but was possessed of a very strong, clear and vigorous mind. He always attracted the riveted attention of the House when he spoke; his manner of speech as well as thought was original . . . his anecdotes were always exceedingly apt and pointed, and socially he always kept his company in a roar of laughter."

Lincoln's ability to win the respect of others, to earn their trust and even devotion, would prove essential in his rise to power. There was something mysterious in his persona that led countless men, even old adversaries, to feel bound to him in admiration.

• • •

TAKING UP HIS LAW PRACTICE once more, Lincoln began to feel, he later remarked, that he "was losing interest in politics." The likely reality was that his position on the Mexican War had temporarily closed the door to political office. Furthermore, this withdrawal from office was never complete. He worked to secure political posts for fellow Illinoisans, and joined in a call for a convention to reorganize the Whig Party. Through his lengthy eulogies for several Whig leaders, he spoke out on national issues, referring to slavery as "the one *great* question of the day." And he never missed an opportunity to criticize Stephen Douglas, now a leading national figure.

In the interim, he resolved to work at the law with "greater earnestness." His Springfield practice flourished, providing a steady income. Mary was able to enlarge their home, hire additional help with the household chores, and entertain more freely. These years should have been happy ones for Mary, but death intervened to crush her spirits. In the summer after Lincoln returned from Washington, Mary's father died during a cholera epidemic. He was only fifty-eight at the time, still vigorous and actively involved in politics; in fact, he was running for a seat in the Kentucky Senate when he succumbed to the epidemic. Six months later, Eliza Parker, Mary's beloved maternal grandmother, died in Lexington. To this grandmother, the six-year-old Mary had turned for love and consolation when her mother died.

February 1, 1850, brought Mary's most terrible loss: the death of her second son, three-year-old Eddie, from pulmonary tuberculosis. That destiny had branded her for misery became her conviction. For seven weeks, Mary had worked to arrest the high fever and racking cough that accompanied the relentless disease. Despite her ministrations, Eddie declined until he fell into unconsciousness and died early on the morning of the 1st. Neighbors recalled hearing Mary's inconsolable weeping. For days, she remained in her bed, refusing to eat, unable to stop crying. Only Lincoln, though despairing himself, was able to reach her. "Eat, Mary," he begged her, "for we must live."

Finally, Mary found some solace in long conversations with the pastor of the First Presbyterian Church, James Smith, who had conducted the funeral service for Eddie. So comforting was the pastor's faith in an eternal life after death that Mary was moved to join his congregation and renew her religious faith. A grateful Lincoln rented a family pew at the First Presbyterian and occasionally accompanied Mary to church, though he remained unable to share her thought that Eddie awaited their reunion in some afterlife.

Though Mary became pregnant again a month after Eddie's death, giving birth to a third son, William Wallace, in December 1850, and a fourth son, Thomas, in April 1853, Eddie's death left an indelible scar on her psyche—deepening her mood swings, magnifying her weaknesses, and increasing her fears. Tales of her erratic behavior began to circulate, stories of "hysterical outbursts" against her husband, rumors that she chased him through the yard with a knife, drove him from the house with a broomstick, smashed his head with a chunk of wood. Though the outbursts generally subsided as swiftly as they had begun, her instability and violent episodes unquestionably caused great upheavals in the family life.

When Mary fell into one of these moods, Lincoln developed what one neighbor called "a protective deafness," which doubtless exasperated her fury. Instead of engaging Mary directly, he would lose himself in thought, quietly leave the room, or take the children for a walk. If the discord continued, he would head to the state library or his office, where he would occasionally remain through the night until the emotional storm had ceased.

Had his marriage been happier, Lincoln's friends believed, he would have been satisfied as a country lawyer. Had he married "a woman of more angelic temperament," Springfield lawyer Milton Hay speculated, "he, doubtless, would have remained at home more and been less inclined to mingle with people outside."

Though a tranquil domestic union might have made Lincoln a happier man, the supposition that he would have been a contented homebody, like Edward Bates, belies everything we know of Lincoln's fierce ambition and extraordinary drive—an ambition that drove him to devour books in every spare moment, memorize his father's stories in order to captivate his friends, study law late into the night after a full day's work, and run for office at the age of twenty-three. Indeed, long before his political career even took shape, he had been determined to win the veneration of his fellow men by "rendering [himself] worthy" of their esteem.

Even as Lincoln focused his attention on the law, he was simply waiting for events to turn, waiting for the right time to reenter public life.

•   •   •

IF LINCOLN'S AMBITIONS appeared to have stalled, the careers of Seward and Chase gathered new momentum. Zachary Taylor's triumph at the polls created a Whig majority in the New York state legislature for the first time in many years. Because U.S. senators at the time were elected by state legislatures rather than by popular vote, Thurlow Weed focused his magic on the legislature to propel Seward into the U.S. Senate. His task was complicated by the division of the state's Whig Party into two distinct factions. Millard Fillmore, bolstered by his election as vice president, led the conservative wing, composed of merchants, capitalists, and cotton manufacturers who preferred to defuse the slavery issue. Weed and Seward represented the liberal wing.

Weed's difficulties were compounded when New York papers reported a fiery speech Seward delivered in Cleveland, putting him at odds with the

more moderate stance of the new administration. "There are two antagonistical elements of society in America," Seward had proclaimed, "freedom
and slavery. Freedom is in harmony with our system of government and
with the spirit of the age, and is therefore passive and quiescent. Slavery is
in conflict with that system, with justice, and with humanity, and is therefore organized, defensive, active, and perpetually aggressive." Free labor,
he said, demands universal suffrage and the widespread "diffusion of
knowledge." The slave-based system, by contrast "cherishes ignorance because it is the only security for oppression." Sectional conflict, Seward
warned, would inevitably arise from these two intrinsically different economic systems, which were producing dangerously divergent cultures, values, and assumptions.

Seward stood before his Cleveland audience and called for the abolition
of the black codes that prevented blacks from voting, sitting on juries, or
holding office in Ohio. Slavery, he conceded, was once the sin of all the
states. "We in New York are guilty of slavery still, by withholding the right
of suffrage from the race we have emancipated. You in Ohio are guilty in
the same way, by a system of black-laws still more aristocratic and odious."
Seward's support that day for the black vote, black presence on juries, and
black officeholding was startlingly radical for a mainstream politician. Even
a full decade later, during his debates with Stephen Douglas, Abraham Lincoln would maintain that he had never been in favor "of making voters or
jurors of negroes, nor of qualifying them to hold office, nor to intermarry."

Although the difference in their positions was due largely to the con-
trasting political environments of the more progressive New York and the
conservative, Southern-leaning Illinois, Seward was more willing than
Lincoln to employ language designed to ignite the emotions of particular
crowds, tailoring his rhetoric to suit the convictions of his immediate audience. Knowing that his audience in the Western Reserve was likely far
more progressive than many Eastern audiences, Seward ventured further
toward abolitionism than he had in the past. Even so, the *Cleveland Plain
Dealer* charged, Seward fell short of the antislavery zeal that put the Reserve a decade ahead of the East Coast.

Nor did Seward stop with his condemnation of the Black Laws, he proceeded to deliver a powerful attack against the Fugitive Slave Law, written,
he claimed, in violation of divine law. He brought his speech to a close with
a stirring appeal intended to rouse his audience to act. " 'Can nothing be
done for freedom because the public conscience is inert?' Yes, much can be
done—everything can be done. Slavery can be limited to its present
bounds, it can be ameliorated, it *can* be and *must* be abolished and you and
I can and must do it."

Seward's speech worried Weed. Though he agreed that slavery was "a political crime and a national curse—a great moral and political evil," he predicted that "this question of slavery, when it becomes a matter of political controversy, will shake, if not unsettle, the foundations of our Government. It is too fearful, and too mighty, in all its bearings and consequences, to be recklessly mixed up in our partisan conflicts."

At a time when professed abolitionists remained an unpopular minority, subjected in some Northern cities to physical assault, Weed warned Seward that his provocative language would place him in the same camp with extremist figures such as William Lloyd Garrison and Wendell Phillips. Seward weighed Weed's concerns, acknowledging that the emancipation issue had not fully "ripened." In the weeks that followed, he muted his stridency on slavery, allowing Weed the space necessary to carry his protégé to the next level. Weed ingratiated Seward with the legislators one by one. He rounded up the liberals and assured the moderates that when Seward talked about slavery, he "wanted to level society up, not down." Furthermore, he promised the Taylor administration that Seward would loyally follow the moderate party line. Despite the split in the party and Fillmore's rising star, Weed managed to corral a majority and send his friend Seward to the Senate.

"Probably no man ever yet appeared for the first time in Congress so widely known and so warmly appreciated," declared the *New York Tribune* after his election. Seward arrived with an aura of celebrity, even notoriety. Yet Weed proved correct when he anticipated that Seward's radical speech in Cleveland would come back to haunt him. Not long after the young New Yorker was sworn into the Senate, a Southern senator rose from his seat and read aloud the peroration in which Seward told his audience that slavery "can and must be abolished." It was said that "a shudder" ran through the chamber. "If we ever find you in Georgia," one letter writer warned Seward, "you will forfeit your odious neck."

• • •

SALMON CHASE'S BID for success through a viable antislavery party came to fruition in 1849. Thirteen Free-Soilers had been elected to the seventy-two-member Ohio state legislature, which would choose the next U.S. senator. Neither the Whigs nor the Democrats had a controlling majority, which gave the tiny Free Soil bloc enormous leverage. Though many assumed that former Whig Joshua Giddings, who had championed the antislavery cause in Congress for more than a decade, had earned the right to be considered the front-runner, Chase managed to gain the seat for himself. Ironically, his winning tactics in pursuit of this goal would shadow his career and ultimately bring him the lasting enmity of many important figures in his own state.

Most of the Free-Soilers were former Whigs who would not vote with the Democrats. They favored Giddings. Two independents, meanwhile, vacillated: Dr. Norton Townshend, once a Democrat, who had been a member of the Liberty Party; and John F. Morse, formerly a "conscience Whig." The decisions of these two men would prove pivotal. Working behind the scenes, Chase drafted a deal with Samuel Medary, the boss of the Democratic Party in Ohio. If Chase delivered Townshend and Morse to the Democrats, Medary would see to it that Chase became the new U.S. senator. In addition, the Democrats would vote to repeal the Black Laws, a condition Morse insisted upon before he would agree to the deal. In return, the Democrats would have the House speakership and control of the extensive patronage that office enjoyed. For Medary, control of the state was far more important than naming a senator.

Chase worked ceaselessly to deliver Townshend and Morse to the Democrats. While Giddings remained in Washington, Chase journeyed to Columbus and took a room at the Neil House close to the state Capitol so he could attend Free Soil caucuses at night and negotiate with individual Democrats during the day. He planted articles in key newspapers, praising not only himself but Townshend and Morse. He lent money to more than one paper, and when the needs of the Free Soil weekly, the Columbus *Daily Standard*, exceeded his means, he reassured its editor: "After the Senatorial Election, whether the choice falls on me or another, I can act more efficiently, and you may rely on me." He advanced money to the *Standard* and later agreed to a loan but refused to take a mortgage on the newspaper as security because he did not want his name publicly connected, "which could not be avoided in case of a mortgage to myself."

Knowing that Morse was introducing a bill to establish separate schools for blacks, Chase enlisted the editor of the *Standard* to help get it passed. "It is really important," he urged, "and if it can be got through with the help of democratic votes, will do a great deal of good to the cause generally & our friend Morse especially." Certainly, it would do a great deal of good for the career of Salmon Chase, who sanctimoniously told Morse that the only consideration in determining the next senator should be ability to best advance the cause: "Every thing, but sacrifice of principle, for the Cause, and nothing for men except as instruments of the Cause." Advancement of self and advancement of the cause were intertwined in Chase's mind. In Chase's mind, both were served when Morse and Townshend voted with the Democrats to organize the legislature and the victorious Medary swung his new Democratic majority to Chase for senator.

The unusual circumstances of Chase's election provoked negative comment in the press. "Every act of his was subsidiary to his own ambition," charged the *Ohio State Journal:* "He talked of the interests of Free Soil, he *meant* His Own." This judgment by a hostile paper was perhaps unduly harsh, for the deal with the Democrats did indeed end up promoting the Free Soil cause. As Medary had promised, the Democrats voted to repeal the hated Black Laws. And when Chase reached the Senate, he would become a stalwart leader in the antislavery cause.

Nonetheless, fallout from Chase's Senate election eventually found its way into the widely circulated pages of Horace Greeley's *New York Tribune*. Editorializing on the machinations involved, Greeley declared that he did "not see how men who desire to maintain a decent reputation can countenance or profit by it." Indeed, the suspicions and mistrust engendered by the peculiar circumstances of the Senate election would never be wholly erased. "It lost to him at once and forever the confidence of every Whig of middle age in Ohio," a fellow politician observed. "Its shadow never wholly dispelled, always fell upon him, and hovered near and darkened his pathway at the critical places in his political after life." The Whigs, and their later counterparts, the Republicans, would deny Chase the united support of the Ohio delegation so vital to his hopes for the presidential nomination in 1860. And Chase, for his part, would never forgive them.

Showing little intuitive sense of how others might view his maneuvering, Chase failed to appreciate that with each party shift, he betrayed old associates and made lifelong enemies. Certainly, his willingness to sever bonds and forge new alliances, though at times courageous and visionary, was out of step with the political custom of the times.

Though troubled by the criticism attending his election, Chase was thrilled with his victory. So was Charles Sumner, who would join Chase two years later in the Senate by way of a similar alliance between Free-Soilers and independent Democrats in Massachusetts. "I can hardly believe it," Sumner wrote. "It does seem to me that this is 'the beginning of the end.' Your election must influence all the Great West. Still more your presence in the Senate will give an unprecedented impulse to the discussion of our cause."

When Chase took his seat in the handsome Senate chamber in March 1849, nearly twenty years had elapsed since his early days as a poor teacher living on the margins of the city's social whirl. Now, as a renowned political organizer, prominent lawyer, and fabled antislavery crusader, Chase could claim a place in the first tier of Washington society. William Wirt would have been proud. For a brief moment, Chase's relentless need "to be first wherever I may be" was sated.

As the 1840s drew to a close, William Henry Seward and Salmon P. Chase had moved toward the summit of political power in the United States Senate. Edward Bates, though spending most of his days at his country home with his ever-growing family, had become a widely respected national figure, considered a top prospect for a variety of high political posts. Abraham Lincoln, by contrast, was practicing law, regaling his fellow lawyers on the circuit with an endless stream of anecdotes, and reflecting with silent absorption on the great issues of the day.

Seattle

Portland
Salem

OREGON
TERRITORY,
1848

Columbia R.

Cascade Range

Snake R.

Rocky Mountains

Missouri R.

NEBRASKA
TERRITORY

Missouri R.

Platte R.

Sacramento R.

Sacramento

San Francisco

Great Salt Lake

Salt Lake City

UTAH TERRITORY

Colorado R.

KANSAS TERRITORY

Arkansas R.

CALIFORNIA

Missouri Compromise line 36° 30'

NEW MEXICO
TERRITORY

Rio Grande

Santa Fe

Canadian R.

Red R.

Oklahoma
City

INDIAN
TERRITORY

Dallas •

TEXAS

Austin •

Pacific

Ocean

MEXICO

Sierra Madre

Rio Grande

0 Miles   500

0 Kilometers   500

Legal Boundary Against the Spread of Slavery,
Drawn by Congress in 1820 (Missouri Compromise)

States (& the District of Columbia)
Where Slavery Existed by Law in 1856

UNITED STATES, CIRCA 1856 .

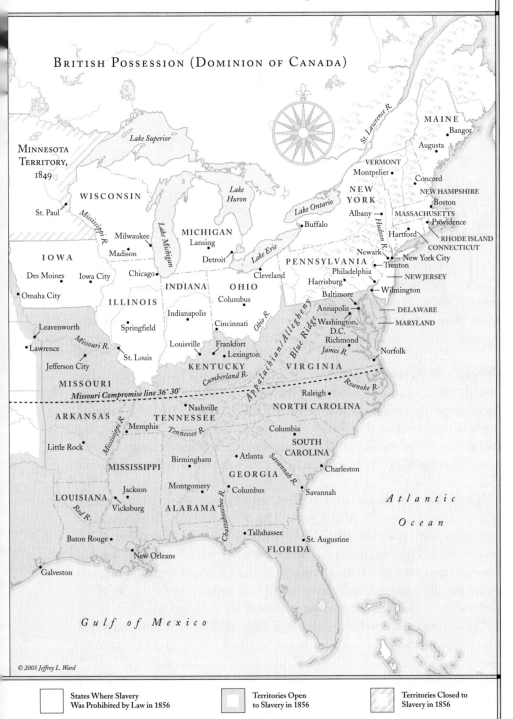

BRITISH POSSESSION (DOMINION OF CANADA)

MINNESOTA TERRITORY, 1849

Lake Superior

WISCONSIN

St. Paul

Mississippi R.

Milwaukee

MICHIGAN
Lansing

Lake Huron

Madison

Lake Michigan

Detroit

Lake Erie

Cleveland

MAINE
Bangor
Augusta

VERMONT
Montpelier

Concord

NEW HAMPSHIRE
Boston

St. Lawrence R.

NEW YORK

Albany

Lake Ontario

Buffalo

MASSACHUSETTS

Providence

RHODE ISLAND
CONNECTICUT

Hartford

IOWA
Des Moines   Iowa City
Chicago

Omaha City

ILLINOIS

Leavenworth

Lawrence

Missouri R.

Jefferson City

MISSOURI

INDIANA   OHIO
Columbus

Indianapolis

Springfield

Ohio R.

Cincinnati

Louisville   Frankfort
St. Louis   Lexington

KENTUCKY

Cumberland R.

Hudson R.

PENNSYLVANIA

Harrisburg
Philadelphia

Baltimore

Newark   New York City
Trenton

NEW JERSEY

Wilmington

DELAWARE

Annapolis
Washington, D.C.
Richmond   MARYLAND

James R.

Norfolk

VIRGINIA

Appalachian/Allegheny
Blue Ridge

Missouri Compromise line 36° 30'

ARKANSAS

Little Rock

Mississippi R.

TENNESSEE
Memphis

Tennessee R.

Nashville

Roanoke R.

Raleigh

NORTH CAROLINA

Columbia

SOUTH CAROLINA

Charleston

MISSISSIPPI

Birmingham

Atlanta

Savannah R.

Jackson

Montgomery

GEORGIA
Columbus

Savannah

LOUISIANA
Red R.

Vicksburg

ALABAMA

Chattahoochee R.

Atlantic Ocean

Baton Rouge

Tallahassee

St. Augustine

New Orleans

FLORIDA

Galveston

Gulf of Mexico

© 2005 Jeffrey L. Ward

| States Where Slavery Was Prohibited by Law in 1856 | Territories Open to Slavery in 1856 | Territories Closed to Slavery in 1856 |

CHAPTER 5

THE TURBULENT FIFTIES

HE AMERICA OF 1850 was a largely rural nation of about 23 million people in which politics and public issues—at every level of government—were of consuming interest. Citizen participation in public life far exceeded that of later years. Nearly three fourths of those eligible to vote participated in the two presidential elections of the decade.

The principal weapon of political combatants was the speech. A gift for oratory was the key to success in politics. Even as a child, Lincoln had honed his skills by addressing his companions from a tree stump. Speeches on important occasions were exhaustively researched and closely reasoned, often lasting three or four hours. There was demagoguery, of course, but there were also metaphors and references to literature and classical history and occasionally, as with some of Lincoln's speeches, a lasting literary glory.

The issues and declamations of politics were carried to the people by newspapers—the media of the time. The great majority of papers were highly partisan. Editors and publishers, as the careers of Thurlow Weed and Horace Greeley illustrate, were often powerful political figures. Newspapers in the nineteenth century, author Charles Ingersoll observed, "were the daily fare of nearly every meal in almost every family; so cheap and common, that, like air and water, its uses are undervalued."

"Look into the morning trains," Ralph Waldo Emerson marveled, which "carry the business men into the city to their shops, counting-rooms, workyards and warehouses." Into every car the newsboy "unfolds his magical sheets,—twopence a head his bread of knowledge costs—and instantly the entire rectangular assembly, fresh from their breakfast, are bending as one man to their second breakfast." A European tourist was amazed at the central role newspapers played in the life of the new nation. "You meet newspaper readers everywhere; and in the evening the whole city knows what lay twenty-four hours ago on newswriters' desks. . . . The few who cannot read can hear news discussed or read aloud in ale- and-oyster houses."

Seventeen years before the decade had begun, President Andrew Jackson had prophesied: "The nullifiers in the south intend to blow up a storm on the slave question . . . be assured these men would do any act to destroy this union and form a southern confederacy bounded, north, by the Potomac river."

And now the storm had come.

The slavery issue had been a source of division between North and South from the beginning of the nation. That difference was embodied in the Constitution itself, which provided that a slave would be counted as three fifths of a person for purposes of congressional representation and which imposed an obligation to surrender fugitive slaves to their lawful masters. Although slavery was not named in the Constitution, it was, as antislavery Congressman John Quincy Adams said, "written in the bond," which meant that he, like everyone else, must "faithfully perform its obligations."

The constitutional compromise that protected slavery in states where it already existed did not apply to newly acquired territories. Thus, every expansion of the nation reignited the divisive issue. The Missouri Compromise had provided a temporary solution for nearly three decades, but when Congress was called upon to decide the fate of the new territories acquired in the Mexican War, the stage was set for the renewal of the national debate. "If by your legislation you seek to drive us from the territories of California and New Mexico, purchased by the common blood and treasure of the whole people," Robert Toombs of Georgia warned, "*I am for disunion.*" Mississippi called for a convention of Southern states to meet in Nashville for the defense of Southern rights.

The issue of slavery could no longer be put aside. It would dominate the debates in Congress. As Thomas Hart Benton once colorfully observed: "We read in Holy Writ, that a certain people were cursed by the plague of frogs, and that the plague was everywhere! You could not look upon the table but there were frogs, you could not sit down at the banquet but there were frogs, you could not go to the bridal couch and lift the sheets but there were frogs!" A similar affliction infested national discourse as every other topic was subsumed by slavery. "We can see nothing, touch nothing, have no measures proposed, without having this pestilence thrust before us. Here it is, this black question, forever on the table, on the nuptial couch, everywhere!"

Of course, slavery was not the only issue that divided the sections. The South opposed protective tariffs designed to foster Northern manufacturing and fought against using the national resources for internal improvements in Northern transportation. But issues like these, however hard fought, were subject to political accommodation. Slavery was not. "We must concern ourselves with what is, and slavery exists," said John Randolph of Virginia early in the century. Slavery "is to us a question of life and death." By the 1850s, Randolph's observation had come to fruition. The "peculiar institution" now permeated every aspect of Southern society—economically, politically, and socially. For a minority in the North, on the other hand, slavery represented a profoundly disturbing moral issue. For many more Northerners, the expansion of slavery into the territories threatened the triumph of the free labor movement. Events of the 1850s would put these "antagonistical elements" on a collision course.

"It is a great mistake," warned John Calhoun in 1850, "to suppose that disunion can be effected by a single blow. The cords which bind these States together in one common Union are far too numerous and powerful for that. Disunion must be the work of time. It is only through a long process . . . that the cords can be snapped until the whole fabric falls asunder. Already the agitation of the slavery question has snapped some of the most important." If these common cords continue to rupture, he predicted, "nothing will be left to hold the States together except force."

The spiritual cords of union—the great religious denominations—had already been fractured along sectional lines. The national political parties, the political cords of union, would be next, splintered in the struggle between those who wished to extend slavery and those who resisted its expansion. Early in the decade the national Whig Party, hopelessly divided on slavery, would begin to diminish and then disappear as a national force. The national Democratic Party, beset by defections from Free Soil Democrats, would steadily lose ground, fragmenting beyond repair by the end of the decade.

The ties that bound the Union were not simply institutions but a less tangible sense of nationhood—shared pride in the achievements of the revolutionary generation, a sense of mutual interests and common aspirations for the future. The chronicle of the 1850s is, at bottom, a narrative of the increasing strain placed upon these cords, their gradual fraying, and their final rupture. Abraham Lincoln would correctly prophesy that a house divided against itself could not stand. By the end of the decade, as Calhoun had warned, only force would be left to sustain the Union.

Was this outcome inevitable? It is not a question that can be answered in the abstract. We must begin with the historical realities and ask if the same actors with the same convictions, emotions, and passions could have behaved differently. Possibly, but all we can know for certain is that they felt what they felt, believed as they believed, and did as they would do. And so they moved the country inexorably toward Civil War.

· · ·

As THE 31ST CONGRESS OPENED, the rancorous discord boiled to the surface. All eyes turned to the seventy-three-year-old Henry Clay, who, Lincoln later said, was "regarded by all, as *the* man for a crisis." Henry Clay had saved the Union once before. Now, thirty years after the Missouri Compromise, the Congress and nation looked to him once again. Already Clay suffered from the tuberculosis that would take his life two years later. He could not even manage the stairs leading up to the Senate chamber. Nonetheless, when he took the floor to introduce the cluster of resolutions that would become known as the Compromise of 1850, he mustered, the *New York Tribune* marveled, "the spirit and the fire of youth."

He began by admitting he had never been "so anxious" facing his colleagues, for he believed the country stood "at the edge of the precipice." He beseeched his colleagues to halt "before the fearful and disastrous leap is taken in the yawning abyss below, which will inevitably lead to certain and irretrievable destruction." He prophesied that dissolution would bring a war "so furious, so bloody, so implacable and so exterminating" that it would be marked forever in the pages of history. To avoid catastrophe, a compromise must be reached.

His first resolution called for admitting the state of California immediately, leaving the decision regarding the status of slavery within its borders to California's new state legislature. As it was widely known that a majority of Californians wished to prohibit slavery entirely, this resolution favored the North. He then proposed dividing the remainder of the Mexican accession into two territories, New Mexico and Utah, with no restrictions on slavery—a provision that favored the South. He called for an end to the slave trade within the boundaries of the national capital, but called on Congress to strengthen the old Fugitive Slave Law of 1793 to facilitate the recapture of runaway slaves. Fugitives would be denied a jury trial, commissioners would adjudicate claims, and federal marshals would be empowered to draft citizens to hunt down escapees.

Clay recognized that the compromise resolutions demanded far greater concessions from the North than he had asked from the slave states, but he appealed to the North to sustain the Union. Northern objections to slavery were based on ideology and sentiment, rather than on the Southern concerns with property, social intercourse, habit, safety, and life itself. The North had nothing tangible to lose. Finally, he implored God that "if the direful and sad event of the dissolution of the Union shall happen, I may not survive to behold the sad and heart-rending spectacle." This prayer was answered. He died two years later, nearly a decade before the Civil War began.

Frances Seward was in the overcrowded gallery on February 5, 1850, when Henry Clay rose from his desk to speak. She had come to Washington to help her husband get settled in a spacious three-story brick house on the north side of F Street. "He *is* a charming orator," Frances confessed to her sister. "I have never heard but one more impressive speaker—and that is *our* Henry (don't say this to anybody)." But Clay was mistaken, she claimed, if he believed the wound between North and South could be sutured by his persuasive charm. Though he might make "doughfaces out of half the Congress," his arguments had not convinced her. Most upsetting was Clay's claim that "Northern men were only activated by policy and party spirits. Now if Henry Clay has lived to be 70 years old and still thinks slavery is opposed only from such motives I can only say he knows much less of human nature than I supposed."

Four weeks later, the galleries were once again filled to hear South Carolina's John Calhoun speak. Although unsteady in his walk and enveloped in flannels to ward off the chill of pneumonia that had plagued him all winter, the sixty-seven-year-old arch defender of states' rights appeared in the Senate with the text of the speech he intended to deliver. He rose with great difficulty from his chair and then, recognizing that he was too weak to speak, handed his remarks to his friend Senator James Mason of Virginia to read.

The speech was an uncompromising diatribe against the North. Calhoun warned that secession was the sole option unless the North conceded the Southern right to bring slavery into every section of the new territories, stopped agitating the slave question, and consented to a constitutional provision restoring the balance of power between the two regions. Making much the same argument he had utilized in the early debates surrounding the Wilmot Proviso, he warned that additional free states would tilt the power in the Senate, as well as in the House of Representatives, and destroy "the equilibrium between the two sections in the Government, as it stood when the constitution was ratified." This final address to the Senate concluded, Calhoun retired to his boardinghouse, where he would die before the month was out.

Daniel Webster of Massachusetts, the third of the "great triumvirate"(as Clay, Calhoun, and Webster were called), was scheduled to speak on the 7th of March. The Senate chamber was "crammed" with more men and women, a Washington newspaper reported, than on any previous occasion. Anticipation soared with the rumor that Webster had decided, against the fervent hopes of his overwhelmingly antislavery constituents, to support Clay's Southern-leaning compromise. Frances Seward was watching when the senator rose.

"I wish to speak to-day, not as a Massachusetts man, nor as a northern man, but as an American," Webster began. "I speak to-day for the preservation of the Union. 'Hear me for my cause.' " He proceeded to stun many in the North by castigating abolitionists, vowing never to support the Wilmot Proviso, and coming out in favor of every one of Clay's resolutions—including the provision to strengthen the hateful Fugitive Slave Law. Many in New England found Webster's new stand particularly abhorrent. "Mr Webster has deliberately taken out his name from all the files of honour," Ralph Waldo Emerson wrote. "He has undone all that he spent his years in doing."

Frances found the speech greatly disappointing. The word "compromise," she told her sister, "is becoming hateful to me." Acknowledging that Webster was "a forcible speaker," particularly when he extolled the Union, she found him "much less eloquent than Henry Clay because his heart is decidedly colder—people must have feeling themselves to touch others." Despite such criticisms, the speech won nationwide approval from moderates who desperately wanted a peaceful settlement of the situation. A few antislavery Whigs expressed a fear that Seward might hesitate when the time came to deliver his own speech, scheduled three days later. "How little they know his nature," Frances wrote. "Every concession of Mr. Webster to Southern principles only makes Henry advocate more strongly the cause which he thinks just."

Frances was right. Antislavery advocates had no need to worry about her husband. For weeks, Seward had been working hard on his maiden address to the Senate, delivered on March 11, 1850. He had talked at length with Weed and rehearsed various drafts before Frances. The Capitol of the 1850s offered no private office space, so Seward wrote at home, rising early in the morning and working long past the midnight hour.

As he began his Senate oration, Seward spoke somewhat hesitantly. Reading from his manuscript without dramatic gestures, he quoted Machiavelli, Montesquieu, and the ancient philosophers in a voice so low that it seemed he was talking to himself rather than addressing the chamber and the galleries. His words were so powerful, however, that Webster was riveted; while John Calhoun, attending one of his final sessions in the chamber, was "restless at first" but "soon sat still."

Seward began by maintaining flatly that he was opposed to compromise, "in any and all the forms in which it has been proposed." He refused to strengthen the Fugitive Slave Law. "We are not slaveholders. We cannot . . . be either true Christians or real freemen," he continued, "if we impose on another a chain that we defy all human power to fasten on ourselves." He declared that a ban on the slave trade in the District was insufficient: slavery itself must be abolished in the capital. Finally, staunchly affirming the Wilmot Proviso, he refused to accept the introduction of slavery anywhere in the new territories.

As he moved into the second hour of his speech, his conviction gave him ease and confidence. Step by step, he laid the foundation for the "higher law" doctrine that would be forever associated with his name. Not only did the Constitution bind the American people to goals incompatible with slavery, he asserted, "but there is a higher law than the Constitution, which regulates our authority over the domain, and devotes it to the same noble purposes. The territory is a part . . . of the common heritage of mankind, bestowed upon them by the Creator of the universe. We are his stewards."

With this single speech, his first national address, Seward became the principal antislavery voice in the Senate. Tens of thousands of copies of the speech were printed and distributed throughout the North. The *New York Tribune* predicted that it would awaken the nation, that his words would "live longer, be read with a more hearty admiration, and exert a more potential and pervading influence on the National mind and character than any other speech of the Session."

• • •

ARRIVING ON THE NATIONAL SCENE at this same dramatic moment, Chase expected to take a leading role in the fight. He, too, labored over his speech for weeks, poring through old statute books and exchanging ideas with fellow crusader Charles Sumner. The bond between Chase and Sumner would continue to grow through the years, providing both men with emotional support in the face of the condemnation they suffered due to their strong antislavery views. "I find no man so congenial to me as yourself," Chase confided in Sumner. For his part, Sumner considered Chase "a tower of strength" whose election to the Senate would "confirm the irresolute, quicken the indolent and confound the trimmers."

"I cannot disguise the deep interest with which I watch your movements," Sumner wrote Chase shortly before he was to give his speech. "I count confidently upon an exposition of our cause which will toll throughout the country." When Chase took the floor on March 26, for the first part of his five-hour address, however, Seward had already delivered the celebrated address that outlined most of the positions Chase intended to take and had instantly made the fiery New Yorker the foremost national voice among the antislavery forces.

Nor did Chase possess Seward's compelling speaking style. If, over the years, constant practice had improved his range and delivery, he was unable to eradicate the slight lisp that remained from his boyhood days. Although his arguments were thoughtful and well reasoned, the chamber emptied long before he finished speaking. Writing home, he admitted great disappointment with the result, which was "infinitely below my own standards . . . and fell below those of my friends who expected much."

"You know I am not a rousing speaker at best," he conceded in a letter to a friend. He wanted it understood, however, that the speech was delivered "under very great disadvantages": the first chapter of the celebrated Benton-Foote confrontation, "which so engaged the attention of everybody," occurred on the very same day, so that "I had hardly any chance of attention, and in fact, received not much."

Chase was referring to a dramatic argument that broke out on the Senate floor between Senator Thomas Hart Benton of Missouri and Senator Henry Foote of Mississippi. Benton had called Foote a coward, leading Foote to recall an earlier histrionic incident when Benton himself had behaved in cowardly fashion. In response to this personal attack, Benton rose from his chair and rushed forward menacingly. Foote retreated behind a desk and then drew and cocked a pistol. "I disdain to carry arms!" Benton shouted. "Let him fire! . . . Stand out of the way, and let the assassin fire!" The melodrama was finally brought to a peaceful close when Foote was persuaded to hand over his pistol to a fellow senator and Benton returned to his chair.

Chase's disappointment over his failure was compounded by Sumner's praise for Seward's compelling maiden effort, which, Sumner told Chase, had filled him with gratitude. "Seward is with us," Sumner exulted. "You mistake when you say 'Seward is with us,' " Chase replied, with a heat not unmixed with resentment. While Seward "holds many of our Anti Slavery opinions," he continued, his loyalty to the Whig Party made him untrustworthy. "I have never been able to establish much sympathy between us," he explained in a follow-up letter. "He is too much of a politician for me."

Over the course of the previous decade, Seward and Chase had maintained a dialogue on the most effective methods to promote the antislavery cause. Despite their divergent views on whether or not to join a third party, Chase had always held Seward in the highest esteem and looked forward to working with him on antislavery issues in the Senate.

The alteration in his attitude was likely spurred by jealousy, an emotion the introspective Chase begrudged in others yet could never subdue in himself. "I made this resolution today," he had confided in his diary when he was twenty-three years old. "I will try to excel in all things yet if I am excelled, without fault of mine, I will not be mortified. I will not withhold from any one the praise which I think his due; nor will I allow myself to envy another's praise or to feel jealousy when I hear him praised. May God help me to keep it." His best intentions, however, could not assuage the invidious envy that possessed him at the realization that, given an identical opportunity, Seward had emerged the acclaimed leader of the antislavery forces. A rift developed between the two men that would last long into the Lincoln administration, with far-reaching consequences for the country.

Even as Seward basked in the applause of the antislavery community, however, he found himself excoriated in both Southern editorials and conservative papers throughout the North. "Senator Seward is against all compromise," the *New York Herald* observed, "so are the negroes of New York. . . . [His] views are those of the extreme fanatics of the North, looking forward to the utter destruction of the institutions of the South." Seward was initially untroubled by such criticism from expected sources and remained convinced he had "spoken words that will tell when I am dead." Frances had never been prouder of her husband. When she looked at him, she told her sister, she felt almost overwhelmed by her love and respect for him.

Such elation was soon tempered by a disquieting letter from Weed, who feared that Seward had overreached when enunciating a "higher law" than the Constitution. Though Weed had seen earlier versions, he had not read the final draft. "Your speech . . . sent me to bed with a heavy heart," Weed confessed to Seward. "A restless night and an anxious day have not relieved my apprehensions." Weed's criticism distressed Seward, who recognized that his mentor's political instincts were usually better than his own. Indeed, the implications of Weed's critical letter left Seward sunk in "despondency . . . covered with sorrow and shame," apprehensive that he had jeopardized not only his own career but that of his mentor as well.

Seward's status was further shaken when President Zachary Taylor, who had admitted both Weed and Seward to his inner circle, developed a fatal gastronomical illness after attending Fourth of July festivities on the grounds of the unfinished Washington Monument. Taylor's sudden death brought Seward's conservative rival, Millard Fillmore, into the presidency.

With Fillmore in the White House, the antislavery contingent had no prospect of stopping the Compromise. Under the skillful leadership of Illinois senator Stephen Douglas, Clay's omnibus bill was broken up into a series of separate pieces of legislation, which passed in both the House and Senate in September.

The Compromise of 1850 seemed to end the crisis. Stephen Douglas regarded the bill as a "final settlement," urging his colleagues on both sides to "stop the debate, and drop the subject." Upon its passage, the leading hotels in the capital were illuminated and a salute of one hundred guns was sounded. Serenaders, accompanied by a large crowd of spectators, honored Clay, Webster, and Douglas, singing "Hail Columbia" and "The Star-Spangled Banner" under the windows of their residences. "The joy of everyone seemed unbounded," the *New York Tribune* noted. The Southern-leaning Lewis Cass exulted: "The crisis is passed—the cloud is gone." While the nation hailed the Compromise, however, a Georgia editor warned prophetically: "The elements of that contest are yet all alive and they are destined yet to outlive the Government. There is a feud between the North and the South which may be smothered, but never overcome."

. . .

In Springfield, tracing the unfolding drama in the newspapers, Abraham Lincoln appeared to be satisfied that a peaceful solution had been reached. While he was unhappy about the provision bolstering the Fugitive Slave Law, he understood, he later said, that "devotion to the Union rightfully inclined men to yield somewhat, in points where nothing could have so inclined them." Rejecting Seward's concept of a "higher law," he preferred to rest his own opposition to slavery in the Constitution and the Declaration of Independence.

During the relative calm that followed the passage of the Compromise, Lincoln rode the legal circuit, a pursuit that proved congenial to his personality as well as his finances. He relished the convivial life he shared with the lawyers who battled one another fiercely during the day, only to gather as friends in the taverns at night. The arrival of the judge and lawyers generally created a stir in each town on their circuit. Villagers traveled from miles around, anticipating the courtroom drama as hundreds of small cases were tried, ranging from disputed wills, divorce, and bastardy proceedings to slander and libel suits, from patent challenges and collection of debts to murder and robbery.

"The local belles came in to see and be seen," fellow circuit rider Henry Whitney recalled, "and the court house, from 'early morn till dewy eve,' and the tavern from dewy eve to early morn, were replete with bustle, business, energy, hilarity, novelty, irony, sarcasm, excitement and eloquence." In some villages, the boardinghouses were clean and comfortable and the food was excellent; in others, there were "plenty of bedbugs" and the dirt was "half an inch thick." The lawyers generally slept two to a bed, with three or four beds in a room. While most of the traveling bar regularly bemoaned the living conditions, Lincoln savored the rollicking life on the circuit.

He was singularly good at his work, earning the respect and admiration of his fellow lawyers. Several of these associates became great friends and supporters, among them Circuit Judge David Davis. In letters to his wife, Sarah, Davis spoke not only of Lincoln's exceptional skill in addressing juries but of his "warm-hearted" nature and his "exceeding honesty & fairness." Davis had come to Illinois from Maryland when he was twenty-one, after graduating from Kenyon College and New Haven Law School. In his late twenties he was elected to the state legislature and considered a career in politics, but his wife, whom he loved "too well to thwart her views," was vehemently opposed. Instead, he ran for circuit judge, a position that offered the camaraderie of the circuit six months a year, yet enabled him to devote sufficient energy to business ventures that he eventually accumulated a substantial fortune.

The evolution of a warm and intimate friendship with Lincoln is evident in the judge's letters home. The two men took lazy strolls along the river, shared accommodations in various villages, read books in common, and enjoyed long conversations on the rides from one county to the next. No lawyer on the circuit was better loved than Lincoln, a fellow lawyer recalled. "He arrogated to himself no superiority over anyone—not even the most obscure member of the bar. . . . He was remarkably gentle with young lawyers. . . . No young lawyer ever practised in the courts with Mr. Lincoln who did not in all his after life have a regard for him akin to personal affection."

At mealtimes, all those with an interest in the various cases at hand would eat together at the same long table. Judge Davis would preside, surrounded by the lawyers, the members of the jury, the witnesses, the bailiffs, and the prisoners out on bail. Once the meal was done, everyone would gather before the blazing fire or in Judge Davis's quarters to talk, drink, smoke, and share stories. Though Lincoln did not drink, smoke tobacco, use profane language, or engage in games of chance, he never condescended to those who did. On the contrary, when he had addressed the Springfield Temperance Society at the height of the temperance crusade, he had insisted that "such of us as have never fallen victims, have been spared more from the absence of appetite, than from any mental or moral superiority over those who have."

No sooner had everyone settled in than the call would come for Lincoln to take center stage. Standing with his back to the fire, he juggled one tale after another, Herndon recalled, keeping his audience "in full laugh till near daylight." His "eyes would sparkle with fun," one old-timer remembered, "and when he had reached the point in his narrative which invariably evoked the laughter of the crowd, nobody's enjoyment was greater than his."

One of Lincoln's favorite anecdotes sprang from the early days just after the Revolution. Shortly after the peace was signed, the story began, the Revolutionary War hero Ethan Allen "had occasion to visit England," where he was subjected to considerable teasing banter. The British would make "fun of the Americans and General Washington in particular and one day they got a picture of General Washington" and displayed it prominently in the outhouse so Mr. Allen could not miss it. When he made no mention of it, they finally asked him if he had seen the Washington picture. Mr. Allen said, "he thought that it was a very appropriate [place] for an Englishman to Keep it. Why they asked, for said Mr. Allen there is Nothing that Will Make an Englishman Shit So quick as the Sight of Genl Washington."

Another story, relayed years later by John Usher, centered on a man "who had a great veneration for Revolutionary relics." Learning that an old woman still possessed a dress that "she had worn in the Revolutionary War," he traveled to her house and asked to see it. She took the dress from a bureau and handed it to him. He was so excited that he brought the dress to his lips and kissed it. "The practical old lady rather resented such foolishness over an old piece of wearing apparel and she said: 'Stranger if you want to kiss something old you had better kiss my ass. It is sixteen years older than that dress.' "

But Lincoln's stories provided more than mere amusement. Drawn from his own experiences and the curiosities reported by others, they frequently provided maxims or proverbs that usefully connected to the lives of his listeners. Lincoln possessed an extraordinary ability to convey practical wisdom in the form of humorous tales his listeners could remember and repeat. This process of repetition is central to the oral tradition; indeed, Walter Benjamin in his essay on the storyteller's art suggests that repetition "is the nature of the web in which the gift of storytelling is cradled."

"Would we do nothing but listen to Lincoln's stories?" Whitney was asked. "Oh! yes, we frequently talked philosophy, politics, political economy, metaphysics and men; in short, our subjects of conversation ranged through the universe of thought and experience." Years later, Whitney recalled a lengthy discussion about George Washington. The question for debate was whether the first president was perfect, or whether, being human, he was fallible. According to Whitney, Lincoln thought there was merit in retaining the notion of a Washington without blemish that they had all been taught as children. "It makes human nature better to believe that one human being was perfect," Lincoln argued, "that human perfection is possible."

When the court closed on Saturday afternoons, most of the lawyers traveled home to rejoin their families, returning on Sunday night or Monday morning. Davis later recalled that Lincoln was the exception to the rule, often remaining on the circuit throughout the weekend. At first they all "wondered at it," Davis said; but they "soon learned to account for his strange disinclination to go home"—while "most of us had pleasant, inviting homes" to return to, Lincoln did not. With the traveling bar, Lincoln was "as happy as *he* could be . . . and happy no other place." Herndon agreed, arguing that Lincoln stayed on the circuit as long as he could because "his home was *Hell.* . . . Absence from home was his *Heaven.*"

Such withering commentary on Lincoln's marriage and home life was made years afterward, when both Davis and Herndon had developed a deep hostility to Mary. The letters Davis wrote to Sarah at the time reveal quite a different story. "Lincoln speaks very affectionately of his wife & children," Davis told Sarah in 1851. On other occasions, Davis described a letter Lincoln had received from Mary reporting nursing troubles with Willie, and a conversation in which Lincoln had confided that both he and Mary were hoping for a girl before Tad was born. Nothing in these letters hint that Davis detected marital discord in the Lincoln home.

The specter of some domestic hell is not necessary to justify Lincoln's devotion to his law career. Life on the circuit provided Lincoln the time and space he needed to remedy the "want of education" he regretted all his life. During his nights and weekends on the circuit, in the absence of domestic interruptions, he taught himself geometry, carefully working out propositions and theorems until he could proudly claim that he had "nearly mastered the Six-books of Euclid." His first law partner, John Stuart, recalled that "he read hard works—was philosophical—logical— mathematical—never read generally."

Herndon describes finding him one day "so deeply absorbed in study he scarcely looked up when I entered." Surrounded by "a quantity of blank paper, large heavy sheets, a compass, a rule, numerous pencils, several bottles of ink of various colors, and a profusion of stationery," Lincoln was apparently "struggling with a calculation of some magnitude, for scattered about were sheet after sheet of paper covered with an unusual array of figures." When Herndon inquired what he was doing, he announced "that he was trying to solve the difficult problem of squaring the circle." To this in-soluble task posed by the ancients over four thousand years earlier, he de-voted "the better part of the succeeding two days . . . almost to the point of exhaustion."

In addition to geometry, Lincoln's solitary researches allowed him to study the astronomy, political economy, and philosophy that his fellow lawyers had learned in college. "Life was to him a school," fellow circuit rider Leonard Swett observed, "and he was always studying and mastering every subject which came before him."

Lincoln's time on the circuit was certainly difficult for Mary; his long absences from home were "one of the greatest hardships" of their mar-riage. For Lincoln, circuit life was invaluable. Beyond the congeniality of boardinghouse life and the opportunity to continue his lifelong education, these travels provided the chance to walk the streets in dozens of small towns, eat at local taverns in remote corners of the state, and gain a first-hand knowledge of the desires, fears, and hopes of thousands of ordinary people in Illinois—the people who would become his loyal base of support in the years ahead when the time came to return to his first love: politics.`

• • •

WHILE LINCOLN was productively engaged on the circuit, Seward was dispirited by what he perceived as a reactionary turn in the country's mood. "If I muzzle not my mouth on the subject of slavery," he wrote Frances, "I shall be set down as a disturber, seeking to disturb the Whig Administration and derange the Whig party." Responding to the public mood, he muted his strident voice on slavery and turned his attention to the less controversial issues of education, internal improvements, and for-eign policy. Progress on emancipation, he endeavored to convince himself, could come only with the gradual enlightenment of the American public. When both Henry Clay and Daniel Webster died in 1852, he delivered such glowing eulogies on the Senate floor that his more radical friends took offense. "They cannot see," Seward complained to Frances, "how much of the misery of human life is derived from the indulgence of wrath!"

The idealistic Frances accepted her husband's rationale for the eulogies but could not countenance his reluctance to resist the reactionary zeal that enveloped the country after the Compromise. When it appeared that the 1852 Whig Convention was on the verge of endorsing the Compromise in an attempt to create a moderate platform for its presidential candidate, General Winfield Scott, Frances begged her husband to come home. "I do not wish you to be held responsible for the doings of that Convention if they are to endorse the Compromise in any manner or degree," she wrote. "It will be a sad disappointment to men who are true to liberty."

Nor did she spare him whenever she detected a blatantly conciliatory tone in his speeches or writings. While she conceded that "worldly wisdom certainly does impel a person to 'swim with the tide'—and if they can judge unerringly which way the tide runs, may bring them to port," she continued to argue for "a more elevated course" that would "reconcile one to struggling against the current if necessary."

In Charles Sumner, Frances found a politician who consistently chose the elevated course she favored, even though he was often isolated as a result. Sumner, a bachelor, who, like Chase, was said to look like a statesman, with imperious, well-chiseled features, would often dine with the Sewards when Frances was in town. When she returned to Auburn, they kept up a rich correspondence. Sumner valued her unflagging confidence particularly during his early days in the Senate when his unyielding position on slavery provoked anger and ridicule. Though his attempt to repeal the Fugitive Slave Act in August 1852 garnered only 4 votes in the Senate, not including Seward's—who, like other antislavery men, refused to support it on the grounds that it would torpedo Scott's chances for the presidency— Frances stood loyally by her friend. "This fearless defense of Freedom must silence those cavilers who doubted your sincerity," she wrote. "It is a noble plea for a righteous cause."

That November, when the Southerners' candidate, Franklin Pierce, crushed Scott in what Northern Whigs considered "a Waterloo defeat," Frances fell into a state of despair. Her confidence in the mainstream political system gone, she was tempted, she told her husband, to join the abolitionists. Seward persuaded her to hold back, arguing that it would do "more harm than good" if the Seward name were attached to the abolitionist cause.

Try as he might, Seward could not persuade Frances to stay with him for more than a few months at a time in Washington. Her decision to remain in upstate New York, especially in the wretched summer months, was not unusual, but even when the weather began to cool as autumn set in, Frances remained in Auburn. "Would that I were nearer to you," he lamented from Washington on his fifty-fourth birthday; but he accepted that his "widened spheres of obligation and duty" prevented him from realizing his wishes.

Had Frances Seward enjoyed good health, the course of their marriage might have been different; everywhere Seward went he rented sumptuous homes, hopeful that she and the children might join him. Burdened with a fragile constitution, Frances was increasingly debilitated by a wide range of nervous disorders: nausea, temporary blindness, insomnia, migraines, mysterious pains in her muscles and joints, crying spells, and sustained bouts of depression. A flashing light, a bumpy carriage ride, or a piercing sound was often sufficient to send her to bed. As her health deteriorated, she found it more and more difficult to leave her "sanctuary" in Auburn, where she was attended by her solicitous extended family.

Doctors could not pinpoint the physical origin of the various ailments that conspired to leave Frances a semi-invalid. A brilliant woman, Frances once speculated whether the "various nervous afflictions & morbid habits of thought" that plagued so many women she knew had their origin in the frustrations of an educated woman's life in the mid-nineteenth century. Among her papers is a draft of an unpublished essay on the plight of women: "To share in any kind of household work is to demean herself, and she would be thought mad, to run, leap, or engage in active sports." She was permitted to dance all night in ballrooms, but it "would be deemed un-womanly" and "imprudent" for her to race with her children "on the com-mon, or to search the cliff for flowers." Reflecting on "the number of invalids that exist among women exempted from Labour," she suggested that the "want of fitting employment—real purpose in their life" was re-sponsible.

Seward himself recognized that his marriage was built upon contradic-tions. "There you are at home all your life-long. It is too cold to travel in winter and home is too pleasant in summer to be foresaken. The children cannot go abroad and must not be left at home. Here I am, on the contrary, roving for instruction when at leisure, and driven abroad continually by my occupation. How strange a thing it is that we can never enjoy each oth-ers cares and pleasures, except at intervals."

The Sewards' relationship was sustained chiefly through the long, lov-ing letters they wrote to each other day after day, year after year. In her let-ters, which number in the thousands, Frances described the progress of the garden and the antics of the children. She offered advice on political mat-ters, critiqued his speeches, and expressed her passionate opinions about slavery. She encouraged his idealism, pressing him repeatedly to consider what *should* be done rather than what *could* be done. In his letters, he ana-lyzed the personalities of his colleagues, confessed his fears, discussed his reactions to the books he was reading, and told her repeatedly how he loved her "above every other thing in the world." He conjured images of the moon, whose "silver rays" they shared as they each sat in their separate homes "writing the lines" that would cross in the mail. He recollected pleasures of home, where the children played in the smoke from his cigar, and husband and wife were engaged in free and open conversation, so different from the talk of politicians.

Yet in the end, it was the talk of politicians he craved. As a result, the Sewards, to a far greater extent than the Lincolns, spent much of their married life apart.

· · ·

CHASE, TOO, found himself in a dispirited state in the months that followed the Compromise. "Clouds and darkness are upon us at present," he wrote Sumner. "The Slaveholders have succeeded beyond their wildest hopes twelve months ago." It seemed as if, temporarily at least, the wind had been taken out of the sails of the antislavery movement.

Moreover, Chase was isolated in the Senate, the regular Democratic Party having shut him out of committee work and political meetings. Nor could he rely on the camaraderie of the Free-Soilers, who believed he had sacrificed them to achieve his position. With time heavy on his hands, he spent hours writing to Kate at her boarding school in New York, where she had been sent when his third wife, Belle, contracted the tuberculosis that took her life.

The long years away from home must have been bleak and often difficult for the motherless child. Located at Madison Avenue and Forty-ninth Street, Miss Haines's School held the girls to a strict routine. They rose at 6 a.m. to study for an hour and a half before breakfast and prayers. A brisk walk outside, with no skipping permitted, preceded classes in literature, French, Latin, English grammar, science, elocution, piano, and dancing. At midafternoon, they were taken out once again for an hour-long walk. In the evenings, they attended study hall, where, "without [the teacher's] permission," one student recalled, "we could hardly breathe." Only on weekends, when they attended recitals or the theater, was the routine relaxed.

Living ten months a year under such regimented circumstances, Kate yearned to see the one person she loved: her father. Though he wrote hundreds of letters to her, his correspondence lacked the playful warmth of Seward's notes to his own children. In cold, didactic fashion, Chase alternately praised and upbraided her, instructing her in the art of letter writing and admonishing her to cultivate good habits. If her letters were well written, he critiqued her penmanship. If the penmanship was good, he criticized her flat style of expression. If both met his standards, he complained that she had waited too long to write.

"Your last letter . . . was quite well written," he told her when she was ten years old. "I should be glad, however, to have you describe more of what you see and do every day. Can't you tell me all about your schoolmates one by one. . . . Take pains, use your eyes, reflect." "I wish you could put a little more life into your letters." Four years later, he was still urging improvement. "Your nice letter, my darling child, came yesterday," he wrote, "but I must say that it had rather a sleepy air. The words seemed occasionally chosen and arranged under the influence of the drowsy God."

"It will be a great advantage to you to cultivate a *noticing habit,*" he advised. "Accustom yourself to talk of what you see and to write details, and in a conversational, & even narrative style. There is the greatest possible difference in charm between the same narrative told by one person and by another. . . . No doubt a large part of this difference is to be ascribed to constitutional differences of temperament, but any intelligent person can greatly increase facility of apprehension & expression by careful self culture." The ascetic refrain of Chase's instruction to Kate is that an effort of will can surmount most obstacles and self-denial can lead to its own gratifications: "I know you do not like writing. . . . You can overcome if you will. . . . I dislike for example to bathe myself all over with cold water in the morning especially when the thermometer is so low as at present: but I find I can when I determine to do so overcome my feeling of dislike and even substitute a certain pleasurable sensation."

In his efforts to discipline and educate his daughter, Chase did not spare Kate his own morbid thoughts about death. "Remember, my dear child, that the eye of a Holy God is upon you all the time, and that not an act or word or thought is unnoticed by Him. Remember too, that you may die soon. . . . Already eleven years of your life are passed. You may not live another eleven years. . . . How short then is this life! And how earnest ought to be our preparation for another!" To illustrate his point, he described the death of a little girl just Kate's age, the daughter of a fellow senator. The Monday before her death, he had seen her in the capital, "strong, robust, active, intelligent; the very impersonation of life and health. A week after and she had gone from earth. What a lesson was here. Lay it to heart, dear Katie, and may God give you grace."

If Kate's school reports were unfavorable, Chase refused to allow her to return home for vacation. "I am sorry that you feel so lonely," he told her one summer. "I wish I could feel it safe to allow you to visit more freely, but your conversations with Miss Haines have made known to you the reasons why." He urged her to understand: "you have it in your power greatly to promote my happiness by your good conduct, and greatly to destroy my comfort and peace by ill conduct."

More often she excelled, relying on her nearly encyclopedic memory and hard work to please her exacting father. If unsparing in his criticism, he was extravagant in his praise. "To an affectionate father" nothing was more gratifying, he told her—not even the thought that he might someday "be made President"—than "a beloved child, improving in intelligence, in manners, in physical development, and giving promise of a rich and delightful future."

He rewarded her with invitations to Washington, visits she vividly recalled years later. "I knew Clay, Webster and Calhoun," she proudly told a reporter when she was in her fifties. As a small girl, she was particularly impressed by Clay, so tall that "he had to unwind himself to get up." At ease with children, Clay "made much of me and I liked him." Daniel Webster appeared to Kate an "ideal of how a statesman ought to look," the very words later used to describe her father. "He seldom laughed, yet he was very kind and he used to send me his speeches. I don't suppose he thought I would read them, but he wanted to compliment me and show that he remembered me and I know that I felt very proud when I saw Daniel Webster's frank upon pieces of mail which came to me at the New York school."

Of all her father's Senate colleagues, Charles Sumner was her favorite, as he was of Frances Seward. "He was warm-hearted and sensitive," Kate recalled. "He was full of anecdotes and was a brilliant talker." When Sumner, in turn, spoke well of little Kate, Chase was overjoyed. "You cannot think, my precious child, how much pleasure it gives me to hear you praised."

Buoyant at such moments with satisfied expectations, Chase shared with her intimate chronicles of his life in Washington, long descriptions of the protocol followed when a senator visited the president in his office, detailed accounts of dinners at the White House, amusing reports of late-night sessions in the Senate chamber, when all too many of his colleagues "have visited the refectory a little too often, and are not as sober as they should be."

"The sun shines warm and clear," he wrote one beautiful June day. "The wind stirs the trees and fans the earth. I sit in my room and hear the rustle of branches; the merry twitter and song of the birds; the chirp of insects." "I should like to have you with me and we should take a ramble together."

Not surprisingly, Kate cherished the prospect of living in the nation's capital, accompanying her father wherever he went, assisting him in his daily tasks. Chase understood her desire and was careful to assuage her fear that he might remarry and deprive her of her rightful place by his side. Describing a visit to the Elliotts, a Quaker family with two remarkable daughters, he confessed that "Miss Lizzie is the best looking of them all, and is really a very superior woman, with a great deal of sense and a great deal of heart. You need not however be alarmed for me, for a gentleman in New York is said to be her accepted lover, and I look only for *friends* among ladies as I do among gentlemen."

• • •

OF THE FOUR future presidential candidates, Edward Bates was the only one who supported the Compromise wholeheartedly. At last, with what he called the "African mania" finally subdued, he felt the American people might focus their energies once more on the vast economic opportunities provided by the ever-expanding frontier.

With equal ire, he denounced both "the lovers of free negroes in the North & the lovers of slave negroes in the South," believing that the argument over slavery was simply "a struggle among politicians for sectional supremacy," with radicals like Seward and Chase in the North, and Calhoun and Toombs in the South, exploiting the issue for personal ambition.

He specifically condemned Seward's *"higher law"* supposition invoked to invalidate the Fugitive Slave Law, arguing that "in Civil government, such as we have, there can be no law *higher* than the Constitution and the Statutes. And he would set himself above these, claiming some transcendental authority for his disobedience, must be, as I deliberately think, either a Canting hypocrite, a presumptuous fool, or an arbitrary designing knave."

He exhibited similar scorn for Calhoun, who would shatter "the world's best hope of freedom for the white man, because he is not allowed to have his own wayward will about negro slaves! . . . Poor man, he is greatly to be pitied! . . . It is truly a melancholy spectacle to behold his sun going down behind a cloud so black."

In the early fifties, Bates still believed that the West could refrain from taking sides, trusting that "if we stood aloof from the quarrel & pressed the even tenor of our way, for the public good, both of those factions would soon sink to the level of their intrinsic insignificance." His hopes would quickly prove futile, for the settlement was destined to last only four years.

• • •

"A HUMAN BEING," the novelist Thomas Mann observed, "lives out not only his personal life as an individual, but also, consciously or subconsciously, the lives of his epoch and his contemporaries . . . if the times, themselves, despite all their hustle and bustle," do not provide opportunity, he continued, "the situation will have a crippling effect."

More than a decade earlier, speaking to the Springfield Young Men's Lyceum, Lincoln had expressed his concern that his generation had been left a meager yield after the "field of glory" was harvested by the founding fathers. They were a "forest of giant oaks," he said, who faced the "task (and nobly they performed it) to possess themselves, and through themselves, us, of this goodly land," and to build "upon its hills and its valleys, a political edifice of liberty and equal rights." Their destinies were *"inseparably* linked" with the experiment of providing the world, "a practical demonstration" of *"the capability of a people to govern themselves.* If they succeeded, they were to be immortalized; their names were to be transferred to counties and cities, and rivers and mountains; and to be revered and sung, and toasted through all time."

Because their experiment succeeded, Lincoln observed, thousands "won their deathless names in making it so." What was left for the men of his generation to accomplish? There was no shortage of good men "whose ambition would aspire to nothing beyond a seat in Congress, a gubernatorial or a presidential chair; but *such belong not to the family of the lion, or the tribe of the eagle."* Such modest aspirations, he argued, would never satisfy men of "towering genius" who scorned "a beaten path."

In 1854, the wheel of history turned. A train of events that mobilized the antislavery North resulted in the formation of the Republican Party and ultimately provided Lincoln's generation with a challenge equal to or surpassing that of the founding fathers. The sequence began when settlers in Kansas and Nebraska called upon Congress to grant them territorial status, raising once again the contentious question of extending slavery into the territories. As chairman of the Committee on Territories, Illinois senator Stephen Douglas introduced a bill that appeared to provide an easy solution to the problem by allowing the settlers themselves the "popular sovereignty" to decide if they wished to become free or slave states. This solution proved anything but simple. Since both Kansas and Nebraska lay north of the old 36° 30' line, the passage of the Kansas-Nebraska Act would mean that the Missouri Compromise was null and void, opening the possibility of slavery to land long since guaranteed to freedom.

The debate over the Kansas-Nebraska Act opened against increased antislavery sentiment in the North. Enforcement of the fugitive slave provisions contained in the Compromise of 1850 had aroused Northern ire. Near riots erupted when slaveholders tried to recapture runaway slaves who had settled in Boston and New York. Ralph Waldo Emerson expressed a common sentiment among Northerners: "I had never in my life up to this time suffered from the Slave Institution. Slavery in Virginia or Carolina was like Slavery in Africa or the Feejees, for me. There was an old fugitive law, but it had become, or was fast becoming a dead letter, and, by the genius and laws of Massachusetts, inoperative. The new Bill made it operative, required me to hunt slaves, and it found citizens in Massachusetts willing to act as judges and captors. Moreover, it discloses the secret of the new times, that Slavery was no longer mendicant, but was becoming aggressive and dangerous."

Northern sentiment had been inflamed further by the publication of Harriet Beecher Stowe's *Uncle Tom's Cabin*. Less than a year after its publication in March 1852, more than three hundred thousand copies of the novel had sold in the United States, a sales rate rivaled only by the Bible. Abolitionist leader Frederick Douglass later likened it to "a flash" that lit "a million camp fires in front of the embattled hosts of slavery," awakening such powerful compassion for the slave and indignation against slavery that many previously unconcerned Americans were transformed into advocates for the antislavery cause.

Until the introduction of the Kansas-Nebraska Act, there was no signal point around which the antislavery advocates could rally. As the Senate debate opened, Northerners were stirred into action "in greater numbers than ever," the historian Don Fehrenbacher has written, fighting "with all the fierceness of an army defending its homeland against invasion."

Passions in the South were equally aroused. To Southerners, the issue of Kansas was not merely an issue of slavery, but whether they, who had helped create and enlarge the nation with their "blood and treasure," would be entitled to share in the territories held in common by the entire country. "The day may come," said Governor Thomas Bragg of North Carolina, "when our Northern brethren will discover that the Southern States intend to be equals in the Union, or independent out of it!"

This time Salmon Chase assumed the leadership of the antislavery forces. Seward understood that the bill was "a mighty subject" that "required research and meditation," but he was distracted by a multitude of issues and the demands of Washington's social life. With "the street door bell [ringing] every five minutes," the popular New Yorker was unable to find the time to construct a great speech or to marshal the opposition. Consequently, while Seward's speeches against the Nebraska bill were simply "essays against slavery," Stephen Douglas later said, "Chase of Ohio was the leader."

Chase, along with Sumner and Ohio congressman Joshua Giddings, conceived the idea of reaching beyond the Senate to the country at large with an open "Appeal of the Independent Democrats in Congress to the People of the United States." The "Appeal" was originally printed in *The National Era*, the abolitionist newspaper that had first serialized *Uncle*

Tom's Cabin. Deemed by historians "one of the most effective pieces of political propaganda ever produced," the Appeal was reprinted in pamphlet form to organize opposition to the Kansas-Nebraska Act.

"We arraign this bill as a gross violation of a sacred pledge," the Appeal began, charging that a rapacious proslavery conspiracy was determined to subvert the old Missouri compact, which forever had excluded slavery in all the territory acquired from France in the Louisiana Purchase. Passage of the Nebraska Act would mean that "this immense region, occupying the very heart" of the continent, would, in "flagrant disregard" of a "sacred faith," be transformed into "a dreary region of despotism, inhabited by masters and slaves." The manifesto urged citizens to protest by any means available. Its authors promised to call on their constituents "to come to the rescue of the country from the domination of slavery . . . for the cause of human freedom is the cause of God."

"Chase's greatest opportunity had at last come to him," his biographer Albert Hart observes, "for in the Kansas-Nebraska debate he was able to concentrate all the previous experience of his life." By the time he rose to speak on the Senate floor on February 3, 1854, the country was aroused and prepared for a great battle. "By far the most numerous audience of the season listened to Mr. Chase's speech," the *New York Times* reported. "The galleries and lobbies were densely crowded an hour before the debate began, and the ladies even crowded into and took possession of, one-half the lobby seats on the floor of the Senate."

In the course of the heated debate, Chase accused Douglas of sponsoring the bill to aid his quest for the presidency, an allegation that brought the Illinois senator to such a "high pitch of wrath" that he countered, accusing Chase of entering the Senate by a corrupt bargain. "Do you say I came here by a corrupt bargain?" Chase demanded to know. "I said the man who charged me with having brought in this bill as a bid for the Presidency did come here by a corrupt bargain," Douglas replied. "Did you mean me? If so, I mean you."

Seated beside his friend, Sumner watched with rapturous attention as Chase refuted Douglas's claim that the concept of "popular sovereignty" would provide a final settlement of all territorial questions. On the contrary, Chase predicted, "this discussion will hasten the inevitable reorganization of parties." Moreover, he asked, "What kind of popular sovereignty is that which allows one portion of the people to enslave another portion? Is that the doctrine of equal rights? . . . No, sir, no! There can be no real democracy which does not fully maintain the rights of man, as man."

At midnight, Douglas began his concluding speech, which lasted nearly four hours. At one point, Seward interrupted to ask for an explanation of something Douglas had said. "Ah," Douglas retorted, "you can't crawl behind that free nigger dodge." In reply, Seward said: "Douglas, no man will ever be President of the United States who spells 'negro' with two gs."

"Midnight passed and the cock crew, and daylight broke before the vote was taken," the *New York Tribune* reported. The all-night session was marked by "great confusion, hard words between various Senators and intense excitement in which the galleries participated." Many of the senators were observed to be "beastly drunk," their grandiloquence further inflated by "too frequent visits to one of the ante-chambers of the Senate room."

When the Senate majority cast its votes in favor of the bill at 5 a.m. on the morning of March 4, the antislavery minority was crushed. "The Senate is emasculated," Senator Benton exclaimed. As Chase and Sumner descended the sweeping steps of the Capitol, a distant cannonade signaled passage of the bill. "They celebrate a present victory," Chase said, "but the echoes they awake will never rest until slavery itself shall die."

"Be assured, be assured, gentlemen," *New York Tribune* reporter James Pike warned the Southerners, that "you are sowing the wind and you will reap the whirlwind. . . . No man can stand in the North in that day of reckoning who plants himself on the ground of sustaining the repeal of the Missouri Compromise. . . . [Here is] the opening of a great drama that . . . inaugurates the era of a geographical division of political parties. It draws the line between North and South. It pits face to face the two opposing forces of slavery and freedom."

In the weeks that followed, mass protest meetings spread like wildfire throughout the North, fueled by the enormous reach of the daily newspaper. "The tremendous storm sweeping the North seemed to gather new force every week," writes the historian Allan Nevins. Resolutions against the law were signed by tens of thousands in Connecticut, New Hampshire, Ohio, Indiana, Iowa, Massachusetts, and Pennsylvania. In New York, the *Tribune* reported, two thousand protesters marched up Broadway, "led by a band of music, and brilliant with torches and banners." On college campuses and village squares, in town halls and county fairgrounds, people gathered to make their voices heard.

•   •   •

LINCOLN WAS RIDING the circuit in the backcountry of Illinois when the news reached him of the passage of the Kansas-Nebraska Act. A fellow lawyer, T. Lyle Dickey, sharing a room with Lincoln, reported that "he sat on the edge of his bed and discussed the political situation far into the night." At dawn, he was still "sitting up in bed, deeply absorbed in thought." He told his companion—"I tell you, Dickey, this nation cannot exist half-slave and half-free."

Lincoln later affirmed that the successful passage of the bill roused him "as he had never been before." It permanently recast his views on slavery. He could no longer maintain that slavery was on course to ultimate extinction. The repeal of the Missouri Compromise persuaded him that unless the North mobilized into action against the proslavery forces, free society itself was in peril. The Nebraska Act "took us by surprise," Lincoln later said. "We were thunderstruck and stunned." The fight to stem the spread of slavery would become the great purpose Lincoln had been seeking.

Before speaking out against the Nebraska Act, Lincoln spent many hours in the State Library, studying present and past congressional debates so that he could reach back into the stream of American history and tell a clear, reasoned, and compelling tale. He would express no opinion on anything, Herndon observed, until he knew his subject "inside and outside, upside and downside." Lincoln told Joshua Speed, "I am slow to learn and slow to forget that which I have learned. My mind is like a piece of steel, very hard to scratch any thing on it and almost impossible after you get it there to rub it out."

Lincoln delivered his first great antislavery speech in Springfield at the annual State Fair before a crowd of thousands on October 4, 1854. Farmers and their families had journeyed to the capital from all over the state, filling every hotel room, tavern, and boardinghouse. Billed as the largest agricultural fair in the history of the state, the exhibition featured the most advanced farm implements and heavy machinery, including a "world-renowned" plow. Residents took pride in what was considered the finest display of livestock ever assembled in one place. Games and amusements, music and refreshments were provided from morning until night, ensuring, as one reporter wrote, that "a jolly good time ensued."

The previous day, Lincoln had heard Stephen Douglas hold forth for three hours before the same audience. Douglas, stunned by the widespread hostility in northern Illinois to his seminal role in passing the controversial Kansas-Nebraska Act, had chosen the State Fair as the best forum for a vigorous defense of the bill. Rain forced the event into the house of representatives chamber, but the change of venue didn't diminish the impact of Douglas's speech. Sharpening arguments he had made in the Senate, Douglas emphasized that his bill rested on the unassailable principle of self-government, allowing the people themselves to decide whether or not to allow slavery into their own territorial lands.

The expressive face of "the Little Giant," as the short, stocky Douglas was called, was matched by his stentorian voice. "He had a large head, surmounted by an abundant mane," one reporter observed, "which gave him the appearance of a lion prepared to roar or crush his prey." In the midst of speaking, he would "cast away his cravat" and undo the buttons on his coat, captivating his audience with "the air and aspect of a half-naked pugilist." "He was frequently interrupted by cheers and hearty demonstrations of applause," the *Peoria Daily Press* reported, "thus showing that a large majority of the meeting was with him." When he finished, Lincoln jumped up and announced to the crowd that a rebuttal would be delivered the following day.

The next afternoon, with Douglas seated in the front row, Lincoln faced most likely the largest audience of his life. He appeared "awkward" at first, in his shirtsleeves with no collar. "He began in a slow and hesitating manner," the reporter Horace White noted. Yet, minutes into his speech, "it was evident that he had mastered his subject, that he knew what he was going to say, and that he knew he was right." White was only twenty at the time but was aware even then, he said, that he was hearing "one of the world's masterpieces of argumentative power and moral grandeur." Sixty years later, that conviction remained. The initial impression was "overwhelming," White told an audience in 1914, "and it has lost nothing by the lapse of time."

Although Lincoln's voice was "thin, high-pitched," White observed, it had "much carrying power" and "could be heard a long distance in spite of the bustle and tumult of the crowd." As Lincoln hit his stride, "his words began to come faster." Gesturing with his "body and head rather than with his arms," he grew "very impassioned" and "seemed transfigured" by the strength of his words. "Then the inspiration that possessed him took possession of his hearers also. His speaking went to the heart because it came from the heart. I have heard celebrated orators who could start thunders of applause without changing any man's opinion. Mr. Lincoln's eloquence was of the higher type, which produced conviction in others because of the conviction of the speaker himself."

While Douglas simply asserted his points as self-evident, Lincoln embedded his argument in a narrative history, transporting his listeners back to their roots as a people, to the founding of the nation—a story that still retained its power to arouse strong emotion and thoughtful attention. Many of his arguments were familiar to those who had followed the Senate debate and had read Chase's masterly "Appeal"; but the structure of the speech was so "clear and logical," the *Illinois Daily Journal* observed, the arrangement of facts so "methodical," that the overall effect was strikingly original and "most effective."

At the State Fair, and twelve nights later, by torchlight in Peoria, where the debate over the Kansas-Nebraska Act was repeated, Lincoln presented his carefully "connected view" for better than three hours. In order to make his argument, Lincoln decided to begin with nothing less than an account of our common history, the powerful narrative of how slavery grew with our country, how its growth and expansion had been carefully contained by the founding fathers, and how on this fall night in 1854 the great story they were being told—the story of the Union—had come to such an impasse that the exemplary meaning, indeed, the continued existence of the story, hung in the balance.

For the first time in his public life, his remarkable array of gifts as historian, storyteller, and teacher combined with a lucid, relentless, yet always accessible logic. Instead of the ornate language so familiar to men like Webster, Lincoln used irony and humor, laced with workaday, homespun images to build an eloquent tower of logic. The proslavery argument that a vote for the Wilmot Proviso threatened the stability of the entire Union was reduced to absurdity by analogy—"because I may have refused to build an addition to my house, I thereby have decided to destroy the existing house!" Such flashes of figurative language were always available to Lincoln to drive home a point, gracefully educating while entertaining— in a word, *communicating* an enormously complicated issue with wit, simplicity, and a massive power of moral persuasion.

At the time the Constitution was adopted, Lincoln pointed out, "the plain unmistakable spirit of that age, towards slavery, was hostility to the *principle*, and toleration, *only by necessity*," since slavery was already woven into the fabric of American society. Noting that neither the word "slave" nor "slavery" was ever mentioned in the Constitution, Lincoln claimed that the framers concealed it, "just as an afflicted man hides away a wen or a cancer, which he dares not cut out at once, lest he bleed to death; with the promise, nevertheless, that the cutting may begin at the end of a given time." As additional evidence of the framers' intent, Lincoln brought his audience even further back, to the moment when Virginia ceded its vast northwestern territory to the United States with the understanding that slavery would be forever prohibited from the new territory, thus creating a "happy home" for "teeming millions" of free people, with "no slave amongst them." In recent years, he said, slavery had seemed to be gradually on the wane until the fateful Nebraska law transformed it into "a sacred right," putting it "on the high road to extension and perpetuity"; giving it "a pat on its back," saying, " 'Go, and God speed you.' "

Douglas had argued that Northern politicians were simply manufacturing a crisis, that Kansas and Nebraska were destined, in any event, to become free states because the soil and climate in both regions were inhospitable to the cultivation of staple crops. Labeling this argument "a *lullaby*," Lincoln exhibited a map demonstrating that five of the present slave states had similar climates to Kansas and Nebraska, and that the census returns for 1850 showed these states held one fourth of all the slaves in the nation.

Finally, as the greatest bulwark against the Nebraska Act and the concept of "popular sovereignty," Lincoln invoked the Declaration of Independence. He considered the Nebraska Act simply a legal term for the perpetuation and expansion of slavery and, as such, nothing less than the possible death knell of the Union and the meaning of America. "The doctrine of self government is right—absolutely and eternally right," he argued, but to use it, as Douglas proposed, to extend slavery perverted its very meaning. "No man is good enough to govern another man, *without that other's consent*. I say this is the leading principle—the sheet anchor of American republicanism." If the Negro was a man, which Lincoln claimed he most assuredly was, then it was "a total destruction of self-government" to propose that he be governed by a master without his consent. Allowing slavery to spread forced the American people into an open war with the Declaration of Independence, depriving "our republican example of its just influence in the world."

By appealing to the moral and philosophical foundation work of the nation, Lincoln hoped to provide common ground on which good men in both the North and the South could stand. "I am not now combating the argument of *necessity*, arising from the fact that the blacks are already amongst us; but I am combating what is set up as *moral* argument for allowing them to be taken where they have never yet been." Unlike the majority of antislavery orators, who denounced the South and castigated slaveowners as corrupt and un-Christian, Lincoln pointedly denied fundamental differences between Northerners and Southerners. He argued that "they are just what we would be in their situation. If slavery did not now exist amongst them, they would not introduce it. If it did now exist amongst us, we should not instantly give it up. . . . When it is said that the institution exists; and that it is very difficult to get rid of it, in any satisfactory way, I can understand and appreciate the saying. I surely will not blame them for not doing what I should not know how to do myself." And, finally, "when they remind us of their constitutional rights, I acknowledge them . . . and I would give them any legislation for the reclaiming of their fugitives."

Rather than upbraid slaveowners, Lincoln sought to comprehend their position through empathy. More than a decade earlier, he had employed a similar approach when he advised temperance advocates to refrain from

denouncing drinkers in "thundering tones of anathema and denunciation," for denunciation would inevitably be met with denunciation, "crimination with crimination, and anathema with anathema." In a passage
directed at abolitionists as well as temperance reformers, he had observed
that it was the nature of man, when told that he should be "shunned and
despised," and condemned as the author "of all the vice and misery and
crime in the land," to "retreat within himself, close all the avenues to his
head and his heart."

Though the cause be "naked truth itself, transformed to the heaviest
lance, harder than steel," the sanctimonious reformer could no more
pierce the heart of the drinker or the slaveowner than "penetrate the hard
shell of a tortoise with a rye straw. Such is man, and so *must* he be understood by those who would lead him." In order to "win a man to your
cause," Lincoln explained, you must first reach his heart, "the great high
road to his reason." This, he concluded, was the only road to victory—to
that glorious day "when there shall be neither a slave nor a drunkard on the
earth."

Building on his rhetorical advice, Lincoln tried to place himself in the
shoes of the slaveowner to reason his way through the sectional impasse,
by asking Southerners to let their own hearts and history reveal that they,
too, recognized the basic humanity of the black man. Never appealing like
Seward to a "higher law," or resorting to Chase's "natural right" derived
from "the code of heaven," Lincoln staked his argument in reality. He
confronted Southerners with the contradictions surrounding the legal status of blacks that existed in their own laws and social practices.

In 1820, he reminded them, they had "joined the north, almost unanimously, in declaring the African slave trade piracy, and in annexing to it the
punishment of death." In so doing, they must have understood that selling
slaves was wrong, for they never thought of hanging men for selling
horses, buffaloes, or bears. Likewise, though forced to do business with the
domestic slave dealer, they did not "recognize him as a friend, or even as an
honest man. . . . Now why is this?" he asked. "You do not so treat the man
who deals in corn, cattle or tobacco." Finally, he observed, over four hundred thousand free blacks in the United States had been liberated at "vast
pecuniary sacrifices" by white owners who understood something about
the human rights of Negroes. "In all these cases it is your sense of justice,
and human sympathy, continually telling you" that the slave is a man who
cannot be considered "mere merchandise."

As he wound to a close, Lincoln implored his audience to re-adopt the
Declaration of Independence and "return [slavery] to the position our fathers gave it; and there let it rest in peace." This accomplishment, he

pledged, would save the Union, and "succeeding millions of free happy people, the world over, shall rise up, and call us blessed, to the latest generations." When he finished, the enthusiastic audience broke out in "deafening applause." Even the editors of the Democratic paper felt "compelled" to say that they had "never read or heard a stronger anti-Nebraska speech."

From that moment on, propelled by a renewed sense of purpose, Lincoln dedicated the major part of his energies to the antislavery movement. Conservative and contemplative by temperament, he embraced new positions warily. Once he committed himself, however, as he did in the mid-fifties to the antislavery cause, he demonstrated singular tenacity and authenticity of feeling. Ambition and conviction united, "as my two eyes make one in sight," as Robert Frost wrote, to give Lincoln both a political future and a cause worthy of his era.

CHAPTER 6

THE GATHERING STORM

S 1854 GAVE WAY TO 1855, Abraham Lincoln's long-dormant dream of high political office was reawakened, now infused with a new sense of purpose by the passage of the Nebraska Act. He won a seat in the Illinois State Assembly, then promptly declared himself a candidate for the U.S. Senate. In the Illinois state elections the previous fall, the loose coalition of antislavery Whigs and independent Democrats had gained a narrow majority over the Douglas Democrats in the legislature. The victory was "mainly attributed" to Lincoln's leadership, observed state legislator Joseph Gillespie. With the new legislature set to convene in late January to choose the next U.S. senator from Illinois, Lincoln was "the first choice" of the overwhelming majority of anti-Nebraska members. His lifelong dream of achieving high political office seemed about to be realized at last.

On January 20, 1855, however, the worst blizzard in more than two decades isolated Springfield from the rest of the state, preventing a quorum from assembling in the state legislature. Immense snowdrifts cut off trains coming in from the North, and mail was halted for more than a week. While Springfield's children relished "the merry sleigh bells" jingling through the snow, the "pulsation of business" was "nearly extinct." Finally, the weather improved sufficiently for the legislature to convene.

On Thursday morning, February 8, long before the balloting opened at three o'clock, the Capitol was "a beehive of activity." Representatives caucused and whispered in every corner. The anti-Nebraska caucus, composed mainly of Whigs, voted, as expected, to support Lincoln, but a small group of five anti-Nebraska Democrats was ominously absent. The Douglas Democrats, meanwhile, had decided to support the incumbent senator, James Shields, on the early ballots. If Shields's campaign faltered, due to his outspoken endorsement of the Nebraska bill, they had devised a plan to switch their support to the popular Democratic governor, Joel Matteson, who had not taken an open position on the bill. In this way, the Democrats believed, they might win over some members of the anti-Nebraska caucus.

By noon, the "lobby and the galleries of the Hall of the House of Representatives began to fill with senators, representatives and their guests." Notable among the ladies in the gallery were Mary Todd Lincoln and her friend Julia Jayne Trumbull, wife of Democrat Lyman Trumbull, who had recently been elected to Congress on an anti-Nebraska platform. The wife and daughter of Governor Matteson were also in attendance. Some weeks earlier, Lincoln had bought a stack of small notebooks to record, with Mary's help, all hundred members of the two houses, identifying the party affiliation of each, as well as his stance on the Nebraska bill. Their calculations gave reason to hope, but the situation was complicated. To reach a majority of 51 votes, Lincoln would have to hold together the fragile coalition comprised of former rivals in the Whig and Democratic camps who had only recently joined hands against the Nebraska bill.

Led by the governor, the senators marched into the House chamber at the appointed hour. When all were sworn in, the balloting began. On the first ballot, Lincoln received 45 votes, against 41 for the Douglas Democrat, James Shields, and 5 for Congressman Lyman Trumbull. The five anti-Nebraska Democrats who voted for Trumbull were led by Norman Judd of Chicago. They had no personal animosity toward Lincoln, but "having been elected as Democrats . . . they could not sustain themselves at home," they claimed, if they voted for a Whig for senator.

In the ballots that followed, as daylight gave way to gaslights in the great hall, Lincoln reached a high point of 47 votes, only 4 shy of victory.

Nonetheless, the little Trumbull coalition refused to budge, denying Lincoln the necessary majority. Finally, after nine ballots, Lincoln concluded that unless his supporters shifted to Trumbull, the Douglas Democrats, who had, as expected, switched their allegiance to Matteson, would choose the next senator.

Unwilling to sacrifice all the hard work of the antislavery coalition, Lincoln advised his floor manager, Stephen Logan, to drop him for Trumbull. Logan refused at first, protesting the injustice of the candidate with the much larger vote giving in to the candidate with the smaller vote. Lincoln was adamant, insisting that if his name remained on the ballot, "you will lose both Trumbull and myself and I think the cause in this case is to be preferred to men."

When Logan rose to speak, the tension in the chamber was so great that the "spectators scarcely breathed." In a sad voice, he announced that it was "the purpose of the remaining Whigs to decide the contest." Obeying his directions, Lincoln's supporters switched their votes to Trumbull, giving him the 51 votes needed for victory. Lincoln's friends were inconsolable, believing that this was "perhaps his last chance for that high position." Logan put his hands over his face and began to cry, while Davis stormily announced that had he been in Lincoln's situation, "he never would have consented to the 47 men being controlled by the 5."

In public, Lincoln expressed no hard feelings toward either Trumbull or Judd. He deliberately showed up at Trumbull's victory party, with a smile on his face and a warm handshake for the victor. Consoled that the Nebraska men were "worse whipped" than he, Lincoln insisted that Matteson's defeat "gives me more pleasure than my own gives me pain. . . . On the whole, it is perhaps as well for our general cause that Trumbull is elected."

Lincoln's magnanimity served him well. While Seward and Chase would lose friends in victory—Seward by neglecting at the height of his success his old friend Horace Greeley, and Chase by not understanding the lingering resentments that followed in the wake of his 1849 Senate victory—Lincoln, in defeat, gained friends. Neither Trumbull nor Judd would ever forget Lincoln's generous behavior. Indeed, both men would assist him in his bid for the U.S. Senate in 1858, and Judd would play a critical role in his run for the presidency in 1860.

Mary Lincoln was unable to be so gracious. Convinced that Trumbull had acted with "cold, selfish, treachery," she never spoke another word to Trumbull's wife, Julia, who had been a bridesmaid at her wedding and one of her closest friends. Though intermediaries tried in succeeding years to bring the two women together, the ruptured friendship never healed. Neither could Mary forgive Norman Judd for his role in supporting Trumbull. Though Judd, along with Davis, would do more than anyone else to assure Lincoln's nomination at the Chicago convention, Mary did everything she could to blackball him from a cabinet post after her husband's election.

Despite the dignity of Lincoln's public demeanor, he privately suffered a brutal disappointment, describing the ordeal as an "agony." Though he had engineered Trumbull's victory for the sake of the anti-Nebraska cause, it was difficult to accept the manner of his loss. "He could bear defeat inflicted by his enemies with a pretty good grace," he told his friend Gillespie, "but it was hard to be wounded in the house of his friends." After all the hard work, the interminable nights and weekends on the hustings, the conversations with fellow politicians, the hours spent writing letters to garner support, after so many years of patient waiting and hopefulness, he seemed as far from realizing his ambition as ever. Fate seemed to take a curious delight in finding new ways to shatter his dreams.

• • •

IN THE SUMMER OF 1855, disappointment piled upon disappointment. Six months after his loss to Trumbull, Lincoln's involvement in a celebrated law case forced him to recognize that his legal reputation, secure as it might have been in frontier Illinois, carried little weight among the preeminent lawyers in the country.

The story began that June with the arrival in Springfield of Peter Watson, a young associate in the distinguished Philadelphia firm headed by George Harding, a nationally renowned patent specialist. Harding had been hired by the John Manny Company of Rockford, Illinois, to defend its mechanical reaping machine against a patent infringement charge brought by Cyrus McCormick, the original inventor of the reaper. *McCormick v. Manny*, better known as the "Reaper" suit, was considered an important test case, pitting two outstanding patent lawyers, Edward Dickerson of New York and former Attorney General Reverdy Johnson for McCormick, against Harding for Manny. Since the case was to be tried before a judge in Chicago, Harding decided to engage a local lawyer who "understood the judge and had his confidence," though, from his Eastern perspective, he condescendingly expressed doubt he could find a lawyer in Illinois "who would be of real assistance" in arguing the case.

Watson was sent to Springfield to see if Abraham Lincoln, whose name had been recommended, was the right man for the position. His initial impression was not positive. Neither the small frame house on Eighth Street nor Lincoln's appearance at the door with "neither coat nor vest" indicated a lawyer of sufficient standing for a case of this magnitude. After talking with Lincoln, however, Watson decided he might be "rather effective" after all. He paid Lincoln a retainer and arranged a substantial fee when the work was completed. Lincoln was thrilled with both the fee and the opportunity to test himself with the renowned Reverdy Johnson. He began working on the legal arguments for the case, understanding that Harding would present the scientific arguments.

Not long after Watson's Springfield visit, Harding received word that the case had been transferred from Chicago to Cincinnati. The change of venue to Ohio "removed the one object" for employing Lincoln, allowing Harding to team up with the man he had wanted in the first place—the brilliant Edwin Stanton. Unaware of the changed situation, Lincoln continued to develop his case. "At our interview here in June," he wrote Watson in late July, "I understood you to say you would send me copies of the Bill and Answer . . . and also of depositions . . . I have had nothing from you since. However, I attended the U.S. Court at Chicago, and while there, got copies . . . I write this particularly to urge you to forward on to me the additional evidence as fast as you can. During August, and the remainder of this month, I can devote some time to the case, and, of course, I want all the material that can be had. During my day at Chicago, I went out to Rockford, and spent half a day, examining and studying Manny's Machine."

Though Lincoln never heard from Watson, he pieced together what he needed and in late September set out for Cincinnati with a lengthy brief in his hands. Arriving at the Burnet House where all the lawyers were lodged, he encountered Harding and Stanton as they left for the court. Years later, Harding could still recall the shock of his first sight of the "tall, rawly boned, ungainly back woodsman, with coarse, ill-fitting clothing, his trousers hardly reaching his ankles, holding in his hands a blue cotton umbrella with a ball on the end of the handle." Lincoln introduced himself and proposed, "Let's go up in a gang." At this point, Stanton drew Harding aside and whispered, "Why did you bring that d——d long armed Ape here . . . he does not know any thing and can do you no good." With that, Stanton and Harding turned from Lincoln and continued to court on their own.

In the days that followed, Stanton "managed to make it plain to Lincoln" that he was expected to remove himself from the case. Lincoln did withdraw, though he remained in Cincinnati to hear the arguments. Harding never opened Lincoln's manuscript, "so sure that it would be only trash." Throughout that week, though Lincoln ate at the same hotel, Harding and Stanton never asked him to join them for a meal, or accompany them to or from court. When Judge John McLean hosted a dinner for the lawyers on both sides, Lincoln was not invited.

The hearing continued for a week. The sophisticated arguments were "a revelation" to Lincoln, recalled Ralph Emerson, one of Manny's partners. So intrigued was he by Stanton's speech, in particular, that he stood in "rapt attention . . . drinking in his words." Never before, Emerson realized, had Lincoln "seen anything so finished and elaborated, and so thoroughly prepared." When the hearing was over, Lincoln told Emerson that he was going home "to study law." Emerson did not understand at first what Lincoln meant by this, but Lincoln explained. "For any rough-and-tumble case (and a pretty good one, too), I am enough for any man we have out in that country; but these college-trained men are coming West. They have had all the advantages of a life-long training in the law, plenty of time to study and everything, perhaps, to fit them. Soon they will be in Illinois . . . and when they appear I will be ready."

As Lincoln prepared to leave Cincinnati, he went to say goodbye to William Dickson, one of the few people who had shown him kindness that week. "You have made my stay here most agreeable, and I am a thousand times obliged to you," Lincoln told Dickson's wife, "but in reply to your request for me to come again I must say to you I never expect to be in Cincinnati again. I have nothing against the city, but things have so happened here to make it undesirable for me ever to return here."

After returning to Springfield, Lincoln received a check in the mail for the balance of his fee. He returned it, saying he had not earned it, never having made any argument. When Watson sent the check a second time, Lincoln cashed it.

Unimaginable as it might seem, after Stanton's bearish behavior, at their next encounter six years later, Lincoln would offer Stanton "the most powerful civilian post within his gift"—the post of secretary of war. Lincoln's choice of Stanton would reveal, as would his subsequent dealings with Trumbull and Judd, a singular ability to transcend personal vendetta, humiliation, or bitterness. As for Stanton, despite his initial contempt for the "long armed Ape," he would not only accept the offer but come to respect and love Lincoln more than any person outside of his immediate family.

Stanton's surly condescension toward Lincoln must be considered in the context of his anxiety over the Reaper trial, which had assumed crucial importance for him. Ever since the death of his father when he was only thirteen, Stanton had been obsessed with financial security. Until his father, a successful physician, died from apoplexy at the age of forty, young

Edwin had led a pampered existence in Steubenville, Ohio, surrounded by a loving family in a stately, two-story brick house with a large yard and fruitful garden. Taught to read when he was only three years old, the precocious child had ready access to his father's large collection of books and received an excellent education at the Old Academy in Steubenville. But when his father died, leaving no estate, Edwin was forced to leave school to help support his widowed mother and three younger siblings. First came the forced sale of the house, then the sale of his father's library, and finally, the necessity to move to much smaller quarters. Apprenticed to a bookseller, Stanton read books in every spare moment he could find and spent his evenings preparing for entrance to nearby Kenyon College, headed by Chase's uncle Philander. An excellent student, he enjoyed two happy years at Kenyon before his family's scarce resources required that he return to work, this time in a Columbus bookstore.

The following year, Stanton returned to Steubenville and secured an apprenticeship in a law office, where he simultaneously studied law and helped his mother with the younger children. In later years, his adoring sister Pamphila recalled Stanton's critical role in anchoring the entire family, tenderly nursing his ailing mother, sending his brother Darwin to Harvard Medical School, and encouraging his younger sisters to memorize dozens of poems by Byron and Whittier, all the while reading Plutarch's *Lives* and other works of history. Success in the law came quickly, the result of an intuitive mind, a prodigious capacity for work, and a forceful courtroom manner.

When he fell in love with Mary Lamson, he enjoyed what he much later called the "happiest hours of his life." A marvelously intellectual young woman, Mary shared his passion for reading and study, coupled with a feminist determination that women could *"regenerate the world"* if only they were rightly educated. When their marriage produced a daughter, Lucy, and a son, Edwin Junior, Stanton had every reason to believe that fortune was smiling on him. His sister Pamphila later recalled that her brother seemed perpetually "bright and cheery." As his practice grew, he had the means not only to take care of his own family but to provide for his mother and younger siblings as well.

Stanton looked upon Mary as his life companion. They both loved history, literature, and poetry. Together, they read Gibbon, Carlisle, Macaulay, Madame de Staël, Samuel Johnson, Bancroft, and Byron. "We years ago were lovers," he wrote her after the children were born. "We are now parents; a new relation has taken place. The love of our offspring has opened up fresh fountains of love for each other. We look forward now to life, not for ourselves only, but for our children. I loved you for your beauty, and grace and loveliness of your person. I love you now for the richness and surpassing excellence of your mind. One love has not taken the place of the other, but both stand side by side. I love you now with a fervor and truth of affection which speech cannot express."

His happiness was short-lived: his daughter Lucy died after an attack of scarlet fever; three years later, in March, 1844, his beloved Mary developed a fatal bilious fever and died at the age of twenty-nine. Stanton was so brokenhearted, his grief "verged on insanity." Before he would allow her burial, he had a seamstress fashion a wedding dress for her. "She is my bride and shall be dressed and buried like a bride." After the funeral, he could not bring himself to work for months. Since he was involved in almost every case that came before the court in Jefferson County, Ohio, no court was held that spring. For months, he laid out Mary's nightcap and gown on her pillow. His sister, Pamphila, who had come to stay with him, would never forget the horror of the long nights when, "with lamp in hand," he searched for Mary through every room of the house, "with sobs and tears streaming from his eyes," screaming over and over, "Where is Mary?"

Stanton's responsibilities to his family eventually brought him back to his law practice, but he could not let go of his sorrow. Fearful that his son, then only two years old, would have no memories of the mother he had lost, he spent his nights writing a letter of over a hundred pages to the boy. He described his romance with Mary from its earliest days and included extracts from all the letters they had exchanged over the years. His words were penned with an unsteady hand, he confessed, with "tears obscuring his vision" and an "anguish of heart" driving him periodically from his chair. He would have preferred to wait until the boy was older and better able to understand; "but time, care, sickness, and the vicissitudes of life, wear out and efface the impression of the mind. Besides life is uncertain. I may be called from you. . . . You might live and die without knowing of the affection your father and mother bore for you, and for each other."

Stanton's miseries multiplied when his younger brother, Darwin, who completed his studies at Harvard Medical School, developed a high fever that impaired his brain. Unhinged by his acute illness, the young doctor, who was married with three small children, took a sharp lance-head and punctured his throat. "He bled to death in a few moments," a family friend recalled. His mother watched helplessly as "the blood spouted up to the ceiling." Neighbors were sent to fetch Edwin, who lived nearby. When he witnessed the aftermath of the gruesome spectacle, he reportedly "lost self-control and wandered off into the woods without his hat or coat." Fearful that he, too, might commit suicide, neighbors pursued, restrained, and escorted him home, where they took turns watching over him.

This horrific train of events transformed Stanton's spirit. His natural ebullience faded. "Where formerly he met everybody with hearty and cheerful greeting," said a friend, "he now moved about in silence and gloom, with head bowed and hands clasped behind." Though he remained a tender father to his son and a loving brother to his younger sisters, he became increasingly aggressive in court, intimidating witnesses unnecessarily, antagonizing fellow lawyers, exhibiting rude and irascible behavior.

He derived his only satisfaction from his growing reputation and his increasing wealth, which allowed him to care for his son, his widowed mother, his sisters, and his dead brother's wife and children. The Reaper case was the biggest case of his career, "the most important Patent cause that has ever been tried," he told a friend, "and more time, labor, money and brains have been expended in getting it ready for argument, than any other Patent case ever has had bestowed upon it." If all went well, it would open doors for Stanton at the highest level of his profession.

When he arrived at the Burnet House, he discovered that Harding "had been unwell for several days" and might not be in a position to go to court. Terrified that in addition to the legal argument he had fully prepared, he might now have to present the "scientific part of the case to which [he] had given no attention," Stanton stayed up all night in preparation. He was greatly relieved when Harding recovered, but anxiety and lack of sleep compounded the irascibility that had marked his demeanor since the multiple deaths in his family.

Beyond the breaking pressures of the case, Stanton had become involved in a turbulent courtship. The young woman, Ellen Hutchison, the daughter of a wealthy Pittsburgh businessman, was the first woman who had attracted his interest since the death of his wife more than a decade earlier. Tall, blond, and blue-eyed, Ellen was, by Stanton's description, "radiant with beauty and intellect." While Stanton was smitten with Ellen immediately, she was slow to respond to his affections. She still suffered from a romantic disappointment that had left her heart in "agony" and convinced her that she could not love again.

Stanton understood, he told her, that "the trouble of early love fell like a killing frost upon the tree of your life," but he was confident that "enough life still remains to put forth fresh blossoms." Despite his encouragement, Ellen was vexed by some of the qualities others noted in Stanton: his obsessive concentration on work, his impatience and lack of humor, and, most worrisome, "his careless[ness] and indifferen[ce] to the feelings of all."

Addressing these concerns, Stanton admitted that "there is so much of the hard and repulsive in my—(I will not say nature, for that I think is soft and tender) but in the temper and habit of life generated by adverse circumstances, that great love only can bear with and overlook." If the last decade of his life had been different, he assured her, if he had been "blessed with the companionship of a woman whose love would have pointed out and kindly corrected my errors, I would have escaped the fault you condemn."

After the successful conclusion of the Reaper trial, Ellen was finally persuaded to marry Edwin on June 25, 1856. Happier years followed for Stanton. The Manny patent was sustained not only by the Cincinnati court but by the U.S. Supreme Court on appeal. With this huge victory behind him, Stanton moved his practice to Washington, D.C., where he argued important cases before the Supreme Court, achieved substantial financial security, and built a brick mansion for his new wife.

• • •

As LINCOLN'S OWN HOPES were repeatedly frustrated, he wistfully watched the progress of others, in particular, Stephen Douglas, his great rival with whom he had often debated around the fire of Speed's general store. "Twenty-two years ago Judge Douglas and I first became acquainted," he confided in a private fragment later discovered in his papers. "We were both young then; he a trifle younger than I. Even then, we were both ambitious; I, perhaps, quite as much so as he. With *me* the race of ambition has been a failure—a flat failure; with *him* it has been one of splendid success. His name fills the nation; and is not unknown, even, in foreign lands. I affect no contempt for the high eminence he has reached. So reached, that the oppressed of my species, might have shared with me in the elevation, I would rather stand on that eminence, than wear the richest crown that ever pressed a monarch's brow."

At this juncture, some have suggested, Lincoln was sustained by his wife's unflagging belief that a glorious destiny awaited him. "She had the fire, will and ambition," his law partner John Stuart observed. When Mary was young and still being courted by many beaux, she had told a friend who had taken an old, wealthy husband, "I would rather marry a good man—a man of mind—with a hope and bright prospects ahead for position—fame and power than to marry all the houses—gold and bones in the world." Stephen Douglas, who had been among her suitors, she considered "a very little, *little* giant, by the side of my tall Kentuckian, and intellectually my husband towers above Douglas just as he does physically." Quite simply, in Mary's mind, her husband had "no equal in the United States."

In an era when, as Mary herself admitted, it was "unladylike" to be so interested in politics, she avidly supported her husband's political ambitions at every stage. Although she undoubtedly fortified his will at difficult moments, however, Lincoln's quest for public recognition and influence was so consuming, it is unlikely he would have abandoned his dreams, whatever the circumstances.

• • •

ONCE AGAIN, at a moment when Lincoln's career appeared to have come to a halt, Seward and Chase were moving forward. Chase's leadership during the political uprising in the North that followed the passage of the Nebraska Act had proved, in the words of Carl Schurz, to be "the first bugle call for the formation of a new party." Under the pressure of mounting sectional division, both national parties—the Whigs and the Democrats—had begun to fray. The Whig Party—the party of Clay and Webster, Lincoln, Seward, and Bates—had been the first to decline as "conscience Whigs," opposed to slavery, split from "cotton Whigs," who desired an accommodation with slavery. In the 1852 election, the divided Whig Party had been buried in a Democratic landslide. But the passage of the Nebraska Act brought serious defections in the Democratic Party as well, as Northerners unwilling to sanction the extension of slavery looked for a new home, leaving the party in control of the Southern Democrats.

The political upheaval was enormously complicated by the emergence of the Know Nothing Party, which had formed in reaction to an unprecedented flood of immigration in the 1840s and 1850s. In 1845, about 20 million people inhabited the United States. During the next decade, nearly 3 million immigrants arrived, mainly from Ireland and Germany. This largely Catholic influx descended on a country that was mostly native-born Protestant, anti-Catholic in sympathy. The Know Nothings fought to delay citizenship for the new immigrants and bar them from voting. In the early 1850s, they won elections in several cities, swept to statewide victory in Massachusetts, and gained surprising ground in New York. Newspapers and preachers assaulted "popery"; there were bloody anti-Catholic riots in several Northern cities.

Lincoln had nothing but disdain for the discriminatory beliefs of the Know Nothings. "How can any one who abhors the oppression of negroes, be in favor of degrading classes of white people?" he queried his friend Joshua Speed. "Our progress in degeneracy appears to me to be pretty rapid. As a nation, we began by declaring that '*all men are created equal.*' We now practically read it 'all men are created equal, *except negroes.*' When the Know-Nothings get control, it will read 'all men are created equal, except negroes, *and foreigners, and catholics.*' When it comes to this I should prefer emigrating to some country where they make no pretence of loving liberty—to Russia, for instance."

But this party, too, was soon to founder on the issue of slavery. Many Northern Know Nothings were also antislavery, and finally the anti-Nebraska cause proved more compelling, of more import, than resistance to foreign immigration. The split between the party's Northern and Southern factions would diminish its strength, though the nativist feelings that had fueled its birth would continue to influence the political climate even after the party itself collapsed and died.

With the Whigs disappearing and the Democrats under Southern domination, all those opposed to the extension of slavery found their new home in what eventually became the Republican Party, comprised of "conscience Whigs," "independent Democrats," and antislavery Know Nothings. In state after state, new coalitions with different names came into being—the Fusion Party, the People's Party, the Anti-Nebraska Party. In Ripon, Wisconsin, an 1854 gathering of antislavery men proposed the name "Republican Party," and other state conventions soon followed suit.

In Illinois, Lincoln held back, still hoping that the Whig Party could become the antislavery party. In New York, Seward hesitated as well, finding it difficult to sever friendships and relationships built over three decades. Salmon Chase, however, was unhindered by past loyalties. He was ready to commit himself wholeheartedly to the task of forging a new party under the Republican banner. He had always been willing to move on when new political arrangements offered richer prospects for himself and the cause. Beginning as a Whig, he had joined the Liberty Party. He had abandoned that party for the Free-Soilers and then had gone to the Senate as an independent Democrat. Now, with his Senate term coming to an end, and with little chance of being nominated by the Democrats for a second term, he was happy to become a Republican.

In Ohio, as in New York and Illinois, the new movement was complicated by the strength of nativist sentiment. A delicate balance would be required to court the old Know Nothings without forfeiting support in the immigrant German-American community, which was passionate in its hatred of slavery. Chase accomplished this feat by running for governor on a Republican platform endorsing no specific Know Nothing proposals, but including eight Know Nothing candidates for all the important offices on the statewide ticket.

It was a hard-fought canvass, and the indefatigable Chase left nothing to chance. Traveling by railroad, horseback, hand car, canoe, and open wagon, he spoke at fifty-seven different places in forty-nine counties.

Campaigning in the sparsely settled sections of Ohio proved to be an adventure. To reach the town of Delphos, he wrote Kate, he was driven along the railroad tracks "on a hand car" operated by two men who "placed themselves at the cranks." Though the stars provided light, "it was rather dangerous for who could tell but we might meet a train or perhaps another hand car."

Chase's strenuous work paid off, making him the first Republican governor of a major state. "The anxiety of the last few days is over," Sumner wrote from Boston. "At last I breathe freely!" Reading the news under the telegraphic band at breakfast, the Massachusetts senator could barely contain his excitement, predicting that his friend's victory would do more than anything else for the antislavery cause.

In New York, Seward faced a more difficult challenge than Chase in trying to placate the Know Nothings, who had never forgiven his proposal to extend state funds to Catholic schools. Indeed, they were determined to defeat Seward for reelection to the Senate in 1855. Facing the enmity of both the Know Nothings and the proslavery "cotton Whigs," he concluded that he could not risk moving to a new, untested party.

Seward's only hope for reelection lay in Weed's ability to cobble together an antislavery majority from among the various discordant elements in the state legislature. In the weeks before the legislature was set to convene, Weed entertained the members in alphabetical groups, angling for every possible vote, including a few Know Nothings who might put their antislavery principles above their anti-Catholic sentiments. At one of these lavish dinners, the story is told, three or four Know Nothings on a special tour of Weed's house confronted a portrait of Weed's good friend New York's bishop John Hughes. The stratagem would be doomed if the identity of the man in the portrait was known, so they were told that it was George Washington in his Continental robes, presented to Weed's father by Washington himself!

Working without rest, Weed somehow stitched together enough votes to reelect Seward to a second term in the Senate. "I snatch a minute from the pressure of solicitations of lobby men, and congratulations of newly-made friends, to express, not so much my deep, and deepened gratitude to you," Seward wrote Weed, "as my amazement at the magnitude and complexity of the dangers through which you have conducted our shattered bark." In Auburn, a great celebration followed the news of Seward's reelection. "I have never known such a season of rejoicing," Frances happily reported to her son Augustus. "They are firing 700 cannons here—a salute of 300 was given in Albany as soon as the vote was made known."

Once Seward was securely positioned for six additional years in the

Senate, he and Weed were liberated to join the Republican Party. Two state conventions, one Whig, one Republican, were convened in Syracuse in late September 1855. When Seward was asked by a friend which to attend, he replied that it didn't matter. Delegates would enter through two doors, but exit through one. The Whig delegates assembled first and adopted a strong antislavery platform. Then, led by Weed, they marched into the adjoining hall, where the Republicans greeted them with thunderous applause. From the remnants of dissolving parties, a new Republican Party had been born in the state of New York.

"I am so happy that you and I are at last on the same platform and in the same political pew," Sumner told Seward. That October, Seward announced his allegiance to the Republican Party in a rousing speech that traced the history of the growth of the slave power, illustrating the constant march to acquire new slave states and thereby ensure for slaveholders the balance of power in the Congress. "What, then, is wanted?" he asked. "Nothing but organization." The task before the new Republican Party was to consolidate its strength until it gained control of the Congress and secured the power to forbid the extension of slavery in the territories.

• • •

IN EARLY 1856, Lincoln decided that Illinois should follow New York and Ohio in organizing the various anti-Nebraska elements into the new Republican Party. Through his efforts, the call went out for an anti-Nebraska state convention to be held on May 29, 1856. Lincoln proceeded carefully in the weeks leading to the convention, recognizing the complexities of reconciling the disparate opponents of the Nebraska bill into a unified party. Despite the success of Weed and Chase in their respective states, Lincoln worried that the convention call would attract only the more radical elements of the coalition, providing too narrow a base for a viable new party.

Dramatic events in Kansas helped rally support for Lincoln's cause. A guerrilla war had broken out between Northern emigrants desiring to make Kansas a free state under the "popular sovereignty" provision of the Nebraska Act, and so-called "border ruffians," who crossed the river from Missouri and cast illicit votes to make Kansas a slave state. During the debate over the Nebraska Act, Seward had told the slave states that the North would "engage in competition for the virgin soil of Kansas, and God give the victory to the side which is stronger in numbers as it is in right." In the South, the *Charleston Mercury* responded: "When the North presents a sectional issue, and tenders battle upon it, she must meet it, or abide all the consequences of a victory easily won, by a remorseless and eager foe." As the violence spiraled, "Bleeding Kansas" became a new rallying cry for the antislavery forces. Kansas was not merely a contest between settlers but a war between North and South.

Moderate antislavery sentiment was further aroused when shocking news from Washington reached Illinois the week before the convention. On the Senate floor, South Carolina's Preston Brooks had savagely bludgeoned Charles Sumner in return for Sumner's incendiary antislavery speech. Sumner had begun unremarkably enough, presenting familiar arguments, laced with literary and historical references, against admitting Kansas as a slave state. The mood of the Senate chamber instantly shifted, however, when Sumner launched into a vituperative attack directed particularly against two of his fellow senators, Stephen Douglas of Illinois and Andrew Butler of South Carolina. He likened Butler to the aging, feeble Don Quixote, who imagined himself "a chivalrous knight," sentimentally devoted to his beloved "harlot, Slavery . . . who, though ugly to others, is always lovely to him." Riding forth by Butler's side, Douglas was "the squire of Slavery, its very Sancho Panza, ready to do all its humiliating offices."

In the days before delivering the speech, Sumner had read a draft to Frances Seward. She strongly advised him to remove the personal attacks, including a reference to Butler's slight paralysis that slurred his speech. In this instance Sumner did not heed her advice; when he finished speaking, Senator Lewis Cass of Michigan characterized the speech as "the most un-American and unpatriotic that ever grated on the ears of the members of this high body—as I hope never to hear again here or elsewhere."

Two days later, Butler's young cousin Congressman Preston Brooks entered the Senate chamber armed with a heavy cane. Walking up to Sumner, who was writing at his desk, Brooks reportedly said, "You have libelled South Carolina and my relative, and I have come to punish you." Before Sumner could speak, Brooks brought the cane down upon his head, cudgeling him repeatedly as Sumner futilely tried to rise from his desk. Covered with blood, Sumner fell unconscious and was carried from the floor.

News of the brutal assault, which left Sumner with severe injuries to his brain and spinal cord and kept him out of the Senate for three years, galvanized antislavery sentiment in the North. "Knots of men" on street corners pronounced it "a gross outrage on an American Senator and on freedom of speech," reported the *Boston Daily Evening Transcript*. Even the moderate supporters of the Nebraska bill "expressed themselves as never so much aroused before by the slave power." Mass public meetings, so crowded that thousands were unable to gain entrance, convened in cities and towns to protest the caning. Truly to *"see* the slave aggression," one of

Sumner's supporters wrote, the North had first to see "one of its best men Butchered in Congress." Other antislavery men had been assaulted, the *New York Tribune* observed, "but the knocking-down and beating to bloody blindness and unconsciousness of an American Senator while writing at his desk in the Senate Chamber is a novel illustration of the ferocious Southern spirit." The beating reached into the people's hearts and minds, which political events rarely touch, the historian William Gienapp has argued. It "proved a powerful stimulus in driving moderates and conservatives into the Republican party."

If Sumner became a hero in the North, Brooks was equally lionized in the South, where the press almost universally applauded the assault. The *Richmond Enquirer* spoke for many when it pronounced the act "good in conception, better in execution, and best of all in consequence." Celebratory gatherings were held everywhere, and in Columbia, South Carolina, the governor presented Brooks with a silver goblet and walking stick in honor of his good work.

More ominous still was the reaction of the distinguished *Richmond Whig*, a professed opponent of extremism on sectional issues. *"We are rejoiced at this,"* the *Whig* proclaimed. "The only regret we feel is, that Mr. Brooks did not employ a horsewhip or a cowhide upon his slanderous back, instead of a cane. *We trust the ball may be kept in motion. Seward and others should catch it next."* The *Petersburg [Virginia] Intelligencer* sounded a similar theme. "If thrashing is the only remedy by which the foul conduct of the Abolitionists can be controlled . . . *it will be very well to give Seward a double dose at least every other day* until it operates freely on his political bowels . . . his adroit demagoguism and damnable doctrines are infinitely more dangerous to the country than the coarse blackguardism of the perjured wretch, Sumner." The antipodal reactions of North and South, David Donald notes, made it "apparent that something dangerous was happening to the American Union when the two sections no longer spoke the same language, but employed rival sets of clichés to describe the Brooks-Sumner affair."

With emotions running high in Illinois, "all shades of antislavery opinion" flocked to the Bloomington convention—"old-line Whigs, bolting Democrats, Free-Soilers, Know Nothings, and abolitionists." Lincoln's fears were put to rest. Every faction seemed willing to concede something to create a party that all could stand behind.

The adopted platform united disparate factions on the issue of slavery extension without giving in to the bigoted views of the Know Nothings. Lincoln then delivered a powerful speech, full of "fire and energy and force," that further fortified the jarring factions into a united front. "That is the greatest speech ever made in Illinois," state auditor Jesse Dubois said, "and puts Lincoln on the track for the presidency." So enthralled were those in the audience that reporters cast aside their pens so as to concentrate on what Lincoln said, and the unrecorded speech has become known to history as the famous "Lost Speech." Lincoln was now the acknowledged leader of the new Republican Party in Illinois.

• • •

BY THE LATE SPRING of 1856, branches of the Republican Party had already been organized in at least twenty-two states and the District of Columbia, a remarkable beginning for a new party, giving hope to the leaders that this time, with the Whig Party all but dissolved and the Democratic Party split in two, they stood a solid chance in the presidential election. On June 17, when energized Republicans assembled in Philadelphia for their first national convention, both Seward and Chase had their hearts set on the nomination.

In Republican circles, Chase's gubernatorial election had earned him such tremendous prestige that he was convinced he was destined for the presidency. Writing to a friend just ten days after his Ohio victory, Chase suggested that his success in uniting liberal nativists with antislavery German-Americans demonstrated the key to Republican victory in the future. Where Republicans challenged the Know Nothing Party, as they did in Massachusetts, they found defeat. Chase seemed to feel that he was now entitled to the Republican presidential nomination in 1856.

Chase had journeyed to Francis Blair's country home in Maryland the previous December for the legendary Christmas conclave called to organize the Republican Party on a national basis. Francis Blair, the patriarch of the Blair family, wielded great power in party politics because of his old ties to the Democratic Party and his newfound antislavery views. Chase arrived to find Sumner in attendance, along with his old friend Gamaliel Bailey, the abolitionist editor of *The National Era*; New York congressman Preston King; and Massachusetts politician Nathaniel Banks. Seward had been invited, but, uncertain of how he would proceed on a national scale, he had sent Blair a note "approving of his activity, but declining his invitation." After an elegant dinner, served, ironically, by Blair's household slaves, the group sat down to discuss the future of the Republican Party.

At Chase's suggestion, the gathering agreed to hold an organizational meeting the following month in Pittsburgh. Inevitably, the conversation turned to potential candidates for the upcoming presidential election. Blair's suggestion of John Charles Frémont, the celebrated explorer who had played a central role in the conquest of California during the Mexican

War, met with general approval. The discussion undoubtedly disappointed Chase, who believed up to the moment of Frémont's nomination at the Philadelphia convention on June 19 that "if the unvarnished wishes of the people" prevailed, he would be chosen.

Chase's certainty was insufficient to mobilize the wrangling elements at the convention in support of his candidacy. Not only had he neglected to appoint a manager, but he failed to unite his own state behind him on the first ballot. The questionable deals he had made to secure his Senate seat eight years earlier had created permanent enemies within his home state. "I know that if Ohio had united on you instead of dividing her votes between [John] McLean & Fremont & you," Chase's friend Hiram Barney wrote, "your nomination would have been a matter of necessity; or if a tithe of the pains which were taken to urge Fremont had been employed for your nomination, it would have been accomplished."

Before the convention met, Seward had greater reason for hope than Chase, for clearly, he was the first choice of Republican voters and politicians. Weed kept him from running, however, insisting that the party was not yet sufficiently organized to win a national election. Better to wait four years than to be tarred with failure.

While the Republican Convention was in progress, Lincoln was staying at the American House in Urbana, Illinois, attending court. He was in high spirits, recalled Henry Whitney, having engaged in one of the practical jokes of which he was so fond. He had hidden the loud and annoying gong that summoned his fellow boarders to dinner. When the loss was discovered, Whitney entered the dining room and saw Lincoln sitting "awkwardly in a chair tilted up after his fashion, looking amused, silly and guilty." When Judge Davis told him he must put it back, Lincoln took the gong from its hiding place and returned it, "after which he bounded up the stairs, two steps at a time."

Within a day or two, the merry prankster received word that in the balloting for vice president, he had received 110 votes, second only to the eventual nominee, William Dayton of New Jersey. "Davis and I were greatly excited," Whitney recalled. Lincoln did not take it seriously at first, remarking only that "there's another great man in Massachusetts named Lincoln, and I reckon it's him." His casual response aside, it is probable that this unexpected event stimulated Lincoln's aspiration for higher office.

Unlike Seward, Chase, and Lincoln in 1856, Edward Bates refused to desert the divided and much-diminished Whig Party. While he joined with Republicans in vigorous opposition to the Kansas-Nebraska Act and the repeal of the sacred Missouri Compromise, he feared that the Republican focus on slavery would lead to an irreparable divide between North and South. After some indecision, he agreed to preside over the shrunken Whig National Convention of July 1856. The Whigs gathered in Baltimore and ultimately decided to support Millard Fillmore for president. Fillmore ran as a member of the American Party (a more palatable title for the old Know Nothing Party) on a platform that denounced both Republicans and Democrats for agitating the slavery issue at the risk of the nation's peace.

Though not a fanatical nativist, Bates considered the American Party, with its emphasis on issues other than slavery and a support base drawn from all sections of the country, the best hope for preserving the Union. "I am neither North nor South," he said in a final plea before the convention, "I repudiate political geography. . . . I am a man believing in making laws and then whether the law is exactly to my liking or not, enforcing it—whether it be to catch a runaway slave and bring him back to his master or to quell a riot in a disordered territory."

The general election resulted in a three-way race between the Republican Frémont, the Southern-leaning Democrat James Buchanan, and American Party candidate Millard Fillmore. When the votes were counted, Weed's advice to Seward proved correct. Though the Republican Party showed considerable strength throughout the North in its first national effort, winning eleven states, the South threw its strength behind Democrat James Buchanan, who emerged the victor. In addition to his overwhelming strength in the South, Buchanan captured four Northern states—Illinois, Indiana, Pennsylvania, and New Jersey—the states destined to be the battleground in the 1860 election. Fillmore and the American Party captured only tiny Maryland.

• • •

As THE DAY of Buchanan's inauguration approached, the Supreme Court was drafting a decision in the case of *Dred Scott v. Sandford*, which had originated in Missouri eleven years earlier. Scott, a slave, was suing for his freedom on the grounds that his master, an army doctor, had removed him for several years to military bases in both the free state of Illinois and the Wisconsin Territory before returning to the slave state of Missouri. The case wound its way through state and federal courts until it finally reached the Supreme Court for argument in 1856, with Francis Blair's son, Montgomery, representing Dred Scott and the celebrated Reverdy Johnson from the slave state of Maryland representing Scott's owners. The court was headed by Chief Justice Roger Taney of Maryland, "an uncompromising supporter of the South and slavery and an implacable foe of racial equality, the Republican Party, and the antislavery movement."

Seward was among the thousands of spectators gathered at the Capitol on March 4, 1857, to witness James Buchanan's inauguration. "Bright skies and a deliciously bland atmosphere" relieved the blustery weather of the previous two days. In his inaugural address, Buchanan conceded that a "difference of opinion" had arisen over the question of extending slavery into the territories. However, this vital question, which had figured in the formation of the Republican Party, was not a political issue, he claimed, but "a judicial question, which legitimately belongs to the Supreme Court of the United States." A decision in the *Dred Scott* case bearing on this very issue was pending before that august body. To that decision, Buchanan pledged: "I shall cheerfully submit, whatever this may be." All evidence suggests that Buchanan was already aware of the substance of the decision.

Two days later, on March 6, the historic decision was read by the seventy-nine-year-old Taney in the old Supreme Court chamber, one flight below the Senate. The 7–2 decision was breathtaking in its scope and consequences. The Court ruled that blacks "are not included, and were not intended to be included, under the word 'citizens' in the Constitution." Therefore, Scott had no standing in federal court. This should have decided the case, but Taney went further. Neither the Declaration of Independence nor the Constitution had been intended to apply to blacks, he said. Blacks were "so far inferior that they had no rights which the white man was bound to respect." But the Chief Justice did not stop even there; he went on to say that Congress had exceeded its authority when it forbade slavery in the territories by such legislation as the Missouri Compromise, for slaves were private property protected by the Constitution. In other words, the Missouri Compromise was unconstitutional. The act itself, of course, had already been repealed by the Nebraska Act, meaning that the Court was pronouncing on an issue that was not before it.

One of the justices later asserted that Taney had "become convinced that it was practicable for the Court to quiet all agitation on the question of slavery in the territories by affirming that Congress had no constitutional power to prohibit its introduction." But the fierce sectional conflict of the age, the question that had given birth to the Republican Party, could not be quieted by a divided judicial fiat. The *Dred Scott* case, Supreme Court Justice Felix Frankfurter later said, was "one of the Court's great self-inflicted wounds."

Initially, the decision appeared to be a stunning victory for the South. For more than a decade, the *Richmond Enquirer* proclaimed, antislavery forces had claimed for the federal government the right of prescribing the boundaries of slavery in the territories. Now the territorial prize for which the two sides had "often wrestled in the halls of Congress, has been awarded at last, by the proper umpire, to those who have justly won it." The decision of the Supreme Court, "the accredited interpreter of the Constitution and arbiter of disagreements between the several States," the *Enquirer* continued, has destroyed "*the foundation* of the theory upon which their warfare has been waged against the institutions of the South." Antislavery men were staggered, the *Enquirer* claimed, left "nonplused and bewildered, confounded and confused."

"Sheer blasphemy," Republicans responded. The ruling was "entitled to just so much moral weight as would be the judgment of a majority of those congregated in any Washington bar-room." The *New York Tribune* argued that the Supreme Court had forfeited its stature as "an impartial judicial body," and predicted that its attempt to derail the Republican Party, which had come so close to victory in the previous presidential election, would fail. "Judge Taney can do many things," Frederick Douglass observed, "but he cannot . . . change the essential nature of things—making evil good, and good, evil." Frances Seward hoped that the blatantly unethical decision would galvanize the national will of the North. It "has aroused many to the encroachments of the slave power," she happily reported to Sumner.

The furor broke yet another bond of union by involving the Supreme Court, the common guarantor of both North and South, in sectional conflict. Dred Scott was sold to a Mr. Taylor Blow, who promptly freed him. He would die within a year, a free man whose name would leave a deeper mark on American history than those of the justices who had consigned him to slavery.

Speaking in Springfield, Lincoln attacked the decision in characteristic fashion, not by castigating the Court but by meticulously exposing flaws of logic. The Chief Justice, Lincoln said, "insists at great length that negroes were no part of the people who made, or for whom was made, the Declaration of Independence, or the Constitution." Yet in at least five states, black voters acted on the ratification of the Constitution and were among the "We the People" by whom the Constitution was ordained and established. The founders, he acknowledged, did not "declare all men equal *in all respects*. They did not mean to say all were equal in color, size, intellect, moral developments, or social capacity." But they did declare all men "equal in 'certain inalienable rights, among which are life, liberty, and the pursuit of happiness.' . . . They meant simply to declare the *right*, so the *enforcement* of it might follow as fast as circumstances should permit."

• • •

SEWARD, TOO, would condemn the *Dred Scott* decision in a sensational oration on the Senate floor, accusing the administration of having engaged in a corrupt conspiracy with the Supreme Court. "The day of inauguration came," Seward said. The innocent crowd gathered for the ceremony were "unaware of the import of the whisperings carried on between the President and the Chief Justice." While the Chief Justice looked on and the members of the Senate watched in silence, Seward continued, President Buchanan proclaimed his complete support for the forthcoming, and supposedly yet unknown, Supreme Court ruling on the status of blacks under the Constitution. When "the pageant ended," Seward cried scornfully, "the judges, without even exchanging their silken robes for courtiers' gowns, paid their salutations to the President, in the Executive palace. Doubtlessly the President received them as graciously as Charles I did the judges who had, at his instance, subverted the statutes of English liberty."

While Seward's charges were echoed and acclaimed throughout the North, they provoked a violent reaction in the South and within the administration. President Buchanan was so enraged by the conspiracy charge that he forbade Seward access to the White House. Chief Justice Taney was even more infuriated, declaring later that if Seward had become president in 1861, he would "have refused to administer to him the official oath, and thereby proclaim to the nation that he would not administer that oath to such a man."

Six months later, Seward delivered another provocative speech that, like the "higher law" speech, would be indelibly linked to his name. Catering to the emotions of an ardent Republican gathering overflowing in Corinthian Hall in Rochester, New York, Seward argued that the United States was divided by two "incompatible" political and economic systems, which had developed divergent cultures, values, and assumptions. The free labor system had uneasily coexisted with slave labor, he observed, until recent advances in transportation, communication, and commerce increasingly brought the two "into closer contact." A catastrophic "collision" was inevitable. "Shall I tell you what this collision means?" he asked his audience. "They who think that it is accidental, unnecessary, the work of interested or fanatical agitators, and therefore ephemeral, mistake the case altogether. It is an *irrepressible conflict* between opposing and enduring forces, and it means that the United States must and will, sooner or later, become either entirely a slaveholding nation, or entirely a free-labor nation."

Frances Seward was thrilled with her husband's speech, believing its radical tone completely warranted by the increasingly aggressive stance of the South. Indeed, for all those fighting against slavery, the words "irrepressible conflict" provided a mighty battle cry. Seward had defined the sectional conflict as driven by fundamental differences rather than the machinations of extremists who exaggerated discord for their own political ends. He had taken his stand on an issue, Kenneth Stampp suggests, "that troubled the politicians of his generation as it has since troubled American historians: Was the conflict that ultimately culminated in the Civil War *repressible* or *irrepressible?*"

The speech produced an uproar in opposition papers. The Albany *Atlas and Argus* claimed that Seward was no longer content with restricting slavery to its present domain, but threatening to end slavery in South Carolina and Georgia. With this speech, the *New York Herald* claimed, Seward had thrown off his mask to reveal a "more repulsive abolitionist, because a more dangerous one, than Beecher, Garrison or [Massachusetts minister Theodore] Rev. Dr. Parker."

Seward, in fact, was not an abolitionist. He had long maintained that slavery in the states where it already existed was beyond the reach of national power. When he told of a nation without slavery, he referred to long-run historical forces and the inevitable triumph of an urbanizing, industrializing society. To Southerners, however, Seward seemed to be threatening the forced extinction of slavery and the permanent subjugation of the South. Seward, the historian William Gienapp suggests, "never comprehended fully the power of his words." He failed to anticipate the impact that such radical phrases as "higher law" and "irrepressible conflict" would have on the moderate image he wished to project. Long after the incendiary words had been spoken, Seward conceded that "if heaven would forgive him for stringing together two high sounding words, he would never do it again."

Ironically, while Seward was applauded in the antislavery North for his radical rhetoric, he was by temperament fundamentally conciliatory, eager to use his charisma and good-natured manner to unify the nation and find a peaceful solution to the sectional crisis. From his earliest days in politics, Seward had trusted the warmth and power of his personality to bridge any divide, so long as he could deal one-on-one with his adversaries. When his first election to the Senate was greeted with "alarm and apprehension" throughout the South, he remained placid. Although his positions on immigration, public education, the protective tariff, internal improvements, and above all, slavery made him a symbol of everything the South abhorred about the North, Seward's confidence was unshaken. "This general impression only amuses me," he wrote, "for I think that I shall prove as gentle a lion as he who played that part before the Duke, in the 'Midsummer Night's Dream.' "

He remained true to his resolve. "Those who assailed him with a view to personal controversy were disturbed by continual failures to provoke his anger," a contemporary recalled. The story was told and retold of a Southern senator who delivered an abusive speech against Seward, labeling him "an infidel and a traitor." When the senator resumed his seat, "heated and shaken with the fierce frenzy" of his own ire, Seward walked over to his chair and "sympathetically offered him a pinch of snuff."

Within the Washington community, Seward's extravagant dinner parties were legendary, attended by Northerners and Southerners alike. No one showed greater acumen in reconciling the most contentious politicians in a relaxing evening atmosphere. Throughout the 1850s, the New Yorker used such dinners to maintain cordial relations with everyone, from Jefferson Davis of Mississippi and John Crittenden of Kentucky to Charles Sumner and Charles Francis Adams of Massachusetts. Seward was a superb master of ceremonies, putting all at ease with his amiable disposition. Though an inveterate storyteller himself, he would draw the company into lively conversations ranging from literature and science to theater and history.

A woman who was present at one of these feasts recalled that seventeen courses were served, beginning with turtle soup. The plates were changed with each serving of fish, meat, asparagus, sweetbreads, quail, duck, terrapin, ice cream, and "beautiful pyramids of iced fruits, oranges, french kisses." By each place setting there stood wineglasses, "five in number, of different size, form and color, indicating the different wines to be served." After dinner, coffee was served to the women in the parlor while the men gathered in the study to enjoy after-dinner liqueurs, and cigars ordered specially from Cuba. Through these Bacchanalian feasts, "by the juice of the grape, and even certain distillations from peaches and corn," Seward endeavored, one reporter suggested, "to give his guests good cheer, and whether they are from the North or South, keep them in the bonds of good fellowship. Strange rumors have often crept out from Washington and startled the people, to the effect, that fire-eaters have been known to visit the house of the great New Yorker, and come away mellow with the oil of gladness, purple with the essence of the fruit of the wine."

Seward's social engagements did not lessen when Congress was out of session. The summer after the *Dred Scott* decision was handed down, he invited Francis Blair, Sr., and his wife, Eliza, to accompany him on a trip through Canada. Joining the party were Seward's son Fred and Fred's young wife, Anna. Though he understood that the Blairs were far more conservative than he, Seward trusted that his charm would win their support for the nomination in 1860.

The "voyage of discovery," as Blair later described the trip, took the travelers through Niagara Falls, Toronto, and the Thousand Islands to the coast of Labrador. The sprightly Blairs, who seemed far younger than their years, enjoyed the adventure thoroughly. In an exuberant letter of thanks, Blair told Seward he was the "very best traveling companion," who not only made every stop "doubly interesting" by his gifts as a storyteller, but had taken pains to remove all the hardships of the voyage, providing secure sleeping arrangements, a comfortable fishing boat that traversed rough waters without inducing seasickness, and elegant meals. It was a trip they would never forget. But when the time came for hard decisions, the Blair family would back the man more closely aligned with their political views—Edward Bates.

• • •

WHILE SEWARD WAS A NATURAL in social situations, Governor Chase struggled through the dinners and receptions he organized to further his political ambitions, possessing none of Seward's social grace. Chase's greatest resource was his seventeen-year-old daughter, Kate, who flourished in her role as her father's hostess. "At an age when most girls are shy and lanky," the *Cincinnati Enquirer* noted, "she stepped forth into the world an accomplished young woman, able to cross swords with the brightest intellects of the nation."

A child less strong-willed and high-spirited than Kate might have been crushed by the vicissitudes of her father's demanding love, which he bestowed or denied depending on her performance. In her case, however, the unremitting stress on good habits, fine manners, and hard work paid off. By the time she returned to Columbus, she had acquired an excellent education, a proficiency in several languages, an ability to converse with anyone, and, her biographer observes, "a scientific knowledge of politics that no woman, and few men, have ever surpassed."

Tall and willowy, Kate was celebrated far and wide as one of the most captivating women of her age. "Her complexion was marvellously delicate," a contemporary recalled, "her hair a wonderful color like the ripe corn-tassel in full sunlight. Her teeth were perfect. Poets sang then, and still sing, to the turn of her beautiful neck and the regal carriage of her head." Friends and acquaintances were struck by the extraordinary similarity in looks between the handsome Chase and his stunning daughter. Indeed, when they made an entrance, a hush invariably fell over the room, as if a king and his queen stood in the doorway.

Kate's return to Columbus prompted her father to settle in a house of his own. Devastated by the loss of three young wives, Chase had never summoned the energy to buy and furnish a home, shuttling instead between rented homes, boardinghouses, and hotel suites. Now, with both Kate and Nettie at home, he bought the stately Gothic mansion on Sixth Street, leaving most of the decorating decisions to Kate. He sent her to Cincinnati to select the wallpaper, carpets, draperies, and sideboards. "I feel I am trusting a good deal to the judgment of a girl of 17," Chase told her, "but I am confident I may safely trust yours" . . . "you have capacity and will do very well."

Assuming the role of Ohio's first lady, Kate wrote out the invitations and oversaw arrangements for scores of receptions, soirées, and dinners. "I knew all of the great men of my time," she later recalled. "I was thrown upon my own resources at a very early age." William Dean Howells, working then as a cub reporter in Columbus, never forgot his invitation to an elegant Thanksgiving party at the governor's house. It was his first dinner "in society," the first time he had seen individual plates placed before guests "by a shining black butler, instead of being passed from hand to hand among them." After dinner, the company was invited to a game of charades, which promised mortification for the shy young Howells. Kate immediately allayed his fears, he gratefully recalled, by "the raillery glancing through the deep lashes of her brown eyes which were very beautiful." Kate's dynamic grace and intellect made her the most interesting woman in any gathering, as well as a critical force behind her father's drive for the presidency.

While Kate projected a mature poise, she was yet a spirited young girl with a rebellious streak. Her craving for excitement and glamour led to a tryst with a wealthy young man who had recently married the daughter of a well-known Ohio journalist. The dashing figure reportedly "began his attentions by little civilities, then mild flirtations," building familiarity to take Kate for carriage rides and call on her in the Governor's Mansion. When Chase learned of these encounters, he banished Kate's admirer from the house. Nonetheless, the young couple continued meeting, signaling each other with handkerchiefs from the window. One day Chase apparently arrived home unexpectedly, to find the "enamored Benedict" in his drawing room. Chase used his horsewhip to put an end to the relationship.

Kate once again settled into her role as her father's helpmate, working with him side by side as he set his sights on a presidential run in 1860. Like Seward and Lincoln, Chase regarded the *Dred Scott* decision as part of a conspiracy aimed at free institutions, which only a Republican victory could stop. He had offered his services to Scott's defenders, but in the end had not taken part in the case. His true service to the nation, he believed, could best be served in the White House. "I find that many are beginning to talk about the election of 1860," he wrote his friend Charles Cleveland in November 1857, "and not a few are again urging my name. . . . Some imagine that I can combine more strength than any other man."

• • •

WHILE SEWARD AND CHASE eyed the presidency, Lincoln prepared for another bid for the U.S. Senate. As chief architect of the Republican Party in his state, Lincoln had first claim to run against Stephen Douglas in 1858. Recognizing the sacrifice he had made three years earlier to ensure Trumbull's election, hundreds of party workers stood ready to do everything they could to ensure that this time Lincoln had every chance to realize his dream. In addition to David Davis, Leonard Swett, and Billy Herndon, stalwart friends in 1855, he could count on Norman Judd, whose refusal to abandon Trumbull had contributed mightily to his earlier defeat.

Once again fate threatened to disrupt his plans as events in Kansas took an ominous turn. Although an overwhelming majority of the settlers were opposed to slavery and wanted to join the Union as a free state, a rump group of proslavery forces met in Lecompton, drafted a proslavery constitution, and applied for statehood. The Buchanan administration, hoping to appease Southern mainstays of the Democratic Party, endorsed the Lecompton Constitution, calling on Congress to admit Kansas as a slave state. A new wave of outrage swept the North.

At this juncture, Stephen Douglas stunned the political world by breaking with his fellow Democrats. In an acrimonious session with President Buchanan, he told him he would not support the Lecompton Constitution. The man who had led the Democratic fight for the Nebraska Act was now siding with the Republicans in open opposition to his own administration. "My objection to the Lecompton constitution did not consist in the fact that it made Kansas a slave State," he later explained. He cared not whether slavery was voted up or down; but the decision "was not the act and deed of the people of Kansas, and did not embody their will." To Douglas, the clash with the Buchanan administration must have seemed unavoidable. Support for Lecompton would have betrayed his own doctrine of "popular sovereignty," on which he had staked his political future, and seriously diminished his chances for reelection to the Senate from Illinois.

With Douglas on their side, Republicans were thrilled, believing they now had a chance to keep Kansas from entering the Union as a slave state.

"What can equal the caprices of politics?" Seward queried his wife the day after Douglas made his dramatic announcement. Throughout the entire decade, Seward explained, "the triumph of slavery . . . could not have occurred but for the accession to it of Stephen A. Douglas, the representative of the West." His defection, Seward exulted, was "a great day for freedom and justice." Old party enmities were forgotten as Eastern Republicans rushed to embrace Douglas as an ally in the fight against slavery. In the *Tribune*, Horace Greeley called on Illinois Republicans to cross party lines and endorse Douglas for senator in the upcoming race.

Lincoln at once understood the catastrophic implications for his own political prospects. Furthermore, knowing Douglas as he did, Lincoln believed that his "break" with the administration was but a temporary squabble over the facts of the situation in Kansas, rather than a change of heart on principle. Once the Kansas matter was settled, Lincoln suspected, Douglas would resume his long-standing alliance with the proslavery Democrats. In the meantime, duped Republican voters would have reelected Douglas, destroyed the Republican Party in Illinois, and ceded their voice in the Senate to a fundamentally proslavery politician.

Everywhere he went, lamented Lincoln, he was "accosted by friends" asking if he had read Douglas's speech. "In every instance the question is accompanied with an anxious inquiring stare, which asks, quite as plainly as words could, 'Can't you go for Douglas now?' Like boys who have set a bird-trap, they are watching to see if the birds are picking at the bait and likely to go under."

"What does the New-York Tribune mean by it's constant eulogising, and admiring, and magnifying [of] Douglas?" Lincoln demanded of Trumbull. "Have they concluded that the republican cause, generally, can be best promoted by sacraficing us here in Illinois?" Even in his bleakest moods, Lincoln characteristically refused to attribute petty motives to Greeley, whom he considered "incapable of corruption." While he recognized that Greeley would rather "see Douglas reelected over me or any other republican," it was not because Greeley conspired with Douglas, but because "he thinks Douglas' superior position, reputation, experience, and *ability*, if you please, would more than compensate for his lack of a pure republican position." Lincoln felt much the same about Seward's enthusiasm for Douglas's reversal, despite the hazard it posed to his own chances.

To Lincoln's immense relief, the interference of the Eastern Republicans only served to strengthen the determination of his friends and supporters. At hastily called conventions all over the state, resolutions were passed declaring that "Abraham Lincoln is the first and only choice of the

Republicans of Illinois for the United States Senate." In an unprecedented move, since the ultimate decision would be made by the state legislature elected that fall, a statewide Republican convention in Springfield was called in June to officially nominate Lincoln for senator. "Lincoln's rise from relative obscurity to a presidential nomination," Don Fehrenbacher has convincingly argued, "includes no more decisive date than June 16, 1858," when the convention met in Springfield and enthusiastically endorsed Lincoln as its "first and only choice . . . for the United States Senate, as the successor of Stephen A. Douglas."

"A house divided against itself cannot stand," Lincoln said, echoing the Gospels of Mark and Matthew, as he began his now famous acceptance speech at Springfield. Straightaway, he set forth an instantly accessible image of the Union as a house in danger of collapse under the relentless pressure of the slavery issue. "I believe this government cannot endure, permanently half *slave* and half *free,*" he continued. "I do not expect the house to *fall*—but I *do* expect it will cease to be divided. It will become *all* one thing, or *all* the other."

Supporters and opponents alike believed that with his image of a house that could not "endure, permanently half *slave* and half *free,*" Lincoln had abandoned the moderate approach of his Peoria speech four years earlier in favor of more militant action. His argument, however, remained essentially unchanged: slavery had seemed on the road to gradual extinction until the fateful passage of the Nebraska bill gave it new momentum. His call for action was no more radical than before—to "arrest the further spread" of slavery and "place it where the public mind shall rest in the belief" that it was back where the framers intended it, "in course of ultimate extinction." The true change since the Peoria speech was not in Lincoln's stance but in the designs of proslavery Democrats, who, he charged, had cunningly erected a new proslavery edifice to destroy the framers' house of democracy.

Lincoln deftly illustrated what he, like Seward, considered a plot to overthrow the Constitution. Whereas Seward cited the days of the English king, Charles I, with an oblique reference to the Roman emperor Nero, to present a tableau of a tyrant's coronation, Lincoln delineated the conspiracy with an everyday metaphor. "When we see a lot of framed timbers, different portions of which we know have been gotten out at different times and places by different workmen—Stephen, Franklin, Roger and James, for instance," Lincoln explained, "and when we see these timbers joined together, and see they exactly make the frame of a house . . . all the lengths and proportions of the different pieces exactly adapted to their respective places . . . we find it impossible to not *believe* that Stephen and Franklin and Roger and James all understood one another from the beginning, and all worked upon a common *plan* or *draft* drawn up before the first lick was struck." With these timbers in place, Lincoln warned, only one other "nice little niche" needed to be "filled with another Supreme Court decision," declaring that the constitutional protection of private property prevented states as well as territories from excluding slavery from their limits. Then, in one fell swoop, all laws outlawing slavery in the Northern states would be invalidated.

If "the point of this rather elaborate [house] metaphor seems obscure today," the historian James McPherson observes, "Lincoln's audience knew exactly what he was talking about." The four conniving Democratic carpenters were Stephen Douglas, architect of the lamentable Nebraska law and vocal defender of the *Dred Scott* decision; Franklin Pierce, the outgoing president who had used his last annual message to underscore the *"weight and authority"* of Supreme Court decisions even before the Court had completed its deliberations in the *Dred Scott* case; Roger Taney, the Chief Justice who had authored the revolutionary decision; and James Buchanan, the incoming president who had strongly urged compliance with the Supreme Court decision a full two days before the opinion was made public. Working together, these four men had put slavery on a path to "become alike lawful in *all* the States, *old* as well as *new—North* as well as *South.*"

Reminding his audience that Douglas had always been among the foremost carpenters in the Democratic plan to nationalize slavery, Lincoln made it clear that the Republican cause must be "intrusted to, and conducted by its own undoubted friends—those whose hands are free, whose hearts are in the work" of shoring up the frame first raised by the founding fathers. While Douglas might be "a very *great* man," and the "largest of *us* are very small ones," he had consistently used his influence to distort the framers' intentions regarding slavery, exhibiting a moral indifference to slavery itself. "Clearly, he is not *now* with us," Lincoln stated, "he does not *pretend* to be—he does not *promise* to *ever* be."

The image of America as an unfinished house in danger of collapse worked brilliantly because it provided a ringing challenge to the Republican audience, a call for action to throw out the conspiring carpenters, unseat the Democratic Party, and recapture control of the nation's building blocks—the laws that had wisely prevented the spread of slavery. Only then, Lincoln claimed, with the public mind secure in the belief that slavery was once more on a course to eventual extinction, would the people in all sections of the country live together peaceably in the great house their forefathers had built.

In the campaign that followed, Douglas would strenuously deny that he had ever conspired with Taney and Buchanan before the *Dred Scott* decision. "What if Judge Douglas never did talk with Chief Justice Taney and the President," replied Lincoln. "It can only show that he was *used* by conspirators, and was not a *leader* of them." This charge reflected his agreement with Seward and Chase that—whether there was an explicit conspiracy—there was a mutual intent by the slave power to extend slavery. Edward Bates also feared that Southern radicals "planned to seize control of the federal government and nationalize slavery."

* * *

SO THE STAGE WAS SET for a titanic battle, arguably the most famous Senate fight in American history, a clash that would make Lincoln a national figure and propel him to the presidency while it would, at the same time, undermine Douglas's support in the South and further fracture the Democratic Party.

In keeping with political strategy followed to this day, Lincoln, the challenger, asked Douglas to campaign with him so they could debate the issues. The incumbent, Douglas, who boasted a national reputation and deep pockets, had little to gain from debating Lincoln and initially refused the challenge, but eventually felt compelled to participate in the seven face-to-face debates known to history as the Lincoln-Douglas Debates.

In the course of the campaign, both men covered over 4,000 miles within Illinois, delivering hundreds of speeches. The northern part of the state was Republican territory. In the southern counties, populated largely by migrants from the South, the proslavery sentiment dominated. The election would be decided in the central section of Illinois, where the debates became the centerpiece of the struggle. With marching bands, parades, fireworks, banners, flags, and picnics, the debates brought tens of thousands of people together with "all the devoted attention," one historian has noted, "that many later Americans would reserve for athletic contests."

Attending the debate in Quincy, the young Republican leader Carl Schurz recounted how "the country people began to stream into town for the great meeting, some singly, on foot or on horseback, or small parties of men and women, and even children, in buggies or farm wagons; while others were marshaled in solemn procession from outlying towns or districts. . . . It was indeed the whole American people that listened to those debates," continued Schurz, later remarking that "the spectacle reminded one of those lays of ancient times telling us of two armies in battle array, standing still to see their two principal champions fight out the contested

Abraham Lincoln photographed at age forty-eight in Chicago
on February 28, 1857. The lawyer's political star had begun to
rise at last. A year later, accepting his party's nomination
for U.S. senator, he would utter the famous words
"A house divided against itself cannot stand."

2

Mary Todd Lincoln, shown here at twenty-eight, after four years of marriage. Upon their first meeting, Lincoln told Mary: "I want to dance with you in the worst way." And, Mary laughingly told her cousin later that night, "he certainly did."

3

The Lincolns were indulgent parents, believing that "love is the chain whereby to lock a child to its parent." Robert was the eldest *(above)*, followed by Willie *(left)* and Tad *(right)*. Another son, Eddie, died of tuberculosis in 1850 at the age of three.

4

5

6
7

When William H. Seward, shown here at age forty-three *(left)*, married
Frances Miller *(right)*, the daughter of a wealthy judge, in 1824, he
acquired wealth, professional connections, and the stately mansion in
Auburn, New York *(below)*, that would become his lifelong home.

8

9

Possessed of a powerful intellect and strong moral convictions, Frances Seward (*above*) served as her husband's political conscience. Young Fanny Seward, shown with her father, adored her mother but idolized her father, thinking him one of the greatest men in the country.

10

"A vale of misery" descended upon Salmon P. Chase *(above left and below)* after he lost three wives, including Catherine *(above right)* and Sarah Bella *(below)*, in slightly over a decade.

14

Chase thereafter sought companionship with political friends such as
Edwin M. Stanton *(above)*, whose own life had been marred by family
tragedy. Only when he became governor of Ohio did Chase settle
into a home of his own in Columbus *(below)*.

15

16 17

Julia Bates (*above left and below*) provided Edward Bates (*above right*) with what their friends uniformly described as an ideal home life. Through four decades of married life and the birth of seventeen children their intimacy remained strong.

18

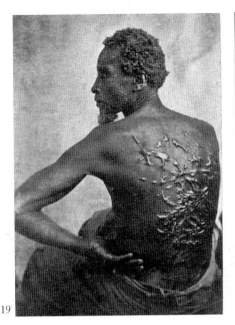

19

20

In the 1850s, Northern sentiment was inflamed by the publication of
Uncle Tom's Cabin, with its disturbing scenes of slavery's violence *(left)*,
and by the landmark *Dred Scott* decision. Scott *(right)* had sued for his
freedom, but the Supreme Court, led by Roger B. Taney *(below)*, decreed
that he "had no rights which the white man was bound to respect."

21

22

Lincoln's gift for making and keeping friends, such as Joshua Speed *(above)* and David Davis *(below)*, played a critical role in both his personal happiness and professional advancement.

23

24

25

Lincoln forged lasting friendships while riding the "circuit" with fellow lawyers, including William Herndon *(left)* and Ward Lamon *(right)*. In these convivial settings *(below)*, Lincoln's never-ending stream of stories made him the center of attention, while he, in turn, gained firsthand knowledge of the voters throughout Illinois.

26

27

28

Neither Lyman Trumbull *(left)* nor Norman Judd *(right)* would ever forget Lincoln's magnanimity when conceding defeat in his 1855 bid for the Senate. Both men would help Lincoln at the 1860 Republican National Convention in Chicago *(below)*.

29

THE REPUBLICAN WIGWAM AT CHICAGO.

30

31

Thurlow Weed *(right)* failed to win the Republican nomination for his protégé, William Seward. An act of betrayal by Horace Greeley *(left)*, who bore an old political grudge against Seward, contributed to the defeat. Editorial humor of the day cast Seward in the role of an assassinated Julius Caesar and depicted Greeley as a vengeful Brutus *(below)*.

32

33

"A profound stillness fell upon the Wigwam" *(above)* as the results of the crucial third ballot hung in the balance. Seward awaited the news from Chicago in the garden of his Auburn home *(below)*.

34

35

Residents of Springfield congregated before Lincoln's home for a campaign rally
after his unexpected capture of the Republican nomination over
Seward, Chase, and Bates.

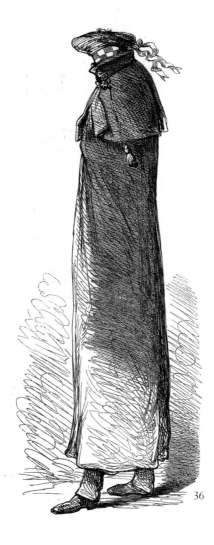

36

Assassination threats prompted President-elect Lincoln to enter
Washington at the crack of dawn. A scurrilous rumor that he had
disguised himself in a Scotch plaid cap and military cloak circulated
widely in the media, causing him much embarrassment.

cause between the lines in single combat." The debates, said Lincoln in Quincy, "were the successive acts of a drama . . . to be enacted not merely in the face of audiences like this, but in the face of the nation."

"On the whole," Schurz observed, "the Democratic displays were much more elaborate and gorgeous than those of the Republicans, and it was said that Douglas had plenty of money to spend for such things. He himself also traveled in what was called in those days 'great style,' with a secretary and servants and a numerous escort of somewhat loud companions, moving from place to place by special train with cars specially decorated for the occasion, all of which contrasted strongly with Lincoln's extreme modest simplicity."

Each debate followed the same rules. The first contestant spoke for an hour, followed by a one-and-a-half-hour response, after which the man who had gone first would deliver a half-hour rebuttal. The huge crowds were riveted for the full three hours, often interjecting comments, cheering for their champion, bemoaning the jabs of his opponent. Newspaper stenographers worked diligently to take down every word, and their transcripts were swiftly dispatched throughout the country.

"No more striking contrast could have been imagined than that between those two men as they appeared upon the platform," one observer wrote. "By the side of Lincoln's tall, lank, and ungainly form, Douglas stood almost like a dwarf, very short of stature, but square-shouldered and broad-chested, a massive head upon a strong neck, the very embodiment of force, combativeness, and staying power."

The highly partisan papers concocted contradictory pictures of crowd response and outcome. At the end of the first debate, the Republican Chicago *Press and Tribune* reported that "when Mr. Lincoln walked down from the platform, he was seized by the multitude and borne off on their shoulders, in the center of a crowd of five thousand shouting Republicans, with a band of music in front." Observing the same occasion, the Democratic *Chicago Times* claimed that when it was over, Douglas's "excoriation of Lincoln" had been so successful and "so severe, that the republicans hung their heads in shame."

The people of Illinois had followed the careers of Douglas and, to a lesser extent, Lincoln for nearly a quarter of a century as they represented opposing parties in the State House, in Congress, and on the campaign trail. Indeed, in the opening debate at Ottawa, Douglas spoke of his first acquaintance with Lincoln when they were "both comparatively boys, and both struggling with poverty in a strange land," when Lincoln was "just as good at telling an anecdote as now. He could beat any of the boys wrestling, or running a foot race, in pitching quoits or tossing a copper, could ruin more liquor than all the boys of the town together, and the dignity and impartiality with which he presided at a horse race or fist fight, excited the admiration and won the praise of everybody," as well as the lifelong epithet "Honest Abe."

The amiable tone was laced with innuendo as Douglas described Lincoln's climb from "flourishing grocery-keeper" (meaning that Lincoln sold liquor, a curious charge from the notoriously hard-drinking Douglas) to the state legislature, where they had served together in 1836, till Lincoln was "submerged . . . for some years," turning up again in Congress, where he "in the Senate . . . was glad to welcome my old friend," for he had neither friends nor companions. "He distinguished himself by his opposition to the Mexican war, taking the side of the common enemy against his own country; and when he returned home he found that the indignation of the people followed him everywhere, and he was again submerged or obliged to retire into private life, forgotten by his former friends. He came up again in 1854, just in time to make this Abolition or Black Republican platform, in company with Giddings, Lovejoy, Chase, and Fred Douglass for the Republican party to stand upon." With this, the crowd broke into laughter, shouting: "Hit him again."

Lincoln readily conceded that Douglas was far better known than he. As he outlined the advantages of Douglas's stature, however, his audience laughed with glee. "All the anxious politicians of his party," Lincoln told a crowd at Springfield, "have been looking upon him as certainly, at no distant day, to be the President of the United States. They have seen in his round, jolly, fruitful face, postoffices, landoffices, marshalships, and cabinet appointments, chargeships and foreign missions, bursting and sprouting out in wonderful exuberance ready to be laid hold of by their greedy hands." When the cheers and laughter drawn forth by this comical image subsided, Lincoln went on, "Nobody has ever expected me to be President. In my poor, lean, lank face, nobody has ever seen that any cabbages were sprouting out. These are disadvantages all, taken together, that the Republicans labor under. *We* have to fight this battle upon principle and upon principle, alone."

Douglas asserted that Lincoln dare not repeat his antislavery principles in the southern counties of Illinois. "The very notice that I was going to take him down to Egypt made him tremble in the knees so that he had to be carried from the platform. He laid up seven days, and in the meantime held a consultation with his political physicians." Lincoln promptly responded, "Well, I know that sickness altogether furnishes a subject for philosophical contemplation, and I have been treating it in that way, and I have really come to the conclusion (for I can reconcile it no other way), that the Judge is crazy." There was "not a word of truth" to the claim that he had ever had to be carried prostrate from a platform, although he had been hoisted aloft by enthusiastic supporters. "I don't know how to meet that sort of thing. I don't want to call him a liar, yet, if I come square up to the truth, I do not know what else it is." Amid cheers and laughter, Lincoln closed: "I suppose my time is nearly out, and if it is not, I will give up and let the Judge set my knees to trembling—if he can."

Throughout the debates, Lincoln carried a small notebook that contained clippings relevant to the questions of the day sent to him by his law partner, William Herndon, along with the opening lines of his own "House Divided" speech and the paragraph of the Declaration of Independence proclaiming that "all men are created equal, that they are endowed by their Creator with certain unalienable Rights, that among these are Life, Liberty and the pursuit of Happiness." It was on the meaning of the Declaration that battle lines were drawn.

As Lincoln repeatedly said in many forums, slavery was a violation of the Declaration's "majestic interpretation of the economy of the Universe," allowed by the founders because it was already among us, but placed by them in the course of ultimate extinction. Although unfulfilled in the present, the Declaration's promise of equality was "a beacon to guide" not only "the whole race of man then living" but "their children and their children's children, and the countless myriads who should inhabit the earth in other ages."

For Douglas, the crux of the controversy was the right of self-government, the principle that the people in each territory and each state should decide for themselves whether to introduce or exclude slavery. "I care more for the great principle of self-government, the right of the people to rule, than I do for all the negroes in Christendom."

Lincoln agreed that "the doctrine of self government is right—absolutely and eternally right," but argued that "it has no just application" to slavery. "When the white man governs himself," he asserted, "that is self-government; but when he governs himself, and also governs *another* man, that is *more* than self-government—that is despotism. If the negro is a *man*, why then my ancient faith teaches me that 'all men are created equal'; and that there can be no moral right in connection with one man's making a slave of another."

While it did not matter to Douglas what the people of Kansas decided, so long as they had the right to decide, for Lincoln, the substance of the decision was crucial. "The difference between the Republican and the Democratic parties on the leading issue of this contest," declared Lincoln, "is, that the former consider slavery a moral, social and political wrong, while the latter *do not* consider it either a moral, social or political wrong; and the action of each . . . is squared to meet these views."

                              • • •

DOUGLAS UNDERSTOOD from the outset that his primary goal, more important than debating or defining his own position, was to cast Lincoln as a radical, bent on abolishing all distinctions between the races. The question of black equality—in the modern sense—was not controversial in Illinois, or in the nation as a whole. Almost every white man was against it, even most abolitionists. Douglas was certain that no candidate who professed a belief in the social or political equality of blacks and whites could possibly carry Illinois, where a long-standing set of Black Laws prevented blacks from voting, holding political office, giving testimony against whites, and sitting on juries.

At every forum, therefore, Douglas missed no opportunity to portray Lincoln as a Negro-loving agitator bent on debasing white society. "If you desire negro citizenship," Douglas baited his audience, "if you desire them to vote on an equality with yourselves, and to make them eligible to office, to serve on juries, and to adjudge your rights, then support Mr. Lincoln and the Black Republican party." The crowd responded as Douglas hoped: "Never, never." Cheers nearly drowned out his voice as he shouted his opinion that "the signers of the Declaration of Independence had no reference to negroes at all when they declared all men to be created equal. They did not mean negro, nor the savage Indians, nor the Fejee Islanders, nor any other barbarous race. They were speaking of white men. . . . I hold that this government was established . . . for the benefit of white men and their posterity forever, and should be administered by white men, and none others." Cries of "that's the truth" erupted from the agitated throng amid raucous applause.

In response, Lincoln avowed that he had "no purpose to introduce political and social equality between the white and the black races." He had never been in favor "of making voters or jurors of negroes, nor of qualifying them to hold office, nor to intermarry." He acknowledged "a physical difference between the two" that would "probably forever forbid their living together upon the footing of perfect equality." But "notwithstanding all this," he said, taking direct aim at the Supreme Court's decision in the *Dred Scott* case, "there is no reason in the world why the negro is not entitled to all the natural rights enumerated in the Declaration of Independence. . . . I agree with Judge Douglas he is not my equal in many respects—certainly not in color, perhaps not in moral and intellectual endowment. But in the right to eat the bread, without leave of anybody else, which his own hand earns, he is my equal and the equal of Judge Douglas, and the equal of every living man."

It is instructive, political philosopher Harry Jaffa perceptively notes, that the only unequivocal statement of white supremacy Lincoln ever made was as to "color"—the assertion of an obvious difference. Had he advocated political and social equality for blacks, he unquestionably would have lost the election in a state where the legislature not only supported the discriminatory Black Laws but had gone even further by passing a special law making it a criminal offense to bring into the boundaries of Illinois "a person having in him one-fourth negro blood, whether free or slave." And this same law essentially barred blacks and mulattos from entering the state to take up residence.

Nonetheless, Lincoln's implied support for the Black Laws stands in contrast to the bolder positions adopted by both Seward and Chase. Chase had long since adopted a liberal stance on race far in advance of the general public, and had been instrumental in removing some but not all of Ohio's discriminatory Black Laws. Seward, too, had spoken out vehemently against the Black Laws, and in favor of black suffrage, coming from the more progressive state of New York.

However, neither Seward nor Chase advocated full social and political equality for blacks. "Seward did not believe," his biographer concludes, "that the black man in America was the equal of the white, or that he was capable of assimilation as were the Irish and German immigrants. But he did believe that the Negro was a man, and as such deserved and should have all the privileges of the whites." Nor did Salmon Chase think that "the two races could live together." He told Frederick Douglass that he thought "separation was in everyone's best interests." He believed that blacks would find "happier homes in other lands." So long as they were here, however, he championed measures to fight discrimination.

These statements of Seward and Chase, coming from the leaders of the antislavery cause, reveal that racism, the belief in white supremacy, was deeply embedded in the entire country. It is only in this context that the statements of Lincoln and his contemporaries can be judged.

Less than two decades earlier, Alexis de Tocqueville, who was deeply opposed to slavery and believed emancipation to be inevitable, had written: "The most dreadful of all the evils that threaten the future of the United States arises from the presence of blacks on its soil." Even in the states where slavery had been eradicated and where suffrage had been granted, he observed, countless obstacles had been placed in the way of the black man. "If he presents himself to vote, he runs a risk to his life. Oppressed, he can complain, but he finds only whites among his judges. . . .

His son is excluded from the school where the descendants of Europeans come to be instructed. In theaters he cannot buy for the price of gold the right to be placed at the side of one who was his master; in hospitals he lies apart. The black is permitted to beseech the same God as whites, but not to pray to him at the same altar. He has his own priests and churches. One does not close the doors of Heaven to him; yet inequality hardly stops at the boundary of the other world. When the Negro is no longer, his bones are cast to one side, and the difference of conditions is still found even in the equality of death." Even when abolition should come, Tocqueville predicted, Americans would "have still to destroy three prejudices much more intangible and more tenacious than it: the prejudice of the master, the prejudice of race, and finally the prejudice of the white."

The dilemma faced by advocates of emancipation was the place of free blacks in American society. The opposition to assimilation was almost universal. Blacks were already barred from entering the borders of many free states. Confronting such barriers, what "in the name of humanity," Henry Clay asked, "is to become of them—where are they to go?"

"My first impulse," Lincoln had said before, "would be to free all the slaves, and send them to Liberia,—to their own native land." Lincoln had long supported the same implausible plan endorsed by Edward Bates and Henry Clay, the notion of compensating slaveowners and returning freed slaves to their homeland. Without such a program, "colonizers" argued, Southern whites would never accept the idea of emancipation. Still, Lincoln took note of the staggering administrative and economic difficulties. More than 3 million blacks lived in the South, representing 35 percent of the entire Southern population. The overwhelming majority had no desire to go to Africa, and only a few spokesmen, not including Lincoln, advocated forced deportation. They were here to stay.

"What then?" Lincoln asked. "Free them all, and keep them among us as underlings? Is it quite certain that this betters their condition?" But once freed, could they be made "politically and socially, our equals? My own feelings will not admit of this; and if mine would, we well know that those of the great mass of white people will not. Whether this feeling accords with justice and sound judgment, is not the sole question. . . . A universal feeling, whether well or ill-founded, can not be safely disregarded."

Lincoln understood that the greatest challenge for a leader in a democratic society is to educate public opinion. "With public sentiment, nothing can fail; without it nothing can succeed," he said. "Consequently he who moulds public sentiment, goes deeper than he who enacts statutes or pronounces decisions." This statement goes to the heart of his disagreement with Douglas; when such an influential leader as Mary's "Little

Giant" insisted that blacks were not included in the Declaration, he was molding public opinion and bending history in the wrong direction. "He is blowing out the moral lights around us," Lincoln warned, borrowing a phrase from his hero Henry Clay, "eradicating the light of reason and the love of liberty in this American people."

Lincoln's goal was to rekindle those very beacons, constantly affirming the revolutionary promises made in the Declaration. When the authors of the Declaration spoke of equality, Lincoln insisted, "they did not mean to assert the obvious untruth, that all were then actually enjoying that equality. . . . They meant to set up a standard maxim for free society, which should be familiar to all, and revered by all; constantly looked to, constantly labored for, and even though never perfectly attained, constantly approximated, and thereby constantly spreading and deepening its influence, and augmenting the happiness and value of life to all people of all colors everywhere."

He hoped to "penetrate the human soul" until, as he said, "all this quibbling about this man and the other man—this race and that race and the other race being inferior" could be discarded, until all Americans could "unite as one people throughout this land," providing true meaning to the phrase "all men are created equal." His comments on race here and throughout the debates reveal a brooding quality, as if he was thinking aloud, balancing a realistic appraisal of the present with a cautious eye toward progress in the future.

History demonstrates that Lincoln and his contemporaries were not overestimating the depth of racial bigotry in America. A century would pass before legal apartheid was outlawed in the South, before separate schools were deemed unconstitutional, before blacks were finally guaranteed the right to vote. Moreover, each of these steps toward what Frederick Douglass called the "practical recognition of our Equality" met with fierce white resistance and were made possible only by the struggles of blacks themselves, forcing the issue upon largely hostile or indifferent whites.

There is no way to penetrate Lincoln's personal feelings about race. There is, however, the fact that armies of scholars, meticulously investigating every aspect of his life, have failed to find a single act of racial bigotry on his part. Even more telling is the observation of Frederick Douglass, who would become a frequent public critic of Lincoln's during his presidency, that of all the men he had met, Lincoln was "the first great man that I talked with in the United States freely, who in no single instance reminded me of the difference between himself and myself, of the difference of color." This remark takes on additional meaning when one realizes that Douglass had met dozens of celebrated abolitionists, including Wendell

Phillips, William Lloyd Garrison, and Salmon Chase. Apparently, Douglass never felt with any of them, as he did with Lincoln, an "entire freedom from popular prejudice against the colored race."

•   •   •

THE SEVENTH AND LAST debate took place at Alton, a town on the Mississippi River in southwest Illinois, before an audience Lincoln described as "having strong sympathies southward by relationship, place of birth, and so on." By the middle of the day, the "whole town" was "alive and stirring with large masses of human beings." Gustave Koerner, a leader of the German-Americans, was among the throng that came to witness the show. "More than a thousand Douglas men," Koerner wrote, "had chartered a boat to attend the Alton meeting," while Lincoln "had come quietly down from Springfield with his wife that morning, unobserved. . . . He was soon surrounded by a crowd of Republicans; but there was no parade or fuss, while Douglas, about noon, made his pompous entry, and soon afterwards the boat from St. Louis landed at the wharf, heralded by the firing of guns and the strains of martial music." When Koerner reached Lincoln's hotel, he found him seated in the lobby. No sooner had they said hello than Lincoln suggested that they go together to "see Mary." Apparently, Mary was "rather dispirited" about his chances for victory, and Lincoln hoped that Koerner would lift her mood. Koerner told Mary that he was "certain" the Republicans would carry the state in the popular vote, "and tolerably certain of our carrying the Legislature."

Although there was little new in the Alton debate, Koerner believed that Lincoln's speech included "some of the finest passages of all the speeches he ever made." The "real issue," Lincoln argued, the issue that would continue long after the "tongues of Judge Douglas and myself shall be silent," was "the eternal struggle between . . . right and wrong"; the "common right of humanity" set against "the divine right of kings. . . .

"It is the same spirit that says, 'You work and toil and earn bread, and I'll eat it.' No matter in what shape it comes, whether from the mouth of a king who seeks to bestride the people of his own nation and live by the fruit of their labor, or from one race of men as an apology for enslaving another race, it is the same tyrannical principle." With this, Lincoln took his seat, Douglas made his concluding remarks, and the great debates came to an end.

In this race, as in all others, Lincoln was his own political manager. He drew up for his supporters a detailed battle plan, examining every district in the state and listing those he regarded as lost, those "we take to ourselves," and those "to be struggled for." Between his speeches, he drafted letters of instruction to key supporters, telling Koerner, for example, "We are in great danger in Madison. It is said half the Americans are going for Douglas. . . . Nothing must be left undone. Elsewhere things look reasonably well. Please write me."

Though Eastern Republicans stayed out of the race, Chase came to Illinois to stump for the Republican ticket. He believed that Lincoln was a man who could be trusted on the antislavery issue, while at the same time he recognized that the prairie lawyer could be helpful to him in the upcoming presidential convention. More clearly than Seward or Greeley, Chase saw from the start that Douglas would never truly stand with the antislavery forces. For eight days, traveling to Chicago, Galena, Warren, Rockford, and Mendota, Chase spoke to thousands on behalf of Lincoln and the Republican ticket in Illinois—a gesture Lincoln would not forget.

It was a dreary day, November 2, 1858, when the voters of Illinois went to the polls. The names of Lincoln and Douglas did not appear on the ballots, since the state legislature would choose the next senator. That evening, Lincoln anxiously awaited the returns with his friends in the telegraph office. Once again, he would be sorely disappointed. Though the Republicans had won the popular vote, the Democrats had retained control of the state legislature, thereby ensuring Douglas's reelection. Lincoln's supporters were disconsolate and angry, blaming an unfair apportionment scheme. Koerner charged that "by the gerrymandering the State seven hundred Democratic votes were equal to one thousand Republican votes." Republicans in Illinois bewailed the lack of support from Eastern Republicans and bitterly resented a last-minute intervention by the respected Whig leader and Kentucky senator John Crittenden, who had penned a series of highly publicized letters to Illinois, urging old Whigs and American supporters to vote for Douglas to repay his Lecompton stance. "Thousands of Whigs dropped us just on the eve of the election, through the influence of Crittenden," Herndon complained.

Two days later, still feeling the sting of his defeat, Lincoln wrote Crittenden. He suppressed his justifiable resentment, exhibiting as he had with Greeley, and earlier with Trumbull and Judd, a magnanimity rare in the world of politics. "The emotions of defeat, at the close of a struggle in which I felt more than a merely selfish interest, and to which defeat the use of your name contributed largely, are fresh upon me," he told Crittenden, "but, even in this mood, I can not for a moment suspect you of anything dishonorable."

Yet this defeat left Lincoln far less disheartened than his loss four years earlier. He had won the vote of the people. The ambition he had outlined in his very first public address at the age of twenty-three—to render himself worthy of his fellow citizens' esteem—had been realized.

"I am glad I made the late race," he wrote his Springfield friend Dr. Anson Henry on November 19. "It gave me a hearing on the great and durable question of the age, which I could have had in no other way. . . . I believe I have made some marks which will tell for the cause of civil liberty long after I am gone." That cause, he vowed to Henry Ashbury, "must not be surrendered at the end of *one*, or even, one *hundred* defeats." There was no reason for despondency, he told another friend, Dr. Charles Ray, who continued to brood over Lincoln's defeat. "You will soon feel better. Another 'blow-up' is coming; and we shall have fun again."

CHAPTER 7

COUNTDOWN TO
THE NOMINATION

A s 1859 OPENED, Lincoln remained guardedly optimistic about the future, knowing he had run a solid campaign for the Senate and made a good name for himself. Well aware that he had only an outside chance at the presidential nomination in 1860, he nevertheless worked to build his reputation nationally. He was always careful to conceal his ambitions. Whenever he was asked about the upcoming election, he would speak with well-modulated enthusiasm of other candidates. Yet all his actions were consistent with a cautious and politically skillful pursuit of the nomination. Indeed, no other period in his prepresidential life better illustrates his consummate abilities as a politician.

Unlike Seward, he had no experienced political manager to guide his efforts. He would have to rely on himself, as he had from his early days on the frontier and throughout his career as shopkeeper, lawyer, and politician. A month earlier, Jesse Fell, secretary of the Illinois Republican state central committee, had expressed his "decided impression" in a letter to Lincoln that Lincoln's tremendous fight against Douglas had given him a national platform. If the details of his early life and his "efforts on the slavery question" could be "sufficiently brought before the people," he could be made "a formidable, if not a successful candidate for the presidency." Skeptical, Lincoln noted that Seward and Chase and others were "so much better known." With an equivocal modesty, he asked: "Is it not, as a matter of justice, due to such men, who have carried this movement forward to its present status, in spite of fearful opposition, personal abuse, and hard names? I really think so." As for a campaign biography, he curtly answered, "there is nothing in my early history that would interest you or anybody else."

Although refusing to confuse flattery with fact, he recognized nonetheless that Fell's argument had force. Lincoln's gradually evolving political strategy began with an awareness that while each of his three rivals had first claim on a substantial number of delegates, if he could position himself as the second choice of those who supported each of the others, he might pick up votes if one or another of the top candidates faltered.

As a dark horse, he knew it was important not to reveal his intentions too early, so as to minimize the possibility of opponents mobilizing against him. On April 16, 1859, when the Republican editor of the *Rock Island Register* proposed to call on other editors to make "a simultaneous announcement of your name for the Presidency," Lincoln replied: "I certainly am flattered, and gratified, that some partial friends think of me in that connection; but I really think it best for our cause that no concerted effort, such as you suggest, should be made." He added that he "must, in candor, say I do not think myself fit for the Presidency." By "fit," the self-confident Lincoln meant only to suggest that he did not necessarily have the credentials or experience appropriate to the office, not that he lacked the ability. It was important that any efforts on his behalf be squelched until the timing was right. And Lincoln, as would be evidenced throughout his presidency, was a master of timing.

•   •   •

WHILE LINCOLN MOVED CAREFULLY, step by step, Seward, Chase, and even Bates had grown so eager for the presidential nomination that they made a number of costly errors as they headed down the final stretch.

In the crucial months before the nomination, Seward, at Weed's rare misguided suggestion, took an extended tour of Europe. Certain that Seward had the nomination locked up so long as he refrained from the radical statements that frightened more moderate elements of the party, Weed recommended that his protégé remove himself from the increasingly contentious debate at home by traveling overseas for eight months. "All our discreet friends unite in sending me out of the country to spend the recess of Congress," Seward joked.

Fourteen-year-old Fanny Seward, at home with her mother, was desolate at the prospect of an eight-month separation from her father. In the days before his ship was set to sail from New York, she could think of nothing else, she confided in her diary, but his approaching departure. An intelligent, plain girl, Fanny had been encouraged from an early age to read broadly and to write. Beyond her daily journal, she tried her hand at poetry and plays, determined, she once vowed, never to marry, so that she could live at home and devote herself to a literary career. While extremely close to her mother, a relationship she described as " 'my affinity' with whom I *think* instead of speak," she idolized her father. The night before he left for Europe, she could barely contain her tears.

In Europe, Seward was entertained by politicians and royalty alike, who assumed that he would be the next president. He met with Queen Victoria, Lord Palmerston, William Gladstone, King Victor Emmanuel of Italy, King Leopold I of Belgium, and Pope Pius IX. Moving from one dazzling social occasion to the next, Seward was ebullient. His letters home revealed the great pleasure he took in his sojourn, which carried him to Egypt and the Holy Land. Yet in the countdown to the presidential nomination, eight months was a critical absence.

Upon his return to Washington for the new congressional session that began after the New Year in 1860, Seward took Weed's advice and prepared a major address. Designed to reassure Northern conservatives and moderate Southerners that he was a man who could be trusted to hold the Union together, the speech was to be delivered on the Senate floor on February 29, 1860. The reporter Henry Stanton later recalled that Seward showed it to him beforehand and asked him to write it up for the *New York Tribune*, with an accompanying description of the scene in the Senate chamber as he was speaking. "The description was elaborate," Stanton claimed, "the Senator himself suggesting some of the nicer touches, and every line of it was written and on its way to New York before Mr. Seward had uttered a word in the Senate Chamber." Seward was in "buoyant spirits," assuring Stanton that with this speech they would "go down to posterity together."

Frances Seward was less enthusiastic, perhaps fearing that her husband would bend too far to placate the moderates. "I wish it were over," she told her son Will on the morning of the speech. Fanny, however, seated in the gallery directly opposite her father, was thrilled to witness the great event. "The whole house of Reps were there," she gushed, "the galleries soon filled, alike with those of North and South, ladies and gentlemen, even the doorways were filled." When the three-hour speech started, Fanny recorded, "no Republican member left his seat . . . the house was very still." Everyone understood that this speech could influence the Republican nomination.

Seward took as his theme the enduring quality of the national compact. Though he maintained his principled opposition to slavery, he softened his tone, referring to the slave states as "capital States," while the free states became the "labor States." His language remained tranquil throughout, with no trace of the inflammatory phrases that had characterized his great speeches in the past. It seemed, one historian observed, that " 'the irrepressible conflict' between slavery and freedom had graciously given way to the somewhat repressible conflict of the political aspirants."

Departing from the bold assertions of his Rochester speech, Seward now claimed that "differences of opinion, even on the subject of slavery, with us are political, not social or personal differences. There is not one disunionist or disloyalist among us all. . . . We have never been more patient, and never loved the representatives of other sections more, than now. . . . The people of the North are not enemies but friends and brethren of the South, faithful and true as in the days when death has dealt his arrows promiscuously among them on the common battle-fields of freedom."

The Republican Party in the North, he pledged, did not "seek to force, or even to intrude, our system" upon the South. "You are sovereign on the subject of slavery within your own borders." The debate revolved only around the expansion of slavery in new and future states. Retreating from the larger vision of the nation's future manifest destiny in some of his earlier speeches, he promised that Republicans did not harbor any ulterior motive "to introduce negro equality" in the nation at large.

Seward's powerful conclusion—an altered form of which would appear in Lincoln's inaugural address—was an impassioned testimony to the Union. The nation could never be sundered, for its bonds were not simply "the written compact," or even the radiating network of roads, train tracks, trade routes, and telegraph lines that facilitated "commerce and social intercourse." Rather, Seward urged his audience to conceive of the strongest bonds holding the Union together as "the millions of fibers of millions of contented, happy human hearts," linked by affection and hope to their democratic government, "the first, the last, and the only such one that has ever existed, which takes equal heed always of their wants."

The speech produced deafening applause in the galleries and widespread praise in the press. Reprinted in pamphlet form, more than half a million copies were circulated throughout the country. Some, of course, considered Seward's tone too conciliatory, lacking the principle and fire of his previous addresses. That speech *"killed Seward with me forever,"* the abolitionist Cassius Clay reportedly said. Charles Sumner wrote to a friend that "as an intellectual effort," Seward's oration was "most eminent," but that there was "one passage"—perhaps the one disclaiming any intention to support black equality—which he "regretted, & [Seward's] wife agrees with me."

Nevertheless, Seward's goal had not been to rally the faithful but to disarm the opposition and placate uneasy moderates. "From the stand-point of Radical Abolitionism, it would be very easy to criticize," Frederick Douglass observed in his monthly paper, but "it is a masterly and triumphant effort. It will reassure the timid wing of his party, which has been rendered a little nervous by recent clamors against him, by its coolness of temper and conservatism of manner. . . . We think that Mr. Seward's prospects for the Chicago nomination will be essentially brightened by the wide circulation of this speech." Seward, he concluded, was "the ablest man of his party," and "as a matter of party justice," he deserved the nomination.

"I hear of ultra old Whigs in Boston who say they are ready to take up Mr. Seward upon his recent speech," a Massachusetts delegate told Weed. "All the New England delegates, save Connecticut's, will be equally satisfactory." And in Ohio, Salmon Chase admitted that there "seems to be at present a considerable set toward Seward." Seward himself believed that the speech had been a great success, the final step in his long journey to the presidency.

In the heady weeks that followed, Weed assured him that everything was in readiness for a victory at the convention. By trading legislative charters to build city railroads for campaign contributions, Weed had assembled what one observer called "oceans of money," a campaign chest worth several hundred thousand dollars.

As the convention approached, overconfidence reigned in the Seward camp and poor judgment set in. Despite Weed's generally keen political intuition, he failed to anticipate the damage Seward would suffer as a consequence of a rift with Horace Greeley. Over the years, Greeley had voiced a longing for political office, for both the monetary compensation it would provide and the prestige it promised. On several occasions, Greeley later claimed, he had made this desire clear to Seward and Weed. They never took his political aspirations seriously, believing that his strength and usefulness lay in writing, not in practical politics and public office. Greeley had written a plaintive letter to Seward in the autumn of 1854, in which he catalogued a long list of grievances and announced the dissolution of the political firm of Seward, Weed, & Greeley. He recalled the work he had done to secure Seward's first victory as governor, only to discover that jobs had been dispensed "worth $3000 to $20,000 per year to your friends and compatriots, and I returned to my garret and my crust, and my desperate battle with pecuniary obligations." With the exception of a single term in Congress, Greeley charged, Weed had never given him a chance to be nominated for any office. Despite hundreds of suggestions that he run for governor in the most recent election, Weed had refused to support the possibility, claiming that his candidacy would hurt Seward's chances for the Senate. But the most humiliating moment had come, Greeley revealed, when Weed handed the nomination for lieutenant governor that year to Henry Raymond, editor of the *New York Times*, the *Tribune's* archrival.

Seward was distressed to read Greeley's letter, which he characterized as "full of sharp, pricking thorns," but he mistakenly assumed that Greeley's pique was temporary, akin to the anger, he said, that one of his sons might display if denied the chance to go to the circus or a dancing party. After showing it to his wife, Seward cast the letter aside. Frances read it more accurately. Recognizing the "mortal offense" Greeley had taken, she saved the letter, preserving a record of the tangled web of emotions that led Greeley in 1860 to abandon one of his oldest friends in favor of Edward Bates, a man he barely knew.

Week after week, through his columns in the *Tribune*, Greeley laid the groundwork for the nomination of Bates. Seward's supporters were incensed when he subtly began to sabotage the New Yorker's campaign. Henry Raymond remarked that Greeley "insinuated, rather than openly uttered, exaggerations of local prejudice and animosity against him; hints that parties and men hostile to him and to the Republican organization must be conciliated and their support secured; and a new-born zeal for nationalizing the party by consulting the slave-holding states in regard to the nomination." The influence of the *Tribune* was substantial, and with each passing day, enthusiasm for Bates's candidacy grew.

At some point that spring, Weed had a long talk with Greeley and came away with the mistaken conviction that Greeley was "all right," that despite his editorial support for Bates, he would not play a major role at the convention. The conversation mistakenly satisfied Weed that ties of old friendship would keep Greeley from taking an active role against Seward once the convention began.

Overconfidence also played a role in Weed's failure to meet with Pennsylvania's powerful political boss, Simon Cameron, before the convention opened. In mid-March, Cameron told Seward that he wanted to see Weed in either Washington or Philadelphia "at any time" convenient to Weed. Seward relayed the message to his mentor, but Weed, certain that Cameron would deliver Pennsylvania to Seward by the second ballot, as he thought he had promised, never managed to make the trip.

Weed's faith in Cameron was due partly to Seward's report of a special visit he had made to Cameron's estate, Lochiel, near Harrisburg, Pennsylvania. Shortly before leaving for Europe the previous spring, Seward had spent a day with Cameron and had returned certain that Cameron was pledged to his candidacy. "He took me to his home, told me all was right," Seward told Weed. "He was for me, and Pa. would be. It might want to cast a first ballot for him or might not. . . . He brought the whole legislature of both parties to see me—feasted them gloriously and they were in the main so free, so generous as to embarrass me." Reports of this lavish reception persuaded reporters and politicians alike that a deal had been brokered.

In the months that followed, even as gossip spread that Cameron did not have control of his entire delegation, Weed continued to believe that the Pennsylvania boss, so like himself in many ways, would do whatever was necessary to fulfill his pledge and deliver his state. After all, to Cameron was attributed the oft-quoted definition: "an honest politician is one who, when he is bought, stays bought."

Cameron had been quicker than Weed to exploit the lucrative potential of politics. Through contracts with canal companies, railroads, and banks, he amassed "so much money," he later boasted, that he might have become "the richest man in Pennsylvania" had he not pursued elective office. Unlike Weed, who remained behind the scenes, Cameron secured for himself two terms in the U.S. Senate; in 1844 and again in 1855. He began his political life as a Democrat but became frustrated by Democratic positions on slavery and, more important, on the tariff, which was his "legislative child." In 1855, he was instrumental in establishing Pennsylvania's Republican Party, initially called the People's Party.

At the People's Party state convention in February 1860, Cameron received the expected favorite-son nod for the presidency, but Andrew Curtin, a magnetic young politician who was challenging Cameron for control in the state, was nominated for governor. Though Cameron received a majority vote at the convention, a substantial number of district delegates remained to be chosen, eventually producing a split between the rival forces of Cameron and Curtin. Curtin was uncommitted to any candidate when the Republican Convention opened, yet it was known that he questioned Seward's electability. Seward's name on the ticket might hamstring his own election, for the anti-Catholic Know Nothings, who still exerted considerable power in Pennsylvania, had never forgiven Seward for his liberalism toward immigrants and his controversial support for parochial education. Boss Cameron might have been able to resolve these obstacles with Boss Weed in private conversation before the convention. Since that meeting never took place, Weed was left to navigate the countervailing forces of the Pennsylvania state delegation without Cameron's guidance.

• • •

SEWARD'S LEISURELY SOJOURN abroad afforded Chase the opportunity to actively secure pledges and workers for his nomination. Never the most astute of politicians, Chase made curiously little use of the precious months of 1859 to better his chances. Sure of the power and depth of his support, he once again, as in 1856, assumed he would somehow gain the nomination without much personal intervention. News to the contrary Chase dismissed out of hand, even when the intelligence came from his close friend Gamaliel Bailey.

Bailey and Chase had become acquainted in Cincinnati when Bailey was editing *The Philanthropist*. Later on, when Bailey became publisher of *The National Era* and moved his family to Washington, they warmly welcomed the lonely Chase into their home. When the Senate was in session, Chase lived for months at a time at their house, forming friendships with Bailey's wife, Margaret, and the entire Bailey clan. On Saturday evenings, the Baileys' home became "a salon in European tradition," replete with dinner and the word games at which Chase excelled.

Throughout their long friendship, Bailey had always been frank with Chase, castigating him in 1856 for his temporizing attitude toward the "detestable" Know Nothings. Nonetheless, Bailey remained loyal and supportive of his old friend, assuring him on numerous occasions that he would rather see him "in the presidential chair than any other man." Yet, as Bailey assessed the temper of the country in early 1859, conversing with many people, "observing the signs of the times and the phases of public opinion," he concluded in a long, candid letter to Chase that he thought it best to support Seward in 1860. The time for Chase would come again four years later.

"He and you are the two most prominent representative men of the party," Bailey wrote on January 16, 1859, "but he is older than you." His friends believe it is *"now or never"* with him, "to postpone him now is to postpone him forever . . . you are in the prime of life and have the promise of continuing so—you have not attained your full stature or *status—he has*—every year adds to your strength, and in 1864, you will be stronger than in 1860. . . . To be urgent now against the settled feeling of Seward's numerous friends, would provoke unpleasant and damaging discords, and tend hereafter to weaken your position." Bailey suspected that Chase might disagree with his recommendation, but "I know you will not question my integrity or my friendship."

"I do not doubt your friendship," Chase testily replied, "but I do think that if our situations were reversed I should take a different method of showing mine for you. . . . The suggestion 'now or never' [with regard to Seward] is babyish . . . how ridiculous . . . but to sum up all in brief . . . let me say it cannot change my position. I have no right to do so. . . . A very large body of the people—embracing not a few who would hardly vote for any man other than myself as a Republican nominee—seem to desire that I shall be a candidate in 1860. No effort of mine, and as far as I know none of my immediate personal friends has produced this feeling. It seems to be of spontaneous growth."

Bailey responded that he presumed Chase's characterization of the "now or never" position of Seward's supporters as "babyish" was "a slip of your pen. . . . It may be erroneous, groundless, but . . . it is entitled to consideration. It has reference not only to age, & health, but other matters. . . . Governor Seward will be fifty-nine in May, 1860. . . . Should another be nominated, and elected, the chances would be in favor of a renomination— which would postpone the Governor eight years—until he should be sixty- seven, in the shadow of seventy. . . . You are still growing [Chase had just turned fifty-one]—you are still increasing in reputation—four years hence . . . your chances of nomination & election to the Presidency would be greater than they are now." Bailey assured Chase that he would never work against him. "All I desired was to apprise you, as a friend."

Deluded by flattery, Chase preferred the unrealistic projections of New York's Hiram Barney, who thought his strength in New York State was growing so rapidly that it was possible he might receive New York's vote on the first ballot. So heroic was his self-conception, Chase believed that doubtful supporters would flock to his side once they understood the central role he had played as the guardian of the antislavery tradition and father of the Republican Party.

Failing once again to appoint a campaign manager, Chase had no one to bargain and maneuver for him, no one to promise government posts in return for votes. He rejected an appeal from a New Hampshire supporter who proposed to build a state organization. He never capitalized on the initial support of powerful Chicago *Press and Tribune* editor Joseph Medill. He turned down an invitation to speak at Cooper Union in a lecture series organized by his supporters as a forum for candidates other than Seward. Refusing even to consider that his own state might deny him a united vote on the first ballot, he failed to confirm that every delegate appointed to the convention was pledged to vote for him. Indeed, his sole contribution to his own campaign was a series of letters to various supporters and journalists around the country, reminding them that he was the best man for the job.

Frustrated supporters tried to shake him into more concerted action. "I now begin to fear that Seward will get a majority of the delegates from Maryland," Chase's loyal backer James Ashley warned. "He and his friends *work—work*. They not only work—but *he works.*" The willful Chase was blind to troubling signs, convinced that if the delegates voted their conscience, he would ultimately prevail.

"I shall have nobody to push or act for me at Chicago," Chase boasted to Benjamin Eggleston, a delegate from Cincinnati, "except the Ohio delegation who will, I doubt not, faithfully represent the Republicans of the State." While a large majority of the Ohio state delegation indeed supported Chase, Senator Ben Wade had his own devoted followers. "The Ohio delegation does not seem to be anywhere as yet," delegate Erastus Hopkins warned. Heedless, Chase remained positive that the entire Ohio delegation would come around, given everything he had done and sacrificed for his state. To support any other candidate would put one "in a position no man of honor or sensibility would care to occupy."

A month before the convention, Kate convinced her father that a journey to Washington would shore up his support among various congressmen and senators. Lodging at the Willard Hotel, they made the rounds of receptions and dinners. Seward was very kind to them, Chase admitted to his friend James Briggs. The genial New Yorker hosted a dinner party in their honor at which "all sides were pretty fairly represented" and "there was a good deal of joking." The next evening, former Ohio congressman John Gurley organized a party to honor both Chase and Ohio's new governor, William Dennison. Seward was invited to join the Ohio gathering, which included former Whig leader Tom Corwin and Senator Ben Wade.

Writing home after the dinner, Seward joshingly noted that he "found much comfort" in the discovery that Ohio was home to at least three candidates for the presidency, "all eminent and excellent men, but each preferring anybody out of Ohio, to his two rivals within." While Seward immediately intuited signals that Ben Wade, in particular, coveted the nomination, Chase remained oblivious, refusing to believe that Ohio would not back its most deserving son. On the Chases' last evening in Washington, the Blairs threw them a lavish party at their country estate in Silver Spring.

As usual, Kate left a deep impression on everyone. Seward afterward told Frances that she was quite "a young lady, pleasant and well-cultivated." Chase wrote Nettie how pleased he was that many showed "attention to Katie," and many were "kind to me." He returned home convinced that his trip had accomplished a great deal. "Everybody seems to like me and to feel a very gratifying degree of confidence in me," he reported to a Cincinnati friend. Confusing hospitality with hard allegiance, he told one of his supporters that "a great change seemed to come over men's minds while I was in Washington."

• • •

THE BEGINNING of the pre-presidential year found the backers of Edward Bates more active in the pursuit of his nomination than the candidate himself. While Bates would gradually warm to the idea, he found himself, as always, conflicted about plunging into politics. Without the encouragement of the powerful Blairs, it is unlikely that he would have put his name forward. Once he agreed to stand, he was confronted with a political dilemma. His strength lay among old Whigs and nativists concentrated in the border states, and conservatives in the North and Northwest. To have a genuine chance for the nomination, he would have to prove himself acceptable to moderate Republicans as well.

Had he used the months prior to the nomination to travel to the very different states of Illinois, Indiana, Massachusetts, Connecticut, or Maryland, he might have acquainted himself with the wide range of views that comprised the new party. But he never left his home state, preferring to rely on intelligence received from colleagues and supporters who came to visit him. Not only did he keep to Missouri, he rarely left his beloved home, noting in his diary when he was forced to stay overnight in St. Louis that it was "the first that I have slept in town for about two years." Four decades of marriage had not diminished his bond with Julia.

Secluding himself at home, Bates never developed a clear understanding of the varied constituencies that had to be aligned, a deficit that resulted in a number of missteps. While his distance from the fierce arguments of the fifties was considered beneficial to his candidacy, his long absence from politics made him less familiar with the savage polarization created by the slavery issue. In late February 1859, he answered the request of the Whig Committee of New York for his "views and opinions on the politics of the country." The New York Whigs had passed a resolution calling for an end to agitation of "the Negro question" so that the country might focus on "topics of general importance," such as economic development and internal improvements, that would unite rather than fracture the nation. In his letter, which was published nationwide, Bates declared that he had always considered "the Negro question" to be "a pestilent question, the agitation of which has never done good to any party, section or class, and never can do good, unless it be accounted good to stir up the angry passions of men, and exasperate the unreasoning jealousy of sections." He believed that those who continued to press the issue, "after the sorrowful experience of the last few years," must be motivated by "personal ambition or sectional prejudice."

Lauded by Whigs and nativists, the letter provoked widespread criticism in Republican circles. Schuyler Colfax, who backed Bates for president, warned him that his comments "denouncing the agitation of the negro question" sounded like "a denunciation of the Rep[ublica]n party, and would turn many against [him]." Bates disagreed. "If my letter had been universally acceptable to the Republicans, that fact alone might have destroyed my prospects in two frontier slave states, Md. and Mo., and so I would have no streng[t]h at all but the Republican party," where Seward and Chase, he knew, were far better positioned. Maryland congressman Henry Winter Davis, the leading member of the American Party in the House, confirmed Bates's views, advising him that he was poised to secure majority approval and should not attempt to further define his views— "write no more public letters—let well enough alone."

As the new year opened, Bates believed his chances were growing "brighter every day." Supporters in the key battleground states of Indiana and Pennsylvania assured him that large percentages of the delegates appointed to the Chicago convention were "made up of 'Bates men.'" A visitor from Illinois told him that much "good feeling" existed in the southern part of the state, "but first (on a point of State pride,) they must support Lincoln." This was the first time in his daily entries that Bates so much as mentioned Lincoln's name as a presidential aspirant. In Illinois, Lincoln was keenly aware of Bates, answering an inquiring letter about how Illinois regarded the various candidates by saying that Bates "would be the best man for the South of our State, and the worst for the North of it," while Seward was "the very best candidate we could have for the North of Illinois, and the very *worst* for the South of it." With amusing self-serving logic, Lincoln suggested that neither Bates nor Seward could command a majority vote in Illinois.

On the last day of February 1860, the very day of Seward's conciliatory speech in the Senate, a great Opposition Convention comprised of Whigs and Americans met in Jefferson City, Missouri, and "enthusiastically" endorsed Bates for president. Two weeks later, Bates received a second endorsement from the Republican state convention in St. Louis. The Missouri Republicans, however, were in a carping mood, particularly the German-American contingent, which threatened to block the endorsement, still troubled by Bates's open support for the nativist party in 1856. To satisfy both the more ardent Republicans and the German-American community, Frank Blair suggested that Bates agree to outline his positions in answer to a questionnaire drawn up by the German-American press.

The questionnaire posed a difficult problem for Bates. He had to assuage the doubts of Republicans who felt, like editor Joseph Medill of Chicago, that it was better to be "beaten with a representative man" who placed himself squarely on the Republican platform than to "triumph with a 'Union-saver' " and "sink into the quicksands." However, if he moved too far to the left to satisfy the passionate Republicans, he would risk his natural base among the old Whigs and Americans. Though once noted for his deft touch in harmonizing opposing forces, Bates plunged into his answers without calculating the consequences.

Asked to render his opinions on the extension of slavery into the territories, he announced that Congress had the power to decide the issue, a position that directly contradicted the *Dred Scott* decision. He felt, moreover, that "the spirit and the policy of the Government ought to be against its extension." He advocated equal constitutional rights for all citizens, native-born or naturalized, claiming to endorse "no distinctions among Americans citizens," and adding that the "Government is bound to protect all the citizens in the enjoyment of all their rights every where." Beyond this, he favored colonizing former slaves in Africa and Central America, a Homestead Act, a Pacific Railroad, and the admission of Kansas as a free state.

His statement met with approval in traditional Republican enclaves in the Northeast and Northwest, but in the border states, where his advantage was supposed to reside, it proved disastrous. The *Lexington [Missouri] Express* wrote that the published letter came "as a clap of thunder from a clear sky," placing Bates so blatantly in the Black Republican camp that he should no longer expect support from the more conservative border states. By subscribing to every article of the Republican creed, the *Louisville Journal* complained, Bates became "just as good or bad a Republican as Seward, Chase or Lincoln is. . . . He has by a single blow severed every tie of confidence or sympathy which connected him with the Southern Conservatives." Only four years earlier, the *Memphis Bulletin* observed, Bates had denounced Black Republicans as "agitators," labeling them "dangerous enemies to the peace of our Union." Now he had become one of them. Bates himself recognized the backlash his letter had created, lamenting "the simultaneous abandonment of me by a good many papers" in the border states.

The attempt to pacify the anxious German-Americans had diminished his hold on what should have been his natural base, without bringing a commensurate number of Republicans to his side. Though the Bates camp maintained faith that their man was bound to win the nomination, Bates confided in his diary that "knowing the fickleness of popular favor, and on what small things great events depend, I shall take care not so to set my heart upon the glittering bauble, as to be mortified or made at all unhappy by a failure."

•   •   •

NOT HINDERED by the hubris, delusions, and inconsistencies that plagued his three chief rivals, Abraham Lincoln gained steady ground through a combination of hard work, skill, and luck. While Seward and Bates felt compelled in the final months to reposition themselves toward the center of the party, Lincoln never changed his basic stance. He could remain where he had always been, "neither on the left wing nor the right, but very close to dead center," as Don Fehrenbacher writes. From the time he had first spoken out against the extension of slavery into the territories in the wake of the Kansas-Nebraska Act, Lincoln had insisted that while the spread of slavery must be "fairly headed off," he had no wish "to interfere with slavery" where it already existed. So long as the institution was contained, which Lincoln considered a sacred pledge, it was "in course of ultimate extinction." This position represented perfectly the views of the moderate majority in the Republican Party.

Though a successful bid for the nomination remained unlikely, a viable candidacy was no longer an impossible dream. Slowly and methodically, Lincoln set out to improve his long odds. He arranged to publish his debates with Douglas in a book that was read widely by Republicans. As more and more people became familiar with him through the newspaper stories of the debates, invitations to speak at Republican gatherings began to pour in. Not yet an avowed candidate, Lincoln delivered nearly two dozen speeches in Iowa, Ohio, Wisconsin, Indiana, and Kansas in the four months between August and December 1859.

While Seward was still touring Europe and the Middle East, Lincoln was introducing himself to tens of thousands of Westerners. "I think it is a mistake," a leading New Yorker wrote Lincoln, "that Senator Seward is not on his own battlefield, instead of being in Egypt surveying the route of an old Underground Rail Road, over which Moses took, one day, a whole nation, from bondage into Liberty." Lincoln capitalized on Seward's absence. The crowds that greeted him grew with every stop along the way. Most of his audiences had never laid eyes on him, and he invariably forged an indelible impression. Once he began speaking, the *Janesville Gazette* reported, "the high order of [his] intellect" left a permanent impact upon his listeners, who would remember his "tall, gaunt form" and "his points and his hits" for "many a day."

Speaking not as a candidate but as an advocate for the Republican cause, Lincoln sharpened his attacks on the Democrats and, in particular, on the party's front-runner, Stephen Douglas, who preceded him at many of the same locations. "Douglasism," he wrote Chase, "is all which now stands in the way of an early and complete success of Republicanism." In this way, ironically, Douglas's national reputation continually increased the attention paid to Lincoln.

Perhaps Lincoln's most rewarding stop was Cincinnati, which he had vowed never again to visit after the humiliating Reaper trial. This time, he was "greeted with the thunder of cannon, the strains of martial music, and the joyous plaudits of thousands of citizens thronging the streets." He arrived at the Burnet House and was put up "in princely style," delighted to find that the most prominent of Cincinnati's residents were vying to meet the "rising star."

Lincoln addressed the Southern threats that the election of a Republican president would divide the Union, directing his remarks particularly to the many Kentuckians who had crossed the Ohio River to listen to him. "Will you make war upon us and kill us all? Why, gentlemen, I think you are as gallant and as brave men as live; that you can fight as bravely in a good cause, man for man, as any other people living . . . but, man for man, you are not better than we are, and there are not so many of you as there are of us. You will never make much of a hand at whipping us. If we were fewer in numbers than you, I think that you could whip us; if we were equal it would likely be a drawn battle; but being inferior in numbers, you will make nothing by attempting to master us." The next day, his speech was described in the *Cincinnati Gazette* "as an effort remarkable for its clear statement, powerful argument and massive common sense," and possessed of "such dignity and power as to have impressed some of our ablest lawyers with the conclusion that it was superior to any political effort they had ever heard."

Lincoln's crowded schedule allowed him no time to accept Joshua Speed's invitation to visit him in Kentucky for the opening of the national racecourse, "when," his old friend promised, "we expect to have some of the best horses in America to compete for the purses. In addition we think we can show the prettiest women," adding, "if you are not too old to enjoy either the speed of the horses or the beauty of the women come." If his speaking tour caused Lincoln to forgo speedy horses and beautiful women, it greatly increased his stature among western Republicans. "Your visit to Ohio has excited an extensive interest in your favor," former congressman Samuel Galloway told him. "We must take some man not hitherto corrupted with the discussion upon Candidates. Your name has been again and again mentioned. . . . I am candid to say you are my choice."

Rapidly becoming a national spokesman for the fledgling Republican Party, Lincoln sought to preserve the unity of the still-fragile coalition. He wished, he wrote Schuyler Colfax, "to hedge against divisions in the Republican ranks." An anti-immigrant movement in Massachusetts "failed to see that tilting against foreigners would ruin us in the whole North-West," while attempts in both Ohio and New Hampshire to thwart enforcement of the Fugitive Slave Law might "utterly overwhelm us in Illinois with the charge of enmity to the constitution itself. . . . In a word, in every locality we should look beyond our noses; and at least say *nothing* on points where it is probable we shall disagree."

Colfax appreciated Lincoln's "kind & timely note," which underscored the need to enlist in the Republican cause "men of all shades & gradations of opinion from the Conservative . . . to the bold radical." To be victorious in 1860, he wrote, "we must either win this Conservative sentiment, with its kindred sympathizers, represented under the title of North Americans, Old Line Whigs &c, to our banners" without alienating the radicals, "or by repelling them must go into the contest looking for defeat." In this cause of unity, Colfax assured Lincoln, "your counsel carries great weight . . . there is no political letter that falls from your pen, which is not copied throughout the Union." Lincoln's ability to bridge these divisions would prove of vital importance to his campaign.

On October 16, 1859, as Lincoln prepared for a trip to Kansas, the remaining bonds of union were strained almost to the point of rupture when the white abolitionist John Brown came to Virginia, in the words of Stephen Vincent Benét, "with foolish pikes/And a pack of desperate boys to shadow the sun." Brown and his band of thirteen white men and five blacks seized the federal arsenal at Harpers Ferry with a bold but ill-conceived plan of provoking a slave insurrection. The arsenal was swiftly recaptured and Brown taken prisoner by a federal force under the command of Colonel Robert E. Lee, accompanied by Lieutenant J. E. B. Stuart.

Brown was tried and sentenced to death. "I am waiting the hour of my public *murder* with great composure of mind, & cheerfulness," Brown wrote his family, "feeling the strongest assurance that in no other possible way could I be used to so much advance the cause of God; & of humanity." In the month between the sentence and his hanging, the dignity and courage of his conduct and the eloquence of his statements and letters made John Brown a martyr/hero to many in the antislavery North. His death, when it came, was mourned by public assemblies throughout the Northern states. "Church bells tolled," the historian David Potter writes, "black bunting was hung out, minute guns were fired, prayer meetings assembled, and memorial resolutions were adopted."

Brown's motivations, psychological profile, and strategy would be probed by historians, poets, and novelists for generations. The immediate impact of the intrepid raid, which "sent a shiver of fear to the inmost fiber of every white man, woman, and child" in the South, was unmistakable.

While antislavery fervor in the North was intensified, Southern solid
and rhetoric reached a new level of zealotry. "Harper's Ferry," wrote ...c
Richmond Enquirer, "coupled with the expression of Northern sentiment in
support . . . have shaken and disrupted all regard for the Union; and there
are but few men who do not look to a certain and not distant day when dissolution must ensue." The raid at Harpers Ferry, one historian notes, was
"like a great meteor disclosing in its lurid flash the width and depth of that
abyss," which cut the nation in two. Herman Melville, in his poem "The
Portent," would use the same metaphor, calling "Weird John Brown/ The
meteor of the war"—the tail of his long beard trailing out from under the
executioner's cap.

Throughout the South, heightened fear of slave insurrection led to severe restrictions on the expression of antislavery sentiments. "I do not exaggerate in designating the present state of affairs in the Southern country
as a reign of terror," the British consul in Charleston wrote. "Persons are
torn away from their residences and pursuits . . . letters are opened at the
Post Offices; discussion upon slavery is entirely prohibited under penalty
of expulsion. . . . The Northern merchants and Travellers are leaving in
great numbers." In Norfolk, Virginia, the *St. Louis News* reported, a grand
jury indicted a merchant "for seditious language, because he declared that
John Brown was a good man, fighting in a good cause."

Leading Southern politicians were quick to indict the Republican Party
and, by extension, the entire North. The Tennessee legislature resolved
that the raiders at Harpers Ferry were "the natural fruits of this treasonable 'irrepressible conflict' doctrine, put forth by the great head of the
Black Republican party, and echoed by his subordinates." A man representing "one hundred gentlemen" published a circular that offered a
$50,000 reward *"for the head of William H. Seward,"* along with the consid-
erably smaller sum of $25 for the heads of a long list of "traitors," includ-
ing Sumner, Greeley, Giddings, and Colfax. Lincoln was not included in
the list of enemies.

Democratic papers in the North joined in, targeting Seward for special
condemnation. "The first overt act in the great drama of national disruption which has been plotted by that demagogue, Wm. H. Seward, has just
closed at Harper's Ferry," the *New York Herald* charged. "No reasoning
mind can fail to trace cause and effect between the bloody and brutal manifesto of William H. Seward [the "irrepressible conflict" speech a year ear-
lier] . . . and the terrible scenes of violence, rapine and death, that have
been enacted at the confluence of the Potomac and the Shenandoah."

Republicans, naturally, countered Democratic attempts to implicate
their party. Seward himself stated that although Brown was a sympathetic

figure, his execution was "necessary and just." Weed's *Albany Evening Journal* also took a decided stance against the futile raid, deeming Brown's men guilty of treason for "seeking to plunge a peaceful community into the horrors of a servile insurrection." They "justly deserve, universal condemnation."

In Missouri, Bates concluded that "the wild extravagance and utter futility of his plan" proved that Brown was "a madman." He discussed the incident at length with his young friend Lieutenant J. E. B. Stuart, who had come to stay at Grape Hill for several days with his wife, Flora, his child, and two free black servants. "He tells me a good deal about 'Old Brown,' " Bates wrote in his diary. "He was at his capture—and has his [dagger]."

For Chase, the situation presented particular problems. Though he publicly denounced Brown's violation of law and order, his younger daughter, Nettie, later conceded that "for a household accustomed to revere as friends of the family such men as Sumner, Garrison, Wendell Phillips, Whittier, and Longfellow," it was impossible not to sympathize with "the truly good old man who was about to die for others." She and her friends built a small fort in the conservatory and "raised a flag on which was painted . . . defiantly 'Freedom forever; slavery never.' " When friends warned Chase that such open support of Brown could not be countenanced, he had to explain to his daughter that "a great wrong" could not be righted "in the way poor old John Brown had attempted to do." The little fort was dismantled.

At the time of Brown's execution on December 2, 1859, Lincoln was back on the campaign trail, telling an audience in Leavenworth, Kansas, that "the attempt to identify the Republican party with the John Brown business was an electioneering dodge." He wisely sought the middle ground between the statements of radical Republicans, like Emerson, who believed that Brown's execution would "make the gallows as glorious as the cross," and conservative Republicans, who denounced Brown for his demented, traitorous scheme. He acknowledged that Brown had displayed "great courage" and "rare unselfishness." Nonetheless, he concluded, "that cannot excuse violence, bloodshed, and treason. It could avail him nothing that he might think himself right."

•   •   •

WHEN HE RETURNED from his canvassing, Lincoln focused on the approaching meeting of the Republican National Committee, to be held on December 21, 1859, at the Astor House in New York. Committee members from nearly all the free states were gathered to decide where the Republican Convention would be held. Supporters of Seward, Chase, and

Bates argued in turn that the convention should be placed in New York, Ohio, or Missouri. Though Lincoln had not yet committed himself publicly to run for the nomination, he wrote to Norman Judd, a member of the selection committee, to press the claims of Illinois, to satisfy friends who "attach more consequence" to the location than either he or Judd had originally done.

Judd waited patiently as the claims of Buffalo, Cleveland, Cincinnati, St. Louis, Indianapolis, and Harrisburg were put forth. When no agreement could be reached, he shrewdly suggested Chicago as "good neutral ground where everyone would have an even chance." Although Lincoln was known to most of the committee members at this point, none considered him a serious candidate for the presidency. Judd "carefully kept 'Old Abe' out of sight," observed Henry Whitney, "and the delegates failed to see any personal bearing the place of meeting was to have on the nomination." The choice finally narrowed down to St. Louis and Chicago. Judd "promised that the members of the Convention and all outsiders of the Republican faith should have a hospitable reception," that sufficient accommodations would be provided "for feeding and lodging the large crowd," and that "a hall for deliberation should be furnished free." Ultimately, Chicago beat St. Louis by a single vote.

Once Chicago was selected, Judd, a railway lawyer, persuaded the railroad companies to provide "a cheap excursion rate from all parts of the State," so that lack of funds would not keep Lincoln supporters from attending the convention. Concealed from his rivals, Lincoln had taken an important step toward the nomination.

So confident were Seward's friends about his chances that they had no problem with the Chicago selection. "I like the place & the tenor of the call," New York editor John Bigelow wrote Seward at the time. "I do not see how either could be bettered, nor how it is possible to take exception to it." But Charles Gibson, Bates's friend and supporter, was not so sanguine; he recognized that it was a blow to the Bates candidacy. "Had the convention been held in St. Louis," Gibson later wrote, "Lincoln would not have been the nominee."

As Lincoln's candidacy became a real prospect, he attended to the request made by Jesse Fell a year earlier for a short history of his life to be published and distributed. After warning Fell that "there is not much of it, for the reason, I suppose, that there is not much of me," Lincoln detailed, without a hint of self-pity, the facts of his early life, growing up in "a wild region, with many bears and other wild animals still in the woods."

"If any thing be made out of it, I wish it to be modest," Lincoln told Fell. "Of course it must not appear to have been written by myself." This simple sketch written in his own hand would be used later in Republican efforts to romanticize Lincoln's humble beginnings.

• • •

LINCOLN'S HOPES for making himself better known outside the West received an immense boost when he received the invitation from Chase supporter James Briggs to speak as part of a lecture series in Brooklyn. The lecture was eventually scheduled for February 27, 1860. Chase, as we saw, had declined the opportunity to speak in the same series, despite word that its organizers were men seeking an alternative to Seward. Upon his arrival in New York, Lincoln sought out Henry Bowen, editor of the antislavery *New York Independent*, who had helped arrange the event. "His clothes were travel-stained and he looked tired and woe-begone," Bowen recalled. "In this first view of him, there came to me the disheartening and appalling thought of the great throng which I had been so instrumental in inducing to come." But Bowen's initial impression of Lincoln softened after Lincoln admitted that the long journey had worn him out, and said, "if you have no objection I will lie down on your lounge here and you can tell me about the arrangements for Monday night."

At the Astor House, Lincoln met Mayson Brayman, a fellow lawyer who had lived in Springfield for some years before returning to his native New York. "Well, B. how have you fared since you left Illinois?" Lincoln asked. "I have made one hundred thousand dollars and lost all," Brayman ruefully replied; "how is it with you, Mr. Lincoln?"

"Oh, very well," Lincoln said. "I have the cottage at Springfield and about $8,000 in money. If they make me Vice-President with Seward, as some say they will, I hope I shall be able to increase it to $20,000, and that is as much as a man ought to want." Lincoln's sights, however, were not trained on the vice presidency, and politics, not riches, were his object.

That February afternoon, Lincoln paid a visit to the studio of the photographer Mathew Brady on Broadway. When Brady was posing him, he urged Lincoln to hike up his shirt collar. Lincoln quipped that Brady wanted "to shorten [his] neck." The resulting three-quarter-length portrait shows the fifty-one-year-old Lincoln standing before a pillar, the fingers of his left hand spread over a book. Prominent cheekbones cast marked shadows across his clean-shaven face. The delicate long bow of his upper lip contrasts with the full lower lip, and the deep-set gaze is steady and melancholy. This photograph, circulated widely in engravings and lithographs in the Northeast, was the first arresting image many would see of Abraham Lincoln.

Nearly fifteen hundred people came to hear "this western man" speak in the great hall at Cooper Union. He had bought a new black suit for the occasion, but it was badly wrinkled from the trip. An observer noticed that "one of the legs of his trousers was up about two inches above his shoe; his hair was disheveled and stuck out like rooster's feathers; his coat was altogether too large for him in the back, his arms much longer than his sleeves." Yet once he began to speak, people were captivated by his earnest and powerful delivery.

Lincoln had labored to craft his address for many weeks, extensively researching the attitudes of the founding fathers toward slavery. He took as the text for his discourse a speech in which Senator Douglas had said of slavery: *"Our fathers, when they framed the Government under which we live, understood this question just as well, and even better, than we do now."* Fully endorsing this statement, Lincoln examined the beliefs and actions of the founders, concluding that they had marked slavery *"as an evil not to be extended, but to be tolerated and protected only because of and so far as its actual presence among us makes that toleration and protection a necessity."*

In the preceding months, tensions between North and South had continued to escalate, with each section joining in a "hue and cry" against the other. The troubling scenario that Lincoln had observed nearly two decades earlier, during the battle over temperance, had come to pass. Denunciation was being met by denunciation, "crimination with crimination, and anathema with anathema." To have expected either side to respond differently once the rhetoric had heated up, Lincoln warned during that earlier battle, "was to expect a reversal of human nature, which is God's decree, and never can be reversed."

At Cooper Union, as he had done in his celebrated Peoria speech six years earlier, Lincoln attempted to cut through the rancor of the embattled factions by speaking directly to the Southern people. While his faith in Southern responsiveness had seriously dimmed by this time, he hoped the fear and animosity of slaveholders might be assuaged if they understood that the Republicans desired only a return to the "old policy of the fathers," so "the peace of the old times" could once more be established. Denying charges of sectionalism, he said Republicans were the true conservatives, adhering "to the old and tried, against the new and untried."

Turning to his fellow Republicans, he entreated, *"let us do nothing through passion and ill temper. Even though the southern people will not so much as listen to us, let us calmly consider their demands, and yield to them if, in our deliberate view of our duty, we possibly can."* Though the approach was moderate, Lincoln spoke with such passion and certainty about the unifying principle of the Republican Party—never to allow slavery "to spread into the National Territories, and to overrun us here in these Free States"—

that even the most radical Republicans in the audience were captivated. When he came to the dramatic ending pledge—"LET US HAVE FAITH THAT RIGHT MAKES MIGHT, AND IN THAT FAITH, LET US, TO THE END, DARE TO DO OUR DUTY AS WE UNDERSTAND IT"—the audience erupted in thunderous applause.

After Lincoln spoke, several of the event organizers took the platform. Chase supporter James Briggs predicted that "one of three gentlemen will be our standard bearer"—William Henry Seward, Salmon Chase, or "the gallant son of Kentucky, who was reared in Illinois, and whom you have heard tonight." Lincoln's still-unannounced candidacy had taken an enormous step forward.

"When I came out of the hall," one member of the audience said, "my face glowing with an excitement and my frame all aquiver, a friend, with his eyes aglow, asked me what I thought of Abe Lincoln, the rail-splitter. I said, 'He's the greatest man since St. Paul.' "

Once the speech was reported in the papers, Lincoln was in demand across New England. He answered as many requests as possible, undertaking an exhausting tour of New Hampshire, Rhode Island, and Connecticut, repeating and modifying the arguments of his Cooper Union address. He was forced to decline invitations from outside New England but hoped "to visit New-Jersey & Pa. before the fall elections."

Writing to Mary from Exeter Academy in New Hampshire, where their son Robert was completing a preparatory year before entering Harvard College, Lincoln admitted that the Cooper Union speech, "being within my calculation before I started, went off passably well and gave me no trouble whatever. The difficulty was to make nine others, before reading audiences who had already seen all my ideas in print."

In Hartford, Connecticut, on March 5, Lincoln first met Gideon Welles, an editorial writer for the *Hartford Evening Press* who would become his secretary of the navy. Arriving by train in the afternoon, Lincoln had several hours to spare before his speech that evening. He walked up Asylum Street to the bookstore of Brown & Gross, where he encountered the fifty-eight-year-old Welles, a peculiar-looking man with a curly wig perched on his outsize head, and a flowing white beard. Welles had attended Norwich University and studied the law but then devoted himself to writing, leaving the legal profession at twenty-four to take charge of the Democratic *Hartford Times*. A strong supporter of Andrew Jackson, Welles had represented his town of Glastonbury in the state legislature for eight years. He remained a loyal Democrat until the mid-fifties, when he became troubled by his affiliation to "the party of the Southern slaveocracy."

Like many antislavery Democrats, he joined the Republican Party, though he still held fast to the frugal fiscal policies of the Democrats.

With the convention only two months away, Welles had settled on Chase, whom he had met four years earlier while visiting Cincinnati. While Welles held less radical views on slavery, he was comforted by Chase's similar sentiments regarding government spending and states' rights. Seward, by contrast, frightened Welles. For years, the former Whig and the former Democrat had been at loggerheads over government spending; Welles was convinced that Seward belonged "to the New York school of very expensive rulers." Moreover, Welles was appalled by Seward's talk of a "higher law" than the Constitution and his predictions of an "irrepressible conflict." He was ready to support any candidate but Seward, despite the fact that Seward was the most popular among the Republicans.

That afternoon, Lincoln and Welles spent several hours conversing on a bench in the front of the store. Welles had read accounts of Lincoln's debates with Douglas and had noted the extravagant reviews of his Cooper Union speech. There is no record of their conversation that day, but the prairie lawyer left a strong imprint on Welles, who watched that evening as he delivered a two-hour speech before an overflowing crowd at City Hall.

Though he retained much of his Cooper Union speech, Lincoln developed a new metaphor in Hartford to perfectly illustrate his distinction between accepting slavery where it already existed while doing everything possible to curtail its spread. Testing his image in Hartford, he would refine it further in subsequent speeches. "If I saw a venomous snake crawling in the road," Lincoln began, "any man would say I might seize the nearest stick and kill it; but if I found that snake in bed with my children, that would be another question. I might hurt the children more than the snake, and it might bite them. . . . But if there was a bed newly made up, to which the children were to be taken, and it was proposed to take a batch of young snakes and put them there with them, I take it no man would say there was any question how I ought to decide! . . . The new Territories are the newly made bed to which our children are to go, and it lies with the nation to say whether they shall have snakes mixed up with them or not."

The snake metaphor acknowledged the constitutional protection of slavery where it legally existed, while harnessing the protective instincts of parents to safeguard future generations from the venomous expansion of slavery. This homely vision of the territories as beds for American children exemplified what James Russell Lowell described as Lincoln's ability to speak "as if the people were listening to their own thinking out loud." When Seward reached for a metaphor to dramatize the same danger, he warned that if slavery were allowed into Kansas, his countrymen would have "introduced the Trojan horse" into the new territory. Even if most of his classically trained fellow senators immediately grasped his intent, the Trojan horse image carried neither the instant accessibility of Lincoln's snake-in-the-bed story nor its memorable originality.

The morning after his City Hall speech, Lincoln met with Welles again in the office of the *Hartford Evening Press*. When they parted after an hour of discussion, Welles was favorably impressed. "This orator and lawyer has been caricatured. He is not Apollo, but he is not Caliban," he wrote in the next edition of his paper. "He is [in] every way large, brain included, but his countenance shows intellect, generosity, great good nature, and keen discrimination. . . . He is an effective speaker, because he is earnest, strong, honest, simple in style, and clear as crystal in his logic."

Preparing to return to Springfield, Lincoln had accomplished more than he ever could have anticipated. No longer the distant frontiersman, he had made a name in the East. His possible candidacy was now widely discussed. "I have been sufficiently astonished at my success in the West," Lincoln told a Yale professor who had praised his speech highly. "But I had no thought of any marked success at the East, and least of all that I should draw out such commendations from literary and learned men." When James Briggs told him, "I think your chance for being the next President is equal to that of any man in the country," Lincoln responded, "When I was East several gentlemen made about the same remarks to me that you did to-day about the Presidency; they thought my chances were about equal to the best."

Now there was work to be done at home. A successful bid would require the complete support of the Illinois delegation. To accomplish this, Lincoln would need to bridge the often rancorous divisions within the Republican ranks, a task that would demand all his ample and subtle political skills.

At the end of January 1859, Lyman Trumbull, concerned that the increasingly popular Lincoln might contest his reelection to the Senate, had apprised him of an article "said to have been prepared by Col. John Wentworth," the Republican mayor of Chicago, "the object of which evidently is, to stir up bad feeling between Republicans who were formerly Whigs, & those who were Democrats." The piece suggested bad faith on the Democrats' part, singling out Norman Judd and Trumbull himself, in 1855, and again in 1858, when Lincoln ran a second time against Douglas. "Any effort to put enmity between you and me," Lincoln reassured Trumbull, "is as idle as the wind . . . the republicans generally, coming from the old democratic ranks, were as sincerely anxious for my success in the late contest, as I myself. . . . And I beg to assure you, beyond all possible cavil, that you can scarcely be more anxious to be sustained two years hence than I am that you shall be so sustained. I can not conceive it possible for me to be a rival of yours.

"A word now for your own special benefit," Lincoln warned in a follow-up note. "You better write no letters which can possibly be distorted into opposition, or quasi opposition to me. There are men on the constant watch for such things out of which to prejudice my peculiar friends against you. While I have no more suspicion of you than I have of my best friend living, I am kept in a constant struggle against suggestions of this sort."

It would require more effort to defuse the increasingly bitter feud between Norman Judd and John Wentworth. In public forums, Wentworth would drag out past wrongs, continuing to accuse Judd and his former Democratic allies of conspiring to defeat Lincoln in 1855, of "bungling" Lincoln's campaign in 1858, and of working now "to advance Trumbull as a presidential candidate, at Lincoln's expense."

Lincoln hastened to reassure Judd, who hoped to run for governor, that the "vague charge that you played me false last year, I believe to be false and outrageous." In 1855, "you did vote for Trumbull against me; and, although I think, and have said a thousand times, that was no injustice to me, I cannot change the fact, nor compel people to cease speaking of it. Ever since that matter occurred, I have constantly labored, as I believe you know, to have all recollection of it dropped." Finally, "as to the charge of your intriguing for Trumbull against me, I believe as little of that as any other charge." If such charges were made, Lincoln promised, they would not "go uncontradicted."

The controversy erupted into public view when Judd brought a libel suit against Wentworth, who tried to retain Lincoln as his counsel, claiming that the "very reason that you may assign for declining my offer is the very one that urges me to write you. You are friendly to us both. I prefer to put myself in the hands of mutual friends rather than . . . in the hands of those who have a deep interest in keeping up a quarrel." Of course, Lincoln had no intention of entangling himself in such explosive litigation, but he did help to mediate the altercation. The dispute was resolved without a court fight. Consequently, both Wentworth and Judd remained close to Lincoln and would support his efforts to control the Illinois delegation.

"I am not in a position where it would hurt much for me to not be nominated on the national ticket; but I am where it would hurt some for me to not get the Illinois delegation," Lincoln wrote Judd, knowing that the former Democrat had influence with the Chicago *Press and Tribune*, which covered the northern part of the state. "Can you not help me a little in this matter, in your end of the vineyard?" A week later, the *Tribune* published a resounding editorial on behalf of Lincoln's candidacy. "You saw what the Tribune said about you," Judd said to Lincoln. "Was it satisfactory?"

On May 10, 1860, the Illinois state Republicans assembled in Decatur. Buoyed by the noisy enthusiasm his candidacy elicited at the state convention, Lincoln nonetheless recognized that some of the delegates chosen to go to the national convention, though liking him, probably favored Seward or Bates. To head off possible desertions, Lincoln's friends introduced a resolution on the second day of the meeting: "That Abraham Lincoln is the choice of the Republican party of Illinois for the Presidency, and the delegates from this State are instructed to use all honorable means to secure his nomination by the Chicago Convention, and to vote as a unit for him."

With the Republican National Convention set to begin the following week, Lincoln could rest easy in the knowledge that he had used his time well. Though he often claimed to be a fatalist, declaring that "what is to be will be, and no prayers of ours can reverse the decree," his diligence and shrewd strategy in the months prior to the convention belied his claim. More than all his opponents combined, the country lawyer and local politician had toiled skillfully to increase his chances to become the Republican nominee for president.

CHAPTER 8

SHOWDOWN IN CHICAGO

ORTY THOUSAND VISITORS descended upon Chicago in the middle of May 1860, drawn by the festive excitement surrounding the Republican National Convention. Dozens of trains, mechanical marvels of the age, carried the delegates and supporters of America's youngest political party to America's fastest-growing city. All along the routes, as trains roared past the Niagara, up across the majestic Ohio River, and troubled the air of the western frontier, crowds gathered at every bunting-draped station, sounding their enthusiasm for the Republican cause with brass bands and volleys of cannon fire. Even at crossroads, reporters observed, "small groups were assembled to lend their countenances to the occasion, and from farm houses the ladies waved their kerchiefs, and farmers in the fields swung their hats."

Of all the trains bound for Chicago, none attracted more attention than the one that began its journey at the Suspension Bridge in Buffalo, New York, and swept to Chicago in an astonishing record time of sixteen hours. The unprecedented speed of the massive train was said to amaze every passenger. A reporter recalled that "when 'a mile a minute' was accomplished, the 'boldest held his breath,' and the timid ones trembled in their boots." Every seat was occupied: in addition to delegates, the train carried dozens of newspapermen, professional applauders, henchmen, office seekers, and prizefighters hired "to keep the peace," recalled one young passenger, "for in those hot days men's opinions often cost them broken heads." Amenities included a carload of "such refreshments," one reporter noted, "as lead inevitably to the conclusion that the majority of delegates are among the opponents" of temperance laws.

With boosterish pride, young Chicago was determined to show its best face to the world during the convention. Chicago's growth in previous decades had been "almost ridiculous," a contemporary magazine suggested. Indeed, "growth is much too slow a word," an English visitor marveled to describe the explosion Chicago had experienced since an 1830 guidebook depicted "a military post and fur station," with wolves prowling the streets at night, and a meager population of twelve families who would bunk together in the town's well-defended fort for safety each winter. Thirty years later, Chicago boasted a population of more than a hundred thousand, and the distinction of being "the first grain market in the world," surpassing not only Odessa, "the great grain market of Russia, but all of Europe." It had supplanted St. Louis as the chief marketplace for the vast herds of cattle that grazed the northwest prairies, and had become "the first lumber-market in the world." Newcomers to the bustling city were dazzled by its "miles of wharves crowded with shipping . . . long lines of stately ware-houses," and "crowds of men busy in the active pursuit of trade." Only recently, its streets had been raised from the mud and water by a bold deci-sion to elevate every building and roadway to a level of twelve feet above Lake Michigan.

"Our city has been chosen, here to throw to the winds the broad banner of Republicanism," the *Press and Tribune* proclaimed, "and here to name the leader who shall lead all our hosts to victory." Lavish preparations were made to give the arriving trains a reception to remember. Chicagoans who lived on Michigan Avenue were asked to illuminate their houses. "A most magically beautiful effect was the result," one reporter noted, "the lights flashing back from and multiplied countlessly in the waters of the Lake shore basin." Thousands of spectators lined the shore of the lake, and as the trains moved along the pier, "half minute guns were fired by the Chicago Light Artillery, and rockets shot off from the foot of Jackson Street." No one present, the reporter observed, would forget the effect of "artillery pealing, the flight of the rockets, the gleaming windows from the entire res-idence front of our city, the vast depot edifice filled with the eager crowd."

Hotels and boardinghouse proprietors had spent weeks sprucing up their establishments; private citizens were asked to open their homes; and restaurants promised hearty meals at low prices. The most popular lunch-eon in town included a glass of four-year-old ale and a ham sandwich for ten cents. As packed trains continued to steam into the thronged city, the number of eager Republican visitors on Chicago's streets climbed to forty thousand.

"I thought the city was crowded yesterday," one amazed reporter ex-claimed on the day before the convention was set to open, "but it was as loose and comfortable as a last year's shoe beside the wedging and packing of today. The streets are full, and appear very like conduits leading off the overflowings of the hotels, where huge crowds are constantly pouring out as if they were spouted up from below in some popular eruption."

Even billiard rooms were enlisted to accommodate the staggering crowds. At a certain hour each evening, the games were brought to an abrupt halt as mattresses were laid across the tables to create beds for the sleepy visitors. Looking in on one such establishment at midnight, a reporter saw 130 people stretched out on billiard tables "with a zest, from the fatigues of the day, that would have excited the sympathy of the most unfeeling bosom."

"The city is thronged with Republicans," wrote the *Chicago Evening Journal.* "Republicans from the woods of Maine and the green valleys of all New England; Republicans from the Golden Gate and the old plantation, Republicans from everywhere. What seems a brilliant festival is but the rallying for a battle. It is an army with banners!" Amid "this murmur of the multitude, thought reverts to a time long past," the *Journal* reminded readers, "when a single car and one small chamber could have conveyed them all," when the antislavery principle that "now blossoms white over the land was deemed the vision of enthusiasts, ridiculed, shunned and condemned."

By 1860, the Republican Party had clearly become the dominant force in Northern politics. Its growth and momentum had absorbed two parties, the Whigs and the Know Nothings, and ruptured a third—the Democratic Party. If this new party could carry three of the four conservative Northern states it had lost in 1856—Illinois, Indiana, Pennsylvania, and New Jersey—it could win the presidency. These battleground states lay along the southern tier of the North; they all bordered on slave states; they would play a decisive role in choosing a nominee.

● ● ●

IN THE EARLY HOURS of Wednesday, May 16, the streets surrounding the newly built convention hall swarmed with excited citizens "who crowded around the doors and windows, congregated upon the bridge, sat on the curb stones, and, in fine, used every available inch of standing room." When the big doors of the Wigwam—"so called," it was said, "because the chiefs of the Republican party were to meet there"—were finally opened to the assembled multitude, thousands of ticket holders raced forward to fill the center seats and the more exclusive side galleries, where gentlemen were allowed only if accompanied by a lady. Desperate men had scoured the streets for women—schoolgirls, washerwomen, painted ladies—anyone wearing a skirt and willing to be their date for the afternoon. Within minutes, every seat and nook of the Wigwam was occupied as ten thousand party members waited expectantly for the proceedings to begin.

Exactly at noon, New York's governor Edwin Morgan, chairman of the Republican National Committee, lowered his gavel, and the convention officially began. In his opening address, Morgan told the cheering crowd that "no body of men of equal number was ever clothed with greater responsibility than those now within the hearing of my voice. . . . Let me then invoke you to act in a spirit of harmony, that by the dignity, the wisdom and the patriotism displayed here you may be enabled to enlist the hearts of the people, and to strengthen them in [their] faith."

The work of the convention began. In the course of the first two days, credential battles were settled, and an inclusive platform, keyed to Northern interests, was enthusiastically adopted. While opposition to the extension of slavery remained as central as it had been in 1856, the 1860 platform also called for a Homestead Act, a protective tariff, a railroad to the Pacific, protection for naturalized citizens, and government support for harbor and river improvements—a far broader range of issues designed to attract a larger base.

After much debate, the delegates rejected a provision requiring a two-thirds vote to secure the nomination. Their decision that a simple majority was sufficient to nominate appeared to be a victory for Seward. Coming into Chicago as the best known of all the contenders, he already had nearly a majority of pledges. "The great body of ardent Republicans all over the country," James Pike observed, "desired to elevate to the Presidency the man who had begun so early and had labored so long in behalf of their cardinal doctrines." Indeed, when business came to a close at the end of the second day, a move was made to proceed directly to the presidential balloting. Had votes been cast at that moment, many believe, Seward would have emerged the victor. Instead, the secretary of the convention informed the delegates that the papers necessary for keeping the tally had not yet been prepared, and they adjourned until ten o'clock the next morning.

For those concerned that Seward was too radical on slavery and too liberal on immigration to win battleground states—Indiana, Illinois, New Jersey, and Pennsylvania—the central question was whether the opposition could be unified behind one man. A Committee of Twelve was formed by the prominent representatives of the four critical states to see if a consensus could be reached. By 10 p.m., twelve hours before the balloting was set to begin, no one had been agreed upon. "The time had been consumed in talking," a member of the opposition committee lamented, as each delegation argued stubbornly for its favorite son.

Shortly before midnight, Horace Greeley visited the committee to see if any agreement had been reached. Having surprised Weed by gaining entrance to the convention by representing Oregon as a proxy, Greeley planned to promote Bates and defeat Seward. Disappointed to learn that no agreement had been reached, Greeley sent a telegraph to the *Tribune*, concluding that since the opposition "cannot concentrate on any candidate," Seward "will be nominated." Murat Halstead of the *Cincinnati Commercial* telegraphed the same message to his paper at the same time, reporting that "every one of the forty thousand men in attendance upon the Chicago Convention will testify that at midnight of Thursday–Friday night, the universal impression was that Seward's success was certain." In the rooms shared by the New York delegation, great cheers were heard. "Three hundred bottles of champagne are said to have been cracked," reported Halstead; "it flowed freely as water."

Still, the night was young, the battle only just begun.

• • •

As the hours passed, Weed must have sensed growing opposition among politicians in the conservative battleground states, many of whom feared that supporting Seward's candidacy would hurt their own chances in state elections. However, he never altered his original strategy: before each delegation, he simply asserted that in this perilous time, Seward was, without question, the best man for the job. His love and devotion to his friend of more than thirty years blinded him to the inner dynamics at work since the convention began, the serious doubts that were surfacing about Seward's availability, which meant, bluntly, his ability to win.

"Four years ago we went to Philadelphia to name our candidate," Weed told one delegation after another, "and we made one of the most inexcusable blunders. . . . We nominated a man who had no qualification for the position of Chief Magistrate. . . . We were defeated as we probably deserved to be. . . . We are facing a crisis; there are troublous times ahead of us. . . . What this country will demand as its chief executive for the next four years is a man of the highest order of executive ability, a man of real statesmanlike qualities, well known to the Country, and of large experience in national affairs. No other class of men ought to be considered at this time. We think we have in Mr. Seward just the qualities the Country will need. . . . We expect to nominate him . . . and to go before the Country full of courage and confidence."

No sooner did Weed leave each chamber than Horace Greeley came in and addressed the delegates: "I suppose they are telling you that Seward is the be all and the end all of our existence as a party, our great statesman, our profound philosopher, our pillar of cloud by day, our pillar of fire by night, but I want to tell you boys that in spite of all this you couldn't elect Seward if you could nominate him. You must remember as things stand today we are a sectional party. We have no strength outside the North, practically we must have the entire North with us if we hope to win. . . .

He cannot carry New Jersey, Pennsylvania, Indiana, or Iowa, and I will bring to you representative men from each of these states who will confirm what I say." Greeley proceeded to do just that, one delegate recalled, introducing Governor Samuel Kirkwood of Iowa, and gubernatorial candidates Andrew Curtin of Pennsylvania and Henry Lane of Indiana, "each of whom confirmed what Greeley had said."

"I know my people well," Pennsylvania's Henry Lane argued. "In the south half of my State a good proportion of my people have come from Slave States. . . . They will not tolerate slavery in Indiana or in our free territories but they will not oppose it where it is. . . . They are afraid Seward would be influenced by that abolition element of the East and make war on slavery where it is."

Greeley's spearheading of the anti-Seward forces was all the more credible because few were aware of his estrangement from Seward. Delegates accepted his arguments as those of a friend who simply feared Seward would not bring their party the presidency. "While professing so high a regard for Mr. Seward," one reporter later recognized, "there was rankling in the bosom of Greeley a hatred of the great statesman as bitter as that ever entertained by the most implacable of his political enemies. The feeling had been pent up for years, gathering strength and fury for an occasion when a final explosion could be had with effect. The occasion was afforded at Chicago. The match was lit—the combustible material was ignited, the explosion came. . . . Horace Greeley had his revenge."

Nor was Seward the only target of the late-night gatherings. Gustave Koerner, the leader of the German-Americans—an important component of the Republican constituency in the West—had never forgiven Bates for supporting Fillmore's Know Nothing Party in 1856. In his memoirs, Koerner described rushing into a crowded meeting of delegates from Pennsylvania and Indiana. Frank Blair was just finishing an eloquent speech for Bates when Koerner took the floor. "In all candor," he said, "if Bates [is] nominated," even if he were to win his home state of Missouri, which was doubtful, "the German Republicans in the other States would never vote for him; I for one would not, and I would advise my countrymen to the same effect."

Bates was further handicapped by the fact that he never really represented the middle of the party, however much the Blairs and Greeley tried to position him there. He was much too conservative for liberal Republicans, who might welcome him into their party but would never accord him chief command of an army in which he had never officially enlisted. At the same time, the letter he had written to prove his credentials to the Republicans had diminished the previous enthusiasm of conservatives and former Know Nothings.

Nor was all going well for Salmon Chase. Besides Seward, Chase was the most renowned Republican aspirant. Though more zealously committed to the black man than Seward, Chase was not hampered by Seward's radical reputation; his words had not become emblazoned on the banner of the antislavery movement. In contrast to Seward's reputation as a liberal spender, which hurt in battleground states, he was an economic conservative. And, unlike Seward, he had never openly attacked the Know Nothings.

Moreover, as the third largest delegation at the convention, Ohio wielded substantial power. "If united," observed Halstead, "it would have a formidable influence and might throw the casting votes between candidates, holding the balance of power between the East and the West." But Ohio would not unite behind Chase, as some delegates held out for Ben Wade or Judge McLean. The many enemies Chase had made and failed to conciliate over the years came back to haunt him at this critical juncture. Any hope of persuading McLean to turn over his votes had been lost long before as a consequence of his manipulations to gain his Senate seat. Chase, McLean remarked, "is selfish, beyond any other man. And I know from the bargain he has made in being elected to the Senate, he is ready to make any bargain to promote his interest."

"There was no unity of action, no determination of purpose," one Chase supporter later lamented; there was "a weakness in the spinal column in the Ohio delegation at Chicago, most pitiable to behold." Ohio's inability to settle firmly on Chase, another delegate told him, proved catastrophic. "If the Ohio delegation had been true . . . you would have been nominated. . . . I mingled freely with many of the delegations—they stood ready as a second choice . . . to give you their votes—would have done so if Ohio had . . . [been] relied upon."

Nor had Chase learned from his mistakes four years earlier. Once again, he failed to appoint a set of trusted managers who could guide his campaign, answer objections, cajole wavering delegates, and, at the right moment, make promises to buoy supporters and strengthen wills. "There are lots of good feeling afloat here for you," one of Chase's friends told him, "but there is no set of men in earnest for you . . . I think the hardest kind of death to die is that occasioned by indecisive, or lukewarm friends."

•   •   •

MEANWHILE, THROUGHOUT this night of a thousand knives, the opposition to Seward grew more vociferous, even frantic. "Men gather in little groups," observed Halstead, "and with their arms about each other, and chatter and whisper as if the fate of the country depended upon their immediate delivery of the mighty political secrets with which their imaginations are big." Rumors multiplied with each passing hour; "things of incalculable moment are communicated to you confidentially, at intervals of five minutes."

The rumor was deliberately circulated "that the Republican candidates for governor in Indiana, Illinois and Pennsylvania would resign if Seward were nominated." No one challenged Seward's ability; no one questioned his credentials as statesman of the party. He was opposed simply because it was thought he would damage the prospects of the Republican Party and hurt Republican candidates in local elections. Still, Halstead admiringly observed: "Amid all these cries of distress, the Sewardites are true as steel to their champion, and they will cling to 'Old Irrepressible,' as they call him, until the last gun is fired and the big bell rings."

All along, the main question among the gathering ranks of the "stop Seward" movement had been whether the opposition would be able to concentrate its strength on a single alternative, or be crippled by its own divisions.

For this eventuality, Lincoln had long prepared. Though he understood he could not positively count on the unanimous support of any delegation beyond Illinois, he knew he had earned widespread respect and admiration throughout the North. "You know how it is in Ohio," he wrote a friend from the Buckeye State two weeks before the convention. "I am certainly not the first choice there; and yet I have not heard that any one makes any positive objection to me. It is just so everywhere so far as I can perceive. Everywhere, except in Illinois, and possibly Indiana, one or another is prefered to me, but there is no positive objection."

To reach his goal of becoming everyone's second choice, Lincoln was careful not to disparage any other candidate. Nor was it in his nature to do so. His committed team of workers—including Judge David Davis, Leonard Swett, Norman Judd, and Stephen Logan—understood this, resolving from the start "to antagonize no one." They did not need to, for Greeley and candidates for governor in the doubtful states had that task well in hand. Nor, as Kenneth Stampp writes, did they need to win support based upon Lincoln's "relative ability compared with other candidates. . . . Their appeal was based on availability and expediency; they urged the delegates to nominate the man who could win."

"No men ever worked as our boys did," Swett later claimed. "I did not, the whole week I was there, sleep two hours a night." Although some of Lincoln's men had political ambitions of their own, Henry Whitney observed, "Most of them worked *con amore*, chiefly from love of the man, his lofty moral tone, his pure political morality." Working in his "typically me-thodical way," Davis designated specific tasks to each member of his team. Maine's Leonard Swett was charged with making inroads in the Maine del-egation. Samuel Parks, a native Vermonter, was dispatched to the delega-tion of the Green Mountain State. In the spring elections in New England, the Republicans had suffered setbacks, leading Lincoln to observe that the election result would be seen as "a drawback upon the prospects of Gov. Seward," opening the door for one of his rivals. Stephen Logan and Richard Yates were given Kentucky, while Ward Lamon was assigned his home state of Virginia. In each of these states, the Lincoln men worked to pick off individual delegates to keep Seward from sweeping the field on the first ballot.

"It all worked to a charm," boasted Swett. "The first State approached was Indiana." Even before the convention had opened, Lincoln got word that "the whole of Indiana might not be difficult to get" and had urged Davis to concentrate on the Hoosier State. Though Indiana contained twenty thousand or more former Know Nothings who likely preferred Bates, the Indiana politicians were fearful that Bates was not strong enough to challenge Seward for the nomination. And if Seward headed the ticket, gubernatorial candidate Henry Lane never tired of warning, the radical image he projected and his unpopularity with the Know Nothings would jeopardize the entire state ticket.

Claims have been made that Davis made a deal with Indiana's chairman, Caleb Smith, to bring him into the cabinet in return for Indiana's vote. No deal was needed, however; Smith had admired Lincoln since their days in Congress and had agreed, even before the balloting, to second Lincoln's nomination. The Indiana delegates' decision to back Lincoln on the first ballot was more likely a practical decision based on the best interests of their own state.

By securing Indiana's pledge, the Lincoln men gained a decided ad-vantage in the Committee of Twelve, which had remained deadlocked at midnight in its attempts to agree on a common candidate to oppose Seward—prompting Greeley and Halstead to predict a Seward victory. As the committee members continued to talk in the early-morning hours, someone proposed a straw vote to determine the opposition candidate with the greatest strength. In this impromptu poll, since Lincoln already had the support of both Illinois and Indiana, two of the four key states, he emerged as the strongest candidate. According to one committee member, "Mr. Dudley of New Jersey then proposed that for the general good of the party," Pennsylvania should give up its favorite son after the first ballot, as would New Jersey. The proposition was generally agreed upon, but Pennsylvania required further negotiations to ratify the agreement.

According to Henry Whitney, Davis had previously sent a telegram to Lincoln informing him that if Cameron were promised a space in the cabinet, Pennsylvania might be procured. Lincoln scribbled his answer in the margin of a newspaper, which an emissary carried to the convention. *"Make no contracts that will bind me."* When the message arrived, Whitney writes, "Everybody was mad, of course. Here were men working night and day to place him on the highest mountain peak of fame, and he pulling back all he knew how. What was to be done? The bluff Dubois said: 'Damn Lincoln!' The polished Swett said, in mellifluous accents: 'I am very sure if Lincoln was aware of the necessities . . .' The critical Logan expectorated viciously, and said: 'The main difficulty with Lincoln is . . .' Herndon ventured: 'Now, friend, I'll answer that.' But Davis cut the Gordian knot by brushing all aside with: 'Lincoln ain't here, and don't know what we have to meet, so we will go ahead, as if we hadn't heard from him, and he must ratify it.' "

Moreover, Davis undoubtedly understood that other candidates were making pledges of their own. The Blairs had supposedly promised Cassius Clay the post of secretary of war if he would endorse Bates. And doubtless Weed could promise not only cabinet posts but the "oceans of money" he had accumulated for the Republican cause. Nonetheless, Davis's biographer concludes that no direct pledge was ever made to Cameron. Davis promised only that he would "get every member of the Illinois delegation to recommend Cameron's appointment," which the Cameron men mistook for a guaranteed pledge.

Whether or not explicit deals were made, the Lincoln men worked hard to convince Cameron's contingent that Pennsylvania would be treated generously if Lincoln received their votes. "My assurance to them," Swett later wrote Lincoln, was that despite the fact that Pennsylvania had not supported Lincoln from the start, "they should be placed upon the same footing as if originally they had been your friends. Now, of course, it is unpleasant for me to write all this *stuff* and for you to read it. Of course I have never feared you would unintentionally do anything unfair towards these men. I only write to suggest the very delicate situation I am placed towards them so that you might cultivate them as much as possible."

By adding the votes of Indiana, Pennsylvania, and New Jersey, three of the four doubtful states, to those of Illinois, Davis and Swett had achieved what many considered impossible: they had made possible the nomination of Abraham Lincoln.

• • •

As THE DAY of the balloting dawned, the Seward men, confident of victory, gathered at the Richmond House for a celebratory march to the convention hall. "A thousand strong," Murat Halstead observed, and accompanied by a "magnificent band, which was brilliantly uniformed—epaulets shining on their shoulders," they prolonged "their march a little too far." Upon reaching the Wigwam, they were dismayed to find that some of their number could not get in—Lincoln's partisans had manufactured duplicate tickets the evening before and had filed into the hall as soon as the doors opened.

Recognizing that "it was part of the Seward plan to carry the Convention" by bringing more supporters to Chicago than any other candidate, Lincoln's managers had mustered friends and supporters from all over the state. The nominations became the initial test of strength. New York's William Evarts was the first to rise, asking the convention to place Seward's name in nomination. His words were met "by a deafening shout." The applause was "loud and long," as supporters continued to stand, waving handkerchiefs in frenzied excitement. Lincoln's man, Leonard Swett, confessed that the level of enthusiasm "appalled us a little."

Nonetheless, Lincoln's contingent was ready when Norman Judd placed the name of Illinois's favorite son in nomination. "If Mr. Seward's name drew forth thunders of applause," one reporter noted, "what can be said of the enthusiastic reception of [Lincoln's] name. . . . The audience, like a wild colt with [a] bit between his teeth, rose above all cry of order, and again and again the irrepressible applause broke forth and resounded far and wide." To Seward's supporters, this "tremendous applause" was "the first distinct impression in Lincoln's favor." Though Chase and Bates were also nominated to loud applause, the responses were "cold when compared" to the receptions for Seward and Lincoln.

When the seconding nominations proceeded, the "trial of lungs" intensified. Determined to win the battle, Seward's adherents rallied when Austin Blair of Michigan rose to second his nomination. "The shouting was absolutely frantic," Halstead reported. "No Comanches, no panthers ever struck a higher note, or gave screams with more infernal intensity." Once again, the Lincoln men rose to the challenge. When Indiana's Caleb Smith seconded Lincoln's nomination, "five thousand people at once" jumped to their feet, Leonard Swett reported. "A thousand steam whistles, ten acres of hotel gongs . . . might have mingled in the scene unnoticed." A voice rose from the crowd: "Abe Lincoln has it by the sound, let us ballot!" The efforts of Lincoln's men to corral more supporters had paid off.

"This was not the most deliberate way of nominating a President," Swett later confessed, but "it had its weight."

The convention finally settled down and the balloting began. Two hundred thirty-three votes would decide the Republican presidential nomination. The roll call opened with the New England states, which had been considered solidly for Seward. In fact, a surprising number of votes went for Lincoln, as well as a scattering for Chase. Lincoln's journey through New England after the Cooper Union speech had apparently won over a number of delegates. As expected, New York gave its full 70 votes to Seward, allowing him to leap far ahead. The Seward men relaxed until Virginia, which had also been considered solid for Seward, split its 22 votes between Seward and Lincoln. Chase had assumed that Ohio, which came next, would give him its full 46 votes, but the delegation was divided in its vote, giving 34 to Chase and the remaining 12 to Lincoln and McLean. Perhaps the greatest surprise was Indiana, which Bates had assumed was his territory; instead, Lincoln gathered all 26 votes. "This solid vote was a startler," reported Halstead, "and the keen little eyes of Henry S. Lane glittered as it was given."

At the end of the first ballot, the tally stood: Seward 173½; Lincoln 102; Chase 49; Bates 48. The Bates managers were downhearted to realize, as the historian Marvin Cain writes, that "no pivotal state had gone for Bates, and the sought-after votes of the Iowa, Kentucky, Minnesota and Ohio delegations had not been delivered." Disappointment was equally evident in the faces of the Chase men, for they were keenly aware that the division within the Ohio delegation was probably fatal. Lincoln's camp was exhilarated, for with his total of 102 votes, Lincoln had emerged as the clear-cut alternative to Seward. Although taken aback by the unexpected defections, Weed still hoped that Seward would win on the second ballot. The 48 votes Cameron had supposedly promised from Pennsylvania would put Seward within striking distance of the victory number of 233.

The second ballot revealed a crucial shift in Lincoln's favor. In New England he picked up 17 more votes, while Delaware switched its 6 votes from Bates to Lincoln. Then came the biggest surprise of all, "startling the vast auditorium like a clap of thunder": Pennsylvania announced 44 votes for Lincoln, boosting his total to 181, only 3½ votes behind Seward's new total of 184½. Chase and Bates both lost ground on the second ballot, essentially removing them from contention. The race had narrowed to Seward and Lincoln.

Tension in the Wigwam mounted. The spectators sat on the edge of their seats as the third ballot began. Lincoln gained 4 additional votes from Massachusetts and 4 from Pennsylvania, also adding 15 votes from Ohio.

His total reached 231½, only 1½ votes shy of victory. "There was a pause," Halstead recorded. "In about ten ticks of a watch," David K. Cartter of Ohio stood and announced the switch of 4 votes from Chase to Lincoln. "A profound stillness fell upon the Wigwam," one eyewitness wrote. Then the Lincoln supporters "rose to their feet applauding rapturously, the ladies waving their handkerchiefs, the men waving and throwing up their hats by thousands, cheering again and again."

For the Sewardites, the defeat was devastating. "Great men wept like boys," one New Yorker observed, "faces drawn, white and aged as if ten years had passed in that one night of struggle." Everyone looked to Thurlow Weed, but there was no solace he could give. The work of his lifetime had ended in defeat, and he, too, could not restrain his tears. His failure to serve his country by making his good friend president, Weed later acknowledged, was "the great disappointment of his life."

All across the chamber, representatives rose, clamoring to change their votes so that Lincoln could achieve a unanimous victory. Their emotional tone revealed that the defeated Seward still had a great hold on their hearts. When Michigan shifted its votes to Lincoln, Austin Blair confessed that his state was laying down "her first, best loved candidate . . . with some bleeding of the heart, with some quivering in the veins; but she does not fear that the fame of Seward will suffer," for his story will be "written, and read, and beloved long after the temporary excitement of this day has passed away, and when Presidents are themselves forgotten." In similar fashion, Carl Schurz of Wisconsin predicted that Seward's ambition would be fulfilled "with the success of the cause which was the dream of his youth," and that his name would "remain in history, an instance of the highest merit uncrowned with the highest honor."

The most poignant moment came when New York's chairman, William Evarts, stood up. "Mounting a table, with grief manifest in his countenance, his hands clenched nervously," he delivered a powerful tribute to Seward: "Gentlemen, it was from Governor Seward that most of us learned to love Republican principles and the Republican party." He finally requested that New York shift its votes to Lincoln. So moving was his speech, one reporter noted, that "the spectator could not fail to be impressed with the idea that a man who could have such a friend must be a noble man indeed."

Once the vote was made unanimous, the celebration began in earnest. A man stationed on the roof of the Wigwam shouted the news of Lincoln's nomination, along with that of Hannibal Hamlin of Maine for vice president, to the thousands waiting on the street. Cannons were fired and "between 20,000 and 30,000 outside were yelling and shouting at once." The festivities continued through the night. "The Press and Tribune building," one of the paper's reporters wrote, "was illuminated from 'turret to foundation,' by the brilliant glare of a thousand lights which blazed from windows and doors." Shouldering the symbolic fence rails that Lincoln had supposedly split, Republicans paraded through the streets to the music of a dozen bands.

• • •

SEWARD RECEIVED THE NEWS of his loss while sitting with friends in his country garden at Auburn. A rider on a swift horse had waited at the telegraph office to dash through the crowded streets the moment a telegram arrived. When the totals of the first ballot came in, the messenger had galloped to Seward's house and handed the telegram to him. When the news of Seward's large lead was repeated to guests at his house and to the crowds on the street, great cheers went up. When the totals of the second ballot came in, Seward retained his optimism. "I shall be nominated on the next ballot," he predicted to the boisterous audience on the lawn, and a great cheer resounded from the streets. Long, anxious moments followed. When no further news arrived, Seward "rightly [judged] that . . . there was no news that friends would love to bring." Finally, the unwelcome telegram announcing Lincoln's nomination on the third ballot arrived. Seward turned "as pale as ashes." He understood at once, as did his supporters, his son Fred would remember, "that it was no ordinary political defeat, to be retrieved in some subsequent campaign. It was . . . final and irrevocable."

"The sad tidings crept through the vast concourse," one reporter noted. "The flags were furled, the cannon was rolled away, and Cayuga county went home with a clouded brow." Later that night, writing in his diary in Washington, Charles Francis Adams could not stop thinking of his defeated friend, "of his sanguine expectations, of his long services, of his large and comprehensive philosophy, and of his great ambition—all now merged for a time in a deep abyss of disappointment. He has too much of alloy in his composition to rise above it. Few men can."

Yet "he took the blow as a champion should," his biographer notes, putting on "a brave front before his family and the world." In her diary, sixteen-year-old Fanny Seward noted simply that "Father told Mother and I in three words, Abraham Lincoln nominated. His friends feel much distress—he alone has a smile—he takes it with philosophical and unselfish coolness." Informed that the editor of the local evening paper could find no one in the disconsolate town willing to write and comment on the news announcing Lincoln and Hamlin's nominations, Seward took up his own pen. "No truer or firmer defenders of the Republican faith could have been found in the Union," he graciously stated, "than the distinguished and esteemed citizens on whom the honors of the nomination have fallen."

Before he retired that night, Seward wrote to Weed: "You have my unbounded gratitude for this last, as for the whole life of efforts in my behalf. I wish that I was sure that your sense of the disappointment is as light as my own." A week later, in a public letter, Seward pledged his support to the Republican ticket and said he hoped his friends who had "labored so long" by his side would not allow their "sense of disappointment . . . to hinder or delay . . . the progress of that cause."

Beneath his graceful facade, Seward was angry, hurt, and humiliated. "It was only some months later," the biographer Glyndon Van Deusen writes, "when the shock had worn off and hope of a sort had revived, that he could say half ruefully, half whimsically, how fortunate it was that he did not keep a diary, for if he had there would be a record of all his cursing and swearing" when the news arrived.

If Seward managed to project a willed equanimity, Chase could not hide his bitterness at his defeat, nor his fury at the Ohio delegation that had failed to support him unanimously. "When I remember what New York did for Seward, what Illinois did for Lincoln and what Missouri did for Bates," Chase told a friend, "and remember also that neither of these gentlemen ever spent a fourth part—if indeed a tithe of the time labor and means for the Republican Party in their respective states that I have spent for our party in Ohio; & then reflect on the action of the Ohio delegation in Chicago towards me; I confess I have little heart to write or think about it. . . . I must say that had [Senator Ben Wade] received the same expression from Ohio which was given to me, and had I been in his place, I would have suffered my arm to be wrenched from my body, before I would have allowed my name to be brought into competition with his."

For years, Chase was racked by the thought that had Ohio remained loyal, he would have won the nomination. Even in a congratulatory letter to Lincoln, he could not refrain from citing his own situation. Supposing that the "adhesion of the Illinois delegation" yielded Lincoln "a higher gratification" even than "the nomination itself," Chase confessed that the perfidy of his own delegation was unbearable. "In this . . . I am quite sure you must participate," he sounded Lincoln, "for I err greatly in my estimate of your magnanimity, if you do not condemn as I do the conduct of delegates, from whatever state, who disregard . . . the clearly expressed preference of their own State Convention." Lincoln responded graciously without taking the bait.

Carl Schurz contemplated Chase's torment in the dark hours following the nomination. "While the victory of Mr. Lincoln was being announced to the outside world," he wrote, "my thoughts involuntarily turned to Chase, who, I imagined, sat in a quiet office room at Columbus with a telegraph near by clicking the news from Chicago. . . . Not even his own State had given him its full strength. No doubt he had hoped, and hoped, and hoped against hope . . . and now came this disastrous, crushing, humiliating defeat. I saw that magnificent man before me, writhing with the agony of his disappointment, and I sympathized with him most profoundly."

As the news of Chase's defeat filtered into the streets of Columbus, the dray readied to haul the cannon to the corner of Third and State streets, to announce his victory with a roar of thunder, was used instead to honor Lincoln's nomination. After the short "melancholy ceremony" was concluded, the dray hauled the cannon back to its shed, and the city went to sleep.

Bates accepted defeat with the composure that had marked his character from the outset. "As for me, I was surprised, I own, but not at all mortified, at the result at Chicago," he wrote Greeley. "I had no claim—literally none—upon the Republicans as a party, and no right to expect their party honors; and I shall cherish, with enduring gratitude, the recollection of the generous confidence with which many of their very best men have honored me. So far from feeling beaten and depressed, I have cause rather for joy and exultation; for, by the good opinion of certain eminent Republicans, I have gained much in standing and reputation before the country—more, I think, than any mere private man I have ever known."

In his private journal, however, Bates admitted to a sense of irritation. "Some of my friends who attended the Convention assure me that the nomination of Mr. Lincoln took every body by surprise: That it was brought about by accident or trick, by which my pledged friends had to vote against me. . . . The thing was well planned and boldly executed. A few Germans—Schurz of Wisconsin and Koerner of Illinois, with their truculent boldness, scared the timid men of Indiana into submission. Koerner went before the Indiana Delegation and assured them that if Bates were nominated, the *Germans* would bolt!"

The platform, he continued, "is exclusive and defiant, not attracting but repelling assistance from without. . . . It lugs in the lofty generalities of the Declaration of Independence, for no practical object that I can see, but needlessly exposing the party to the specious charge of favoring negro equality. . . . I think they will soon be convinced, if they are not already, that they have committed a fatal blunder—They have denationalized their Party; weakened it in the free states, and destroyed its hopeful beginnings in the border slave states."

While the melancholy spirit of defeated expectations settled upon the streets of Auburn, Columbus, and St. Louis, Springfield was euphoric. The legendary moment when Lincoln learned of his nomination has spawned many versions over the years. Some claim Lincoln was standing in a shop, purchasing some items that Mary had requested, when cheers were heard from the telegraph office, followed by the shouts of a boy rushing through the crowd: "Mr. Lincoln, Mr. Lincoln, you are nominated." Others maintain that he was talking with friends in the office of the *Illinois State Journal* when he received the news. Handed the scrap of paper that reported his victory, he "looked at it long and silently, not heeding the noisy exultation of all around." Shaking hands with everyone in the room, he remarked quietly, "I knew this would come when I saw the second ballot." Leaving the *Journal* office, Lincoln plunged into a crowd of well-wishers on the street. "My friends," he said, "I am glad to receive your congratulations, and as there is a little woman down on Eighth street who will be glad to hear the news, you must excuse me until I inform her." When he reached his home, Ida Tarbell reports, he found that Mary "already knew that the honor which for twenty years and more she had believed and stoutly declared her husband deserved . . . at last had come."

The tumult in Springfield that evening was recorded by a young journalist, John Hay, who would later become Lincoln's aide. He reported that "the hearty western populace burst forth in the wildest manifestations of joy . . . Lincoln banners, decked in every style of rude splendor, fluttered in the high west wind." The church bells tolled. Thousands assembled in the rotunda of the Capitol for a festive celebration replete with victory speeches. When the meeting adjourned, the happy throngs converged on Lincoln's house. His appearance at the door was "the signal for immense cheering." Modestly, Lincoln insisted that "he did not suppose the honor of such a visit was intended particularly for himself as a private citizen but rather as the representative to a great party."

• • •

FOR GENERATIONS, people have weighed and debated the factors that led to Lincoln's surprising victory. Many have agreed with the verdict of Murat Halstead, who wrote that "the fact of the Convention was the defeat of Seward rather than the nomination of Lincoln." Seward himself seemed to accept this analysis. When asked years later why Lincoln had won, he said: "The leader of a political party in a country like ours is so exposed that his enemies become as numerous and formidable as his friends." Abraham Lincoln, by contrast, "comparatively unknown, had not to contend with the animosities generally marshaled against a leader."

There is truth to this argument, but it tells only part of the story, for the question remains: why was Lincoln the beneficiary of Seward's downfall rather than Chase or Bates?

Some have pointed to luck, to the fact that Lincoln lived in a battle-ground state the Republicans needed to win, and to the fact that the convention was held in Chicago, where the strength of local support could add weight to his candidacy. "Had the Convention been held at any other place," Koerner admitted, "Lincoln would not have been nominated."

Others have argued that he was positioned perfectly in the center of the party. He was less radical than Seward or Chase, but less conservative than Bates. He was less offensive than Seward to the Know Nothings, but more acceptable than Bates to the German-Americans.

Still others have argued that Lincoln's team in Chicago played the game better than anyone else, conceiving the best strategy and cleverly using the leverage of promises to the best advantage. Without doubt, the Lincoln men, under the skillful leadership of David Davis, performed brilliantly.

Chance, positioning, and managerial strategy—all played a role in Lincoln's victory. Still, if we consider the comparative resources each contender brought to the race—their range of political skills, their emotional, intellectual, and moral qualities, their rhetorical abilities, and their determination and willingness to work hard—it is clear that when opportunity beckoned, Lincoln was the best prepared to answer the call. His nomination, finally, was the result of his character and his life experiences—these separated him from his rivals and provided him with advantages unrecognized at the time.

Having risen to power with fewer privileges than any of his rivals, Lincoln was more accustomed to rely upon himself to shape events. From beginning to end, he took the greatest control of the process leading up to the nomination. While Seward, at Weed's suggestion, spent eight months wandering Europe and the Middle East to escape dissension at home, Lincoln earned the goodwill and respect of tens of thousands with a strenuous speaking tour that left a positive imprint on Republicans in five crucial Midwestern states. While Chase unwisely declined his invitation to speak at the lecture series in New York at Cooper Union, Lincoln accepted with alacrity, recognizing the critical importance of making a good impression in Seward's home territory. In addition, Chase refused invitations to travel to New England and shore up his support. Ironically, despite repeated pledges in his diary to do anything necessary to achieve honor and fame, Chase showed a lack of resolution in the final weeks before the convention.

When ardent Republicans heard Lincoln speak, they knew that if their beloved Seward could not win, they had in the eloquent orator from Illinois a man of considerable capacity whom they could trust, one who would hold fast on the central issue that had forged the party—the fight against extending slavery into the territories. Though Lincoln had entered the antislavery struggle later than Seward or Chase, his speeches possessed unmatched power, conviction, clarity, and moral strength.

At the same time, his native caution and precision with language—he rarely said more than he was sure about, rarely pandered to his various audiences—gave Lincoln great advantages over his rivals, each of whom tried to reposition himself in the months before the convention. Seward disappointed liberal Republicans when he tried to soften his fiery rhetoric to placate moderates. Bates infuriated conservatives with his strongly worded public letter. And Chase fooled no one when he tried to shift his position on the tariff at the last moment. Lincoln remained consistent throughout.

Nor, as the Chicago *Press and Tribune* pointed out, was "his avoidance of extremes" simply "the result of ambition which measures words or regulates acts." It was, more accurately, "the natural consequence of an equable nature and a mental constitution that is never off its balance."

In his years of travel on the circuit through central Illinois, engaging people in taverns, on street corners, and in shops, Lincoln had developed a keen sense of what people felt, thought, needed, and wanted. Seward, too, had an instinctive feeling for people, but too many years in Washington had dulled those instincts. Like Lincoln, Chase had spent many months traveling throughout his home state, but his haughty demeanor prevented him from truly connecting with the farmers, clerks, and bartenders he met along the way. Bates, meanwhile, had isolated himself for so long from the hurly-burly of the political world that his once natural political savvy was diminished.

It was Lincoln's political intuition, not blind luck, that secured the convention site in Chicago. To be sure, the fact that Lincoln was "comparatively unknown" aided Norman Judd in landing the venue in Illinois. However, it was part of Lincoln's strategy to hold his name back as long as possible and to "give no offence to others—leave them in a mood to come to us, if they shall be compelled to give up their first love." It was Lincoln who first suggested to Judd that it might be important to secure Chicago. And it was Lincoln who first pointed out to his managers that Indiana might be won. Indeed, his guidance and determination were evident at every step along the way to the nomination.

Lincoln, like Seward, had developed a cadre of lifelong friends who were willing to do anything in their power to ensure his nomination. But unlike Seward, he had not made enemies or aroused envy along the way. It

256TEAM OF RIVALS

is hard to imagine Lincoln letting Greeley's resentment smolder for years as Seward did. On the contrary, he took pains to reestablish rapport with Judd and Trumbull after they had defeated him in his first run for the Senate. His ability to rise above defeat and create friendships with previous opponents was never shared by Chase, who was unable to forgive those who crossed him. And though Bates had a warm circle of friends in St. Louis, most of them were not politicians. His campaign at the convention was managed by a group of men who barely knew him. Without burning personal loyalty, they had simply picked him as a potential winner, dropping him with equal ease when the path to his nomination proved bumpy.

Finally, Lincoln's profound and elevated sense of ambition—"an ambition," Fehrenbacher observes, "notably free of pettiness, malice, and overindulgence," shared little common ground with Chase's blatant obsession with office, Seward's tendency toward opportunism, or the ambivalent ambition that led Bates to withdraw from public office. Though Lincoln desired success as fiercely as any of his rivals, he did not allow his quest for office to consume the kindness and openheartedness with which he treated supporters and rivals alike, nor alter his steady commitment to the antislavery cause.

In the end, though the men who nominated Abraham Lincoln in Chicago may not have recognized all these qualities, they chose the best man for the supreme challenge looming over the nation.

CHAPTER 9

"A MAN KNOWS
HIS OWN NAME"

T HE NEWS THAT Lincoln had defeated Seward came as a shock
to much of the country, especially to the Eastern Republican establishment. On Capitol Hill, word of Lincoln's nomination
"was received with general incredulity," conceded Charles Francis Adams,
"until by repeated announcements from different quarters it appeared that
he had carried the day by a union of all the anti-Seward elements. . . . The
House was in such a state of confusion that it was clear no business would
be done, so we adjourned."

Since people were unaware of the skill with which he had crafted his
victory, Lincoln was viewed as merely the accidental candidate of the consolidated anti-Seward forces. Still an obscure figure, he was referred to by
half the journals representing his own party as "Abram" rather than "Abraham." Pointing out that when Lincoln had visited the Historical Library at
Hartford the previous March, he signed the visitors' book as "Abraham
Lincoln," the Democratic *New York Herald* caustically noted that "it is but
fair to presume that a man knows his own name." Lincoln wrote to George
Ashmun, the Republican chairman of the acceptance committee: "It seems
as if the question whether my first name is 'Abraham' or 'Abram' will never
be settled. It is *'Abraham.'* "

Exulting in Lincoln's lack of national experience, Democratic newspapers had a field day ridiculing his biography. He is "a third rate Western
lawyer," the *Herald* gloated. "The conduct of the republican party in this
nomination is a remarkable indication of a small intellect, growing
smaller." Rejecting Seward and Chase, "who are statesmen and able men,"
the *Herald* continued, "they take up a fourth rate lecturer, who cannot
speak good grammar," and whose speeches are "illiterate compositions . . .
interlarded with coarse and clumsy jokes." Not content to deride his intel-

lect, hostile publications focused on his appearance. "Lincoln is the lean-est, lankest, most ungainly mass of legs, arms and hatchet-face ever strung upon a single frame. He has most unwarrantably abused the privilege which all politicians have of being ugly."

More violent attacks appeared in the *Charleston Mercury*, which scorn-fully asked: "After him what decent white man would be President?" Sew-ard, the paper insisted, had been "thrust aside" because he "lacked the necessary nerve to carry through measures of Southern subjugation." Lin-coln, on the other hand, was "the *beau ideal* of a relentless, dogged, freesoil border-ruffian." He was "an illiterate partizan," claimed the influential *Richmond Enquirer,* "possessed only of his inveterate hatred of slavery and his openly avowed predilections for negro equality."

The venom of such attacks reflected the growing discord and apprehen-sion among Southern Democrats. As Lincoln prepared for the election campaign, his prospects of victory had been enhanced considerably by the splintering of the Democratic Party, which was now the only party with supporters in both the North and South. Meeting in Charleston, South Carolina, before Lincoln's nomination, the Democratic National Conven-tion had ended in chaos. A majority of delegates, comprised of Stephen Douglas's supporters, had presented a platform designed to paper over the slavery issue. Unfortunately for Douglas, the time when the slavery issue could be veiled had passed. Recent events, including the *Dred Scott* deci-sion and the raid on Harpers Ferry by John Brown had hardened the posi-tion of many Southern leaders. The moderate positions acceptable in the past were rejected by radical Southern politicians who now condemned all compromise, demanding complete freedom to bring slaves into all the ter-ritories and explicit congressional protection for those slaves. They dis-missed the doctrine of "popular sovereignty," once widely acceptable, as an abandonment of Southern principle.

When the convention approved the moderate Douglas platform, the representatives from Alabama walked out, followed first by Mississippi and then the other Southern states. As the Mississippi delegation rose to walk out, one incensed delegate climbed on a chair for a rousing farewell speech, predicting that "in less than sixty days there would be a United South." With this, observer Murat Halstead recorded, "the South Car-olinians cheered loud and long," the applause mounting as each state bolted. That night, "there was a Fourth of July feeling in Charleston. . . . There was no mistaking the public sentiment of the city. It was over-whelmingly and enthusiastically in favor of the seceders."

Unable to secure a two-thirds vote for any nominee, the deadlocked Charleston convention was forced to reconvene in Baltimore after Lincoln had been nominated by the Republicans. There Douglas would finally receive the nomination he had long pursued. It was too late, however, to reassemble the pieces of the last national party. The positions of the Northern and Southern Democrats were now irreconcilable, shattered by the same forces that had destroyed the Whigs and the Know Nothings.

With Douglas the Democratic nominee, Southern seceders reconvened to nominate John C. Breckinridge of Kentucky, a staunch believer that slavery could not constitutionally be excluded from the territories. North Carolina–born senator Joseph Lane was chosen as the vice presidential nominee. To complicate matters further, the new Constitutional Union Party, composed of old-line Whigs and remnant Know Nothings, held its own convention, nominating John Bell of Tennessee and Edward Everett of Massachusetts on a platform rooted in the illusory hope that the dissolution of the Union could be avoided by ignoring the slavery question altogether.

"The great democratic organization has finally burst into pieces," Charles Francis Adams rejoiced in a diary entry of June 23, "and the two sections have respectively nominated candidates of their own." Two weeks later, Lincoln informed a friend that he figured "the chances were more than equal, that we could have beaten the Democracy *united*. Divided, as it is, it's chance appears very slim." Nonetheless, he cautioned, "great is Democracy in resources; and it may yet give it's fortunes a turn."

While the Democrats were splintering, a committee came to Springfield to notify Lincoln formally of his nomination. "Mr. Lincoln received us in the parlor of his modest frame house," wrote Carl Schurz, Seward's avid supporter and a leading spokesman for the German-Americans. In the "rather bare-looking room," Lincoln "stood, tall and ungainly in his black suit of apparently new but ill-fitting clothes, his long tawny neck emerging gauntly from his turn-down collar, his melancholy eyes sunken deep in his haggard face." Ashmun spoke for the committee, and Lincoln "responded with a few appropriate, earnest, and well-shaped sentences." Afterward, everyone relaxed into a more general conversation, "partly of a jovial kind, in which the hearty simplicity of Lincoln's nature shone out." As the committee members left, Mr. Kelley of Pennsylvania remarked to Schurz: "Well, we might have done a more brilliant thing, but we could hardly have done a better thing." Still, Schurz acknowledged, other members of the committee "could not quite conceal their misgivings as to how this single-minded man, this child of nature, would bear himself in the contact with the great world."

Another visitor, Thurlow Weed, detected an unexpected sophistication and political acumen in Lincoln. Still nursing wounds from Seward's defeat, Weed traveled to Springfield at the invitation of Swett and Davis shortly after the convention. The two master politicians analyzed "the prospects of success, assuming that all or nearly all the slave States would be against [them]," determining which states "were safe without effort . . . which required attention," and which "were sure to be vigorously contested." Lincoln exhibited, Weed later wrote, "so much good sense, such intuitive knowledge of human nature, and such familiarity with the virtues and infirmities of politicians, that I became impressed very favorably with his fitness for the duties which he was not unlikely to be called upon to discharge." Weed departed, ready to "go to work with a will."

As Weed and Lincoln plotted election strategy, it must have been apparent to both men that there would, in actuality, be two elections. In the free states, the contest would pit Lincoln against Douglas, while the Southern Democrat, Breckinridge, would battle border-state Bell for the slave states. Douglas, once the defender of Southern principles, the author of the infamous Kansas-Nebraska Act, was, by 1860, reviled throughout the South as a traitor or closet abolitionist. "Now what difference is it to the people whether Lincoln or Douglas shall be elected?" one Southern newspaper asked. "The same ends are sought by each, and we do not see any reason to choose between them."

A Lincoln victory would require at least 152 electoral votes. Anything short of a majority would throw the election into the turbulent chamber of the House of Representatives, which might well prove unable to elect anyone. The choice of vice president would be left to the Southern-dominated Senate, which might well elect Joseph Lane, Breckinridge's running mate, to occupy the vacant presidential chair. Lincoln, therefore, would have to capture virtually the entire North, including those states that had voted for the Democrat Buchanan in the last election.

In three of these "must win" states—Indiana, Pennsylvania, and Ohio—Douglas had considerable strength, especially in their southern counties, populated largely by settlers from the South. Although slavery was an issue everywhere, it was not always the dominant concern. Pennsylvanians were more interested in tariff protection, while voters in Indiana, Ohio, and elsewhere in the Northwest wanted free land for settlers and internal improvements to expand commerce there. In addition, remnants of the anti-immigrant American Party lingered everywhere. The antislavery vote would undoubtedly go Republican, but that alone could not build a majority among such diverse constituencies.

• • •

LINCOLN'S FIRST TASK was to secure his hold on the Republican Party by conciliating and enlisting those who had fought him for the nomination—Chase, Seward, and Bates.

Chase was first approached to speak on behalf of Lincoln in the form of *"a mere printed circular."* He felt, he later admitted, "not a little hurt & [his] first impulse was not to reply at all." Then a personal letter from Lincoln arrived. Ignoring newspaper reports that Chase was "much chagrined and much dissatisfied with the nomination of so obscure a man as Mr. Abe Lincoln," Lincoln graciously chose to construe Chase's formal congratulatory letter as a symbol of his willingness to help. "Holding myself the humblest of all whose names were before the convention," Lincoln wrote Chase, "I feel in especial need of the assistance of all; and I am glad—very glad—of the indication that you stand ready." His ego soothed, Chase spoke at numerous Republican gatherings in Ohio, Indiana, and Michigan during the weeks that followed. Though he harbored a lasting bitterness toward the Ohio delegation, he affirmed his hopes for the nation, arguing "first, that the Republican party is an inevitable party; secondly, that it grows out of the circumstances of the country; thirdly, that it proposes no measure which can be injurious to the true interests of the people."

The formation of the Constitutional Union Party had made the support of Edward Bates vital to Lincoln. The party had enlisted many of the Missouri statesman's old Whig supporters, and included many old Know Nothings. To engage the elder statesman's support, Lincoln's old friend Orville Browning called on Bates at his St. Louis home. Browning was in the best position to persuade Bates to help the Republican cause, since he had supported Bates's presidential bid until the Illinois delegation, of which he was a member, had pledged itself to Lincoln. During their conversation, Bates "declined to take the stump" but promised to pen a public letter supporting Lincoln, even though he was aware, he said later, that in doing so, he would "probably give offense to some members of the *Constitutional Union party.*"

True to his word, Bates produced a letter for Browning to publish in which he praised Lincoln lavishly, positioned him as a conservative, and affirmed his own determination to support the Republican ticket. "I give my opinion freely in favor of Mr. Lincoln," Bates wrote. "I consider Mr. Lincoln a sound, safe, national man. He could not be sectional if he tried. His birth, his education, the habits of his life, and his geographical position, compel him to be national." What was more, Bates continued, Lincoln had "earned a high reputation for truth, courage, candor, morals and ability so that, as a man, he is most trustworthy. And in this particular, he is

more entitled to our esteem [than] some other men, his equals, who had
far better opportunities and aids in early life." Later in the campaign Bates
wrote of Lincoln: "His character is marked by a happy mixture of amiabil-
ity and courage; and while I expect him to be as mild as Fillmore, I equally
expect him to be as firm as Jackson."

While Lincoln worked to enlist the cooperation of all his rivals, he
knew that the active support of William Henry Seward would be pivotal to
his campaign. Seward's following among Republicans had brought him to
the edge of nomination. His reverberant phrase making—"irrepressible
conflict," "higher law than the Constitution"—though too flammable for
some, had emblazoned the banners and helped define the Republican
cause. The 35 electoral votes in his home state of New York might well
prove the key to victory. And for Lincoln it did not bode well that Seward
had returned to New York in the wake of the convention to find many of
his supporters disillusioned and dispirited by the prospect of any other
candidate.

"The campaign started heavily," Kansas delegate Addison Procter recalled. "Enthusiasm was lacking and conditions were getting more and
more desperate." Hoping to organize a Lincoln Club in Kansas, Procter
approached one of the state's most respected Republicans and asked him to
preside. The man vehemently refused: "You fellows knew at Chicago what
this country is facing. . . . You knew that it will take the very best ability we
can produce to pull us through. You knew that above everything else, these
times demanded a statesman and you have gone and given us a *rail splitter.*
No, I will not preside or attend."

"My personal feelings have been so much disturbed by the result at
Chicago," Charles Sumner wrote, "that I cannot yet appreciate it as a public act." There is but "one & only one thing consoles me," Michigan Republican George Pomeroy told Seward—"our chance of being defeated
this time and *your* sure chance of a nomination in '64." Treasury agent
William Mellen of Ohio expressed his disbelief to Frances Seward that
Abraham Lincoln was presented as "the suitable man for the Presidency.
The rail-candidate forsooth! I confess to a disposition to *rail* at him, &
much more at the Convention for its self-stultification. . . . What is to be
feared is the utter disintegration of the Republican party as a consequence
of this abandonment of principle for mere expediency."

Though Seward had pledged his support to the Republican ticket in
a public letter, he was so dejected in the aftermath of his defeat that he
considered resigning immediately from the Senate. Without the onerous
demands of the congressional session, he could remain in Auburn, surrounded by his loving family and consoling friends. "When I went out to

market this morning," he told one friend, "I had the rare experience of a man walking about town, after he is dead, and hearing what people would say of him. I confess I was unprepared for so much real grief, as I heard expressed at every corner."

But he understood that a decision to resign would look petulant and would, as his friend Israel Washburn warned, "give the malignants" an opportunity to damage him further. In the end, he determined to return to Washington in late May to complete his Senate term. The journey back to Capitol Hill "in the character of a leader deposed by [his] own party" was agonizing for him, however, as he admitted in a long letter to Frances. "I arrived here on Tuesday night. Preston King, with a carriage, met me at the depot, and conveyed me to my home. It seemed sad and mournful." Even the pictures hanging on the wall, "Dr. Nott's benevolent face, Lord Napier's complacent one, Jefferson's benignant one, and Lady Napier's loving one, seemed all like pictures of the dead." When he reached the Senate, "good men came through the day to see me. . . . Their eyes fill with tears. . . . They console themselves with the vain hope of a day of 'vindication;' and my letters all talk of the same thing. But they awaken no response in my heart." His only solace, he told her, was the realization that "responsibility has passed away from me, and that the shadow of it grows shorter every day."

Frances was delighted at the thought of her husband's permanent return to their Auburn home when his Senate term ended the following March. "You have earned the right to a peaceful old age," she assured him; "35 years of the best part of a mans life is all that his country can reasonably claim." This was not the time, however, for Seward to fade contentedly from public life. Weed's report of his visit with Lincoln perhaps roused Seward's own resolve. To withdraw from this fight would be an abdication of his fierce political ambition and his belief in the Republican cause.

In the weeks that followed the convention, Seward was overwhelmed with speaking requests from dozens of Republican committees throughout the North. "Your services are more necessary to the cause than they ever were," Charles Francis Adams wrote. "And your own reputation will gain more of permanency from the becoming manner with which you meet this disappointment, than it would from all the brilliancy of the highest success."

"I am content to quit with the political world, when it proposes to quit with me," Seward told Weed in late June. "But I am not insensible to the claims of a million of friends, nor indifferent to the opinion of mankind. All that seems to me clear, just now, is that it would not be wise to rush in at the beginning of the canvass, and so seem, most falsely, to fear that I shall be forgotten. Later in the canvass, it may be seen that I am wanted for the public interest." So he delayed, while entreaties to join streamed in, finally committing himself to an electioneering tour in nine states in late August and early September. The announcement that Seward "was about to take the platform and open the campaign for Lincoln," Addison Procter recalled, "was our first gleam of sunshine from out of the depths of discouragement."

• • •

WHILE SEWARD PREPARED for his grand tour, Lincoln remained in Springfield. In deference to political tradition and to his own judgment that further public statements could only damage his prospects, he decided against a personal speaking tour. Recognizing that his cluttered law office could not accommodate the flood of visitors eager to see him, he moved his headquarters to the governor's reception room at the State House.

Initially, Lincoln's sole assistant was John Nicolay, a twenty-eight-year-old German-American immigrant who had worked for three years as a clerk in the secretary of state's office. Lincoln had often visited the serious-minded Nicolay when searching out the latest election figures maintained in the office. After the convention, Lincoln had asked Nicolay to be his private secretary, "a call to service," Nicolay's daughter, Helen, later noted, "that lasted until his hair grew white and the powers of life ran down."

With Nicolay's help, Lincoln answered letters, received hundreds, perhaps thousands, of visitors from all parts of the North, talked with politicians, and contributed to a short campaign biography that sold more than a million copies. From his impromptu headquarters at the State House, Lincoln would engineer many aspects of his campaign. The telegraph wires allowed for fairly swift communication to political battlegrounds. Confidential messages were sent by mail, carried by personal emissaries, and given to political visitors. Most of these meetings are lost to history, but those that were recorded reveal Lincoln as a skillful politician, formulating and guiding his own campaign strategy.

"He sat down beside me on the sofa," wrote a correspondent from Utica, New York, "and commenced talking about political affairs in my own State with a knowledge of details which surprised me. I found that he was more conversant with some of our party performances in Oneida County than I could have desired." He "can not only discuss ably the great democratic principle of our Government," wrote a newspaperman from Missouri, "but at the same time tell how to navigate a vessel, maul a rail, or even to dress a deer-skin." Each correspondent's impression was quickly forwarded to the newspapers, the principal conduits between candidates and the public.

To counter the savage caricatures of Lincoln in Democratic papers as semiliterate, ignorant, an uncultured buffoon, homely, and awkward, Republican journalists were dispatched to Springfield to write positive stories about Lincoln, his educated wife, Mary, and their dignified home. Newspapers that had supported Seward swiftly transferred their allegiance to the new leader of the Republican Party, and utilized every occasion to extol their candidate and attack the opposition.

Lincoln and his team doubtless controlled the "line" out of Springfield that reverberated in Republican papers across the nation. After spending an evening at the Lincoln home, the correspondent from the *Utica Morning Herald* reported that "an air of quiet refinement pervaded the place. You would have known instantly that she who presided over that modest household was a true type of the American lady." As for Lincoln, "he has all the marks of a mind that scans closely, canvasses thoroughly, concludes deliberately, and holds to such conclusions unflinchingly."

"Ten thousand inquiries will be made as to the looks, the habits, tastes and other characteristics of Honest Old Abe," the Chicago *Press and Tribune* wrote. "We anticipate a few of them. . . . Always clean, he is never fashionable; he is careless but not slovenly. . . . In his personal habits, Mr. Lincoln is as simple as a child . . . his food is plain and nutritious. He never drinks intoxicating liquors of any sort. . . . He is not addicted to tobacco. . . . If Mr. Lincoln is elected President, he will carry but little that is ornamental to the White House. The country must accept his sincerity, his ability and his honesty, in the mould in which they are cast. He will not be able to make as polite a bow as Frank Pierce, but he will not commence anew the agitation of the Slavery question by recommending to Congress any Kansas-Nebraska bills. He may not preside at the Presidential dinners with the ease and grace which distinguish the 'venerable public functionary,' Mr. Buchanan; but he will not create the necessity" for a congressional committee to investigate corruption in his administration.

The visiting correspondents from Republican papers had nothing but praise for Mary. "Whatever of awkwardness may be ascribed to her husband, there is none of it in her," a journalist from the *New York Evening Post* wrote. "She converses with freedom and grace, and is thoroughly *au fait* in all the little amenities of society." Frequent mention was made of her distinguished Kentucky relatives, her sophisticated education, her ladylike courtesy, her ability to speak French fluently, her son's enrollment in Harvard College, and her membership in the Presbyterian Church. Mrs. Lincoln is "a very handsome woman, with a vivacious and graceful manner," another reporter observed; "an interesting and often sparkling talker."

Reporters were fascinated by the contrast between a cultured woman from a refined background and the self-made rough-hewn Lincoln. Party leaders began to cultivate the legend of Lincoln that would permeate the entire campaign and, indeed, evolve into the present day. He was depicted as "a Man of the People," an appealing political title after the rustic Andrew Jackson first supplanted the Eastern elites who had occupied the presidency for the forty years from Washington through John Quincy Adams.

The log cabin was emblematic of the dignity of honest, common, impoverished origins ever since William Henry Harrison had been triumphantly dubbed the "log-cabin, hard-cider" candidate twenty years earlier. Harrison had merely been posed in front of a log cabin. Lincoln had actually been born in one. One Republican worker wrote: "It has also afforded me sincere pleasure to think of Mr. Lincoln taking possession of the White House; he, who was once the inmate of the log cabin—were he the pampered, effeminated child of fortune, no such pleasing emotions would be inspired." Answering the charge that Lincoln would be a "nullity," the *New York Tribune* suggested that a "man who by his own genius and force of character has raised himself from being a penniless and uneducated flat boatman on the Wabash River to the position Mr. Lincoln now occupies is not likely to be a nullity anywhere."

This aura of the Western man, the man of the prairie, had been reinforced during the Chicago convention, when Republicans paraded through the streets carrying the rails Lincoln had supposedly split. Although Lincoln—Honest Abe—was careful not to verify that any particular rail had been his handiwork, in one interview he held a rail aloft and said: "here is a stick I received a day or two since from Josiah Crawford. . . . He writes me that it is a part of one of the rails that I cut for him in 1825."

Lincoln was aware that being "a Man of the People" was an advantage, especially in the raw and growing Western states critical to the election of a Republican candidate. Prior to the campaign, he had reinforced this politically potent image with descriptions of his poor schooling, years of poverty, and manual labor. Although his grim beginnings held no fascination for him, Lincoln was astute enough to capitalize upon this invaluable political asset.

From the outset, he decided that "it would be both imprudent, and contrary to the reasonable expectation of friends for me to write, or speak anything upon doctrinal points now. Besides this, my published speeches contain nearly all I could willingly say." When his friend Leonard Swett asked his approval of a letter expressing the candidate's sentiments, Lincoln replied, "Your letter, written to go to N.Y. is . . . substantially right." However, he advised, "Burn this, not that there is any thing wrong in it; but because it is best not to be known that I write at all." He recognized that anything he said would be scanned scrupulously for partisan purposes. The slightest departure from the printed record would be distorted by friends as well as enemies. Even his simple reiteration of a previous position might, in the midst of a campaign, give it new emphasis. He preferred to point simply to the party platform that he had endorsed. His few lapses justified his fears. A facetious comment to a Democratic reporter that "he would like to go into Kentucky to discuss issues but was afraid of being lynched" was made into a campaign issue.

Underlying this policy of self-restraint was another important but unvoiced political reality: Lincoln had to maintain the cohesion of the new Republican Party, a coalition of old Democrats, former Whigs, and members of the nativist American Party. Informing a Jewish friend that he had never entered a Know Nothing lodge, as accused by Democrats, he cautioned that "our adversaries think they can gain a point, if they could force me to openly deny this charge, by which some degree of offence would be given to the Americans. For this reason, it must not publicly appear that I am paying any attention to the charge." Although Lincoln himself had disavowed any sympathy with the nativists, and had actually invested in a German paper, many Republicans remained hostile to immigrants, and their support was essential.

Lincoln knew this election would not be determined by a single issue. While opposition to slavery extension had led to the creation of the Republican Party and dominated the national debate, in many places other issues took precedence. In Pennsylvania, the leading iron producer in the nation, and in New Jersey, the desire for a protective tariff was stronger than hostility to slavery. In the West, especially among immigrant groups, multitudes hoped for homestead legislation providing free or cheap land to new settlers, many of whom had been hard hit by the Panic of 1857. "Land for the Landless" was the battle cry. And when, in the midst of the campaign, President Buchanan vetoed a mild Homestead Act, many in Indiana and throughout the West turned to Lincoln. All of these issues had been carefully addressed in the Republican Party platform. Had the election been fought on the single issue of slavery, it is likely that Lincoln would have lost.

• • •

WHILE LINCOLN KEPT a strategic silence in Springfield, Seward stepped forward to speak on public issues and provide the drama and excitement of the campaign. Traveling by train, steamboat, and carriage with an entourage (which included Fanny and her friend Ellen Perry; Charles Francis Adams and his son, Charles Junior; along with a contingent of politicians), Seward opened his tour in Michigan. From there, he proceeded west to Wisconsin and Minnesota, south to Iowa and Kansas, and east to Illinois and Ohio.

At every stop, Seward was met with "cannons, brass bands, and processions of torch-bearing 'Wide Awakes' "—young Republicans dressed in striking oilcloth capes and caps—who generated enthusiasm for the party. They created a circus atmosphere at Republican rallies, surrounding the perimeter of crowds and marching in meandering, illuminated processions. One such march took several hours to pass the Lincoln house in Springfield. "Viewed from an elevated position, it wound its sinuous track over a length of two miles, seeming, in its blazing lights and glittering uniforms, like a beautiful serpent of fire," wrote John Hay. "The companies . . . ignited vast quantities of Roman candles, and as the drilled battalions moved steadily on, canopied and crowded with a hissing and bursting blaze of fiery splendor . . . the enthusiasm of the people broke out in wild cheerings." Other candidates mustered marching clubs, but with less success. One group of Douglas partisans designated themselves the "Choloroformers," ready and able to "put the Wide Awakes to sleep."

Fifty thousand people gathered to hear Seward speak in Detroit, and the fervor only increased as his tour moved west. Thousands waited past midnight for the arrival of his train in Kalamazoo, and when he disembarked, crowds followed him along the streets to the place where he would sleep that night. The next day, thousands more assembled on the village green to enjoy a brilliant "procession of young men and women on horseback, all well mounted, children with banners, men with carts and wagons," that preceded the formal speeches. Still craving more, the crowd followed the entourage back to the train station, where Seward appeared at the window to speak again. To the discomfort of the elder Charles Francis Adams, Seward suggested that he, too, stick his head out of the window for some final words. "All of this reminded me of a menagerie," Adams confessed in his diary, "where each of the beasts, beginning with the lion, is passed in review before a gaping crowd."

In St. Paul, Minnesota, a correspondent reported, Seward's arrival was "a day ever memorable in the political history of our State." Early in the morning, the streets were "alive with people—the pioneer, the backwoodsman, the trapper, the hunter, the trader from the Red River," all of them standing in wonder as a "magnificent Lincoln and Hamlin pole" was raised. A procession of bands and carriages heralded the arrival of Seward, who spoke for nearly two hours on the front steps of the Capitol.

Reporters marveled at Seward's ability to make every speech seem spontaneous and vital, "without repetition of former utterances," surpassing "the ordinary stump speech in fervency . . . literary quality, elevation of thought, and great enthusiasm on the part of the auditors." It often appeared "the whole population of the surrounding country had turned out to greet him," one correspondent noted. "Gov. Seward, you are doing more for Lincoln's election than any hundred men in the United States," a judge on board the Mississippi boat told him. "Well, I ought to," Seward replied.

Charles Francis Adams, Jr., who was twenty-five at the time, could not figure "where, when, or how" Seward was able to prepare "the really remarkable speeches he delivered in rapid succession," for "the consumption of liquors and cigars" during the journey was excessive. "When it came to drinking, Seward was, for a man of sixty, a free liver; and at times his brandy-and-water would excite him, and set his tongue going with dangerous volubility; but I never saw him more affected than that—never approaching drunkenness. He simply liked the stimulus." Amazingly, Adams remarked, despite Seward's drinking, his capacity for work was unimpaired.

Young Adams was mesmerized by Seward, whom he considered the most "delightful traveling companion" imaginable. "The early morning sun shone on Seward, wrapped in a strange and indescribable Syrian cashmere cloak, and my humble self, puffing our morning cigars," Adams recorded in his diary after an overnight journey by rail to Quincy, Illinois. The two smokers had adjourned to the baggage car, "having rendered ourselves," in Seward's words, " 'independent on this tobacco question.' "

Seward's grand tour received extensive coverage, complete with excerpts from his speeches, in newspapers across the land. From Maine, Israel Washburn wrote that he was astonished at the "integrity & versatility" of the speeches. He considered the speech in Detroit "the most perfect & philosophical—the St. Paul the broadest, the Dubuque the warmest, the Chicago the most practical & effective . . . but, of all the speeches . . . I like the short one at Madison—it seems to me to be the most comprehensive & complete, the grandest & highest."

At home in Auburn, Frances Seward received dozens of letters praising her husband's performance. "I am sure you must be most happy," Seward's old friend Richard Blatchford wrote. "He has shown throughout a depth of power, eloquence & resonance of thought and mind, which we here who know him so well, are not a little taken a-back by." Sumner told

Frances that as he read each speech, he "marveled more & more. I know nothing like such a succession of speeches by any American." Frances took pride in her husband's accomplishments but simultaneously recognized that his great success had eclipsed the possibility he would soon retire to private life in Auburn. "Yes Henry is very popular now," she wrote Sumner. "He is monopolized by the public and I am at last—resigned—Is that the word."

On October 1, en route to Chicago, Seward's train made a brief stop in Springfield. "There was a rush into and about the windows of the car in which Mr. Seward was seated," observed a correspondent. Lincoln and Trumbull had waited with the crowd and came aboard to pay their respects. Lincoln "was a revelation," young Adams recorded in his diary. "There he was, tall, shambling, plain and good-natured. He seemed shy to a degree, and very awkward in manner; as if he felt out of place, and had a realizing sense that properly the positions should be reversed. Seward too appeared constrained." Adams undoubtedly ascribed his own feelings to Lincoln, who most likely did not feel "out of place" at all.

This was the first time Lincoln and Seward had met since the evening they spent together in Massachusetts in 1848. "Twelve years ago you told me that this cause would be successful," Lincoln told him, referring to the antislavery crusade, "and ever since I have believed that it would be."

During their conversation, Lincoln asked Seward if he would be willing in his upcoming Chicago speech to address a certain problematic subject: John Wentworth, now the mayor of Chicago, was continually making references to an argument the party was trying to avoid—that a Republican win would bring an eventual end to slavery altogether. Knowing Wentworth was set to introduce Seward, Lincoln asked the New Yorker to reassure the audience that Republicans "would not interfere with slavery where it already existed." Seward readily agreed and made it clear in his speech that Republicans were not attacking slavery in the South, that securing freedom for the territories need not interrupt ordinary intercourse with the South. In distancing themselves from Northern abolitionists, the Lincoln team was far more concerned with reassuring Northern conservatives than with conciliating the South.

Seward's tour came to a triumphant close on October 6. His train pulled into Auburn, where a "noisy throng" gave him a warm welcome home. "Seward, in fact, never appeared so well as at home," young Adams observed. "He walked the streets exchanging greetings with everyone." His responses were "all genuine, the relations were kindly, unaffected, neighborly." Seward's return created "an impression of individuality approaching greatness." It was a journey Adams would never forget.

Although Lincoln himself made no public statements or speeches, he labored constantly on his campaign and fully justified Weed's appraisal of his political acumen. He strove to hold his coalition together, while disrupting efforts of his opponents to unite on fusion tickets. He sent emissaries to his supporters with instructions to solve campaign problems and heal divisions. Indirectly, he sought to clarify his position on important issues without breaking his vow of silence. He rigorously abstained from making patronage commitments. Responding to Senator Trumbull's suggestion that he make some pledges in New York, Lincoln replied, "Remembering that Peter denied his Lord with an oath, after most solemnly protesting that he never would, I will not swear I will make no committals; but I do think I will not."

Despite the unremitting, consuming labor of organizing his campaign, Lincoln somehow found time to write a humorous fictional dialogue between Breckinridge and Douglas. He also answered many of the endless letters he received, writing personal, unpretentious replies to supporters and well-wishers of every kind. An author wishing to dedicate his new legal work to Lincoln was answered: "I give the leave, begging only that the inscription may be in modest terms, not representing me as a man of great learning, or a very extraordinary one in any respect." In mid-October, he replied to eleven-year-old Grace Bedell, who had recommended that he grow a beard, "for your face is so thin" and "all the ladies like whiskers." After lamenting the fact that he had no daughter of his own, he wondered: "As to the whiskers, having never worn any, do you not think people would call it a piece of silly affection if I were to begin it now?" Nonetheless, he proceeded to grow a beard. By January 1861, John Hay would pen a witty couplet: "Election news Abe's hirsute fancy warrant—Apparent hair becomes heir apparent."

Recognizing that much of the positive news he received from friends was biased, Lincoln implored his supporters to give straightforward accounts of his prospects in each state. He worried about reports from Maine, New York, and Chicago, and brooded over the lack of solid information from Pennsylvania. His political objectives in the Keystone State were to establish his soundness on the tariff issue and heal the ominous divisions between the followers of Cameron and Curtin, the gubernatorial candidate. Lincoln always understood the importance of what he described as "the dry, and irksome labor" of building organizations to get out the vote, while most politicians preferred "parades, and shows, and monster meetings."

He enthusiastically supported Carl Schurz's "excellent plan" for mobilizing the German-American vote, and assured Schurz that "your having supported Gov. Seward, in preference to myself in the convention, is not even remembered by me for any practical purpose . . . to the extent of our limited acquaintance, no man stands nearer my heart than yourself." A large part of the German-American vote would go to Lincoln, aiding his victories in the Northwest.

Although concerned with progress in all the Northern states, he focused his attention primarily on the critical West. He urged Caleb Smith to do his utmost in Indiana, believing that nothing would affect the November results in Illinois more strongly than the momentum provided by an Indiana victory in the October state elections. In July, he sent Nicolay to an Indiana supporter who wished to prevent a Bell ticket from being placed on the ballot. "Ascertain what he wants," Lincoln instructed Nicolay. "On what subjects he would converse with me. And the particulars if he will give them. Is an interview indispensable? Tell him my motto is 'Fairness to all,' but commit me to nothing."

Having pledged to make no new statement on public issues, Lincoln had surrogates present excerpts from his previous speeches to reinforce his positions. He had Judge Davis show Cameron selections of pro-tariff speeches he had made in the 1840s, and then cautioned Cameron: "Before this reaches you, my very good friend, Judge Davis, will have called upon you, and, perhaps, shown you the 'scraps.' . . . Nothing about these, must get into the news-papers." This tone reveals Lincoln's keen awareness that notes from unpublished thirteen-year-old speeches stretched his vow of silence, but he hoped the assurances they provided would corral Cameron's powerful influence in Pennsylvania. Cameron replied that he was pleased by the content of Lincoln's earlier writings.

To a correspondent who sought his intervention in the discord between Cameron and Curtin, Lincoln replied: "I am slow to listen to criminations among friends, and never expose their quarrels on either side . . . allow by-gones to be by-gones, and look to the present & future only." Yet at the same time, he informed Leonard Swett, who was preparing a trip to Pennsylvania, that he was very concerned about former congressman Joseph Casey's disclosures that the Cameron faction lacked confidence in the Pennsylvania Central Committee, controlled by Curtin. "Write Mr. Casey," Lincoln urged, "suggest to him that great caution and delicacy of action, is necessary in that matter." Meanwhile, Republican money flowed into Pennsylvania. "After all," wrote Republican National Committeeman John Goodrich of Massachusetts, "Pennsylvania is the Sebastopol we must take."

Lincoln turned his political attention to every state where his campaign experienced difficulty. Hearing that two Republican seats might be lost in Maine's September elections, he told his vice presidential mate, Hannibal Hamlin, that "such a result . . . would, I fear, put us on the down-hill track, lose us the State elections in Pennsylvania and Indiana, and probably ruin us on the main turn in November. You must not allow it." In August, troubled by a letter received from Rhode Island "intimating that Douglas is inlisting some rich men there, who know how to use money, and that it is endangering the State," Lincoln asked Rhode Island's senator James Simmons, "How is this? Please write me." In the end, the September elections in New England favored the Republicans, preparing the way for the great October contests in the West.

Lincoln was not alone in his assessment that the October state elections in Indiana and Pennsylvania would prove critical to the fortunes of the Republican Party. On the eve of the state elections, Judge Davis told his son that "tomorrow is the most important day in the history of the Country." Lincoln's camp was elated by the positive results as large Republican majorities piled up in both states. When Judge Davis first heard the exciting news, Ward Lamon reported back to Lincoln, "he was trying an important criminal case, which terminated in his Kicking over the Clerk's desk, turned a double somersault and adjourned court until after the presidential Election." If the three-hundred-pound Davis actually performed such a stunt, it was a miracle second only to Lincoln's nomination. But there was no question that Davis was thrilled. "We are all in the highest glee on acct of the elections," he wrote his wife, Sarah. "Mr. Lincoln will evidently be the next Pres't." That Saturday night, Davis traveled to Springfield to celebrate with the Lincolns, Trumbull, and Governor Corwin. "I never was better entertained," he rejoiced, though he confessed that Mary was still "not to my liking." She appears to be "in high feather," he continued. "I am in hopes that she will not give her husband any trouble."

Mary reveled in her newfound celebrity. She delighted in the crowds of visitors coming to her house, the artists pleading to paint her husband's portrait, the prominent politicians waiting for the chance to converse with the presidential nominee. With pride, and perhaps a shade of spite toward the man who had so often bested her husband, she noted that a reception for Stephen Douglas in Springfield had attracted only thirty people when hundreds were expected. "This rather looks as if his greatness had passed away," she commented to a friend.

Still, Mary remained terribly anxious that ultimate success might once again prove elusive. "You used to be worried, that I took politics so cooly," she confessed to her friend Hannah Shearer; "you would not do so, were you to see me now. Whenever I *have time*, to think, my mind is sufficiently exercised for my comfort . . . I scarcely know, how I would bear up, under defeat. I trust that we will not have the trial."

For weeks, Stephen Douglas had been barnstorming the country, having decided immediately after his nomination to defy custom. Disregarding criticism that his unbecoming behavior diminished the "high office of the presidency . . . to the level of a county clerkship," he stumped the country, from the New England states to the Northwest, from the border states to the South, becoming "the first presidential candidate in American history to make a nationwide tour in person."

Douglas was in Cedar Rapids, Iowa, when he heard the news of the Republican victories in Indiana and Pennsylvania, which destroyed any hope he might have had for victory. "Mr. Lincoln is the next President," he declared. "We must try to save the Union. I will go South." It was a courageous move, his "finest hour," according to Allan Nevins. Exhausted from his nonstop weeks of campaigning, Douglas faced one hostile audience after another as he moved into the Deep South. No longer hoping to gain support for his candidacy, he campaigned for the survival of the Union. "I believe there is a conspiracy on foot to break up this Union," he warned an audience in Montgomery, Alabama. "It is the duty of every good citizen to frustrate the scheme . . . if Lincoln is elected, he must be inaugurated."

Douglas understood what the Republicans failed to see—that Southerners were serious in their threats to secede from the Union if Lincoln won the election. "The cardinal error of the Republicans," Nevins writes, was their failure to deal candidly with "the now imminent danger of secession." Their dismissal of the looming possibility of secession was in part, but only in part, a deliberate tactic to ignore the threat so that voters would not be scared away from the Republican ticket. Beyond that, they simply did not believe that the threat was serious. After all, the South had made similar threats intermittently for the past forty years. Charles Francis Adams, Jr., later admitted, "we all dwelt in a fool's Paradise." Though Northern Republicans had undoubtedly seen the threatening editorials in Southern newspapers, they continued to believe, as Lincoln told a journalist friend, that the movement was simply "a sort of political game of bluff, gotten up by politicians, and meant solely to frighten the North."

In mid-August, Lincoln assured one of his supporters, John Fry, that "people of the South have too much of good sense, and good temper, to attempt the ruin of the government." Many in the South were equally skeptical. A Tennessee editor later admitted that "the cry of disunion had been raised so often that few had taken it seriously during the campaign. Evidently the 'Northern sectionalists' had believed it to be 'all talk' . . . while most intelligent Southerners had assumed that it was 'an idle menace, made to sway Northern sentiment.' "

Bates likewise shrugged off Southern threats as the desperation of belligerent politicians, while Seward openly scorned the taunts of secession: "they cry out that they will tear the Union to pieces . . . 'Who's afraid?' Nobody's afraid." His audience echoed: "Nobody!" Among Lincoln's colleagues, only Frank Blair, Jr., recognized that the distortions of Lincoln's speeches in the Southern papers and the "misrepresentations" of extremists who intimated the Republicans intended an attack on the South had created "a large and influential class who are even now ready to apply the torch which will light the fires of civil discord." Still, Blair believed, these extremists would not succeed and "this glorious Union" would not "be sundered in consequence of the triumph of our party." Even John Breckinridge, the South's standard-bearer, sought to distance himself from Southern extremists. His sole campaign speech refuted charges that he favored splitting up the Union.

The realization that the "irrepressible conflict" might prove more than rhetoric came too late. The divided house would indeed fall. These phrases, intended by Seward and Lincoln as historical prophecies, were perceived by many in the South as threats—imminent and meant to be answered.

With the October elections, the campaign had gained decisive momentum, but it was not yet over. With four candidates dividing the vote, Lincoln would have to capture New York's pivotal 35 electoral votes to win an electoral majority and avoid throwing the election into the House. He relied on Thurlow Weed to manage the campaign in New York, but continued to seek other perspectives and intelligence. "I have a good deal of news from New-York," Lincoln told former congressman John Pettit, "but, of course, it is from *friends*, and is one-sided. . . . It would seem that assurances to this point could not be better than I have. And yet it *may* be delusive."

The Empire State posed unique problems for Republicans. New York was home to large numbers of traditionally Democratic Irish immigrants who were unfriendly to the antislavery cause. In addition, New York City contained an influential class of merchants and manufacturers who viewed Republicanism as a threat to their commercial relations with the South. If these groups united against Lincoln, and if, as the Douglas people believed, Seward's partisans remained unreconciled to Lincoln's nomination, New York could easily be lost.

Lincoln recognized these complications from the outset, warning Weed in August that "there will be the most extraordinary effort ever

made, to carry New-York for Douglas." He feared that Douglas was "managing the Bell-element with great adroitness," and might well obtain a fusion of the two forces, thereby keeping the state from the Republicans.
Less worried than Lincoln, Weed nonetheless left nothing to chance. He
wrote to Seward in late October from the Astor House in New York City:
"Can you afford to make a *soothing* speech in this city? . . . A speech in the
spirit that you delivered last in the Senate, showing that it is the business of
Republicans and the mission of the Republican Party to preserve the
Union . . . that there is not an aggressive Plank in the Republican Platform. . . . I think it would finish the work." Seward agreed to come to New
York at once. His speech, even in this Democratic stronghold, was punctu-
ated by wild applause, and when he finished, "the whole audience broke
forth into the most tumultuous cheering."

• • •

ON ELECTION DAY, November 6, 1860, the citizens of Springfield were
awakened at sunrise by cannonade and rousing band music "to stir whatever sluggish spirits there might be among the populace." Lincoln spent
the morning in his quarters at the State House, receiving and entertaining
visitors. Samuel Weed of the *New York Times* long remembered the atmosphere in the room that morning. Lincoln "was chatting with three or four
friends as calmly and as amiably as if he had started on a picnic." Tipping
his armchair backward to prop his long legs atop the woodstove, he made
such detailed inquiry into all the local races that "one would have concluded that the District Attorneyship of a county of Illinois was of far more
importance than the Presidency."

Lincoln had originally declined to vote himself, believing that "the candidate for a Presidential office ought not to vote for his own electors," but
Herndon insisted that if he cut off the presidential electors at the top, he
could still vote for all the state and local offices. Warming to the idea, Lincoln headed over at about three o'clock to the polling place at the courthouse. His appearance drew a large crowd, "who welcomed him with
immense cheering, and followed him in dense numbers along the hall and
up stairs into the Court room," where he was hailed with another wild
"burst of enthusiasm."

At five, he headed home to have supper with Mary and the boys, returning to the State House at seven, accompanied by Judge Davis and a few
friends. An immense crowd followed him into the Capitol, leading one
supporter to suggest that he ask everyone but his closest friends to withdraw. "He said he had never done such a thing in his life, and wouldn't
commence now." When the polls had closed, the first dispatches began to

filter into the telegraph office. A correspondent from the *Missouri Democrat* noted that throughout the evening, "Lincoln was calm and collected as ever in his life, but there was a nervous twitch on his countenance when the messenger from the telegraphic offices entered that revealed an anxiety within that no coolness from without could repress." The first dispatch, indicating a strong Republican win in Decatur, Illinois, was "borne into the Assembly hall as a trophy of victory, to be read to the crowd," who responded with great shouts of joy. Though the early returns were incomplete, it was observed that Lincoln "seemed to understand their bearing on the general result in the State and commented upon every return by way of comparison with previous elections."

By nine o'clock, as tallies were relayed from distant states, Lincoln, Davis, and a few friends gathered at the telegraph office for immediate access to the returns. While Lincoln reclined on a sofa, the telegraph tapped out good news all around. New England, the Northwest, Indiana, and Pennsylvania had all come into the Republican camp. When ten o'clock arrived, however, with no word from New York, Lincoln grew fretful. "The news would come quick enough if it was good," he told his cohorts that "and if bad, he was not in any hurry to hear it."

Finally, at 11:30, a message came from New York. "We have made steady gains everywhere throughout the State, but the city returns are not sufficiently forward to make us sure of the result, although we are quite sanguine a great victory has been won." The dispatch produced tremendous cheers. Minutes later, Lyman Trumbull came running into the room: "Uncle Abe, you're the next President, and I know it." Lincoln was still uncertain, for if the Democrats piled up huge majorities in New York City, the Republican votes in the rest of the state could be offset. "Not too fast, my friends," he said. "Not too fast, it may not be over yet."

At midnight, Lincoln attended a "victory" supper prepared by the Republican ladies. While everyone else was in high spirits, assured of victory, Lincoln remained anxious about New York. Too often in the past his dreams had collapsed at the last moment. Without New York's 35 electoral votes, his total of 145 electoral votes would be 7 short of a majority.

Lincoln's concerns proved groundless, for Thurlow Weed's unparalleled organization had been at work since dawn, rounding up Republican voters in every precinct. "Don't wait until the last hour," Weed had instructed his workers. "Consider every man a 'delinquent' who doesn't vote before 10 o'clock." He left his organization plenty of time to prod, push, and, if necessary, carry voters to the polls.

Soon after midnight, the returns from New York and Brooklyn came in, revealing that Democratic control of New York City was not enough to counter the Republican vote throughout the state. Celebrations could begin in earnest, for Lincoln's victory was accomplished.

Church bells began to ring. Cheers for "Old Abe" resounded through the streets. Lincoln was jubilant, admitting that he was "a very happy man . . . who could help being so under such circumstances?" Pocketing the final dispatch, he headed home to tell Mary, who had been waiting anxiously all day. "Mary, Mary," he cried out, *we are elected!*"

CHAPTER 10

"AN INTENSIFIED CROSSWORD PUZZLE"

B Y THE TIME LINCOLN got to bed, it was two o'clock. He was exhausted but could not sleep. "The excitement which had kept him up through the campaign had passed away," he later recalled to Gideon Welles, "and he was oppressed with the load of responsibility that was upon him." Outside his windows, he could hear the citizens of Springfield partying in the streets, laughing, singing, and marching until they could carry on no longer. With the arrival of dawn, they finally dispersed to their homes.

Undoubtedly, Lincoln shared the elation of his neighbors. From his earliest days in politics, he had craved the opportunity to accomplish important deeds that would benefit his fellows. In modern parlance, he wanted to make a difference and now he had the opportunity to do so. Yet, keenly aware of both the fractious nature of the youthful Republican Party and the ominous threats from the South, he understood that his country was entering a most perilous time.

"I began at once to feel that I needed support," he noted later; "others to share with me the burden." As the exhausted townsfolk shuffled back to their homes and the city sank "into its usual quietness," Lincoln began to compose his official family—the core of his administration. "This was on Wednesday morning," he revealed, "and before the sun went down, I had made up my Cabinet. It was almost the same as I finally selected."

On a blank card he wrote the names of the seven men he wanted. At the center of his list stood his chief rivals for the nomination—Seward, Chase, and Bates. The list also included Montgomery Blair, Gideon Welles, and Norman Judd, all former Democrats, as well as William Dayton of New Jersey, a former Whig. While several months would pass before the cabinet was assembled, subjecting Lincoln to intense pressures from all sides, he resolved that day to surround himself with the strongest men from every faction of the new Republican Party—former Whigs, Free-Soilers, and antislavery Democrats.

The stillness of this first day that allowed Lincoln to contemplate the formulation of his ideal cabinet proved to be the calm before the storm. Soon, "the mad scramble" for the lesser positions began. With letters of recommendation stuffed in their pockets and fervent hopes in their hearts, hordes of office seekers descended on Springfield. Some arrived with "muddy boots and hickory shirts," while others were dressed in their finest linen and woolens. All were graciously welcomed by Lincoln.

He decided to hold two receptions a day, the first in the morning, the second in the late afternoon. The receptions were held in the Governor's Room in the State House, a chamber far too small for the constant crush of visitors pushing their way through the narrow doorway, guided by Lincoln's "clear voice and often ringing laughter." *New York Tribune* correspondent Henry Villard, although initially skeptical of Lincoln's qualifications to be president, observed that the president-elect "showed remarkable tact" with every caller. Listening patiently to each applicant, Lincoln revealed a quick-witted "adaptation to individual characteristics and peculiarities. He never evaded a proper question, or failed to give a fit answer." What most impressed Villard was Lincoln's remarkable ability to tell a humorous story or deliver an appropriate anecdote "to explain a meaning or enforce a point, the aptness of which was always perfect."

While the opposition papers derided Lincoln's penchant for telling stories, imagining that he babbled on from the moment he awakened—at mealtimes, on the street, in his office, in stores, even in his sleep (with Mary beside him in her nightcap)—the perceptive Villard understood that the president-elect's perpetual supply of stories "helped many times to heal wounded feelings and mitigate disappointments." Everyone Lincoln dealt with, Villard concluded, agreed that "he is the very embodiment of good temper and affability. They will all concede that he has a kind word, an encouraging smile, a humorous remark for nearly everyone that seeks his presence, and that but few, if any, emerge from his reception room without being strongly and favorably impressed with his general disposition."

At this juncture, Lincoln was sorely in need of a second assistant. Nicolay recommended twenty-two-year-old John Hay, the young journalist and Brown University graduate who had become actively involved in the campaign and had written pro-Lincoln columns for the *Missouri Democrat*. Nicolay had originally met Hay in private school. When Nicolay asked his boyhood friend to help with the overflowing correspondence, the gregarious young man was delighted. Though Hay was preparing for the bar in the Springfield office of his uncle Milton Hay, he was passionate about literature. On Class Day at Brown, he had delivered a poem that was remembered for years afterward. He had hoped quixotically to make his living as a poet upon graduation, but had reluctantly settled for a career in law. He leaped at the chance to work in the White House.

For Mary, Willie, and Tad, it was an exciting time. At night, after the formal receptions were over, visitors, sketch artists, and friends flocked to their home. Mary flourished in her role as hostess, while the boys regaled visitors with laughter and stories of their own. The ardent political conversations of celebrated men surely reminded Mary of childhood evenings when her father entertained congressmen and senators, including Henry Clay, in the parlor of his Kentucky mansion. To be sure, there were unpleasant moments, as when mud was tracked into the house, or when callers would point to Mary and boisterously ask: "Is that the old woman?" But Mary seemed to take it all in stride. Her delight in victory overshadowed such small aggravations.

Even as the Lincolns entertained their colorful parade of callers, the president-elect never lost sight of the intricate task he faced in building a cabinet that would preserve the integrity of the Republican Party in the North, while providing the fairest possible representation from the South. To help with his deliberations, he asked Hannibal Hamlin, his vice president–elect, to meet him in Chicago. Once the arrangements were made, he invited his old friend Joshua Speed to join him, and suggested that he bring his wife, Fanny, to keep Mary company. Traveling by train with a small party of journalists and friends, the Lincolns took up quarters at the Tremont House, which had lodged Davis and Swett six months earlier when they managed the unexpected nomination.

Although Hamlin had been a senator when Lincoln was in the House, this was the first time they would meet. Hamlin recalled listening to a speech Lincoln delivered that "was so full of good humor and sharp points" that the entire chamber "was convulsed with laughter." Born in Maine the same year as Lincoln, Hamlin was a tall, powerfully built man with a swarthy complexion. He had entered politics as a Jacksonian Democrat at a young age, serving first in the Maine state legislature, then in the U.S. House of Representatives, and finally in the Senate.

The two men began their discussions in Lincoln's room in the Tremont House, but news of their meeting soon brought "a great throng of visitors," necessitating a public reception and a round of dinners. The following day, however, their dialogue resumed privately at a friend's house, where Lincoln made clear his determination to create "a compact body" by drawing his former rivals into "his official household." Hamlin apparently agreed with this notion, and the conversation turned to selecting a representative from New England. Lincoln's original choice, Gideon Welles, was mentioned, along with Nathaniel Banks and Charles Francis Adams, Jr. Hamlin objected to Banks but agreed to look into the availability and feasibility of both Adams and Welles.

Amid the flood of political aspirants and tactical discussions, Lincoln must have coveted his time with Speed. He arranged for Fanny to visit with Mary so that he might speak with his old friend in private. Speed later recalled that Lincoln "threw himself on the bed" and said: "Speed what are your pecuniary Conditions—are you rich, or poor." Understanding the import of the question, Speed replied: "I think I know what you wish. I'll Speak Candidly to you—My pecuniary Conditions are good—I do not think you have any office within your gift that I can afford to take." Though Speed's resolve never wavered, the two friends would maintain contact during the war, and Speed would play an important role in keeping Kentucky in the Union.

While Lincoln was preoccupied with selecting his cabinet, Mary had a splendid time. She visited the scene of her husband's triumph at the Wigwam, toured the Custom House and the Post Office, and maintained her poise and charm at the large public reception accorded the president-elect and his wife.

Returning home, Lincoln corresponded with a wide range of politicians and listened carefully to their suggestions for his cabinet. In the end, however, he alone would solve what Nicolay's daughter, Helen, later described as "an intensified crossword puzzle in which party loyalty and service, personal fitness, geographical location and a dozen other factors have to be taken into account and made to harmonize."

From the start, Lincoln determined to give the highest place to Seward, "in view of his ability, his integrity, and his commanding influence." The presidency now unavailable, Seward never questioned that he deserved the premier post as secretary of state. Not only had he been the overwhelming favorite for the nomination, but he had vigorously campaigned for Lincoln in the general election and had helped to bring the critical state of New York to Lincoln's side.

"*Of course*, Mr. Lincoln will offer you the chief place in his Cabinet," Charles Francis Adams wrote Seward. "I trust no considerations will deter you from accepting it. . . . I know of no such faith existing in the competency of any other person." From Pennsylvania, Simon Cameron tendered a similar prediction. "You will be offered the State Dept. within a few days and you *must not* refuse it. The whole victory achieved by the labor of so many years, will be lost if you run away now. My whole ambition is to see you in the Presidency."

Lincoln agreed wholeheartedly with the presumption that Seward deserved first consideration. Seward, however, harbored more elaborate ambitions. While Lincoln desired a cabinet that stitched together the various factions of the Republican Party, Seward believed the cabinet should be dominated by former Whigs like himself. The Whig Party had provided nearly two thirds of Lincoln's total vote. Lesser posts could be given to the leading representatives of the other factions, but the former Whigs, Seward believed, deserved all the top prizes. Furthermore, Seward intended, with Weed's help, to have a major role in choosing the remaining cabinet members, thus acquiring a position in the new government more commanding than that of Lincoln himself.

To set this in motion, Thurlow Weed invited Lincoln shortly after the election to join him at Seward's home in Auburn so the three men might deliberate about the cabinet. As precedent, he invoked the journey of President-elect William Harrison to Lexington, Kentucky, in 1841 to confer with his rival Henry Clay. Lincoln wisely declined. When Weed suggested meeting in a more neutral setting, Lincoln again declined. While more than willing to consult with Weed and Seward on his cabinet selections, Lincoln wanted it known that the ultimate decisions would emanate from Springfield and would be his alone.

Lincoln's careful maneuvering with Weed did not indicate any hesitation to make Seward his secretary of state. On the contrary, Lincoln responded testily to a warning from a conservative Kentucky judge that "if obnoxious men like Seward, Cassius M. Clay, &c were put in the Cabinet," the citizens of Kentucky might feel compelled to follow South Carolina in its call for a secession convention. "In what speech," Lincoln asked, had Seward or any prominent Republican "ever spoken menacingly of the South?" The problem was not what the Republicans said or believed but the manner in which Southerners "persistently bespotted and bespattered every northern man by their misrepresentations to rob them of what strength they might otherwise have."

In fact, after newspapers had speculated that Seward had no interest in a cabinet post, and that, even if he did, Lincoln did not want to offer him one, Lincoln resolved to act quickly. Early in December, he directed Hamlin to ascertain Seward's state of mind. When Hamlin approached Seward's friend Preston King, King suggested that the vice president–elect should deal directly with Seward. Knowing this would be equivalent "to a tender of a place," Hamlin again sought Lincoln's instructions.

Lincoln concluded the time had come to make the offer official. In reply to Hamlin, he enclosed two letters for Seward and directed Hamlin, after consulting with Trumbull in Washington, to deliver them to Seward "at once." On the afternoon of December 10, after the Senate had adjourned, Hamlin caught up with Seward on the street. Reaching the Washington House on the corner of Third Street and Pennsylvania Avenue where Hamlin was staying, the vice president–elect invited Seward in to talk. Asked if he would, in truth, reject the position of secretary of state, Seward was guarded. "If that is what you have come to talk to me about, Hamlin, we might as well stop here," he replied. "I don't want the place, and if I did, I have reason to know that I could not get it; therefore let us have no more talk about it."

"Very well," Hamlin said, "but before you express yourself to others as plainly as you have done to me, let me present you with this letter from Mr. Lincoln." Seward "trembled" and appeared "nervous" as he took the first letter, dated December 8, which contained the formal invitation. "With your permission," Lincoln wrote, "I shall, at the proper time, nominate you to the Senate, for confirmation, as Secretary of State, for the United States. Please let me hear from you at your own earliest convenience."

At first, Seward said little, perhaps suspecting this was the pro forma offer that the papers had predicted all along. Moments later, he opened the second letter, labeled private and confidential, which was brilliantly designed to soothe Seward's ego. "Rumors have got into the newspapers," Lincoln wrote, "to the effect that the Department, named above, would be tendered you, as a compliment, and with the expectation that you would decline it. I beg you to be assured that I have said nothing to justify these rumors. On the contrary, it has been my purpose, from the day of the nomination at Chicago, to assign you, by your leave, this place in the administration. . . . I now offer you the place, in the hope that you will accept it, and with the belief that your position in the public eye, your integrity, ability, learning, and great experience, all combine to render it an appointment pre-eminently fit to be made."

His face "pale with excitement," Seward grasped Hamlin's hand. "This is remarkable, Mr. Hamlin; I will consider the matter, and, in accordance with Mr. Lincoln's request, give him my decision at the earliest practicable moment." Three days later, on December 13, Seward wrote Lincoln a gracious note, explaining that it was an honor to have received the offer, but that he needed "a little time" to think about whether he had "the qualifications and temper of a minister, and whether it is in such a capacity that my friends would prefer that I should act if I am to continue at all in the public service." He wished, he said, that he could confer directly with Lincoln on these questions, but he did not see how such a meeting "could prudently be held under existing circumstances." While there was little doubt that Seward desired the post, he still wished to test the extent of his influence in selecting congenial (pro-Seward) colleagues.

•   •   •

AFTER TENDERING THE OFFER to Seward, Lincoln turned his attention to Bates. Through Frank Blair, arrangements were made for Bates to visit Lincoln in Springfield on December 15. Arriving the evening before, Bates took a room at the Chenery House, where he encountered John Nicolay the next morning at breakfast. Nicolay was somewhat taken aback by the elder statesman's appearance. "He is not of impressive exterior; his hair is grey, and his beard quite white," Nicolay recorded, "and his face shows all the marks of age quite strongly." Nonetheless, he found "his flow of words in conversation" to be "very genial and easy." After breakfast, Bates walked over to Lincoln's room at the State House. Since Lincoln had not yet arrived, Nicolay gave Bates the morning paper and hastened to Lincoln's house to inform him that Bates was waiting. Shortly, the two former Whigs settled down for what Bates described as a "free conversation—till interrupted by a crowd" of callers. In order to speak privately, Lincoln suggested that they adjourn to Bates's room in the hotel, where they spent much of the afternoon together.

Lincoln took little time in assuring Bates that "from the time of his nomination, his determination was, in case of success, to invite [him] into the Cabinet." In fact, Bates proudly noted in his diary, Lincoln told him that he deemed his participation in his administration "necessary to its complete success." Lincoln acknowledged that several of Bates's friends had urged his appointment as secretary of state, but he believed he "should offer that place to Mr. Seward," not only "as a matter of duty to the party, and to Mr. Sewards many and strong friends," but also because "it accorded perfectly with his own personal inclinations." However, "he had not yet communicated with Mr. Seward, and did not know whether he would accept the appointment—as there had been some doubts expressed about his doing so." While Lincoln may have deliberately chosen the word "communicated" to allow Bates the belief he was the first approached, he actually meant that Seward had not yet responded affirmatively to his letter. Bates understood it to mean that he was the first man to whom Lincoln had spoken about a cabinet position. Lincoln explained that although he could not offer Bates the premier slot as secretary of state, he could extend "what he supposed would be most congenial, and for which he was certainly in every way qualified, viz: the Attorney Generalship."

Bates told Lincoln that if "peace and order prevailed in the country," he would decline the honor much as he had refused the post of secretary of war under President Fillmore in 1850. Only two months earlier, acknowledging in his diary that "everybody expects Mr. Lincoln to offer me one of his Departments," he had vowed to decline the position. "My pecuniary circumstances (barely competent) and my settled domestic habits make it very undesirable for me to be in high office with low pay—it subjects a man to great temptations to live above his income, and thus become dishonest; and if he have the courage to live economically, it subjects his family to ridicule."

With the country "in trouble and danger," however, he "felt it his duty to sacrifice his personal inclinations, and if he could, to contribute his labor and influence to the restoration of peace in, and the preservation of his country." Lincoln knew he had his man, either for U.S. Attorney General, or, if Seward should decline, for secretary of state. When Bates suggested several days later that "a good effect might be produced on the public mind—especially in the border slave States" by leaking the news of his offer, Lincoln agreed. "Let a little editorial appear in the Missouri Democrat," he wrote Bates, revealing that he had accepted a place in the cabinet, though "it is not yet definitely settled which Department." The announcement of Bates's appointment received positive marks almost everywhere. Indeed, the appointment of Bates would require the least maneuvering of all Lincoln's selections.

Meanwhile, after receiving Lincoln's offer, Seward consulted Weed, as he had at every critical juncture in his long career. Weed had already established a strong working relationship with Leonard Swett, who had assured him after the election that "we all feel that New York and the friends of Seward have acted nobly. . . . We should be exceedingly glad to know your wishes and your views, and to serve you in any way in our power." Weed now contacted Swett to secure an invitation to discuss Seward's thoughts on the design of the cabinet with Lincoln. "Mr. Lincoln would be very glad to see you," Swett informed Weed on December 10. "He asks me to tell you so. . . . Mr. Lincoln wants your advice about his Cabinet, and the general policy of his administration."

With Weed en route to Illinois, Seward wrote to inform Lincoln of his conversations with Weed, who would convey his "present unsettled view of the subject upon which you so kindly wrote me a few days ago." Weed arrived in Springfield on December 20. For weeks, reporters representing New York papers had been scanning the guest lists of the local Springfield hotels for signatures of any of their fellow New Yorkers. They were about to conclude that the Eastern establishment was deliberately shunning Lincoln when they uncovered the name of Thurlow Weed on the register at the Chenery House: "The renowned chief of the Albany lobby—the maker and destroyer of political fortunes—the unrivaled party manager—the once almighty Weed," a newspaper in Rochester noted, has "migrated towards the rising sun!"

Lincoln and Weed settled down opposite each other in Lincoln's parlor, with Swett and Davis in attendance. Swett would never forget the image of the two men, who "took to each other" so strongly, both "remarkable in stature and appearance," with "rough, strongly marked features," both having "risen by their own exertions from humble relations to the control of a nation." Despite their mutual respect, Lincoln's resolve regarding his cabinet choices undoubtedly dismayed Weed, who had assumed that he and Seward would have a critical role in the composition of the entire body. To Lincoln's appointment of Bates, Weed did not object; neither did he complain when the conversation turned to Caleb Smith of Indiana and Simon Cameron. Though Cameron was a former Democrat, Weed understood that Pennsylvania deserved an appointment. Besides, Cameron was a practical man, a politician after his own heart. When mention was made, however, of Salmon Chase, Gideon Welles, and Montgomery Blair—all former Democrats, all unfriendly to Seward—Weed "made strong opposition."

Chase, Weed argued, was an abolitionist. Welles and his Democratic colleagues in Connecticut had been thorns in the side of Weed and Seward for years. To Welles, "more than any one, perhaps, Weed attributed the defeat of Mr. Seward at Chicago," for the Connecticut delegation was "unanimously opposed to Mr. Seward" and set the tone for other New England states. Far better than Welles, Weed recommended, would be Charles Francis Adams or George Ashmun, both former Whigs and good friends of both Seward and Weed. Lincoln somewhat disingenuously claimed that since Hamlin was from New England, where so much shipping was located, the vice president–elect had been designated to choose the New England representative for the Navy Department. Since Hamlin had chosen Welles, "the only question was as to whether he [Welles] was unfit personally." In fact, Hamlin and Lincoln had discussed various men for the post, including Welles. Hamlin preferred Charles Francis Adams, but Lincoln wanted the former Democrat Welles to help balance the Whig members of his cabinet. Indeed, several years later, in a conversation with Welles, Lincoln claimed that his mind was "fixed" on Welles from the start. Though his choice was "confirmed" by Hamlin and others, recalled Lincoln, "the selection was my own, and not theirs."

Understanding that Lincoln would not be swayed from Welles, Weed playfully suggested a fanciful alternative for secretary of the navy. The president-elect could purchase "an attractive figure-head, to be adorned with an elaborate wig and luxuriant whiskers, and transfer it from the prow of a ship to the entrance of the Navy Department," which would be "quite as serviceable as his secretary, and less expensive." Lincoln immediately appreciated the humor in the resemblance between Weed's image of a wigged, bewhiskered figurehead and Father Neptune, as he would later call Welles. He reckoned, however, he needed "a live secretary of the navy."

Next, Lincoln brought up the name of Montgomery Blair. "Has he been suggested by any one except his father, Francis P. Blair, Sr.?" Weed mocked. The question prompted from Lincoln an amusing anecdote that made it all too clear to Weed that Blair was Lincoln's choice. Still, Weed argued that Lincoln would eventually regret his selection. Lincoln explained that he needed a representative from the border states. Montgomery's appointment would ensure support both in Maryland and through his brother, Frank, in Missouri. Weed suggested instead John Gilmer of North Carolina, a loyal Union man. Lincoln knew Gilmer and liked him, but doubted if any Southerner would accept a post. Nonetheless, he conceded that if Gilmer were contacted and agreed, and if "there was no doubt of his fidelity, he would appoint him."

As the conversation was drawing to an end, Weed pointed out that the inclusion of Chase, Cameron, Welles, and Blair in the cabinet along with Seward, Bates, and Smith would give the Democrats a majority, slighting the Whigs who made up the major portion of the Republican Party. "You seem to forget," Lincoln replied, "that *I* expect to be there; and counting me as one, you see how nicely the cabinet would be balanced and ballasted."

Weed returned to Albany convinced that Lincoln was "capable in the largest sense of the term." In the *Albany Evening Journal*, he wrote: "his mind is at once philosophical and practical. He sees all who go there, hears all they have to say, talks freely with everybody, reads whatever is written to him; but thinks and acts by himself and for himself."

While publicly praising Lincoln's independence, Weed was privately so chagrined by the complexion of the cabinet that he was no longer certain Seward should accept. "In one aspect *all* is gone," Weed wrote Seward on Christmas Day, likely indicating Welles, "nor do I know how much can be saved in the other," probably referring to Blair.

The following evening, Seward sent a note to Charles Francis Adams, asking him to call in the morning. With a tone of sorrow in his voice, Seward told Adams he had imagined that when Lincoln offered him the premier position in the cabinet, he "would have consulted him upon the selection of the colleagues with whom he was to act"; but Weed had returned from Springfield empty-handed. He had hoped Adams would be awarded the Treasury, but the likely choice of Welles would fill New England's quota, closing the door on Adams. "This was not such a Cabinet," Seward confided to Adams, "as he had hoped to see, and it placed him in great embarrassment what to do. If he declined, could he assign the true reasons for it, which was the want of support in it? If he accepted, what a task he had before him!" Adams replied that "in this moment of great difficulty and danger, there was no alternative for him but acceptance." This is probably what Seward wanted to hear all along, after he had expressed his distress at not being able to bring his friend Adams along.

The next day, Seward wrote to Lincoln that "after due reflection and with much self distrust," he had "concluded; that if I should be nominated to the Senate . . . it would be my duty to accept." That evening, he wrote to his wife, "I have advised Mr. L. that I will not decline. It is inevitable. I will try to save freedom and my country." Frances was not surprised by her husband's acceptance. Though she wanted him to close the curtain on his political career and come home to his family in Auburn, when huge worshipful crowds met his whirlwind summer tour for Lincoln, she had foreseen that his driving ambition would never be satisfied in tranquil Auburn. Nor was she surprised by his grandiose claim that he would try to save freedom and his country. She often saw her man with a clearer eye than he saw himself.

• • •

WITH ACCEPTANCES from Seward and Bates in hand, Lincoln turned his attention to his third rival, Salmon Chase. Knowing that Chase would never accept a subordinate position, Lincoln had slated him for the Treasury Department. As soon as he received Seward's written acceptance, he wrote to Chase: "In these troublous times, I would [much] like a conference with you. Please visit me here at once." The pieces of the puzzle were beginning to fall into place.

But Lincoln's plans for Chase were temporarily waylaid by intense pressure for the appointment of Pennsylvania's Simon Cameron as secretary of the treasury. Exactly what promises Swett and Davis had made to Cameron's men at the convention for their switch to Lincoln on the second ballot went unrecorded. We know from Swett's letter to Lincoln, however, that he had given his word to the Cameron men that "they should be placed upon the same footing as if originally they had been your friends." The lobbying for Cameron began days after Lincoln's election with a deluge of letters "from very strong and unexpected quarters." Lincoln had understood from the start the importance of satisfying Pennsylvania. Initially, he had hoped Pennsylvania would accept New Jersey's William Dayton, who, like Cameron, was a staunch protectionist. As testimonials to Cameron poured in, however, Lincoln dispatched Swett to Harrisburg to invite Cameron to Springfield.

"The unexpected arrival of [Cameron] was somewhat of a stunner," Henry Villard confessed, "not only to your correspondent but to a majority of the political schemers and intriguants in Springfield." Considering Lincoln's "well known rigid adherence to honesty," it seemed impossible to Villard that Honest Abe would besmirch his cabinet with someone of Cameron's unsavory reputation. For years, charges of bribery and bad dealings with the Winnebago Indians had sullied Cameron's name. However compromised his reputation, the campaign on the Pennsylvanian's behalf was organized with great skill and effectiveness.

As soon as Cameron reached the Chenery House on December 30, he sent a note to Lincoln. "Shall I have the honor of waiting on you,—or will you do me the favor to call here?" Lincoln told him to come to his office, where they spoke for several hours. The conversation continued that evening at the Chenery House. Their talks were candid and enjoyable, for even those opposed to Cameron acknowledged his winning personality, shrewd understanding of politics, and repertoire of intriguing stories. At the end of the interview, Lincoln told Cameron he would appoint him to the cabinet, as either secretary of the treasury or secretary of war. The wily Cameron asked Lincoln to put the offer in writing, which Lincoln somewhat impulsively did, on the promise that it remain confidential. Unfortunately, when Cameron returned home, he brandished the offer among his friends like "an exuberant school boy."

As word of the probable appointment leaked out, opposition flared. "There is an odor about Mr. C. which would be very detrimental to your administration," Trumbull warned Lincoln in a letter that probably reached Springfield shortly after Cameron left. "Not a Senator I have spoken with, thinks well of such an appointment." Then, on January 3, 1861, Alexander McClure, representing one of Pennsylvania's anti-Cameron factions, came to Springfield carrying papers that purportedly revealed Cameron's lack of moral fitness, particularly inappropriate for stewardship of the Treasury. Recognizing that he had acted too hastily, Lincoln sent a private note to Cameron on January 3: "Since seeing you things have developed which make it impossible for me to take you into the cabinet. You will say this comes of an interview with McClure; and this is partly, but not wholly true. The more potent matter is wholly outside of Pennsylvania." To save face, Lincoln suggested that Cameron decline the appointment, in which case Lincoln would "not object to its being known that it was tendered you."

Hopeful that Cameron would cooperate, Lincoln looked forward to his meeting with Chase, who arrived in Springfield on Friday, January 4, "travel-stained and weary after two days on the cramped, stuffy cars of the four different railroads he took from Columbus." Ever meticulous about his appearance, Chase barely had time to wash up before being notified that Lincoln was downstairs in the lobby of the Chenery House. Though discomfited by the awkwardness of their introduction, Chase was immediately disarmed by Lincoln's warm expression of thanks for Chase's support in 1858 during his failed Senate campaign against Douglas.

Lincoln then directly addressed the point of the meeting. "I have done with you," he said, "what I would not perhaps have ventured to do with any other man in the country—sent for you to ask you whether you will accept the appointment of Secretary of the Treasury, without, however, being exactly prepared to offer it to you." The problem, Lincoln explained, would be garnering acceptance for Chase's appointment in Pennsylvania, a prospect complicated by the unresolved Cameron situation and by Chase's previous support for free trade that had enraged industrial Pennsylvania. Lincoln's straightforward manner impressed Chase, even as it irritated him. "I frankly said to him that I desired no position & could not easily reconcile myself to the acceptance of a subordinate one; but should gladly give to his admn., as a Senator, all the support which a sincere friend . . . could give." [Chase had once again been elected to the U.S. Senate by the Ohio legislature.]

As the interview continued, however, Chase began to relax. Lincoln explained that had Seward declined the State Department, he would have "without hesitation" offered it to Chase, certain that Seward and Chase deserved the two top positions in his cabinet. His dignity restored, Chase promised to consider the contingent Treasury offer "under the advice of friends." He and Lincoln continued their discussion on Saturday, and Chase attended Sunday church with the Lincoln family.

After this long weekend meeting, Lincoln considered Chase's inclusion in the cabinet essential. But what of Cameron, who had refused to withdraw from consideration? Early that Sunday morning, Lincoln walked over to the Chenery House, where Gustave Koerner was still in bed. Lincoln rounded up Judd and returned to Koerner's room. Speaking in an agitated voice, Lincoln said: "I am in a quandary. Pennsylvania is entitled to a cabinet office." He had received "hundreds of letters, and the cry is 'Cameron, Cameron!' . . . The Pennsylvania people say: 'If you leave out Cameron you disgrace him.' " Nonetheless, he had his mind "already fixed on Chase, Seward and Bates, my competitors at the convention." Koerner and Judd expressed themselves strongly against Cameron but were unable to solve Lincoln's dilemma.

By Monday morning, as Chase left for Columbus, Lincoln had reached a tentative solution. He would not offer Cameron the Treasury but would hold open the possibility of another post. "It seems to me not only highly proper, but a *necessity*," he confided in Trumbull that day, "that Gov. Chase shall take [the Treasury]. His ability, firmness, and purity of character, produce the propriety." As for the necessity, his name alone would reconcile the merchant class in New York who had long opposed Seward. "But then comes the danger that the protectionists of Pennsylvania will be dissatisfied; and, to clear this difficulty, Gen. C. must be brought to co-operate." The solution was to persuade him to take the lesser position of the War Department.

Moving carefully, Lincoln wrote a conciliatory letter to Cameron, admitting that his first letter was written "under great anxiety," and begging him to understand that he "intended no offence." He promised that if he made a cabinet appointment for Pennsylvania before he arrived in the capital, he would not do so without talking to Cameron, "and giving all the weight to your views and wishes which I consistently can."

Uncertain about Lincoln's complex plans, Chase left Springfield with some ambivalence. Although he had to admit that his conversations with Lincoln "were entirely free & unreserved," he had not been given the firm offer he coveted, even as he claimed a preference to remain in the Senate. On the train back to Ohio, he penned notes urging several friends to visit

Lincoln and support his case. "What is done must be done quickly & done judiciously," he told Hiram Barney, "with the concurrence of our best men & by a deputation to Springfield."

Chase's friends appealed to Lincoln, but the trouble occasioned by his impulsive letter to Cameron had convinced Lincoln to make no more official offers until he reached Washington in late February. Uncertainty left Chase increasingly agitated. "I think that in allowing my name to be *under consideration* . . . and to be tossed about in men's mouths and in the press as that of a competitor for a seat which I don't want, I have done all that any friends can reasonably ask of me," he wrote Elizabeth Pike. "And it is my purpose by a note to Mr. Lincoln within the present week to put my veto on any further *consideration* of it. If he had thought fit to tender me the Treasury Department with the same considerate respect which was manifested toward Mr. Seward and Mr. Bates I might have felt under a pretty strong obligation to defer to the judgment of friends and accept it." In the end, Chase never did send a note requesting Lincoln to withdraw his name from further cabinet consideration. His desire for position and glory, as Lincoln shrewdly guessed, would allow Lincoln alone to determine the time and place of his appointment.

• • •

WHILE LINCOLN WAS PREOCCUPIED with the construction of his official family, the country was tearing itself apart. On December 20, 1860, the same day that Lincoln met with Thurlow Weed, South Carolina held a state convention in the wake of the Republican victory and passed an ordinance to secede from the Union. The vote was unanimous. Throughout the Deep South, such "a snowballing process" began that over the next six weeks, six additional states followed suit—Mississippi, Louisiana, Florida, Alabama, Georgia, Texas.

For Southern radicals, a correspondent for the *Charleston Courier* observed, Lincoln's victory opened the door to the goal "desired by all true hearted Southerners, viz: a Southern Confederacy." The night after the election, the citizens of Charleston had turned out in droves for a torchlight parade featuring an effigy of Lincoln, with a placard in its hand reading: "Abe Lincoln, First President Northern Confederacy." Two slaves hoisted the figure to a scaffold, where it was set afire and "speedily consumed amid the cheers of the multitude."

As the various secession ordinances made clear, the election of a "Black Republican" was merely the final injury in a long list of grievances against the North. These documents cited attempts to exclude slaveholders from the new territories; failure to enforce the Fugitive Slave Act; continued agitation of the slavery question that held Southerners up to contempt and mockery; and the fear of insurrection provoked by the John Brown raid.

Though Southern newspapers had long threatened that secession would follow fast upon a Lincoln victory, the rapidity and vehemence of the secession movement took many in the North, including President Buchanan, by surprise. The bachelor president was attending a young friend's wedding reception when he heard news of South Carolina's secession. A sudden disturbance heralded the entrance of South Carolina congressman Lawrence Keitt. Flourishing his state's secession ordinance over his head, he shouted: "Thank God! Oh, thank God! . . . I feel like a boy let out from school." When Buchanan absorbed the news, he "looked stunned, fell back, and grasped the arms of his chair." No longer able to enjoy the festivities, he left immediately.

For Lincoln, who would not take office until March 4, it was a time of mounting anxiety and frustration. He strongly believed, he told John Nicolay, that the government possessed "both the authority and the power to maintain its own integrity," but there was little he could do until he held the reins of power. While he was "indefatigable in his efforts to arrive at the fullest comprehension of the present situation of public affairs," relying not simply on the newspapers he devoured but on "faithful researches for precedents, analogies, authorities, etc.," it was hard to stand by while his country was disintegrating. He declared at one point that he would be willing to reduce his own life span by "a period of years" equal to the anxious months separating his election and the inauguration.

Besieged with requests to say something conciliatory, Lincoln refused to take "a position towards the South which might be considered a sort of an apology for his election." He was determined to stand behind the Republican platform, believing that any attempt to soften his position would dishearten his supporters in the North without producing any beneficial impact on the South. When asked by the editor of a Democratic paper in Missouri to make a soothing public statement that would keep Missouri in the Union, Lincoln replied: "I could say nothing which I have not already said, and which is in print and accessible to the public. Please pardon me for suggesting that if the papers, like yours, which heretofore have persistently garbled, and misrepresented what I have said, will now fully and fairly place it before their readers, there can be no further misunderstanding. . . . I am not at liberty to shift my ground—that is out of the question. . . . The secessionists, *per se* believing they had alarmed me, would clamor all the louder."

As panic began to affect the stock market and the business community in the North, Lincoln reluctantly agreed to insert an authorized passage in a speech Trumbull was scheduled to make in Chicago. He simply repeated that once he assumed power, "each and all of the States will be left in as complete control of their own affairs respectively, and at as perfect liberty to choose, and employ, their own means of protecting property, and preserving peace and order within their respective limits, as they have ever been under any administration."

Just as Lincoln had predicted, however, the speech had no positive impact. "On the contrary," he wrote the *New York Times*'s Henry Raymond, "the Boston Courier, and its' class, hold me responsible for the speech, and endeavor to inflame the North with the belief that it foreshadows an abandonment of Republican ground by the incoming administration; while the Washington Constitution, and its' class hold the same speech up to the South as an open declaration of war against them." The South, he claimed, "has eyes but does not see, and ears but does not hear."

Although increasingly infuriated by Southern misrepresentations of his positions, Lincoln confined expression of his anger to private letters. Upon hearing from the *New York Times*'s Henry Raymond that one of his correspondents, a wealthy Mississippi gentleman named William Smedes, had justified the state's "blaze of passion" for secession on the grounds that Lincoln was "pledged to the ultimate extinction of slavery, holds the black man to be the equal of the white, & stigmatizes our whole people as immoral & unchristian," Lincoln issued a blistering reply. As evidence, Smedes had cited an "infamous" speech Lincoln had purportedly given on the occasion when Chase was presented with his silver pitcher by the free blacks of Cincinnati. For such a speech, Smedes proclaimed, he would "regard death by a stroke of lightning to Mr. Lincoln as but a just punishment from an offended deity."

"What a very mad-man your correspondent, Smedes is," Lincoln replied, countering that he "was never in a meeting of negroes in [his] life; and never saw a pitcher presented by anybody to anybody." Moreover, he went on, "Mr. Lincoln is not pledged to the ultimate extinctincton of slavery; does not hold the black man to be the equal of the white, unqualifiedly as Mr. S. states it; and never did stigmatize their white people as immoral & unchristian."

However justifiable Lincoln's anger at what he rightly called a "forgery out and out," his response reveals the gulf still separating him from Chase on the issue of race. Although Lincoln's views on racial equality reflected the majority position in the North, Chase regarded his call at the pitcher ceremony to eradicate the Black Laws one of the proudest moments of his life.

• • • •

WHILE OUTRAGED BY the South's willful distortions of his positions, Lincoln was far more troubled by the growing rancor splitting his own party. Conciliators believed that with the proper compromises, the eight remaining slaveholding states could be kept in the Union, hoping that without expansion, the secession movement would ultimately die out. Hard-liners, meanwhile, ranged from those who thought compromise would only embolden the South to extremists who believed that military force alone would bring the South back to the Union fold. As president-elect, Lincoln had to balance two emerging poles of the Republican Party, a task made all the more difficult by the over 700 miles that separated Springfield from Washington.

Yet, almost unnoticed, Lincoln managed through a series of complex and subtle maneuvers to keep the Republican Party intact through the "Great Secession Winter." Whatever conciliatory measures he might consider, Lincoln was adamant, he told Trumbull, that there must be "no compromise on the question of *extending* slavery. If there be, all our labor is lost, and, ere long, must be done again. . . . Stand firm. The tug has to come, & better now, than any time hereafter." If the door were opened to slavery in any of the new territories, Lincoln feared that the South would eventually try to annex Cuba or invade Mexico, thereby restarting the long struggle.

Though Lincoln remained inflexible on the territorial question, he was willing, he told Seward, to compromise on "fugitive slaves, District of Columbia, slave trade among the slave states, and whatever springs of necessity from the fact that the institution is amongst us." Knowing that two parallel committees in the House and Senate were set to address the sectional crisis, Lincoln relayed a confidential message to Seward that he had drafted three short resolutions. He instructed Seward to introduce these proposals in the Senate Committee of Thirteen without indicating they issued from Springfield. The first resolved that "the Constitution should never be altered so as to authorize Congress to abolish or interfere with slavery in the states." The second would amend the Fugitive Slave Law "by granting a jury trial to the fugitive." The third recommended that all state personal liberty laws in opposition to the Fugitive Slave Law be repealed.

Seward agreed to introduce Lincoln's resolutions without revealing their source, though he was of the opinion that they would do nothing to stop the secession movement. The best option, he told Lincoln, was to focus on keeping the border states in the Union, though he feared "nothing could *certainly* restrain them" short of adopting the series of proposals authored by Kentucky's John Crittenden. The Crittenden Compromise, among other provisions, offered to extend the Missouri Compromise line to the Pacific, thereby initiating the very extension of slavery into the territories Lincoln had pledged to prevent.

Lincoln's clear resolve never to accept any measure extending slavery prevented the wavering Seward and other like-minded Republicans from backing the Crittenden Compromise. As one Southern state after another withdrew from the Union, Seward came to believe that only conciliation could save the Union. With Lincoln's iron hand guiding the way in this matter, however, Seward conceded that there was not "the slightest" chance that the Republican side would adopt the Compromise. Still, Seward retained his characteristic optimism, assuring Lincoln that with the passage of time, "sedition will be growing weaker and Loyalty stronger."

Events soon eclipsed the slender hope that time would bring about a peaceful solution to the sectional crisis. There were three federal forts in South Carolina: Fort Moultrie, under the command of Major Robert Anderson; Fort Sumter; and Castle Pinckney. South Carolina announced that all three were in its domain and that three commissioners of the new "republic" had been named to negotiate the matter with the Buchanan administration. "From the first," John Nicolay reported, it was apparent that "the Carolinians intended somehow to get possession of these fortifications, as it was the only means by which they could make any serious resistance to the federal government."

In late December, a rumor reached Springfield that Buchanan had instructed Major Anderson "to surrender Fort Moultrie if it is attacked." When Lincoln heard the news, he told Nicolay: "If that is true they ought to hang him!" Straightaway, he sent a message to General Scott through his friend Congressman Washburne, to be prepared at the time of the inauguration "to either *hold*, or *retake*, the forts, as the case may require."

In fact, the ever-vacillating Buchanan had not decided to surrender the forts. The issue produced an open rift in his already compromised cabinet. Treasury Secretary Howell Cobb of Georgia had resigned and departed for his native state, but several secessionists remained, "vying . . . for Buchanan's ear" with staunch Unionists Secretary of State Jeremiah Black and Postmaster General Joseph Holt. In the midst of the cabinet crisis, Black prevailed on Buchanan to offer the attorney generalship to his good friend Edwin Stanton, who was still practicing law in Washington. Black also pressured Stanton to accept the post, adding a third ally to bolster Buchanan's will. While Buchanan waffled over the proper course of action, Anderson preempted his decision on the night of December 26, 1860, by deciding to move his troops from Fort Moultrie to the less vulnerable Fort

Sumter. The next day, South Carolina took possession of the abandoned Fort Moultrie as well as Castle Pinckney.

Under the influence of Black, Holt, and Stanton, Buchanan agreed to send reinforcements to Anderson at Sumter. In early January, the same day that Lincoln met with Chase in Springfield, an unarmed merchant vessel, the *Star of the West*, headed for Charleston Harbor equipped with men and supplies. The mission failed when the weaponless vessel was fired upon by shore batteries. The *Star of the West* turned back immediately and headed north.

These dramatic events created what Seward called "a feverish excitement" in Washington. No one felt more apprehensive than the newest member of Buchanan's cabinet, Edwin Stanton. Thoroughly loyal to the Union, excitable and suspicious by nature, he became convinced that secessionists planned to seize the nation's capital and prevent Lincoln's inauguration. From his position inside the government, Stanton feared that "every department in Washington then contained numerous traitors and spies." He discovered that the army had been deployed in far-flung places and that treasonous officers had shifted arms and guns from arsenals in the North to various places in the South. If Maryland and Virginia could be provoked into secession, Stanton believed secessionists would be in a position to take Washington. With the essentially defenseless capital captured, they would possess "the *symbols* of government, the seals and the treaties— the treasuries & the apparent right to control the army & the navy." Stanton was driven to distraction when President Buchanan could not "*be made to believe*, the existence of this danger," and would not credit the treasonous plot, which, Stanton feared, would include an attempt to assassinate Lincoln before his inauguration.

At this juncture, his co-biographers report, Stanton "came to a momentous decision: he decided to throw party fealty and cabinet secrecy to the winds and to work behind the President's back." With the White House paralyzed and the Democratic Party at loggerheads, he determined that "Congress and its Republican leaders were the last hope for a strong policy, the last place for him to turn." Stanton knew that becoming an informer violated his oath of office, but concluded that his oath to support the Constitution was paramount.

Seeking the most powerful conduit for his information, Stanton chose Seward. Knowing they could not openly communicate, fearful that secessionists lurking on every corner would report the meetings in newspapers, Stanton prevailed on Peter Watson—the same Watson who had initially interviewed Lincoln for the Reaper trial—to act as his middleman. Almost every evening, Watson would call on Seward at his home to deliver oral and written messages from Stanton. Watson would then return to Stanton with Seward's responses. "The question what either of us could or ought to do at the time for the public welfare was discussed and settled," Seward later recalled.

The first meeting between Seward and Watson likely took place on December 29, prompting the flurry of private letters that Seward penned late that night. "At length I have gotten a position in which I can see what is going on in the Councils of the President," Seward wrote Lincoln. "It pains me to learn that things are even worse than is understood. . . . A plot is forming to seize the Capitol on or before the 4th of March. . . . Believe that I know what I write. In point of fact the responsibilities of your administration must begin before the time arrives. I therefore renew the suggestion of your coming here earlier than you otherwise would. . . . I trust that by this time you will be able to know your correspondent without his signature, which for prudence is omitted." That same evening, Seward confided in Frances that "treason is all around and amongst us," and warned Weed, whose presence in Washington he would welcome, that a plot to seize the government had "abettors near the President."

Seward assumed that Stanton was communicating with him alone. In fact, the cunning Stanton secretly spread word of the danger to several other Republicans, including Charles Sumner, Salmon Chase, and Congressman Henry Dawes. "By early disclosure," Dawes later wrote, Stanton was able to thwart some of the attempts by treasonous officers to turn supplies and arms over to "the enemies of their country." Increasingly paranoid, Stanton invited Sumner to his office and then led him through a half-dozen different rooms before feeling safe to talk for a few minutes. Arrangements were made for papers to be "found and read by the light of the street lamp at night, and then returned to the place of deposit."

Unaware of these other communications, Seward assumed it was on his shoulders to save the Union, that he "held the key to all discontent." After his appointment as secretary of state was made public on January 10, 1861, when he "came to be regarded somewhat extensively as a person representing the incoming administration and the Republican party," the pressure of his position was immense. "By common consent," Seward's admirer Henry Adams later wrote, "all eyes were turned on him, and he was overwhelmed by entreaties from men in all sections of the country to do something to save the Union." As members of Congress, the cabinet, and hundreds of nervous citizens approached him "with prayers and tears," Seward became "virtually the ruler of the country." Or so he thought.

Intuiting that the country needed a clear, strong Republican voice, Seward announced that he would deliver a major speech in the Senate on Janu-

ary 12. "Never in the history of the American Congress has there been witnessed so intense an anxiety to hear a speech as that which preceded the
delivery of Mr. Seward's," a reporter for the Chicago *Tribune* wrote.
"What gave so much interest and weight to the Senator's words, was the
belief that it was equivalent to a speech from Lincoln himself."

"The families of nearly all the Senators and Cabinet officers were present," another correspondent reported, and the crush to get in was so great
that "extravagant prices were offered to the various doorkeepers to obtain
admission." As Seward began to speak, senators on both sides of the aisle
sat in rapt attention, including Mississippi's Jefferson Davis, who would
soon resign the Senate to become the president of the Southern Confederacy. "No man was as usual engaged in writing letters, no one called for
pages, no one answered messages," a witness observed, "and every ear in
the vast assembly was strained to catch his every word."

Seward's chief purpose was "to set forth the advantages, the necessities
to the Union to the people . . . and the vast calamities to them and to the
world which its destruction would involve." He warned that disunion
would give rise to a state of "perpetual civil war," for neither side would
tolerate an imbalance of strength or power. Opportunistic foreign nations
would then move in, preying on the bickering factions. "When once the
guardian angel has taken flight," he predicted, "everything is lost."

Listening from the packed galleries, a Boston reporter confessed that it
was "difficult to restrain oneself from tears, when at the allusion of Seward
to the great men of the country now dead and gone, and at his vivid portrayal of the horrors and evils of dissolution and civil war, we saw the venerable Senator Crittenden, who sat directly in front of Seward, shedding
tears, and finally, overcome by his feelings, cover his face with his handkerchief."

As he moved into the second hour of his speech, Seward offered the concessions he hoped might stem the tide of secession. He endeavored "to meet
prejudice with conciliation, exaction with concession which surrenders no
principle, and violence with the right hand of peace." He began with
Lincoln's resolutions calling for a constitutional amendment to prevent any
future Congress from interfering with slavery where it already existed and
suggesting a repeal of all personal liberty laws in opposition to the Fugitive
Slave Law. He then added several resolutions of his own, including the
prospect of a Constitutional Convention "when the eccentric movements
of secession and disunion shall have ended" to consider additional changes
to the Constitution. When, after nearly two hours, he concluded his emotional remarks, the galleries erupted in thunderous applause.

As Seward no doubt anticipated, his speech had little impact on the seven states of the Deep South, where the secession movement continued its course. The following week, five Southern senators, including Jefferson Davis, rose to deliver farewell speeches to their colleagues before resigning their seats and heading south. Davis delivered the most wrenching farewell. Unable to sleep for days, he appeared "inexpressibly sad," very ill, and "in a state of mind bordering on despair."

"I am sure I feel no hostility to you, Senators from the North," he began. "I am sure there is not one of you, whatever sharp discussion there may have been between us, to whom I cannot now say, in the presence of my God, I wish you well." The friendships forged over the years were not easily discarded. Seward himself had visited Davis every day during a painful illness several years earlier, when it seemed that Davis might lose his eyesight. Seated by Davis's side, Seward would recount all the speeches delivered that day by both Democrats and Republicans. The ever-genial Seward told how at one point, "Your man outtalked ours, you would have liked it, but I didn't." The families of the senators likewise suffered as Southerners prepared for departure. Old Man Blair's daughter, Elizabeth Blair Lee, and Varina Davis had been close friends for years. "Mrs Jef asked me if I was going down south to fight her," Elizabeth told her husband, Phil. "I told her no. I would kiss & hug her too tight to let her break any *bonds* between us."

As the senators from the seceded states packed up their belongings to return to their hometowns, it was clear that a "regime had ended in Washington." The mansions of the old Southern aristocracy were closed; the clothes, papers, china, rugs, and furniture that embellished their lives were stowed in heavy trunks and crates to be conveyed by steamers to their Southern plantations.

Seward understood the momentum in the Deep South. His words and hopes that winter were directed at the border states. His "great wish," young Henry Adams observed, "was to gain time," to give the Union men in the border states "some sign of good-will; something, no matter what, with which they could go home and deny the charges of the disunionists." In this respect, he seemed to succeed.

"As an indication of the *spirit* in which the Administration of Mr. Lincoln will be conducted," a *New York Times* editorial concluded, the speech "must convince every candid man that its predominant and paramount aim will be to perpetuate the Union,—that it will consult, with scrupulous care, the interests, the principles, and the sentiments of every section." While none of the concessions would recall the seceded states back into the Union, "many are sanguine in the hope that its wide diffusion through the border Slave States will stay the tide of secession."

During the tumultuous time from Lincoln's election in November 1860 to his inauguration in March 1861, Seward "fought," Henry Adams judged, "a fight which might go down to history as one of the wonders of statesmanship." In the weeks that followed, "the Union men in the South took new courage." In the critical state of Virginia, the Union party prevailed. Its members defeated the secessionists by a large margin, and proposed a Peace Convention to be held in Washington with the implied promise that no further action would be taken until the convention had completed its work. Days later, Tennessee and Missouri followed suit. "Secession has run its course," the New York diarist George Templeton Strong happily noted, betraying the false optimism throughout the North.

Seward was in the best of spirits after the speech, believing, as he told his wife, that without surrendering his principles, he had gained time "for the new Administration to organize and for the frenzy of passion to subside." Unfortunately, hard-liners read Seward's speech differently. Charles Sumner, Thaddeus Stevens, and Salmon Chase were outraged by his conciliatory tone in the face of what they considered treason on the part of the secessionist states. Animosity toward Seward was planted in the hearts of the more radical Republicans that would haunt him for the rest of his life. "I deplore S[eward]'s speech," Sumner wrote to a friend. He "read me his speech 4 days before its delivery. When he came to his propositions, I protested, with my whole soul—for the sake of our cause . . . & his own good name, & I supplicated him to say no such thing."

Thaddeus Stevens, the fiery abolitionist congressman from Pennsylvania, was beside himself. Writing to Chase, who had already spoken out against the adoption of any compromise measure, Stevens warned that if Lincoln "seeks to purchase peace by concession, and ignoring platforms, *á la mode* Seward, I shall give up the fight, being too old for another seven (or thirty) years war."

The speech was particularly disappointing to those, like Carl Schurz, who had long considered Seward the leader of the great antislavery cause. "What do you think of Seward, my child?" Schurz asked his wife. "The mighty is fallen. He bows before the slave power. He has trodden the way of compromise and concession, and I do not see where he can take his stand on this back track. . . . That is hard. We believed in him so firmly and were so affectionately attached to him. This is the time that tries men's souls, and many probably will be found wanting."

In the heated atmosphere of Washington, the realization that members of his own party had lost faith in him took a heavy toll on Seward. Visiting the Capitol after the speech, Charles Francis Adams, Jr., was stunned by Seward's altered appearance since their journey together on the campaign train the previous September. "There he was, the same small, thin, sallow man, with the pale, wrinkled, strongly marked face—plain and imperturbable—the thick, guttural voice and the everlasting cigar. Yet it was immediately apparent that his winter's cares had told on him, for he looked thin and worn, and ten years older than when I had left him at Auburn."

While his conciliatory address cost him the esteem of many longtime supporters, Seward still believed that offering his hand in peace in the attempt to prevent a civil war was the right judgment. His wife, Frances, profoundly disagreed. The final speech had reached her in Auburn by telegraph hours after it was delivered. She wrote her husband a blistering letter. "Eloquent as your speech was it fails to meet the entire approval of those who love you best," she began. "You are in danger of taking the path which led Daniel Webster to an unhonored grave ten years ago. Compromises based on the idea that the preservation of the Union is more important than the liberty of nearly 4,000,000 human beings cannot be right. The alteration of the Constitution to perpetuate slavery—the enforcement of a law to recapture a poor, suffering fugitive . . . these compromises cannot be approved by God or supported by good men. . . ."

"No one can dread war more than I do," she continued; "for 16 years I have prayed earnestly that our son might be spared the misfortune of raising his hand against his fellow man—yet I could not to day assent to the perpetuation or extension of slavery to prevent war. I say this in no spirit of unkindness . . . but I must obey the admonitions of conscience which impel me to warn you of your dangers."

Stung deeply by her denunciation, Seward admitted that "I am not surprised that you do not like the 'concessions' in my speech. You will soon enough come to see that they are not compromises, but explanations, to disarm the enemies of Truth, Freedom, and Union, of their most effective weapons."

Perhaps no one understood Seward's painful position better than his oldest friend, Thurlow Weed. Weed loved the speech. "It will do to live and die by and with," he said. Still, he realized that Seward had opened himself to continuing attack. "In the cars, most of the night," Weed wrote, "I was thinking of the ordeal you are to pass. It is to be [a] great trial of Wisdom and Temper; in Wisdom you will not fail; but of our Tempers, at sixty, we are not so sure. . . . You had both once, and they made you strong. How much more you need them now when hemmed in and hedged in by envy, jealousies and hatreds."

Seward retained his equanimity amid the onslaught due largely to his belief that Lincoln not only endorsed but had covertly orchestrated his actions, for Lincoln himself had confidentially suggested several of the compromises that Seward had offered. Furthermore, in a private letter, Lincoln encouraged him: "Your recent speech is well received here; and, I think, is doing good all over the country." Meeting in the Capitol with Charles Francis Adams a few weeks after the speech, Seward confided that "he had heard from Mr. Lincoln, who approved his course, but was so badgered at Springfield that he felt compelled to keep uncommitted on it at present."

The president-elect was engaged in a more intricate game of political engineering than Seward realized. While undoubtedly pleased that Seward's conciliatory tone had produced a calming effect on the border states, Lincoln knew that if he personally called for compromise, he would lose the support of an important wing of the Republican Party. Instead, he maintained firmness through silence while Seward absorbed the backlash for what might prove an advantageous posture of conciliation.

When Carl Schurz visited Lincoln in Springfield after Seward's speech, Lincoln told the idealistic young man that "Seward made all his speeches without consulting him," a technically accurate if undeniably misleading statement. "[Lincoln] is a whole man," Schurz assured his wife, "firm as a stone wall and clear as crystal. . . . He himself will not hear of concessions and compromises, and says so openly."

In the end, though Lincoln's role was not fully recognized at the time, he was the one who kept his fractious party together when an open rupture might easily have destroyed his administration before it could even begin. By privately endorsing Seward's spirit of compromise while projecting an unyielding public image, President-elect Lincoln retained an astonishing degree of control over an increasingly chaotic and potentially devastating situation.

CHAPTER 11

"I AM NOW
PUBLIC PROPERTY"

A S THE CONFUSION and turmoil of secession swept Washington, the Lincolns made final preparations for their departure from Springfield. In early January 1861, Mary journeyed to New York, both to spend time with her son Robert, whom she had been *"wild* to see" since he had left for the East Coast a year earlier, and to shop for a wardrobe befitting a first lady. Staying at the Astor Hotel, she was fêted by merchants eager to sell her fancy bonnets, richly textured shawls, kid gloves, and bolts of the finest antique silk for fashionable dresses. The store owners happily extended her credit, encouraging an extravagant spree, the first of many. After years of making do on a limited budget, this woman who was raised in a wealthy household took great pleasure in acquiring everything she wanted, even to the point of outspending her wealthier sisters.

"Buying was an intoxication with her," her biographer Ruth Randall writes, "it became an utterly irrational thing, an obsession." Mary's desire for elegant clothes reflected more than vanity, however. She was undoubtedly aware of the whispering comments about her plain looks and her husband's lack of breeding: "Could he, with any honor, fill the Presidential Chair?" one guest at an elegant restaurant was overhead saying. "Would his western gaucherie disgrace the Nation?" Her fighting spirit stimulated, she was determined to show the world that the civility of the West was more than equal to that of the East.

Entranced by her experience in New York, Mary stayed three extra days without notifying her husband, who plunged vainly through sleet and snow three nights running to meet her train. When she did return, Mary was in the best of spirits, as was her handsome, well-dressed son, whose "outward appearance" was said to present "a striking contrast to the loose, careless, awkward rigging of his Presidential father."

The Lincolns decided to rent out their house on Eighth Street, selling some of the furnishings and putting the rest into storage. Before packing their belongings, however, they held a farewell levee in the twin parlors of their home. Mary was in her element as she graciously welcomed a crowd of seven hundred Springfield friends. It was, Villard commented, "the most brilliant affair of the kind witnessed here in many years."

Mary was thrilled by the attention and relished the lavish gifts presented by office seekers. Nonetheless, she became increasingly apprehensive about her husband. Shortly before she left for New York, she received an unwelcome present from South Carolina—a painting depicting Lincoln "with a rope around his neck, his feet chained and his body adorned with tar and feathers." For Mary, terrified of thunderstorms and fearing death with every illness, the gruesome painting undoubtedly left her cold with foreboding.

For Lincoln, the hours of his remaining Springfield days must have seemed too short. The never-ending procession of office seekers and the hard work of packing left little time or space for the most important task of all—the composition of his inaugural address. Unable to concentrate either in his home or in the governor's office, he sought places to isolate himself and be undisturbed. For several precious hours each morning, he wrote and honed the words that were awaited anxiously by both the conciliators and the non-compromisers alike.

As the time for departure drew near, Lincoln appeared "unusually grave and reflective," saddened by the prospect of "parting with this scene of joys and sorrows during the last thirty years and the large circle of old and faithful friends." He journeyed to Farmington for an emotional farewell to his beloved stepmother, Sarah, and to visit his father's grave. Returning home, he called on Billy Herndon, his law partner for sixteen years. He wanted to assure Herndon that his election would only interrupt their partnership in the firm. "If I live I'm coming back some time, and then we'll go right on practising law as if nothing had ever happened."

The day of February 11 was damp and biting as Lincoln, accompanied by family and friends, headed for the Western Railroad Depot. The circuitous twelve-day trip to Washington, D.C., would permit contact with tens of thousands of citizens. He had packed his own trunk, tied it with a rope, and inscribed it simply: "A. Lincoln, White House, Washington, D.C." His oldest son, Robert, would accompany his father on the entire trip, while Mary and the two younger boys would join them the following day.

Arriving at the train station, Lincoln discovered that more than a thousand people had gathered to bid him farewell. He stood in the waiting room, shaking hands with each of his friends. "His face was pale, and quivered with emotion so deep as to render him almost unable to utter a single word," a reporter for the *New York Herald* noted. Just before 8 a.m., Lincoln was escorted to the platform of his private car. He took off his hat, requested silence, and began to speak: "My friends—No one, not in my situation, can appreciate my feeling of sadness at this parting. To this place, and the kindness of these people, I owe every thing. Here I have lived a quarter of a century, and have passed from a young to an old man. Here my children have been born, and one is buried. I now leave, not knowing when, or whether ever, I may return, with a task before me greater than that which rested upon Washington. . . . I hope in your prayers you will commend me, I bid you an affectionate farewell."

Many eyes, including Lincoln's, were filled with tears as he delivered his short but moving remarks. "As he turned to enter the cars three cheers were given," the *Herald* reporter observed, "and a few seconds afterwards the train moved slowly out of the sight of the silent gathering." Lincoln would never return to Springfield.

Neither the luxurious presidential car, decorated with dark furniture, crimson curtains, and a rich tapestry carpet, nor the colorful flags and streamers swaying from its paneled exterior could lift the solemn mood of the president-elect. For most of the ride to the first major stop in Indianapolis, Villard noted, Lincoln "sat alone and depressed" in his private car, "forsaken by his usual hilarious good spirits."

Lincoln understood that his country faced a perilous situation, perhaps the most perilous in its history. That same morning, Jefferson Davis was beginning a journey of his own. He had bade farewell to his wife, children, and slaves, heading for the Confederacy's new capital at Montgomery, Alabama. To the cheers of thousands and the rousing strains of the "Marseillaise," he would be inaugurated president of the new Confederacy. Alexander Stephens, Lincoln's old colleague from Congress, would be sworn in as his vice president.

Lincoln's spirits began to revive somewhat as he witnessed the friendly crowds lined up all along the way, buoyed by "the cheers, the cannon, and the general intensity of welcome." When he reached Indianapolis, thirty-four guns sounded before he alighted to face a wildly enthusiastic crowd of more than twenty thousand people. They lined the streets, waving flags and banners as he made his way to the Bates House, where he was scheduled to spend the night. Knowing that here in Indianapolis, he was expected to deliver his first public speech since election, he had carefully crafted its language before leaving Springfield.

From the balcony of the Bates House, he delivered a direct, powerful talk, one of the few substantive speeches he would make during the long journey. He began by illustrating the word "coercion." If an army marched into South Carolina without the prior consent of its people, that would admittedly constitute "coercion." But would it be coercion, he asked, "if the Government, for instance, but simply insists upon holding its own forts, or retaking those forts which belong to it?" If such acts were considered coercion, he continued, then "the Union, as a family relation, would not be anything like a regular marriage at all, but only as a sort of free-love arrangement." His words provoked loud cheers, sustained applause, and hearty laughter. The speech was considered a great success.

As the train rolled into Cincinnati the next day, John Hay noted that Lincoln had "shaken off the despondency which was noticed during the first day's journey, and now, as his friends say, looks and talks like himself. Good humor, wit and geniality are so prominently associated with him in the minds of those who know him familiarly, that to see him in a melancholy frame of mind, is much as seeing Reeve or Liston in high tragedy would have been." (Reeve and Liston were celebrated comic actors in Shakespeare's plays.) It is interesting to note that Hay considered Lincoln's despondency an aberration rather than the rule.

The following day, as Lincoln was fêted in the state Capitol at Columbus, Ohio, he received a telegram that the electors had met in Washington to count the votes and make his election official. For weeks, Seward and Stanton had worried that secessionists would choose this day to besiege the capital and prevent the electors from meeting. The day, Lincoln learned, had passed peacefully. "The votes have been counted," Seward's son Fred reported to his wife, Anna, "and the Capital is not attacked. Gen. Scott had his troops all under arms, out of sight but ready, with guns loaded, horses harnessed and matches lighted so that they could take the field at a moments notice. But there was no enemy."

Seward himself was immensely relieved to "have passed the 13th safely," believing, he wrote home, that "each day brings the people apparently nearer to the tone and temper, and even to the policy I have indicated. . . . I am, at last, out of direct responsibility. I have brought the ship off the sands, and am ready to resign the helm into the hands of the Captain whom the people have chosen." Despite his stated intentions, Seward would make one later effort to resume the helm.

In Columbus, a great celebration followed news of the official counting of the votes. In the late afternoon, Lincoln was presented at a "full evening dress" reception at Governor Dennison's home for members of the legislature; following dinner, he attended a lavish military ball, where it was said that he danced with Chase's lovely daughter, Kate, much to the irritation of Mary. The image of Lincoln dancing with the twenty-year-old beauty, tall, slim, and captivating, was spoken of in hushed tones for many years afterward. In fact, the charismatic young belle could not have danced with Lincoln that evening, for she was absent from the city when the Lincolns arrived. In an interview with a reporter more than three decades later, Kate maintained that "Mrs. Lincoln was piqued that I did not remain at Columbus to see her, and I have always felt that this was the chief reason why she did not like me at Washington."

For the rest of the trip, as the train wended its way through Pennsylvania, New York, and New Jersey, Lincoln said little to elaborate his position. Never comfortable with extemporaneous speech, he was forced to speak at dozens of stops along the way. He was determined not to foreshadow his inaugural address or to disturb the tenuous calm that seemed to have descended upon the country. He chose, therefore, to say little or nothing, projecting an optimistic tone that belied the seriousness of the situation. Lincoln repeatedly ignored conflicting statements in both his own "House Divided" speech and Seward's "Irrepressible Conflict" speech, assuring his audiences that "there is really no crisis except an *artificial one!* . . . I repeat it, then—*there is no crisis* excepting such a one as may be gotten up at any time by designing politicians. My advice, then, under such circumstances, is to keep cool. If the great American people will only keep their temper, on both sides of the line, the troubles will come to an end."

Throughout his journey, Lincoln endeavored to avoid any suggestion that might inflame or be used to destabilize the country before he could assume power. He simply acknowledged the cheers of the crowds, relying upon his good humor to divert attention from serious political discussion. In Ashtabula, Ohio, he playfully answered calls for Mrs. Lincoln by suggesting that "he should hardly hope to induce her to appear, as he had always found it very difficult to make her do what she did not want to." In Westfield, New York, he kissed Grace Bedell, the little girl who had encouraged him to grow a beard.

For Mary and the boys, the trip was "a continuous carnival," with "rounds of cheers, salvos of artillery, flags, banners, handkerchiefs, enthusiastic gatherings—in short, all the accessories of a grand popular ovation." Every glimpse of Mary or the children through the windows drew wild applause, as did the image of her smoothing her husband's ruffled hair and giving him a kiss before they disembarked in New York City.

To those who listened attentively for any revelation of the incoming administration's intentions, the speeches were a great disappointment. In his diary, Charles Francis Adams lamented that Lincoln's remarks on his journey toward Washington "are rapidly reducing the estimate put upon him. I am much afraid that in this lottery we may have drawn a blank. . . . They betray a person unconscious of his own position as well as of the nature of the contest around him. Good natured, kindly, honest, but frivolous and uncertain."

In fact, Lincoln was not oblivious to the abyss that could easily open beneath his feet. While he "observed the utmost caution of utterance and reticence of declaration," John Nicolay noted, "the shades of meaning in his carefully chosen sentences were enough to show how alive he was to the trials and dangers confronting his administration." In Trenton, for example, while he asserted that "the man does not live who is more devoted to peace than I am," he recognized that it might "be necessary to put the foot down firmly." At this point, Hay noted, he "lifted his foot lightly, and pressed it with a quick, but not violent, gesture upon the floor." The audience erupted with such sustained applause that for several minutes Lincoln was unable to continue his remarks.

Lincoln again revealed his strength of will in his short address at the Astor Hotel in New York City. While he opened with a conciliatory tone, promising that he would never of his own volition "consent to the destruction of this Union," he qualified his promise with "unless it were to be that thing for which the Union itself was made." Two days later, speaking in Independence Hall in Philadelphia, he clarified what he meant by those portentous words. Moved by a keen awareness that he was speaking in the hall where the Declaration of Independence was adopted, he asserted that he had "never had a feeling politically that did not spring from the sentiments embodied in the Declaration. . . . It was not the mere matter of the separation of the colonies from the mother land; but something in that Declaration" that provided "hope to the world for all future time. It was that which gave promise that in due time the weights should be lifted from the shoulders of all men, and that *all* should have an equal chance." If the Union could "be saved upon that basis," he would be among "the happiest men in the world"; but if it "cannot be saved without giving up that principle," he maintained, he "would rather be assassinated on this spot than to surrender it."

Lincoln's ominous mention of assassination may have been prompted by the previous day's report of a plot to kill him during his scheduled stop in Baltimore, a city rampant with Southern sympathizers. Lincoln first received word of the plot through the detective Allan Pinkerton, responsible for guarding him on the trip, who advised him to leave Philadelphia at once and pass through Baltimore on a night train ahead of schedule to confound the conspirators. "This," according to Ward Lamon, who accompanied Lincoln on the trip, "he flatly refused to do. He had engagements with the people, he said, to raise a flag over Independence Hall in the morning, and to exhibit himself at Harrisburg in the afternoon."

That same afternoon, Seward's son Fred was in the Senate gallery when a page summoned him to speak with his father at once. Meeting in the lobby, Seward handed Fred a note from General Winfield Scott carrying a similar warning of trouble in Baltimore. "I want you to go by the first train," Seward directed his son. "Find Mr. Lincoln, wherever he is. Let no one else know your errand." Fred immediately boarded a train and arrived at the Continental Hotel in Philadelphia, where Lincoln was staying, after ten that night.

"I found Chestnut street crowded with people, gay with lights, and echoing with music and hurrahs," Fred recalled. Lincoln was encircled by people, and Fred was forced to wait several hours to deliver his message. "After a few words of friendly greeting with inquiries about my father and matters in Washington," Fred remembered, "he sat down by the table under the gas-light to peruse the letter I had brought." After a few moments, Lincoln spoke: "If different persons, not knowing of each other's work, have been pursuing separate clews that led to the same result, why then it shows there may be something in it. But if this is only the same story, filtered through two channels, and reaching me in two ways, then that don't make it any stronger. Don't you see?" Then, Fred related, "noticing that I looked disappointed at his reluctance to regard the warning, he said kindly: 'You need not think I will not consider it well. I shall think it over carefully, and try to decide it right; and I will let you know in the morning.'"

The next morning, Lincoln agreed to leave Philadelphia for Washington on the night train as soon as his engagement in Harrisburg was completed. Pinkerton insisted, against Mary's judgment, that she and the boys should remain behind and travel to Washington in the afternoon as scheduled. Wearing a felt hat in place of his familiar stovepipe, Lincoln secretly boarded a special car on the night train, accompanied by Ward Lamon and Detective Pinkerton. All other trains were to be "side-tracked" until Lincoln's had passed. All the telegraph wires were to be cut between Harrisburg and Washington until it was clear that Lincoln had arrived in the capital. At 3:30 a.m., the train passed through Baltimore without mishap and proceeded straight to Washington. "At six o'clock," a relieved Lamon recalled, "the dome of the Capitol came in sight."

It was an inauspicious beginning for the new president. Though he arrived safely, critics, including Edwin Stanton, spoke maliciously of the manner in which Lincoln had "crept into Washington." A scurrilous rumor spread that he had entered the train in a Scotch plaid cap, Scottish kilts, and a long military cloak. "It's to be hoped that the conspiracy can be proved beyond cavil," wrote George Templeton Strong in his diary. "If it cannot be made manifest and indisputable, this surreptitious nocturnal dodging or sneaking of the President-elect into his capital city, under cloud of night, will be used to damage his moral position and throw ridicule on his Administration." Lincoln regretted ever heeding General Scott and Detective Pinkerton.

The question of Lincoln's accommodations in Washington for the ten days until his inauguration had been debated for weeks. In early December, Montgomery Blair had issued the Lincolns an invitation to stay at the Blair House on Pennsylvania Avenue, offering the very room "Genl Jackson intended to occupy after leaving the White house," and insisting that the Blairs "would be delighted for you to begin where he left." In the meantime, Senator Trumbull and Congressman Washburne had rented a private house for the Lincolns several blocks from the White House. When Lincoln had passed through Albany on his roundabout tour, however, Weed strongly objected. He advised Lincoln that he was "now public property, and ought to be where he can be reached by the people until he is inaugurated."

Lincoln agreed. "The truth is, I suppose I am now public property; and a public inn is the place where people can have access to me." A suite of rooms was reserved at the celebrated Willard Hotel, which stood at the corner of 14th Street and Pennsylvania Avenue, within sight of the White House.

• • •

SEWARD AND ILLINOIS CONGRESSMAN WASHBURNE were appointed to greet Lincoln and escort him to the Willard. Accounts vary, however, as to whether Seward was actually there to meet the train. He wrote his wife that "the President-elect arrived *incog.* at six this morning. I met him at the depot." Nevertheless, Washburne later claimed that Seward had overslept and arrived at the Willard two minutes after Lincoln, "much out of breath and somewhat chagrined to think he had not been up in season to be at the depot on the arrival of the train."

What is certain is that Seward greeted the president-elect with "a virtuoso performance," attempting to control his every movement and make himself indispensable to the relative newcomer. The two men breakfasted together that morning in the Willard, choosing from an elaborate menu of "fried oysters, steak and onions, blanc mange and *pâté de foie gras.*" Then, after breakfast, Seward escorted Lincoln to the White House to meet with President Buchanan and his cabinet. Lincoln's surprise call disconcerted Harriet Lane, Buchanan's niece, who had brilliantly performed the role of hostess for her bachelor uncle. The appearance of Buchanan's successor signaled the end of her days in the White House. Afterward, she had few kind words to say about the new couple who would occupy her former home. She likened Lincoln to the "tall awkward Irishman who waits on the door," but insisted that the doorman was "the best looking." About Mary, Harriet claimed, she had heard only that she "is awfully *western*, loud & unrefined."

From the White House, Seward shepherded Lincoln to see General Scott. An inch taller than Lincoln and twice his weight, the old hero of the Mexican War was now scarcely able to walk. After the conversation with Scott, Seward and Lincoln drove together for an hour through the streets of Washington. Pressing issues, particularly the still-unfinished cabinet, required immediate attention. Months earlier, Lincoln had promised Weed and Seward that if John Gilmer of North Carolina would accept a seat, he would offer him a position. Seward considered the inclusion of a Unionist Southerner vital in retaining the border states, and Lincoln also considered Gilmer the best choice due to his *"living* position in the South." Gilmer had failed to respond to Lincoln's invitation to visit him in Springfield, however, and Seward had been unable to secure a positive reply.

Simon Cameron remained a candidate whom Seward considered a necessary ingredient in the cabinet. Five weeks earlier, Seward had warned Lincoln that "to grieve as well as disrespect [Cameron] would produce great embarrassment. . . . I should dread exceedingly the army of Cameron's friends in hostility." In fact, after much painful deliberation, Lincoln had decided to offer Cameron a place. During his train trip through Pennsylvania, he had met with a delegation of Cameron supporters who assured him they were authorized to speak for Governor Curtin and Alexander McClure. All the charges against Cameron had been withdrawn, they told Lincoln; the state now stood strongly behind him. Apparently the fear that Pennsylvania might have no representation in the administration had brought warring factions to agree on Cameron. Telling the delegation that "the information relieved him greatly," Lincoln remained unwilling to make his decision until he reached Washington. The problem was that Cameron still insisted on the Treasury position, which Lincoln had resolved to give to Chase. Only when Cameron realized he was not in a position to dictate what he wanted did he grudgingly accept the War Department.

When his carriage ride with Seward ended, Lincoln rested for an hour in his suite before receiving his old adversary Stephen Douglas at two-thirty. Then, while Seward went to the train station to greet Mary, he welcomed the Blairs, Francis Senior and Montgomery. "The Blairs," Hay wrote in his diary, "have to an unusual degree the spirit of a clan. Their family is a close corporation. . . . They have a way of going with a rush for anything they undertake." Lincoln understood all this, but he liked and trusted the old man and knew that he needed former Democrats and hardliners to counterbalance Seward.

The Blairs had been appalled by Seward's conciliatory speech. Old Man Blair warned Lincoln that Seward's compromises resembled Mr. Buchanan's approach and would only invite more aggression from the South. Indeed, the Blairs so violently championed their hard-line position that they effectively advocated war. Monty contended that so long as the Southerners continued to believe "that one Southern man is equal to half a dozen Yankees," they would never submit to anything without a "decisive defeat" on the field. "It will show the Southern people that they wholly mistake the quality of the men they are taught by demagogues to despise." Only as magnanimous victors could Northerners afford to conciliate. Beyond Seward's premature willingness to compromise, Francis Blair, Sr., cautioned that the New Yorker would prove a perpetual thorn in Lincoln's side. "In your cabinet his restless vanity & ambition would do nothing but mischief. He would set himself up as a rival . . . & make an influence to supplant all aspirants for the succession."

While Lincoln generally respected the opinions of Old Man Blair, he had long since determined that he needed Seward for the premier post in his administration. He also hoped, however, to include Monty Blair in his cabinet. While the availability of a true Southerner would have left no room for the border-state Blair, the attempt to enlist Gilmer had apparently failed. Lincoln was prepared to offer Monty a position, most likely as U.S. Postmaster General.

As Lincoln was conversing with the Blairs, Seward made his way through the large crowd at the train depot. Unaware that Lincoln had arrived earlier that day, the throng had gathered to welcome him on the special four o'clock train. When the train finally arrived, one reporter noted, "four carriages were driven up to the rear car, from which Mr. Seward soon emerged with Mrs. Lincoln" and her sons. Once it became clear that the president-elect was not aboard, the assembled citizens began to voice their dismay. "The rain was pouring down in torrents, there was no escape, and the crowd indulged in one or two jokes, a little whistling, and considerable swearing." This was not the welcome Mary had expected. Leaning upon

Seward's arm as she alighted at the Willard, she was anxious. She had distrusted Seward from the start, fearing that he would be a continuing rival to her husband; now she was forced to depend on him during her less than triumphant entry into the city that would be her new home.

That evening Lincoln visited Seward's home for a dinner hosted by Fred's wife, Anna, who served as mistress of the household while Frances remained in Auburn to complete some ongoing work on her home. Although Frances would visit several times a year, she never made Washington her home, leaving all the social duties to her husband, son, and daughter-in-law.

Lincoln returned to the Willard for a nine o'clock reception with the members of the Peace Convention, called by Virginia to attempt a compromise before Congress adjourned on March 4. As the convention members from both South and North assembled, one of the delegates, Lucius Chittenden, representing Vermont, called upon Lincoln in his suite to brief him on the workings of the convention. Chittenden knew that many of the Southern delegates had come simply "to scoff" or "to nourish their contempt for the 'rail-splitter.'" He could not imagine how Lincoln, who had traveled for ten days and "just escaped a conspiracy against his life," could face a gathering in which so many were openly hostile. Yet Lincoln's "wonderful vivacity surprised every spectator," Chittenden marveled. "He spoke apparently without premeditation, with a singular ease of manner and facility of expression."

Representing Ohio was Salmon Chase, whom Lincoln had not seen since their meeting in Springfield. Still uncertain whether he would have a place in the cabinet, Chase stiffly assumed the responsibility of introducing Lincoln to the members of the delegation. Lincoln, Chittenden recalled, "had some apt observation for each person ready the moment he heard his name." The introductions complete, a lively discussion ensued.

In the end, the Peace Convention produced no proposal that could command a majority in Congress, indicating that the time for compromise had passed. That evening at the Willard, however, the delegates had gotten a revelatory glimpse of the president-elect. "He has been both misjudged and misunderstood by the Southern people," William Rives of Virginia said. "They have looked upon him as an ignorant, self-willed man, incapable of independent judgment, full of prejudices, willing to be used as a tool by more able men. This is all wrong. He will be the head of his administration, and he will do his own thinking." Judge Thomas Ruffin of North Carolina considered Lincoln's unwillingness to make concessions on the territorial issue a great "misfortune," but was relieved to hear of his hearty support of the Constitution.

The next morning, a "clear and blustering" day with "a wind that sweeps over this city with mighty power," Seward escorted Lincoln to St. John's Episcopal Church; then, returning to Seward's house, they conferred for two hours. "Governor Seward, there is one part of my work that I shall have to leave largely to you," Lincoln said. "I shall have to depend upon you for taking care of these matters of foreign affairs, of which I know so little, and with which I reckon you are familiar." At some point that morning, Lincoln handed Seward a draft of his inaugural address and asked for his suggestions.

The following day, Seward and Lincoln made an informal visit to the House and the Senate. Senators from all parties congregated to greet Lincoln. Even firebrand Southerners who refused to acknowledge his presence were consumed with curiosity. Virginia's James Mason, one reporter noted, "affected *nonchalance* and pretended to be writing, but for the life of him he could not help looking askance, from time to time; and it may be doubted if what he wrote could be translated into plain English."

One reporter commented that Lincoln's "face has not yet become familiar enough to be popularly recognized here," so "he passed to and from the Capitol yesterday without catching the attention of the multitude." His informal visit, the *New York Times* noted, was "without a precedent. His illustrious predecessors . . . deemed it incompatible with the stately dignity of the Executive of the Union, to visit the coordinate departments of the Government. Clearly, the Railsplitter has, in following the dictates of his own feelings, rightly interpreted the proprieties of his position."

In the days ahead, Lincoln confirmed two more positions for his cabinet. He chose Caleb Smith, his old Whig colleague, over Schuyler Colfax for the Department of the Interior, despite widespread support for Colfax. In a gracious letter to Colfax, he explained: "I had partly made up my mind in favor of Mr. Smith—not conclusively of course—before your name was mentioned in that connection. When you were brought forward I said 'Colfax is a young man—is already in position—is running a brilliant career, and is sure of a bright future in any event. With Smith, it is now or never.' I considered either abundantly competent, and decided on the ground I have stated." Mentioning that Colfax had not supported him during his Senate campaign against Douglas, Lincoln begged him to "not do me the injustice to suppose, for a moment, that I remembered any thing against you in malice."

At one point, Norman Judd had been in consideration for a cabinet appointment, but the opposition to him in Illinois from Lincoln's campaign manager, David Davis, and a host of others was very strong. Mary Lincoln herself had written to Davis as an ally in the cause against Judd, charging that "*Judd* would cause trouble & dissatisfaction, & if Wall Street testifies correctly, his business transactions, have not always borne inspection." Mary, unlike her husband, was unable to forgive Judd's role in Trumbull's victory over Lincoln in 1855. In the end, Lincoln decided he alone would provide sufficient representation for his state of Illinois. Instead, he offered Judd a ministry post in Berlin, which was more agreeable to Judd's wife, Adeline.

For weeks, the newspapers had been reporting that Gideon Welles was the most likely candidate from New England. Though bitterly opposed by Seward and Weed, Welles had the full confidence of the more hard-line members of the party. Nonetheless, Welles was "in an agony of suspense during that last week in February," as he waited in Hartford for positive word. When his son Edgar eagerly wrote from Yale that he would love to accompany his father to Washington for the inauguration, Welles replied: "It is by no means certain, my son, that I shall go myself . . . if not invited [by Lincoln] I shall not go at all."

Finally, on March 1, Welles received a telegram from Vice President–elect Hannibal Hamlin in Washington: "I desire to see you here forthwith." In his hurry to catch the train the next day, he discovered he had left his toiletries behind. More disconcerting, he arrived at the Willard to find the corridors so crowded that his trunks were temporarily mislaid, forcing him to remain in his rumpled clothes. Fortunately, Lincoln was dining elsewhere that evening, and a meeting was called for the following day. Lincoln offered him the navy portfolio.

With hard-liners Blair and Welles on board to balance Cameron and Bates, Lincoln still faced a difficult problem. He had resolved from the start to bring both Seward and Chase into his cabinet, but as the inauguration approached, each man's supporters violently opposed the appointment of the other. "The struggle for Cabinet portfolios waxes warmer, hourly," the *Evening Star* reported on March 1. Seward's delegation met with Lincoln on March 2, claiming that Chase would make the cabinet untenable for Seward. Hoping Lincoln would agree to forsake Chase, they were dismayed when, instead, Lincoln countered that although he still preferred a cabinet with both men, he might consider offering State to William Dayton and giving Seward the ministry to Great Britain.

After receiving the report of his friends, and beleaguered by the strength of the opposition to him, Seward sent a note to Lincoln asking to withdraw his earlier acceptance of the State portfolio. Lincoln waited two days to answer. "I can't afford to let Seward take the first trick," he told Nicolay. Nonetheless, his gracious manner again soothed a troubled situation. In his reply to Seward's withdrawal note, he wrote: "It is the subject of most painful solicitude with me; and I feel constrained to beg that you will countermand the withdrawal. The public interest, I think, demands that you should; and my personal feelings are deeply inlisted in the same direction."

Never genuinely desiring to withdraw, but hoping to pressure Lincoln to drop Chase, Seward rescinded his decision and accepted. In a letter to Frances, the New Yorker portrayed his waffling reversals in the most honorable light: "The President is determined that he will have a compound Cabinet; and that it shall be peaceful, and even permanent. I was at one time on the point of refusing—nay, I did refuse, for a time to hazard myself in the experiment. But a distracted country appeared before me; and I withdrew from that position. I believe I can endure as much as any one; and may be that I can endure enough to make the experiment successful. At all events I did not dare to go home, or to England, and leave the country to chance."

All that remained was for Lincoln to secure Chase's acceptance. He had not exchanged a single word with Chase about the appointment since his arrival in Washington. Now, without consulting the proud Ohioan, Lincoln sent Chase's nomination as treasury secretary to the Senate. Chase was on the Senate floor when a number of his colleagues came over to congratulate him. "Ever conscious of his own importance and overly sensitive to matters of protocol," he promptly called on the president to express his anger and his decision to decline the appointment. In the course of their ensuing conversation, Chase later recalled, Lincoln "referred to the embarrassment my declination would occasion him." Chase promised to consider the matter further, and, as Lincoln hoped, he "finally yielded."

In the end, Lincoln had unerringly read the character of Chase and slyly called Seward's bluff. Through all the countervailing pressures, he had achieved the cabinet he wanted from the outset—a mixture of former Whigs and Democrats, a combination of conciliators and hard-liners. He would be the head of his own administration, the master of the most unusual cabinet in the history of the country.

His opponents had been certain that Lincoln would fail in this first test of leadership. "The construction of a Cabinet," one editorial advised, "like the courting of a shrewd girl, belongs to a branch of the fine arts with which the new Executive is not acquainted. There are certain little tricks which go far beyond the arts familiar to the stump, and the cross-road tavern, whose comprehension requires a delicacy of thought and subtlety of perception, secured only by experience."

In fact, as John Nicolay later wrote, Lincoln's "first decision was one of great courage and self-reliance." Each of his rivals was "sure to feel that the wrong man had been nominated." A less confident man might have surrounded himself with personal supporters who would never question his authority. James Buchanan, for example, had deliberately chosen men who thought as he did. Buchanan believed, Allan Nevins writes, that a president "who tried to conciliate opposing elements by placing determined agents of each in his official family would find that he had simply strengthened discord, and had deepened party divisions." While it was possible that his team of rivals would devour one another, Lincoln determined that "he must risk the dangers of faction to overcome the dangers of rebellion."

Later, Joseph Medill of the *Chicago Tribune* asked Lincoln why he had chosen a cabinet comprised of enemies and opponents. He particularly questioned the president's selection of the three men who had been his chief rivals for the Republican nomination, each of whom was still smarting from the loss.

Lincoln's answer was simple, straightforward, and shrewd. "We needed the strongest men of the party in the Cabinet. We needed to hold our own people together. I had looked the party over and concluded that these were the very strongest men. Then I had no right to deprive the country of their services."

Seward, Chase, Bates—they were indeed strong men. But in the end, it was the prairie lawyer from Springfield who would emerge as the strongest of them all.

PART II

MASTER AMONG MEN

In this composite, Lincoln has taken over Seward's central position in the Republican Party, becoming the clear leader of a most unusual team of rivals.

Dressing Room

A. Lincoln's Bedroom

Bedroom

Mary's Bedroom

Prince of Wales Room (where Willie died)

Central Hall

Family Library

Bedroom

Corridor to North Window

Office Reception

Bedroom

Office Vestibule

Lincoln's Office

Nicolay's Office

Office Waiting Room

Nicolay & Hay's Bedroom

Hay's Office

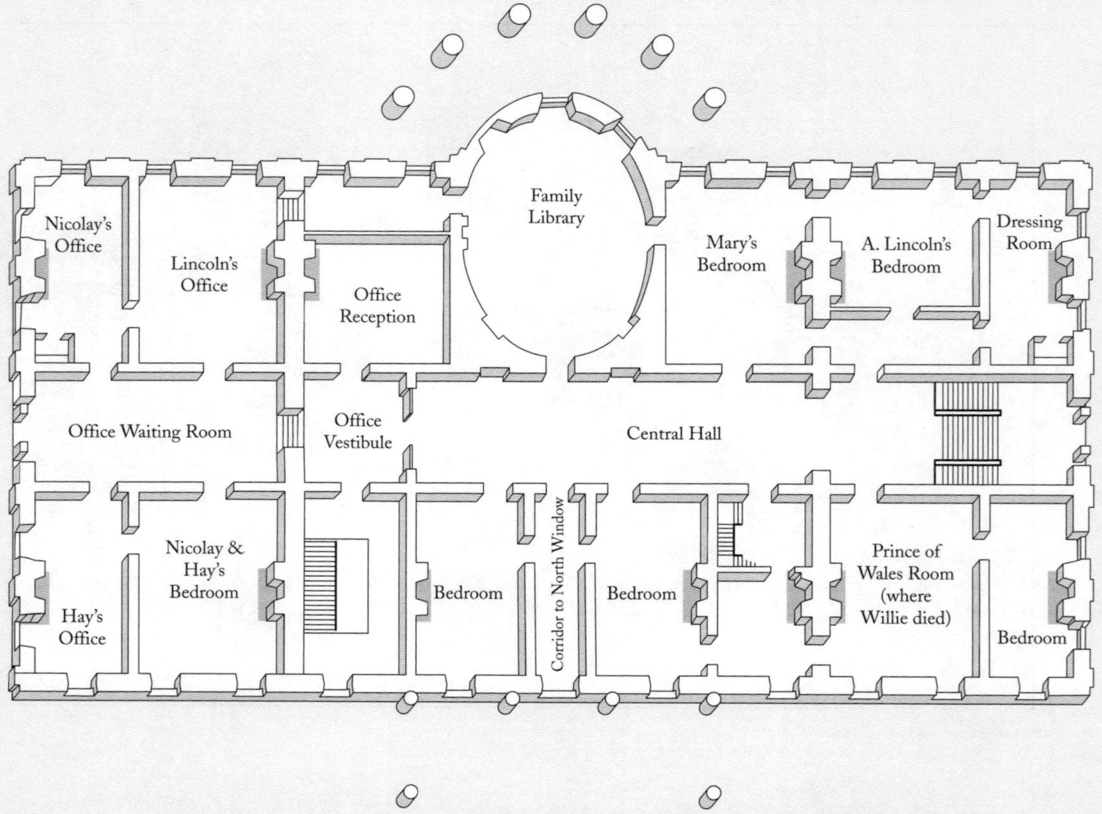

© 2005 Jeffrey L. Ward

CHAPTER 12

"MYSTIC CHORDS
OF MEMORY"

O N THE NIGHT BEFORE her husband's March 4 inauguration, Mary Lincoln was unable to sleep. She stood by her window in the Willard Hotel and watched strangers swarming in the darkened streets below. Though all the major hotels had laid out mattresses and cots in every conceivable open space, filling parlors, reception rooms, and lobbies, thousands were still left to wander the streets and wait for the great day to dawn.

Lincoln rose before sunrise to look over the inaugural address he had been crafting in his peculiar fashion. According to Nicolay, "Lincoln often resorted to the process of cumulative thought." He would reduce complex ideas to paragraphs and sentences, and then days or weeks later return to the same passage and polish it further "to elaborate or to conclude his point or argument." While Seward or Chase would consult countless books, drawing from ancient to modern history to illustrate and refine their arguments, Lincoln built the armature of his inaugural out of four documents: the Constitution, Andrew Jackson's nullification proclamation, Daniel Webster's memorable "Liberty and Union Forever" speech, and Clay's address to the Senate arguing for the Compromise of 1850.

Lincoln faced a dual challenge in this long-awaited speech, his first significant public address since his election. It was imperative that he convey his staunch resolution to defend the Union and to carry out his responsibilities as president, while at the same time mitigating the anxieties of the Southern states. Finding the balance between force and conciliation was not easy, and his early draft tilted more toward the forceful side. Among the first people to see the draft was Orville Browning. Browning had intended to accompany Lincoln on the train from Springfield to Washington, but finding "such a crowd of hangers on gathering about him," he decided to end the journey in Indianapolis. Before Browning left, Lincoln handed him a copy of his draft.

Browning focused on one imprudent passage that he feared would be seen in the South as a direct "threat, or menace," and would prove "irritating even in the border states." Lincoln had pledged: "All the power at my disposal will be used to reclaim the public property and places which have fallen; to hold, occupy and possess these, and all other property and places belonging to the government...." Browning suggested he delete the promise to reclaim what had already fallen, such as Fort Moultrie or Castle Pinckney, limiting himself to "hold, occupy, and possess" what was still in Union hands. "In any conflict which may ensue between the government and the seceding States," Browning argued, "it is very important that the traitors shall be the aggressors, and that they be kept constantly and palpably in the wrong." Though in a number of private conversations during the long secession winter Lincoln had expressed his determination to take back the fallen properties, he accepted Browning's argument and took out the promise to reclaim places that the seceding states had already taken.

Of all who read the draft, it was Seward who had the largest impact on Lincoln's inaugural address. Seward had read the initial draft with a heavy heart. Though he believed Lincoln's argument for the perpetuity of the Union was "strong and conclusive," he felt that the bellicose tone of the text would render useless all the hard work, all the risks taken during the previous weeks to stop the secession movement from expanding. Working on the draft for hours, seated in his favorite swivel chair, Seward wrote a long, thoughtful letter to Lincoln that contained scores of revisions. Taken together, his suggested changes softened the tone of the draft, made it more conciliatory toward the South.

Lincoln's text had opened on a forceful note, pledging himself "bound by duty . . . upon the plainest grounds of good faith" to abide by the Chicago platform, without "liberty to shift his position." Since many seceders considered the Chicago platform one of the touchstones of their withdrawal from the Union, this was clearly a provocative beginning. Even Bates had lambasted the Chicago platform as "exclusive and defiant . . . needlessly exposing the party to the specious charge of favoring negro equality." Seward argued that unless Lincoln eliminated his words pledging strict adherence to the platform, he would "give such advantages to the Disunionists that Virginia and Maryland will secede, and we shall within ninety, perhaps within sixty, days be obliged to fight the South for this capital. . . . In that case the dismemberment of the republic would date from the inauguration of a Republican Administration." Lincoln agreed to delete the reference to the Chicago platform entirely.

Seward also criticized Lincoln's pledge to reclaim fallen properties and to hold those still belonging to the government. He suggested that the text refer more "ambiguously" to "the exercise of power." Lincoln had already planned to change the text as Browning advised, so he ignored this overly compromising suggestion and retained his pledge to "hold, occupy and possess" the properties still belonging to the federal government, including Fort Sumter.

Seward's revisions are evident in nearly every paragraph. He qualified some, removed rough edges in others. Where Lincoln had referred to the secession ordinances and the acts of violence as "treasonable," Seward substituted the less accusatory "revolutionary." With the *Dred Scott* decision in mind, Lincoln warned against turning the "government over to the despotism of the few men [life officers] composing the court." Seward deleted the word "despotism" and elevated the Court to read "that eminent tribunal."

Lincoln had decried the idea of an amendment to the Constitution to ensure that Congress could never interfere with slavery in the states where it already existed. "I am, rather, for the old ship," he had written, "and the chart of the old pilots." Lincoln's stance put Seward in a difficult position; at Lincoln's behest, he had introduced the controversial resolution that called for the amendment in the first place. Lincoln's reversal now would leave Seward exposed. Treading carefully, Seward suggested that Lincoln acknowledge a diversity of opinion surrounding the proposed amendment, and that his own views would only "aggravate the dispute." As it happened,

Lincoln went further than Seward had suggested. In the early hours of the night before the inauguration, Congress, in its final session, had passed the proposed amendment "to the effect that the federal government, shall never interfere with the domestic institutions of the States." In light of this action, Lincoln reversed his position yet again. He revised his passage to say that since Congress had proposed the amendment, and since he believed "such a provision to now be implied constitutional law, I have no objection to its being made express, and irrevocable."

Seward's greatest contribution to the tone and substance of the inaugural address was in its conclusion. Lincoln's finale threw down the gauntlet to the South: "With *you*, and not with *me*, is the solemn question of 'Shall it be peace, or a sword?' " Seward recommended a very different closing, designed "to meet and remove prejudice and passion in the South, and despondency and fear in the East. Some words of affection—some of calm and cheerful confidence." He suggested two alternate endings. Lincoln drew upon Seward's language to create his immortal coda.

Seward suggested: "I close. We are not we must not be aliens or enemies but fellow countrymen and brethren. Although passion has strained our bonds of affection too hardly they must not, I am sure they will not be broken. The mystic chords which proceeding from so many battle fields and so many patriot graves pass through all the hearts and all the hearths in this broad continent of ours will yet again harmonize in their ancient music when breathed upon by the guardian angel of the nation."

Lincoln proceeded to recast and sharpen Seward's patriotic sentiments into a concise and powerful poetry: "I am loth to close. We are not enemies, but friends. We must not be enemies. Though passion may have strained, it must not break our bonds of affection. The mystic chords of memory, stretching from every battle-field, and patriot grave, to every living heart and hearthstone, all over this broad land, will yet swell the chorus of the Union, when again touched, as surely they will be, by the better angels of our nature." Most significant, Seward's "guardian angel" breathes down on the nation from above; Lincoln's "better angels" are inherent in our nature as a people.

· · ·

AFTER PLACING HIS FINISHING TOUCHES on the final draft, Lincoln read the speech to his family. Then he asked to be left alone. Several blocks away, Seward had finished reading the morning newspapers and was getting ready to go to the Capitol when a chorus of voices outside attracted his attention. Hundreds of devoted followers were assembled in front of his house. Moved by the spirit of the serenade, Seward spoke to them with emotion. "I have been a representative of my native State in the Senate for twelve years, and there is no living being who can look in my face and say that in all that time I have not done my duty toward all—the high and the low, the rich and the poor, the bond and the free."

Perhaps this show of popular support softened the wrenching realization that his chance had come and gone. When a congressman argued with him that a certain politician would be disappointed if he didn't get an appointment in the new administration, Seward lost his composure: "Disappointment! You speak to me of disappointment. To me, who was justly entitled to the Republican nomination for the presidency, and who had to stand aside and see it given to a little Illinois lawyer!"

As the clock struck noon, President Buchanan arrived at the Willard to escort the president-elect to the ceremony. Lincoln, only fifty-two, tall and energetic in his shiny new black suit and stovepipe hat, presented a striking contrast to the short and thickset Buchanan, nearly seventy, who had a sorrowful expression on his aged face. As they moved arm in arm toward the open carriage, the Marine Band played "Hail to the Chief." The carriage made its way up Pennsylvania Avenue, while cheering crowds and hundreds of dignitaries mingled uneasily with the hundreds of troops put in place by General Scott to guard against an attempted assassination. Sharpshooters looked down from windows and rooftops. Cavalry were placed strategically throughout the entire route.

Along the way, an ominous sound was heard. "A sharp, cracking, rasping sort of detonation, at regular intervals of perhaps three seconds" set everyone's nerves on edge, the Washington *Evening Star* reported. The perplexed police finally identified the sound as issuing from the New England delegation. They wore their customary "pegged" shoes, with heavy soles designed for the ice and snow of the north country. In the more temperate climate of Washington, the "heat and dryness of the atmosphere" had apparently "shrunk the peg timber in the foot-gear excessively, occasioning a general squeaking with every movement, swelling in the aggregate" when the delegation marched in step.

As the day brightened, Washington, according to one foreign observer, "assume[d] an almost idyllic garb." Though the city "displayed an unfinished aspect"—with the monument to President Washington still only one third of its intended height, the new Capitol dome two years away from completion, and most of the streets unpaved—the numerous trees and gardens were very pleasing, creating the feel of "a large rural village."

The appearance of Lincoln on the square platform constructed out from the east portico of the Capitol was met with loud cheers from more than thirty thousand spectators. Mary sat behind her husband, their three sons beside her. In the front row, along with Lincoln, sat President Buchanan, Senator Douglas, and Chief Justice Taney, three of the four men Lincoln had portrayed in his "House Divided" speech as conspiring carpenters intent on destroying the original house the framers had designed and built.

Lincoln's old friend Edward Baker, who had moved to Oregon and won a seat in the Senate, introduced the president-elect. Lincoln made his way to the little table from which he was meant to speak. Noting Lincoln's uncertainty as to where to place his stovepipe hat, Senator Douglas reached over, took the hat, and placed it on his own lap. Then Lincoln began. His clear high voice, trained in the outdoor venues of the Western states, could be heard from the far reaches of the crowd.

Having dropped his opening pledge of strict fealty to the Chicago platform, Lincoln moved immediately to calm the anxieties of the Southern people, quoting an earlier speech in which he had promised that he had "no purpose, directly or indirectly, to interfere with the institution of slavery in the States where it exists. I believe I have no lawful right to do so, and I have no inclination to do so." He turned then to the controversial Fugitive Slave Law, repeating his tenet that while "safeguards" should be put in place to ensure that free men were not illegally seized, the U.S. Constitution required that the slaves "shall be delivered upon claim of the party to whom such service or labor may be due." Although he understood that the Fugitive Slave Law offended "the moral sense" of many people in the North, he felt compelled, under the Constitution, to enforce it.

Lincoln went on to make his powerful case for continued federal authority over what he insisted, "in view of the Constitution and the laws," was an "unbroken" Union. While "there needs to be no bloodshed," he intended to execute the laws, "to hold, occupy, and possess the property, and places belonging to the government, and to collect the duties and imposts; but beyond what may be necessary for these objects, there will be no invasion—no using of force against, or among the people anywhere. . . .

"Physically speaking, we cannot separate," Lincoln declared, prophetically adding: "Suppose you go to war, you cannot fight always; and when, after much loss on both sides, and no gain on either, you cease fighting, the identical old questions, as to terms of intercourse, are again upon you. . . .

"In *your* hands, my dissatisfied fellow countrymen, and not in *mine*, is the momentous issue of civil war. The government will not assail *you*. You can have no conflict, without being yourselves the aggressors."

He closed with the lyrical assurance that "the mystic chords of memory . . . will yet swell the chorus of the Union, when again touched, as surely as they will be, by the better angels of our nature."

At the end of the address, Chief Justice Taney walked slowly to the table. The Bible was opened, and Abraham Lincoln was sworn in as the sixteenth President of the United States.

•   •   •

"THE MANSION was in a perfect state of readiness" when the Lincolns arrived, Mary's cousin Elizabeth Grimsley observed. "A competent chef, with efficient butler and waiters, under the direction of the accomplished Miss Harriet Lane, had an elegant dinner prepared." As Buchanan bade farewell, he said to Lincoln, "If you are as happy, my dear sir, on entering the house as I am in leaving it and returning home, you are the happiest man in this country." After some hasty unpacking, the Lincolns dressed for the Inaugural Ball, held in the rear of the City Hall, in a room referred to as the Muslim Palace of Aladdin "because of the abundance of white draperies trimmed with blue used in its decoration." Brightened by five enormous chandeliers, the room accommodated two thousand people, though the hooped crinolines worn by the women took up a good deal of space. Seward was there with his daughter-in-law Anna. Chase was accompanied by the lovely Kate. Still, this night Mary shone as the brightest star. "Dressed all in blue, with a necklace and bracelets of gold and pearls," she danced the quadrille with her old beau Stephen Douglas and remained at the ball for several hours after the departure of her exhausted husband.

While the party was still in full swing, word of Lincoln's inaugural speech was making its way across the country, carried by telegraph and printed in dozens of evening newspapers. In Auburn, Frances and Fanny waited in suspense throughout the night for the paper to arrive. Finally, Fanny heard a sound downstairs and raced to find out the news. "What an inappreciable relief," Fanny wrote in her diary when she read that the ceremony went off without violence. "For months I have felt constant anxiety for Father's safety—& of course joined in the fears so often expressed that Lincoln would never see the 5th of March." The news traveled more slowly west of St. Joseph, Missouri, where the telegraph lines stopped. Dozens of pony express riders, traveling in relays, carried the text of the address to the Pacific Coast. They did their job well. In a record time of "seven days and seventeen hours," Lincoln's words could be read in Sacramento, California.

Reactions to his speech varied widely, depending on the political persuasion of the commentators. Republican papers lauded the address as "grand and admirable in every respect," and "convincing in argument, concise and pithy in manner." It was "eminently conciliatory," the *Philadelphia Bulletin* observed, extolling the president's "determination to secure the rights of the whole country, of every State under the Constitution." The *Commercial Advertiser* of New York claimed that the inaugural was "the work of Mr. Lincoln's own pen and hand, unaltered by any to whom he confided its contents."

In Northern Democratic papers, the tone was less charitable. A "wretchedly botched and unstatesmanlike paper," the *Hartford Times* opined. "It is he that is the nullifier," the Albany *Atlas and Argus* raged. "It is he that defies the will of the majority. It is he that initiates Civil War." Not surprisingly, negative reactions were stronger in the South. The *Richmond Enquirer* argued that the address was "couched in the cool, unimpassioned, deliberate language of the fanatic . . . pursuing the promptings of fanaticism even to the dismemberment of the Government with the horrors of civil war." In ominous language, the Wilmington, North Carolina, *Herald* warned that the citizens of America "might as well open their eyes to the solemn fact that war is inevitable."

But beneath the blustery commentary in the majority of Southern papers, the historian Benjamin Thomas notes, the address "won some favorable comment in the all-important loyal slave states" of Virginia and North Carolina. This was the audience Seward had targeted when he told Lincoln to soften the tone of his speech. Indeed, Seward was greatly relieved, not only because he realized many of his suggestions had been adopted, but because Lincoln's conciliatory stance had given him cover with his critics in Congress. He could now leave the Senate, he told his wife, "without getting any bones broken," content with having provided a foundation "on which an Administration can stand."

Likewise, Charles Francis Adams, Sr., felt that a great burden had been lifted from his shoulders when Lincoln accepted the controversial amendment that prevented Congress from ever interfering with slavery. Having sponsored the amendment in the House, to the great dismay of the hard-liners, Adams now felt that he had "been fully justified in the face of the country by the head of the nation as well as of the Republican party. . . . Thus ends this most trying period of our history. . . . I should be fortunate if I closed my political career now. I have gained all that I can for myself and I shall never have such another opportunity to benefit my country."

Of the reactions to the inaugural speech, perhaps the most portentous came from within the Republican Party itself. Radicals and abolitionists were disheartened by what they considered an appeasing tone. The news of Lincoln's election had initially provided some desperately needed hope to the black abolitionist Frederick Douglass.

The dramatic life of the former slave who became an eloquent orator and writer was well known in the North. He had been owned by several cruel slaveholders, but his second master's kindly wife had taught him to read. When the master found out, he stopped the instruction immediately, warning his wife that "it was unlawful, as well as unsafe, to teach a slave to read . . . there would be no keeping him. It would forever unfit him to be a slave. . . . It would make him . . . discontented and unhappy." These words proved prescient. Young Douglass soon felt that "learning to read had been a curse rather than a blessing. It had given me a view of my wretched condition, without the remedy." He fervently wished that he were dead or perhaps an animal—"Any thing, no matter what, to get rid of thinking!" Only the faraway hope of escaping to freedom kept him alive. While waiting six years for his chance, he surreptitiously learned to write.

At the age of twenty, Douglass managed to escape from Maryland to New York, eventually becoming a lecturer with the Massachusetts Anti-Slavery Society, headed by William Lloyd Garrison. His autobiography made him a celebrity in antislavery circles, allowing him to edit his own monthly paper in Rochester, New York. Throughout all his writings, the historian David Blight argues, there was "no more pervasive theme in Douglass' thought than the simple sustenance of *hope* in a better future for blacks in America."

Douglass believed that the election of a Republican president foretold a rupture in the power of the slaveocracy. "It has taught the North its strength, and shown the South its weakness. More important still, it has demonstrated the possibility of electing, if not an Abolitionist, at least an *anti-slavery reputation* to the Presidency." But when Douglass read the inaugural, beginning with Lincoln's declaration that he had "no lawful power to interfere with slavery in the States," and worse still, no *"inclination"* to do so, he found little reason for optimism. More insufferable was Lincoln's readiness to catch fugitive slaves, "to shoot them down if they rise against their oppressors, and to prohibit the Federal Government *irrevocably* from interfering for their deliverance." The whole tone of the speech, Douglass claimed, revealed Lincoln's compulsion to grovel "before the foul and withering curse of slavery. Some thought we had in Mr. Lincoln the nerve and decision of an Oliver Cromwell; but the result shows that we merely have a continuation of the Pierces and Buchanans."

• • •

THE WHITE HOUSE FAMILY QUARTERS were then confined to the west
end of the second floor. Lincoln chose a small bedroom with a large dressing room on the southwest side. Mary took the more spacious room adjacent to her husband's, while Willie and Tad occupied a bedroom across the
hall. Beyond the ample sleeping quarters, there was only one other private
space—an oval room, filled with bookcases, that Mary turned into the
family's library. At the east end of the same floor was a sleeping chamber
shared by Nicolay and Hay and a small, narrow workspace that opened
onto the president's simply furnished office. The rest of the mansion was
largely open to the public. In the first few weeks, Seward reported to his
wife, "the grounds, halls, stairways, closets" were overrun with hundreds
of people, standing in long winding lines and waving their letters of introduction in desperate hope of securing a job.

For Willie and Tad, now ten and almost eight, respectively, the early
days in the White House were filled with great adventures. They ran from
floor to floor, inspecting every room. They talked with everyone along
the way, "from Edward, the door keeper, Stackpole, the messenger, to
the maids and scullions." Willie was "a noble, beautiful boy," Elizabeth
Grimsley observed, "of great mental activity, unusual intelligence, wonderful memory, methodical, frank and loving, a counterpart of his father,
save that he was handsome." Willie spent hours memorizing railroad
timetables and would entertain his friends by conducting "an imaginary
train from Chicago to New York with perfect precision" and dramatic flair.
He was an avid reader, a budding writer, and generally sweet-tempered, all
reminiscent of his father.

Tad, to whom Willie was devoted, bore greater resemblance to his
mother. Healthy and high-spirited, he had a blazing temper, which disappeared as quickly as it came. He was a "merry, spontaneous fellow, bubbling over with innocent fun, whose laugh rang through the house, when
not moved to tears." Irrepressible and undisciplined, never hesitant to interrupt his father in the midst of a cabinet meeting, he was "the life, as also
the worry of the household." A speech impediment made it hard for anyone outside his family to understand his words, but he never stopped talking. He had, John Hay recalled, "a very bad opinion of books and no
opinion of discipline."

The boys harried the staff at the executive mansion, racing through the
hallways, playing advocate for the most anguished office seekers, organizing little plays in the garret, and setting off all the servants' bells at the
same time. Fearing that her boys would grow lonely and isolated, Mary
found them two lively companions in twelve-year-old Horatio Nelson
"Bud" Taft and his eight-year-old brother, Halsey, nicknamed "Holly."

Together with their older sister, Julia, who later wrote a small book recording their adventures in the White House, the Taft children quickly formed a tight circle with Willie and Tad. "If there was any motto or slogan of the White House during the early years," Julia recalled, "it was this: 'Let the children have a good time.' "

Mary, too, seemed happy at first, surrounded by friends and relatives, who stayed on for weeks after the inauguration. Her confidence that she could handle the demands of first lady was buoyed by the great success of the first evening levee on the Friday after they moved in. Seward had proposed that he would lead off the social season from his own mansion, but Mary immediately took exception. Like her husband, Mary had no desire "to let Seward take the first trick." She insisted that the new administration's first official entertainment take place at the White House. Though she had little time to prepare, she arranged an unforgettable event. "For over two hours," Nicolay wrote his fiancée, Therena, "the crowd poured in as rapidly as the door would admit them, and many climbed in at the windows." The president and first lady shook hands with as many of the five thousand "well dressed and well behaved" guests as they could. Even the blue-blood Charles Francis Adams was impressed by Mary's poise, though he found Lincoln to be wholly ignorant of formal "social courtesy." Nonetheless, according to Nicolay, the levee "was voted by all the 'oldest inhabitants' to have been the most successful one ever known here."

Mary was thrilled. "This is certainly a very charming spot," she wrote her friend Hannah Shearer several weeks later, "& I have formed many delightful acquaintances. Every evening our *blue room*, is filled with the elite of the land, last eve, we had about 40 to call in, to see us *ladies*, from Vice. P. Breckinridge down. . . . I am beginning to feel so perfectly at home, and enjoy every thing so much. The conservatory attached to this house is so delightful." Scarcely concealing her pride at having outdone her older sister Elizabeth, she told Hannah that Elizabeth had so enjoyed herself at the festivities that she "cannot settle down at home, since she has been here."

• • •

A "LIGHT AND CAPRICIOUS" SLEEPER, Lincoln generally awakened early in the morning. Before breakfast he liked to exercise, often by walking around the spacious White House grounds. After a simple meal, usually a single egg and a cup of coffee, he made his way down the corridor to his office, where on cool days a fire blazed in the white marble fireplace with a big brass fender. His worktable stood between two tall windows that faced the south lawn, affording a panorama of the incomplete Washington

Monument, the red-roofed Smithsonian, and the Potomac River. An arm-chair nearby allowed him to read in comfort, his long legs stretched before him or crossed one over the other.

In the center of the chamber, which doubled as the Cabinet Room, stood a long oak table around which the members arranged themselves in order of precedence. Old maps hung on the wall, and over the mantel, a portrait of President Andrew Jackson. A few sofas and an assortment of chairs completed the furnishings. The musty smell of tobacco, lodged in the draperies from the heavy cigar smoke of the previous president and the new secretary of state, conveyed the atmosphere of the traditional men's club.

When Lincoln entered his office on the first morning after his inaugu-ration, he was confronted with profoundly disturbing news. On his desk, "the very first thing placed in his hands" was a letter from Major Anderson at Fort Sumter. The communication estimated, Lincoln later recalled, "that their provisions would be exhausted before an expedition could be sent to their relief." The letter carried General Winfield Scott's endorse-ment: "I now see no alternative but a surrender."

The immediacy of this crisis posed great difficulties for Lincoln. His revised inaugural had no longer contained a promise to "reclaim" fallen properties, but Lincoln had most definitely pledged to "hold, occupy and possess" all properties still in Federal hands. No symbol of Federal author-ity was more important than Fort Sumter. Ever since Major Anderson, in the dead of night on December 26, had surreptitiously moved his troops from Fort Moultrie to the better-protected Sumter, he had become a ro-mantic hero in the North. Surrender of his garrison would be humiliating. Still, the president felt bound by his vow to his "dissatisfied fellow country-men" that the new "government will not assail *you*. You can have no con-flict, without being yourselves the aggressors."

The president needed time to think, but scarcely had a moment "to eat or sleep" amid the crush of office seekers. Hundreds, perhaps thousands, pressed in as soon as the doors were opened, ignoring the barriers set up to keep them in line. As Lincoln moved throughout the house to take his lunch—which was generally limited to bread, fruit, and milk—"he had lit-erally to run the gantlet through the crowds." Each aspirant had a story to tell, a reason why a clerkship in Washington or a job in their local post office or customs house would allow their family to survive. Time and again, Lincoln was faulted for wasting his energies. "You will wear yourself out," Senator Henry Wilson of Massachusetts warned. "They don't want much," Lincoln replied, "they get but little, and I must see them."

Such openheartedness indicated incompetence to many, or, worse, a sign of terrible weakness. He "has no conception of his situation," Sumner told Adams. "He is ignorant, and must have help," Adams agreed, citing Seward as "our only security now." The *New York Times* reproved Lincoln repeatedly, writing disdainfully that he "owes a higher duty to the country . . . than to fritter away the priceless opportunities of the Presidency in listening to the appeals of competing office-hunters." Seward, too, was critical. "The President proposes to do all his work," he wrote home. "Of course he takes that business up, first, which is pressed upon him most."

Somehow Lincoln managed, despite the chaos, to focus upon the crisis at Sumter. Late at night, he would sit in the library, clothed in his "long-skirted faded dressing-gown, belted around his waist," his large leather Bible beside him. He liked to read and think in "his big chair by the window," observed Julia Taft, "in his stocking feet with one long leg crossed over the other, the unshod foot slowly waving back and forth, as if in time to some inaudible music."

Unwilling to accept Scott's assumption that Sumter must be evacuated, Lincoln penned a note to the old general, asking for more specifics. Exactly how long could Anderson hold out? What would it take to resupply him and to reinforce Sumter? Scott's reply laid out a bleak prospect indeed. With the government of South Carolina now preventing the garrison from resupplying in Charleston, Anderson could hold out, Scott estimated, for only twenty-six days. It would require "six to eight months" to assemble the "fleet of war vessels & transports, 5,000 additional regular troops & 20,000 volunteers" necessary to resupply and reinforce the garrison.

Rumors spread that Sumter would soon be surrendered, but Lincoln "was disinclined to hasty action," Welles recorded in his diary, "and wished time for the Administration to get in working order and its policy to be understood." Repeatedly, he called his cabinet into session to discuss the situation. He met with Francis Blair, who, like his son, Monty, believed passionately that the surrender of Sumter "was virtually a surrender of the Union unless under irresistible force—that compounding with treason was treason to the Govt."

At Monty Blair's suggestion, Lincoln met with his brother-in-law, Gustavus Fox, a former navy officer who had developed an ingenious plan for relief by sea. Bread and supplies could be loaded onto two sturdy tugboats, shadowed by a large steamer conveying troops ready to fire if the tugs were opposed. Intrigued, Lincoln asked Fox to present his plan; and the next day, March 15, the cabinet gathered around the long table to discuss the stratagem. Lincoln seldom took his seat, pacing up and down as he spoke. After the meeting, he sent a memo to each of the members, asking for a written response to the following question: "Assuming it to be possible to now provision Fort-Sumpter, under all the circumstances, is it wise to attempt it?"

Seward, who had exerted himself in the previous months trying to mollify the Union's remaining slave states, found the idea of provisioning Sumter and sending troops to South Carolina detestable. From his suite in the old State Department, a two-story brick building containing only thirty-two rooms, Seward drafted his reply, while his son Frederick, who had been confirmed by the Senate as assistant secretary of state, handled the crowds downstairs. In his lengthy reply to the president, Seward reiterated that without the conciliation measures that had solidified the Unionist sentiment in the South, Virginia, North Carolina, Arkansas, and the border states would have joined the Confederacy. The attempt to supply Fort Sumter with armed forces would inevitably provoke the remaining slave states to secede and launch a civil war—that "most disastrous and deplorable of national calamities." Far better, Seward advised, to assume a defensive position, leaving "the necessity for action" in the hands of "those who seek to dismember and subvert this Union. . . . In that case, we should have the spirit of the country and the approval of mankind on our side." His emphatic negative reply probably reached Lincoln within minutes, for the State Department was adjacent to the northern wing of the Treasury Department and connected by a short pathway to the White House.

Chase did not return his answer until the following day, repairing that evening to his suite at the Willard Hotel. Considering his hard-line credentials, Chase returned a surprisingly evasive and equivocal reply: "If the attempt will so inflame civil war as to involve an immediate necessity for the enlistment of armies and the expenditure of millions I cannot advise it." Better, he later explained, to consider "the organization of actual government by the seven seceded states *as an accomplished revolution*—accomplished through the complicity of the late admn.—& letting that confederacy try its experiment." Still, he concluded in his answer to Lincoln, "it seems to me highly improbable" that war will result. "I return, therefore, an affirmative answer."

Every other cabinet officer save Blair rejected the possibility of sustaining Fort Sumter. Bates argued that he was loath "to do any act which may have the semblance, before the world of beginning a civil war." Cameron contended that even if Fox's plan should succeed, which he considered doubtful, the surrender of the fort would remain "an inevitable necessity." Thus, "the sooner it be done, the better." Welles, writing from his second-floor suite in the Navy Department on 17th Street, reasoned that since the "impression has gone abroad that Sumter is to be evacuated and the shock caused by that announcement has done its work," it would only cause further damage to follow "a course that would provoke hostilities." And if it did not succeed, "failure would be attended with untold disaster." In like fashion, Interior Secretary Caleb Smith concluded that while the plan might succeed, "it would not be wise under all the circumstances."

Only Montgomery Blair delivered an unconditional yes, arguing that "every new conquest made by the rebels strengthens their hands at home and their claim to recognition as an independent people abroad." So long as the rebels could claim *"that the Northern men are deficient in the courage necessary to maintain the Government,"* the secession momentum would continue. Just as President Jackson stopped the attempted secession of South Carolina in 1833 by making it clear that punishment would follow, so Lincoln must now take "measures which will inspire respect for the power of the Government and the firmness of those who administer it."

In the end, five cabinet members strongly opposed the resupply and reinforcement of Sumter; one remained ambiguous; one was in favor.

•   •   •

IN THE DAYS THAT FOLLOWED the cabinet vote, Lincoln appeared to waver. Weed later insisted that on at least three occasions, the president said if he could keep Virginia in the Union, he would give up Sumter. Seward urged that so long as Fort Pickens in Florida remained in Union hands, Sumter's evacuation would matter little. Pickens was fully provisioned and, situated in Pensacola Bay, would be easier than Sumter to defend. Orders had already been issued to reinforce the garrison. However, Lincoln felt that the surrender of Sumter would be "utterly ruinous . . . that, at home, it would discourage the friends of the Union, embolden its adversaries, and go far to insure to the latter, a recognition abroad."

Desiring more information, Lincoln sent Fox to talk directly to Major Anderson and determine exactly how long his supplies would last. Through the intervention of an old friend who was close to the governor of South Carolina, Fox received permission to enter Sumter and meet with Anderson. If his men went on half-rations, Anderson told him, he could last until April 15. At the same time, Lincoln sent Stephen Hurlbut, whom he had known well in Springfield, to Charleston. Hurlbut had grown up in Charleston, and his sister still lived there. Speaking privately to old friends, he could test Seward's assumption that Unionist sentiment throughout the South would continue to strengthen so long as the government refrained from any provocative action or perceived aggression. Hurlbut spent two days in his native city. He returned with "no hesitation in reporting as unquestionable" that Unionist sentiment in both city and state was dead, "that separate nationality is a fixed fact."

While Lincoln was learning more about the facts of the situation, his cabinet colleagues were engaged in a series of petty feuds. Chase considered Smith "a cypher" and Bates "a humdrum lawyer." Seward was furious when Chase and Bates insisted on two appointments in his own district and stated that would be "humiliating" to him. "I would sooner attack either of those gentlemen in the open street," Seward indignantly wrote Lincoln, "than consent to oppose any local appointment they might desire to make in their respective states." From his Treasury Department office overlooking the White House grounds, Chase complained to Lincoln that Seward would "certainly have no cause to congratulate himself if he persists in denying the only favor he *can* show me." Blair Senior, echoing the sentiment of his son, grumbled to Chase that all the best missions abroad had been given to Seward's old Whig friends. "I believe our Republican Party will not endure, unless there is a fusion of the Whig & Democratic element," he noted ruefully.

While the cabinet members squabbled over patronage, they united in their resentment of Seward's preeminent position. They were irritated that he was the one who called the cabinet into session, and the time he spent with Lincoln inspired jealousy. Finally, with Chase as their "spokesman," they requested that cabinet meetings be held at regular times. Lincoln agreed, designating Tuesdays and Fridays at noon.

Still, Seward was recognized as the man who had the president's ear. William Russell of *The Times* in London capitalized on this intimacy when he first arrived in Washington. Russell was then forty-one, a spectacled, lively, rotund Englishman whose sparkling reports from the Crimean War had made him a celebrity in London. At a dinner party on March 26, he was fascinated by Seward, "a subtle, quick man, rejoicing in power . . . fond of badinage, bursting with the importance of state mysteries." The next day, Seward arranged for Russell to slip into a White House reception for the Italian minister. Russell recalled that Lincoln "put out his hand in a very friendly manner, and said, 'Mr. Russell, I am very glad to make your acquaintance, and to see you in this country. The London *Times* is one of the greatest powers in the world—in fact, I don't know anything which has much more power—except perhaps the Mississippi.' "

Russell attended the Lincolns' first state dinner that evening. Arriving at the White House, he noted that Mary "was already seated to receive her guests." He found her features "plain, her nose and mouth of an ordinary type, and her manners and appearance homely, stiffened, however, by the consciousness that her position requires her to be something more than plain Mrs. Lincoln, the wife of the Illinois lawyer; she is profuse in the introduction of the word 'sir' in every sentence."

Once acquainted with all the cabinet officers and the various guests, Russell rated Chase, with his "fine forehead" and his "face indicating energy and power," as "one of the most intelligent and distinguished persons in the whole assemblage." He was particularly taken with Kate Chase, whom he described as "very attractive, agreeable, and sprightly." Kate was in her element, talking "easily, with a low melodious voice . . . her head tilted slightly upward, a faint, almost disdainful smile upon her face, as if she were a titled English lady posing in a formal garden for Gainsborough or Reynolds." As her father's hostess, Kate stood fourth in official Washington society. Her only real rival was Mrs. Lincoln, since neither Ellen Hamlin nor Frances Seward had any desire for social aggrandizement. "In reality, there was no one in Washington to compare with Kate Chase," one of Kate's intimate friends later told the *Cincinnati Enquirer.* "She was the queen of society. Men showered adulation upon her and went on their knees to her. I have never seen a woman who has so much personal charm and magnetism." The possibly apocryphal story spread of Kate's introduction to Mary that night. "I shall be glad to see you any time, Miss Chase," Mary said. Kate replied: "Mrs. Lincoln, I shall be glad to have *you* call on *me* at any time." Though Mary would later manifest intense jealousy of Kate, it is doubtful that Kate's remark spoiled her pleasure that glittering evening.

At the formal dinner, "there was a Babel of small talk," Russell observed, "except when there was an attentive silence caused by one of the President's stories . . . for which he is famous." As he reeled off one humorous anecdote after another, no one could have guessed that earlier that day, Lincoln had received devastating news from General Scott. In a written memorandum, Scott had advised that it was now unlikely, "according to recent information from the South, whether the voluntary evacuation of Fort Sumter alone would have a decisive effect upon the States now wavering between adherence to the Union and secession." Fort Pickens would also have to be abandoned, Scott argued, in order to "give confidence to the eight remaining slave-holding States."

Shortly before the state dinner ended, Lincoln called his cabinet colleagues aside and asked them to follow him into a different room. Montgomery Blair would long remember Lincoln's agitation as he revealed the contents of Scott's report. "A very oppressive silence succeeded," Blair recalled, interrupted only by his own angry retort that Scott was playing "politician and not General," a comment directed at Seward's influence with Scott. Like his son, Blair Senior had long believed that Lincoln should have announced the reinforcement of Sumter at the time of his in-auguration and he blamed Seward for Lincoln's "timid temporizing policy." It was Andrew Jackson's motto, he reminded, that "if you temporize, you are lost."

• • •

THAT NIGHT, Lincoln was unable to sleep. The time for musing and assessment was at an end. He must make the decision between a surrender that might compromise the honor of the North and tear it apart, or a reinforcement that might carry the country into civil war. Later he confessed to Browning, "of all the trials I have had since I came here, none begin to compare with those I had between the inauguration and the fall of Fort Sumpter. They were so great that could I have anticipated them, I would not have believed it possible to survive them."

At noon the next day, the cabinet convened. Lincoln presented all the intelligence he had gathered, including Fox's report on Major Anderson's situation and Hurlbut's conclusion that Unionism was essentially dead in South Carolina. Once more the members were asked to submit their opinions in writing. This time, shaped no doubt by Lincoln's presentation and General Scott's disturbing memo, the majority opinion—with only Seward and Smith clearly dissenting—advised that both Sumter and Pickens should be resupplied and reinforced.

Evidence suggests that Lincoln had reached a decision before the cabinet met, for he had already requested that Fox send a list of the "ships, men, and supplies he would need for his expedition." Several hours after the cabinet adjourned, he also implemented a drastic restructuring of his daily schedule. Much as he wanted to give office seekers their due, he needed time and space to consider the grave problems facing the country. He ordered Nicolay to limit visiting hours from 10 a.m. to 3 p.m., ending the hectic burden of twelve-hour days that Nicolay knew "would be impossible to sustain for a great length of time."

For Seward, Lincoln's decision to reinforce Sumter was shattering. He was in his house on the evening of March 29 when George Harrington, assistant secretary of the treasury, knocked at the door. Harrington had just left the White House, where Welles, Blair, and Fox had met with Lincoln, and "it was finally determined, with the President's approval to reinforce Fort Sumter."

"Thunder, George! What are you talking about?" Seward asked. "It cannot be." When Harrington repeated his news, Seward was irate. "I want no more at this time of the Administration which may be defeated. We are not yet in a position to go to war." Seward's success in getting Lincoln to soften the tone of his inaugural address, coupled with the cabinet vote on March 15, decisively echoing his own advice to evacuate Sumter, had left him with the mistaken conviction that he was the power behind a weak president.

Flattering letters from the South had compounded Seward's erroneous assumption. Frederick Roberts in North Carolina assured him that everyone was looking to him for "a peaceful adjustment of the difficulties." While Lincoln, the letter continued, was considered throughout the state as "a 3rd rate man," Seward was looked upon as "the Hector or Atlas of not only his Cabinet, but the giant intellect of the whole north." Another admirer swore that "Unionists look to yourself, and only to you Sir, as a member of the Cabinet—*to save the country*." With these judgments of both the president's failings and his own stature, Seward wholeheartedly agreed. He confided to Adams that Lincoln had "no conception of his situation—much absorption in the details of office dispensation, but little application to great ideas." Adams needed little convincing. Despite accepting the high-ranking appointment as minister to Great Britain, he remained dismissive of Lincoln, writing in his diary: "The man is not equal to the hour." The only hope, he repeatedly wrote, lay in the secretary of state's influence with the president.

For weeks, Seward had acted under "two supreme illusions": first, that he was in reality the man in charge; and second, that Southerners would be appeased by the abandonment of Sumter and would eventually return to the Union. He had risked his good name on his conviction that Lincoln would follow his advice and surrender Sumter. Three commissioners had been sent to Washington by the Confederacy to negotiate, among other issues, the question of the forts. Lincoln, however, had refused to allow any dealings with them on the grounds that direct communication would legitimize the seceded states. Stifled, Seward had resorted to an indirect link through Alabama's John Campbell, who had remained on the Supreme Court despite the secession of his state. After the March 15 cabinet meeting, Seward, believing that his vote to evacuate would soon be confirmed by Lincoln, had sent a message that Campbell relayed to the commissioners, who reported to the Confederacy's capital, then located in Montgomery, Alabama: Sumter "would be evacuated in the next five days."

Desperate to save his own honor and prevent the country from drifting into war, while the administration established no clear-cut policy, Seward composed an extraordinary memo that would become the source of great criticism and controversy. During the afternoon of April 1, Fred Seward recalled, his father wrote "Some thoughts for the President's consideration." Since his "handwriting was almost illegible," he asked Fred to copy it over and bring it personally to Lincoln, not allowing it "to be filed, or to pass into the hands of any clerk."

"We are at the end of a month's Administration, and yet without a policy either domestic or foreign," the contentious memo began. Seward proceeded to reiterate his argument for abandoning Fort Sumter, placing new emphasis on reinforcing Fort Pickens. He asserted that focusing on Fort Pickens rather than on Sumter would allow Lincoln to retain "the symbolism of Federal authority" with far less provocation. Seward's mistake was not the diabolical plot that some critics later charged, but a grave misreading of the situation and a grave misunderstanding of Lincoln.

Seward continued under the heading of "For Foreign Nations," suggesting that Lincoln deflect attention from the domestic crisis by demanding that Spain and France explain their meddling in the Western Hemisphere and that Great Britain, Canada, and Russia account for their threats to intervene in the American crisis. If the explanations of any country proved unsatisfactory, war should be declared. In fact, some such explanations were eventually demanded, convincing European leaders to be more careful in their response to the American situation. It was Seward's wilder proposal of declaring war, if necessary, that would arouse the harsh rebuke of biographers and historians.

Nor did Seward's overreaching end there. The previous February, Seward had informed a German diplomat "that there was no great difference between an elected president of the United States and an hereditary monarch." Neither truly ran things. "The actual direction of public affairs belongs to the leader of the ruling party." Seward had conceived of himself as a prime minister, with Lincoln the figurehead. Testing this presumptuous notion, Seward closed with the idea that "whatever policy we adopt, there must be an energetic prosecution of it. . . . Either the President must do it himself . . . or DEVOLVE it on some member of his Cabinet. . . . It is not in my especial province. But I neither seek to evade nor assume responsibility." As Nicolay later wrote, "had Mr. Lincoln been an envious or a resentful man, he could not have wished for a better occasion to put a rival under his feet." Seward's effrontery easily could have provoked a swift dismissal. Yet, as happened so often, Lincoln showed an "unselfish magnanimity," which was "the central marvel of the whole affair."

The president immediately dashed off a reply to Seward that he would never send, probably preferring to respond in person. Buried in Lincoln's papers, the document was not unearthed until decades later, as Nicolay and Hay labored on their massive Lincoln biography. Lincoln's response was short but pointed. Concerning the assertion that the administration was "without a policy," Lincoln reminded Seward of his inaugural pledge that "the power confided to me will be used to hold, occupy, and possess the property and places belonging to the government." This was the "exact domestic policy" that Seward called for, "with the single exception, that it does not propose to abandon Fort Sumpter." As for the charge that the administration lacked a foreign policy, "we have been preparing circulars, and instructions to ministers . . . without even a suggestion that we had no foreign policy." The idea of engineering a foreign war to reunify the country did not even rate a response.

Lincoln responded most emphatically to Seward's suggestion that perhaps the secretary of state was needed to design and pursue a vigorous policy where the president had not. In unmistakable language, Lincoln wrote: "I remark that if this must be done, *I* must do it."

Undaunted, Seward worked furiously to complete his plans for reinforcing Fort Pickens, hopeful that Lincoln might change his mind before the Fox expedition to Fort Sumter was launched. The previous day, he had sent an urgent summons to Captain Montgomery Meigs to come to his house. Recognizing that time was short, Seward requested Meigs "to put down upon paper an estimate & project for relieving & holding Fort Pickens" and "to bring it to the Presidents before 4 p.m." Lincoln was happy to receive the army captain's report, though in his mind, reinforcing Pickens did not mean choosing between the two garrisons. "Tell [Scott]," the president said, "that I wish this thing done & not to let it fail unless he can show that I have refused him something he asked for as necessary. I depend upon you gentlemen to push this thing through."

Lincoln was cautioned by Seward that the army's expedition to Pickens should be kept from naval authorities, given the number of navy men who were openly disloyal to the Union. Lincoln signed orders on April 1 to Andrew Foote, the commandant of the Navy Yard in Brooklyn, to "fit out the *Powhatan* without delay" for a secret mission to Pensacola under the command of Lieutenant David Porter. The *Powhatan* was the U.S. Navy's most powerful warship. "Under no circumstances" should "the fact that she is fitting out" be disclosed to the Navy Department, Lincoln emphasized. Both Navy Secretary Welles and Captain Fox, whose plans for the relief of Sumter depended on the *Powhatan*, remained unaware of the secret orders. With its mighty guns and three hundred sailors, the *Powhatan* was supposed to play an essential role in backing up the tugboats carrying supplies to Sumter.

Lincoln had failed to peruse the orders carefully and inadvertently assigned the *Powhatan* simultaneously to both Pickens and Sumter. In the confusion of the first weeks, it was not unusual for Lincoln to sign documents from Seward without reading them. Fred Seward later recalled that when he brought papers over to the White House for signature, Lincoln would say: "Your father says this is all right, does he? Well, I guess he knows. Where do I put my name?"

Still ignorant of the mix-up, Welles wrote to Samuel Mercer, the current commander of the *Powhatan*, on April 5, instructing him to "leave New York with the Powhatan in time to be off Charleston bar" by the morning of the 11th. If the supply boats were permitted to land at Fort Sumter, he should return to New York at once. If their entry was opposed, then the *Powhatan* and its support ships should be used "to open the way." Should the "peaceable" supply mission fail, "a reinforcement of the garrison" should be attempted by "disposing of your force," as needed. The orders from Welles to Mercer were read to the president that same day and authorized.

The next day, Lincoln drafted a letter for Cameron to send through a messenger to the governor of South Carolina: "I am directed by the President of the United States to notify you to expect an attempt will be made, to supply Fort-Sumpter with provisions only; and that, if such attempt be not resisted, no effort to throw in men, arms, or ammunition, will be made without further notice." Lincoln had devised a means to separate the peaceful supply mission from the more controversial issue of reinforcement, forging, at least for the record, a final alternative to war.

While Lincoln's strategy was creative, its execution was fatally bungled. Learning that the Pickens expedition was "embarrassed by conflicting orders from the Secretary of the Navy," Captain Meigs had telegraphed Seward for an explanation. Placed in an awkward situation, Seward knew he would have to reveal the secret Pickens mission to Welles. Sometime after 11 p.m., Seward and Fred took a short walk to the Willard to talk with Welles. Earlier that evening, Welles, assuming that the *Powhatan* and its accompanying ships had already set sail for Sumter, had congratulated himself on accomplishing so much in such a short time.

Seward showed Welles the telegram, explaining that it must relate to the *Powhatan*, which was now under command of David Porter and on its way to Pensacola. Welles insisted that was impossible. The *Powhatan* was "the flagship" of the mission to Sumter. They decided to consult the president at once. Though midnight was approaching, Lincoln was still awake. Upon hearing the problem, he "looked first at one and then the other, and declared there was some mistake." Once the error was clear, he told Seward to send Porter a telegram, ordering him to "return the Powhatan to Mercer without delay," so that the Sumter expedition could proceed. Seward tried to champion the Pickens expedition, but Lincoln "was imperative," insisting that the telegram go out that night.

To the astonishment of Welles, Lincoln "took upon himself the whole blame—said it was carelessness, heedlessness on his part—he ought to have been more careful and attentive." In fact, Welles continued, Lincoln "often declared that he, and not his Cabinet, was in fault for errors imputed to them." Seward reluctantly sent the telegram; but Porter had already set sail for Florida. A fast ship was dispatched to catch up with the *Powhatan*, but when Porter read the telegram, bearing Seward's signature instead of the president's, he continued to Florida, on the assumption that the previous order signed by the president had priority.

When Gustavus Fox reached Charleston, he spent hours futilely searching for the *Powhatan*, having no clue the vessel had been misrouted. Nor did he know that Confederate authorities in Montgomery had intercepted his plans and ordered the commander in Charleston, Brigadier General Pierre Beauregard, to attack the fort before the *Powhatan* and Union convoy were due to arrive. At 3:30 a.m. on April 12, Beauregard sent a note to Anderson announcing his intent to commence firing in one hour. Anderson's small garrison of sixty men returned fire but were quickly overwhelmed by the Confederate force of nine thousand. They had no chance, Fox lamented, without the *Powhatan*'s men, howitzers, and "fighting launches." Abner Doubleday, an officer on Anderson's staff, recalled that "the conflagration was terrible and disastrous. . . . One-fifth of the fort was on fire, and the wind drove the smoke in dense masses into the angle where we had all taken refuge."

Thirty-four hours after the fighting began, Major Anderson surrendered. In a gesture that forever endeared him to the North, he brought his men together and fired a dignified fifty-round salute to the shredded American flag before hauling it down and leaving the fort. Incredibly, only one Union soldier died, the result of an accidental explosion of gunpowder during the salute to the flag. Beauregard, who had been been a student of Anderson's at West Point and had great respect for him, waited until Anderson had departed before entering the fort, as "it would be an unhonorable thing . . . to be present at the humiliation of his friend."

Captain Fox was inconsolable. Convinced that his mission would have been successful with the missing *Powhatan*, he believed that for a failure that was not his fault, he had lost his "reputation with the general public." Lincoln, once more, assumed the blame, assuring him that "by an accident, for which you were in no wise responsible, and possibly I, to some extent was, you were deprived of a war vessel with her men, which you deemed of great importance to the enterprize. I most cheerfully and truly declare that the failure of the undertaking has not lowered you a particle, while the qualities you developed in the effort, have greatly heightened you, in my estimation.

"You and I," he continued, "both anticipated that the cause of the country would be advanced by making the attempt to provision Fort-Sumpter, even if it should fail; and it is no small consolation now to feel that our anticipation is justified by the result."

Critics later claimed that Lincoln had maneuvered the South into beginning the war. In fact, he had simply followed his inaugural pledge that he would "hold" the properties belonging to the government, "but beyond what may be necessary" to accomplish this, "there will be no invasion—no using of force." Fort Sumter could not be held without food and supplies. Had Lincoln chosen to abandon the fort, he would have violated his pledge to the North. Had he used force in any way other than to "hold" government properties, he would have breached his promise to the South.

The Confederates had fired the first shot. A war had begun that no one imagined would last four years and cost greater than six hundred thousand lives—more than the cumulative total of all our other wars, from the Revolution to Iraq. The devastation and sacrifice would reach into every community, into almost every family, in a nation of 31.5 million. In proportion to today's population, the number of deaths would exceed five million.

CHAPTER 13

"THE BALL HAS OPENED"

N EWS OF THE CONFEDERATE ATTACK on Fort Sumter spread
throughout the North that weekend. Walt Whitman recalled
hearing the shouts of newsboys after he emerged from an opera
on 14th Street and was strolling down Broadway late Saturday night. At
the Metropolitan Hotel, "where the great lamps were still brightly blazing," the news was read to a crowd of thirty or forty suddenly gathered
round. More than twenty years later, he could "almost see them there now,
under the lamps at midnight again."

The "firing on the flag" produced a "volcanic upheaval" in the North,
Whitman observed, "which at once substantially settled the question of
disunion." The *National Intelligencer* spoke for many Northerners: "Our
people now, one and all, are determined to sustain the Government and
demand a vigorous prosecution of the war inaugurated by the disunionists.
All sympathy with them is dead."

The fevered excitement in the North was mirrored in the South. "The ball has opened," a dispatch from Charleston, South Carolina, began. "The excitement in the community is indescribable. With the very first boom of the guns thousands rushed from their beds to the harbor front, and all day every available place has been thronged by ladies and gentlemen, viewing the spectacle through their glasses."

On Sunday, Lincoln returned from church and immediately called his cabinet into session. He had decided to issue a proclamation to the North, calling out state militias and fixing a time for Congress to reconvene. The number of volunteer soldiers to be requested came under debate. Some wanted 100,000, others 50,000; Lincoln settled on 75,000. The timing of the congressional session also posed a difficult question. While the executive branch needed Congress to raise armies and authorize spending, Lincoln was advised that "to wait for 'many men of many minds' to shape a war policy would be to invite disaster." Seward was particularly adamant on this point, believing that "history tells us that kings who call extra parliaments lose their heads." Lincoln and his cabinet set the Fourth of July as the date for Congress to reconvene, relying on "their patriotism to sanction the war measures taken prior to that time by the Executive."

John Nicolay made a copy of the president's proclamation and delivered it to the secretary of state, who stamped the great seal and sent it for publication the following day. That afternoon, Lincoln took a carriage ride with his boys and Nicolay, trying for a moment to distract himself from the increasingly onerous events. Upon his return, he welcomed his old rival Stephen Douglas for a private meeting of several hours. Douglas was not well; a lifetime of alcohol and frenetic activity had taken its toll. In two months' time, he would be dead. Nevertheless, he offered his solid support to Lincoln, afterward publicly declaring himself ready "to sustain the President in the exercise of his constitutional functions to preserve the Union, and maintain the Government." His statement proved tremendously helpful in mobilizing Democratic support. "In this hour of trial it becomes the duty of every patriotic citizen to sustain the General Government," one Douglas paper began. Another urged "every man to lay aside his party bias . . . give up small prejudices and go in, heart and hand, to put down treason and traitors."

"The response to the Proclamation at the North," Fred Seward recalled, "was all or more than could be anticipated. Every Governor of a free State promptly promised that his quota should be forthcoming. An enthusiastic outburst of patriotic feeling—an 'uprising of the North' in town and country—was reported by telegraph." Northern newspapers described massive rallies, with bands blaring and volunteers marching in support of the Union. Old party lines seemed to have evaporated. "We begin to look like a United North," George Templeton Strong recorded in his diary, prophesying that the Democratic *New York Herald* would soon "denounce Jefferson Davis as it denounced Lincoln a week ago."

The enthusiastic solidarity of the North dangerously underestimated the strength and determination of the South. Seward predicted that the war would be over in sixty days. John Hay expressed the condescending wish that it would "be bloody and short, in pity to the maniac South. They are weak, ignorant, bankrupt in money and credit. Their army is a vast mob, insubordinate and hungry. . . . What is before them but defeat, poverty, dissensions, insurrections and ruin."

Ominous signals from the South soon deflated these facile forecasts. North Carolina, Tennessee, and Kentucky refused to send troops "for the wicked purpose of subduing [their] sister Southern States." Then, on April 17, citing the president's call to arms, the vital state of Virginia seceded from the Union. The historian James Randall would designate this act "one of the most fateful events in American history." News of Virginia's decision provoked jubilation throughout the South. "We never saw our population so much excited as it was yesterday afternoon, when the glorious news spread all over town as wildfire, that Virginia, the 'Mother of Presidents,' had seceded at last," the New Orleans *Daily Picayune* reported. "Citizens on the sidewalks, were shaking each other by the hand, our office was overcrowded, the boys were running to and fro, unable to restrain their delight, and now and then venting their enthusiasm by giving a hearty hurrah."

In their excitement, Southerners fell victim to the same hectic misjudgment that plagued the North, overstating their own chances as they underestimated their opponent's will. "And now we are eight!" the *Picayune* exulted, predicting they would soon be fifteen when all the remaining slave states followed Virginia's lead. In fact, the Old Dominion's action prodded only three more states to join the Confederacy—North Carolina, Arkansas, and Tennessee. For many agonizing months, however, Lincoln would remain apprehensive about the border states of Maryland, Missouri, and Kentucky.

The day after Virginia seceded, Francis Blair, Sr., invited Colonel Robert E. Lee to his yellow house on Pennsylvania Avenue. A graduate of West Point, the fifty-four-year-old Lee had served in the Mexican War, held the post of superintendent at West Point, and commanded the forces that captured John Brown at Harpers Ferry. General Scott regarded him as "the very best soldier I ever saw in the field." Lincoln had designated Blair to tender Lee the highest-ranking military position within the president's power to proffer.

"I come to you on the part of President Lincoln," Blair began, "to ask whether any inducement that he can offer will prevail on you to take command of the Union army?" Lee responded "as candidly and as courteously" as he could: "Mr. Blair, I look upon secession as anarchy. If I owned the four millions of slaves in the South I would sacrifice them all to the Union; but how can I draw my sword upon Virginia, my native state?"

When the meeting ended, Lee called upon old General Scott to discuss the dilemma further. Then he returned to his Arlington home to think. Two days later, he contacted Scott to tender his resignation from the U.S. Army. "It would have been presented at once," Lee explained, "but for the struggle it has cost me to separate myself from a service to which I have devoted all the best years of my life & all the ability I possessed. During the whole of that time, more than 30 years, I have experienced nothing but kindness from my superiors, & the most cordial friendship from my companions. . . . I shall carry with me to the grave the most grateful recollections of your kind consideration, & your name & fame will always be dear to me."

That same day, a distraught Lee wrote to his sister: "Now we are in a state of war which will yield to nothing." Though he could apprehend "no necessity for this state of things, and would have forborne and pleaded to the end for redress of grievances, real or supposed," he was unable, he explained, "to raise my hand against my relatives, my children, my home. I have, therefore, resigned my commission in the Army, and save in defense of my native State (with the sincere hope that my poor services may never be needed) I hope I may never be called upon to draw my sword." Shortly thereafter, Lee was designated commander of the Virginia state forces.

While Lee wrestled with the grim personal consequences of his decision, Lincoln's brother-in-law Benjamin Hardin Helm confronted a painful decision of his own. Helm, a native of Kentucky and a graduate of West Point, had married Mary's half sister Emilie in 1856. While conducting business in Springfield, he had stayed with the Lincolns. According to his daughter Katherine, he and Lincoln "formed a friendship which was more like the affection of brothers than the ordinary liking of men." Two weeks after Sumter, Lincoln brought Helm, a staunch "Southern-rights Democrat," into his office. "Ben, here is something for you," Lincoln said, placing a sealed envelope in his hands. "Think it over and let me know what you will do." The letter offered Helm the rank of major and the prestigious position of paymaster in the Union Army. That afternoon, Helm encountered Lee, whose face betrayed his anxiety. "Are you not feeling well, Colonel Lee?" Helm asked. "Well in body but not in mind," Lee replied. "In the prime of life I quit a service in which were all my hopes and expectations in this world." Helm showed Lee Lincoln's offer and asked for advice, saying, "I have no doubt of his kindly intentions. But he cannot control the elements. There must be a great war." Lee was "too much disturbed" to render advice, urging Helm to "do as your conscience and your honor bid."

That night, Emilie Helm later recalled, her husband was unable to sleep. The next day, he returned to the White House. "I am going home," he told Lincoln. "I will answer you from there. The position you offer me is beyond what I had expected, even in my most hopeful dreams. You have been very generous to me, Mr. Lincoln, generous beyond anything I have ever known. I had no claim upon you, for I opposed your candidacy, and did what I could to prevent your election. . . . Don't let this offer be made public yet. I will send you my answer in a few days." When Helm reached Kentucky and spoke with General Simon Bolivar Buckner and his friends, he realized he must decline Lincoln's offer and "cast his destinies with his native southland." The time spent in drafting his reply to Lincoln proved to be, he told a friend, "the most painful hour of his life." Soon after, he received a commission in the Confederate Army, where he eventually became a brigadier general.

• • •

EACH DAY BROUGHT NEW conflicts and decisions as Lincoln struggled to stabilize the beleaguered Union. In a contentious cabinet meeting, Seward argued that a blockade of Southern ports should be instituted at once. Recognized by the law of nations, the blockade would grant the Union the power to search and seize vessels. Gideon Welles countered that to proclaim a blockade would mistakenly acknowledge that the Union was engaged in a war with the South and encourage foreign powers to extend belligerent rights to the Confederacy. Better to simply close the ports against the insurrection and use the policing powers of municipal law to seize entering or exiting ships. The cabinet split down the middle. Chase, Blair, and Bates backed Welles, while Smith and Cameron sided with Seward. Lincoln concluded that Seward's position was stronger and issued his formal blockade proclamation on April 19. Welles, despite his initial hesitation, would execute the blockade with great energy and skill.

The commencement of war found Welles and the Navy Department in a grave situation. Southerners, who had made up the majority of navy officers in peacetime, resigned in droves every day. Treason was rampant.

Early in April, Lincoln had graciously attended a wedding celebration for the daughter of Captain Frank Buchanan, the commandant of the Navy Yard in Washington, D.C. Two weeks later, expecting that his home state of Maryland "would soon secede and join the Confederacy," Buchanan resigned his commission, vowing that he would "not take any part in the defence of this Yard from this date."

Meanwhile, the secession of Virginia jeopardized the Norfolk Navy Yard. With its strategic location, immense dry dock, great supply of cannons and guns, and premier vessel, the *Merrimac*, the Norfolk yard was indispensable to both sides. Welles had encouraged Lincoln to reinforce the yard before Sumter fell, but Lincoln had resisted any action that would provoke Virginia. This decision would seriously compromise the Union's naval strength. By the time Welles received orders to send troops to Norfolk, it was too late. The Confederates had secured control of the Navy Yard. The calamitous news, Charles Francis Adams recorded in his diary, sent him into a state of "extreme uneasiness" about the future of the Union. "We the children of the third and fourth generations are doomed to pay the penalties of the compromises made by the first."

The first casualties of the war came on April 19, 1861, the same day the blockade was announced. When the Sixth Massachusetts Regiment reached Baltimore by rail en route to defend Washington, the men were attacked by a secessionist mob. "The scene while the troops were changing cars was indescribably fearful," the Baltimore *Sun* reported. The enraged crowd, branding the troops "nigger thieves," assaulted them with knives and revolvers. Four soldiers and nine civilians were killed. As George Templeton Strong noted in his diary: "It's a notable coincidence that the first blood in this great struggle is drawn by Massachusetts men on the anniversary" of the battles of Lexington and Concord that touched off the Revolutionary War.

The president immediately summoned the mayor of Baltimore and the governor of Maryland to the White House. Still hoping to keep Maryland in the Union, Lincoln agreed to "make no point of bringing [further troops] *through* Baltimore" where strident secessionists were concentrated, but insisted that the troops must be allowed to go *"around* Baltimore." Shortly after midnight, an angry committee of delegates from Baltimore arrived at the White House to confront Lincoln. John Hay took them to see Cameron, but kept them from the president until morning. The delegation demanded that troops be kept not only out of Baltimore but out of the entire state of Maryland. Lincoln adamantly refused to comply. "I must have troops to defend this Capital," he replied. "Geographically it lies surrounded by the soil of Maryland. . . . Our men are not moles, and can't dig under the earth; they are not birds, and can't fly through the air. There is no way but to march across, and that they must do."

The day the war claimed its first casualties was also the day when "the censorship of the press was exercised for the first time at the telegraph office," a veteran journalist recalled. "When correspondents wished to telegraph the lists of the dead and wounded of the Massachusetts Sixth they found a squad of the National Rifles in possession of the office, with orders to permit the transmission of no messages." Infuriated, the correspondents rode to Seward's house to complain. The secretary of state argued that if they sent "accounts of the killed and wounded," they "would only influence public sentiment, and be an obstacle in the path of reconciliation." The issue became moot when reporters learned that secessionists had cut all the telegraph wires in Baltimore and demolished all the railroad bridges surrounding the city. Washington was isolated from all communication with the North.

For the next week, with wires cut and mails stopped, the residents of Washington lived in a state of constant fear. Visitors abandoned the great hotels. Stores closed. Windows and doors were barricaded. "Literally," Villard noted, "it was as though the government of a great nation had been suddenly removed to an island in mid-ocean in a state of entire isolation." Anxious citizens crowded the train station every day, hopeful to greet an influx of the Northern troops needed to protect the vulnerable city. Rumors spread quickly. Across the Potomac, the campfires of the Confederate soldiers were visible. It appeared they were ready to lay siege to Washington. Waiting for the attack, War Secretary Cameron slept in his office. "Here we were in this city," Nicolay wrote his fiancée, "in charge of all the public buildings, property and archives, with only about 2000 *reliable* men to defend it."

Elsewhere in the North, anxiety was nearly as great. "No despatches from Washington," Strong reported from New York. "People talked darkly of its being attacked before our reinforcements come to the rescue, and everyone said we must not be surprised by news that Lincoln and Seward and all the Administration are prisoners." Kate and Nettie Chase were in New York visiting Chase's wealthy friend Hiram Barney, who had received the powerful post of collector of customs in New York. Reflecting a general fear that the "rebels are at Washington or near it," Barney insisted that the girls stay in New York until the capital was out of danger. For Kate, so passionately attached to her father, these were difficult hours. "I can see that K. is anxious for her father," Barney wrote Chase; "it may be seen in many ways—in spite of her efforts to be calm & conceal it." Kate leaped at the chance to accompany Major Robert Anderson, who had just arrived in New York from Fort Sumter and was heading to Washington to report to the president.

The little party made its way to Philadelphia and then caught a steamer from Perryville to Annapolis, bypassing the blocked railroad tracks in Baltimore. En route, however, they were approached by an enemy vessel, which fired a warning shot. Fearing that the Confederates had intelligence that Anderson was on board and were intending to capture him, the captain placed a cannon in position and "crowded on steam." While Kate and Nettie remained below with the hatches closed, the steamer churned ahead, eventually gaining enough ground that its adversary "ran up a black flag, changed her course, and was soon out of sight." From Annapolis, they reached Washington and were reunited with their relieved father.

These "were terrible days of suspense" for the Seward family in Auburn as well. Young Will Seward, now twenty-two, made nightly forays to the local telegraph office, hoping in vain for news from his father. In daily letters, Frances entreated her husband to let her join him. "It is hard to be so far from you when your life is in danger," she pleaded. No reply came to her appeal.

In public, Lincoln maintained his calm, but the growing desperation of the government's position filled him with dread. Late one night, after "a day of gloom and doubt," John Hay saw him staring out the window in futile expectation of the troops promised by various Northern states, including New York, Rhode Island, and Pennsylvania. "Why don't they come!" he asked. "Why don't they come!" The next day, visiting the injured men of the Massachusetts Sixth, he was heard to say: "I don't believe there is any North. The Seventh Regiment [from New York] is a myth. R. Island is not known in our geography any longer. *You* [Massachusetts men] are the only Northern realities."

For days, the rioting in Baltimore continued. Fears multiplied that the Maryland legislature, which had convened in Annapolis, was intending to vote for secession. The cabinet debated whether the president should bring in the army "to arrest, or disperse the members of that body." Lincoln decided that "it would *not* be justifiable." It was a wise determination, for in the end, though secessionist mobs continued to disrupt the peace of Maryland for weeks, the state never joined the Confederacy, and eventually became, as Lincoln predicted, "the first of the redeemed."

Receiving word that the mobs intended to destroy the train tracks between Annapolis and Philadelphia in order to prevent the long-awaited troops from reaching the beleaguered capital, Lincoln made a controversial decision. If resistance along the military line between Washington and Philadelphia made it "necessary to suspend the writ of Habeas Corpus for the public safety," Lincoln authorized General Scott to do so. In Lincoln's words, General Scott could "arrest, and detain, without resort to the ordinary processes and forms of law, such individuals as he might deem dangerous to the public safety." Seward later claimed that he had urged a wavering Lincoln to take this step, convincing him that "perdition was the sure penalty of further hesitation." There may be truth in this, for Seward was initially put in charge of administering the program.

Lincoln had not issued a sweeping order but a directive confined to this single route. Still, by rescinding the basic constitutional protection against arbitrary arrest, he aroused the wrath of Chief Justice Taney, who was on circuit duty in Maryland at the time. Ruling in favor of one of the prisoners, John Merryman, Taney blasted Lincoln and maintained that only Congress could suspend the writ.

Attorney General Bates, though reluctant to oppose Taney, upheld Lincoln's suspension. Over a period of weeks, he drafted a twenty-six-page opinion, arguing that "in a time like the present, when the very existence of the Nation is assailed, by a great and dangerous insurrection, the President has the lawful discretionary power to arrest and hold in custody, persons known to have criminal intercourse with the insurgents."

Lincoln later defended his decision in his first message to Congress. As chief executive, he was responsible for ensuring "that the laws be faithfully executed." An insurrection "in nearly one-third of the States" had subverted the "whole of the laws . . . are all the laws, *but one*, to go unexecuted, and the government itself go to pieces, lest that one be violated?" His logic was unanswerable, but as Supreme Court Justice Thurgood Marshall argued in another context many years later, the "grave threats to liberty often come in times of urgency, when constitutional rights seem too extravagant to endure." Welles seemed to understand the complex balancing act, correctly predicting to his wife that the "government will, doubtless, be stronger after the conflict is over than it ever has been, and there will be less liberty."

Finally, after a week of mounting uneasiness, the Seventh Regiment of New York arrived in Washington. The *New York Times* reported that the "steps and balconies of the hotels, the windows of the private houses, the doorways of the stores, and even the roofs of many houses were crowded with men, women and children, shouting, and waving handkerchiefs and flags." In the days that followed, more regiments arrived. Mary and her friends watched the regimental parades from a window in the mansion. The presence of the troops considerably lightened Lincoln's mood. He blithely told John Hay that in addition to assuring the safety of the capital, he would eventually "go down to Charleston and pay her the little debt we are owing her." Hay was so happy to hear these words that he "felt like letting off an Illinois yell."

Frances Seward was greatly relieved when she received a letter from her husband confirming that more than eight thousand troops were in Washington. He did not, however, grant her request to join him there. His daughter-in-law, Anna, had almost completed decorating their new house on Lafayette Square. The carpets were down, and hundreds of books already lined the library shelves. They would move in at the end of April. Unlike Frances, Anna loved the bustle of Seward's life. "For six or eight nights we had visitors at all hours," she cheerfully reported. Perhaps Seward, anticipating the trials such a hectic environment would cause his wife, deemed it better for her to stay in their tranquil house in Auburn.

Furthermore, he knew they would argue about the purpose of the war. Frances, unlike her husband, had already decided that the principal goal was to end slavery. She recognized that the war might last years and entail "immense sacrifice of human life," but the eradication of slavery justified it all. "The true, strong, glorious North is at last fairly roused," she wrote her husband, "the enthusiasm of the people—high & low rich & poor . . . all enlisted at last in the cause of human rights. No concession from the South now will avail to stem the torrent.—No compromise will be made with slavery of black or white. God has heard the prayer of the oppressed and a fearful retribution awaits the oppressors."

In her all-embracing vision of the war, Frances stood at this point in opposition not only to her husband but to most of the cabinet and a substantial majority of Northerners. Still certain it would be a quick war with an easy reconciliation, Seward told a friend, "there would be no serious fighting after all; the South would collapse and everything be serenely adjusted." Bates wanted a limited war so as "to disturb as little as possible the accustomed occupations of the people," including Southern slaveholding. Blair agreed, counseling Lincoln that it would be a "fatal error" if the contest became "one between the whole people of the South and the people of the North."

To Lincoln's mind, the battle to save the Union contained an even larger purpose than ending slavery, which was after all sanctioned by the very Constitution he was sworn to uphold. "I consider the central idea pervading this struggle," he told Hay in early May, "is the necessity that is upon us, of proving that popular government is not an absurdity. We must settle this question now, whether in a free government the minority have the right to break up the government whenever they choose. If we fail it will go far to prove the incapability of the people to govern themselves."

The philosopher John Stuart Mill shared Lincoln's spacious understanding of the sectional crisis, predicting that a Southern victory "would give courage to the enemies of progress and damp the spirits of its friends all over the civilized world." From the opposite point of view, a member of the British nobility expressed the hope that with "the dissolution of the Union," men would "live to see an aristocracy established in America."

In his Farewell Address, George Washington had given voice to this transcendent idea of Union. "It is of infinite moment," George Washington said, "that you should properly estimate the immense value of your national union to your collective and individual happiness; that you should cherish a cordial, habitual, and immovable attachment to it; accustoming yourselves to think and speak of it as of the palladium of your political safety and prosperity." Foreseeing the potential for dissension, Washington advised vigilance against "the first dawning of every attempt to alienate any portion of our country from the rest or to enfeeble the sacred ties which now link together the various parts."

It was this mystical idea of popular government and democracy that propelled Abraham Lincoln to call forth the thousands of soldiers who would rise up to defend the sacred Union created by the Founding Fathers.

• • •

IN THE DAYS BEFORE the troops arrived, rumors spread that the White House would be targeted for a direct attack. Late one evening, an agitated visitor arrived to inform the president that "a mortar battery has been planted on the Virginia heights commanding the town." John Hay recorded in his diary that he "had to do some very dexterous lying to calm the awakened fears of Mrs. Lincoln in regard to the assassination suspicion." Only when troops appeared in force was she able to relax. "Thousands of soldiers are guarding us," she wrote a friend in Springfield, "and if there is safety in numbers, we have every reason, to feel secure." Mary's cousin Elizabeth Grimsley was equally relieved. "The intense excitement has blown over," she told a friend. "Washington is very quiet and pleasant. We enjoy the beautiful drives around the city."

With little understanding of the peril threatening the city and their well-being, Willie and Tad found the period of Washington's isolation exhilarating. Tad boasted at Sunday School that he had no fear of the "plug-uglies," as the rowdy secessionists in Baltimore were called. "You ought to see the fort we've got on the roof of our house. Let 'em come. Willie and I are ready for 'em." Though the fort consisted of only "a small log" symbolizing a cannon and several decommissioned rifles, the Lincoln boys developed elaborate plans to defend the White House from the roof. And they loved visiting the troops quartered in the East Room of the White House and in the Capitol, where Hay noted the contrast "between the grey haired dignity" that had previously prevailed in the Senate and the young soldiers, "scattered over the desks chairs and galleries some loafing, many writing letters, slowly and with plough hardened hands."

The Taft boys and their sixteen-year-old sister, Julia, were now almost daily guests at the White House. Like Willie, Bud was "rather pale and languid, not very robust," but a "pretty good" student. Holly, as described by his father, Judge Taft, resembled Tad—"all motion and activity, never idle, impatient of restraint, quick to learn when he *tries*, impetuous, all 'go ahead.'" In Bud and Holly, Willie and Tad each found a best friend. Julia, meanwhile, formed a friendship with Mary Lincoln. For the rest of her life, Julia retained warm memories of both the first lady and the president. "More than once," she recalled, Mary had said to her: "I wish I had a little girl like you, Julia." Mary even shared her memories of the death of her son Edward, and they "wept together." In the evenings, when the president unwound in the family sitting room, the four boys would beg him to tell a story. Julia long remembered the scene, as the president launched into one of his amusing tales: "Tad perched precariously on the back of the big chair, Willie on one knee, Bud on the other, both leaning against him," while Holly sat "on the arm of the chair."

As a proper young lady, Julia was appalled by some of the boys' antics. She refused to join in when she found the four of them sitting on the president, attempting to pin him to the floor. She was embarrassed when they interrupted cabinet meetings to invite members and the president to attend one of their theatrical performances in the attic. Though Lincoln himself never seemed to mind, taking great pleasure in their fun, Julia felt she was responsible for curbing their youthful exuberance. Sometimes Willie would help to restore order. He was, Julia wrote, "the most lovable boy" she had ever known, "bright, sensible, sweet-tempered and gentle-mannered." More often he would simply retreat to his mother's room, where he loved to read poetry and write verses.

Despite Julia's great affection for Mary, she was stunned by the first lady's overbearing need to get "what she wanted when she wanted it," regardless of how others might be hurt or inconvenienced. A curious example of such behavior took place when Julia's mother attended a White House concert, decked out in one of her fashionable bonnets. When Mary greeted her, she looked closely at the beautiful purple strings on the bonnet and then took Mrs. Taft aside. Watching the scene, Julia was "puzzled at the look of amazement" on her mother's face, not fathoming why she "should look so surprised at a passing compliment." It turned out that

Mary's milliner had created a purple-trimmed bonnet but lacked sufficient purple ribbon for the strings. Mary hoped to acquire Mrs. Taft's purple strings!

Few recognized the insecurity behind Mary's outlandish behavior, the terrible needs behind the ostentation and apparent abrasiveness. While initially thrilled to move into the White House, Mary soon found herself in the compromising situation of having one full brother, three half brothers, and three brothers-in-law in the Confederate Army. From the start, she was not fully trusted in the North. As the wife of President Lincoln, she was vilified in the South. As a Westerner, she did not meet the standards of Eastern society. Feeling pressure on all sides, she was determined to present herself as an accomplished and sophisticated woman; in short, the most elegant and admired lady in Washington.

Driven by the need to prove herself to society, Mary Lincoln became obsessed with recasting her own image and renovating that of her new home, the White House. Unattended for years, the White House had come to look like "an old and unsuccessful hotel." Elizabeth Grimsley was stunned to find that "the family apartments were in a deplorably shabby condition as to furniture, (which looked as if it has been brought in by the first President)." The public rooms, too, were in poor shape, with threadbare, tobacco-stained rugs, torn curtains, and broken chairs.

The sorry condition of the White House provided the energetic Mary with a worthy ambition. She would restore the people's home to its former elegance as a symbol of her husband's strength and the Union's power. In another era, this ambition might have been applauded, but in the midst of a civil war, it was regarded as frivolous.

In the middle of May, Mary went on a shopping trip to Philadelphia and New York, taking along her cousin Elizabeth Grimsley and William Wood, the commissioner of public buildings. Having discovered that each president was allotted a $20,000 allowance to maintain the White House, she bought new furniture, elegant curtains, and expensive carpets for the public rooms to replace their worn predecessors. For the state guest room, she purchased what later became known as the "Lincoln bed," an eight-foot-long rosewood bedstead with an ornate headboard carved with "exotic birds, grapevines and clusters of grapes." Again, merchants at the clothing stores were more than willing to extend the first lady credit. The press exaggerated her shopping spree, claiming she had purchased thousands of dollars of merchandise in stores she had never even visited. Exaggeration notwithstanding, when she returned to Washington, the bills added up. She received a $7,500 invoice for curtain materials and trimmings, and owed $900 for a new carriage. And the redecorating process to make the nation's house a fit emblem for the country and for herself had just begun.

Never one to be outdone, Kate Chase was hard at work decorating her father's new home—a large three-story brick mansion at Sixth and E Street NW. Though the secretary of the treasury worried constantly about money, he understood the importance of having an elegant home with expansive public rooms appropriate for entertaining senators, congressmen, diplomats, and generals. In the years ahead, he intended to gather friends and associates who would be ready to back him when the time came for the next presidential election. The lease on the house came to $1,200 a year; when the furnishing costs were added on, Chase found himself in debt. Unable to sell off his Cincinnati and Columbus properties in the depressed real estate market that prevailed in Ohio, he was forced to borrow $10,000 from his old friend Hiram Barney. It must have been painfully awkward for the straitlaced model of probity to request the loan, particularly since Barney, as collector of customs in New York, was technically his subordinate. Nevertheless, Chase persuaded himself that a person in his position, who had given so much to the public for so many years, deserved to live in a distinguished home.

So, like Mary Lincoln, Kate traveled to New York and Philadelphia to purchase carpets, draperies, and furniture. The house, complete with six servants, would prove perfect for entertaining, although Chase later complained that the distance from the White House, in comparison with Seward's new lodgings at Lafayette Square, denied him an equal intimacy with the president. He apparently never considered that Lincoln might simply find Seward more lively and amiable company.

None of her father's social demeanor or leaden eminence hindered Kate. As the mistress of his Washington household, she managed "in a single season" to be "as much at home in the society of the national capital as if she had lived there for a lifetime." Dozens of young men paid court to her. A contemporary reporter noted that "no other maiden in Washington had more suitors at her feet." Yet, he continued, "it was early noticed that among all the young men who flocked to the Chase home, and who were eager to obey her slightest nod, there was not one who seemed to obtain even the remotest hold upon her affections"—until Rhode Island's young governor, William Sprague, came to Washington and drew her attention.

Kate had first met the fabulously wealthy Sprague, whose family owned one of the largest textile manufacturing establishments in the country, the previous September in Cleveland. Sprague had come to Ohio at the head of an official delegation to dedicate a statue of Rhode Island native Commodore Oliver Perry, which was to be placed in the public square. Introduced at the festive ball that followed the ceremony, the two immediately hit it off. "For the rest of the evening," one observer recalled, "whenever we saw one of them we were pretty sure to see the other."

For his part, Sprague would never forget his first sight of Kate, "dressed in that celebrated dress," when "you became my gaze and the gaze of all observers, and you left the house taking with you my admiration and my appreciation, but more than all my *pulsations*. I remember well how I was possessed that night and the following day." Years later, he assured her he could "recall the sensation better than if it was yesterday."

Ten years Kate's senior, William Sprague had assumed responsibility for the family business at an early age. When William was thirteen, his father, Amasa Sprague, was shot down on the street as he walked home from his cotton mill one evening. The elder Sprague had been involved in a nasty fight over the renewal of a liquor license. The owner of the gin mill shut down by Sprague was arrested and hanged for the murder. Control of the company passed to William's uncle, who determined that young William should cut short his education to learn the business from the bottom up. "I was thrust into the counting-room, performing its lowest drudgeries, raising myself to all of its highest positions," he later recalled. When his uncle died of typhoid fever, William, at twenty-six, took over.

As the largest employer in Rhode Island, with more than ten thousand workers, young Sprague wielded enormous political influence. He capitalized on his resources when he ran for governor in 1860 and won on the Democratic ticket, spending over $100,000 of his own money. After the attack on Fort Sumter, Sprague organized the First Rhode Island Regiment, providing the state with "a loan of one hundred thousand dollars to outfit the troops," while his brother supplied the artillery battery with ninety-six horses. When the lavishly supplied volunteer regiment arrived in the threatened capital, the men were received as heroes. On April 29, the regiment was officially sworn in before the president and General Scott after a dress parade from its headquarters at the Patent Office to the White House. "The entire street was filled with spectators from Seventh to Ninth street," the *Evening Star* reported, "and many were the complimentary remarks made by the multitude upon the general appearance and movements of the regiment."

All the members of the cabinet were present at the ceremony, joining in the rousing greeting for the resplendent troops. Though Sprague stood only five feet six inches tall, his military uniform and his "yellow-plumed hat" undoubtedly increased his stature. John Hay commented after meeting the young man with brown wavy hair, gray eyes, and a thin mustache that while he appeared at first "a small, insignificant youth, who bought his place," he "is certainly all right now. He is very proud of his Company of its wealth and social standing." Hay, too, was impressed by the number of eminent young men in Sprague's regiment. "When men like these leave their horses, their women and their wine, harden their hands, eat crackers for dinner, wear a shirt for a week and never black their shoes,—all for a principle, it is hard to set any bounds to the possibilities of such an army." Washingtonians nicknamed the First Rhode Island "the millionaires' regiment" and dubbed Sprague the most eligible bachelor in the city.

It was only a matter of days before Sprague called on Kate. Unlike earlier tentative suitors, intimidated perhaps by Kate's beauty and brains, Sprague moved confidently to establish a place in her heart, becoming "the first, the only man," she said afterward, "that had found a lodgment there." Years later, writing to Kate, Sprague vividly recalled their earlier courtship days. "Do you remember the hesitating kiss I stole, and the glowing, blushing face that responded to the touch. I well remember it all. The step forward from the Cleveland meeting, and the enhanced poetical sensation, for it was poetry, if there ever is such in life."

For Kate, who acknowledged that she was "accustomed to command and be obeyed, to wish and be anticipated," Sprague's cocksure attitude must have presented a welcome challenge. In the weeks that followed, the young couple saw each other frequently. By summer's end, Nettie Chase told Kate that she liked Sprague "very much" and hoped the two would marry. Nettie's hopes were put on hold, however, as the war continued to escalate, changing the course of countless lives throughout the fractured nation.

The tragedies of war came home to the Lincolns with the death of Elmer Ellsworth on May 24, 1861. Young Ellsworth had read law in Lincoln's office and had become so close to the family that he made the journey from Springfield to Washington with them, catching the measles from Willie and Tad along the way. Once in the capital, Ellsworth joined the war effort by organizing a group of New York firemen into a Zouave unit, distinguished by their exotic and colorful uniforms. After Virginia seceded from the Union, Ellsworth's Zouaves were among the first troops to cross the Potomac River into Alexandria, a town counting ardent secessionists among its residents, including the proprietor of the Marshall House. Spying a Confederate flag waving above the hotel, Ellsworth dashed up to the roof to confiscate it. Having captured the flag, Ellsworth met the armed hotel manager, secessionist James Jackson, on his way down the stairs. Jackson killed Ellsworth on the spot, only to be shot by Ellsworth's men.

Ellsworth's death, as one of the first casualties of the war, was national news and mourned across the country. The bereaved president wrote a personal note of condolence to Ellsworth's parents, praising the young man whose body lay in state in the East Room. Nicolay confessed that he had been "quite unable to keep the tears out of my eyes" whenever he thought of Ellsworth. After the funeral, Mary was presented with the bloodied flag for which Ellsworth had given his life; but the horrified first lady, not wanting to be reminded of the sad event, quickly had it packed away.

• • •

WITH MORE THAN ENOUGH TROUBLES to occupy him at home, Lincoln faced a tangled situation abroad. A member of the British Parliament had introduced a resolution urging England to accord the Southern Confederacy belligerent status. If passed, the resolution would give Confederate ships the same rights in neutral ports enjoyed by Federal ships. Britain's textile economy depended on cotton furnished by Southern plantations. Unless the British broke the Union blockade to ensure a continuing supply of cotton, the great textile mills in Manchester and Leeds would be forced to cut back or come to a halt. Merchants would lose money, and thousands of workers would lose their jobs.

Seward feared that England would back the South simply to feed its own factories. While the "younger branch of the British stock" might support freedom, he told his wife, the aristocrats, concerned more with economics than morality, would become "the ally of the traitors." To prevent this from happening, he was "trying to get a bold remonstrance through the Cabinet, before it is too late." He hoped not only to halt further thoughts of recognition of the Confederacy but to ensure that the British would respect the Union blockade and refuse, even informally, to meet with the three Southern commissioners who had been sent to London to negotiate for the Confederacy. To achieve these goals, Seward was willing to wage war. "God damn 'em, I'll give 'em hell," he told Sumner, thrusting his foot in the air as he spoke.

On May 21, Seward brought Lincoln a surly letter drafted for Charles Francis Adams to read verbatim to Lord John Russell, Britain's foreign secretary. Lincoln recognized immediately that the tone was too abrasive for a diplomatic communication. While decisive action might be necessary to prevent Britain from any form of overt sympathy with the South, Lincoln had no intention of fighting two wars at once. All his life, he had taken care not to send letters written in anger. Now, to mitigate the harshness of the draft, he altered the tone of the letter at numerous points. Where Seward had claimed that the president was "surprised and grieved" that no protest had been made against unofficial meetings with the Southern commissioners, Lincoln wrote simply that the "President regrets." Where Seward threatened that "no one of these proceedings [informal or formal recognition, or breaking the blockade] will be borne," Lincoln shifted the phrase to "will *pass unnoticed.*"

Most important, where Seward had indicated that the letter be read directly to the British foreign secretary, Lincoln insisted that it serve merely for Adams's guidance and should not *"be read, or shown to any one."* Still, the central message remained clear: a warning to Britain that if the vexing issues were not resolved, and Britain decided "to fraternize with our domestic enemy," then a war between the United States and Britain "may ensue," caused by "the action of Great Britain, not our own." In that event, Britain would forever lose "the sympathies and the affections of the only nation on whose sympathies and affections she has a natural claim."

Thus, a threatening message that might have embroiled the Union in two wars at the same time became instead the basis for a hard-line policy that effectively interrupted British momentum toward recognizing the Confederacy. Furthermore, France, whose ministers had promised to act in concert with Britain, followed suit. This was a critical victory for the Union, preventing for the time being the recognition that would have conferred legitimacy on the Confederacy in the eyes of the world, weakened Northern morale, and accorded "currency to Southern bonds."

History would later give Secretary of State Seward high marks for his role in preventing Britain and France from intervening in the war. He is considered by some to have been "the ablest American diplomatist of the century." But here, as was so often the case, Lincoln's unseen hand had shaped critical policy. Only three months earlier, the frontier lawyer had confessed to Seward that he knew little of foreign affairs. His revisions of the dispatch, however, exhibit the sophisticated prowess of a veteran statesman: he had analyzed a complex situation and sought the least provocative way to neutralize a potential enemy while making crystal-clear his country's position.

Seward was slowly but inevitably coming to appreciate Lincoln's remarkable abilities. "It is due to the President to say, that his magnanimity is almost superhuman," he told his wife in mid-May. "His confidence and sympathy increase every day." As Lincoln began to trust his own abilities, Seward became more confident in him. In early June, he told Frances: "Executive skill and vigor are rare qualities. The President is the best of us; but he needs constant and assiduous cooperation." Though the feisty New Yorker would continue to debate numerous issues with Lincoln in the years ahead, exactly as Lincoln had hoped and needed him to do, Seward would become his most faithful ally in the cabinet. He committed himself "to his chief," Nicolay and Hay observed, "not only without reserve, but with a sincere and devoted personal attachment."

Seward's mortification at not having received his party's nomination in 1860 never fully abated, but he no longer felt compelled to belittle Lincoln to ease his pain. He settled into his position as secretary of state, and his optimistic and gregarious nature reasserted itself. Once more, his elaborate parties and receptions became the talk of Washington. Five days after the dispatch was sent, Seward hosted "a brilliant assemblage" at his new home. All the rooms were full, with dancing in one, drinks in another, and good conversation all around. Seward was "in excellent spirits," moving easily among cabinet members, military officers, diplomats, and senators. Even white-haired Secretary Welles, who, it was mockingly remarked, should have died, "to all intents and purposes, twenty years ago," was having such a good time that he seemed "good for, at least, twenty years more."

• • •

LINCOLN LOOKED TO CHASE for guidance on the complex problem of financing a war at a time when the government was heavily in debt. The economic Panic of 1857, corruption in the Buchanan administration, and the partial dismemberment of the Union had taken a massive toll on the government coffers. With Congress not in session to authorize new tariffs and taxes, Chase was forced to rely on government loans to sustain war expenditures. Banks held back at first, demanding higher interest rates than the government could afford to pay, but eventually, Chase cobbled together enough revenue to meet expenses until Congress convened.

Chase later noted proudly that in the early days of the war, Lincoln relied on him to carry out functions that ordinarily belonged to the War Department. According to Chase, he assumed "the principal charge" of preventing the key border states of Kentucky, Missouri, and Tennessee from falling into secessionist hands. He authorized a loyal state senator from Kentucky to muster twenty companies. He drew up the orders that allowed Andrew Johnson, the only senator from a Confederate state who remained loyal to the Union, "to raise regiments in Tennessee." He believed himself instrumental in keeping Kentucky and Missouri in the Union, seriously underestimating Lincoln's critical role.

Indeed, Chase would never cease to underestimate Lincoln, nor to resent the fact that he had lost the presidency to a man he considered his inferior. In late April, he presumptuously sent Lincoln a *New York Times* article highly derogatory of the administration. "The President and the Cabinet at Washington are far behind the people," the *Times* argued.

"They are like a person just aroused from sleep, and in a state of dreamy half-consciousness." This charge, Chase informed Lincoln, "has too much truth in it." Lincoln did not reply, well understanding Chase's implacable yearning for the presidency. But for now he needed the Ohioan's enormous talents and total cooperation.

Cameron, meanwhile, found the task of running the War Department unbearable. Unable to manage his vast responsibilities, he turned to both Seward and Chase for help. "Oh, it was a terrible time," Cameron remembered years later. "We were entirely unprepared for such a conflict, and for the moment, at least, absolutely without even the simplest instruments with which to engage in war. We had no guns, and even if we had, they would have been of but little use, for we had no ammunition to put in them—no powder, no saltpetre, no bullets, no anything." The demands placed on the War Department in the early days of the war were indeed excruciating. Not only were weapons in short supply, but uniforms, blankets, horses, medical supplies, food, and everything necessary to outfit the vast numbers of volunteer soldiers arriving daily in Washington were unobtainable. It would have taken thousands of personnel to handle the varied functions of the quartermaster's department, the ordnance office, the engineering department, the medical office, and the pay department. Yet, in 1861, the entire War Department consisted of fewer than two hundred people, including clerks, messengers, and watchmen. As Cameron lamented afterward: "I was certainly not in a place to be envied."

Lincoln later explained that with "so large a number of disloyal persons" infiltrating every department, the government could not rely on official agents to manage contracts for manufacturing the weapons and supplies necessary to maintain a fighting force. With the cabinet's unanimous consent, he directed Chase to dispense millions of dollars to a small number of trusted private individuals to negotiate and sign contracts that would mobilize the military. Acting "without compensation," the majority of these men did their utmost under the circumstances. A few, including Alexander Cummings, one of Cameron's lieutenants, would bring shame to the War Department.

• • •

As SPRING GAVE WAY to the stifling heat of a Washington summer, Lincoln began work on the message he would deliver to Congress when the House and Senate assembled in special session on July 4. Needing time to think, he placed an "embargo" on all office seekers, "so strict" that they were not even allowed entry into the White House. As he labored in his newfound quiet, congressmen and senators gathered at Willard's and Brown's hotels, exchanging greetings and trading stories. They all anticipated, one reporter stated, that they would "soon ascertain the exact intentions of the Administration, through the medium of the President's message."

Lincoln worked long hours on the text, shifting words, condensing, deleting sentences. Even Senator Orville Browning, his old friend from Illinois who had come to see him, was told he was busy, but Lincoln overheard Browning talking and sent for him. It was after 9 p.m. on July 3, and he had just that moment finished writing. "He said he wished to read it to me, and did so," Browning recorded in his diary. "It is an able state paper and will fully meet the expectations of the Country."

Lincoln did not personally deliver his address on Capitol Hill. President Thomas Jefferson had denounced presidential appearances before Congress, considering them a monarchical remnant of the English system where kings personally opened parliamentary sessions. Since Jefferson, presidents had submitted their written messages to be read by a clerk. Yet, if the practice lacked theatricality, Lincoln's arguments against secession and for the necessity of executive action in the midst of rebellion left an indelible impression. He traced the history of the struggle and called on Congress to "give the legal means for making this contest a short, and a decisive one."

He asked for "at least four hundred thousand men, and four hundred millions of dollars . . . a less sum per head, than was the debt of our revolution." A "right result, at this time, will be worth more to the world, than ten times the men, and ten times the money," he assured Congress. For "this issue embraces more than the fate of these United States. It presents to the whole family of man, the question, whether a constitutional republic, or a democracy—a government of the people, by the same people—can, or cannot, maintain its territorial integrity, against its own domestic foes. . . .

"This is essentially a People's contest," the president asserted. "On the side of the Union, it is a struggle for maintaining in the world, that form, and substance of government, whose leading object is, to elevate the condition of men—to lift artificial weights from all shoulders—to clear the paths of laudable pursuit for all—to afford all, an unfettered start, and a fair chance, in the race of life." As evidence of the capacity of free institutions to better the "condition" of the people, "beyond any example in the world," he cited the regiments of the Union Army, in which "there is scarcely one, from which could not be selected, a President, a Cabinet, a Congress, and perhaps a Court, abundantly competent to administer the government itself."

Northern newspapers generally praised the message, though some failed to appreciate the rigor of Lincoln's appeal and the clear grace of his language. "In spite of obvious faults in style," the *New York Times* correspondent conceded, "I venture to say it will add to the popularity of the Rail-splitter. It is evidently the production of an honest, clear-headed and straightforward man; and its direct and forcible logic and quaint style of illustration will cause it to be read with peculiar pleasure by the masses of the people." More important, the Congress responded with alacrity. Its members authorized more money and an even larger mobilization of troops than the president had requested. In addition, they provided retroactive authority for nearly all of Lincoln's executive actions taken before they convened, remaining silent only on his suspension of habeas corpus. With the Southern Democrats gone, the Republicans had a substantial majority. And, for the moment, Northern Democrats also acceded, their dislike of Republicans overshadowed by patriotic fervor.

Not everyone was pleased. Abolitionists and radical Republicans found the message disheartening. "No mention is, at all, made of slavery," Frederick Douglass lamented. "Any one reading that document, with no previous knowledge of the United States, would never dream from anything there written that we have a slaveholding war waged upon the Government . . . while all here know that *that* is the vital and animating motive of the rebellion."

Radicals tended to blame Seward for Lincoln's reluctance to emphasize the role of slavery. "We have an honest President," Wendell Phillips, the abolitionist editor, proclaimed before a celebratory crowd on the Fourth of July, "but, distrusting the strength of the popular feeling behind him, he listens overmuch to Seward." Men like Phillips, Thaddeus Stevens, and Charles Sumner could never forgive Seward for apparently lowering the antislavery banner he had once carried so triumphantly. Seward was accustomed to criticism, however, and while he had the president beside him, he remained secure in his position.

Meanwhile, the events of the war itself began to reshape the old order in ways few realized. At Fort Monroe, at the tip of the peninsula in Virginia, a bold decision by General Benjamin Butler proved a harbinger of things to come. One night, three fugitive slaves arrived at the fort after escaping from the Confederate battery that their master had ordered them to help build. When an agent of their owner demanded their return, Butler refused. The rebels were using slaves in the field to support their troops, Butler argued. The slaves were therefore contraband of war, and the federal government was no longer obliged to surrender them to their masters.

Coming from Butler, a conservative Democrat from Massachusetts who had run for governor on the Breckinridge ticket in 1860, the decision delighted Republican stalwarts who had previously objected to Butler's high position. Butler himself would soon be equally delighted by Lincoln's magnanimity in making him a brigadier general. "I will accept the commission," Butler gratefully told Lincoln, but "there is one thing I must say to you, as we don't know each other: That as a Democrat I opposed your election, and did all I could for your opponent; but I shall do no political act, and loyally support your administration as long as I hold your commission; and when I find any act that I cannot support I shall bring the commission back at once, and return it to you."

Lincoln replied, "That is frank, that is fair. But I want to add one thing: When you see me doing anything that for the good of the country ought not to be done, come and tell me so, and why you think so, and then perhaps you won't have any chance to resign your commission." Had Butler known Lincoln, he would have been less astonished. The president commissioned officers with the same eye toward coalition building that he displayed in constructing his cabinet.

Butler's order was approved by both Lincoln and Cameron, and eventually, the Congress passed a confiscation law ending the rights of masters over fugitive slaves utilized to support the Confederate troops. Even conservative Monty Blair applauded Butler. "You were right when you declared *secession* niggers contraband of war," he told his fellow Democrat. "The Secessionists have used them to do all their fortifying."

Blair's approval of Butler's measure as an act of war did not mean that he advocated emancipation. On the contrary, he advised Butler to "improve the code by restricting its operations to working people, leaving the Secessionists to take care of the non working classes." The Union should provide safe harbor only to the "pick of the lot," the strong-bodied slaves who were helping the rebels in the field. Women and children and other "unproductive laborers" should be left for their Southern masters to house and feed.

Lincoln, as usual, was slowly formulating his own position on the slavery question. He told Blair that Butler's action raised "a very important subject . . . one requiring some thought in view of the numbers of negroes we were likely to have on hand in virtue of this new doctrine." Indeed, in the weeks that followed, hundreds of courageous slaves worked their way into Union lines. The situation worried Lincoln; at this juncture, he still favored compensated emancipation and voluntary colonization, allowing blacks who wished to do so to return to their original homeland in Africa. Most important, he knew that any hint of total, direct emancipation would alienate the border states, whose continued loyalty was essential for victory, and would shatter the Republicans' fragile alliance with Northern Democrats.

By shying from emancipation in these early months of the war, Lincoln aligned himself with the majority of the Northern people, the Republican Congress, and the whole of his cabinet. Two weeks into its session, the House passed a resolution declaring that the purpose of the war was "to preserve the Union," not to eliminate slavery. Even Chase, the most fervent antislavery man in the cabinet, agreed that at this time the "sword" of total abolition should be left "in the sheath." If the conflict were drawn out, however, he told the historian John Motley, if "we find it much more difficult and expensive in blood and treasure to put it down than we anticipated," then the sword would be drawn. "We do not wish this, we deplore it, because of the vast confiscation of property, and of the servile insurrections, too horrible to contemplate, which would follow. We wish the Constitution and Union as it is, with slavery, as a municipal institution, existing till such time as each State in its wisdom thinks fit to mitigate or abolish it . . . but if the issue be distinctly presented—death to the American Republic or death to slavery, slavery *must die.*"

•　•　•

By MID-JULY, the outcry in the North for some form of significant action against the rebels reached fever pitch. "Forward to Richmond!" blared the headline in the *New York Tribune.* Senator Trumbull introduced a resolution calling for "the immediate movement of the troops, and the occupation of Richmond before the 20th July," the date set for the Confederate Congress to convene. General Scott hesitated, believing the army still unprepared for a major offensive, but Lincoln feared that without action, the morale of both the troops and the general public would diminish. European leaders would interpret Northern inaction as a faltering resolve in the Union.

General Irvin McDowell, a brigadier general from Ohio, devised a plan to engage the rebel forces under command of General Beauregard at Manassas, twenty-six miles southwest of Washington. It was an intelligent plan. Many Northerners had come to see Manassas as "a terrible, unknown, mysterious something . . . filled by countless thousands of the most ferocious warriors," poised to attack Washington, D.C. "Foreigners do not understand," Bates confided to a friend, "why we should allow a hostile army to remain so long almost in sight of the Capitol, if we were able to drive them off." With 30,000 Union troops at his disposal, McDowell could overrun Beauregard's forces so long as Union general Robert Patterson prevented the 9,000 Confederate troops under General Joseph Johnston at

Winchester, Virginia, from joining Beauregard. On June 29, Lincoln and his cabinet approved McDowell's plan.

The Battle of Bull Run, as it later became known in the North, began in the early-morning hours of Sunday, July 21. As the "roar of the artillery" reached the White House, Elizabeth Grimsley recalled, "the excitement grew intense." As far away as the Blair estate in Silver Spring, Monty's sister, Elizabeth, took a walk in the woods to "stop the *roar* in [her] ears," but the sound of the guns only increased. As soldiers on both sides of the battlefield were discovering the gruesome carnage of war, hundreds of Washingtonians hastily prepared picnic baskets filled with bread and wine. They raced to the hill at Centreville and the fields below to witness what most presumed would be an easy victory for the North. Senators, congressmen, government employees, and their families peered through opera glasses to survey the battlefield. After "an unusually heavy discharge," the British journalist William Russell overheard one woman exclaim: "That is splendid. Oh, my! Is not that first-rate? I guess we will be in Richmond this time to-morrow."

While Lincoln attended church, the Union troops pressed forward, forcing the rebels farther south into the woods. At midday, news of what seemed a complete Union victory reached Lincoln and the members of his cabinet at the telegraph office in the War Department. In the crowded space that housed the telegraph instruments, operators found it hard to focus on their responsibilities. Each new dispatch, the *New York Times* noted, was posted and read aloud to hundreds of people gathered in front of the Willard Hotel. The jubilant throng "cheered vehemently, and seemed fairly intoxicated with joy."

Even as the crowds celebrated in the streets, the fiercest stage of the fighting was just beginning. The Confederates refused to give up, rallied by the steadfast General Thomas Jackson. "There is Jackson with his Virginians, standing like a stone wall," General Barnard Bee reportedly shouted to inspire his troops, and both Confederate and Union soldiers thereafter referred to Jackson as "Stonewall" Jackson. The two sides fought valiantly in the blazing sun as the line of battle shifted back and forth. At 3 p.m., Lincoln was in the telegraph office studying the maps on the wall and waiting anxiously for the updated bulletins, which arrived in fifteen-minute intervals. The telegraph line stretched only as far as the Fairfax Court House. News from the battlefront farther south was relayed to Fairfax by a troupe of mounted couriers established by the young Andrew Carnegie, who then worked with the U.S. Military Telegraph Corps. Noting some confusion in the battlefield reports, Lincoln crossed over to General Scott's headquarters, "a small three-storied brick house" jammed with officers and clerks. Waking Scott from a nap, Lincoln expressed his concern. Scott, Nicolay reported, simply confirmed "his confidence in a successful result, and composed himself for another nap when the President left."

Succeeding dispatches became uniformly positive, conveying assurances that the Confederate lines had broken. At about 4:30, the telegraph operator proclaimed that "the Union Army had achieved a glorious victory." Lincoln decided to take his usual carriage ride, accompanied by Tad, Willie, and Secretary Bates. As they rode together to the Navy Yard to talk with John A. Dahlgren, one of Lincoln's favorite naval officers, Bates confided his anxiety for his son, Coalter, who was soon to be sent into battle. When young Coalter departed to join his regiment, Bates wrote, it was "the first time he ever left home." The carriage ride came to a close with Bates feeling a new intimacy with his president.

As Lincoln relaxed with Bates in his carriage, the tide of battle turned against the Union. Confederate general Johnston's forces had escaped General Patterson's grasp, and by midafternoon, nine thousand fresh Confederate troops arrived to reinforce Beauregard. McDowell had no reserve troops left. "A sudden swoop, and a body of [Confederate] cavalry rushed down upon our columns," Edmund Stedman reported from the battlefield. "They came from the woods . . . and infantry poured out behind them."

Exhausted Union infantrymen, including Sprague's First Rhode Island Regiment, broke ranks. An uncontrolled retreat toward Washington began, further confused by the panicked flight of horrified spectators. Indeed, an acquaintance of Chase's who had witnessed the battle "never stopped until he reached New-York." Young Stedman was appalled by the raging scene: "Army wagons, sutlers' teams, and private carriages, choked the passage, tumbling against each other, amid clouds of dust, and sickening sights and sounds." Muskets and small arms were discarded along the way. Wounded soldiers pled for help. Horses, running free, exacerbated the human stampede.

The shocking news reached Washington in Lincoln's absence. "General McDowell's army in full retreat through Centerville," the dispatch read; "the day is lost. Save Washington and the remnants of the Army." Seward grabbed the telegram and ran to the White House. With "a terribly frightened and excited look" on his face, he asked Nicolay for the latest news. Lincoln's secretary read him an earlier exultant dispatch. "Tell no one. That is not so. The battle is lost," Seward revealed. "Find the President and tell him to come immediately to Gen. Scott's."

When Lincoln returned, his young aides relayed Seward's message.

"He listened in silence," they later reported, "without the slightest change of feature or expression, and walked away to army headquarters." He remained there with Scott and his cabinet until a telegram from McDowell verified the loss. Immediate reinforcements were summoned to defend the capital. With no further recourse, the disconsolate team dispersed.

"Oh what a sad long weary day has this sabbath been," Elizabeth Blair told her husband. For Simon Cameron, the day brought a sharper personal grief. His brother James, in the service of Colonel William Sherman's brigade, was among the nearly nine hundred soldiers killed. "I loved my brother," Cameron wrote Chase, "as only the poor and lonely can love those with whom they have toiled & struggled up the rugged hill of life's success—but he died bravely in the discharge of his duty."

Seward stayed up past midnight composing a letter to Frances. "Every thing is being done that mortal man can do. Scott is grieved and disappointed. . . . What went out an army is surging back toward Washington as a disorganized mob. They fought well, did nobly, and apparently had gained the day, when some unreasonable alarm started a retreat. If the officers had experience and the men discipline, they could be rallied, and could be marched clear back to the field."

Lincoln returned to the White House, where he watched the returning soldiers straggle down the street, listened to the mournful sounds of ambulances, and sat for hours with various senators and congressmen who had witnessed the battle from the hill. Early the following morning, with rain pouring down, General Scott arrived, urging Mary to take the children to the North until Washington was deemed safe from capture. Elizabeth Grimsley recollected the exchange as Mary turned to her husband: "Will you go with us?" she asked. "Most assuredly I will not leave at this juncture," he replied. "Then I will not leave you at this juncture," she answered with finality.

Lincoln did not sleep that dreadful night. Finding his only comfort in forward motion, he began drafting a memo incorporating the painful lessons of Bull Run into a coherent future military policy. Understanding that the disorder of the newly formed troops had contributed to the debacle, he called for the forces to "be constantly drilled, disciplined and instructed." Furthermore, when he learned that soldiers preparing to end their three months of service had led the retreat, Lincoln proposed to let all those short-termers "who decline to enter the longer service, be discharged as rapidly as circumstances will permit." Anticipating European reactions to the defeat, he determined to move "with all possible despatch" to make the blockade operative. That night, a telegram was also sent to General George McClellan in western Virginia with orders to come to

Washington and take command of the Army of the Potomac. Lincoln then devised a strategy consisting of three advances: a second stand at Manassas; a move down the Mississippi toward Memphis; and a drive from Cincinnati to East Tennessee.

"If there were nothing else of Abraham Lincoln for history to stamp him with," Walt Whitman reflected, "it is enough to send him with his wreath to the memory of all future time, that he endured that hour, that day, bitterer than gall—indeed a crucifixion day—that it did not conquer him—that he unflinchingly stemmed it, and resolved to lift himself and the Union out of it."

Recriminations were plentiful. The Democratic *New York Herald* placed responsibility on "a weak, inharmonious and inefficient Cabinet." General Patterson was blamed for failing to keep Johnston's troops from joining Beauregard. "Two weeks ago," Chase self-righteously complained to a friend, "I urged the sending of Fremont to this command; and had it been done we should now have been rejoicing over a great victory." Still, the historian James Rawley concludes that "public censure touched too lightly on Lincoln," who should have held back the assault until the troops were ready.

"The sun rises, but shines not," Whitman wrote of the dismal day after the defeat. Rain continued to fall as the defeated troops flooded into Washington. From his window at Willard's, Russell observed these bedraggled soldiers. "Some had neither great-coats nor shoes, others were covered with blankets." Nettie Chase recalled being "awakened in the gray dawn by the heavy, unwonted, rumbling of laden wagons passing along the street below." Thinking at first they were bound for market, she was sickened to realize they were filled with wounded soldiers heading for the hospital nearby. To relieve the crowded hospital wards, Chase opened his spacious home to nearly a dozen wounded men. Bishop McIlvaine, a friend visiting from Ohio who happened to be staying with Chase at the time, tended to the sick and dying. Nettie recalled the bishop's uneasiness when one of the wounded men cursed loudly with each pain. "Just let me swear a bit," the young man entreated the stunned bishop, "it helps me stand the hurting."

"The dreadful disaster of Sunday can scarcely be mentioned," Stanton wrote to former president Buchanan five days after Bull Run. "The imbecility of this Administration culminated in that catastrophe," he pronounced with a sycophantic nod to his former boss, calling the fiasco "the result of Lincoln's 'running the machine' for five months. . . . The capture of Washington seems now to be inevitable—during the whole of Monday and Tuesday it might have been taken without any resistance. . . . Even now I doubt whether any serious opposition to the entrance of the Confederate forces could be offered."

Historians have long pondered the reluctance of the Confederates to capitalize on their victory by attacking Washington. Jefferson Davis later cited "an overweening confidence" after the initial victory that led to lax decisions. General Johnston observed that hundreds of volunteers, believing the war already won, simply left their regiments and returned home to "exhibit the trophies picked up on the field." Other soldiers melted into the countryside, accompanying wounded comrades to faraway hospitals. Perhaps the most straightforward explanation of both the dismal Union retreat and the Confederate failure to march into Washington is manifest in the plain assessment Nancy Bates posted to her young niece Hester: "Well we fought all day Sunday. Our men were so tired that they had to come away from Manassa I expect that the others were very tired too or they would have followed our men."

While Lincoln brooded in private, confiding in Browning that he was "very melancholy," he maintained a stoic public image. He refrained from answering Horace Greeley's acerbic letter, written in "black despair" after the *Tribune* editor had endured a week without sleep. "You are not considered a great man," Greeley charged, adding that if the Confederacy could not be defeated, Lincoln should "not fear to sacrifice [himself] to [his] country." Despite a blizzard of such indictments, Lincoln listened patiently to reports from the field of what went wrong. He told humorous stories to provide relief. And in the days that followed, with Seward by his side, he visited a number of regiments, raising spirits at every stop along the way.

At Fort Corcoran, on the Virginia side of the Potomac, he asked Colonel William T. Sherman if he could address the troops. Sherman was delighted, though he asked Lincoln to "discourage all cheering." After the boasts that preceded Bull Run, he explained, "what we needed were cool, thoughtful, hard-fighting soldiers—no more hurrahing, no more humbug." Lincoln agreed, proceeding to deliver what Sherman considered "one of the neatest, best, and most feeling addresses" he had ever heard. Lincoln commented on the lost battle but emphasized "the high duties that still devolved on us, and the brighter days yet to come." At various points, "the soldiers began to cheer, but [Lincoln] promptly checked them, saying: 'Don't cheer, boys. I confess I rather like it myself, but Colonel Sherman here says it is not military; and I guess we had better defer to his opinion.'"

The president closed his graceful speech with a pledge to provide the troops with all they needed, and even encouraged them to call on him "personally in case they were wronged." One aggrieved officer took him at his word, revealing that, as a three-month volunteer, he had tried to leave, but Sherman had "threatened to shoot" him. In a "stage-whisper," Lincoln counseled the officer: "Well, if I were you, and he threatened to shoot, I would not trust him, for I believe he would do it." The response produced gales of laughter among the men while upholding Sherman's discipline.

Northern public opinion reflected Lincoln's firm resolve. Republican newspapers across the land reported a "renewed patriotism," bringing thousands of volunteers to sign up for three years. "Let no loyal man be discouraged by the reverse," the *Chicago Tribune* proclaimed. "Like the great Antaeas, who, when thrown to the ground, gathered strength from the contact with mother earth and arose refreshed and stronger than before, to renew the contest, so of the Sons of Liberty; the loss of this battle will only nerve them to greater efforts." Several papers compared the Bull Run disaster to George Washington's early defeats in the Revolutionary War, which eventually resulted in triumph at Yorktown. "The spirit of the people is now thoroughly aroused," the *New York Times* announced, "and, what is equally important, it has been chastened and moderated by the stern lessons of experience."

With the stunning reversal and rout at Bull Run, however, Northern delusions of easy triumph dissolved. "It is pretty evident now that we have underrated the strength, the resources and the temper of the enemy," the *Times* conceded. "And we have been blind, moreover, to the extraordinary nature of the country over which the contest is to be waged,—and to its wonderful facilities for defence." Yet the harrowing lessons of Bull Run generated a perverse confidence that the North could "take comfort" in already knowing the worst that could happen. It was unimaginable in the anxious chaos following the first major battle of the Civil War that far worse was yet to come.

CHAPTER 14

"I DO NOT INTEND TO BE SACRIFICED"

"NOTHING BUT A PATENT PILL was ever so suddenly famous," it was said of George B. McClellan when he arrived in Washington on July 27, 1861, to take command of the Army of the Potomac. "That dear old domestic bird, the Public," an essayist later wrote, "was sure she had brooded out an eagle-chick at last." Among the Union's youngest generals at thirty-four, the handsome, athletic McClellan seemed to warrant the acclaim and great expectation. He was the scion of a distinguished Philadelphia family. His father graduated from Yale College and the University of Pennsylvania Medical School. His mother was elegant and genteel. Educated in excellent schools, including West Point, McClellan had served on the staff of General Scott in the Mexican War.

Most important, to a public looking for deliverance, he had recently defeated a guerrilla band in western Virginia, handing the North its only victory, albeit a small one.

To the nerve-worn residents of Washington, McClellan seemed "the man on horseback," just the leader to mold the disorganized Union troops into a disciplined army capable of returning to Manassas and defeating the enemy. Within days of his arrival, one diarist noted, Washington itself had assumed "a more martial look." Hotel bars no longer overflowed with drunken soldiers, nor did troops wander the city late at night in search of lodgings. The young general seemed able to mystically project his own self-confidence onto the demoralized troops, restoring their faith in themselves and their hope for the future. "You have no idea how the men brighten up now, when I go among them—I can see every eye glisten," he wrote proudly to his wife, Mary Ellen. "Yesterday they nearly pulled me to pieces in one regt. You never heard such yelling."

Lincoln hoped that between Scott's seasoned wisdom as general-in-chief and McClellan's vitality and force, he would finally have a powerfully effective team. From the start, however, McClellan viewed Scott as "the great obstacle" to both his own ambition for sole authority and to his larger strategy in the war. Less than two weeks after assuming command of the Army of the Potomac, McClellan questioned Scott's belief that the rush of reinforcements to Washington had secured the capital. In a letter to General Scott, which he copied to the president, he argued that his army was "entirely insufficient for the emergency," for "the enemy has at least 100,000 men in our front." Scott was furious that his judgment had been called into question, correctly insisting that McClellan was grossly exaggerating the opposition forces. It would not be the last of the imperious general's miscalculations.

Lincoln temporarily defused the animosity by asking McClellan to withdraw his offending letter, but the discord between the two generals continued to escalate. Scott wanted to employ "concentric pressure" on the rebels in different theaters of war. McClellan declared that only with an overwhelming force concentrated on Virginia could he put an end to hostilities. All other engagements he considered secondary, dispersing resources needed to "crush the rebels in one campaign."

In his almost daily letters to his wife, McClellan recognized that his disagreements with Scott might "result in a mortal enmity on his part against me." Justifying his unwillingness to make peace with Scott, he referred frequently to his sense of destiny. It was his conviction that "God has placed a great work in my hands." He felt that "by some strange operation of magic" he had "become *the* power of the land" and if "the people call upon me to save the country—I *must* save it & cannot respect anything that is in the way." McClellan told her that he received "letter after letter" begging him to assume the presidency or become a dictator. While he would eschew the presidency, he would "cheerfully take the Dictatorship & agree to lay down my life when the country is saved."

Frustrated by the lack of response to his constant calls for more troops and equipment, McClellan insisted that Scott was "a perfect imbecile," a *"dotard,"* even possibly "a *traitor."* Refusing to acknowledge that the dispute represented an honest clash of opinions, McClellan insisted that the root of contention with Scott was the veteran's "eternal jealousy of all who acquire any distinction."

As the row between the two men intensified, McClellan decided to ignore Scott's communications, though the chain of command required that he inform his superior officer of his position and the number of troops at his disposal. Scott was indignant. "The remedy by arrest and trial before a Court Martial, would probably, soon cure the evil," Scott told Secretary of War Cameron, but he feared a public conflict "would be highly encouraging to the enemies, and depressing to the friends of the Union. Hence my long forbearance." Instead, he proposed that as soon as the president could make other arrangements, he himself would gladly retire, "being, as I am, unable to ride in the saddle, or to walk, by reason of dropsy in my feet and legs, and paralysis in the small of the back."

For two months, Lincoln tried to restore harmony between his commanders. He spent many hours at General Scott's headquarters, listening to the old warrior and attempting to mollify him. He made frequent visits to McClellan's headquarters, situated in a luxurious house at the corner of Lafayette Square, not far from Seward's new home. The upstairs rooms were reserved for McClellan's private use. The parlors downstairs were occupied by the telegraph office, with dozens of staff "smoking, reading the papers, and writing." Sometimes McClellan welcomed Lincoln's visits; on other occasions, he felt them a waste of time: "I have just been interrupted here by the Presdt & Secty Seward who had nothing very particular to say, except some stories to tell." Observers noted with consternation that McClellan often kept Lincoln waiting in the downstairs room, "together with other common mortals." British reporter William Russell began to pity the president, who would call only to be told that the general was "lying down, very much fatigued." Nonetheless, so long as he believed in McClellan's positive influence on the army, Lincoln tolerated such flagrant breaches of protocol.

The first public dissatisfaction with McClellan's performance began to emerge as the autumn leaves began to fall. While Washingtonians delighted in his magnificent reviews of more than fifty thousand troops marching in straight columns to the sounds of hundred-gun salutes, with "not a mistake made, not a hitch," they grew restive with the failure of the troops to leave camp. Undeterred, McClellan insisted to his wife that he would not move until he was certain that he was completely ready to take on the enemy. "A long time must yet elapse before I can do this, & I expect all the newspapers to abuse me for delay—but I will not mind that."

Radical Republicans who had initially applauded McClellan's appointment began to turn on him when they learned he had issued "a slave-catching order" requiring commanders to return fugitive slaves to their masters. McClellan repeatedly emphasized that he was "fighting to preserve the integrity of the Union & the power of the Govt," and that to achieve that overriding goal, the country could not "afford to raise up the negro question." Coming under attack, he sought cover from his Democratic friends. "Help me to dodge the nigger," he entreated Samuel Barlow of New York, "we want nothing to do with him."

At the first whiff of censure, McClellan shifted blame onto any other shoulder but his own—onto Scott's failure to muster necessary resources, onto the incompetence of the cabinet, "some of the greatest geese . . . I have ever seen—enough to tax the patience of Job." He considered Seward "a meddling, officious, incompetent little puppy," Welles "weaker than the most garrulous old woman," and Bates "an old fool." He was disgusted by the "rascality of Cameron," and though he commended Monty Blair's courage, he did not "altogether fancy him!" Only Chase was spared his scorn, perhaps because the treasury secretary had sent a flattering letter before McClellan was called to Washington in which he claimed that he was the one responsible for the general's promotion to major general.

Impatience with McClellan mounted when one of his divisions suffered a crushing defeat at a small engagement on October 21, 1861. Having learned that the rebels had pulled back some of their troops from Leesburg, Virginia, McClellan ordered General Charles P. Stone to mount "a slight demonstration on your part" in order "to move them." Stone assumed that he would have the help of a neighboring division, which McClellan had ordered back to Washington without informing Stone. Colonel Edward Baker, Lincoln's close friend from Illinois, was killed in action, along with forty-nine of his men when the Confederates trapped them at the river's edge at Ball's Bluff. Many more were seriously wounded, including the young Oliver Wendell Holmes, Jr., who was brought to Chase's spacious home to recover.

Baker was mourned by the entire Lincoln family. Lincoln later told the journalist Noah Brooks that "the death of his beloved Baker smote upon him like a whirlwind from a desert." The day before Baker was killed, the two old friends had talked together on the White House grounds. A passing officer recalled the poignant scene: "Mr. Lincoln sat on the ground leaning against a tree; Colonel Baker was lying prone on the ground his head supported by his clasped hands. The trees and the lawns were gorgeous in purple and crimson and scarlet, like the curtains of God's tabernacle." Not far away, ten-year-old Willie "was tossing the fallen leaves about in childish grace and abandon." When the time came for Baker to take his leave, he shook Lincoln's hand and then took Willie into his arms and kissed him.

Twenty-four hours later, Captain Thomas Eckert, in charge of the telegraph office at McClellan's headquarters, received word of Baker's death and the defeat at Ball's Bluff. Instructed to deliver all military telegrams directly to McClellan, Eckert searched for the commanding general. Finding him at the White House talking with Lincoln, he handed the general the wire and withdrew. McClellan chose not to reveal its contents to the president. Afterward, when Lincoln dropped in at the telegraph office to get the latest news from the front, he discovered the dispatch. A correspondent seated in the outer room observed Lincoln's reaction. He walked "with bowed head, and tears rolling down his furrowed cheeks, his face pale and wan, his heart heaving with emotion." He stumbled through the room and "almost fell as he stepped into the street."

Mary was similarly distraught. She had named her second son, Edward, in honor of Edward Baker. Now both her child and his dear namesake were lost. Willie and Tad, who had likewise adored Baker, were heartbroken. For Willie, much like his father, writing provided some measure of solace. He composed a small poem, "On the Death of Colonel Edward Baker," which was published in the *National Republican*. After two stanzas recalling Baker's patriotic life and celebrated oratorical skills, he wrote:

> *No squeamish notions filled his breast,*
>   The Union *was his theme.*
> "No surrender and no compromise,"
>   *His day thought and night's dream.*
>
> *His country has* her *part to play,*
>   *To'rds those he has left behind,*
> *His widow and his children all,—*
>   *She must always keep in mind.*

The child's homage to a cherished friend reflected a depressingly common circumstance as the war left mounting casualties and desolation in its wake. Ten-year-old Willie's words would be echoed in his father's memorable plea in the Second Inaugural Address, when he urged the nation "to care for him who shall have borne the battle, and for his widow, and his orphan."

McClellan straightaway denied responsibility for the defeat at Ball's Bluff, characteristically insisting that the "disaster was caused by errors committed" by the leaders at the front. "The whole thing took place some 40 miles from here without my orders or knowledge," he told his wife; "it was entirely unauthorized by me & I am in no manner responsible for it." The person "*directly* to blame," McClellan said, was Colonel Baker, who had exceeded General Stone's orders by crossing the river. Rumors then began to spread that Stone himself would be court-martialed.

When frustrated congressional leaders, many of whom were longtime friends of Baker, decried the defeat at Ball's Bluff and the general stagnation of the Union troops, the president defended McClellan. When these same leaders approached McClellan, he unleashed a diatribe against Scott, accusing him of placing obstacles at every step along his way. The congressional delegation left, vowing to remove Scott. "You may have heard from the papers etc of the small row that is going on just now between Genl Scott & myself," McClellan wrote his wife, "in which the vox populi is coming out strongly on my side. . . . I hear that off[icer]s & men all declare that they will fight under no one but 'our George,' as the scamps have taken it into their heads to call me."

On November 1, Lincoln regretfully accepted the veteran's request for retirement. The newspapers released General Scott's resignation letter along with Lincoln's heartfelt reply. The president extolled Scott's "long and brilliant career," stating that Americans would hear the news of his departure from active service "with sadness and deep emotion." At the same time, Lincoln designated McClellan to succeed Scott as general-in-chief of the Union Army.

Two days later, his objective accomplished, McClellan confessed to conflicted emotions when he accompanied Scott to the railroad station for his departure from Washington. "I saw there the end of a long, active & ambitious life," he wrote his wife, "the end of the career of the first soldier of his nation—& it was a feeble old man scarce able to walk—hardly any one there to see him off but his successor." The truth, as the newspapers reported, was that a large crowd had assembled at the depot, despite the train's leaving at 5 a.m. in a drenching rain. All the members of Scott's staff were there, along with McClellan's complete staff and a cavalry escort. Secretaries Chase and Cameron had come to join the general on his journey to Harrisburg. Moreover, "quite a number of citizens" had gathered to pay their respects, belying the ignominious farewell that McClellan depicted. Once again, the young Napoleon erred in his calculations.

As winter approached, public discontent with the inaction of the Union Army intensified. "I do not intend to be sacrificed," the new general-in-chief wrote his wife. Now that McClellan could no longer blame Scott for his troubles, he shifted his censure to Lincoln for denying him the means to confront the rebel forces in Virginia, whose numbers, he insisted, were at least three times his own. In letters home, he complained about Lincoln's constant intrusions, which forced him to hide out at the home of fellow Democrat Edwin Stanton, "to dodge all enemies in shape of 'browsing' Presdt etc." He reported a visit to the White House one Sunday after tea, where he found "the *original gorrilla*," as he had taken to describing the president. "What a specimen to be at the head of our affairs now!" he ranted. "I went to Seward's, where I found the 'Gorilla' again, & was of course much edified by his anecdotes—ever apropos, & ever unworthy of one holding his high position."

On Wednesday night, November 13, Lincoln went with Seward and Hay to McClellan's house. Told that the general was at a wedding, the three waited in the parlor for an hour. When McClellan arrived home, the porter told him the president was waiting, but McClellan passed by the parlor room and climbed the stairs to his private quarters. After another half hour, Lincoln again sent word that he was waiting, only to be informed that the general had gone to sleep. Young John Hay was enraged. "I wish here to record what I consider a portent of evil to come," he wrote in his diary, recounting what he considered an inexcusable "insolence of epaulettes," the first indicator "of the threatened supremacy of the military authorities." To Hay's surprise, Lincoln "seemed not to have noticed it specially, saying it was better at this time not to be making points of etiquette & personal dignity." He would hold McClellan's horse, he once said, if a victory could be achieved.

Though Lincoln, the consummate pragmatist, did not express anger at McClellan's rebuff, his aides fumed at every instance of such arrogance. Lincoln's secretary, William Stoddard, described the infuriating delay when he accompanied Lincoln to McClellan's anteroom. "A minute passes, then another, and then another, and with every tick of the clock upon the mantel your blood warms nearer and nearer its boiling-point. Your face feels hot and your fingers tingle, as you look at the man, sitting so patiently over there . . . and you try to master your rebellious consciousness." As time went by, Lincoln visited the haughty general less frequently.

If he wanted to talk with McClellan, he sent a summons for him to appear at the White House.

• • •

DURING THESE TENSE DAYS, Mary tried to distract her husband. If old friends were in town, she would invite them to breakfast and dispatch a message to his office, calling the president to join the gathering. Initially irritated to be taken from his work, Lincoln would grudgingly sit down and begin exchanging stories. His "mouth would relax, his eye brighten, and his whole face lighten," Elizabeth Grimsley recalled, "and we would be launched into a sea of laughter." Mary had also introduced a therapeutic "daily drive," insisting that the two of them, and sometimes the children, take an hour-long carriage ride at the end of the afternoon, to absorb "the fresh air, which he so much needed."

More than most previous first ladies, Mary enjoyed entertaining. She had never lost her taste for politics. On many nights, while her husband worked late in his office, the first lady held soirées in the Blue Room, to which she invited a mostly male circle of guests. Her frequent visitors included Daniel Sickles, the New York congressman who recently had murdered the son of the composer of "The Star-Spangled Banner," Philip Barton Key, who was having an affair with Sickles's wife. Defended by a team of lawyers including Edwin Stanton, Sickles had been found innocent by reason of "temporary insanity."

Another flamboyant figure at Mary's salons was Henry Wikoff, who had published an account of his picaresque adventures in Europe. He had been a spy for Britain and had spent time in jail for kidnapping and seducing a young woman. Mary enjoyed people with scandalous backgrounds, and delighted in the lively conversation, which ranged from "love, law, literature, and war" to "gossip of courts and cabinets, of the *boudoir* and the *salon*, of commerce and the Church, of the peer and the pauper, of Dickens and Thackeray."

While Mary charmed guests in her evening salons, she gained respect for the energy and aplomb with which she hosted the traditional White House receptions for the public. She believed that these social gatherings helped to sustain morale. Most important, her husband was proud of both her social skills and her appearance. "My wife is as handsome as when she was a girl," he said at one White House levee, "and I a poor nobody then, fell in love with her and once more, have never fallen out."

When Prince Napoleon, the cousin of Napoleon Bonaparte III, visited Washington in early August, Mary organized an elaborate dinner party. She found the task of entertaining much simpler than it had been in

Springfield days. "We only have to give our orders for the dinner, and *dress* in proper season," she wrote her friend Hannah Shearer. Having learned French when she was young, she conversed easily with the prince. It was a "beautiful dinner," Lizzie Grimsley recalled, "beautifully served, gay conversation in which the French tongue predominated." Two days later, her interest in French literature apparently renewed, Mary requested Volume 9 of the *Oeuvres de Victor Hugo* from the Library of Congress.

Nor did Mary Lincoln confine her abundant energies to social ventures. A month after the French dinner, she strenuously pressured her husband on a matter of state—the pending execution of William Scott. A soldier from Vermont, Scott had fallen asleep during picket duty. His dereliction of duty had occurred during the predawn hours of his second straight night of standing guard. As the story was told, he had volunteered the first night to replace a sick friend, and then was called to duty the next night on his own. According to Lizzie Grimsley, the severity of the soldier's sentence distressed both Tad and his mother. "Think," Tad entreated, "if it was your own little boy who was just tired after fighting, and marching all day, that he could not keep awake, much as he tried to." Mary joined in, begging her husband to show mercy to the young soldier. The situation was not easy for Lincoln. While he understood the human circumstances that led to the soldier's lapse, he also recognized that his intervention might undermine military discipline. In the end, Mary's arguments apparently swayed him.

The day before the scheduled execution, Lincoln walked over to McClellan's office and asked him to issue a pardon, "suggesting," the general recollected, "that I could give as a reason in the order that it was by request of the 'Lady President.' " Vermont senator Lucius Chittenden, who had also interceded on young Scott's behalf, apologized for the imposition, recognizing "that it was asking too much of the President" to intervene "in behalf of a private soldier." Lincoln put Chittenden's mind at ease, assuring him that "Scott's life is as valuable to him as that of any person in the land. You remember the remark of a Scotchman about the head of a nobleman who was decapitated. 'It was a small matter of a head, but it was valuable to him, poor fellow, for it was the only one he had.' "

The renovation of the White House and its surrounding landscape engaged Mary throughout the summer and fall of 1861. She raved to a friend that she had "the most beautiful flowers & grounds imaginable, and company & excitement enough, to turn a wiser head than my own." Yet with each passing month, she spent less time with her husband, whose every hour was preoccupied with the war. Though he still took the afternoon drives she had prescribed, he often invited Seward along so the two men could talk. In late August, when Seward's wife and daughter arrived in

Washington to spend several weeks, Lincoln took them for drives nearly every afternoon. Frances took an immediate liking to the president, whom she described as "a plain unassuming farmer—not awkward or ungainly," who talked with equal ease about "the war & the crops." Fanny was captivated. "I liked him very much," she recorded in her diary. She was especially delighted when the president showed her the kittens her father had given to Willie and Tad and told her that "they climb all over him."

During these pleasant interludes with the Seward family, Lincoln stopped to visit the various encampments in the surrounding countryside. Halting the carriages, he and Seward would talk with the soldiers. A veteran reporter who had watched every president since Jackson wrote that he had never seen anyone go through the routine of handshaking with the "*abandon* of President Lincoln. He goes it with both hands, and hand over hand, very much as a sailor would climb a rope." The affable Seward was equally at ease. Fanny took particular delight in watching them greet troops from the 23rd Pennsylvania Regiment. "With one impulse" the men cheered Lincoln's appearance so loudly that the horses were "somewhat startled"; then they "began cheering for 'Secretary Seward' passing his name from mouth to mouth." Fanny proudly confided in her diary that "I love to remember all Father says and does."

Frances Seward was happy to be reunited with her husband for the first extended period in almost a year, but she found the frantic pace of wartime Washington life enervating. Nor did she feel at home in the "palatial" house her husband had taken on Lafayette Square. In a letter to her sister, she wistfully confessed that Henry was never "more pleased with a home— it accommodates itself marvelously to his tastes & habits—such as they are at this day." She praised Fred and Anna, who were so "gifted in making their surroundings . . . tasteful & attractive." But it was a home designed for the three of them—her husband, son, and daughter-in-law—not for her. It perfectly fitted the constant round of entertaining that Seward so enjoyed. And Anna was far better suited to the role of hostess than Frances—confined to her bed by migraines for several days every week— could ever hope to be.

As she readied herself to return to Auburn, Frances was concerned that she had not yet called on Mary Lincoln. The first lady had just come back from a three-week vacation in upstate New York and Long Branch, New Jersey, and Frances felt it her duty to visit, "especially as I went to see her husband." On the Monday before Frances was due to leave, word came that Mary would receive her and her family that evening. After dinner, John Nicolay arrived to escort the Sewards to the White House. The little group included Henry, Frances, Fred, Anna, and Fanny, as well as Seward's youngest son, Will, and his new bride, Jenny. They were shown into the Blue Parlor by Edward, the Irish doorkeeper who had worked in the White House for nearly two decades. "Edward drew a chair for Mrs. L.," Fanny recalled, and then arranged the chairs for the rest of the party, before leaving to inform Mary that her guests had arrived. "Well there we sat," Fanny recorded, until "after a lapse of some time the usher came and said Mrs. Lincoln begged to be excused, she was *very* much engaged."

"The truth," Fanny wrote, "was probably that she did not want to see Mother—else why not give general direction to the doorkeeper to let no one in? It was certainly very rude to have us all seated first." Referring to Mary's celebrated salons, Fanny archly added that it was "the only time on record that she ever refused to see company in the evening." In fact, Mary detested Seward and had most likely contrived to snub the entire Seward family. From the outset, she had resisted Seward's appointment to the cabinet, fearing that his celebrity would outshine her husband's. "If things should go on all right," she warned, "the credit would go to *Seward*—if they went wrong—the blame would fall upon my husband." Contrary to Mary's suspicions, it was Seward who received much of the censure incurred by the administration, as his fellow cabinet members tended to blame him more than Lincoln for whatever displeased them. Long after Seward had come to respect Lincoln's authority, however, many observers, including Mary, mistakenly assumed that the secretary of state was the mastermind of the administration. "It makes me mad to see you sit still and let that hypocrite, Seward, twine you around his finger as if you were a skein of thread," Mary fumed to her husband.

Furthermore, Mary resented the long evenings Lincoln spent at Seward's Lafayette Square mansion rather than remaining home with her. Warmed by Seward's fireplace and gregarious personality, Lincoln could unwind. Though he himself neither drank nor smoked, he happily watched Seward light up a Havana cigar and pour a glass of brandy. And while Lincoln rarely swore, he found Seward's colorful cursing amusing. On one occasion, as Lincoln and Seward were en route to review the troops, the driver lost control of his team and began swearing with gusto. "My friend, are you an Episcopalian?" Lincoln asked. The teamster replied that he was, in fact, a Methodist. "Oh, excuse me," Lincoln said with a laugh. "I thought you must be an Episcopalian for you swear just like Secretary Seward, and he's a churchwarden!"

Lincoln and Seward talked of many things besides the war. They debated the historical legacies of Henry Clay, Daniel Webster, and John Quincy Adams. Seward argued that neither Clay's nor Webster's would live "a tithe as long as J. Q. Adams." Lincoln disagreed, believing that

"Webster will be read for ever." They explored the concept of "personal courage." When Lincoln spoke admiringly of the intensity of a particular soldier's desire to take on the enemy in person, Seward disagreed. "He had always acted on the opposite principle, admitting you are scared and assuming that the enemy is." They traded stories and teased each other.

One night when John Hay was also present, another guest brought up the Chicago convention. Hay feared that reminding Seward of his loss was in "very bad taste," but Lincoln used the remark to tell a humorous story about 1860. At one point, he related, the mayor of Chicago, John Wentworth, had feared that Lincoln was oblivious to shifting opinion in Illinois. "I tell you what," Wentworth advised, referring to Thurlow Weed. "You must do like Seward does—get a feller to run you." Both Lincoln and Seward found the story "vastly amusing."

Lincoln's buoyant mood plummeted an hour or so later that evening when he received General Thomas W. Sherman's request for more troops before his advance upon Port Royal, South Carolina. Frustrated by repeated calls from every general for reinforcements, he told Seward he would refuse Sherman's request and would telegraph him to say he didn't have "much hope of his expedition anyway." Now it was Seward's turn to moderate the president's reply, much as Lincoln had softened Seward's language in the famous May 21 dispatch. "No," Seward replied, "you wont say discouraging things to a man going off with his life in his hand." Lincoln rejected Sherman's request for more troops but expressed no pessimism about the mission.

The long evenings of camaraderie at Seward's, where interesting guests wandered in and out, probably rekindled memories of Lincoln's convivial days on the circuit, when he and his fellow lawyers gathered together before the log fire to talk, drink, and share stories. Between official meetings and private get-togethers, Lincoln spent more time with Seward in the first year of his presidency than with anyone else, including his family. It was not therefore surprising that the possessive Mary felt rancor toward Seward and his family.

• • •

WHILE LINCOLN ENDURED complaints about the lack of forward movement in the East, he was forced to confront an equally thorny situation in the West, where the fighting between secessionists and Unionists in Missouri threatened to erupt into civil war. Though a majority of the state supported the Union, the new governor, Claiborne Jackson, commanded a sizable number of secessionists intent upon bringing the state into the Confederacy. Missouri initially succeeded in thwarting the rebel guerrillas, largely through the combined efforts of Frank Blair, who had left Congress to become a colonel, and his good friend, General Nathaniel Lyon. They had prevented rebel troops from seizing the St. Louis arsenal, and ingeniously captured Fort Jackson, where the Confederate troops were headquartered. Lyon had entered the rebel camp on a scouting mission, disguised as the familiar figure of Frank's mother-in-law, a well-respected old lady in St. Louis. He wore a dress and shawl, with a "thickly veiled sunbonnet," to hide his red beard. Hidden in his egg basket were revolvers in case he was recognized. The following day, with knowledge of the camp and seven thousand troops, Lyon marched in and took the fort.

In spite of these early successes, daring rebel raids soon destroyed bridges, roads, and property, and threw the state into a panic. To take charge of this perilous situation and command the entire Department of the West, Lincoln appointed General John C. Frémont, the dashing hero whose exploits in 1847 in the liberation of California from Mexico had earned him the first Republican nomination for president in 1856. Lincoln later recalled that it was upon the "earnest solicitation" and united advocacy of the powerful Blair family that he made Frémont a major general and sent him to Missouri.

Frémont's appointment was initially greeted with enthusiasm. "He is just such a person as Western men will idolize and follow through every danger to death or victory," John Hay wrote. "He is upright, brave, generous, enterprising, learned and eminently practical." Frémont's staunch antislavery principles found favor among the German-Americans who comprised a large portion of the St. Louis population. "There was a sort of romantic halo about him," Gustave Koerner recalled. His name alone had "a magical influence," inducing thousands of volunteers from the Western states to join the Union Army.

Within weeks of Frémont's arrival, however, stories filtered back to Washington of "recklessness in expenditures." Tales circulated that the Frémonts had set themselves up in a $6,000 mansion, where bodyguards deterred unwanted visitors, including Hamilton Gamble, the former Unionist governor of Missouri and brother-in-law of Edward Bates. Some worried that Frémont, like McClellan, had chosen to stay in the city to prepare for a move against the rebels rather than join his troops in the field. These unsettling rumors were followed by the shocking news of General Lyon's death in a struggle at Wilson's Creek on August 10. Weeks later, the Union forces suffered another devastating defeat when they were forced to surrender Lexington to the rebels. Among Missouri's loyalists morale plummeted.

In late August, realizing he must act before the situation deteriorated further, Frémont issued a bold proclamation. Without consulting Lincoln, he declared martial law throughout the state, giving the military the authority to try and, if warranted, shoot any rebels within Union lines who were found "with arms in their hands." Union troops were directed to confiscate all property, including slaves, of all persons "who shall be directly proven to have taken an active part with their enemies in the field." These slaves, Frémont proclaimed, "are hereby declared freemen." Frémont's policy far exceeded the Confiscation Act passed by the Congress earlier that month, which applied only to slaves supporting Confederate troops and did not spell out their future status.

Lincoln learned of Frémont's proclamation by reading it in the newspapers along with the rest of the nation. With this announcement, Frémont had unilaterally recast the struggle to preserve the Union as a war against slavery, a shift that the president believed would lead Kentucky and the border states to join the Confederacy. Lincoln wrote a private letter to Frémont, expressing his "anxiety" on two points: "First, should you shoot a man, according to the proclamation, the Confederates would very certainly shoot our best man in their hands in retaliation; and so, man for man, indefinitely." Even more troubling, he saw "great danger" in "liberating slaves of traiterous owners," a move that would certainly "alarm our Southern Union friends, and turn them against us—perhaps ruin our rather fair prospect for Kentucky. Allow me therefore to ask, that you will as of your own motion, modify that paragraph so as to conform" to the recent Confiscation Act of Congress. Lincoln was anxious that Frémont change the language of his own accord, so that the president would not be officially forced to override him. He understood that if the controversy became public, radical Republicans, whose loyalty was crucial to his governing coalition, might side with Frémont rather than with him.

Moreover, as Lincoln later explained to Orville Browning, "Fremont's proclamation, as to confiscation of property, and the liberation of slaves, is *purely political*, and not within the range of *military* law, or necessity." As chief executive, he could not allow a general in the field to determine the "permanent future condition" of slaves. Seward fully supported Lincoln on principle as well as policy. "The trouble with Fremont was, that he acted without authority from the President," Seward later maintained. "The President could permit no subordinate to assume a responsibility which belonged only to himself."

Lincoln's fears about the reaction to Frémont's proclamation in the border states were justified. Within days, frantic letters reached Washington from Unionists in Kentucky. Joshua Speed wrote to Lincoln that Frémont's proclamation had left him "unable to eat or sleep—It will crush out every vestage of a union party in the state—I perhaps & a few others will be left alone." He reminded his old friend that there were "from 180 to 200000 slaves" in Kentucky, of whom only 20,000 belonged to rebels. "So fixed is public sentiment in this state against freeing negroes & allowing negroes to be emancipated & remain among us," he continued, "that you had as well attack the freedom of worship in the north or the right of a parent to teach his child to read—as to wage war in a slave state on such a principle."

Meanwhile, events in Missouri took a strange turn. On September 1, the same day that Frémont made his proclamation public, Colonel Frank Blair penned a long letter to his brother, Montgomery, that would lead to the colonel's arrest and imprisonment two weeks later. "I know that you and I are both in some sort responsible for Fremonts appointment," he admitted, but "my decided opinion is that he should be relieved of his command." Blair was not reacting to the proclamation, as was assumed by contemporaries and historians alike. On the contrary, he told Monty he agreed with the proclamation, believing that stringent measures, including the liberation of slaves, were necessary to dispel the illusions of impunity the marauding bands of rebel guerrillas seemed to harbor. He wished only that the proclamation had been issued earlier, when Frémont "had the power to enforce it & the enemy no power to retaliate."

But since Frémont had taken command, Frank told his brother, the situation in Missouri had grown increasingly desperate. Through "gross & inexcusable negligence," the rebels had accumulated a substantial following. "Oh! for one hour of our dead Lyon," he lamented, adding that many now ascribed Lyon's death to Frémont's failure to reinforce him. Moreover, in the camps around St. Louis, there was "an active want of discipline" reminiscent of the disorganization in Washington that led to Bull Run. If his brother had information absolving Frémont, Frank continued, if the government knew more of Frémont's plans than he, then Montgomery should "burn this paper and say that I am an *alarmist*"; but at this moment, his faith was shaken "to the very foundations."

Monty Blair showed his brother's frank letter to Lincoln and added a letter of his own. He asserted that he himself had reluctantly concluded that Frémont must be dismissed. He acknowledged that he had sponsored Frémont at the start, having enjoyed a warm friendship with the celebrated explorer, "but being now satisfied of my mistake duty requires that I should frankly admit it and ask that it may be promptly corrected." Like Frank, he took no issue with the proclamation, believing a show of strength was necessary. Frémont's removal, he concluded, was "required by public interests."

Hearing similar testimony from other sources in Missouri, Lincoln sent General Meigs and Montgomery Blair on September 10 to talk with Frémont and "look into the affair." At this point, the president still had not received confirmation from Frémont that he would modify the proclamation as requested.

That evening, Frémont's spirited wife, Jessie, the daughter of former senator Thomas Benton, arrived in Washington after a three-day trip on a dusty, cramped train to hand-deliver Frémont's delayed response. She sent Lincoln a card asking when she could see him and received the peremptory response: "A. Lincoln. Now." Straightaway, Jessie left her room at the Willard in the wrinkled dress she had worn during her sweltering trip. As she later reported, when the president came into the room, he "bowed slightly" but did not speak. Nor did he offer her a seat. She handed him her husband's letter, which he read standing. To Lincoln's fury and dismay, Frémont had refused his private request to modify the proclamation, insisting that the president must publicly order him to do so. "If I were to retract of my own accord," the general argued, "it would imply that I myself thought it wrong and that I had acted without the reflection which the gravity of the point demanded. But I did not do so."

When Lincoln remarked that Frémont clearly knew what was expected of him, Jessie implied that Lincoln did not understand the complex situation in Missouri. Nor did he appreciate that unless the war became one of emancipation, European powers were more than likely to recognize the Confederacy. "You are quite a female politician," Lincoln remarked. He later recalled that Jessie Frémont had "taxed me so violently with many things that I had to exercise all the awkward tact I have to avoid quarelling with her. . . . She more than once intimated that if Gen Fremont should conclude to try conclusions with me he could set up for himself." As Jessie left, she asked Lincoln when she might return to receive his reply. He told her he would send for her when he was ready.

The next morning, Lincoln wrote his reply. This time, he issued "an open order" to Frémont to revise his proclamation to conform to the provisions of the Confiscation Act. Rather than allow Jessie to hand-deliver it, he sent it to be mailed. In keeping with Frémont's own tactics, he made the reply public before Frémont would receive it.

While Jessie waited vainly at the Willard for word from Lincoln, Francis Blair, Sr., visited her room. "He had always been fond of me," Jessie recalled, "I had been like a child in their family; but Mr. Blair was now very angry." He told her that she and her husband had made a great mistake in incurring the enmity of the president. Talking too freely over a two-hour period, the elder Blair revealed that Frank had sent a letter to Monty describing the situation in Missouri, and that the president had sent Monty to St. Louis to "examine into that Department."

Jessie was infuriated, assuming that Frank's letter had precipitated the investigation. She "threatened the old man that Fremont should hold Frank personally responsible expecting that she could make [him] quail at the thought of losing the son of whom [he] is most proud in a duel with a skilled duellist." Blair Senior told her "that the Blairs did not shrink from responsibility." Frank's sister, Lizzie, who, like the rest of the family, adored her high-spirited brother, believed her father had been "most incautious" in discussing Frank's letter with Jessie, rightly fearing that the Frémonts would retaliate.

Meanwhile, Meigs and Monty Blair had assessed affairs in Missouri and were heading home. Meigs had come to the clear conclusion that Frémont was not fit to command the Department of the West. "The rebels are killing and ravaging the Unionmen throughout the state," he wrote; "great distress and alarm prevail; In St. Louis the leading people of the state complain that they cannot see him; he does not encourage the men to form regiments for defence." Monty Blair agreed. After what he described to Lincoln as "a full & plain talk with Fremont," he claimed that the general "Seems Stupefied & almost unconscious, & is doing absolutely nothing." Rumors circulated that Frémont was an opium-eater. "No time is to be lost, & no mans feelings should be consulted," Blair concluded.

The day after Monty Blair and Meigs departed for Washington, Frémont imprisoned Frank Blair, claiming that the letter he had written his brother on September 1 was an act of insubordination. By criticizing his commanding officer "with a view of effecting his removal," Frank was guilty of conduct "unbecoming an officer and a gentleman."

Frémont and Jessie had concluded that the Blairs had betrayed them. Monty interceded, writing a conciliatory letter to Frémont that led to Frank's release from jail. Frank insisted on fighting the charges, however, and was soon arrested again. Opinion in Missouri was equally divided between Frank Blair and General Frémont, each intent on destroying the other. General Scott had finally stepped in, ordering a suspension of Frank's arrest and postponing the trial, which would never take place. But the quarrel between the two old allies would have serious consequences in the years ahead.

Lincoln's public abrogation of Frémont's proclamation produced a sigh of relief in the border states but, as Lincoln had apprehended, it profoundly disappointed radical Republicans and abolitionists. Only days earlier, Frances Seward had happily asked her sister, "Were you not pleased with Fremont's proclamation?" Now Lincoln had once again dashed her

hopes. In Chicago, Joseph Medill lamented that Lincoln's letter "has cast a
funeral gloom over our patriotic city. . . . It comes upon us like a killing
June frost—which destroys the comming harvest. It is a *step backwards.*"
Senator Ben Wade blamed Lincoln's "poor white trash" background for
his revolting decision, while Frederick Douglass despaired: "Many blunders have been committed by the Government at Washington during this
war, but this, we think, is the largest of them all."

While radicals hoping to make emancipation the war's focus rallied behind Frémont, his antislavery credentials could not compensate for his flagrant mismanagement of the Department of the West. On September 18,
Monty Blair and Meigs delivered their negative report to the cabinet. Still,
Lincoln hesitated. The president "is determined to let Fremont have a
chance to win the State of Missouri," the frustrated postmaster general
told Francis Blair, Sr. Bates, too, was irritated by the president's lack of resolution. With much of his large family still in Missouri, Bates had followed
the state's troubles closely. He had spoken against Frémont on numerous
occasions in the cabinet, certain that Frémont was doing "more damage
to our cause than half a dozen of the ablest generals of the enemy can
do." Having assured Unionist friends in his home state that Frémont's removal was imminent, Bates felt "distressed & mortified" by the president's
inaction.

Anxious about Missouri's troubles and anguished by the illness of his
wife, Julia, who had suffered a slight paralytic stroke, Bates uncharacteristically lashed out at Lincoln. "Immense mischief is caused by his lack of
vim," he wrote his brother-in-law, the former governor of Missouri; "he
has no will, no power to command—He makes no body afraid of him. And
hence discipline is relaxed, & stupid inanity takes the place of action."

Frank Blair was more scathing in his criticisms of Lincoln and his cabinet. "I think God has made up his mind to ruin this nation," he wrote his
brother Monty. "The only way to save it is to kick that pack of old women
who compose the Cabinet into the sea. I never since I was born imagined
that such a lot of poltroons & apes could be gathered together from the
four quarters of the Globe as Old Abe has succeeded in bringing together
in his Cabinet." His anger was focused on Seward and Cameron, and indirectly, of course, on Lincoln himself.

In fact, Lincoln had already dispatched Secretary of War Simon
Cameron, accompanied by Adjutant General Lorenzo Thomas, to St.
Louis to examine the situation once more and deliver, at his discretion, "a
letter directing [Frémont] to surrender his command to the officer next
below him." When Cameron arrived in St. Louis, he talked with Brigadier
General Samuel R. Curtis, who "spoke very freely of [Frémont's] qualities

and conduct" and warned the secretary of war that Missouri's safety could be guaranteed only by the termination of Frémont's command. Upon receiving the letter of dismissal, Frémont "was very much mortified." He told Cameron that "he was now in pursuit of the enemy, whom he believed were now within his reach, and that to recall him at this moment would not only destroy him, but render his whole expenditure useless." Cameron was swayed to withhold the order until he returned to Washington and talked with the president.

By this point, Lincoln had little doubt that Frémont should be discharged. In addition to the impressions of Meigs, Monty Blair, and Cameron, he had received a blistering report from Adjutant General Thomas detailing the sorry "constitution of Fremont's army, its defective equipment and arming, its confusion and imbecility, its lack of transportation," a catalogue of items leading to the unassailable conclusion that "its head is wholly incompetent and unsafe to be instructed with its management." Yet Lincoln still "yielded to delay," Bates angrily confided in his diary, holding Seward responsible when the president hesitated a few days longer. "The President still hangs in painful and mortifying doubt," Bates wrote. "And if we persist in this sort of impotent indecision, we are very likely to share his fate—and, worse than all, *deserve it.*"

The Attorney General's impatience was understandable, but Lincoln's reasoning behind the delay was far shrewder than Bates realized. Two days after Bates made his angry entry, Lincoln dispatched his friend Leonard Swett to hand-carry a removal order to Frémont. Before Swett reached St. Louis, however, the War Department released the damning report of Adjutant General Thomas to the press. Published on October 31, the detailed report was considered by the *New York Times* "the most remarkable document that has seen the light since the beginning of the present war." So damning were the revelations about Frémont, the *Times* continued, that it was mystifying why the Lincoln administration had allowed their publication.

In fact, the decision to publicize the report was both calculated and canny. By the time the message was delivered to Frémont, the public had been primed with powerful arguments for his dismissal. Had Lincoln acted earlier, people might have concluded that Frémont was sacrificed to the Blairs or, worse still, cashiered because of his proclamation emancipating the slaves. By leaking the facts in the report, Lincoln had adroitly prepared public opinion to support his decision.

When Swett reached Missouri, he wisely anticipated that Frémont would suspect his mission and refuse him entry into camp. So he gave the dismissal order to an army captain, who disguised himself as a farmer.

With the document sewed into the lining of his coat, the messenger reached Frémont in person shortly after dawn on November 1, the same day that General Scott's resignation was announced. When Frémont opened the order, the captain recalled, a "frown came over his brow, and he slammed the paper down on the table and exclaimed, 'Sir, how did you get admission into my lines?' "

By November 2, when the news was made public, the general reaction was that Lincoln was "justified" in his decision. Frémont no longer had "apologists or defenders" in Washington, the correspondent for the *New York Times* wrote; "the evidences of his unfitness for command have naturally so accumulated here—the headquarters of the army—that no defence of him is possible." The *Philadelphia Inquirer* agreed. "Slowly and reluctantly we are forced to the conviction that General Fremont is unequal to the command of the Western army. The report of Adjutant-General Thomas, which we publish this morning, settles the question in our judgment." In an unusually pro-administration editorial, the Democratic *New York Herald* noted with approval that while "Lincoln is not the man to deal unjustly or ungenerously with any public officer," his firing of Frémont "had become a public necessity, to which the President could no longer shut his eyes; and this tells the whole story."

Even Chase had to admit that Lincoln had handled the tangled situation admirably. "I am thoroughly persuaded," he wrote a friend, "that in all he has done [concerning] Gen. F. the Prest. has been guided by a true sense of publ[ic] duty."

• • •

ONE WEEK AFTER the resignation of General Scott and the dismissal of General Frémont, the administration faced a pressing new dilemma. Seward had received word that the Confederacy had dispatched two prominent Southerners, James Mason and John Slidell, to England to argue its case for formal recognition. Seward hoped to intercept the Confederate ship carrying the two former senators, but they had escaped the Union blockade in Charleston and reached Cuba, where they boarded the *Trent*, a British mail ship. On November 8, Union captain Charles Wilkes, in command of an armed sloop, encountered the *Trent*. Acting without official orders, he fired a shot across the bow and then proceeded to search the vessel. When Mason and Slidell were found, they were courteously escorted back to the Union sloop *San Jacinto* and taken to prison at Fort Warren in Boston. The British ship was allowed to continue its journey.

Captain Wilkes became a national hero to a North desperate for good news. "We do not believe the American heart ever thrilled with more genuine delight than it did yesterday, at the intelligence of the capture of Messrs. Slidell and Mason," the *New York Times* reported. "If we were to search the whole of Rebeldom, no persons so justly obnoxious to the North, could have been found." Wilkes was fêted at Faneuil Hall in Boston, and a great banquet was given in his honor. Cameron appeared before a throng of happy Washingtonians and led "three cheers for Captain Wilkes." Bates recorded "great and general satisfaction" in his diary, while Chase reportedly said he regretted only that the captain had not gone one step further and seized the British ship.

Lincoln, too, seemed pleased at first. In a letter to Edward Everett, he spoke happily of "the items of news coming in last week," first the Union victory at Port Royal, and "then the capture of Mason & Slidell!" His gratification was soon mingled with anxiety, however, when Britain's furious reaction to the incident became known. It took nearly three weeks for news of Mason and Slidell's capture to reach London, but, as *The Times* reported, the "intelligence spread with wonderful rapidity." The complex situation was promptly reduced to a slogan: "Outrage on the British flag—the Southern Commissioners Forcibly Removed From a British Mail Steamer." The London press fulminated against the incident as an explicit violation of the law of nations, demanding "reparation and apology." Fabricated details of the capture depicted a brutal removal of the Southern commissioners.

Looking to give the supposed transgression a face, the British press focused upon Seward. Though the secretary of state told British officials confidentially that Wilkes had "acted without any instructions from the Government," thereby sparing the government "the embarrassment which might have resulted if the act had been specially directed by us," he decided not to speak publicly on the matter. The first public response should come from the British government, Seward maintained. Seward's silence troubled Thurlow Weed, whom Seward had sent to Europe as an unofficial representative. In one of his daily letters to Washington, Weed warned his oldest friend that "if the taking of the rebels from under the protection of the British flag was intended, and is avowed, and maintained, *it means war.*" Newspapers reported that steamers in every dockyard were being equipped with troops and supplies, ready to leave at the government's order. The press continued "fanning the popular flame by promising to clear the sea of the American navy in a month; acknowledge the Southern Confederacy; and, by breaking the blockade, letting out cotton, and letting in British manufactures." Secessionists in Europe, Weed reported, were "certainly jubilant."

Moreover, Weed anxiously wrote, word circulated in "high places" that

Seward hoped "to provoke a war with England for the purpose of getting
Canada." Animosity toward Seward was widespread, he continued, "how
created or why, I know not. It has been skillfully worked. I was told yesterday, repeatedly, that I ought to write the President demanding your dismissal."

Agitated by the vituperative attacks by the British press, Seward burst
into Lincoln's office on Sunday afternoon, December 15. Orville Browning, who was taking tea with the president at the time, dismissed Seward's
worries, insisting that England would not do "so foolish a thing" as to declare war. Lincoln was not so sure. He recalled a ferocious bulldog in his
hometown. While neighbors convinced themselves that they had nothing
to fear, one wise man observed: "I know the bulldog will not bite. You
know he will not bite, but does the bulldog know he will not bite?"

The American press hounded Seward with questions about the affair,
but both he and Lord Lyons, the British minister to Washington, remained silent as they awaited the official British response. On December
19, nearly six weeks after the initial incident, "Her Majesty's Government"
finally declared the seizure of the envoys from the British ship "an affront
to the national honor," which could be restored only if the prisoners were
freed and returned to "British protection." In addition, Britain demanded
"a suitable apology for the aggression." If the United States did not agree
within a few days, Lyons and the entire British delegation were to pack
up and return to Britain. Lyons carried the document to the secretary of
state's office, where he discussed the inflamed situation with Seward. Before presenting the document formally, he agreed to leave a copy so that
the secretary and the president might have more time to consider their response. "You will perhaps be surprised to find Mr. Seward on the side of
peace," Lord Lyons wrote to the British foreign minister.

Fred Seward recalled that his father shut himself off from all visitors
and "devoted one entire day" to drafting a reply. The astute secretary understood the dilemma perfectly. As a practical matter, the United States
could not afford to go to war with Britain. "With England as an auxiliary to
rebellion," Weed had forewarned, "we are 'crushed out.'" It was necessary
that the government release the prisoners and allow them to continue their
journey to England. Yet, overwhelming popular support in the North for
the seizure of the rebels had to be taken into consideration. "They can
never be given up," one newspaper protested. "The country would never
forgive any man who should propose such a surrender." Lincoln himself,
though resolved to avoid war with England, was reportedly unhappy about
submitting to the British demands, which many considered humiliating.

Seward composed an ingenious response, arguing that while Captain

Wilkes had acted lawfully in searching the *Trent*, the legality of seizing contraband prisoners should have been decided by an American Prize Court. He recognized, he wrote, that he appeared to be taking "the British side" of the dispute "against my own country," but he was "really defending and maintaining, not an exclusively British interest, but an old, honored, and cherished American cause." The principle of referring such disputes to a legal tribunal, he reminded Britain, had been established nearly six decades earlier by Secretary of State James Madison when Britain had seized contraband from American ships in similar fashion. To "deny the justice" of the present British claim would be to "reverse and forever abandon" the very rationale upon which the United States had proudly stood in those earlier disputes. Therefore, in defense of "principles confessedly American," the government would "cheerfully" free the prisoners and turn them over to Lord Lyons.

Seward presented his arguments in an extraordinary cabinet session on Christmas morning. The discussion continued for four hours. "There was great reluctance on the part of some of the members of the cabinet—and even the President himself" to accept Seward's argument, Bates recorded. They feared "the displeasure of our own people—lest they should accuse us of timidly truckling to the power of England." The prospect of returning the prisoners was "gall and wormwood" to Chase. "Rather than consent to the liberation of these men," he wrote, "I would sacrifice everything I possess." Only Monty Blair, the consummate realist, stood firmly with Seward at the start. At Lincoln's invitation, Charles Sumner joined the session. As chairman of the Committee on Foreign Relations, he had conferred with Lincoln frequently during the crisis, asserting that the government should not risk war with England. Sumner had read letters from two respected London officials to Lincoln and Seward, revealing that Britain did not want war and that "if the present dispute were settled amicably Britain would not interfere further in the North's problems." The presentations by Seward and Sumner gained some support; but the cabinet, unable to reach a conclusion, decided to meet again the following day to hear Seward present a new draft.

As the meeting adjourned, Lincoln turned to his secretary of state. "Governor Seward, you will go on, of course, preparing your answer, which, as I understand it, will state the reasons why they [the prisoners] ought to be given up. Now I have a mind to try my hand at stating the reasons why they ought *not* to be given up. We will compare the points on each side."

Seward finished his twenty-six-page dispatch that night and read it to Chase at his house the next morning before the cabinet convened. After brooding through the night, Chase had concluded that Seward was right. "I am consoled by the reflection that while nothing but severest retribution is due to them, the surrender under existing circumstances, is but simply doing right," he recorded in his diary.

When the cabinet met the following day, Seward presented his final draft. Though disturbed by the prospect of surrendering the prisoners, the members were relieved that no apology had been rendered and, as Seward boasted, "a great point was gained for our Government." The dispatch was unanimously adopted. After the meeting, Seward asked Lincoln why he had not presented "an argument for the other side?" With a smile, Lincoln replied, "I found I could not make an argument that would satisfy my own mind, and that proved to me your ground was the right one."

The following night, Seward hosted a dinner party to which he invited Senators Crittenden and Conkling and their wives, Orville Browning, Charles Sumner, Preston King, and English novelist Anthony Trollope, whom Fanny described as "a great homely, red, stupid faced Englishman, with a disgusting beard of iron grey." The conversation at dinner was lively and contentious. Kentucky's Crittenden became enraged when Seward pronounced John Brown "a hero." Fanny was upset when Crittenden criticized Florence Nightingale, the celebrated British nurse of the Crimean War, saying, "he thought it a very unwomanly thing for a gentle lady to go into a hospital of wounded men." Fanny saved her retort for her diary. "That was enough of you, Mr. C. if I hadn't seen you at the table turn your head an[d] spit on the floor cloth." After dinner, Seward took the men into the cloakroom, where he read his *Trent* dispatch. The listeners generally commended Seward's handling of the crisis, though at the end of the reading, Crittenden "swore vehemently." Everyone assumed the public would be infuriated by the decision and that the publication of the dispatch would "doom [Seward] to unpopularity."

In the end, the public greeted the dispatch with relief, not anger. Compared to the prospect of fighting both a civil war and a foreign war at the same time, the release of the two prisoners seemed inconsequential. "The general acquiescence in this concession is a good sign," George Templeton Strong observed. "It looks like willingness to pass over affronts that touch the democracy in its tenderest point for the sake of concentrating all our national energies on the trampling out of domestic treason."

Lincoln himself finally recognized both the diplomatic logic and the absolute necessity of giving up the prisoners. And he was willing to admit that, in this case, his secretary of state had pursued the right course all along—a characteristic response that Fred Seward fully appreciated. "Presidents and Kings are not apt to see flaws in their own arguments," he wrote, "but fortunately for the Union, it had a President, at this critical juncture, who combined a logical intellect with an unselfish heart."

• • •

WITH THE RETURN OF CONGRESS for the winter session, the pace of social life in Washington quickened. "Houses are being fitted for winter gayeties, rich dresses and laughing faces pass on every side," reported *Iowa State Register* columnist Mrs. Cara Kasson, wife of the assistant postmaster general, who wrote under the pseudonym of "Miriam." The city is "thronged with strangers, every nook and corner is occupied with . . . lookers-on at this swiftly-moving Panorama of life in the Capital."

The crowds who streamed into the White House receptions that winter found a mansion transformed by Mary Lincoln's tireless efforts. Peeling walls had been stripped and covered with elegant Parisian wallpaper. New sets of china adorned the tables. Magnificent new rugs replaced their threadbare predecessors. Even one of Mary's severest critics, Mary Clemmer Ames, grudgingly admitted that the new rugs were magnificent. She considered the velvet one in the East Room the "most exquisite carpet ever" to cover the historic floor. "Its ground was of pale sea green, and in effect looked as if [the] ocean, in gleaming and transparent waves, were tossing roses at your feet." A California journalist praised the finished product highly: "The President's house has once more assumed the appearance of comfort and comparative beauty."

The historian George Bancroft reported favorably to his wife about a visit with the first lady, who was able with equal charm to discuss her plans for the "elegant fitting up of Mr. Lincoln's room" and to "discourse eloquently" on a recent military review. Bancroft "came home entranced." Mary "is better in manners and in spirit than we have generally heard: is friendly and not in the least arrogant."

As the bills came in, however, Mary discovered that she had overspent the $20,000 allowance by more than $6,800. Afraid to inform her husband, she inveigled John Watt, the White House groundskeeper, to inflate his expense accounts and funnel the extra money over to her. She had replaced her first Commissioner of Public Buildings after he refused to pay for an elaborate White House dinner from the manure account. She exchanged her patronage influence for reduced bills, and accepted gifts from wealthy donors. At one point, she asked John Hay to turn over the White House stationery fund for her use, and later to pay her as the White House steward. "I told her to kiss mine," Hay jokingly informed Nicolay. "Was I right?" Mary was irate when Hay denied her requests. She tried to have him fired, forever losing his goodwill. "The devil is abroad, having great wrath," he confided to Nicolay. "His daughter, the Hell-Cat . . . is in 'a state of mind' about the Steward's salary."

Despite her finagling, Mary found herself in trouble shortly before the New Year when more bills arrived with no money left in the account. She had no recourse but to tell her husband what had happened and to beg him to ask for an additional appropriation. To bolster her case, she asked Benjamin French, the new Commissioner of Public Buildings, to speak with her husband. French caught up with the president shortly after he returned home from a memorial service in the Senate for Edward Baker. The juxtaposition between the moving eulogies for his old friend and the unpleasant topic of decorating bills provoked in Lincoln an unusual display of anger.

The president was "inexorable," French recalled; "he said it would stink in the land to have it said that an appropriation of $20,000 for furnishing the house had been overrun by the President when the poor freezing soldiers could not have blankets, & he *swore* he would never approve the bills for *flub dubs for that damned old house!*" Moreover, Lincoln angrily pointed out, the place was "furnished well enough when they came—better than any house *they* had ever lived in—& rather than put his name to such a bill he would pay it out of his own pocket!"

French was nonetheless determined to aid Mary's cause. He liked her "better and better the more I see of her," he admitted, "and think she is an admirable woman. She bears herself, in every particular, like a lady and, say what they may about her, I will defend her." He succeeded in convincing a friendly congressman to hide a deficiency appropriation in a complex list of military appropriations. The crisis was resolved, at least temporarily, until Mary's continued spending produced another round of bills.

Mary was not alone in her worries about money. In the fall of 1861, Kate spent several weeks in Philadelphia and New York on a mission to purchase new furnishings for her father's mansion. Merchants gladly extended lines of credit for Kate as they had for Mary, creating great anxiety in her father's mind. "I need hardly caution you to avoid extravagance, as it is going to be hard work to make both ends meet here; and if any circumstances should compel me to resign before long my expences shall have far exceeded my income. It does seem a little hard that one who has so much & such important work to do as I have had for the past twelve years should all the time have to pay such a large part of his own expences."

The sense of injustice Chase felt in having to bear the burdens of public life lured him into a questionable relationship with a wealthy Philadelphia banker, Jay Cooke, who had been granted a lucrative contract from the Treasury Department for the sale of government bonds. Perceiving both

Chase's financial strain and his aggrieved pride, Cooke began to send valuable gifts to the Chase household, including an elegant open carriage for Kate and a set of bookcases for the parlor. As the relationship warmed, Chase borrowed money from Cooke, and eventually, Cooke took it upon himself to set up his own investment account for Chase. "I will take great pains to lay aside occasionally some choice 'tid bits' managing the investments for you and not bothering your head with them." If all went well, Cooke hoped, the profit earned would make up "the deficiency" between Chase's salary and his expenses, "for it is a shame that you should go 'behind hand' working as you do." In the smooth Philadelphia banker, the Chases had found what Mary Lincoln unsuccessfully sought—a reliable source to fund the high cost of being a leader of society in wartime Washington.

•   •   •

BY THE END OF 1861, Lincoln realized that he had made a serious mistake in placing Simon Cameron at the head of the War Department. For many decades, Cameron had maintained his power base in Pennsylvania through the skillful use of patronage to reward loyalists and punish opponents. Unfortunately, the expertise of a wily political boss proved inadequate to the tremendous administrative challenge of leading the War Department in the midst of a civil war. A central system of civilian command was essential to construct a machine capable of providing strategy, supplies, logistics, and training for an army that had grown from 16,000 in March to 670,000 in December. Careful record keeping was indispensable when contracts worth millions had to be negotiated for rifles, cannons, horses, uniforms, food, and blankets.

As Lincoln confided to Nicolay, Cameron was "incapable either of organizing details or conceiving and advising general plans." His primitive filing system consisted mainly of scribbled notes. According to Ohio congressman Albert Riddle, when Cameron was asked about the progress of a particular matter, "he would look about, find a scrap of paper, borrow your pencil, make a note, put the paper in one pocket of his trousers and your pencil in the other."

The war was less than two months old when detailed accusations of corruption and inefficiency in the War Department began to surface in newspapers. In July, the Congress appointed a committee to investigate charges that middlemen had made off with scandalous profits on contracts for unworkable pistols and carbines, blind horses, and knapsacks that disintegrated when it rained. Though Cameron was not charged with pocketing the money himself, several of his political cronies had grown rich, vast public funds had been wasted, and the lives of Union soldiers had been jeopardized. As the charges multiplied, Republican newspapers began to call for his resignation, lest the entire administration become tainted by the scandal. "It is better to lose a mortified finger of the right hand at once," the *New York Times* declared, "than to cherish it till the arm is full of disease, and the whole system threatened with dissolution."

Determined to protect his position, Cameron sought to ingratiate himself with the increasingly powerful radical Republicans in Congress, led by Massachusetts's Charles Sumner, Ohio's Ben Wade, Indiana's George Julian, and Maine's William Fessenden. Though known as a conservative on the issue of slavery, Cameron began by degrees to embrace the radicals' contention that the central purpose of the war was to bring the institution of human bondage to an end. While he had allied himself initially with Seward, Cameron turned increasingly to Chase, the single cabinet member at the time not only in favor of allowing fugitive slaves to stay within Union lines but also of enlisting and arming them. "*We* agreed," Chase later recalled, "that the necessity of arming them was inevitable; but we were alone in that opinion."

Acting without Lincoln's approval, Cameron publicly endorsed the position of an army colonel who had sanctioned seizing slaves and using them for military service as one step in a more general policy of deploying "extremist measures against the rebels, even to their absolute ruin." In cabinet sessions and at private dinners, he instigated heated arguments with Bates, Blair, and Smith, who fiercely assailed his position. Cameron maintained that black soldiers would add an essential weapon in the quest for victory. Blair claimed that Cameron was riding the "nigger hobby" for his own political advantage.

The situation came to a head in early December. Each department customarily presented an annual report to the president as he prepared his own yearly message. While drafting the War Department report, the war secretary resolved to officially advocate arming slaves who came into Union lines. Well aware that he would ignite controversy, Cameron read his draft to a series of friends, most of whom urged him to keep silent on the contentious issue.

At this point, Cameron recalled, "I sought out another counsellor,—one of broad views, great courage, and of tremendous earnestness. It was Edwin Stanton." Cameron had called on Stanton during the summer and fall for legal advice on various contracts. This matter, however, was more delicate. Stanton "read the report carefully," according to Cameron, and "gave it his unequivocal and hearty support." In fact, he suggested his own provocative logic, which served to strengthen the argument for arming slaves: "It is clearly a right of the Government to arm slaves when it may become necessary," the addition read, "as it is to take gunpowder from the enemy."

It remains unclear whether Stanton offered his deliberately incendiary advice to encourage the war secretary openly to defy Lincoln, hoping that if Cameron were dismissed, he, Stanton, might be called upon to replace him. Perhaps he was "an abolitionist at heart," simply waiting for the right moment to reveal his honest convictions. He had, after all, given his boyhood pledge to his father that he would fight slavery until the end of his life, and had expressed similar sentiments to Chase in the bloom of their friendship in Ohio. More significant, Charles Sumner considered Stanton "my *personal* friend," who "goes as far [as] I do in directing the war against Slavery." Yet when Stanton talked with fellow Democrats during this same period of time, including McClellan and his former cabinet colleague Jeremiah Black, he expressed decidedly more conservative views on the issue of slavery. Whatever Stanton's purpose, his approval emboldened Cameron, who sent out advance copies of his report to a number of newspapers before submitting it to the president.

When the government printer brought the War Department report to the president for approval, Lincoln discovered the inflammatory paragraph. "This will never do!" he said. "Gen. Cameron must take no such responsibility. That is a question which belongs exclusively to me!" He deleted the paragraph and issued orders to seize every copy already sent. While Lincoln understood that the slaves coming into Union hands "must be provided for in some way," he did not believe, he later wrote, that he possessed the constitutional authority to liberate and arm them. The only way that such actions, "otherwise unconstitutional, might become lawful," was if those measures were deemed "indispensable" for "the preservation of the nation," and therefore for "the preservation of the constitution" itself. At this juncture, he was not convinced that arming seized slaves was "an indispensable necessity." Moreover, he was undeniably aware that such a measure at this time would alienate the moderate majority of his coalition.

Lincoln informed Cameron of his action at the next cabinet meeting, emphasizing, as he had with Frémont, that any decision regarding the future of slavery rested with the president, not with a subordinate official. Although Cameron immediately conceded and agreed to delete the vetoed language, he complained that his excised recommendation was no different from the suggestion Welles had made in his annual report. "This was the moment that Welles dreaded most," his biographer observed. Like the secretary of war, the secretary of the navy had felt compelled to make some provision for fugitive slaves who "have sought our ships for refuge and protection." In such cases, Welles declared, the slaves "should be cared for and employed" by either the navy or the army (depending on which branch had greater need), and "if no employment could be found for them in the public service, they should be allowed to proceed freely and peaceably, without restraint, to seek a livelihood."

Certain that he, too, would be commanded to revise his report, Welles resolved that he would resign before doing so. But to his bewilderment, Lincoln allowed the navy report to be printed without change. Shrewdly, Lincoln had recognized at once the political difference between the two situations: the army occupied territory in the border states, while the navy did not. Allowing blacks to find employment on naval ships or in surrounding harbors on the coast was fundamentally different from providing weapons to blacks in the slave states of Kentucky or Missouri, whose continued loyalty was critical to the Union. Lincoln still believed that such a step would drive the loyal citizens of these states into the Confederacy.

In fact, the president had developed his own policy for the increasing numbers of fugitive slaves who had come into Union lines. As members of Congress gathered on Capitol Hill for the opening of the winter session, he outlined his ideas in his annual message. He recognized, he wrote, that under the Confiscation Act, when Union armies secured territory where slaves had been used by their masters "for insurrectionary purposes," the legal rights of the slaveholders were "forfeited"; slaves "thus liberated" had to be "provided for in some way." He was hopeful that some of the loyal border states might soon "pass similar enactments." If such actions were taken, Lincoln recommended that the Congress compensate the states for each freed slave.

Lincoln still believed that both classes of freed slaves should be colonized on a purely voluntary basis, "at some place, or places, in a climate congenial to them. It might be well to consider, too,—whether the free colored people already in the United States could not, so far as individuals may desire, be included in such colonization."

So long as Lincoln remained hopeful that the Union could be restored before the conflict "degenerate[d] into a violent and remorseless revolutionary struggle," he was unwilling, he said, to sanction "radical and extreme measures" regarding slavery. Despite this assertion, he closed his message with a graceful and irrefutable argument against the continuation of slavery in a democratic society, the very essence of which opened "the way to all," granted "hope to all," and advanced the "condition of all." In this "just, and generous, and prosperous system," he reasoned, "labor is prior to, and independent of, capital." Then, reflecting upon the vicissitudes of his own experience, Lincoln added: "The prudent, penniless be-ginner in the world, labors for wages awhile, saves a surplus with which to buy tools or land for himself; then labors on his own account another while, and at length hires another new beginner to help him." Clearly, this upward mobility, the possibility of self-realization so central to the idea of America, was closed to the slave unless and until he became a free man.

Abolitionists condemned Lincoln's message. "Away with the unstates-manlike scheme of Colonization, thrust so unfortunately into the face of the nation at this juncture!" the abolitionist Worthington G. Snethen wrote Chase. "Let the sword make a nation of four millions of black men free, and let them be free, as free as the white man." Frederick Douglass was so outraged both by the idea of colonizing freed slaves, and by the president's refusal to enlist blacks into the army, that he was close to losing all faith in Lincoln. The president did not understand that the black man was an American with no desire to live elsewhere; "his attachment to the place of his birth is stronger than iron." Moreover, why such fearful con-cern about the destiny of the freed slave? "Give him wages for his work, and let hunger pinch him if he don't work," Douglass declared. "He is used to [work], and is not afraid of it. His hands are already hardened by toil, and he has no dreams of ever getting a living by any other means than by hard work."

Since the beginning of the war, Douglass had avowed that nothing would terrify the South like the vision of thousands of former slaves wield-ing weapons on behalf of the Union Army. "One black regiment alone would be, in such a war, the full equal of two white ones. The very fact of color in this case would be more terrible than powder and balls." Predict-ing that a "lenient war" would be "a lengthy war and therefore the worst kind of war," Douglass contended that the survival of the nation depended upon enlisting the "slaves and free colored people" into the army. In a speech in Philadelphia, he proclaimed: "We are striking the guilty rebels with our soft, white hand, when we should be striking with the iron hand of the black man, which we keep chained behind us. We have been catch-ing slaves, instead of arming them. . . . We pay more attention to the ad-vice of the half-rebel State of Kentucky, than to any suggestion coming from the loyal North."

While the radical press criticized Lincoln's message, moderate and con-servative Republicans lauded his tact. "It appeals to the judgment,—the solid convictions of the people, rather than their resentments or their im-patient hopes and aspirations," the *New York Times* concluded, and as "the moderate men compose nine-tenths of the population of the country, the message will doubtless meet with popularity." Even the normally critical

New York Tribune conceded that the "country and the world will not fail to mark the contrast" between the magnanimity of Lincoln's message and a recent "truculent" address by Jefferson Davis. Though Davis was "commonly presumed the abler of the two" statesmen, and "certainly the better grammarian," the *Tribune* observed, the address of the Confederate chief was "boastful, defiant, and savage," whereas Lincoln "breathes not an unkind impulse" and "deals in no railing accusations."

CHAPTER 15

"MY BOY IS GONE"

THE LINCOLNS HOSTED the traditional New Year's Day reception to mark the advent of 1862. The day was "unusually beautiful," the *New York Times* reported, "the sky being clear and bright, and the air soft and balmy, more like May than January." Frances Seward, who had joined her husband for the holidays, found the festive atmosphere reassuring. "For the first time since we have been here," she told her sister, "the carriages are rolling along the streets as they used to do in old times." Bates, too, was braced by the glorious day. "All the world was out," he noted. Thousands of citizens streamed into the White House when the gates were opened at noon. The Marine Band played as mem-

bers of the public shook hands with the president and first lady. They mingled with Supreme Court justices, senators, congressmen, foreign ministers, military officers, and cabinet officials. At long last, Fanny met the first
lady, whom she described as "a compact little woman with a full round
face," wearing "a black silk, or brocade, with purple clusters in it—and
some appropriate velvet head arrangement."

Though Lincoln cordially greeted every guest, he was under great pressure. In the ninth month of the war, tales of corruption and mismanagement in the War Department combined with lack of progress on the
battlefield to prevent Chase from raising the funds the Treasury needed to
keep the war effort afloat. As public impatience mounted, Lincoln feared
that "the bottom" was "out of the tub." While the disgruntled public
might focus on various members of the military and the cabinet, the president knew that he would ultimately be held responsible for the choices of
his administration. "If the new year shall be only the continuation of the
faults, the mistakes, and the incapacities prevailing during 1861," diarist
Count Gurowski warned, "then the worst is to be expected."

Lincoln had been so reticent during the summer and fall, when
Cameron was first criticized for his lax administration and questionable
contracts, that Seward questioned whether the president was sufficiently
attentive to the unsavory situation. Then, one night in January, the secretary of state recalled, "there was a ring at my door-bell." The president entered, seated himself on the sofa, "and abruptly commenced talking about
the condition of the War Department. He soon made it apparent that he
had all along observed and known as much about it as any of us . . . his
mind was now settled, and he had come to consult me about a successor to
Mr. Cameron."

Choosing the right successor to Cameron was vital. Lincoln's initial
preferences may have included Joseph Holt, Buchanan's war secretary who
had crucially supported the Union during the secession crisis, or West
Point graduate Montgomery Blair. According to Welles, Blair "had exhibited great intelligence, knowledge of military men, sagacity and sound
judgment" during cabinet discussions. Instead of either man, in a decision
that would prove most significant to the course of the war, Lincoln selected Edwin Stanton, the gruff lawyer who had humiliated him in Cincinnati six years earlier and whose disparaging remarks about his presidency
were well known in Washington circles.

Washington insiders attributed the choice to the combined influence of
Seward and Chase. These two rivals rarely agreed on policy or principle,
but each had his own reasons for advocating Stanton. Seward would never
forget Stanton's contribution as his informant during the last weeks of the

Buchanan tenure. The intelligence provided by Stanton had helped root out traitors and keep Washington safe from capture. It had also fortified Seward's role as the central figure in the critical juncture between Lincoln's election and inauguration. Chase's far more intimate friendship with Stanton had grown from their earlier days in Ohio when Stanton had assured Chase that "to be loved by you, and be told that you value my love is a gratification beyond my power to express." Equally important, Chase believed that Stanton would be a steadfast ally in the struggle against slavery.

Lincoln had his own recollections of Stanton, not all of which were negative. He had watched Stanton at work on the Reaper trial and had been impressed instantly by the powerful reasoning of Stanton's arguments, the passion of his delivery, and the unparalleled energy he had devoted to the case. "He puts his whole soul into any cause he espouses," one observer noted. "If you ever saw Stanton before a jury," you would see that "he toils for his client with as much industry as if his case was his own . . . as if his own life depended upon the issue." Energy and force were desperately needed to galvanize the War Department, and Stanton had both in abundance.

On Saturday, January 11, the president sent an uncharacteristically brusque letter to Cameron. In light of the fact that the war secretary had previously "expressed a desire for a change of position," he wrote, "I can now gratify you, consistently with my view of the public interest," by "nominating you to the Senate, next monday, as minister to Russia." After receiving the dismissal letter on Sunday, Cameron is said to have wept. "This is not a political affair," he insisted, "it means personal degradation."

After dinner that night, Cameron went to see Chase. They apparently talked over the troubled situation and decided to enlist Seward's help. Chase drove Cameron back to Willard's and then went alone to Seward's house. As planned, Cameron came in soon after, brandishing the president's letter, which, he said, was "intended as a dismissal, and, therefore, discourteous." Cameron was finally convinced "to retain the letter till morning, and then go and see the President." Later that night, Chase confided in his diary: "I fear Mr. Seward may think Cameron's coming into his house pre-arranged, and that I was not dealing frankly." As usual, however, so long as the high-minded Chase was certain that he had "acted right, and with just deference to all concerned," he was able to rationalize his machinations.

The next day, presumably briefed by Seward and Chase, Lincoln agreed to withdraw his terse letter and substitute a warm note indicating that Cameron had initiated the departure. Since the desirable post at St. Petersburg was vacant, the president would happily "gratify" Cameron's desire.

"Should you accept it, you will bear with you the assurance of my undiminished confidence, of my affectionate esteem, and of my sure expectation that . . . you will be able to render services to your country, not less important than those you could render at home." He also asked Cameron to recommend a successor. Cameron expressed his fervent opinion that his fellow Pennsylvanian Stanton was the best man for the job. In fact, Lincoln had already made his decision, but Cameron left believing he was responsible for Stanton's selection. In the end, each of the three men—Seward, Chase, and Cameron—assumed he was instrumental in Lincoln's appointment of the new secretary of war.

After settling matters with Cameron, Lincoln asked George Harding, whom he had made head of the Patent Office, to bring his old law partner Stanton to the White House. Stanton was then forty-seven, though the grizzled brown hair and beard made him look older, as did the glasses that hid his bright brown eyes. Harding was afraid that disagreeable recollections from the Reaper trial would cast a pall on the meeting. Both Lincoln and Stanton seemed to have put the past behind them, however, leaving Harding "the most embarrassed of the three."

The urgency of the situation left Stanton little time to deliberate. He consulted his wife, Ellen, who, according to her mother, "objected to his acceptance." The move to the War Department would substantially diminish the lifestyle of the Stanton family, slashing a legal income of over $50,000 a year to $8,000. Stanton, too, tormented all his life by fears of insolvency, must have been concerned about the drastic diminution of income. Nevertheless, he could not refuse to serve as secretary of war in the midst of a great civil war. And if he served with distinction, his life, however short in years, might be made "long by noble deeds," as Chase had once prophesied. He accepted the post, on the condition that he could retain Peter Watson, his old friend and assistant on the Reaper trial, "to take care of the contracts," for he realized he would "be swamped at once" without Watson's aid.

The announcement of Cameron's resignation and Stanton's appointment took the majority of the cabinet by surprise. "Strange," Bates confided in his diary, that "not a hint of all this" was discussed at the cabinet council the previous Friday, "and stranger still," the president had sent for no one but Seward over the weekend. Welles heard the dramatic news from Monty Blair, whom he met on the street. Neither one of them, Welles confessed, had been "taken into Lincoln's confidence." Indeed, Welles had never even met Stanton. Stanton's nomination dismayed radical Republicans on Capitol Hill. The powerful William Fessenden, fearful that Stanton's Democratic heritage would incline him toward a soft policy on both slavery and the South, worked to delay the Senate confirmation until he ascertained more about Stanton's position. He conferred with Chase, who assured Fessenden that "he, Secretary Chase, was responsible for Mr. Stanton's selection," and that he would arrange a meeting that very evening between the Maine senator and Stanton. Seward's role in the selection was not publicized, allowing the radicals to assume that Chase, their man in the cabinet, was the chief architect of the appointment. After a lengthy conversation with Stanton, Fessenden told Chase that he was thoroughly convinced that Stanton was "just the man we want." The senator was delighted to find that he and Buchanan's former Attorney General concurred "on every point," including "the conduct of the war" and "the negro question." The Senate confirmed Stanton's nomination the next day.

News of Stanton's replacement for Cameron met with widespread approval. The public generally assumed that Cameron had retired voluntarily. "Not only was the *press* completely taken by surprise," Seward told his wife, "but with all its fertility of conjecture, not one newspaper has conceived the real cause." Cameron's reputation was preserved until the House Committee on Contracts published its 1,100-page report in February 1862, detailing the extensive corruption in the War Department that had led to the purchase of malfunctioning weapons, diseased horses, and rotten food. According to one newspaper report, the committee "resolved to advise the immediate passage of a bill to punish with death any person who commits a fraud upon the Government, whereby a soldier is bodily injured, as for instance in the sale of unsound provisions." Though Cameron was never charged with personal liability, the House voted to censure him for conduct "highly injurious to the public service."

Cameron was devastated, knowing that he would never recover from the scandal. Lincoln, however, made a great personal effort to assuage his pain and humiliation. He wrote a long public letter to Congress, explaining that the unfortunate contracts were spawned by the emergency situation facing the government in the immediate aftermath of Fort Sumter. Lincoln declared that he and his entire cabinet "were at least equally responsible with [Cameron] for whatever error, wrong, or fault was committed."

Cameron would never forget this generous act. Filled with gratitude and admiration, he would become, Nicolay and Hay observed, "one of the most intimate and devoted of Lincoln's personal friends." He appreciated the courage it took for Lincoln to share the blame at a time when everyone else had deserted him. Most other men in Lincoln's situation, Cameron wrote, "would have permitted an innocent man to suffer rather than incur responsibility." Lincoln was not like most other men, as each cabinet member, including the new war secretary, would soon come to understand.

On his first day in office, the energetic, hardworking Stanton instituted "an entirely new *régime*" in the War Department. Cameron's department had been so inundated by office seekers and politicians that officials had little time to answer letters or file telegraphs they received. As a result, requests for military supplies were often delayed for weeks. Stanton decreed that "letters and written communications will be attended to the first thing in the morning when they are received, and will have precedence over all other business." While Cameron had welcomed congressmen and senators every day but Sunday, Stanton announced that the War Department would be closed to all business unrelated to military matters from Tuesdays through Fridays. Congressmen and senators would be received on Saturdays; the general public on Mondays.

Stanton quickly removed many of Cameron's people and surrounded himself with men much like himself, full of passion, devotion, and drive. He made it clear from the beginning that he would not tolerate unmerited requests for even the smallest job. The day after he took office, Stanton later recalled, he met with a man he instinctively judged to be "one of those indescribable half loafers, half gentlemen," who carried with him "a card from Mrs. Lincoln, asking that the man be made a commissary." Stanton was furious. He ripped up the note and sent the man away. The very next day, the man returned with an official request from Mary that he be given the appointment. Stanton did not budge, dismissing the job seeker once again. That afternoon, Stanton called on Mrs. Lincoln. He told her that "in the midst of a great war for national existence," his "first duty is to the people" and his "next duty is to protect your husband's honor, and your own." If he appointed unqualified men simply to return favors, it would "strike at the very root of all confidence." Mary understood his argument completely. "Mr. Stanton you are right," she told him, "and I will never ask you for anything again." True to her word, Stanton affirmed, "she never did."

Under Stanton's altered regime, the War Department opened early in the morning and the gas lamps remained lit late into the night. "As his carriage turned from Pennsylvania Avenue into Seventeenth Street," one of his clerks recalled, "the door-keeper on watch would put his head inside and cry, in a low, warning tone, 'The Secretary!' The word was passed along and around till the whole building was traversed by it, and for a minute or two there was a shuffling of feet and a noise of opening and shutting of doors, as the stragglers and loungers everywhere fled to their stations."

Stanton kept his meetings brief and pointed. He was "fluent without wordiness," George Templeton Strong wrote, "and above all, earnest, warm-hearted, and large-hearted." His tireless work style invigorated his colleagues. "Persons at a distance," a correspondent in the capital city wrote, "cannot well realize what a revolution has been wrought in Washington by the change of the head of the War Department. The very atmosphere of the city breathes of change; the streets, the hotels, the halls of Congress speak it."

After nearly a year of disappointment with Cameron, Lincoln had found in Stanton the leader the War Department needed.

• • •

EARLY IN FEBRUARY 1862, Mary Lincoln pioneered a new form of entertainment at the White House. Instead of the traditional public receptions, which allowed anyone to walk in off the street, or the expensive state dinners, designed for only a small number, she sent out some five hundred invitations for an evening ball to be held at the White House on February 5. Since the party was not open to the public, an invitation became a mark of prestige in Washington society. Those who were not on the original list, according to Nicolay, "sought, and almost begged their invitations."

Mary prepared for her gala with great enthusiasm. She arranged for the Marine Band to play in the corridor and brought in a famous New York catering firm to serve the midnight supper. She had her black seamstress, Elizabeth Keckley, create a beautiful white satin gown with black trimming, a long train, and a low-cut neckline that instantly attracted Lincoln's eye. He laughingly suggested that "if some of that tail was nearer the head, it would be in better style."

Meanwhile, Willie and Tad had settled into a happy routine. They worked with their tutor in the mornings and played with the two Taft boys in the afternoons and evenings, either at the White House or at the Taft home. Judge Taft became "much attached" to both Lincoln boys. He believed that Willie "had more judgment and foresight than any boy of his age that [he had] ever known." The four boys built a cabin on the mansion's flat roof, which was protectively encircled by "a high stone Ballistrade." They named their makeshift fortification the "Ship of State," and equipped it with a spyglass that enabled them to watch the movement of boats on the Potomac and troops on the shore. They invited guests to theatrical performances in the attic. Riding the pony given Willie as a gift became another favorite pastime. In mid-January, when Robert came home on vacation from Harvard College, the family was complete.

Then, a few days before Mary's grand party, Willie came down with a fever. Illness had been prevalent in Washington that January, as snow was followed by sleet and rain that left the ground covered with a thick layer of foul-smelling mud. Smallpox and typhoid fever had taken many lives. "There is a good deal of alarm in the City on account of the prevalence of the Small pox," Judge Taft recorded in his diary. "There are cases of it in almost every Street in the City."

Illness had struck the Stantons, the Sewards, and the Chases. Stanton's youngest son, James, had become critically ill after a smallpox vaccination caused "a dreadful eruption" on all parts of the baby boy's body. The illness continued for six weeks, during which time he was "not expected to live." In this same period, Fanny Seward, who had gone to Philadelphia with her mother, contracted what was first suspected to be smallpox but was probably typhoid. Her "burning fever," back pains, and "ulcerated" throat lasted for nearly two weeks. Seward left Washington in alarm to be with Fanny, one of the few departures from his work during the entire war. Nettie Chase was also seriously ill, having contracted scarlet fever on her way to boarding school in Pennsylvania.

Mary thought it best to cancel the party because of Willie's illness, but Lincoln hesitated, since the invitations had already been sent out. He called in Dr. Robert Stone, who was considered "the dean of the Washington medical community." After examining Willie, the renowned doctor concluded that the boy was "in no immediate danger" and "that there was every reason for an early recovery." Relieved by the diagnosis, the Lincolns decided to hold the ball.

The carriages began arriving at the brilliantly lit White House around 9 p.m. All the Washington elite were present—the cabinet members and their wives, generals and their high staff, the members of the diplomatic corps, senators and congressmen, lawyers and businessmen. McClellan, in dress uniform, attracted much attention, as did the new secretary of war. The Green, Red, and Blue parlors were open for inspection, along with the East Room, where the Lincolns received their guests. Society reporters commented on both the "exquisite taste with which the White House has been refitted under Mrs. Lincoln's directions" and the magnificence of the women's attire. The "violet-eyed" Kate Chase was singled out, as usual. "She wore a dress of mauve-colored silk, without ornament," one reporter wrote admiringly. "On her small, classically-shaped head a simple wreath of minute white flowers mingled with the blond waves of her sunny hair, which was arranged in a Grecian knot behind."

At midnight, the crowd began to move toward the closed dining room. During a slight delay occasioned by a steward who had temporarily misplaced the key, someone exclaimed, "I am in favor of a forward movement," and everyone laughed, including General McClellan. The doors were thrown open to reveal a sumptuous banquet, which was to be served with excellent wine and champagne. "The brilliance of the scene could not dispel the sadness that rested upon the face of Mrs. Lincoln," Elizabeth Keckley, the seamstress who had become a close confidante, recalled. "During the evening she came up-stairs several times, and stood by the bedside of the suffering boy."

Despite Mary's worry and watchfulness, the ball was a triumph. "Those who were here," Nicolay told his fiancée, "will be forever happy in the recollection of the favor enjoyed, because their vanity has been tickled with the thought that they have attained something which others have not." Although there was some caviling about "frivolity, hilarity and gluttony, while hundreds of sick and suffering soldiers" were "within plain sight," reviews in the capital city were overwhelmingly favorable. The Washington *Evening Star* pronounced the event "a brilliant spectacle," while *Leslie's Illustrated Newspaper* described Mary as "our fair 'Republican Queen,' " garbed in a "lustrous white satin robe" and black and white headdress "in perfect keeping with her regal style of beauty."

The success of the White House ball was followed by two Union victories in Tennessee, the captures of Fort Henry on the Tennessee River and Fort Donelson on the Cumberland. These twin victories shifted the defensive struggle in the West to an offensive war and brought national recognition to a new hero: General Ulysses S. Grant. A West Point graduate whose weakness for alcohol had contributed to his resignation from the army eight years earlier, Grant was struggling to support his family as a leather salesman in Galena, Illinois, when the Civil War began. He volunteered to serve immediately, and was put in charge of a regiment in Missouri. From the start, Grant understood that a southward movement from Missouri was essential, but he was unable to persuade General Henry Halleck, Frémont's successor, to authorize the move. Hearing rumors that the unkempt, bewhiskered Grant still drank too much, Halleck was unwilling to trust him with an important mission. Finally, on February 1, after the navy's Admiral Andrew Foote agreed to a joint army-navy expedition, Halleck gave the go-ahead for Grant "to take and hold Fort Henry."

Grant and Foote set out at once. The navy gunboats opened a blistering attack, forcing the retreat of 2,500 rebel troops to the more heavily reinforced Fort Donelson, twelve miles away. The remaining troops surrendered. "Fort Henry is ours," Grant telegraphed Halleck in the terse, straightforward style that would become his trademark. "I shall take and destroy Fort Donelson on the 8th." Though a severe rainstorm delayed the eastward march to Donelson, Grant remained confident. Writing to his sister, he assured her that her "plain brother however has, as yet, had no reason to feel himself unequal to the task." This was not a boast, he said, but "a presentiment" that proved accurate a few days later when he surrounded the rebel forces at Fort Donelson and began his successful assault. After many had died, the Confederate commander, Kentucky native General Simon Buckner, proposed a cease-fire "and appointment of commissioners to settle terms of capitulation." On February 16, Grant telegraphed back the historic words that would define both his character and career: "No terms except unconditional and immediate surrender can be accepted." Buckner and fifteen thousand Confederate soldiers were taken prisoner.

More than a thousand troops on both sides were killed and three times that number wounded. It was "a most bloody fight," a young Union soldier told his father, so devastating to his company that despite the victory, he remained "sad, lonely and down-hearted." Only seven of the eighty-five men in his unit survived, but "the flag was brought through."

The North was jubilant upon receiving news of Grant's triumph at Donelson, the first substantial Union victory in the war. Hundred-gun salutes were fired in celebrations across the land. The capital city was "quite wild with Excitement." In the Senate, "the gallery rose *en masse* and gave three enthusiastic cheers." Elaborate plans were made to illuminate the capital's public buildings in joint celebration of the double victory and George Washington's birthday.

The day after Grant's victory at Donelson, the president signed papers promoting him to major general. Lincoln had been following the Western general since he had read the gracious proclamation Grant issued when he had marched into Paducah, Kentucky, the previous fall. "I have come among you, not as an enemy," he told the Kentuckians, "but as your friend and fellow-citizen." Reports that "Grant had taken the field with only a spare shirt, a hair brush, and a tooth brush" made comparisons between "Western hardihood" and McClellan's "Eastern luxury" inevitable; it was well known that "six immense four-horse wagons" had arrived at McClellan's door to carry his clothes and other items to the front.

Fort Donelson's capture provided the Union with a strategic foothold in the South. After a ghastly battle at Shiloh two months later left twenty thousand casualties on both sides, the Union would go on to secure Memphis and the entire state of Tennessee. These victories would soon be followed by the capture of New Orleans.

• • •

THE COUNTRY'S EXULTATION at Grant's victory at Donelson found no echo in the White House. Willie's condition had grown steadily worse since the White House ball, and Tad, too, had become ill. It is believed

that both boys had contracted typhoid fever, likely caused by ¹
tary conditions in Washington. The White House drew its w
from the Potomac River, along the banks of which tens of thousands of
troops without proper latrines were stationed. Perhaps because his constitution had been weakened by his earlier bout with scarlet fever, Willie was
affected by the bacterial infection more severely than his brother Tad. He
"grew weaker and more shadow-like" as the debilitating symptoms of his
illness took their toll—high fever, diarrhea, painful cramps, internal hem-
orrhage, vomiting, profound exhaustion, delirium.

Tending to both boys, Mary "almost wore herself out with watching,"
Commissioner French observed. She canceled the customary Saturday receptions and levees. For Lincoln, too, it was an agonizing period. Nicolay
reported that the president gave "pretty much all his attention" to his sons,
but the grim business of conducting the war could not be avoided.

Slipping in and out of consciousness, Willie would call for his friend
Bud Taft, who sat by his bedside day and night. Late one evening, seeing
Bud at his son's side, Lincoln "laid his arm across Bud's shoulder and
stroked Willie's hair." Turning to Bud, he said quietly, "You ought to go to
bed, Bud," but Bud refused to leave, saying, "If I go he will call for me."
Returning later, Lincoln "picked up Bud, who had fallen asleep, and carried him tenderly to bed."

As news of the boy's critical condition spread through Washington,
most of the celebratory illuminations were canceled. The *Evening Star*
wrote that "the President and Mrs. Lincoln have deep sympathy in this
community in this hour of their affliction." Though work continued in the
offices of the White House, staffers walked slowly down the corridors "as
if they did not wish to make a noise." Lincoln's secretary, William Stoddard, recalled the question on everyone's lips: "Is there no hope? Not any.
So the doctors say."

At 5 p.m. on Thursday, February 20, Willie died. Minutes later, Lincoln
burst into Nicolay's office. "Well, Nicolay," he said, "my boy is gone—he is
actually gone!" He began to sob. According to Elizabeth Keckley, when
Lincoln came back into the room after Willie's body had been washed and
dressed, he "buried his head in his hands, and his tall frame was convulsed
with emotion." Though Keckley had observed Lincoln more intimately
than most, she "did not dream that his rugged nature could be so moved."

Mary Lincoln was "inconsolable," Keckley recorded. "The pale face of
her dead boy threw her into convulsions." She had frequently said of her
blue-eyed, handsome son that "if spared by Providence, [he] would be the
hope and stay of her old age." She took to her bed with no way to sleep or
ease her grief.

Meanwhile, Tad was now critically ill. With Mary in no condition to care for him, Lincoln sought help. He sent his carriage to the Brownings, who came at once and spent the night at Tad's bedside. He asked Gideon Welles's young wife, Mary Jane, to sit with the boy. Julia Bates, recovered from her stroke, also watched over him. Clearly, Tad required professional care around the clock. Lincoln turned to Dorothea Dix, the tireless crusader who had been appointed by the secretary of war as Superintendent of Women Nurses. She was a powerful woman with set ideas, among them the belief that women's corsets had a baneful effect on their health. She would routinely lecture young women on the subject. One girl refused to listen, insisting that she would rather "be dead than so out of fashion." To this, Dix rejoined, "My dear . . . if you continue to lace as tightly as you do now, you will not long have the privilege of choice. You will be *both* dead and out of fashion."

Asked to recommend a nurse, Dix chose Rebecca Pomroy, a young widow who had worked on typhoid wards in two Washington hospitals. Introducing Nurse Pomroy to Lincoln, Dix assured the president that she had "more confidence" in her than any other nurse, even those twice her age. Lincoln took Pomroy's hand and smiled, saying: "Well, all I want to say is, let her turn right in."

While Willie's body lay in the Green Room and Mary remained in bed under sedation, Nurse Pomroy tended Tad. Whenever possible, the president brought his work into Tad's room and sat with his son, who was "tossing with typhoid." Always curious and compassionate about other people's lives, Lincoln asked the new nurse about her family. She explained that she was a widow and had lost two children. Her one remaining child was in the army. Hearing her painful story, he began to cry, both for her and for his own stricken family. "This is the hardest trial of my life," he said. "Why is it? Oh, why is it?" Several times during the long nights Tad would awaken and call for his father. "The moment [the president] heard Taddie's voice he was at his side," unmindful of the picture he presented in his dressing gown and slippers.

On the Sunday after Willie's death, Lincoln drove with Browning to Oak Hill Cemetery in Georgetown to inspect the vault where his son's body would lie until his final burial in Springfield. The funeral service was scheduled for 2 p.m. in the East Room the following day. Though scores of people were invited, Mary asked Mrs. Taft to "keep the boys home the day of the funeral; it makes me feel worse to see them." Nonetheless, without consulting his distraught wife, Lincoln "sent for Bud to see Willie before he was put in the casket." "He lay with his eyes closed," the essayist Nathaniel Parker Willis recalled, "his brown hair parted as we had known it—pale in the slumber of death; but otherwise unchanged, for he was dressed as if for the evening." At noontime, the president, the first lady, and Robert entered the Green Room to bid farewell to Willie before the casket was closed. Commissioner French was told that the Lincolns wanted "no spectator of their last sad moments in that house with their dead child," and that Mary was so overcome she could not attend the East Room service.

Congress had adjourned so that members could attend the service. Many of those present had attended the ball just nineteen days earlier— the vice president, the cabinet, the diplomatic corps, General McClellan and his staff. As the funeral guests filed in, a frightful storm arose. Heavy rain and high winds uprooted trees, destroyed a church, and tore the roofs off many houses. After the service was concluded, a long line of carriages made its way through the tempest to the cemetery chapel where Willie was laid to rest temporarily inside the vault. Lincoln, who had so agonized whenever the stormy weather had pelted the grave of his first love, Ann Rutledge, perhaps found some solace that his son's body was now sheltered from the rain and howling wind.

In the weeks that followed, Lincoln worried about Mary, who remained in her bed, unable to cope with daily life. Though Tad eventually recovered, Mary found it difficult to endure his company, which only intensified her sense of Willie's absence. Nor could she bear to see Bud and Holly Taft. She never invited them back to the White House, leaving Tad utterly isolated. Understanding the situation, the president tried to keep his son by his side, often carrying the boy to his own bed at night.

Mary seemed to find some small comfort in her conversations with Rebecca Pomroy and Mary Jane Welles. The latter, who spent many nights keeping vigil at Tad's bedside, had lost five children of her own and could relate to Mary's sorrow. In her talks with Mrs. Pomroy, Mary tried to understand how the widow could bear to nurse the children of strangers after the devastation of her own family. Mary knew that she should surrender to God's will, but found she could not. Looking back on Willie's bout with scarlet fever two years earlier, she concluded that he was spared only "to try us & wean us from a world, whose chains were fastening around us," but "when the blow came," she was still "unprepared" to face it. "Our home is very beautiful," she wrote a friend three months after Willie's death, "the world still smiles & pays homage, yet the charm is dispelled— everything appears a mockery, the idolised one, is not with us."

Indeed, the luxury and vanity in which she had indulged herself now seemed to taunt her. She plunged deeper into guilt and grief, speculating that God had struck Willie down as punishment for her overweening pride in her family's exalted status. "I had become, so wrapped up in the world, so devoted to our own political advancement that I thought of little else," she acknowledged. She knew it was a sin to think thus, but she believed that God must have "foresaken" her in taking away "so lovely a child."

Nor could she fully accept the comfort Mary Jane Welles found in the belief that her children awaited her in heaven. If only she had faith that Willie was "far happier" in an afterlife than he had been "when on earth," Mary suggested to Mary Jane, she might accept his loss. Although in later years she would come to trust that *"Death, is only a blessed transition"* to a place "where there are no more partings & and *no more* tears shed," her faith at this juncture was not strong enough to provide solace.

Crippled by her sadness, Mary was drawn to the relief offered by the spiritualist world. Through Elizabeth Keckley, she was introduced to a celebrated medium who helped her, said Mary, pierce the "veil" that "separates us, from the 'loved & lost.' " During several séances, some conducted at the White House, she believed she was able to see Willie. Spiritualism would reach epic proportions during the Civil War, fueled perhaps by the overwhelming casualties. Mediums could offer comfort to the bereaved, assuring them "the spirits of the dead do not pass from this earth, but remain here amongst us unseen." One contemporary commented that it seemed as if "one heard of nothing but of spirits and of mediums. All tables and other furniture seemed to have become alive." Some mediums communicated by producing rapping or knocking sounds; others made tables tip and sway; still others channeled voices of the dead. Whatever method they used, one scholar of the movement observes, they "offered tangible evidence that the most refractory barrier on earth, the barrier of death, could be transcended by the power of sympathy."

Mary's occasional glimpses of Willie provided only temporary relief. His death had left her "an altered woman," Keckley observed. "The mere mention of Willie's name would excite her emotion, and any trifling memento that recalled him would move her to tears." She was unable to look at his picture. She sent all his toys and clothes away. She refused to enter the guest room in which he died or the Green Room in which he was laid out.

Outwardly, the president appeared to cope with Willie's death better than his wife. He had important work to engage him every hour of the day. He was surrounded by dozens of officials who needed him to discuss plans, make decisions, and communicate them. Yet, despite his relentless duties, he suffered an excruciating sense of loss. On the Thursday after his son died, and for several Thursdays thereafter, he closed himself off in the Green Room and gave way to his terrible grief. "That blow overwhelmed me," he told a White House visitor; "it showed me my weakness as I had never felt it before."

Like Mary, Lincoln longed for Willie's presence, a longing fulfilled not through mediums but in his active dream life. Three months after Willie's death, while reading aloud a passage from Shakespeare's *King John* in which Constance grieves over the death of her son, Lincoln paused; he turned to a nearby army officer and said: "Did you ever dream of some lost friend, and feel that you were having a sweet communion with him, and yet have a consciousness that it was not a reality? . . . That is the way I dream of my lost boy Willie."

While Mary could not tolerate to see physical reminders of Willie, Lincoln cherished mementos of his son. He placed a picture Willie had painted on his mantelpiece so he could show it to visitors and tell stories about his beloved child. One Sunday after church, he invited Browning to the library to show him a scrapbook he had just found in which Willie kept dates of various battles and programs from important events. Maintaining vivid consciousness of his dead child was essential for a man who believed that the dead live on only in the minds of the living. Ten months later, when he wrote young Fanny McCullough shortly after her father's battle-field death, he closed with the consolation of remembrance. In time, he promised her, "the memory of your dear Father, instead of an agony, will yet be a sad sweet feeling in your heart, of a purer, and holier sort than you have known before."

Now, more than ever before, Lincoln was able to identify in a profound and personal way with the sorrows of families who had lost their loved ones in the war.

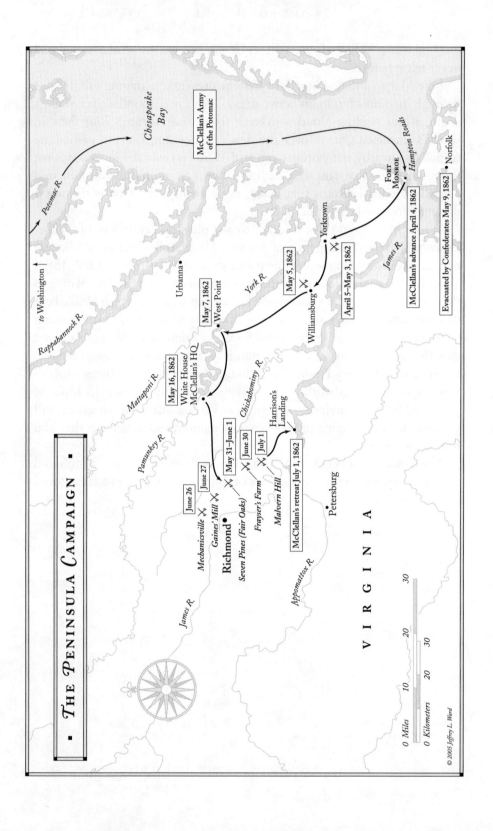

THE PENINSULA CAMPAIGN

VIRGINIA

to Washington

Potomac R.

Rappahannock R.

Chesapeake Bay

McClellan's Army of the Potomac

Hampton Roads

Fort Monroe

Norfolk

Evacuated by Confederates May 9, 1862

McClellan's advance April 4, 1862

James R.

Yorktown

April 5–May 3, 1862

May 5, 1862

Urbanna

May 7, 1862

West Point

York R.

Williamsburg

Mattaponi R.

May 16, 1862

White House/ McClellan's HQ

Chickahominy R.

Harrison's Landing

Pamunkey R.

May 31–June 1

June 30

July 1

June 26

June 27

Mechanicsville

Gaines' Mill

Seven Pines (Fair Oaks)

Frayser's Farm

Richmond

Malvern Hill

McClellan's retreat July 1, 1862

Petersburg

Appomattox R.

James R.

0 Miles 10 20 30

0 Kilometers 20 30

© 2005 Jeffrey L. Ward

CHAPTER 16

"HE WAS SIMPLY
OUT-GENERALED"

TWO DAYS AFTER Willie's death, General McClellan sent a private note expressing his heartfelt sympathy for the "sad calamity" that had overtaken the Lincoln family. "You have been a kind true friend to me," the general told the president, "your confidence has upheld me when I should otherwise have felt weak." Then, referring to the capture of Forts Henry and Donelson in the West as "an auspicious commencement" of his own forward campaign in the East, he beseeched Lincoln not to "allow military affairs to give [him] one moment's trouble," for "nothing shall be left undone" in pursuit of victory.

McClellan's assurances of forward movement provided Lincoln little comfort. The general had made similar promises for many months, while the great Army of the Potomac sat idle. Criticism of the general, previously confined to newspapers, found a powerful voice in the newly created Congressional Joint Committee on the Conduct of the War. Dominated by radicals from both houses, including Ben Wade, Michigan's Zachariah Chandler, and Indiana's George Julian, the committee detested McClellan both for his failure to prosecute the war vigorously and for his conservative views on slavery. From late December to mid-January, McClellan had remained in bed with typhoid. Suspicious that the general was using his illness as a cover for his continuing inaction, the committee held a contentious meeting with Lincoln and his cabinet. During the session, Congressman Julian recorded, it became disturbingly clear "that neither the President nor his advisers seemed to have any definite information . . . of General McClellan's plans."

More astonishing, according to Julian, "Lincoln himself did not think he had any *right* to know, but that, as he was not a military man, it was his duty to defer to General McClellan." Bates strenuously objected to

Lincoln's deferential stance, urging him repeatedly to "organize a *Staff* of his own, and assume to be in fact, what he is in law," the commander in chief, with a duty to "command the commanders." This opinion, voiced by the conservative, trustworthy Bates, struck Lincoln forcefully. He borrowed General Halleck's book on military strategy from the Library of Congress and told Browning a few days later that "he was thinking of taking the field himself."

Though his statement may not have reflected a literal intention, Lincoln had clearly resolved that he must energize the army at once. "The bottom is out of the tub," he confided in General Meigs, repeating a favorite phrase. The nearly bankrupt Treasury could no longer sustain the enormous expense of providing food, clothing, and shelter for hundreds of thousands of immobile soldiers. Without some forward progress, Chase told the president, he would get no additional funds from a discontented public. Meigs suggested that Lincoln convene a war council with his other generals to formulate a decisive course of action. Receiving news of this, McClellan suddenly recovered sufficiently to attend the meeting on the following day. Still reluctant to expose his plans, McClellan told Meigs that the president "can't keep a secret, he will tell them to Tadd."

Finally, Lincoln lost his vaunted patience. On January 27, 1862, he issued his famous General War Order No. 1, setting February 22 as "the day for a general movement of the Land and Naval forces of the United States against the insurgent forces." Lincoln correctly believed that, given the North's superior numbers, they should attack several rebel positions at the same time. The order prompted McClellan to submit his plans for a roundabout movement that developed into the Peninsula Campaign. The plan called for the troops to move by ship down the Potomac River to the Chesapeake Bay, with a turn into Urbanna on the south shore of the Rappahannock River. From there McClellan planned to march southwest to Richmond.

Lincoln, backed by Stanton and several generals, including McDowell, proposed a different strategy. Troops would march overland through nearby Manassas, pushing the rebel army farther and farther back toward Richmond, "destroying him by superior force." This straightforward approach would shield Washington, keeping the Union Army between the capital and the Confederates. Under McClellan's circuitous plan, it was feared that the Confederates might willingly sacrifice Richmond to capture Washington. If the South occupied the seat of the Union, foreign recognition of the Confederacy would undoubtedly follow. In the end, Lincoln reluctantly acquiesced to the Peninsula plan, but not before imposing a written order requiring that a sufficient force be left "in, and about Washington," to keep the capital safe from attack.

February 22, the date designated for the advance, arrived and went with Lincoln deeply preoccupied by Willie's death and Tad's grievous illness. A disheartened Stanton noted that "there was no more sign of movement on the Potomac than there had been for three months before." When he first took his cabinet position, Stanton later explained, he "was, and for months had been the sincere and devoted friend of General McClellan," but he had quickly grown disenchanted. After less than two weeks as secretary of war, he told a friend that "while men are striving nobly in the West, the champagne and oysters on the Potomac must be stopped." Stanton's remark alluded to the sumptuous dinners McClellan hosted each evening for nearly two dozen guests, many of whom were prominent figures in Washington's Southern-leaning society.

Stanton was further disgruntled when McClellan kept him waiting on a number of occasions. Unlike Lincoln, the proud war secretary did not ignore the arrogance of the general in chief. After one particularly galling experience, when he had been forced to wait for an hour after stopping by McClellan's headquarters on his way to the War Department, Stanton angrily announced: "That will be the last time General McClellan will give either myself or the President the waiting snub." A few weeks later, Stanton delivered orders to transfer the telegraph office from McClellan's headquarters to a room adjoining his office in the War Department. Dispatches from the miraculous new system that connected Washington with army officials, camps, and forts throughout the entire North would no longer be funneled through McClellan. McClellan was furious, considering the transfer "his humiliation." He had, indeed, lost significant influence, for the adjacent telegraph office not only allowed Stanton to exercise control over all military communications, but ensured that Lincoln would now spend many daily hours with his war secretary rather than his general in chief.

Still, McClellan had powerful allies in the cabinet, including the influential Montgomery Blair. The Democratic press largely credited the "young Napoleon" for the victories at Forts Henry and Donelson, as if Grant and the troops were merely puppets with McClellan pulling the strings from Washington. Stanton noted satirically that the image portrayed in the papers of a heroic McClellan, seated at the telegraph office, "organizing victory, and by sublime military combinations capturing Fort Donelson *six hours after* Grant and Smith had taken it," was "a picture worthy of *Punch*."

As it turned out, the victories in the West increased the pressure on McClellan to act. At last, on the weekend of March 8, the massive Army of the Potomac prepared to break camp. Anticipating the move, the Confederates began to pull their batteries back from Manassas to the banks of the Rappahannock. Hearing reports of the fallback, McClellan led his armies on a short foray to catch the remaining troops. But once there, he found to his great embarrassment that the entire Confederate force had already departed with their tents, supplies, and weapons. Still more humiliating, the supposedly impregnable fortifications that had deterred him for months turned out to be simply wooden logs painted black to resemble cannons. Had McClellan attacked anytime in the previous months, he would have had superiority in numbers and weapons.

The "Quaker gun" affair, as the stage-prop guns were called, provoked the wrath of radicals. "We shall be the scorn of the world," Senator Fessenden wrote his wife. "It is no longer doubtful that General McClellan is utterly unfit for his position. . . . And yet the President will keep him in command." The embarrassing situation should have been expected, Fessenden lamented, for "we went in for a railsplitter, and we have got one." Echoing Fessenden's dismay, the Committee on the Conduct of the War demanded McClellan's resignation. When Lincoln asked who they proposed to replace McClellan, one of the committee members growled, "Anybody." Lincoln's reply was swift. "*Anybody* will do for you, but not for me. I must have *somebody*."

Lincoln was convinced that something had to be done. On March 11, he issued a war order that relieved McClellan from his post as general in chief but left him in charge of the Army of the Potomac. Lincoln gave Halleck command of the Department of the Mississippi and, in a move that delighted the radicals, reinstated Frémont to take charge of a newly created Mountain Department. The post of general in chief was not filled, leaving Lincoln and Stanton to determine overall strategy. McClellan later recalled that he "learned through the public newspapers that [he] was displaced." Claiming that "no one in authority had ever expressed to [him] the slightest disapprobation," he was infuriated. Lincoln sent Ohio's Governor Dennison to his camp to assure him that this was not a demotion. The president, Dennison explained, simply wanted General McClellan to focus his full energies on the all-important Army of the Potomac, whose actions would most likely determine the result of the war.

Lincoln anticipated that his postmaster general, Monty Blair, would stridently oppose McClellan's removal from high command. The conservative Blair family were staunch McClellan supporters, a loyalty that would continue in the months ahead. Referring to his radical detractors,

Francis Blair, Sr., warned the general "not to let the Carpet Knights in Congress," who would sacrifice anyone's blood but their own, "hurry or worry him into doing anything." Meanwhile, Washington gossip spread that Monty Blair was openly berating his fellow cabinet colleague Stanton for his failure to support McClellan. While conservatives vilified Stanton, radicals upbraided the Blairs as "preservers of slavery" for defending the inert McClellan at Stanton's expense.

Already troubled by McClellan's loss of central control, the powerful Blair family was enraged by Lincoln's decision to reinstall Frémont in a position of command. Monty Blair privately considered Frémont's appointment "unpalatable" and warned his father that it would be "mortifying to Frank," who had been humiliated by his arrest and imprisonment by Frémont. Lizzie Blair told her husband it was "urged by Chase—& Stanton who has his revenges, too," and that her brother Frank felt it intensely. Only four days earlier, with the backing of Democrats and conservative Republicans, Frank Blair had delivered a blistering attack against Frémont on the floor of the House. Frémont had come to Washington at the request of the Committee on the Conduct of the War. For weeks, radicals on the committee had pressured Lincoln to give "the Emancipator," as they called Frémont, a second chance. Congressman Schuyler Colfax eloquently defended their position when he rose to the floor immediately after Frank Blair to deliver a scorching point-by-point repudiation of Blair's address.

The bitter public quarrel between the Blairs and Frémont must have given Lincoln pause as he considered reinstating Frémont. Though the appointment would thrill the radicals, it might cost him the allegiance of the Blairs and thereby destroy the delicate balance he had worked to foster between the conservatives and the radicals. As it happened, a magnanimous gesture by Lincoln just six days before Frémont's appointment played an important role in resolving the complex situation.

On March 5, Monty Blair had come to the White House in great distress. The *New York Tribune* had just published a private letter that he had written to Frémont the previous summer before the family feud had begun. In the letter, furnished by Frémont to the press in an attempt to embarrass Blair, the postmaster general had complained that Lincoln's past affiliations had brought "him naturally not only to incline to the feeble policy of Whigs, but to give his confidence to such advisers. It costs me a great deal of labor to get anything done because of the inclination of mind on the part of the President."

Elizabeth Blair described her brother's meeting with Lincoln in a note to her husband. "Brother just took the letter up to the P. & asked him to read it." Lincoln refused, "saying he did not intend to read it," as it was published for that very purpose. Monty acknowledged "it was a foolish letter" that he deeply regretted. "It is due to you," he told the president, "to make some amends by resigning my place. . . . I leave the whole thing to you & will do exactly as you wish." The president had no desire to exact retribution or remove Blair. "Forget it," he said, "& never mention or think of it again."

A grateful Monty Blair immediately came to Lincoln's defense regarding the Frémont appointment. Although he had not been consulted about the decision and realized his family would consider it a blatant affront to Frank, he told his father that he understood Lincoln's need to arrest "the spread of factions in the country & prevent divisions at this time," and for that reason, he thought "very well of it." The conservative *New York Times* agreed, approving Frémont's appointment as a necessary "concession to this craving for unity" and "the value of united counsels." In his conduct of the war, the *Times* observed, Lincoln believed "tenaciously" in the "necessity of perfect unity of popular opinion and action" in the North.

More than any other cabinet member, Seward appreciated Lincoln's peerless skill in balancing factions both within his administration and in the country at large. While radicals considered Seward a conservative influence on the president, in truth, he and the president were engaged in the same task of finding a middle position between the two extremes—the radical Republicans, who believed that freeing the slaves should be the primary goal of the war, and the conservative Democrats, who resisted any change in the status of the slaves and fought solely for the restoration of the Union. "Somebody must be in a position to mollify and moderate," Seward told Weed. "That is the task of the P. and the S. of S." In another letter to his old friend, Seward expressed great confidence in Lincoln. "The President is wise and practical," he wrote. His trust in Lincoln was complete, inspiring faith in the eventual success of the Union cause.

From the outside, however, Seward was viewed by radicals as a malevolent influence on Lincoln. Count Gurowski despaired at Seward's supposed ties with McClellan, Blair, and their allies in the conservative press. "Oh! Mr. Seward, Mr. Seward," he queried, "why is your name to be recorded among the most ardent supporters of [McClellan's] *strategy?*" In fact, already by the middle of March, Seward had lost his early faith in McClellan and wondered why Lincoln did not strip him of command. In a private conversation with a friend, Seward scorned McClellan's inflated estimates of enemy strength, suggesting that the Union troops from New York State alone probably outnumbered all the Confederate forces in northern Virginia! Nonetheless, he refrained from airing his doubts in public.

In the wake of the "Quaker gun" affair, Lincoln's confidence in McClellan had also eroded. While acknowledging that the general was a great "engineer," Lincoln noted drolly that "he seems to have a special talent for developing a *'stationary'* engine." The more he studied the general, he confided to Browning, the more he realized that when "the hour for action approached he became nervous and oppressed with the responsibility and hesitated to meet the crisis." For this reason, Lincoln had "given him peremptory orders to move." Finally, twenty-four hours before Lincoln's deadline, McClellan's massive army of nearly a quarter of a million men left the base camps around Washington and headed toward the Potomac, where more than four hundred ships had gathered to carry them to Fort Monroe in Hampton Roads, Virginia. Parading to the refrains of regimental bands, with rifles on their shoulders and new equipment on their backs, the high-spirited, well-disciplined troops presented a sight, one diarist noted, such as "the eye of man has seldom seen." Before the army set sail, McClellan delivered an emotional address. "I will bring you now face to face with the rebels," he told his beloved troops, "ever bear in mind that my fate is linked with yours. . . . I am to watch over you as a parent over his children, and you know that your General loves you from the depths of his heart."

When most of the force had reached Fort Monroe, Stanton later recalled, "information was given to me by various persons that there was great reason to fear that no adequate force had been left to defend the Capital," despite Lincoln's "explicit order that Washington should, by the judgment of *all* the commanders of Army corps, be left entirely secure." Stanton referred the matter to Lorenzo Thomas, the adjutant general, who, after surveying the circumstance, concluded that the president's order had most definitely *not* been obeyed. McClellan had left behind "less than 20,000 raw recruits with not a single organized brigade," a force utterly incapable of defending Washington from sudden attack. Enraged, Stanton carried the damning report to the president at midnight. Lincoln promptly withdrew General McDowell's 1st Corps from McClellan's command so that Washington would be protected. That withdrawal, Stanton later recalled, "provoked [McClellan's] wrath, and the wrath of his friends."

With immense forces still at his disposal, McClellan advanced from Fort Monroe to the outskirts of Yorktown, roughly fifty miles from Richmond. Once again, mistakenly insisting that the rebel force outnumbered his, McClellan kept his army in a state of perpetual preparation. His engineers spent precious weeks constructing earthworks so his big guns could quash rebel defenses before the infantry assault. On April 6, Lincoln telegraphed McClellan: "You now have over one hundred thousand troops. . . . I think you better break the enemies' line from York-town to Warwick River, at once. They will probably use *time*, as advantageously as you can." The following day, McClellan scorned the president's admonition, informing his wife that if Lincoln wanted the enemy line broken, "he had better come & do it himself."

Still, McClellan persisted in his baffling inaction. He notified Stanton that "the enemy batteries are stronger" than anticipated. Stanton was livid: "You were sent on purpose to *take* strong batteries," he reminded McClellan. Later that day, Lincoln telegraphed the general, warning that further delay would only allow the enemy to summon reinforcements from other theaters. "It is indispensable to *you* that you strike a blow," Lincoln advised his commander on April 9. "The country will not fail to note—is now noting—that the present hesitation to move upon an intrenched enemy, is but the story of Manassas repeated. I beg to assure you that I have never written you, or spoken to you, in greater kindness of feeling than now. . . . *But you must act.*"

Two more weeks passed without any sign of movement. "Do not misunderstand the apparent inaction here," McClellan wired Lincoln; "not a day, not an hour has been lost, works have been constructed that may almost be called gigantic—roads built through swamps & difficult ravines, material brought up, batteries built." In another letter to his wife, he rationalized his continuing delay with the dubious contention that the more troops the enemy gathered in Yorktown, "the more decisive the results will be." A few days later, McClellan formulated yet another justification for postponement, arguing that he had been "compelled to change plans & become cautious" without McDowell's 1st Corps that had been taken from him to protect Washington. This left him "unexpectedly weakened & with a powerful enemy strongly entrenched in my front." Therefore, he was not "answerable for the delay of victory."

As it happened, Confederate general Joe Johnston, after keeping McClellan at bay for a month with substantially inferior numbers, had decided in early May to withdraw twelve miles up the peninsula toward Richmond. Hearing that a fallback was under way, McClellan finally moved on Yorktown to discover that, in a repeat of his experience at Manassas, the rebels were gone. Though he tried to claim the rebel retreat as a great bloodless victory, the public was unconvinced, and the question remained: why had he kept idle for a month? Had he moved on Yorktown with his greater numbers, he could have done serious damage to the rebel army. In the meantime, just as Lincoln had forewarned, the long delay had allowed the rebels to bring additional forces from various theaters into the peninsula, where, under General Johnston's command, they prepared for a counteroffensive.

· · ·

ANXIETY SURROUNDING the impending battle did little to curtail the spring social season in Washington. If anything, the pace of social life accelerated, as Washingtonians sought relaxation and entertainment in the traditional round of calls, receptions, soirées, musicales, and dinners. Once the air turned "soft and balmy," the *National Republican* reported, the public squares came alive with "crowds of visitors, who either tread its graveled walks, or seat themselves beneath the trees," listening to the songs of birds and the joyful shouts of children rolling "their hoops over the ground."

Mary remained in mourning for Willie, however, and the traditional spring receptions in the White House were canceled, along with the Marine Band concerts on the lawn. In the social vacuum, Kate Chase took command of the Washington social scene, making her a powerful asset to her father. Her intermittent romance with the Rhode Island–based Sprague did not diminish her signal commitment to her father, whose household she managed with matchless style.

Her social supremacy derived in part from her striking appearance, enhanced by the simple but elegant wardrobe assembled during her many trips to New York in pursuit of furnishings for her father's mansion. She was "more of a professional beauty than had at that time ever been seen in America," noted Mary Adams French, the wife of the famed sculptor Daniel Chester French, "with a beauty and a regal carriage which we called 'queenly,' but which no real queen ever has." In an era when "the universal art of being slim had not been discovered," Mrs. French continued, the "tall and slim" Kate seemed otherworldly. She had "an unusually long white neck, and a slow and deliberate way of turning it when she glanced around her. Wherever she appeared, people dropped back in order to watch her." Fanny Villard, wife of the journalist Henry Villard, was one of many who looked with awe on Kate: "I a simple young home body from New England never before had seen so beautiful and brilliant a creature as Kate Chase; and it seemed to me then that nothing could blight her perfection."

And yet Kate's grace and beauty accounted for only a small part of her social success. Her emergence as the foremost lady of Washington society resulted as much from hard work and meticulous planning as from her natural assets. She met each morning with her household servants, giving detailed instructions for the day's activities. Continuing the ritual she had established in Columbus, she and her father hosted regular breakfast parties for out-of-town guests. Her correspondence reveals the elaborate preparations these affairs entailed. A letter to her father's friend, the Philadelphia banker Jay Cooke, requests that he "stop at Van Zant's where you find the best fruit and have a basketful of the best and *prettiest* grapes, pears, oranges, apples etc. sent me by Adams Express . . . so that they may arrive here without fail early Tuesday morning." She regretted the imposition, but she "could not think of anyone who would do it quite so well," and was "especially anxious" to make this "an attractive and agreeable occasion."

In addition to these early-morning breakfasts, Kate presided over weekly receptions known as "Cabinet calling" days. Every Monday, a contemporary Washingtonian wrote, "the wives of the Cabinet officers receive their friends; also Mrs. McClellan is at home on this same day." Through the late morning and early afternoon, regardless of rain, mud, or snow, the ladies of Washington made the rounds, visiting in turn each cabinet member's home. "First to Mrs. Seward's," columnist Cara Kasson reported, where Anna Seward officiated in the absence of Frances. A black doorman delivered their card to yet another servant, "who places it in the silver-card receiver, at the same moment ushering us in (names clearly pronounced), to the presence of Mrs. Seward." Greetings were exchanged and refreshments served, before proceeding to the next reception at Mrs. Caleb Smith's. There they found "an elegantly set table, salads and all good things." After visiting Mrs. Welles, who always entertained "in her friendly manner," the ladies would "take a glass of wine at Mrs. Blair's, admire the queenly dignity of Miss Chase, enjoy a delightful talk with the kindly family of Mrs. Bates, and then drive on to pay our respects to Mrs. McClellan and Mrs. Stanton."

While Kate hosted the weekly cabinet receptions with elegance and grace, she devoted her greatest efforts to the celebrated candlelight dinners she held each Wednesday evening. With exacting care, she drew up the guest lists, prepared the menus, and arranged seating. With her father occupying the head of the table, she would help maintain lively, entertaining conversation from her place at the other end. After dinner, a band would play and dancing would begin. "Diplomats and statesmen felt it an honor to be her guests, and men of letters found that they needed their keenest wits to be her match in conversation," one reporter noted. "Her drawing-room was a salon, and it has been paralleled only in the ante-revolutionary days of the French monarchy, when women ruled the empire of the Bourbons."

Over time, the Chase home increasingly became a forum for critics of the Lincoln administration. In the relaxed atmosphere of Kate's private dinner parties, William Fessenden could freely condemn Lincoln's reluctance to confront the emancipation question. The members of the Committee on the Conduct of the War could censure General McClellan more harshly than public statement would safely allow. Over coffee and dessert in the parlor, the women could spread disdainful gossip about Mary Lincoln. Kate clearly understood the role that "parlor politics" could play in cementing alliances and consolidating power in furtherance of her father's irrepressible political ambitions. She was determined to create nothing less than a "rival court" to the White House that could help catapult Chase to the presidency. In the spring of 1862, she reigned supreme.

The most compelling conversations in the Chase drawing room that balmy spring swirled around the proclamation of General David Hunter, an old friend of Lincoln's who commanded the Department of the South, which encompassed South Carolina, Georgia, and Florida. In early May, acting without prior approval from the White House, Hunter had issued an official order declaring "forever free" all slaves in the three states under his jurisdiction. Chase's circle was exultant, for Hunter's proclamation went beyond even General Frémont's attempt of the previous August. "It seems to me of the highest importance," Chase wrote to Lincoln, "that this order not be revoked. . . . It will be cordially approved, I am sure, by more than nine tenths of the people on whom you must rely for support of your Administration." Lincoln's reply to Chase was swift and blunt: "No commanding general shall do such a thing, upon *my* responsibility, without consulting me."

By repudiating Hunter's proclamation, Lincoln understood that he would give "dissatisfaction, if not offence, to many whose support the country can not afford to lose." He firmly believed, however, that any such proclamation must come from the commander in chief, not from a general in the field. "Gen. Hunter is an honest man," Lincoln told a delegation after officially revoking Hunter's order. "He was, and I hope, still is, my friend. . . . He expected more good, and less harm from the measure, than I could believe would follow."

While Seward and Stanton supported Lincoln's decision, Chase publicly disagreed. In conversations with Sumner and others, he openly denounced Lincoln's action, fanning talk "among the more advanced members" of the Republican Party about Lincoln's "pusillanimity." Chase's defiance earned him plaudits from the *New York Tribune*, "all the more warmly appreciated," Chase told Horace Greeley, given the influential editor's "earlier unfavorable judgments" of his public career. Chase maintained to Greeley that he had "not been so sorely tried by anything here—though I have seen a great deal in the shape of irregularity, assumptions beyond law, extravagance, & deference to generals and reactionists which I could not approve,—as by the nullifying of Hunter's proclamation." Rumors began to surface that the controversy would cause an open rupture in the cabinet and precipitate Chase's departure. Still, so long as Lincoln believed Chase was the right man for the Treasury, he had no intention of requesting his resignation. As for Chase, so long as he could garner radical support by publicly opposing Lincoln on this critical issue, he would productively remain in the cabinet until the time was right to make a break.

• • •

IN THE FIRST WEEK OF MAY, Lincoln resolved to end months of frustration with McClellan by personally visiting Fort Monroe. Stanton had suggested that a presidential journey to the tip of the Peninsula might finally spur McClellan to act. On the evening of Monday, May 5, the president arrived at the Navy Yard and boarded the *Miami*, a five-gun Treasury cutter, accompanied by Stanton, Chase, and General Egbert Viele. "The cabin," Viele recalled, "was neat and cozy. A center table, buffet and washstand, with four berths, two on each side, and some comfortable chairs, constituted its chief appointments." Since the *Miami* was a Treasury ship, Chase "seemed to feel that we were his guests," General Viele observed. The treasury secretary even brought his own butler to serve meals, and "treated us as if we were in his own house."

Both Chase and Stanton began the twenty-seven-hour journey anxious about all the work they had left behind. As the hours passed by, however, they warmed to Lincoln's high-spirited discourse and began to relax. General Viele marveled how Lincoln was always the center of the circle gathered on the quarterdeck, keeping everyone engrossed for hours as he recited passages from Shakespeare, "page after page of Browning and whole cantos of Byron." Talking much of the day, he interspersed stories and anecdotes from his "inexhaustible stock." Many, as usual, were directly applicable to a point made in conversation, but some were simply jokes that set Lincoln laughing louder than all the combined listeners. One of his favorite anecdotes told of a schoolboy "called up by the teacher to be disciplined. 'Hold out your hand!' A paw of the most surprising description was extended, more remarkable for its filthiness than anything else." The schoolmaster was so stunned that he said, " 'Now, if there were such another dirty thing in the room, I would let you off.' '*There it is*,' quoth the unmoved culprit, drawing *the other hand* from behind his back."

While the presidential party lounged on the deck, Lincoln playfully demonstrated that in "muscular power he was one in a thousand," possessing "the strength of a giant." He picked up an ax and "held it at arm's length at the extremity of the [handle] with his thumb and forefinger, continuing to hold it there for a number of minutes. The most powerful sailors on board tried in vain to imitate him."

After the Tuesday luncheon table was cleared, the president and his advisers pored over maps and analyzed the army positions in and around Virginia. Union forces at Fort Monroe occupied the northern shore of Hampton Roads, which connected the Chesapeake to three rivers. Confederate forces on the southern shore still held Norfolk and the Navy Yard. Two months earlier, the rebels had used this strategic foothold to great advantage by sending the powerful nine-gun *Merrimac*, a scuttled Union ship that they had raised and covered with iron plates, into a series of devastating engagements. In the space of five hours, the ironclad had managed to sink, capture, and incapacitate three ships and two Union frigates.

The news had terrified government officials, who feared that the invincible *Merrimac* might sail up the Potomac to attack Washington or even continue on to New York. "It is a disgrace to the country that the rebels, without resources, have built a vessel with which we cannot cope," General Meigs had grumbled. An emergency cabinet meeting was convened, during which Stanton unfairly faulted Welles for the disaster. His attack was so personal, according to Welles's biographer, that the navy secretary "found it very difficult for a time even to be civil in [Stanton's] presence."

In fact, the navy had been more than adequately prepared to deal with the *Merrimac*. The very next day, the *Monitor*, a strange ironclad vessel resembling a "cheese box on a raft," engaged the *Merrimac* in battle. Though the little *Monitor* seemed "a pigmy to a giant," it proved far more maneuverable. Commanded by Lieutenant John L. Worden, who directed two large guns from a revolving turret, the *Monitor* fought the *Merrimac* to a draw and sent the Confederate vessel back to the harbor. When Stanton learned that Worden might lose one eye as a result of the struggle, he said: "Then we will fill the other with diamonds."

To Herman Melville, as to many others, the battle of the two ironclads marked the beginning of a new epoch in warfare. "The ringing of those plates on plates/Still ringeth round the world," he wrote. "War yet shall be, but warriors/Are now but operatives."

As the president and his advisers huddled over maps of Fort Monroe, Norfolk, and the surrounding area, they could not understand why McClellan had not ordered an attack on Norfolk immediately after his occupation of Yorktown. The Confederate retreat up the Peninsula had left the city and the Navy Yard vulnerable. Though the *Monitor* had held its own against the

Merrimac, there was no assurance that this feat would be repeated. If Norfolk were captured, perhaps the *Merrimac* could be captured as well. With McClellan and his troops about twenty miles away, Lincoln and his little group came to a decision of their own. If General John E. Wool, commander of Fort Monroe, had sufficient forces at his disposal, an *immediate* attack should be made on Norfolk. Disconcerted by the prospect, the seventy-eight-year-old General Wool insisted on consulting Commodore Louis Goldsborough, since the navy's warships would have to immobilize the Confederate batteries before any troops could be safely landed.

In the black of night, the *Miami* could not easily pull aside the *Minnesota*, Goldsborough's flagship, so Lincoln's party climbed into a tugboat and approached the port side of the *Minnesota*. The steps leading up to the deck were very "narrow," Chase wrote, "with the guiding ropes on either hand, hardly visible in the darkness. It seemed to me *very* high and a little fearsome. But etiquette required the President to go first and he went. Etiquette required the Secretary of the Treasury to follow." Stanton, climbing immediately behind Chase, must have overcome even greater trepidation, for an accident when he was younger had left one leg permanently damaged and he suffered, besides, from frequent attacks of vertigo. Fortunately, they all made it aboard without mishap. Though Lincoln was probably unfamiliar with Commodore Goldsborough, Chase had known him for several decades—the distinguished naval officer had won the hand of William Wirt's daughter, Elizabeth, at a time when Chase had not been deemed an appropriate suitor.

Goldsborough approved the idea of attack in theory, but feared that so long as the *Merrimac* was still a factor, it was too risky to carry troops across the water. Lincoln disagreed, and orders were given to begin shelling the Confederate batteries. Before long, "a smoke curled up over the woods," Chase recalled, "and each man, almost, said to the other, 'There comes the *Merrimac*,' and, sure enough, it was the *Merrimac*." However, upon spying the *Monitor*, accompanied by a second powerful ship, "the great rebel terror paused—then turned back." The next day, Lincoln, Chase, and Stanton each personally surveyed the shoreline to determine the best landing place for the troops. Under a full moon, Lincoln went ashore in a rowboat. He walked on enemy soil and then returned to the *Miami*. Once the best spot was chosen, Chase pushed for an immediate attack, worried that McClellan might appear and delay the attack. The next night, the convoys headed for shore.

They discovered that the rebels had decided to evacuate Norfolk and scuttle the *Merrimac* to keep it out of Union hands soon after the shelling began. As the Union troops moved uncontested into the city, Chase, accompanying Generals Wool and Viele, heard the soldiers shouting "cheer after cheer." In the city center, they were met by a delegation of civilian authorities who formally surrendered Norfolk to General Viele. The general remained in City Hall as military governor of the region.

It was after midnight when Chase and General Wool finally returned to the *Miami*. Lincoln and Stanton, after waiting nervously all evening for their return, had just retired to their rooms. "The night was very warm," Lincoln recalled, "the moon shining brightly,—and, too restless to sleep, I threw off my clothes and sat for some time by the table, reading." Hearing a knock at Stanton's door, which was directly below his own, he guessed that "the missing men" had come back at last. Minutes later, Chase and General Wool came to Lincoln's room. Eschewing ceremony, Wool happily announced: "Norfolk is ours!" Stanton, who had "burst in, just out of bed, clad in a long nightgown," was so jubilant over the news that "he rushed at the General, whom he hugged most affectionately, fairly lifting him from the floor in his delight." Lincoln recognized that the scene "must have been a comical one," with Stanton clad in a nightgown that "nearly swept the floor" and he himself having just undressed. Nevertheless, they "were all too greatly excited to take much note of mere appearances." Beside the capture of Norfolk, the destruction of the fearsome *Merrimac* would open the supply lines from Washington to the peninsula.

When the triumphant trio returned to Washington, reporters noted that Stanton was "conveyed home seriously ill." Physicians feared at first that he was suffering from one of the bouts of vertigo that immobilized him for days at a time. He soon recovered, however, and enjoyed the sweetness of victory in what the Civil War historian Shelby Foote has called "one of the strangest small-scale campaigns in American military history."

Unusually buoyant, Chase expressed greater admiration for the president than he ever had before or ever would again. "So has ended a brilliant week's campaign of the President," Chase wrote, "for I think it quite certain that if he had not come down, Norfolk would still have been in possession of the enemy, and the *Merrimac*, as grim and defiant and as much a terror as ever. The whole coast is now virtually ours."

Not surprisingly, McClellan refused to credit the president for the return of Norfolk to the Union. "Norfolk is in our possession," he flatly declared to his wife; "the result of my movements."

• • •

THE DAY AFTER Lincoln's triumphant return, Navy Secretary Welles invited Seward, Bates, and their families to join him and his wife for a six-day cruise along the coast of Virginia, now cleared of rebel forces and the menacing *Merrimac*. "We had two pilots and thirteen sailors," Fred Seward informed his mother. "Wormley and his cook and waiters, two howitzers, and two dozen muskets, coal and provisions for a week, field glasses and maps." The armed navy steamer took them to Norfolk and the Gosport Navy Yard, where they viewed the ruins of the *Merrimac*. They proceeded up York River to McClellan's new headquarters at West Point, thirty miles from Richmond. The cabinet colleagues enjoyed an easy camaraderie as the steamer moved from one river to the next. They consumed hearty meals, sang patriotic songs to the music of a navy band, and joked with one another. When Seward discovered that rats had eaten a tie and socks belonging to Bates, he composed a humorous poem, complete with sketches, to commemorate the occasion.

By day, they went ashore and wandered through the seaboard towns now in possession of the Union armies. "Virginia is sad to look upon," Seward wrote to his wife, "not merely the rebellion, but society itself, is falling into ruin. Slaves are deserting the homes intrusted to them by their masters, who have gone into the Southern armies or are fleeing before ours. There is universal stagnation, and sullenness prevails everywhere." Like Lincoln, Seward was always sensitive to the devastation of war. Despite his satisfaction at the recent Union successes that had subdued this part of Virginia, he was disquieted by the bleakness he encountered. "We saw war, not in its holiday garb," he told Fanny, "but in its stern and fearful aspect. We saw the desolation that follows, and the terror that precedes its march."

The steamer reached McClellan's camp at about 3 p.m. on May 13. Approaching the shore, Fred Seward was amazed to find that "a clearing in the woods" had been "suddenly transformed into a great city of a hundred thousand people, by the advent of McClellan's Army and its supporting fleet." McClellan escorted the party ashore, where they reviewed thousands of his troops and discussed the general's plans.

Though McClellan considered such visits "a nuisance," he convinced his official guests that, if properly reinforced, he would soon prevail in a decisive fight "this side of Richmond," which would be "one of the great historic battles of the world." McClellan's high-spirited, well-disciplined troops and the gigantic size of the operation were impressive to all. "At night," Fred Seward observed, "the long lines of lights on the shore, the shipping and bustle in the river made it almost impossible to believe we were not in the harbor of Philadelphia or New York."

After the meeting with McClellan, Seward advised Lincoln by telegraph that McDowell's forces should be sent to the York River to reinforce McClellan "as soon as possible." Lincoln and Stanton agreed. McDowell was ordered to move his entire force from the vicinity of Washington to the peninsula. For weeks, McClellan's Democratic supporters had publicly criticized the president and secretary of war for retaining McDowell's force out of irrational fear for Washington. Yet now that McClellan stood to have his demands met, he told Lincoln that he wouldn't receive McDowell's men unless it was clear that he would have absolute authority over them. McClellan considered McDowell a radical on the issue of slavery and despised him personally, calling him an "animal" in a letter to his wife. Lincoln assured McClellan by telegraph that he was in command.

The day after Lincoln ordered McDowell to prepare for the move south, he made an impromptu visit, accompanied by Stanton and Dahlgren, to McDowell's headquarters at Fredericksburg. The trip was arranged so suddenly that Captain Dahlgren had no chance to bring food or beds aboard the steamboat that was to carry them to Aquia Landing. Despite the makeshift accomodations, Lincoln relaxed at once, reading aloud from the works of a contemporary poet, Fitz-Greene Halleck, then considered "the American Byron." Lincoln chose that night to read *Marco Bozzaris*, a lengthy poem celebrating the death of a Greek hero in the war against Turkey. Lincoln was drawn to the poet's vision of a lasting greatness, of deeds that would resound throughout history. Because of such achievements in life, both Greece, in which "there is no prouder grave," and the mother "who gave thee birth," can speak "of thy doom without a sigh":

> *For thou art Freedom's now, and Fame's;*
> *One of the few, the immortal names,*
> *That were not born to die.*

When Lincoln and his party reached Aquia Creek shortly after dawn, they were driven to McDowell's camp in what Dahlgren described as "a common baggage car, with camp-stools for the party." McDowell was eager to show the little group his army's accomplishments in having rebuilt bridges and repaired telegraph lines, creating a direct link between Washington and Fredericksburg. The general was particularly proud of a new trestle bridge that spanned a creek and deep ravine at a height of a hundred feet. Though "there was nothing but a single plank for us to walk on," Dahlgren recalled, Lincoln impulsively said: "Let us walk over." So the president, followed by McDowell, and then poor Stanton, understandably fearful of heights, and finally Dahlgren, began the hazardous journey. "About half-way," Dahlgren wrote, "the Secretary said he was dizzy and feared he would fall. So he stopped, unable to proceed. I managed to step by him, and took his hand, thus leading him over, when in fact my own head was somewhat confused by the giddy height."

After breakfast, the president and McDowell mounted horses and spent the day inspecting the troops. Enduring a hot sun without the protection of a hat, Lincoln reviewed "one division after another, all in fine order, the men cheering tremendously." After a simple meal, the presidential party returned to Aquia Creek, departing for Washington sometime after 10 p.m. Lincoln "was in good spirits," according to Dahlgren. Once again, he read poetry aloud, and they all retired to their makeshift beds. Before falling asleep, Stanton confided to Dahlgren that "he did not think much of McDowell!"

Troublesome news reached Washington the following day that General Stonewall Jackson had been sent to attack Union forces in the Shenandoah Valley, hoping to prevent McDowell from moving south. The goal was realized. After Jackson attacked Front Royal, forcing General Banks to hastily retreat north to Winchester, the president telegraphed McClellan: "I have been compelled to suspend Gen. McDowell's movement to join you." He followed up with a telegram explaining that with Jackson chasing Banks farther and farther north, Washington was again endangered. "Stripped bare, as we are here, it will be all we can do to prevent [the enemy] crossing the Potomac at Harper's Ferry, or above. . . . If McDowell's force was now beyond our reach, we should be utterly helpless." Moreover, while Jackson and his forces made their way north, Lincoln reasoned, Richmond must be vulnerable. "I think the time is near when you must either attack Richmond or give up the job and come to the defence of Washington. Let me hear from you instantly."

McClellan replied at 5 p.m.: "Independently of it the time is very near when I shall attack Richmond." He then haughtily informed his wife that he had "just finished [his] reply to his Excellency," and complained, "it is perfectly sickening to deal with such people & you may rest assured that I will lose as little time as possible in breaking off all connection with them—I get more sick of them every day—for every day brings with it only additional proofs of their hypocrisy, knavery & folly."

James McPherson concludes that "Lincoln's diversion of McDowell's corps to chase Jackson was probably a strategic error—perhaps even the colossal blunder that McClellan considered it." For as soon as Jackson had managed to divert the Union forces bound for Richmond, he turned back southward to join in the defense of the Confederate capital. Still, McPherson adds, "even if McDowell's corps had joined McClellan as planned, the latter's previous record offered little reason to believe that he would have moved with speed and boldness to capture Richmond."

In the end, though McClellan had advanced to a position only four miles from Richmond by the end of May, he still refused to take the initiative, and his troops were surprised by a Confederate attack at Fair Oaks. Though the battle was inconclusive and the rebels suffered heavier losses than the Union, McClellan was so devastated by the toll of nearly five thousand Union dead and wounded that he lost whatever momentum he had created. "McClellan keeps sending word that he will attack Richmond very soon,—but every day brings some new excuse," reported Christopher Wolcott, Stanton's brother-in-law, now assistant secretary of war. The rain, a legitimate excuse during the first ten days of June, had stopped five days earlier. Nevertheless, Wolcott noted, "he has not stirred."

McClellan's catalogue of gripes and concerns was endless. There were bridges to be built, bad roads, regiments to be reorganized. When Lincoln eventually ordered McDowell to reinforce him, the general continued to protest that "if I cannot fully control all his [McDowell's] troops I want none of them, but would prefer to fight the battle with what I have and let others be responsible for the results." Finally, he confided in his wife, "utmost prudence" was essential. "I must not unnecessarily risk my life—for the fate of my army depends upon me & they all know it."

McClellan's chronic delays allowed General Lee to take the initiative once again. During the last week in June, the Confederates launched a brutal attack on Union forces that became known as the Seven Days Battles. The bloody series of engagements on the plains and in the swamps and forests surrounding the Chickahominy River left 1,734 Federals dead, 8,066 wounded, and 6,055 missing or captured. At the end of the first day's fighting, McClellan telegraphed Stanton to warn that he was up against "vastly superior odds." He calculated that the rebels had 200,000 troops when in fact they had fewer than half that figure. He would carry on without the reinforcements he had repeatedly requested, but, he continued, if his "great inferiority in numbers" caused "a disaster the responsibility cannot be thrown on my shoulders—it must rest where it belongs." Irked, Lincoln replied that McClellan's talk of responsibility "pains me very much. I give you all I can . . . while you continue, ungenerously I think, to assume that I could give you more if I would."

As the fighting intensified in the days that followed, neither McClellan nor Lincoln was able to sleep. Success alternated between the two forces during the first two days. Then, on June 27, the Confederates scored a critical victory at Gaines' Mill, forcing McClellan to retreat. "I now know the full history of the day," McClellan telegraphed Stanton shortly after midnight. "I have lost this battle because my force was too small. I again repeat that I am not responsible for this." The president "is wrong in regarding me as ungenerous when I said that my force was too weak. I merely intimated a truth which to-day has been too plainly proved." Finally, he vindictively added: "If I save this Army now, I tell you plainly that I owe no thanks to you or to any other persons in Washington. You have done your best to sacrifice this army." When the supervisor of telegrams at the War Department read this defiant message, he was so appalled by the insubordinate tone and the extraordinary charge against the government that he directed his staff to strike the last sentence before relaying it to Stanton.

Even the revised telegram conveyed the accusation that would be leveled by McClellan and his supporters for years to come: victory would have been achieved but for the government's failure to reinforce an overpowered McClellan. Even after the defeat at Gaines' Mill, however, McClellan's troops remained a strong and resilient force. In the days that followed, they fought hard and well, inflicting more than five thousand casualties at Malvern Hill while suffering only half that number. In truth, McClellan was psychologically defeated. "He was simply out-generaled," Christopher Wolcott concluded. Instead of counterattacking, he continued to retreat from Richmond until his exhausted troops reached a safe position eight miles down the James at Harrison's Landing. Equally depleted, Lee's troops returned to Richmond, and the Peninsula Campaign came to an end. The Confederates had successfully secured their capital and gained an important strategic victory. It would take nearly three more years and hundreds of thousands more deaths for the Union forces to come as close to Richmond as they had been in May and June 1862.

CHAPTER 17

"WE ARE IN
THE DEPTHS"

T HE DEFEAT ON THE Peninsula devastated Northern morale. "We are in the depths just now," George Templeton Strong admitted on July 14, 1862, "permeated by disgust, saturated with gloomy thinking." In Washington, columnist Cara Kasson observed the frustration written on every face, manifesting an anxiety greater than the aftermath of Bull Run, "for the present repulse is more momentous." Count Gurowski agreed, calling the Fourth of July holiday "the gloomiest since the birth of this republic. Never was the country so low." Even the normally stoical John Nicolay confided to his fiancée, Therena, that "the past has been a very blue week. . . . I don't think I have ever heard more croaking since the war began."

For the irrepressibly optimistic Seward, who had fervently hoped the capture of Richmond might signal an end to the war, the turn of events was shattering. "It is a startling sight to see the mind of a great people, sad-dened, angered, soured, all at once," he confided to Fanny, who was in Auburn with her mother for the summer. "If I should let a shade of this popular despondency fall upon a dispatch, or even rest upon my own countenance," he realized, "there would be black despair throughout the whole country." He begged her for letters detailing daily life at home—the flowers in bloom and the hatching of eggs—anything but war and defeat. "They bring no alarm, no remonstrances, no complaints, and no re-proaches," he explained. "They are the only letters which come to me, free from excitement. . . . Write to me then cheerfully, as you are wont to do, of boys and girls and dogs and horses, and birds that sing, and stars that shine and never weep, and be blessed for all your days, for thus helping to sustain a spirit."

Chase was equally shaken and despondent. "Since the rebellion broke out I have never been so sad," he told a friend. "We ought [to have] won a victory and taken Richmond." Furthermore, Kate, who had gone to Ohio to visit her grandmother, was not in Washington to console him. "The house seemed very dull after you were gone," he told her in one of many long letters cataloguing the events of that summer. He described his sojourn to see General McDowell, who had been knocked unconscious by a bad fall from his horse; told her of an unusual cabinet meeting, a pleasant dinner party at Seward's with the Stantons and the Welles, a meeting with Jay Cooke, and a visit from Bishop McIlvaine. He queried her about her summer clothes, her lace veil, and a diamond she had ordered. In addition to commonplace matters, he provided her with confidential military intel-ligence about the Peninsula Campaign, delineating the flow of the Chicka-hominy and the position of the various divisions so she could visualize the course of the battle.

Kate was thrilled by her father's lengthy epistles, which she interpreted as "a mark of love and confidence." Her appreciation, he replied, was "more than ample reward for the time & trouble of writing." She must trust that she would always have his love and that he would continue to "confide greatly in [her] on many points." He was pleased, as well, with the quality of her letters, which finally seemed to meet his exacting standards. "All your letters have come and all have been good—some very good."

However, Kate's letters that summer concealed her unhappiness over the troubled course of her romance with William Sprague. The young couple had been close to an engagement before Sprague received some nasty letters retelling and likely embellishing the story of Kate's dalliance with the young married man in Columbus who had become obsessed with her when she was sixteen. Though Sprague was guilty of far greater indiscretions himself, having fathered a child during his twenties, it seems he was so taken aback by the rumors of Kate's behavior that he broke off the relationship. "Then came the blank," he later recalled. "Wherever there is day there must be night. In some countries the day is almost constant, but the night cometh. So with us it came."

Kate, unaccustomed to defeat and ignorant of Sprague's reasons for ending the courtship, was plunged into dejection. Sensing that something was wrong, Chase told Kate that if anything disappointed him, it was her failure to disclose her deepest personal concerns, to confide in him as he confided in her. "My confidence will be entire when you entirely give me yours and when I . . . am made by your acts & words to feel that nothing is held back from me which a father should know of the thoughts, sentiments & acts of a daughter. Cannot this entire confidence be given me? You will, I am sure be happier and so will I."

Hoping to raise her spirits, Chase arranged for Kate and Nettie to visit the McDowells' country home, Buttermilk Farm, in upstate New York. The quiet routine of country life did not suit Kate, who craved distraction from her sorrows. Mrs. McDowell, observing that Kate's "health and spirit" were suffering, kindly agreed to let her accompany friends to Saratoga in search of a more active social life. "Trust nothing I have said will alarm you," she assured Chase upon Kate's departure; but he, of course, could not help fretting over his beloved daughter.

Even more than Chase or Seward, Edwin Stanton was afflicted with troubles in the summer of '62. "The first necessity of every community after a disaster, is a *scapegoat*," the *New York Times* noted. "It is an immense relief to find some one upon whom can be fastened all the sins of a whole people, and who can then be sent into the wilderness, to be heard of no more." In the secretary of war, disgruntled Northerners found their scapegoat. "Journals of all sorts," the *Times* reported, "demand his instant removal."

The drumbeat began with McClellan, who told anyone who would listen that Stanton was to blame for the Peninsula defeat. "So you want to know how I feel about Stanton, & what I think of him now?" he wrote Mary Ellen in July. "I think that he is the most unmitigated scoundrel I ever knew, heard or read of; I think that . . . had he lived in the time of the Saviour, Judas Iscariot would have remained a respected member of the fraternity of the Apostles & that the magnificent treachery & rascality of E. M. Stanton would have caused Judas to have raised his arms in holy horror & unaffected wonder." A week later, McClellan wrote that he had "*the proof that the Secy reads all my private telegrams."* In fact, he took pleasure in the thought that "if he has read my private letters to you also his ears must have tingled somewhat." Nor did his suspicions stop him from reiterating his loathing for the former friend whom he now considered "the most depraved hypocrite & villain."

Democrats, unwilling to fault McClellan, were the loudest in their denunciations of Stanton. Spearheaded by the Blairs, conservatives charged that Stanton had abandoned both his Democratic heritage and his old friendship with McClellan. Two navy officers, speaking with Samuel Phillips Lee, Elizabeth Blair's husband, claimed "there had been treachery at the bottom of our Richmond reverse," spurred by "Stanton's political opposition to McClellan." Democrat John Astor could not refrain from cursing at the mere mention of Stanton's name. "He for one believes," Strong reported, "that Stanton willfully withheld reinforcements from McClellan lest he should make himself too important, politically, by a signal victory." Sanitary Commission member Frederick Law Olmsted expressed similar emotions. "If we could help to hang Stanton by resigning and posting him as a liar, hypocrite and knave," he wrote, "I think we should render the country a far greater service that we can in any other way."

The *New York Times* promised not to engage in the "very fierce crusade" against Stanton, but begged the president, "if we are to have a new Secretary of War, to give us a Soldier—one who knows what war is and how it is to be carried on. . . . If Mr. Stanton is to be removed, the country will be reassured, and the public interest greatly promoted, by making Gen. McClellan his successor. Even those who cavil at his leadership in the field, do not question his mastery of the art of war." As the weeks went by, and the pressure to replace him mounted, Stanton must have wondered how long Lincoln would continue to support him.

Beyond the distracting personal attacks, Stanton was tormented by the long lines of ambulances that rolled into the city each morning carrying the injured and the dead from the peninsula. All his life, Stanton had been unnerved in the presence of death. Now he was surrounded by it at every turn. Sometimes he took it upon himself to deliver the news to stricken families. Mary Ellet Cabell, whose father, Colonel Charles Ellet, was fatally wounded in Memphis, long recalled the moment when Stanton appeared at her family's home in Georgetown to tell of Ellet's heroism during the battle. "I have heard that this powerful War Minister was harsh and unfeeling; but I can never forget the tenderness of his manner" as he delivered the news with "tears to his eyes."

Stanton's own family was touched by death as well. In early July, his youngest son, James, entered the final stage of the smallpox precipitated by an inoculation six months earlier. The Stantons had planned to spend the Fourth of July holiday on a cruise with General Meigs and his family, but their child's illness occupied Ellen Stanton night and day. On July 5, a messenger called on Stanton in the War Department to report that "the baby was dying." He immediately began the three-mile drive to the country house where his family was staying for the summer. The child clung to life for several days, finally succumbing on July 10. For Stanton, who loved his children passionately, the death was devastating, particularly bitter in light of the overwhelming pressures at work that had kept him from his family for many weeks. Under the weight of public censure and private tragedy, his own health began to suffer.

• • •

WHILE HIS CABINET REELED in the aftermath of the Peninsula defeat, Lincoln was faced with the grim knowledge that the ultimate authority had been his alone. Nonetheless, as Whitman had observed following the debacle at Bull Run, Lincoln refused to surrender to the gloom of defeat: "He unflinchingly stemm'd it, and resolv'd to lift himself and the Union out of it." While the battle was still ongoing, Lincoln had found time to write a letter to a young cadet at West Point, the son of Mary's cousin Ann Todd Campbell. The boy was miserable at the academy and his mother was worried. "Allow me to assure you it is a perfect certainty that you will, very soon, feel better—quite happy—if you only stick to the resolution you have taken to procure a military education. I am older than you, have felt badly myself, and *know*, what I tell you is true. Adhere to your purpose and you will soon feel as well as you ever did. On the contrary, if you falter, and give up, you will lose the power of keeping any resolution, and will regret it all your life." The boy stayed at West Point, graduating in 1866.

Now, in the wake of the Peninsula battle, confronted with public discontent, diminishing loan subscriptions and renewed threats that Britain would recognize the Confederacy, Lincoln demonstrated that his own purpose remained fixed. He decided to call for a major expansion of the army. Two months earlier, Stanton, assuming that victory would soon be achieved, had made the colossal mistake of shutting down recruiting offices. To call for more troops now on the heels of defeat, Lincoln realized, might well create "a general panic." But the troops were essential. Seward devised an excellent solution. He journeyed to New York, where a conference of Union governors was taking place. After consulting privately with the governors and securing their agreement, he drafted a circular that they would endorse *asking* the president to call for three hundred thousand additional troops. The president would be responding to a patriotic appeal rather than initiating a call on his own.

While Seward worked out the details from his suite at the Astor House, he was kept abreast of the military situation by telegrams from Lincoln. Fearing that their recruiting efforts might prove insufficient, Seward telegraphed Stanton for permission to promise each new recruit an advance of twenty-five dollars. The money "is of vital importance," he wrote. "We fail without it." Stanton hesitated at first. "The existing law does not authorize an advance," he replied. But finally, trusting Seward's judgment, he decided to make the allocation on his own responsibility.

That summer, Seward traveled throughout the North to help build up the Union Army. He set a precedent within his own department by entreating all those between eighteen and forty-five to volunteer, pledging that their positions would be waiting for them when they returned. A large percentage answered Seward's call. In Auburn, the Sewards' twenty-year-old-son, William Junior, was appointed secretary of the war committee responsible for raising a regiment in upstate New York. A half century later, William remembered "the Mass Meetings held in all the principal towns," the fervent appeals for volunteers, the quickened response once the government announced that unfilled quotas would by met by a draft. New recruits "filled the hotels and many private houses, occupied the upper floors of the business blocks, leaned against the fences, sat upon the curb stone," he recalled. They came on foot and in horse-drawn wagons. "The spectacle was so novel and inspiring that our citizens gave them a perfect ovation as they passed, canons were fired—bells rung and flags displayed from almost every house on the line of march."

Young William Seward had no intention of recruiting others without volunteering himself. His decision to enlist aroused trepidation in the Seward household, for William's new wife, Jenny, was expecting their first child in September. Jenny assured her husband that she would "be able to pass through her troubles," but she worried that his departure might jeopardize his mother's fragile health. In fact, although Frances had been heartbroken years before when Gus, now an army paymaster in Washington, had joined the Mexican War, her passionate feelings against slavery now outweighed her maternal anxiety. "As it is obvious all men are needed I made no objection," Frances told Fred.

While the call was out for fresh reserves, Lincoln decided to make a personal visit to bolster the morale of the weary troops who had fought the hard battles on the Peninsula. Accompanied by Assistant Secretary of War Peter Watson and Congressman Frank Blair, he left Washington aboard the *Ariel* early on the morning of July 8, 1862, beginning the twelve-hour journey to McClellan's new headquarters at Harrison's Landing on the James River. "The day had been intensely hot," an army correspondent noted, the temperature climbing to over 100 degrees. Even soldiers who lay in the shade of the trees found small respite from the "almost overpowering" heat. By 6 p.m., however, when General McClellan and his staff met the president at Harrison's Landing, the setting sun had yielded to a pleasant, moonlit evening.

News of the president's arrival spread quickly through the camp. Soldiers in the vicinity let out great cheers whenever they glimpsed him "sitting and smiling serenely on the after deck of the vessel." Lincoln's calm visage, however, masked his deep anxiety about McClellan and the progress of the war.

Equally troubled, the defeated McClellan had spent the hours before Lincoln's arrival drafting what he termed a "strong frank letter" delineating changes necessary to win the war. "If he acts upon it the country will be saved," he told his wife. McClellan handed the letter to Lincoln, who read it as the two sat together on the deck. Known to history as the "Harrison's Landing" letter, the document imperiously outlined for the president what the policy and aims of the war should be. "The time has come when the government must determine upon a civil and military policy," McClellan brazenly began, warning that without a clear-cut policy defining the nature of the war, "our cause will be lost." Somewhat resembling in attitude Seward's April 1 memo of fifteen months earlier, the presumptuous memo was even more astonishing in tone, as it came from a military officer.

"It should not be at all a war upon population," McClellan proclaimed, and all efforts must be made to protect "private property and unarmed persons." In effect, slave property must be respected, for if a radical approach to slavery were adopted, the "present armies" would "rapidly disintegrate." To carry out this conservative policy, the president would need "a Commander-in-Chief of the Army—one who possesses your confidence." While he did not specifically request that position for himself, McClellan made it clear that he was more than willing to retake the central command.

To McClellan's disappointment and disgust, Lincoln "made no comments upon [the letter], merely saying, when he had finished it, that he was obliged to me for it." Clearly, the president did not remain silent because he failed to grasp the political significance of the general's propositions. In the days that followed, his actions would manifest his rejection of the general's political advice. For the moment, however, Lincoln had come to see and support the troops, not to debate policy with his general.

For three hours, the president reviewed one division after another, riding slowly along the long lines of cheering soldiers. He was relieved to find the army in such high spirits after the bloody weeklong battle, which had decimated their ranks, leaving 1,734 dead and 8,066 wounded. "Mr. Lincoln rode at the right of Gen. McClellan," an army correspondent reported, "holding with one hand the reins which checked a spirited horse, and with the other a large-sized stove-pipe hat" that he repeatedly tipped to acknowledge the cheers of the troops. His attempts to coordinate the reins and doff his tall hat were not entirely successful. His legs almost became "entangled with those of the horse he rode . . . while his arms were apparently liable to similar mishap." One soldier admitted in a letter home that he had to lower his cap over his face "to cover a smile that overmastered" him at the "ludicrous sight." Still, he added, the troops loved Lincoln. "His benignant smile as he passed on was a real reflection of his honest, kindly heart; but deeper, under the surface of that marked and not all uncomely face, were the unmistakable signs of care and anxiety. . . . In fact, his popularity in the army is and has been universal."

As Lincoln approached each division, the "successive booming of salutes made known his progress," until finally, "his tall figure, like Saul of old," came into view, provoking wild applause. The tonic of the president's unexpected visit to the enervated regiments was instantaneous. As Lincoln reviewed the "thinned ranks of some of the divisions" and came upon regimental colors "torn almost to shreds by the balls of the enemy," the *Times* noted, he "more than once exhibited much emotion," affording the fatigued soldiers "the assurance of the nation's hearty sympathy with their struggle."

Returning to the steamer, Lincoln conferred again with McClellan. Making no mention of McClellan's letter, which remained in his pocket, he set sail for Washington the next morning. "On the way up the Potomac," the *New York Herald* reported, "the boat was aground for several hours on the Kettle Shoals, and the whole party, including the President, availed themselves of the opportunity to take a bath and swim in the river."

The visit invigorated the spirits of all who accompanied Lincoln. Frank Blair's sister Elizabeth noted that "Frank was as heart sick as man could be when he went off to the Army but he & the President came back greatly cheered." Despite Lincoln's enthusiasm for the mettle of the soldiers, however, his opinion of General McClellan had not improved. Less than forty-eight hours after his return, he summoned General Henry Halleck to Washington to assume the post of general in chief that McClellan had hoped would be his. Halleck's victories in the West, largely due to Grant, had made him a logical choice for the post. Known as "Old Brains," he had written several books on military strategy that were widely respected.

Even before McClellan heard the news, he suspected an unwelcome turn of events. "I do not know what paltry trick the administration will play next," he wrote his wife on the day after Lincoln's visit. "I did not like the Presdt's manner—it seemed that of a man about to do something of which he was much ashamed. A few days will however show, & I do not much care what the result will be. I feel that I have already done enough to prove in history that I am a General."

Although Halleck's appointment met with widespread approval, the clamor for further changes was undiminished. Radicals called for McClellan's dismissal, while conservatives continued their assault on Stanton. The arguments on both sides were heated. In a hotel lobby, Senator Chandler of Michigan called McClellan a "liar and coward," provoking a friend of McClellan's to angrily counter: "It is you who are the liar and the coward." The charges against Stanton were equally caustic, portraying him as brusque, domineering, and unbearably unpleasant to work with. Nonetheless, Lincoln was determined, as Browning advised, to "make up his mind calmly [and] deliberately," to "adhere firmly to his own opinions, and neither to be bullied or cajoled out of them."

In fact, not once during the vicious public onslaught against the secretary of war did Lincoln's support for Stanton waver. During the hours he had spent each day awaiting battlefront news in the telegraph office, Lincoln had taken his own measure of his high-strung, passionate secretary of war. He concluded that Stanton's vigorous, hard-driving style was precisely what was needed at this critical juncture. As one War Department employee said of Stanton, "much of his seeming harshness to and neglect of individuals" could be explained by the "concentration and intensity of his mind on the single object of crushing the rebellion."

And, as always, the president refused to let a subordinate take the blame for his own decisions. He insisted to Browning "that all that Stanton had done in regard to the army had been authorized by him the President." Three weeks later, Lincoln publicly defended the beleaguered Stanton before an immense Union meeting on the Capitol steps. All the government departments had closed down at one o'clock so that everyone could attend. Commissioner French believed he had "never seen more persons assembled in front of the Capitol except at an inauguration, which it very much resembled." Lincoln sat on the flag-draped platform with the members of his cabinet, including Chase, Blair, and Bates, as "the ringing of bells, the firing of cannon, and music from the Marine Band" heralded the speakers.

After a speech by Treasury Registrar Lucius Chittenden, Lincoln turned to Chase, who sat beside him. " 'Well! Hadn't I better say a few words and get rid of myself?' Hardly waiting for an answer, he advanced at once to the stand."

"I believe there is no precedent for my appearing before you on this occasion," he affably began, "but it is also true that there is no precedent for your being here yourselves." Reminding his audience that he was reluctant to speak unless he might "produce some good by it," Lincoln declared that something needed to be said, and it was "not likely to be better said by some one else," for it was *a matter in which we have heard some other persons blamed for what I did myself.*" Addressing the charge that Stanton had withheld troops from McClellan, he explained that every possible soldier available had been sent to the general. "The Secretary of War *is not to blame for not giving when he had none to give.*" As the applause began to mount, he continued, *"I believe he is a brave and able man*, and I stand here, as justice requires me to do, *to take upon myself what has been charged on the Secretary of War.*"

French was profoundly moved by Lincoln's speech. "He is one of the best men God ever created," he asserted. Chase, too, was impressed by the "originality and sagacity" of the address. "His frank, genial, generous face and direct simplicity of bearing, took all hearts." The great rally concluded to the strains of "Yankee Doodle Dandy" and a salute of sixty-eight guns, two for each state in the Union. Reported fully in every newspaper, Lincoln's defense of his beleaguered secretary brought the campaign against Stanton to an end.

•   •   •

AS THE SUMMER PROGRESSED, Lincoln and his family found some respite from the pressure and grief that had seemed so relentless throughout the cruel spring. At last, Mary's intense depression began to lift. Reporters noted that she had begun riding with her husband once more in the late afternoons. On Sundays, she returned to Dr. Gurley's church, though a parishioner seated behind her observed that "she was so hid behind her immense black veil—and very deep black flounces—that one could scarcely tell she was there."

Commissioner French reported that "she seemed to be in excellent spirits" as she prepared to take up residence for the summer at the Soldiers' Home, situated on almost 300 acres in the hills three miles north of the city. Created in the 1850s as a retirement community for disabled veterans, the Soldiers' Home consisted of a main building that could accommodate 150 boarders, an infirmary, a dining hall, and administrative offices. The property also encompassed a number of spacious cottages, including the two-story brick house where the Lincoln family would stay. Known as the Anderson Cottage, it had served as a country residence for George Riggs, founder of the Riggs Bank, before the federal government purchased the property.

Buchanan had been the first president to summer at the Soldiers' Home, where the cooling breeze brought relief from the oppressive heat of the city. Surrounded by abundant flowers, shrubs, and trees, it seemed almost "an earthly paradise," one visitor recalled. The beautiful gravel walks and winding carriage ways, all of which were open to the public, had become a choice destination for Washingtonians out for weekend rides in their carriages. Another visitor in the summer of 1862 claimed he had seen nothing in the capital more charming than "this quiet and beautiful retreat," from which "we look down upon the city and see the whole at a glance"—the Capitol dome, "huge, grand, gloomy, ragged and unfinished, like the war now waging for its preservation," the Potomac River, "stretching away plainly visible for twelve miles, Alexandria, Arlington, Georgetown, and the long line of forts that bristle along the hills."

At Mary's urging, Lincoln agreed to settle in with his family for the summer, riding his horse the three miles to the White House each morning and returning at night. "We are truly delighted, with this retreat," Mary wrote her friend Fanny Eames, "the drives & walks around here are delightful, & each day, brings its visitors. Then too, our boy Robert [home from Harvard], is with us, whom you may remember. We consider it a 'pleasant time' for us, when his vacations, roll around, he is very companionable, and I shall dread when he has to return to Cambridge." For Tad, whose companionship and daily routine had been obliterated by the death of his brother and the banishment of the Taft boys, the Soldiers' Home was a godsend. His lively, cheerful disposition earned him the affection of the soldiers assigned to guard his father. They dubbed him a "3rd Lieutenant," allowing him to join in their drills during the day and their meals around the campfire at night.

In the evenings, the Lincolns could entertain guests on the wide porch overlooking the grounds or in a formal parlor illuminated by gas lamps. Relaxing in his slippers, Lincoln was fond of reciting poetry or reading aloud from favorite authors. Though intermittent cannonfire was audible in the distance, the idyllic retreat provided precious privacy and space for conversation among family and friends. For Lincoln, the historian Matthew Pinsker observes, the soldiers assigned to his security detail "helped him recreate some of the spirit of fraternity that he had once enjoyed as a younger politician and circuit-riding attorney in Illinois."

It was during this restorative summer that Mary formed what one news-paper termed a "daily habit of visiting the hospitals in the District." The hospitals became her refuge, allowing her a few hours of reprieve from her private grief. "But for these humane employments," a friend who often ac-companied her to the hospital wards recalled her saying, "her heart would have broken when she lost her child." It is clear in the recollections of Walt Whitman, who worked as a nurse in the hospital wards, that the har-rowing experience made one's "little cares and difficulties" disappear "into nothing." After ministering each day to the hundreds of young men who had endured ghastly wounds, submitted to amputations without anesthe-sia, and often died without the comfort of family or friends, Whitman wrote, "nothing of ordinary misfortune seems as it used to."

In the days after the Peninsula Campaign, the *New York Daily Tribune* reported, the numbers of sick and wounded pouring into the city were enough "to form an immense army." Every morning, steamers arrived at the Sixth Street Wharf carrying hundreds of injured soldiers, many "horri-bly wounded." As crowds gathered around, the soldiers disembarked, some carried on stretchers, others stumbling along on crudely made crutches. Ambulances stood by, ready to transport them to the dozen or more hastily outfitted hospitals that had sprung up in various parts of the capital.

In the effort to meet the soaring demand for hospital space, the federal government had embarked on a massive project of converting hotels, churches, clubs, school buildings, and private residences into military hos-pitals. The old Union Hotel, where congressmen and senators had boarded during earlier administrations, became the Union Hotel Hospi-tal. A visitor noted that "the rooms in which the politicians of the old school used to sit and sup their wine" were now crowded with patients lying on cots. Louisa May Alcott, who worked there as a nurse, observed that "many of the doors still bore their old names; some not so inappropri-ate as might be imagined, for my ward was in truth a *ball-room*, if gunshot wounds could christen it." The Braddock House, where it was said that "General George Washington held his Councils of War," was also pressed into service, with some of the same old chairs and desks.

The second floor of the Patent Office, under the guidance of Interior Secretary Caleb Smith's wife, Elizabeth, was likewise transformed into a hospital ward accommodating hundreds of patients. It presented "a curi-ous scene," Whitman noted, with rows of "sick, badly wounded and dying soldiers" lying between "high and ponderous glass cases, crowded with models in miniature of every kind of utensil, machine or invention." In ad-dition, "a great long double row" of cots ran "up and down through the middle of the hall," with extra beds placed in the gallery. Especially "at night, when lit up," the impromptu ward presented a bizarre spectacle with its "glass cases, the beds, the sick, the gallery above and the marble pavement under foot."

In mid-June, the Methodist Episcopal Church on 20th Street offered its chapel for conversion to a hospital. Five days later, government carpenters and mechanics were hard at work covering pews with timbers to support a new floor upon which hundreds of beds would be placed. As in other church hospitals, the pulpit and assorted furnishings were safely stored under the floor, while the basement was turned into a laboratory and kitchen. Taken together, these makeshift government hospitals accommodated more than three thousand patients, still only a fraction of the beds that would be needed in the months and years ahead.

In preparation for her hospital visits, Mary filled her carriage with baskets of fruit, food, and fresh flowers. She cleaned out the strawberries in the White House garden and procured a donation from a wealthy merchant, impressed by "the quiet and unostentatious manner" of her ministrations, for $300 worth of lemons and oranges, so necessary to prevent scurvy. For hours, she would distribute the fruit and delicacies, placing fresh flowers on the pillows of wounded men to mask the pervasive stench of disinfectant and decay.

She sat by the side of lonely soldiers, talked with them about their experiences, read to them, and helped them write letters to their families at home. One wounded soldier discovered the identity of the kindly woman who had written to his mother explaining that he had been "quite sick," but was recovering, only after Mary's letter had reached his home with the first lady's signature.

For the soldiers, the need to communicate with their families was tantamount to their need to survive. Alcott told the story of a valiant soldier named John, a young man of "commanding stature," with a handsome face and "the serenest eyes" she had ever seen. A ball had pierced his left lung, making it almost impossible for him to breathe. Although the doctors deemed his condition hopeless, he clung to life for days, hoping to hear from home. "Unsubdued by pain," he never uttered a complaint, "tranquilly [observing] what went on about him." When he died, "many came to see him," paying respect to the quiet courage that had impressed both the hospital staff and his fellow soldiers. While Louisa May Alcott stood by his bed, the ward master handed her a letter from John's mother that had arrived the night before, "just an hour too late to gladden the eyes that had longed and looked for it so eagerly."

The emotional narratives of Whitman and Alcott testify to the enormous fortitude demanded by hospital work. Whitman told his mother that while he kept "singularly cool" during the days, he would "feel sick and actually tremble" at night, recalling the "deaths, operations, sickening wounds (perhaps full of maggots)," and the "heap of feet, arms, legs" that lay beneath a tree on some hospital grounds. Alcott confessed that she found it difficult to keep from weeping at "the sight of several stretchers, each with its legless, armless, or desperately wounded occupant" coming into her ward. Workers and visitors were also exposed to contagion, as soldiers with typhoid lay side by side with patients dying of pneumonia or diphtheria. The thirty-year-old Alcott developed a severe case of typhoid after only two months and was forced to return to her home in Concord, Massachusetts.

Watching the countless young men suffer and die around her, Mary must have found it difficult to dwell solely upon the loss of her own child. "Death itself has lost all its terrors," Whitman wrote. "I have seen so many cases in which it was so welcome and such a relief." Yet somehow the triumphs of life, humor, and love were also evident amid the horrors of the hospitals. One soldier, whose body "was so blackened and burned by a powder explosion that some one remarked, 'There is not much use bringing him in,' " showed such a fierce determination to live that he eventually recovered. Another youth, who had lost one leg and was soon to lose an arm, amazed onlookers when he joked about his condition, imagining the "scramble there'll be for arms and legs, when we old boys come out of our graves, on the Judgment Day." In ward after ward, recovering patients even organized impromptu bands to entertain their fellow bedmates with music and song.

Observing Mary as she departed for her regular round of hospital visits, William Stoddard wondered why she didn't publicize her efforts. "If she were worldly wise she would carry newspaper correspondents, from two to five, of both sexes, every time she went, and she would have them take shorthand notes of what she says to the sick soldiers and of what the sick soldiers say to her." This, more than anything, he surmised, would "sweeten the contents of many journals" that had frequently derided the first lady's receptions and redecorating projects. The *New York Independent* had been particularly relentless in its attacks on Mary. "While her sister-women scraped lint, sewed bandages, and put on nurses' caps," Mary Clemmer Ames wrote, "the wife of its President spent her time in rolling to and fro between Washington and New York, intent on extravagant purchases for herself and the White House."

Yet Mary continued her hospital trips without any publicity. Some physicians objected to further interruption in an already chaotic situation, while others thought it improper for ladies to associate with common soldiers in various states of undress. Under such circumstances, Mary decided to carry on her work discreetly.

So it happened that while newspapers regularly praised the work of other society women, referring to Mrs. Caleb Smith as "our ever-bountiful benefactress & friend," and to Mrs. Stephen Douglas, who had converted her mansion into a hospital, as "an angel of mercy," Mary Lincoln received scant credit for her steadfast attempts to comfort Union casualties. She found something more gratifying than public acknowledgment. For in the hours she spent with these soldiers she must have sensed their unwavering belief in her husband and in the Union for which they fought. Such a faith was not readily found elsewhere—not in the cabinet, the Congress, the press, or the social circles of the city.

• • •

WHILE WASHINGTON SWELTERED through the long, hot summer, Lincoln made the momentous decision on emancipation that would define both his presidency and the course of the Civil War.

The great question of what to do about slavery had provoked increasingly bitter debates on Capitol Hill for many months. Back in March, as foreshadowed in a message to Congress, Lincoln had asked the legislature to pass a joint resolution providing federal aid to any state willing to adopt a plan for the gradual abolition of slavery. The resolution called upon states to stipulate that all slaves within their borders would be freed upon attaining a certain age or specify a date after which slavery would no longer be allowed. Lincoln had calculated that "less than one half-day's cost of this war would pay for all the slaves in Delaware at four hundred dollars per head," and that eighty-seven days' expenses would buy all the slaves in all the other border states combined. He believed that nothing would bring the rebellion to an end faster than a commitment by the border slave states "to surrender on fair terms their own interest in Slavery rather than see the Union dissolved." If the rebels were deprived of hope that these states might join the Confederacy, they would lose heart.

The proposal depended upon approval by the border-state representatives, who would have to promote the plan in their state legislatures. Except for Frank Blair, however, who had long advocated compensated emancipation coupled with colonization, they refused to endorse the proposal. Even when Lincoln personally renewed his plea to them on July 12, they argued that "emancipation in any form" would lengthen, not shorten, the war; it "would further consolidate the spirit of rebellion in the seceded states and fan the spirit of secession among loyal slaveholders in the Border

States." They insisted that the measure would unjustly punish those who remained loyal to the Union, forcing them to relinquish their slaves while the rebellious states retained theirs. They would face an uproar among their own citizens, and the proposal would cost far more than the federal government could pay.

Meanwhile, the Republican majority in Congress, freed from the domination of the Southern bloc, began to push their own agenda on slavery. In April, Congress passed a bill providing for the compensated emancipation of slaves in the District of Columbia. The bill met Lincoln's wholehearted approval, for he had "never doubted the constitutional authority of congress to abolish slavery" in areas that fell under the jurisdiction of the federal government, and, indeed, Lincoln had drafted his own proposal to free slaves in the District when he had been in Congress fourteen years earlier. Frederick Douglass was ecstatic. "I trust I am not dreaming," he wrote Charles Sumner, "but the events taking place seem like a dream." As slaves in the District gained their freedom, slaveholders in surrounding Maryland and northern Virginia, fearful that their own slaves would grow restive, began selling them to owners farther south.

Francis Blair, Sr., who had already assured his slaves that they could "go when they wished," proudly affirmed that "all but one declined the privilege," electing to stay on as servants at Silver Springs, where they lived together in their own "quarters" that resembled those on Southern plantations. One servant, Henry, declared he "was used to quality all his days" and wanted to remain with the Blairs for the rest of his life. Nanny, another servant, agreed. She was "well off," had no thought of moving on, but was "delighted that her children are free."

The situation became more complex when the radical bloc in Congress began to address slavery in the seceded Southern states where it already existed and was protected by the Constitution. In July, despite the vehement protests of Democrats and conservative Republicans, the radical majority passed a new confiscation bill. Broader than the bill passed the previous year, which had limited the federal government to confiscating and freeing only those fugitive slaves employed by rebels in the field, the new act emancipated all slaves of persons engaged in rebellion, regardless of involvement in military affairs. The bill was ill considered, providing no workable means of enforcement and no procedure to determine whether the owner of a slave crossing Union lines was actually engaged in insurrection. "It was," the historian Mark Neely writes, "a dead letter from the start." But it stirred the hearts of all those, like Charles Sumner, who believed that slavery was a "disturbing influence which, so long as it exists, will keep this land a volcano, ever ready to break anew."

It was rumored in Washington that Lincoln would veto the controversial bill. Indeed, Browning carried a copy of it to the White House as soon as it passed, pleading with Lincoln to veto it. If approved, he warned, "our friends" in the border states "could no longer sustain themselves there." The bill would "form the basis upon which the democratic party would again rally, and reorganize an opposition to the administration." Lincoln's decision, Browning insisted, would "determine whether he was to control the abolitionists and radicals, or whether they were to control him." The key moment had arrived when "the tide in his affairs had come and he ought to take it at its flood."

Chase presented the diametrically opposed prediction, which maintained that if Lincoln vetoed the bill, it "will be an end of him." The Republican majority in Congress would break ranks with the administration, and Lincoln would be openly castigated on the floor. Worried that he, too, might be tainted by a presidential veto, Chase told his friends to spread word that he had not been consulted, "nor so far as he knew [had] a single member of his cabinet" been involved. While he would willingly answer for his actions as treasury secretary, Chase refused to take the blame "for other people's blunders or errors of policy."

Rumors that Lincoln would veto the bill proved incorrect. The next morning, Browning found the president working in his library. He "looked weary, care-worn and troubled," Browning noted, "and there was a cadence of deep sadness in his voice." The president had made his decision, which he knew would distress his friend. Still, before signing the bill that would become known as the Second Confiscation Act, Lincoln listed his objections in writing and obtained a revised bill that made it more likely to pass constitutional muster.

As was customary on the last day of the session, the president traveled to the Capitol, stationing himself in the vice president's office, where he signed the spate of bills rushed through in the final days of the term. It had been an extraordinarily productive session. Relieved of Southern opposition, the Republican majority was able to pass three historic bills that had been stalled for years: the Homestead Act, which promised 160 acres of free public land largely in the West to settlers who agreed to reside on the property for five years or more; the Morrill Act, providing public lands to states for the establishment of land-grant colleges; and the Pacific Railroad Act, which made the construction of a transcontinental railroad possible. The 37th Congress also laid the economic foundation for the Union war effort with the Legal Tender bill, which created a paper money known as "greenbacks." A comprehensive tax bill was also enacted, establishing the Internal Revenue Bureau in the Department of the Treasury and levying a federal income tax for the first time in American history.

At that time, the far-reaching impact of this epoch-making home front legislation was overshadowed by the continuing slavery controversy, which preoccupied both sides of the aisle. Referring to the endless hours the Republican stalwarts spent rehashing the issue, Seward jokingly told foreign diplomats over dinner that "he had lately begun to realize the value of a Cromwell," and sometimes longed for "a Coup d'etat for our Congress." As the summer progressed, his level of frustration with Congress grew. "I ask Congress to authorize a draft," he complained to Frances. "They fall into altercation about letting slaves fight and work. Every day is a day lost, and every day lost is a hazard to the whole country. What if I should say, that I concede all they want about negroes? . . . One party has gained another partisan; the country has lost one advocate."

Within the cabinet as well as on Capitol Hill, the rancor over slavery infected every discourse. The debates had grown "so bitter," according to Seward, that personal and even official relationships among members were ruptured, leading to "a prolonged discontinuance of Cabinet meetings." Though Tuesdays and Fridays were still designated for sessions, each secretary remained in his department unless a messenger arrived to confirm that a meeting would be held. Seward recalled that when these general discussions were still taking place, Lincoln had listened intently but had not taken "an active part in them." For Lincoln, the problem of slavery was not an abstract issue. While he concurred with the most passionate abolitionists that slavery was "a moral, a social and a political wrong," as president, he could not ignore the constitutional protection of the institution where it already existed.

The devastating reverses on the Peninsula, which made it clear that extraordinary means were necessary to save the Union, gave Lincoln an opening to deal more directly with slavery. Daily reports from the battlefields illuminated the innumerable uses to which slaves were put by the Confederacy. They dug trenches and built fortifications for the army. They were brought into camps to serve as teamsters, cooks, and hospital attendants, so that soldiers were freed to fight in the fields. They labored on the home front, tilling fields, raising crops, and picking cotton, so their masters could go to war without fearing that their families would go hungry. If the rebels were divested of their slaves, who would then be free to join the Union forces, the North could gain a decided advantage. Seen in this light, emancipation could be considered a military necessity, a legitimate exercise of the president's constitutional war powers. The border states had refused his idea of compensated emancipation as a voluntary first step, insisting that any such action should be initiated in the slave states. A historic decision was taking shape in Lincoln's mind.

Lincoln revealed his preliminary thinking to Seward and Welles in the early hours of Sunday, July 13, as they rode together in the president's carriage to the funeral of Stanton's infant son. The journey to Oak Hill Cemetery, where Stanton's child was to be buried, must have evoked painful memories of Willie, whose body remained there in the private vault awaiting final interment in Springfield. Despite such personal torment, the country's peril demanded Lincoln's complete concentration. During the journey, Welles recorded in his diary, the president informed them that he was considering "emancipating the slaves by proclamation in case the Rebels did not cease to persist in their war." He said that he had "dwelt earnestly on the gravity, importance, and delicacy" of the subject and had "come to the conclusion that it was a military necessity absolutely essential for the salvation of the Union, that we must free the slaves or be ourselves subdued." Thus, the constitutional protection of slavery could and would be overridden by the constitutionally sanctioned war powers of the president.

This was, Welles clearly recognized, "a new departure for the President, for until this time, in all our previous interviews . . . he had been prompt and emphatic in denouncing any interference by the General Government with the subject." The normally talkative Seward said merely that the "subject involved consequences so vast and momentous that he should wish to bestow on it mature reflection before giving a decisive answer," though he was inclined to think it "justifiable."

So the matter rested until Monday morning, July 21, when messengers were dispatched across Washington with notices of a special cabinet meeting to be held at 10 a.m. "It has been so long since any consultation has been held that it struck me as a novelty," Chase wrote in his diary. Earlier that day, Chase had shared breakfast in his home with Count Gurowski, whose acute frustration with Lincoln's hesitancy regarding emancipation had been evident for many months. In Gurowski's mind, Seward was the primary obstacle to progress, while Chase represented the best hope for spurring Lincoln forward. An inveterate gossip, Gurowski related to Chase the story of Seward's comments on Cromwell and the Congress, which, he claimed, had been received with marked disapproval by the diplomats in attendance.

When the cabinet convened, all members save the postmaster general were in attendance. Montgomery Blair was in Maryland, where he had recently built an elegant country estate, Falkland, in Silver Spring near his parents' estate. For this special meeting, the cabinet was summoned to the second-floor library rather than the president's official office. There, sur-rounded by the curved bookshelves that Mary had recently filled with splendidly bound sets of Shakespeare and Sir Walter Scott's novels, the president began with an admission that he was "profoundly concerned at the present aspect of affairs, and had determined to take some definitive steps in respect to military action and slavery." The members listened as Lincoln read several orders he was contemplating. One would authorize Union generals in Confederate territory to appropriate any property nec-essary to sustain themselves in the field; another would sanction the pay-ment of wages to blacks brought into the army's employ. Taken together, these orders signaled a more vigorous prosecution of the war. When the discussion moved to address the possible arming of those blacks in the army's employ, Stanton and Chase were in favor. Lincoln, Chase recorded, was "not prepared to decide the question."

When the preliminary discussions had run long, the president sched-uled another cabinet session the following day, July 22, to reveal his pri-mary purpose in calling the meeting. This second session was likely held in Lincoln's office, as depicted in Francis Carpenter's famous painting, *First Reading of the Emancipation Proclamation*. There, surrounded by evidence of the ever-expanding war, with battlefield maps everywhere—rolled in standing racks, placed in folios on the floor, and reclining up against the walls—the conversation from the previous day continued.

The desultory talk abruptly ended when Lincoln took the floor and an-nounced he had called them together in order to read the preliminary draft of an emancipation proclamation. He understood the "differences in the Cabinet on the slavery question" and welcomed their suggestions after they heard what he had to say; but he wanted them to know that he "had resolved upon this step, and had not called them together to ask their ad-vice." Then, removing two foolscap sheets from his pocket and adjusting his glasses on his nose, he began to read what amounted to a legal brief for emancipation based on the chief executive's powers as commander in chief.

His draft proclamation set January 1, 1863, little more than five months away, as the date on which all slaves within states still in rebellion against the Union would be declared free, "thenceforward, and forever." It re-quired no cumbersome enforcement proceedings. Though it did not cover the roughly 425,000 slaves in the loyal border states—where, without the use of his war powers, no constitutional authority justified his action—the proclamation was shocking in scope. In a single stroke, it superseded legis-lation on slavery and property rights that had guided policy in eleven states for nearly three quarters of a century. Three and a half million blacks who had lived enslaved for generations were promised freedom. It was a daring

move, Welles later said, "fraught with consequences, immediate and remote, such as human foresight could not penetrate."

The cabinet listened in silence. With the exception of Seward and
Welles, to whom the president had intimated his intentions the previous
week, the members were startled by the boldness of Lincoln's proclamation. Only Stanton and, surprisingly, Bates declared themselves in favor of
"its immediate promulgation." Stanton instantly grasped the military
value of the proclamation. Having spent more time than any of his colleagues contemplating the logistical problems facing the army, he understood the tremendous advantage to be gained if the massive workforce of
slaves could be transferred from the Confederacy to the Union. Equally
important, he had developed a passionate belief in the justice of emancipation.

Bates, as one of the more conservative members of the cabinet, surprised his colleagues with his enthusiastic approval of the proclamation.
He had previously registered disapproval of the more limited emancipation measures attempted by the military and had expressed grave misgivings about the confiscation legislation. His sudden support of this far more
radical step can be traced, in part, to the terrible division that slavery and
the war had wrought upon his family.

In a scenario common to many border-state homes torn by divided loyalties, the Bates brothers had joined opposing sides in the war. Twenty-
eight-year-old Fleming Bates had enlisted in the Confederate Army and
was serving under Major General Sterling Price. Fleming faced the prospect of going into battle against any of four brothers. His older brother
Julian, a surgeon, had been made a colonel in the Missouri militia. His
younger brother Coalter was with the Army of the Potomac and would
fight at Antietam, Fredericksburg, Chancellorsville, and Gettysburg. Another brother, Richard, was clerking for his father but would soon join the
Union navy; while the family's youngest son, Charles Woodson, was a
cadet at West Point. For Bates, who valued his family above all else, nothing could be more heartbreaking than the possibility of his sons facing one
another on the battlefield. He had long favored gradual emancipation, but
if the president's proclamation could bring the war to a speedier conclusion, he would give it his "very decided approval."

Bates based his approval, however, on the condition that the freed slaves
would be deported to someplace in Central America or Africa. Unlike Lincoln, who insisted that any emigration must be voluntary, Bates believed it
should be mandatory. Bates "was fully convinced," Welles later recalled,
"that the two races could not live and thrive in social proximity." He believed that assimilation was impossible without amalgamation, and that

amalgamation would inevitably bring "degradation and demoralization to the white race." Although he conceded that "among our colored people who have been long free, there are many who are intelligent and well advanced in arts and knowledge," he could not imagine former slaves, "fresh from the plantations of the South, where they have been long degraded by the total abolition of the family relation, shrouded in artificial darkness, and studiously kept in ignorance," living on an equal footing with whites. Far better for everyone, he argued, if the government established treaties granting aid to foreign governments willing to accept and settle freed slaves. He was hopeful that such treaties would "provide for the just and humane treatment of the emigrants—e.g. ensuring an honest livelihood by their own industry . . . and guaranteeing to them 'their liberty, property and the religion which they profess.' "

Gideon Welles remained silent after Lincoln presented his proclamation. He later admitted that the prospect of emancipation involved such unpredictable results, "carrying with it a revolution of the social, civil, and industrial habits and condition of society in all the slave States," that he was oppressed by the "solemnity and weight" of the decision. He feared that, far from shortening the war, emancipation would generate an "energy of desperation on the part of the slave-owners" and "intensify the struggle." Yet, while he privately questioned the "extreme exercise of war powers" involved, Welles held his tongue and later loyally supported Lincoln.

Caleb Smith kept silent as well, though he, too, had serious reservations. John Usher, the assistant secretary of the Interior Department, later recalled Smith telling him that if Lincoln issued the proclamation, he would "resign and go home and attack the administration."

The division of sentiment within the cabinet was manifest as Blair, Chase, and Seward spoke. Arriving late, after Lincoln's announcement that he had already resolved to issue the proclamation, Blair spoke up vigorously in opposition and asked to file his objections. While he supported the idea of compensated, gradual emancipation linked to colonization, he feared that the president's radical proclamation would cause such an outcry among conservatives and Democrats that Republicans would lose the fall elections. More important, it would "put in jeopardy the patriotic element in the border States, already severely tried," and "would, as soon as it reached them, be likely to carry over those States to the secessionists." Lincoln replied that while he had considered these dangers, he had tried for months to get the border states "to move in this matter, convinced in his own mind that it was their true interest to do so, but his labors were in vain." The time had come to move ahead. He would, however, willingly let Blair file his written objections.

Perhaps the most astonishing response came from Salmon Chase. No cabinet member had more vehemently promoted emancipation, and none could match his lifelong commitment to the abolitionist cause. Yet when faced with a presidential initiative that, he admitted, went "beyond anything I have recommended," he recoiled. According to Stanton's notes, Chase argued that it was "a measure of great danger—and would lead to universal emancipation." He feared that widespread disorder would engulf the South, leading to "depredation and massacre on the one hand, and support to the insurrection on the other." Chase recommended a quieter, more incremental approach, "allowing Generals to organize and arm the slaves" and "directing the Commanders of Departments to proclaim emancipation within their Districts as soon as practicable." Still, since he considered the proclamation better than no action at all, he would support it.

Although Chase's argument that the army might better control the pace of emancipation was legitimate, it is difficult not to suspect personal considerations behind his failure to wholeheartedly endorse the president's proclamation. Chase had seen his bright hopes for the presidency vanish in 1856 and 1860. No president since Andrew Jackson had been reelected, and the next election was only two years away. Chase's strongest claim to beat Lincoln for the nomination in 1864 lay with the unswerving support he had earned among the growing circle of radical Republicans frustrated by Lincoln's slowness on the slavery issue. The bold proclamation threatened to undercut Chase's potential candidacy, for, as Welles astutely recognized, it "placed the President in advance of [Chase] on a path which was his specialty."

Stanton feared that Chase's arguments would deter Lincoln from issuing his proclamation, letting the "golden moment" slip away. Should this come to pass, Stanton's brother-in-law, Christopher Wolcott, wrote, then "Chase must be held responsible for delaying or defeating the greatest act of justice, statesmanship, and civilization, of the last four thousand years." Lincoln later maintained, however, that not a single argument had been presented that he "had not already fully anticipated and settled in [his] own mind, until Secretary Seward spoke."

William Henry Seward's mode of intricate analysis produced a characteristically complex reaction to the proclamation. After the others had spoken, he expressed his worry that the proclamation might provoke a racial war in the South so disruptive to cotton that the ruling classes in England and France would intervene to protect their economic interests. As secretary of state, Seward was particularly sensitive to the threat of European intervention. Curiously, despite his greater access to intelligence from abroad, Seward failed to grasp what Lincoln intuitively understood: that once the Union truly committed itself to emancipation, the masses in Europe, who regarded slavery as an evil demanding eradication, would not be easily maneuvered into supporting the South.

Beyond his worries about intervention, Seward had little faith in the efficacy of proclamations that he considered nothing more than paper without the muscle of the advancing Union Army to enforce them. "The public mind seizes quickly upon theoretical schemes for relief," he pointedly told Frances, who had long yearned for a presidential proclamation against slavery, "but is slow in the adoption of the practical means necessary to give them effect." Seward's position, in fact, was nearly identical to that held by Chase. His preference, he said, "would have been to confiscate all rebel property, including slaves, as fast as the territory was conquered." Only an immediate military presence could assure escaped slaves of protection. Yet Seward's practical focus underestimated the proclamation's power to unleash the moral fervor of the North and keep the Republican Party united by making freedom for the slaves an avowed objective of the war.

Despite his concerns about the effect of the proclamation, Seward had no thought of opposing it. Once Lincoln had made up his mind, Seward was steadfast in his loyalty to him. He demurred only on the issue of timing. "Mr. President," he said, "I approve of the proclamation, but I question the expediency of its issue at this juncture. The depression of the public mind, consequent upon our repeated reverses, is so great that I fear . . . it may be viewed as the last measure of an exhausted government, a cry for help . . . our last *shriek*, on the retreat." Better to wait, he grandiloquently suggested, "until the eagle of victory takes his flight," and buoyed by military success, "hang your proclamation about his neck." Seward's argument was reinforced later that day by Thurlow Weed, who met with Lincoln on a visit to Washington.

"The wisdom of the view of the Secretary of State struck me with very great force," Lincoln later told the artist Francis Carpenter. "It was an aspect of the case that, in all my thought upon the subject, I had entirely overlooked. The result was that I put the draft of the proclamation aside, as you do your sketch for a picture, waiting for a victory."

•   •   •

As JULY GAVE WAY TO AUGUST, however, Lincoln's thoughts never strayed from his proclamation. Repeatedly, he returned to edit his draft, "touching it up here and there, anxiously watching the progress of events." Having resolved to present it for publication upon the first military success, he set out to educate public opinion, to prepare the ground for its acceptance. Lincoln had long believed, as we have seen, that "with public sentiment, nothing can fail; without it nothing can succeed." He understood that one of the principal stumbling blocks in the way of emancipation was the pervasive fear shared by whites in both the North and the South that the two races could never coexist peacefully in a free society. He thought that a plan for the voluntary emigration of freed slaves would allay some of these fears, fostering wider acceptance of his proclamation.

On August 14, Lincoln invited a delegation of freed slaves to a conference at the White House, hoping to inspire their cooperation in educating fellow blacks on the benefits of colonization. "You and we are different races," he began. "We have between us a broader difference than exists between almost any other two races." Lincoln acknowledged that with slavery, the black race had endured "the greatest wrong inflicted on any people." Still, he continued, "when you cease to be slaves, you are yet far removed from being placed on an equality with the white race. You are cut off from many of the advantages which the other race enjoy. The aspiration of men is to enjoy equality with the best when free, but on this broad continent, not a single man of your race is made the equal of a single man of ours." Meanwhile, the evil consequences of slavery upon the white race were manifest in a calamitous civil war that found them "cutting one another's throats." Far "better for us both, therefore, to be separated," Lincoln reasoned, informing the delegates that "a sum of money had been appropriated by Congress, and placed at his disposition" to aid in establishing a colony somewhere in Central America. He needed a contingent of intelligent, educated blacks, such as the men present, to promote the opportunity among their own people.

A discussion followed and the meeting came to a close. "We were entirely hostile to the movement until all the advantages were so ably brought to our views by you," the delegation chief wrote Lincoln two days later, promising to consult with prominent blacks in Philadelphia, New York, and Boston who he hoped would "join heartily in Sustaining Such a movement." His hope was misplaced. The black leaders responded swiftly with widespread antipathy to the proposal. As the *Liberator* eloquently argued, the nation's 4 million slaves "are as much the natives of the country as any of their oppressors. Here they were born; here, by every consideration of justice and humanity, they are entitled to live; and here it is for them to die in the course of nature." One might "as well attempt to roll back Niagara to its source, or to cast the Allegheny mountains into the sea, as to think of driving or enticing them out of the country." How pathetic, the *Liberator* noted, that the president of a country "sufficiently capacious to contain the present population of the globe," a nation that "proudly boasts of being the refuge of the oppressed of all nations," should consider exiling "the entire colored population . . . to a distant shore."

Reports of Lincoln's dialogue with the black delegation provoked Frederick Douglass to his most caustic assault yet on the president. While acknowledging that this was the first time blacks had been invited for a hearing at the White House, he accused Lincoln of making "ridiculous" comments showing a "pride of race and blood" and a "contempt for negroes." The president "ought to know," Douglass argued, "that negro hatred and prejudice of color are neither original nor invincible vices, but merely the offshoots of that root of all crimes and evils—slavery. If the colored people instead of having been stolen and forcibly brought to the United States had come as free immigrants, like the German and the Irish, never thought of as suitable objects of property, they never would have become the objects of aversion and bitter persecution."

Lincoln's remarkable empathy had singularly failed him in this initial approach to the impending consequences of emancipation. Though he had tried to put himself in the place of blacks and suggest what *he* thought was best for them, his lack of contact with the black community left him unaware of their deep attachment to their country and sense of outrage at the thought of removal. In time, Lincoln's friendship with Frederick Douglass and personal contact with hundreds of black soldiers willing to give up their lives for their freedom would create a deeper understanding of his black countrymen that would allow him to cast off forever his thoughts of colonization.

Even as he addressed the black delegation that August, Lincoln may not have been convinced that colonization was a feasible option. He recognized, however, that the mere suggestion of the plan might provide the "drop of honey" to make the prospect of emancipation more palatable. Chase would accept no such concession. "How much better would be a manly protest against prejudice against color!—and a wise effort to give freemen homes in America!" he wrote in his diary after reading Lincoln's colonization discussion. Count Gurowski was even harsher in his condemnation, characterizing Lincoln's talk of racial incompatibility as cheap "clap-trap," revealing a disturbing "display of ignorance or of humbug, or perhaps of both," unworthy of a president.

The most sensational criticism, however, came from Horace Greeley. He published an open letter to the president in the *New York Tribune* on August 20, which he entitled "The Prayer of Twenty Millions." Claiming to speak for his vast readership, he decried the policy Lincoln seemed "to be pursuing with regard to the slaves," which, "unduly influenced by the counsels . . . of certain fossil politicians hailing from the Border Slave States," failed to recognize that "all attempts to put down the Rebellion and at the same time uphold its inciting cause [slavery] are preposterous and futile."

Lincoln decided to reply to Greeley's letter, seizing the opportunity to begin instructing the public on the vital link between emancipation and military necessity. "As to the policy I 'seem to be pursuing' as you say, I have not meant to leave anyone in doubt," he began. "My paramount object in this struggle *is* to save the Union, and is *not* either to save or to destroy slavery. If I could save the Union without freeing *any* slave I would do it, and if I could save it by freeing *all* the slaves I would do it; and if I could save it by freeing some and leaving others alone I would also do that. What I do about slavery, and the colored race, I do because it helps to save the Union; and what I forbear, I forbear because I do *not* believe it would help to save the Union. I shall do *less* whenever I shall believe what I am doing hurts the cause, and I shall do *more* whenever I shall believe doing more will help the cause."

Having already decided upon emancipation, Lincoln hoped that his letter would soften the public impact of what he knew would be a controversial proclamation. Abolitionists, unaware that Lincoln had already committed himself to a path that would "do *more*" than even they had hoped, were infuriated by his response. "I am sorry the President answered Mr. Greeley," Frances Seward complained to her husband; "his letter hardly does him justice . . . he gives the impression that the mere keeping together a number of states is more important than human freedom."

Seward had argued this very issue with his zealous wife for many months. At home in June, he had apparently suggested that the preservation of republican institutions must supersede the immediate abolition of slavery. Though he had fought slavery all his life, Seward hesitated when faced with the possibility that moving too precipitously toward abolition might destroy the republic itself and all that it stood for on the stage of world history. He had no doubt that slavery would eventually be brought to an end. Indeed, he believed the future of slavery had been "killed years ago" by the progress of civilization. "But suppose, for one moment," he later explained, "the Republic destroyed. With it is bound up not alone the destiny of a race, but the best hopes of all mankind. With its overthrow the sun of liberty, like the Hebrew dial, would be set back indefinitely. The magnitude of such a calamity is beyond our calculation. The salvation of the nation is, then, of vastly more consequence than the destruction of slavery."

Frances profoundly disagreed with this balancing equation, asserting there could be no "truly republican" institutions with slavery intact—"they are incompatible." Sometime during that long, anxious summer, she recorded her exhortations in a note to her husband. "Whatever may be the principles in the determination of the President in this matter," she wrote, "you owe it to yourself & your children & your country & to God to make your record clear." If the president refused to act on slavery, "it would be far better for you to resign your place tomorrow than by continuing there seem to give countenance to a great moral evil."

Frances had no intimation that Lincoln's views on the relationship between emancipation and republican institutions had already evolved beyond those of her husband. For despite the continued criticism of his inaction on slavery, Lincoln kept his proclamation concealed until victory could offer the propitious moment. Everything depended on the success of his army.

CHAPTER 18

"MY WORD IS OUT"

L INCOLN PINNED HIS HOPES for the victory that would allow him to issue his Emancipation Proclamation on the newly assembled Army of Virginia, headed by General John Pope. In the Western theater, Pope had demonstrated the aggression McClellan lacked. Early August 1862, Halleck ordered McClellan to withdraw his entire army by steamship from Harrison's Landing to Aquia Creek and Alexandria, thus ending the Peninsula Campaign. Once there, McClellan was to rendezvous with Pope, who would be pushing south from Manassas toward Richmond along the interior route Lincoln had initially favored.

Joined together, the two armies would substantially outnumber General Lee's forces.

But McClellan stalled, fearing that Pope would be placed in charge of the merged army. He argued ferociously against the move, warning Halleck it would "prove disastrous in the extreme." His only hope, he confided to his wife, was that he might "induce the enemy to attack" before he reached Washington and was relieved of his command. After delaying for ten days with strategic protests and claims of insufficient transports, he grudgingly began his withdrawal on August 14, not reaching Aquia Creek until August 24.

Realizing that he would be overpowered by the combined armies, General Lee moved north from Richmond to engage Pope before McClellan reached him. By August 18, the Confederate forces, under Generals Stonewall Jackson and James Longstreet, had come within striking distance of Pope. Only the Rappahannock River, midway between Washington and Richmond, separated the two forces. From the security of the northern riverbank, Pope waited in vain for McClellan's troops to reinforce what everyone hoped would be a major offensive.

Lee capitalized brilliantly on McClellan's delay. Leaving Longstreet's forces in front of Pope, he sent Jackson behind Pope's lines to capture the Union's supply base at Manassas Junction and then assemble in the woods near the old Bull Run battlefield. In a state of confusion, Pope left the Rappahannock and headed north, where he would encounter the combined forces of Lee, Longstreet, and Jackson. "What is the stake?" Seward wrote Frances. "They say that it is nothing less than this capital; and, as many think, the *cause also.*" While soldiers on both sides waited for the fighting to begin, a comet appeared in the northern sky. Lincoln, so familiar with Shakespeare, doubtless recalled Calpurnia's ominous warning to Caesar: "When beggars die there are no comets seen/The heavens themselves blaze forth the death of princes."

Although McClellan agreed to send two corps to Pope, he continued to delay, awaiting word on his own status as commander. If his troops were integrated into Pope's army, he told his wife on August 24, he would "try for a leave of absence!" Everything would change, however, if "Pope is beaten, in which case they may want me to save Washn again."

The Second Battle of Bull Run began in earnest on Friday, August 29. When the wind blew from the west, "the smell of the gunpowder was quite perceptible," the *Evening Star* reported, and the "distant thunder" of cannonfire was plainly audible throughout Washington. Crowds gathered on street corners and huddled in the great hotels. In the absence of reliable information from the front, rumors flew. At one moment, newsboys announced that "Stonewall Jackson was captured with 16,000 of his men." Minutes later, it was said that Jackson had crushed Pope and was heading north to capture Washington. Stories of victory and defeat for each side "alternated in about equal proportions."

These were disquieting days for the president. The manager of the War Department telegraph office recalled that Lincoln spent long hours in the crowded second-floor suite awaiting bulletins from the front, "prepared to stay all night, if necessary." He wired various generals, including McClellan, who had set up his headquarters at Alexandria, requesting news from Manassas. McClellan responded immediately, providing advice rather than information. The president now had only two options, McClellan counseled. Either he must "concentrate all our available forces to open communication with Pope," or he should "leave Pope to get out of his scrape & at once use all our means to make the capital perfectly safe."

On Saturday morning, John Hay met the president at the Soldiers' Home and rode with him to the White House. During the ride, Lincoln "was very outspoken in regard to McClellan's present conduct," saying that "it really seemed to him that McC wanted Pope defeated." He was particularly incensed, Lincoln told Hay, by McClellan's advice to "leave Pope to get out of his own scrape."

Lincoln's condemnation was mild, however, compared to the rage Stanton directed toward the general he now considered a traitor. McClellan's delay in bringing his troops to Pope's defense prompted the secretary of war to approach General Halleck for an official report. He asked Halleck to specify the exact date upon which McClellan had received orders to withdraw from the James, and to render an opinion as to whether the order was obeyed with a promptness commensurate with national safety. Halleck replied that the order given on August 3 "was not obeyed with the promptness I expected and the national safety, in my opinion, required."

Armed with Halleck's report, Stanton took Chase into his confidence. The two old friends decided that McClellan must be removed at once, and that they would have to force Lincoln's hand. Agreeing that verbal arguments with Lincoln were "like throwing water on a duck's back," they decided that "a more decisive expression must be made and that in writing." Stanton volunteered to draft a remonstrance against McClellan, to be signed, if possible, by a majority of the cabinet. They would present it to Lincoln with the inference that General McClellan's continued command would lead to the resignation of some cabinet members, and even the dissolution of the administration. Meanwhile, Stanton and Chase journeyed to Bates's F Street home, hoping to enlist his support. Finding that he was out, they left word for him to call on Chase the following morning.

When Bates stopped by the Treasury office early Saturday morning, Chase was delighted to learn that he was in full agreement regarding McClellan. "Never before was there such a grand army, composed of truly excellent materials, and yet," Bates complained, "so poorly commanded." To his mind, McClellan had "but one of the three Roman requisites for a general, he is young. I fear not brave, and surely not fortunate." Moreover, Bates agreed with Chase and Stanton that "unless there be very soon a change for the better, we [the administration] must sink into contempt." Certain now that Bates was a staunch ally in the cause of McClellan's dismissal, Chase proceeded to the War Department, where Stanton had completed a first draft of the letter.

The scathing document, written in Stanton's distinctive back-sloping script with words added and erased, declared that the undersigned were "unwilling to be accessory to the waste of natural resources, the protraction of the war, the destruction of our armies, and the imperiling of the Union which we believe must result from the continuance of George B. McClellan in command." It charged McClellan with willful "disobedience to superior orders," which had "imperiled the army commanded by General Pope." Chase made several suggestions for changes, affixed his signature above Stanton's, and promised to bring it to Bates, Smith, and Welles.

Having long since lost faith in McClellan, Smith was persuaded immediately to add his signature. Climbing the narrow stairs to the navy secretary's second-floor office later that afternoon, Chase reached him just as he was preparing to leave for the day. After reading the document, Welles assured Chase that he believed McClellan's "withdrawal from any command was demanded," but he "did not choose to denounce McC. for incapacity or declare him a traitor," as the document seemed to proclaim. Even when Chase repeated the damning facts of McClellan's fatal delay in moving to reinforce Pope, Welles hesitated. He pointedly asked whether Blair had seen the document. Chase replied that his "turn had not come." At that very moment, while Welles still held the document, Blair walked in. Sensing Chase's alarm, Welles kept the paper close to his chest until Blair departed only a few minutes later. With the postmaster general out of earshot, Chase entreated Welles not to mention the document to Blair or anyone else.

While Chase was performing his part in the intrigue, Stanton had invited Lincoln and Hay to his K Street home for an impromptu dinner. No clear information on the course of the battle was yet available, though preliminary reports suggested that Pope had gained the advantage. "A pleasant little dinner," Hay recorded, "and a pretty wife as white and cold and motionless as marble, whose rare smiles seemed to pain her." In conversation with Lincoln, Stanton was "unqualifiedly severe upon McClellan," charging that "nothing but foul play could lose us this battle & that it rested with McC. and his friends." Both Stanton and Lincoln expressed their strong belief in General Pope.

After dinner, the president and Hay went to army headquarters, where General Halleck appeared "quiet and somewhat confident" about the direction of what he considered "the greatest battle of the Century." Proceeding to Stanton's office, they found he had dispatched "a vast army of Volunteer Nurses out to the field" to help care for the sick and wounded. "Every thing seemed to be going well," Hay reported, "& we went to bed expecting glad tidings at sunrise."

For Stanton, however, much work was in store that evening. If Pope managed to win without McClellan's aid, it would only strengthen the argument for the young Napoleon's ouster. When Welles stopped by to get an update from the front, he found Stanton with Smith. Stanton launched into a long diatribe against McClellan, reaching back to the winter doldrums, the "Quaker gun" affair, and the blunders on the Peninsula. When Smith left, Welles recalled, Stanton lowered his voice to a whisper. He had previously learned from Chase that Welles had refused to sign the document. Welles explained that while he, by and large, agreed that McClellan must be removed, he "disliked the method and manner of proceeding." It seemed "discourteous and disrespectful to the President." The president, he declared, "had called us around him as friends and advisers to counsel and consult . . . not to enter into combinations against him."

Agitated, Stanton exclaimed that "he knew of no particular obligations he was under to the President who had called him to a difficult position and imposed upon him labors and responsibilities which no man could carry, and which were greatly increased by fastening upon him a commander who was constantly striving to embarrass him. . . . He could not and would not submit to a continuance of this state of things." Welles sympathized but was highly reluctant to join what seemed a cabal against the president.

The next morning, bleak news from the battlefield discredited the optimistic reports of the previous day. Pope's army had been crushed. John Hay recorded in his diary that at "about Eight oclock the President came to my room as I was dressing and calling me out said, 'Well John we are whipped again, I am afraid.' " Once again, as in the aftermath of the First Battle of Bull Run, Washington braced for attack. As rumors spread that General Jackson was crossing the Potomac at Georgetown, thousands of frightened residents began to flee the city. Soldiers straggled in from the front with tales of a demoralized army and units unwilling to fight under

Pope. The losses were immense—out of 65,000 men, the Federals had suffered 16,000 casualties. Momentum now clearly belonged to the Confederacy. At the end of June, the *New York Times* pointed out, "Jeff. Davis, from his chamber at Richmond, listened to the thunder of the cannon of hostile armies battling before his capital." At the end of August, "Lincoln, from the White House, heard the deep peals of the artillery of the contending hosts which, having now changed location, are struggling for supremacy before the National Capital."

The devastating defeat put the president in an untenable position. The more he contemplated McClellan's delay in sending his troops to Pope, the angrier he became. Yet there was no time to indulge in anger while Washington itself was threatened and he sorely needed the best forces at his disposal. He still believed McClellan was best equipped to reorganize the demoralized troops. During his inspection tours at Fort Monroe and Harrison's Landing, Lincoln had witnessed the soldiers' devotion to their commander. "There is no man in the army who can man these fortifications and lick these troops of ours into shape half as well as he," Lincoln told Hay. "Unquestionably he has acted badly toward Pope! He wanted him to fail. That is unpardonable. But he is too useful just now to sacrifice." When Halleck recommended restoring McClellan's command over both the Army of Virginia and the Army of the Potomac, Lincoln agreed.

In ignorance of Lincoln's deliberations, the cabinet vigorously pursued their machinations to oust McClellan. Bates rewrote the protest to soften its tone. Stanton, Chase, Smith, and Bates signed the new document, which Chase again presented to Welles on Monday, September 1. Welles agreed that the new draft was "an improvement," but still disliked the idea of "combining to influence or control the President." Chase admitted that the course of action "was unusual, but the case was unusual." They had to impress upon Lincoln that "the Administration must be broken up, or McC. dismissed." Furthermore, Chase told Welles that "McClellan ought to be shot, and should, were he President, be brought to a summary punishment." Welles granted that McClellan "was not a fighting general," and that "some recent acts indicate delinquencies of a more serious character." While he would not sign the demand, he told the "disappointed" Chase, he would speak up with "no hesitation" at the cabinet meeting the next day to tell Lincoln that he agreed McClellan should go. Accordingly, Stanton and Chase resolved to withhold their confrontation with Lincoln until the following day.

All the cabinet members, save Seward, gathered at noon on Tuesday the 2nd. The secretary of state had departed for Auburn the previous week for a long-awaited vacation. Welles, perpetually suspicious of Seward, believed "there was design in his absence," certain he had left town to avoid the messy controversy over McClellan. More likely, personal considerations dictated the timing of Seward's journey. Jenny was expecting his first grandchild any day. Will was scheduled to leave with his regiment as soon as the baby was born. And Frances's favorite aunt, Clara, was dying. When he heard about the defeat at Bull Run, however, he cut his vacation short. He was on his way back to Washington as the cabinet meeting convened.

The session had barely begun when the president was called out for a brief interval. In his absence, Stanton took the floor. Speaking "in a suppressed voice, trembling with excitement," he informed his colleagues that "McClellan had been ordered to take command of the forces in Washington." The members were stunned. Lincoln returned shortly and explained his decision, which he had communicated to McClellan at 7 a.m. that morning. "McClellan knows this whole ground," Lincoln said, and "can be trusted to act on the defensive." He knew all too well that McClellan had the "slows," but maintained that there was "no better organizer." Events, he believed, would justify his judgment.

In the general discussion that followed, Welles recorded in his diary, "there was a more disturbed and desponding feeling" than he had ever witnessed in any cabinet meeting. Lincoln was "extremely distressed," as were Stanton and Chase. Chase predicted that "it would prove a national calamity," while Stanton, recognizing that the protest was a dead letter, returned to the War Department "in the condition of a drooping leaf." The episode produced an estrangement between Stanton and Lincoln that persisted for weeks.

Lincoln was deeply troubled by the knowledge that his cabinet opposed him on a question of such vital importance. According to Bates, he "seemed wrung by the bitterest anguish—said he felt almost ready to hang himself." The cabinet debacle regarding McClellan, Pope's defeat, and the gruesome, protracted war itself pressed upon him with an appalling weight, leading him to meditate. "In great contests," he wrote in a fragment found among his pages, "each party claims to act in accordance with the will of God. Both *may* be, and one *must* be wrong. God can not be *for*, and *against* the same thing at the same time. In the present civil war it is quite possible that God's purpose is something different from the purpose of either party," and that God had willed "that it shall not end yet."

Lincoln's distress may have been assuaged somewhat by Seward's return to Washington. Lincoln could speak more frankly with his secretary than with any other member of his cabinet. Reaching the capital on the evening of September 3, Seward drove immediately to the Soldiers' Home. Unfortunately, Fred Seward wrote, "there were visitors, whose presence prevented private talk."

"Governor," Lincoln proposed, "I'll get in and ride with you a while." For the next few hours, the two friends drove along the winding carriage ways, "while Seward detailed what he had found at the North, and the President in turn narrated the military events and Cabinet conferences during his absence."

Seward may have revealed to Lincoln the sad, world-wise reflections he expressed to John Hay two days later. "What is the use of growing old?" he asked. "You learn something of men and things but never until too late to use it." Referring to the antagonism between McClellan and Pope that had contributed to the disaster at Bull Run, Seward admitted that he had "only just now found out what military jealousy is. . . . It had never occurred to [him] that any jealousy could prevent these generals from acting for their common fame and the welfare of the country." As an old seasoned politician, perhaps, he reflected, he "should have known it."

Though Seward was temporarily unnerved by the events at Bull Run, he remained confident that the North would ultimately prevail—a contagious confidence that must have bolstered Lincoln's spirits. Whenever faced with desolating prospects, Seward turned to history for guidance and comfort. Recalling the difficult days of the Revolutionary War before independence "enables me," he once said, "to cherish and preserve hopefulness." Moreover, unlike his colleagues in the cabinet, Seward did not question that Lincoln possessed the prudence, wisdom, and magnanimity needed to carry the country "safely through the sea of revolution." Seward's ability to empathize with Lincoln's unenviable position must have afforded Lincoln some real measure of comfort. Unlike Stanton and Chase, Seward clearly understood that a president had to work with the tools at his disposal. At this moment, McClellan was one of those tools.

Meanwhile, McClellan smugly returned to his old headquarters on the corner next to Seward's house. "Again I have been called upon to save the country," he wrote his wife. "It makes my heart bleed to see the poor shattered remnants of my noble Army of the Potomac, poor fellows! and to see how they love me even now. I hear them calling out to me as I ride among them—'George—don't leave us again!' 'They *shan't* take you away from us again.' "

McClellan had been restored to command for only two days when Lee, emboldened by his twin victories on the Peninsula and at Bull Run, crossed the Potomac to begin an invasion of Maryland. The Confederate commander mistakenly assumed that the residents of the slave state would rise up in support of his army. In fact, the Marylanders greeted the rebel army with disdain and reserved their enthusiastic welcome for McClellan's bluecoats, clapping and waving flags as the Federal troops marched through their countryside to engage Lee in battle. When the two armies met, McClellan had another distinct advantage. General Lee's battle plans had been discovered. A careless courier had used the orders to wrap three cigars and left them behind.

On September 17, the Battle of Antietam began. "We are in the midst of the most terrible battle of the age," McClellan wrote Mary Ellen in midafternoon as the fighting raged. By day's end, 6,000 soldiers on both sides were dead and an additional 17,000 had been wounded, a staggering total four times the number of Americans who would lose their lives on D-day during World War II. In the end, the Union Army prevailed, forcing Lee to retreat. "Our victory was complete," McClellan joyfully reported. "I feel some little pride in having with a beaten and demoralized army defeated Lee so utterly, & saved the North so completely."

Lincoln was thrilled by initial reports that indicated Lee's army might be destroyed. Subsequent telegrams, however, revealed that McClellan, flush with victory, had failed to pursue the retreating rebels and allowed Lee to cross the Potomac into Virginia, where he could regroup and replenish men and supplies.

Still, Antietam was a sorely needed victory for the demoralized North. "At last our Generals in the field seem to have risen to the grandeur of the National crisis," the *New York Times* noted. "Sept. 17, 1862, will, we predict, hereafter be looked upon as an epoch in the history of the rebellion, from which will date the inauguration of its downfall."

The statement would prove prescient for reasons the *Times* could not have surmised. The victory, incomplete as it was, was the long-awaited event that provided Lincoln the occasion to announce his plans to issue an Emancipation Proclamation the following January. On September 22, he convened a cabinet meeting to reveal his decision. As Chase and Stanton settled on his right and the others sat down on his left, Lincoln attempted to lighten the mood with a reading from the Maine humorist Charles Farrar Browne. Seward alone readily appreciated the diversion, laughing uproariously along with Lincoln at the antics of Artemus Ward. Chase assumed a forced smile, while Stanton's face betrayed impatience and irritation.

Once his humorous story was done, Lincoln took on "a graver tone," reminding his colleagues of the emancipation order he had drafted and read to them earlier. He told them that when Lee's army was in Maryland, he had decided "as soon as it should be driven out" of the state, he would issue his proclamation. "I said nothing to any one; but I made the promise to myself, and (hesitating a little) to my Maker." While Lincoln rarely ac-knowledged the influence of faith or religious beliefs, "there were occa-sions when, uncertain how to proceed," remarked Gideon Welles, "he had in this way submitted the disposal of the subject to a Higher Power, and abided by what seemed the Supreme Will." The president made clear he was not seeking "advice about the main matter," for he had already consid-ered their views before reaching his decision; but he would welcome any suggestions on language. Lincoln then began to read the document that he had revised slightly in recent weeks to strengthen the rationale of military necessity.

Stanton "made a very emphatic speech sustaining the measure," and Blair reiterated his concerns about the border states and the fall elections, though in the end he filed no objection. Seward alone suggested a substan-tive change. Wouldn't it be stronger, he asked, if the government promised not only to recognize but to "maintain" the freedom of the former slaves, leaving "out all reference to the act being sustained during the incumbency of the present President"? Lincoln answered that he had thought about this, but "it was not my way to promise what I was not entirely *sure* that I could perform." When Seward "insisted that we ought to take this ground," Lincoln agreed, striking the limiting reference to the present ad-ministration.

The preliminary proclamation, published the following day, brought a large crowd of cheering serenaders to the White House. Though it would not take effect until Lincoln issued the final proclamation on January 1, 1863, giving the rebellious states one last chance to return to the Union, it had changed the course of the war. "I can only trust in God I have made no mistake," Lincoln told well-wishers from an upstairs window. "It is now for the country and the world to pass judgment on it." He then called at-tention to the brave soldiers in the field. While he might be "environed with difficulties" as president, these were "scarcely so great as the difficul-ties of those who, upon the battle field, are endeavoring to purchase with their blood and their lives the future happiness and prosperity of this coun-try. Let us never forget them."

The serenaders proceeded to Chase's house at Sixth and E, where the large crowd listened "in a glorious humor" as Chase spoke. Afterward, an excited group, including Bates and "a few old fogies," remained inside, drinking wine. "They all seemed to feel a sort of new and exhilarated life," John Hay observed. "They gleefully and merrily called each other and themselves abolitionists, and seemed to enjoy the novel sensation of ap-propriating that horrible name."

Many radicals, including Count Gurowski and William Fessenden, remained wary of Lincoln. Gurowski complained that the proclamation was written "in the meanest and the most dry routine style; not a word to evoke a generous thrill," while Fessenden remarked that it "did not and could not affect the status of a single negro." Nevertheless, Frederick Douglass, whose criticism of Lincoln had been implacable, understood the revolutionary impact of the proclamation. "We shout for joy that we live to record this righteous decree," he wrote in his *Monthly*. Anticipating the powerful opposition it would encounter, he asked: "Will it lead the President to reconsider and retract." "No," he concluded, "Abraham Lincoln, will take no step backward." Intuitively grasping Lincoln's character, though they were not yet personally acquainted, Douglass explained that "Abraham Lincoln may be slow . . . but Abraham Lincoln is not the man to reconsider, retract and contradict words and purposes solemnly proclaimed over his official signature. . . . If he has taught us to confide in nothing else, he has taught us to confide in his word." Lincoln confirmed this assessment when he told Massachusetts congressman George Boutwell, "My word is out to these people, and I can't take it back."

Opposition came from the expected sources: conservatives feared the proclamation would "render eternal the hatred between the two sections," while Democrats predicted it would demoralize the army. Needless to say, an outcry arose in the South. The *Richmond Enquirer* charged Lincoln with inciting an insurrection that would inevitably lead, as with Nat Turner's uprising, to slaves being hunted down "like wild beasts" and killed. "Cheerful and happy now, he plots their death," the paper accused. None of this surprised Lincoln. Analyzing the range of editorial opinion, he "said he had studied the matter so long that he knew more about it than they did." When Vice President Hannibal Hamlin wrote that the proclamation would "be enthusiastically approved and sustained" and would "stand as the great act of the age," Lincoln replied that "while commendation in newspapers and by distinguished individuals is all that a vain man could wish, the stocks have declined, and troops come forward more slowly than ever. This, looked soberly in the face, is not very satisfactory."

• • •

As McClellan rested his troops in the vicinity of Antietam, he pondered his situation. Convinced that his military reputation had been fully restored by the recent victory, he believed it was his prerogative to insist that "Stanton must leave & that Halleck must restore my old place to me." If these two demands were not met, he told his wife, he would resign his commission. Furthermore, he could not bear the idea of fighting for "such an accursed doctrine" as the Emancipation Proclamation, which he considered an "infamous" call for "a servile insurrection." Indignant, McClellan drafted a letter of protest to Lincoln, declaring himself in opposition. After old friends, including Monty Blair and his father, warned him that it would be ruinous not to submit to the president's policy, he ultimately decided not to send the letter.

McClellan had overestimated his newfound clout. Though Stanton and Chase were so discouraged by the general's apparently unassailable position that they both considered resigning, Lincoln had made another private decision. If McClellan did not mobilize in pursuit of General Lee, which, as September gave way to October, he showed no sign of doing, he would be relieved from duty.

Hoping that a personal visit would inspire McClellan to action, Lincoln journeyed by train to the general's headquarters early in October. Though Halleck, fearing danger, opposed the idea, Lincoln was determined to "slip off . . . and see my soldiers." As always, he was fortified by his interactions with the troops. As the regiments presented arms to the beating of drums, the president, accompanied by McClellan, slowly rode by, lifting his hat. "The review was a splendid affair throughout," one correspondent noted. "The troops, notwithstanding their long marches and hard fighting, presented a fine appearance, for which they were highly complimented. The President indulged in a number of humorous anecdotes, which greatly amused the company."

Sharing McClellan's quarters for meals and occupying the adjoining tent at night, Lincoln quietly but candidly prompted his general to discard his "over-cautiousness" and plan for future movement. While McClellan conceded in a letter to his wife that Lincoln "was very affable" and "very kind personally," he rightly suspected that the "real purpose of his visit is to push me into a premature advance into Virginia."

Lincoln headed back to Washington on Saturday afternoon in high spirits, encouraged by the good condition of the troops. His train stopped at the tiny town of Frederick along the way, where he was greeted by a large crowd of cheering citizens, eager to demonstrate Maryland's loyalty to the Union. Called upon to speak, Lincoln replied cheerfully that "if I were as I have been most of my life, I might perhaps, talk amusing to you for half an hour," but as president, "every word is so closely noted" that he must avoid any "trivial" remarks. Nevertheless, before the train pulled away, he delivered a brief, eloquent speech from the platform of his car, thanking soldiers and citizens alike for their fidelity to the Union's cause. "May our children and our children's children to a thousand generations," he said in closing, "continue to enjoy the benefits conferred upon us by a united country, and have cause yet to rejoice under those glorious institutions bequeathed us by Washington and his compeers."

To ensure that McClellan would not misconstrue their conversations, Lincoln had Halleck telegraph him the following Monday that "the President directs that you cross the Potomac and give battle to the enemy or drive him south. Your army must move now while the roads are good." Weeks went by, however, and McClellan found all manner of excuses for inaction—lack of supplies, lack of shoes, tired horses. At this last excuse, Lincoln could no longer contain his irritation. "Will you pardon me for asking what the horses of your army have done since the battle of Antietam that fatigue anything?"

"Our war on rebellion languishes," a frustrated George Templeton Strong wrote on October 23. "McClellan's repose is doubtless majestic, but if a couchant lion postpone his spring too long, people will begin wondering whether he is not a stuffed specimen after all." The army's inaction combined with conservative resentment against the Emancipation Proclamation to produce what Seward called an "ill wind" of discontent when voters headed to the polls for the midterm November elections. The results were devastating to the administration. Though Republicans retained a slight majority in Congress, the so-called "Peace Democrats," who favored a compromise that would tolerate slavery, gained critical offices in Illinois, New York, Pennsylvania, Ohio, and Indiana. Asked how he felt about the Republican losses, Lincoln said: "Somewhat like that boy in Kentucky, who stubbed his toe while running to see his sweetheart. The boy said he was too big to cry, and far too badly hurt to laugh."

The following day, with the midterm elections behind him, Lincoln relieved McClellan of his command of the Army of the Potomac. Though the young Napoleon had finally crossed the Potomac, he had immediately stalled again. "I began to fear he was playing false—that he did not want to hurt the enemy," Lincoln told Hay. "I saw how he could intercept the enemy on the way to Richmond. I determined to make that the test. If he let them get away I would remove him. He did so & I relieved him."

McClellan received the telegram in his tent at 11 p.m., in the company of the man Lincoln had chosen to succeed him: General Ambrose Burnside. Known as a fighting general, Burnside had commanded a corps under McClellan on the Peninsula and at Antietam. "Poor Burn feels dreadfully, almost crazy," McClellan told his wife. "Of course I was much surprised," he admitted, but "not a muscle quivered nor was the slightest expression of feeling visible on my face."

"More than a hundred thousand soldiers are in great grief to-night," the correspondent for the *National Intelligencer* reported as General McClellan bade farewell to his staff and his troops. With all his officers assembled around a large fire in front of his tent, he raised a glass of wine. "Here's to the Army of the Potomac," he proposed. "And to its old commander," one of his officers added. "Tears were shed in profusion," both at the final toast and when McClellan rode past the lines of his troops. "In parting from you," he told them, "I cannot express the love and gratitude I bear for you. As an Army you have grown up under my care. . . . The glory you have achieved, our mutual perils & fatigues, the graves of our comrades fallen in battle & by disease, the broken forms of those whom wounds & sickness have disabled—the strongest associations which can exist among men, unite us still by an indissoluble tie."

Lincoln's choice of Burnside proved unfortunate. Though he was charismatic, honest, and industrious, he lacked the intelligence and confidence to lead a great army. He was said to possess "ten times as much *heart* as he has *head*." On December 13, against Lincoln's advice, the new commander led about 122,000 troops across the Rappahannock to Fredericksburg, where General Lee waited on the heavily fortified high ground. Caught in a trap, the Union forces suffered 13,000 casualties, more than twice the Confederate losses, and were forced into a humiliating withdrawal.

Lincoln tried to mitigate the impact of the defeat, issuing a public letter of commendation to the troops: "The courage with which you, in an open field, maintained the contest against an entrenched foe . . . [shows] that you possess all the qualities of a great army, which will yet give victory to the cause of the country and of popular government." Even as he did the "awful arithmetic" of the relative losses, Lincoln realized, as he told William Stoddard, "that if the same battle were to be fought over again, every day, through a week of days, with the same relative results, the army under Lee would be wiped out to its last man, the Army of the Potomac would still be a mighty host, the war would be over, the Confederacy gone."

• • •

THE TRAIN OF RECRIMINATIONS that followed the Fredericksburg defeat led to a crisis for the administration that left Lincoln "more depressed," he said, "than by any event of [his] life." Radical Republicans on Capitol Hill began to insist that unless a more vigorous prosecution of the war were adopted, conservative demands for a compromise peace would multiply and the Union would be restored with slavery intact. The midterm elections, they argued, demonstrated growing public dissatisfaction with current tactics—the writing, clearly, was on the wall.

On the afternoon of Tuesday, December 16, all the Republican senators caucused in the high-ceilinged Senate reception room, hoping to devise a unified response to the disastrous situation. Without sweeping changes in the administration, they agreed, "the country was ruined and the cause was lost." Hesitant to publicly attack Lincoln in the midst of war, they focused their fury on the man they considered the malevolent power behind the throne—William Henry Seward. For months, Chase had claimed "there was a back stairs & malign influence which controlled the President, and overruled all the decisions of the cabinet," a hardly veiled reference to Seward. In private letters that had quickly become public knowledge, Chase had repeatedly griped about Lincoln's failure to consult the cabinet "on matters concerning the salvation of the country," intimating that his own councils would have averted the misfortunes now facing the country and the party.

In Republican circles, word spread that Seward was a "paralizing influence on the army and the President." He was rumored to be the "President *de facto*," responsible for the long delay in dismissing McClellan that led to stagnation and loss on the battlefield. Seward was said to have hindered Lincoln's intention to make the war a crusade for emancipation, and was deemed responsible for the resurgence of the conservatives in the midterm elections. In sum, Seward's insidious presence "kept a sponge saturated with chloroform to Uncle Abe's nose."

In the minds of the majority of the Republicans gathered together in the reception room that December afternoon, these rumors had congealed into facts. As one senator after another rose to speak of Seward's "controlling influence upon the mind of the President," Ben Wade suggested that they "should go in a body and demand of the President the dismissal of Mr Seward." Duty dictated that they exercise their constitutional power, as William Fessenden professed, to demand "that measures should be taken to make the Cabinet a unity and to remove from it any one who did not coincide heartily with our views in relation to the war." As the rhetoric grew more heated, Senator James W. Grimes of Iowa introduced a resolution proclaiming "a want of confidence in the Secretary of State" and concluding that "he ought to be removed from the Cabinet."

Fessenden asked for a vote, which clearly indicated that an overwhelming majority of the thirty-one senators were in favor. Seward's friend New York senator Preston King objected that the resolution was not only "hasty and unwise" but also "unjust to Mr. Seward, as it was predicated on mere rumors." Several others agreed. Orville Browning argued that he "had no evidence the charges were true," and therefore could not vote for the resolution. Moreover, this "was not the proper course of proceeding" and would likely provoke a "war between Congress and the President, and the knowledge of this antagonism would injure our cause greatly." Recognizing that "without entire unanimity our action would not only be without force but productive of evil," Fessenden agreed to adjourn until the following afternoon to "give time for reflection."

Though the proceedings were to be kept secret, Preston King felt compelled to acquaint Seward with the situation. That evening, he went to Seward's house. Finding his old colleague in the library, he sat down beside him and told him all that had transpired. Seward listened quietly and then said, "They may do as they please about me, but they shall not put the President in a false position on my account." Asking for pen and paper, he wrote out his resignation as secretary of state and asked his son Fred and King to deliver it to the White House.

Lincoln scanned the resignation "with a face full of pain and surprise, saying 'What does this mean?' " After listening to Senator King's description of the overwrought emotions that had created "a thirst for a victim," Lincoln walked over to Seward's house. The meeting was painful for both men. Masking his anguish, Seward told Lincoln that "it would be a relief to be freed from official cares." Lincoln replied: "Ah, yes, Governor, that will do very well for you, but I am like the starling in [Laurence] Sterne's story, 'I can't get out.' "

Lincoln straightaway understood that he was the true target of the radicals' wrath. "They wish to get rid of me, and I am sometimes half disposed to gratify them," he told Browning two days later. He described the chatter setting forth Seward's controlling influence over him as "a lie, an absurd lie," that one "could not impose upon a child." Seward was the one man in the cabinet Lincoln trusted completely, the only one who fully appreciated his unusual strengths as a leader, and the only one he could call an intimate friend. Still, he could scarcely afford to antagonize the Republican senators so essential to his governing coalition. He had to think through his options. He had to learn more about the dynamics of the situation.

Seward was greatly "disappointed," Welles sensed, "that the President did not promptly refuse to consider his resignation." The hesitation compounded the pain of the unexpected assault from his old colleagues on the Hill, leaving him noticeably "wounded, mortified, and chagrined." Fortunately, Frances had journeyed to Washington the week before to look after their son Will, who had contracted typhoid fever in his army camp six miles from the capital. Fanny, who had just turned eighteen, remained in Auburn with Jenny and the baby. The two women were due to leave Auburn for Washington a few days later to join the family for Christmas.

As Fanny and Jenny were packing their things, Fred sent a hurried

telegram to Fanny: "Do not come at present." F
resignation as assistant secretary of state, and Fi.
gram with a letter telling Fanny that her father "th
serve his country at present by resigning," and that the,
shortly for Auburn. Disconcerted by her father's abrupt dep
worried greatly. "It seemed to me that if he were to leave," she i.
diary, "the distracted state of affairs would prey upon his spirit.
more. I had a vague fear that he would come home ill, and longed to
him with my own eyes, safe. Spent a restless & uncomfortable night."

In some ways, Seward had exacerbated his own situation. His gratuitous comments about the radicals had made him enemies on Capitol Hill. Charles Sumner was particularly offended by a careless remark in one of the secretary's dispatches to London, suggesting that the mind-set of the men in Congress was not so different from that of the Confederates. Furthermore, it is not unlikely that Seward's pridefulness had led him occasionally to make immodest claims regarding his influence in the administration. Yet, despite such indiscretions, he was steadfast and loyal to the president. Having relinquished his own future ambitions, he had fought tirelessly to advance the fortunes of his chief and serve the country he loved.

When the Republican senators convened again Wednesday afternoon, Ira Harris of New York offered a substitute resolution that received unanimous approval. Rather than name Seward directly as the intended target, the resolution stated simply that "the public confidence in the present administration would be increased by a reconstruction of the Cabinet." When fears arose that Chase might lose his position as well, the resolution was amended to call for a "partial reconstruction of the Cabinet." Senator John Sherman of Ohio expressed doubt that any change in the cabinet would have an effect, since Lincoln "had neither dignity, order, nor firmness." Still, believing that they must take action, the caucus selected a Committee of Nine to call on the president and present the resolution. A meeting was set for 7 p.m. Thursday night, December 18.

Orville Browning came to the White House to see Lincoln shortly before the meeting began. "I saw in a moment that he was in distress," Browning recorded in his diary, "that more than usual trouble was pressing upon him." When Lincoln asked, "What do these men want?," Browning bluntly replied that they were "exceedingly violent towards the administration," and that the resolution adopted "was the gentlest thing that could be done." Furthermore, although Seward was "the especial object of their hostility," they were "very bitter" toward the president as well. Lincoln admitted that he had been enormously upset since receiving word about

.ucus proceedings. "I can hardly see a ray of hope," he confided to
.ning.

Concealing his distress, Lincoln greeted the Committee of Nine with
s accustomed civility, affording them ample opportunity to speak their
minds during a three-hour session. Jacob Collamer of Vermont opened
the proceedings with a recitation of their primary contention that a president's cabinet council should jointly endorse principles and policy, "that all
important public measures and appointments should be the result of their
combined wisdom and deliberation." Since this was hardly the current
state of affairs, the cabinet should be reconstructed to "secure to the country unity of purpose and action." In the conversation that followed, the
senators argued that the prosecution of the war had been left too long "in
the hands of bitter and malignant Democrats," like McClellan and Halleck, while the antislavery generals, like Frémont and Hunter, "had been
disgraced."

This grim arraignment was attributed to Seward's domination of policy
and his "lukewarmness in the conduct of the war." While the Republican
senators professed belief in the president's honesty, Lincoln later said,
"they seemed to think that when he had in him any good purposes, Mr.
S[eward] contrived *to suck them out of him unperceived.*" Lincoln worked to
defuse the anger and tension. He confessed that the movement against
Seward "shocked and grieved him," maintaining that while his cabinet had
been at loggerheads on certain issues, "there had never been serious disagreements." Rumors that Seward exercised some perfidious influence in
opposition to the majority of the cabinet were simply not true. On the contrary, the cabinet had acted with great accord on most matters. Indeed, in
his most trying days, "he had been sustained and consoled" by their "mutual and unselfish confidence and zeal." As the conversation continued,
Lincoln seemed to sense that the committee members were "earnest and
sad—not malicious nor passionate." He "expressed his satisfaction with
the tone and temper" of the conversation, promised to examine the prepared paper with care, and left them with the feeling that he was "pleased
with the interview."

Aware that "he must work it out by himself" with no adviser to consult,
Lincoln "thought deeply on the matter." By morning, he had devised a
plan of action. He sent notices to all of his cabinet members except Seward, requesting a special meeting at 10:30 a.m. When all were seated
around the familiar oak table, Lincoln asked them to keep secret what he
had to say. He informed them of Seward's letter of resignation, told them
about his meeting with the Committee of Nine, and read aloud the paper
the committee members had presented to him. He reiterated the state-

ments he had made to the committee, emphasizing how his compound cabinet had worked together "harmoniously, whatever had been their previous party feelings," and that during the "overwhelming troubles of the country, which had borne heavily upon him," he had counted on their loyalty and "good feeling." He "could not afford to lose" any of them and declared that it would not be "possible for him to go on with a total abandonment of old friends."

Knowing that, when personally confronted, the cabinet members would profess they had worked well together, Lincoln proposed a joint session later that evening with the cabinet and the Committee of Nine. Presumably, they would disabuse the senators of their notions of disunity and discord in the cabinet. Chase was panicked at the thought of the joint meeting, since tales of the malfunctioning cabinet had originated largely with his own statements to the senators. Chase argued vehemently against the joint meeting, but when everyone else agreed, he was forced to acquiesce.

On the evening of December 19, when the members of the Committee of Nine arrived at the White House, Lincoln began the unusual session by reading the resolutions of the senators and inviting a candid discussion of the issues raised. He acknowledged that cabinet meetings had not been as regular as he might have liked, given the terrible time pressures that faced his administration. Nonetheless, he believed that "most questions of importance had received a reasonable consideration," and that "all had acquiesced in measures when once decided." He went on to defend Seward against the committee's charge that he had "improperly interfered" with decisions and had not been "earnest in the prosecution of the war." He specifically cited Seward's full concurrence in the Emancipation Proclamation.

The senators renewed their demand that "the whole Cabinet" must "consider and decide great questions," with no one individual directing the "whole Executive action." They noted with approval that John Quincy Adams adhered to the majority vote of his cabinet even when he disagreed with them. In like fashion, "they wanted united counsels, combined wisdom, and energetic action."

Blair followed with a long argument that "sustained the President and dissented most decidedly from the idea of a plural Executive." Though he "had differed much with Mr. Seward," he nonetheless "believed him as earnest as any one in the war; thought it would be injurious to the public service to have him leave the Cabinet, and that the Senate had better not meddle with matters of that kind." Bates expressed wholehearted agreement with Blair, as did Welles. As he contemplated the discussion, Welles wrote the next day, he realized that while he had likewise differed with Seward on numerous occasions, Seward's faults were "venial." Moreover, "no party or faction should be permitted to dictate to the President in regard to his Cabinet."

The course of the conversation had seriously compromised Chase's position. He noted irritably, recalled Fessenden, that "he should not have come here had he known that he was to be arraigned before a committee of the Senate," but he felt compelled to uphold Lincoln and his colleagues. Stating equivocally that he wished the cabinet had more fully considered every measure, Chase endorsed the president's statement that there had been accord on most measures. He grudgingly admitted that "no member had opposed a measure after it had once been decided on." As for the Emancipation Proclamation, Chase conceded that Seward had suggested amendments that substantially strengthened it. Neither Stanton nor Smith said a word.

After nearly five hours of open conversation, sensing he was making headway, Lincoln asked each of the senators if he still desired to see Seward resign his position. Though four, including Lyman Trumbull, reaffirmed their original position, the others had changed their minds. When the meeting adjourned at 1 a.m., the senators suspected that no change in the cabinet would be made.

The disappointed senators now turned their wrath upon Chase, whose duplicitous behavior infuriated them. When Collamer was asked how Chase could have presented such a different face when confronted in the meeting, the Vermont senator answered succinctly, "He lied." Lincoln agreed that Chase had been disingenuous, but not on that night. On the contrary, after months of spreading false stories about Seward and the cabinet, Chase had finally been compelled to tell the truth! Lincoln's political dexterity had enabled him to calm the crisis and expose the duplicity of his secretary of the treasury.

The next day, Welles paid an early call on the president. He said that he had "pondered the events" of the previous night and concluded that it would be a grievous mistake for Lincoln to accept Seward's resignation. The senators' presumption in their criticisms of Seward, "real or imaginary," was "inappropriate and wrong." In order to "maintain the rights and independence of the Executive," Lincoln must reject the senator's attempts to interfere with internal cabinet matters. Welles hoped that Seward would not press Lincoln to accept his resignation. Delighted by these comments, Lincoln asked Welles to talk with Seward.

Welles went at once to Seward's house, where he found Stanton conversing with the secretary of state. While Stanton had probably joined

Chase in airing his frustrations, most particularly when McClellan was restored to command, he had come to see the necessity for solidarity. The cabinet, he said, was like a window. "Suppose you allowed it to be understood that passers-by might knock out one pane of glass—just one at a time—how long do you think any panes would be left in it?"

When Stanton departed, Welles told Seward that he had advised the president not to accept his resignation. This "greatly pleased" Seward, who had been distraught over the whole episode. In short order, another visitor knocked on Seward's door and Monty Blair entered, also to object to the idea of Seward's resignation. So Lincoln had brought the cabinet to rally around one of their own. Like family members who would fault one another within the confines of their own household while fiercely rejecting external criticism, the cabinet put aside its quarrel with Seward, based largely on jealousy over his intimacy with Lincoln, to resist the interference of outsiders.

Still, Lincoln's troubles were not over. The news of Seward's offer of resignation had produced widespread comment, particularly among radicals who hoped that his departure would signal a first step toward a reconstructed cabinet purged of conservative influences. To refuse Seward's offer now that its tender was public knowledge would be interpreted as a slap against the radicals. The delicate balance Lincoln had struggled to maintain in his cabinet would be damaged.

Ironically, Salmon Chase unwittingly provided a perfect solution to Lincoln's difficulty. When Welles returned to Lincoln's office after speaking with Seward, he found Chase and Stanton waiting to see the president. Humiliated after the previous night, Chase had decided to hand in his own resignation. Word had already leaked out that he had been instrumental in the movement to remove Seward "for the purpose of obtaining and maintaining control in the cabinet." Were he to remain after Seward's departure, he told a friend, he would face the hostility of Seward's many friends. Yet a public offer to join Seward in resigning would put the onus on Lincoln to request Chase's continued service and "relieve him from imputations of Seward's friends and clear his future course of difficulties."

Discovering Chase, Stanton, and Welles in his office, Lincoln invited them all to sit with him before the fire. Chase said he "had been painfully affected by the meeting," which had come as "a total surprise" to him. He informed the president he had written out his resignation. "Where is it?" Lincoln asked, "his eye lighting up for a moment." When Chase said he had brought it with him, Lincoln leaped up, exclaiming, "Let me have it." Stretching out to snatch it, Lincoln pulled the paper from Chase, who now seemed "reluctant" to let it go. With "an air of satisfaction spread over his countenance," Lincoln said, "This . . . cuts the Gordian knot." As he began reading the note, he added, "I can dispose of this subject now without difficulty."

Chase gave Welles a "perplexed" look, suggesting he was not pleased that his colleague was a witness to this upsetting encounter. At this point, Stanton also offered to submit his resignation. "I don't want yours," Lincoln immediately replied. Then, indicating Chase's letter, he added, "This . . . is all I want—this relieves me—my way is clear—the trouble is ended. I will detain neither of you longer."

As soon as they left, Lincoln wrote a letter to both Seward and Chase, acknowledging that he had received their resignations, but that "after most anxious consideration," he had determined that the "public interest" required both men to remain in office. "I therefore have to request that you will resume the duties of your Departments respectively," he concluded. Welles immediately fathomed Lincoln's insistence on keeping the two rivals close despite their animosity: "Seward comforts him,—Chase he deems a necessity." By retaining both men, Lincoln kept the balance in his cabinet. When Senator Ira Harris called on him shortly after he had received Chase's resignation, Lincoln was in a buoyant mood. "Yes, Judge," he said, employing a metaphor shaped by his rural childhood, "I can ride on now, I've got a pumpkin in each end of my bag!"

Seward responded to Lincoln with alacrity. "I have cheerfully resumed the functions of this Department in obedience to your command," he replied. That afternoon, a relieved Fanny received a telegram from Fred instructing her and Jenny to "come as soon as possible" to Washington. Chase, meanwhile, had far more difficulty in determining how to respond. His first reaction was to draft a letter refusing Lincoln's wish. "Will you allow me to say," he wrote, "that something you *said* or looked, when I handed you my resignation this morning, made on my mind the impression, that, having received the resignations of both Gov. Seward and myself, you felt you could relieve yourself from trouble by declining to accept either and that the feeling was one of gratification." He then went on to express the opinion that he and Seward could "both better serve you and the country, at this time, as private citizens, than in your cabinet." When Chase received a note from Seward announcing his decision to resume his duties, however, he felt compelled to follow suit. While letting Lincoln know that his original desire to resign remained unchanged, Chase promised that he would do Lincoln's bidding and return to the Treasury.

At the next cabinet meeting, Welles noted, "Seward was feeling very happy," while "Chase was pale, and said he was ill, had been for weeks." Seward magnanimously invited Chase to dine with his family on Christmas Eve. Having achieved what Nicolay termed "a triumph over those who attempted to drive him out," Seward hoped that he and Chase could now make their peace. Though Chase declined the invitation, he sent a gracious note begging that his "unwilling absence" be excused, for he was "too really sick . . . to venture upon his hospitality."

For Lincoln, the most serious governmental crisis of his presidency had ended in victory. He had treated the senators with dignity and respect and, in the process, had protected the integrity and autonomy of his cabinet. He had defended the executive against a legislative attempt to dictate who should constitute the president's political family. He had saved his friend Seward from an unjust attack that was really directed at him, and, simultaneously, solidified his own position as master of both factions in his cabinet.

Mary Lincoln did not share her husband's gratification in the outcome. She told Elizabeth Blair that "she regretted the making up of the family quarrel—that there was not a member of the Cabinet who did not stab her husband & the Country daily," with the exception of Monty Blair. Her protective suspicions were reaffirmed during a visit to a Georgetown spiritualist on New Year's Eve. Mrs. Laury's revelations combined comforting communications from Willie with political commentary on affairs of the day. In particular, the spiritualist warned "that the cabinet were all the enemies of the President, working for themselves, and that they would have to be dismissed, and others called to his aid before he had success."

Lincoln listened patiently to Mary's concerns, but he knew that he had now balanced his team of rivals and consolidated his leadership. "I do not now see how it could have been done better," he told Hay. "I am sure it was right. If I had yielded to that storm & dismissed Seward the thing would all have slumped over one way & we should have been left with a scanty handful of supporters. When Chase gave in his resignation I saw that the game was in my own hands & I put it through."

The happy resolution of the crisis provided an upbeat ending to a very difficult year.

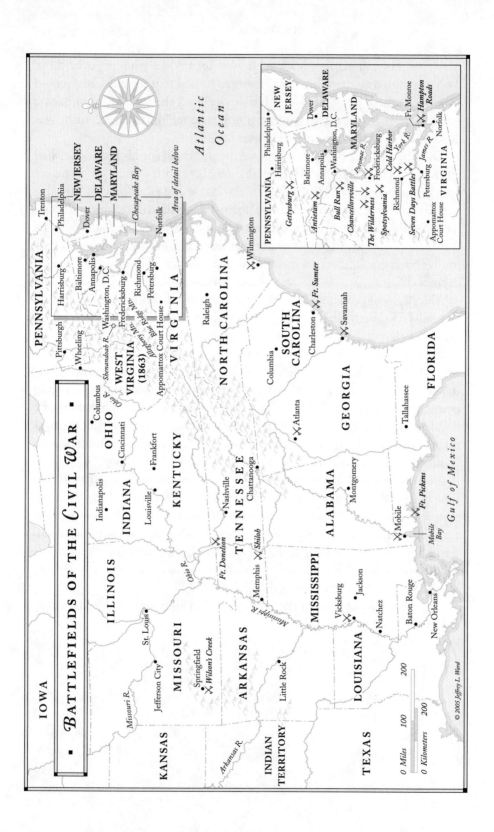

BATTLEFIELDS OF THE CIVIL WAR

IOWA

ILLINOIS

MISSOURI
Jefferson City •
• St. Louis
Springfield •
✗ Wilson's Creek
Missouri R.

KANSAS

INDIAN TERRITORY

ARKANSAS
• Little Rock
Arkansas R.

TEXAS

LOUISIANA
• Baton Rouge
• New Orleans

INDIANA
Indianapolis •
Louisville •

OHIO
Columbus •
Cincinnati •

KENTUCKY
• Frankfort

TENNESSEE
• Nashville
Chattanooga •
Memphis •
✗ Ft. Donelson
✗ Shiloh
Ohio R.

MISSISSIPPI
Vicksburg ✗
Jackson •
• Natchez
Mississippi R.

ALABAMA
Montgomery •
Mobile ✗
✗ Ft. Pickens
Mobile Bay

GEORGIA
Atlanta ✗
• Tallahassee

FLORIDA

Gulf of Mexico

WEST VIRGINIA (1863)
Wheeling •
Pittsburgh •
Ohio R.

PENNSYLVANIA
Harrisburg •
• Trenton
Philadelphia •

NEW JERSEY

DELAWARE
• Dover

MARYLAND
• Baltimore
Annapolis •
Washington, D.C. •
Chesapeake Bay

VIRGINIA
Fredericksburg •
Richmond •
Petersburg •
Appomattox Court House •
Shenandoah R.
Allegheny Mts.
Blue Ridge Mts.
Norfolk

Atlantic Ocean

Area of detail below

NORTH CAROLINA
• Raleigh
Wilmington ✗

SOUTH CAROLINA
• Columbia
Charleston ✗
✗ Ft. Sumter
✗ Savannah

Inset map (Area of detail)

PENNSYLVANIA
• Philadelphia
Harrisburg ✗
Gettysburg ✗
Antietam ✗

NEW JERSEY

DELAWARE
Dover •

MARYLAND
• Baltimore
Annapolis •
Washington, D.C. •
Potomac R.

Bull Run ✗
Chancellorsville ✗
The Wilderness ✗
Spotsylvania ✗
Seven Days Battles ✗
Richmond ✗
Petersburg ✗
Appomattox Court House
Fredericksburg ✗
Cold Harbor ✗
York R.
James R.
Ft. Monroe
✗ Hampton Roads
Norfolk

VIRGINIA

0 Miles   100   200
0 Kilometers   100   200

© 2005 Jeffrey L. Ward

CHAPTER 19

"FIRE IN THE REAR"

A s the first day of January 1863 approached, the public evinced a "general air of doubt" regarding the president's intention to follow through on his September pledge to issue his Emancipation Proclamation on New Year's Day. "Will Lincoln's backbone carry him through?" a skeptical George Templeton Strong asked. "Nobody knows."

The cynics were wrong. Despite repeated warnings that the issuance of the proclamation would have harmful consequences for the Union's cause, Lincoln never considered retracting his pledge. As Frederick Douglass had perceived, once the president staked himself to a forward position, he did not give up ground. The final proclamation deviated from the preliminary document in one major respect. The document still proclaimed that "all persons held as slaves" within states and parts of states still in rebellion "are, and henceforward shall be free"; but Lincoln, for the first time, officially authorized the recruitment of blacks into the armed forces. Stanton and Chase had advocated this step for many months, yet Lincoln, knowing that it would provoke serious disaffection in his governing coalition, had hesitated. Now, as the public began to comprehend the massive manpower necessary to fight a prolonged war, he believed the timing was right.

The cabinet members suggested a few changes that Lincoln cheerfully adopted, most notably Chase's proposal to conclude the legalistic document with a flourish, invoking "the considerate judgment of mankind, and the gracious favor of Almighty God . . . upon this act."

On the morning he would deliver the historic proclamation, Lincoln rose early after a fitful sleep. He walked over to his office to make final revisions and sent the document by messenger to the State Department, where it was put into legal form. He then met with General Burnside, who had readied his army for "another expedition against the rebels along the Rappahannock," only to be restrained by the president. Lincoln explained

that several of Burnside's division commanders had made forceful objections to the new plan. Troubled by the realization that he had lost the confidence of his officers, Burnside offered to resign. Lincoln managed to
assuage the discord temporarily, but three weeks later, he would replace
Burnside with "Fighting Joe" Hooker. A West Point graduate who had
fought in the Mexican War, Hooker had served under McClellan in the
Peninsula Campaign and at Antietam.

Seward returned from the State Department with the formally copied
proclamation shortly before 11 a.m. Lincoln read it over once more and
made ready to sign it when he noticed a technical error in the format. The
document had to be returned to the State Department for correction.
Since the traditional New Year's reception was about to begin, the signing
would have to be delayed until midafternoon.

The first hour of the three-hour reception was reserved for Washington
officials—diplomats, senators, representatives, justices, and high officers in
the armed forces. All the cabinet members and their families were there,
with the exception of Caleb Smith, who had recently resigned his Department of Interior post to become a district judge in Indiana. Young Fanny
Seward anxiously anticipated the occasion, for she had just passed her
eighteenth birthday and this was her "coming out" day. Outfitted in blue
silk with a white hat and an ivory fan, Fanny was thrilled when the president and first lady remembered her. Between the "full court dress" of the
diplomatic corps and the dazzling costumes of the ladies, "the scene,"
Fanny recalled, was "very brilliant." She recorded in her diary that Mary
"wore a rich dress of black velvet, with lozenge formed trimming on the
waist," but she was especially captivated by Kate Chase, "looking like a
fairy queen" in her lace dress: "Oh how pretty she is."

At noon, the cabinet members left to prepare for their own receptions
and the gates to the White House were opened to the general public. The
immense and disorderly crowd surged into the mansion at the cost of torn
coattails and lost bonnets. The journalist Noah Brooks was relieved when
he finally reached the Blue Room, where a single line formed to shake the
president's hand. He had recently noted how Lincoln's appearance had
"grievously altered from the happy-faced Springfield lawyer" he had first
met in 1856. "His hair is grizzled, his gait more stooping, his countenance
sallow, and there is a sunken, deathly look about the large, cavernous eyes."
Nonetheless, the president greeted every visitor with a smile and a kind remark, "his blessed old pump handle working steadily" to ensure that his
"People's Levee" would be a success. Benjamin French, standing beside
Mary during the first part of the public reception, noted her doleful appearance. "Oh Mr. French," she said, "how much we have passed through

since last we stood here." This was the first reception since Willie's death, and Mary was "too much overcome by her feelings to remain until it ended."

After mingling with the crowd, Noah Brooks took his California friends "a-calling" at the homes of various cabinet members. It was a beautiful, sunny day, and the streets were jammed with carriages. At Chase's mansion, they were greeted by a "young gentleman of color who had a double row of silver plated buttons from his throat to his toes." Handing their "pasteboards" to the doorkeeper, they were brought into the crowded parlor, where they shook hands with the secretary and his "very beautiful" daughter. Chase was "gentlemanly in his manners," Brooks noted, "though he has a painful way of holding his head straight, which leads one to fancy that his shirt collar cuts his ears." Their next stop was Seward's Lafayette Square house, where Brooks's eye, initially drawn to the elegant furnishings in the upstairs parlor, came to rest on "the prodigious nose" of the secretary, who greeted each visitor "with all of his matchless *suaviter in modo.*"

Of all the receptions that day, the Stantons' was the most elaborate. Brooks was overwhelmed by the abundant supply of "oysters, salads, game pastries, fruits, cake, wines . . . arranged with a most gorgeous display of china, glass, and silver." Remarking on Stanton's "little, aristocratic wife," Ellen, Brooks wondered if her lavish style was depleting the fortune Stanton had accumulated during his years as a lawyer. His observation was perceptive: while Stanton's salary had been reduced markedly by his decision to leave private practice, Ellen continued to spend money as though large retainers were still coming in. Yet Stanton refused to puncture Ellen's dreams, even as his rapidly diminishing wealth stirred old worries about bankruptcy.

At 2 p.m., Lincoln, wearily finished with his own reception, returned to his office. Seward and Fred soon joined him, carrying the corrected proclamation in a large portfolio. Not wishing to delay any longer, Lincoln commenced the signing. As the parchment was unrolled before him, he "took a pen, dipped it in ink, moved his hand to the place for the signature," but then, his hand trembling, he stopped and put the pen down.

"I never, in my life, felt more certain that I was doing right, than I do in signing this paper," he said. "If my name ever goes into history it will be for this act, and my whole soul is in it." His arm was "stiff and numb" from shaking hands for three hours, however. "If my hand trembles when I sign the Proclamation," Lincoln said, "all who examine the document hereafter will say, 'He hesitated.' " So the president waited a moment and then took up the pen once more, "slowly and carefully" writing his name. "The signature proved to be unusually bold, clear, and firm, even for him," Fred

Seward recalled, "and a laugh followed, at his apprehensions." The secretary of state added his own name and carried it back to the State Department, where the great seal of the United States was affixed before copies were sent out to the press.

In cities and towns all across the North, people had anxiously waited for word of Lincoln's action. Count Gurowski was in despair as the day dragged on without confirmation that the proclamation had been signed. "Has Lincoln played false to humanity?" he wondered. At Tremont Temple in Boston, where snow covered the ground, an audience of three thousand had gathered since morning, anticipating "the first flash of the electric wires." Frederick Douglass was there, along with two other antislavery leaders, John S. Rock and Anna Dickinson. At the nearby Music Hall, another expectant crowd had formed, including the eminent authors Henry Wadsworth Longfellow, Ralph Waldo Emerson, John Greenleaf Whittier, Harriet Beecher Stowe, and Oliver Wendell Holmes. "Every moment of waiting chilled our hopes, and strengthened our fears," Douglass recalled. "A line of messengers" connected the telegraph office with the platform at Tremont Temple, and although the time was passed with speeches, as it reached nine and then ten o'clock without any word, "a visible shadow" fell upon the crowd.

"On the side of doubt," Douglass recalled, "it was said that Mr. Lincoln's kindly nature [toward the South] might cause him to relent at the last moment." It was rumored that Mary Lincoln, "coming from an old slaveholding family," might have stayed his hand, persuading him to "give the slaveholders one other chance." These speculations, which "had absolutely no foundation," hurt Mary "to the quick," her niece Katherine noted. In fact, Mary had rushed a photograph of her husband to Sumner's abolitionist friend Harvard president Josiah Quincy, hoping it would "reach him, by the 1st of Jan" to mark the joyous occasion.

Finally, at roughly 10 p.m., when the anxiety at Tremont Temple "was becoming agony," a man raced through the crowd. "It is coming! It is on the wires!!" Douglass would long remember the "wild and grand" reaction, the shouts of "joy and gladness," the audible sobs and visible tears. The happy crowd celebrated with music and song, dispersing at dawn. A similar elation poured forth in the Music Hall. "It was a sublime moment," Quincy's daughter, Eliza, wrote Mary; "the thought of the millions upon millions of human beings whose happiness was to be affected & freedom secured by the words of President Lincoln, was almost overwhelming. . . . I wish you & the President could have enjoyed it with us, here."

In Washington, a crowd of serenaders gathered at the White House to applaud Lincoln's action. The president came to the window and silently bowed to the crowd. The signed proclamation rendered words unnecessary. While its immediate effects were limited, since it applied only to enslaved blacks behind rebel lines, the Emancipation Proclamation changed forever the relationship of the national government to slavery. Where slavery had been protected by the national government, it was now "under its ban." The armed forces that had returned fugitive slaves to bondage would be employed in securing their freedom. "Whatever partial reverses may attend its progress," the *Boston Daily Evening Transcript* predicted, "Slavery from this hour ceases to be a political power in the country . . . such a righteous revolution as it inaugurates never goes backward." Ohio congressman-elect James Garfield agreed, though he retained a low opinion of Lincoln, doubtless shaped by his close friendship with Chase. "Strange phenomenon in the world's history," he wrote, "when a second-rate Illinois lawyer is the instrument to utter words which shall form an epoch memorable in all future ages."

Lincoln did not need any such confirmation of the historic nature of the edict. "Fellow-citizens," he had said in his annual message in December, "*we* cannot escape history. We of this Congress and this administration, will be remembered in spite of ourselves. No personal significance, or insignificance, can spare one or another of us. The fiery trial through which we pass, will light us down, in honor or dishonor, to the latest generation."

When Joshua Speed next came to visit, Lincoln reminded his old friend of the suicidal depression he had suffered two decades earlier, and of his disclosure that he would gladly die but that he "had done nothing to make any human being remember that he had lived." Now, indicating his Emancipation Proclamation, he declared: "I believe that in this measure . . . my fondest hopes will be realized."

• • •

GRAVE QUESTIONS REMAINED: Had Lincoln chosen the right moment to issue his revolutionary edict? Would the Union cause be helped or hindered? Even Republican papers worried that the edict would create "discord in the North and concord in the South," strengthening "the spirit of the rebellion" while it diminished "the spirit of the nation." Lincoln's most intimate counselor, Seward, repeatedly warned that the situation demanded "union and harmony, in order to save the country from destruction."

All his life, Lincoln had exhibited an exceptionally sensitive grasp of the limits set by public opinion. As a politician, he had an intuitive sense of when to hold fast, when to wait, and when to lead. "It is my conviction," Lincoln later said, "that, had the proclamation been issued even six months earlier than it was, public sentiment would not have sustained it." If the question of "*slavery and quiet*" as opposed to war and abolition had been placed before the American people in a vote at the time of Fort Sumter, Walt Whitman wrote, the former "would have triumphantly carried the day in a majority of the Northern States—in the large cities, leading off with New York and Philadelphia, by tremendous majorities." In other words, the North would not fight to end slavery, but it would and did fight to preserve the Union. Lincoln had known this and realized that any assault on slavery would have to await a change in public attitudes.

The proposition to enlist blacks in the armed forces had required a similar period of preparation. "A man watches his pear-tree day after day, impatient for the ripening of the fruit," Lincoln explained. "Let him attempt to *force* the process, and he may spoil both fruit and tree. But let him patiently *wait*, and the ripe pear at length falls into his lap!" He had watched "this great revolution in public sentiment slowly but *surely* progressing." He saw this gradual shift in newspaper editorials, in conversations with people throughout the North, and in the views expressed by the troops during his own visits to the field. He had witnessed the subtle changes in the opinions of his cabinet colleagues, even those who represented the more conservative points of view. Although he knew that opposition would still be fierce, he believed it was no longer "strong enough to defeat the purpose."

Events soon tested Lincoln's belief. In the weeks that followed the issuance of the proclamation, the tenuous coalition of Democrats and Republicans that had supported the war showed signs of disintegration. In New York, the newly elected Democratic governor Horatio Seymour denounced emancipation in his inaugural message. In Kentucky, Governor James Robinson recommended that the state legislature reject the proclamation. Heavily Democratic legislatures in Illinois and Indiana threatened to sever ties with abolitionist New England and ally their states with the states of the lower Mississippi in order to end the war with slavery intact. "Every Democratic paper in Indiana is teeming with abuse of New England," Indiana governor Oliver Morton warned Stanton. "They allege that New England has brought upon us the War by a fanatical crusade against Slavery." As reports filtered into the White House, John Nicolay feared that "under the subterfuge of opposing the Emancipation Proclamation," a portion of the Democratic Party was "really organizing to oppose the War."

The "fire in the rear," in Lincoln's phrase, was fed by the lack of military progress. Heavy rains in January followed by a succession of snowstorms in February and March forced the demoralized Army of the Potomac into winter quarters on the north side of the Rappahannock. Nature conspired against Grant's Army of the Tennessee as well. Between February and March, four different attempts to capture Vicksburg failed, preventing the Union from gaining control of the Mississippi River. "This winter is, indeed, the Valley Forge of the war," one officer wrote.

In the Congress, the Peace Democrats, popularly known as Copperheads, thought war measures had strayed too far from simply repressing the rebellion and restoring the Union as it had been, and thus vigorously opposed legislation to reform the banking system, emancipate the slaves, and curtail civil liberties. They especially railed against the conscription law, which authorized provost marshals in every congressional district to enroll men between twenty and forty-five for a term of three years. As the March 4 date of adjournment neared, they engaged in a variety of tactics to suppress votes on all of these key measures. They hid out in the House lobbies and cloakrooms during quorum calls, attached unacceptable amendments onto each of the bills, and kept the Senate up day and night with filibusters.

In the House, Copperhead Clement Vallandigham, a lame duck congressman from Ohio, took the lead. He delivered a series of violent antiwar speeches that attracted national attention. As he warmed to his theme, Noah Brooks observed, his face "fearfully changed," his agreeable smile gave way to "a vindictive, ghastly grin," his smooth voice rose "higher and higher" until it reached a piercing shriek that echoed through the chamber. "Ought this war to continue?" Vallandigham thundered, depicting a war purportedly waged to defend the Union, now become "a war for the negro." He answered: "no—not a day, not an hour." The time had come for the soldiers on both sides to go home. Let the Northwest and the Old South come together in compromise. If New England did not want to remain in a Union with slavery intact, then let her go.

In the Senate, Willard Saulsbury of Delaware took to the floor to prevent a vote sustaining the administration on the suspension of habeas corpus. He could hardly keep his footing during a liquor-fueled harangue, while he inveighed against the president "in language fit only for a drunken fishwife," calling him "an imbecile" and claiming that he was "the weakest man ever placed in a high office." Called to order by Vice President Hamlin, he refused to take his seat. When the sergeant at arms approached to take Saulsbury into custody, he pulled out his revolver. "Damn you," he said, pointing the pistol at the sergeant's head, "if you touch me I'll shoot you dead." The wild scene continued for some time before Saulsbury was removed from the Senate floor.

The brouhaha on Capitol Hill troubled Lincoln less than repeated reports of growing disaffection in the army. Admiral Foote claimed that the proclamation was having a "baneful" impact on the troops, "damping their zeal and ardor, and producing discontent at the idea of fighting only for the negro." Orville Browning, who considered the proclamation a fatal mistake, warned Lincoln that recruiting new volunteers would be nearly impossible and that "an attempt to draft would probably be made the occasion of resistance to the government." Browning had talked with some friends upon their return from the front, where they had "conversed with a great many soldiers, all of whom expressed the greatest dissatisfaction, saying they had been deceived—that the[y] volunteered to fight for the Country, and had they known it was to be converted into a war for the negro they would not have enlisted. They think that scarcely one of the 200,000 whose term of service is soon to expire will re enlist."

Patiently, Lincoln weathered criticisms from Browning and a host of others. He listened carefully when David Davis, who, more than anyone, had helped engineer his victory at the Chicago convention and whom he had recently appointed to the Supreme Court, warned him about "the alarming condition of things." Yet when Davis told Lincoln to alter his policy of emancipation "as the only means of saving the Country," Lincoln told him it was "a fixed thing." And when Browning raised the specter that "the democrats would soon begin to clamor for compromise," Lincoln replied that if they moved toward concessions, "the people would leave them." Through the worst days of discord and division, Lincoln never lost his confidence that he understood the will and desires of the people.

"The resources, advantages, and powers of the American people are very great," he wrote the workingmen of London when they congratulated him on emancipation, "and they have, consequently, succeeded to equally great responsibilities. It seems to have devolved upon them to test whether a government, established on the principles of human freedom, can be maintained."

While his anxious friends observed only the rancor on Capitol Hill, Lincoln noted that before Congress adjourned on March 4, the people's representatives had passed every single one of the administration's war-related bills. They had supported the vital banking and currency legislation that would provide the financial foundation for a long and costly war, as well as the conscription bill, called by the *New York Times* "the grandest pledge yet given that our Government means to prevail."

Moreover, with Lincoln's blessings, monster mass rallies in city after city throughout the North were organized to express popular support for the war against the defeatism of the Copperheads. In New York, the *Times* reported, the "largest popular gathering ever held in this City" thronged

Madison Square to hear General Scott speak and to "cheer with hearty voice each testimony of fealty to the land of the free and the home of the brave." In Washington, Lincoln and his cabinet attended a giant Union rally at the Capitol, hailed as "the greatest popular demonstration ever known in Washington." A journalist noted that while Lincoln was dressed more plainly than the others on the platform, with "no sign of watch chain, white bosom or color . . . he wore on his breast, an immense jewel, the value of which I can form no estimate." She was speaking of little Tad, snuggled against his father's chest. Though he occasionally grew restless during the long speeches and jumped off his father's lap to wander along the platform, Tad quickly returned to the security of his father's embrace.

Scheduled for early April, the congressional and state elections in Connecticut, Rhode Island, and New Hampshire would be a test case in the battle for the heart of the North. Lincoln sent a telegram to Thurlow Weed at the Astor House in New York, requesting that he take the first train to Washington. Weed arrived the next morning, had breakfast with Seward, and met with Lincoln at the White House. "Mr. Weed, we are in a tight place," Lincoln explained. "Money for legitimate purposes is needed immediately; but there is no appropriation from which it can be lawfully taken. I didn't know how to raise it, and so I sent for you." The amount needed was $15,000. Weed returned to New York on the next train. Before the night had ended, "the Dictator" had persuaded fifteen New Yorkers to contribute $1,000 each. Although Weed later claimed that he was ignorant of the purpose of the secret fund, it is most likely, as Welles speculated, that it helped finance a plan worked out between Seward and Lincoln "to influence the New Hampshire and Connecticut elections."

It was money well spent. Voters in both states defeated the Copperhead candidates by clear majorities, ensuring that the great war measures would be sustained in the next House of Representatives. The results were "a stunning blow to the Copperheads," the *New York Times* noted. The surprising triumph "puts the Administration safely round the cape, and insures it clear seas to the end." John Hay reveled in the thought that the elections had "frightened" and "disheartened" the rebels and their sympathizers, who had expected war weariness to depress voter sentiment. "I rejoiced with my whole heart in your loyal victory," Stanton told an administration supporter in Connecticut. "It was in my judgement the most important election held since the War commenced."

"The feeling of the country is I think every day becoming more hopeful and buoyant," Nicolay told his fiancée, "a very healthy reaction against Copperheadism becoming everywhere manifest." Noah Brooks detected a similar shift in mood. "The glamour which the insidious enemies of the

Union had for a while cast over the minds of the people of the North is disappearing," he noted. The Copperheads "find that they have gone too fast and too far" in talking of a compromise peace, "and they have brought upon themselves the denunciations" of Republicans and loyal "War Democrats" alike.

This was precisely what Lincoln had anticipated in the dark days of January when he told Browning that "the people" would never sustain the Copperheads' call for peace on any terms. He had let the reaction against the defeatist propositions grow, then worked to mobilize the renewed Union spirit.

•   •   •

AMID THE CLAMOROUS OPPOSITION in Congress, the continued threats of intervention from abroad, and the stalemate in the war, Lincoln remained remarkably calm, good-natured, and self-controlled. While Chase confessed to an unremitting anxiety and Stanton suffered from repeated bouts of exhaustion, Lincoln found numerous ways to sustain his spirits. No matter how brutally trying his days, he still found time in the evenings to call at Seward's house, where he was assured of good conversation and much-needed relaxation.

Seward appreciated Lincoln's original mind and his keen wit. Fanny told of an intimate evening in their parlor when Lincoln engaged the entire family with an amusing tale about young women during the War of 1812 who made belts with engraved mottoes to give their lovers departing for battle. When one young girl suggested "Liberty or Death!," her soldier protested that the phrase was "rather strong." Couldn't she make it "Liberty or *be crippled*" instead? Although Seward laughed as uproariously as Lincoln, it is certain that neither Chase nor the serious-minded Stanton would have enjoyed such broad humor. Nor would either have approved of the grim levity of Lincoln's response to a gentleman who had waited for weeks to receive a pass to Richmond. "Well," said Lincoln, "I would be very happy to oblige you, if my passes were respected: but the fact is, sir, I have, within the past two years, given passes to two hundred and fifty thousand men to go to Richmond, and not one has got there yet."

Like Lincoln, Seward usually possessed a profound self-assurance that enabled him to withstand an endless, savage barrage of criticism. Noah Brooks noted that he was unfailingly cheerful, "smoking cigars always, ruffled or excited never, astute, keen to perceive a joke, appreciative of a good thing, and fond of 'good victuals.' " Newsmen loved to hear Seward's stories and he loved to tell them. At one dinner party, he talked nonstop from five-thirty to eleven o'clock. What left the deeper impression upon his listeners, however, was Seward's unconditional love for Lincoln, whom he praised "without limitation" as "the best and wisest man he [had] ever known."

On the nights he did not spend with Seward, Lincoln found welcome diversion in the telegraph office, where he could stretch his legs, rest his feet on the table, and enjoy the company of the young telegraph operators. He sought out Captains Dahlgren and Fox, whose conversation always cheered him. Describing a pleasant evening in Captain Fox's room, Dahlgren remarked that "Abe was in good humor, and at leaving said, 'Well I will go home; I had no business here; but, as the lawyer said, I had none anywhere else.' "

Occasionally, late at night, Lincoln would rouse John Hay. Seated on the edge of his young aide's bed, or calling him into the office, the president would read aloud favorite passages ranging from Shakespeare to the humorist Thomas Hood. Hay recorded one occasion, "a little after midnight," when Lincoln, with amused gusto, read a portion of Hood, "utterly unconscious that he with his short shirt hanging about his long legs & setting out behind like the tail feathers of an enormous ostrich was infinitely funnier than anything in the book he was laughing at. What a man it is! Occupied all day with matters of vast moment . . . he yet has such a wealth of simple bonhommie & good fellow ship that he gets out of bed & perambulates the house in his shirt to find us that we may share with him the fun of one of poor Hoods queer little conceits."

Lincoln's evening rambles suggest that Mary's continuing depression over Willie precluded easy relaxation at home. "Only those, who have passed through such bereavements, can realize, how the heart bleeds," Mary admitted to Mary Jane Welles. Yet despite the desolation that still tormented her, Mary had gamely resumed her duties as first lady, telling Benjamin French that she felt responsible to "receive the world at large" and would endeavor "to bear up" under her sorrow. French, in turn, marveled at the "affable and pleasant" demeanor the first lady regularly displayed in public. "The skeleton," he noted, "is always kept out of sight."

As the anniversary of Willie's death approached, Robert came down from Harvard to spend a few weeks with his family. Encountering him at a number of parties, Fanny Seward found him to be a delightful young man, "much shorter than his father," with "a good, strong face," though not an especially handsome one. "I talked some time with him. He is ready and easy in conversation—having, I fancy, considerable humor in his composition."

With the official mourning period behind them, the Lincolns resumed the weekly public receptions they both enjoyed despite the exhausting rounds of handshaking. In gratitude to Rebecca Pomroy, the nurse who had cared for Tad after Willie died, Mary arranged for all the nurses, officers, and soldiers at Pomroy's hospital to attend a grand White House reception in early March. Mrs. Pomroy instructed the soldiers "to provide themselves with clean white gloves, and to look their best." The White House that night was "brilliantly lighted and decorated with flowers in the greatest profusion." Pomroy was certain that her soldiers would remember this night, declaring that if they survived the war, "they will tell their children's children" of their enchanting evening at the White House.

The abolitionist Jane Grey Swisshelm had initially been reluctant to join her friends at one of these Saturday receptions. She had no interest in meeting Mary Lincoln after the tales suggesting the first lady's sympathy with the Confederate cause. Yet when she was actually introduced to Mary, she realized at once that the stories were slanderous gossip. "When I came to Mrs. Lincoln, she did not catch the name at first, and asked to hear it again, then repeated it, and a sudden glow of pleasure lit her face, as she held out her hand and said how very glad she was to see me. I objected to giving her my hand because my black glove would soil her white one; but she said: 'Then I shall preserve the glove to remember a great pleasure, for I have long wished to see you.' " Over time, as the two women developed a close friendship, Swisshelm came to believe that Mary was "more staunch even than her husband in opposition to the Rebellion and its cause."

In February, Mary was delighted and surprised by Lincoln's impulsive agreement to attend a séance in Georgetown featuring a celebrated medium, Nettie Colburn. The good-looking young woman's sessions attracted many distinguished people, including Joshua Speed, who described Nettie and a fellow medium to Lincoln as "very choice spirits, themselves. It will I am sure be some relief from the tedious round of office seekers to see two such agreeable ladies." When the president and first lady arrived, the host said: "Welcome, Mr. Lincoln . . . you were expected." Lincoln stopped short. "Expected! *Why, it is only five minutes since I knew that I was coming.*" The guests settled into chairs for the presentation, which, according to the Philadelphia banker S. P. Kase, included a piano that "began to move up and down in accord with the rise and fall of the music." Intrigued by the mechanics behind such spectacles, Lincoln told one of the soldiers present to sit on the piano to weigh it down. When it continued to move, the president himself "stepped to the end of the piano and added his weight to that of the soldiers." When the rise and fall of the piano persisted, Lincoln "resumed his seat in one of the large horse hair easy chairs of the day."

At this juncture, Nettie Colburn entered the room, and Lincoln addressed her cheerfully: "Well, Miss Nettie, do you think you have anything to say to me to-night?" There is no evidence that Lincoln believed in spiritualism. On the contrary, after hearing the mysterious clicking sounds in the presence of another medium the previous summer, he had asked the head of the Smithsonian, Joseph Henry, to discover how the noises were produced. Henry interviewed the medium, Lord Colchester, who, unsurprisingly, revealed nothing. Not long afterward, Henry happened to be seated on a train beside a young man who revealed that he manufactured telegraphic devices for spiritualists. Placed around the biceps, the instrument produced telegraphic clicks when the medium stretched his muscle. Asked if he had sold one to Lord Colchester, the young man said yes. Lincoln was reportedly "pleased to learn the secret."

Lincoln's lack of belief did not prevent him, however, from enjoying the evening's entertainment. Nettie was an accomplished actress, ably mimicking the booming baritone of Daniel Webster or the frail voice of an Indian maiden. She spoke for an hour, channeling one voice and then another as she related historical episodes from the landing of the Pilgrims to the current war. Her oration, which carried a passionate abolitionist message, seemed to S. P. Kase "the grandest" he had ever heard. When the spirits left her, she departed as abruptly as she had arrived. All was silent for a while, then "the President turned in his seat, threw his long right leg over the arm of his chair," and exclaimed, "Was not this wonderful?" He seemed to have viewed Nettie's performance with the same pleasure he derived from the theater—respite from the cares of the day.

● ● ●

CHASE, UNLIKE LINCOLN, was never able to forgo his statesmanlike persona and simply enjoy conversations and lighter amusements. He was inclined to let things fester, brooding over perceived slights and restlessly calculating the effect of every incident on his own standing. Weeks after the cabinet crisis had been resolved, he questioned his own decision to stay on board. "I have neither love nor taste for the position I occupy," he told Horace Greeley, "and have only two great regrets connected with it—one, that I ever took it; the other, that having resigned it I yielded to the counsels of those who said I must resume it."

Chase became physically ill during the tumultuous debate on Capitol Hill over his banking bill, terrified that the measures necessary to finance the war would not make it through. When the bills passed and the new greenbacks were ready for distribution, he momentarily basked in the knowledge that the Treasury was full for the first time since the war began.

He was also pleased by the fact that his own handsome face would appear in the left-hand corner of every dollar bill. He had deliberately chosen to place his picture on the ubiquitous one-dollar bill rather than a bill of a higher denomination, knowing that his image would thus reach the greatest number of people. His mood quickly darkened when he contemplated his own strained finances, however, and feared that his personal investments with Jay Cooke and his brother, Henry, might be misconstrued. Their virtual monopoly over the government bond business was beginning to attract negative newspaper comment, though they had succeeded brilliantly in selling the war bonds to the public.

The stormy and irascible secretary of war also seemed unable to relax or distract himself from the incessant pressures of his office. Stanton's clerk, Charles Benjamin, recalled that "a word or a gesture would set [Stanton] aflame in an instant. He would dash the glasses before his eyes far up on his forehead, as though they pained or obstructed his vision; the muscles of his face would become agitated, and his voice would tremble and grow intense, without elevation." Though "the storm would pass away as quickly as it came," and though Stanton would quickly make amends to victims of his ill humor, the employees in the War Department, while respecting Stanton greatly, never loved him as Lincoln's aides loved their president.

Stanton also lacked Lincoln's ability to put grudges behind him. When asked why he disliked the Sanitary Commission, which had done so much to promote healthy conditions in the army camps, Stanton replied that the commission had persuaded the president and the Senate to appoint a surgeon general against his vigorous objections. "I'm not used to being beaten, and don't like it," he said, "and therefore I am hostile to the Commission." In fact, Stanton admitted, he "detested it."

Those who worked with Stanton attributed his "nervous irritability" to the combination of overwork and poor health. At times, his asthma became so severe that he collapsed in "violent fits of strangulation." Still, he refused to take a break. When doctors pleaded with him to get some rest and exercise, he insisted that he wanted only to be kept alive until the war ended and then, and only then, would he consent to seek rest. Though he loved good conversation and had built his large house in order to gather interesting people around his table, he stayed in the War Department day and night, rarely enjoying the convivial evenings that replenished Seward and Lincoln or that Kate provided for Chase. And while he enjoyed reading novels, with a special preference for Dickens, Stanton seldom found the time to unwind with a book. Instead, one of his clerks recalled, when he wanted "an hour's rest," he would lock his door, lie on his couch, and peruse English periodicals sympathetic to the Confederate cause, endeavoring to better understand the British attitude to the war.

Unlike Seward, who had promptly brought Fred into the State Department and relished the professional and personal support of his own son, Stanton had no family member or intimate friend to rely upon for daily counsel. Except for the initial appointment of his brother-in-law Christopher Wolcott as assistant secretary of war, Stanton refused to bring any of his relatives into his department. When Senator Ben Wade recommended an appointment for Stanton's capable cousin William, the secretary angrily declared that no relative would have any "office in his gift" so long as he remained at his post. John Hay went so far as to remark that he "would rather make the tour of a small-pox hospital" than be forced to ask Stanton for a favor. Even when Stanton's own son, Edwin Junior, wanted to serve as his private secretary after graduating from Kenyon, Stanton refused to bend. Only after months of unpaid labor for an assistant secretary did the boy receive his father's consent to an official appointment.

Stanton rarely returned to Steubenville during the war. During the winter of 1862, Christopher Wolcott had become seriously ill. When he died in April 1863, Stanton and his son boarded a special train to join Stanton's sister for the funeral in Ohio. Pamphila's conviction that her husband had died from overwork must have made Stanton's attempts at consolation difficult. Though he tried to relax on his old home ground, revisit the places he had loved, Stanton returned to Washington more exhausted than restored.

As the pressure on all the key administration officials mounted, Lincoln, with the hardest task of all, maintained the most generous and even-tempered disposition. Even he, however, was sorely tried on occasion. After recommending that the War Department utilize the services of a meteorologist, Francis Capen, Lincoln was exasperated when none of Capen's presumably scientific predictions proved correct. "It seems to me Mr. Capen knows nothing about the weather, in advance," Lincoln wrote three days after Capen had assured him it would not rain for five or six days. "It is raining now & has been for ten hours. I can not spare any more time to Mr. Capen." He was more irritated when warring factions in Missouri refused to reconcile. He informed the recalcitrant groups that their continuing feud was "very painful" for him. "I have been tormented with it beyond endurance for months, by both sides. Neither side pays the least respect to my appeals to your reason. I am now compelled to take hold of the case."

But Lincoln refused to let resentments rankle. Discovering that a hastily written note to General Franz Sigel had upset the general, he swiftly followed up with another. "I was a little cross," he told Sigel, "I ask pardon. If I do get up a little temper I have no sufficient time to keep it up." Such gestures on Lincoln's part repaired injured feelings that might have escalated into lasting animosity.

The story is told of an army colonel who rode out to the Soldiers' Home, hopeful of securing Lincoln's aid in recovering the body of his wife, who had died in a steamboat accident. His brief period of relaxation interrupted, Lincoln listened to the colonel's tale but offered no help. "Am I to have no rest? Is there no hour or spot when or where I may escape this constant call? Why do you follow me out here with such business as this?" The disheartened colonel returned to his hotel in Washington. The following morning, Lincoln appeared at his door. "I was a brute last night," Lincoln said, offering to help the colonel in any way possible.

Republican stalwart Carl Schurz relates an equally remarkable encounter in the wake of an unpleasant written exchange that initially seemed to threaten his friendship with Lincoln. Discouraged by the lack of progress in the war, Schurz had blamed Lincoln's misguided appointment of Democrats "whose hearts" were not fully "in the struggle" to top positions in the field. Lincoln had responded testily, telling Schurz that he obviously wanted men with "heart in it." The question was "who is to be the judge of hearts, or of 'heart in it?' If I must discard my own judgment, and take yours, I must also take that of others; and by the time I should reject all I should be advised to reject, I should have none left, Republicans or others—not even yourself." Schurz, at the army camp in Centreville, Virginia, where he led the Third Division of the 11th Corps, detected in Lincoln's long reply "an undertone of impatience, of irritation, unusual with him." Though he had been encouraged by the president to correspond freely, he feared that his letter had transgressed.

Several days later, a messenger arrived at Schurz's encampment with an invitation from Lincoln "to come to see him as soon as my duties would permit." Obtaining permission to leave that same day, Schurz reached the White House at seven the next morning. He found Lincoln upstairs in his comfortable armchair, clad in his slippers. "He greeted me cordially as of old and bade me pull up a chair and sit by his side. Then he brought his large hand with a slap down on my knee and said with a smile: 'Now tell me, young man, whether you really think that I am as poor a fellow as you have made me out in your letter!' " Flustered, Schurz hesitantly explained the reason behind his tirade. Lincoln listened patiently and then delineated his own situation, explaining that his terse reply had been provoked by a hailstorm of criticism that had been pelting down on him. "Then, slapping my knee again, he broke out in a loud laugh and exclaimed: 'Didn't I give it to you hard in my letter? Didn't I? But it didn't hurt, did it? I did not mean to, and therefore I wanted you to come so quickly.' " Lincoln and Schurz talked for an hour, at the end of which Schurz asked whether his letters were still welcome. " 'Why, certainly,' he answered; 'write me whenever the spirit moves you.' We parted as better friends than ever."

• • •

To CELEBRATE Tad's tenth birthday on Saturday, April 4, Mary Lincoln proposed a family excursion by steamer and train to the Army of the Potomac headquarters in Falmouth, Virginia. Delighted by the chance to escape from Washington, Lincoln organized a small traveling party, including his old Illinois friend Dr. Anson Henry, Noah Brooks, and, at Henry's suggestion, Edward Bates. Dr. Henry had maintained a friendship with Bates over the years and considered him "one of the purest and best men in the world." Bates agreed to the foray, hoping to visit his son Coalter, who was with Hooker's army; as it happened, Coalter had just left to pay a final visit to the family in Washington before the expected spring battles began.

The little party left the White House in the midst of a furious blizzard. Gale winds blew clouds of dust and snow in all directions as they boarded the steamer *Carrie Martin* at sunset. They headed south past Alexandria and Mount Vernon, where, according to the custom of the river, a bell tolled a salute in honor of George Washington. The steamer was due to reach the army supply depot at Aquia Creek that evening, but the escalating storm required them to cast anchor in a protected cove for the night. Undeterred by the falling snow and the howling winds that drove everyone else to the warm comfort of the cabin, Tad remained on deck with his fishing line, determined to provide food for supper. Racing in to announce every bite to his parents, Tad finally caught a small fish that, much to his delight, was added to the dinner menu. Brooks marveled at the simplicity of the scene, watching "the chief magistrate of this mighty nation" relax with family and friends, "telling stories" and conversing in "a free and easy way," with no servant standing by and no guard on deck. Had the rebels known their whereabouts, Brooks mused, they "might have gobbled up the entire party without firing a shot."

The snowstorm was "at its height" when the *Carrie Martin* pulled into the busy dock at Aquia Creek, where, on Easter morning, the presidential party boarded a special train for Falmouth Station. Along the way, with "snow piled in huge drifts" and "the wind whistling fiercely over the hills," they passed one army camp after another. Each encampment along the thirty miles had hundreds of campfires surrounded by tents, fortifications, and stockades. Disembarking at Falmouth Station, they were taken by closed carriage over rough roads to Hooker's headquarters a half mile away. Situated about three miles from the Rappahannock, the headquarters resembled a small city, complete with telegraph office, printing establishment, bakery, post office, and accommodations for more than 133,000 soldiers.

General Hooker, tall and broad-shouldered, awaited them in front of his tent, which stood at the end of a wide street flanked with officers' tents on both sides. He greeted the party of six and beckoned them into his comfortable quarters, furnished with a large fireplace, two beds, chairs for the entire party, and a long table covered with papers and books.

Lincoln liked and respected Hooker. When he had tendered him command of the Army of the Potomac ten weeks earlier, he had sent along a remarkable letter of advice. "I believe you to be a brave and a skillful soldier," the letter began. "You have confidence in yourself, which is valuable, if not an indispensable quality. You are ambitious, which, within reasonable bounds, does good rather than harm. But I think that during Gen. Burnside's command of the Army, you have taken counsel of your ambition, and thwarted him as much as you could, in which you did a great wrong to the country, and to a most meritorious and honorable brother officer." Lincoln continued with an admonition about Hooker's recent comments suggesting the need for a dictator to assume command of "both the Army and the Government." He informed Hooker that "it was not *for* this, but in spite of it, that I have given you the command. Only those generals who gain successes, can set up dictators. What I now ask of you is military success, and I will risk the dictatorship." The president closed with shrewd words of guidance: "Beware of rashness, but with energy, and sleepless vigilance, go forward, and give us victories." Aside from the wisdom of the advice, the letter clearly manifests Lincoln's growing confidence in his own powers.

Hooker took the advice in stride. In fact, he was so moved by the kind-hearted tone of the letter that over the next few days he read it aloud to various people, including Noah Brooks and Dr. Henry, who thought it should be printed in gold letters. "That is just such a letter as a father might write to his son," Hooker fervently told Brooks as the young journalist sat with him before a fire in his tent. "It is a beautiful letter," Hooker continued, "and, although I think he was harder on me than I deserved, I will say that I love the man who wrote it."

Reporters noted Mary's curiosity about every aspect of camp life; they commented on her simple attire and speculated that this was her first experience sleeping in a tent. In fact, the first couple's tent was far more elaborately outfitted than an ordinary one. It boasted a plank floor, a stove, and beds especially constructed for the occasion, complete with real sheets, blankets, and pillowcases. As the days went by, the weariness that had marked Mary's face upon arrival began to fade, and "the change seemed pleasant to her." Brooks reported badinage between husband and wife occasioned by a photograph of a Confederate officer with an inscription on the back: "A rebellious rebel." Mary suggested that this meant he "was a rebel against the rebel government." Lincoln smiled, countering that perhaps the officer "wanted everybody to know that he was not only a rebel, but a rebel of rebels—'a double-dyed-in-the-wool sort of rebel.'"

Stormy weather postponed the first grand review from Sunday to Monday afternoon, leaving the president and first lady free to talk at length with the members of Hooker's staff. The irrepressible Tad, meanwhile, inspected every facility in the compound, zealously racing from one place to another. A reporter present at the meetings with Hooker's officers and aides noted that "Lincoln was in unusual good humor," lightening the atmosphere "by his sociability and shafts of wit."

The roar of artillery at noon the next day signaled the start of the cavalry review. With General Hooker by his side, Lincoln rode along serried ranks that stretched for miles over the rolling hills. The soldiers cheered and shouted when they saw the president and cheered even louder when they saw Master Tad Lincoln bravely attempting to keep up, "clinging to the saddle of his pony as tenaciously as the best man among them," his gray cloak flapping "like a flag or banneret."

The boy's "short legs stuck straight out from his saddle," Brooks noted, "and sometimes there was danger that his steed, by a sudden turn in the rough road, would throw him off like a bolt from a catapult." Much to the relief of onlookers, Tad made it through "safe and sound," his reckless riding steadied by a young orderly who remained faithfully by his side. "And thereby hangs a tale," noted a *New York Herald* reporter. The orderly was a thirteen-year-old boy, Gustave Shuman, who had left home when the war began to accompany the New Jersey Brigade. General Philip Kearny had made him his bugler. The boy rode in front of the troops throughout the Peninsula Campaign. When General Kearny was killed in the late summer of 1862, the new commander, Daniel Sickles, retained the boy as bugler. So, though not much older than the president's son, Gustave was a hardened veteran, quite capable of containing the impulsive Tad. Reporters noted that from that first review on, the two boys became inseparable, roaming about the camp like brothers.

Over the next few hours, tens of thousands of troops passed in front of the president and first lady, sweeping one after another "like waves at sea." From atop the little knoll on which the Lincolns were stationed, the endless tiers provided a majestic vista. When the sun came out, one reporter observed, "the sunbeams danced on the rifles and bayonets, and lingered in the folds of the banners." At the review of the infantry and artillery, artists sketched the spectacle of sixty thousand men, "their arms shining in the distance and their bayonets bristling like a forest on the horizon as they disappeared far away."

Lincoln so enjoyed mingling with the men—who appeared amazingly healthy and lavishly outfitted with new uniforms, arms, and equipment—that he extended his visit until Friday. After one review, someone remarked that the regulars could be easily distinguished from the volunteers, for "the former stood rigidly in their places without moving their heads an inch as he rode by, while the latter almost invariably turned their heads to get a glimpse of him." Quick to defend the volunteers, Lincoln replied, "I don't care how much my soldiers turn their heads, if they don't turn their backs."

During a break from the reviews, several members of the presidential party, including Noah Brooks, journeyed down to the Rappahannock for a glimpse of the rebel camps across the river. With the naked eye, they could see the houses and steeples of Fredericksburg. The wooded hills and the renowned plain that had become "a slaughter pen for so many men" in the December battle were also clearly visible. Binoculars allowed a view of the ridge on which thousands of unmarked graves had been dug. Beyond the ridge, smoke rose from the rebel camps with elaborate earthworks, a myriad of white tents, and the flag of stars and bars. At the shoreline, the Union pickets paced their rounds mirrored by rebel sentries across the narrow river. Honoring the "tacit understanding" that sentries would not fire at each other, they bandied comments across the water, hailing each other as "Secesh" or "Yank," and conversing "as amiably as though belonging to friendly armies." At one point, Brooks noted, a Confederate officer "came down to the water's edge, doubtless to see if Uncle Abraham was of our party. Failing to see him, he bowed politely and retired."

Both sides knew that as soon as the weather cleared, the brutal fighting would resume. "It was a saddening thought," Brooks remarked after one impressive review, "that so many of the gallant men whose hearts beat high as they rode past must, in the course of events, be numbered with the slain before many days shall pass." Yet despite the awareness that a major engagement was not far off, "all enjoyed the present after a certain grim fashion and deferred any anxiety for the morrow until that period should arrive." Before he departed, Lincoln issued one final directive to Hooker and his second in command, General Darius Couch. "Gentlemen, in your next battle *put in all your men.*"

Tremendously heartened by the splendid condition of the army and the high spirits and reception of the troops, Lincoln boarded the *Carrie Martin* at sunset on Friday for the return trip to Washington. The *Herald* noted that he "received a salute from all the vessels in port and locomotives on shore, whistles being blown, bells run, and flags displayed."

• • •

LINCOLN RETURNED to the White House to find Blair enraged with Stanton, Welles feuding with Seward, and Chase threatening once again to resign. The Blairs, father and son, were defending James S. Pleasants, a Union man from Maryland who was related to Confederate John Key. Key had sought refuge at Pleasants's house, begging food and shelter. Reluctantly, the loyal Marylander had allowed him to stay at his home. Stanton insisted that such treason deserved the gallows. "The skirmish was sharp & long," Elizabeth Blair told her husband, but finally, the president commuted the sentence to imprisonment. Furthermore, when Lincoln learned of the man's poor health, he agreed, at the Blairs' request, to reduce the sentence. All of this left Stanton "very bitter."

The quarrel between Seward and Welles concerned an English ship captured in neutral waters by a blockade runner. Suspecting that the cargo aboard was meant for the Confederacy, the Union Navy sent the *Peterhoff* to New York for disposition by a prize court. Long-standing tradition dictated that the ship's mail be opened by the court to determine the true destination of the vessel and its cargo. The controversy had aroused strong protest from Britain regarding the sanctity of its mails. Seward, wanting to avoid British intervention at all cost, had agreed to surrender the mails unopened. Furious, Welles claimed that surrender was in violation of international law and would set a terrible precedent. Moreover, Seward had no basis meddling in this issue, since jurisdiction belonged to the Navy Department.

For days, as the unresolved matter led to rumors of war with England, the two colleagues argued the case before Lincoln. They visited him late at night armed with letters explaining their positions, argued in cabinet council, and solicited allies. Sumner backed Welles in the fray, maintaining that England would never go to war over this issue. The president, however, concurred with Seward that at this juncture good relations with England must supersede the legal questions surrounding the mails. Sumner left much disgruntled, considering Lincoln "very ignorant" about the precedents involved. Welles agreed, blaming Seward for "daily, and almost hourly wailing in [Lincoln's] ears the calamities of a war with England," thus diverting the president "from the real question." Montgomery Blair also sided with Welles, telling him after a cabinet meeting that Seward "knows less of public law and of administrative duties than any man who ever held a seat in the Cabinet." In the end, as Seward had advised, the president determined that the mails would be returned unopened to the British government.

Chase's disaffection also weighed heavily on Lincoln that spring. For the third time in five months, Chase threatened to resign his position in the Treasury. His first resignation during the cabinet crisis had been repeated in March when Lincoln, bowing to pressure from a Connecticut senator, had decided not to renominate one of Chase's appointees for collector of internal revenue in Hartford. Livid, Chase informed the president that unless his authority over his own appointments could be established, he could not continue in the cabinet: "I feel that I cannot be useful to you or the country in my present position." Lincoln managed once again to placate Chase, only to receive another threat in short order. This squabble was provoked by Lincoln's removal of one of Chase's appointees in the Puget Sound district who had been accused of speculating in land. Enraged that he was not consulted, Chase argued that he could not function in his department if decisions were made "not only without my concurrence, but without my knowledge." If the president could not respect his authority, Chase wrote, "I will, unhesitatingly, relieve you from all embarrassment so far as I am concerned by tendering you my resignation."

Understanding that "Chase's feelings were hurt," Lincoln set about once again to sooth his ruffled pride. That evening, he later recounted, he called at Chase's house with the resignation in hand. Placing his long arms on Chase's shoulders, he said: "Chase, here is a paper with which I wish to have nothing to do; take it back, and be reasonable." He then explained why he had felt compelled to make the decision, which had taken place in Chase's absence from the city, and promised his touchy secretary that he would have complete authority to name the removed appointee's successor. "I had to plead with him a long time, but I finally succeeded," Lincoln happily noted.

Though irritated by Chase's haughty yet fundamentally insecure nature, Lincoln recognized the superlative accomplishments of his treasury secretary. In the two months since Congress had adjourned, Chase had sold more than $45 million in bonds, and the demand for the bonds was steadily increasing. "Never before did the finances of any nation, in the midst of a great war, work so admirably as do ours," the *New York Times* noted in a laudatory article on Chase. Even as Lincoln deferred to Chase, however, he placed his prickly secretary's third resignation letter on file for future reference.

Monty Blair, meanwhile, resented Chase and showed little respect for his remaining colleagues. He considered Seward "an unprincipled liar" and Stanton "a great scoundrel." In fact, Blair thought the entire cabinet save Welles, and perhaps Bates, whom he liked but did not consider a stalwart ally, should be replaced, and that his father, "the ablest and best informed politician in America," should become Lincoln's "private counsellor." And so one personal struggle succeeded another, complicating the president's job, absorbing his energies.

Lincoln's uneasiness about his warring cabinet colleagues paled in comparison, however, to his disquietude about the impending movements of the Army of the Potomac. On April 13, 1863, three days after Lincoln returned from his trip, Hooker took the first step in what would become known as the Battle of Chancellorsville. He dispatched ten thousand cavalrymen under General George Stoneman to head south and insert themselves between Lee's army and Richmond. With the Confederate supply lines to Richmond severed, Hooker intended to cross the Rappahannock, draw the enemy away from Fredericksburg, and engage him in battle. Heavy rains and impassable roads delayed the advance, but finally, during the last week of April, Hooker's men began crossing the river.

For Lincoln and his cabinet, anxious days followed. "We have been in a terrible suspense here," Nicolay wrote his fiancée on Monday, May 4. Fighting had begun, but there was no "definite information" on the battle's progress. Welles joined Lincoln in the War Department to wait for news that did not come. Bates was particularly tense, knowing that his son John Coalter was with Hooker "in the most active and dangerous service." Lincoln admitted to Francis Blair, Sr., that nobody seemed to know what was going on. Welles found it odd that "no reliable intelligence" was reaching them, correctly surmising that this boded ill. "In the absence of news the President strives to feel encouraged and to inspire others," he wrote, "but I can perceive he has doubts and misgivings, though he does not express them."

"While I am anxious, please do not suppose I am impatient, or waste a moment's thought on me, to your own hindrance, or discomfort," Lincoln had written Hooker at the outset of the campaign. Even when disturbing fragments filtered in, Lincoln refused to pressure Hooker. "God bless you, and all with you. I know you will do your best," he wired his general on the morning of May 6. "Waste no time unnecessarily, to gratify our curiosity with despatches."

At 3 p.m. that afternoon, the suspense ended with an unwelcome telegram from Hooker's chief of staff. The Union forces had been defeated. The army had retreated to its original position on the north side of the Rappahannock, and seventeen thousand Union soldiers were dead, wounded, or missing. Hooker's second in command, General Darius Couch, later claimed that Hooker was simply "outgeneraled" by Lee. Assuming that Lee would "fall back without risking battle," Fighting Joe was "demoralized" by the fierceness of the Confederate attack. Had he committed all his troops, as Lincoln had directed him to do, the course of the battle might have been different. By immediately assuming a defensive stance, however, Hooker gave the initiative to Lee and never regained his footing. An injury sustained on the battlefield further dulled Hooker's perceptions. Though his subordinates wanted to press the battle, he issued the order to retreat.

Noah Brooks was with Lincoln when the news came. "I shall never forget that picture of despair," he later wrote. "Had a thunderbolt fallen upon the President he could not have been more overwhelmed." His beloved army, so healthy and spirited weeks earlier, had been "driven back, torn and bleeding, to our starting point, where the heart-sickening delay, the long and tedious work of reorganizing a decimated and demoralized army would again commence." Observing the president's "ashen" face, Brooks "vaguely took in the thought" that his complexion "almost exactly" matched the French gray wallpaper in the room. "Clasping his hands behind his back, he walked up and down the room, saying, 'My God! my God! What will the country say! What will the country say!' "

The news traveled fast. The president informed Senator Sumner, who rushed to tell Welles. "Lost, lost, all is lost!" Sumner exclaimed, lifting both hands as he entered the navy secretary's office. Welles went to the War Department, where Seward was with Stanton. "I asked Stanton if he knew where Hooker was. He answered curtly, No. I looked at him sharply, and I have no doubt with some incredulity, for he, after a moment's pause, said he is on this side of the river, but I know not where." As the afternoon wore on and endless casualty lists began streaming in, Stanton could no longer hide his despair. "This is the darkest day of the war," he lamented. At the Willard Hotel, Brooks observed, secessionists suddenly "sprang to new life and animation and with smiling faces and ill-suppressed joy" moved openly through the gloomy crowds.

Within the hour of receiving the news, Lincoln ordered a carriage to drive him to the Navy Yard. Accompanied by General Halleck, he boarded a steamer bound for Hooker's headquarters, a grim counterpoint to his joyous April visit. Once again, Lincoln found some redemption in the resolute determination of his troops. "All accounts agree," one reporter wrote from army headquarters, "that the troops on the Rappahannock came out of their late bloody fight game to the backbone." Though "fresh from all the horrors of the battlefield, with ranks decimated, and almost exhausted with exposure and fatigue," they remained "undaunted and erect, composed and ready to turn on the instant and follow their leaders back into the fray."

Moreover, while the Confederates had lost 4,000 fewer men, their casualty list of 13,000 represented a larger percentage of their total forces. In addition, they had lost one of their greatest generals: Thomas "Stonewall" Jackson. Returning from a reconnaissance mission, Jackson had been mistaken for an enemy and was fired upon by some of his own men. His left arm was amputated in a nearby field hospital, but he died of pneumonia eight days later. The South went into mourning. "Since the death of Washington," the *Richmond Whig* proclaimed, "no similar event has so profoundly and sorrowfully impressed the people of Virginia as the death of Jackson."

Lincoln remained at army headquarters for only a few hours. Before leaving, he handed Hooker a letter expressing confidence in the continuing campaign. "If possible," the president wrote, "I would be very glad of another movement early enough to give us some benefit from the fact of the enemies communications being broken, but neither for this reason or any other, do I wish anything done in desperation or rashness." Lincoln made it clear that he stood ready to assist Hooker in the development of a new plan of action. As he had done so many times before, Lincoln withstood the storm of defeat by replacing anguish over an unchangeable past with hope in an uncharted future.

CHAPTER 20

"THE TYCOON
IS IN FINE WHACK"

N o sooner had Lincoln returned from his May 7 visit to the troops than he was confronted by a colossal political uproar over the arrest and imprisonment of former Ohio congressman Clement Vallandigham on the charge of treason.

The arrest was ordered by General Burnside, who had assumed command of the Department of the Ohio after his replacement by Hooker. Responding to tumultuous peace demonstrations where speakers openly advocated the defeat of the Union's cause, Burnside issued General Orders No. 38, proclaiming that "the habit of declaring sympathy for the enemy will not be allowed in this department." All persons committing "treason, expressed or implied," would be arrested and tried by a military court. In deliberate defiance, Vallandigham incited a large crowd to a frenzy with his passionate denunciations of a failed war. This demagogue of defeat railed that the conflict would end only if soldiers deserted en masse and the people acted to "hurl King Lincoln from his throne."

After reading a transcript of Vallandigham's remarks, Burnside sent his soldiers to arrest him at his home in the middle of the night. "The door resisted the efforts of the soldiers," a local journalist wrote, "and Vallandigham flourished a revolver at the window, and fired two or three shots," but the soldiers made their entry through a side entrance. With unprecedented speed, a military tribunal found him guilty and sentenced him to prison for the remainder of the war. His application for a writ of habeas corpus was denied. When the *Chicago Times* exacerbated the incident with its incendiary coverage, Burnside, on his own authority, shut the paper down.

Learning of these events in the morning newspaper, Lincoln found himself in a difficult position. While he later admitted that the news of the arrest brought him pain, he felt compelled to uphold Burnside. Nonetheless, he anticipated the damaging political fallout. Criticism came not only from Copperheads and Democrats but from loyal Republicans. Thurlow Weed deplored the arrest. Senator Trumbull warned Browning that if such arbitrary arrests continued, "the civil tribunals will be completely subordinated to the military, and the government overthrown." A friend of Seward cautioned him that "by a large and honest portion of the community," the arrest was considered an "invasion of a great principle—the right of free speech," and that it might well precipitate civil war within the loyal states. Seward agreed. Indeed, in a moment of rare accord, every member of the cabinet united in opposition to the Vallandigham arrest.

Lincoln, searching for compromise, publicly supported Vallandigham's arrest but commuted the sentence to banishment within the Confederate lines. There, it was playfully remarked, his Copperhead body could go "where his heart already was." The *New York Times* recorded "general satisfaction" at the solution, which "so happily meets the difficulties of the case—avoiding the possibility of making him a martyr, and yet effectually destroying his power for evil." Escorted by Union cavalry holding a flag of truce, Vallandigham was removed to Tennessee. In an act that further diminished his reputation, he quickly escaped to Canada. Meanwhile, Stanton revoked Burnside's suspension of the *Chicago Times* and informed local officials that they were not to suppress newspapers.

Thus, Lincoln was able to maintain his support for General Burnside while minimizing any violation of civil liberties necessitated by war. Asked months later by a radical to "suppress the infamous 'Chicago Times,'" Lincoln told her, "I fear you do not fully comprehend the danger of abridging the *liberties* of the people. Nothing but the very sternest necessity can ever justify it. A government had better go to the very extreme of toleration, than to do aught that could be construed into an interference with, or to jeopardize in any degree, the common rights of its citizens."

After he dealt with Vallandigham, Lincoln's next priority was to comfort Burnside. Upon hearing that the entire cabinet had opposed his action, the general had offered to resign. Lincoln not only refused the resignation but insisted that while "the cabinet regretted the necessity" of the arrest, once it was done, "all were for seeing you through with it."

Finally, knowing that the public would ultimately be the judge of the administration's actions on the home front, Lincoln began drafting a document that would put the complex matter of military arrests into perspective. He had contemplated the subject for months, but his delineation of his ideas assumed new urgency with the public outrage at the arrest of Vallandigham. "Often an idea about it would occur to me which seemed to have force and make perfect answer to some of the things that were said and written about my actions," he later told a visitor. "I never let one of those ideas escape me, but wrote it on a scrap of paper." Now he would have to cobble those scraps into a cogent argument that the American public would accept.

Furthermore, Lincoln needed the proper forum in which to present his ideas. It came in late May, when a meeting of New York Democrats passed a set of resolutions condemning his military arrests as unconstitutional. Lincoln's extensive response to the Democratic resolutions took "less time than any other of like importance" because he had already "studied it from every side." In early June, the president read his draft to the cabinet. "It has vigor and ability," a delighted Welles noted. Blair advised the president to emphasize that "we are Struggling against a Conspiracy to put down popular Govt." Blair realized that Lincoln had often reiterated this theme, but as Thomas Hart Benton used to say, the "ding dong" proved to be "the best figure in Rhetoric."

The finished letter, addressed to New York Democrat Erastus Corning, was released to the *New York Tribune* on June 12. Conceding that in ordinary times, military arrests would be unconstitutional, Lincoln reminded his critics that the Constitution specifically provided for the suspension of the writ of habeas corpus "in cases of Rebellion or Invasion." He went on to say that Vallandigham was not arrested for his criticism of the administration but "because he was laboring, with some effect, to prevent the raising of troops, to encourage desertions from the army, and to leave the rebellion without an adequate military force to suppress it."

Pointing out that "long experience has shown that armies can not be maintained unless desertion shall be punished by the severe penalty of death," Lincoln posed a question that was soon echoed by supporters everywhere: "Must I shoot a simple-minded soldier boy who deserts, while I must not touch a hair of a wiley agitator who induces him to desert? This is none the less injurious when effected by getting a father, or brother, or friend, into a public meeting, and there working upon his feelings, till he is persuaded to write the soldier boy, that he is fighting in a bad cause, for a wicked administration of a contemptable government, too weak to arrest and punish him if he shall desert."

The president's letter garnered extravagant praise throughout the North. "It is full, candid, clear and conclusive," the *New York Times* affirmed. Even Democrats were impressed. While Edward Everett told Lincoln he would not have advocated Vallandigham's arrest, he considered the president's "defence of the step complete." Supporters were thrilled. "It is a grand document, strong, plain, simple, without one sparkle of tinsel ornament," Stoddard enthused, "yet dignified as becomes the ruler of a great people when the nation is listening to what he says. It should be printed in every Northern paper, and read by every citizen." In fact, Lincoln took every step to ensure that his words would shape public opinion. Printed in a great variety of formats, the letter eventually reached an astonishing 10 million people in their homes and workplaces, on isolated farms and in the cities. And as the American people absorbed the logic of Lincoln's argument, popular sentiment began to shift.

• • •

WITH THE APPROACH OF SUMMER, the tempers of the cabinet ministers grew shorter. Welles noted with disapproval that Stanton attended only half the cabinet meetings and said little when present. "Not unfrequently he has a private conference with the President in the corner of the room, or with Seward in the library," griped Welles. Seward, too, would turn up when a session commenced, speak privately with the president, then leave his son, Fred Seward, to represent his department. Stanton, who claimed he would never raise "any important question, when an assistant is present," was infuriated. Blair, frustrated by the superior access granted Seward and Stanton, often lingered after cabinet meetings in hopes of a private word with Lincoln.

"At such a time as this, it would seem there should be free, full and constant intercourse and interchange of views," fumed Welles. Bates, also discontented, agreed. "There is now no mutual confidence among the members of the Govt.—and really no such thing as a C.[abinet] C.[ouncil]," he grumbled. "The more ambitious members, who seek to control— Seward—Chase—Stanton—never start their projects in C. C. but try *first* to commit the Prest., and then, if possible, secure the *apparent* consent of the members." Chase found the lack of collective deliberation demeaning. "But how idle it seems to me to speculate on Military affairs!" he complained to David Dudley Field. "The President consults only Stanton & Halleck in the management of the War. I look on from the outside and, as well as I can, furnish the means." If he were president, Chase assured Congressman Garfield, surely he "would have a system of information which should at least keep my Secretary of the Treasury advised of every thing of importance."

More strongly than Chase, Blair decried the lack of more formal meetings, attributing the cabinet's failings to the machinations of Seward and Stanton. They had also been responsible, he believed, for Lincoln's unwillingness to replace Halleck, whom Blair despised, and restore McClellan. In Blair's mind, both Seward and Chase were "scheming for the succession. Stanton would cut the President's throat if he could." Blair's hatred for Stanton was so virulent that he refused to set foot in the War Department, the primary source of military information. Talking with Welles one evening at the depot, Blair admitted that Lincoln's behavior puzzled him. "Strange, strange," he exclaimed, "that the President who has sterling ability should give himself over so completely to Stanton and Seward."

Certainly, Lincoln was not oblivious to the infighting of his colleagues. He remained firmly convinced, however, that so long as each continued to do his own job well, no changes need be made. Moreover, he had no desire for contentious cabinet discussions on tactical matters, preferring to rely on the trusted counsel of Seward and Stanton. Still, he understood the resentment this provoked in neglected members of his administration; and through many small acts of generosity, he managed to keep the respect and affection of his disgruntled colleagues.

Recognizing Blair's desire for more personal influence, Lincoln kept his door open to both Monty and his father. Monty Blair, despite his frustrations, was ultimately loyal and had accomplished marvels as postmaster general, utterly transforming a primitive postal system without letter carriers, mailboxes on streets, or free delivery. Modernizing the postal service was particularly important for the soldiers, who relied on letters, newspapers, and magazines from home to sustain morale. To this end, Blair created a special system of army post offices, complete with army postmasters and stamp agents. His innovations provided the means for soldiers to send mail without postage so long as the recipient paid three cents on delivery of each letter. Even when foul weather and muddy roads made the delivery of mails to the army camps nearly impossible, inordinate efforts allowed the mail to get through.

Lincoln was also careful to reserve time for private conversation with Welles. He would often catch up with his "Neptune" on the pathway leading from the White House to the War and Navy Departments or call him aside as they awaited news in the telegraph office. In his written correspondence, the president was equally thoughtful. When he felt compelled to issue Welles an order regarding the instructions of naval officers at neutral ports, he assured Welles that "it is not intended to be insinuated that you have been remiss in the performance of the arduous and responsible duties of your Department, which I take pleasure in affirming has, in your hands, been conducted with admirable success."

So, in the end, the feuding cabinet members, with the exception of Chase, remained loyal to their president, who met rivalry and irritability with kindness and defused their tensions with humor. A particularly bitter argument arose between Chase and Monty Blair when Blair claimed that the Fugitive Slave Law still applied in loyal states and should be employed to return a runaway to his owner; Chase demanded instead that the slave be placed into military service. Lincoln mediated the dispute, assuring them both that this very issue had long bedeviled him. "It reminded him," Welles recorded in his diary, "of a man in Illinois who was in debt and terribly annoyed by a pressing creditor, until finally the debtor assumed to be crazy whenever the creditor broached the subject. I, said the President, have on more than one occasion, in this room when beset by extremists on this question, been compelled to appear to be very mad."

During another tense session, Lincoln cited the work of the humorist Orpheus C. Kerr, which he especially relished, even though it often lampooned him and the members of the cabinet. "Now the hits that are given to you, Mr. Welles or to Chase I can enjoy, but I dare say they may have disgusted you while I was laughing at them. So *vice versa* as regards myself."

• • •

WHILE WORKING TO SUSTAIN the spirits of his cabinet, Lincoln also tried to soothe the incessant bickering and occasional resentment among his generals. Learning that William Rosecrans, headquartered in Nashville, had taken umbrage at a note he had sent, Lincoln replied at once. "In no case have I intended to censure you, or to question your ability," he wrote. "I frequently make mistakes myself, in the many things I am compelled to do hastily." He had merely intended to express concern over Rosecrans's action regarding a particular colonel. And when Lincoln felt compelled to remove General Samuel Curtis from command in Missouri, he assured him that his removal was necessary only "to somehow break up the state of things in Missouri," where Governor Gamble headed one quarreling faction and Curtis another. "I did not mean to cast any censure upon you, nor to indorse any of the charges made against you by others. With me the presumption is still in your favor that you are honest, capable, faithful, and patriotic."

Despite Lincoln's diplomacy, the quarrels in Missouri continued, eliciting a note from Governor Gamble complaining that the language in one of Lincoln's published letters had been "grossly offensive" to him. When Hay presented the note to Lincoln, he was told "to put it away." Lincoln explained to Gamble that as he was "trying to preserve [his] own temper, by avoiding irritants, so far as practicable," he had decided not to read what his secretary had described as a "*cross*" letter. Having made his point, Lincoln assured the wounded Gamble: "I was totally unconscious of any malice, or disrespect towards you, or of using any expression which should offend you."

Lincoln's patience had its limits, however. When Major General Robert H. Milroy railed about "the blind unreasoning hatred" of Halleck that he claimed had supposedly led to his suspension from command, Lincoln was unyielding. "I have scarcely seen anything from you at any time, that did not contain imputations against your superiors," Lincoln replied. "You have constantly urged the idea that you were persecuted because you did not come from West-Point, and you repeat it in these letters. This, my dear general, is I fear, the rock on which you have split."

Likewise, when Rosecrans grumbled that his request for a predated commission to secure a higher rank had been denied, Lincoln was unsympathetic: "Truth to speak, I do not appreciate this matter of rank on paper, as you officers do. The world will not forget that you fought the battle of 'Stone River' and it will never care a fig whether you rank Gen. Grant on paper, or he so, ranks you."

As he was forced to deal with quarreling generals on almost every front, it is little wonder that Lincoln developed such respect and admiration for Ulysses S. Grant. Steadily and uncomplainingly, Grant had advanced toward Vicksburg, the Confederate stronghold whose capture would give the Union control of the Mississippi River and split the Confederacy. By the middle of May, after five successive victories, Grant had come within striking distance of Vicksburg. After two direct assaults against John Pemberton's forces failed on May 19 and May 22, he settled into a siege designed to starve the Confederates out.

"Whether Gen. Grant shall or shall not consummate the capture of Vicksburg," Lincoln wrote a friend on May 26, "his campaign from the beginning of this month up to the twenty second day of it, is one of the most brilliant in the world." During the troubling weeks with Hooker's army in the East, news from Grant's army in the West had sustained Lincoln. In March, Stanton had sent Charles Dana, the newspaperman who would later become assistant secretary of war, to observe General Grant and report on his movements. Dana had developed a powerful respect for Grant that was evident in his long, detailed dispatches. Lincoln's own estimation of his general steadily increased as reports revealed a terse man of character and action. Requesting that General Banks join forces with him in the final drive to open the Mississippi, Grant assured Banks that he "would gladly serve under him as his superior in rank or simply cooperate with him for the benefit of the common cause if he should prefer that course."

Despite his growing regard for Grant, there were instances that required Lincoln to intervene with his most successful general. In a misguided effort to stop peddlers from illegally profiteering in cotton in areas penetrated by Union armies, Grant had issued an order expelling "the

Jews, as a class," from his department. The discriminatory order, which contained no provision for individual hearings or trials, forced all Jewish people to depart within twenty-four hours, leaving horses, carriages, and other valuables behind.

When a delegation of Jewish leaders approached Lincoln, it was clear that he was not fully informed about the matter. He responded to their plight with a biblical allusion: "And so the children of Israel were driven from the happy land of Canaan?" The delegation leader answered: "Yes, and that is why we have come unto Father Abraham's bosom, asking protection." Lincoln replied quickly: "And this protection they shall have at once." He took his pen and wrote a note to Halleck, ordering immediate cancellation of the order. Halleck reluctantly complied after assuring Grant that "the President has no objection to your expelling traitors and Jew peddlers, which, I suppose, was the object of your order; but, as it in terms proscribed an entire religious class, some of whom are fighting in our ranks, the President deemed it necessary to revoke it."

Lincoln was also confronted by continuing rumors of Grant's relapse into excessive drinking. Tales of drunkenness were not confined to Grant. Elizabeth Blair heard that during the Battle of Chancellorsville, Hooker "was drunk all the time," while Bates was told that "General H.[alleck] was a confirmed *opium-eater,*" a habit that contributed to his "watery eyes" and "bloated" appearance. In Grant's case, the gossip reached Lincoln by way of the puritanical Chase, who had received a letter from Murat Halstead. The respected journalist warned Chase that Grant was "most of the time more than half drunk, and much of the time idiotically drunk."

In fact, Lincoln and Stanton had already heard similar complaints. After dispatching investigators to look into General Grant's behavior, however, they had concluded that his drinking did not affect his unmatched ability to plan, execute, and win battles. A memorable story circulated that when a delegation brought further rumors of Grant's drinking to the president, Lincoln declared that if he could find the brand of whiskey Grant used, he would promptly distribute it to the rest of his generals!

• • •

WHILE THE SIEGE of VICKSBURG tightened in the West, a deceptive quiet settled on the Rappahannock. After visiting Hooker's headquarters in mid-May, Senators Wade and Chandler told Lincoln that the pickets on both sides of the river had resumed "their old pastime of bandying wit and repartee . . . 'I say Yank,' shouted over one of the Rebels, 'where is fightin' Joe Hooker, now?' 'Oh, he's gone to Stonewall Jackson's funeral,' shouted 'Yank' in reply."

During this interlude on the Eastern front, Seward accompanied Frances and Fanny back to Auburn, where they were planning to spend the summer. For a few precious days, he entertained old friends, caught up on his reading, and tended his garden. The sole trying event was the decision to fell a favorite old poplar tree that had grown unsound. Frances could not bear to be present as it was cut, certain that she "should feel every stroke of the axe." Once it was over, however, she could relax in the beautiful garden she had sorely missed during her prolonged stay in Washington. On June 1, when Seward boarded the train to return to the capital, Fanny wrote that their home seemed "very lonely" without him.

No sooner had Seward departed Auburn than Frances and Fanny began hearing troubling rumors that Lee intended to invade Washington, Maryland, or Pennsylvania. "We have again been anxious about Washington," Fanny told her father. "Although I don't consider myself a protection, Washington seems safer to me when I am there." Reassuring his daughter, Seward noted that during his stay in Auburn, he, too, had remained "in constant uneasiness" over all manner of rumors that proved groundless upon his return to the capital. "Certainly the last thing that any one here thinks of, now-a-days, is an invasion of Washington."

On Monday, June 8, Mary and Tad left the capital for a two-week vacation in Philadelphia, where they took a suite at the Continental Hotel. After they had gone, Welles spoke with Lincoln about a "delicate" matter concerning Mary. In the aftermath of Willie's death the previous year, she had canceled the weekly Marine Band summer concerts on the White House lawn. Welles warned that if the public were deprived of the entertainment for yet another season, the "grumbling and discontent" of the previous summer would only increase. Lincoln hesitated at first. Willie had loved the weekly concerts with their picniclike festivities, but "Mrs. L. would not consent, certainly not until after the 4th of July." When Welles persisted, Lincoln finally agreed to let him do whatever he "thought best." That night, most likely unsettled by the conversation about Willie, Lincoln had a nightmare about Tad's recently acquired revolver. "Think you better put 'Tad's' pistol away," he wired Mary the next morning. "I had an ugly dream about him."

In the days that followed, reports that Lee's army was heading north through the Shenandoah Valley to invade Maryland and Pennsylvania multiplied. On June 15, Seward sent a telegram to his son Will, suggesting he had better cut short his leave to return to his regiment in Washington. "Oh! what a disappointment!" Fanny lamented. Will had just arrived in Auburn for a twenty-day sojourn with both his own family and Jenny's. Many plans would be canceled, including "a double family pic-nic to the

Lake." Writing to Frances that same day, Seward sought to set her mind at ease. Though it now seemed certain that Lee had crossed the Rappahannock, she must "not infer that there is any increase of danger for any of us in this change." On the contrary, "the near approach of battles toward us brings disadvantages to the enemy, and adds to our strength."

In similar fashion, Lincoln reassured Mary when a headline in a Northern paper blared: *"Invasion! Rebel Forces in Maryland and Pennsylvania."* "It is a matter of choice with yourself whether you come home," he told her. "I do not think the raid into Pennsylvania amounts to anything at all." When each day brought reports of further Confederate advances, however, Mary decided to rejoin her husband in Washington.

"The country, now, is in a blaze of excitement," Benjamin French recorded on June 18. "Some of the Rebel troops have crossed into the upper part of Pennsylvania, & the North is wide awake." While Welles worried that "something of a panic pervades the city," Lincoln remained quietly confident that the Union troops, fighting on home ground, would achieve the signal victory so long denied. Capitalizing on the intense patriotism inspired by the invasion, he called out a hundred thousand troops from the militias in Pennsylvania, Maryland, Ohio, and the new state of West Virginia.

"I should think this constant toil and moil would kill him," French marveled, yet the resilient president seemed "in excellent spirits." Inspired by Lincoln's steadfast nature, French added, "the more I see of him the more I am convinced of his superlative goodness, truth, kindness & Patriotism."

In the tense atmosphere of Washington, the committee charged with planning the Fourth of July celebrations considered suspending their preparations. "Don't you stop!" Mary Lincoln ordered White House secretary William Stoddard, promising to personally help make the anniversary celebrations a success. Reflecting her husband's unruffled confidence, she assured Stoddard of her husband's certainty that "the crisis has come and that all the chances are on our side. This move of Lee's is all he could ask for."

Lincoln's primary concern was that Hooker would again be "outgeneraled" by Lee. His worry escalated in the last weeks of June when he "observed in Hooker the same failings that were witnessed in McClellan after the Battle of Antietam. A want of alacrity to obey, and a greedy call for more troops which could not, and ought not to be taken from other points." When Hooker delivered a prickly telegram asking to be relieved of command, Lincoln and Stanton replaced him with General George Meade, who had participated in the Peninsula Campaign, Second Bull Run, and Chancellorsville. The surprising move distressed Chase. He had long championed Hooker and had recently returned from spending the day with him in the field. When Lincoln informed his cabinet that the change was already accomplished, Welles noted that "Chase was disturbed more than he cared should appear." The following day, Chase wrote to Kate, who was in New York. "You must have been greatly astonished for the relieving of General Hooker; but your astonishment cannot have exceeded mine."

• • •

THREE DAYS LATER, in Pennsylvania, the three-day Battle of Gettysburg began. "The turning point of the whole war seems to be crowding itself into the present," wrote John Nicolay. "It seems almost impossible to wait for the result. Hours become days and days become months in such a suspense." If Lee achieved victory at Gettysburg, he could move on to Philadelphia, Baltimore, and Washington. His aura of invincibility might, it was feared, eventually lead the British and French to recognize the independence of the Confederacy and bring the war to an end.

Telegraph service from the front was "poor and desultory," according to operator David Bates. Lincoln remained a constant fixture in the telegraph office, resting fitfully on the couch. At intervals, Stanton, Seward, Welles, and Senators Sumner and Chandler drifted in and out. Senator Chandler would "never forget the painful anxiety of those few days when the fate of the nation seemed to hang in the balance; nor the restless solicitude of Mr. Lincoln, as he paced up and down the room, reading dispatches, soliloquizing, and often stopping to trace the map which hung on the wall." Sketched on the map were the generals and places that would later be engraved in history: James Longstreet and George Pickett, Winfield Hancock and Joshua Chamberlain, Little Round Top and Cemetery Ridge.

After inconclusive fighting on the first day, a dispatch from Meade on Thursday night, July 2, reported that "after one of the severest contests of the war," the rebels had been "repulsed at all points." Still, given recent reversals and the protracted uncertainty in the present, everyone held their breath. As of 9 p.m. the following night, the *New York Times* reported, "no reliable advices have been received here from the Pennsylvania battlefield. It is generally felt that this is the crisis of the war. Intense anxiety prevails." At midnight, a messenger handed Welles a telegram from a Connecticut editor named Byington, who had left the battlefield a few hours earlier and reported that "everything looked hopeful." Welles assured Lincoln that Byington was "reliable," but the hours of uncertainty continued until shortly after dawn, July 4, when a telegram from Meade reported that the battle had been successfully concluded. The rebels were withdrawing after severe losses. Casualties were later calculated at 28,000, nearly a third of Lee's army.

General Abner Doubleday described the tenacious fighting, which cost 23,000 Union casualties, "as being the most desperate which ever took place in the world." He told a reporter that "nothing can picture the horrors of the battlefield around the ruined city of Gettysburg. Each house, church, hovel, and barn is filled with the wounded of both armies. The ground is covered with the dead."

On the morning of the Fourth of July, Lincoln issued a celebratory press release that was carried by telegram across the country. For young Fanny Seward, waiting anxiously in Auburn, the day had started as "the gloomiest Fourth" she had ever known. "No public demonstration here—No ringing of bells." Everything changed in the late afternoon when the "extra" arrived, carrying the tidings of victory. Fireworks were set off to glorify simultaneously the country's independence and the long-awaited victory.

In New York City, George Templeton Strong exulted in the colorful newspaper accounts of Lee's retreat. "The results of this victory are priceless," he wrote. "Government is strengthened four-fold at home and abroad. Gold one hundred and thirty-eight today, and government securities rising. Copperheads are palsied and dumb for the moment at least."

Triumphant news from Vicksburg followed on the heels of victory at Gettysburg. Grant's forty-six-day siege had finally forced Pemberton to surrender his starving troops. Welles had received the first tiding that Vicksburg had surrendered to Grant in a dispatch from Admiral David Porter. The bespectacled, "slightly fossilized" Welles hurried to the White House, dispatch in hand. Reaching the room where Lincoln was talking with Chase and several others, Welles reportedly "executed a double shuffle and threw up his hat by way of showing that he was the bearer of glad tidings." Lincoln affirmed that "he never before nor afterward saw Mr. Welles so thoroughly excited as he was then."

The elated president "caught my hand," recorded Welles, "and throwing his arm around me, exclaimed: 'what can we do for the Secretary of the Navy for this glorious intelligence—He is always giving us good news. I cannot, in words, tell you my joy over this result. It is great, Mr. Welles, it is great!'" With the fall of Vicksburg, as Lincoln later said, "The Father of Waters again goes unvexed to the sea."

Dana described the surrender in a telegram to Stanton the next day. "The rebel troops marched out and stacked arms in front of their works while Genl. Pemberton appeared for a moment with his staff upon the parapet of the central post. . . . No troops remain outside—everything quiet here. Grant entered the city at 11 o'clock and was rec'd by Pemberton," whom he treated with great "courtesy & dignity." Dana estimated the number of prisoners, for whom rations were being distributed, to be about thirty thousand.

Lincoln expressed his joyful appreciation to Grant in a remarkable letter. "I write this now as a grateful acknowledgment for the almost inestimable service you have done the country," he began. He conceded that while he had approved most of the general's maneuvers during the long struggle, he had harbored misgivings over Grant's decision to turn "Northward East of the Big Black" instead of joining General Banks. "I now wish to make the personal acknowledgment that you were right, and I was wrong."

Word of Vicksburg's surrender unleashed wild celebrations throughout the North. In Washington, a large crowd, led by the 34th Massachusetts Regimental Band, formed at the National Hotel and marched to the White House to congratulate the president. Lincoln appeared before the cheering multitude, revealing the preliminary thoughts that would coalesce in his historic Gettysburg Address. "How long is it—eighty odd years—since on the Fourth of July for the first time in the history of the world a nation, by its representatives, assembled and declared as a self-evident truth that 'all men are created equal.' " He went on to recall the signal events that had shared the anniversary of the nation's birth, beginning with the twin deaths of Thomas Jefferson and John Adams on July 4, and ending with the Union's twin victories at Gettysburg and Vicksburg on the same day. "Gentlemen," the president declared, "this is a glorious theme, and the occasion for a speech, but I am not prepared to make one worthy of the occasion." Instead, he spoke of the "praise due to the many brave officers and soldiers who have fought in the cause of the Union."

The band played some patriotic airs, and the crowd pressed on to the War Department, where Stanton paid generous tribute to General Grant. Although several more speeches followed and songs were played, the people had not exhausted their euphoria. Marching to Lafayette Square, they joined another throng at Seward's house, cheering for the secretary to appear. The indefatigable Seward happily obliged, delivering a long, animated speech tracing the conflict from its troubled early days to its recent triumphs, which, he assured them, foretold "the beginning of the end."

The following day, little work was accomplished in the offices of government. In every building, Noah Brooks reported, the official bulletins were read "over and over again," producing "cheer upon cheer from the crowds of officers and clerks." On the streets, "Union men were shaking hands wherever they met, like friends after a long absence," while the Copperheads had "retired to their holes like evil beasts at sunrise."

The joyous occasion was marred for the Lincolns by a serious carriage accident that took place on the second day of the Gettysburg battle. As Rebecca Pomroy related the events, the Lincolns were returning to the White House from the Soldiers' Home. Lincoln was riding on horseback while Mary followed behind in their carriage. The night before, presumably targeting the president, an unknown assailant had removed the screws fastening the driver's seat to the body of the carriage. When the vehicle began to descend from a winding hill, the seat came loose, throwing the driver to the ground. Unable to restrain the runaway horses, Mary tried to leap from the carriage. She landed on her back, hitting her head against a sharp stone. The wound was dressed at a nearby hospital, but a dangerous infection set in that kept her incapacitated for several weeks. With the Battle of Gettysburg in full swing, Lincoln was unable to minister to Mary's needs. He brought Mrs. Pomroy to the Soldiers' Home to nurse his wife round the clock. Robert Lincoln believed that his mother "never quite recovered from the effects of her fall," which exacerbated the debilitating headaches that she already endured.

• • •

IN THE WAKE OF the triumphs at Gettysburg and Vicksburg, Lincoln anticipated a quick end to the rebellion. General Meade, he told Halleck, had only to "complete his work, so gloriously prosecuted thus far, by the literal or substantial destruction of Lee's army." In the days that followed, both Halleck and Lincoln urged Meade to go after Lee, to attack him vigorously, to capture his army before he could escape into Virginia. Robert Lincoln later said that his father had sent explicit orders to Meade "directing him to attack Lee's army with all his force immediately, and that if he was successful in the attack, he might destroy the order, but if he was unsuccessful he might preserve it for his vindication." The order has never been found. If Meade did receive it, he nonetheless failed to move against Lee. As the days passed, Lincoln began "to grow anxious and impatient."

Lincoln's worst fears were realized on July 14, when he received a dispatch from Meade reporting that Lee's army had escaped his grasp by successfully crossing the Potomac at Williamsport, Maryland, into Virginia. At the cabinet meeting that day, Stanton was reluctant to share the news, though his face clearly revealed that he "was disturbed, disconcerted." Welles recorded that, when asked directly if Lee had escaped, "Stanton said abruptly and curtly he knew nothing of Lee's crossing. 'I do,' said the President emphatically, with a look of painful rebuke to Stanton." Lincoln revealed what he had learned and suggested that the cabinet meeting be

adjourned. "Probably none of us were in a right frame of mind for deliberation," Welles wrote. Certainly, he added, the president "was not."

Lincoln caught up with Welles as his navy secretary was leaving and
walked with him across the lawn. His sorrow that Lee had once again managed to escape was palpable. "On only one or two occasions have I ever
seen the President so troubled, so dejected and discouraged," Welles wrote.
"Our Army held the war in the hollow of their hand & they would not close
it," Lincoln said later. "We had gone through all the labor of tilling &
planting an enormous crop & when it was ripe we did not harvest it."

Later that afternoon, Lincoln wrote a frank letter to General Meade.
While expressing his profound gratitude for "the magnificent success" at
Gettysburg, he acknowledged that he was "distressed immeasurably" by
"the magnitude of the misfortune involved in Lee's escape. He was within
your easy grasp, and to have closed upon him would, in connection with
our other late successes, have ended the war. As it is, the war will be prolonged indefinitely." Before sending the letter, which he knew would leave
Meade disconsolate, Lincoln held back, as he often did when he was upset
or angry, waiting for his emotions to settle. In the end, he placed the letter
in an envelope inscribed: "To Gen. Meade, never sent, or signed."

Lincoln later told Connecticut congressman Henry C. Deming that
Meade's failure to attack Lee after Gettysburg was one of three occasions
when "better management upon the part of the commanding general
might have terminated the war." The other two command failures he
attributed to McClellan during the Peninsula Campaign and Hooker at
Chancellorsville. Still, he acknowledged, "I do not know that I could have
given any different orders had I been with them myself. I have not fully
made up my mind how I should behave when minie-balls were whistling,
and those great oblong shells shrieking in my ear. I might run away."

Troubling events in New York City soon diverted the nation's attention.
For weeks, authorities had worried about the potential for violence on July
11. On that date, the names of all the men eligible for the first draft in
American history would be placed in a giant wheel and drawn randomly
until the prescribed quota was filled. The unpopular idea of coercing men
to become soldiers had provided traction for Copperhead politicians.
Speaking on July 4, Governor Seymour had told an immense crowd that
the federal government had exceeded its constitutional authority by forcing men into an "ungodly conflict" waged on behalf of the black man.
The antagonistic *Daily News,* read by the majority of working-class Irish,
claimed that the purpose of the draft was to "kill off Democrats."

A provision in the Conscription Act that allowed a draftee to either pay
$300 or provide a substitute provoked further discontent. Both Stanton

and Lincoln had objected to this feature of the bill, but Congress had insisted. Opponents of the draft gained powerful ammunition that this was "a rich man's war and a poor man's fight." Still, the first day of the draft proceeded peacefully, leaving the city woefully unprepared for the violent uprising that accompanied the spinning of the wheel on the second day. "Scarcely had two dozen names been called," the *New York Times* reported, "when a crowd, numbering perhaps 500," stormed the building "with clubs, stones, brickbats and other missiles." Entering through the broken windows, they stoned the drafting officers, smashed the giant wheel, shredded the lists and records, and then set the building on fire.

Returning to the street, the mob, composed mainly of poor Irish immigrants, turned its vengeance against anyone it encountered. "It seemed to be an understood thing," the *Times* reporter noted, "that the negroes should be attacked wherever found, whether they offered any provocation or not. As soon as one of these unfortunate people was spied, whether on a cart, a railroad car, or in the street, he was immediately set upon by a crowd of men and boys." Terror unfolded as the rioters beat their victims to death and then strung their bodies on trees. An orphanage for black children was burned to the ground, hundreds of stores were looted, and dozens of policemen lost their lives. More than a thousand people were killed or wounded.

The riots continued unchecked for five days, becoming "the all engrossing topic of conversation" in Washington. The inability of the authorities to restore law and order prompted Chase to announce his desire to "have the power for a week." The mob violence finally ended when a regiment of soldiers, returning from Pennsylvania, entered the city. Although some advised Lincoln to suspend the draft indefinitely, he insisted that it go forward.

The turmoil in New York created foreboding throughout the North as other cities prepared to commence their own drafts. In the days preceding Auburn's draft on July 23, Frances Seward lived "in daily apprehension of a riot." In frequent letters to her husband, she reported that Copperheads were spreading "malicious stories" blaming Seward's "higher law" for the riots in New York. Tensions in Auburn escalated when several Irishmen fought with blacks, resisted arrest, and threatened to destroy the Seward home. Frances awoke one morning to find that a large rock had been thrown into the room where she regularly sat to read. After discovering the damage, she advised her daughter-in-law to remove anything she considered valuable. "So that afternoon," Jenny recalled, "I took my husband's photograph down to my mother's house, it being, to my mind, the most valuable thing that I possessed."

From Washington, Seward sought to placate his wife. "Do not give yourself a thought about the house. There will hardly be any body desperate enough to do you personal harm, and if the country, in its unwonted state of excitement, will destroy our home, the sacrifice will be a small one for our country, and not without benefit." Frances persevered, retaining her calm during these difficult days, as she had done years before during the trial of William Freeman. "As to personal injury," she told her husband, "I fear more for the poor colored people than for others—They cannot protect themselves and few persons are willing to assist them."

On the morning of Auburn's draft, Frances reported to her son Fred that while everyone was "somewhat anxious," she was feeling "more secure" since the local citizenry had organized a volunteer police force. The *New York Times* reported the successful results of the efforts in Auburn. "The best of order was observed and the best spirit was manifested" by the two thousand citizens who had gathered to witness the draft. As local officials addressed patriotic speeches to the crowd, the drafted men cheered for "The Union," "Old Abe," "The Draft," and "Our recent victories."

Even before such reassuring accounts reached him, Seward had predicted that the disturbances in New York, like a "thunder shower," would "clear the political skies, of the storms" that the Copperheads had been "gathering up a long time." His words proved prescient, for when the loss of life and property was tallied in the wake of the New York riots, public opinion turned against Governor Seymour. His incendiary Fourth of July speech was seen by many as a direct "incitement to the people to resist the government." John Hay learned from a visiting New Yorker that Seymour was "in a terrible state of nervous excitement," precipitated "both by the terrible reminiscence of the riots" and the virulent condemnation by the press for his handling of the situation. The news that Seymour had "lost ground immensely with a large number of the best men" engendered great satisfaction in the Lincoln administration. And when the draft was eventually resumed in New York City, everything went smoothly.

"The nation is great, brave, and generous," Seward confidently told Frances. "All will go on well, and though not without the hindrance of faction at every step, yet it will go through to the right and just end. How differently the nation has acted, thus far in the crisis, from what it did in 1850 to 1860!"

Within twenty-four distressing hours, the president had learned of both Lee's escape and the disgraceful riots in New York. Nonetheless, he was able to shake off his gloom within a matter of days. On Sunday morning, July 19, Hay reported that the "President was in very good humour." He had written a humorous verse mocking the "pomp, and mighty swell" with which Lee had gone forth to "sack Phil-del." While he remained fully cognizant of the consequences of Lee's escape, he had willed himself to reconsider his outlook on General Meade and the Battle of Gettysburg. "A few days having passed," he assured one of Meade's commanding generals, "I am now profoundly grateful for what was done, without criticism for what was not done. Gen. Meade has my confidence as a brave and skillful officer, and a true man."

Oddly enough, Lincoln's good spirits that Sunday morning were due in part to the six straight hours he had spent with Hay the previous day reviewing one hundred courts-martial. Whereas the young secretary was "in a state of entire collapse" after the ordeal, Lincoln found relief and renewed vigor as he exercised the power to pardon. As they went through the cases, Hay marveled "at the eagerness with which the President caught at any fact which would justify him in saving the life of a condemned soldier."

Confronted with soldiers who had been sentenced to death for cowardice, Lincoln typically reduced the sentence to imprisonment or hard labor. "It would frighten the poor devils too terribly, to shoot them," he said. One case involved a private who was sentenced to be shot for desertion though he had later re-enlisted. Lincoln simply proposed, "Let him fight instead of shooting him." Lincoln acknowledged to General John Eaton that some of his officers believed he employed the pardoning power "with so much freedom as to demoralize the army and destroy the discipline." Although "officers only see the force of military discipline," he explained, he tried to comprehend it from the vantage of individual soldiers—a picket so exhausted that "sleep steals upon him unawares," a family man who overstayed his leave, a young boy "overcome by a physical fear greater than his will." He liked to tell of a soldier who, when asked why he had run away, said: "Well, Captain, it was not my fault. I have got just as brave a heart as Julius [Caesar] but these legs of mine will always run away with me when the battle begins."

Rather than fearing that he had overused his pardoning power, Lincoln feared he had made too little use of it. He could not bear the sound of gunshot on the days when deserters were executed. Only "where meanness or cruelty were shown" did he exhibit no clemency.

Yet even as he plowed through one court-martial after another, Lincoln's humor remained intact. At one point, he was handed the case of a captain charged with "looking thro keyholes & over transoms at a lady undressing." He laughingly suggested that the captain "be elevated to the peerage" so that he could be accorded the appropriate title "Count Peeper."

• • •

THE SUMMER OF 1863 brought the hottest weather Washington had suffered in many years. "Men and horses dropping dead in the streets every
day," Hay reported to Nicolay, who had escaped to the Rocky Mountains.
"The garments cling to the skin," one resident observed, "shirt collars are
laid low; moisture oozes from every object, standing in clammy exudation
upon iron, marble, wood, and human flesh; the air is pervaded with a faint
odor as of withered bouquets and dead mint juleps, and the warm steam of
a home washing day is over everything."

Stanton found the "hot, dusty weather, the most disagreeable" he had
ever experienced. "Burning sun all day, sultry at night." Ellen Stanton had
escaped with her children for the summer, leaving her husband alone in
Washington. Writing to her at a mountain retreat in Bedford, Pennsylvania, Stanton acknowledged that "all is silent and lonely, but there is consolation in knowing that you and the children are free from the oppressive
heat and discomfort of Washington."

"Nearly everybody except the members of the unfortunate Can't-get-
away Club has gone to the seaside or countryside," Noah Brooks reported.
"Truly the season is one of languor, lassitude, and laziness," and even "the
reporters have nearly all followed the example of better men and have likewise skeddadled from the heat."

As soon as Mary felt well enough to travel, she, too, fled the capital with
both Tad and Robert, commencing a two-month sojourn in New York,
Philadelphia, and the White and Green Mountains. The cool breezes of
New Hampshire and Vermont would prove beneficial to young Tad,
whose health remained fragile, while the lure of a resort hotel in the
mountains kept Robert by her side through most of August. A correspondent who caught up with her at "Tiptop," Mount Washington, was delighted with her "very easy, agreeable" manner and her "very fair, cheerful,
smiling face."

Only a dozen short telegrams between the Lincolns remain from that
summer. In these brief communications, Lincoln talked about the heat,
shared news of the Kentucky elections, and asked her to let "dear Tad"
know that his nanny goat had run away and left his father "in distress about
it." Only in mid-September, as the time drew near for Mary's return, did
Lincoln admit that he had missed her, repeating in two separate telegrams
his eagerness to be reunited with her and with Tad. Mary understood that
he was "not *given* to letter writing," and so long as she was assured of his
good health, she remained content.

The Lincolns' undemonstrative communications stand in marked con-

trast to the effusive letters the Sewards exchanged all summer, openly sharing their feelings about the family, the war, and the country. "I wish I could
gain from some other source the confidence with which you inspire me
when I am with you," Frances told her husband. "I need it in these disastrous times. . . . The loyalty of the people is now to be put to the test."
Seward urged her to be calm and confident: "Every day since the war
broke out we have drawn on the people for a thousand men, and they have
gone to the field." To her husband, Frances acknowledged that while the
country rejoiced over the victories at Gettysburg and Vicksburg, she despaired when she "read the lists of killed & wounded." Only with Frances
could the stalwart Seward reveal his own distress, confusion, and exhaustion.

While Lincoln spent hours writing letters to keep generals and politicians on an even keel, he apparently never found the solace Seward and
Chase took in their extensive family correspondence. Nor did his wife and
children write regularly. Tad, a slow learner, may not have developed the
skill to easily compose letters. Robert, then entering his junior year at Harvard, surely was capable of penning descriptions of his days in the mountains. Very different in temperament, Lincoln and his eldest son never
seemed to develop a close relationship. During Robert's childhood, Lincoln had been absent for months at a time, traveling the circuits of both
politics and law. At sixteen, Robert entered boarding school in New
Hampshire, and he was a student at Harvard when his father became president. "Thenceforth," Robert noted sadly, "any great intimacy between us
became impossible. I scarcely even had ten minutes quiet talk with him
during his Presidency, on account of his constant devotion to business."

For Lincoln, it was enough to know that his wife and sons were happily
ensconced at the Equinox House in Manchester, Vermont, then considered "a primary summer resort," providing access to fishing, nature walks,
gardens, swimming holes, concerts, croquet, archery, and excellent dining
facilities. During the visit, Mary climbed a mountain, socialized with General Doubleday and his wife, and enjoyed the clear, refreshing air.

• • •

KATE CHASE WOULD REMEMBER the summer of 1863 less for its record-
breaking heat than for her rekindled romance with William Sprague,
elected earlier in the year to the U.S. Senate. When the young millionaire
came to Washington to take his seat, he called on Kate, and their troubled
past was soon forgotten. "We did again join hands, and again join fortunes," Sprague later said. In early May, Sprague invited Kate to visit his
estate in Providence, Rhode Island, so that she would meet his family and

see his immense manufacturing company. Running at full tilt, the company's 10,000 employees could turn out "35,000 pieces of print-cloth" weekly, with the 280,000 spindles and 28 printing machines in the factories. "I want to show you how to make calico from cotton," he told Kate. "You are a statesman's daughter, will doubtless be a statesman's wife, and who if not you, should know how things are done, not how only they are undone or destroyed."

Shortly after they returned to Washington, Sprague asked Chase for Kate's hand in marriage. "The Gov and Miss Kate have consented to take me into their fold," Sprague proudly reported to a friend in New York. Sprague's adoration for Kate is clear from the flood of letters he wrote during the first months of their engagement. "The business which takes my time, my attention, my heart, my all," he wrote, "is of a certain young lady who has become so entwined in every pulsation, that my former self has lost its identity." Without her, he confessed, his life seemed "a wilderness, a blank." He kept her miniature by his side and waited for her return letters "as a drowning man [seizing] at anything to sustain him." A five-day separation seemed "an age" to him, so "strong a hold" had she gained upon his heart. Even when they were both in Washington, he sent her loving notes from his room at the Willard Hotel. "I am my darling up & in sympathy with the sunshine," he wrote early one morning. And another morning, "I hope my darling you are up feeling fresh and happy. Knowing that you are so is happiness to me. I kiss you good morning and adieu."

Kate's attachment to Sprague, however, did not indicate a readiness to leave her father. Nor was Chase, despite his claims, prepared to relinquish his hold on Kate. The impending marriage set in motion a curious series of machinations as to where the young couple should reside. Still harboring the illusory hope that closer proximity to Lincoln would beget greater influence, Chase opened the discussion by suggesting that Kate and William "take the house just as it is and let me find a place suited to my purpose nearer the President's." He assured Sprague that he was not among those fathers "who wish to retain the love & duty of daughters even in larger measure that they are given to their husbands." On the contrary, he wrote, "I want to have Katie honor & love you with an honor & love far exceeding any due to me."

Kate, however, was not persuaded by such protestations. She thought her father would be lost without her daily devotions and her consummate grace in orchestrating his social life. Under her supervision, the parties at the Chase mansion had become legendary. "Probably no woman in American history has had as brilliant a social career," one journalist observed of Kate. "Even the achievements of Dolly Madison pale into insignificance compared with her successes." Fanny Seward considered herself lucky to receive an invitation to one of Kate's parties. "Scarcely a person there whom it was not a pleasure to meet," she bubbled. "I don't know whether it was Miss Chase being so charming herself that made the party pass so pleasantly, but I think so sweet a presence must have lent a charm to the whole."

Unwilling to abandon her role in forwarding Chase's dreams, Kate persuaded William that they should all reside under the same roof. Approaching her father, she insisted that both she and William desired a united household. Though Chase had undoubtedly longed for this very arrangement, he made a show of reluctantly abandoning his "idea of taking a house or apartment near the Presidents" to suit their wishes. "Life is short and uncertain and I am not willing to do anything which will grieve my children," he wrote. "So I yield the point." They agreed that Chase would continue to pay the rent and the servants while William would cover the food and entertainment, assume half the stable expenses, and renovate the house to suit the needs of both a senator and a cabinet official.

Recognizing "the delicate link which has so long united father & daughter," Sprague wisely decided to "respect and honor" their relationship. "I am not afraid that the tenacious affection of a daughter will detract from that she owes to one she accepts for her life companion," he wrote Kate. "I am not so silly as not to see & feel that it is a surer garuantee of a more permanent and enduring love." While he bristled at the discovery that Kate allowed her father to read all of Sprague's letters to her, he was gratified by the praise his writing drew from the ever critical Chase. "Katie showed me yesterday your letters to her," Chase told William, "and I cannot refrain from telling you how much they delighted me." Making no mention of misspellings or grammatical mistakes, as he usually did with Kate and Nettie, Chase assured Sprague that the "manly affection breathed in them satisfied me that I had not given my daughter to one [who] did not fully appreciate her, or to whom she could not give the full wealth of her affections."

For Chase, William's desire to assume "as much of the pecuniary burden as possible" was timely, indeed. The engagement allowed him to divest himself of his financial ties to the Cooke brothers, whose private loans and gifts had assisted him over the years. Recent months had brought mounting criticism over the virtual monopoly the Cookes enjoyed in the lucrative sale of Treasury bonds, but Chase had not felt free to dispense with the arrangement. On June 1, however, he informed Jay Cooke that his compensation for the sale of the bonds would henceforth be reduced. "I have a duty to the country to perform," he sanctimoniously wrote, "which forbids me to pay rates which will not be approved by all right-minded men." The following day, he returned a check for $4,200 that he had received from Cooke as profit on the sale of a stock that he had not paid for. "In order to be able to render most efficient service to our country it is essential for me to *be* right as well as *seem* right & to *seem* right as well as *be* right."

Late in July, Chase joined Kate and Nettie for a few days' vacation in Rhode Island, where Sprague had secured rooms near the shore at South Pier. With a carriage provided by Sprague and good dining in the resort hotels on Narragansett Bay, the hardworking secretary relaxed for the first time in months. Leaving the girls at the seashore, he returned to Washington on August 7. Alone in the big house, he complained to Nettie that his only companion was their dog, Nellie, who "comes to see me every evening after dinner and puts her nose up in my face in a sort of sympathetic way." A sullen irritability is evident in his letters to both girls that summer. He chastised Nettie for her "somewhat ragged looking letter," pointing out how much her carelessness pained him, and he reprimanded Kate for failing to inform him when she borrowed money for the vacation expenses.

In his loneliness, Chase resumed a warm correspondence with Charlotte Eastman, the widow of a former congressman. Handsome and intelligent, she had enjoyed a sporadic friendship with Chase over the years. When the relationship had promised to develop into a romance, however, Kate had disapproved, going "so far as to intercept her letters." Chase had been unwilling to defy his daughter. Now, in Kate's absence, the two wrote to each other again. With inviting detail, Mrs. Eastman described her house on the Massachusetts seashore. She evinced little hope that Chase would join her, however. She suspected that her letters gave him "little satisfaction, as they can do but nothing to advance the object for which it seems to me you live for—Now shall I be frank? and perhaps offend you and tell you I am jealous! and of whom and what, of your Ambition and through that of yourself; for dont Ambition make the worshipper the God of his own idolatry?"

"What a sweet letter you have sent me," Chase replied from his desk at the Treasury. "I have read and reread it. What a charming picture you draw of the old house. . . . It made [me] half feel myself with you & quite wish to be. . . . I am so sorry that you & Katie—one so dear to me as a friend and the other as a daughter don't exactly *jee.*" As for her remarks on his ambition, he acknowledged that he was, in fact, driven in ways that sometimes led him to neglect "duties of friendship & charity." She should understand, however, that he would always "try to direct my ambition to public ends and in honorable ways." It would amuse her to know, he concluded, how many times he had been interrupted while writing this letter, which he had to bring to a close in order to attend to the president.

While the heat enervated most of official Washington, Lincoln thrived on the long days, the relative freedom from office seekers, and the lack of family interference with his work. "The Tycoon is in fine whack," John Hay reported on August 7. "I have rarely seen him more serene & busy. He is managing this war, the draft, foreign relations, and planning a reconstruction of the Union, all at once. I never knew with what tyrannous authority he rules the Cabinet, till now. The most important things he decides & there is no cavil. I am growing more and more firmly convinced that the good of the country absolutely demands that he should be kept where he is till this thing is over. There is no man in the country, so wise so gentle and so firm. I believe the hand of God placed him where he is."

With Mary out of town, Lincoln found John Hay a ready companion. Smart, energetic, and amusing, the twenty-five-year-old Hay had become far more intimately connected to the president than his own eldest son. Their conversation moved easily from linguistics to reconstruction, from Shakespeare to Artemus Ward. Hay had a good sense of humor and, according to William Stoddard, could "tell a story better than most boys of his age." Stoddard long recalled an occasion when he and Nicolay were rocked with laughter at one of Hay's humorous tales. Hearing the noise, Lincoln came to the door. "His feet had made no sound in coming over from his room, or our own racket had drowned any foot-fall, but here was the President." If the young secretaries feared that Lincoln would chastise them for the interruption, he quickly dissipated their concern. He sat down in a chair and demanded that Hay repeat his tale. When the story was done, "down came the President's foot from across his knee, with a heavy stamp on the floor, and out through the hall went an uproarious peal of fun."

On Sunday, August 9, Hay accompanied the president to Alexander Gardner's photo studio at the corner of Seventh and D streets. The pictures taken that day do not reflect what Hay characterized as the president's "very good spirits." Rigidly posed, with one hand on a book and the other at his waist, Lincoln was forced to endure the lengthy process of the photograph, which almost invariably produced a grim, unsmiling portrait. Subjects would be required to sit absolutely still while the photographer removed the cap from the lens to expose the picture. "Don't move a muscle!" the subject would be told, for the slightest twitch would blur the image. Moreover, since "contrived grinning in photographs had not yet become obligatory," many faces, like Lincoln's, took on a melancholy cast.

Lincoln retained his high spirits through much of the summer, buoyed by the thought that "the rebel power is at last beginning to disintegrate." In his diary, Hay described a number of pleasant outings, including an evening journey to the Observatory. They viewed the moon and the star Arcturus through a newly installed telescope before driving out to the Soldiers' Home, where Lincoln read Shakespeare to Hay—"the end of Henry VI and the beginning of Richard III till my heavy eye-lids caught his considerate notice & he sent me to bed."

The route Lincoln traveled to and from the Soldiers' Home took him down Vermont Avenue past the lodgings of Walt Whitman. "I see the President almost every day," Whitman wrote. "None of the artists or pictures has caught the deep, though subtle and indirect expression of this man's face. There is something else there. One of the great portrait painters of two or three centuries ago is needed." Whitman proudly noted that "we have got so that we exchange bows, and very cordial ones. Sometimes the President goes and comes in an open barouche. The cavalry always accompany him, with drawn sabers. Often I notice as he goes out evenings—and sometimes in the morning, when he returns early—he turns off and halts at the large and handsome residence of the Secretary of War, on K Street."

All summer, Stanton harbored hopes that he and Lincoln might escape to the mountains of Pennsylvania. "The President and I have been arranging to make a trip to Bedford," he told Ellen, "but something always turns up to keep him or me in Washington. He is so eager for it that I expect we shall accomplish it before the season is over." In fact, though Stanton finally joined his wife during the first week of September, Lincoln journeyed no farther that summer than the Soldiers' Home.

The president was rarely alone, however. In addition to Hay and Stanton, he could rely on Seward for good companionship. John Hay witnessed a typically wide-ranging conversation between them as the three rode to the Capitol on August 13 to view a sculptural work, *The Progress of Civilization*, recently installed in the eastern pediment of the north wing of the Capitol. The conversation opened on the topic of slavery, slipped back to the time of the Masons and anti-Masons, then turned to the Mexican War. Both Seward and Lincoln agreed that "one fundamental principle of politics is to be always on the side of your country in a war. It kills any party to oppose a war." As, indeed, Lincoln knew from his own experience in opposing the Mexican War.

The following day, Seward left for a two-week tour of upstate New York with foreign ministers, including those from England, France, Spain, Germany, and Russia. Seward had engineered the trip to counter the impression abroad that the lengthy war was starting to exhaust the resources of the North. With Seward as their guide, members of the diplomatic corps journeyed up the Hudson, stopping in Albany, Schenectady, and Cooperstown. They sailed on the Finger Lakes, visited Niagara Falls, and spent the night in Auburn, where they were joined by Seward's neighbors and friends for a picnic on the lake.

"All seemed to be enjoying themselves very much," Frances noted. Seward, extroverted as always, provided a sparkling commentary, excellent food, abundant drink, and good cheer. After months of tense wrangling over the status of the Confederacy, the European ministers saw a different side of Seward and enjoyed his easy camaraderie. "When one comes really to know him," Lord Lyons reported to Lord Russell, "one is surprised to find much to esteem and even to like in him."

More important, the tour allowed the skeptical ministers to witness the boundless resources of the North. "Hundreds of factories with whirring wheels," Fred Seward wrote, "thousands of acres of golden harvest fields, miles of railway trains, laden with freight, busy fleets on rivers, lakes and canals"—all presaged the inevitable triumph of the Union. This clear perception of the Union's strength contributed to the successful resolution of a troubling controversy with Great Britain and France. Since the previous autumn, the administration had been bedeviled by knowledge that the Confederacy had contracts with European shipbuilders for armored vessels vastly superior to anything in the Union fleet. For months, Seward had coupled diplomatic efforts with strident warnings of war should the ironclads leave Europe. Not until September, several weeks after the diplomatic tour, did he receive trustworthy assurances from the governments of England and France that the rams would not be delivered.

With Seward in upstate New York, Stanton in the mountains of Pennsylvania, Nicolay out west, and Hay setting out for a week's vacation in Long Branch, New Jersey, Lincoln was left in relative solitude. "The White House," Stoddard noted, "is deserted, save by our faithful and untiring Chief Magistrate, who, alone of all our public men, is *always* at his post." Notwithstanding, Stoddard observed, "he looks less careworn and emaciated than in the spring, as if, living only for his country, he found his own vigor keeping pace with the returning health of the nation."

CHAPTER 21

"I FEEL TROUBLE
IN THE AIR"

T HE SUMMER OF 1863 marked a crucial transformation in the
Union war effort—the organization and deployment of black
regiments that would eventually amount to 180,000 soldiers, a
substantial proportion of eligible black males. The struggle to open the
door for black recruits had finally ended when Lincoln's Emancipation
Proclamation flatly declared that blacks would "be received into the armed
service of the United States." Three weeks later, Stanton authorized Massachusetts governor John Andrew to raise two regiments of black troops.
Since Massachusetts had only a small black population, Andrew called on
Major George L. Stearns to head a recruitment effort that would reach

into New York and other Northern states. Stearns approached Frederick Douglass for help.

Douglass was overjoyed. He had long believed that the war would not be won so long as the North refused "to employ the black man's arm in suppressing the rebels." He wrote stirring appeals in his *Monthly* magazine and traveled throughout the North, speaking at large meetings in Albany, Syracuse, Buffalo, Philadelphia, and many other cities, offering a dozen answers to the question: "Why should a colored man enlist?" Nothing, he assured them, would more clearly legitimize their call for equal citizenship: "You will stand more erect, walk more assured, feel more at ease, and be less liable to insult than you ever were before. He who fights the battles of America may claim America as his country—and have that claim respected."

The black soldiers who initially answered Douglass's call became part of the famed 54th Massachusetts Regiment. Captained by Robert Gould Shaw, the son of wealthy Boston abolitionists, this first black regiment from the North included two of Frederick Douglass's own sons, Charles and Lewis. On May 28, thousands of Bostonians poured into the streets cheering the men as they marched past the State House and the Common. At the parade ground, they were reviewed by the governor and various high-ranking military officials. "No single regiment has attracted larger crowds," the *Boston Daily Evening Transcript* reported. "Ladies lined the balconies and windows of the houses," waving their handkerchiefs as the brass band led the proud regiment to the parade ground.

Frederick Douglass attended the ceremonies, proudly extolling the "manly bearing" and "admirable marching" of the men he had worked hard to recruit. After bidding his sons farewell, he returned to the task of recruiting with renewed zeal.

Lincoln was in full accord with this drive to build black regiments. Though he had initially resisted proposals to arm blacks, he was now totally dedicated. He urged Banks, Hunter, and Grant to speed the enlisting process and implored Governor Andrew Johnson of Tennessee to raise black troops. "The colored population is the great *available* and yet *unavailed* of, force for restoring the Union," Lincoln wrote. "The bare sight of fifty thousand armed, and drilled black soldiers on the banks of the Mississippi, would end the rebellion at once." Chase, who had argued more strongly than any other cabinet member for black soldiers, took great satisfaction in Lincoln's newfound commitment. "The President is now thoroughly in earnest in this business," he wrote a friend, "& sees it much as I saw it nearly two years ago."

In his efforts to recruit black soldiers, Douglass encountered a series of obstacles forged by white prejudice: black soldiers received less pay than white soldiers, they were denied the enlistment bounty, and they were not allowed to be commissioned as officers. Still, Douglass insisted, "this is no time for hesitation. . . . Once let the black man get upon his person the brass letters, U.S.; let him get an eagle on his button, and a musket on his shoulder, and bullets in his pocket," he told a mass audience in Philadelphia, "and there is no power on the earth or under the earth which can deny that he has earned the right of citizenship in the United States. I say again, this is our chance, and woe betide us if we fail to embrace it."

When the newly organized black troops went into battle—at Port Hudson, Milliken's Bend, and Fort Wagner—they earned great respect from white soldiers and civilians alike for their "bravery and steadiness." If captured, however, they ran the risk of losing their freedom or their lives, for the Confederate Congress had passed an ordinance "dooming to death or slavery every negro taken in arms, and every white officer who commands negro troops."

As word of the unique dangers they faced spread through the black community, Douglass found that the size and enthusiasm of his audiences were swiftly diminishing, as was the number of black enlistments. He blamed Lincoln for not speaking out against the Confederate ordinance. "What has Mr. Lincoln to say about this slavery and murder? What has he said?—Not one word. In the hearing of the nation he is as silent as an oyster on the whole subject." The time for patience with the president had come and gone, he argued. Until he "shall interpose his power to prevent these atrocious assassinations of negro soldiers, the civilized world will hold him equally with Jefferson Davis responsible for them."

Lincoln's failure to speak out and protect the Union's black soldiers convinced Douglass that he could no longer persuade men to enlist in good conscience. "When I plead for recruits, I want to do it with my heart, without qualification," he explained to Major Stearns. "I cannot do that now. The impression settles upon me that colored men have much over-rated the enlightenment, justice and generosity of our rulers at Washington."

In fact, Lincoln was already formulating a response. During the last week of July 1863, he asked Halleck to prepare an Order of Retaliation, which was issued on July 30. The order made clear that "the law of nations and the usages and customs of war as carried on by civilized powers, permit no distinction as to color in the treatment of prisoners of war." The Confederate ordinance represented "a relapse into barbarism" that required action on the part of the Union. "It is therefore ordered that for every sol-

dier of the United States killed in violation of the laws of war, a rebel soldier shall be executed; and for every one enslaved by the enemy or sold
into slavery, a rebel soldier shall be placed at hard labor."

The order was "well-written," the antagonistic Count Gurowski conceded, "but like all Mr. Lincoln's acts it is done almost too late, only when
the poor President was so cornered by events, that shifting and escape became impossible." Douglass agreed but acknowledged that the president,
"being a man of action," might have been waiting "for a case in which he
should be required to act."

Although the retaliatory order alleviated one major concern, Douglass
feared that the lack of "fair play" in the handling of black enrollees would
continue to hamper recruiting. Major Stearns suggested that Douglass
should go to Washington and explain the situation to the president. Having never visited the nation's capital, Douglass experienced an inexpress-
ible "tumult of feeling" when he entered the White House. "I could not
know what kind of a reception would be accorded me. I might be told to go
home and mind my business. . . . Or I might be refused an interview altogether."

Finding a large crowd in the hallway, Douglass expected to wait hours
before gaining an audience with the president. Minutes after presenting
his card, however, he was called into the office. "I was never more quickly
or more completely put at ease in the presence of a great man than in that
of Abraham Lincoln," he later recalled. The president was seated in a chair
when Douglass entered the room, "surrounded by a multitude of books
and papers, his feet and legs were extended in front of his chair. On my approach he slowly drew his feet in from the different parts of the room into
which they had strayed, and he began to rise." As Lincoln extended his
hand in greeting, Douglass hesitantly began to introduce himself. "I know
who you are, Mr. Douglass," Lincoln said. "Mr. Seward has told me all
about you. Sit down. I am glad to see you." Lincoln's warmth put Douglass
instantly at ease. Douglass later maintained that he had "never seen a more
transparent countenance." He could tell "at a glance the justice of the popular estimate of the President['s] qualities expressed in the prefix 'honest' to
the name of Abraham Lincoln."

Douglass laid before the president the discriminatory measures that
were frustrating his recruiting efforts. "Mr. Lincoln listened with earnest
attention and with very apparent sympathy," he recalled. "Upon my ceasing to speak [he] proceeded with an earnestness and fluency of which I had
not suspected him." Lincoln first recognized the indisputable justice of the
demand for equal pay. When Congress passed the bill for black soldiers, he
explained, it "seemed a necessary concession to smooth the way to their

employment at all as soldiers," but he promised that "in the end they shall have the same pay as white soldiers." As for the absence of black officers, Lincoln assured Douglass that "he would sign any commission to colored soldiers whom his Secretary of War should commend to him."

Douglass was particularly impressed by Lincoln's justification for delaying the retaliatory order until the public mind was prepared for it. Had he acted earlier, Lincoln said, before the recent battles "in which negroes had distinguished themselves for bravery and general good conduct," he was certain that "such was the state of public popular prejudice that an outcry would have been raised against the measure. It would be said—Ah! we thought it would come to this. White men were to be killed for negroes." In fact, he confessed to grave misgivings that, "once begun, there was no telling where it would end; that if he could get hold of the Confederate soldiers who had been guilty [of killing black prisoners] he could easily retaliate, but the thought of hanging men for a crime perpetrated by others was revolting to his feelings." While Douglass disagreed, believing the order essential, he respected the "humane spirit" that prompted Lincoln's concerns.

Before they parted, Lincoln told Douglass that he had read a recent speech in which the fiery orator had lambasted "the tardy, hesitating and vacillating policy of the President of the United States." Though he conceded that he might move with frustrating deliberation on large issues, he disputed the accusation of vacillation. "I think it cannot be shown that when I have once taken a position, I have ever retreated from it." Douglass would never forget his first meeting with Lincoln, during which he felt "as though I could . . . put my hand on his shoulder."

Later that same day, Douglass met with Stanton. "The manner of no two men could be more widely different," he observed. "His first glance was that of a man who says: 'Well, what do you want? I have no time to waste upon you or anybody else.' " Nonetheless, once Douglass began to outline much the same issues he had addressed with the president, "contempt and suspicion and brusqueness had all disappeared from his face," and Stanton, too, promised "that justice would ultimately be done." Indeed, Stanton had already implored Congress to remove the discriminatory wage and bounty provisions, which it would eventually do. Impressed by Douglass, Stanton promised to make him an assistant adjutant general assigned to Lorenzo Thomas, then charged with recruiting black soldiers in the Mississippi Valley. The War Department followed up with an offer of a $100-a-month salary plus subsistence and transportation, but the commission was not included. Douglass declined: "I knew too much of

37

President Abraham Lincoln,
photographed by Mathew Brady in 1862.

38

Lincoln's office in the White House *(above)* doubled as the cabinet's meeting room. Late at night, he liked to relax and share stories with his two secretaries, John Nicolay *(below left)* and John Hay *(below right)*, who became almost like sons to him.

39

40

41

Seventy-five-year-old General Winfield Scott *(below)*, veteran of the War of 1812 and the Mexican War, commanded the U.S. Army when Lincoln took office. Shown here with the cabinet *(above)*, Scott suffered from a variety of ailments that limited his active role in military planning.

42

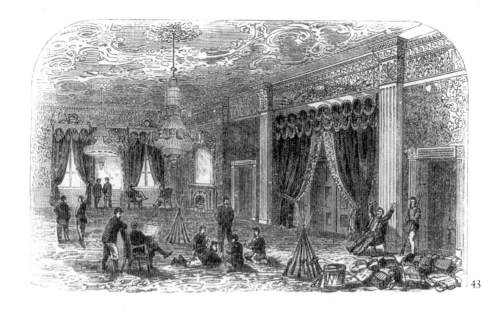

43

Even during the Civil War, ordinary people had nearly unlimited access
to the White House. Volunteer troops bivouacked in the East Room
in May 1861 *(above)*, while large public receptions *(below)* attracted
a "living tide of humanity" who poured in to shake hands
with the president and first lady.

44

45

46

In February 1862, while Mary Lincoln *(left)* hosted a triumphant
reception downstairs, her twelve-year-old son, Willie, lay dying upstairs.
After Mary fell into a depression *(right)*, Lincoln was left to care
for their youngest son, Tad *(below)*, who was
equally devastated by Willie's death.

47

48

49

When Seward became secretary of state *(left)*, he installed his son Fred as his second in command *(above, far right)* and settled his close-knit family, including Augustus *(below, standing)*, Fred *(left)*, Fanny *(right)*, and Fred's wife, Anna *(foreground)*, into an elegant mansion on Lafayette Square.

50

51

Treasury Secretary Salmon Chase *(above)* craved the presidency with every fiber of his being, an ambition shared by his beautiful daughter Kate *(below left, and seated, right)*. Rumors circulated that her 1863 marriage to William Sprague *(below, right)* "was a coldly calculated plan to secure the Sprague millions" to finance her father's 1864 campaign.

52

53

54

55

When his first war secretary, Simon Cameron *(left)*, resigned under fire,
Lincoln called on Edwin M. Stanton *(right)*, who overcame his initial
contempt for the president to embrace a deep friendship.
The Lincoln and Stanton families spent their summers
together at the Soldiers' Home *(below)*.

SOLDIER'S HOME, WASHINGTON, D.C.

56

Francis P. Blair and his wife, Eliza *(middle)*, presided over a political dynasty that included their sons, Postmaster General Montgomery Blair *(bottom right)* and Union general Frank *(bottom left)*. Daughter Elizabeth's *(top right)* voluminous letters to her husband, Captain Samuel P. Lee *(top left)*, left a vivid record of life in Washington during the Civil War.

62

In addition to their cabinet duties, both Navy Secretary Gideon
Welles *(above)* and Attorney General Edward Bates *(below)*
kept detailed diaries that recorded the inner workings
of the Lincoln administration.

63

64

In letters to his wife, Mary Ellen *(right)*, General George B. McClellan regularly derided Lincoln, his cabinet, and most of the hierarchy in the Union army, while crediting himself with every success. Admirers hailed him as a young Napoleon *(below)*.

65

67

66

Lincoln went through a succession of generals, including Ambrose E.
Burnside *(below left)* and Joseph Hooker *(below right)*, before he found
a winning team in Ulysses S. Grant *(above left)* and
William T. Sherman *(above right)*.

69

68

70

71

Antislavery leader Frederick Douglass *(left)* and Senator Charles
Sumner *(right)* urged Lincoln to bring blacks into the Union army.
Ultimately, almost two hundred thousand black men served,
including this young soldier *(below)*.

72

Lincoln took more than a dozen trips to the front, both to consult with his generals and to inspire the troops *(above)*. Scenes of the dead littered on the battlefield *(below)* tore at his heart.

Lincoln and his son Tad walked through the Confederate capital of Richmond on April 4, 1865. Freed slaves crowded the streets, shouting, "Glory! Hallelujah!" when Lincoln came into view.

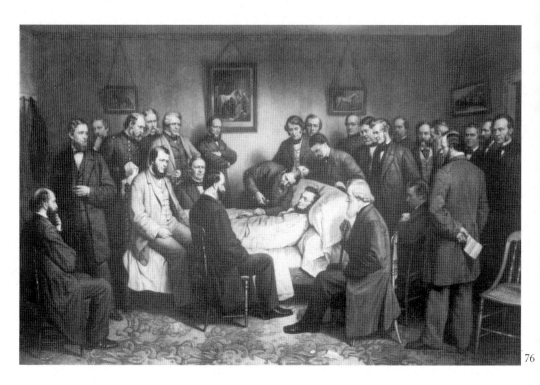

76

As Lincoln lay dying in the Petersen boardinghouse, he was surrounded
by family, members of his cabinet, congressmen, senators, and military
officials. When Lincoln died at 7:22 A.M. on April 15, 1865,
Stanton proclaimed: "Now he belongs to the ages."

camp life and the value of shoulder straps in the army to go into the service without some visible mark of my rank."

Douglass and Lincoln had established a relationship that would prove important for both men in the weeks and months ahead. In subsequent speeches, Douglass frequently commented on his gracious reception at the White House. "Perhaps you may like to know how the President of the United States received a black man at the White House," he would say. "I will tell you how he received me—just as you have seen one gentleman receive another." As the crowd erupted into "great applause," he continued, "I tell you I felt big there!"

•   •   •

IN THE RELATIVE QUIET that followed, Lincoln immersed himself in the task of composing another public letter. This letter was addressed to James Conkling, the old Springfield friend in whose office he had anxiously awaited news from Chicago during the Republican nominating convention. As a leading Illinois Republican, Conkling had invited Lincoln to attend a mass meeting in Springfield on September 3, organized to rally loyal Unionists in a show of strength against the Copperhead influence, which remained strong in the Northwest. Union victories at Gettysburg and Vicksburg had created a deceptive feeling that peace was close at hand. False rumors circulated that Lincoln had received and rejected several viable peace proposals. It was essential to derail these damaging stories and halt Copperhead momentum in its tracks. While he doubtless would have been received with adoration in his hometown, Lincoln decided to remain in Washington and compose a comprehensive letter for Conkling to read at the meeting and then have printed for mass distribution.

After completing an early draft, Lincoln searched out someone to listen as he read it aloud. It was a Sunday night, and the mansion was nearly vacant. Entering the library, the president was delighted to find William Stoddard. "Ah! I'm glad you're here," Lincoln said. "Come over into my room." Stoddard followed him into his office. "Sit down," Lincoln urged. "What I want is an audience. Nothing sounds the same when there isn't anybody to hear it and find fault with it." Stoddard expressed doubt that he would be inclined to criticize the president's words. "Yes, you will," Lincoln good-humoredly replied. "Everybody else will. It's just what I want you to do." Then, taking the sheets of foolscap paper from the end of the cabinet table on which he had been writing, he began to read.

Warming to the task, Lincoln allowed his voice to rise and fall as if he were speaking to an audience of thousands. When he finished, he asked

Stoddard's impression. Stoddard's sole objection was to fault Lincoln's metaphor—"Uncle Sam's web-feet"—for the navy gunboats that plied the rivers and bayous. "I never saw a web-footed gunboat in all my life," Stoddard said. "They're a queer kind of duck." Lincoln laughed. "Some of 'em did get ashore, though. I'll leave it in, now I know how it's going to sound." Then, thanking Stoddard, he bade him good night.

The address was designed to curb the "deceptive and groundless" rumors that Lincoln had secretly rejected peace proposals. If any legitimate propositions should be received, he pledged, they would not be kept a secret from the people he was elected to serve. "But, to be plain," he went on, "you are dissatisfied with me about the negro. . . . You dislike the emancipation proclamation; and, perhaps, would have it retracted." On this point there would be no compromise: "it can not be retracted, any more than the dead can be brought to life," for "the promise being made, must be kept." Furthermore, black soldiers had become so integral to the war effort that "some of the commanders of our armies in the field who have given us our most important successes, believe the emancipation policy, and the use of colored troops, constitute the heaviest blow yet dealt to the rebellion. . . .

"Peace does not appear so distant as it did," Lincoln concluded. "And then, there will be some black men who can remember that, with silent tongue, and clenched teeth, and steady eye, and well-poised bayonet, they have helped mankind on to this great consummation; while, I fear, there will be some white ones, unable to forget that, with malignant heart, and deceitful speech, they have strove to hinder it."

Lincoln continued to refine his letter over the next ten days, stealing what time he could from his public duties. He finally sent it, accompanied with a personal note to Conkling: "You are one of the best public readers. I have but one suggestion. Read it very slowly." An immense crowd was expected, drawn "from the farm and the workshop," the local newspaper reported, "from the office and the counting-room," to prove to the Copperheads that behind the soldiers already in the field were "hundreds of thousands more who are willing to offer their services whenever the country calls."

Confident in his final composition, Lincoln anticipated a positive reception on September 3 when it would be read to the crowd and then given to newspapers for publication the following day. When he awoke on the morning of the mass meeting, however, he was furious to see a truncated version of his letter printed in the Washington *Daily Chronicle*. Lincoln immediately complained to the editor, John Forney. Don't blame us, Forney explained to Lincoln, we got it from the Associated Press, and it's in daily newspapers around the country. Provoked, Lincoln telegraphed

Conkling in Springfield. "I am mortified this morning to find the letter to you, botched up, in the Eastern papers, telegraphed from Chicago. How did this happen?"

Hearing nothing that day from Conkling, Lincoln remained testy. When a petitioner tried to solicit his help in securing property for a Memphis woman whose husband was in the Confederate Army, the president uncharacteristically replied that he had "neither the means nor time" to consider the request and that "the impropriety of bringing such cases to me, is obvious to any one."

The following morning, a message arrived from Conkling. Apparently, he had telegraphed the letter in advance, with "strict injunctions not to permit it to be published before the meeting or make any improper use of it." He was "mortified" that someone had broken faith, but trusted that "no prejudicial results have been experienced as the whole Letter was published the next day."

In fact, the publication of the entire letter received excellent reviews. "Disclaiming the arts of the diplomatist, the cunning of the politician, and the graces of rhetoric, he comes straight to the points he wants to discuss," praised the *New York Daily Tribune*. "The most consummate rhetorician never used language more pat to the purpose," the *New York Times* declared, "and still there is not a word in the letter not familiar to the plainest plowman." While "felicity of speech" was usually linked to "high culture," the *Times* continued, Lincoln, "in his own independent, and perhaps we might say very peculiar, way," exhibits a "felicity of speech far surpassing" stylistic preference. He possesses a far more valuable "felicity of thought," which "invariably gets at the needed truth of the time," hitting "the very nail of all others which needs driving." The *Philadelphia Inquirer* had regarded Lincoln's unconventional habit of writing public letters with skepticism, but granted that his recent letters, including this one, "have dispelled the doubt. If he is as felicitous in the future, we hope he will continue to write."

"His last letter is a great thing," Hay told Nicolay a few days later. "Some hideously bad rhetoric—some indecorums that are infamous—yet the whole letter takes its solid place in history, as a great utterance of a great man. The whole Cabinet could not have tinkered up a letter which could have been compared with it. He can snake a sophism out of its hole, better than all the trained logicians of all schools."

In its fulsome praise of the letter to Conkling, the *New York Times* also commended a long line of Lincoln's writings, including his inaugural, the letters to McClellan made public by the congressional Committee on the Conduct of the War, and his published letters to Greeley and Corning, which revealed "the same fitness to the occasion, and the same effectiveness in its own direction." Taken together, these remarkable documents had made Lincoln "the most popular man in the Republic. All the denunciations and all the arts of demagogues are perfectly powerless to wean the people from their faith in him."

"I know the people want him," Hay wrote to Nicolay, looking forward to the next election. "There is no mistaking that fact. But politicians are strong yet & he is not their 'kind of a cat.' I hope God wont see fit to scourge us for our sins by any one of the two or three most prominent candidates on the ground."

•   •   •

BY THE MIDDLE of September 1863, all the members of Lincoln's cabinet had returned from their summer sojourns. Seward came back invigorated by his trip through the lake region with the diplomatic corps. Bates was back from Missouri in time to celebrate his seventieth birthday, grateful that his long life had "been crowned with many blessings, and, comparatively few crosses." He noted with pride that, as a public figure, he had achieved a reputation "for knowledge and probity, quite as good as I deserve." Stanton, too, had enjoyed a much-needed vacation with his family in the mountains of Pennsylvania. Chase, in characteristic fashion, had allowed himself scant respite from work, leaving his daughters at the seashore and then peevishly awaiting their return. Welles was gratified to return from his ten-day visit to the Navy Yards, noting in his diary that all his colleagues seemed "glad to see me,—none more so than the President, who cordially and earnestly greeted me. I have been less absent than any other member and was therefore perhaps more missed." Lincoln himself still enjoyed leisurely nights at the Soldiers' Home and looked forward to Mary's homecoming from the Green Mountains.

Grim news from Tennessee deflated the genial, relaxed mood of the president and his cabinet. After the victories at Gettysburg and Vicksburg, Lincoln and Stanton had hoped that General Rosecrans, with the Army of the Cumberland, could deliver the "finishing blow to the rebellion." He was positioned to push the enemy from Chattanooga and Knoxville, Tennessee, with an eye to advancing on Georgia. However, after Rosecrans delivered "a great and bloodless victory at Chattanooga" as the enemy fled from the city before advancing troops, the Confederates regrouped and "unexpectedly appeared in force, on the south bank of [the] Chicamauga." A furious battle commenced on Saturday, September 19. Within thirty-six hours, the telegrams from the field indicated a stunning Confederate victory. "Chicamauga is as fatal a name in our history as Bull

Run," Dana wired Stanton. Union casualties totaled sixteen thousand men. "We have met with a serious disaster," Rosecrans acknowledged. "Enemy overwhelmed us, drove our right, pierced our center and scattered troops there."

Lincoln told Welles that the dispatches reached him "at the Soldiers' Home shortly after he got asleep, and so disturbed him that he had no more rest, but arose and came to the city and passed the remainder of the night awake and watchful." At daybreak, the president wandered into Hay's room, where, seated on the bed, he broke the news to his young aide. "Well, Rosecrans has been whipped, as I feared. I have feared it for several days. I believe I feel trouble in the air before it comes."

Later that same day, perhaps hoping that the presence of his family might lift his spirits, Lincoln telegraphed Mary. "The air is so clear and cool, and apparently healthy, that I would be glad for you to come. Nothing very particular, but I would be glad [to] see you and Tad." Mary responded immediately, saying she was "anxious to return home" and had already made plans to do so.

As further reports filtered in, the fallout of the battle proved "less unfavorable than was feared," a relieved Chase noted. General George Thomas's corps had held its ground, and the rebels had lost even more troops than the Federals. Chattanooga "still remains in our hands," Charles Dana wired to Stanton and, with reinforcements of twenty to thirty thousand troops "can be held by this army for from fifteen to twenty days." Without the additional troops, however, the outnumbered Federals would have to abandon Chattanooga or face another potentially disastrous battle. Everything hinged on whether this massive movement of troops would reach Tennessee in time. Shortly before midnight on Wednesday, Stanton came up with a bold idea that required the president's approval.

Unwilling to waste the remainder of the night, Stanton dispatched messengers to bring Lincoln, Halleck, Seward, and Chase to a secret meeting in his office. Chase had just retired for the night when the courier rang his bell. "The Secretary of War desires that you will come to the Department immediately & has sent a carriage for you," he announced. Chase "hastily rose & dressed," terrified that the enemy had captured Rosecrans and his entire army. John Hay was sent to the Soldiers' Home to summon Lincoln, who, like Chase, was already in bed. As Lincoln rose to dress, "he was considerably disturbed," saying that "it was the first time Stanton had ever sent for him." Guided by the light of the moon, Lincoln and Hay then rode back to the War Department.

When the five men were assembled around the table, the austere Stanton said: "I have invited this meeting because I am thoroughly convinced that something must be done & done immediately." He proceeded to out-line an audacious proposal to remove twenty thousand men from General Meade's Army of the Potomac to Nashville and Chattanooga under Gen-eral Hooker's command. The plan struck both Halleck and Lincoln as dangerous and impractical. Halleck protested that it would take at least forty days to reach Tennessee. The troops would arrive too late, and Meade would be left vulnerable on the Rappahannock. The president agreed. "Why," he quipped, "you cant get one corps into Washington in the time you fix for reaching Nashville." A humorous anecdote he em-ployed to illustrate his point "greatly annoyed" Stanton, who remarked that "the danger was too imminent & the occasion [too] serious for jokes." He said that "he had fully considered the question of practicability & should not have submitted his proposition had he not fully satisfied him-self" as to its feasibility.

After further discussion, Chase suggested taking a break for the refresh-ments Stanton had prepared. "On returning," Chase recalled, "Mr. Seward took up the subject & supported Mr. Stantons proposition with ex-cellent arguments." Chase believed that Seward's support for the proposal was instrumental. Sensing his advantage, Stanton immediately sent an or-derly to find Colonel D. C. McCallum, director of the Department of Mil-itary Railroads. Stanton had briefed McCallum earlier in the evening and directed him to prepare an estimate of the time necessary to transfer the troops by rail if all available trains were put at his disposal. When McCal-lum entered, Lincoln described the proposition and asked him to estimate how long it would take to achieve the goal. Without disclosing that he had received prior notice to consider the matter, McCallum asked for a mo-ment to "make a few figures." Seated at a desk with timetables spread before him, he worked for some time while the room remained silent. Fi-nally, he stood up and said: "I can complete it in seven days."

"Good!" Stanton exclaimed, turning contemptuously to Halleck. "I told you so! I knew it could be done! Forty days! Forty days indeed, when the life of the nation is at stake!" He then addressed McCallum: "Go ahead; begin now." At this point, Lincoln interrupted. "I have not yet given my consent," he reminded the secretary of war. "Colonel McCal-lum, are you sure about this?" Lincoln asked. "There must be no mistake." When McCallum said he would "pledge [his] life to accomplish it inside of seven days," Lincoln was satisfied. "Mr. Secretary, you are the captain. Give the necessary orders and I will approve them."

Relentlessly, Stanton worked for more than forty-eight hours straight, commandeering trains for military use, telegraphing railroad managers along the route, determining the various gauges of the tracks. He acquired the provisions necessary for soldiers and horses to travel straight across the Alleghenies into East Tennessee without a stop to resupply.

The first train left Washington at 5 p.m. on September 25, with departures every hour until 23,000 men and 1,100 horses, 9 batteries, and hundreds of wagons, tents, and supplies arrived in Tennessee ready to join Rosecrans in defense of Chattanooga. Monitoring reports from every station along the way, Stanton refused to go home. When exhaustion overtook him, he would collapse on his couch for a few hours, a cologne-moistened handkerchief tied around his forehead. Only when it became clear that the movement would succeed within the promised seven days did he agree to leave his post. "It was an extraordinary feat of logistics," James McPherson writes, "the longest and fastest movement of such a large body of troops before the twentieth century."

The immediate peril was past, but Dana's reports in the following weeks indicated that the rebels had cut off supply routes into Chattanooga and that the troops had lost confidence in Rosecrans. Lincoln and Stanton decided that the time had come for a change in command. Stanton telegraphed Grant to leave Cairo, Illinois, for Louisville, Kentucky, where he would "meet an officer of the War Department" and receive new instructions. When Grant reached Indianapolis, he discovered that the War Department officer was Stanton himself. This was the first meeting between the two men.

Stanton presented Grant with a choice between two orders. Both offered him command of a new "Military Division of the Mississippi" encompassing the Departments of the Cumberland, the Ohio, and the Tennessee. The first left the departmental commanders in place. Grant chose the second order, which replaced Rosecrans with Thomas. Stanton spent a day with Grant discussing the overall military situation before the general departed for Chattanooga. There, under his leadership, the Federals eventually drove the rebels from Tennessee after a stunning victory at Missionary Ridge.

In his memoirs, Grant credits Stanton for playing an important role in saving Chattanooga. The unprecedented troop movement prevented a retreat that, Grant acknowledged, "would have been a terrible disaster." Chase, too, lauded Stanton. "The country does not know how much it owes Edwin M. Stanton for that nights work."

It was this indomitable drive that Lincoln had sought when he put aside any resentment at the humiliation Stanton had inflicted years earlier in Cincinnati. The bluntness and single-minded intensity behind Stanton's brusque dismissal of Lincoln at that first acquaintance were the qualities the president valued in his secretary of war—whom he would affectionately call his "Mars."

Those who observed the improbable pair in the little room adjoining the telegraph office noted the "esteem and affection" that characterized their relationship. "It was an interesting and a pleasant sight," clerk Charles Benjamin recalled, "that of Mr. Lincoln seated with one long leg crossed upon the other, his head a little peaked and his face lit up by the animation of talking or listening, while Mr. Stanton would stand sidewise to him, with one hand resting lightly on the high back of the chair in the brief intervals of that everlasting occupation of wiping his spectacles." Should Lincoln rise from the writing desk that Stanton arranged for him, "the picturesqueness of the scene" would give way to laughter, for "the striking differences in height and girth at once suggested the two *gendarmes* in the French comic opera."

"No two men were ever more utterly and irreconcilably unlike," Stanton's private secretary, A. E. Johnson, observed. "The secretiveness which Lincoln wholly lacked, Stanton had in marked degree; the charity which Stanton could not feel, coursed from every pore in Lincoln. Lincoln was for giving a wayward subordinate seventy times seven chances to repair his errors; Stanton was for either forcing him to obey or cutting off his head without more ado. Lincoln was as calm and unruffled as the summer sea in moments of the gravest peril; Stanton would lash himself into a fury over the same condition of things. Stanton would take hardships with a groan; Lincoln would find a funny story to fit them. Stanton was all dignity and sternness, Lincoln all simplicity and good nature . . . yet no two men ever did or could work better in harness. They supplemented each other's nature, and they fully recognized the fact that they were a necessity to each other."

Johnson believed that "in dealing with the public, Lincoln's heart was greater than his head, while Stanton's head was greater than his heart." The antithetical styles are typified in the story of a congressman who had received Lincoln's authorization for the War Department's aid in a project. When Stanton refused to honor the order, the disappointed petitioner returned to Lincoln, telling him that Stanton had not only countermanded the order but had called the president a damned fool for issuing it. "Did Stanton say I was a d——d fool?" Lincoln asked. "He did, sir," the congressman replied, "and repeated it." Smiling, the president remarked: "If Stanton said I was a d——d fool, then I must be one, for he is nearly always right, and generally says what he means. I will step over and see him."

As Stanton came to know and understand Lincoln, his initial disdain turned to admiration. When George Harding, his old partner in the Reaper trial, assumed that Stanton was the author of the "remarkable passages" in one of Lincoln's messages, Stanton set him straight. "Lincoln wrote it—every word of it; and he is capable of more than that, Harding, no men were ever so deceived as we at Cincinnati."

"Few war ministers have had such real personal affection and respect for their king or president as Mr. Stanton had for Mr. Lincoln," a contemporary observed. Both had suffered great personal losses, and both were haunted all their days by thoughts of mortality and death. When Stanton was eighteen, a cholera epidemic had spread through the Midwest. Victims were buried as quickly as possible in an effort to contain the plague. Learning that a young friend had been buried within hours of falling ill, Stanton panicked, fearing that "she had been buried alive while in a faint." He raced to the grave, where, with the help of a medical student friend, he exhumed her body to determine if she was truly dead. Contact with the body led to his own infection and near death from cholera. When his beloved wife, Mary, died ten years later, he insisted on including her wedding ring, valuable pieces of her jewelry, and some of his correspondence in her casket. He spent hours at her gravesite, and when he could not be there, he sent an employee to stand guard.

That Lincoln was also preoccupied with death is clear from the themes of many of his favorite poems that addressed the ephemeral nature of life and reflected his own painful acquaintance with death. He particularly cherished "Mortality," by William Knox, and transcribed a copy for the Stantons.

> *Oh! Why should the spirit of mortal be proud?*
> *Like a swift-fleeting meteor, a fast-flying cloud,*
> *A flash of lightning, a break of the wave,*
> *He passeth from life to his rest in the grave.*

He could recite from memory "The Last Leaf," by Oliver Wendell Holmes, and once claimed to the painter Francis Carpenter that "for pure pathos" there was "nothing finer . . . in the English language" than the six-line stanza:

> *The mossy marbles rest*
> *On lips that he has prest*
> *In their bloom,*
> *And the names he loved to hear*
> *Have been carved for many a year*
> *On the tomb.*

Yet, beyond sharing a romantic and philosophical preoccupation with death, the commander in chief and the secretary of war shared the harrowing knowledge that their choices resulted in sending hundreds of thousands of young men to their graves. Stanton's Quaker background made the strain particularly unbearable. As a young man, he had written a passionate essay decrying society's exaltation of war. "Why is it," he asked, that military generals "are praised and honored instead of being punished as malefactors?" After all, the work of war is "the making of widows and orphans—the plundering of towns and villages—the exterminating & spoiling of all, making the earth a slaughterhouse." Though governments might argue war's necessity to achieve certain objectives, "how much better might they accomplish their ends by some other means? But if generals are useful so are butchers, and who will say that because a butcher is useful he should be honored?"

Three decades after writing this, Stanton found himself responsible for an army of more than 2 million men. "There could be no greater madness," he reasoned, "than for a man to encounter what I do for anything less than motives that overleap time and look forward to eternity." Lincoln, too, found the horrific scope of the burden hard to fathom. "Doesn't it strike you as queer that I, who couldn't cut the head off of a chicken, and who was sick at the sight of blood, should be cast into the middle of a great war, with blood flowing all about me?"

Like Stanton, the president tried to console himself that the Civil War, however terrible, represented a divine will at work in human affairs. The previous year, he had granted an audience to a group of Quakers, including Eliza Gurney. "If I had had my way," he reportedly said during the meeting, "this war would never have been commenced; if I had been allowed my way this war would have been ended before this, but we find it still continues; and we must believe that He permits it for some wise purpose of his own, mysterious and unknown to us; and though with our limited understandings we may not be able to comprehend it, yet we cannot but believe, that He who made the world still governs it."

He understood the terrible conflict suffered by the Friends, he wrote Mrs. Gurney later. "On principle, and faith, opposed to both war and oppression, they can only practically oppose oppression by war." Their support and their prayers, even as they endured their own "very great trial," would never be forgotten. "Meanwhile," he continued, "we must work earnestly in the best light He gives us, trusting that so working still conduces to the great ends He ordains. Surely He intends some great good to follow this mighty convulsion, which no mortal could make, and no mortal could stay."

• • •

As the friendship between Stanton and Lincoln deepened, Chase, who had been Stanton's most intimate companion, was increasingly marginalized. Chase maintained a warm relationship with the secretary of war, however. Stanton still wrote affectionate notes to him. "I return your knife which by some means found its way into my pocket," Stanton had written Chase the previous winter. "Let me add that, 'if you love me like I love you no knife can cut our love in two.'" A year later, Stanton would ask Chase to stand as godfather to his newborn child. Nevertheless, the balance of power between the two men had shifted. Stanton was now a happily married man with four children. The overworked secretary of war no longer begrudged the lack of time Chase was able to spend with him. On the contrary, it was Chase who now had to pay court to Stanton. Deprived of access to vital military decisions, Chase was forced to rely on the war secretary for the latest intelligence. Stanton had once yearned to spend entire evenings in Chase's study; now Chase was lucky to obtain a private conversation with his old friend when he joined the crowd that gathered in the telegraph office at the end of the working day.

"It is painful for one to be so near the springs of action and yet unable to touch them," Chase admitted to an acquaintance. "It is almost like the nightmare in oppressiveness, and worse because there is no illusion. I can only counsel; and that without any certainty of being understood, or, if understood, of being able to obtain concurrence, or, even after concurrence, action."

Chase's frustration with his position was alleviated only by his dreams of future glory, by his dogged hope that he, rather than Lincoln, would be the Republican nominee in 1864. In an era when single-term presidencies were the rule, he believed that if he could outflank Lincoln on Reconstruction—an issue most dear to radical Republicans—he could capture the nomination. The recent victories at Gettysburg and Vicksburg had created an illusion in the North that the end of the war was at hand. Questions of how the rebel states should be brought back into the Union began to dominate discussions in the halls of Congress, at dinner parties, in newspaper editorials, and in the smoke-filled bar of the Willard Hotel.

The issue divided the Republican Party. Radicals insisted that only those who had never displayed even indirect support for the Confederacy should be allowed to vote in the redeemed states. Lawyers and teachers who had not been staunch Unionists should not be allowed to resume their professions. Slavery should be immediately abolished without compensation, and newly freed blacks should be allowed to vote in some cases. Conservative Republicans preferred compensated emancipation and a lenient definition of who should gain suffrage. They argued that in every Southern state, a silent majority of non-slaveholders had been dragged into secession by the wealthy plantation owners. It would be unjust to exclude them in the new order so long as they would take an oath to uphold both the Union and emancipation.

It was assumed in political circles that Lincoln would be the "standard-bearer for the Conservatives," while Chase would be "the champion of the Radicals." The state elections in the fall would presumably serve as the opening round of the presidential race. It was expected that Chase would aggressively promote the candidacies of fellow radicals, who, in turn, would be indebted to him the following year. While Chase's desire for the presidency was no less worthy a pursuit than Lincoln's, Noah Brooks observed, Chase's decision to pursue that ambition from within the president's cabinet rather than resign his seat and openly proclaim his campaign struck many as disingenuous.

Chase's strategy was to approach potential supporters without expressly acknowledging that he would run. Late at night in his study, he wrote hundreds of letters to local officials, congressional leaders, generals, and journalists, citing the failures of the Lincoln administration. "I should fear nothing," he wrote the editor of the *Cincinnati Gazette*, "if we had An *Administration* in the first sense of the word guided by a bold, resolute, farseeing, & active mind, guided by an honest, earnest heart. But this we have not. Oh! for energy & economy in the management of the War."

A similar style prevailed in all of his letters. After detailing the flaws in Lincoln's leadership, Chase would suggest the differences that would characterize his own presidency. He denied that he coveted the position, but said he would accept the burden if pressed by his countrymen. "If I were myself controlled merely by personal sentiments I should prefer the re-election of Mr. Lincoln," Chase explained, but "I think that a man of different qualities from those the President has will be needed for the next four years. I am not anxious to be regarded as that man; but I am quite willing to refer that question to the decision of those who agree in thinking that some such man should be had."

As in 1860, Chase took great pains to cultivate the press, not recognizing that it was too early to extract binding commitments. He was thrilled by Horace Greeley's letter in late September, telling him that he knew no one "better qualified for President than yourself, nor one whom I should more cordially support." Chase apparently discounted Greeley's closing caveat that in six months, events might dictate the need to concentrate on another candidate. Similarly, while Chase elicited assurance from Hiram

Barney, the head of the New York Custom House, that he was his "first choice for the presidency," Barney insisted on deciding only when the time came "whether yourself, the President, or some other person should receive it."

Lincoln was fully aware of what Chase was doing. Governor Dennison alerted him that Chase was "working like a beaver," and Seward cautioned that several organizations were "fixing to control delegate appointments for Mr. Chase." Ohio congressman Samuel Cox warned the White House that Chase had tied up "nearly the whole strength of the New England States." A Pennsylvanian politician informed the White House that Chase had so ardently campaigned for his support that he could see the "Presidency glaring out of both eyes." John Hay learned that Chase had called on the New York journalist Theodore Tilton, working "all a summer's day" to maneuver the influential *Independent* to his side.

Whereas Lincoln's loyal young secretary was disturbed by "Chase's mad hunt after the Presidency," Lincoln was amused. Chase's incessant presidential ambitions reminded him of the time when he was "plowing corn on a Kentucky farm" with a lazy horse that suddenly sped forward energetically to "the end of the furrow." Upon reaching the horse, he discovered "an enormous chin-fly fastened upon him, and knocked him off," not wanting "the old horse bitten in that way." His companion said that it was a mistake to knock it off, for "that's all that made him go."

"Now," Lincoln concluded, "if Mr. [Chase] has a presidential chin-fly biting him, I'm not going to knock him off, if it will only make his department go." Lincoln agreed that his secretary's tactics were in "very bad taste," and "was sorry the thing had begun, for though the matter did not annoy him his friends insisted that it ought to." Lincoln's friends could not understand why the president continued to approve appointments for avid Chase supporters who were known to be "hostile to the President's interests." Lincoln merely asserted that he would rather let "Chase have his own way in these sneaking tricks than getting into a snarl with him by refusing him what he asks." Moreover, he had no thought of dismissing Chase while he was hard at work raising the resources needed to support the immense Union Army.

Lincoln's response to Chase was neither artless nor naive. His old friend Leonard Swett maintained that there never was a greater mistake than the impression that Lincoln was a "frank, guileless, unsophisticated man." In fact, "he handled and moved man *remotely* as we do pieces upon a chessboard." Nor did Lincoln's posture toward Chase imply a tepid desire for a second term. Swett was correct in supposing that Lincoln "was much more eager for it, than he was for the first one." The Union, emancipation, his reputation, his honor, and his legacy—all depended on the outcome of the ongoing war. But he recognized it was safer to keep Chase as a dubious ally within the administration rather that to cut him loose to mount a full-blown campaign. Meanwhile, so long as Chase remained in the cabinet, Lincoln insisted on treating him with respect and dignity.

That Chase was disconcerted by Lincoln's warmth is evident in a letter he wrote to James Watson Webb, the former editor who was now the American minister to Brazil. After criticizing Lincoln's "disjointed method of administration" and admitting that he had "been often tempted to retire," Chase acknowledged that "the President has always treated me with such personal kindness and has always manifested such fairness and integrity of purpose, that I have not found myself free to throw up my trust. . . . So I still work on."

Lincoln told a worried Hay that he had "all along clearly seen [Chase's] plan of strengthening himself. Whenever he [sees] that an important matter is troubling me, if I am compelled to decide it in a way to give offense to a man of some influence he always ranges himself in opposition to me and persuades the victim that he has been hardly dealt by and that he (C.) would have arranged it very differently. It was so with Gen. Fremont—with Genl. Hunter when I annulled his hasty proclamation—with Gen. Butler when he was recalled from New Orleans." Recognizing the truth of Lincoln's words, Hay speculated that "Chase would try to make capital out of this Rosecrans business," though Lincoln had simply relieved the general from command of the Department of the Tennessee at Grant's request. Lincoln drolly replied: "I suppose he will, like the bluebottle fly, lay his eggs in every rotten spot he can find."

In late September, as the rift within Missouri's Republican Party threatened to erupt into open warfare, Chase continued his divisive plotting. Lincoln sought to keep radicals and conservatives united against the rebels. Chase aligned himself with the radicals. The struggle centered on Reconstruction. Since the Emancipation Proclamation did not extend to the loyal border states, the people of Missouri were left to determine the fate of slavery independently in their state. The conservatives, led by Frank Blair and Bates's brother-in-law Governor Hamilton Gamble, were in favor of a gradual emancipation that provided protection to slaveholders during a transitional period. Radical leaders such as B. Gratz Brown, Charles Drake, and Henry Blow favored changes in the state constitution that would immediately extinguish slavery.

So flammable had the dispute become that Governor Gamble worried the radicals intended to overthrow the elected state government. For their part, the radicals had come to believe that General John M. Schofield, the military commander of Missouri whom Lincoln had put in place as a neutral figure, had become a conservative partisan. He was accused of abusing his authority by arresting leading radicals and suppressing radical papers under the guise of military necessity.

On September 30, a delegation of radicals led by Charles Drake journeyed to Washington to demand Schofield's removal. The night before the scheduled meeting, Lincoln talked with Hay about the tense situation. He acknowledged Hay's argument that "the Radicals would carry the State and it would be well not to alienate them." Moreover, he believed that "these Radical men have in them the stuff which must save the state and on which we must mainly rely." They would never abandon the cause of emancipation, "while the Conservatives, in casting about for votes to carry through their plans, are tempted to affiliate with those whose record is not clear." If he had to choose, Lincoln told his aide, "if one side *must* be crushed out & the other cherished," he would "side with the Radicals." On another occasion, he had expressed this affinity more strongly, stating that "they are nearer to me than the other side, in thought and sentiment, though bitterly hostile personally." While they might be "the unhandiest devils in the world to deal with . . . their faces are set Zionwards."

Nevertheless, Lincoln refused to be coerced into choosing one faction or the other, and resented the radicals' demand that he treat Gamble, Frank Blair, and the conservatives "as copperheads and enemies to the Govt." rather than as mere political opponents. "This is simply monstrous," Lincoln declared, to denounce men who had courageously upheld the Union in the early days, when that affiliation threatened not only their political futures but their very lives. By contrast, the delegation's vociferous leader, Charles Drake, was originally a Southern-leaning Democrat who had delighted in railing against Black Republicans. "Not that he objected to penitent rebels being radical: he was glad of it: but fair play: let not the pot make injurious reference to the black base of the kettle: he was in favor of short statutes of limitations." Welles understood Lincoln's dilemma. "So intense and fierce" were these radicals, he wrote in his diary, that they might well "inflict greater injury—on those Republicans . . . who do not conform to their extreme radical and fanatical views than on the Rebels in the field." Such vindictiveness, he lamented, was "among the saddest features of the times."

Lincoln assured Hay that if the radicals could "show that Schofield has done anything wrong & has interfered to their disadvantage with State politics," he would consider their case. But if Schofield had "incurred their ill will by refusing to take sides with them," then it would be an entirely different matter. Indeed: "I cannot do anything contrary to my convictions to please these men, earnest and powerful as they may be."

No sooner had the delegates settled themselves at the Willard Hotel than they received an invitation to spend the evening at Chase's home. When Bates learned of the invitation, he told Gamble he was "surprised and mortified" that Chase had extended his hand to those men he considered mortal enemies, and "still more surprised" when Chase invited him as well. He immediately declined. "I refuse flatly to hold social, friendly intercourse with men, who daily denounce me and all my friends, as traitors." Gamble replied that Bates should hardly be shocked by Chase's willingness to entertain "these ~~dogs~~ persons," for "Mr. Chase is the author of our troubles here." His "criminal ambition" for the presidency had led him to incite the struggle, and he would undoubtedly have the support of every radical paper in the state if he were to decide to run against Lincoln.

The president's meeting with the Missourians lasted over two hours. Drake read his list of demands "as pompously as if it were full of matter instead of wind," noted John Hay. Lincoln listened attentively, allowing his critics to enumerate their grievances. He knew well that these men would be important in the coming presidential canvass, but felt their call for Schofield's dismissal was misguided. He explained his position clearly, calmly, and forcefully, both at the meeting that day and in a letter drafted a few days later. While he acknowledged their version of the turmoil facing Missouri, he was not convinced that Schofield was "responsible for that suffering and wrong." On the contrary, he suggested, all the troubles they described could be explained by the fact that during a civil war, confusion abounds: "Deception breeds and thrives. Confidence dies, and universal suspicion reigns." Until he received evidence that Schofield had used his powers arbitrarily for or against a particular faction, he could not, in good conscience, remove him from command. That evidence had not been provided.

"The President never appeared to better advantage in the world," Hay noted proudly in his diary. "Though He knows how immense is the danger to himself from the unreasoning anger of that committee, he never cringed to them for an instant. He stood where he thought he was right and crushed them with his candid logic." Lincoln emerged from the meeting "in a good humor," Bates observed. "Some of them he said, were not as bad as he supposed." Yet, while clarifying the fact that "whoever commands in Missouri, or elsewhere" was responsible to him, "and not to either radicals or conservatives," Lincoln once again moved to defuse the situation without alienating vital constituents. On the day the radicals left town, he wrote to remind Schofield that his authority to "arrest individuals, and suppress assemblies, or newspapers" was limited only to those who were "working *palpable* injury to the Military."

Indeed, several months later, when Lincoln became convinced that Schofield was actually leaning toward the conservatives instead of using "his influence to harmonize the conflicting elements," he decided to replace him with Rosecrans, a man long favored by the radicals. But even then, he engineered the transfer in a manner that protected Schofield's good name, while preserving his own presidential authority to determine when and where to change his commanders.

At this juncture, Frank Blair seriously aggravated matters. That October, returning to Missouri after heroic duty with Grant and Sherman at Vicksburg, the soldier-politician escalated the dissension with an explosive speech. Before an overflowing crowd at Mercantile Library Hall in St. Louis, he proclaimed his firm opposition to every one of the radicals' Reconstruction ideas. Condemning their call for the immediate emancipation of Missouri's slaves, he insisted that no action should be taken until the war was won. He argued that Missourians should focus solely on supporting the Union, deferring all issues regarding slavery. He warned that if the radicals gained control, the country would "degenerate into a revolution like that which afflicted France." They would set themselves up as "judges, witnesses and executioners alike." They would send to the guillotine "men who come back grimed all over with powder from our battle fields" but who happen to disagree with them on Reconstruction.

Blair then turned his ire on Chase, fully aware that the treasury secretary was hoping to ride the radicals' support to the White House. Loyalty to Lincoln and hatred for Chase combined to produce a vitriolic rant in which Blair accused the secretary of manipulating Treasury regulations that governed the cotton trade between North and South to benefit his radical friends and prevent conservative merchants, who "were among the first men to come forward and clothe and arm the troops," from receiving the cotton they desperately needed. As a friendly audience roared its approval, Blair accused Chase of using his cabinet post to create a political machine designed to unseat Lincoln in the next election. In sum, the treasury secretary was a traitor and blackguard indistinguishable from Jefferson Davis himself.

Blair's speech outraged the radicals, who promptly denounced *him* as a Copperhead and a traitor. The *Liberator* criticized his vindictive language, observing that "his style of address does him no honor, and will not advance the ideas of public policy which he advocates." Even his sister, Elizabeth, remarked that he could "not let even a great man set his small dogs on him without kicking the dog & giving his master some share of his resentment."

Lincoln was dismayed by the whole affair, realizing that Frank, whom he liked a great deal, had seriously compromised his future. He wrote a letter to Monty, offering advice as if the tempestuous Frank "were my brother instead of yours." He warned that by "a misunderstanding," Frank was "in danger of being permanently separated from those with whom only he can ever have a real sympathy—the sincere opponents of slavery." By allowing himself to be provoked into personal attacks, he could end up exiled from "the house of his own building. He is young yet. He has abundant talent—quite enough to occupy all his time, without devoting any to temper." If Frank decided to resume his seat in the House when the new Congress assembled, he should bear this in mind. Otherwise, he would "serve both the country and himself more profitably" by returning to the military, where his recent promotion to corps commander proved that he was "rising in military skill and usefulness."

Lincoln's counsel to Frank was echoed in a gentle letter of reprimand to another young man whose intemperate words had made him vulnerable. Captain James Cutts, Jr., had been court-martialed for using "unbecoming language" in addressing a superior officer and for publicly derogating his superior's accomplishments to the point where a duel almost took place. Young Cutts was the brother of Adele Cutts, Stephen Douglas's second wife. In remitting the sentence, Lincoln wrote, "You have too much of life yet before you, and have shown too much of promise as an officer, for your future to be lightly surrendered." He tried to impart some of the measured outlook that had served him so well: "No man resolved to make the most of himself, can spare time for personal contention. Still less can he afford to take all the consequences, including the vitiating of his temper, and the loss of self-control. Yield larger things to which you can show no more than equal right; and yield lesser ones, though clearly your own. Better give your path to a dog, than be bitten by him in contesting for the right. Even killing the dog would not cure the bite."

Frank Blair's battle against Chase in Missouri was carried forward by Monty Blair in Maryland, where a similar struggle over Reconstruction had arisen. Chase again intervened, lending his support to the radical Henry Winter Davis as a candidate for Congress. Davis was a proponent of immediate uncompensated emancipation and rigorous standards for defining eligibility to vote. Monty voiced his opposition at Rockville in early October, flaying the radicals' program, and arguing that the "ultra-abolitionists" were as despotic as the old slaveocrats. If they succeeded in their draconian measures toward the rebel states, he warned, it would be "fatal to republican institutions." He excoriated Sumner's proposition that the rebel states had forfeited their rights to equal participation in the Union by committing suicide by secession. Although Blair's speech met with approval from his partisan audience, it aroused deep hostility in Congress. Fifty congressmen signed a petition calling on Lincoln to remove Blair from his cabinet.

Once again, Lincoln was forced to balance the interests of contentious factions. Many assumed incorrectly that Blair was speaking for the White House. In fact, Lincoln refused to support Blair's candidate against Winter Davis, insisting that a Union convention had nominated Davis and it "would be mean to do anything against him." In the end, the president's most vital objective for Maryland was realized in the election—a dramatic Republican victory over the Copperheads, ensuring that the former slave state stood firmly behind the Union's cause. Noah Brooks attended a mass rally in Baltimore to celebrate the triumph of Winter Davis and the entire Republican ticket. As he surveyed the festive banners proclaiming: "Slavery is dead," he marveled at the thought that not long before, the state "was almost coaxed into open rebellion against the government, in simulated defense of slavery." The enthusiastic crowd signaled that "a great and momentous revolution" had occurred in the hearts and minds of the people. "Do we dream," marveled Brooks, "or do we actually hear with our own ears loyal Marylanders making speeches in favor of immediate emancipation and a loyal crowd of Baltimoreans applauding to the echo the most radical utterances."

Chase was a featured speaker at the celebration, and, according to Brooks, "his simple words of sympathy and cheer for the struggling sons of freedom in Maryland were received with wildest enthusiasm." The complete triumph of the emancipationists was read as a sharp rebuke to Monty Blair and his "fossil theories." Chase was elated, telling Greeley that he attached "a great deal of importance" to the occasion, for it suggested "the time is ripe" for a "great unconditional Union Party, with *Emancipation as a Cardinal principle*"—a party with Salmon Chase, presumably, at its head.

Worried that Lincoln's adversaries were successfully eclipsing him by appealing to the "radical element," Leonard Swett recommended that the president call for a constitutional amendment abolishing slavery. "I told him if he took that stand, it was an outside position and no one could maintain himself upon any measure more radical," Swett recalled, "and if he failed to take the position, his rivals would." Lincoln, too, could see the "time coming" for a constitutional amendment, and then whoever "stands in its way, will be run over by it"; but the country was not yet ready. The "discordant elements" of the great coalition still had to be held together to ensure victory in the war. Moreover, he objected, "I have never done an official act with a view to promote my own personal aggrandizement, and I don't like to begin now."

Herein, Swett concluded, lay the secret to Lincoln's gifted leadership. "It was by ignoring men, and ignoring all small causes, but by closely calculating the tendencies of events and the great forces which were producing logical results." John Forney of the Washington *Daily Chronicle* observed the same intuitive judgment and timing, arguing that Lincoln was "the most truly progressive man of the age, because he always moves in conjunction with propitious circumstances, not waiting to be dragged by the force of events or wasting strength in premature struggles with them."

CHAPTER 22

"STILL IN WILD WATER"

A S THE FALL 1863 ELECTIONS in the crucial states of Ohio and Pennsylvania approached, Lincoln was visibly unsettled. Recalling the disastrous midterm elections of the previous autumn, he confided to Welles in October that his anxiety was greater than during his presidential race in 1860.

If the antiwar Democrats had gained ground since the previous year, it would signal that Northern support for the war was crumbling. Such results would dispirit the army and invigorate rebel morale. While recent battlefield victories augured well for Republican chances, the divisive issues of civil liberties, slavery, and Reconstruction threatened to erode support in many places. Civil liberties was also a divisive issue in the Confederacy, which had suspended habeas corpus, imposed martial law, and instituted conscription. The former Confederate secretary of state Robert Toombs accused "that scoundrel Jeff Davis" of pursuing "an illegal and unconstitutional course" that "outraged justice" and brought a "tide of despotism" upon the South. People in both North and South were becoming increasingly restive.

Lincoln was particularly concerned about Ohio, where Democrats had chosen Copperhead Clement Vallandigham as their gubernatorial candidate against the pro-Union John Brough. Conducting his campaign from exile in Canada, Vallandigham was running on a platform condemning the war as a failure and calling for "peace at any price"—even if slavery was maintained and the Union divided. Lincoln was disheartened that the historic Democratic Party had selected "a man [such] as Vallandigham" for "their representative man." Whatever votes he received would be "a discredit to the country."

In Pennsylvania, the Democrats were running George Woodward, an archly conservative judge, against Republican governor Andrew Curtin. Though not as incendiary as Vallandigham's, Woodward's opinions were well known. "Slavery," he had once said, "was intended as a special blessing to the people of the United States." The contest tightened when the Woodward campaign received a welcome letter of support from George McClellan, written from his residence in New Jersey. If he were voting in Pennsylvania, McClellan wrote, he would "give to Judge Woodward my voice & my vote."

Lincoln, however, had learned from the bitter election of the previous year and took steps to ensure better results. Any government clerk from Ohio or Pennsylvania who wanted to go home to vote was given a fifteen-day leave and provided with a free railroad pass for the trip. Recognizing that the absence of the army vote had been devastating to Republicans in 1862, the president also arranged for soldiers in the field to receive furloughs to return home to vote.

A week before the election, Chase called on Lincoln with a suggestion. If the president granted him a leave of absence from the Treasury, he, like his clerks, would go home to vote the Union ticket. Lincoln had no doubt that Chase would use the campaign trip to bolster his own drive for the presidency. Nevertheless, Chase's presence in Ohio might well help the Union ticket.

To ensure publicity, Chase invited the journalist Whitelaw Reid to accompany him on the train to Columbus and write regular dispatches for the *Cincinnati Gazette* and the Associated Press as they traveled around the state. Advance word of the train's arrival was circulated, and an enormous crowd greeted Chase in Columbus at 2 a.m. The delighted secretary was met with "prolonged cheering, and shouts of 'Hurrah for our old Governor,' 'How are you, old Greenbacks?' 'Glad to see you home again.' " Chase indicated his gratitude for this "most unexpected welcome," and proceeded to give a speech that ostensibly praised the president as a man who "is honestly and earnestly doing his best," even though the war was not being prosecuted "so fast as it ought." With a different leader, he hinted, "some mistakes might have been avoided—some misfortunes averted."

At each stop in his swing through Ohio, Chase encountered huge crowds of supporters. "I come not to speak, but to vote," he insisted, before launching into a series of self-promoting speeches laced with subtle denigration of Lincoln. Military bands followed him through the streets, creating a festival-like atmosphere. In Cincinnati, a long procession and a military escort accompanied Chase, seated in a carriage drawn by six white horses, to the Burnet House, the site of Lincoln's unpleasant encounter with Stanton during the Reaper trial. From the balcony of the elegant hotel, he delivered a few words, followed by a lengthy address that evening before a packed audience at Mozart Hall. With slavery and Reconstruction as his themes, he once again covertly criticized the president. He acknowledged that the Emancipation Proclamation was "the great feature of the war," without which "we could not achieve success," but hastened to add that "it would have been even more right, had it been earlier, and without exceptions."

Lincoln had calculated correctly by giving Chase permission for the trip. His tour helped draw record numbers of pro-Union supporters to the polls. In public squares lit by bonfires and torchlights, the former governor called upon his fellow Ohioans to regard the election as "the day of trial for our Country. All eyes turn to Ohio." On the Monday before the voting, he begged his audiences "to remember that to-morrow is the most important of all the three hundred and sixty-five days in the year."

On Election Day, Lincoln took up his usual post in the crowded telegraph office. By midnight, everything indicated good results in both Ohio and Pennsylvania. Still, the president refused to retire until he was certain. At 1:20 a.m., a welcome telegram arrived from Chase: "The victory is complete, beyond all hopes." Chase predicted that Brough's margin over Vallandigham would be at least 50,000, and would rise higher still when the soldiers' vote was counted. By 5 a.m., Brough's margin had widened to 100,000. *"Glory to God in the highest,"* Lincoln wired to the victorious governor-elect. *"Ohio has saved the Nation."* The results from Pennsylvania, where Governor Curtin defeated his antiwar challenger, produced another jubilant outburst in the telegraph office. "All honor to the Keystone State!" Stanton wired to John Forney. In July, he wrote, the state "drove rebel invaders from her soil; and, now, in October, she has again rallied for the Union, and overwhelmed the foe at the ballot-box."

When Welles called on the president to congratulate him, he found him "in good spirits." Republicans had crushed Copperheads in the two bellwether states, boding well for the congressional elections the following month. Chase had been instrumental in achieving these signal victories. If his journey home to Ohio had also advanced the secretary's presidential aspirations, so be it. Lincoln understood Chase's thirst for the presidency. "No man knows what *that gnawing* is till he has had it," he said. Should Chase become president, he told Hay, "all right. I hope we may never have a worse man."

Lincoln might "shut his eyes" to Chase's stratagems so long as Chase remained a good secretary, but members of his cabinet possessed less tolerance. "I'm afraid Mr. Chase's head is turned by his eagerness in pursuit of the presidency," Bates recorded in his diary. "That visit to the west is generally understood as [his] opening campaign." Perusing newspaper accounts of Chase's speeches, the Attorney General noted derisively that his colleague had attributed "the salvation of the country to his own *admirable financial system*"—much as Cicero had sworn, "By the immortal Gods, I have saved my country." Chase ought to have focused solely on his cabinet position, Bates observed, but "it is of the nature of ambition to grow prurient, and run off with its victim." Like Bates, Welles believed that Chase's presidential aspirations had "warped" his judgment, leading him to divisively exploit the Reconstruction issue to consolidate the radical wing of the party behind him. Yet these critiques were moderate compared to the scathing indictments the Blairs poured forth in daily correspondence to their friends.

Chase remained oblivious to the ire of his colleagues. He had found the trip immensely gratifying. "I little imagined the reception that awaited me," he proudly told a friend. "Such appreciation & such manifestation of warm personal esteem—moved me deeply." Chase apparently never considered that he owed a good part of his tremendous reception to the president he represented and to the victories of the Union armies at Gettysburg and Vicksburg. All personal praise and flattering letters he accepted as his just due. "The late election in this City & State, to you, more than to any other living man was a personal triumph," he was told by James Baker, stationed in St. Louis. "I feel hopeful now for you in the contest of '64." After a few more fawning remarks, Baker proceeded to request a job as a collector, explaining that months "in the saddle" had produced a bad case of hemorrhoids, leaving him unfit for active duty.

Chase also basked in the extravagant praise from the radical press. "To him, more than any other man in the cabinet," the *Liberator* wrote, "are we indebted for the Presidents' proclamation, and the other executive acts which have struck the diabolical system of slavery." The *Liberator* supposed Chase's victory over Seward's influence had finally allowed the proclamation to be issued. "If in any one month of Mr. Seward's administration, he had chosen strenuously to urge upon Abraham Lincoln the abolition of slavery throughout the country on the ground that the conflict *is* irrepressible," the *Liberator* maintained, then "the war would have ended in our victory within six months thereafter." The public should carefully consider "whether a vote for old Abe will not choose Seward to be again acting President."

• • •

No one understood better than Seward the absurdity of the claim that he was the acting president. By the fall of 1863, he had both accepted and respected Lincoln's consummate control of his cabinet, and the relationship between the two men "had grown very close and unreserved," Fred Seward observed. "Thrown into daily companionship, they found, not only cordial accord in most of their political opinions but a trait in common not shared by all their contemporaries. That was their disposition to take a genial, philosophical view of human nature, and of national destiny." Such intimate cooperation benefited not only both men but the country at large.

"As they sat together by the fireside, or in the carriage," Seward's son continued, "the conversation between them, however it began, always drifted back into the same channel—the progress of the great national struggle. Both loved humor, and however trite the theme, Lincoln always found some quaint illustration from his western life, and Seward some case in point, in his long public career, that gave it new light."

Fred Seward recounted the events of one morning in October 1863 when his father called on Lincoln. "They say, Mr. President, that we are stealing away the rights of the States. So I have come to-day to advise you, that there is another State right I think we ought to steal." Raising his head from his pile of papers, Lincoln asked, "Well, Governor, what do you want to steal now?" Seward replied, "The right to name Thanksgiving Day!" He explained that at present, Thanksgiving was celebrated on different days at the discretion of each state's governor. Why not make it a national holiday? Lincoln immediately responded that he supposed a president "had as good a right to thank God as a Governor."

Seward then presented Lincoln with a proclamation that invited citizens "in every part of the United States," at sea, or abroad, "to set apart and observe the last Thursday of November" to give thanks to "our beneficent Father." The proclamation also commended to God's care "all those who have become widows, orphans, mourners or sufferers," and called on Him "to heal the wounds of the nation" and restore it to "peace, harmony, tranquillity and Union." These sentiments would reappear in Lincoln's second inaugural, where once again, as with Seward's "mystic chords" in his First Inaugural Address, Lincoln would transform Seward's language into a powerfully resonant poetry.

Their mutual faith in each other helped sustain both Lincoln and Seward through the continuing attacks of radicals and conservatives. Under political fire, both men remained remarkably calm. Lincoln told Nicolay that before his meeting with the Missouri radicals, Seward had asked him to prepare his response without saying "a word to him on the subject," lest anyone claim he had influenced the president on the controversial matter. Despite their precautions, said Lincoln, Wendell Phillips gave a passionate speech decrying the White House response and stating "that Seward had written the whole of that letter."

As the November congressional elections approached, both men hoped that the North would overwhelmingly support the administration, the Union, and the war. They knew that these elections would set the stage for the presidential contest the following year. In one of their fireside conversations, Seward assured Lincoln that his own hopes for the presidency were "all past and ended." He desired only that Lincoln be his "own successor," for when the rebels "find the people reaffirming their decision to have you President, I think the rebellion will collapse."

Two days before the November 3 elections, Seward left for Auburn. He had worried for weeks about the condition of his son Will, who had returned home on convalescent leave after contracting typhoid in the army. Will suffered fever and terrible stomach pains. As the illness progressed, he had to be carried from his bed to a chair where he could sit up for only short periods of time. The elections offered Seward a chance to attend to his son and rally support among New York voters as well.

Lincoln, too, was concerned about young Will, whom he had come to like and respect. The previous spring, he had ordered Will, then stationed with the army in Virginia, to report to the White House for a special assignment. As Will later recalled, the road to the capital was "exceedingly muddy" that day. He appeared at the president's door "covered with mud" and looking "more like a tramp than a soldier." He was "well known to the old porter at the door," however, and was quickly ushered into the president's library. Lincoln greeted him warmly, handing him a secret dispatch for delivery to General Banks in Louisiana. He would have to travel through "hostile" areas, Lincoln warned, so he would "have to take the chances of riding alone." The dispatch was "of great importance and must not fall into the enemy's hands," so he should commit it to memory. Will left that night and delivered his intelligence safely.

Seward arrived at home to find Will in stable condition. On election eve, he delivered a speech to the citizens of Auburn. He began with the sanguine prediction that the rebellion "will perish . . . and slavery will perish with it." While his optimism might provoke criticism in some quarters, he explained, "as in religion, so in politics, it is faith, and not despondency, that overcomes mountains and scales the heavens." His faith, he predicted, would be confirmed by the Unionist triumph in the coming elections. "The object of this election," he said, "is the object of the war. It is to make Abraham Lincoln President *de facto*" in the South as he is in the North.

"There can be no peace and quiet, until Abraham Lincoln is President of the whole United States." Then, arousing the wrath of radicals, Seward extended his hand to the South, saying, "I am willing that the prodigal son shall return. The doors, as far as I am concerned, shall always be open to him."

As the voters went to the polls on Tuesday, Lincoln telegraphed Seward. "How is your son?" he inquired. "Thanks. William is better," Seward replied. "Our friends reckon on (25,000) majority in the state." New York did even better than that, reversing the losses of the previous year to give a 30,000 majority to the administration. In every state with the exception of New Jersey, Seward reported, "the Copperhead spirit is crushed and humbled."

• • •

A FESTIVE ATMOSPHERE enveloped the nation's capital after the elections as official Washington prepared for the social event of the decade: the wedding of Kate Chase and William Sprague. Fifty guests, including the president, the entire cabinet, and selected congressmen, senators, and generals, were invited to the wedding ceremony on Thursday evening, November 12, in the parlor of the Chase mansion. Five hundred additional invitations had been delivered for the reception immediately following the exchange of vows.

For weeks, the newspapers were filled with gossip about the wedding. It was said that Sprague had given Kate a diamond tiara worth $50,000. Women readers relished details "about the bridal *trousseau*—the robes, the pearls, the diamonds, the lace, the silver, and all the magnificent gifts of this Millionaire Wedding." Curiosity seekers noted the arrival of eminent guests at the Willard Hotel. The spectacle offered a brief respite from the endless sorrows of the war—the casualty reports, the scenes of suffering in the hospitals, the rumors of impending military engagements.

For Salmon Chase, the imminent marriage brought a welter of conflicting emotions. Writing frankly to Sprague thirteen days before the wedding, he acknowledged that he was beginning "to realize how changed every thing will be when she is gone." His life had long been occupied with "the solicitous care" of his beloved daughter, who had "constantly become more thoughtful, more affectionate, more loving; and, at this hour, is dearer than ever." Though they would share the same Washington household, Chase understood that he would no longer enjoy Kate's undivided attention. By return mail, Sprague reassured Chase that he fully appreciated their "high & holy relation" and would "never be happier than when contributing to continue the same relations between father & daughter—

that has heretofore existed." Referring most likely to his drinking problem, Sprague admitted that in the past he had "neglected both mind & body," but promised henceforth to take care of himself, and "with good health and a proper exercise of the talent God has been pleased to give me, I hope to do something usefull for my day and generation."

Those close to Kate remarked that her emotions ran high as the marriage drew near. John Hay recounted that she cried "like a baby" just weeks before the wedding when he took her to see Maggie Mitchell in *The Pearl of Savoy*. The play revolves around the romantic travails of Marie, a peasant girl whose innocent love for a peasant boy is thwarted by a lecherous aristocrat determined to possess the lovely young girl. Through the wealthy suitor's machinations, Marie's family stand to lose their farm unless she gives herself to him. Torn between her devotion to her noble father and her love for the young peasant boy, Marie goes mad. Perhaps Kate shed so many tears over the melodrama because she identified with the tormented heroine's devotion to her father.

Over the years, as the Cinderella match would culminate in tragedy and poverty for Kate, journalists and historians have subjected Kate's feelings for Sprague to considerable analysis. Many have speculated that her decision to marry "was a coldly calculated plan to secure the Sprague millions," thereby to advance the "two great passions in her life—her father and politics." It was said that "in her eyes all other men sank into insignificance when compared with her father," and that no one else had "even the remotest hold upon her affections." Her marriage to Sprague would relieve her father from further financial worries and provide abundant means for an all-out presidential campaign in 1864.

Even journalists at the time noted that outside of his fortune, Sprague possessed few attractive qualities. Having left school early for the cotton mill, he was "wholly innocent of even an approximate understanding of the arts or sciences, polite or vulgar literature." Furthermore, he was "small, thin and unprepossessing in appearance." Still, if he was not physically attractive, the *Brooklyn Daily Eagle* noted, "pecuniarily, he is—several millions." And, as Gideon Welles recorded in his diary, "Miss Kate has talents and ambition sufficient for both."

Henry Adams was among those who deemed Kate's marriage a sacrifice for her father. He spoke of her as Jephthah's daughter, referring to the biblical warrior who promised God that if he gained success in battle, "whatsoever" greeted him at his victorious return would be sacrificed as "a burnt offering." Jephthah arrived home triumphant and was greeted at his door by his daughter, his only child. As the anguished father prepared the sacrificial pyre, his daughter comforted him with assurances that she accepted her fate, for a promise made to God could not be broken.

The sacrificial nature of this scenario is belied by Kate's own words, later confided to her diary as the fifth anniversary of her wedding approached. Thinking back to the night before her marriage, she wrote: "Memory has been busy with the hopes and dreams on a calm moonlight night five years ago of a woman, then in the full flush of social influence and triumph whose career had been curiously independent and successful, surrounded by some kind friends and many more ready to flatter and do her homage, accustomed to command and be obeyed, to wish and be anticipated, successful beyond any right or dessert of her own to claim, and yet stood ready, without a sigh of regret, to lay all these and more upon the altar of her love in exchange for a more earnest and truer life: one long dream of happiness and love."

She remembered spending that evening praying that she might fill her role of loving wife "to completeness," that she "might become, his companion, friend and advocate, that he might be in a word—a husband satisfied. All there is of love and beauty, nobleness & gentleness were woven with this fair dream & I believed no future brighter than that our united lives spread open before us." When folded in William's "loving arms," she continued, "oh the sense of ineffable rest, joy & completeness." She felt like "a child, in security and trust. A lover won, a protector found, a husband to be cherished. . . . Not a reserve in my heart, not a hidden corner he might not scan, the first, the only man that had found a lodgment there."

In the hours before the nuptials began, "a large crowd of all sexes, ages and conditions" gathered around the Chase mansion to watch the procession of guests. The eager crowd was "very good-natured," the Washington *Daily Chronicle* reported, exchanging congenial remarks as the occupants of the long line of carriages stepped down and proceeded inside. One by one the cabinet secretaries arrived; all but Monty Blair, who refused to attend, though his eighty-year-old father thoroughly enjoyed himself and was "quite the belle of the occasion." The entrance of Lord Lyons and the French minister Count Henri Mercier attracted attention, as did the arrivals of Generals Halleck, McDowell, and Robert C. Schenck.

"Much anxiety was manifested for the appearance of President Lincoln," the *Chronicle* reported. At 8:30 p.m., minutes before the ceremony was scheduled to start, Lincoln pulled up in his carriage, unescorted, and without Mrs. Lincoln by his side. As Mary later said, she refused to "bow in reverence" to the twin "Gods, *Chase & daughter.*" Predictably, Mary's absence at the wedding was noticed by the press. Noah Brooks later reported

that Lincoln "stayed two and half hours 'to take the cuss off' the meager-
ness of the presidential party."

All eyes were on Kate, however, as she descended the staircase in "a gorgeous white velvet dress, with an extended train, and upon her head wore a
rich lace veil," encircled by her new pearl and diamond tiara. As the wedding party approached the Episcopal bishop of Rhode Island, the Marine
Band played a march composed specifically for the occasion. When the
vows were completed, "Chase was the first to kiss the newly made wife." A
lavish meal was served, followed by dancing in the dining room, which
lasted until midnight.

John Hay thought it "a very brilliant" affair, noting that Kate "had lost
all her old severity & formal stiffness of manner, & seemed to think she
had *arrived.*" The young couple left the next morning for New York,
where their presence at the Fifth Avenue Hotel drew crowds of women
eager to see the young bride in person, having followed all the details of
her wedding in the papers.

Marriage did not diminish the regular flow of letters between father
and daughter. "Your letter—so full of sweet words and good thoughts—
came yesterday," Chase wrote Kate less than a week after the wedding,
"and I need not tell you how welcome it was." His new son-in-law, to
Chase's delight, also proved to be a good correspondent. "My heart is full
of love for you both," Chase replied to Sprague, "and I rejoice as I never
expected to rejoice in the prospects of happiness opening before both of
you. I feared some inequalities of temper—some too great love of the
world, either of its possessions or its shows—something I hardly know
about. But I find that you each trust the other fully . . . and above all that
you both look to God for his blessing & guidance."

Chase expressed but a single qualm: "I fear that Katie may be a little too
anxious about my political future. She must not be so." He insisted to
Sprague that nothing could be "so uncertain as the political future of any
man: and especially as the future which must be determined by popular
preferences founded quite as much on sentiment as on reason." While he
suggested to his new son-in-law that the country needed a leader other
than Lincoln, Chase ingenuously asserted that he would never allow himself "to be drawn into any hostile or unfriendly position as to Mr. Lincoln.
His course towards me has always been so fair & kind; his progress towards
entire agreement with me on the great question of slavery has been so constant, though rather slower than I wished for; and his general character is
so marked by traits which command respect & affection; that I can never
consent to anything, which he himself could or should consider as incompatible with perfect honor & good faith."

• • •

AT A TUESDAY CABINET MEETING shortly after Kate's wedding, Lincoln informed his colleagues that he would leave for Gettysburg that Thursday, November 19, 1863. He had been asked to say a few words to consecrate the cemetery grounds set aside so that the Union soldiers who had been interred near the battlefield and hospitals the previous July could be "properly buried." Edward Everett, the noted orator and former president of Harvard, was scheduled to give the main address, after which the president would speak. Lincoln told his cabinet that he hoped they would accompany him to the dedication. Seward, Blair, and John Usher readily agreed, but the other members feared they could not spare the time from their duties, particularly since their annual reports to Congress were due in a couple of weeks.

Lincoln was uneasy about the trip. He had been "extremely busy," he told Ward Lamon, and had not been able to carve out the solitary time he needed to compose his address. He "greatly feared he would not be able to acquit himself with credit, much less to fill the measure of public expectation." Stanton had arranged a special train for the presidential party to depart on the morning of the dedication and return home around midnight that same day. Lincoln, however, rescheduled it to leave on Wednesday. "I do not wish to so go that by the slightest accident we fail entirely," he explained, "and, at the best, the whole to be a mere breathless running of the gauntlet." Perhaps he also hoped that an early departure from the White House would allow him more time to work on his address.

The day before setting out, Lincoln told a friend he had "found time to write about half of his speech." Various accounts suggest that he labored over the speech during the four-hour trip. One young man, peering through the window when the train was temporarily stopped at Hanover Junction, distinctly recalled the president at work on some document, "the top of his high hat serving as a makeshift desk." Others swear that he jotted notes on an envelope as the train roared along. Nicolay, who was there, insists that he wrote nothing during the trip, choosing instead to relax and engage his fellow riders with good conversation and humorous stories.

When Lincoln arrived at Gettysburg, he was escorted to the home of David Wills, the event organizer, where he would spend the night along with Governor Andrew Curtin and Edward Everett. "All the hotels as well as the private houses were filled to overflowing," the *New York Times* reported. "People from all parts of the country seem to have taken this opportunity to pay a visit to the battle-fields which are hereafter to make the name of Gettysburgh immortal."

After supper, while Lincoln settled himself in his room to complete his draft, a crowd gathered in front of the house to serenade him. He came to the door to thank them, but said he would make no remarks for the simple reason that "I have no speech to make. In my position it is somewhat important that I should not say any foolish things." His reluctance elicited the snide comment from a member of the audience: "If you can help it." Lincoln's swift rejoinder delighted the crowd. "It very often happens that the only way to help it is to say nothing at all."

Returning to his room, Lincoln sent a servant downstairs to fetch a few additional sheets of paper. A telegram arrived from Stanton with welcome news. Tad had been ill when Lincoln left that morning. The boy's condition had frightened Mary, but now the report that Tad was better eased Lincoln's mind, allowing him to focus on his speech. He went over each line, revising the ending, which was not yet satisfactory.

Meanwhile, the crowd surged over to Robert Harper's house on the public square, where Seward was staying. Seward responded to the serenade with a heartfelt speech, concluding with thanks to the Almighty "for the hope that this is the last fratricidal war which will fall upon this country—the richest, the broadest, the most beautiful, and capable of a great destiny, that has ever been given to any part of the human race." Afterward, inside the house, the convivial secretary held sway for hours in such a lucid manner that Benjamin French, a fellow boarder, averred he had "seldom, if ever, met with a man whose mind is under such perfect discipline, and is so full of original and striking matter as Secretary Seward's. His conversation, no matter on what subject, is worthy of being written down and preserved, and if he had a Boswell to write, as Boswell did of Johnson, one of the most interesting and useful books of the age might be produced from the conversations and sayings of William H. Seward. He is one of the greatest men of this generation."

Sometime after 11 p.m., Lincoln came downstairs, the pages of his speech in his hands. He wanted to talk with Seward, perhaps to share his draft with the colleague whose judgment he most respected and trusted. He walked over to the Harper house and remained there with Seward for about an hour before returning to his room and retiring. The huge, boisterous crowd on the public square, however, did not retire so easily. "They sang, & hallooed, and cheered," French recalled. Listening from his window, he heard a full chorus of the popular refrain "We are coming Father Abraham, three hundred thousand more."

After breakfast the next morning, Lincoln made his final revisions, carefully folded the speech, and placed it in his coat pocket. Mounting a chestnut horse, he joined the procession to the cemetery. He was accompanied by nine governors, members of Congress, foreign ministers, military officials, and the three cabinet officers. Marine lieutenant Henry Clay Cochrane recalled that Seward, riding to Lincoln's right, was "entirely unconscious" that his trousers had pulled up above his shoes, revealing "homemade gray socks" unbefitting the occasion.

An audience of roughly nine thousand stretched away from the platform in a half circle. Lincoln was seated in the front row between Everett and Seward. For two hours, Everett delivered his memorized address, superbly recounting the various battles that had taken place over the three dramatic days. Lincoln reportedly "leaned from one side to the other and crossed his legs, turning his eyes full upon the speaker. Somewhat later he again shifted his position and rested his chin in the palm of his right hand." Another member of the audience remembered Lincoln removing his speech and glancing over it before returning it to his pocket.

French lauded Everett's speech, believing it "could not be surpassed by mortal man." Several correspondents were less enthusiastic. "Seldom has a man talked so long and said so little," wrote the editor of the *Philadelphia Age*. "He gave us plenty of words, but no heart. . . . He talked like a historian, or an encyclopaedist, or an essayist, but not like an orator."

As Everett started back to his seat, Lincoln stood to clasp his hand and warmly congratulate him. George Gitt, a fifteen-year-old who had stationed himself beneath the speaker's stand, later remembered that the "flutter and motion of the crowd ceased the moment the President was on his feet. Such was the quiet that his footfalls, I remember very distinctly, woke echoes, and with the creaking of the boards, it was as if some one were walking through the hallways of an empty house."

Lincoln put on his steel-rimmed spectacles and glanced down at his pages. Though he had had but a brief time to prepare the address, he had devoted intense thought to his chosen theme for nearly a decade. As Garry Wills observes in his classic study of the address: "He had spent a good part of the 1850s repeatedly relating all the most sensitive issues of the day to the Declaration's supreme principle." During the debates with Stephen Douglas, Lincoln had frequently reminded his audiences of the far-reaching promises contained in the Declaration of Independence. Someday, he said, "all this quibbling about . . . this race and that race and the other race being inferior" would be eliminated, giving truth to the phrase "all men are created equal."

Twenty months before the Emancipation Proclamation, the president had told Hay that "the central idea pervading this struggle is the necessity that is upon us, of proving that popular government is not an absurdity," predicting that "if we fail it will go far to prove the incapability of the people to govern themselves." Now tens of thousands had died in pursuit of that purpose. At Gettysburg, he would express that same conviction in far more concise and eloquent terms.

"Four score and seven years ago," he began,

> our fathers brought forth upon this continent, a new nation, conceived in Liberty, and dedicated to the proposition that all men are created equal.
>
> Now we are engaged in a great civil war, testing whether that nation, or any nation so conceived, and so dedicated, can long endure. We are met on a great battle-field of that war. We have come to dedicate a portion of that field, as a final resting place for those who here gave their lives, that that nation might live. It is altogether fitting and proper that we should do this.
>
> But, in a larger sense, we can not dedicate—we can not consecrate—we can not hallow—this ground. The brave men, living and dead, who struggled here, have consecrated it, far above our poor power to add or detract. The world will little note, nor long remember, what we say here, but it can never forget what they did here. It is for us, the living, rather, to be dedicated here to the unfinished work which they who fought here, have, thus far, so nobly advanced. It is rather for us to be here dedicated to the great task remaining before us—that from these honored dead we take increased devotion to that cause for which they here gave the last full measure of devotion—that we here highly resolve that these dead shall not have died in vain—that this nation, under God, shall have a new birth of freedom—and that, government of the people, by the people, for the people, shall not perish from the earth.

When Lincoln finished, "the assemblage stood motionless and silent," according to the awestruck George Gitt. "The extreme brevity of the address together with its abrupt close had so astonished the hearers that they stood transfixed. Had not Lincoln turned and moved toward his chair, the audience would very likely have remained voiceless for several moments more. Finally there came applause." Lincoln may have initially interpreted the audience's surprise as disapproval. As soon as he finished, he turned to Ward Lamon. "Lamon, that speech won't *scour*! It is a flat failure, and the people are disappointed." Edward Everett knew better, and expressed his wonder and respect the following day. "I should be glad," he wrote Lincoln, "if I could flatter myself that I came as near to the central idea of the occasion, in two hours, as you did in two minutes."

Lincoln had translated the story of his country and the meaning of the war into words and ideas accessible to every American. The child who would sleeplessly rework his father's yarns into tales comprehensible to any boy had forged for his country an ideal of its past, present, and future that would be recited and memorized by students forever.

• • •

LINCOLN RETURNED FROM GETTYSBURG to find a vexing letter from Zachariah Chandler, the radical Michigan senator who had made a fortune in dry goods and real estate before entering politics. Chandler had been a thorn in Lincoln's side, constantly criticizing his conduct of the war, his reliance on overly cautious, conservative generals, and his tardiness on emancipation. "Your president is unstable as water," Chandler had warned Trumbull the previous September. "For God & country's sake, send someone to stay with [him] who will controll & hold him."

Now, without having seen a word of the president's upcoming message to Congress, which Lincoln had only begun drafting, Chandler was anticipating a disaster. Having read in the press that Thurlow Weed and New York governor Edwin Morgan had come to the White House to urge a "bold conservative" stance in the message, Chandler warned the president that if he acquiesced, he would jeopardize all the gains made in the fall elections. The president must realize that in each of the victorious states, radical platforms had carried the day. He could be the "master of the Situation," Chandler patronizingly suggested, only if he could *"Stand firm"* against the influences of men like Weed, Seward, and Blair. "They are a millstone about Your neck." If he dropped them, "they are politically ended for ever." The success of the radical canvass proved that. "Conservatives and Traitors are buried together, for Gods sake dont exhume their remains in Your Message. They will smell worse than Lazarus did after he had been buried three days."

Ordinarily, Lincoln would have shelved Chandler's arrogant letter until his temper cooled. This time, however, he did not stifle his anger. Apparently, Chandler had struck a nerve by insinuating that Lincoln did not know his own mind. Although the president listened to the opinions of many, he took pride in arriving at his own decisions in his own way. Nor would he countenance Chandler's slanderous assertion that men like Seward, Weed, and Blair deserved the dishonorable grave of traitors.

"My dear Sir," Lincoln began his cold reply. "I have seen Gov. [Edwin D.] Morgan and Thurlow Weed, separately, but not together, within the last ten days; but neither of them mentioned the forthcoming message, or said anything, so far as I can remember, which brought the thought of the

Message to my mind. I am very glad the elections this autumn have gone favorably, and that I have not, by native depravity, or under evil influences, done anything bad enough to prevent the good result. I hope to 'stand firm' enough not to go backward, and yet not go forward fast enough to wreck the country's cause."

Lincoln's impatience with Chandler may have been aggravated by the fact that he was coming down with a mild case of smallpox. The illness would last for several weeks and fray his self-restraint, yet it left his humor intact. "Yes, it is a bad disease, but it has its advantages," he told some visitors. "For the first time since I have been in office, I have something now to *give* to everybody that calls." The enforced bedrest that attended his sickness allowed Lincoln the quiet he needed to complete his message to Congress. The pause in his frenetic life proved helpful as he laid out his own views on the knotty problem of Reconstruction, which he considered "the greatest question ever presented to practical statesmanship."

Most everyone assumed, Noah Brooks wrote, "that the President would either ignore reconstruction altogether," as the conservatives suggested, or follow the radicals' advice and "give an elaborate and decisive program." No one predicted "such an original message," which cleverly mollified both wings of his divided party. John Hay was present when the message was read. "I never have seen such an effect produced by a public document," he recorded in his diary that night. "Chandler was delighted, Sumner was beaming, while at the other political pole [James] Dixon and Reverdy Johnson said it was highly satisfactory."

Radicals were thrilled with the stipulation that before the president would pardon any rebel or restore the rights of property, he must not only swear allegiance to the Union but also accept emancipation. To abandon the laws and proclamations promising freedom to the slaves would be "a cruel and an astounding breach of faith," Lincoln said, adding that "while I remain in my present position I shall not attempt to retract or modify the emancipation proclamation; nor shall I return to slavery any person who is free by the terms of that proclamation, or by any of the acts of Congress." By this statement, Sumner enthused, "He makes Emancipation the corner-stone of reconstruction." The Missouri radical Henry Blow agreed. Though he recently had castigated Lincoln, he now lauded him. "God bless Old Abe," he said. "I am one of the Radicals who have always believed in the President."

Once again the radicals' doubts about Lincoln's firmness on slavery had proved unfounded. Early in August, he had written a letter to Nathaniel Banks, the general in charge of occupied Louisiana, delineating his thoughts on Reconstruction and emancipation. While not desiring to dictate to the Creole state, Lincoln "would be glad for her to make a new Constitution recognizing the emancipation proclamation, and adopting emancipation in those parts of the state to which the proclamation does not apply. And while she is at it, I think it would not be objectionable for her to adopt some practical system by which the two races could gradually live themselves out of their old relation to each other, and both come out better prepared for the new. Education for young blacks should be included in the plan."

Agreeing that no rebellious state could be reconstructed without emancipation, Lincoln still refused to tolerate the radicals' desire to punish the South. He offered full pardons to all those who took the oath, excepting those who had served at high levels in the Confederate government or the army. When the number of loyal men taking the oath reached 10 percent of the votes cast in the 1860 election, they could "re-establish a State government" recognized by the United States. The names and boundaries of the states would remain as they were.

Conservatives hailed the 10 percent plan, believing it effectively destroyed Sumner's scheme to consider the defeated states as territories that Congress could rename and reorganize as it wished. Nevertheless, Sumner told a fellow radical that Lincoln's "theory is identical with ours," for he, too, required Reconstruction before the "subverted" rebel states could rejoin the Union, "although he adopts a different nomenclature."

In presenting his 10 percent plan, Lincoln assured members of Congress that it was not fixed in stone. He would listen to their ideas as the process evolved. He hoped simply to give the Southern states "a rallying point," bringing them "to act sooner than they otherwise would." He recognized that it would devastate Confederate morale to see Southern citizens declare their fealty to the Union and their support for emancipation.

Though the happy accord would not last long, Lincoln had succeeded for the moment in uniting the Republican Party. When the Blairs, Sumner, and the Missouri radicals "are alike agreed to accept" the president's message, Brooks observed, "we may well conclude that the political millennium has well-nigh come, or that the author of the message is one of the most sagacious men of modern times." The president, announced Congressman Francis Kellogg of Michigan, "is the great man of the century. There is none like him in the world. He sees more widely and more clearly than anybody."

Lincoln's old friend Norman Judd called on the president the evening of the annual address. He speculated that, given the radical tone of the document, Blair and Bates "must walk the plank." On the contrary, Lincoln assured him, both "acquiesced in it without objection. The only member of the Cabinet who objected to it was Mr. Chase."

Chase had obstinately demanded a requirement for states to prove their "sincerity" by changing their constitutions to perpetuate emancipation. This legitimate objection had the felicitous effect of allowing Chase to stay in front of Lincoln on Reconstruction in order to cement his standing in radical circles. While Republicans of all stripes praised the message, Chase expressed disappointment. Writing to the abolitionist Henry Ward Beecher, he said he had tried but failed to get Lincoln to make it "more positive and less qualified. . . . But I suppose I must use Touchstone's philosophy & be thankful for skim milk when cream is not to be had."

• • •

LINCOLN APPROACHED the Christmas season in high spirits. As he said in his annual message, he detected a more hopeful mood in the country after the "dark and doubtful days" following the Emancipation Proclamation. The fall elections had been "highly encouraging"; the rebels had been defeated in a series of recent battles; and the opening round in the debate over Reconstruction had gone surprisingly well.

Early in December, Lincoln translated his rhetoric about forgiveness and reconciliation into action when he invited his sister-in-law, Emilie Helm, to stay at the White House. Emilie's husband, Ben, had disappointed Lincoln in the early days of the war by taking a commission in the Confederate Army instead of Lincoln's offer of the Union Army paymaster's position. Helm was fatally wounded in Tennessee at the Battle of Chickamauga, where he commanded the First Kentucky Brigade. Judge Davis saw Lincoln shortly after he received the news of Helm's death. "I never saw Mr. Lincoln more moved than when he heard that his young brother-in-law, Ben Hardin Helm, scarcely thirty-two years of age, had been killed," Davis said. "I saw how grief-stricken he was . . . so I closed the door and left him alone."

Emilie had been living with her young daughter in Selma, Alabama, when she learned that her wounded husband had been taken to Atlanta. She reached the hospital minutes too late. Alone in Atlanta, she had no desire to return to Selma, where she had moved only for its proximity to her husband's post. Now she desperately wanted to see her mother in Kentucky. Confederate general Braxton Bragg unsuccessfully sought through Grant to secure a pass for her through Union lines. Helm's father then wrote to Betsy Todd, Mary's stepmother, in Lexington, Kentucky. "I am totally at a loss to know how to begin. Could you or one of your daughters write to Mrs. Lincoln and through her secure a pass?"

Four days later, Lincoln personally issued a pass allowing Mrs. Todd "to go south and bring her daughter . . . with her children, North to Kentucky." When Emilie arrived at Fort Monroe, however, the officials demanded that she take the oath of allegiance to the United States. Unable to contemplate such a momentous step so soon after her husband's death in the Confederate cause, she refused. The officials sent a telegram to the president, explaining the dilemma. They received a prompt directive: "Send her to me."

After weeks of uncertainty, the young widow was received at the White House by the president and first lady "with the warmest affection." The three of them, Emilie wrote in her diary, were "all too grief-stricken at first for speech." The Lincolns had lost Willie, Emilie had lost her husband, and the two sisters had lost three brothers in the Confederate Army—Sam Todd at Shiloh, David Todd from wounds at Vicksburg, and little Alexander, Mary's favorite baby brother, at Baton Rouge.

Families rent apart by the Civil War abounded in border states such as Missouri or Kentucky, the ancestral home of the Todds. The reality of "brother fighting brother" lent an intimate horror to the idea of a nation divided. "Often the boundaries separating people of opposing loyalties," the historian John Shaffer writes, "were nothing more than the property line between two farms, or a table over which members of the same family argued and ultimately chose sides."

That night, as Mary and Emilie dined alone, they carefully avoided mention of the war, which "comes between us," Emilie acknowledged, "like a barrier of granite closing our lips." They talked instead of old times and of old friends. Emilie marveled at Mary's "fine tact," which allowed her to "so quickly turn a dangerous subject into other channels." In the days that followed, Mary did her utmost to deflect her sister's mind from her sorrow. She gave her the Prince of Wales guest room, took her for long carriage rides, made sure Emilie's little daughter was entertained, and sat with her at night in the drawing room before the light and warmth of a blazing fire.

Emilie's visit provided solace for both sisters. One night after Emilie had gone to her room, Mary knocked on the door, intending to share an experience that she could not readily discuss with others. She wanted Emilie to know that in her own grief over Willie's death, she now was comforted by the belief that his spirit was still present. "He comes to me every night," she told Emilie, "with the same sweet, adorable smile he has always had; he does not always come alone; little Eddie is sometimes with him and twice he has come with our brother Alec, he tells me he loves his Uncle Alec and is with him most of the time."

The vision of spiritual harmony between Willie and Alec seemed to promise a day when the Todd family would again be united, and the devastating divisions between North and South would be dissolved by history. Then Mary herself would no longer be "the scape-goat" for both sides. "You cannot dream of the comfort this gives me," she told her sister, speaking "with a thrill in her voice" that Emilie would long remember.

Sadly for Mary, her reconciliation with her Confederate sister had some troubling consequences. Lincoln had tried to keep Emilie's visit a secret, knowing that it would give rise to intense criticism at a time when Northerners were still punished for fraternizing with the enemy. On December 14, he confided her presence to Browning but cautioned that "he did not wish it known." When two of Mary's friends, General Daniel Sickles and Senator Ira Harris, called on her one night, however, Mary let down her guard and invited Emilie to join them. Both men were loyal to Lincoln and had been regulars at Mary's drawing room salons. Lincoln had personally attended Sickles when Sickles returned to Washington after losing a leg at Gettysburg. Sickles had been in severe pain at the time, but Lincoln's cheerful presence at his bedside had helped to restore his spirits. Mary also considered Harris a special friend, recalling years later how he invariably brightened her drawing room with his merriment.

Still, neither Sickles nor Harris could tolerate the presence of a traitor in the home of the commander in chief. Emilie recorded the events in her diary. No sooner had she entered the room than Senator Harris turned to her, a triumphant tone in his voice. "Well, we have whipped the rebels at Chattanooga and I hear, madam, that the scoundrels ran like scared rabbits." Emilie replied, "It was the example, Senator Harris, that you set them at Bull Run and Manassas."

The conversation degenerated rapidly. Mary's face "turned white as death" when Senator Harris asked why Robert Lincoln had not joined the army. "If fault there be, it is mine," Mary replied. "I have insisted that he should stay in college a little longer." She did not state her underlying terror that she would lose another son. "I have only one son and he is fighting for his country," Harris countered. "And, Madam," he said, turning to Emilie, "If I had twenty sons they should all be fighting the rebels."

"And if I had twenty sons," Emilie coldly replied, "they should all be opposing yours." This brought the evening to an abrupt close. Emilie fled the room with Mary close behind. The sisters threw their arms around each other and wept. The hot-tempered General Sickles insisted on reporting directly to Lincoln on what had happened. John Stuart, who was present, recalled that after Lincoln heard the tale, his "eyes twinkled," and he told the general, "The child has a tongue like the rest of the Todds."

Lincoln's remark apparently infuriated Sickles, who said "in a loud, dictatorial voice, slapping the table with his hand, 'You should not have that rebel in your house.' "

"Excuse me, General Sickles," Lincoln replied, "my wife and I are in the habit of choosing our own guests. We do not need from our friends either advice or assistance in the matter."

The nasty confrontation in the Red Room prompted Emilie to leave, despite the protestations of Lincoln and Mary. "Oh, Emilie," Mary lamented, "will we ever awake from this hideous nightmare?"

. . .

LINCOLN REFUSED TO LET the unpleasant experience destroy his good humor. As Emilie and Mary said their goodbyes, he took Nicolay and Hay to Ford's Theatre to see James Hackett play Falstaff in *Henry IV.* Afterward, he engaged his aides in a lively conversation about the play. The next day, at the regular Tuesday cabinet meeting, Welles found him "in fine spirits." Eager for distraction, Lincoln returned to Ford's Theatre two days later for *The Merry Wives of Windsor.* The following evening, he "was greeted with loud applause" at Willard's Hall as he arrived for a lecture on Russia by the diplomat Bayard Taylor.

The next week, Lincoln related a peculiarly pleasant dream. He was at a party, he told Hay, and overheard one of the guests say of him, "He is a very common-looking man." In the dream, he relished his reply: "The Lord prefers Common-looking people that is the reason he makes so many of them." His dreamed response still amused him as he recalled it the next day.

The holiday season found most of the cabinet in cheerful spirits as well. Seward entertained the members of the visiting Russian fleet in his usual lavish style: a four-course meal, served with an unlimited supply of the best wine. As the ladies took tea in the parlor, the men adjourned to the sitting room, where Fred Seward recalled that "the conversation would often be continued for two or three hours in a cloud of smoke."

Edward Bates, too, had reason to be gladdened. Though he remained despondent over the defection of his son Fleming to the Confederate Army, the rest of his large brood were doing well. Coalter had fought at Chancellorsville and Gettysburg, and remained on General Meade's staff. Woodson would soon graduate from West Point. Barton and Julian were both in Missouri, where Barton was a judge of the state Supreme Court and Julian a surgeon in the Missouri militia. His two daughters lived with the family at home. Even Dick, his troubled eighth child, who had struggled with alcoholism, seemed to be improving.

Of all the causes for holiday thanksgiving, Bates was most grateful for his wife's complete return to health after her stroke. After forty years of marriage, he still believed that "no man has been more blessed." He was proud to make the rare claim that "in all that time," Julia had never committed "an unkind act" toward him, nor spoken a disparaging word against him. On Christmas Day, he attended a funeral for the wife of one of his closest friends. The couple had been married for more than half a century. "I know not how he can bear the loss of such a companion," he wrote, speaking for himself as well as for his friend. "I am prepared to see him sink rapidly and die soon."

Christmas Day found Welles rejoicing at his son Edgar's return from Kenyon College, though holiday festivities immediately brought back memories of the children he had lost. "The glad faces and loving childish voices that cheered our household with 'Merry Christmas' in years gone by are silent on earth forever." His mood was lightened, however, by the situation in the country. "The year closes more satisfactorily than it commenced," he wrote; "the heart of the nation is sounder and its hopes brighter." Although the president still faced "trying circumstances," Welles predicted that his leadership would "be better appreciated in the future than now."

The Stantons' domestic life had brightened with the birth of a new baby girl, Bessie, eleven months after the death of their infant son, James. As Ellen prepared for the baptismal celebration, Stanton spent Christmas visiting wounded soldiers. He shared with the men his renewed faith that "when the next anniversary of the day you are now celebrating occurs, this war will be ended, and you will have returned to your homes and your firesides. When you shall have so returned, you will be considered as honored guests of the nation."

Lincoln invited Stanton to accompany him "down the river" to visit the Union prison camp at Point Lookout, Maryland. He had heard that a significant number of the rebel prisoners had expressed willingness to take the oath of allegiance to the United States, and swear acceptance of emancipation in return for a full presidential pardon. The general in charge of the prison confirmed this hopeful intelligence when Lincoln and Stanton arrived, prompting Stanton to make plans for carrying Lincoln's "10% plan" into the Deep South, where it might spur further disaffection in Confederate strongholds.

As 1863 drew to a close, even the carping Count Gurowski had to admit that the Union's position had improved. "Oh! dying year! you will record that the American people increased its sacrifices in proportion to its dangers; that blood, time, and money were cheerfully thrown into the balance against treason—inside and outside. And brighter hopes dawn." The surly count remained unwilling to acknowledge the president's role in the improved situation, but other former critics revealed a new appreciation of Lincoln. Charles Francis Adams, the American minister to Britain, had been unimpressed by his first encounter with Lincoln in 1861, describing him as "a tall, illfavored man, with little grace of manner or polish of appearance." After several awkward meetings, the haughty Adams had concluded that Lincoln did not belong to the same "sphere of civilization" as the rest of official Washington. The first six months of the administration further confirmed this low estimation. Adams saw in Lincoln no "heroic qualities" whatsoever and was convinced that he was "not equal to the gravity of his position." But by the end of 1863, Adams had drastically altered his assessment.

At a festive dinner for loyal Americans in St. James's Hall in London, Adams delivered an eloquent speech praising Lincoln's leadership. He reminded his listeners of the dire situation the new president had faced arriving in Washington when "the edifice of Government seemed crumbling around him." Treachery reigned in every department. Traitors at Treasury had undermined the country's credit, the foreign service was replete with secessionists, and both the army and the navy had to be completely rebuilt. Few believed that this novice, who "came to his post with less of practical experience in the Government than any individual," was equal to the task. Nevertheless, the past three years had seen treason excised from the government; European nations had come to look upon the North with respect; the Treasury was flush with funds to support the armed forces; the army had grown to "half a million men," and the navy was now "respected upon every sea in all parts of the globe." All this had been accomplished, Adams acknowledged, with a remnant tinge of condescension, not because Lincoln possessed "any superior genius" but because he, "from the beginning to the end, impressed upon the people the conviction of his honesty and fidelity to one great purpose."

James Russell Lowell, a Harvard professor considered the "foremost American man of letters in his time," revealed a more incisive view of Lincoln's qualities. In a long article for the *North American Review*, which Lincoln read with pleasure, Lowell traced the progress of the Lincoln administration. "Never did a President enter upon office with less means at his command," he began. "All that was known of him was that he was a good stump-speaker, nominated for his *availability*,—that is, because he had no history." For many months, Lowell observed, the untried president seemed too hesitant—on military engagements, on emancipation, on recruiting black troops. Increasingly, it was becoming evident that this Abraham Lincoln was "a character of marked individuality and capacity for affairs." In a democratic nation, Lowell added, "where the rough and ready understanding of the people is sure at last to be the controlling power, a profound common-sense is the best genius for statesmanship." Lincoln had demonstrated a perfectly calibrated touch for public sentiment and impeccable timing in his introduction of new measures. While some thought he had delayed his decision on emancipation too long, he undoubtedly had a "sure-footed understanding" of the American people. Similarly, when the first black regiments were formed, many feared that "something terrible" would happen, "but the earth stood firm."

"Mr. Lincoln's perilous task has been to carry a rather shackly raft through the rapids, making fast the unrulier logs as he could snatch opportunity," concluded Lowell, "and the country is to be congratulated that he did not think it his duty to run straight at all hazards, but cautiously to assure himself with his setting-pole where the main current was, and keep steadily to that."

Despite the remarkable transformations of the previous three years, Lowell understood that the raft was "still in wild water." So, of course, did Lincoln. The president recommended the Lowell piece to Gideon Welles, telling him it presented a "very excellent" discussion of the administration's policy, but that it "gave him over-much credit."

CHAPTER 23

"THERE'S A MAN IN IT!"

NEW YEAR'S DAY, 1864, dawned "fearfully cold and windy," Noah Brooks recorded, and "the morning newspaper and the milkman were alike snapped up by the nipping frosts." Eventually, a bright sun scattered the clouds, and a mood of good cheer enveloped the city as the *National Republican* headlined the long list of Union victories during the previous year—"Murfreesboro, Vicksburg, Morris Island, Gettysburg, Port Hudson, Chattanooga, Knoxville."

"History does not furnish a year's victories by the armies of any country in any war that will excel these," the *National Republican* boasted. "We have a right to be somewhat gay and festive here at the national metropolis. No one wishes to deny that we have had a rebellious storm, and that the political horizon is still somewhat muggy; but our gallant old ship of State, with

Abraham Lincoln at the helm, has weathered the gale." William Stoddard echoed these sentiments in a published dispatch. "The instinct of all, rather than the reasoning, teaches us, as it has the rest of the country, that once and for all the danger is over."

At 10 a.m., official Washington began arriving at the White House for the traditional New Year's reception. At noon, when the gates opened to the general public, eight thousand people streamed in—"a human kalei-descope, constantly changing," of "diplomats and dragoons, exquisites from the Atlantic cities and hardy backwoodsmen, contented contractors and shoddy swindlers, ingenious patentees and persevering petitioners."

Lincoln considered his meetings with the general public his *"public-opinion baths."* They "serve to renew in me a clearer and more vivid image of that great popular assemblage out of which I sprung," he told a visitor, "and though they may not be pleasant in all their particulars, the effect, as a whole, is renovating and invigorating to my perceptions of responsibility and duty."

"European democrats go into ecstasies over so palpable a sign of our universal equality," Stoddard noted, while "European aristocrats, attaches of legations, tourists, and the like, turn up their noses somewhat scornfully at so singularly American a custom." Visitors noted that Lincoln "appeared to be in excellent health and spirits, and whatever perplexities his generals may give him, he possesses the happy faculty of leaving them in his office upstairs, when he comes down to receive the salutations of the people. His clear eyes beamed with good humor, and he not only cordially returned the pressure of each offered hand, but generally said a pleasant word or two." Noah Brooks noted that Mary Lincoln "never looked better," having replaced her black "mourning garb" with a rich purple velvet dress.

"We seem to have reached a new stage in the war," Fred Seward wrote home. "Gayety has become as epidemic in Washington this winter, as gloom was last winter. There is a lull in political discussions; and people are inclined to eat, drink, and be merry. The newspapers can furnish nothing more interesting to their readers, than accounts of parties, balls and theaters, like so many Court Journals. Questions of etiquette are debated with gravity. People talk of 'society,' who never before knew or cared about it."

The winter social calendar followed a prescribed order. The president's receptions were on Tuesday evenings, the first lady's matinées on Saturday afternoons, the soirées of the Speaker of the House on Friday nights. No cards of invitation were required for these events. Since the president and speaker held their offices at the will of the people, their homes were open to the public at large. In contrast, invitations were necessary, and highly coveted, for the elegant parties at the dwellings of cabinet officers. Access to the drawing rooms of Seward and Chase were prized most of all.

Social columnists attributed the legendary success of the parties held by the secretary of state to both his genial wit and the "grace and elegance" of his daughter-in-law, Anna, "who with such rare art groups those of congenial tastes, and makes all truly 'at home.' " For young belles, there was added mystique in the presence of the diplomatic corps, which held out the titillating prospect of attracting a titled foreigner. For those fascinated by fashion and etiquette, nothing compared to the impeccable manners and gorgeous dress of the diplomats, bespangled with ribbons and garters denoting different orders of knighthood. "Who wonders that the House of Gov. Seward is a favorite resort," one columnist asked, "and who that enjoys his hospitality does not wish that he might be Secretary of State forever, and be 'at home' once a week."

At the Chase mansion, Kate Sprague continued to be the "observed of all observers." Whether dressed in blue brocade, gray, or simple black, she impressed congressmen, senators, and generals alike with her interest in politics and familiarity with military affairs. Holding court at the entrance, she had an appropriate greeting for every guest. Benjamin French thought her "one of the most lovable women" he had ever seen. Noah Brooks was likewise smitten, at once recognizing the delightful contrast to her "frosty" father, who "looked uncomfortable and generally bothered" at these affairs. Chase's nearsightedness had grown so extreme that he was unable to recognize anyone without "a very close examination." Nevertheless, he still refused to wear glasses.

The Washington elite preferred the fancy dinner parties at the Seward and Chase mansions to the public levees at the White House, where bonnets were crushed and cloaks occasionally stolen in the chaos. During the winter, Mary found it necessary to put durable brown coverings over her elegant French carpets to protect them from the muddy tramp of the "human tide" that poured in to shake hands with the president. Many visitors were ill dressed and bedraggled, as after a long dusty ride, and some still carried their carpetbags. The elegant furnishings that Mary had so lovingly and expensively put in place took a beating. Brooks noted that "the lace curtains, heavy cords, tassels, and damask drapery have suffered considerably this season from the hands of relic-hunting vandals who actually clip off small bits of the precious stuff to carry home as mementoes." Desperate to preserve their experience, some even lifted the brown covering and cut out pieces of the French carpet "as large as a man's hand."

For Mary, who relished her position as first lady, it was galling to read in the papers that Seward, not she, would inaugurate "the fashionable 'season.'" He was to host an exclusive party for the visiting members of the National Academy of Science, along with "the heads of the foreign Legations, the Cabinet, the Justices of the Supreme Court, the presiding officers of the two Houses of Congress and the Committees on Foreign Relations, with their families." That same week, the *New York Herald* noted, the White House reception was "not so largely attended as usual." Benjamin French, who was Mary's customary escort at public functions, saw that she was "disappointed." The Sewards hosted three more receptions in January 1864, accounted the "grandest," "most elegant," and "most brilliant" affairs of the season, with guest lists including barons, counts, lords, ladies, and young Robert Lincoln, home for vacation.

Mary's wounded pride increased her feelings of resentment toward Seward. She continued to begrudge the intimacy he shared with her husband, the many nights Lincoln chose to spend with Seward instead of her. Fred Seward records a pleasant evening that January when Lincoln walked over to Seward's with John Hay to share a humorous language guidebook, *English as She is Spoke*. "As John Hay read aloud its queer inverted sentences, Lincoln and Seward laughed heartily, their minds finding a brief but welcome relief from care." Though Seward had long since ceased to be a political threat to her husband, Mary could not relinquish her suspicions. She told their family friend Anson Henry that Seward and his friends were behind the various "scandalous reports in circulation about her." Dr. Henry dismissed her fears, saying that the nasty rumors probably originated in "the Treasury Department," for he had "traced many of them" to Chase's friends and supporters.

Indeed, by early 1864, Chase's presidential ambitions were widely known and frequently discussed in political circles. Mary's anger toward Chase grew "very bitter," Elizabeth Keckley recalled: she "warned Mr. Lincoln not to trust him," but Lincoln continued to insist that Chase was "a patriot." As Mary planned for her first state dinner of the year, traditionally held for the members of the cabinet, justices of the Supreme Court, and their families, she decided to take matters into her own hands. She perused the guest list compiled by John Nicolay, and crossed out the names of Kate Chase and William Sprague. Certain the "snub" would become public and reflect badly on Lincoln, Nicolay appealed to his boss to reinstate the Spragues. Lincoln immediately agreed, sending Mary into a rage.

"There soon arose such a rampage as the House hasn't seen for a year," Nicolay confided to an absent Hay, "and I am again taboo. How the thing is to end is yet as dark a problem as the Schleswig-Holstein difficulty." Mary directed her wrath toward Nicolay, banishing him from the dinner and eschewing his customary help with the arrangements. "Things ran on thus till the afternoon of the dinner," Nicolay reported, when Mary "backed down, requested my presence and assistance—apologizing, and explaining that the affair had worried her so she hadn't slept for a night or two."

The dinner "was pleasant," Welles recorded in his diary. "A little stiff and awkward on the part of the some of the guests [perhaps referring to Chase], but passed off very well." Welles, however, was unable to share the capital's renewed delight in parties, receptions, and fairs. It all seemed inappropriate, "like merry-making at a funeral," he wrote his son Edgar.

Not every occasion was merely a frivolous distraction. The hosts and partygoers did not forget the imperiled men in the armed forces. Where once "the old secession or semi-secesh element" reigned in Washington society, injured soldiers and sailors became the stars of every occasion. Admiral Dahlgren's twenty-one-year-old son, Ulric, had lost a leg at Gettysburg. When he appeared at a Washington party, he was surrounded by pretty girls. They stayed by his side all night, refusing to dance, in tribute to the handsome colonel who had been known as an expert waltzer.

In late January, Copperhead congressman Fernando Wood of New York, who had often and bitterly denounced the Republican administration and the war, threw a great party to which he invited Republicans as well as fellow Democrats. Republicans were expected to stay away, but many actually attended, as did "Abolitionists of the most ultra stripe." Stoddard found it "one of the charming features of life in Washington" that "political animosities" were not carried "into social life," that people who publicly savaged one another could still be "commendably cordial and friendly in all personal intercourse."

In keeping with that tradition, Mary Lincoln sent a bouquet of flowers to Mrs. Wood. The Woods exaggerated the courtesy by placing cards that read: "Compliments of Mrs. A. Lincoln" beside all the many flower vases, making it appear that Mary had supplied the entire array. Newspapers played up the story, citing the supposedly lavish display as evidence of Mary's Southern sympathies. Stung by the criticism, Mary wrote her influential friend General Sickles: "I am pleased to announce to you my entire innocence. . . . With the exception of two political public receptions, they [the Woods] have not entered the [White] house—all of my, friends, who know my detestation of disloyal persons will discredit the rumor—You know me too well to believe it."

Still, slander against the president and first lady continued to fill the columns of opposition papers. In December, when Emilie Todd Helm had come through Union lines after her husband's death, she had been accompanied north by another sister, Martha Todd White. After Emilie left the White House, Lincoln issued a pass to Martha, allowing her to return to the Confederacy. Such passes were not unusual, but the false story spread that Lincoln, presumably at his wife's request, had granted a special permit allowing Martha to bring her bags through without inspection. Some opposition papers claimed that she was, in fact, a Confederate spy and had used her privilege to smuggle contraband through Union lines. It was bruited that when she arrived at Fort Monroe and was told to open her trunks, she waved the president's permit in General Butler's face, defiantly proclaiming: "Here (pushing it under their noses) here is the positive order of your master."

Ordinarily, Lincoln took little heed of scurrilous rumors, but in this case, he directed Nicolay to ascertain the facts from General Butler. Butler replied that the smuggling story was spurious. Mrs. White's bags had undergone the usual search. Nothing untoward had been found. Nicolay used Butler's letter to document a public rebuttal of the fraudulent story. Butler was surprised that the White House would even bother to respond to something so "silly," but after the Wood affair had cast doubt on his wife's loyalty, Lincoln may have wanted to nip the new round of rumors in the bud. Nor did he want his soldiers to think that he would ever facilitate the Confederacy's access to contraband items that might sustain the rebel cause.

It is scarcely surprising that Lincoln not long afterward showed little patience when his old friend Orville Browning requested a favor for a loyal Unionist who owned a cotton plantation in Mississippi. When the Union Army overran her home and took her slaves, she had fallen into poverty. She asked if the government could provide her an equal number of Negroes whom she would pay to work her farm. Lincoln "became very much excited," according to Browning, and "said with great vehemence he had rather take a rope and hang himself than to do it." When Browning argued for "some sort of remuneration" for the lost property, Lincoln countered that "she had lost no property—that her slaves were free when they were taken." Puzzled by Lincoln's sharp reaction, Browning "left him in no very good humor."

As was usually the case with Lincoln's rare episodes of pique, other strains had contributed to the sharp rejoinder. Earlier that day, he had visited the sickbed of Illinois congressman Owen Lovejoy, whom he considered "the best friend [he] had in Congress." The fifty-three-year-old Lovejoy was suffering from a debilitating liver and kidney ailment that would soon take his life. Lincoln was distraught over Lovejoy's misery and seemed to internalize the grim prospects facing his friend. "This war is eating my life out," he told the dying Lovejoy. "I have a strong impression that I shall not live to see the end."

On the night of February 10, a fire alarm rang in the White House. Smoke was seen issuing from the president's private stables, which stood between the mansion and the Treasury building, and Lincoln raced to the scene. "When he reached the boxwood hedge that served as an enclosure to the stables," a member of his bodyguard, Robert McBride, recalled, "he sprang over it like a deer." Learning that the horses were still inside, Lincoln, "with his own hands burst open the stable door." It was immediately apparent that the fast-moving fire, the work of an arsonist, prevented any hope of rescue. "Notwithstanding this," McBride observed, "he would apparently have tried to enter the burning building had not those standing near caught and restrained him."

Six horses burned to death that night. When McBride returned to the White House, he found Lincoln in tears. Ten-year-old Tad "explained his father's emotion": one of the ponies had belonged to his brother, Willie. A coachman who had been fired by Mary that morning was charged with setting the fire. The following day, Lincoln had collected himself and moved forward. He called Commissioner French to his office and instructed him to consult contractors, estimate the cost, and "bring the matter to the attention of Congress to-day, if possible, that measures might be taken to have it rebuilt."

• • •

LINCOLN'S GIFT FOR MANAGING men was never more apparent than during the presidential boomlet for Chase that peaked in the winter months of 1864. While Chase's supporters prematurely showed their hand, Lincoln, according to the Pennsylvania politician Alexander McClure, "carefully veiled his keen and sometimes bitter resentment against Chase, and waited the fullness of time when he could by some fortuitous circumstance remove Chase as a competitor, or by some shrewd manipulation of politics make him a hopeless one."

The game had begun in earnest early in January. Friends of Chase, including Jay and Henry Cooke, contributed thousands of dollars to the publisher of the *American Exchange and Review*, a small Philadelphia magazine, so he would print a flattering biographical sketch of the treasury secretary. Chase's friend William Orton warned him that "no matter how able or 'faithful' the biography may be," its publication in a "seedy" magazine with a reputation for selling its space to whomever could pay enough would be seen "as a flimsy political trick." Orton's note elicited no direct reply, but at some point the president had apparently questioned the involvement of the Cooke brothers, who were still official agents for selling government bonds. The president's questions elicited a long, emotional letter from Chase.

Chase opened his letter with the assertion that his actions, as always, proceeded from the purest of motives. He claimed he had "never, consciously & deliberately, injured one fellow man." He had been told that the publisher intended to print a series of sketches about prominent figures, starting with him. "How could I object?" Treasury business so occupied him that he had paid no further attention to the matter. "What Mr. H. D. Cooke did about the unfortunate biography was done of his own accord without any prompting from me," Chase insisted. Had Cooke or his brother sought his consent, he would have stopped them. "Not that any wrong was intended or done; but because the act was subject to misconstruction. . . . You will pardon me if I write as one somewhat moved. It makes me hate public life when I realize how powerless are the most faithful labors and the most upright conduct to protect any man from carping envy or malignant denunciations."

Embarrassment over the circumstances surrounding the *Exchange and Review* piece did not stop Chase from writing twenty-five long letters that winter to the Boston writer John Trowbridge. His missives were designed to provide the foundation for a small inspirational book about his life, *The Ferry-Boy and the Financier*. An excerpt appeared that spring in the *Atlantic Monthly*. These letters were but a small part of a massive campaign to extol his own virtues at Lincoln's expense. From early morning until late at night, Chase toiled to maintain his stream of correspondence with friends and supporters. "So far," he told a friend in Cincinnati, "I think I have made few mistakes. Indeed, on looking back over the whole ground with an earnest desire to detect error and correct it, I am not able to see where, if I had to do my work all over again, I could in any matter do materially otherwise than I have."

With Kate married and Nettie away at school, Chase resumed his sporadic correspondence with Charlotte Eastman. "I think of you constantly," he assured her, "and—if any feeling is left in me—with the sincerest affection. . . . How I wish you were here in our house—in this little library room—and that we could talk, instead of this writing by myself, while you are—where?" Such romantic inclinations were probably never consummated. Similarly, though he enjoyed the company of Susan Walker, an educated "bluestocking" from Cincinnati, the relationship never seemed to deepen. "*I wish* you could come to Washington," he wrote Miss Walker in late January, "though I could probably see so little of you that it would be difficult to tell which would be greater, the pleasure of seeing you, or the sensation of not seeing you enough." Though Chase obviously admired both Eastman and Walker, his intense focus on his ambition for the presidency kept him from ever making the time to unbend in their company.

The second push in Chase's race for the presidential nomination opened with the public announcement of a "Chase for President" committee. The committee, headed by Kansas senator Samuel Pomeroy and a successful railroad agent, James Winchell, was another enterprise backed by Jay Cooke. In this case, however, Chase's son-in-law, William Sprague, contributed the largest share of the funds. Pomeroy and Winchell were both committed abolitionists who believed Chase would best protect the rights of blacks. Their appearance of altruistic principle was compromised by the fact that they stood to benefit financially if Chase released funds for the construction of the Kansas-Pacific Railroad in which both held a large interest.

Lincoln's old friend Judge David Davis was incensed that Chase was "eating a man's bread and stabbing him at the same time." Chase, unsurprisingly, viewed things differently. Since one-term presidencies had become the rule, Chase felt justified in presenting himself as an alternative. While the committee was being organized, Chase busied himself lining up support in Ohio, determined to avoid the humiliation he had suffered in 1860, when his own state had withheld its support.

Optimistic that he might defeat Lincoln, Chase told his old law partner Flamen Ball that he was immensely "gratified" by the newly formed committee and the quality of the people supporting his candidacy, for they tended to be "men of great weight." Much would depend on the Buckeye State, for "if Ohio should express a preference for any other person, I would not allow my name to be used." Should all go well, Chase believed he would put up a good fight against the president, for, sad to say, the prairie lawyer was simply not up to the job. "If to his kindliness of spirit and good sense he joined strong will and energetic action, there would be little left to wish for in him. As it is, I think that he will be likely to close his first term with more honor than he will the second, should he be reelected."

Nor did Chase confine his criticisms of Lincoln to conversation and correspondence with trusted friends. Speaking with Gideon Welles early in February, he "lamented the want of energy and force by the President, which he said paralyzed everything." Disregarding Welles's silence, he went on to suggest that the president's "weakness was crushing" the nation. When Welles still "did not respond to this distinct feeler," Chase finally let the matter drop. Chase was equally indiscreet with Bates, seeming not to recognize that while the Attorney General occasionally criticized the president, he "immeasurably" preferred him to any other candidate.

Lincoln seemed unfazed by the machinations surrounding the race. Welles reported with delight an exchange with a "fair plump lady" who appeared in the hallway just before a cabinet meeting. She said she lived in Iowa and had come to get a look at the president. Hearing her story, Lincoln invited her into his office. "Well, in the matter of looking at one another," said he with a smile and a chuckle, "I have altogether the advantage."

In February, the Pomeroy Committee distributed a confidential circular to one hundred leading Republicans throughout the North. Intended to mobilize support for Chase, the circular opened with a slashing critique of the president, claiming that "even were the reelection of Mr. Lincoln desirable, it is practically impossible," given the widespread opposition. Furthermore, "should he be reelected, his manifest tendency toward compromises and temporary expedients of policy will become stronger during a second term than it has been in the first." The war would "continue to languish," the country would be bankrupted, and "the dignity of the nation" would suffer. Therefore, in order to win the war, establish the peace, and "vindicate the honor of the republic," it was essential that Republicans unite in nominating the one man with "more of the qualities needed in a President, during the next four years, than are combined in any other available candidate"—Salmon P. Chase.

When the Pomeroy circular was leaked to the press, it created a political explosion. Lincoln's friends were furious, while Democrats celebrated the open division in Republican ranks. "No sensible man here is in doubt that Chase was privy to this," David Davis told a friend. "They did not expect that it wd see the light so soon. . . . I wd dismiss him [from] the cabinet if it killed me."

In a state of panic, Chase sent Lincoln a letter in which he claimed he "had no knowledge" of the circular until it was printed in the *Constitutional Union* on February 20. Though he had been approached by friends to use his name in the coming election, he had not been consulted about the formation of the Pomeroy Committee and was unfamiliar with its members. "You are not responsible for acts not your own," he reminded Lincoln, "nor will you hold me responsible except for what I do or say myself." Yet, he proclaimed, "if there is anything in my action or position which, in your judgment, will prejudice the public interest under my charge I beg you to say so. I do not wish to administer the Treasury Department one day without your entire confidence."

It is unlikely that Lincoln believed Chase's protestations of innocence. Indeed, a decade later, the circular's author, James Winchell, testified that Chase had been fully informed about everything and had personally affirmed "that the arraignment of the Administration made in the circular was one which he thoroughly indorsed, and would sustain." Still, Lincoln restrained his anger and carefully gauged his response, taking a dispassionate view of the situation. He understood the political landscape, he assured Bates. There was a number of malcontents within his own party who "would strike him at once, if they durst; but they fear that the blow would be ineffectual, and so, they would fall under his power, as *beaten enemies.*" So long as he remained confident that he had the public's support, he could afford to let the game play out a little longer. Keeping Chase in suspense, Lincoln simply acknowledged receipt of the letter and promised to "answer a little more fully when I can find time to do so." Then he sat back to measure the reaction of the people to the circular.

It did not take long. The morning it was printed, Welles correctly predicted: "Its recoil will be more dangerous I apprehend than its projectile. That is, it will damage Chase more than Lincoln." Even papers friendly to Chase lamented the circular's publication. "It is unworthy of the cause," the *New York Times* proclaimed. "We protest against the spirit of this movement." Four days later, Nicolay happily informed his fiancée, Therena, that the effect of the circular had been the opposite of what its authors intended, for "it has stirred up all Mr. Lincoln's friends to active exertion," seriously diminishing Chase's prospects. In state after state, Republicans met and passed unanimous resolutions in favor of Lincoln's renomination. Even in Pomeroy's home state of Kansas, a counter-circular was distributed among Republicans that denounced the efforts to carry the state for Chase and rallied support for Lincoln.

Noting the "long list" of state legislatures that had come out for Lincoln, the *Times* acknowledged that the "universality of popular sentiment in favor of Mr. Lincoln's reelection, is one of the most remarkable developments of the time. . . . The faith of the people in the sound judgment and honest purpose of Mr. Lincoln is as tenacious as if it were a veritable instinct. Nothing can overcome it or seriously weaken it. This power of attracting and holding popular confidence springs only from a rare combination of qualities. Very few public men in American history have possessed it in an equal degree with Abraham Lincoln." *Harper's Weekly* agreed. In an editorial endorsing the president's reelection, it claimed that "among all the prominent men in our history from the beginning none have ever shown the power of understanding the popular mind so accurately as Mr. Lincoln." In moving gradually toward emancipation, as he had done, the *Harper's* editor observed, Lincoln understood that in a democracy, "every step he took must seem wise to the great public mind." Thus, he had wisely nullified the premature proclamations issued by Frémont and Hunter, waiting until "the blood of sons and brothers and friends would wash clear a thousand eyes that had been blinded." In his grudging fashion, even Lincoln's critic Count Gurowski acknowledged the president's hold on the people's affections. "The masses are taken in by Lincoln's *apparent* simplicity and good-naturedness, by his awkwardness, by his vulgar jokes, and, in the people's belief, the great shifter is earnest and honest."

The fatal blow to the Chase campaign came again in Ohio, as it had four years before. Although Chase's friends in the Union caucus of the state legislature had previously blocked attempts to endorse Lincoln's re-election, the publication of the Pomeroy circular, a Chase ally conceded, "brought matters to a crisis. . . . It arrayed at once men agt each other who had been party friends always; & finally produced a perfect convulsion in the party." The end result was the unanimous passage of a resolution in favor of Lincoln. "As matters now stand here, with so many states already declared for Lincoln," Chase's friend Cleveland attorney Richard Parsons warned, "prolonging a contest that will in the end array our 'house against itself,' & bring no good to our party at last, seems to me one of the gravest character."

Perceiving this turn of events, Lincoln decided the time was right to answer Chase's letter. He informed Chase that the circular had not surprised him, for he "had knowledge of Mr. Pomeroy's Committee," and of its "secret issues" and "secret agents," for a number of weeks. However, he did not intend to hold Chase responsible. "I fully concur with you that neither of us can be justly held responsible for what our respective friends may do without our instigation or countenance; and I assure you, as you have assured me, that no assault has been made upon you by my instigation, or with my countenance." As to whether Chase should remain as treasury secretary, Lincoln would decide based solely on "my judgement of the public service." For the present, he wrote, "I do not perceive occasion for a change."

A few days later, Chase withdrew his presidential bid. In a public letter to an influential state senator in Ohio, he reminded his fellow Ohioans that he had determined to withdraw from the race if he did not gain the support of his home state. With the legislature's support of Lincoln, "it becomes my duty therefore,—and I count it more a privilege than a duty,—to ask that no further consideration be given to my name."

Trying as ever to explain his action as an unselfish move, Chase told his daughter Nettie that he had withdrawn from the race, though "a good many of the best and most earnest men of the country desired to make me a candidate," because "it was becoming daily more & more clear that the continuance of my name before the people would produce serious discords in the Union organization and might endanger the success of the measures & the establishment of the principles I thought most indispensable to the welfare of the country." Attorney General Bates suggested a less patriotic explanation: "It proves only that the *present* prospects of Mr. Lincoln are too good to be openly resisted."

Discipline and keen insight had once again served Lincoln most effectively. By regulating his emotions and resisting the impulse to strike back at Chase when the circular first became known, he gained time for his friends to mobilize the massive latent support for his candidacy. Chase's aspirations were crushed without Lincoln's direct intrusion. He had known all along that his treasury secretary was no innocent, but by seeming to accept Chase's word, he allowed the secretary to retain some measure of his dignity while the country retained his services in the cabinet. Lincoln himself would determine the appropriate time for Chase's departure.

· · ·

LINCOLN'S ABILITY TO RETAIN his emotional balance in such difficult situations was rooted in an acute self-awareness and an enormous capacity to dispel anxiety in constructive ways. In the most difficult moments of his presidency, nothing provided Lincoln greater respite and renewal than to immerse himself in a play at either Grover's or Ford's. Leonard Grover estimated that Lincoln had visited his theater "more than a hundred times" during his four years as president. He was most frequently accompanied by Seward, who shared Lincoln's passion for drama and was an old friend of Mr. Grover's. But his three young assistants, Nicolay, Hay, and Stoddard, also joined him on occasion, as did Noah Brooks, Mary, and Tad. On many nights, Lincoln came by himself, delighted at the chance to sink into his seat as the gaslights dimmed and the action on the stage began.

"It gave him an hour or two of freedom from care and worry," observed Brooks, "and what was better, freedom from the interruption of office-seekers and politicians. He was on such terms with the managers of two of the theaters that he could go in privately by the stage door, and slip into the stage boxes without being seen by the audience." More than anything else, Stoddard remarked how "the drama by drawing his mind into other channels of thought, afforded him the most entire relief." At a performance of *Henry IV: Part One*, Stoddard noted how thoroughly Lincoln enjoyed himself. "He has forgotten the war. He has forgotten Congress. He is out of politics. He is living in Prince Hal's time."

It is not surprising that the theater offered ideal refreshment for a man who regularly employed storytelling to ease tensions. The theater held all the elements of a perfect escape. Enthralled by the live drama, the costumes and scenery, the stagecraft, and the rhetorical extravagances, he was transported into a realm far from the troubling events that filled the rest of his waking hours.

In the mid-nineteenth century, developments with gaslight had vastly improved the experience of theatergoers. Managers had learned "to dim or brighten illumination" by manipulating the valves that fed the gas to the jets. A setting sun, a full moon, or a misty evening could be achieved by placing "colored glass mantles" over the lamps. Technicians stationed above the balcony could illuminate individual actors as they made their entrance onto the stage.

"To envision nineteenth-century theater audiences correctly," the cultural historian Lawrence Levine suggests, "one might do well to visit a contemporary sporting event in which the spectators not only are similarly heterogeneous but are also . . . more than an audience; they are participants who can enter into the action on the field, who feel a sense of immediacy and at times even of control, who articulate their opinions and feelings vocally and unmistakably." Though different classes occupied different areas of the theater—the wealthy in the first-tier boxes, the working class in the orchestra, and the poor in the balcony—the entire audience shared a fairly intimate space. Indeed, Frances Trollope complained that in American theaters she encountered men without jackets, their sleeves rolled to their elbows, and their breath smelling of "onions and whiskey." Though Lincoln was seated in his presidential box, he could still enjoy the communal experience, which allowed him to feel the pulse of the people, much as he had done when he traveled the circuit in his early days.

The years surrounding the Civil War have been called the golden age of American acting. During those years, one historian claims, "the American theatre was blessed with a galaxy of performers who have never been excelled"—including Edwin Forrest, John McCullough, Edwin Booth, Laura Keene, and Charlotte Cushman. It was said of Miss Cushman, who was lionized in both Europe and America for her role as Lady Macbeth, that "she was not a great actress merely, but she was a great woman." She had a magnetic personality and "when she came upon the stage she filled it with . . . the brilliant vitality of her presence." A liberated woman, far ahead of her time, she had lovers but never married. Her work was her chief passion.

Seward and Miss Cushman had met in the 1850s and become great friends. Whenever she was in Washington, she stayed at the Seward home.

The celebrated actress forged a close relationship with young Fanny, who idolized her. Miss Cushman offered a glimpse of the vital and independent life Fanny hoped to lead someday, if her dream to become a writer came true. "Imagine me," Fanny wrote her mother after one of Miss Cushman's visits, "full of the old literary fervor and anxious to be at work, to try hard—& at the same time 'learn to labor, & to wait' I mean, improve in the work which I cannot choose but take . . . I am full of hope that I may yet make my life worth the living and be of some use in the world."

In honor of the star guest, Seward organized a series of dinner parties, inviting members of foreign legations and cabinet colleagues. For her part, Miss Cushman regarded Seward as "the greatest man this country ever produced." Fanny believed that Cushman understood her noble father better than almost anyone outside their family.

Fred Seward recalled that Lincoln made his way to their house almost every night while Miss Cushman visited. Seward had introduced Cushman to the president in the summer of 1861. She had hoped to ask Lincoln for help in obtaining a West Point appointment for a young friend, but the scintillating conversation distracted her from the purpose of her visit. And Lincoln was undoubtedly riveted by the celebrated actress of his beloved Shakespeare.

Unlike Seward, who had been attending theater since he was a young man, Lincoln had seen very few live performances until he came to Washington. So excited was he by his first sight of Falstaff on the stage that he wrote the actor, James Hackett: "Perhaps the best compliment I can pay is to say, as I truly can, I am very anxious to see it again." Although he had not read all of Shakespeare's plays, he told Hackett that he had studied some of them "perhaps as frequently as any unprofessional reader. Among the latter are Lear, Richard Third, Henry Eighth, Hamlet, and especially Macbeth. I think nothing equals Macbeth. It is wonderful. Unlike you gentlemen of the profession, I think the soliloquy in Hamlet commencing 'O, my offence is rank' surpasses that commencing, 'To be, or not to be.' But pardon this small attempt at criticism." When Hackett shared the president's letter with friends, it unfortunately made its way into opposition newspapers. Lincoln was promptly ridiculed for his attempt to render dramatic judgments. An embarrassed Hackett apologized to Lincoln, who urged him to have "no uneasiness on the subject." He was not "shocked by the newspaper comments," for all his life he had "endured a great deal of ridicule without much malice."

The histories and tragedies of Shakespeare that Lincoln loved most dealt with themes that would resonate to a president in the midst of civil war: political intrigue, the burdens of power, the nature of ambition, the relationship of leaders to those they governed. The plays illuminated with stark beauty the dire consequences of civil strife, the evils wrought by jealousy and disloyalty, the emotions evoked by the death of a child, the sundering of family ties or love of country.

Congressman William D. Kelley of Pennsylvania recalled bringing the actor John McDonough to the White House on a stormy night. Lincoln had relished McDonough's performance as Edgar in *King Lear* and was delighted to meet him. For his part, McDonough was "an intensely partisan Democrat, and had accepted the theory that Mr. Lincoln was a mere buffoon." His attitude changed after spending four hours discussing Shakespeare with the president. Lincoln was eager to know why certain scenes were left out of productions. He was fascinated by the different ways that classic lines could be delivered. He lifted his "well-thumbed volume" of Shakespeare from the shelf, reading aloud some passages, repeating others from memory. When the clock approached midnight, Kelley stood up to go, chagrined to have kept the president so long. Lincoln swiftly assured his guests that he had "not enjoyed such a season of literary recreation" in many months. The evening had provided an immensely "pleasant interval" from his work.

Of all the remarkable stage actors in this golden time, none surpassed Edwin Booth, son of the celebrated tragedian Junius Booth and elder brother to Lincoln's future assassin, John Wilkes Booth. "Edwin Booth has done more for the stage in America than any other man," wrote a drama critic in the 1860s. The soulful young actor captivated audiences everywhere with the naturalness of his performances and his conversational tone, which stood in contrast to the bombastic, stylized performances of the older generation.

In late February and early March 1864, Edwin Booth came to Grover's Theatre for a three-week engagement, delivering one masterly performance after another. Lincoln and Seward attended the theater night after night. They saw Booth in the title roles of Hamlet and Richard III. They applauded his performance as Brutus in *Julius Caesar* and as Shylock in *The Merchant of Venice*.

On Friday evening, March 11, Booth came to dinner at the Sewards'. Twenty-year-old Fanny Seward could barely contain her excitement. She had seen every one of his performances and had been transfixed by his "magnificent dark eyes." At dinner, Seward presumed to ask Booth if he might advise the thespian how "his acting might be improved." According to Fanny, Booth "accepted Father's criticisms very gracefully—often saying he had felt those defects himself." Seward focused particularly on

Booth's performance in Bulwer-Lytton's *Richelieu*, where he thought he had made the crafty cardinal "too old and infirm." Long identified as the power behind the throne himself, Seward perhaps wanted a younger, more vibrant characterization for Richelieu. When Seward told Booth he thought his performance as Shylock was perfect, Booth disagreed, saying he "had a painful sense of something wanting—could compare it to nothing else but the want of body in wine."

Detained at the White House, Lincoln missed the enjoyable interchange with Booth. A few days earlier, anticipating Booth's Hamlet, Lincoln had talked about the play with Francis Carpenter, the young artist who was at work on his picture depicting the first reading of the Emancipation Proclamation. In the course of the conversation, Lincoln recited from memory his favorite passage, the king's soliloquy after the murder of Hamlet's father, "with a feeling and appreciation unsurpassed by anything I ever witnessed upon the stage."

What struck Carpenter most forcefully was Lincoln's ability to appreciate tragedy and comedy with equal intensity. He could, in one sitting, bring tears to a visitor's eyes with a sensitive rendering from *Richard III* and moments later induce riotous laughter with a comic tall tale. His "laugh," Carpenter observed, "stood by itself. The 'neigh' of a wild horse on his native prairie is not more undisguised and hearty." Lincoln's ability to commingle joy with sorrow seemed to Carpenter a trait the president shared with his favorite playwright. "It has been well said," Carpenter noted, "that 'the spirit which held the woe of "Lear," and the tragedy of "Hamlet," would have broken, had it not also had the humor of the "Merry Wives of Windsor," and the merriment of "Midsummer Night's Dream."'"

No other cabinet member went to the theater as regularly as Lincoln and Seward. Chase and Bates considered it a foolish waste of time, perhaps even a "Satanic diversion," while Stanton came only once to Grover's playhouse, with the sole intention of buttonholing Lincoln about some pressing matter. Seated with Lincoln in his box, Grover had been startled when Stanton arrived a half hour late, sidled up to Lincoln, and engaged him in a long conversation. Lincoln listened attentively but kept his eyes on the stage. Frustrated, Stanton "grasped Mr. Lincoln by the lapel of his coat, slowly pulled him round face to face, and continued the conversation. Mr. Lincoln responded to this brusque act with all the smiling geniality that one might bestow on a similar act from a favorite child, but soon again turned his eyes to the stage." Finally, Stanton despaired utterly of conducting his business. He "arose, said good night, and withdrew."

According to Grover, Tad loved the theater as much as his father. John

Hay noted that Tad would laugh "enormously whenever he saw his father's eye twinkle, though not seeing clearly why." Often escorted to Grover's by his tutor, Tad "felt at home and frequently came alone to the rehearsals, which he watched with rapt interest. He made the acquaintance of the stage attachés, who liked him and gave him complete liberty of action." Tad would help them move scenery, and on one occasion, he actually appeared in a play. For the lonely boy, who broke down in tears when the appearance of Julia Taft at a White House reception recalled his happier days with Willie and the Taft boys, the camaraderie of the playhouse must have been immensely comforting.

●   ●   ●

ULYSSES S. GRANT, the hero of Vicksburg and Chattanooga, arrived in the nation's capital on March 8, 1864, to take command of all the Union armies. A grateful Congress had revived the grade of lieutenant general, not held since George Washington, and Lincoln had nominated Grant to receive the honored rank. With Grant's promotion, Halleck became chief of staff, and Sherman assumed Grant's old command of the Western armies.

Grant's entrance into Washington was consistent with his image as an unpretentious man of action, the polar opposite of McClellan. He walked into the Willard Hotel at dusk, accompanied only by his teenage son, Fred. Unrecognized by the desk clerk, he was told that nothing was available except a small room on the top floor. The situation was remedied only when the embarrassed clerk looked at the signature in the register— U. S. Grant and son, Galena, Illinois—and immediately switched the accommodations. After freshening up, Grant took his son to the dining room at the lobby level. His slim build, "stooping shoulders, mild blue eyes, and light brown hair and whiskers" attracted little notice until someone began pointing at his table. Suddenly, "there was a shout of welcome from all present, an immense cheer going up from the crowd," who banged their fists on the tops of the tables until he finally stood up and took a bow.

After readying his son for bed, Grant walked over to the White House, where a large crowd had gathered for the president's weekly reception. Horace Porter, a young colonel who would later become Grant's aide-de-camp, was standing near Lincoln in the Blue Room when "a sudden commotion near the entrance to the room attracted general attention." The cause was the appearance of General Grant, "walking along modestly with the rest of the crowd toward Mr. Lincoln." Meeting Grant for the first time, Lincoln's face lit up with a broad smile. Not waiting for his visitor to reach him, the president "advanced rapidly two or three steps," taking Grant by the hand. "Why, here is General Grant! Well, this is a great pleasure."

Porter was struck by the physical contrast between the two men. From his uncommon height, the president "looked down with beaming countenance" upon Grant, who stood eight inches shorter. The collar on Lincoln's evening dress was "a size too large," his necktie "awkwardly tied." He seemed to Porter "more of a Hercules than an Adonis." Yet Porter noted the "merry twinkle" in his gray eyes and "a tone of familiarity" that instantly set people at ease. Watching the two men together, Welles, who was also present, was slightly disconcerted by Grant's demeanor, remarking on his lack of soldierly presence, "a degree of awkwardness."

After talking with Grant, Lincoln referred him to Seward, knowing that his gregarious secretary could best help the general navigate the crowds of admirers shouting his name and rapidly descending upon him. So frantic was the cheering throng to draw near the conquering hero that "laces were torn, crinoline mashed, and things were generally much mixed." Seward rapidly maneuvered Grant into the East Room, where he persuaded the general to stand on a sofa so that everyone could see his face. "He blushed like a girl," the *New York Herald* correspondent noted. "The handshaking brought streams of perspiration down his forehead and over his face." Grant later remarked that the reception was "his warmest campaign during the war."

The president was delighted by the crowd's embrace of Grant. He willingly ceded to the unassuming general his own customary place of honor, fully aware that the path to victory was wide enough, as Porter phrased it, for the two of them to "walk it abreast." Lincoln's reception of Grant might have been more calculated if he had thought the general intended to compete for the presidency, but he had ascertained from a trustworthy source that Grant wanted nothing more than to successfully complete his mission to end the war. "My son, you will never know how gratifying that is to me," Lincoln had told J. Russell Jones, the emissary who carried a letter from Grant affirming that not only did he have no desire for the presidency but he fully supported "keeping Mr. Lincoln in the presidential chair."

After mingling with the excited crowd for an hour, the indefatigable Seward and the exhausted general made their way back to Lincoln, who was waiting with Stanton in the drawing room. They talked over the details of the ceremony the next day, when Grant would be given his commission. To help him prepare his response, Lincoln handed the general a copy of the remarks he would deliver before Grant was expected to speak. Returning to his room at the Willard, Grant wrote out his statement in pencil on a half sheet of paper. When the time came the following afternoon to speak, he seemed, according to Nicolay, "quite embarrassed by the occasion, and finding his own writing so very difficult to read," he stumbled through his speech.

After the ceremony, Lincoln and Grant went upstairs to talk in private. Lincoln explained that while "procrastination on the part of commanders" had led him in the past to issue military orders from the White House, "all he wanted or had ever wanted was some one who would take the responsibility and act," leaving to him the task of mobilizing "all the power of the government" to provide whatever assistance was needed.

On Thursday, Grant journeyed by rail to the headquarters of the Army of the Potomac to consult with General Meade. Upon Grant's return, Lincoln informed him that Mrs. Lincoln was planning a dinner in his honor that Saturday. When Grant begged off, arguing that he wanted to get back to the field as soon as possible, Lincoln laughingly said: "But we can't excuse you. It would be the play of 'Hamlet' with *Hamlet* left out." Still, Grant insisted. "I appreciate fully the honor," he said, "but—time is very precious just now—and—really, Mr. President, I believe I have had enough of the *'show'* business!"

Grant's visit to Washington that March solidified his image as a man of the people. The public had already heard stories of his aversion to what Congressman Elihu Washburne called the "trappings and paraphernalia so common to many military men." While the bill to establish the new rank of lieutenant general was being debated in Washington, Washburne recounted spending six days on the road with Grant, who "took with him neither a horse nor an orderly nor a servant nor a camp-chest nor an overcoat nor a blanket nor even a clean shirt." Carrying only a toothbrush, "he fared like the commonest soldier in his command, partaking of his rations and sleeping upon the ground with no covering except the canopy of heaven." Noting his preference for pork and beans, the *New York Times* speculated that caterers who had previously served "the delicate palates" of officers were "in spasms." Everything Grant did during his four-day stay in Washington, from his unheralded entrance to his early departure, "was done exactly right," the historian William McFeely concludes. "He was consummately modest and quietly confident; the image held for the rest of his political career—and beyond, into history."

•   •   •

THE SPRING OF 1864 was "unusually backward," Bates recorded in his diary. Trees that normally blossomed in early April did not "put out their leaves" until the end of the month. To those waiting anxiously for the army's spring campaign to begin, it seemed that the "stormy and inclement" weather, which brought "torrents" of rain day after day, was nature's attempt to forestall the inevitable bloodshed. Stoddard speculated that Grant was detained by the same "old enemy" that had stymied McClellan, obstructed Burnside, and allowed Lee to escape after Gettysburg: "the red mud of the Old Dominion."

Lincoln remained convinced that in Ulysses S. Grant he had finally found the commander he needed. At a White House reception in late March, held in the midst of "the toughest snowstorm" of the year, Benjamin French reported that the president was "as full of fun and story as ever I saw him." Three weeks later, on another stormy day, Lincoln was still "as pleasant and funny as could be," entertaining an immense crowd of visitors at his Saturday levee. The following Sunday, he strolled into John Hay's room, "picked up a paper and read the Richmond Examiners recent attack on Jeff. Davis. It amused him. 'Why,' said he 'the Examiner seems abt. as fond of Jeff as the World is of me.' "

That Jefferson Davis was under attack in his own house was not surprising. In the spring of 1864, the Confederacy was "a beleaguered nation," in James Randall's words. "Finances were shaky; currency was unsound; the foreign outlook was never bright." Though rebel convictions remained remarkably steady, there was "real suffering among the people." A letter intended to be sent overseas fell into the hands of a *New York Times* correspondent. The writer, a Virginian, acknowledged the harsh impact of the blockade and rampant inflation upon daily life. "Refined and graceful ladies, who have been used to drink Chambertin, and to eat the rich beef and mutton . . . are reduced to such a state that they know not tea nor coffee, and are glad to put up daily with a slice or two of the coarsest bacon." Furthermore, the "mass of misery" increased exponentially "as one goes down in the social scale." Food riots had broken out in Richmond and Atlanta, and clothing was in such short supply that shops were vandalized.

Davis's health gradually succumbed to the strain; his innate despondency deepened. Friends noticed a withdrawn air about him, and his evening rides were often companionless. Only the company of his wife, Varina, and his family let him truly relax and replenish his energies. Much like Lincoln, he spoiled his children, letting them interrupt grave cabinet meetings and enjoying their games.

Tragedy struck the Davis household on the last day of April 1864.

Varina Davis had left five-year-old Joseph and his seven-year-old brother, Jeff Junior, for a few moments while she brought lunch to her husband in his second-floor office. Little Joe had climbed onto the balcony railing and lost his balance. He died when his head hit the brick pavement below. His parents were inconsolable. It was said that Varina's screams could be heard for hours, while Davis isolated himself on the top floor. The "tramp" of his feet pacing up and down, recalled the diarist Mary Chesnut, wife of Confederate general James Chesnut, produced an eerie echo in the drawing room below. The relentless pace of the war allowed little time for mourning, for Davis understood, as did Lincoln, that it was only a matter of days before the spring campaign would begin.

By the first week of May, William Stoddard observed, Washington was filled with an "oppressive sense of something coming," almost like the "pause and hush before the coming of the hurricane." Although the trees were finally "full of buds and blossoms" and "a few adventurous birds" had begun to sing, "the day had no spring sunshine in it, nor any temptations to make music," for everyone knew that ominous events were imminent. While confidence in Grant remained high, many people, Nicolay conceded, were "beginning to feel superstitious" about his prospects, since previous spring campaigns had "so generally been failures."

Aware that communications would be sporadic once Lieutenant General Grant launched his assault on Lee, Lincoln wrote him a letter that Hay described as "full of kindness & dignity at once." He conveyed his "entire satisfaction with what you have done," and promised that "if there is anything wanting which is within my power to give," it would be provided. Grant graciously replied that he had thus far "been astonished at the readiness with which every thing asked for has been yielded." The final line of Grant's letter illustrated the profound difference between his character and McClellan's. "Should my success be less than I desire, and expect, the least I can say is, the fault is not with you."

Lincoln had heartily approved Grant's plan to move in three directions at once: the Army of the Potomac would strike Lee head-on, forcing him to retreat south toward Richmond; Sherman would move through Georgia from west to east, with the aim of capturing Atlanta; Butler, meanwhile, would move northeast against Richmond from the James River. "This concerted movement," Lincoln reminded Hay, was what he had wanted all along, "so as to bring into action to our advantage our great superiority in numbers." Still, on the eve of battle, Lincoln felt great "solicitude" for his lieutenant general, telling Browning that while he had complete confidence in Grant, he feared that "Lee would select his own ground, and await an attack, which would give him great advantages."

Lincoln's fears proved prescient. As Grant moved south, Lee awaited him in an area just west of Fredericksburg known as the Wilderness—an unforgiving maze of craggy ravines and slippery bogs, dense with vines and thorn bushes. The gloomy terrain provided cover for Lee's earthworks and prevented Grant's superb artillery from being used: it effectively negated the Union's superiority of numbers. Nonetheless, Grant pushed relentlessly south to Spotsylvania and Cold Harbor, slightly northeast of Richmond, engaging Lee in a hideous struggle. Men on both sides had to climb over the dead and dying, "lying in some places in piles three and four deep." Grant's biographer calls the campaign "a nightmare of inhumanity," resulting in 86,000 Union and Confederate casualties in the space of seven weeks. "The world has never seen so bloody and so protracted a battle as the one being fought," Grant told his wife at the end of the first nine days, "and I hope never will again." He later admitted in his memoirs that he "always regretted that the last assault at Cold Harbor was ever made."

Grant buried the dead and sent the wounded to Washington, where they arrived by the thousands. Noah Brooks recorded the heartbreaking scene as steamers reached the city wharves, carrying the "shattered wrecks" of brave soldiers. "Long trains of ambulances are in waiting, and the suffering heroes are tenderly handled and brought out upon stretchers, though with some of them even the lightest touch is torture and pain." The ghastly scene, repeated day after day, was hard for Washingtonians to bear. Judge Taft was present at the wharves one morning when three thousand wounded soldiers disembarked, "some with their heads bound up and some with their arms in a Sling," others limping along. As each steamer landed, crowds gathered around, hoping to recognize in "a maimed and battle-stained form, once so proud and manly," a husband, son, or brother. Elizabeth Blair fled the city, admitting that "the lines [of] ambulances & the moans of their poor suffering men were too much for my nerves."

"The carnage has been unexampled," a depressed Bates lamented in his diary. Even the optimistic Seward acknowledged in his European circular that "it seems to myself like exaggeration, when I find, that, in describing conflict after conflict, in this energetic campaign, I am required always to say of the last one, that it was the severest battle of the war." The immense tension in the War Department, where the cabinet colleagues gathered each night to await the latest news, made it impossible to carry out ordinary business. "The intense anxiety is oppressive," Welles conceded, "and almost unfits the mind for mental activity." John Nicolay wrote to Therena that he was "more nervous and anxious" during these weeks than he had been "for a year previous." Still, he added, "if my own anxiety is so great, what must be [the president's] solicitude, after waiting through three long, weary years of doubt and disaster."

There were, indeed, nights when Lincoln did not sleep. One of these nights, Francis Carpenter "met him, clad in a long morning wrapper, pacing back and forth . . . his hands behind him, great black rings under his eyes, his head bent forward upon his breast." There were moments when he was overwhelmed with sorrow at the appalling loss of life. As the leader of his cabinet and the leader of his country, however, he understood the need to remain collected and project hope and confidence to his colleagues and his people. Between anxious hours at the War Department awaiting news from the front, Lincoln made time to get to the theater, attend a public lecture on Gettysburg, and see an opera. "People may think strange of it," he explained, "but I *must* have some relief from this terrible anxiety, or it will kill me."

Schuyler Colfax came to visit one Sunday during the Battle of the Wilderness. "I saw [Lincoln] walk up and down the Executive Chamber, his long arms behind his back, his dark features contracted still more with gloom; and as he looked up, I thought his face the saddest one I had ever seen." But, Colfax added, "he quickly recovered," and suddenly spoke of Grant with such confidence that "hope beamed on his face." An hour later, greeting a delegation of congressional visitors, he managed to tell "story after story," which hid "his saddened heart from their keen and anxious scrutiny."

Lincoln never lost faith in Grant. He realized that whereas "any other General" would have retreated after sustaining such terrible losses, Grant somehow retained "the dogged pertinacity . . . that wins." Lincoln hugged and kissed a young reporter on the forehead who arrived at the White House with a verbal message from the general that said, "there is to be no turning back." His spirits rose further when he read the words in Grant's famous dispatch on May 11: "I propose to fight it out on this line if it takes all summer." When a visitor asked one day about the prospects of the army under Grant, Lincoln's face lit up "with that peculiar smile which he always puts on when about to tell a good story." The question, he said, "reminds me of a little anecdote about the automaton chessplayer, which many years ago astonished the world by its skill in that game. After a while the automaton was challenged by a celebrated player, who, to his great chagrin, was beaten twice by the machine. At the end of the second game, the player, significantly pointing his finger at the automaton, exclaimed in a very decided tone. *'There's a man in it!'* " That, he explained, referring to Grant, was "the secret" to the army's fortunes.

*   *   *

IN EARLY JUNE, when the Republican Convention was set to open in Baltimore, Salmon Chase grew restless. Though he had withdrawn his name from the race the previous March, he still retained the hope that events might turn in his favor. Thurlow Weed had repeatedly warned the president that Chase's withdrawal was simply a "shrewd dodge" that would allow him "to turn up again with more strength than ever." The well-informed political boss had compiled a long list of Treasury employees who were devoting all their energies to the Chase campaign. More troubling still, Weed had heard from myriad sources that corrupt Treasury agents were exchanging army supplies for Confederate cotton in violation of the congressional law that forbade any trade between the free and slave states without an express permit from the Treasury. Weed believed that Chase's son-in-law, Sprague, was a beneficiary of one of these schemes. He could not fathom Lincoln's refusal to fire Chase, predicting that if the president "goes into the canvass with this mill-stone tied to him, he will inevitably sink."

Meanwhile, the smoldering feud between Chase and the Blairs erupted into full public view. With the army in winter quarters the previous January, Frank Blair had resigned his commission and retaken his seat in Congress. He intended to return to Sherman's command in time for the march to Atlanta, but first, he had a score to settle with Chase. A Chase partisan had publicly accused Blair of swindling the government by charging $8,000 for a personal shipment of liquor and tobacco. Blair knew the document in question was spurious and suspected that it had been forged in the Treasury Department. He asked a congressional committee to investigate the matter. The resulting report fully exonerated Blair. The accusing document was, indeed, a forgery penned by a Treasury agent. Although there was no suggestion of Chase's personal involvement, Blair waited for the issuance of the committee's report before rising to speak on the floor.

Addressing a packed audience the day before his scheduled departure for Sherman's army, he began by calmly summarizing the report's findings. His self-control swiftly vanished, however, as he turned his anger on Chase. "These dogs have been set on me by their master, and since I have whipped them back into their kennel I mean to hold their master responsible for this outrage and not the curs who have been set upon me." Speaker Colfax admonished Blair to stick to the committee report, but Blair's supporters insisted that he be allowed to continue. He accused Chase of corruption, treachery against Lincoln, lack of patriotism, and sordid ambition for the presidency.

Elizabeth Blair, present in the galleries, believed the speech "a complete triumph" in the short run but worried about its livid tone. "Anger is the poorest of counselors," she conceded, "& revenge is suicide." She was right to worry, for the speech inflamed the ongoing war between Chase and Blair that would end by damaging both men. Chase's friends reacted quickly, labeling the accusations against the treasury secretary "mendacious slanders."

Gideon Welles considered the speech "violent and injudicious" and feared that it would ultimately hurt the president. The wise navy secretary was dismayed by the continuing feud between Chase and the Blairs, believing both sides shared the blame. "Chase is deficient in magnanimity and generosity. The Blairs have both, but they have strong resentments. Warfare with them is open, bold and unsparing. With Chase it is silent, persistent, but regulated with discretion."

Chase was told about the speech later that night as he boarded a train to the Sanitary Fair in Baltimore. His friend Congressman Albert Riddle joined him in his private car. "He was alone," Riddle recalled, "and in a frightful rage, and controlled himself with difficulty while he explained the cause. The recital in a hoarse, constrained voice, seemed to rekindle his anger and aggravate his intensity. The spacious car fairly trembled under his feet." Chase felt certain that "all this, including the speech, had been done with the cordial approval of the President." Ohio congressman James Garfield agreed with this assessment. He considered Frank Blair Lincoln's "creature," sent to the House for the "special purpose" of destroying Chase's reputation. With this accomplished, Garfield charged, Lincoln would simply renew Blair's commission and return him to the front, "thus ratifying all he said and did while here." Chase told Riddle that unless Lincoln repudiated Blair, he would feel honor-bound once again to tender his resignation.

Riddle and another friend of Chase's, Rufus Spalding, called on the president. They warned him that "Chase's abrupt resignation now would be equal in its effects to a severe set-back of the army under Grant." Explaining that the coincidence of Blair's vicious speech and the president's renewal of his commission "seemed as if planned for dramatic effect, as parts of a conspiracy against a most important member of the Cabinet," they demanded to know if Lincoln had known ahead of time the nature of Blair's remarks.

Lincoln had prepared well for the encounter. The last thing he wanted was for Chase to resign on a point of honor. The rift between the radicals and conservatives in the Republican Party might then become irreparable. He gave the visitors his usual undivided attention. When they finished, Riddle recalled, "he arose, came round, and with great cordiality took each of us by the hand and evinced the greatest satisfaction at our presence." Then, taking up a stack of papers on his desk, he inquired if either of them had seen his letter to Chase two months earlier when the secretary had offered to resign over his implication in the humiliating Pomeroy circular. Determining that Riddle had not, Lincoln read aloud the lines where he concurred with Chase that neither of them should be "held responsible for what our respective friends may do without our instigation or countenance."

He explained that while he had great respect for Frank Blair, he "was annoyed and mortified by the speech." He had, in fact, warned Blair against "pursuing a personal warfare." As soon as he heard of Blair's rant, Lincoln knew that *"another beehive was kicked over"* and considered canceling "the orders restoring him to the army and assigning him to command." After assessing how much General Sherman valued Frank's services, however, he had decided to let the orders stand.

In making his case, Riddle recalled, Lincoln "was plain, sincere, and most impressive." Riddle and Spalding were "perfectly satisfied" and assured Lincoln that Chase would be, too. Once again, Lincoln had sutured a potentially dangerous wound within his administration and his party.

• • •

IT WAS A WARM DAY on June 7, 1864, when Republicans gathered in Baltimore to choose their candidates for president and vice president. Noah Brooks was moved by the sight of the people's representatives gathering "in the midst of a civil war and in the actual din of battle" to perform the most precious function of democracy. The Democrats would also meet that summer, though they delayed their convention until the end of August to give themselves a better chance to react to the latest events on the battlefield.

As the delegates from twenty-five states flocked to the Republican Convention, which was relabeled the National Union Convention, Lincoln's renomination was assured. So certain was the outcome that David Davis, who had been instrumental in guiding Lincoln to the nomination four years earlier, chose not to attend. He had originally planned to go, he told Lincoln, "but since the New York & Ohio Conventions, the necessity for doing so is foreclosed—I have kept count of all the States that have instructed, & you must be nominated by acclamation—if there had been a speck of opposition, I wd have gone to Baltimore—But the opposition is so utterly beaten, that the fight is not even interesting, and the services of no one is necessary." In Judge Davis's stead, Lincoln sent John Nicolay as his personal emissary to the convention.

Even Horace Greeley, while holding out for an alternative, acknowledged that the president had earned an honored place in the hearts of his fellow Americans. "The People think of him by night & by day & pray for him & their *hearts* are where they have made so heavy investments." Long before the convention opened its doors, the official nominating committee said, "popular instinct had plainly indicated [Lincoln] as its candidate," and the work of the convention was simply to register "the popular will." While politicians in Washington may have entertained other prospects, Brooks observed, "the country at large really thought of no name but Lincoln's."

There were, of course, some pockets of resistance. At the end of May, several hundred malcontents had gathered in Cleveland's Chapin Hall to nominate John Frémont for president on a third-party ticket. Frémont had never forgiven Lincoln for relieving him of command in 1861. Though he had eventually been offered another commission, he had refused upon learning that he would report to another general. His supporters were a mix of radicals, abolitionists, disappointed office seekers, and Copperheads. They hoped to split the Republican Party with a platform calling for a constitutional amendment ending slavery. They demanded that Congress, rather than the president, take the lead on Reconstruction, and pressed for the "confiscation of the lands of the rebels, and their distribution among the soldiers."

Lincoln had been in the telegraph office when reports of the Frémont convention came over the wires. Hearing that the attendance was a mere four hundred of the expected thousands, he was reminded of a passage in the Bible. Opening his Bible to I Samuel 22:2, he read aloud: "And every one that was in distress, and every one that was in debt, and every one that was discontented, gathered themselves unto him; and he became a captain over them: and there were with him about four hundred men."

The night before the Baltimore convention, Lincoln talked with Noah Brooks. When Brooks observed that his "renomination was an absolute certainty," Lincoln "cheerfully conceded that point without any false modesty." Understanding that there were several candidates for vice president, including the incumbent Hannibal Hamlin, New York's Daniel Dickinson, and Tennessee's military governor, Andrew Johnson, Lincoln declined to express his preference. He did say, however, that "he hoped that the convention would declare in favor of the constitutional amendment abolishing slavery," and he asked Brooks to report back to him all "the odd bits of gossip" that a good reporter would pick up.

As expected, the convention was initially confronted with two contesting delegations from Missouri: an anti-Blair radical delegation pledged to vote for Grant as a means of expressing displeasure with Lincoln, and a pro-Blair conservative delegation pledged to Lincoln. With the president's approval, the radical delegation was seated. Lincoln understood the importance, as one delegate put it, of integrating "all the elements of the Republican party—including the impracticables, the Pharisees, the better-than-thou declaimers, the long-haired men and the short-haired women." Moreover, the radicals had tacitly agreed that they would switch their votes to Lincoln after the first ballot, making the president's nomination unanimous.

Nothing better indicated the nation's transformation since the Chicago convention four years earlier than the tumultuous applause that greeted the third resolution of the platform: "*Resolved*, That as Slavery was the cause, and now constitutes the strength, of this Rebellion . . . [we] demand its utter and complete extirpation from the soil of the Republic." While upholding the president's proclamation, which "aimed a death-blow at this gigantic evil," the resolution continued: "we are in favor, furthermore," of a constitutional amendment to "forever prohibit the existence of slavery" in the United States.

Resounding applause also greeted the resolution thanking soldiers and sailors, "who have periled their lives in defense of their country"; but the crowd's greatest demonstration was reserved for the resolution endorsing Lincoln's leadership. "The enthusiasm was terrific," Brooks noted, "the convention breaking out into yells and cheers unbounded as soon as the beloved name of Lincoln was spoken." The only discordant note was the passage of a radical plank aimed at conservative Montgomery Blair, calling for "a purge of any cabinet member" who failed to support the platform in full. "Harmony was restored" when the roll call nominating Lincoln was completed, at which point, the *National Republican* noted, "the audience rose *en masse*, and such an enthusiastic demonstration was scarcely ever paralleled. Men waved their hands and hats, and ladies, in the galleries, their kerchiefs," while the band played "The Star-Spangled Banner."

The next order of business was the nomination of a vice president. Though Thurlow Weed was not a delegate, his towering presence played a central role in the selection of Andrew Johnson. Always alive to the interests of his oldest friend, Seward, Weed at once understood that if New

York's Daniel Dickinson received the vice presidential nod, Seward might not retain his position as secretary of state. An unwritten rule dictated that two significant posts could not be allotted to a single state. Weed had initially supported Hamlin but soon saw that the growing sentiment for a War Democrat would result in the nomination of either Dickinson or Johnson. He placed the Weed-Seward machine behind the victorious Johnson.

The results of the convention were routed through the telegraph office at the War Department. It was "Stanton's theory," his secretary explained, that *"everything* concerned his own Department," and he had centralized into his office "the whole telegraphic system of the United States." Lincoln was present in the late afternoon when a clerk handed him a dispatch reporting Johnson's nomination. Having not yet heard his own nomination confirmed, Lincoln was startled. "What! do they nominate a Vice-President before they do a President?" Is that not putting "the cart before the horse"? The embarrassed operator explained that the dispatch about the president's nomination had come in several hours earlier, while Lincoln was at lunch, and had been sent directly to the White House. "It is all right," replied Lincoln. "I shall probably find it on my return."

The following day, a committee appointed by the delegates arrived at the White House to officially notify Lincoln of his nomination. In response to their laudatory statement, Lincoln said he did not assume that the convention had found him to be "the best man in the country; but I am reminded, in this connection, of a story of an old Dutch farmer, who remarked to a companion once that 'it was not best to swap horses when crossing streams.' " Later that night, when the Ohio delegation came to serenade him at the White House, he humbly directed their attention to the soldiers in the field. "What we want, still more than Baltimore conventions or presidential elections, is success under Gen. Grant," he said. "I propose that you help me to close up what I am now saying with three rousing cheers for Gen. Grant and the officers and soldiers under his command."

A visitor to the White House at this time told Lincoln that "nothing could defeat him but Grant's *capture of Richmond,* to be followed by [the general's] nomination at Chicago"—where the Democratic Convention was scheduled to take place later that summer. "Well," said Lincoln, "I feel very much like the man who said he didn't want to die particularly, but if he had got to die, that was precisely the disease he would like to die of."

CHAPTER 24

"ATLANTA IS OURS"

UNION HOPES FOR imminent victory faded as the spring of 1864 gave way to summer. "Our troops have suffered much and accomplished but little," Gideon Welles recorded in his diary on June 20. "The immense slaughter of our brave men chills and sickens us all." Unable to dislodge Lee's troops, who displayed what the White House secretary William Stoddard called an awe-inspiring "steady courage," Grant settled in for a siege at Petersburg. Meanwhile, Sherman was encountering tough resistance as he moved slowly through Georgia.

Daily reports of the brutal battles in Virginia and Georgia provoked a particular dread in the Sewards, the Blairs, the Bates, and the Welleses, all of whom had loved ones at the front. For the Sewards, whose youngest son, William, nearly lost his life at Cold Harbor, there were many sleepless nights. "I cannot yet bring myself to the contemplation of your death or of your suffering as others have done," Frances Seward told Will, though she considered that he was "fighting for a holy cause" in a "righteous" conflict, unlike the Mexican War, which she had vigorously opposed when her older son, Augustus, had been in the army.

Elizabeth Blair had become "so nervous" with her husband in the navy and her brother Frank moving toward Atlanta with Sherman that she "quake[d] all night with terror." Even her normally cheerful father was perpetually "grave & anxious," certain that if Frank were taken prisoner, the Confederates "would be as eager to kill him physically—as the Radicals are politically." Bates feared for his twenty-one-year-old son, Coalter, who was with General Meade and the Army of the Potomac, and Welles was pained "beyond what I can describe" when his eighteen-year-old son, Thomas, departed "with boyish pride and enthusiasm" to join General Grant. "It was uncertain whether we should ever meet again," he recorded in his diary, "and if we do he may be mutilated, and a ruined man." His anxiety left Welles "sad, and unfit for any labor." The painful apprehension within the administration mirrored the fears experienced in hundreds of thousands of homes throughout the country.

Lincoln knew the ravages of this most bloody war had touched every town and household of America. The time had come to revive the oppressed spirits of the people. In mid-June, he found the perfect forum for a public speech when he journeyed to the Great Central Fair in Philadelphia, designed to benefit the Sanitary Commission. Thousands of citizens had come from the surrounding area to enjoy the collections of art, statuary, and flowers, the zoological garden, restaurants, raffles, and games that covered a two-mile concourse and were said to offer "miracles as many as Faust saw in his journey through the world of magic."

At seven o'clock on the morning of June 16, Lincoln, Mary, and Tad left for Philadelphia by train. Word of their journey had spread. At every depot along the way, cheering crowds gathered for a glimpse of the first family. Arriving before noon, they were escorted in an open carriage up Broad Street to Chestnut Street and the Continental Hotel. The streets were "lined with citizens" and the windows "crowded with ladies waving their handkerchiefs." The unbounded ardor and spontaneous applause was such, one reporter noted, "as has not been heard for many a day in Philadelphia." Lincoln declined to speak at the hotel or at the fairgrounds that afternoon, preferring to wait until the dinner that evening. Perhaps he knew that his remarks, which he had carefully drafted, would be recorded more accurately in that setting.

"War, at the best, is terrible, and this war of ours, in its magnitude and in its duration, is one of the most terrible," he began. "It has destroyed property, and ruined homes; it has produced a national debt and taxation unprecedented. . . . It has carried mourning to almost every home, until it can almost be said that the 'heavens are hung in black.' " Nonetheless, he reminded his listeners, "We accepted this war for an object, a worthy object, and the war will end when that object is attained. Under God, I hope it never will until that time." The force of his words and the unshakable determination they embodied instantly uplifted and emboldened his audience.

A few days later, in order to stem his own "intense anxiety" about the stalemate in Virginia, Lincoln decided to visit Grant at his headquarters at City Point. Welles strongly disapproved of the decision. "He can do no good," he predicted. "It can hardly be otherwise than to do harm, even if no accident befalls him. Better for him and the country that he should remain at his post here." The navy secretary failed to understand the importance of these trips to Lincoln, who needed the contact with the troops to lift his own spirits so that he, in turn, could better buoy the spirits of those around him.

Accompanied by Tad and Assistant Navy Secretary Gustavus Fox, Lincoln left the Washington Navy Yard aboard the river steamer *Baltimore* in the early evening of June 20. The journey to City Point, which was about 180 miles farther south by water than Aquia Creek, took more than sixteen hours. Horace Porter, Grant's aide-de-camp, recalled that when the steamer arrived at the wharf, Lincoln "came down from the upper deck . . . and reaching out his long, angular arm, he wrung General Grant's hand vigorously, and held it in his for some time," as he expressed great appreciation for all that Grant had been through since they last met in Washington. Introduced to the members of Grant's staff, the president "had for each one a cordial greeting and a pleasant word. There was a kindliness in his tone and a hearty manner of expression which went far to captivate all who met him."

Over a "plain and substantial" lunch, typical of "the hero of Vicksburg," noted the *Herald* correspondent, Lincoln conversed entertainingly and delivered "three capital jokes" that provoked hilarity. When the meal was finished, Grant suggested a ride to the front ten miles away. Porter noted that Lincoln made an odd appearance on his horse as his "trousers gradually worked up above his ankles, and gave him the appearance of a country farmer riding into town wearing his Sunday clothes." The sight "bordered upon the grotesque," but the troops he passed along the way "were so lost in admiration of the man that the humorous aspect did not seem to strike them . . . cheers broke forth from all the commands, and en-thusiastic shouts and even words of familiar greeting met him on all sides."

Reaching the front, the president took "a long and lingering look" at the sights of Petersburg, where Lee's armies were gathered behind formidable earthworks. On the return trip, they passed a brigade of black soldiers, who rushed forward to greet the president, "screaming, yelling, shouting: 'Hurrah for the Liberator; Hurrah for the President.'" Their "spontaneous outburst" moved Lincoln to tears, "and his voice was so broken by emotion" that he could hardly reply.

That evening, Porter recalled, as Lincoln sat for hours with General Grant and his staff, "we had an opportunity of appreciating his charm as a talker, and hearing some of the stories for which he had become celebrated." The young aide-de-camp observed what so many others had seen before, that Lincoln "did not tell a story merely for the sake of the anecdote, but to point a moral or clench a fact." Seated on "a low camp-chair," with his long legs wrapped around each other "as if in an effort to get them out of the way," he used his arms to accompany his words and "joined heartily with the listeners in the laugh which followed." Discussion of a new form of gunpowder prompted a story of two competing powder merchants in Springfield. The sight of a newly patented artillery trace led to the recitation of a line from a poem: "Sorrow had fled, but left her traces there." Reference to the electoral college brought forth the quaint observation that "the Electoral College is the only one where they choose their own masters." When the convivial evening came to a close, the president walked with Porter to his tent, taking a peek inside, "from curiosity, doubtless, to see how the officers were quartered," before returning to his stateroom on the *Baltimore*.

The next morning, "in excellent spirits," Lincoln steamed up the James River with Grant to visit General Butler and Admiral Samuel Phillips Lee, Elizabeth Blair's husband. Talking with Butler about Grant, he observed that "When Grant once gets possession of a place, he holds on to it as if he had inherited it." After lunch, it was time to return to Washington. On taking leave, General Grant took Lincoln aside, assuring him with a rousing pledge that the president would repeat and cite in the weeks ahead: "You will never hear of me farther from Richmond than now, till I have taken it. I am just as sure of going into Richmond as I am of any future event. It may take a long summer day, but I will go in."

On the morning of June 23, John Hay reported that Lincoln returned to the White House "sunburnt and fagged but still refreshed and cheered. He found the army in fine health good position and good spirits." The next day, at the regular Friday cabinet meeting, the skeptical Welles conceded that the trip to the front had "done him good, physically, and strengthened him mentally in confidence in the General and army." And of signal importance, Lincoln could now better project his own renewed hope to the anxious public, lauding Grant's "extraordinary qualities as a commander" to one reporter, and speaking to another "of the condition of army matters in the very highest terms of confidence."

Acutely aware of his own emotional needs, Lincoln had chosen exactly the right time to review the troops, for his conversations with Grant and his interactions with the soldiers sustained and inspired him during the troubling days ahead. "Having hope," writes Daniel Goleman in his study of emotional intelligence, "means that one will not give in to overwhelming anxiety, a defeatist attitude, or depression in the face of difficult challenges or setbacks." Hope is "more than the sunny view that everything will turn out all right"; it is "believing you have the will and the way to accomplish your goals." More clearly than his colleagues, Lincoln understood that numerous setbacks were inevitable before the war could be brought to a close. Yet in the end, he firmly believed the North would prevail. "We are today further ahead than I thought one year and a half ago we should be," he told Noah Brooks that June, "and yet there are plenty of people who believe that the war is about to be substantially closed. As God is my judge I shall be satisfied if we are over with the fight in Virginia within a year."

• • •

BY THE LAST WEEK of June, the forbearance Lincoln had long shown toward his ambitious secretary of the treasury was finally exhausted. The dramatic upheaval in the cabinet began when John Cisco, assistant treasurer of New York, announced his resignation. Cisco had held the prestigious post through three different administrations and was well respected by all factions. Lincoln was anxious that his replacement satisfy both wings of New York's Republican Party. For several months, the president had been bombarded by complaints from friends in New York, including Thurlow Weed and Senator Edwin Morgan, that Chase was filling all the customs house positions with his own partisans—former Democrats who were now radical Republicans supporting Chase's own presidential hopes.

Sensitive to Weed's concerns, Lincoln told Chase to consult with Senator Morgan and ensure that his selection was satisfactory to all sides. Chase discussed the matter with the powerful New York senator but then proceeded, over Morgan's strong objection, to send Lincoln a formal nomination for Maunsell Field. A Democratic journalist with ties to New York society, Field was serving as third assistant secretary of the treasury, a post

Chase had designed especially to compensate Field for the access he had provided Chase to the inner circles of New York literary and social life. The appointment was stunning, recalled the treasury registrar, Lucius Chittenden, for Field "had no financial or political standing, and his natural abilities were of a literary rather than an executive character."

Undeterred, Chase apparently assumed that his own services were so indispensable that Lincoln would sanction a controversial nominee rather than risk a messy squabble when the financial health of the nation was at stake. Chase awoke the morning after sending the Field nomination to the White House and cheerfully undertook his daily reading of the Bible, which on that summer morning included a letter St. Paul sent to the Ephesians imploring them to "Stand therefore, having your loins girt about with truth, and having on the breastplate of righteousness." When he reached the department, however, he found a disturbing note from the president on his desk. "I can not, without much embarrassment, make this appointment," Lincoln informed him, "principally because of Senator Morgan's very firm opposition to it." It would "really oblige" him, he said, if Chase and Senator Morgan could agree on another nominee.

Still confident that he could change the president's mind, Chase wrote an immediate request for a personal interview. When Lincoln did not respond, Chase decided to resolve the difficulty on his own. He telegraphed Cisco in New York and pleaded with him to withdraw his resignation and stay on for another three months. Before obtaining Cisco's answer, he received Lincoln's reply to his interview request. "The difficulty," wrote Lincoln, "does not, in the main part, lie within the range of a conversation between you and me." Lincoln went on to explain the criticism he had faced in the previous months over treasury appointments in New York, and noted that to disregard Morgan's judgment in this instance might trigger "open revolt."

Cisco's agreement to stay on should have ended the matter; but Chase, peeved at Lincoln's refusal to meet in person and bent on reestablishing his authority over his own appointments, could not rest. He decided to chasten the president with what was essentially his fourth letter of resignation, certain it would again be rejected. He began his letter by enclosing Cisco's telegram withdrawing his resignation, which, he acknowledged, "relieves the present difficulty." But then he went on: "I cannot help feeling that my position here is not altogether agreeable to you; and it is certainly too full of embarrassment and difficulty and painful responsibility to allow in me the least desire to retain it. I think it my duty therefore to enclose to you my resignation."

Lincoln was seated at his desk in his office, he later recalled, when a messenger handed him a letter from the Treasury Department. "I opened it, recognized Chase's handwriting, read the first sentence, and inferred from its tenor that this matter was in the way of satisfactory adjustment. I was truly glad of this, and, laying the envelope with its inclosure down upon the desk, went on talking. People were coming and going all the time till three o'clock, and I forgot all about Chase's letter. At that hour it occurred to me that I would go down stairs and get a bit of lunch. My wife happened to be away, and they had failed to call me at the usual time [Mary was in Massachusetts for Robert's graduation from Harvard]. While I was sitting alone at table my thoughts reverted to Chase's letter, and I determined to answer it just as soon as I should go up stairs again.

"Well, as soon as I was back here, I took pen and paper and prepared to write, but then it occurred to me that I might as well read the letter before I answered it. I took it out of the envelope for that purpose, and, as I did so, another inclosure fell from it upon the floor. I picked it up, read it, and said to myself, '*Halloo, this is a horse of another color!*' It was his resignation. I put my pen into my mouth, and *grit my teeth* upon it. I did not long reflect."

Lincoln quickly perceived that Chase was essentially saying: "You have been acting very badly. Unless you say you are sorry, & ask me to stay & agree that I shall be absolute and that you shall have nothing, no matter how you beg for it, I will go." This presumption the president could not and would not countenance. He took his pen from his mouth and began to write.

"Your resignation of the office of Secretary of the Treasury," he tersely opened, "is accepted. Of all I have said in commendation of your ability and fidelity, I have nothing to unsay; and yet you and I have reached a point of mutual embarrassment in our official relation which it seems can not be overcome, or longer sustained, consistently with the public service."

Early the next morning, Lincoln called John Hay into his office and asked him to deliver the news of Chase's resignation to the Senate as soon as it convened, along with his recommendation of former Ohio governor David Tod as his successor. "It is a big fish," he said. "I thought I could not stand it any longer." Though worried that the president was making a costly mistake, the loyal Hay proceeded to the Capitol, reaching the Senate just as the chaplain recited the opening prayer.

Still ignorant of the president's letter, Chase went about his daily business, anticipating Lincoln's penitent request for him to continue his duties. Perhaps Lincoln would personally visit his office, put his arm around him, and again tell him how much he was needed. After breakfast, Chase went to his office, where he received word that Senator Fessenden of Maine wanted to see him immediately at the Capitol. Riding in his carriage, he surmised that the chairman of the Finance Committee wanted to discuss the various financial bills currently before him. In the midst of his conversation with Fessenden, a messenger arrived to tell the senator of David Tod's nomination. "Have you resigned?" the distraught Fessenden asked. "I am called to the Senate & told that the President has sent in the nomination of your successor." Stunned, Chase explained that he had indeed sent in his resignation, but did not know that it had been accepted.

Returning at once to the department, Chase found the letter from Lincoln. Reaching the part where Lincoln spoke of "mutual embarrassment" in their relations, Chase was dumbfounded. "I had found a good deal of embarrassment from him," he recorded in his diary that night, "but what he had found from me I could not imagine, unless it has been created by my unwillingness to have offices distributed by spoils or benefits with more regard to the claims of divisions, factions, cliques and individuals, than to fitness of selection." Blinded by self-righteousness and donning what Nicolay and Hay termed "his full armor of noble sentiments," Chase refused to see that in choosing the inexperienced Field, he, not the president, was filling an office on the basis of faction rather than fitness.

The startling news spread quickly on Capitol Hill. "The Senators were struck dumb with amazement," Noah Brooks reported. The members of the Senate Finance Committee convened an emergency meeting and decided to go as a body to the White House to lodge a vehement protest. "Fessenden was frightened," Lincoln later told Hay; "Conness [of California] was mad." Lincoln listened patiently to their concerns about losing Chase at this perilous time and their doubts about Tod as a viable successor. Then, reaching into his desk, he pulled out Chase's previous letters of resignation and read them aloud to his visitors, along with the gracious replies that had kept Chase in the cabinet each time. Moreover, though he agreed that "Mr. Chase had a full right to indulge in his ambition to be President," he suggested that the indiscretions of Chase's friends had so complicated matters that the two of them "disliked to meet each other" in person. In fact, in recent weeks, Chase had declined to attend most of the regular cabinet meetings. The situation had become "unendurable," Lincoln concluded, this most recent controversy being simply "the last straw." Though the committee left dissatisfied, they at least departed with a true picture of the long history behind the final break.

Chase's friend Massachusetts congressman Samuel Hooper came in to see the president later that afternoon. He said he felt "very nervous & cut up" by Chase's departure. Treasury Registrar Lucius Chittenden was equally distraught, telling Lincoln that the loss of Chase was "worse than another Bull Run defeat," for there was not a single man in the country who could replace him. "I will tell you," Lincoln said, "how it is with Chase. It is the easiest thing in the world for a man to fall into a bad habit. Chase has fallen into two bad habits. . . . He thinks he has become indispensable to the country. . . . He also thinks he ought to be President; he has no doubt whatever about that." These two unfortunate tendencies, Lincoln explained, had made Chase "irritable, uncomfortable, so that he is never perfectly happy unless he is thoroughly miserable."

At this point, according to Chittenden, Lincoln paused. "And yet there is not a man in the Union who would make as good a chief justice as Chase," he continued, "and, if I have the opportunity, I will make him Chief Justice of the United States." Chittenden concluded that this extraordinary want of vindictiveness toward someone who had caused him such grief proved that Lincoln "must move upon a higher plane and be influenced by loftier motives than any man" he had ever known. Yet while Lincoln did indeed possess unusual magnanimity, he was also a shrewd politician. He mentioned the chief justiceship to Chittenden knowing that when Chase learned of it, the prospect might dampen his public opposition. Lincoln made a similar remark to Congressman Hooper. In a relaxed conversation, he expressed his "esteem" for the secretary and his sincere "regret" that the two of them had become so "awkward" and "constrained" when they got together. When Hooper relayed these comments to his friend, Chase was moved, suggesting that "had any such expressions of good will" been tendered before his resignation, he might have acted differently. Unfortunately, it was too late.

The news of Chase's resignation was met with dismay and regret in the country. He was "the great magician of the treasury," the *Chicago Tribune* wrote; "his name will be handed down to history as the greatest financier of his century." Greeley's *Tribune* went even further, claiming that "Mr. Chase is one of the very few great men left in public life since the almost simultaneous decease of Messrs. Clay, Webster and Calhoun."

Choosing a worthy successor was vital, and it was not clear that David Tod was up to the task. Any concerns Lincoln might have had about his hasty choice were alleviated, however, when he received a telegram from the former governor declining the post for reasons of health. According to Francis Carpenter, Lincoln "laid awake some hours, canvassing in his mind the merits of various public men." By morning, he had found the ideal solution, a candidate so perfect he should have considered him from the start: William Pitt Fessenden. "*First,*" he told Hay the next morning, "he knows the ropes thoroughly: as Chairman of the Senate Committee on Finance he knows as much of this special subject as Mr. Chase. *2nd* he is a man possessing a national reputation and the confidence of the country.

3d He is a radical—without the petulant and vicious fretfulness of many radicals."

In a far better humor, Lincoln handed Hay his official nomination of Fessenden to carry to the Senate. When Hay told him that Fessenden was in the reception room waiting to see him, Lincoln said: "Send him in & go at once to the Senate." Understanding that Fessenden might be reluctant, and perhaps remembering that three years earlier he had sent in Chase's nomination before securing his acceptance, the president hoped that a fait accompli would once again move the process forward.

Lincoln greeted Fessenden warmly and listened politely for a few minutes as the senator suggested a few names for the vacant Treasury post. Smiling, Lincoln finally interrupted and told Fessenden there was no need to continue. He had found his man, and the nomination of Fessenden was already en route to the Senate. "You must withdraw it, I cannot accept," Fessenden cried out, jumping to his feet. He explained that his health was not good, and he was certain that the pressures of the new job would kill him. "If you decline," Lincoln said, "you must do it in open day: for I shall not recall the nomination." Fessenden left with a promise that he would think on it further, though his acceptance was doubtful.

Returning to the Senate, Fessenden discovered that his colleagues had unanimously approved his nomination. Encircled by the warmth of their good wishes and congratulations, he began to waver. "Telegrams came pouring in from all quarters," he later recalled, insisting that he accept for the good of the nation, that he was an inspired choice for the critical post. It was both the most rewarding and "the most miserable" day of his life, for he still feared that the duties of the post would be his death. "Very well," the always blunt Stanton told him, "you cannot die better than in trying to save your country."

As he was driven to the White House the next morning, however, Fessenden carried with him a letter declining the nomination. It took all of the president's persuasive powers to change his mind. "He said the crisis was such as demanded any sacrifice, even life itself," Fessenden recalled, "that Providence had never deserted him or the country, and that his choice of me was a special proof that Providence would not desert him. All this and more." In the end, Fessenden felt he "could not decline but at the risk of danger to the country."

Fessenden's appointment received universal praise. "He is a man of undoubted financial ability, and of unsurpassed personal integrity," the *Chicago Tribune* wrote, reflecting the sentiment of many Northern papers. Radicals felt he was one of their own, while conservatives applauded his intelligence and experience. "He is honest," Elizabeth Blair told her husband, "& as Mrs Jeff [Davis] once said the ablest of all the Republican Senators." The business world, long familiar with his work on the Senate Finance Committee, breathed a sigh of relief. "I am the most popular man in my country," Fessenden wryly noted several days after his acceptance.

"So my official life closes," Chase recorded in his diary on the last day of June. Sadness pervades the entry, written when the oppressive heat of Washington was such, observed Bates, that "even the trees in the streets are wilting." Chase believed he had "laid broad foundations" to secure financial support for the troops, but he knew the job was still unfinished. From this point on, he would not have any real influence.

If Chase had hoped his resignation would produce consternation and regret among his cabinet colleagues, he was disappointed. On the night his departure was announced, Blair and Bates called on Welles to talk over the startling event. While they were all surprised, none was sorry to see him go. "I look upon it as a blessing," Welles said. On numerous occasions Welles had confided doubts about Chase's character to his diary, observing that he lacked "the courage and candor to admit his errors," and that "his jokes are always clumsy—he is destitute of wit." Bates greeted Chase's retirement with "a vague feeling of relief from a burden, and a hope of better things," observing that Chase's relations with his fellow cabinet ministers had long since failed "to be cordial." And Monty Blair, whose family regarded Chase as a mortal enemy, was thrilled. Old Man Blair happily informed Frank that Chase had "dropped off at last like a rotten pear unexpectedly to himself & every body else." Seward, unlike his other colleagues, expressed no personal pleasure in Chase's demise. He simply informed Frances of his relief that the "Cabinet crisis" did not engender a "severe shock" in the country. He traced the origin of the present upheaval back to "the first day of the Administration," when, against his advice, Lincoln had created his compound cabinet.

As Chase prepared to leave Washington, he noted sadly that Stanton, "warm & cordial as ever," was the only former colleague who came to see him "—no other Head of Dept. has called on me since my resignation." If Chase believed the powerful war secretary might feel the slightest compulsion to resign his own place in solidarity with his old friend, however, he was mistaken.

In his misery, Chase searched for reasons why Lincoln had so abruptly accepted his resignation. His answers betray an unwillingness to take the slightest responsibility for his own missteps. "I can see but one reason," he wrote, "that I am too earnest, too antislavery, &, say, too radical to make him willing to have me connected with the Admn., just as my opinion that he is not earnest enough; not antislavery enough; not radical enough,—but goes naturally with those hostile to me." As his melancholy deepened, he generated another explanation that displayed the obtuseness that had always proved his undoing as a politician. "The root of the matter," he told his friend Whitelaw Reid, "was a difficulty of temperament. The truth is that I have never been able to make a joke out of this war."

To Kate, who remained at the Sprague mansion in Narragansett through the summer, he confessed that he was "oppressed" by anxiety. "You know how much I have endured rather than run counter to those friends who have insisted that I should remain in my place." He should have resigned earlier, he told her, right after Frank Blair's attack. Then he might have departed while heroically defending the radicals against the conservatives, but now "I am reproached with having left my post in the hour of danger." And though "the crushing load is off my shoulders," there is the regret that "I cannot finish what I began."

Chase's gloom was mirrored by the distress of his daughter, whose marriage to William Sprague was in trouble. Kate had seemed to hold "the balance of power" throughout the courtship, yet William now believed he had a right to control his high-spirited wife. Though he had made her responsible for redecorating his several multimillion-dollar households, he angrily rebuked her in private and in public for exorbitant spending. "Can it be," she later lamented in her diary, "that he would keep this hateful thought of my dependence ever before me, forcing me to believe that every dollar given or expended upon his home is begrudged?" She worried that, "reared in a pinched, prejudiced narrow atmosphere," with the thought of the "insatiable Moloch—money" always before him, he had vested in it "all the power when after all it is only a tributary. . . . My father was, in comparison with my husband, a poor man, but he felt himself rich when he was enabled to bestow a benefit upon the needy or a pleasure upon those he loved & a treasure laid up in his home was money well invested."

Though she was proud of her new husband's "worldly success" as both a senator and businessman, she had hoped to be a partner in all his endeavors, as she had been with her father. She "would gladly follow all his interests with sympathy & encouragement," she wrote, "but I cannot make them mine for his effort would seem to be to show me that I have no part in them." In fact, he rebuffed her when she tried to talk of business or politics, complaining in public that she had "different ideas & ways of life, from his own."

Most hurtful of all, Sprague had started drinking again. He would lash out at her when drunk, provoking bitter arguments that would take days to resolve. Kate could not restrain herself from replying to his insults with

"harsh and cruel words" of her own. When sober, Sprague would vow reform, pledging "to fill & occupy his place, in the home circle he has created . . . as well as the position he has secured for himself in the world."
These resolves were short-lived, and Kate began to fear that he did not seriously contemplate a worthy future, that his only thought was "to slip
through these obligations in life" with the least effort possible. "God forgive me," she later confessed, "that I had so often wished that I had found
in my husband a man of more intellectual resources, even with far less material wealth."

Though she acknowledged occasionally loathing her husband, she also
believed that "few men were loved" as much as she loved him. Perhaps she,
too, was at fault. "My hopes were too high," she confessed. "Proud, passionate and intolerant, I had never learned to submit." Chase witnessed a
fight between the young couple at Narragansett but mistakenly interpreted the problem as a simple "misunderstanding" that time and patience
would make right. His hopes seemed justified a few weeks later when he
learned that Kate was pregnant with her first child.

· · ·

THE GOODWILL ENGENDERED among congressional radicals by Lincoln's appointment of Fessenden was swiftly eroded by his refusal to sign
the punitive Reconstruction bill that passed the Congress in the final hours
of July 2, 1864, before it adjourned for the summer. Sponsored by Ben
Wade and Henry Winter Davis, the bill laid down a rigid formula for
bringing the seceded states back into the Union. The process differed in
significant ways from the more lenient plan Lincoln had announced the
previous December. Lincoln had proposed to rehabilitate individual states
as quickly as possible, hoping their return would deflate Southern morale
and thereby shorten the war. The Wade-Davis bill, in contrast, postponed
any attempts at Reconstruction until all fighting had ceased. It required
that a majority of a state's citizens, not simply 10 percent, take an oath of
allegiance to the Constitution before the process could begin. In addition,
suffrage would be denied to all those who had held civil or military office in
the Confederacy and who could not prove they had borne arms involuntarily. Finally, the bill imposed emancipation by congressional fiat where
Lincoln believed that such a step overstepped constitutional authority and
instead proposed a constitutional amendment to ensure that slavery could
never return.

Rather than veto the bill outright, Lincoln exercised a little-known provision called the pocket veto, according to which unsigned bills still on the
president's desk when Congress adjourns do not become law. In a written

proclamation, he explained that while he would not protest if any individual state adopted the plan outlined in the bill, he did not think it wise to require every state to adhere to a single, inflexible system. Talking with Noah
Brooks, he likened the Wade-Davis bill to the infamous bed designed by
the tyrant Procrustes. "If the captive was too short to fill the bedstead, he
was stretched by main force until he was long enough; and if he was too
long, he was chopped off to fit the bedstead."

Lincoln understood that he would be politically damaged if the radicals
"choose to make a point upon this." Nevertheless, he told John Hay, "I
must keep some consciousness of being somewhere near right: I must keep
some standard of principle fixed within myself." He would rely on this
conviction in the days ahead when Wade and Davis published a bitter
manifesto against him. He was not surprised by their anger at the suppres-
sion of their bill, but he was stung by their vitriolic tone and their suggestion that his veto had been prompted by crass electoral concerns. "To be
wounded in the house of one's friends," he told Brooks, "is perhaps the
most grievous affliction that can befall a man," the same sentiment he had
expressed when he lost his first Senate race in 1855. Now personal sorrow
was compounded by the realization that radical opposition might divide
the Republican Party, undoing the unity he had struggled to maintain
through the turbulent years of his presidency.

During the first week of July, rumors spread that a rebel force of unde-
termined strength was moving north through the Shenandoah Valley toward Washington. The rumors alarmed Elizabeth Blair, who feared that
the Confederate troops would come through Silver Spring, Maryland, exposing both her parents' home and that of her brother Monty to direct
danger. She cautioned her father, but his mind was elsewhere. For weeks
he and Monty had been planning a hunting and fishing trip to the Pennsylvania mountains, and he was eager to get started. In a letter to Frank on
July 4, the seventy-three-year-old Blair happily anticipated the two-week
vacation. Two grandsons were coming along; their grandfather hoped "to
give them a taste for woodcraft and to amuse & invigorate them." Meanwhile, the womenfolk were heading to Cape May. "Your mother & I enjoy
our young progeny's happiness as our own," Blair told his son, "& look on
it as a prolongation of our enjoyment of the earth, through a remote future."

Elizabeth's admonitions concerned Monty at first, but after the War
Department erroneously told him that the Confederate force had been
stopped at Harpers Ferry, he and his father set off for the Pennsylvania
countryside. Unable to prevent their departure, Elizabeth tried to convince her mother to remove the silver and other valuables to their city

home before leaving for Cape May. Eliza Blair refused, telling her daughter "she would not have the house pulled to pieces."

Elizabeth Blair's fears proved justified. Grant's decision to move south of Richmond and attack Petersburg from the rear had inspired Lee to send General Jubal Early and fifteen thousand troops north, hoping to catch Washington unawares. If a panic like that which prevailed at the time of Bull Run could be induced, Grant might have to withdraw some of his troops from Virginia. For several weeks, Early's movements remained undetected, and on July 5 he crossed the Potomac into Maryland. At this point, only miscellaneous troops under the command of General Lew Wallace, later to become famous as the author of *Ben Hur*, barred the path to the nation's capital. Wallace understood that with only half as many men as Early, he could not push the enemy back, but hoped he might hinder Early's progress while Washington prepared itself for attack.

The two sides met at Monocacy River on July 9. Young Will Seward, a colonel now, participated in the fierce engagement. "The battle lasted most of the day," he proudly recalled years later, "and every inch of the ground was hotly contested, until our men were finally overwhelmed by superior numbers." During the fighting, Will's horse was shot from under him, hurling the young colonel to the ground and breaking his leg. Encircled by rebels when he fell, Will was assumed to have been captured.

Secretary Seward spent a tense night at the War Department waiting for news of his son. He had just returned home after midnight when Stanton appeared with a discouraging report from General Wallace that Will had been wounded and taken prisoner. "None of us slept much the rest of the night," Fred Seward recalled, and in the morning, "it was arranged that Augustus should go over in the first train to Baltimore to make inquiries." At 3 p.m., Augustus telegraphed more hopeful news. Though Will's injury was confirmed, he had not been captured. "God be praised for the safety of our boy," Frances exclaimed. "With the help of one of his men," Will somehow "reached a piece of woods; where mounting a mule, and using his pocket-handkerchief for a bridle, he succeeded, after a painful ride of many miles during the night, in rejoining the forces."

The routing of the Federals at Monocacy gave Early an unobstructed path to Washington. As the rebel troops ranged through the countryside, they destroyed railroad tracks, stores, mills, and houses, much as the Union men under David Hunter had done in Virginia. Reaching Silver Spring, they came upon Monty's Falkland mansion. Blair's carpenter reported that the troops had immediately "commenced the work of wholesale destruction, battering the doors, robbing all the bookcases, breaking or carrying off all the chinaware, and ransacking the house from top to bottom." The next night, they torched the house, leaving only a "black-ened ruin."

At the nearby home of Monty's father, the patriarch, the soldiers scat-tered papers, documents, and books. They rummaged through the wine cellar and the bedrooms, littering the lawn with furniture and clothing. Elizabeth Blair was told that "one man dressed in Betty's riding habit, pants & all—another in Fathers red velvet wrapper." Still others donned assorted coats and uniforms, dancing with "great frolic" on the lawn.

The "perfect saturnalia" that Elizabeth decried was brought to an im-mediate halt when Generals Jubal Early and John Breckinridge arrived. Cursing the marauding soldiers, Breckinridge made them return stolen items. He retrieved the scattered papers and documents and sent them away for safekeeping. He asked Early to station a guard on the grounds to preserve the trees, grapery, shrubs, horses, and crops.

When Early inquired why he would "fret about one house when we have lost so much by this proceeding," Breckinridge replied that "this place is the only one I felt was a home to me on this side of the Mts." He explained that some years earlier, during a difficult period in his life, the old gentleman had taken him in, providing a "place of refuge & of rest." A neighbor told Blair Senior that Breckinridge "made more fuss" about pre-serving the house and its possessions "than if they had belonged to Jeff Davis."

When the older Blairs eventually returned home, they found a note on the mantel: "a confederate officer, for himself & all his comrades, regrets exceedingly that damage & pilfering was committed in this house. . . . Es-pecially we regret that Ladies property has been disturbed." In this man-ner, Elizabeth marveled, "bread cast upon the waters came back to us."

The time the Confederates lost during the Battle of Monocacy and the frolic at Silver Spring allowed Washington to mobilize its defenses. In his initial panic, Stanton had sent his secretary to take his bonds and gold from a War Department safe and place them under his mattress at home. He took heart from Lincoln's calm demeanor, however, and thereafter, the two worked together as one during the crisis. They telegraphed Grant, who put his highly respected Sixth Corps on a fast route to the capital. They called up the militia, supplied government clerks with muskets, and ordered "all convalescents capable of defending the forts and rifle-pits" to report for duty.

Throughout the tense days, Lincoln remained "in a pleasant and confi-dent humor," observed John Hay, not seeming to be "in the least con-cerned about the safety of Washington. With him the only concern seems to be whether we can bag or destroy this force in our front." Welles noted approvingly that Stanton "exhibits none of the alarm and fright I have seen in him on former occasions." As nervous farmers with homes in the Confederate path poured into Washington, the president and the war secretary drove together through the streets in a open carriage, "to *show* the *people*," one resident thought, "that *they* were not *frightened*." Such calm evinced by the administration had a salutary effect, allowing the residents of Washington, who had despaired in the wake of Bull Run, a measure of solace. Some "could even appreciate," as Fred Seward noted, "the grim humour of their predicament, in being thus suddenly attacked from the north, after having sent their available troops to the south."

By the time the Capitol dome was visible to the rebel force, the opportunity for a successful attack had receded. "Before even the first brigade of the leading division was brought into line," General Early later acknowledged, "a cloud of dust from the direction of Washington" revealed that Grant's reinforcements had arrived. Furthermore, inspection of the Union fortifications revealed them "to be exceedingly strong . . . with a tier of lower works in front of each pierced for an immense number of guns." Stretching "as far as the eye could reach," the earthworks appeared in many places to be "impregnable."

Still, Early refused to withdraw. He was determined to show the North how close he had come and sent a small force to engage the Union troops at Fort Stevens, about five miles from the White House. The skirmishing continued for several days, during which time Lincoln witnessed the action from a parapet, accompanied by Mary on one occasion, by Seward and Welles on another. The tall president's presence in the line of fire made a vivid impression upon those who were there. "The President evinced a remarkable coolness and disregard of danger," recalled General Horatio G. Wright. Even after a surgeon standing by his side was shot, "he still maintained his ground till I told him I should have to remove him forcibly. The absurdity of the idea of sending off the President under guard seemed to amuse Lincoln, but in consideration of my earnestness in the matter, he agreed to compromise by sitting behind the parapet instead of standing upon it."

Still, Lincoln would periodically stand, provoking concern on the part of a young captain who shouted, "Get down, you fool!" Years later, the captain, Oliver Wendell Holmes, Jr., son of the poet whom Lincoln greatly admired and himself to become a distinguished Supreme Court justice, would recall this unusual incident. For the normally sedentary Gideon Welles, to witness live action "was exciting and wild," until the sight of dead soldiers carried away on stretchers instantly sobered his mind. "In times gone by I had passed over these roads little anticipating scenes like this, and a few years hence they will scarcely be believed to have occurred."

Having made his point, Early retired as swiftly and mysteriously as he had come, leaving behind a spate of recriminations. The misguided command signals in Washington that allowed him to escape constituted "an egregious blunder," acknowledged Stanton's aide, Charles Dana. Blame was generally attributed to General Halleck, though Welles knew that in the eyes of the public, the entire administration appeared "contemptible."

Mary Lincoln, sensing her husband's profound disappointment that the rebels had escaped, turned on Stanton during a conversation at the Soldiers' Home. "Mrs. Lincoln," Stanton remarked with rare levity, "I intend to have a full-length portrait of you painted, standing on the ramparts at Fort Stevens overlooking the fight!"

"That is very well," Mary replied, "and I can assure you of one thing, Mr. Secretary, if I had had a few *ladies* with me the Rebels would not have been permitted to get away as they did!"

Mary was not alone in her indignation. The sight of his ruined home provoked Monty Blair into openly defiant rants against the command structure in Washington directed by Halleck. His diatribes were reported to Halleck, who immediately wrote a furious letter to Stanton. "I am informed by an officer of rank," he began, "that the Hon. M. Blair, Post Master Genl, in speaking of the burning of his house in Maryland, this morning said, in effect, that 'the officers in command about Washington are poltroons; that there were not more than five hundred rebels on the Silver Spring road and we had a million of men in arms; that it was a disgrace.' " On behalf of those officers "who have devoted their time and energies night and day, and have periled their lives," Halleck demanded to know whether "such wholesale denouncement & accusation by a member of the cabinet receives the sanction and approbation of the President of the United States. If so the names of the officers accused should be stricken from the rolls of the Army; if not, it is due to the honor of the accused that the slanderer should be dismissed from the cabinet."

Stanton sent the letter to Lincoln, who replied the same day. "Whether the remarks were really made I do not know; nor do I suppose such knowledge is necessary to a correct response. If they were made I do *not* approve them; and yet, under the circumstances, I would not dismiss a member of the Cabinet thereof. I do not consider what may have been hastily said in a moment of vexation at so severe a loss, is sufficient ground for so grave a step." Moreover, he concluded, "I propose continuing to be myself the judge as to when a member of the Cabinet shall be dismissed." Then, to further underscore his authority in the matter, Lincoln composed a note to his cabinet colleagues, stating categorically that only he would decide when the time had come to let one of them go. "It would greatly pain me to discover any of you endeavoring to procure anothers removal, or, in any way to prejudice him before the public. Such endeavor would be a wrong to me; and much worse, a wrong to the country. My wish is that on this subject, no remark be made, nor question asked, by any of you, here or elsewhere, now or hereafter."

Lincoln's restrained reaction was validated by Blair's conduct once the shock of seeing his gutted homestead wore off. Learning that Ben Butler had torched a Confederate officer's house in retaliation for the burning of Falkland, Monty implored the general to avoid any more like actions. "If we allow the military to invade the rights of private property on any other grounds than those recognized by civilized warfare," he cautioned, "there will soon cease to be any security whatever for the rights of civilians on either side." When friends offered to raise funds for him to rebuild, he graciously declined their help. "The loss is a very great one to me it is true," but it did not compare "to the losses suffered by the unknown millions in this great struggle for the life of the nation. Could I consent to have my house rebuilt by friends, whilst my neighbor a poor old blacksmith is unrelieved[?]" Monty Blair had confirmed Lincoln's faith in him as a man and as a responsible public figure. The postmaster general would retain his post until Lincoln himself decided it was time for him to go.

• • •

"The month of August does not open cheerfully," Noah Brooks reported. The steady progression of unfavorable events—the shocking slaughter at Petersburg, the raid on Washington, and the failure to capture Jubal Early's troops—had created a mood of widespread despondency throughout the North. In addition, the president's mid-July call for five hundred thousand additional volunteers had disturbed many Republicans, who feared negative repercussions on the fall elections. Lincoln himself acknowledged the "dissatisfaction" with his new recruiting effort but emphasized that "the men were needed, and must be had, and that should he fall in consequence, he would at least have the satisfaction of going down with the colors flying."

Meanwhile, dispatches from Grant revealed a continuing stalemate in the siege against Petersburg. An ingenious attempt by a regiment of former coal miners to mine under the Confederate earthworks and blow a hole in the enemy lines had resulted in a spectacular tragedy instead. In the confusion after the explosion, Union soldiers advanced into the 32-foot-deep crater itself, rather than circle around it, and had become trapped.

"Piled on top of each other like frightened sheep," they were easy targets for slaughter. By day's end, Grant had lost nearly four thousand men. "It was the saddest affair I have witnessed in the war," Grant wired Halleck. "Such opportunity for carrying fortifications I have never seen and do not expect again to have."

The appalling event left Gideon Welles in a depressed state, "less however from the result, bad as it is, than from an awakening apprehension that Grant is not equal to the position assigned him. . . . A blight and sadness comes over me like a dark shadow when I dwell on the subject, a melancholy feeling of the past, a foreboding of the future." Edward Bates shared his colleague's despair. In his diary he admitted feeling heartsick when he contemplated "the obstinate errors and persistent blunders of certain of our generals."

Unlike Welles or Bates, Lincoln refused to let the incident shake his faith in Grant. The day after the Battle of the Crater, he met with Grant at Fort Monroe, where the two men looked resolutely toward the future. Grant had received intelligence that the hard-riding Early had once again crossed the Potomac, spreading fear and devastation in Chambersburg, Pennsylvania. He dispatched General Philip Sheridan, one of his best commanders, to the Shenandoah Valley with instructions to find Early "and follow him to the death. Wherever the enemy goes let our troops go also." Lincoln, as determined as Grant to take the battle directly to the enemy without respite, replied: "This, I think, is exactly right."

A few days later, Commissioner French enjoyed "a long and very pleasant talk" with Lincoln. "He said we must be patient, all would come out right—that he did not expect Sherman to take Atlanta in a day, nor that Grant could walk right into Richmond,—but that we should have them both in time." Lincoln's confidence was not now shared by the country. The ongoing disasters had combined to create "much wretchedness and great humiliation in the land," a doleful Welles noted. "The People are wild for Peace," Thurlow Weed cautioned Seward.

Even before this train of events, Horace Greeley had taken it upon himself to counsel Lincoln. Greeley had received word that "*two Ambassadors*" representing Jefferson Davis had come to Niagara Falls in Canada "*with full & complete powers for a peace.*" Urging the president to meet with them immediately, he reminded Lincoln that "our bleeding, bankrupt, almost dying country also longs for peace—shudders at the prospect of fresh conscriptions, of further wholesale devastations, and of new rivers of human blood. And a wide-spread conviction that the Government . . . [is] not anxious for Peace, and do not improve proffered opportunities to achieve it, is doing great harm."

Though fairly certain that the so-called "ambassadors" had not been authorized by Jefferson Davis, Lincoln nonetheless discussed the matter with Seward and commissioned Horace Greeley to go to Niagara Falls. If the Confederate envoys were genuinely carrying legitimate propositions for peace, Greeley should offer them "safe conduct" and escort them to Washington. In addition, Lincoln dispatched John Hay to join Greeley at Niagara Falls and deliver a handwritten, confidential note to the envoys. "To Whom it may concern," the note read. "Any proposition which embraces the restoration of peace, the integrity of the whole Union, and the abandonment of slavery . . . will be met by liberal terms on other substantial and collateral points."

As Lincoln suspected, the two envoys had "no credentials whatever" and could offer no assurances that Jefferson Davis was ready to stop the war. He hoped the failed mission would demonstrate to Greeley and others the absurdity of the claims that *he* was the one preventing peace. Unfortunately, his intention backfired when the Confederate envoys sent Lincoln's confidential letter to the newspapers, falsely proclaiming that Lincoln's inadmissible demand for abolition had torpedoed the negotiations. Democratic newspapers embellished the story, accusing Lincoln of continuing the war for the sole purpose of freeing the slaves.

Leading Republicans were also upset by the president's "To Whom it may concern" letter. Looking simply for restoration of the Union, Thurlow Weed complained, the people "are told that the President will only listen to terms of Peace on condition Slavery be 'abandoned.' " Deeply disheartened, Weed and other leading Republicans became convinced that their party would be defeated in November. Weed journeyed to Washington during the first week in August and told Lincoln "that his re-election was an impossibility." Leonard Swett felt compelled to inform his friend of a growing movement to "call a convention and supplant him." A date for the new convention had been set for September 22 in Cincinnati, three weeks after the Democratic Convention. Swett warned Lincoln that a "most alarming depression" had overtaken his erstwhile supporters, and that unless something were done "to stem the tide," the situation was hopeless.

Dissatisfaction was rife inside the cabinet as well. Both Gideon Welles and Montgomery Blair were mystified by Lincoln's decision to "impose conditions" that were "inadmissible" by their very nature. Knowing that only Seward and Fessenden had been privy to his plan, Welles questioned the president's right "to assume this unfortunate attitude without consulting his Cabinet."

Henry Raymond, editor of the *New York Times* and chairman of the Re-

publican National Party, added to Lincoln's woes. "I am in active correspondence with your staunchest friends in every state and from them all I
hear but one report," wrote Raymond in late August. "The tide is setting
strongly against us." Raymond went on to predict that if the election were
held immediately, Lincoln would be beaten in Illinois, Pennsylvania, and
Indiana. Raymond ascribed two causes for "this great reaction in public
sentiment,—the want of military successes, and the impression in some
minds, the fear and suspicion in others" that the Confederates were ready
for reunion and peace, but for the absolute demand that slavery be abandoned. He recognized the inaccuracy of this perception but argued that it
could "only be expelled by some authoritative act, at once bold enough to
fix attention." He recommended sending a commissioner to meet with Jefferson Davis *"to make distinct proffers of peace . . . on the sole Condition of acknowledging the supremacy of the Constitution,"* leaving all remaining issues to
be settled later.

Lincoln's response to these extraordinary pressures reveals much about
his character. "I confess that I desire to be re-elected," he told Thaddeus
Stevens and Simon Cameron that August. "I have the common pride of
humanity to wish my past four years administration endorsed; and besides
I honestly believe that I can better serve the nation in its need and peril
than any new man could possibly do. I want to finish this job of putting
down the rebellion, and restoring peace and prosperity to the country."

Yet he forthrightly faced the likelihood of defeat and resolved to do his
utmost in the remaining months both to win the war on the North's terms
and to bring as many slaves as possible into Union lines before newly
elected Democratic leaders could shut the door forever. In the third week
of August, Lincoln asked all cabinet members to sign—without having
read—a memorandum committing the administration to devote all its
powers and energies to help bring the war to a successful conclusion. The
presumption was that no Democrat would be able to resist the immense
pressure for an immediate compromise peace. Slavery would thus be allowed to remain in the South, and even independence might be sanctioned.

"This morning, as for some days past," the blind memo began, "it seems
exceedingly probable that this Administration will not be re-elected. Then
it will be my duty to so co-operate with the President elect, as to save the
Union between the election and the inauguration; as he will have secured
his election on such ground that he can not possibly save it afterwards."

In these same weeks, Colonel John Eaton recalled, Lincoln "was considering every possible means by which the Negro could be secured in his

freedom." He knew that Eaton had come into contact with thousands of slaves who had escaped as the Union troops advanced. Tens of thousands more remained in the South. Lincoln asked Eaton if he thought Frederick Douglass "could be induced to come to see him" and discuss how these slaves could be brought into freedom. Eaton was aware that Douglass had recently criticized the president vehemently, denouncing the administration's insufficient retaliatory measures against the Confederacy for its blatant refusal to treat captured black soldiers as prisoners of war. He also knew, however, that Douglass respected Lincoln and was certain that he would lend his hand.

Douglass met with the president on August 19. In an open conversation that Douglass later recounted, Lincoln candidly acknowledged his fear that the "mad cry" for peace might bring a premature end to the war, "which would leave still in slavery all who had not come within our lines." He had thought the publication of his Emancipation Proclamation would stimulate an exodus from the South, but, he lamented, "the slaves are not coming so rapidly and so numerously to us as I had hoped." Douglass suggested that "the slaveholders knew how to keep such things from their slaves, and probably very few knew of his proclamation." Hearing this, Lincoln proposed that the federal government might underwrite an organized "band of scouts, composed of colored men, whose business should be somewhat after the original plan of John Brown, to go into the rebel states, beyond the lines of our Armies, and carry the news of emancipation, and urge the slaves to come within our boundaries." Douglass promised to confer with leaders in the black community on the possibility of such a plan.

There was yet another subject Lincoln wanted to discuss with Douglass. Three days earlier, Wisconsin's former governor Alexander Randall had hand-delivered a heartfelt letter from Charles Robinson, the editor of a Democratic paper in Wisconsin. "I am a War Democrat," Robinson began. "I have sustained your Administration. . . . It was alleged that because I and my friends sustained the Emancipation measure, we had become abolitionized. We replied that we regarded the freeing of the negroes as sound war policy, in that the depriving the South of its laborers weakened the strength of the Rebellion. That was a good argument, and was accepted by a great many men who would have listened to no other. It was solid ground on which we could stand, and still maintain our position as Democrats." Now the Niagara Falls declaration that "no steps can be taken towards peace, from any quarter, unless accompanied with an abandonment of slavery," left him with "no ground to stand upon." He was not writing "for the purpose of finding fault . . . but with the hope that you may suggest some interpretation of it, as well as make it tenable ground on which we War Democrats may stand."

Lincoln shared a draft of his reply with Douglass and requested his advice on whether or not to send it. "To me it seems plain," the draft began, "that saying reunion and abandonment of slavery would be considered, if offered, is not saying that nothing *else* or *less* would be considered." Having written these evasive words, however, he at once emphasized that as a "matter of morals" and a "matter of policy," it would be ruinous to recant the promise of freedom contained in his proclamation "as it seems you would have me to do. . . . For such a work, another would have to be found." Nonetheless, he acknowledged that if the rebels agreed to "cease fighting & consent to reunion" so long as they could keep their slaves, he would be powerless to continue the war for the sole purpose of abolition. The people would not support such a war; their congressional representatives would cut off supplies. All such figuring was irrelevant, in any case, for "no one who can control the rebel armies has made the offer supposed."

Douglass saw clearly that Lincoln was trying "to make manifest his want of power to do the thing which his enemies and pretended friends professed to be afraid he would do." Regardless of his personal convictions, he seemed to be saying, he "could not carry on the war for the abolition of slavery. The country would not sustain such a war, and [he] could do nothing without the support of Congress." Douglass emphatically urged Lincoln not to send the letter. "It would be given a broader meaning than you intend to convey; it would be taken as a complete surrender of your anti-slavery policy, and do you serious damage."

After listening carefully to the impassioned advice of Douglass, Lincoln turned the conversation to other topics. While they were talking, a messenger informed Lincoln that the governor of Connecticut wished for an audience. "Tell Governor Buckingham to wait, I want to have a long talk with my friend Douglass," Lincoln instructed. Douglass could barely "suppress his excitement" when he encountered John Eaton later that day. "He treated me as a man; he did not let me feel for a moment that there was any difference in the color of our skins! The President is a most remarkable man. I am satisfied now that he is doing all that circumstances will permit him to do." Eaton believed that Douglass "had seen the situation for the first time as it appeared to Mr. Lincoln's eyes." For his part, Lincoln told Eaton that "considering the conditions from which Douglass rose, and the position to which he had attained, he was . . . one of the most meritorious men in America."

That same night, perhaps buoyed by his conversation with Douglass, Lincoln invited Governor Randall and Judge Joseph Mills to the Soldiers' Home for a further discussion of the Robinson letter. "The President was free & animated in conversation," Mills recorded in his diary. "I was astonished at his elasticity of spirits." Lincoln admitted from the outset that he could not help "but feel that the weal or woe of this great nation will be decided in the approaching canvas." This was not "personal vanity, or ambition," but rather a firm belief that the Democrats' strategy of mollifying the South with a promise to renounce abolition as a condition for peace would "result in the dismemberment of the Union." He pointed out that there were "between 1 & 200 thousand black men now in the service of the Union." If the promise of freedom were rescinded, these men would rightly give up their arms. "Abandon all the posts now possessed by black men surrender all these advantages to the enemy, & we would be compelled to abandon the war in 3 weeks."

Lincoln's tone grew more fervent as he continued, as if he were arguing with himself against sending the reply to Robinson. "There have been men who have proposed to me to return to slavery the black warriors of Port Hudson & Olustee to their masters to conciliate the South. I should be damned in time & in eternity for so doing." Those who accused him of "carrying on this war for the sole purpose of abolition" must understand that "no human power can subdue this rebellion without using the Emancipation lever. . . . Let them prove by the history of this war, that we can restore the Union without it."

Mills, who had been initially skeptical of Lincoln, was overwhelmed by "his transparent honesty" and the depth of his convictions. "As I heard a vindication of his policy from his own lips, I could not but feel that his mind grew in stature like his body, & that I stood in the presence of the great guiding intellect of the age." His confidence in the justice of the Union cause "could not but inspire me with confidence." The visitors stood to leave, but Lincoln entreated them to stay so that he might entertain them with a mix of stories, jokes, and "reminiscences of the past."

His momentary ambivalence over a peace compromise put to rest by his own logic, Lincoln permanently shelved the draft of his letter to Robinson. Nor did he accede to Raymond's suggestion that he dispatch a commissioner to Richmond and sound out Jefferson Davis's conditions for peace. He played with the idea for a few days, even drafting a letter allowing Raymond to proceed to Richmond with authority to say that "upon the restoration of the Union and the national authority, the war shall cease at once, all remaining questions [including slavery] to be left for adjustment by peaceful modes." But he soon discarded the idea. The Raymond letter, like the reply to Robinson, was placed in an envelope and "slept undisturbed" for over two decades until unearthed by Nicolay and Hay when writing their biography of Lincoln.

Through these difficult days that Nicolay deemed "a sort of political Bull Run," Lincoln was sustained most of all by his "ever present and companionable" secretary of state. Mary and Tad had once again escaped the summer heat, spending August and early September in Manchester, Vermont. Seward had hoped to get away but did not feel he should leave Lincoln in this trying period, when "one difficulty no sooner passes away than another arises." His presence buoyed Lincoln, for he never lost faith that all would be well. While Seward agreed that "the signs of discontent and faction are very numerous and very painful," he refused to panic, believing that "any considerable success would cause them all to disappear." So long as ordinary people retained their faith in the cause, a faith evidenced by new enlistments in the army, Seward remained "firm and hopeful," convinced that Lincoln would see the country through.

Stanton provided additional reassurance to the beleaguered president. The relationship among Lincoln, Seward, and Stanton had strengthened over the years. Welles observed that "the two S's" had developed "an understanding" enabling them to act in concert supporting the president. Though Stanton lacked the genial temperament that won both Lincoln and Seward countless friends, he believed passionately in both the Union and the soldiers who were risking their lives to support it. Though he regularly argued with Lincoln over minor matters and peremptorily dismissed favor seekers from his office, the sight of a disabled soldier would command his immediate attention. In the mind of this brilliant, irascible man, there could be no peace without submission by the South.

On August 25, Lincoln invited Raymond to the White House and explained why, after careful consideration, he had decided that sending a commissioner to Richmond "would be utter ruination." Raymond was already in Washington, chairing a meeting of the Republican National Committee. The committee members charged with organizing support for Lincoln in the upcoming election had been so dubious about his chances that, as yet, they had done nothing to mobilize the party.

John Nicolay believed the president's meeting with Raymond and his colleagues could prove "the turning-point in our crisis." As the group gathered that morning, Nicolay wrote to John Hay, who was visiting his family in Illinois, "If the President can infect R. and his committee with some of his own patience and pluck, we are saved." If the committee members were unmoved after talking with Lincoln, however, hope for the election would fade.

Nicolay was relieved to see that Lincoln had invited Seward, Stanton, and Fessenden, "the stronger half of the Cabinet," to join the meeting. The results exceeded Nicolay's fondest hopes. In a memo written that same day, Nicolay delightedly noted that the president and his cabinet colleagues had managed to convince Raymond "that to follow his plan of sending a commission to Richmond would be worse than losing the Presidential contest—it would be ignominiously surrendering it in advance." Nicolay was convinced that the meeting had done "great good." The president's iron will impressed the committee members. They returned home "encouraged and cheered," with renewed belief that the election could be salvaged.

Two days later, a revealing item appeared in Raymond's *New York Times*. Noting that the members of the Republican National Committee would remain in Washington for another day to complete their plans for the presidential canvass, the *Times* declared: "Every member is deeply impressed with the belief that Mr. Lincoln will be reelected; and regards the political situation as most hopeful and satisfactory for the Union party."

Even before the approaching military success in Atlanta, which would transform the public mood, Lincoln had alleviated his own discouragement by refocusing his intense commitment to the twin goals of Union and freedom. He gave voice to these ideals in late August with an emotional address to the men of an Ohio regiment returning home to their families. "I happen temporarily to occupy this big White House," he said. "I am a living witness that any one of your children may look to come here as my father's child has. It is in order that each of you may have through this free government which we have enjoyed, an open field and a fair chance for your industry, enterprise and intelligence; that you may all have equal privileges in the race of life, with all its desirable human aspirations. It is for this the struggle should be maintained, that we may not lose our birthright. . . . The nation is worth fighting for, to secure such an inestimable jewel."

• • •

THE PRESIDENT'S REELECTION CAMPAIGN received a significant boost when the long-delayed Democratic Convention finally met on August 29, 1864. Until this moment, when a candidate would be chosen and a platform written, Nicolay wrote, anxious Republicans had imagined "giants in the airy and unsubstantial shadows of the opposition." Brooks, who had traveled to Chicago to cover the convention, agreed. He attributed the despondent mood that had overtaken Republicans in July and August to the fact that "we have had nothing to solidify and compact us; a platform and candidate from here will materially change all this."

Although Democrats had cheerfully capitalized all summer long on dissensions within the Republican camp, their own party was rent by the anger between War Democrats who supported a continuation of the war until reunion (though not abolition) was assured and Peace Democrats, who called for an immediate armistice at any cost. "They have a peace leg and a war leg," *New York Herald* editor James Gordon Bennett noted, "but, like a stork by a frog pond, they are as yet undecided which to rest upon." When the convention opened, Noah Brooks reported, it seemed as if the Peace Democrats had the upper hand. "It was noticeable that peace men and measures and sentiments were applauded to the echo, while patriotic utterances, what few there were, received no response from the crowd." The playing of "Dixie" was cheered, while Union tunes were met with virtual silence.

Though the peace wing commanded the emotions at the convention hall, it was generally assumed that War Democrat George McClellan would be the nominee. "His partisans are united and have plenty of money," Brooks observed, "while his opponents are divided as to their own choice." The peace wing, led by New York governor Horatio Seymour, Congressman Fernando Wood, and former congressman Clement Vallandigham, who had returned from his exile in Canada, floated several possible names but with no consensus. As a result, when the balloting began, McClellan easily won.

If McClellan's victory "was expected," George Templeton Strong confided to his diary, "the baseness of the platform on which he is to run was unexpected. Jefferson Davis might have drawn it. The word 'rebel' does not occur in it. It contemplates surrender and abasement." Pressed upon the party by the peace contingent, the platform declared that "after four years of failure to restore the Union by the experiment of war," the time had come to "demand that immediate efforts be made for a cessation of hostilities." Strong predicted that if McClellan agreed to represent this dishonorable platform, "he condemns his name to infamy." Indeed, it was rumored that he would "decline a nomination on such terms." For Democrats, the capitulation called for in their platform proved to be exceedingly ill timed.

Three days later came the stunning news that Atlanta had fallen. "Atlanta is ours, and fairly won," Sherman wired Washington on September 3. This joyous news, which followed on the heels of Admiral David

Farragut's capture of Mobile Bay, Alabama, prompted Lincoln to order that one hundred guns be fired in Washington and a dozen other cities to celebrate the victories. Jubilant headlines filled Northern newspapers. "Atlanta is ours," the *New York Times* repeated. "The foundries, furnaces, rolling-mills, machine-shops, laboratories and railroad repair-shops; the factories of cannon and small arms; of powder, cartridges and percussion caps; of gun carriages, wagons, ambulances, harnesses, shoes and clothing, which have been accumulated at Atlanta, are ours now"—although, unbeknownst to the *Times*, the departing Confederates had set fire to nearly "everything of military value." Still, George Templeton Strong instantly understood the importance of Atlanta's fall. "Glorious news this morning," he exulted, "it is (coming at this political crisis) the greatest event of the war."

Seward received the news from the War Department while seated in his library in Auburn, where he had finally escaped for a few days to see his family. He had barely finished reading Stanton's telegram before a crowd gathered at his house to celebrate. As the news spread, the crowd swelled until it spilled over to the park adjoining his residence. "Flags were hoisted in all parts of the city," a local correspondent reported, "all the bells commenced ringing, and a salvo of one hundred guns was fired." At the request of the spirited assemblage, which included "several hundred volunteers, who were waiting to be mustered in," Seward delivered a spontaneous talk that lasted more than an hour.

Seward's extemporaneous words were considered by one reporter present to be "one of his most impressive and effective speeches." He remarked that the twin victories should help inspire the three hundred thousand more men—"volunteers, if you will, drafted men if we must"—necessary "to end the war." He paid homage not only to the sailors and soldiers but to "the wisdom and the energy of the war Administration," pointing out that "Farragut's fleet did not make itself, nor did he make it. It was prepared by the Secretary of the Navy. And he that shall record the history of this war impartially will write that, since the days of Carnot [the military organizer of the French Revolution], no man has organized war with ability equal to that of Stanton." Seward ended with a moving tribute to his friend and president, telling the crowd that nothing was more important than Lincoln's reelection. "If we do this, the rebellion will perish and leave no root." The crowd roared its approval.

When Gideon Welles read Seward's speech, with its generous praise for the Navy Department, he professed himself delighted. "For a man of not very compact thought . . . often loose in the expressions of his ideas," Seward had set forth an argument, Welles believed, that would serve as "the keynote" of the upcoming campaign. Welles understood that Atlanta's fall would wreak havoc on the plans of his old party, the Democrats. "This intelligence will not be gratifying to the zealous partisans who have just sent out a peace platform, and declared the war a failure. . . . There is a fatuity in nominating a general and warrior in time of war on a peace platform."

McClellan, meanwhile, remained secluded at his home in Orange, New Jersey. He found himself under tremendous pressure from both factions of his divided party as he tried to draft his letter of acceptance. War Democrats warned that unless he repudiated the peace platform, his candidacy would be stillborn. Peace Democrats threatened that if he wavered on the proposed armistice, they might "withdraw their support." He went through six drafts before he finally delivered his letter to the Democratic Nominating Committee at midnight on September 8.

He began with a nod to the peace wing. Had the war been conducted for the sole purpose of preserving the Union, McClellan argued, "the work of reconciliation would have been easy, and we might have reaped the benefits of our many victories on land and sea." Were he in power, he would "exhaust all the resources of statesmanship" to yield peace. This said, he went on to disavow aspects of the strident demand for peace at any cost, insisting that hostilities would not end without the restoration of the Union. "I could not look in the face of my gallant comrades of the Army and Navy, who have survived so many bloody battles, and tell them that their labors, and the sacrifice of so many of our slain and wounded brethren had been in vain." The peace men were furious but had no alternative candidate. The stage was set for the fall election.

The fall of Atlanta produced a remarkable transformation in the mood of Republicans. "We are going to win the Presidential election," Lincoln's longtime critic Theodore Tilton wrote Nicolay. "All divisions are going to be healed. I have never seen such a sudden lighting up of public mind as since the late victory at Atlanta. This great event, following the Chicago platform—a most villainous political manifesto known to American history!—has secured a sudden unanimity for Mr. Lincoln." Even he, "never having been a partisan for Mr. Lincoln's re-election, but the reverse," was intending to advise everyone he knew "to unite on Mr. Lincoln."

Leonard Swett, who only weeks before had warned Lincoln that his re-election looked doubtful, believed that God had given the Union its glorious victory to make the floundering ship of state "right itself, as a ship in a storm does after a great wave has nearly capsized it." Relieved, Thurlow Weed informed Seward that with military success, the "conspiracy against Mr. Lincoln collapsed."

The changed public mood took Salmon Chase by surprise. He had spent the summer traveling through New England, meeting with abolitionist friends, including Ralph Waldo Emerson, Massachusetts governor John Andrew, the writer Richard Henry Dana, Jr., and Congressman Samuel Hooper. He had maintained contact with organizers of the secret meetings being held to pursue the possibility of a new convention to draft an alternative to Lincoln. He had done his best, according to Gideon Welles, "to weaken the President and impair confidence in him . . . expressing his discontent, not in public speeches but in social intercourse down East." Now that support for Lincoln had revived, Welles observed, Chase "is beginning to realize that the issue is made up, and no new leaders are to be brought forward, and he will now support Lincoln."

Deciding to return to Washington to offer his services to Lincoln, Chase stopped en route in New York. There, he had an unsettling conversation with a "gentleman who thought Lincoln very wise—if more radical would have offended conservatives—if more conservative the radicals." Would this, Chase asked himself, be the "judgment of history?"

When he reached the capital, Chase called on Fessenden, who told him the president would like to see him. News of their meeting spread quickly. "Mr. Chase had a long confab in his visit to the President yesterday after abusing him every where at the north," Elizabeth Blair told her husband. Two days later, Chase accompanied Stanton to the Soldiers' Home, where he once again spoke with Lincoln. "I have seen the President twice since I have been here," Chase told Kate. "Both times third persons were present & there was nothing like private conversation. His manner was evidently intended to be cordial & so were his words: and I hear of nothing but good will from him."

Graciousness did not satisfy Chase, however. He wanted the president to be more "demonstrative" toward him after an absence of two months. Chase still acknowledged no responsibility for sundering their relationship, believing it was he who had been "wronged and hurt" by the events surrounding his resignation. "I never desired any thing else than his complete success," Chase insisted, "and never indulged a personal feeling incompatible with absolute fidelity to his Administration."

Proud of his own magnanimity, Chase professed a "conviction that the cause I love & the general public interests will be best promoted by his election, and I have resolved to join my efforts to those of almost the whole body of my friends in securing it."

In the weeks that followed, Chase remained true to his word. He traveled by train, boat, and horseback to Ohio, Kentucky, Pennsylvania, Michigan, Illinois, and Missouri, delivering dozens of speeches in support of Lincoln's reelection before overflowing crowds. Meanwhile, the state elections in Vermont and Maine revealed larger Union majorities than the previous year. After the Vermont election, Nicolay wrote a cheery letter to Therena: "Three weeks ago, our friends everywhere were despondent, almost to the point of giving up the contest in despair. Now they are hopeful, jubilant, hard at work and confident of success."

More good news greeted Republicans on September 19, when Philip Sheridan, having finally caught up with Jubal Early in the Shenandoah Valley, fought a brutal but successful battle that destroyed more than a quarter of Early's army. The "shouting of Clerks" could be heard in every government department when the news became known. "This will do much to encourage and stimulate all Union loving men," Welles recorded in his diary.

• • •

MILITARY SUCCESS MAY have substantially cleared Lincoln's road to victory, but a serious obstacle remained in the form of John Frémont's candidacy. Time and again, a divided party had lost elections when a third-party candidate swayed the final result. To ensure party unity, Lincoln needed the support of the radicals. His task was made difficult by the dissatisfaction of men like Wade and Davis over his conciliatory policy on Reconstruction. In addition, the radicals objected to the continuing presence of Montgomery Blair in the cabinet while Chase had been allowed to resign.

Blair was aware that he had become the target of the radicals' wrath. When the Baltimore convention passed its resolution essentially calling for his dismissal, he had offered his resignation to Lincoln. Later that summer, his father had repeated Monty's offer during a visit with Lincoln at the Soldiers' Home. He assured Lincoln that to heal the party, Monty "would very willingly be a martyr to the Radical phrenzy or jealousy, that would feed on the Blairs, if that would help." At the time, Lincoln had declined to take action, saying that "he did not think it good policy to sacrifice a true friend to a false one or an avowed enemy." But the pressure to remove Blair continued to build. Henry Wilson warned Lincoln in early September that "tens of thousands of men will be lost to you or will give a reluctant vote on account of the Blairs."

The feud between the Blairs and the radicals had rendered cabinet life increasingly unbearable. Monty Blair detested Stanton. He believed the war secretary was in league with Wade and Davis against both the Blair family and the president. He spoke publicly of Stanton with what John Hay considered "unbecoming harshness," calling him "a liar" and "a thief." When these intemperate words reached Stanton, he refused to sit in cabinet meetings if Blair was present. In mid-August, Welles observed that the two embittered colleagues had not "interchanged words for weeks."

Lincoln had no patience for such personal contention. He had warned his cabinet members in July to refrain from criticizing one another in public. He decided that when the opportunity arose, he would take Monty Blair up on his offer to resign. That moment arose when Michigan senator Zachariah Chandler informed him that Blair's resignation would elicit the support of Wade and Davis for Lincoln's reelection. Chandler later asserted that the radical senator and congressman were only part of a larger bargain that included Frémont's agreement to withdraw his candidacy if Blair were removed. Historians have debated the extent of Chandler's influence on Frémont. By September, the Pathfinder had no hope of winning in any case and realized that his reputation would be sullied if he stayed in the race.

Two facts are clear: On September 22, Frémont announced his withdrawal from the race. Then, on the morning of September 23, Lincoln sent a letter to Monty's office asking for his resignation. "You have generously said to me more than once," he began, "that whenever your resignation could be a relief to me, it was at my disposal. The time has come. You very well know that this proceeds from no dissatisfaction of mine with you personally or officially. Your uniform kindness has been unsurpassed by that of any friend." Moreover, "in the three years and a half during which you have administered the General Post-Office, I remember no single complaint against you in connection therewith."

Despite his offer to resign, Blair was surprised to find the dismissal letter on his desk. Later that morning, he encountered Welles and Bates coming out of the White House. "I suppose you are both aware that my head is decapitated," he told them. "I am no longer a member of the Cabinet." Welles was so stunned that he asked Blair to repeat himself, at which point Blair took the letter from his pocket and read it aloud to his two colleagues. Blair said "he had no doubt he was a peace-offering to Frémont and his friends." Welles was uncertain, telling Blair that while "pacifying the partisans of Frémont might have been brought into consideration . . . the President would never have yielded to that." Welles thought it more likely that Blair had been sacrificed to restore balance to the cabinet after Chase's resignation. Chase's partisans clearly "felt wounded" that their man was gone while his assailant remained. The removal of Blair would allow Lincoln to "reconcile all parties, and rid the Administration of irritating bickerings." Lincoln chose the former governor of Ohio, William Dennison, to succeed Blair.

Welles was saddened by Blair's departure. "In parting with Blair,"

Welles recorded in his diary, "the President parts with a true friend, and he leaves no adviser so able sagacious. Honest, truthful and sincere, he has been wise, discriminating and correct." In the days that followed, Welles came to view "the removal of Montgomery from our counsels as the greatest misfortune that had befallen the Cabinet." Bates was equally distressed. Though he did not consider himself so intimate with Blair, he respected his straight-speaking colleague and believed Lincoln had erred in making a bargain for Wade and Davis. "I think Mr. Lincoln could have been elected without them and in spite of them. In that event, the Country might have been governed, free from their *malign influences.*"

Although Blair was hurt by a dismissal that he felt was "an unnecessary mortification," he remained certain, he told his wife, that Lincoln had acted "from the best motives" and that "it is for the best all around." His father wholeheartedly agreed. "In my opinion it is all for the best," he told Frank, no doubt worried that his fiery son would make some regrettable public remark. The patriarch suggested that Monty himself had "pressed this matter" by intimating to Frémont's friends that he would resign if Frémont withdrew. In the end, the senior Blair concluded, "if it tends to give a greater certainty of the defeat of McClellan, which I look upon as the salvation of the Republic, it is well. . . . I hope you will concur with the views I have taken. The true interests of the Country require the reelection of Lincoln."

Frank eventually did concur with his father, though, like his brother, he at first found it "somewhat mortifying to reflect that this triumph has been given to those who are equally the enemies of the President & 'the Blairs.' " On the other hand, he was certain that "a failure to re-elect Mr. Lincoln would be the greatest disaster that could befall the country and the sacrifice made by [Monty] to avert this is so incomparably small that I felt it would not cost him a penny to make."

Elizabeth Blair, hearing the noble sentiments of the men, believed that she and Monty's wife, Minna, were "more hurt than anybody else." As far as Monty's loyal sister was concerned, Lincoln should have stuck with his "first view—of the poor policy of sacrificing his friends to his enemies." She was impressed, however, by her brother's "fine manly bearing," which he illustrated repeatedly in the days ahead as he took to the stump on behalf of Abraham Lincoln. Speaking to large conservative gatherings, Monty insisted that the request for his resignation had not proceeded from any unkindness on Lincoln's part. On the contrary, the president "has at least the support of those who are nearer to me than all other people on this earth. I retired by the recommendation of my own father to the President."

John Hay returned from Illinois just at the time of Blair's resignation. He noted that Blair was behaving "very handsomely and is doing his utmost" to reelect Lincoln. Monty would never forget that Lincoln had stood by him after the mortifying publication of his private letter to Frémont three years earlier, which contained passages demeaning the president. He knew that his father had never been turned away when he requested a private audience with Lincoln, and that his sister, Elizabeth, was always welcome at the White House. His entire family would forever appreciate Lincoln's support for Frank during his continuing battle with the radicals in Congress. Indeed, Lincoln's countless acts of generosity and kindness had cemented a powerful connection with the close-knit Blair family that even Monty's forced resignation could not break. In the end, Lincoln gained the withdrawal of Frémont and the backing of the radicals without losing the affection and support of the conservative and powerful Blairs.

* * *

BOTH REPUBLICANS AND DEMOCRATS considered the state elections in Ohio, Pennsylvania, and Indiana on October 11 harbingers of the presidential election in November. Not only would the results reveal public sentiment, but the party that gained the governor's offices in those states would have "a grand central rallying point" for its partisans. That evening, Lincoln made his customary visit to the telegraph office in the War Department to read the dispatches as they came over the wire. Stanton was there, as was his assistant secretary, Charles Dana, and Thomas Eckert, chief of the telegraph office. Early reports from Cincinnati and Philadelphia looked hopeful, but reliable figures were unbearably slow in coming.

To defuse the tension, Dana recalled, Lincoln took from his pocket "a thin yellow-covered pamphlet" containing the latest writings of the humorist Petroleum V. Nasby. "He would read a page or a story, pause to con[sider] a new election telegram, and then open the book again and go ahead with a new passage." John Hay, who had accompanied Lincoln, found the selections "immensely amusing" and mistakenly thought Stanton felt the same way. During a break in the readings, however, the solemn war secretary signaled Dana to follow him into the adjoining room. "I shall never forget," Dana later recalled, "the fire of his indignation at what seemed to him to be mere nonsense." Stanton found it incomprehensible that "when the safety of the Republic was thus at issue, when the control of an empire was to be determined by a few figures brought in by the telegraph, the leader, the man most deeply concerned, not merely for himself but for his country, could turn aside to read such balderdash and to laugh at such frivolous jests." Stanton never would understand the indispensable role that laughter played in sustaining Lincoln's spirits in difficult times.

As the night wore on, the news from Ohio and Indiana proved better than anyone expected. The Republicans in Ohio gained twelve congressional seats, and the state provided a fifty-thousand-vote Republican majority. In Indiana, the Republican candidate for governor, Oliver Morton, won by a large margin, and Republicans captured eight of the eleven congressional seats.

The results in Pennsylvania were less decisive. Sometime after midnight, Lincoln sent a telegram to Simon Cameron. "Am leaving office to go home," he wrote. "How does it stand now?" No answer was received from Cameron, which seemed "ominous" to Hay. It turned out that the margin was so close that neither party could declare victory. Only when the absentee soldier vote was tallied in the days ahead could the Republicans claim a slight margin.

Welles observed that "Seward was quite exultant over the elections—feels strong and self gratified. Says this Administration is wise, energetic, faithful and able beyond any of its predecessors. That it has gone through trials which none of them has ever known." Lincoln, characteristically, reacted with more caution than his debonair colleague. Though delighted by Ohio and Indiana, he found the close vote in Pennsylvania sobering.

Two nights after the state elections, appearing "unusually weary," Lincoln returned to the telegraph office in the War Department to calculate the probability of his election in November. Taking a blank sheet of telegraph paper, he made two neat columns. The one on the left represented his estimate of the electoral votes McClellan would win; the one on the right tabulated the states he thought would be his. The cipher operator David Homer Bates noted that he wrote "slowly and deliberately, stopping at times in thoughtful mood to look out of the window for a moment or two, and then resuming his writing." The president guessed he would lose both New York and Pennsylvania, which meant his best hope was to squeak through by a total of only 3 electoral votes: 117 to 114. If these calculations were correct, he lamented, "the moral effect of his triumph would be broken and his power to prosecute the war and make peace would be greatly impaired."

During the anxious four-week period that stretched between the state and presidential elections, Lincoln received the heartening news that voters in Maryland had ratified a new constitution officially terminating slavery in their state. The margin had been perilously close, with the absentee soldier vote making the difference. "Most heartily do I congratulate you, and Maryland, and the nation, and the world, upon the event," Lincoln told a group of serenaders. Speaking that same day with Noah Brooks, he said: "I had rather have Maryland upon that issue than have a State twice its size upon the Presidential issue; it cleans up a piece of ground." Brooks admired the "frank homeliness" of Lincoln's choice of words: "Any one who has ever had to do with 'cleaning up' a piece of ground, digging out vicious roots and demolishing old stumps, can appreciate the homely simile applied to Maryland, where slavery has just been cleaned up effectually."

It was clear to both parties that the absentee vote could prove critical in the presidential election. Democrats, remembering the fanatical devotion McClellan had inspired among his men, believed their man would receive an overwhelming majority of the soldier vote. "We are as certain of two-thirds of that vote for General McClellan as that the sun shines," the Democratic publisher Manton Marble jauntily predicted.

Lincoln thought differently. He trusted the bond he had developed with his soldiers during his many trips to the front. After every defeat, he had joined them, riding slowly along their lines, boosting their spirits. He had wandered companionably through their encampments, fascinated by the smallest details of camp life. Sitting with the wounded in hospital tents, he had taken their hands and wished them well. The humorous stories he had told clusters of soldiers had been retold to hundreds more. The historian William Davis estimates that "a quarter-million or more had had some glimpse of him on their own." In addition, word of his pardons to soldiers who had fallen asleep on picket duty or exhibited fear in the midst of battle had spread through the ranks. Most important of all, through his eloquent speeches and public letters he had given profound meaning to the struggle for which they were risking their lives.

Provisions for soldiers to cast absentee ballots in the field had recently been introduced in thirteen states. Four other states allowed soldiers to vote by proxy, placing their ballots in a sealed envelope to be sent or carried for deposit in their hometowns. In several crucial states, however, soldiers still had to be in their hometowns on Election Day to cast their ballots. In an attempt to remedy this situation before the October state elections, Lincoln had wired General Sherman about Indiana, "whose soldiers cannot vote in the field. Any thing you can safely do to let her soldiers, or any part of them, go home and vote at the State election, will be greatly in point." He emphasized that "this is, in no sense, an order," but merely a request.

Stanton followed up, making certain that furloughs were liberally granted wherever possible. "All the power and influence of the War Department . . . was employed to secure the re-election of Mr. Lincoln,"

Charles Dana later asserted. When Thurlow Weed alerted the White House that among the sailors "on Gun Boats along the Mississippi," there were "several thousand" New Yorkers ready to vote if the government could provide a steamer to reach them and gather their ballots, Lincoln asked Welles to put a navy boat "at the disposal of the New York commission to gather votes."

As the election drew close, Lincoln told a visitor: "I would rather be defeated with the soldier vote behind me than to be elected without it." It is likely that McClellan shared Lincoln's sentiment. The election would tell which man had won the hearts and minds of the more than 850,000 men who were fighting for the Union.

• • •

On Election Day, November 8, 1864, the *New York Times* editorialized that "before this morning's sun sets, the destinies of this republic, so far as depends on human agency, are to be settled for weal or for woe." To elect Lincoln was to choose "war, tremendous and terrible, yet ushering in at the end every national security and glory." To choose McClellan was to choose "the mocking shadow of a peace . . . sure to rob us of our birthright, and to entail upon our children a dissevered Union and ceaseless strife."

In Washington, it was "dark and rainy." Arriving at the White House about noon, Noah Brooks was surprised to find the president "entirely alone." Seward and Usher had gone home to vote, as had William Dennison, Blair's replacement as postmaster general. This would be the tenth time Seward had cast a presidential ballot in Auburn; he had voted in more than half of the nineteen presidential elections since the beginning of the country. Fessenden was in New York working out the details of a new government loan, while Stanton was at home with a fever. Lincoln could not vote that day, for Illinois required voters to be present in the state.

Lincoln felt no need to conceal his anxiety from Brooks. "I am just enough of a politician to know that there was not much doubt about the result of the Baltimore convention; but about this thing I am very far from being certain. I wish I were certain." Brooks remained with Lincoln through most of the afternoon, noting that the president "found it difficult to put his mind on any of the routine work of his office." The only respite he found was in telling a humorous story about Tad, whose pet turkey apparently roamed at will among the Pennsylvania soldiers quartered at the White House. When the day had come for the Bucktail soldiers to cast their absentee ballots before their state's commission, Tad had excitedly rushed into his father's office so they could watch the voting from the window. Teasing his son, Lincoln had asked if the turkey, too, intended to vote. Tad's clever reply delighted his father. "No," he said. "He is not of age." Brooks noted that Lincoln so "dearly loved the boy" that "for days thereafter he took pride in relating this anecdote illustrative of Tad's quick-wittedness."

As the clock struck seven, the president, accompanied by John Hay, walked over to the telegraph office to begin the long vigil. "It is a little singular," Lincoln remarked to Hay, "that I who am not a vindictive man, should have always been before the people for election in canvasses marked for their bitterness." The lights of the War Department, bursting with dozens of orderlies and clerks, provided a welcome contrast to the murky night.

The muddy grounds had caused Thomas Eckert to fall on his face, which, "of course," Hay noted, "reminded the Tycoon" of a story. "For such an awkward fellow," Lincoln began, "I am pretty sure-footed. It used to take a pretty dextrous man to throw me. I remember, the evening of the day in 1858, that decided the contest for the Senate between Mr. Douglas and myself, was something like this, dark, rainy & gloomy. I had been reading the returns, and had ascertained that we had lost the Legislature and started to go home. The path had been worn hog-backed & was slippering. My foot slipped from under me, knocking the other one out of the way, but I recovered myself & lit square: and I said to myself, *'It's a slip and not a fall.'* " Even at the time Lincoln had understood that his defeat for the Senate was "a slip and not a fall." Little could he then have imagined, however, that on another dreary night six years later, he would be waiting to hear if he had been elected to a second presidential term.

The early returns were positive, revealing larger Republican majorities than in the state elections. Lincoln asked to have the good news carried to Mary at the White House. "She is more anxious than I," he commented. Shortly afterward, Welles and Fox arrived. Fox was thrilled to hear that Winter Davis had been defeated in Maryland. "You have more of that feeling of personal resentment than I," Lincoln said. "A man has not time to spend half his life in quarrels. If any man ceases to attack me, I never remember the past against him."

The returns, including those from Pennsylvania, continued to be promising, though New York, with its large number of traditionally Democratic Irish immigrants, remained in doubt. By the hour of midnight, however, when a supper of fried oysters was served, Lincoln's victory was assured, though his lopsided electoral college win would not be known for several days. In the end, he would win all but three states—New Jersey, Delaware, and Kentucky—giving him 212 electoral votes against McClellan's 21. The popular vote was closer; the two candidates were separated by about 400,000 votes. Nonetheless, the results were far better than Lincoln had predicted. The Republican/Union Party had gained thirty-seven seats in Congress and placed twelve governors in office. It had also seized control of most of the state legislatures with the power to name the next round of U.S. senators.

It was after 2 a.m. when Lincoln left the telegraph office. The rain had stopped, and along Pennsylvania Avenue, an impromptu crowd had gathered, "singing 'The Battle Cry of Freedom' at the tops of their voices." As he went to sleep that night, Lincoln carried with him the knowledge, as Brooks put it, that "the verdict of the people was likely to be so full, clear, and unmistakable that there could be no dispute," thereby affording him the chance to continue the war until both liberty and Union were secured.

Most impressive, the soldier vote had swung overwhelmingly in his favor. In the armies of the West, he won eight out of ten votes, and even in McClellan's Army of the Potomac, Lincoln earned the votes of seven out of every ten soldiers. Many of these soldiers still admired McClellan but could not countenance the defeatist Democratic platform or the fact that the Confederacy was obviously hoping the young Napoleon would win. But there was something else, something Democrats had failed to understand. Over the years, Lincoln had inspired an almost mystical devotion among his troops. "The men had come to regard Mr. Lincoln with sentiments of veneration and love," noted an Illinois corporal. "To them he really was 'Father Abraham,' with all that the term implied." By supporting Lincoln, the soldiers understood that they were voting to prolong the war, but they voted with their hearts for the president they loved and the cause that he embodied.

CHAPTER 25

"A SACRED EFFORT"

ON THURSDAY NIGHT, November 10, 1864, an immense crowd, "gay with banners and resplendent with lanterns," gathered on the White House lawn to congratulate the president on his re-election. "Martial music, the cheers of people, and the roar of cannon, shook the sky." When the joyful throng demanded his appearance, Lincoln spoke to the crowd from a second-floor window. Acknowledging that the recent canvass had been marred by "undesirable strife," he nonetheless felt it had "demonstrated that a people's government can sustain a national election, in the midst of a great civil war. Until now it has not been known to the world that this was a possibility."

When Lincoln drew his little speech to a close, the revelers moved on to Seward's Lafayette Square home. They found the secretary of state, who had just returned from Auburn, "in an exceedingly jocose frame of

mind." He predicted that the time was near when "we will all come together again . . . when the stars and stripes wave over Richmond," and
"you will have to look mighty sharp to find a man who was a secessionist,
or an aider of the rebellion." He recollected that when he was a boy in the
early 1800s, his parents had told of "the vast number of tories" who opposed the government during the American revolution; yet, thirty years
later, "there was not a tory to be found in the whole United States."

Seward's good humor infected the crowd, who responded with cheers
and laughter. In closing, he observed that the night was young. "I advise
you to go and see Mr. Fessenden, for if he gets discouraged we shall
all come to grief; also be good enough to poke up Mr. Stanton; he needs
poking up, for he has been seriously sick, I hear, for several days past. You
cannot do better also than to call upon my excellent friend Gideon Welles,
and ask him if he cannot make the blockade off Wilmington more stringent, so that I shall not need to have so much trouble with my foreign relations."

Seward's playful remarks about his colleagues reflected the improved
atmosphere in the cabinet now that Chase and Blair were gone. Both men
had symbolized the animosity between radicals and conservatives in the
country at large; their clashing emotions had long reverberated through
the cabinet. The periodic jealousy Welles felt over the superior access
Seward and Stanton enjoyed with the president had been intensified a
hundredfold so long as Blair was there to fuel the flames. Likewise, when
Stanton was angry with Lincoln over pardons or appointments, Chase had
eagerly lent an approving ear to his complaints. Never initiated into this
contentious drama, Fessenden and Dennison brought cooperation and
amity to the cabinet. Strife abated, and Welles even acknowledged that his
relations with Seward had grown more "amicable" and that Stanton was
sounding more reasonable and less radical regarding Reconstruction.

Rumormongers had speculated that Lincoln would now want to replace
his entire cabinet. It was positively asserted that Seward would give way to
Charles Francis Adams, that General Butler would replace Stanton, and
that Welles and Bates had outlived their usefulness. It was surmised that
Lincoln would prefer more controllable colleagues. The busy, hypotheti-
cal cabinetmakers did not understand that Lincoln had no wish to disturb
the rhythm of his relationships with his colleagues, which, to his mind,
worked exceedingly well.

Lincoln's friendship with Seward had deepened with each passing year.
"His confidence in Seward is great," observed Welles that autumn. Seward
"spends more or less of every day with the President." On subjects "of the
gravest importance," Seward was the president's "only confidant and ad-

viser." Whenever Lincoln bounced an idea off Seward, he received straightforward advice. When a plan to foster Union sentiment in the South through confidential government purchase of a controlling share in a number of failing Southern newspapers was presented to Lincoln, he turned to Seward for advice. "It seems to me very judicious and wise," Seward responded. It would provide a forum for Union men to help sway the opinion of fellow Southerners. If government funds were not readily available, he suggested that Thurlow Weed "might find money by contribution."

Though some still considered the talkative New Yorker the "power behind the throne," Seward had long since understood that Lincoln was the master. "There is but one vote in the Cabinet," asserted Seward, "and that is cast by the President." Two days after the election, Seward told a crowd of supporters, "Henceforth all men will come to see him, as you and I have seen him. . . . Abraham Lincoln will take his place with Washington and Franklin, and Jefferson, and Adams, and Jackson, among the benefactors of the country and of the human race."

Lincoln's partnership with his volatile secretary of war, though not as intimate and leisurely, was equally effective. Stanton was only fifty in the fall of 1864, but he "looked older," his clerk Benjamin recalled, "by reason of the abundant tinging of his originally brown hair and beard with iron-gray." The war had taken a toll on his constitution, already weakened by the lifelong struggle with asthma that caused periodic "fits of strangulation." The illness that kept him in bed on election eve lasted for nearly three weeks. For a time it seemed he would not rally. His doctor begged him to take a leave of absence from his post. "Barnes," Stanton replied, "keep me alive till this rebellion is over, and then I will take a rest . . . a long one, perhaps." In a letter to Chase written shortly after Lincoln's reelection, he acknowledged that his health could be restored only by "absolute rest and relief from labor and care," though nothing could keep him from his post until he had brought the soldiers home in peace.

By late November, Stanton was back working fifteen-hour days at his stand-up desk, directing his subordinates with a steely determination. The complex relationship between the president and his secretary of war was not easy to comprehend. At times it seemed as if Stanton controlled the president; at other times it was clear that Lincoln was the dominant force in dictating policy. In fact, there was an unwritten code between the two powerful men: "Each could veto the other's acts, but Lincoln was to rule when he felt it necessary."

Lincoln used his veto over Stanton sparingly, as two of his congressional friends learned to their dismay. Having obtained the president's assent to a military appointment for one of their constituents, they carried the endorsed application to Stanton. Stanton flatly refused to consider it. "The position is of high importance," Stanton explained. "I have in mind a man of suitable experience and capacity to fill it." When informed that Lincoln wanted this man, Stanton bellowed, "I do not care what the President wants; the country wants the very best it can get. I am serving the country . . . regardless of individuals."

The two congressmen walked back to the White House, assuming the president would override his secretary, but Lincoln refused: "Gentlemen, it is my duty to submit. I cannot add to Mr. Stanton's troubles. His position is one of the most difficult in the world. Thousands in the army blame him because they are not promoted and other thousands out of the army blame him because they are not appointed. The pressure upon him is immeasurable and unending. He is the rock on the beach of our national ocean against which the breakers dash and roar, dash and roar without ceasing. He fights back the angry waters and prevents them from undermining and overwhelming the land. Gentlemen, I do not see how he survives, why he is not crushed and torn to pieces. Without him I should be destroyed. He performs his task superhumanly. Now do not mind this matter, for Mr. Stanton is right and I cannot wrongly interfere with him."

At the same time, Lincoln expected Stanton to be aware of the special burdens he faced as president. For weeks, Lincoln wrote Stanton, he had been pressed by relatives of "prisoners of war in our custody, whose homes are within our lines, and who wish . . . to take the oath and be discharged." He believed that "taking the oath" was an act of honor, that "none of them will again go to the rebellion," though he acknowledged that "the rebellion again coming to them, a considerable per centage of them, probably not a majority, would rejoin it." With "a cautious discrimination," however, "the number so discharged would not be large enough to do any considerable mischief." Moreover, looking forward to the day when the two sides would once again be united, he thought the government "should avoid planting and cultivating too many thorns in the bosom of society." With all these considerations in mind, it would provide "relief from an intolerable pressure" if he could have Stanton's "cheerful assent to the discharge of those names I may send, which I will only do with circumspection." Stanton replied the following day: "Your order for the discharge of any prisoners of war, will be cheerfully & promptly obeyed."

Lincoln's liberal use of his pardoning power created the greatest tension between the two men. Stanton felt compelled to protect military discipline by exacting proper punishment for desertions or derelictions of duty, while Lincoln looked for any "good excuse for saving a man's life." When he found one, he said, "I go to bed happy as I think how joyous the signing of my name will make him and his family and his friends."

Stanton would not allow himself such leniency. A clerk recalled finding Stanton one night in his office, "the mother, wife, and children of a soldier who had been condemned to be shot as a deserter, on their knees before him pleading for the life of their loved one. He listened standing, in cold and austere silence, and at the end of their heart-breaking sobs and prayers answered briefly that the man must die. The crushed and despairing little family left and Mr. Stanton turned, apparently unmoved, and walked into his private room." The clerk thought Stanton an unfeeling tyrant, until he discovered him moments later, "leaning over a desk, his face buried in his hands and his heavy frame shaking with sobs. 'God help me to do my duty; God help me to do my duty!' he was repeating in a low wail of anguish." On such occasions, when Stanton felt he could not afford to set a precedent, he must have been secretly relieved that the president had the ultimate authority.

When Stanton thought he was right, however, he tenaciously pursued his purpose. When a group of Pennsylvania politicians received the president's assent for discharging some prisoners of war in their district who were willing to take the oath and join the Union army fighting Indians in the West, Stanton flatly refused to execute the order. The order specified that the discharged prisoners would receive a bounty and be credited against Pennsylvania's draft quota, thus reducing the number of troops required of the Keystone State. "Mr. President, I cannot do it," he asserted. "The order is an improper one, and I cannot execute it." Lincoln was equally firm in his reply: "Mr. Secretary, it will have to be done." And so it was.

When the order was publicized, a storm of criticism descended upon Stanton. To give a bounty to soldiers who were already in government custody seemed wasteful and wrong, as did counting the discharged prisoners against the quota that Pennsylvania, like every other state, was required to supply. Lincoln learned that Grant, too, was unhappy and blamed Stanton. "I send this," Lincoln promptly wrote Grant, "to do justice to the Secretary of War." He then explained that he had responded to the idea "upon pressing application . . . and the thing went so far before it came to the knowledge of the Secretary of War that in my judgment it could not be abandoned without greater evil than would follow it's going through. I did not know, at the time, that you had protested against that class of thing being done; and I now say that while this particular job must be completed, no other of the sort, will be authorized, without an understanding with you, if at all. The Secretary of War is wholly free of any part in this blunder."

In this instance, Stanton was transparently blameless, but Lincoln protected his volatile secretary even when criticism was justified, when "his firmness degenerated, at times, into sheer obstinacy; his enthusiasm, into intolerance; his strength of will, into arrogance." Even the equitable George Templeton Strong acknowledged that it was "hard to vote for sustaining an Administration of which Stanton is a member. He is a ruffian."

Implacable and abrasive as Stanton could be, his scrupulous honesty, energy, and determination were invaluable to Lincoln. When one caller complained bitterly about Stanton's bearish style, Lincoln stopped him cold: "Go home my friend, and read attentively the tenth verse of the thirtieth chapter of Proverbs!" The verse reads as follows: "Accuse not a servant to his master, lest he curse thee, and then be found guilty." When people speculated about cabinet changes after his reelection, Lincoln made it clear that Stanton would not be leaving. "Folks come up here and tell me that there are a great many men in the country who have all Stanton's excellent qualities without his defects," he commented. "All I have to say is, I have n't met 'em! I don't know 'em!"

Nor did Lincoln consider dismissing his "Neptune," Gideon Welles. Reserved by nature, Welles did not enjoy the easy camaraderie with Lincoln that Seward did. The discreet New Englander looked askance at the curious pleasure both Lincoln and Seward took in talking with "the little newsmongers" and hearing "all the political gossip." And he was often vexed by the odd intimacy between Lincoln and Stanton. Unlike Chase, however, he confined his complaints to his diary and remained totally loyal to the president whose natural sagacity he greatly admired.

Moreover, Lincoln recognized that Welles had accomplished a Herculean task—he had built a navy almost from scratch, utterly revamping a department initially paralyzed by subversion and strife. Even the normally critical *Times* of London was forced to concede the extraordinary growth of the American navy under the leadership of Gideon Welles. When Welles took office, there were only 76 vessels flying the American flag; four years later, there were 671. The number of seamen had increased from 7,600 to 51,000. In the span of only four years, the American navy had become "a first class power."

A shrewd judge of character, Welles had assembled an excellent team, including his dynamic assistant secretary, Gustavus Vasa Fox, and the industrious commandant of the Navy Yard, John Dahlgren. Welles had opposed the blockade but, once overruled, had enforced it with determination and skill. He had fought Lincoln on the admission of West Virginia as a state and the suspension of the writ of habeas corpus, but he had never publicly vented his objections.

With Seward, Stanton, and Welles secure in their cabinet places, the resignation of Edward Bates provided the only opening for change in the immediate aftermath of the election. The seventy-one-year-old Bates had contemplated resigning the previous spring, after suffering through a winter of chronic illness. In May, his son Barton had pleaded with him to return to St. Louis. "The situation of affairs is such that you are not required to sacrifice your health and comfort for any good which you may possibly do," urged Barton. "As to pecuniary matters, I know well that you have but little to fall back on . . . for the present at least make your home at my house & Julian's, going from one to the other as suits your convenience. . . . You've done your share of work anyhow, & it is time the youngsters were working for you. If you had nothing at all, Julian and I could continue to take good care of you and Ma and the girls; & you know that we would do it as cheerfully as you ever worked for us, and we would greatly prefer to do it rather than you should be wearing yourself out as now with labor and cares unsuited to your age."

The prospect of going home to children and grandchildren was attractive, especially to Julia Bates, whose wishes remained paramount with her husband after forty-one years of marriage. On their anniversary in late May, Bates happily noted that "our mutual affection is as warm, and our mutual confidence far stronger, than in the first week of marriage. This is god's blessing."

However, during the dark period that preceded the fall of Atlanta, when Bates believed "the fate of the nation hung, in doubt & gloom," he did not feel he could leave his post. Nor did he wish to depart until Lincoln's reelection was assured. "Now, on the contrary," he wrote to Lincoln on November 24, 1864, "the affairs of the Government display a brighter aspect; and to you, as head & leader of the Government all the honor & good fortune that we hoped for, has come. And it seems to me, under these altered circumstances, that the time has come, when I may, without dereliction of duty, ask leave to retire to private life."

Bates went on to express his profound gratitude to Lincoln "not only for your good opinion which led to my appointment, but also for your uniform & unvarying courtesy & kindness during the whole time in which we have been associated in the public service. The memory of that kindness & personal favor, I shall bear with me into private life, and hope to retain in my heart, as long as I live."

Bates had served his president and his country faithfully. In his first months as Attorney General, though he had been uncomfortable confronting Justice Taney on the issue of arbitrary arrests, he had composed an elaborate opinion justifying Lincoln's suspension of the writ of habeas corpus. When McClellan had refused to divulge his plans in early 1862, Bates had urged Lincoln to assume control of his commanders, advising him that the authority of the presidency stood above that of his generals, even on military matters. When the president read his first draft of the Emancipation Proclamation to the cabinet in July 1862, Bates had been one of the first to speak favorably. Though Bates never fully escaped from the racial prejudices formed in his early years—he continued to believe until the end of his life that emancipation should be accompanied by colonization—his ideas had evolved to the point where he supported some very progressive measures. When asked in 1864 to deliver a legal opinion on the controversial question of the unequal pay scale for black soldiers, he declared "unhesitatingly" that "persons of color" who were performing in the field the same duties as their white counterparts should receive "the same pay, bounty, and clothing."

Abolitionists applauded this opinion along with an earlier one declaring blacks to be citizens of the United States. The citizenship issue had arisen when a commercial schooner plying the coastal trade was detained because its captain was a black man. The *Dred Scott* decision had declared that blacks were not citizens, and naval law required one to be a citizen to command a ship flying the American flag. When the question was put to him, Bates carefully researched definitions of citizenship dating back to Greek and Roman times. After much consideration, he concluded that place of birth, not color of skin, determined citizenship. The *Dred Scott* decision was wrong; free blacks were citizens of the United States.

Bates's decision did not cover the status of slaves, nor did it suggest that citizenship implied the right of suffrage or the right to sit on juries. Nonetheless, as a local Washington paper noted at the time of his resignation: "Though esteemed by many as more conservative than the majority of his countrymen at the present day, Mr. Bates has given opinions involving the rights of the colored race which have been quite abreast with the times, and which will henceforth stand as landmarks of constitutional interpretation."

From their first acquaintance, the relationship between Bates and Lincoln had been marked by warmth and cordiality. On occasion, Bates's diary reveals frustration with Lincoln's loose management style, which left the administration with "no system—no unity—no accountability—no subordination." He believed Lincoln relied too heavily on Seward and Stanton. He could not fathom why the disloyal Chase had been kept in place for so long or why General Butler was not fired when complaints arose about his arbitrary arrests in Norfolk. In fact, Bates confided in his diary, his "chief fear" was "the President's easy good nature."

Nonetheless, by the end of his tenure as Attorney General, Bates had formed a more spacious understanding of the president's unique leadership style. While troubled at the start by Lincoln's "never-failing fund of anecdote," he had come to realize that storytelling played a central role in the president's ability to communicate with the public. "The character of the President's mind is such," Bates remarked, "that his thought habitually takes on this form of illustration, by which the point he wishes to enforce is invariably brought home with a strength and clearness impossible in hours of abstract argument.

"Mr. Lincoln," Bates told Francis Carpenter, "comes very near being a perfect man, according to my ideal of manhood. He lacks but one thing . . . the element of *will*. I have sometimes told him, for instance, that he was unfit to be intrusted with the pardoning power. Why, if a man comes to him with a touching story, his judgment is almost certain to be affected by it. Should the applicant be a *woman*, a wife, a mother, or a sister,—in nine cases out of ten, her tears, if nothing else, are sure to prevail."

As Bates prepared to leave Washington, each of his colleagues stopped to say goodbye, in contrast to the lonely leave-taking endured by Salmon Chase. Stanton was "especially civil," Bates noted. "Told me to write to my sons, in the army and assure them that he would [do] any thing for them that they would expect me to do." Bates joined Seward, Welles, and Usher in the president's office for a "pleasant" farewell. The departing Attorney General was once again touched by the president's "affable and kind" manner.

Bates left his colleagues and staff "with regret," but with the knowledge that his life was forever connected with the history of his country. Because Lincoln had chosen him as his Attorney General, Edward Bates had been able to "leave a trail which might make known/That I once lived—when I am gone."

To replace Bates, Lincoln felt he had to find a man from one of the border states. "My Cabinet has *shrunk up* North, and I must find a Southern man," he explained to a colleague. "I suppose if the twelve Apostles were to be chosen nowadays the shrieks of locality would have to be heeded." His first choice was Judge Advocate General Joseph Holt. The native Kentuckian had been one of the trio of cabinet members, together with Edwin Stanton and Jeremiah Black, who had stiffened Buchanan's will to resist secession. Lincoln liked and respected Judge Holt, having worked closely with him on court-martial cases. Holt declined the offer, however, recommending instead his fellow Kentuckian James Speed, the older brother of

Lincoln's great friend Joshua. "I can recall no public man in the State of *uncompromising loyalty*," Holt told Lincoln, "who unites in the same degree, the qualifications of professional attainments, fervent devotion to the union, & to the principles of your administration, & spotless points of personal character."

Lincoln followed Holt's recommendation that very day, sending a telegram to Speed. "I appoint you to be Attorney General. Please come on at once." Though taken by surprise, Speed was honored to accept: "Will leave tomorrow for Washington."

James Speed would prove to be an excellent choice. Over the years, he had arrived at a radical position on slavery. The previous spring, he and his brother, Joshua, had been instrumental in forming a new liberal party in conservative Kentucky, the Unconditional Union Party, which supported Lincoln's reelection and emancipation. "I am a thorough Constitutional Abolitionist," James Speed had declared during the fall campaign, meaning he, like Lincoln, was "for abolishing Slavery under the War Power of the National Constitution, and then clinching it by a Constitutional amendment prohibiting it everywhere forever." Though unable to swing the state for Lincoln, the Unconditionalists remained hopeful that they might eventually direct Kentucky's future. "We are less now but true," James Speed had written Lincoln after the election.

To those unfamiliar with the Louisville lawyer, Lincoln explained that Speed was "a man I know well, though not so well as I know his brother Joshua. That, however, is not strange, for I slept with Joshua for four years, and I suppose I ought to know him well." Lincoln's ease in referring to his sleeping arrangement with Joshua Speed is further evidence that theirs was not a sexual relationship. Had it been, historian David Donald suggests, the president would not have spoken of it "so freely and publicly."

"You will find," Lincoln predicted as James Speed set out for Washington, "he is one of those well-poised men, not too common here, who are not spoiled by a big office."

• • •

THE EASE WITH WHICH LINCOLN filled the post of Attorney General was not replicated when Roger Taney's death in mid-October left vacant the seat of Chief Justice of the Supreme Court. Though Lincoln had initially planned to offer Salmon Chase the position, he discovered that three of his most loyal cabinet members—Edwin Stanton, Edward Bates, and Montgomery Blair—desired the honored post for themselves. He decided to postpone his choice until after the election.

Stanton's claim seemed the most compelling. The Chief Justiceship was the only position, observed a longtime friend, "Stanton ever desired." His brilliant legal career had brought him to argue numerous cases before the Supreme Court. Lifetime tenure would secure his family's finances, which had diminished seriously during the war. His unstable health might be restored with the pressures of the war office removed. "You have been wearing out your life in the service of your country & have fulfilled the duties of your very responsible & laborious office with unexampled ability," wrote his friend the Supreme Court justice Robert Grier. Though Grier himself was an obvious choice to fill Taney's position, he believed Stanton deserved the honor. "It would give me the greatest pleasure and satisfaction," he wrote Stanton, "to have you preside on our bench. . . . I think the Pres owes it to you."

Ellen Stanton, doubtless acting at her husband's behest, invited Orville Browning to their house one Sunday night when Stanton was at City Point. "She expressed to me a great desire to have her husband appointed Chief Justice," Browning recorded in his diary, "and wished me to see the President upon the subject. I fear Mr Chase's appointment, and am anxious to prevent it. Mr Stanton is an able lawyer, learned in his profession, and fond of it, of great application, and capacity of endurance in labor— I think a just man—honest and upright, and incapable of corruption, and I, therefore, think would be an appointment most fit to be made. I will see the President upon the subject tomorrow."

Methodist bishop Matthew Simpson also called on Lincoln to urge Stanton's appointment "on the grounds of his fitness, and as a reward for his services and labors." Lincoln "listened attentively" and then, "throwing his leg over a chair, and running his hands through his hair," responded with heartfelt emotion: "Bishop, I believe every word you have said. But where can I get a man to take Secretary Stanton's place? Tell me that, and I will do it."

Like Lincoln, General Grant worried about losing Stanton's indispensable talents in the War Department. At City Point, he urged the secretary to stay at his post. The strain of the situation likely contributed to Stanton's ongoing illness that fall. In the end, Stanton informed Lincoln through a friend that he should no longer be considered "among candidates." He "felt that the completion of the work he had in hand," his sister Pamphila recalled, "was nearer to his heart, and a far higher ambition."

A heartfelt note from Henry Ward Beecher helped to dispel Stanton's disappointment at relinquishing his ambition. "The country cannot spare your services from your present place," wrote the celebrated minister, "or I could wish that you might redeem Taney's place and restore to that Court, the honor and trust of Marshall's day. . . . I regard your administration of the War Department, from whatever point it is viewed, as one of the great-est features of this grand time. Your energy vitalizing industry, and fidelity, but above all, *Your moral vision* . . . are just as sure to give your name honor and fame. . . . If you were to die to-morrow you have done enough for your own fame already."

In an emotional reply, Stanton told Beecher that he was deeply moved by his generous remarks. "Often, in dark hours, you have come before me, and I have longed to hear your voice, feeling that above all other men you could cheer, strengthen, guide, and uphold me in this great battle, where, by God's providence, it has fallen upon me to hold a post and perform a duty beyond my own strength. But being a stranger I had no right to claim your confidence or ask for help. . . . Now, my dear Sir, your voice has reached me, and your hand is stretched forth as to a friend. . . . Already my heart feels renewed strength and is inspired with fresh hope."

Montgomery Blair desired the post of Chief Justice even more fervently than Stanton. He had gracefully acceded to Lincoln's request for his resig-nation, but the high appointment would certainly compensate for the rem-nant wound. His distinguished career as a lawyer had been defined by his eloquent representation of the slave Dred Scott in the case that had forever cast a blight on Justice Taney's name. Monty had powerful backers, includ-ing Seward, Weed, and Welles, all of whom vastly preferred him to Chase. Welles told Lincoln that, of all the candidates, Blair "best conformed to these requirements—that the President knew the man, his ability, his truth-fulness, honesty and courage." Lincoln "expressed his concurrence . . . and spoke kindly and complimentarily of Mr. Blair but did not in any way com-mit himself, nor did I expect or suppose he would."

Lincoln understood that the appointment mattered greatly, not only to Monty but to his father, who had taken his son's forced resignation as a personal blow. A week after Taney died, the elder Blair wrote Lincoln an impassioned plea: "I beg you to indulge me with a little conference with you on paper about a thing which as involving a good deal of egotism, I am ashamed to talk about face to face." He went on to describe the Blairs' enduring loyalty to both the Union and the president. "Now I come," he pressed, "to what I hope you will consider another & higher opportunity of serving you & the Republic by carrying your political principles & the support of your policy expressed in relation to the reconstruction of the Union & the support of the freedman's proclamation, into the Supreme Court. I think Montgomery's unswerving support of your administration in all its aspects coupled with his unfaltering attachment to you personally fits him to be your representative man at the head of that Bench."

When Mary Lincoln warned Old Man Blair that "Chase and his friends are besieging my Husband for the Chief-Justiceship," Blair discarded his embarrassment and requested a personal interview. Lincoln listened graciously as Monty's father suggested that his son "had been tried as a Judge and not found wanting, that his practice in the West had made him conversant with our land law, Spanish law, as well as the common and civil law in which his university studies had grounded him, that his practice in the Supreme Court brought him into the circle of commercial and constitutional questions. That, besides on political issues he sustained him [the President] in every thing," and "when Chase and every other member of [the] Cabinet declined to make war for Sumter, Montgomery stood by him."

Lincoln agreed that Monty would admirably acquit himself as Chief Justice, but he was also aware that the nomination would produce a storm of criticism from his many enemies in the Congress. He had no desire to provoke unnecessary animosity among the radicals, who probably held sufficient power to deny confirmation. Nor did Lincoln trust where Monty Blair's conservative philosophy would lead on issues surrounding Reconstruction and the integration of the country's new black citizens.

The same objections most likely applied to Edward Bates. Believing the post would be "a crowning and retiring honor," Bates had "personally solicited" Lincoln to consider his name. "If not overborne by others," Lincoln told Bates, he would happily consider him for the post, but "Chase was turning every stone, to get it, and several others were urged, from different quarters." Hearing this, Bates declared himself "happy in the feeling that the failure to get the place, will be no painful disappointment for my mind is made up to private life."

In the end, Lincoln returned to his first impulse upon learning of Roger Taney's illness—Salmon P. Chase. "Of Mr. Chase's ability and of his soundness on the general issues of the war there is, of course, no question," he told Chase's friend Henry Wilson. "I have only one doubt about his appointment. He is a man of unbounded ambition, and has been working all his life to become President. That he can never be; and I fear that if I make him chief-justice he will simply become more restless and uneasy and neglect the place in his strife and intrigue to make himself President. If I were sure that he would go on the bench and give up his aspirations and do nothing but make himself a great judge, I would not hesitate a moment." He made a similar comment when Schuyler Colfax gave his word that Chase "would dedicate the remainder of his life to the Bench."

When supporters of other candidates reminded the president of Chase's myriad intrigues against him, Lincoln responded, "Now, I know meaner things about Governor Chase than any of those men can tell me," but "we have stood together in the time of trial, and I should despise myself if I allowed personal differences to affect my judgment of his fitness for the office."

Chase remained in Ohio throughout this tumult, confident that the nomination would be his. Oblivious to Stanton's own hopes, he told the war secretary two days after Taney's death that "within the last three or four months I have been assured that it was the Presidents intention, to offer the place to me in case of a vacancy. I think I should accept it if offered: for I am weary of political life & work." However, when weeks passed with no word from the president, Chase anxiously decided to come to Washington. Fessenden and Sumner assured him that the appointment would be made as soon as the elections were over, but Lincoln waited until December 6 to announce his choice.

That morning, Chase's friend John Alley of Massachusetts had called on the president. "I have something to tell you that will make you happy," Lincoln announced. "I have just sent Mr. Chase word that he is to be appointed Chief-Justice, and you are the first man I have told of it." Alley enthusiastically replied, "Mr. President, this is an exhibition of magnanimity and patriotism that could hardly be expected of any one. After what he has said against your administration, which has undoubtedly been reported to you, it was hardly to be expected that you would bestow the most important office within your gift on such a man."

"To have done otherwise I should have been recreant to my convictions of duty to the Republican party and to the country," Lincoln answered. "As to his talk about me, I do not mind that. Chase is, on the whole, a pretty good fellow and a very able man. His only trouble is that he has 'the White House fever' a little too bad, but I hope this may cure him and that he will be satisfied."

Lincoln later told Senator Chandler that personally he "would rather have swallowed his buckhorn chair than to have nominated Chase," but the decision was right for the country. "Probably no other man than Lincoln," Nicolay wrote to Therena, "would have had, in this age of the world, the degree of magnanimity to thus forgive and exalt a rival who had so deeply and so unjustifiably intrigued against him. It is however only another most marked illustration of the greatness of the President."

Chase got the official word from Kate when he arrived home that night. He immediately sat down to write the president. "I cannot sleep before I thank [you] for this mark of your confidence. . . . Be assured that I prize your confidence & good will more than nomination or office."

On December 15, the Supreme Court was "overflowing with an immense throng of dignitaries of various degrees, ladies, congressmen, foreign ministers, and others who wished to view the simple but impressive ceremony of swearing in the chief judicial officer of the republic." Kate Sprague and her sister, Nettie, were there, "gorgeously dressed," according to Noah Brooks. Secretary Seward was also present, along with Nathaniel Banks, Ben Wade, Reverdy Johnson, and Charles Sumner, whose "handsome features plainly showed his inward glow of gratification." At the usher's solemn announcement, everyone stood as the robed justices entered the room. The senior justice, James W. Wayne, administered the oath, which Chase "read in a clear but tremulous voice." When he finished, Chase "lifted his right hand, looked upward to the beautiful dome of the court-room, and with deep feeling added, 'So help me God.' "

"I hope the President may have no occasion to regret his selection," Gideon Welles confided in his diary, sharing Lincoln's apprehension that Chase would "use the place for political advancement and thereby endanger confidence in the court." Still, Lincoln believed the risk worth taking. He trusted that Chase would help secure the rights of the black man, for which he had fought throughout his career, a belief that outweighed concerns about Chase's restless temperament.

Chase quickly justified Lincoln's confidence in this regard. Within hours of Chase's accession to the Court, John Rock, a black lawyer from Massachusetts, wrote a hopeful letter to Charles Sumner. Rock had been seeking to practice before the Supreme Court for over a year, but his efforts had been denied on the basis of his race. "We now have a great and good man for our Chief Justice, and with him I think my color will not be a bar to my admission," he wrote. Sumner immediately contacted Chase, who was delighted to pursue the cause of opening the Court to its first black barrister.

Six weeks later, Sumner stood before the Supreme Court as Rock's sponsor: "May it please the Court, I move that John S. Rock, a member of the Supreme Court of the State of Massachusetts, be admitted to practice as a member of this Court." Then, with Chase's assent, Rock stepped forward for the oath that would allow him to practice before the highest court in the land. "This event," *Harper's Weekly* observed, represented an "extraordinary reversal" of the decision in the *Dred Scott* case. Rock's admission, *Harper's* predicted, would "be regarded by the future historian as a remarkable indication of the revolution which is going on in the sentiment of a great people."

• • •

MARY LINCOLN TOOK special satisfaction in her husband's reelection. The White House "has been quite a *Mecca* of late," she wrote to her friend Mercy Conkling. "We are surrounded, at all times, by a great deal of company," and "it has been gratifying, from all quarters, to receive so many kind & congratulatory letters, so fraught, with good feeling."

Mary's pleasure in her husband's victory reflected more than simple pride. During the fall election, she had been terrified that his defeat might signal merchants in New York and Philadelphia—to whom she still owed substantial sums—to call in her debt. "I owe altogether about twenty-seven thousand dollars," she confided in Elizabeth Keckley. "Mr. Lincoln has but little idea of the expense of a woman's wardrobe. He glances at my rich dresses, and is happy in the belief that the few hundred dollars that I obtain from him supply all my wants. I must dress in costly materials. The people scrutinize every article that I wear with critical curiosity. The very fact of having grown up in the West, subjects me to more searching observation. To keep up appearances, I must have money—more than Mr. Lincoln can spare for me. He is too honest to make a penny outside of his salary; consequently I had, and still have, no alternative but to run in debt."

Although padded bills and attempts to trade upon her White House influence exposed her to serious scandal, Mary could not curtail her excessive spending habits. "Here is the carriage of Mrs Lincoln before a dry goods Store," Judge Taft noted four weeks after the election, "her footman has gone into the Store. The Clerk is just going out to the carriage (where Mrs L is waiting) with some pieces of goods for her to choose from. I should rather think that she would have a better chance at the goods if she was to go into the Store but then she *might* get jostled and gazed at and that too would be doing just as the common people do. The footman holds the carriage door open. The driver sits on the box and hold[s] the horses. Mrs L. thumbs the goods and asks a great many questions."

A week later, Mary journeyed to Philadelphia for another shopping trip. Not long afterward, she visited New York, where she purchased a new dress, expensive furs, and "300 pairs of kid gloves." When the items she purchased did not measure up to her expectations, her manic sprees quickly gave way to depression and anger. "I can neither wear, or settle with you, for my bonnet without different inside flowers," she threatened a milliner in New York. "I cannot retain or wear the bonnet, as it is—I am certainly taught a lesson, by your acting thus."

Mary's self-conscious attention to the details of her bonnet was not entirely misplaced. Newspaper reports of her evening receptions invariably commented on every piece of her apparel. At the first White House levee of the new winter season, the *National Republican* noted that she "was charmingly and elegantly attired . . . dressed in a rich, plain white silk, with heavy black lace flounce and black lace shawl, and upon her head was a coronet of white and purple flowers—a most tasteful decoration." Her outfit at a state dinner a few weeks later drew equal praise. "Mrs. Lincoln was tastefully attired in a heavy black and white spotted silk, elegantly trimmed with black lace, her headdress and rich set of jewelry harmonizing throughout."

The new season brought new rules of etiquette for visitors at public receptions at the White House: "Overcoats, hats, caps, bonnets, shawls, cloaks &c. should be deposited in the several ante-rooms provided for that purpose, and where they will be in charge of proper persons for safe-keeping." The new arrangement pleased the Washington social elite, who began returning to the open receptions they had shunned. A reporter for the *National Republican* noted on the part of all the guests "a more general observance of the proprieties of dress and demeanor," which seemed to suggest "increasing respect for the President, his family and themselves."

Mary also took great pride in her informal Blue Room receptions, which continued to draw distinguished visitors. She was particularly gratified by the regular appearance of Charles Sumner. The handsome senator, though in his early fifties, was considered one of the most eligible bachelors in Washington. "*I* was pleased," Mary later recalled, "knowing he visited no other lady—His time was so immersed in his business—and that cold & haughty looking man to the world—would insist upon my telling him all the news, & we would have such frequent and delightful conversations & often late in the evening—My darling husband would join us & they would laugh together, like *two* school boys."

However, the prestige and pleasure of her second term as first lady could not assuage Mary's lingering grief over the loss of Willie. Over two years after her son's death, it was still difficult for her to enter the library, which had been one of his favorite rooms. Her "darling Boy!"—"the idolized child, of the household"—was never far from her mind. "I have sometimes feared," she admitted to a friend, "that the *deep waters*, through which we have passed would overwhelm me." In the absence of her gentle son, "*The World*, has lost so much, of its charm. My position, requires my presence, where my heart is *so far* from being."

After Willie's death, Mary had been determined not to allow her oldest son, Robert, to risk his life in the army. But after his graduation from Harvard, she could no longer detain him. In January 1865, Lincoln wrote to General Grant: "Please read and answer this letter as though I was not President, but only a friend. My son, now in his twenty second year, having graduated at Harvard, wishes to see something of the war before it ends. I do not wish to put him in the ranks, nor yet to give him a commission, to which those who have already served long, are better entitled, and better qualified to hold. Could he, without embarrassment to you, or detriment to the service, go into your Military family with some nominal rank, I, and not the public, furnishing his necessary means? If no, say so without the least hesitation, because I am as anxious, and as deeply interested, that you shall not be encumbered."

Grant replied two days later. "I will be most happy to have him in my Military family," he wrote. He suggested that the rank of captain would be most appropriate. So Robert's wish to join the army was granted. Stationed at Grant's headquarters, Robert "soon became exceedingly popular," Horace Porter recalled. "He was always ready to perform his share of hard work, and never expected to be treated differently from any other officer on account of his being the son of the Chief Executive of the nation."

• • •

IN THE FIRST DAYS OF 1865, Gideon Welles was preoccupied with thoughts of "passing time and accumulating years." His wistful contemplation was shared by Salmon Chase. On the first of January, the Chief Justice's last surviving sister, Helen, was buried in Ohio. Of ten siblings, only Chase and his brother Edward, both in their mid-fifties, remained alive. Chase wrote to Lincoln explaining that the death of his sister precluded his attendance at the traditional New Year's reception. "Without your note of to-day," Lincoln promptly replied, "I should have felt assured that some sufficient reason had detained you. Allow me to condole with you in the sad bereavement."

One of the guests at the White House reception noted "a great contrast between this 'New Years' and any previous one for the past three years, four years ago there was a solemn stillness, a burthensome weight hanging upon the minds of all, a fearful foreboding of Evil, a dread of the future. It was but little better *three* years or *two* years ago. . . . Even one year ago we could scarcely see any light. Today all are in good spirits."

The stunning success of Sherman's March to the Sea, which had ended with the capture of Savannah just prior to Christmas, was largely responsible for the ebullience that prevailed in Washington. "Our joy was irrepressible," recalled Assistant Treasury Secretary Hugh McCulloch, "because it was an assurance that the days of the Confederacy were numbered." The president had initially been "*anxious*, if not fearful," about Sherman's plan to abandon his supply lines and trust that his men could forage for necessary food and provisions along the way. The day after Christmas, Lincoln recalled his skepticism in a gracious note to Sherman: "The honor is all yours; for I believe none of us went farther than to acquiesce."

Sherman's March to the Sea proved devastating to Southern property and countryside. Frank Blair, whose troops played a major role in the historic march, rationalized the indiscriminate destruction in a letter to his father: "We have destroyed nearly four hundred miles of Railroad, severing the western from the Eastern part of the Confederacy, and we have burned millions of dollars worth of cotton which is the only thing that enables them to maintain credit abroad & to purchase arms & munitions of war & we have actually 'gobbled' up enough provisions to have fed Lee's army for six months." Though the military gains justified the march in the minds of Union soldiers, the memory of its terrible impact on civilian lives haunts the South to this day.

In his congratulatory note to Sherman, Lincoln also paid tribute to General George Thomas, who had defeated Hood's forces at Nashville ten days earlier. News of the two victories, Lincoln wrote, brought "those who sat in darkness, to see a great light." The telegram announcing Thomas's victory had been carried to Stanton in the middle of the night. "Hurrah," Stanton cried as he hurriedly dressed and rushed to the White House with Thomas Eckert, the chief of the telegraph office. Eckert would long remember the delight on Lincoln's face when he heard the news. Standing at the top of the stairs "in his night-dress, with a lighted candle in his hand," the tall president created an arresting tableau.

The fall of Fort Fisher, which guarded the port of Wilmington, North Carolina, followed in mid-January. Headlines trumpeted the "Combined Work of the Army and Navy!," which had gained the capture of the fort and its seventy-two large-caliber guns. "This glorious work," hailed the *National Republican*, "closes the port of Wilmington, and shuts off supplies to the rebels from abroad." Gideon Welles was ecstatic, recording that at the cabinet meeting that morning, "there was a very pleasant feeling. Seward thought there was little now for the Navy to do. . . . The President was happy." The defeat was shattering to Southern logistics and morale. Confederate vice president Alexander Stephens considered the fall of Fort Fisher "one of the greatest disasters which had befallen our Cause from the beginning of the war—not excepting the loss of Vicksburg or Atlanta." With nearly every other port closed by the naval blockade, the closing of Wilmington signaled "the complete shutting out of the Confederate States from all intercourse by sea with Foreign Countries," bringing an end to the exchange of cotton for vitally needed munitions and supplies.

Stanton was in Savannah, Georgia, for a conference with Sherman when "the rebel flag of Fort Fisher was delivered to [him]." Eager to see the battleground, he journeyed to North Carolina, where he spent the night with General Rufus Saxton and his wife. When he arrived, he warned his hosts that "fatigue would compel him to retire early," but, relaxing before the fire, surrounded by a collection of books, he revived. "Ah, here are old friends," he said, picking up a volume of Macauley's poetry from the table. He asked Mrs. Saxton to read "Horatius at the Bridge," which he followed with "The Battle of Ivry." Midnight found him still seated by the fire, "repeating snatches of poetry." During his stay, Mrs. Saxton noted, "the Titan War Secretary was replaced by the genial companion, the man of letters, the lover of nature—the *real* Stanton." For a few hours, Stanton allowed himself the distraction and the levity he had often decried in Lincoln.

Stanton had journeyed south to confer with Sherman, concerned by reports of the general's hostile behavior toward the black refugees who were arriving by the thousands into his lines. It was said that Sherman opposed their employment as soldiers, drove them from his camp even when they were starving, and manifested toward them "an almost *criminal* dislike." Sherman countered that the movement of his military columns was hindered "by the crowds of helpless negroes that flock after our armies . . . clogging my roads, and eating up our substance." Military success, he felt, had to take precedence over treatment of the Negroes.

In his conversations with Stanton, however, Sherman agreed to issue "Special Field Orders, No. 15," a temporary plan to allocate "a plot of not more than forty acres of tillable ground" to help settle the tide of freed slaves along the coast of Georgia and on the neighboring islands. Stanton returned home feeling more at ease about the situation. In the weeks that followed, Congress followed up by creating a Freedmen's Bureau with authority to distribute lands and provide assistance to displaced refugees throughout the South.

• • •

NOTHING ON THE HOME FRONT in January engaged Lincoln with greater urgency than the passage of the Thirteenth Amendment, abolishing slavery. He had long feared that his Emancipation Proclamation would be discarded once the war came to an end. "A question might be raised whether the proclamation was legally valid," he said. "It might be added that it only aided those who came into our lines . . . or that it would have no effect upon the children of the slaves born hereafter." Passage of a constitutional amendment eradicating slavery once and for all would be "a King's cure for all the evils."

The previous spring, the Thirteenth Amendment had passed in the Senate by two thirds but failed to garner the necessary two-thirds vote in the House, where Republicans had voted aye and Democrats nay along nearly unanimous party lines. In his annual message in December, Lincoln had urged Congress to reconsider the measure. He acknowledged that he was asking the same body to debate the same question, but he hoped the intervening election had altered the situation. Republican gains in November ensured that if he called a special session after March 4, the amendment would pass. Since it was "only a question of *time*," how much better it would be if this Congress could complete the job, if Democrats as well as Republicans could be brought to support its passage in a show of bipartisan unity.

Congressman James M. Ashley of Ohio reintroduced the measure into the House on January 6, 1865. Lincoln set to work at once to sway the votes of moderate Democrats and border-state Unionists. He invited individual House members to his office, dealing gracefully and effectively with each one. "I have sent for you as an old whig friend," he told Missouri's James Rollins, "that I might make an appeal to you to vote for this amendment. It is going to be very close, a few votes one way or the other will decide it." He emphasized the importance of sending a signal to the South that the border states could no longer be relied upon to uphold slavery. This would "bring the war," he predicted, "rapidly to a close." When Rollins agreed to support the amendment, Lincoln jumped from his chair and grasped the congressman's hands, expressing his profound gratitude. The two old Whigs then discussed the leanings of the various members of the Missouri delegation, determining which members might be persuaded. "Tell them of my anxiety to have the measure pass," Lincoln urged, "and let me know the prospect of the border state vote."

He assigned two of his allies in the House to deliver the votes of two wavering members. When they asked how to proceed, he said, "I am President of the United States, clothed with great power. The abolition of slavery by constitutional provision settles the fate, for all coming time, not only of the millions now in bondage, but of unborn millions to come—a measure of such importance that *those two votes must be procured*. I leave it to you to determine how it shall be done; but remember that I am President of the United States, clothed with immense power, and I expect you to procure those votes." It was clear to his emissaries that his powers extended to plum assignments, pardons, campaign contributions, and government jobs for relatives and friends of faithful members. Brooklyn Democrat Moses F. Odell agreed to change his vote; when the session ended, he was given the lucrative post of navy agent in New York. Elizabeth Blair noted that her father had successfully joined in the lobbying effort, persuading several members.

Ashley learned that the Camden & Amboy Railroad could secure the vote of two New Jersey Democrats if Senator Sumner could be convinced to postpone a bill he had introduced to end the monopoly the railroad enjoyed. Unable to move Sumner, Ashley asked Lincoln to intervene. Lincoln regretfully replied that he could "do nothing with Mr. Sumner in these matters," and feared if he tried, Sumner "would be all the more resolute."

As the vote neared, pressure intensified. The leader of the opposition was McClellan's running mate, Democrat George Pendleton of Ohio. "Though he had been defeated in the election," observed Senator James Blaine, "he returned to the House with increased prestige among his own political associates." Democrats who considered changing their vote were made to understand that dire consequences would follow if they failed to maintain the party line on an issue compromising the sanctity of states' rights and effecting a fundamental shift in the Constitution.

Both sides knew that the outcome would be decided by the thinnest of margins. "We are like whalers," Lincoln observed, "who have been long on a chase: we have at last got the harpoon into the monster, but we must now look how we steer, or with one 'flop' of his tail he will send us all into eternity." On the morning of the scheduled vote, Ashley feared that the entire effort would collapse. Rumors circulated that Confederate Peace Commissioners were on the way to Washington or had already arrived in the capital. "If it is true," Ashley urgently wrote to the president, "I fear we shall [lose] the bill." The Democratic leadership would prevail upon wavering party members, arguing that the amendment would lead the commissioners to abort the peace talks. "Please authorize me to contradict it, if not true," Ashley entreated.

"So far as I know," Lincoln promptly replied, "there are no peace Commissioners in the City, or likely to be in it." Ashley later learned that Lincoln, in fact, had been informed that three Peace Commissioners were en route to Fort Monroe, but he could honestly, if insincerely, claim that no commissioners were *in* the capital city. Without this cunning evasion, Ashley believed, "the proposed amendment would have failed."

As the debate opened, Ashley acknowledged that "never before, and certain I am that never again, will I be seized with so strong a desire to give utterance to the thoughts and emotions which throbbed my heart and brain." The amendment's passage would signal "the complete triumph of a cause, which at the beginning of my political life I had not hoped to live long enough to see."

Ashley recalled, "Every available foot of space, both in the galleries and on the floor of the House, was crowded at an early hour, and many hundred could not get within hearing." Chief Justice Chase and the members of the Supreme Court were present, along with Seward, Fessenden, and

Dennison representing the cabinet. Dozens of senators had come to witness the historic debate, as had members of most foreign ministries.

Ashley wisely decided to yield his time to the small band of Democrats who would support the amendment but needed to justify their shift to constituents. He called first on Archibald McAllister. The Pennsylvania congressman explained that he had changed his mind when he saw that the only way to achieve peace was to destroy "the corner-stone of the Southern Confederacy." His remarks brought forth applause from the galleries, as did those of his colleague Alexander Coffroth. "If by my action to-day I dig my political grave," the congressman from Somerset County proclaimed, "I will descend into it without a murmur."

After every Democrat who wanted to speak had been heard, the voting began. "Hundreds of tally sheets had been distributed on the floor and in the galleries," Ashley recorded. It appeared at first that the amendment had fallen two or three votes short of the requisite two-thirds margin. The floor was in tumult when Speaker Colfax stood to announce the final tally. His voice shaking, he said, "On the passage of the Joint Resolution to amend the Constitution of the United States the ayes have 119, the noes 56. The constitutional majority of two thirds having voted in the affirmative, the Joint Resolution has passed." Without the five Democrats who had changed their votes, the amendment would have lost.

"For a moment there was a pause of utter silence," Noah Brooks reported, "as if the voices of the dense mass of spectators were choked by strong emotion. Then there was an explosion, a storm of cheers, the like of which probably no Congress of the United States ever heard before."

"Before the members left their seats," Congressman Arnold recalled, "the roar of artillery from Capitol Hill announced to the people of Washington that the amendment had passed." Ashley brought to the War Department a list of all those who had voted in favor. Stanton ordered three additional batteries to "fire one hundred guns with their heaviest charges" while he slowly read each name aloud, proclaiming, "History will embalm them in great honor."

Lincoln's friends raced to the White House to share the news. "The passage of the resolution," recalled Arnold, "filled his heart with joy. He saw in it the complete consummation of his own great work, the emancipation proclamation." The following evening, Lincoln spoke to celebrants gathered at the White House. "The occasion was one of congratulation to the country and to the whole world," he said. "But there is a task yet before us—to go forward and consummate by the votes of the States that which Congress so nobly began." The audience responded with cheers. "They will do it" was the confident cry. And, indeed, the legislatures in twenty states acted almost immediately. Before the year 1865 was out, the requisite three quarters had spoken putting a dramatic end to the slavery issue that had disturbed the nation's tranquillity from its earliest days.

No praise must have been more welcome to Lincoln than that of his old critic, the fiery abolitionist William Lloyd Garrison. "And to whom is the country more immediately indebted for this vital and saving amendment of the Constitution than, perhaps, to any other man?" Garrison asked a cheering crowd at the Boston Music Hall. "I believe I may confidently answer—to the humble railsplitter of Illinois—to the Presidential chain-breaker for millions of the oppressed—to Abraham Lincoln!"

• • •

THE STORY OF the Peace Commissioners, whose presence had almost derailed the vote on the new amendment, had begun with Francis Preston Blair. Lincoln's reelection had convinced the old editor that another attempt at peace might be successful. Lincoln remained unconvinced that talks at this juncture would be effective, but Blair was so anxious to try that Lincoln gave him a pass for Richmond. It was understood, however, that he was proceeding on his own, without authority to speak for the president.

After leaving Lincoln, Blair wrote two letters to Jefferson Davis. The first, designed for public consumption, requested simply "the privilege of visiting Richmond" to inquire about the papers Blair had lost when General Early's troops took possession of his Silver Spring house. The second revealed that his "main purpose" in coming was to discuss "the state of the affairs of our country." He promised to "unbosom [his] heart frankly & without reserve," hopeful that some good might result.

On January 11, 1865, the seventy-three-year-old Blair arrived in Richmond, where he was greeted warmly by numerous old friends. Jefferson Davis's wife, Varina, "threw her arms around him" and said, "Oh you Rascal, I am overjoyed to see you." Seated with President Davis in the library of the Confederate White House, Blair conceded his proposal "might be the dreams of an old man," but he was confident of Davis's "practical good sense" and "utmost frankness." He reminded Davis of his own deep attachment to the South. "Every drop" of his own blood and his children's sprang from "a Southern source." Davis responded with equal warmth, assuring Blair that he "would never forget" the many "kindnesses" exhibited by the Blairs toward the Davis family, and that "even when dying they would be remembered in his prayers."

Blair presented his proposal, which would essentially postpone the war between the North and the South while the armies allied against the

French, who had invaded Mexico and installed a puppet regime in viola- tion of the Monroe Doctrine. Davis agreed that nothing would better heal the raw emotions on both sides "than to see the arms of our countrymen from the North and the South united in a war upon a Foreign Power." The specifics of this improbable and unauthorized plan, reminiscent of Seward's proposal four years earlier, were not discussed, though Davis agreed to send Peace Commissioners to Washington "with a view to se- cure peace to the two Countries."

Though tired from his arduous journey back to Washington by carriage, train, and steamer, Blair rushed to the White House and deliv- ered the Davis letter to the president. Lincoln consulted Stanton, who pointedly noted: "There are not two countries . . . and there never will be two countries. Tell Davis that if you treat for peace, it will be for this one country; negotiations on any other basis are impossible." Lincoln im- mediately agreed. "You may say to him," Lincoln directed Blair, "that I have constantly been, am now, and shall continue, ready to receive any agent . . . with the view of securing peace to the people of our one com- mon country."

Blair returned straightaway to Richmond with Lincoln's response, and Davis called a cabinet meeting at his home to discuss his next move. His advisers recognized the irreconcilable conflict between the concepts of "two countries" and "one common country," but the insistent clamor for peace had convinced Davis to send three commissioners to Fort Monroe—Vice President Alexander Stephens, former United States sena- tor R. M. T. Hunter, and former Supreme Court Justice John A. Camp- bell.

On Sunday, January 29, a flag of truce flown at Petersburg announced the arrival of the commissioners. "By common consent all picket firing was suspended," the *New York Herald* reported, "and the lines of both armies presented the appearance of a gala day." Viewed as "harbingers of peace," the three gentlemen elicited "prolonged and enthusiastic" applause from both sides, revealing the depth of the soldiers' desire to end the fighting and return to their families and homes. One reporter noted that when rival songs were played by Southern and Northern bands—"Dixie" and "Yan- kee Doodle Dandy"—each side responded only to its own patriotic air, "but when the band struck up 'Home Sweet Home,' the opposing camps forgot their hostility, and united in vociferous tribute to the common sen- timent."

A Union colonel escorted the commissioners to Grant's headquarters at City Point. "It was night when we arrived," Alexander Stephens later recalled. "There was nothing in [Grant's] appearance or surroundings which indicated his official rank. There were neither guards nor aids about him. . . . I was instantly struck with the great simplicity and perfect naturalness of his manners, and the entire absence of everything like affectation, show, or even the usual military air or *mien* of men in his position. He was plainly attired, sitting in a log-cabin, busily writing on a small table, by a Kerosene lamp. . . . His conversation was easy and fluent, without the least effort or restraint." After talking for a while, Grant escorted them to the steamship *Mary Martin*, where he had arranged "comfortable quarters" for his three distinguished visitors. Though Grant was not authorized to discuss the peace mission itself, Stephens got the impression that he was very anxious for "the return of peace and harmony throughout the country."

Meanwhile, at Lincoln's request, Seward headed south to meet with the commissioners. "You will make known to them that three things are indispensable," Lincoln wrote: "The restoration of the national authority. . . . No receding, by the Executive of the United States on the Slavery question. . . . No cessation of hostilities short of an end of the war." If these three conditions were accepted, he was to tell them that all other propositions would be met with "a spirit of sincere liberality." After riding the train to Annapolis, Seward boarded Grant's flagship, the *River Queen*, and proceeded to Fort Monroe.

Before Seward could interview the commissioners, word reached Lincoln that President Davis had instructed them to negotiate peace for *two* countries. The president felt he had no choice but to recall Seward, until an urgent telegram from Grant changed his mind. Grant was "convinced," he had written to Stanton, after talking with the three men "that their intentions are good," and he believed that "their going back without any expression from any one in authority will have a bad influence." Given the complexity of the situation, Grant wished that the president could meet with them personally. "Induced by a despatch of Gen. Grant," Lincoln promptly telegraphed Seward and Grant, "Say to the gentlemen I will meet them personally at Fortress-Monroe, as soon as I can get there."

Accompanied by a single valet and an overnight bag, the president left Washington two hours later on a train headed to Annapolis. There, the steamer *Thomas Collyer*, "supposed to be the fastest in the world," stood ready to take him to Fort Monroe. "Upon getting out of the bay," noted a *Herald* correspondent who had boarded the vessel before the president arrived, "we encountered large fields of ice, through which we passed slowly." The steamer finally arrived at Fort Monroe a little past ten that evening, and Lincoln joined Seward on the *River Queen*.

The four-hour meeting, known as the Hampton Roads Conference, took place the next day in the saloon of the *River Queen*, which had been lashed to the *Mary Martin* the night before and "gaily decked out with a superabundance of streamers and flags." After everyone was introduced, Stephens opened the conversation with warm memories of his days as Lincoln's congressional colleague nearly two decades earlier. The president "responded in a cheerful and cordial manner," Stephens recalled, "as if the remembrance of those times . . . had awakened in him a train of agreeable reflections." They talked for several minutes of old acquaintances before Stephens asked, "Well, Mr. President, is there no way of putting an end to the present trouble, and bringing about a restoration of the general good feeling and harmony *then* existing between the different States and Sections of the country?"

The conversation that followed, Seward later wrote, "was altogether informal. There was no attendance of secretaries, clerks, or other witnesses. Nothing was written or read." The only other person who entered the room was the "steward, who came in occasionally to see if anything was wanted, and to bring in water, cigars, and other refreshments."

In reply to the question posed by Stephens, Lincoln attested that "there was but one way that he knew of, and that was, for those who were resisting the laws of the Union to cease that resistance." Stephens countered with the hope for a temporary solution that would integrate their respective armies to fight the French "until the passions on both sides might cool."

"I suppose you refer to something Mr. Blair has said," Lincoln replied. "Now it is proper to state at the beginning, that whatever he said was of his own accord. . . . The restoration of the Union is a *sine qua non* with me." There could be no substantive talk of an armistice or postponement until "the resistance ceased and the National Authority was recognized." Attempting to circumvent this declaration, Hunter recalled that Charles I of England had entered repeatedly into arrangements with his adversaries despite ongoing hostilities. "I do not profess to be posted in history," Lincoln answered. "On all such matters I will turn you over to Seward. All I distinctly recollect about the case of Charles I, is, that he lost his head in the end."

Judge Campbell then turned the conversation to the question of "how restoration was to take place, supposing that the Confederate States were consenting to it." This opened a discussion of slavery, which Seward addressed by reciting verbatim from Lincoln's annual address in which he had said that he would not "attempt to retract or modify the Emancipation Proclamation, nor . . . return to slavery any person who is free by the terms of that Proclamation." Moreover, Seward said, he felt obliged to inform the commissioners that Congress had just passed a constitutional amendment banning slavery throughout the entire United States.

They had clearly reached an impasse, but the conversation continued in an amicable tone. Lincoln let the commissioners know that "he would be willing to be taxed to remunerate the Southern people for their slaves." He was fairly confident "the people of the North" would sustain him with "an appropriation as high as Four Hundred Millions of Dollars for this purpose." On the question of some sort of postponement of hostilities prior to the end of the war, Lincoln was immovable. The conference drew to a close without agreement on any issue.

Before any outcome was made public, the radicals had worked themselves into "a fury of rage," certain that the president "was about to give up the political fruits which had been already gathered from the long and exhausting military struggle." Fearing Lincoln would turn his back on emancipation, Thaddeus Stevens excoriated him on the floor of the House. In the Senate, "the leading members of the Committee on the Conduct of the War" roundly castigated the very idea of the conference, predicting that "we shall be sold out, and that the Peace we shall obtain, if any we do, will dishonor us." Both branches passed a resolution calling for a full report on the proceedings. Even Stanton worried that the president's kindheartedness "might lead him to make some admission which the astute Southerners would wilfully misconstrue and twist to serve their purpose."

Lincoln's report on the conference, complete with the telegrams and documents preceding it, was "read amidst a breathless silence in the hall, every member being in his seat. A low gush of satisfaction broke out when the phrase 'one common country' was read in the Blair letter, and an involuntary burst followed the annunciation of the three conditions of peace, given to Seward." Noah Brooks observed that "as the reading of the message and documents went on, the change which took place in the moral atmosphere of the hall of the House was obvious. The appearance of grave intentness passed away, and members smilingly exchanged glances as they began to appreciate Lincoln's sagacious plan for unmasking the craftiness of the rebel leaders." When the presentation was done, "there was an instant and irrepressible storm of applause . . . it was like a burst of refreshing rain after a long and heartbreaking drought." Representatives vied with one another to praise the president. Even Thaddeus Stevens "paid a high tribute to the sagacity, wisdom, and patriotism of President Lincoln."

"Indeed," *Harper's Weekly* observed, "nothing but the foolish assumption of four years ago, that Mr. Lincoln was unfit for his office," could explain the fatuous predictions that he would "flinch and falter" before the Southern delegates. "If there is any man in the country who comprehends the scope of the war more fully than the President, who is he? . . . We venture to say that there is no man in our history who has shown a more felicitous combination of temperament, conviction, and ability to grapple with a complication like that in which this country is involved than Abraham Lincoln."

Jefferson Davis pragmatically employed the failed conference to incite greater effort on the battlefield, pledging that "he would be willing to yield up everything he had on earth" before acceding to Northern demands. He predicted that before another year had passed, the South would be able to secure peace on its own terms, with separation and slavery intact. "I can have no 'common country' with the Yankees," he announced. "My life is bound up in the Confederacy; and, if any man supposes that, under any circumstances, I can be an agent of reconstruction of the Union, he has mistaken every element of my nature!"

Still, Lincoln did not relinquish hope that he might somehow bring the war to an honorable end before tens of thousands more young men had to die. Following his Hampton Roads suggestion of compensated emancipation, he drafted a proposal that Congress empower him "to pay four hundred millions of dollars" to the Southern states, distributed according to "their respective slave populations." The first half would be paid if "all resistance to the national authority" came to an end by April 1; the second half would be allocated if the Thirteenth Amendment were ratified by July 1. At that point, with the armed rebellion at an end, the Union restored, and slavery eradicated, "all political offences will be pardoned" and "all property, except slaves, liable to confiscation or forfeiture, will be released." Furthermore, "liberality will be recommended to congress upon all points not lying within executive control."

The proposition met with unanimous disapproval from the cabinet, all of whom were present except Seward. "The earnest desire of the President to conciliate and effect peace was manifest," Welles recorded, "but there may be such a thing as so overdoing as to cause a distrust or adverse feeling." Usher believed that the radicals in Congress "would make it the occasion of a violent assault on the President." Stanton had long maintained that it was unnecessary and wasteful to talk about compensation for slaves already freed by the Emancipation Proclamation. Fessenden declared "that the only way to effectually end the war was by force of arms, and that until the war was thus ended no proposition to pay money would come from us."

Lincoln pointed out that the sum he proposed was simply the cost of continuing the war for another one or two hundred days, "to say nothing of the lives lost and property destroyed." Still, the cabinet was adamant. "You are all against me," Lincoln said, his voice filled with sadness. "His heart was so fully enlisted in behalf of such a plan that he would have followed it if only a single member of his Cabinet had supported him," Usher thought. Had Seward been there, Usher mused, "he would probably have approved the measure." Without a trace of support among his colleagues at the table, Lincoln felt compelled to forsake his proposition, which, in any event, as Jefferson Davis had made clear, was unacceptable to the Confederacy. So the war would continue until the South capitulated.

• • •

MEANWHILE, THE WAR FRONT continued to generate good news for the Union. After capturing Savannah, Sherman had headed north to Columbia, reaching the state capital of South Carolina on February 17. Columbia's fall led to the evacuation of Charleston. Stanton ordered "a national salute" fired from "every fort arsenal and army headquarters of the United States, in honor of the restoration of the flag of the Union upon Fort Sumter." In Washington, the *National Republican* noted, "the flash and smoke were visible from the tops of buildings on the avenue, and the thunder of the guns was heard in all parts of the city." That evening, Lincoln was in "cheerful" spirits as he relaxed with Seward, Welles, and General Hooker in his office. "General H. thinks it the brightest day in four years," Welles recorded in his diary.

The following day, however, Browning found Lincoln "more depressed" than he had seen him in the four years of his presidency. His low spirits were probably caused by the pending execution of John Yates Beall, a former Confederate captain who had been tried and found guilty as a spy. In the fall of 1864, when Confederate agents based in Canada were pursuing plots to disrupt the draft and influence the elections, Beall had led a team of raiders in a daring and elaborate scheme to commandeer Union ships in the Great Lakes area, destroy railroad lines, and liberate Confederate prisoners in Ohio. The commander of the army in New York State, General John A. Dix, was unyielding in his belief that Beall must be executed as an example to others.

But Beall came from a prominent Virginia family, and a wide array of supporters petitioned Lincoln for clemency, including Orville Browning, Monty Blair, eight dozen congressmen, and six United States senators. They argued that Beall was acting as a commissioned officer in the Confederate army and should not be treated as "a robber, brigand, and pirate." The case troubled Lincoln greatly, but he felt compelled to support General Dix. "I had to stand firm," he told an acquaintance a few weeks later, "and I even had to turn away his poor sister when she came and begged for his life, and let him be executed, and he was executed, and I can't get the distress out of my mind yet."

The week before his second inaugural on March 4, Lincoln announced that he would "not receive callers (except members of the Cabinet) for any purpose whatever, between the hours of three and seven o'clock p.m." He needed solitude to work on his inaugural speech. "The hopeful condition of the Union cause" had brought thousands of visitors to Washington, the *National Republican* reported. They were anxious not only to partake of the inaugural revelries but to share in the general elation that pervaded the capital. The city was so overcrowded that the parlors of all the leading hotels "were occupied by ladies and gentlemen, sitting up all night because no beds could be found for them."

Frederick Douglass decided to join "in the grand procession of citizens from all parts of the country." Blacks had been excluded from previous inaugural festivities, but with soldiers of both races "mingling their blood," it seemed to him that "it was not too great an assumption for a colored man to offer his congratulations to the President with those of other citizens." The evening before the inauguration, he visited Chase's Sixth Street home. There, he later recalled, he helped Kate "in placing over her honored father's shoulders the new robe then being made in which he was to administer the oath to the reelected President." As he looked at the new Chief Justice, Douglass recollected the "early anti-slavery days" of their first acquaintance. Chase had "welcomed [him] to his home and his table when to do so was a strange thing."

The steady rain on the morning of March 4 did not dampen the spirits of the estimated fifty thousand citizens gathered at the Capitol to witness the inauguration. Invited guests poured into the Senate chamber for the first part of the ceremony, which included a farewell address by the outgoing vice president, Hannibal Hamlin, and the swearing in of Andrew Johnson. Shortly before noon, a stir in the galleries revealed the arrival of the "notables"—generals, governors, the justices of the Supreme Court, the cabinet members, led by Seward, and finally, the president himself, whose chair was positioned in the middle of the front row. Mary Lincoln was seated in the Diplomatic Gallery, surrounded by members of the foreign ministries. "One ambassador was so stiff with gold lace," Noah Brooks observed, "that he could not sit down except with great difficulty and had to unbutton before he could get his feet on the floor."

After Hamlin delivered a graceful farewell address, Andrew Johnson rose to take the oath. His face was "extraordinarily red," his balance precarious. He appeared to observers to be "in a state of manifest intoxication." For twenty long minutes, he spoke incoherently, repeatedly declaring his plebeian background and his pride that such a humble man "could rise from the ranks, under the Constitution, to the proud position of the second place in the gift of the people." Pivoting to face the Supreme Court justices, he reminded them that they also derived their "power from the people." Then he spoke to the members of the cabinet, insisting they, too, were "creature[s]" of the people. He addressed each secretary by name—Mr. Seward, Mr. Stanton, and down the ranks—until he reached Gideon Welles, whose name he could not remember. Seemingly non-plused, he turned to someone near him and loudly inquired, "What's the name of the Secretary of the Navy?" Continuing his tirade, he ignored Hamlin's pointed reminder that "the hour for the inauguration ceremony had passed."

The crowd stirred uneasily, and the men on the dais tried with varying success to conceal their dismay. "Stanton looked like a petrified man," Noah Brooks observed. "All this is in wretched bad taste," Speed whispered to Welles. "The man is certainly deranged." Welles whispered to Stanton that "Johnson is either drunk or crazy." Dennison, the new post-master general, "was red and white by turns," while Justice Samuel Nelson's jaw "dropped clean down in blank horror." Seward and Lincoln alone appeared unruffled. Seward remained as "serene as summer," charitably suggesting to Welles that Johnson's performance was a by-product of "emotion on returning and revisiting the Senate." Lincoln listened in silence, "patiently waiting" for the harangue to end, his eyes shut so that no one could discern his discomfort. "You need not be scared," he said a few days later; Johnson had "made a bad slip" but was not "a drunkard."

When Johnson finished at last, the audience proceeded outside to the east front of the Capitol for the inaugural ceremony. As the president appeared on the platform, observed Noah Brooks, "the sun, which had been obscured all day, burst forth in its unclouded meridian splendor and flooded the spectacle with glory and light." It seemed to many, including the superstitious Lincoln, an auspicious omen, as did the appearance of the newly completed Capitol dome, topped with the statue of Freedom.

If the spirited crowd expected a speech exalting recent Union victories, they were disappointed. In keeping with his lifelong tendency to consider all sides of a troubled situation, Lincoln urged a more sympathetic under-standing of the nation's alienated citizens in the South. There were no un-bridgeable differences, he insisted: "Both read the same Bible, and pray to the same God; and each invokes His aid against the other. It may seem strange that any men should dare to ask a just God's assistance in wringing their bread from the sweat of other men's faces; but let us judge not that we be not judged. The prayers of both could not be answered; that of neither has been answered fully. The Almighty has His own purposes."

In his Springfield speech a decade earlier, Lincoln had maintained that he could not condemn the South for an inability to end slavery when he himself knew of no easy solution. Now the president suggested that God had given "to both North and South, this terrible war" as punishment for their shared sin of slavery. Speaking with "the eloquence of the prophets," he continued, "Fondly do we hope—fervently do we pray—that this mighty scourge of war may speedily pass away. Yet, if God wills that it continue, until all the wealth piled by the bond-man's two hundred and fifty years of unrequited toil shall be sunk, and until every drop of blood drawn with the lash, shall be paid by another drawn with the sword, as was said three thousand years ago, so still it must be said 'the judgments of the Lord, are true and righteous altogether.' "

Drawing upon the rare wisdom of a temperament that consistently displayed uncommon magnanimity toward those who opposed him, he then issued his historic plea to his fellow countrymen: "With malice toward none; with charity for all; with firmness in the right, as God gives us to see the right, let us strive on to finish the work we are in; to bind up the nation's wounds; to care for him who shall have borne the battle, and for his widow, and his orphan—to do all which may achieve and cherish a just, and a lasting peace, among ourselves, and with all nations."

More than any of his other speeches, the Second Inaugural fused spiritual faith with politics. While Lincoln might have questioned the higher force that shaped human ends, "as he became involved in matters of the gravest importance," his friend Leonard Swett observed, "a feeling of religious reverence, and belief in God—his justice and overruling power—increased upon him." If his devotion were determined by his lack of "faith in ceremonials and forms," or by his failure "to observe the Sabath very scrupulously," Swett added, "he would fall far short of the standard." However, if he were judged "by the higher rule of purity of conduct, of honesty of motive, of unyielding fidelity to the right," or by his powerful belief "in the great laws of truth, the rigid discharge of duty, his accountability to God," then he was undoubtedly "full of natural religion," for "he believed in God as much as the most approved Church member."

His address completed, the president turned to Chief Justice Salmon Chase, who administered the oath of office. The crowd cheered loudly, the artillery fired a round of salutes, the band played, and the peaceful ceremony drew to a close.

That evening the gates of the White House were opened for a public reception attended by "the largest crowd that has been here yet," according to Nicolay. The president was reported to be "in excellent spirits" as he tirelessly shook the hands of the more than five thousand people who came to show their respect and affection. "It was a grand ovation of *the People* to

their President," Commissioner French observed, and Mary vowed "to remain till morning, rather than have the door closed on a single visitor."
French estimated that Lincoln shook hands "at the rate of 100 every 4
minutes."

Frederick Douglass would always remember the events of that evening.
"On reaching the door, two policemen stationed there took me rudely by
the arm and ordered me to stand back, for their directions were to admit
no persons of my color." Douglass assured the officers "there must be
some mistake, for no such order could have emanated from President Lincoln; and that if he knew I was at the door he would desire my admission."
His assumption was later confirmed when he discovered there were "no
orders from Mr. Lincoln, or from any one else. They were simply comply-
ing with an old custom." The impasse continued for a few moments, until
Douglass recognized a gentleman going in and asked him to tell the president that he was unable to gain entry. Minutes later, the word came back to
admit Douglass. "I walked into the spacious East Room, amid a scene of elegance such as in this country I had never before witnessed."

Douglass had no difficulty spotting Lincoln, who stood "like a mountain pine high above the others," he recalled, "in his grand simplicity, and
home-like beauty. Recognizing me, even before I reached him, he exclaimed, so that all around could hear him, 'Here comes my friend Douglass.' Taking me by the hand, he said, 'I am glad to see you. I saw you in the
crowd to-day, listening to my inaugural address; how did you like it?' "
Douglass was embarrassed to detain the president in conversation when
there were "thousands waiting to shake hands," but Lincoln insisted. "You
must stop a little, Douglass; there is no man in the country whose opinion
I value more than yours. I want to know what you think of it?"

For a moment these two remarkable men stood together amid the sea
of faces. Lincoln knew that Douglass would speak his mind, just as he always had. "Mr. Lincoln," Douglass said finally, "that was a sacred effort."
Lincoln's face lit up with delight. "I am glad you liked it!" he replied.

A few days later, Lincoln provided his own assessment to Thurlow
Weed, predicting that the address would "wear as well as—perhaps better
than—any thing" he had written, though he did not believe it would be
"immediately popular. Men are not flattered by being shown that there has
been a difference of purpose between the Almighty and them." Just as Lincoln surmised, the speech drew criticism from several quarters. The Democratic *New York World* faulted Lincoln for his "substitution of religion for
statesmanship," while the *Tribune* charged that the stern biblical overtones
would impede any chance for peace.

Many others, however, recognized the historic weight of the address.

"That rail-splitting lawyer is one of the wonders of the day," Charles Francis Adams, Jr., wrote to his father in London. "The inaugural strikes me in its grand simplicity and directness as being for all time the historical keynote of this war." The London *Spectator*, previously critical of Lincoln, agreed with young Adams, judging the address as "by far the noblest which any American President has yet uttered to an American Congress."

Praise for the speech mingled with praise for Lincoln himself. The *Spectator* suggested that it was "divine inspiration, or providence" that brought the Republican Convention in 1860 to choose Lincoln the "village lawyer" over Seward. Congressman Isaac Arnold overheard a conversation between a celebrated minister and an unidentified New York statesman, who one historian suggests was likely William Henry Seward himself. "The President's inaugural is the finest state paper in all history," the minister declared. "Yes," the New Yorker answered, "and as Washington's name grows brighter with time, so it will be with Lincoln's. A century from to-day that inaugural will be read as one of the most sublime utterances ever spoken by man. Washington is the great man of the era of the Revolution. So will Lincoln be of this, but Lincoln will reach the higher position in history."

Perhaps the most surprising contemporaneous evaluation of Lincoln's leadership appeared in the extreme secessionist paper the *Charleston Mercury*. "He has called around him in counsel," the *Mercury* marveled, "the ablest and most earnest men of his country. Where he has lacked in individual ability, learning, experience or statesmanship, he has sought it, and found it.... Force, energy, brains, earnestness, he has collected around him in every department." Were he not a "blackguard" and "an unscrupulous knave in the end," the *Mercury* concluded, "he would undoubtedly command our respect as a ruler.... We turn our eyes to Richmond, and the contrast is appalling, sickening to the heart."

The editors of the *Mercury* would have been even more astonished if they had an inkling of the truth recognized by those closer to Lincoln: his political genius was not simply his ability to gather the best men of the country around him, but to impress upon them his own purpose, perception, and resolution at every juncture. With respect to Lincoln's cabinet, Charles Dana observed, "it was always plain that he was the master and they were the subordinates. They constantly had to yield to his will, and if he ever yielded to them it was because they convinced him that the course they advised was judicious and appropriate."

CHAPTER 26

THE FINAL WEEKS

A s LINCOLN BEGAN his second term, "he was in mind, body, and nerves a very different man," John Hay observed, "from the one who had taken the oath in 1861. He continued always the same kindly, genial, and cordial spirit he had been at first; but the boisterous laughter became less frequent year by year; the eye grew veiled by constant meditation on momentous subjects; the air of reserve and detachment from his surroundings increased."

Four years of relentless strain had touched Lincoln's spirit and his countenance. The aged, wearied face in the life-mask cast by Clark Mills in the spring of 1865 barely resembled the mold Leonard Volk had taken five years earlier. In 1860, noted John Hay, "the large mobile mouth is ready to speak, to shout, or laugh; the bold, curved nose is broad and substantial, with spreading nostrils; it is a face full of life, of energy, of vivid aspiration." The second life-mask, with its lined brow and cavernous cheeks, has "a look as of one on whom sorrow and care had done their worst . . . the whole expression is of unspeakable sadness and all-sufficing strength."

That inner strength had sustained Lincoln all his life. But his four years as president had immeasurably enhanced his self-confidence. Despite the appalling pressures he had faced from his very first day in office, he had never lost faith in himself. In fact, he was the one who had sustained the spirits of those around him time and again, gently guiding his colleagues with good humor, energy, and steady purpose. He had learned from early mistakes, transcended the jealousy of rivals, and his insight into men and events had deepened with each passing year. Though "a tired spot" remained within that no rest or relaxation could restore, he was ready for the arduous tasks of the next four years.

Settling into his daily routine after the inauguration, Lincoln was determined to avoid the thousands of office seekers who again descended "like Egyptian locusts" upon Washington. "The bare thought of going through again what I did the first year here, would *crush* me," he confessed. In the first months of his presidency, he had been disparaged for allowing office seekers to accost him at all hours, consuming his energy and disrupting his concentration. Nicolay and Hay had tried to get him to be more methodical, to close his door to outsiders for longer periods, but at the time he had insisted that "they don't want much; they get but little, and I must see them." Experience had finally taught him that he must set priorities and concentrate on the vital questions of war and Reconstruction confronting his administration. "I think now that I will not remove a single man, except for delinquency," he told New Hampshire senator Clark. "To remove a man is very easy," he commented to another visitor, "but when I go to fill his place, there are *twenty* applicants, and of these I must make *nineteen* enemies."

With two classes of office seekers, however, he was prepared to take a personal interest—artists and disabled veterans. He expressed to Seward his hope that consul positions could be offered to "facilitate artists a little [in] their profession," mentioning in particular a poet and a sculptor he wished to help. To General Scott, who was working with the Sanitary Commission to find government jobs for disabled veterans, Lincoln emphasized that the Commission should "at all times be ready to recognize the paramount claims of the soldiers of the nation, in the disposition of public trusts."

With his cabinet, he was satisfied. The only change he made after the inauguration was to replace treasury secretary William Pitt Fessenden with the banker Hugh McCulloch. When he had assumed the post the previous summer, Fessenden had been assured that he could leave once the finances of the country were in good shape. By the spring of 1865, the Treasury was stable, and when Maine reelected him to the Senate for a term to begin on March 4, Fessenden felt free to resign.

Lincoln was sorry to lose his brilliant, hardworking secretary. Fessenden, too, "parted from the President with regret." During his tenure at the Treasury, his initial critical attitude toward Lincoln had been transformed into warm admiration. "I desire gratefully to acknowledge the kindness and consideration with which you have invariably treated me," he wrote to the president, "and to assure you that in retiring I carry with me great and increased respect for your personal character and for the ability which has marked your administration." Noting that the "prolonged struggle for national life" was finally nearing a successful conclusion, he went on, "no one can claim to have so largely contributed as the chosen chief magistrate of this great people."

Hugh McCulloch was entirely familiar with Treasury operations, having served as comptroller of the currency. When Lincoln first approached him, however, he was nervous about accepting the position. "I should be glad to comply with your wishes," he told Lincoln, "if I did not distrust my ability to do what will be required of the Secretary of the Treasury." Lincoln cheerfully replied, "I will be responsible for that, and so I reckon we will consider the matter settled." McCulloch would remain at his post for four years and was "never sorry" that he had acceded to Lincoln's wishes. The only other cabinet change Lincoln anticipated was in the Department of the Interior, where, in several months' time, he intended to replace Usher with Senator James Harlan of Iowa.

The time had also come for John Nicolay and John Hay to move on. The two secretaries had served Lincoln exceptionally well, introducing a systematic order into the president's vast correspondence and drafting replies to the great majority of letters he received. In their small offices on the second floor of the White House, they had served as gatekeepers, tactfully holding back the crush of senators, congressmen, generals, diplomats, and office seekers endeavoring to gain access to the president. John Hay was particularly adept at keeping the throngs entertained. "No one could be in his presence, even for a few moments," Hay's college roommate recalled, "without falling under the spell which his conversation and companionship invariably cast upon all who came within his influence."

Lincoln had increased their responsibilities with each passing year. In 1864, Nicolay functioned as the "unofficial manager of Lincoln's reelection campaign" and was dispatched as his personal emissary to ease tensions in Missouri and New York. Hay was chosen to accompany Greeley to

Canada, to carry sensitive messages back and forth to Capitol Hill, and to enroll Confederate voters under Lincoln's plan for the reconstruction of Florida.

More essential to Lincoln than the duties they so faithfully discharged was the camaraderie the young assistants provided him. They were part of his family, like sons during the troubled days and nights of his first term. They would listen spellbound when he recited Shakespeare or told another tale from his endless store. Throughout their years in the White House, they offered Lincoln conversation, undivided loyalty, and love. They were awake late at night when he could not sleep, up early in the morning to share the latest news, offering the lonely president round-the-clock companionship.

At the outset, Hay had been dumbfounded by the haphazard administrative style of the man he nicknamed "the Ancient" or "the Tycoon." Something of an intellectual snob, the young college graduate had betrayed early on a hint of condescension toward his self-taught boss. Proximity to the president soon altered his opinion. He had come to believe by 1863 that "the hand of God" had put the prairie lawyer in the White House. If the "patent leather kid glove set" did not yet appreciate this giant of a man, it was because they "know no more of him than an owl does of a comet, blazing into his blinking eyes."

By the spring of 1865, Nicolay, soon to marry Therena Bates, was contemplating the purchase of a newspaper in Washington or Baltimore, while Hay wanted time for his studies and his active social life, too long constrained by fourteen-hour workdays. While they would both miss Lincoln, they were glad to escape the constant struggles with Mary—the "Hellcat," as they irreverently called her—who still resented their claims on her husband's attention. Indeed, soon after Lincoln's reelection, Mary had enlisted the help of Dr. Anson Henry in an effort to replace Nicolay with the journalist Noah Brooks. Nicolay had apparently tried to talk with Lincoln about his problems with Mary, but the president had refused any such discussion.

Seward found worthy alternatives for both Nicolay and Hay. When the consulate in Paris opened up in March, he recommended Nicolay for the job. The president agreed, understanding the significance of the opportunity for his loyal assistant. "So important an appointment has rarely been conferred on one so young," the *National Republican* commented when the Senate confirmed Nicolay without a dissenting vote. Nicolay was thrilled. The position paid five thousand dollars a year, allowing him to start married life on solid ground.

Once Nicolay was confirmed, Seward turned his attentions to Hay, with whom he had become especially close over the years. Many nights Hay had wandered over to Seward's house, where he was certain to find a good meal, vivid conversation, and a warm welcome. Moreover, in watching Seward and Lincoln together, Hay had recognized that the secretary of state had been the first cabinet member to recognize Lincoln's "personal preeminence."

In mid-March, Seward arranged for Hay to receive an appointment as secretary of the legation in Paris. "It was entirely unsolicited and unexpected," Hay told his brother Charles. "It is a pleasant and honorable way of leaving my present post which I should have left in any event very soon." He had thought of returning to Warsaw, Illinois, but Paris, France, was far more exciting. Hay planned to stay at the White House for another month or so, until arrangements were completed for Noah Brooks to assume his duties. Then he and Nicolay would sail for Europe to begin their new adventures. "It will be exceedingly pleasant," Nicolay said, "for both of us, to be there at the same time."

Spring seemed to revive the spirits of Mary Lincoln, who invariably sank into depression each February, with the anniversary of Willie's death. "We are having charming weather," she wrote to her friend Abram Wakeman on March 20. "We went to the Opera on Saturday eve; Mr Sumner accompanied us—we had a very gay little time. Mr S when he throws off his heavy manner, as he often does, can make himself very very agreeable. Last evening, he again joined our little coterie & tomorrow eve,—we all go again to hear 'Robin Adair,' sung in 'La Dame Blanche' by Habelmann. This is always the pleasant time to me in W. springtime, some few of the most pleasant Senators families remain until June, & all ceremony, with each other is laid aside." A few days later, she wrote a note to Sumner, telling him that she would be sending along a copy of Louis Napoleon's manuscript on Julius Caesar, which she had just received from the State Department and knew he would want to read. "In the coming summer," she promised, "I shall peruse it myself, for I have so sadly neglected the little French, I fancied so familiar to me."

Like his mother, Tad Lincoln possessed "an emotional temperament much like an April day, sunning all over with laughter one moment, the next crying as though [his] heart would break." The painter Francis Carpenter recounted an incident when photographers from Brady's studio set up their equipment in an unoccupied room that Tad had turned into a little theater. Taking "great offence at the occupation of his room without his consent," Tad locked the door and hid the key, preventing the photographers from retrieving their chemicals and supplies. Carpenter pleaded with Tad to unlock the door, but he refused. Finally, the president had to intervene. He left his office and returned a few minutes later with the key. Though Tad "was violently excited when I went to him," Lincoln told Carpenter, "I said, 'Tad, do you know you are making your father a great deal of trouble?' He burst into tears, instantly giving me up the key."

Most of the time, however, Tad was "so full of life and vigor," recalled John Hay, "so bubbling over with health and high spirits, that he kept the house alive with his pranks and his fantastic enterprises." From dawn to dusk, "you could hear his shrill pipe resounding through the dreary corridors of the Executive residence . . . and when the President laid down his weary pen toward midnight, he generally found his infant goblin asleep under his table or roasting his curly head by the open fire-place; and the tall chief would pick up the child and trudge off to bed with the drowsy little burden on his shoulder, stooping under the doors and dodging the chandeliers."

Though Tad never developed a love of books, and "felt he could not waste time in learning to spell," he had a clever, intuitive mind and was a good judge of character. "He treated flatterers and office-seekers with a curious coolness and contempt," marveled Hay, "but he often espoused the cause of some poor widow or tattered soldier, whom he found waiting in the ante-rooms." His enterprising nature and natural shrewdness would augur well for him once his schooling was completed. With all his heart, Lincoln loved his "little sprite."

• • •

In late March, Lincoln, Mary, and Tad journeyed to City Point to visit General Grant. For Lincoln, the eighteen-day sojourn was his longest break from Washington in four years. Grant had issued the invitation at the suggestion of his wife, Julia, who had been struck by constant newspaper reports of "the exhausted appearance of the President." Grant worried at first about the propriety of issuing an invitation when the president could visit without waiting "to be asked," but on March 20, he wrote a note to Lincoln: "Can you not visit City Point for a day or two? I would like very much to see you and I think the rest would do you good."

Delighted with the idea, Lincoln asked the Navy Department to make arrangements for a ship to carry him south. Assistant Secretary Fox was not happy to be assigned the task, for he believed "the President was incurring great risk in making the journey." To minimize danger, he ordered John Barnes, commander of the *Bat*, a fast-moving gunboat, to report to the Washington Navy Yard at once. Work immediately commenced on the interior of the armed ship to make alterations necessary "to insure the personal comfort of the President as long as he desired to make the *Bat* his home." To discuss the meals and amenities Lincoln might require, Fox brought Barnes to the White House. Lincoln told Barnes "he wanted no luxuries but only plain, simple food and ordinary comfort—that what was good for me would be good enough for him." Barnes returned to the Navy Yard to supervise the changes.

The next morning, Lincoln summoned Barnes back to the White House. Embarrassed at the thought that workers had stayed up all night to make alterations that might now require additional work, Lincoln explained apologetically that "Mrs. Lincoln had decided that she would accompany him to City Point, and could the *Bat* accommodate her and her maid servant." Barnes was, "in sailor's phrase, taken 'all aback,'" knowing that the austere gunboat "was in no respect adapted to the private life of womankind, nor could she be made so." He returned to the Navy Yard, where "the alterations to the *Bat* were stopped and the steamer *River Queen* was chartered." The change of plans was particularly upsetting to Fox, who "expressed great regret that the determination of Mrs. Lincoln to accompany the President" had forced the shift to "an unarmed, fragile, river-boat, so easily assailed and so vulnerable." He directed Barnes to follow Lincoln's steamer in the *Bat*, but still could not shake his anxiety. Though aware of the danger, Lincoln remained relaxed and cheerful, talking about the problems of accommodating womenfolk at sea "in very funny terms."

The presidential party, which included army captain Charles B. Penrose, Tad and Mary Lincoln, Mary's maid, and Lincoln's bodyguard, W. H. Crook, departed from the Arsenal Wharf at Sixth Street at 1 p.m. on Thursday, March 23. Stanton had been laid up for several days, but against Ellen's advice, he took a carriage to see Lincoln off, arriving minutes after the *River Queen*'s departure. Anxious about the president's safety, Stanton panicked an hour later when "a hurricane swept over the city." The "terrific squalls of winds, accompanied by thunder and lightning, did considerable damage here," the *Herald*'s Washington correspondent reported. "The roof of a factory on Sixth street was blown off into the street and fell upon a hack, crushing the horses and its driver." In some neighborhoods, trees were felled and houses destroyed, "while down the river the steamboats and sailing craft were dashed about with great violence." Leaving his bed once again, Stanton went to the War Department and telegraphed Lincoln at 8:45 p.m. "I hope you have reached Point Lookout safely notwithstanding the furious gale that came on soon after you started. . . . Please let me hear from you at Point Lookout."

Lincoln, meanwhile, was enjoying himself immensely. While Tad raced around the ship, investigating every nook and befriending members of the crew, Lincoln remained on deck, watching "the city until he could see it no more." Once inside, he listened with relish to the adventures of the *River Queen's* captain, who had chased blockade runners early in the war. "It was nearly midnight when he went to bed," Crook recalled.

Crook, who shared a stateroom with Tad, was "startled out of a sound sleep" by Mary Lincoln. "It is growing colder," she explained, "and I came in to see if my little boy has covers enough on him." Later that night, Crook was awakened by the steamer passing through rough waters, which felt as if it were "slowly climbing up one side of a hill and then rushing down the other." The next morning, still feeling seasick, Crook noted that the turbulent passage had apparently not disturbed Lincoln. On the contrary, the president looked rested, claimed to be "feeling splendidly," and did "full justice to the delicious fish" served at breakfast.

Mary would nostalgically recall her husband's fine humor during this last trip to City Point. "Feeling *so encouraged*" the war "was near its close," and relieved from the daily burdens of his office, "he freely gave vent to his cheerfulness," to such an extent that "he was almost boyish, in his mirth & reminded me, of his original nature, what I had always remembered of him, in our own home—free from care, surrounded by those he loved so well."

Crook recalled that "it was after dark on the 24th" when the *River Queen* reached City Point. He would long remember the beauty of the scene that stretched before him, "the many-colored lights of the boats in the harbor and the lights of the town straggling up the high bluffs of the shore, crowned by the lights from Grant's headquarters at the top."

Newly minted captain Robert Lincoln escorted General and Mrs. Grant to call on the president shortly after he arrived. "Our gracious President met us at the gangplank," Julia Grant recalled, "greeted the General most heartily, and, giving me his arm, conducted us to where Mrs. Lincoln was awaiting." Leaving the two women together, the men went into the president's room for a short consultation, "at the end of which," reported Crook, "Mr. Lincoln appeared particularly happy," reassured by Grant's estimation that the conflict was nearing an end. After the Grants left, Lincoln and Mary, appearing "in very good spirits," talked late into the night.

While the Lincolns were breakfasting the next day on the lower deck, Robert came by to report that the review planned for that morning would have to be postponed. Rebels had initiated an attack on Fort Stedman, only eight miles away. With Grant and Sherman closing in upon him, Lee had decided to abandon Petersburg and move his army south to North Carolina, hoping to join General Joseph Johnston and prevent Sherman from joining Grant. Abandoning Petersburg meant losing Richmond, but it was the only way to save his army. The attack on Fort Stedman, intended to open an escape route, took the Federals by surprise. Nonetheless, within hours, Grant's men succeeded in retaking the fort and restoring the original line.

After breakfast, Lincoln walked up the bluff to Grant's headquarters, where plans were made for a visit to the front. As the presidential party passed by the battle sites, it became clear that the engagement had been more serious than first realized. "The ground immediately about us was still strewn with dead and wounded men," recalled Barnes. The Confederates had suffered nearly five thousand casualties; the Federals over two thousand. Burial parties were already at work as ambulances transported the wounded to the hospital and surgeons attended those still lying in the field. When a long line of captured Confederate soldiers passed by, "Lincoln remarked upon their sad and unhappy condition . . . his whole face showing sympathetic feeling for the suffering about him." On the return trip, he commented "that he had seen enough of the horrors of war, that he hoped this was the beginning of the end, and that there would be no more bloodshed or ruin of homes."

"I am here within five miles of the scene of this morning's action," Lincoln telegraphed Stanton from Meade's headquarters in the field. "I have seen the prisoners myself and they look like there might be the number Meade states—1600." Unsettled by Lincoln's proximity to the front, Stanton replied, "I hope you will remember Gen. Harrison's advice to his men at Tippecanoe, that they 'can see as well a little further off.' " But for the soldiers in the field who greeted him with heartfelt cheers, Lincoln's presence at the scene revealed that "he was not afraid to show himself among them, and willing to share their dangers here, as often, far away, he had shared the joy of their triumphs."

Seated at the campfire that night, Lincoln seemed to Horace Porter much more "grave and his language much more serious than usual." Undoubtedly, the grisly images of the dead and wounded were not easily dismissed. As the night wore on, the president rallied and "entertained the general-in-chief and several members of the staff by talking in a most interesting manner about public affairs, and illustrating the subjects mentioned with his incomparable anecdotes." Toward the end of the evening, Grant asked, "Mr. President, did you at any time doubt the final success of the cause?" "Never for a moment," Lincoln replied.

Grant then turned the conversation to the *Trent* affair. According to Grant, Seward had given "a very interesting account" of the tangled questions involved during his visit the previous summer. " 'Yes,' said the President; 'Seward studied up all the works ever written on international law, and came to cabinet meetings loaded to the muzzle with the subject. We gave due consideration to the case, but at that critical period of the war it was soon decided to deliver up the prisoners. It was a pretty bitter pill to swallow, but I contented myself with believing that England's triumph in the matter would be short-lived, and that after ending our war successfully we would be so powerful that we could call her to account for all the embarrassments she had inflicted upon us."

Lincoln continued, "I felt a good deal like the sick man in Illinois who was told he probably had n't many days longer to live, and he ought to make his peace with any enemies he might have. He said the man he hated worst of all was a fellow named Brown, in the next village. . . . So Brown was sent for, and when he came the sick man began to say, in a voice as meek as Moses's, that he wanted to die at peace with all his fellow-creatures, and he hoped he and Brown could now shake hands and bury all their enmity. The scene was becoming altogether too pathetic for Brown, who had to get out his handkerchief and wipe the gathering tears from his eyes. . . . After a parting that would have softened the heart of a grind-stone, Brown had about reached the room door when the sick man rose up on his elbow and called out to him: 'But see here, Brown; if I should happen to get well, mind, that old grudge stands.' So I thought that if this nation should happen to get well we might want that old grudge against England to stand." Everyone laughed heartily, and the pleasant evening drew to a close.

On Sunday morning, the *River Queen* carried the presidential party downriver to where Admiral Porter's naval flotilla awaited them, "ranged in double line, dressed with flags, the crews on deck cheering." As each vessel passed by, reported Barnes, Lincoln "waved his high hat as if saluting old friends in his native town, and seemed as happy as a schoolboy." After lunch aboard Porter's flagship, the *River Queen* sailed to Aiken's Landing. There, arrangements were made for Lincoln to ride on horse-back with Grant to General Ord's encampment four miles away while Mary Lincoln and Julia Grant followed in an ambulance. "The President was in high spirits," observed Barnes, "laughing and chatting first to General Grant and then to General Ord as they rode forward through the woods and over the swamps." Reaching the parade ground ahead of the ladies, they decided to begin the review without them, since the troops had been waiting for hours and had missed their midday meal. General Ord's wife, Mary, asked if "it was proper for her to accompany the cavalcade" without Mrs. Lincoln and Mrs. Grant. "Of course," she was told. "Come along!"

Meanwhile, the ambulance carrying the women had encountered great discomfort due to the corduroyed road, which jounced them into the air each time a log was struck. Concerned that the agonizingly slow pace would make them late for the review, Mary ordered the driver to go faster. This only made things worse, for the first "jolt lifted the party clear off the seats," striking their heads on the top of the wagon. Mary "now insisted on getting out and walking," recalled Horace Porter, who had been assigned to escort the ladies, "but as the mud was nearly hub-deep, Mrs. Grant and I persuaded her that we had better stick to the wagon as our only ark of refuge."

When Mary finally reached the parade grounds and saw the attractive Mrs. Ord riding beside her husband in the place of honor that should have been her own, she erupted in an embarrassing tirade against Mrs. Ord, calling her "vile names in the presence of a crowd of officers." Mrs. Ord, according to one observer, "burst into tears and inquired what she had done, but Mrs. Lincoln refused to be appeased, and stormed till she was tired. Mrs. Grant tried to stand by her friend, and everybody was shocked and horrified."

That evening Mary continued her harangue at dinner, manifestly aggrieving her husband, whose attitude toward her, marveled Captain Barnes, "was always that of the most affectionate solicitude, so marked, so gentle and unaffected that no one could see them together without being impressed by it." Knowing his wife would awake the next morning humiliated by such a public display of temper, Lincoln had no desire to exacerbate the situation. Perhaps, as Mary's biographer suggests, the blow in the wagon that Mary suffered to her head had initiated a migraine headache, spurring the irrational outburst of wrath. Whether from illness or mortification, she remained sequestered in her stateroom for the next few days.

At this time, General Sherman was on his way to City Point. His army had stopped in Goldsboro, North Carolina, to resupply, leaving him several days to visit Grant and discuss plans for the final push. When Sherman arrived, he and Grant eagerly greeted each other, "their hands locked in a cordial grasp." To Horace Porter, "their encounter was more like that of two school-boys coming together after a vacation than the meeting of the chief actors in a great war tragedy." After talking for an hour, they walked down to the wharf and joined the president on the *River Queen*. Lincoln greeted Sherman "with a warmth of manner and expression" that the general would long remember, and initiated "a lively conversation," intently questioning Sherman about his march from Savannah to Goldsboro.

The talk darkened as Sherman and Grant agreed that "one more bloody battle was likely to occur before the close of the war." They believed Lee's only option now was to retreat to the Carolinas. There, joining forces with

Johnston, he would stage a desperate attack against either Sherman or Grant. "Must more blood be shed?" Lincoln asked. "Cannot this last bloody battle be avoided?" That was not in their hands, the generals explained. All would depend upon the actions taken by Robert E. Lee.

The next morning, March 28, Sherman and Grant, accompanied this time by Admiral Porter, returned to the *River Queen* for a long talk with Lincoln in the upper saloon. With the war drawing to a close, Sherman inquired of Lincoln: "What was to be done with the rebel armies when defeated? And what should be done with the political leaders, such as Jeff. Davis, etc.?" Lincoln replied that "all he wanted of us was to defeat the opposing armies, and to get the men composing the Confederate armies back to their homes, at work on their farms and in their shops." He wanted no retaliation or retribution. "Let them have their horses to plow with, and, if you like, their guns to shoot crows with. I want no one punished; treat them liberally all round. We want those people to return to their allegiance to the Union and submit to the laws."

Regarding Jefferson Davis and his top political leaders, Lincoln privately wished they could somehow "escape the country," though he could not say this in public. "As usual," Sherman recalled, "he illustrated his meaning by a story: 'A man once had taken the total-abstinence pledge. When visiting a friend, he was invited to take a drink, but declined, on the score of his pledge; when his friend suggested lemonade, [the man] accepted. In preparing the lemonade, the friend pointed to the brandy-bottle, and said the lemonade would be more palatable if he were to pour in a little brandy; when his guest said, if he could do so "unbeknown" to him, he would not object.'" Sherman grasped the point immediately. "Mr. Lincoln wanted Davis to escape, 'unbeknown' to him."

Later that afternoon, Sherman left City Point to return to his troops and prepare for the expected battle. Saying goodbye to the president, he "was more than ever impressed by his kindly nature, his deep and earnest sympathy with the afflictions of the whole people," and his "absolute faith in the courage, manliness, and integrity of the armies in the field." To be sure, "his face was care-worn and haggard; but, the moment he began to talk, his face lightened up, his tall form, as it were, unfolded, and he was the very impersonation of good-humor and fellowship." A decade later, Sherman remained convinced of Lincoln's unparalleled leadership. "Of all the men I ever met, he seemed to possess more of the elements of greatness, combined with goodness, than any other."

Lincoln walked to the railroad station early the next morning to bid farewell to Grant, who was heading to the front for what they hoped would be the final offensive against Lee. Oppressed by thoughts of the expected battle, "Lincoln looked more serious than at any other time since he had visited headquarters," recalled Horace Porter; "the lines in his face seemed deeper, and the rings under his eyes were of a darker hue." As the train pulled away from the platform, Grant and his party tipped their hats in honor of the president. Returning the salute, his "voice broken by an emotion he could ill conceal," Lincoln said: "Good-by, gentlemen, God bless you all!"

As Grant was leaving City Point, Seward was heading south to join Lincoln. "I think the President must have telegraphed for him," Welles surmised, "and if so I came to the conclusion that efforts are again being made for peace. I am by no means certain that this irregular proceeding and importunity on the part of the Executive is the wisest course." The *Tribune* concurred: "We presume no person of even average sagacity has imagined that the President of the United States had gone down to the front at such a time as this in quest merely of pleasure, or leisure or health even." That he hoped to "bring peace with him on his return," the editorial suggested, was "too palpable to be doubted."

Though Lincoln clearly would have loved "to bring peace with him on his return," he went to City Point with no intention of engaging in further negotiations. He had, in fact, sought a "change of air & rest," as well as the chance "to escape the unceasing and relentless pressure of visitors." More important, he wanted to underscore his directive that Grant should converse with Lee only with regard to capitulation or solely military concerns. Grant was "not to decide, discuss, or confer upon any political question. Such questions the President holds in his own hands." Lincoln wished to ensure that his lenient policy toward the rebels would not be undercut by a punitive agenda.

He knew that work was accumulating on his desk as his second week of absence from Washington began, but he was not yet ready to return. "I begin to feel that I ought to be at home," he telegraphed Stanton on March 30, "and yet I dislike to leave without seeing nearer to the end of General Grant's present movement. He has now been out since yesterday morning. . . . Last night at 10.15, when it was dark as a rainy night without a moon could be, a furious cannonade, soon joined in by a heavy musketry-fire, opened near Petersburg and lasted about two hours. The sound was very distinct here, as also were the flashes of guns upon the clouds. It seemed to me a great battle, but the older hands here scarcely noticed it, and, sure enough, this morning it was found that very little had been done." Stanton replied promptly, "I hope you will stay to see it out, or for a few days at least. I have strong faith that your presence will have great influence in inducing exertions that will bring Richmond; compared to that no other duty can weigh a feather. . . . A pause by the army now would do harm; if you are on the ground there will be no pause. All well here."

Seward, who had most likely come to keep Lincoln company, remained only two days. On April 1, he accompanied Mary back to Washington. The Lincolns had apparently decided that, after her public outburst, she would be better off in the White House, away from prying reporters. Moreover, Lincoln had related to her a dream in which the White House had caught fire, and Mary wanted to assure herself that all was well. Once she was aboard the steamer heading north, her spirits lifted abruptly. Fellow passenger Carl Schurz talked with her on the voyage. She "was overwhelmingly charming to me," he wrote to his wife. "She chided me for not visiting her, overpowered me with invitations, and finally had me driven to my hotel in her own state carriage. I learned more state secrets in a few hours than I could otherwise in a year. . . . She is an astounding person."

All that day, Lincoln haunted the telegraph office at City Point, anxiously awaiting news from Grant. Returning to the *River Queen*, he could see "the flash of the cannon" in the distance, signaling that the battle for Petersburg had begun. "Almost all night he walked up and down the deck," Crook recalled, "pausing now and then to listen or to look out into the darkness to see if he could see anything. I have never seen such suffering in the face of any man as was in his that night."

The battle was intense, but by early morning, the Federals had broken through Petersburg's outer lines of defense and had almost reached General Lee's headquarters at the Turnbull House. Realizing he could no longer hold on, Lee ordered his troops to withdraw from both Petersburg and Richmond. That evening Lincoln received the news that Grant had "Petersburg completely enveloped from river below to river above," and had taken "about 12,000 prisoners." Grant invited the president to visit him in Petersburg the following day.

Earlier that day, Lincoln had moved from the luxurious *River Queen* to the compact *Malvern*, Admiral Porter's flagship. Concerned by the cramped quarters, Porter had offered Lincoln his bed, "but he positively declined it," Porter recalled, choosing instead "the smallest kind of a room, six feet long by four and a half feet wide." The next morning he insisted he had "slept well," but teasingly remarked that "you can't put a long blade into a short scabbard." Realizing that the president's six-foot-four frame must have overhung the bed considerably, Porter got carpenters to knock down the wall, increasing the size of both the room and the bed. When Lincoln awoke the next morning, he announced with delight that "a greater miracle than ever happened last night; I shrank six inches in length and about a foot sideways."

To reach Grant, who was waiting in "a comfortable-looking brick house with a yard in front" on Market Street in Petersburg, Lincoln had to ride over the battlefields, littered with dead and dying soldiers. Years later, his bodyguard could recall the sight of "one man with a bullet-hole through his forehead, and another with both arms shot away." As Lincoln absorbed the sorrowful scene, Crook noticed that his "face settled into its old lines of sadness." By the time he reached Grant, he had recovered himself. Grant's aide Horace Porter watched as Lincoln "dismounted in the street, and came in through the front gate with long and rapid strides, his face beaming with delight. He seized General Grant's hand as the general stepped forward to greet him, and stood shaking it for some time." Lincoln showed such elation that Porter doubted whether he had "ever experienced a happier moment in his life."

Lincoln and his lieutenant general conferred for about an hour and a half on the piazza in front of the house while curious citizens strolled by. Though no word had arrived yet from Richmond, Grant surmised that, with the fall of Petersburg, Lee had no choice but to evacuate the capital and move west along the Danville Road, hoping to escape to North Carolina, in which case the Federals would attempt to "get ahead of him and cut him off." Grant had hoped to receive word of Richmond's fall while still in the president's company, but when no message arrived, he felt compelled to join his troops in the field.

Lincoln was back at City Point when news reached him that Union troops commanded by General Weitzel had now occupied Richmond. "Thank God that I have lived to see this!" he remarked to Admiral Porter. "It seems to me that I have been dreaming a horrid dream for four years, and now the nightmare is gone."

For Jefferson Davis and the Confederate government, the nightmare was just beginning. Twenty-four hours earlier, the Confederate president had received the devastating news of Lee's evacuation plans. Seated in his customary pew at St. Paul's Church for the Sunday service, Davis had received "a telegram announcing that General Lee could not hold his position longer than till night, and warning [him] that we must leave Richmond, as the army would commence retreating that evening."

"Thereupon," an attendant at the service noted, Davis "instantly arose, and walked hurriedly down the aisle, beneath the questionings of all eyes in the house." Summoning his cabinet to an emergency session, he made preparations for a special train to carry the leading officials and important government papers south and west to Danville, where a new capital could be established. As word of the evacuation of the troops spread, the citizenry panicked, and a general exodus began. In the tumult, a small fire, deliberately set to destroy the tobacco warehouses before the Federals arrived, raged out of control, burning "nearly everything between Main street and the river for about three-quarters of a mile." All the public buildings in its path, including the offices of the Richmond *Examiner* and the *Inquirer*, were destroyed, leaving only the Customhouse and the Spotswood Hotel.

The news of Richmond's capture on April 3, 1865, reached the War Department in Washington shortly before noon. When over the wire came the words "Here is the first message for you in four years from Richmond," the telegraph operator leaped from his seat and shouted from the window, "Richmond has fallen." The news quickly "spread by a thousand mouths," and "almost by magic the streets were crowded with hosts of people, talking, laughing, hurrahing, and shouting in the fullness of their joy." A *Herald* reporter noted that many "wept as children" while "men embraced and kissed each other upon the streets; friends who had been estranged for years shook hands and renewed their vows of friendship."

Gathering at the War Department, the crowd called for Stanton, who had not left his post for several nights. "As he stood upon the steps to speak," recalled his aide A. E. Johnson, "he trembled like a leaf, and his voice showed his emotion." He began by expressing "gratitude to Almighty God for his deliverance of the nation," then called for thanks "to the President, to the Army and Navy, to the great commanders by sea and land, to the gallant officers and men who have periled their lives upon the battle-field, and drenched the soil with their blood." Stanton was "so overcome by emotion that he could not speak continuously," but when he finished, the crowd roared its approval.

Seward, who had been at the War Department awaiting news of Richmond's fall, was urged to speak next. Clearly understanding that the moment belonged to Stanton, he kept his remarks short and humorous. He was beginning to think that it was time for a change in the cabinet, he began. "Why I started to go to 'the front' the other day, and when I got to City Point they told me it was at Hatcher's Run, and when I got there I was told it was not there but somewhere else, and when I get back I am told by the Secretary that it is at Petersburg; but before I can realize that, I am told again that it is at Richmond, and west of that. Now I leave you to judge what I ought to think of such a Secretary of War as this." The crowd erupted in "loud and lusty" cheers, and a "beaming" Stanton led them in a chorus of "The Star-Spangled Banner."

Newspapers raced to issue special editions. "The demand seemed inexhaustible," the *Star* reported, "and almost beyond the power of our lightning press to supply." One hundred *Herald* couriers, "as fleet on foot and as breathless with enthusiasm as Malice with his fiery cross," raced to distribute papers in every section of the city. EXTRA! GLORIOUS! FALL OF RICHMOND! read the headlines, adding that black troops were among the first to enter the city. For anyone who missed the cries of the newsboys, the sound of eight hundred guns, fired at Stanton's order, marked the signal triumph.

That night, with bands playing in the streets, candles sparkling in the windows of government buildings, and flags flying from every housetop, Seward joined a group of guests for dinner at Stanton's house. The evening's joy was diminished only by the anxiety Stanton and Seward shared for Lincoln's safety. Earlier that day, Seward had talked with James Speed about his fear that "if there were to be assassinations, now was the time." With the fall of Richmond, Seward told Speed, "the Southern people would feel as though the world had come to an end." At such moments, history suggested, desperate men might be prompted to take desperate action, and "the President, being the most marked man on the Federal side, was the most liable to attack." Aware that Mary had invited Speed to join her two days later on a return trip to City Point, Seward begged him to "warn the President of the danger."

Stanton, who worried constantly about the president's safety, needed no reminders that the situation was more hazardous than ever. He had tried to keep Lincoln from going to Petersburg, asking him "to consider whether you ought to expose the nation to the consequence of any disaster to yourself," and pointing out that while generals must run such risks "in the line of their duty," political leaders were not "in the same condition." Lincoln was already back from Petersburg when he received Stanton's telegram. He thanked the secretary for his concern and promised to "take care of [himself]," while simultaneously announcing his intended departure for Richmond the next day.

At 8 a.m. on Tuesday morning, April 4, Lincoln set forth on his historic journey to Richmond. When the *Malvern* reached the channel approaching the city, its passage was blocked by "wreckage of all sorts," including "dead horses, broken ordnance, wrecked boats," and floating torpedoes. They were forced to transfer to the captain's barge, which was towed in behind a little tug manned by marines. When the tug went aground, the president's arrival was left to the rowing skills of a dozen sailors. The situation was unnerving to Crook. "On either side," he recalled, "we passed so close to torpedoes that we could have put out our hands and touched them."

"Here we were in a solitary boat," Admiral Porter remembered, "after having set out with a number of vessels flying flags at every mast-head, hoping to enter the conquered capital in a manner befitting the rank of the

President of the United States." Lincoln was not disturbed in the slightest. The situation reminded him, he cheerfully noted, of a man who had approached him seeking a high position as a consulate minister: "Finding he could not get that, he came down to some more modest position. Finally he asked to be made a tide-waiter. When he saw he could not get that, he asked me for an old pair of trousers. But it is well to be humble."

No sooner had the presidential party reached the landing than Lincoln was surrounded by a small group of black laborers shouting, "Bress de Lord! . . . dere is de great Messiah! . . . Glory, Hallelujah!" First one and then several others fell on their knees. "Don't kneel to me," Lincoln said, his voice full of emotion, "that is not right. You must kneel to God only, and thank him for the liberty you will hereafter enjoy." The men stood up, joined hands, and began to sing a hymn. The streets, which had been "entirely deserted," became "suddenly alive" with crowds of black people "tumbling and shouting, from over the hills and from the water-side."

An ever-growing crowd trailed Lincoln as he walked up the street. "It was a warm day," Admiral Porter noted, and Lincoln, whose tall figure "overtopped every man there," was easily visible. From the windows of the houses along the two-mile route, hundreds of white faces looked on with curiosity at the lanky figure, "walking with his usual long, careless stride, and looking about with an interested air and taking in everything."

Lincoln's bodyguard was relieved when they finally reached the safety of General Weitzel's headquarters, for he thought he had glimpsed a figure in Confederate uniform pointing a gun at Lincoln from a window along the route. Weitzel and his officers had occupied the stucco mansion that Jefferson Davis had abandoned only two days earlier. Captain Barnes recalled that when Lincoln walked into the "comfortably furnished" office of the Confederate president, he crossed the room "to the easy chair and sank down in it." To all present, it seemed "a supreme moment," but Lincoln betrayed no sense of exaltation or triumph. His first words, softly spoken, were simply to ask for a glass of water. The water was promptly supplied, along with a bottle of whiskey. An old black servant still at his post told them that "Mrs. Davis had ordered him to have the house in good condition for the Yankees."

Lincoln had already toured the mansion, seeming "interested in everything," and had met with the members of General Weitzel's staff, when the Confederate assistant secretary of war, John Campbell, arrived to see him. Lincoln welcomed Campbell, whom he had met two months earlier at the Hampton Roads Conference. While the details of their conversation were later disputed, it appears that Lincoln, still fearing that Lee might engage in a final battle, agreed to allow the Virginia legislature to convene, on the understanding that they would repeal the order of secession and remove the state's troops from the war.

Riding through the city that afternoon in an open carriage, the president and his entourage found the Confederate statehouse "in dreadful disorder, signs of a sudden and unexpected flight; members' tables were upset, bales of Confederate scrip were lying about the floor, and many official documents of some value were scattered about." When they finally returned to the flagship, both Admiral Porter and William Crook were greatly relieved. Having worried all day about Lincoln's safety, Crook later wrote that it was "nothing short of miraculous that some attempt on [Lincoln's] life was not made. It is to the everlasting glory of the South that he was permitted to come and go in peace."

As Lincoln rested on the *Malvern* that night, all the public buildings in the nation's capital were illuminated by order of the secretary of state. "The city was all alight with rockets, fireworks, and illuminations of every description," observed Noah Brooks, "the streets being one blaze of glory." It seemed "the entire population of Washington" had poured into the streets to share in the triumph and view the brilliant spectacle produced by "thousands of lighted candles."

Though Seward joined in the glorious celebrations, he continued to fret. The following day he told Welles that he had secured a revenue cutter to take him to Richmond with some important papers that required the president's immediate attention. "He is filled with anxiety to see the President," Welles recorded in his diary, "and these schemes are his apology."

Minutes after taking leave of Welles, Seward nearly lost his life in a carriage accident. Fanny and her friend Mary Titus had come to the Department to join her father and brother Fred for their "customary" afternoon ride. As the horses moved up Vermont Avenue, the coachman stopped to close the carriage door, which had not been properly latched. Before he could return to his seat, the horses bolted, "swinging the driver by the reins as one would swing a cat by the tail." Both Fred and Seward jumped out, hoping they could stop the runaway horses. Fred was not hurt, but Seward caught his heel on the carriage as he jumped, and landed "violently upon the pavement," causing him to lose consciousness.

"The horses tore along," Fanny recorded in her diary, and "we seemed to be whirling on to certain destruction." At an alley, they "turned. We brushed against a tree," and headed straight toward the corner of a house, where she feared she would be "crushed to death." Fortunately, a passing soldier got control of the reins and brought an end to the terrifying ride. Rushing back to the place where her father had fallen, Fanny was horrified to find his broken body, "blood streaming from his mouth." At first she feared he was dead.

For two hours after he was carried to his home, Seward remained unconscious. When he came to at last, he was delirious with pain, having suffered a broken jaw and a badly dislocated shoulder. Doctors arrived, and Fanny could hear his agonized cries through the bedroom door. When she was finally allowed to see him, "he was so disfigured by bruises . . . that he had scarcely a trace of resemblance to himself."

Hearing the news, Stanton rushed to Seward's bedside, where, Fanny recalled, he "was like a woman in the sickroom." He ministered carefully to his friend, perhaps remembering childhood days when he had accompanied his father on sick calls. He "wiped his lips" where the blood had caked, "spoke gently to him," and remained by his side for hours. Returning to the War Department, Stanton sent Lincoln a telegram at City Point: "Mr Seward was thrown from his carriage his shoulder bone at the head of the joint broken off, his head and face much bruised and he is in my opinion dangerously injured. I think your presence here is needed."

Receiving the message shortly before midnight, Lincoln advised Grant that Seward's accident necessitated his return to Washington. Meanwhile, Mary and her invited guests, including James Speed, Elizabeth Keckley, Charles Sumner, Senator Harlan, and the Marquis de Chambrun, were steaming toward City Point. At dawn the next morning, Mary sent a telegram to Stanton: "If Mr Seward is not too severely injured—cannot the President, remain until we arrive at City Point." By this time the surgeon general had determined that Seward had suffered no internal injuries. Stanton informed Mary that there was "no objection to the President remaining at City Point." A few hours later, he sent word to Lincoln that Seward was recovering. "I have seen him and read him all the news. . . . His mind is clear and spirits good."

When Mary's party arrived at noon on April 6, Lincoln brought them into the drawing room of the *River Queen* and relayed the latest bulletins, all positive, from Grant. "His whole appearance, pose, and bearing had marvelously changed," Senator Harlan noted. "He was, in fact, transfigured. That indescribable sadness which had previously seemed to be an adamantine element of his very being had been suddenly changed for an equally indescribable expression of serene joy, as if conscious that the great purpose of his life had been attained." Nonetheless, the marquis marveled, "it was impossible to detect in him the slightest feeling of pride, much less of vanity."

While the visitors went off to Richmond, Lincoln remained at City

Point to await further word from Grant. Welcome news soon arrived—a copy of a telegram from Sheridan, reporting a successful engagement with Lee's retreating armies that had resulted in the capture of "several thousand prisoners," including a half-dozen generals. "If the thing is pressed," Sheridan predicted, "I think Lee will surrender." Lincoln rejoined: "Let the *thing* be pressed."

That evening Julia Grant, accompanied by Lincoln's old friend E. B. Washburne, joined the Lincoln party on the *River Queen*. The conversation turned on what should be done with Jefferson Davis if he were apprehended. "Don't allow him to escape the law," one of the group said, "he must be hung." At once Lincoln interjected: "Let us judge not, that we be not judged."

On Saturday morning, Lincoln and his guests visited Petersburg. At a certain spot, the marquis recalled, "he gave orders to stop the carriage." On his previous visit, Lincoln had noticed a "very tall and beautiful" oak tree that he wanted to examine more closely. "He admired the strength of its trunk, the vigorous development of branches," which reminded him of "the great oaks" in the Western forests. He halted the carriage again when they passed "an old country graveyard" where trees shaded a carpet of spring flowers. Turning to his wife, Lincoln said, "Mary, you are younger than I. You will survive me. When I am gone, lay my remains in some quiet place like this." On the train ride back to City Point, Lincoln observed a turtle "basking in the warm sunshine on the wayside." He asked that the train be stopped so that the turtle could be brought into the car. "The movements of the ungainly little animal seemed to delight him," Elizabeth Keckley recalled. He and Tad shared "a happy laugh" all the way back to the wharf.

Such distractions could not forestall the afternoon's grim task. Lincoln visited injured soldiers at City Point, moving "from one bed to another," the marquis recalled, "saying a friendly word to each wounded man, or at least giving him a handshake." At one bed, he held the hand of a twenty-four-year-old captain who had been cited for bravery. "The dying man half-opened his eyes; a faint smile passed over his lips. It was then that his pulse ceased beating." Lincoln remained among the wounded for five hours and returned to the steamer depleted. "There has been war enough," he said when the marquis inquired about troubles with France over Mexico, "during my second term there will be no more fighting."

That evening, as the *River Queen* prepared to return to Washington, Grant's officers and staff came to say farewell. Lincoln had hoped to remain at City Point until Lee's surrender, but he felt he should visit Seward. "As the twilight shadows deepened the lamps were lighted, and the boat was brilliantly illuminated," Elizabeth Keckley recalled, "it looked like an enchanted floating palace." When the military band came aboard, Lincoln asked them to play "La Marseillaise" in honor of the Marquis de Chambrun.

As the *River Queen* steamed toward Washington on Sunday, "the conversation," Chambrun recalled, "dwelt upon literary subjects." Holding "a beautiful quarto copy of Shakespeare in his hands," Lincoln read several passages from *Macbeth*, including the king's pained tribute to the murdered Duncan:

> *Duncan is in his grave;*
> *After life's fitful fever he sleeps well.*
> *Treason has done his worst; nor steel, nor poison,*
> *Malice domestic, foreign levy, nothing,*
> *Can touch him further.*

Lincoln read the lines slowly, marveling "how true a description of the murderer that one was; when, the dark deed achieved, its tortured perpetrator came to envy the sleep of his victim," and when he finished, "he read over again the same scene." Lincoln's ominous selection prompted James Speed to deliver Seward's warning about the increased threat upon his life. "He stopped me at once," Speed recalled, "saying, he had rather be dead than to live in continual dread." Moreover, he considered it essential "that the people know I come among them without fear."

Early that evening, the steamer passed by Mount Vernon, prompting Chambrun to say to Lincoln, "Mount Vernon and Springfield, the memories of Washington and your own, those of the revolutionary and civil wars; these are the spots and names America shall one day equally honor." The remark brought a dreamy smile to Lincoln's face. "Springfield!" he said. "How happy, four years hence, will I be to return there in peace and tranquility."

Years later, Chambrun remained intrigued by Lincoln's temperament. On first impression, he "left with you with a sort of impression of vague and deep sadness." Yet he "was quite humorous," often telling hilarious stories and laughing uproariously. "But all of a sudden he would retire within himself; then he would close his eyes, and all his features would at once bespeak a kind of sadness as indescribable as it was deep. After a while, as though it were by an effort of his will, he would shake off this mysterious weight under which he seemed bowed; his generous and open disposition would again reappear."

Lincoln's bodyguard, William Crook, believed he understood something of the shifting moods that mystified the French aristocrat. He had observed that Lincoln seemed to absorb the horrors of the war into himself. In the course of the two-week trip, Crook had witnessed Lincoln's "agony when the thunder of the cannon told him that men were being cut down like grass." He had seen the anguish on the president's face when he came within "sight of the poor, torn bodies of the dead and dying on the field of Petersburg." He discerned his "painful sympathy with the forlorn rebel prisoners," and his profound distress at "the revelation of the devastation of a noble people in ruined Richmond." In each instance, Lincoln had internalized the pain of those around him—the wounded soldiers, the captured prisoners, the defeated Southerners. Little wonder that he was overwhelmed at times by a profound sadness that even his own resilient temperament could not dispel.

· · ·

DIRECTLY UPON HIS RETURN to Washington, Lincoln went to Seward's bedside. "It was in the evening," Fred Seward recalled, "the gas-lights were turned down low, and the house was still, every one moving softly, and speaking in whispers." His father had taken a turn for the worse. A high fever had developed, and "grave apprehensions were entertained, by his medical attendants, that his system would not survive the injuries and the shock." Frances had hurried down from Auburn to find her husband in a more serious state than she had imagined, his face "so marred and swollen and discolored that one can hardly persuade themselves of his identity; his voice so changed; utterance almost entirely prevented by the broken jaw and the swollen tongue. It makes my heart ache to look at him." His mind was "perfectly clear," however, and he remained, as always, "patient and uncomplaining."

"The extreme sensitiveness of the wounded arm," Fred recalled, "made even the touch of the bed clothing intolerable. To keep it free from their contact, he was lying on the edge of the bed, farthest from the door." When Lincoln entered the room, he walked over to the far side of the bed and sat down near the bandaged patient. "You are back from Richmond?" Seward queried in a halting, scarcely audible voice. "Yes," Lincoln replied, "and I think we are near the end, at last." To continue the conversation more intimately, Lincoln stretched out on the bed. Supporting his head with his hand, Lincoln lay side by side with Seward, as they had done at the time of their first meeting in Massachusetts many years before. When Fanny came in to sit down, Lincoln somehow managed to unfold his long arm and bring it "around the foot of the bed, to shake hands in his cordial way." He related the details of his trip to Richmond, where he had "worked as hard" at the task of shaking seven thousand hands as he had when he sawed wood, "& seemed," Fanny thought, "much satisfied at the labor."

Finally, when he saw that Seward had fallen into a much-needed sleep, Lincoln quietly got up and left the room. Drained by Seward's grievous condition, Lincoln revived when Stanton burst into the White House bearing a telegram from Grant: "General Lee surrendered the Army of Northern Virginia this afternoon upon terms proposed by myself." It was later said that "the President hugged him with joy" upon hearing the news, and then went immediately to tell Mary.

Although it was close to 10 p.m., Stanton knew that Seward would want to be awakened for this news. "God bless you," Seward said when Stanton read the telegram. This was the third time Stanton had come to see Seward that Sunday. "Don't try to speak," Stanton said. "You have made me cry for the first time in my life," Seward replied.

• • •

BOTH GRANT AND LEE had acquitted themselves admirably at the courtly surrender ceremony that afternoon at the Appomattox Court House. "One general, magnanimous in victory," historian Jay Winik writes, "the other, gracious and equally dignified in defeat." Two days earlier, Grant had sent a note to Lee asking him to surrender. In light of "the result of the last week," Grant wrote, he hoped that Lee understood "the hopelessness of further resistance" and would choose to prevent "any further effusion of blood." At first Lee refused to accept the futility of his cause, contemplating one last attempt to escape. But Sunday morning, with his troops almost completely surrounded, Lee sent word to Grant that he was ready to surrender.

As the distinguished silver-haired general dressed for the historic meeting, his biographer writes, he "put on his handsomest sword and his sash of deep, red silk." Thinking it likely he would be imprisoned before day's end, he told General William Pendleton, "I must make my best appearance." He need not have worried, for Grant was determined to follow Lincoln's lenient guidelines. The terms of surrender allowed Confederate officers, after relinquishing their arms and artillery, "to return to their homes, not to be disturbed by the United States authority," on the condition that they never "take up arms" against the Union "until properly exchanged."

As Grant continued to work out the terms, he later recalled, "the thought occurred to me that the officers had their own private horses and effects, which were important to them, but of no value to us; also that it would be an unnecessary humiliation to call upon them to deliver their side arms." He therefore added a provision allowing officers to take their sidearms, as well as their private horses and baggage. This permission, Lee observed, "would have a happy effect upon his army." Before the two men parted, Lee mentioned that "his army was in a very bad condition for want of food." Grant responded immediately, promising to send rations for twenty-five thousand men.

As Lee rode back to his headquarters, word of the surrender spread through the Confederate lines. He tried to speak to his men, but "tears came into his eyes," and he could manage to say only "Men, we have fought the war together, and I have done the best I could for you." If Lee had trouble expressing his grief and pride, his soldiers showed no such reservations. In an overwhelming display of respect and devotion, they spontaneously arranged themselves on "each side of the road to greet him as he passed, and two solid walls of men were formed along the whole distance." When their cheers brought tears to Lee's eyes, they, too, began to weep. "Each group began in the same way, with cheers, and ended in the same way, with sobs, all along the route to his quarters." One soldier spoke for all: "I love you just as well as ever, General Lee!"

At dawn the next day, Noah Brooks heard "a great boom." The reverberation of a five-hundred-gun salute "startled the misty air of Washington, shaking the very earth, and breaking the windows of houses about Lafayette Square." The morning newspapers would carry the details, but "this was Secretary Stanton's way of telling the people that the Army of Northern Virginia had at last laid down its arms."

"The nation seems delirious with joy," noted Welles. "Guns are firing, bells ringing, flags flying, men laughing, children cheering—all, all jubilant. This surrender of the great Rebel captain and the most formidable and reliable army of the Secessionists virtually terminates the Rebellion." A spontaneous holiday was announced in all departments. Employees poured into the streets.

An exuberant crowd of several thousand gathered at the White House. "The bands played, the howitzers belched forth their thunder, and the people cheered," reported the *National Intelligencer.* Despite shouted demands for him to speak, Lincoln hesitated. He was planning a speech for the following evening and did not want to "dribble it all out" before he completed his thoughts. If he said something mistaken, it would make its way into print, and a person in his position, he modestly said, "ought at least try not to make mistakes." Still, the crowd was so insistent that the president finally appeared at the second-story window, where he "was received in the most enthusiastic manner, the people waving their hats, swinging their umbrellas, and the ladies waving their handkerchiefs."

When the assembly quieted down, Lincoln acknowledged their euphoria with a smile of his own. "I am very greatly rejoiced to find that an occasion has occurred so pleasurable that the people cannot restrain themselves." These words drew even wilder cheers. Lincoln then announced a special request for the band. "I have always thought 'Dixie' one of the best tunes I have ever heard," he began. "Our adversaries over the way attempted to appropriate it, but I insisted yesterday that we fairly captured it." This was followed by tumultuous applause. "I presented the question to the Attorney General, and he gave it as his legal opinion that it is our lawful prize. I now request the band to favor me with its performance." In requesting the patriotic song of the South, Lincoln believed that "it is good to show the rebels that with us they will be free to hear it again." The band followed "Dixie" with "Yankee Doodle," and "the crowd went off in high good-humor."

"If possible," Mary wrote, "this is a happier day, than last Monday," when the news of Richmond's capture had reached Washington. Her exhilaration was evident in a note she wrote to Charles Sumner the next morning, inviting him and the marquis to join her in a carriage ride around the city to see the grand illumination and to hear the president speak. "It does not appear to me," she wrote, "that this *womanly* curiosity will be undignified or indiscreet, qu'en pensez vous?"

Illuminated once again, the city was spectacular to behold. The windows of every government building were ablaze with candles and lanterns, and the lights of the newly completed Capitol dome were visible for miles around. "Bonfires blazed in many parts of the city, and rockets were fired" in ongoing celebrations. Knowing the president was going to address the public, Stanton put his men to work decorating the front of the War Department "with flags, corps badges and evergreens."

When Lincoln came to a second-story window on the north side of the White House, "he carried a roll of manuscript in his hand." He had explained to Noah Brooks that "this was a precaution" against colloquial expressions that might offend men such as Charles Sumner, who had objected previously to phrases such as "the rebels turned tail and ran" or "sugar-coated pill." At the sight of the president, the immense crowd's enthusiasm was loosed in "wave after wave of applause," requiring him to stand still for some time until the din subsided.

"The speech," Noah Brooks observed, "was longer than most people had expected, and of a different character." Instead of simply celebrating the moment, Lincoln wanted to address the national debate surrounding the reintroduction of the Southern states into the Union, "the greatest question," he still believed, "ever presented to practical statesmanship."

He acknowledged that in Louisiana, where the process had already begun, some were disappointed that, in the new state constitution, "the elective franchise is not given to the colored man." He felt the right of suffrage should be extended to blacks—to those who were literate and those "who serve our cause as soldiers." On the other hand, the new Louisiana constitution contained a number of remarkable provisions. It emancipated all the slaves within the state and provided "the benefit of public schools equally to black and white." The state legislature, which had already revealed its good intentions by ratifying the Thirteenth Amendment, was empowered specifically "to confer the elective franchise upon the colored man." Were they to cast out the hard work already achieved, Lincoln asked rhetorically, or trust that this was the start of a process that would eventually produce "a complete success"? Relying on a simple, rustic image to convey the complex question, he wondered if "we shall sooner have the fowl by hatching the egg than by smashing it?"

In the crowd that evening was Confederate sympathizer John Wilkes Booth. The younger brother of the famed Shakespearian actor Edwin Booth, whose performances Lincoln so admired, Wilkes had also acquired popularity as an actor. Unlike his older brother, who supported the Union, John Wilkes "had spent the most formative years of his youth in the South" and had developed an abiding passion for the rebels' cause. In recent months, this passion had become a full-blown obsessive hatred for the North. Since the previous summer, he and a small group of conspirators had evolved a plan to kidnap Lincoln and bring him to Richmond, where he could be exchanged for rebel prisoners of war. The capture of Richmond and the surrender of Lee rendered the plan useless, but Booth was not ready to yield. "Our cause being almost lost," he wrote in his diary, "something decisive and great must be done."

Two other conspirators were with Booth in the crowd—drugstore clerk David Herold and former Confederate soldier Lewis Powell, also known as Lewis Payne. When Lincoln spoke of his desire to extend suffrage to blacks, Booth turned to Powell. "That means nigger citizenship. That is the last speech he will ever make," he said. He pleaded with Powell to shoot Lincoln then and there. When Powell demurred, Booth proclaimed, "By God, I'll put him through."

Curiously, Lincoln had recently experienced a dream that carried ominous intimations. "There seemed to be a death-like stillness about me," Lincoln purportedly told Ward Lamon. "Then I heard subdued sobs, as if a number of people were weeping. . . . I went from room to room; no living person was in sight, but the same mournful sounds of distress met me as I passed along. . . . Determined to find the cause of a state of things so mysterious and so shocking, I kept on until I arrived at the East Room, which I entered. There I met with a sickening surprise. Before me was a catafalque, on which rested a corpse wrapped in funeral vestments. Around it were stationed soldiers who were acting as guards; and there was a throng of people, some gazing mournfully upon the corpse, whose face was covered, others weeping pitifully. 'Who is dead in the White House?' I demanded of one of the soldiers. 'The President,' was his answer; 'he was killed by an assassin!' "

Lamon also described what he claimed was the president's attempt to evade the dire portent of the dream. "Don't you see how it will turn out?" Lincoln comforted Lamon. "In this dream, it was not me but some other fellow that was killed. . . . Well, let it go. I think the Lord in His own good time and way will work this out all right. God knows what is best." Historian Don Fehrenbacher is persuasive that Lamon's chronology is confused, which casts doubt on the veracity of the entire story. Yet Lincoln's penchant for portentous dreams and his tendency to relate them to others were remarked on by many of his intimate acquaintances.

While radicals, including Sumner and Chase, believed that universal suffrage should be mandated, rebel leaders should be punished, and the federal government should assume control of the seceded states, "a large majority of the people" approved of Lincoln's speech. "Reunion," according to Noah Brooks, "was then the foremost thought in the minds of men."

Lincoln's support for the quickly assembled imperfect governments in Louisiana and elsewhere drew further criticism from radicals. He believed "there must be courts, and law, and order, or society would be broken up, the disbanded armies would turn into robber bands and guerillas." That same belief had informed his conversations with Judge Campbell in Richmond and his conditional permission for the old Virginia legislature to assemble. At the time of their meeting, five days before Lee's surrender, Lincoln had hoped the Virginians would vote to take back the order of secession and remove Virginia's troops from the war. He also felt that it was sound policy to let "the prominent and influential men of their respective counties . . . come together and undo their own work."

Lincoln's cabinet strongly disagreed with the idea of letting the rebel legislature assemble for any reason. In Seward's absence, Stanton assumed center stage, telling Lincoln "that to place such powers in the Virginia legislature would be giving away the scepter of the conqueror; that it would transfer the result of victory of our arms from the field to the very legislatures which four years before had said, 'give us war'; that it would put the Government in the hands of its enemies; that it would surely bring trouble with Congress." Stanton insisted that "any effort to reorganize the Gov-

ernment should be under Federal authority solely, treating the rebel organizations and government as absolutely null and void."

Attorney General Speed expressed his accord with Stanton's assessment
in the meeting and, afterward, privately with Lincoln. The president confessed to Welles that the opposition of Speed and Stanton troubled him
tremendously. Welles provided no relief. He, too, "doubted the policy of
convening a Rebel legislature," and predicted that, "once convened, they
would with their hostile feelings be inclined perhaps, to conspire against
us." Lincoln still disagreed, maintaining that if "prominent Virginians"
were to come together, they would "turn themselves and their neighbors
into good Union men." Nonetheless, Welles said, "as we had all taken a
different view he had perhaps made a mistake, and was ready to correct it if
he had."

Lincoln's thinking was further influenced by a telegram from Campbell
to General Weitzel, which suggested that Campbell was indeed assuming
more powers for the legislature than he and Lincoln had originally discussed. In the late afternoon of April 12, Lincoln walked over to the War
Department to confer again with Stanton. Stanton's clerk A. E. Johnson
recalled that Lincoln sat on the sofa and listened intently while Stanton,
"full of feeling," reiterated his passionate opposition to allowing the legislature to convene, warning that "the fate of the emancipated millions"
would be left in the hands of untrustworthy men, that "being once assembled, its deliberations could not be confined to any specific acts."

Finally, Lincoln stood up and walked over to Stanton's desk, where he
wrote what would be the final telegram issued under his name from the
War Department. He directed General Weitzel to withdraw the original
permission for the legislature to convene. "Do not now allow them to assemble; but if any have come, allow them safe-return to their homes."
Stanton was pleased, believing "*that* . . . was exactly right."

On Thursday, April 13, Grant journeyed to Washington, where Stanton had planned a celebration in his honor. "As we reached our destination
that bright morning in our boat," Julia Grant recalled, "every gun in and
near Washington burst forth—and such a salvo!—all the bells rang out
merry greetings, and the city was literally swathed in flags and bunting."
Grant went to see the president while Julia, at the Willard Hotel, received
"calls of congratulations all day." Later in the afternoon, she and Ellen
Stanton joined their husbands at the War Department. There, Julia recalled, "Stanton was in his happiest mood, showing me many stands of
arms, flags, and, among other things, a stump of a large tree perforated on
all sides by bullets, taken from the field of Shiloh." He enthusiastically detailed plans for the illumination of his department that night, and "face-

tiously remarked: 'They are going to illuminate at the Navy Department, I know, for they sent and borrowed two or three boxes of candles from my department.' "

For the first time since Willie's death, Mary Lincoln seemed positively carefree. She had received a delightful note from her husband the day before, only "a few lines," but "playfully & tenderly worded, notifying, the hour, of the day, *he* would drive with me!" She wrote a number of letters, all brimming with vitality. "We are rejoicing beyond expression, over our great and glorious victories," she told James Bennett. To her friend Abram Wakeman, she described in detail the "charming time" she had enjoyed at City Point. "I wish very much you had been with us, even our stately dignified Mr Sumner acknowledged himself transformed, into a lad of sixteen." She told Sumner that her new volume of *Julius Caesar* had arrived, and she invited him to join her that evening at the White House for a visit with General Grant.

• • •

GOOD FRIDAY, APRIL 14, 1865, was surely one of Lincoln's happiest days. The morning began with a leisurely breakfast in the company of his son Robert, just arrived in Washington. "Well, my son, you have returned safely from the front," Lincoln said. "The war is now closed, and we soon will live in peace with the brave men that have been fighting against us." He urged Robert to "lay aside" his army uniform and finish his education, perhaps in preparation for a law career. As the father imparted his advice, Elizabeth Keckley observed, "his face was more cheerful than [she] had seen it for a long while."

At 11 a.m., Grant arrived at the White House to attend the regularly scheduled Friday cabinet meeting. He had hoped for word that Johnston's army, the last substantial rebel force remaining, had surrendered to Sherman, but no news had yet arrived. Lincoln told Grant not to worry. He predicted that the tidings would come soon, "for he had last night the usual dream which he had preceding nearly every great and important event of the War." Welles asked him to describe the dream. Turning toward him, Lincoln said it involved the navy secretary's "element, the water—that he seemed to be in some singular, indescribable vessel, and that he was moving with great rapidity towards an indefinite shore; that he had this dream preceding Sumter, Bull Run, Antietam, Gettysburg, Stone River, Vicksburg, Wilmington, etc." Grant remarked that not all those great events had been victories, but Lincoln remained hopeful that this time this event would be favorable.

The complexities of reestablishing law and order in the Southern states dominated the conversation. A few days earlier, Stanton had drafted a plan for imposing a temporary military government on Virginia and North Carolina, until the restoration of civilian rule. "Lincoln alluded to the paper," Stanton later recalled, "went into his room, brought it out, and asked me to read it." A general discussion revealed that most of the cabinet concurred, although Welles and Dennison objected to the idea of undoing state boundaries by uniting two different states into a single military department. Recognizing the validity of this objection, Lincoln asked Stanton to revise his plan to make it applicable to two separate states.

Lincoln said that "he thought it providential that this great rebellion was crushed just as Congress had adjourned," since he and the cabinet were more likely to "accomplish more without them than with them" regarding Reconstruction. He noted that "there were men in Congress who, if their motives were good, were nevertheless impracticable, and who possessed feelings of hate and vindictiveness in which he did not sympathize and could not participate. He hoped there would be no persecution, no bloody work, after the war was over."

As for the rebel leaders, Lincoln reiterated his resolve to perpetrate no further violence: "None need expect he would take any part in hanging or killing those men, even the worst of them." While their continued presence on American soil might prove troublesome, he preferred to "frighten them out of the country, open the gates, let down the bars, scare them off." To illustrate his point, he shook "his hands as if scaring sheep," and said, "Enough lives have been sacrificed. We must extinguish our resentments if we expect harmony and union."

After the cabinet meeting, Stanton and Speed descended the stairs together. "Didn't our Chief look grand today?" Stanton asked. Years later, Speed held fast "to the memory of Lincoln's personal appearance" that day, "with cleanly-shaved face, well-brushed clothing and neatly-combed hair and whiskers," a marked contrast to his usual rumpled aspect. Stanton later wrote that Lincoln seemed "more cheerful and happy" than at any previous cabinet meeting, thrilled by "the near prospect of firm and durable peace at home and abroad." Throughout the discussion, Stanton recalled, Lincoln "spoke very kindly of General Lee and others of the Confederacy," exhibiting "in marked degree the kindness and humanity of his disposition, and the tender and forgiving spirit that so eminently distinguished him."

Later that day, Lincoln put into practice his liberal policy toward the rebel leaders. Intelligence had reached Stanton at the War Department that "a conspicuous secessionist," Jacob Thompson, was en route to Portland, Maine, where a steamer awaited to take him to England. Operating from Canada, Thompson had organized a series of troublesome raids across the border that left Stanton with little sympathy for the Confederate marauder. Upon reading the telegram, Stanton did not hesitate a moment. "Arrest him!" he ordered Assistant Secretary Dana. As Dana was leaving the room, however, Stanton called him back. "No, wait; better to go over and see the President."

Dana found Lincoln in his office. "Halloo, Dana!" Lincoln greeted him. "What's up?" Dana described the situation, explaining that Stanton wanted to arrest Thompson but thought he should first "refer the question" to Lincoln. "Well," said Lincoln, "no, I rather think not. When you have got an elephant by the hind leg, and he's trying to run away, it's best to let him run."

Mary Lincoln's memories of her husband's infectious happiness that day match the recollections of his inner circle. She had never seen him so "cheerful," she told Francis Carpenter, "his manner was even playful. At three o'clock, in the afternoon, he drove out with me in the open carriage, in starting, I asked him, if any one, should accompany us, he immediately replied—'No—I prefer to ride by ourselves to day.' During the drive he was so gay, that I said to him, laughingly, 'Dear Husband, you almost startle me by your great cheerfulness,' he replied, 'and well I may feel so, Mary, I consider *this day*, the war, has come to a close—and then added, 'We must *both*, be more cheerful in the future—between the war & the loss of our darling Willie—we have both, been very miserable.'"

As the carriage rolled toward the Navy Yard, Mary recalled, "he spoke of his old Springfield home, and recollections of his early days, his little brown cottage, the law office, the court room, the green bag for his briefs and law papers, his adventures when riding the circuit." They had traveled an unimaginable distance together since their first dance in Springfield a quarter of a century earlier. Over the years, they had supported each other, irritated each other, shared a love of family, politics, poetry, and drama. Mary's descent into depression after Willie's death had added immeasurably to Lincoln's burdens, and the terrible pressures of the war had further distorted their relationship. His intense focus on his presidential responsibilities had often left her feeling abandoned and resentful. Now, with the war coming to an end and time bringing solace to their grief, the Lincolns could plan for a happier future. They hoped to travel someday—to Europe and the Holy Land, over the Rockies to California, then back home to Illinois, where their life together had begun.

As the carriage neared the White House, Lincoln saw that a group of old friends, including Illinois governor Richard Oglesby, were just leaving. "Come back, boys, come back," he told them, relishing the relaxing com-

pany of friends. They remained for some time, Governor Oglesby recalled. "Lincoln got to reading some humorous book; I think it was by
'John Phoenix.' They kept sending for him to come to dinner. He promised each time to go, but would continue reading the book. Finally he got a
sort of peremptory order that he must come to dinner at once."

The early dinner was necessary, for the Lincolns had plans to see Laura
Keene in *Our American Cousin* at Ford's Theatre that evening. After supper, the president met with Noah Brooks, Massachusetts congressman
George Ashmun, and Speaker Colfax, who was soon to depart for California. "How I would rejoice to make that trip!" Lincoln told Colfax, "but
public duties chain me down here, and I can only envy you its pleasures."
The president invited Colfax to join him at the theater that night, but Colfax had too many commitments.

To Noah Brooks, Lincoln had never seemed "more hopeful and buoyant concerning the condition of the country. . . . He was full of fun and anecdotes, feeling especially jubilant at the prospect before us." His parting
words, Brooks recalled, focused on the country's economic future. "Grant
thinks that we can reduce the cost of the army establishment at least a half
million a day, which, with the reduction of expenditures of the Navy, will
soon bring down our national debt to something like decent proportions,
and bring our national paper up to a par, or nearly so with gold."

Speaker Colfax was among several people who declined the Lincolns'
invitation to the theater that evening. The morning edition of the *National
Republican* had announced that the Grants would join the Lincolns in the
president's box that night, but Julia Grant had her heart set on visiting
their children in New Jersey, so Grant asked to be excused. The Stantons
also declined. Stanton, like Chase, considered the theater a foolish diversion and, more important, a dangerous one. He had fought a losing battle
for months to keep the president from such public places, and he felt that
his presence would only sanction an unnecessary hazard. Earlier that day,
"unwilling to encourage the theater project," Stanton had refused to let
his chief telegrapher, Thomas Eckert, accept Lincoln's invitation, even
though the president had teasingly requested him for his uncommon
strength—he had been known to "break a poker over his arm" and could
serve as a bodyguard.

It was after eight when the Lincolns entered their carriage to drive to
the theater. "I suppose it's time to go," Lincoln told Colfax, "though I
would rather stay." While nothing had provided greater diversion during
the bitter nights of his presidency than the theater, Lincoln required no
escape on this happy night. Still, he had made a commitment. "It has been
advertised that we will be there," he told his bodyguard, Crook, who had

the night off, "and I cannot disappoint the people." Clara Harris—the daughter of Mary's friend Senator Ira Harris—and her fiancé, Major Henry Rathbone, joined the Lincolns in their carriage.

• • •

AS THE LINCOLNS RODE to Ford's Theatre on 10th Street, John Wilkes Booth and three conspirators were a block away at the Herndon House. Booth had devised a plan that called for the simultaneous assassinations of President Lincoln, Secretary of State Seward, and Vice President Johnson. Having learned that morning of Lincoln's plan to attend the theater, he had decided that this night would provide their best opportunity. The powerfully built Lewis Powell, accompanied by David Herold, was assigned to kill Seward at his Lafayette Square home. Meanwhile, the carriage maker George Atzerodt was to shoot the vice president in his suite at the Kirkwood Hotel. Booth, whose familiarity with the stagehands would ensure access, would assassinate the president.

Just as Brutus had been honored for slaying the tyrant Julius Caesar, Booth believed he would be exalted for killing an even "greater tyrant." Assassinating Lincoln would not be enough. "Booth knew," his biographer observes, "that in the end, the Brutus conspiracy was foiled by Marc Antony, whose famous oration made outlaws of the assassins and a martyr of Caesar." William Henry Seward, Lincoln's Mark Antony, must not live. Finally, to throw the entire North into disarray, the vice president must die as well. The triple assassinations were set for 10:15 p.m.

• • •

STILL BEDRIDDEN, Seward had enjoyed his best day since his nearly fatal carriage accident nine days earlier. Fanny Seward noted in her diary that he had slept well the previous night and had taken "solid food for the first time." In the afternoon, he had "listened with a look of pleasure to the narrative of the events of the Cabinet meeting," which Fred, as assistant secretary, had attended in his father's stead. Later in the afternoon, he had listened to Fanny's reading of "Enoch Arden" and remarked on how much he enjoyed it.

The three-story house was full of people. The entire family, except Will and Jenny, were there—Frances, Augustus, Fred, Anna, and Fanny. In addition to the half-dozen household servants and the State Department messenger rooming on the third floor, two soldiers had been assigned by Stanton to stay with Seward. In the early evening, Edwin Stanton had stopped by to check on his friend and colleague. He stayed for a while, chatting with other visitors until martial music in the air reminded him that War Department employees had planned on serenading him that night at his home six blocks away.

After all the guests left, "the quiet arrangements for the night" began. To ensure that Seward was never left alone, the family members had taken turns sitting by his bed. That night Fanny was scheduled to stay with him until 11 p.m., when her brother Gus would relieve her. George Robinson, one of the soldiers whom Stanton had detailed to the household, was standing by. Shortly after 10 p.m., Fanny noticed that her father was falling asleep. She closed the pages of the *Legends of Charlemagne*, turned down the gas lamps, and took a seat on the opposite side of the bed.

Fred Seward later wrote that "there seemed nothing unusual in the occurrence, when a tall, well dressed, but unknown man presented himself" at the door. Powell told the servant who answered the bell that he had some medicine for Mr. Seward and had been instructed by his physician to deliver it in person. "I told him he could not go up," the servant later testified, "that if he would give me the medicine, I would tell Mr. Seward how to take it." Powell was so insistent that the boy stepped aside. When he reached the landing, Fred Seward stopped him. "My father is asleep; give me the medicine and the directions; I will take them to him." Powell argued that he must deliver it in person, but Fred refused.

At this point, Fred recalled, the intruder "stood apparently irresolute." He began to head down the stairs, then "suddenly turning again, he sprang up and forward, having drawn a Navy revolver, which he levelled, with a muttered oath, at my head, and pulled the trigger." This was the last memory Fred would have of that night. The pistol misfired, but Powell brought it down so savagely that Fred's skull was crushed in two places, exposing his brain and rendering him unconscious.

Hearing the disturbance, Private Robinson ran to the door from Seward's bedside. The moment the door was opened, Powell rushed inside, brandishing his now broken pistol in one hand and a large knife in the other. He slashed Robinson in the forehead with his knife, knocking him "partially down," and headed toward Seward. Fanny ran beside Powell, begging him not to kill her father. When Seward heard the word "kill," he awakened, affording him "one glimpse of the assassin's face bending over" before the large bowie knife plunged into his neck and face, severing his cheek so badly that "the flap hung loose on his neck." Oddly, he would later recall that his only impressions were what a fine-looking man Powell was and "what handsome cloth that overcoat is made of."

Fanny's screams brought her brother Gus into the room as Powell advanced again upon Seward, who had been knocked to the floor by the force of the blows. Gus and the injured Robinson managed to pull Powell away, but not before he struck Robinson again and slashed Gus on the forehead and the right hand. When Gus ran for his pistol, Powell bolted down the stairs, stabbing Emerick Hansell, the young State Department messenger, in the back before he bolted out the door and fled through the city streets.

The clamor had roused the entire household. Anna sent the servant to fetch Dr. Verdi, while Private Robinson, though bleeding from his head and shoulders, lifted Seward onto the bed and instructed Fanny about "staunching the blood with clothes & water." Still fearing that another assassin might be hiding in the house, Frances and Anna checked the attic while Fanny searched the rooms on the parlor floor.

Dr. Verdi would never forget his first sight of Seward that night. "He looked like an exsanguinated corpse. In approaching him my feet went deep in blood. Blood was streaming from an extensive gash in his swollen cheek; the cheek was now laid open." So "frightful" was the wound and "so great was the loss of blood" that Verdi assumed the jugular vein must have been cut. Miraculously, it was not. Further examination revealed that the knife had been deflected by the metal contraption holding Seward's broken jaw in place. In bizarre fashion, the carriage accident had saved his life.

"I had hardly sponged his face from the bloody stains and replaced the flap," Verdi recalled, "when Mrs. Seward, with an intense look, called me to her. 'Come and see Frederick,' said she." Not understanding, he followed Frances to the next room, where he "found Frederick bleeding profusely from the head." Fred's appearance was so "ghastly" and his wounds so large that Verdi feared he would not live, but with the application of "cold water pledgets," he was able to stanch the bleeding temporarily.

Once Fred was stabilized, Frances drew Dr. Verdi into another room on the same floor. "For Heaven's sake, Mrs. Seward," asked the befuddled doctor, "what does all this mean?" Verdi found Gus lying on the bed with stab wounds on his hand and forehead, but assured Frances that he would recover. Frances barely had time to absorb these words of comfort before entreating Dr. Verdi to see Private Robinson. "I ceased wondering," Verdi recalled, "my mind became as if paralyzed; mechanically I followed her and examined Mr. Robinson. He had four or five cuts on his shoulders."

"Any more?" Verdi asked, though not imagining the carnage could go on. "Yes," Frances answered, "one more." She led him to Mr. Hansell, "piteously groaning on the bed." Stripping off the young man's clothes, Verdi "found a deep gash just above the small of the back, near the spine."

"And all this," Verdi thought, "the work of one man—yes, of one man!"

•   •   •

IN PREPARING FOR the attack on the vice president, George Atzerodt had taken a room at the Kirkwood Hotel, where Johnson was staying. At 10:15, he was supposed to ring the bell of Suite 68, enter the room by force, find his target, and murder him. When first informed that the original plan to kidnap the president had shifted to a triple assassination, he had balked. "I won't do it," he had insisted. "I enlisted to abduct the President of the United States, not to kill." He had eventually agreed to help, but fifteen minutes before the appointed moment, seated at the bar of the Kirkwood House, he changed his mind, left the hotel, and never returned.

•   •   •

JOHN WILKES BOOTH had left little to chance in his plot to kill the president. Though already well acquainted with the layout of Ford's Theatre, Booth had attended a dress rehearsal the day before to better rehearse his scheme for shooting Lincoln in the state box and then escaping into the alley beside the theater. That morning he had again visited the theater to collect his mail, chatting amiably in the front lobby with the theater owner's brother, Harry Ford. Booth had already taken his place inside the theater when the Lincolns arrived.

The play had started as the presidential party entered the flag-draped box in the dress circle. The notes of "Hail to the Chief" brought the audience to their feet, applauding wildly and craning to see the president. Lincoln responded "with a smile and bow" before taking his seat in a comfortable armchair at the center of the box, with Mary by his side. Clara Harris was seated at the opposite end of the box, while Henry Rathbone occupied a small sofa on her left. Observing the president and first lady, one theatergoer noticed that she "rested her hand on his knee much of the time, and often called his attention to some humorous situation on the stage." Mary herself later recalled that as she snuggled ever closer to her husband, she had whispered, "What will Miss Harris think of my hanging on to you so?" He had looked at her and smiled. "She wont think any thing about it."

During the performance, the White House footman delivered a message to the president. At about twelve minutes after ten, the impeccably dressed John Wilkes Booth presented his calling card to the footman and gained admittance to the box. Once inside, he raised his pistol, pointed it at the back of the president's head, and fired.

As Lincoln slumped forward, Henry Rathbone attempted to grab the intruder. Booth pulled out his knife, slashed Rathbone in the chest, and managed to leap from the box onto the stage fifteen feet below. "As he jumped," one eyewitness recalled, "one of the spurs on his riding-boots caught in the folds of the flag draped over the front, and caused him to fall partly on his hands and knees as he struck the stage." Another onlooker observed that "he was suffering great pain," but, "making a desperate effort, he struggled up." Raising "his shining dagger in the air, which reflected the light as though it had been a diamond," he shouted the now historic words of the Virginia state motto—"Sic semper tyrannis" (Thus always to tyrants)—and ran from the stage.

Until the screams broke forth from the president's box, many in the audience thought the dramatic moment was part of the play. Then they saw Mary Lincoln frantically waving. "They have shot the President!" she cried. "They have shot the President!" Charles Leale, a young doctor seated near the presidential box, was the first to respond. "When I reached the President," he recalled, "he was almost dead, his eyes were closed." Unable at first to locate the wound, he stripped away Lincoln's coat and collar. Examining the base of the skull, he discovered "the perfectly smooth opening made by the ball." Using his finger "as a probe" to remove "the coagula which was firmly matted with the hair," he released the flow of blood, relieving somewhat the pressure on Lincoln's brain. Another doctor, Charles Sabin Taft, Julia Taft's half brother, soon arrived, and the decision was made to remove the president from the crowded box to a room in the Petersen boardinghouse across the street.

By this time, people had massed in the street. The word began to spread that assassins had attacked not only Lincoln but Seward as well. Joseph Sterling, a young clerk in the War Department, rushed to inform Stanton of the calamity. On his way, he encountered his roommate, J. G. Johnson, who joined him on the terrible errand. "When Johnson and I reached Stanton's residence," Sterling recalled, "I was breathless," so when Stanton's son Edwin Jr. opened the door, Johnson was the one to speak. "We have come," Johnson said, "to tell your father that President Lincoln has been shot." Young Stanton hurried to his father, who had been undressing for bed. When the war secretary came to the door, Sterling recalled, "he fairly shouted at me in his heavy tones: 'Mr. Sterling what news is this you bring?' " Sterling told him that both Lincoln and Seward had been assassinated. Desperately hoping this news was mere rumor, Stanton remained calm and skeptical. "Oh, that can't be so," he said, "that can't be so!" But when another clerk arrived at the door to describe the attack on Seward, Stanton had his carriage brought around at once, and against the appeals of his wife, who feared that he, too, might be a target, he headed for Seward's house at Lafayette Square.

The news reached Gideon Welles almost simultaneously. He had already gone to bed when his wife reported someone at the door. "I arose at once," Welles recorded in his diary, "and raised a window, when my messenger, James called to me that Mr. Lincoln the President had been shot," and that Seward and his son had been assassinated. Welles thought the story "very incoherent and improbable," but the messenger assured him that he had already been to Seward's house to check its veracity before coming to see his boss. Also ignoring his wife's protests, Welles dressed and set forth in the foggy night for the Seward house on the other side of the square.

Upon reaching Seward's house, Welles and Stanton were shocked at what they found. Blood was everywhere—on "the white wood work of the entry," on the stairs, on the dresses of the women, on the floor of the bedroom. Seward's bed, Welles recalled, "was saturated with blood. The Secretary was lying on his back, the upper part of his head covered by a cloth, which extended down over his eyes." Welles questioned Dr. Verdi in a whisper, but Stanton was unable to mute his stentorian voice until the doctor asked for quiet. After looking in on Fred's unconscious form, the two men walked together down the stairs. In the lower hall, they exchanged what information they had regarding the president. Welles thought they should go to the White House, but Stanton believed Lincoln was still at the theater. Army quartermaster general Meigs, who had just come to the door, implored them not to go to 10th Street, where thousands of people had gathered. When they insisted, he decided to join them.

Twelve blocks away, in his home at Sixth and E streets, Chief Justice Chase had already retired for the night. Earlier that afternoon, he had taken a carriage ride with Nettie, intending to stop at the White House to remonstrate with Lincoln over his too lenient approach to Reconstruction and his failure to demand universal suffrage. At the last minute, "uncertain how [Lincoln] would take it," Chase had decided to wait until the following day.

He was fast asleep when a servant knocked on his bedroom door. There was a gentleman downstairs, the servant said, who claimed "the President had been shot." The caller was a Treasury employee who had actually witnessed the shooting "by a man who leaped from the box upon the stage & escaped by the rear." Chase hoped "he might be mistaken," but in short order, three more callers arrived. Each "confirmed what I had been told & added that Secretary Seward had also been assassinated, and that guards were being placed around the houses of all the prominent officials, under the apprehension that the plot had a wide range. My first impulse was to rise immediately & go to the President . . . but reflecting that I could not possibly be of any service and should probably be in the way of those who could, I resolved to wait for morning & further intelligence. In a little while the guard came—for it was supposed that I was one of the destined victims—and their heavy tramp-tramp was heard under my window all night. . . . It was a night of horrors."

When Stanton and Welles arrived at the crammed room in the Petersen boardinghouse, they found that Lincoln had been placed diagonally across a bed to accommodate his long frame. Stripped of his shirt, "his large arms," Welles noted, "were of a size which one would scarce have expected from his spare appearance." His devastating wound, the doctors reported with awe, "would have killed most men instantly, or in a very few minutes. But Mr. Lincoln had so *much vitality*" that he continued to struggle against the inevitable end.

Mary spent most of the endless night weeping in an adjoining parlor, where several women friends tried vainly to comfort her. "About once an hour," Welles noted, she "would repair to the bedside of her dying husband and with lamentation and tears remain until overcome by emotion." She could only rotely repeat the question "Why didn't he shoot me? Why didn't he shoot me?" Though everyone in the room knew the president was dying, Mary was not told, out of fear that she would collapse. Whenever she came into the room, Dr. Taft recalled, "clean napkins were laid over the crimson stains on the pillow."

Early on, Mary sent a messenger for Robert, who had remained at home that night in the company of John Hay. He had already turned in when the White House doorkeeper came to his room. "Something happened to the President," Thomas Pendel told Robert, "you had better go down to the theater and see what it is." Robert asked Pendel to get Hay. Reaching Hay's room, Pendel told him, "Captain Lincoln wants to see you at once. The President has been shot." Pendel recalled that when Hay heard the news, "he turned deathly pale, the color entirely leaving his cheeks." The two young men jumped in a carriage, picking up Senator Sumner along the way.

Mary was torn over whether to summon Tad, but was apparently persuaded that the emotional boy would be devastated if he saw his father's condition. Tad and his tutor had gone that night to Grover's Theatre to see *Aladdin*. The theater had been decorated with patriotic emblems, and a poem commemorating Fort Sumter's recapture was read aloud between the acts. An eyewitness recalled that the audience was "enjoying the spectacle of Aladdin" when the theater manager came forward, "as pale as a ghost." A look of "mortal agony" contorted his face as he announced to the stunned audience that the president had been shot at Ford's Theatre.

In the midst of the pandemonium that followed, Tad was seen running "like a young deer, shrieking in agony."

"Poor little Tad," Pendel recalled, returned to the White House in tears. "O Tom Pen! Tom Pen!" Tad wailed. "They have killed Papa dead. They've killed Papa dead!" Pendel carried the little boy into Lincoln's bedroom. Turning down the bedcovers, he helped Tad undress and finally got him to lie down. "I covered him up and laid down beside him, put my arm around him, and talked to him until he fell into a sound sleep."

By midnight the entire cabinet, with the exception of Seward, had gathered in the small room at the Petersen boardinghouse. An eyewitness noted that Robert Lincoln "bore himself with great firmness, and constantly endeavored to assuage the grief of his mother by telling her to put her trust in God." Despite his brave attempts to console others, he was sometimes "entirely overcome" and "would retire into the hall and give vent to most heartrending lamentations." Almost no one was able to contain his grief that night, for as one witness observed, "there was not a soul present that did not love the president."

To Edwin Stanton fell the onerous task of alerting the generals, taking the testimony of witnesses at the theater, and orchestrating the search for the assassins. "While evidently swayed by the great shock which held us all under its paralyzing influence," Colonel A. F. Rockwell noted, "he was not only master of himself but unmistakably the dominating power over all. Indeed, the members of the cabinet, much as children might to their father, instinctively deferred to him in all things."

Throughout the night, Stanton dictated numerous dispatches, which were carried to the War Department telegraph office by a relay team of messengers positioned nearby. "Each messenger," Stanton's secretary recalled, "after handing a dispatch to the next, would run back to his post to wait for the next." The first telegram went to General Grant, requesting his immediate presence in Washington. "The President was assassinated at Ford's Theater at 10.30 to-night and cannot live. . . . Secretary Seward and his son Frederick were also assassinated at their residence and are in a dangerous condition." The dispatch reached Grant in the Bloodgood Hotel, where he was taking supper. He "dropped his head," Horace Porter recalled, "and sat in perfect silence." Noticing that he had turned "very pale," Julia Grant guessed that bad news had arrived and asked him to read the telegram aloud. "First prepare yourself for the most painful and startling news that could be received," he warned. As he made plans to return to Washington, he told Julia that the tidings filled him "with the gloomiest apprehension. The President was inclined to be kind and magnanimous, and his death at this time is an irreparable loss to the South, which now needs so much both his tenderness and magnanimity."

At 1 a.m., Stanton telegraphed the chief of police in New York, telling him to "send here immediately three or four of your best detectives." Half an hour later, he notified General Dix, "The wound is mortal. The President has been insensible ever since it was inflicted, and is now dying." Three hours later, he updated Dix: "The President continues insensible and is sinking." Early eyewitness accounts, Stanton revealed, suggested "that two assassins were engaged in the horrible crime, Wilkes Booth being the one that shot the President."

Shortly after dawn, Mary entered the room for the last time. "The death-struggle had begun," Welles recorded. "As she entered the chamber and saw how the beloved features were distorted, she fell fainting to the floor." Restoratives were given, and Mary was assisted back to the sofa in the parlor, never again to see her husband alive.

No sooner had "the town clocks struck seven," one observer recalled, than "the character of the President's breathing changed. It became faint and low. At intervals it altogether ceased, until we thought him dead. And then it would be again resumed." Lincoln's nine-hour struggle had reached its final moments. "Let us pray," Reverend Phineas D. Gurley said, and everyone present knelt.

At 7:22 a.m., April 15, 1865, Abraham Lincoln was pronounced dead. Stanton's concise tribute from his deathbed still echoes. "Now he belongs to the ages."

When Mary was told that he was gone, she piteously demanded, "Oh, why did you not tell me that he was dying." Her moans could be heard throughout the house. Finally, with Robert's help, she was taken to her carriage, which had waited in front of the house through the long night.

Until the moment of Lincoln's death, Stanton's "coolness and self-possession" had seemed "remarkable" to those around him. Now he could not stop the tears that streamed down his cheeks. In the days that followed, even as he worked tirelessly to secure the city and catch the conspirators, "Stanton's grief was uncontrollable," recalled Horace Porter, "and at the mention of Mr. Lincoln's name he would break down and weep bitterly."

While Stanton's raw grief surprised those who had seen only his gruff exterior, John Hay understood. "Not everyone knows, as I do," he wrote Stanton, "how close you stood to our lost leader, how he loved you and trusted you, and how vain were all the efforts to shake that trust and confidence, not lightly given & never withdrawn. All this will be known some time of course, to his honor and yours."

Salmon Chase was up at dawn. Soldiers had guarded him through the "night of horrors," and he was ready to join his colleagues at Lincoln's side. As he reached 10th Street, however, he encountered Assistant Treasury Secretary Maunsell Field. "Is he dead?" Chase asked. "Yes," Field replied, noting that Chase's "eyes were bloodshot, and his entire face was distorted." The Chief Justice had arrived too late, the president was already dead, and his colleagues had dispersed. Uncertain what to do next, Chase walked to Seward's house. Guards had been stationed to prevent entry, but Chase was recognized and allowed into the lower hall. There, doctors told him that Seward "had partially recovered" and, though still in critical condition, "might live—but that Mr. Frederick Seward's case was hopeless."

Chase headed toward the Kirkwood Hotel to call on the man who represented the future: the soon-to-be president, Andrew Johnson. In Johnson's suite, he encountered his old enemies Montgomery Blair and his father. He took Old Man Blair's hand and "with tearful eyes said 'Mr. Blair I hope that from this day there will cease all anger & bitterness between us.'" The old gentleman responded with equal warmth and kindness.

Perhaps more than any of Lincoln's colleagues, the Southern-born Blairs understood that the assassination was a calamity for the South. "Those of southern sympathies know now they have lost a friend willing— & more powerful to protect & serve them than they can now ever hope to find again," Elizabeth Blair remarked to her husband in a letter later that day. "Their grief is as honest as that of any one of our side." An editorial in the *Richmond Whig* expressed similar sentiments, observing that with Lincoln's death, "the heaviest blow which has ever fallen upon the people of the South has descended."

In distant St. Louis, where his son Barton had found him a new house with a large garden and a comfortable study, Edward Bates was shaken by "the astounding news" that reached him by telegram. In his diary, he remarked that beyond the "calamity which the nation has sustained, my private feelings are deeply moved by the sudden murder of my chief, with and under whom I have served the country, through many difficult and trying scenes, and always with mutual sentiments of respect and friendship. I mourn his fall, both for the country and for myself."

News of Lincoln's death was withheld from Seward. The doctors feared that he could not sustain the shock. On Easter Sunday, however, as he looked out the window toward Lafayette Park, he noticed the War Department flag at half-mast. "He gazed awhile," Noah Brooks reported, "then, turning to his attendant," he announced, "The President is dead." The attendant tried to deny it, but Seward knew with grim certainty. "If he had been alive he would have been the first to call on me," he said, "but he has not been here, nor has he sent to know how I am, and there's the flag at halfmast." He lay back on the bed, "the great tears coursing down his gashed cheeks, and the dreadful truth sinking into his mind." His good friend, his captain and chief, was dead.

"The history of governments," John Hay later observed, "affords few instances of an official connection hallowed by a friendship so absolute and sincere as that which existed between these two magnanimous spirits. Lincoln had snatched away from Seward at Chicago the prize of a laborious life-time, when it seemed within his grasp. Yet Seward was the first man named in his Cabinet and the first who acknowledged his personal preeminence. . . . From the beginning of the Administration to that dark and terrible hour when they were both struck down by the hand of murderous treason, there was no shadow of jealousy or doubt ever disturbed their mutual confidence and regard."

•   •   •

FLAGS REMAINED AT HALF-STAFF in the nation's capital until the last week of May, when citizens from all over the country came to Washington to witness "the farewell march" of nearly two hundred thousand Union soldiers who would soon disband and return to their homes. Stanton had orchestrated the two-day pageant as a final tribute to the brave men who had fought on battlefields from Antietam to Fredericksburg, Gettysburg to Vicksburg, Atlanta to the sea. "Never in the history of Washington," reported Noah Brooks, "had there been such an enormous influx of visitors as at that time. For weeks there had been so vast a volume of applications for accommodations at the hotels and boarding-houses that every available nook and corner had been taken."

Schools and government buildings were closed for the occasion. Reviewing stands had been built all along Pennsylvania Avenue, "from the Capitol to the White House." A covered platform had been erected to seat President Andrew Johnson, General Grant, and an assortment of dignitaries. The weather was beautiful on both days: "The air was bright, clear, and invigorating."

The first day was dedicated to the Army of the Potomac. Hour after hour the troops filed past in review—the cavalry, the mounted artillery, the infantry, the engineering brigades—each with their distinctive uniforms and badges, accompanied by "the clatter of hoofs, the clank of sabers, and the shrill call of bugles." It was, Gideon Welles marveled, a "magnificent and imposing spectacle."

"You see in these armies," Stanton predicted, "the foundation of our

Republic—our future railway managers, congressmen, bank presidents, senators, manufacturers, judges, governors, and diplomats; yes, and not less than half a dozen presidents." (He was very nearly right, for five of the next seven presidents would be Civil War veterans: Ulysses S. Grant, Rutherford B. Hayes, James Garfield, Benjamin Harrison, and William McKinley.)

Over a quarter of a century earlier, in 1838, young Abraham Lincoln had spoken with fervor of the veterans of the Revolutionary War, who were by then mostly gone, the fabled scenes of their great struggle for American independence growing "more and more dim by the lapse of time." In that war, "nearly every adult male had been a participant," he said, "in the form of a husband, a father, a son or a brother," until "a *living history was* to be found in every family." Such he had said was no longer true for his generation.

Now a new "living history" had been forged in the families of nearly three million Union soldiers who had fought to create what their matured leader had called "a new birth of freedom" to ensure that "government of the people, by the people, for the people, shall not perish from the earth." The soldiers marching down Pennsylvania Avenue that warm spring day knew they had accomplished something that would change their lives and their nation forever.

The second day belonged to the Army of the West, marching with solemn dignity behind General Sherman. "The streets were filled with people to see the pageant," Sherman recalled. "When I reached the Treasury-building, and looked back, the sight was simply magnificent. The column was compact, and the glittering muskets looked like a solid mass of steel, moving with the regularity of a pendulum."

When Sherman came to the corner of Lafayette Square, someone pointed to an upper window of a brick house where Seward, still too feeble to walk on his own, had been carried to witness the parade. "I moved in that direction and took off my hat to Mr. Seward," Sherman recalled. "He recognized the salute, returned it, and then we rode on steadily past the President, saluting with our swords."

All of Washington was present, Gideon Welles sadly noted—congressmen, senators, justices, diplomats, governors, military officers, the members of the cabinet, fathers and sons, mothers and daughters. "But Abraham Lincoln was not there. All felt this." None felt that absence more keenly than the members of his cabinet, the remarkable group of rivals whom Lincoln had brought into his official family. They had fiercely opposed one another and often contested their chief on important questions, but, as Seward later remarked, "a Cabinet which should agree at once on every such question would be no better or safer than one counsellor." By calling these men to his side, Lincoln had afforded them an opportunity to exercise their talents to the fullest and to share in the labor and the glory of the struggle that would reunite and transform their country and secure their own places in posterity.

•   •   •

"I HAVE NO DOUBT that Lincoln will be the conspicuous figure of the war," predicted Ulysses S. Grant. "He was incontestably the greatest man I ever knew."

The poet Walt Whitman felt much the same. "I have more than once fancied to myself," Whitman wrote in 1888, "the time when the present century has closed, and a new one open'd, and the men and deeds of that contest have become somewhat vague and mythical." He fancied that at some commemoration of those earlier days, an "ancient soldier" would sit surrounded by a group of young men whose eyes and "eager questions" would betray their sense of wonder. "What! have you seen Abraham Lincoln—and heard him speak—and touch'd his hand?" Though conceding that the future might decide differently about the prairie president, Whitman had no trouble speaking for his own generation: "Abraham Lincoln seems to me the grandest figure yet, on all the crowded canvas of the Nineteenth Century."

Even Whitman might have been amazed by the scope of Lincoln's legacy by the time the new century arrived. In 1908, in a wild and remote area of the North Caucasus, Leo Tolstoy, the greatest writer of the age, was the guest of a tribal chief "living far away from civilized life in the mountains." Gathering his family and neighbors, the chief asked Tolstoy to tell stories about the famous men of history. Tolstoy told how he entertained the eager crowd for hours with tales of Alexander, Caesar, Frederick the Great, and Napoleon. When he was winding to a close, the chief stood and said, "But you have not told us a syllable about the greatest general and greatest ruler of the world. We want to know something about him. He was a hero. He spoke with a voice of thunder; he laughed like the sunrise and his deeds were strong as the rock. . . . His name was Lincoln and the country in which he lived is called America, which is so far away that if a youth should journey to reach it he would be an old man when he arrived. Tell us of that man."

"I looked at them," Tolstoy recalled, "and saw their faces all aglow, while their eyes were burning. I saw that those rude barbarians were really interested in a man whose name and deeds had already become a legend." He told them everything he knew about Lincoln's "home life and youth . . . his habits, his influence upon the people and his physical strength." When he finished, they were so grateful for the story that they presented him with "a wonderful Arabian horse." The next morning, as Tolstoy prepared to leave, they asked if he could possibly acquire for them a picture of Lincoln. Thinking that he might find one at a friend's house in the neighboring town, Tolstoy asked one of the riders to accompany him. "I was successful in getting a large photograph from my friend," recalled Tolstoy. As he handed it to the rider, he noted that the man's hand trembled as he took it. "He gazed for several minutes silently, like one in a reverent prayer, his eyes filled with tears."

Tolstoy went on to observe, "This little incident proves how largely the name of Lincoln is worshipped throughout the world and how legendary his personality has become. Now, why was Lincoln so great that he over-shadows all other national heroes? He really was not a great general like Napoleon or Washington; he was not such a skilful statesman as Gladstone or Frederick the Great; but his supremacy expresses itself altogether in his peculiar moral power and in the greatness of his character.

"Washington was a typical American. Napoleon was a typical French-man, but Lincoln was a humanitarian as broad as the world. He was bigger than his country—bigger than all the Presidents together.

"We are still too near to his greatness," Tolstoy concluded, "but after a few centuries more our posterity will find him considerably bigger than we do. His genius is still too strong and too powerful for the common under-standing, just as the sun is too hot when its light beams directly on us."

• • •

"EVERY MAN IS SAID to have his peculiar ambition," the twenty-three-year-old Abraham Lincoln had written in his open letter to the people of Sangamon County during his first bid for public office in the Illinois state legislature. "Whether it be true or not, I can say for one that I have no other [ambition] so great as that of being truly esteemed of my fellow men, by rendering myself worthy of their esteem. How far I shall succeed in gratifying this ambition, is yet to be developed."

The ambition to establish a reputation worthy of the esteem of his fel-lows so that his story could be told after his death had carried Lincoln through his bleak childhood, his laborious efforts to educate himself, his string of political failures, and a depression so profound that he declared himself more than willing to die, except that "he had done nothing to make any human being remember that he had lived." An indomitable sense of purpose had sustained him through the disintegration of the Union and through the darkest months of the war, when he was called upon again and again to rally his disheartened countrymen, soothe the animosity of his generals, and mediate among members of his often contentious administration.

His conviction that we are one nation, indivisible, "conceived in Liberty, and dedicated to the proposition that all men are created equal," led to the rebirth of a union free of slavery. And he expressed this conviction in a language of enduring clarity and beauty, exhibiting a literary genius to match his political genius.

With his death, Abraham Lincoln had come to seem the embodiment of his own words—"With malice toward none; with charity for all"—voiced in his second inaugural to lay out the visionary pathway to a reconstructed union. The deathless name he sought from the start had grown far beyond Sangamon County and Illinois, reached across the truly United States, until his legacy, as Stanton had surmised at the moment of his death, belonged not only to America but to the ages—to be revered and sung throughout all time.

EPILOGUE

———•———

A GAINST ALL ODDS, Seward and his son Frederick eventually recovered from their frightful injuries, but the "night of horrors" took its ultimate toll on Frances Seward. Six weeks afterward, convinced that she had taken on the afflictions of her loved ones through "vicarious suffering," she collapsed and died. Her funeral in Auburn was said to have brought together "the largest assemblage that ever attended the funeral of a woman in America." In the months that followed, Fanny remained at her father's side, trying to compensate for her departed mother until she herself fell desperately ill from tuberculosis. When she died two months short of her twenty-second birthday, Seward was inconsolable. "Truly it may be said," the *Washington Republican* noted, "that the assassin's blows passed by the father and son and fell fatally on the mother and daughter."

Seward remained secretary of state throughout President Andrew Johnson's term. While his attempts to mediate Johnson's bitter struggles with the radicals in Congress failed, he took great pride in what was originally lampooned as "Seward's Folly"—the purchase of Alaska. After retiring from public office, he spent his last years traveling. With Fred and Anna, he embarked on an eight-month journey to Alaska, California, and Mexico. Returning to Auburn, he immediately made plans for a trip around the world, visiting Japan, China, India, Egypt, Greece, Turkey, and France. He died peacefully in 1872 at the age of seventy-one, surrounded by his family. When his daughter-in-law Jenny asked if he had any deathbed advice to impart, he said simply: "Love one another." Thurlow Weed, who served as a pallbearer, wept openly as the body of his oldest friend was lowered into the grave.

Stanton's remaining days in the cabinet were acrimonious. His sympathy with the congressional radicals on Reconstruction brought him into open conflict with the president, who asked for his resignation. Refusing to honor Johnson's request even after he was handed a removal order, Stanton "barricaded himself" in his office for weeks, taking his meals in the department and sleeping on his couch. He argued that his dismissal violated the Tenure of Office Act, recently passed by congressional radicals over the president's veto, which required Senate consent for the removal of any cabinet officer. Johnson's disregard for the Tenure of Office Act became one of the articles of impeachment lodged against him in 1868. When the impeachment failed by one vote in the Senate, Stanton finally submitted his resignation.

Although exhausted by the ordeal, Stanton had little time to rest. His fortune had been depleted during his tenure in the cabinet. After returning to the practice of law, he was overjoyed when President Grant nominated him to the Supreme Court, the "only office" he had ever desired to hold, in December 1869. His happiness was short-lived. Three days later, as his family gathered for the Christmas holidays, he suffered a severe asthma attack, lapsed into unconsciousness, and died. He had just turned fifty-five. "I know that it is useless to say anything," Robert Todd Lincoln wrote to Stanton's son Edwin, Jr., "and yet when I recall the kindness of your father to me, when my father was lying dead and I felt utterly desperate, hardly able to realize the truth, I am as little able to keep my eyes from filling with tears as he was then."

Edward Bates spent his remaining years with his close-knit family, reunited with his son Fleming, whom he had welcomed home from the Confederate Army once the war ended. When Bates died in 1869 at the age of seventy-six, he was revered as much for his character as for his public accomplishments. Above all, one eulogist noted, "it was in his social and domestic relations that his character shown brightest; it was as a husband, as a father and a friend that he has endeared himself to others by ties which death cannot sever."

After presiding over the impeachment trial of Andrew Johnson, Salmon Chase turned his addicted gaze to the 1868 presidential race, his hopes resting with the Democrats after Grant had secured the Republican nomination. With Kate serving as his campaign manager, he had his name placed before the delegates, but when Ohio announced for New York's Horace Seymour, Chase's candidacy was doomed. Once more, his home state had derailed his ambitions. Four years later, still hoping for the presidential nod, he switched his allegiance to the Liberal Republican Party. Again the nomination eluded him, going instead to Horace Greeley. His physical condition weakened by a heart attack and a stroke, Chase fell into depression, confiding to a friend that he was "too much of an invalid to be more than a cipher. Sometimes I feel as if I were dead." Death came on May 7, 1873, with Kate and Nettie by his side. He was sixty-five.

After her father's death, Kate saw her marriage to Sprague fall apart. An affair with New York senator Roscoe Conkling ended in scandal when Sprague, finding the couple together at his Narragansett mansion, went after Conkling with a shotgun. Following a violent argument during which

Sprague tried to throw Kate from a bedroom window, she sued for divorce. She returned to Washington, where she died in poverty at fifty-eight.

The Blairs returned to the Democratic Party. Though Frank Blair was selected as Seymour's vice presidential candidate in 1868, his intemperate denunciations of opponents cut short what might have been a promising political future. He died from a fall in his house in 1875 at the age of fifty-four. Old Man Blair outlived his son by one year, maintaining "his physical vigor, his mental faculties and his sprightliness of disposition" until his death at eighty-five. Montgomery served as counsel to Democrat Samuel Tilden in the disputed election of 1876, which Republican Rutherford B. Hayes eventually won. Blair was writing a biography of Andrew Jackson when he died in 1883 at the age of seventy.

Gideon Welles supported Andrew Johnson during the impeachment trial, remaining in the cabinet until 1868. Returning to Connecticut, he wrote a series of historical essays and was among the first to depict Lincoln as "a towering figure, coping admirably with herculean tasks." His perceptive diary, which he edited in his last years, remains one of the most valuable sources on the dynamics within the Lincoln administration. Welles was seventy-five when he died from a streptococcus infection in 1878.

John Nicolay and John Hay remained friends until the end of their lives, coauthoring a massive ten-volume study of Lincoln based on his then-unpublished papers. Nicolay was at work on an abridged version of their study when he died in 1901 at sixty-nine. Hay served as secretary of state under Presidents William McKinley and Theodore Roosevelt. Shortly before he died from a blood clot at the age of sixty-six in 1905, he dreamed that he had returned "to the White House to report to the President who turned out to be Mr. Lincoln. He was very kind and considerate, and sympathetic about my illness. . . . He gave me two unimportant letters to answer. I was pleased that this slight order was within my power to obey." Forty years after the assassination of his beloved chief, Hay awoke with an "overpowering melancholy."

Mary Lincoln never recovered from her husband's death. After returning to Illinois, she confided to Elizabeth Blair Lee that "each morning, on awakening, from my troubled slumbers, the utter impossibility of living another day, so wretched, appears to me, as an impossibility." Were it not for her "precious Tad," she told her boy's tutor, she "would gladly welcome death."

Mother and son were nearly inseparable. Tad journeyed with Mary to Europe, demonstrating what John Hay described as "a thoughtful devotion and tenderness beyond his years." Not long after returning to America, Tad suffered what doctors termed "compression of the heart." He died two months later at eighteen. "The modest and cordial young fellow who passed through New York a few weeks ago with his mother will never be known outside the circle of his mourning friends," commented John Hay in a touching obituary written for the *New York Tribune*. "But 'little Tad' will be remembered as long as any live who bore a personal share in the great movements whose center for four years was Washington. He was so full of life and vigor—so bubbling over with health and high spirits, that he kept the house alive with his pranks and his fantastic enterprises."

Mary's misery was compounded by her ever-consuming worries over money. "It is very hard to deal with one who is sane on all subjects but one," Robert confided in Mary Harlan, the young woman who would become his wife. "You could hardly believe it possible, but my mother protests to me that she is in actual want and nothing I can do or say will convince her to the contrary." Her increasingly erratic behavior persuaded Robert to commit her to a state hospital for the insane where she remained for four months until she was released to the care of her sister Elizabeth in Springfield. The episode permanently estranged Mary from her only remaining child. After a final trip to Europe, she lived her remaining years as a virtual recluse in the Edwards mansion, where, in happier days, she and Abraham Lincoln had met and married. She was sixty-three in 1882 when her oft-stated longing for death was fulfilled at last.

ACKNOWLEDGMENTS

A NYONE WRITING on Abraham Lincoln stands on the shoulders of a monumental body of work, including classic volumes by some of our country's finest historians. I am immensely grateful to the many Lincoln scholars who generously welcomed me into their field, sharing sources, discussing ideas, inviting me to their homes, reading parts of my manuscript, and offering access to their rare collections of Lincolniana. They include David Herbert Donald, Douglas L. Wilson, Thomas F. Schwartz, Frank J. Williams, Harold Holzer, John R. Sellers, Virginia Laas, Michael A. Burlingame, Gabor S. Boritt, James O. Hall, Harold M. Hyman, Philip B. Kunhardt III, Peter W. Kuhnhardt, and Louise Taper.

In the course of the last ten years, I have been guided in my search for primary materials by superb staffs at thirty different libraries. I especially wish to thank the remarkably generous Thomas F. Schwartz, Kim Matthew Bauer, Mary Michals, and John Marruffo at the Abraham Lincoln Presidential Library and Museum in Springfield, Illinois.

I owe thanks as well to the following: in California, John Rhodehamel and the staff of the Huntington Library. In Illinois, the Chicago Historical Society; the Newberry Library; the University of Chicago's Special Collections Research Center and Harper Memorial Library; Daniel Weinberg and the Abraham Lincoln Book Shop. In Indiana, the Lincoln Museum. In Iowa, the State Historical Society of Iowa and the University of Iowa Library. In Kentucky, the Eastern Kentucky University Archives. In Louisiana, Judy Bolton and the staff of the Louisiana and Lower Mississippi Valley Collections of the Louisiana State University Library. In Maryland, the Maryland Historical Society.

In Massachusetts, the Boston Public Library's Rare Book and Manuscript Collections; the Concord Public Library; Harvard University's Government Documents and Microfilm Collection, the Houghton Library, the Arthur and Elizabeth Schlesinger Library on the History of Women in America, and Widener Library; and the Massachusetts Historical Society. In Missouri, Dennis Northcott and the staff of the Missouri Historical Society; the St. Louis Art Museum; and the State Historical Society of Missouri. In New Jersey, Don C. Skemer and Anna Lee Pauls at Princeton University's Department of Rare Books and Special Collections.

In New York, the New York State Library; Betty Mae Lewis and Peter A. Wisbey of the Seward House, Auburn; Mary M. Huth and the staff of the University of Rochester Library's Department of Rare Books and Special Collections. In Ohio, the Cincinnati Historical Society; John Haas and the staff of the Ohio Historical Society; the Ohio State House; and the Western Reserve Historical Society. In Pennsylvania, the Dauphin County Historical Society and the Historical Society of Pennsylvania. In Rhode Island, Mary-Jo Kline and Ann Morgan Dodge of Brown University's John Hay Library. In Virginia, the Virginia Historical Society. In Washington, D.C., John Sellers, Clark Evans, and the staff of the Library of Congress; Michael Musick and the staff of the National Archives and Records Administration; James C. Hewes at the Willard Hotel; and the staff at the Blair House. And last, Michael Burlingame, who is for all Lincoln scholars a library unto himself, generously sharing his unparalled knowledge of Lincoln while writing his own monumental Lincoln biography.

I owe an immense debt once again to my great friend and indefatigable assistant, Linda Vandegrift, who has worked at my side on all my projects for the past twenty years.

I am grateful to Nora Titone (currently writing what I am certain will be an extraordinary biography of Edwin Booth, actor and brother to Lincoln's assassin), who did research at Harvard University and in Illinois, the Land of Lincoln. Through our many discussions, she provided invaluable insights into the social, intellectual, and literary milieu of nineteenth-century America.

In Washington, Dr. Michelle Krowl, a brilliant Civil War historian who has published numerous scholarly articles and teaches at Northern Virginia Community College, displayed remarkable energy, intuition, and intelligence in digging through archives and checking source materials at both the Library of Congress and the National Archives.

There are many others who read portions of the manuscript and helped in various ways, including Judith Arnold, Beth Laski, Erik Owens, Louisa Thomas, Chad Callaghan, Michael Goodwin, Lindsay Hosmer, J. Wayne Lee, Phyllis Grann, John Logan, Paul Webb, Kathleen Krowl, Brad Gernand, Karen Needles, and John Hill, and all our good friends at our two favorite watering holes in Concord, Massachusetts—Serafina Ristorante and Walden Grille. To Michael Kushakji, who came to our house day and night when our computers failed, I owe a special debt.

As always, I am grateful to my supportive and enthusiastic literary agent, Binky Urban, and to the men and women at Simon & Schuster who have become almost like family after more than twenty-five years of collaboration: David Rosenthal, Carolyn Reidy, Irene Kheradi, Jackie Seow,

George Turianski, Linda Dingler, Ellen Sasahara, Lisa Healy, Victoria Meyer, and Elizabeth Hayes. For a superb job in copyediting the manuscript, I thank Ann Adelman and Emily Beth Thomas. I owe a special thanks to Roger Labrie, who displayed extraordinary grace under pressure while shepherding the book to meet various deadlines in the final stages.

I have long depended on my incomparable editor, Alice E. Mayhew, but never did her massive contributions weigh more heavily than on this book. No editor has a more profound knowledge of Abraham Lincoln. No editor could have given me better advice from start to finish on structure, tone, and language. She is the absolute best in her profession. I shall be forever grateful to her.

Finally, I owe more than I can ever express to my husband, Richard Goodwin, to whom this book is dedicated. He read and edited every single page, from the earliest drafts to the finished product. His passion for the subject of Abraham Lincoln matches my own. I argued with him, debated with him, and ended up usually following his advice. He has thought as deeply about Lincoln as anyone. This book is his creation as much as mine.

Concord, Massachusetts
July 2005

NOTES

ABBREVIATIONS USED IN THE NOTES:

AL	Abraham Lincoln	JWW	Jesse W. Weik
CS	Charles Sumner	KCS	Kate Chase Sprague
EB	Edward Bates	LW	Lazette M. (Miller) Worden
EBL	Elizabeth Blair Lee	MB	Montgomery Blair
EMS	Edwin M. Stanton	MEM	Mary Ellen McClellan
FAS	Frances A. (Miller) Seward	MTL	Mary Todd Lincoln
FB	Francis Preston ("Frank") Blair, Jr.	SPC	Salmon P. Chase
FPB	Francis Preston Blair, Sr.	SPL	Samuel Phillips Lee
FS	Frances A. ("Fanny") Seward	TB	Therena Bates
FWS	Frederick W. Seward	TW	Thurlow Weed
GBM	George B. McClellan	USG	Ulysses S. Grant
GW	Gideon Welles	WHH	William H. Herndon
JGN	John G. Nicolay	WHS	William H. Seward
JH	John Hay		

CW   *Collected Works of Abraham Lincoln*
HI   *Herndon's Informants*
NR   *National Republican*, Washington, D.C.
NYH   *New York Herald*, New York, N.Y.
NYT   *New York Times*, New York, N.Y.
NYTrib *New York Tribune*, New York, N.Y.
OR   *The War of the Rebellion: A Compilation of the Official Records*
            of the Union and Confederate Armies (128 vols., Washington, D.C.:
            Government Printing Office, 1880–1901)
Star   *Evening Star*, Washington, D.C.

Chase Papers   *The Salmon P. Chase Papers: Microfilm Edition*, ed. John Niven (Frederick, Md.: University Publications of America, 1987)
Lincoln Papers Papers of Abraham Lincoln, Manuscript Division, Library of Congress. Available at *Abraham Lincoln Papers at the Library of Congress*, Manuscript Division (Washington, D.C.: American Memory Project, [2000–01]), http://memory.loc.gov/ammem/alhtml/alhome.html
Nicolay Papers Papers of John G. Nicolay, Manuscript Division, Library of Congress
Seward Papers   *The Papers of William H. Seward* (Woodbridge, Conn.: Research Publications, 1983
Welles Papers   Papers of Gideon Welles, Manuscript Division, Library of Congress

NOTE TO READERS: When quoting from primary documents, original spelling and grammar have been kept.

INTRODUCTION

Page

xv "there is little . . . of Abraham Lincoln": Frederick Douglass, "Oration in Memory of Abraham Lincoln," April 14, 1876, in *Frederick Douglass: Selected Speeches and Writings*, ed. Philip S. Foner, abridged by Yuval Taylor (Chicago: Lawrence Hill Books, 1999), pp. 620–21.

xvi "comparatively unknown . . . such anxious times": Ralph Waldo Emerson, "Abraham Lincoln," in *Miscellanies* (Cambridge, Mass.: Riverside Press, 1904), pp. 330–31.

xvi "very near . . . perfect man": EB, quoted in F. B. Carpenter, *Six Months at the White House with Abraham Lincoln* (New York: Hurd and Houghton, 1866), p. 68.

xix "field of glory": AL, "Address Before the Young Men's Lyceum of Springfield, Illinois," January 27, 1838, in *CW*, I, p. 113.

xix "a new birth of freedom": AL, "Address Delivered at the Dedication of the Cemetery at Gettysburg, November 19, 1863; Edward Everett Copy," in *CW*, VII, p. 21.

CHAPTER 1: FOUR MEN WAITING

Page

5 Lincoln was up early: Henry B. Rankin, *Personal Recollections of Abraham Lincoln* (New York and London: G. P. Putnam's Sons, 1916), p. 187.

5 Chenery House: Paul M. Angle, *"Here I Have Lived": A History of Lincoln's Springfield, 1821–1865* (Springfield, Ill.: Abraham Lincoln Association, 1935), p. 175.

5 Springfield businesses: See advertisements in *Illinois State Journal*, Springfield, Ill., May 18, 1860.

5 first ballot was not due to be called until 10 a.m.: *Press and Tribune*, Chicago, May 19, 1860; *Star*, May 19, 1860.

5 visibly "nervous, fidgety . . . excited": Christopher C. Brown interview, 1865–1866, in Douglas L. Wilson and Rodney O. Davis, eds., *Herndon's Informants: Letters, Interviews, and Statements About Abraham Lincoln* (Urbana and Chicago: University of Illinois Press, 1998), p. 438 [hereafter *HI*].

5 the untidy office: William H. Herndon and Jesse W. Weik, *Herndon's Life of Lincoln*, introduction and notes by Paul M. Angle, new introduction by Henry Steele Commager (Cleveland, Ohio: World Publishing Co., 1942; New York: Da Capo Press, 1983), pp. 254–55.

5 The editorial room: Paul Angle, *Lincoln in Springfield: A Guide to the Places in Springfield which were Associated with the Life of Abraham Lincoln* (Springfield, Ill.: Lincoln Centennial Association, 1927), p. 2.

6 a "complimentary" gesture: Entry of May 19, 1860, in Edward Bates, *The Diary of Edward Bates, 1859–1866*, ed. Howard K. Beale. Vol. IV of the Annual Report of the American Historical Association for the Year 1930 (Washington, D.C.: Government Printing Office, 1933), p. 130.

6 the town clock: *Illinois State Journal*, Springfield, Ill., January 17, 1860.

6 James Conkling: Clinton L. Conkling, "How Mr. Lincoln Received the News of His First Nomination," *Transactions of the Illinois State Historical Society* (1909), p. 64.

6 his singular way of walking . . . needed oiling: Herndon and Weik, *Herndon's Life of Lincoln*, p. 471.

6 "His legs . . . a hard day's work": William E. Doster, *Lincoln and Episodes of the Civil War* (New York and London: G. P. Putnam's Sons, 1915), p. 15.

6 His features . . . "as belong to a handsome man": *Press and Tribune*, Chicago, May 23, 1860.

6 "so overspread with sadness . . . capital of Illinois": Horace White, *Abraham Lincoln in 1854: An Address delivered before the Illinois State Historical Society, at its 9th Annual Meeting at Springfield, Illinois, Jan. 30, 1908* (Springfield, Ill.: Illinois State Historical Society, 1908), p. 19.

6 "his winning manner . . . and gentleness": Ibid.

6 "this expression . . . true friendship": Ibid.

7 "you cease to think . . . awkward": *Utica Morning Herald*, reprinted in *NYTrib*, July 9, 1860.

7 "on a borrowed horse . . . a few clothes": Joshua F. Speed, *Reminiscences of Abraham Lincoln and Notes of a Visit to California* (Louisville, Ky.: John P. Morton & Co., 1884), p. 21.

7 population of Springfield: Harry E. Pratt, *Lincoln's Springfield* (Springfield, Ill.: Abraham Lincoln Association, 1938), p. 2; Octavia Roberts, *Lincoln in Illinois* (Boston: Houghton Mifflin, 1918), p. 94.

7 number of hotels, saloons, etc.: C.S. Williams, comp., *Williams' Springfield Directory City Guide, and Business Mirror, for 1860–61. To Which is Appended a List of Post Offices in the United States and Territories, Corrected up to Date* (Springfield, Ill.: Johnson & Bradford, 1860).

7 "the belle of the town": "Lincoln and Mary Todd," [c. 1880s], reel 11, Herndon-Weik Collection of Lincolniana, Manuscript Division, Library of Congress [hereafter Herndon-Weik Collection, DLC].

7 Mary's education: Ruth Painter Randall, *Mary Lincoln: Biography of a Marriage* (Boston: Little, Brown, 1953), pp. 23, 25, 27, 28; Jean H. Baker, *Mary Todd Lincoln: A Biography* (New York and London: W. W. Norton & Co., 1987), pp. 37–42, 44–45.

7 "I want to dance . . . he certainly did": Katherine Helm, *The True Story of Mary, Wife of Lincoln* (New York and London: Harper & Bros., 1928), p. 74.

7 children born, and one buried in Springfield: AL, "Farewell Address at Springfield, Illinois," February 11,

1861, in *The Collected Works of Lincoln*, Vol. IV, ed. Roy P. Basler (8 vols., New Brunswick, N.J.: Rutgers University Press, 1953), p. 190.

7 "two-story" . . . no garden: *New York Evening Post*, reprinted in *Albany Evening Journal*, May 24, 1860 (quote); *Utica Morning Herald*, reprinted in *NYTrib*, July 9, 1860; Frances Todd Wallace interview, [1865–1866], in *HI*, p. 486.

7 "The adornments . . . chastely appropriate": *Utica Morning Herald*, reprinted in *NYTrib*, July 9, 1860.

7 "the customary little table": Carl Schurz, *The Reminiscences of Carl Schurz. Vol. II: 1852–1863* (New York: McClure Co., 1907), p. 188.

7 "Everything tended to represent . . . showy display": *Springfield [Mass.] Republican*, May 23, 1860.

8 "moving heaven & Earth": David Davis and Jesse K. Dubois to AL, May 15, 1860, Lincoln Papers.

8 "a big brain and a big heart": Mrs. John A. Logan, quoted by Allan Nevins in foreword to Willard L. King, *Lincoln's Manager: David Davis* (Cambridge, Mass.: Harvard University Press, 1960), p. xi.

8 Norman Judd: Ibid., pp. 128–29.

8 he knew Lincoln "as intimately": Leonard Swett, quoted in Osborn H. Oldroyd, *Lincoln's Campaign, or The Political Revolution of 1860* (Chicago: Laird & Lee, 1896), p. 70.

8 the "circuit": Henry Clay Whitney, *Life on the Circuit with Lincoln*, introduction and notes by Paul M. Angle (Caldwell, Idaho: The Caxon Printers, 1940), pp. 61–88; see "Travelling on the Circuit," chapter 15 in Ida M. Tarbell, *The Life of Abraham Lincoln*, Vol. I (New York: S. S. McClure Co., 1895; New York: The Macmillan Company, 1917), pp. 241–56.

8 Lincoln . . . the center of attention: Henry C. Whitney, *Lincoln the Citizen. Vol. I of A Life of Lincoln* (1892; New York: Baker & Taylor Co., 1908), pp. 190–91; William H. Herndon, *A Letter from William H. Herndon to Isaac N. Arnold Relating to Abraham Lincoln, His Wife, and Their Life in Springfield* (privately printed, 1937).

8 crowds of villagers: Francis Fisher Browne, *The Every-Day Life of Abraham Lincoln* (New York: N. D. Thompson Publishing Co., 1886; Lincoln, Nebr., and London: University of Nebraska Press, 1995), p. 158.

8 emboldened his quest for office: David Herbert Donald, *Lincoln* (New York: Simon & Schuster, 1995), p. 106.

8 "broke down . . . mutual trust": Robert H. Wiebe, "Lincoln's Fraternal Democracy," in John L. Thomas, ed., *Abraham Lincoln and the American Political Tradition* (Amherst: University of Massachusetts Press, 1986), p. 19.

8 disparate elements of . . . Republican Party: Theodore Clarke Smith, *The Liberty and Free Soil Parties in the Old Northwest. Harvard Historical Studies*, Vol. VI (New York: Longmans, Green & Co., 1897; New York: Russell & Russell, 1967), p. 1; William Lee Miller, *Lincoln's Virtues: An Ethical Biography* (New York: Alfred A. Knopf, 2002), p. 317.

9 "Of *strange, discordant* . . . fought the battle through": AL, "A House Divided": Speech at Springfield, Illinois, June 16, 1858, in *CW*, II, p. 468.

9 when speech-making prowess: Lawrence W. Levine, *Highbrow / Lowbrow: The Emergence of Cultural Hierarchy in America* (Cambridge, Mass.: Harvard University Press, 1988), p. 36.

9 "from sun-up til sun-down": Christine Ann Fidler, "Young Limbs of the Law: Law Students, Legal Education and the Occupational Culture of Attorneys, 1820–1860." Ph.D. diss., University of California, Berkeley, 1996, p. 165.

9 attendance at Cooper Union speech: Benjamin P. Thomas, *Abraham Lincoln: A Biography* (New York: Alfred A. Knopf, 1952), p. 202.

9 "one of the happiest . . . New York audience": *NYTrib*, February 28, 1860.

9 state convention at Decatur: *Press and Tribune*, Chicago, May 11, 1860; Don E. Fehrenbacher, *Prelude to Greatness: Lincoln in the 1850s* (Stanford, Calif.: Stanford University Press, 1962), p. 148.

9 "the Rail Candidate for President": *NYH*, May 24, 1860.

9 "with no clogs . . . rights of the South": *Press and Tribune*, Chicago, May 15, 1860. The *Press and Tribune* became the *Tribune* on October 25, 1860.

9 "new in the field . . . very great many": AL to Sam Galloway, March 24, 1860, in *CW*, IV, p. 34.

10 "in a mood to come . . . their first love": Ibid.

10 "We are laboring . . . for any result": Nathan M. Knapp to AL, May 14, 1860, Lincoln Papers.

10 "Am very hopeful . . . be Excited": David Davis to AL, May 17, 1860, Lincoln Papers.

10 Lincoln stretched . . . "and practice law": Conkling, "How Mr. Lincoln Received the News," *Transactions* (1909), pp. 64–65.

11 Seward typically rose: Frederick W. Seward, *William H. Seward: An Autobiography from 1801 to 1834, with a Memoir of His Life, and Selections from His Letters, 1831–1846* (New York: D. Appleton & Co., 1877), p. 658 [hereafter Seward, *An Autobiography*]; Frederick W. Seward, *Seward at Washington, as Senator and Secretary of State. A Memoir of His Life, with Selections from His Letters, 1846–1861* (New York: Derby & Miller, 1891), p. 203.

11 description of Seward mansion: Interview with Betty Mae Lewis, curator of Seward House, Auburn, N.Y., 1999 [hereafter Lewis interview]; *The Seward House* (Auburn, N.Y.: The Foundation Historical Association, 1955); *NYH*, August 27, 1860.

11 Seward's interest in gardening: Seward, *An Autobiography*, pp. 368, 657–58.

11 "a lover's interest": WHS to [TW?], April 12, 1835, in ibid., p. 257.

11 "came in to the table . . . that was exhausted": Ibid., pp. 658, 461, 481; Lewis interview.

12 "The cannoneers . . . joyful news": *Auburn Democrat*, reprinted in the *Atlas and Argus*, Albany, N.Y., May 28, 1860.

12 weather conditions: WHS to FAS, December 17, 1834, reel 112, Seward Papers; Patricia C. Johnson, "Sensi-

tivity and Civil War: The Selected Diaries and Papers, 1858–1866, of Frances Adeline [Fanny] Seward." Ph.D. diss., University of Rochester, 1963, pp. 1–2.

12 Visitors had come . . . Weedsport to the north: Henry B. Stanton, *Random Recollections*, 3rd edn. (New York: Harper & Bros., 1887), p. 215.

12 Local restaurants had stocked up: *NYH*, August 27, 1860; *Auburn Democrat*, reprinted in the *Atlas and Argus*, Albany, N.Y., May 28, 1860.

12 the vigorous senator: See Glyndon G. Van Deusen, *William Henry Seward* (New York: Oxford University Press, 1967), pp. 255–57, 263.

12 *New York Herald* . . . "dauntless and intrepid": *NYH*, August 27, 1860.

12 slender frame . . . "most glorious original": Henry Adams to Charles Francis Adams, Jr., December 9, 1860, in *Letters of Henry Adams (1858–1891)*, Vol. I., ed. Worthington Chauncey Ford (Boston and New York: Houghton Mifflin, 1930), p. 63.

12 physical description of Seward: John M. Taylor, *William Henry Seward: Lincoln's Right Hand* (New York: HarperCollins, 1991), p. 17; Burton J. Hendrick, *Lincoln's War Cabinet* (Boston, Little, Brown, 1946), p. 8; Johnson, "Sensitivity and Civil War," pp. 11, 56–57; Frederic Bancroft, *The Life of William H. Seward*, Vol. I (New York: Harper & Bros., 1899; Gloucester, Mass.: Peter Smith, 1967), p. 184.

13 "school-boy elasticity . . . slashing swagger": Murat Halstead, *Three Against Lincoln: Murat Halstead Reports the Caucuses of 1860*, ed. William B. Hesseltine (Baton Rouge: Louisiana State University Press, 1960), p. 120.

13 Every room . . . by Washington Irving: Lewis interview; *The Seward House*, pp. 5–6, 12, 16, 23, 26; Seward, *An Autobiography*, pp. 440, 677; Susan Sutton Smith, "Mr. Seward's Home," *University of Rochester Library Bulletin* 31 (Autumn 1978), pp. 69–93.

13 "the honor in question . . . of its principles": *National Intelligencer*, Washington, D.C., May 19, 1860.

13 "No press has opposed . . . leadership of the man": *Atlas and Argus*, Albany, N.Y., May 19, 1860.

13 valedictory speech to the Senate: Bancroft, *The Life of William H. Seward*, Vol. I, p. 522; Van Deusen, *William Henry Seward*, p. 222; entry for May 13, 1860, Diary of Charles Francis Adams, reel 75, *microfilms of The Adams Papers owned by the Adams Manuscript Trust and deposited in the Massachusetts Historical Society*, Part I (Boston: Massachusetts Historical Society, 1954) [hereafter Charles Francis Adams diary].

13 love of Auburn: Seward, *An Autobiography*, p. 744.

13 "free to act . . . to die": *Auburn Journal*, December 31, 1859, reprinted in *Albany Evening Journal*, Albany, N.Y., January 3, 1860.

14 Auburn in the 1860s: Johnson, "Sensitivity and Civil War," pp. 2–3.

14 Seward had arrived . . . Cayuga County: Van Deusen, *William Henry Seward*, pp. 6–7.

14 description of Frances: Ibid., p. 10; Taylor, *William Henry Seward*, pp. 18–19.

14 death of Cornelia: Van Deusen, *William Henry Seward*, p. 37.

14 slow to take up the Republican banner: Clarence Edward Macartney, *Lincoln and His Cabinet* (New York and London: Charles Scribner's Sons, 1931), pp. 94–95.

14 "would inspire a cow . . . language": Henry Adams to Charles Francis Adams, Jr., December 9, 1860, *Letters of Henry Adams (1858–1891)*, Vol. I, p. 62.

14 the "leader of the political . . . pass-words of our combatants": Schurz, *Reminiscences*, Vol. II, pp. 173–74.

15 his exuberant personality . . . yellow pantaloons: Hendrick, *Lincoln's War Cabinet*, p. 8; Johnson, "Sensitivity and Civil War," p. 57.

15 an aura of inevitability: Halstead, *Three Against Lincoln*, p. 120.

15 "Men might love . . . ignore him": Glyndon G. Van Deusen, "Thurlow Weed: A Character Study," *American Historical Review* XLIX (April 1944), p. 427.

15 "as a hen does its chicks": Hendrick, *Lincoln's War Cabinet*, p. 17.

15 an exceptional team: Richard L. Watson, Jr., "Thurlow Weed, Political Boss," *New York History* 22 (October 1941), p. 415.

15 "Seward is Weed": WHS, quoted in Gideon Welles, *Lincoln and Seward Remarks Upon the Memorial Address of Chas. Francis Adams, on the Late Wm. H. Seward* . . . (New York: Sheldon & Co., 1874), p. 23.

15 Weed certainly understood . . . created jealousy: Van Deusen, *William Henry Seward*, pp. 216, 222–23.

16 Weed believed . . . emerge the victor: TW to WHS, May 20, 1860, reel 59, Seward Papers.

16 Members . . . confirmed Weed's assessment: Mary King Clark, "Lincoln's Nomination As Seen By a Young Girl from New York," *Putnam's Magazine* 5 (February 1909), pp. 536–37.

16 "no *cause* for doubting . . . to the result": James Watson Webb to WHS, May 16, 1860, reel 59, Seward Papers.

16 "Your friends . . . a few ballots": Elbridge Gerry Spaulding to WHS, May 17, 1860, reel 59, Seward Papers.

16 "All right . . . today sure": Telegram from Preston King, William M. Evarts, and Richard M. Blatchford to WHS, May 18, 1860, reel 59, Seward Papers.

16 Gothic mansion . . . State and Sixth Streets: "History of the Chase House," article in the Central Ohio Buildings File, Local History Room, Columbus Metropolitan Library, Columbus, Ohio; William Dean Howells, *Years of My Youth* (New York and London: Harper & Bros., 1916; 1917), p. 153.

16 Brass bands . . . were revealed: *Daily Ohio Statesman*, Columbus, Ohio, May 19, 1860.

17 Chase's height, physical description: Albert Bushnell Hart, *Salmon P. Chase*, introduction by G. S. Boritt. *American Statesmen Series* (Boston: Houghton Mifflin, 1899; New York and London: Chelsea House, 1980), p. 415; Hendrick, *Lincoln's War Cabinet*, p. 32.

17 "looked . . . statesman to look": Schurz, *Reminiscences*, Vol. II, p. 34.

17 "he is one of . . . splendor and brilliancy": *Troy [N.Y.] Times*, October 18, 1860, quoted in *Columbus Gazette*, November 2, 1860.

17 "an arresting duality . . . the world": Thomas Graham Belden and Marva Robins Belden, *So Fell the Angels* (Boston: Little, Brown, 1956), p. 4.

17 dressed with meticulous care: Hart, *Salmon P. Chase*, p. 415.

17 so nearsighted: John Niven, *Salmon P. Chase: A Biography* (New York and Oxford: Oxford University Press, 1995), pp. 79, 173, 193.

17 man of unbending routine: Virginia Tatnall Peacock, *Famous American Belles of the Nineteenth Century* (1900; Freeport, N.Y.: Books for Libraries Press, 1970), p. 211; Demarest Lloyd, "The Home-Life of Salmon Portland Chase," *Atlantic Monthly* 32 (November 1873), pp. 528, 530–31, 536, 538; Niven, *Salmon P. Chase*, pp. 203–05; J. W. Schuckers, *The Life and Public Services of Salmon Portland Chase, United States Senator and Governor of Ohio; Secretary of the Treasury, and Chief-Justice of the United States* (New York: D. Appleton & Co., 1874), p. 595; Schurz, *Reminiscences*, Vol. II, pp. 169–70.

17 On the rare nights: Lloyd, "Home-Life of Salmon Portland Chase," *Atlantic Monthly*, pp. 529 (quote), 531; Peacock, *Famous American Belles of the Nineteenth Century*, pp. 211–12; Ishbel Ross, *Proud Kate: Portrait of an Ambitious Woman* (New York: Harper & Bros., 1953), p. 37.

18 items in Chase home: SPC to KCS, December 3, 4, 5, and 6, 1857, reel 11, Chase Papers.

18 dogs . . . "designed and posed": Doster, *Lincoln and Episodes of the Civil War*, p. 173.

18 description of Columbus in 1860: Howells, *Years of My Youth*, pp. 134, 169, 181 (quote); Francis Phelps Weisenburger, *Columbus during the Civil War* (n.p.: Ohio State University Press for the Ohio Historical Society, 1963), pp. 3–4.

18 new Capitol building: Henry Howe, *Historical Collections of Ohio*, Vol. I, Ohio Centennial Edition (Norwalk, Ohio: Laning Printing Co., 1896), p. 621 (quote); Writers' Program of the Works Projects Administration, comps., *The Ohio Guide*, sponsored by Ohio State Archaeological and Historical Society (New York: Oxford University Press, 1940; 1948), pp. 251, 254.

18 contrast between Seward and Chase: Hendrick, *Lincoln's War Cabinet*, p. 36; Johnson, "Sensitivity and Civil War," pp. 58–59.

18 recoiled from all games of chance: SPC to KCS, September 15, 1854, reel 10, Chase Papers; Lloyd, "Home-Life of Salmon Portland Chase," *Atlantic Monthly*, pp. 529, 531.

18 "he seldom . . . without spoiling it": Lloyd, "Home-Life of Salmon Portland Chase," *Atlantic Monthly*, p. 536.

18 Kate's education: Belden and Belden, *So Fell the Angels*, p. 15; Ross, *Proud Kate*, pp. 19–22, 34.

19 "In a few years . . . anything else": SPC to KCS, December 20, 1853, reel 9, Chase Papers.

19 absolutely essential: Belden and Belden, *So Fell the Angels*, pp. 16, 18, 21–22; Niven, *Salmon P. Chase*, pp. 202–03.

19 "She did everything . . . another Mrs. Chase": Belden and Belden, *So Fell the Angels*, p. 22.

19 Chase treated his . . . younger daughter: Peacock, *Famous American Belles of the Nineteenth Century*, p. 207.

19 Chase was actually more radical than Seward: Hart, *Salmon P. Chase*, pp. 423, 429.

20 "There may have been . . . ideas as he": Ibid., p. 434.

20 "In the long run . . . than did Chase": William E. Gienapp, *The Origins of the Republican Party, 1852–1856* (New York and Oxford: Oxford University Press, 1987), p. 192.

20 "A very large body . . . spontaneous growth": SPC to Gamaliel Bailey, January 24, 1859, reel 12, Chase Papers.

20 "I arrived early . . . he should be President": Schurz, *Reminiscences*, Vol. II, pp. 169–72.

21 "desirable . . . our best men": SPC to Robert Hosea, March 18, 1860, reel 13, Chase Papers.

21 "No man . . . more competent": *Ohio State Journal*, Columbus, Ohio, March 12, 1860.

21 "steady devotion . . . beyond the State": Ibid., May 21, 1860.

21 refused to engage in the practical methods: Niven, *Salmon P. Chase*, pp. 214–17; Hart, *Salmon P. Chase*, p. 428.

21 "if the most cherished . . . could prevail": SPC to Edward S. Hamlin, June 12, 1856, reel 11, Chase Papers.

21 "Now is the time . . . topmost wave": Calvin Ellis Stowe to SPC, March 30, 1858, reel 12, Chase Papers.

21 "There is reason to hope": SPC to James A Briggs, from Wheeling, Va., May 8, 1860, reel 13, Chase Papers.

21 Judge Edward Bates awaited: Marvin R. Cain, *Lincoln's Attorney General: Edward Bates of Missouri* (Columbia, Mo.: University of Missouri Press, 1965), p. 115.

21 Grape Hill: Entry of September 28, 1859, Orville H. Browning, *The Diary of Orville Hickman Browning. Vol. I: 1850–1864*, ed. Theodore Calvin Pease and James G. Randall. *Collections of the Illinois State Historical Library*, Volume XX (Springfield, Ill.: Illinois State Historical Library, 1925), p. 380; Cain, *Lincoln's Attorney General*, p. 59.

21 general information on Bates family: Introduction, *The Diary of Edward Bates, 1859–1866*, pp. xv–xvi; *Missouri Republican*, St. Louis, Mo., March 26, 1869.

22 The judge's orderly life: EB to Julia Bates, January 1, 1835; January 5, 1828; November 7, 1827; Edward Bates Papers, 1778–1872, mss 1 B3184a, Virginia Historical Society, Richmond, Va. [hereafter Bates Papers, ViHi]; entry for April 9, 1860, in *The Diary of Edward Bates, 1859–1866*, p. 120 (quote).

22 description of St. Louis: "Lecture of Edward Bates," *St. Louis Weekly Reveille*, February 24, 1845, typescript copy, St. Louis History Collection, Missouri Historical Society, St. Louis, Mo. [hereafter MoSHi]; William C. Winter, *The Civil War in St. Louis: A Guided Tour* (St. Louis, Mo.: Missouri Historical Society, 1995), p. 3; James Neal Primm, *Lion of the Valley: St. Louis, Missouri, 1764–1980*, 3rd edn. (St. Louis: Missouri Historical Society Press, 1998), pp. 192, 182 (quote).

22 "the quaintest looking . . . youth of twenty": Alban Jasper Conant, "A Visit to Washington in 1861–62," *Metropolitan Magazine* XXXIII (June 1910), p. 313.

22 descriptions of Bates: Hendrick, *Lincoln's War Cabinet*, pp. 46–47; Cain, *Lincoln's Attorney General*, pp. 1, 64.

22 Lincoln noted the striking . . . "more than his head": AL quoted in Hendrick, *Lincoln's War Cabinet*, p. 46.

23 "unaffected by . . . little bonnet": Conant, "A Visit to Washington in 1861–62," *Metropolitan Magazine*, p. 313.

23 "How happy is my lot! . . . so freely gives": Edward Bates diary, November 27, 1851, Edward Bates Papers, Missouri Historical Society, St. Louis, Mo. [hereafter Bates diary].

23 "a very domestic, home, man": Ibid., May 2, 1852.

23 speech at the River and Harbor Convention: "Bates, Edward," *Dictionary of American Biography. Vol. I: Abbe-Brazer*; ed. Allen Johnson (New York: Charles Scribner's Sons, 1927; 1957), p. 48; James Shaw, "A Neglected Episode in the Life of Abraham Lincoln," *Transactions of the Illinois State Historical Society*, no. 29 of the Illinois State Historical Library (1922), pp. 52, 54.

23 as the 1860 election neared: Cain, *Lincoln's Attorney General*, pp. 95–96.

23 dinner at Frank Blair's home: Entry of April 27, 1859, in *The Diary of Edward Bates, 1859–1866*, p. 11; Reinhard H. Luthin, *The First Lincoln Campaign* (Cambridge, Mass.: Harvard University Press, 1944; Gloucester, Mass.: Peter Smith, 1964), pp. 54–55.

23 Blair family details: See Elbert B. Smith, *Francis Preston Blair* (New York: Free Press/Macmillan Publishing Co., 1980), pp. 172–73; William Ernest Smith, *The Francis Preston Blair Family in Politics*, Vol. I (New York: The Macmillan Company, 1933), pp. 185–88, 189–91; Hendrick, *Lincoln's War Cabinet*, pp. 61–69, 388; *Washington Post*, September 14, 1906; *Star*, September 14, 1906; Virginia Jeans Laas, ed., *Wartime Washington: The Civil War Letters of Elizabeth Blair Lee* (Chicago: University of Illinois Press, 1991), pp. 1, 2; William E. Parrish, *Frank Blair: Lincoln's Conservative* (Columbia, Mo., and London: University of Missouri Press, 1998). Francis P. Blair, owner, slave schedule for 5th District, Montgomery County, Maryland, Eighth Census of the United States, 1860 (National Archives Microfilm Publication M653, reel 485), Records of the Bureau of the Census, Record Group [RG] 29, National Archives and Records Administration, Washington, D.C. [hereafter DNA]. Blair owned fifteen slaves in 1860.

24 had settled on the widely respected judge: *Lincoln's Attorney General*, pp. 84–86, 91–92; Primm, *Lion of the Valley*, p. 230; Smith, *Francis Preston Blair*, p. 257; Smith, *The Francis Preston Blair Family in Politics*, Vol. I, pp. 461–62.

25 "I feel . . . of character": Entry of July 5, 1859, in *The Diary of Edward Bates, 1859–1866*, pp. 29–30.

25 "a mere seat . . . member": EB to Julia Coalter Bates, November 7, 1827, Bates Papers, ViHi.

25 "the mania . . . heretofore done": FB, quoted in Parrish, *Frank Blair*, p. 81.

25 "My nomination . . . in vain": Entry of January 9, 1860, in *The Diary of Edward Bates, 1859–1866*, pp. 89–90.

26 days were increasingly . . . first ballot victory: Cain, *Lincoln's Attorney General*, pp. 93, 94, 107.

26 "I have many strong . . . in New York, Pa.": Entry of December 1, 1859, in *The Diary of Edward Bates, 1859–1866*, pp. 71–72.

26 pockets of opposition . . . German-Americans: Cain, *Lincoln's Attorney General*, pp. 103, 106.

26 "There is no question . . . conservative antecedents": *NYTrib*, May 15, 1860.

26 Bates would triumph in Chicago: Cain, *Lincoln's Attorney General*, p. 110.

26 "some of the most moderate and patriotic": EB, *Letter of Hon. Edward Bates, of Missouri, Indorsing Mr. Lincoln, and Giving His Reasons for Supporting the Chicago Nominees* (Washington, D.C.: Printed at the Congressional Globe Office, 1860).

26 "would tend to soften . . . in the border States": Ibid.

CHAPTER 2: THE "LONGING TO RISE"

Page

28 "We find ourselves . . . times tells us": AL, "Address Before the Young Men's Lyceum of Springfield, Illinois," January 27, 1838, in *CW*, I, p. 108.

28 "When both the . . . universal feeling": Alexis de Tocqueville, *Democracy in America*, ed. J. P. Mayer, trans. George Lawrence (New York: Harper & Row, 1966; 1988), p. 629.

29 "any man's son . . . any other man's son": Frances M. Trollope, *Domestic Manners of the Americans* (London: Whittaker, Treacher, & Co., 1832; Barre, Mass.: Imprint Society, 1969), p. 93.

29 thousands of young men to break away: Joyce Appleby, *Inheriting the Revolution: The First Generation of Americans* (Cambridge, Mass., and London: Belknap Press of Harvard University Press, 2000), p. 88.

29 the Louisiana Purchase: See Robert Wiebe, *The Opening of American Society: From the Adoption of the Constitution to the Eve of Disunion* (New York: Alfred A. Knopf, 1984), pp. 131–32; "Louisiana Purchase," in *The Reader's Companion to American History*, ed. Eric Foner and John A. Garraty (Boston: Houghton Mifflin, 1991), p. 682.

29 "Americans are always moving . . . the mountainside": Stephen Vincent Benét, *Western Star* (New York: Farrar & Rinehart, 1943), pp. 3, 7–8.

29 In the South . . . thriving cities: Thomas Dublin, "Internal Migration," in *The Reader's Companion to American History*, ed. Foner and Garraty, pp. 564–65.

29 "Every American . . . to rise": de Tocqueville, *Democracy in America*, ed. Mayer, p. 627.

29 born on May 16, 1801: Van Deusen, *William Henry Seward*, p. 3.

30 Samuel Seward: Seward, *An Autobiography*, pp. 19–20; Bancroft, *The Life of William H. Seward*, Vol. I, pp. 1–2; Taylor, *William Henry Seward*, p. 12.

30 "a considerable . . . destined preferment": Seward, *An Autobiography*, pp. 20, 21.

30 Seward's early education: Ibid., pp. 20, 22; "Biographical Memoir of William H. Seward," *The Works of William H. Seward*, Vol. I, ed. George E. Baker (5 vols., New York: J. S. Redfield, 1853; New York: AMS Press, 1972), pp. xvi–xvii.

30 "at five in the morning . . . politics or religion!": Seward, *An Autobiography*, pp. 21, 22.

NOTES

30 Seward slaves: Ibid., p. 27. The Sewards still owned seven slaves in 1820. See entry for Samuel S. Seward, Warwick, Orange County, N.Y., Fourth Census of the United States, 1820 (National Archives Microfilm Publication M33, reel 64), RG 29, DNA.

30 "loquacious" . . . to fight against slavery: Seward, *An Autobiography*, pp. 27–28.

31 status of slavery in the North after the Revolution: Winthrop D. Jordan, *White Over Black: American Attitudes Toward the Negro, 1550–1812* (New York: W. W. Norton & Co., 1977), p. 345; Leon F. Litwack, *North of Slavery: The Negro in the Free States, 1790–1860* (Chicago and London: University of Chicago Press, 1961), pp. 3, 6.

31 slavery eliminated in New York by 1827: Taylor, *William Henry Seward*, p. 14.

31 enrolled in . . . Union College: Van Deusen, *William Henry Seward*, p. 4.

31 "a magnificent . . . so imposing": Seward, *An Autobiography*, p. 29.

31 "I cherished . . . of my class": Ibid., p. 31.

31 "had determined . . . at Union College": Ibid., p. 35.

31 "all the eminent . . . a broken heart": Ibid., pp. 35, 36–43.

32 "Matters prosper . . . even his notice": WHS to Daniel Jessup, Jr., January 24, 1820, reel 1, Seward Papers.

32 "was received as a student . . . in Washington Hall": Seward, *An Autobiography*, pp. 47–48.

33 friendship with . . . David Berdan: David Berdan," Eulogy read before the Adelphic Society of Union College, July 21, 1828, and published in *The Knickerbocker Magazine* (December 1839), in *The Works of William H. Seward*, Vol. III, pp. 117–27; WHS to the President of the Adelphic Society, Union College, draft copy, September 3, 1827, reel 1, Seward Papers; Taylor, *William Henry Seward*, p. 18.

33 "a genius of the highest order" . . . Seward was devastated: WHS to the President of the Adelphic Society, Union College, draft copy, September 3, 1827, reel 1, Seward Papers.

33 "never again . . . in this world": FAS to WHS, February 15, 1831, reel 113, Seward Papers.

33 "a common feature" . . . passionate romances: E. Anthony Rotundo, *American Manhood: Transformations in Masculinity from the Revolution to the Modern Era* (New York: Basic Books/HarperCollins, 1993), pp. 3, 76 (quote), 86.

34 Relationship with Judge Miller: "Biographical Memoir of William H. Seward," *Works of William H. Seward*, Vol. I, p. xxi.

34 marriage to Frances Miller . . . The judge insisted: Seward, *An Autobiography*, p. 62.

34 Chase's ancestors: Niven, *Salmon P. Chase*, pp. 5–7, 21; Schuckers, *The Life and Public Services of Salmon Portland Chase*, p. 3; Robert B. Warden, *An Account of the Private Life and Public Services of Salmon Portland Chase* (Cincinnati: Wilstach, Baldwin & Co., 1874), pp. 22–27.

34 "the neighboring folk . . . in New England": SPC to John T. Trowbridge, December 27, 1863, reel 30, Chase Papers.

34 "a good man": SPC to Trowbridge, January 19, 1864, reel 31, Chase Papers.

34 "angry word . . . from his lips": SPC to Trowbridge, December 27, 1863, reel 30, Chase Papers.

34 Chase long remembered . . . "& kind looks": SPC to Trowbridge, January 19, 1864, reel 31, Chase Papers.

35 "I was . . . ambitious . . . of my class": SPC to Trowbridge, December 27, 1863, reel 30, Chase Papers.

35 taught by elder sister: Warden, *Private Life and Public Services*, p. 36.

35 retreat to the garden . . . designated passages: SPC to Trowbridge, January 19, 1864, reel 31, Chase Papers.

35 "once repeating . . . a single recitation": Biographical sketch of Salmon P. Chase, quoted in Warden, *Private Life and Public Services*, p. 39.

35 "for the entertainment they afforded": Warden, *Private Life and Public Services*, p. 38.

35 "quite a prodigy . . . and head down": SPC to Trowbridge, January 21, 1864, reel 31, Chase Papers.

35 "sliding down hill" . . . would swear: SPC to Trowbridge, December 27, 1863, reel 30, Chase Papers.

35 made him abhor intemperance: Warden, *Private Life and Public Services*, p. 63.

35 "face forward . . . sufficed to save": SPC to Trowbridge, January 21, 1864, reel 31, Chase Papers.

36 Ithamar's glass venture and financial ruin: SPC to Trowbridge, January 19, 1864, reel 31, Chase Papers; Niven, *Salmon P. Chase*, pp. 7–8.

36 Ithamar Chase's fatal stroke: Niven, *Salmon P. Chase*, p. 8.

36 "He lingered . . . our home": SPC to Trowbridge, January 19, 1864, reel 31, Chase Papers.

36 "almost to suffering": SPC to Trowbridge, February 1, 1864, reel 31, Chase Papers.

36 "ever lamented and deceased father": Janette Ralston Chase to SPC, August 14, 1824, [filed as 1824–1825 correspondence], reel 4, Chase Papers.

36 Salmon sent to Philander Chase: SPC to Trowbridge, January 21 and 31, 1864, reel 31, Chase Papers; Arthur Meier Schlesinger, "Salmon Portland Chase: Undergraduate and Pedagogue," *Ohio Archaeological and Historical Quarterly* [hereafter *OAHQ*] 28 (April 1919), pp. 120–21.

36 Salmon's journey to Worthington: SPC to Trowbridge, January 23, 1864, reel 31, Chase Papers; Niven, *Salmon P. Chase*, pp. 9–11.

36 "was not passive . . . quite tyrannical": SPC to Trowbridge, January 25, 1864, reel 31, Chase Papers.

37 "My memories . . . wish I had not": SPC to Trowbridge, January 27, 1864, reel 31, Chase Papers.

37 Cincinnati College . . . "gave it to reading": SPC to Trowbridge, January 31, 1864, typescript copy, reel 31, Chase Papers.

37 his "life might have been . . . more fun!": Warden, *Private Life and Public Services*, p. 94.

37 first teaching position . . . dismissed: Niven, *Salmon P. Chase*, p. 17.

38 At Dartmouth: Ibid., pp. 18–19; Frederick J. Blue, *Salmon P. Chase: A Life in Politics* (Kent, Ohio, and London: Kent State University Press, 1987), pp. 6–7.

38 two lifelong friendships: Niven, *Salmon P. Chase*, p. 97.

38 "Especially do I . . . have been wasted": SPC to Thomas Sparhawk, July 8, 1827, reel 4, Chase Papers.
38 "the author is doubtless . . . vilest purposes": Entry for September 22, 1829, SPC diary, reel 40, Chase Papers. The editors of the published edition of the Salmon P. Chase Papers identify the author of the novel as Edward Bulwer-Lytton. See note 65 for entry of September 22, 1829, *The Salmon P. Chase Papers.* Vol. I: *Journals, 1829–1872,* ed. John Niven (Kent, Ohio, and London: Kent State University Press, 1993), p. 24 [hereafter *Chase Papers,* Vol. I].
38 established a successful school: SPC to Trowbridge, February 10, 1864, reel 31, Chase Papers; Schlesinger, "Salmon Portland Chase," *OAHQ* (1919), pp. 132–33, 143.
38 distinct classes of society . . . "utter contempt": SPC to Hamilton Smith, May 31, 1827, reel 4, Chase Papers.
38 "I have always thought . . . to achieve": SPC to Hamilton Smith, April 7, 1829, reel 4, Chase Papers.
38 "saw the novelty . . . poor and young": Appleby, *Inheriting the Revolution,* p. 7.
39 wrote to an older brother in 1825 for advice: Alexander R. Chase to SPC, November 4, 1825, reel 4, Chase Papers.
39 Attorney General William Wirt: Warden, *Private Life and Public Services,* pp. 124–25, 175; Fidler, "Young Limbs of the Law," pp. 245, 276. See also Michael L. Oberg, "Wirt, William," *American National Biography,* Vol. XXIII, ed. John A. Garraty and Mark C. Carnes, American Council of Learned Societies (New York and Oxford: Oxford University Press, 1999), pp. 675–76.
39 Wirt welcomed: Entries of January 10, 29, 30, 1829; February 9, 1829; April 8, 20, 1829; *Chase Papers,* Vol. I, pp. 5–9, 13–14; Schuckers, *The Life and Public Services of Salmon Portland Chase,* p. 29.
39 to read and study . . . his students: SPC to Trowbridge, February 13, 1864, reel 31, Chase Papers.
39 "many happy hours . . . the stars": SPC to Trowbridge, February 10, 1864, in *The Salmon P. Chase Papers.* Vol. IV: *Correspondence, April 1863–1864,* ed. John Niven (Kent, Ohio, and London: Kent State University Press, 1997), p. 283.
39 the social gulf . . . discouraged: Elizabeth Goldsborough to Robert Warden, quoted in Warden, *Private Life and Public Services,* p. 126; Niven, *Salmon P. Chase,* pp. 23, 40.
39 "thousands . . . universal scholar": Alexander R. Chase to SPC, November 4, 1825, reel 4, Chase Papers.
39 "Day and night . . . my labours": Entry for March 1, 1830, *Chase Papers,* Vol. I, p. 45.
40 "knowledge may yet . . . be mine": Entry for January 13, 1829, ibid., p. 6.
40 "*You* will be . . . in that walk": William Wirt to SPC, May 4, 1829, reel 4, Chase Papers.
40 "God [prospering] . . . your example": SPC to William Wirt, June 16, 1829, reel 4, Chase Papers.
40 self-designed course of preparation: Niven, *Salmon P. Chase,* pp. 23, 26.
40 "his voice deep . . . of my toils": Entry for February 14, 1829, diary, reel 1, Papers of Salmon P. Chase, Manuscript Division, Library of Congress [hereafter Chase Papers, DLC].
40 "I feel humbled . . . of well-doing": Entry for December 31, 1829, diary, reel 1, Chase Papers, LC.
40 Chase before the bar, 1829: William Cranch, quoted in Niven, *Salmon P. Chase,* p. 27.
40 "study another year" . . . sworn in at the bar: SPC, "Admission to the Bar," June 30, 1853, reel 32, Chase Papers, DLC.
40 "I would rather . . . wherever I may be": SPC to Charles D. Cleveland, February 8, 1830, reel 4, Chase Papers.
41 Cincinnati in 1830: Hart, *Salmon P. Chase,* pp. 13–16.
41 "was covered by the primeval forest": SPC, "On the Dedication of a New State House, January 6, 1857," reel 41, Chase Papers.
41 "a stranger and an adventurer": Entry for September 1, 1830, *Chase Papers,* Vol. I, p. 53.
41 shyness, speech defect: Niven, *Salmon P. Chase,* p. 31.
41 "I wish I was . . . provide the remedy": William Wirt to SPC, May 4, 1829, reel 4, Chase Papers.
41 "awkward, *fishy* . . . little inconvenience": SPC to Charles D. Cleveland, February 8, 1830, reel 4, Chase Papers.
41 "I made this resolution . . . excel in all things": Entry for April 29, 1831, *Chase Papers,* Vol. I, p. 57.
41 "I was fully . . . a 'crown of glory' ": Entry for March 1, 1830, ibid., p. 45.
41 founded a popular lecture series . . . berated himself: Entry for February 8, 1834, diary, reel 40, Chase Papers; Niven, *Salmon P. Chase,* pp. 32, 34–38; Mary Merwin Phelps, *Kate Chase, Dominant Daughter: The Life Story of a Brilliant Woman and Her Famous Father* (New York: Thomas Y. Crowell, 1935), pp. 12, 35.
42 "I confess . . . terminate in this life": Abigail Chase Colby to SPC, April 21, 1832, reel 4, Chase Papers.
42 death of Catherine Garniss Chase: Entries for November 21 and December 1, 1835, *Chase Papers,* Vol. I, pp. 87, 92–93.
42 "so overwhelming . . . has been severed": SPC to Charles D. Cleveland, April 6, 1836, reel 5, Chase Papers.
42 "Oh how I accused . . . tempted me away": Entry for December 25, 1835, *Chase Papers,* Vol. I, p. 94.
42 "that death was within . . . left but clay": Entry for December 1, 1835, ibid., pp. 93–94.
42 "the dreadful calamity . . . care for her": SPC to Charles D. Cleveland, April 6, 1836, reel 5, Chase Papers.
42 doctors had bled her so profusely: Entry for December 26, 1835, *Chase Papers,* Vol. I, p. 96.
42 he delved into textbooks: Entry for December 28, 1835, ibid., p. 99.
42 "Oh if I had not . . . now she is gone": Entry for December 27, 1835, ibid., pp. 97–98.
42 "the bar of God . . . an accusing spirit": Entry for December 28, 1835, ibid., p. 99.
43 a "second conversion": Stephen E. Maizlish, "Salmon P. Chase: The Roots of Ambition and the Origins of Reform," *Journal of the Early Republic* 18 (Spring 1998), p. 62.
43 death of daughter Catherine: Blue, *Salmon P. Chase,* p. 35; Warden, *Private Life and Public Services,* p. 286; Niven, *Salmon P. Chase,* p. 72.
43 "one of the . . . desolation of my heart": SPC to Charles D. Cleveland, February 7, 1840, reel 5, Chase Papers.
43 marriage to Eliza; birth of Kate: Blue, *Salmon P. Chase,* pp. 25–26; Warden, *Private Life and Public Services,* pp. 290–91, 295, 296, 301, 302.

43 "I feel as if . . . we are desolate": SPC to Charles D. Cleveland, October 1, 1845, reel 6, Chase Papers.
43 Marriage to Belle; death of wife and daughter: Blue, *Salmon P. Chase*, p. 74; Warden, *Private Life and Public Services*, pp. 311–12.
43 "What a vale . . . I rise & press on": SPC to CS, January 28, 1850, reel 8, Chase Papers (quote); Niven, *Salmon P. Chase*, p. 135.
43 "to go West and grow up with the country": William F. Switzler, "Lincoln's Attorney General: Edward Bates, One of Missouri's Greatest Citizens—His Career as a Lawyer, Farmer and Statesman," reprinted in Onward Bates, *Bates, et al., of Virginia and Missouri* (Chicago: P. F. Pettibone, 1914), p. 26.
43 His father, Thomas Fleming Bates: For general information on Bates's family and early years, see Cain, *Lincoln's Attorney General*, pp. 1–3, 5; "Bates, Edward," *DAB*, Vol. I, p. 48; James M. McPherson, "Bates, Edward," *American National Biography*, Vol. II, ed. John A. Garraty and Mark C. Carnes, American Council of Learned Societies (New York and Oxford: Oxford University Press, 1999), p. 329; Introduction, *The Diary of Edward Bates, 1859–1866*, p. xi; Bates, *Bates, et al., of Virginia and Missouri*, p. 22; "Death of Edward Bates," *Missouri Republican*, St. Louis, Mo., March 26, 1869; Elie Weeks, "Belmont," *Goochland County Historical Society Magazine* 12 (1980), pp. 36–49; EB to C. I. Walker, February 10, 1859, reprinted in *Collections of the Pioneer Society of the State of Michigan Together with Reports of County Pioneer Societies*, Vol. VIII, 2nd edn. (1886; Lansing, Mich.: Wynkoop Hallenbeck Crawford Co., 1907), pp. 563–64.
44 "as distinctly . . . Western Europe": Charles Gibson, *The Autobiography of Charles Gibson*, ed. E. R. Gibson, 1899, Charles Gibson Papers, Missouri Historical Society, St. Louis, Mo. [hereafter Gibson Papers, MoSHi].
44 English manorial life . . . monetary wealth: James Truslow Adams, *America's Tragedy* (New York and London: Charles Scribner's Sons, 1934), pp. 87–88.
44 "enjoyable living . . . and their manners": Bates, *Bates, et al., of Virginia and Missouri*, p. 20.
44 The flintlock musket . . . "helped to win": Ibid., p. 22.
45 lured by the vast potential . . . Louisiana Purchase: Wiebe, *The Opening of American Society*, pp. 131–32.
45 Over the next three decades: James M. McPherson, *Battle Cry of Freedom: The Civil War Era* (New York: Oxford University Press, 1988; New York: Ballantine Books, 1989), p. 42.
45 "too young . . . a buffalo!": "Lecture by Edward Bates," St. Louis *Weekly Reveille*, February 24, 1845, St. Louis History Collection, MoSHi.
45 "After years of family . . . burned brightly in him": Cain, *Lincoln's Attorney General*, p. 5.
45 passed his bar examination . . . the rest of their family there: EB to Frederick Bates, September 29, 1817; October 13, 1817; June 15, 1818; July 19, 1818; Bates Papers, MoSHi; Cain, *Lincoln's Attorney General*, p. 7.
45 "The slaves sold . . . at $290!": EB to Frederick Bates, September 21, 1817, Bates Papers, MoSHi.
45 expected to realize . . . "full-handed": EB to Frederick Bates, September 29, 1817, Bates Papers, MoSHi.
46 death of his brother Tarleton . . . "by the delay": Cain, *Lincoln's Attorney General*, p. 6; EB to Frederick Bates, June 15, 1818, Bates Papers, MoSHi (quote).
46 "In those days . . . in the country": Samuel T. Glover, "Addresses by the Members of the St. Louis Bar on the Death of Edward Bates," *Minutes of the St. Louis Bar Association* (1869), Bates Papers, MoSHi.
46 "a lazy or squandering fellow": EB to Frederick Bates, July 19, 1818, Bates Papers, MoSHi.
46 if accompanied only by his family: EB to Frederick Bates, September 29, 1817, Bates Papers, MoSHi.
46 "in a tenth part of the time . . . my embarrassment": EB to Frederick Bates, June 15, 1818, Bates Papers, MoSHi.
46 "Mother & Sister . . . occasioned you": EB to Frederick Bates, July 19, 1818, Bates Papers, MoSHi.
46 "friend and benefactor . . . wealth & influence": EB to Frederick Bates, October 13, 1817, Bates Papers, MoSHi.
46 introduced him to the leading figures: Cain, *Lincoln's Attorney General*, p. 4.
46 a partnership with Joshua Barton: Ibid., p. 7.
47 "more in the way . . . his own name": AL, "Autobiography Written for John L. Scripps," [c. June 1860], in *CW*, IV, p. 61 [hereafter "Scripps autobiography"].
47 Thomas had watched: A. H. Chapman statement, ante September 8, 1865, in *HI*, p. 95; Donald, *Lincoln*, p. 21.
47 "very narrow circumstances . . . without education": AL, "Scripps autobiography," in *CW*, IV, p. 61.
47 Nancy Hanks: Dennis F. Hanks to WHH, June 13, 1865, and John Hanks interview, May 25, 1865, in *HI*, pp. 5, 37; Benjamin P. Thomas, *Abraham Lincoln: A Biography* (New York: Alfred A. Knopf, 1952), p. 6. On Nancy Hanks's ancestry, see Paul H. Verduin, "New Evidence Suggest Lincoln's Mother Born in Richmond County, Virginia, Giving Credibility to Planter-Grandfather Legend," *Northern Neck of Virginia Historical Magazine* XXXVIII (December 1988), pp. 4, 354–89.
47 Thomas in relentless poverty: Thomas, *Abraham Lincoln*, p. 5; Kenneth J. Winkle, *The Young Eagle: The Rise of Abraham Lincoln* (Dallas: Taylor Trade Publishing, 2001), p. 13.
47 "Why Scripps, it is . . . 'annals of the poor' ": John L. Scripps to WHH, June 24, 1865, in *HI*, p. 57.
47 "was a woman . . . a brilliant woman": Nathaniel Grigsby interview, September 12, 1865, in ibid., p. 113.
47 "read the good . . . benevolence as well": Dennis F. Hanks to WHH (interview), June 13, 1865, in ibid., p. 40.
47 "beyond all doubt an intellectual woman": John Hanks interview, [1865–1866], in ibid., p. 454.
47 "Remarkable" perception: Dennis F. Hanks to WHH, [December 1865?], in ibid., p. 149.
47 "very smart . . . naturally Strong minded": William Wood interview, September 15, 1865, in ibid., p. 124.
47 "All that I am . . . God bless her": AL, comment to WHH, quoted in Michael Burlingame, *The Inner World of Abraham Lincoln* (Urbana and Chicago: University of Illinois Press, 1994), p. 42.
47 "milk sickness": Philip D. Jordan, "The Death of Nancy Hanks Lincoln," *Indiana Magazine of History* XL (June 1944), pp. 103–10.
47 Thomas and Elizabeth Sparrow: Thomas, *Abraham Lincoln*, pp. 10–11.
48 "I am going away . . . return": Nancy Lincoln, quoted in Robert Bruce, "The Riddle of Death," in Gabor

Boritt, ed., *The Lincoln Enigma: The Changing Faces of an American Icon* (Oxford and New York: Oxford University Press, 2001), p. 132.

48 average life expectancy: Appleby, *Inheriting the Revolution*, p. 63.

48 "He restlessly looked . . . before his gaze": Schurz, *Reminiscences*, Vol. II, p. 187.

48 had a uniquely shattering impact: Bruce, "The Riddle of Death," in *The Lincoln Enigma*, p. 132.

48 "a wild region": AL, "Autobiography written for Jesse W. Fell," December 20, 1859, in *CW*, III, p. 511.

48 "the panther's . . . on the swine": "The Bear Hunt," [September 6, 1846?], in *CW*, I, p. 386.

48 Sarah, did the cooking . . . Dennis Hanks: Dennis F. Hanks to WHH (interview), June 13, 1865, in *HI*, p. 40.

48 a "quick minded woman . . . laugh": Nathaniel Grigsby interview, September 12, 1865, in ibid., p. 113.

48 "wild—ragged and dirty": Dennis F. Hanks to WHH, June 13, 1865, in ibid., p. 41.

48 soaped . . . "more human": Sarah Bush Lincoln interview, September 8, 1865, in ibid., p. 106.

49 "sat down . . . to his grief": Redmond Grigsby, quoted in Burlingame, *The Inner World of Abraham Lincoln*, p. 95.

49 "From then on . . . you might say": John W. Lamar, quoted in ibid.

49 "It is with deep grief . . . ever expect it": AL to Fanny McCullough, December 23, 1862, in *CW*, VI, pp. 16–17.

49 "He was different . . . great potential": Douglas L. Wilson, "Young Man Lincoln," in *The Lincoln Enigma*, p. 35.

49 "clearly exceptional . . . intellectual equal": Donald, *Lincoln*, p. 32.

49 "soared above us . . . guide and leader": Nathaniel Grigsby interview, September 12, 1865, in *HI*, p. 114.

49 "a Boy of uncommon natural Talents": A. H. Chapman statement, ante September 8, 1865, in ibid., p. 99.

49 "His mind & mine . . . if he could": Sarah Bush Lincoln interview, September 8, 1865, in ibid., pp. 108, 107.

50 "He was a strong . . . neighborhood": Leonard Swett, "Lincoln's Story of His Own Life," in *Reminiscences of Abraham Lincoln by Distinguished Men of His Time*, ed. Allen Thorndike Rice (1885; New York and London: Harper & Bros., 1909), p. 71.

50 his great gift for storytelling . . . fireplace at night: Sarah Bush Lincoln interview, September 8, 1865, in *HI*, p. 107; John Hanks interview, [1865–1866], in ibid., p. 454.

50 along the old Cumberland Trail: Thomas, *Abraham Lincoln*, p. 7.

50 Thomas Lincoln would swap tales: Dennis F. Hanks to WHH, June 13, 1865, in *HI*, p. 37.

50 Young Abe listened . . . in his memory: Sarah Bush Lincoln interview, September 8, 1865, in ibid., p. 107.

50 Nothing was more upsetting . . . that was told: Rev. J. P. Gulliver article in *New York Independent*, September 1, 1864, quoted in F. B. Carpenter, *Six Months at the White House with Abraham Lincoln* (New York: Hurd & Houghton, 1866), p. 312.

50 "no small part . . . to comprehend": AL, quoted in ibid., pp. 312–13.

50 having translated the stories . . . young listeners: Dennis F. Hanks to WHH, June 13, 1865, and Dennis F. Hanks interview, September 8, 1865, in *HI*, pp. 42, 104; Sarah Bush Lincoln interview, September 8, 1865, in ibid., p. 107.

50 subscription schools: Donald, *Lincoln*, p. 29.

51 "No qualification . . . wizzard": AL, "Autobiography written for Jesse W. Fell," December 20, 1859, in *CW*, III, p. 511.

51 "by littles" . . . pick up on his own: AL, "Scripps autobiography," in *CW*, IV, p. 62.

51 "he could lay his hands on": Dennis F. Hanks to WHH, June 13, 1865, in *HI*, p. 41; Sarah Bush Lincoln interview, September 8, 1865, in ibid., p. 107; John S. Houghland interview, September 17, 1865, in ibid., p. 130.

51 "a luxury . . . the middle class": Fidler, "Young Limbs of the Law," p. 249.

51 obtained copies of: Thomas, *Abraham Lincoln*, p. 15; Nathaniel Grigsby interview, September 12, 1865, in *HI*, p. 112; Charles B. Strozier, *Lincoln's Quest for Union: Public and Private Meanings* (New York: Basic Books, 1982), p. 231.

51 "his eyes sparkled . . . could not sleep": David Herbert Donald, *Lincoln Reconsidered: Essays on the Civil War Era*, 3rd edn. (New York: Alfred A. Knopf, 1956; New York: Vintage Books, 2001), pp. 67–68.

51 "the great mass . . . to perform": AL, "Second Lecture on Discoveries and Inventions," [February 11, 1859], in *CW*, III, pp. 362–63.

51 "as unpoetical . . . of the earth": AL to Andrew Johnston, April 18, 1846, in *CW*, I, p. 378.

51 "There is no Frigate . . . Lands away": Emily Dickinson, "There is no Frigate like a Book," *The Complete Poems of Emily Dickinson*, ed. Thomas H. Johnson (Boston: Little, Brown, 1960), p. 553.

51 the *Revised Statutes* . . . and political thought: Helen Nicolay, *Personal Traits of Abraham Lincoln* (New York: Century Co., 1912), pp. 66–68.

52 Everywhere he went: Nathaniel Grigsby interview, September 12, 1865, in *HI*, p. 113.

52 "When he came across" . . . memorized: Sarah Bush Lincoln interview, September 8, 1865, in ibid., p. 107.

52 The story is often recounted . . . "on a stalk": Oliver C. Terry to JWW, July 1888, in ibid., p. 662.

52 Lincoln wrote poems . . . Crawford's large nose: Dennis F. Hanks to WHH, June 13, 1865, in ibid., p. 41; A. H. Chapman statement, ante September 8, 1865, in ibid., p. 101.

52 "Josiah blowing his bugle": AL, "Chronicles of Reuben," as paraphrased in Herndon and Weik, *Herndon's Life of Lincoln*, p. 47.

53 Seward had only to pick: Seward, *An Autobiography*, pp. 19–22, 31–35.

53 regarded as odd and indolent: Herndon and Weik, *Herndon's Life of Lincoln*, p. 38; Dennis Hanks interview, September 8, 1865, in *HI*, p. 104.

53 "particular Care . . . of his own accord": Sarah Bush Lincoln interview, September 8, 1865, in ibid., p. 108.

53 When he found . . . could continue: Matilda Johnston Moore interview, September 8, 1865, in ibid., p. 110.

53 destroyed his books . . . abused him: Burlingame, *The Inner World of Abraham Lincoln*, pp. 38–39.

53 father's decision to hire him out: Swett, "Lincoln's Story of His Own Life," in *Reminiscences of Abraham Lincoln*, ed. Rice, p. 70.

53 the "self-made" men in Lincoln's generation: Appleby, *Inheriting the Revolution*, p. 231; Wiebe, *The Opening of American Society*, p. 271.

53 The same "longing to rise": de Tocqueville, *Democracy in America*, p. 627.

54 departed . . . bundled on his shoulder: Swett, "Lincoln's Story of His Own Life," in *Reminiscences of Abraham Lincoln*, ed. Rice, pp. 71–72.

54 New Salem was a budding town: Benjamin P. Thomas, *Lincoln's New Salem* (Springfield, Ill.: Abraham Lincoln Association, 1934; 1947), p. 15.

54 to "keep body and soul together": AL, "Scripps autobiography," in *CW*, IV, p. 65.

54 Lincoln in New Salem: Thomas, *Lincoln's New Salem*, pp. 41–77; Mentor Graham to WHH, May 29, 1865, in *HI*, pp. 9–10; Wilson, *Honor's Voice*, pp. 59–67.

54 "studied with nobody": AL, "Scripps autobiography," in *CW*, IV, p. 65.

54 He buried himself . . . *Equity Jurisprudence:* Donald, *Lincoln*, p. 55; Thomas, *Abraham Lincoln*, p. 43.

54 able to read and reread his books . . . "any other one thing": AL to Isham Reavis, November 5, 1855, in *CW*, II, p. 327.

55 "*I am Anne Rutledge* . . . : Edgar Lee Masters, "Anne Rutledge," in *Spoon River Anthology* (New York: The Macmillan Company, 1914; 1916), p. 220.

55 Lincoln would take . . . "wooded knoll" to read: W. D. Howells, "Life of Abraham Lincoln," in *Lives and Speeches of Abraham Lincoln and Hannibal Hamlin* (New York: W. A. Townsend & Co., and Columbus, Ohio: Follett, Foster & Co., 1860), p. 31.

55 "it is true . . . of her now": Isaac Cogdal interview, 1865–1866, in *HI*, p. 440.

55 "Eyes blue large, & Expressive," auburn hair: Mentor Graham interview, April 2, 1866, in ibid., p. 242.

55 "She was beloved by Every body": Ibid., p. 243.

55 "quick . . . worthy of Lincoln's love": William G. Greene to WHH (interview), May 30, 1865, in ibid., p. 21.

55 that they would marry . . . at Jacksonville: Thomas, *Lincoln's New Salem*, p. 82; Tarbell, *The Life of Abraham Lincoln*, Vol. I, p. 119.

55 details of Ann's death: Rankin, *Personal Recollections of Abraham Lincoln*, pp. 73–74.

55 "*indifferent* . . . woods by him self": Henry McHenry to WHH, January 8, 1866, in *HI*, p. 155.

55 "never seen a man . . . he did": Elizabeth Abell to WHH, February 15, 1867, in ibid., p. 557.

55 "be reconcile[d] . . . temporarily deranged": William G. Greene interview, May 30, 1865, in ibid., p. 21.

56 "reason would desert her throne": Robert B. Rutledge to WHH, ca. November 1, 1866, in ibid., p. 383.

56 he ran "off the track": Isaac Cogdal interview, [1865–1866], in ibid., p. 440.

56 "*I hear the loved survivors tell* . . .": AL to Andrew Johnston, April 18, 1846, in *CW*, I, p. 379.

56 "was not crazy": Elizabeth Abell to WHH, February 15, 1867, in *HI*, p. 557.

56 "Only people . . . and heal them": Leo Tolstoy, *Childhood, Boyhood, Youth*, quoted in George E. Vaillant, *The Wisdom of the Ego* (Cambridge, Mass., and London: Harvard University Press, 1993), p. 358.

56 "I'm afraid . . . last of us": AL to Mrs. Samuel Hill, quoted in Wilson, *Honor's Voice*, p. 83.

56 of any "faith in life after death": Bruce, "The Riddle of Death," in *The Lincoln Enigma*, pp. 137–39. Lincoln wrote to his stepbrother that were his father to die soon, Thomas Lincoln would have a "joyous [meeting] with many loved ones gone before; and where [the rest] of us, through the help of God, hope ere-long [to join] them." AL to John D. Johnston, January 12, 1851, in *CW*, II, p. 97.

56 his "heart was broken" . . . eternal companionship: SPC to Charles D. Cleveland, October 1, 1845, reel 6, Chase Papers.

56 "to a higher world . . . with her mother": Bates diary, November 15, 1846.

57 "I ought to be able . . . in these reflections": WHS to Charlotte S. Cushman, January 7, 1867, Vol. 13, The Papers of Charlotte S. Cushman, Manuscript Division, Library of Congress.

57 his "experiment . . . never saw a sadder face": Speed, *Reminiscences of Abraham Lincoln*, p. 21.

57 Speed had heard Lincoln speak: Ibid., pp. 17–18; Joshua F. Speed statement, 1865–1866, in *HI*, p. 477.

57 "You seem to be . . . 'I am moved!' ": Speed, *Reminiscences of Abraham Lincoln*, pp. 21–22.

57 description of Joshua Speed: See ibid., pp. 3–14; Robert L. Kincaid, *Joshua Fry Speed: Lincoln's Most Intimate Friend*, reprinted from *The Filson Club History Quarterly* 17 (Louisville, Ky.: Filson Club, 1943; Harrogate, Tenn.: Department of Lincolniana, Lincoln Memorial University, 1943), pp. 10–11.

58 Lincoln and Speed shared: For the relationship between Lincoln and Speed, see Speed, *Reminiscences of Abraham Lincoln*; Kincaid, *Joshua Fry Speed*, pp. 13–14.

58 as his "most intimate friend": Kincaid, *Joshua Fry Speed*, pp. 10, 33 n2.

58 "You know my desire . . . to do any thing": AL to Joshua F. Speed, February 13, 1842, in *CW*, I, p. 269.

58 Some have suggested: C. A. Tripp, *The Intimate World of Abraham Lincoln*, ed. Lewis Gannett (New York: Free Press, 2005), pp. 126–29.

58 sharing a bed: Rotundo, *American Manhood*, pp. 84–85; Strozier, *Lincoln's Quest for Union*, p. 43.

58 The room above Speed's store: Michael Burlingame, "A Respectful Dissent," Afterword I, in Tripp, *The Intimate World of Abraham Lincoln*, p. 228.

58 attorneys of the Eighth Circuit . . . for a companion: Whitney, *Life on the Circuit with Lincoln*, pp. 63, 72.

58 the "preoccupation . . . the nineteenth": Donald Yacovone, "Abolitionists and the 'Language of Fraternal Love,' " in *Meanings for Manhood: Constructions of Masculinity in Victorian America*, ed. Mark C. Carnes and Clyde Griffen (Chicago: University of Chicago Press, 1990), p. 94.

CHAPTER 3: THE LURE OF POLITICS

Page

60 "Scarcely have you . . . as to an assembly": Alexis de Tocqueville, *Democracy in America*, ed. and trans. Harvey C. Mansfield and Delba Winthrop (Chicago and London: University of Chicago Press, 2000), p. 232.

61 Noah Webster's *Elementary Spelling Book:* Fidler, "Young Limbs of the Law," pp. 175–76.

61 "Who can wonder . . . hush before his": Ralph Waldo Emerson, "Eloquence," in *The Works of Ralph Waldo Emerson: Society and Solitude*, Vol. VI, Fireside Edition (Boston and New York: n.p., 1870; 1898), p. 65.

61 Bates was the first . . . "form of government": Cain, *Lincoln's Attorney General*, pp. 8–9, 11 (quotes pp. 9, 11); Appleby, *Inheriting the Revolution*, p. 247.

62 "This momentous question . . . of the Union": Thomas Jefferson to John Holmes, April 22, 1820, *The Works of Thomas Jefferson*, Vol. XII, Federal Edition, ed. Paul Leicester Ford (New York and London: G. P. Putnam's Sons/The Knickerbocker Press, 1905), p. 158.

62 Missouri Compromise: "Missouri Compromise," in *The Reader's Companion to American History*, ed. Foner and Garraty, p. 737.

62 *"Great Pacificator"*: Stephen Douglas, quoted by AL, "Speech at Peoria, Illinois," October 16, 1854, in *CW*, II, p. 251.

62 "emerged as one" . . . candidates for state offices: Cain, *Lincoln's Attorney General*, pp. 14–15 (quote p. 14).

62 tensions developed between Senators Barton and Benton: Cain, *Lincoln's Attorney General*, pp. 19–22.

62 The Whigs favored public support: See Michael F. Holt, *The Rise and Fall of the American Whig Party: Jacksonian Politics and the Onset of the Civil War* (New York: Oxford University Press, 1999), pp. 27, 64, 66–70.

63 "a most beautiful woman": John F. Darby, "Mrs. Julia Bates, Widow of the Late Ed. Bates, Esq. For the Republican," reprinted in Bates, *Bates, et al., of Virginia and Missouri*, p. 31.

63 Julia's South Carolina family: Ibid., pp. 31–32.

63 Her surviving letters: Julia Davenport Bates to Caroline Hatcher Bates, April 10, 1850; Julia Davenport Bates to Onward Bates, July 24, 1855, February 14, 1861, Bates Papers, MoSHi.

63 "was calculated . . . domestic circle": Darby, "Mrs. Julia Bates," reprinted in Bates, *Bates, et al., of Virginia and Missouri*, p. 31.

63 When he sought and won a seat: Cain, *Lincoln's Attorney General*, pp. 26–27.

63 "I have never . . . to have it again": EB to Julia Bates, April 11, 1825, Bates Papers, ViHi.

63 Bates's lonely journey to Washington: EB to Julia Bates, November 7, 1827, Bates Papers, ViHi.

63 "something of a melancholy . . . mood": EB to Julia Bates, November 7, 1827, Bates Papers, ViHi.

64 "magic . . . feel it to be true": EB to Julia Bates, November 7, 1827, Bates Papers, ViHi.

64 life in Washington: EB to Julia Bates, January 5 and 22, February 25, March 17, 1828, December 4, 1829, Bates Papers, ViHi.

64 "That man grows . . . associate with him": EB to Julia Bates, February 25, 1828, Bates Papers, ViHi.

64 The main issues that confronted Bates: EB to Julia Bates, March 17, 1828, Bates Papers, ViHi; Cain, *Lincoln's Attorney General*, pp. 28–32.

64 Benton and Barton were antagonists: Cain, *Lincoln's Attorney General*, pp. 28–29.

64 Bates published a pamphlet: EB, *Edward Bates Against Thomas H. Benton* (St. Louis: Charless & Paschall, 1828).

64 "My piece is . . . never be effaced": EB to Julia Bates, December 4, 1829, Bates Papers, ViHi.

64 "roaring disorder . . . magnificent appearance": EB to Julia Bates, February 23, 1829, Bates Papers, ViHi.

64 "As yet I only . . . is in my eye": EB to Julia Bates, January 5, 1828, Bates Papers, ViHi.

65 "O, that I could . . . my sunshine": EB to Julia Bates, February 25, 1828, Bates Papers, ViHi.

65 he lost his bid for reelection: EB to Julia Bates, December 4, 1829, Bates Papers, ViHi.

65 got into a heated argument: Cain, *Lincoln's Attorney General*, pp. 38–39.

65 "The code preserved . . . are well spent": Charles Gibson, *The Autobiography of Charles Gibson*, ed. E. R. Gibson, 1899, Gibson Papers, MoSHi.

65 "as much as any man . . . we possessed": EB to Julia Bates, December 4, 1829, Bates Papers, ViHi.

65 two terms in the state legislature: "Bates, Edward," *DAB*, Vol. I, p. 48.

65 "the ablest . . . of that body": Switzler, "Lincoln's Attorney General," reprinted in Bates, *Bates, et al., of Virginia and Missouri*, p. 27.

65 he decided in 1835: Cain, *Lincoln's Attorney General*, pp. 53, 55, 58.

66 the "curious fact . . . of the frog": Bates diary, September 17, 1847.

66 "bad stammerer . . . more devoted piety": Bates diary, December 15, 1849.

66 "Mistress & Queen": Bates diary, July 10, 1851.

66 "begrudge her the short respite": Bates diary, April 23, 1848.

66 "This day . . . in a large house": Bates diary, November 15, 1851.

67 Every year, on April 29: See, for example, entry for April 29, 1859, in *The Diary of Edward Bates, 1859–1866*, p. 13.

67 "mighty changes . . . of the continent": Entry for April 29, 1859, in ibid.

67 His entries proudly record: Bates diary, November 7, 1847; December 20, 1847; December 9, 1852.

67 a great fire . . . cholera epidemic: Bates diary, May 18; June 14–28; July 1–11, 1849.

67 "in perfect health" . . . fruits and vegetables: Bates diary, July 19, 1849.

67 medical ignorance . . . "two weeks at a time": Bates diary, June 21, 1849.

67 "I am one . . . of a known duty": EB to R. B. Frayser, June 1849, Bates Papers, MoSHi.

67 Bates filled the pages of his diary: Bates diary, May 21, 1847; May 22, 1847; November 22, 1847; December 10, 1847; March 13, 1848; May 6, 1848; March 11, 1849; March 29, 1851 (quote).

67 "the largest Convention . . . the Civil War": Floyd A. McNeil, "Lincoln's Attorney General; Edward Bates," Ph.D. diss., State University of Iowa, 1934, p. 155.
67 5,000 accredited delegates . . . David Dudley Field: Shaw, "A Neglected Episode in the Life of Abraham Lincoln," *Transactions* (1922), p. 54; Albert J. Beveridge, *Abraham Lincoln, 1809–1858*, Vol. II (Boston and New York: Houghton Mifflin/Riverside Press, 1928), pp. 89–90.
68 "Hon. Abraham . . . in the State": *NYTrib*, July 14, 1847.
68 "No one who saw . . . with woolen socks": E. B. Washburne, "Political Life in Illinois," in *Reminiscences of Abraham Lincoln*, ed. Rice, p. 92.
68 "deep astonishment" . . . responsibility for its failure: Bates diary, July 5, 1847.
68 "leaped at one bound . . . prominence": Switzler, "Lincoln's Attorney General," reprinted in Bates, *Bates, et al., of Virginia and Missouri*, p. 28.
68 Lincoln impressed . . . Democrat Field: *Beveridge, Abraham Lincoln, 1809–1859*, Vol. II, p. 91.
68 "too intent . . . of Reporting": *Albany Evening Journal*, July 23, 1847.
68 "No account . . . do it justice": *NYTrib*, July 15, 1847.
68 "between sectional disruption . . . material greatness": Cain, *Lincoln's Attorney General*, p. 63.
69 "he was interrupted . . . in attendance": TW, quoted in Bates, *Bates, et al., of Virginia and Missouri*, p. 30.
69 "the crowning act . . . either house of Congress": Bates diary, July 5, 1847.
69 "The nation cannot . . . and patriotism": *Albany Evening Journal*, July 23, 1847.
69 "the glittering bauble": Entry for February 28, 1860, *The Diary of Edward Bates, 1859–1866*, p. 106.
69 "noble aspirations . . . natural result": EB to TW, August 9, 1847, reprinted in *Albany Evening Journal*, January 11, 1861.
69 "had no ambition . . . business of the country": Seward, *An Autobiography*, pp. 52, 53.
70 Seward and Weed meet: See ibid., pp. 55–56; Thurlow Weed, *Autobiography of Thurlow Weed*, ed. Harriet A. Weed (Boston: Houghton Mifflin, 1883), p. 139.
70 "he printed . . . his own hand": Seward, *An Autobiography*, p. 56.
70 details of Weed's early life: *Autobiography of Thurlow Weed*, ed. Weed; Thurlow Weed Barnes, *Memoir of Thurlow Weed* (Boston: Houghton Mifflin, 1884).
70 He had walked miles: *Autobiography of Thurlow Weed*, ed. Weed, pp. 12–13.
70 "a politician who sees . . . him forever": Barnes, *Memoir of Thurlow Weed*, pp. 26–27.
70 Such measures . . . "extend its dominion": Seward, *An Autobiography*, p. 54.
71 the *Albany Evening Journal*: *Autobiography of Thurlow Weed*, ed. Weed, pp. 360–62.
71 Weed engineered . . . from the seventh district: Seward, *An Autobiography*, p. 80.
71 the youngest member to enter: Taylor, *William Henry Seward*, p. 24.
71 Albany still a small town: John J. McEneny, *Albany: Capital City on the Hudson* (Sun Valley, Calif.: American Historical Press, 1998), p. 76.
71 description of Albany: "Albany Fifty Years Ago," *Harper's New Monthly Magazine* 14 (March 1857), pp. 451–63.
71 "first steam-powered . . . web of tracks": McEneny, *Albany*, p. 16 (quote), 98.
71 The legislature . . . Bemont's Hotel: Seward, *An Autobiography*, pp. 80–81; Frederick W. Seward, *Reminiscences of a War-Time Statesman and Diplomat, 1830–1915* (New York and London: G. P. Putnam's Sons, 1916), p. 2; Taylor, *William Henry Seward*, p. 24.
71 Seward attends alone: Seward, *An Autobiography*, p. 80.
71 "Weed is . . . warmth of feeling": WHS to FAS, January 12, 1831, in ibid., p. 166.
71 "one of the greatest . . . except politics": WHS to FAS, February 6, 1831, in ibid., pp. 179–80.
71 Weed and Seward's mutual interests: Van Deusen, *William Henry Seward*, p. 17; Taylor, *William Henry Seward*, p. 25.
71 "My room is a thoroughfare": WHS to FAS, February 16, 1831, in Seward, *An Autobiography*, p. 182.
72 Albert Haller Tracy: Van Deusen, *William Henry Seward*, p. 17; "Tracy, Albert Haller, 1793–1859," *Biographical Directory of the United States Congress*, http://bioguide.congress.gov (accessed December 2003).
72 "crushed . . . passes in his mind": FAS to LW, March 12, 1832, reel 118, Seward Papers.
72 "He and Henry . . . love with each other": FAS to LW, March 4, 1832, reel 118, Seward Papers.
72 "It shames my . . . since I left Albany": Albert H. Tracy to WHS, February 7, 1831, reel 1, Seward Papers.
72 Seward at first reciprocated: FAS to LW, March 12, 1832, reel 118, Seward Papers.
72 a "rapturous joy . . . I possessed": WHS to Albert H. Tracy, February 11, 1831, typescript copy, Albert Haller Tracy Papers, New York State Library, Albany, New York [hereafter Tracy Papers].
72 "My feelings . . . divided with many": Albert H. Tracy to WHS, June 12, 1832, reel 1, Seward Papers.
72 "Weed has never . . . account for it": FAS to LW, March [?] 1832, reel 118, Seward Papers (quote); FAS to LW, April 5, 1832, reel 118, Seward Papers.
72 "Love—cruel tyrant . . . hallowed affections": Albert H. Tracy to WHS, September 24, 1832, reel 1, Seward Papers.
72 He transferred his unrequited love: FAS to LW, March [?] and September 27, 1832, reel 118, Seward Papers; WHS to FAS, November 28, 1834, reel 112, Seward Papers.
73 "losing my influence . . . differently constituted": FAS to WHS, December 5, 1834, reel 113, Seward Papers.
73 relationship between Tracys and Sewards: FAS to LW, March 12, 24, and undated March, April 9, 1832, reel 118, Seward Papers.
73 "He is a singular . . . shade of difference": FAS to LW, March 12, 1832, reel 118, Seward Papers.
73 "I believe at present . . . should choose": FAS to LW, March [?] 1832, reel 118, Seward Papers.
73 "very glad . . . very much": FAS to LW, November 17, 1833, reel 118, Seward Papers.
73 private emotional intimacy: See Karen Lystra, *Searching the Heart: Women, Men and Romantic Love in Victorian America* (New York: Oxford University Press, 1989), pp. 31–33.

73 a three-month voyage to Europe: Seward, *An Autobiography*, pp. 104–41.
73 "What a romance . . . malicious political warfare": Ibid., pp. 116, 128.
74 spent a long weekend visiting: Ibid., pp. 134–40.
74 When Judge Miller . . . "be so unreasonable": FAS to LW, September 27, 1833, reel 118, Seward Papers.
74 she proffered the letters: WHS to Albert Tracy, quoted in WHS to FAS, December 29, 1834, reel 112, Seward Papers.
74 Seward's first run for governor: Glyndon G. Van Deusen, *Thurlow Weed: Wizard of the Lobby* (Boston: Little, Brown, 1947), pp. 87–89; Taylor, *William Henry Seward*, pp. 35–36.
75 Whigs offered a gallery . . . Henry Clay himself: Seward, *An Autobiography*, p. 238. This same campaign tactic was adopted by the youthful John F. Kennedy in his campaign for the presidency in 1960.
75 Defeat shook . . . jeopardized his marriage: WHS to FAS, November 24 and 28, 1834, reel 112, Seward Papers; Van Deusen, *William Henry Seward*, pp. 28, 33–34.
75 "What a demon . . . are not crushed": WHS to FAS, November 28, 1834, reel 112, Seward Papers.
75 "I am growing womanish . . . happy a lot": WHS to FAS, December 5, 1834, reel 112, Seward Papers.
75 "You reproach yourself . . . the right path": FAS to WHS, December 5, 1834, reel 113, Seward Papers.
76 Seward pledged: WHS to FAS, December 15 and 29, 1834, reel 112, Seward Papers.
76 "to live for you . . . dear boys": WHS to FAS, December 29, 1834, reel 112, Seward Papers.
76 "a partner in . . . cares and feelings": WHS to FAS, December 1, 1834, reel 112, Seward Papers.
76 "count[ing] with eagerness . . . life will commence": WHS to FAS, December 29, 1834, reel 112, Seward Papers.
76 "golden dreams . . . displayed towards you": Albert Tracy to WHS, December 29, 1834, reel 3, Seward Papers.
76 "alienation . . . but without affection": WHS to Albert Tracy, quoted in Seward to FAS, December 29, 1834, reel 112, Seward Papers.
76 If Seward believed: WHS to TW, January 18, 1835, in Seward, *An Autobiography*, p. 249; WHS to unknown recipient, June 1, 1836, in ibid., p. 300.
76 "It is seldom . . . periods of seclusion": WHS to Alvah Hunt, January 25, 1843, quoted in Van Deusen, *William Henry Seward*, p. 99.
77 "keep me informed . . . as a politician": WHS to TW, January 1835, in Seward, *An Autobiography*, p. 249.
77 family expedition to the South: Taylor, *William Henry Seward*, p. 37; Seward, *Reminiscences of a War-Time Statesman and Diplomat*, p. 9.
77 "When I travel . . . and reflection": WHS to Albert H. Tracy, June 23, 1831, Tracy Papers.
77 their letters home extolled: Seward, *An Autobiography*, pp. 272–73; Seward, *Reminiscences of a War-Time Statesman and Diplomat*, pp. 12–13.
77 "teemed with . . . reform of mankind": Introduction to "The Conflict of Cultures," in *The Causes of the Civil War*, 3rd edn., ed. Kenneth M. Stampp (Englewood Cliffs, N.J.: Prentice-Hall, 1959; New York: Touchstone Books, 1991), p. 201.
77 a world virtually unchanged: James M. McPherson, "Modernization and Sectionalism," in ibid., p. 104.
77 "We no longer passed . . . of slaves": Entry for June 12, 1835, WHS journal, quoted in Seward, *An Autobiography*, p. 267.
77 "a waste . . . decaying habitation": Entry for June 12, 1835, WHS journal, in ibid., p. 267.
77 "How deeply . . . decayed as Virginia": WHS to Albert H. Tracy, June 25, 1835, Tracy Papers.
77 Slavery trapped . . . a sizable middle class: McPherson, "Modernization and Sectionalism," in *The Causes of the Civil War*, ed. Stampp, pp. 104–05.
78 "We are told that . . . this injured race": FAS to LW, quoted in Seward, *An Autobiography*, p. 272.
78 "turning the ponderous" . . . any of them again: Seward, *Reminiscences of a War-Time Statesman and Diplomat*, pp. 14–15.
78 "Ten naked little boys . . . themselves to sleep": Seward, *An Autobiography*, p. 271.
78 "Sick of slavery and the South": Entry for June 13, 1835, FAS, "Diary of Trip through Pennsylvania, Virginia, and Maryland, 1835," reel 197, Seward Papers.
78 "the evil effects . . . marring everything": Entry of June 17, 1835, FAS, "Diary of Trip through Pennsylvania, Virginia, and Maryland, 1835," reel 197, Seward Papers.
78 "turned their horses' . . . homeward": Seward, *An Autobiography*, p. 272.
78 indelible images . . . social conscience: Entry for June 15, 1835, WHS journal in Seward, *An Autobiography*, p. 268; FAS to LW, January 15, 1853, reel 119, Seward Papers; WHS, "Speech in Cleveland, Ohio on the Election of 1848," *Works of William H. Seward*, Vol. III, pp. 295–96.
78 a lucrative opportunity . . . Seward did not hesitate: Van Deusen, *William Henry Seward*, pp. 38–39.
79 "more beautiful" . . . invited Weed's seventeen-year-old daughter: WHS to Harriet Weed, September 8, 1836, Thurlow Weed Papers, Department of Rare Books & Special Collections, University of Rochester Library, Rochester, N.Y. [hereafter Weed Papers].
79 "there are a thousand . . . upon them": WHS to FAS, December 21, 1836, in Seward, *An Autobiography*, p. 321.
79 "so vividly remembered . . . a rare event": Seward, *An Autobiography*, p. 162.
79 death of Cornelia from smallpox: Seward, *An Autobiography*, p. 323.
79 "did not think it . . . from their Grandpa": FAS to Harriet Weed, February 9, 1837, Weed Papers.
79 "lightness that was . . . for myself": WHS to FAS, February 12, 1837, in Seward, *An Autobiography*, p. 325.
79 Frances and the boys come to Westfield: Seward, *An Autobiography*, pp. 334–35.
80 "Well, I am here . . . from Tusculum": WHS to TW, July 10, 1837, in ibid., p. 336.
80 "found Westfield . . . missed and loved her": FAS to Harriet Weed, September 6, 1837, Weed Papers.
80 "I am almost in despair . . . almost as helpless": WHS to [FAS], December 17, 1837, in Seward, *An Autobiography*, p. 354.

80 "There is such . . . time to think": WHS to [TW], undated, in ibid., p. 344.
80 "I have been two . . . healthful channels": TW to WHS, November 11, 1837, quoted in Van Deusen, *Thurlow Weed*, p. 95.
80 Weed raised money . . . powerful *New York Tribune: Autobiography of Thurlow Weed*, ed. Weed, pp. 466–67; Seward, *Reminiscences of a War-Time Statesman and Diplomat*, pp. 45, 88.
81 1838 gubernatorial campaign: Van Deusen, *William Henry Seward*, pp. 49–52.
81 received the nomination on the fourth ballot: Seward, *An Autobiography*, p. 373; Van Deusen, *Thurlow Weed*, p. 100.
81 "Well, Seward . . . earnestly to work": TW to WHS, September 15, 1838, reel 5, Seward Papers.
81 the overwhelming victor: Seward, *An Autobiography*, p. 378.
81 "God bless . . . result to him": WHS, quoted in J. C. Derby, *Fifty Years Among Authors, Books and Publishers* (New York: G.W. Carleton & Co., 1884), p. 58.
81 "It is a fearful post . . . a house alone": WHS to TW, November 11, 1838, hereafter Weed Papers.
81 Weed arrived . . . inaugural outfit: WHS to TW, November 28, 1838, Weed Papers; Seward, *An Autobiography*, pp. 381–82 (quote p. 382); Van Deusen, *Thurlow Weed*, p. 102.
81 "it was [his] . . . a cabinet": WHS to Hiram Ketchum, February 15, 1839, reel 8, Seward Papers.
81 "Your letter . . . as it comes up": WHS to [TW], November 23, 1837, in Seward, *An Autobiography*, p. 345.
82 "I had no idea . . . amiable creatures": WHS to TW, December 14, 1838, in ibid., p. 381.
82 "There were never two . . . highest sense": Barnes, *Memoir of Thurlow Weed*, p. 262.
82 told the story of a carriage ride: Seward, *An Autobiography*, p. 395.
82 an ambitious agenda . . . imprisonment for debt: WHS, "Annual Message to the Legislature, January 1, 1839," *The Works of William H. Seward*, Vol. II, pp. 183–211; Seward, *An Autobiography*, pp. 386–87.
82 "Our race is ordained" . . . the engine of Northern expansion: WHS, "Annual Message, 1839," *Works of William H. Seward*, Vol. II, pp. 197–99.
83 to support parochial schools: Ibid., p. 199; WHS, "Annual Message to the Legislature, January 7, 1840," p. 215.
83 "to overthrow republican" . . . the hands of priests: Seward, *An Autobiography*, p. 462.
83 "Virginia Case" . . . governor refused: WHS, "Biographical Memoir of William H. Seward," *Works of William H. Seward*, Vol. I, pp. lxiii–lxvi.
83 "the universal sentiment . . . praiseworthy": George E. Baker, ed., *Life of William H. Seward, with Selections from His Works* (New York: J. S. Redfield, 1855), p. 85.
83 "intermeddling . . . New England fanatic": Seward, *An Autobiography*, pp. 463, 464.
84 This only emboldened Seward's resolve: Ibid., pp. 463–64, 510–11.
84 the "new irritation": Thomas Jefferson to John Holmes, April 22, 1820, in *The Works of Thomas Jefferson*, Vol. XII, ed. Ford, p. 158.
84 number of slaves who escaped to the North: Don E. Fehrenbacher, "The Wilmot Proviso and the Mid-Century Crisis," in Fehrenbacher, *The South and Three Sectional Crises* (Baton Rouge: Louisiana State University Press, 1980), p. 33.
84 "all actions . . . Constitution": William H. Pease and Jane H. Pease, ed. *The Antislavery Argument* (Indianapolis: Bobbs-Merrill, 1965), p. xxx.
84 *"The Empire of Satan"*: Henry Mayer, *All on Fire: William Lloyd Garrison and the Abolition of Slavery* (New York: St. Martin's Press, 1998), p. 188.
84 They proclaimed slavery a "positive good": John C. Calhoun, *Remarks of Mr. Calhoun of South Carolina, on the Reception of Abolition Petitions, delivered in the Senate of the United States, February 1837*, reprinted in Robert C. Byrd, *The Senate, 1789–1989*. Vol. III: *Classic Speeches, 1830–1993*, Bicentennial Edition, ed. Wendy Wolff (Washington, D.C.: Government Printing Office, 1994), p. 177.
84 incited attacks on abolitionist printers: Niven, *Salmon P. Chase*, pp. 47–48.
84 Seward reelected but with a reduced margin: Seward, *An Autobiography*, p. 506.
84 "henceforth be . . . in his life": Horace Greeley article, *Log Cabin*, in ibid., p. 510.
84 "All that can . . . in its history": WHS to Christopher Morgan, [June?] 1841, in ibid., p. 547.
84 "What am I . . . on your affection?": WHS to TW, December 31, 1842, quoted in Barnes, *Memoir of Thurlow Weed*, p. 98.
85 the new Liberty Party: "Liberty Party," in *The Reader's Companion to American History*, ed. Foner and Garraty, p. 657; Taylor, *William Henry Seward*, p. 59.
85 story of black man named William Freeman: Baker, ed., *Life of William H. Seward*, pp. 99–113; "Defence of William Freeman," *Works of William H. Seward*, Vol. I, pp. 409–75.
85 "I trust in the mercy . . . incomprehensible": FAS to WHS, March 1846, in Seward, *An Autobiography*, pp. 787, 786.
85 insanity . . . floggings in jail: Seward, *An Autobiography*, p. 812.
85 "Will anyone defend . . . *until his death!*": Baker, ed., *Life of William H. Seward*, pp. 104, 106.
85 roundly criticized Seward for his decision: WHS to TW, May 29, 1846, quoted in Seward, *An Autobiography*, p. 810.
85 Only Frances stood proudly: Van Deusen, *William Henry Seward*, p. 97.
85 "he will do . . . wrong is perpetrated": FAS to LW, July 1, 1846, reel 119, Seward Papers.
85 "there are few men . . . a peaceful mind": FAS to Augustus Seward, July 19, 1846, reel 114, Seward Papers.
86 she sat in the courtroom: FAS to LW, January–February 1850, reel 119, Seward Papers.
86 summoning five doctors: Seward, *An Autobiography*, pp. 811, 813.
86 "He is still your brother . . . be a man": "Defence of William Freeman," *Works of William H. Seward*, Vol. I, p. 417.

86 "I am not . . . malefactor": Ibid., pp. 414–15.
86 "unexplainable on any principle of *sanity*": WHS to TW, May 29, 1846, in Seward, *An Autobiography*, p. 810.
86 "there is not . . . such a prosecution": "Defence of William Freeman," *Works of William H. Seward*, Vol. I, p. 419.
86 "In due time . . . 'He was Faithful!' ": WHS, quoted in Seward, *An Autobiography*, p. 822.
86 While Seward endured . . . still wider distribution: Seward, *Seward at Washington . . . 1846–1861*, pp. 29, 32, 46.
86 "one of the very first . . . the highest degree": SPC to Lewis Tappan, March 18, 1847, reel 6, Chase Papers.
87 Lincoln's run for legislature from Sangamon County: Thomas, *Abraham Lincoln*, pp. 28–29, 34–35.
87 "Every man . . . very much chagrined": AL, "Communication to the People of Sangamo County," March 9, 1832, in *CW,* I, pp. 8–9.
87 only after being defeated . . . "to try it again": J. Rowan Herndon to WHH, May 28, 1865, in *HI*, p. 7.
87 Lincoln had lost the election: AL, "Communication to the People of Sangamo County," March 9, 1832, in *CW,* I, p. 5n.
87 "made friends everywhere he went": "Conversation with Hon. J. T. Stuart June 23 1875," quoted in John G. Nicolay, *An Oral History of Abraham Lincoln: John G. Nicolay's Interviews and Essays*, ed. Michael Burlingame (Carbondale and Edwardsville: Southern Illinois University Press, 1996), p. 10.
88 "This was the only time . . . of the people": AL, "Scripps autobiography," in *CW,* IV, p. 64.
88 Two years later . . . in the state legislature: Thomas, *Abraham Lincoln*, p. 41.
88 frontier county . . . "consuming the whole afternoon": Robert L. Wilson to WHH, February 10, 1866, in *HI*, pp. 201–02.
88 At Mr. Kyle's store . . . "one Could throw it": Andrew S. Kirk interview, March 7, 1887, in ibid., pp. 602–03.
88 "They came there . . . social club": Speed, *Reminiscences of Abraham Lincoln*, p. 23.
89 Lincoln proved . . . grassroots politician: Thomas, *Abraham Lincoln*, pp. 58, 63, 79.
89 three levels of command . . . "day as possible": "Lincoln's Plan of Campaign in 1840" [c. January 1840], in *CW,* I, p. 180.
89 "Our intention . . . which we are engaged": "Campaign Circular from Whig Committee," January [31?], 1840, in ibid., pp. 201–03. See also "Lincoln's Plan of Campaign in 1840" [c. January 1840], in ibid., pp. 180–81.
90 Lincoln likened . . . internal improvements: James A. Herndon to WHH, May 29, 1865, in *HI*, p. 16.
90 Lincoln had actually . . . "wider and fairer": Carpenter, *Six Months at the White House*, pp. 97–98 (quote p. 97).
90 "to the ideal . . . rise in life": G. S. Boritt, *Lincoln and the Economics of the American Dream* (Memphis, Tenn.: Memphis State University Press, 1978), p. ix.
90 "an unfettered start . . . pursuit for all": AL, "Message to Congress in Special Session," July 4, 1861, in *CW,* IV, p. 438.
91 "DeWitt Clinton of Illinois": Herndon and Weik, *Herndon's Life of Lincoln*, p. 140.
91 "we highly disapprove . . . of the citizens": Resolutions by the General Assembly of the State of Illinois, quoted in note 2 of "Protest in Illinois Legislature on Slavery," March 3, 1837, in *CW,* I, p. 75.
91 he issued a formal protest . . . "people of said District": "Protest in Illinois Legislature on Slavery," March 3, 1837, in ibid., p. 75. Daniel Stone of Springfield co-authored the protest with Lincoln.
91 "if slavery . . . so think, and feel": AL to Albert G. Hodges, April 4, 1864, draft copy, Lincoln Papers.
91 "partly on account . . . that it is now": AL, "Scripps autobiography," in *CW,* IV, pp. 61, 65.
92 In these early years . . . gradually become extinct: For an example of Lincoln stating that he believed slavery would gradually become extinct, see AL, "Speech at Greenville, Illinois," September 13, 1858, in *CW,* III, p. 96.
92 Lincoln defended both slaveowners and fugitive slaves: Donald, *Lincoln*, p. 104.
92 the constitutional requirements . . . could not be evaded: Burlingame, *The Inner World of Abraham Lincoln*, p. 28.
92 a sustained recession . . . sentiment turned: Donald, *Lincoln*, pp. 61–62; Boritt, *Lincoln and the Economics of the American Dream*, p. 28.
92 "stopping a skift . . . go down": AL, "Remarks in the Illinois Legislature Concerning the Illinois and Michigan Canal," January 22, 23, 1840, in *CW,* I, p. 196.
92 "If you make . . . the tighter": AL to Joshua F. Speed, February 25, 1842, in ibid., p. 280 (quote); Boritt, *Lincoln and the Economics of the American Dream*, p. 30.
92 was forced to liquidate . . . deterred from emigrating: *King, Lincoln's Manager*, p. 40.
92 to win a fourth term . . . term was completed: Thomas, *Abraham Lincoln*, p. 77; entry for August 3, 1840, *Lincoln Day by Day: A Chronology, 1809–1865*. Vol. I, ed. Earl Schenck Miers (Washington, D.C.: Lincoln Sesquicentennial Commission, 1960; Dayton, Ohio: Morningside, 1991), p. 142.
92 "He was not very fond of girls": Sarah Bush Lincoln interview, September 8, 1865, in *HI*, p. 108.
92 "He would burst . . . 'clean those girls look' ": AL, quoted in William H. Herndon, "Analysis of the Character of Abraham Lincoln," *Abraham Lincoln Quarterly* I (September 1941), p. 367.
93 "as demoralized . . . out of sight": Whitney, *Life on the Circuit with Lincoln*, p. 59.
93 "a business which I do not understand": AL to Mrs. M. J. Green, September 22, 1860, in *CW,* IV, p. 118.
93 " . . . *when the genius of*": Stephen Vincent Benét, *John Brown's Body* (New York: Henry Holt & Co., 1927; 1990), p. 189.
93 "Lincoln had . . . his terrible passion": WHH to JWW, January 23, 1890, reel 10, Herndon-Weik Collection, DLC.
93 "his Conscience . . . many a woman": David Davis interview, September 20, 1866, in *HI*, p. 350.
93 "handsome . . . much vivacity": Esther Sumners Bale interview, [1866], in ibid., p. 527 (first quote); Nancy G. Vineyard to JWW, February 4, 1887, in ibid., p. 601 (second quote).

93 "a good conversationalist . . . splendid reader": Benjamin R. Vineyard to JWW, March 14, 1887, in ibid., p. 610.

93 would make a good match . . . honor-bound to keep his word: AL to Mrs. Orville H. Browning, April 1, 1838, in *CW*, I, pp. 117–19.

94 "This thing of living . . . Yours, &c.—Lincoln": AL to Mary S. Owens, May 7, 1837, in ibid., pp. 78–79.

94 "mortified almost beyond . . . enough to have me": AL to Mrs. Orville H. Browning, April 1, 1838, in ibid., p. 119.

94 The Edwards mansion . . . drink, and merry conversation: Randall, *Mary Lincoln*, p. 5.

94 "the exact reverse": Herndon and Weik, *Herndon's Life of Lincoln*, p. 165.

94 "physically, temperamentally, emotionally": Rankin, *Personal Recollections of Abraham Lincoln*, p. 160.

94 "her face an . . . passing emotion": Elizabeth Humphreys Norris to Emilie Todd Helm, September 28, 1895, quoted in Randall, *Mary Lincoln*, p. 24.

94 a self-controlled man: Elizabeth and Ninian W. Edwards interview, July 27, 1887, in *HI*, p. 623; MTL to Josiah G. Holland, December 4, 1865, in Justin G. Turner and Linda Levitt Turner, *Mary Todd Lincoln: Her Life and Letters* (New York: Knopf, 1972; New York: Fromm International, 1987), p. 293.

94 "he felt most deeply . . . the least": MTL to Josiah G. Holland, December 4, 1865, in ibid., p. 293.

95 "the very creature of excitement": James C. Conkling to Mercy Ann Levering, September 21, 1840, quoted in ibid., pp. 10–11.

95 "a Bishop forget his prayers": Ninian W. Edwards, quoted in Helm, *The True Story of Mary*, p. 81.

95 "a welcome guest everywhere . . . rarely danced": Tarbell, *The Life of Abraham Lincoln*, Vol. I (New York: Doubleday & McClure Co., 1900), p. 171.

95 "the highest marks . . . the biggest prizes": Helm, *The True Story of Mary*, p. 52.

95 Mary journeyed to . . . " 'Mary's' grave": MTL to Rhoda White, August 30, 1869, in Turner and Turner, *Mary Todd Lincoln*, p. 516.

95 Mary's life in Lexington: See chapters 1–3 in Baker, *Mary Todd Lincoln*.

95 "a violent little Whig": Helm, *The True Story of Mary*, p. 41.

95 "destined to be . . . future President": Elizabeth Todd Edward interview, 1865–1866, in *HI*, p. 443.

95 proudly rode her new pony: Helm, *The True Story of Mary*, pp. 1–2.

95 "I suppose like the rest . . . called in question?": MTL to Mercy Ann Levering, December [15?], 1840, in Turner and Turner, *Mary Todd Lincoln*, p. 21.

95 "the *great cause*": "Campaign Circular from Whig Committee," January [31?], 1840, in *CW*, 1, p. 202.

95 "Old hero": "Communication to the Readers of *The Old Soldier*," February 28, 1840, in ibid., p. 204.

95 death of Mary's mother; father's remarriage: See Baker, *Mary Todd Lincoln*, pp. 20, 22, 24, 28–30.

96 turned "desolate": MTL to Eliza Stuart Steele, May 23, 1871, in Turner and Turner, *Mary Todd Lincoln*, p. 588.

96 her only real home: MTL to Elizabeth Keckley, October 29, 1867, in ibid., p. 447.

96 "an emotional . . . heart would break": Mrs. Woodrow, quoted in Helm, *The True Story of Mary*, p. 32.

96 "either in the garret or cellar": Orville H. Browning, quoted in Nicolay, *An Oral History of Abraham Lincoln*, p. 1.

96 Mary may have precipitated: Abner Y. Ellis to WHH, March 24, 1866, in *HI*, p. 238; Stephen B. Oates, *With Malice Toward None: The Life of Abraham Lincoln* (New York: New American Library Penguin Books, 1977; 1978), p. 60.

96 Elizabeth warned . . . "husband & wife": Elizabeth Todd Edwards interview, 1865–1866, in *HI*, pp. 443, 444.

97 Mary had other suitors: MTL to Mercy Ann Levering, July 23 and December [15?], 1840, in Turner and Turner, *Mary Todd Lincoln*, pp. 18, 20; Baker, *Mary Todd Lincoln*, pp. 84–85.

97 "an agreeable . . . my heart is not": MTL to Mercy Ann Levering, July 23, 1840, in Turner and Turner, *Mary Todd Lincoln*, p. 18.

97 Far more likely, Lincoln's own misgivings: Tarbell, *The Life of Abraham Lincoln*, Vol. I, p. 173; Donald, *Lincoln*, pp. 86–87; Paul M. Angle, Appendix, in Carl Sandburg and Paul M. Angle, *Mary Lincoln, Wife and Widow* (New York: Harcourt, Brace & World, 1932; 1960), p. 331.

97 "in the winter . . . whole heart to me": Joshua F. Speed to WHH, November 30, 1866, in *HI*, p. 430.

97 Lincoln's change of heart . . . Matilda Edwards: Douglas L. Wilson, "Abraham Lincoln and 'That Fatal First of January,' " in Douglas L. Wilson, *Lincoln before Washington: New Perspectives on the Illinois Years* (Urbana and Chicago: University of Illinois Press, 1997), pp. 99–125.

97 "A lovelier girl I never saw": MTL to Mercy Ann Levering, December [15?], 1840, in Turner and Turner, *Mary Todd Lincoln*, p. 20.

97 "aberration of mind . . . violation of his word": Browning, quoted in Nicolay, *An Oral History of Abraham Lincoln*, p. 1.

97 no evidence that Lincoln ever made his feelings known: Elizabeth Todd and Ninian W. Edwards interviews, September 22, 1865, [1865–1866], July 27, 1887, in *HI*, pp. 133, 444, 623.

97 "never bear to leave . . . the strength of it": Jane Bell quoted in Wilson, "Abraham Lincoln and 'That Fatal First of January,' " in Wilson, *Lincoln before Washington*, p. 110.

97 "his ability and Capacity . . . support a wife": Elizabeth Todd Edwards interview, 1865–1866, in *HI*, p. 443.

98 driving up the marriage age: Fidler, "Young Limbs of the Law," pp. 266–67.

98 "is a jealous mistress . . . constant courtship": Joseph Story, "The Value and Importance of Legal Studies. A Discourse Pronounced at the Inauguration of the Author as Dane Professor of Law in Harvard University, August 25, 1829," in *The Miscellaneous Writings of Joseph Story*, ed. William W. Story. *Da Capo Press Reprints in American Constitutional and Legal History*, gen. ed. Leonard W. Levy (Boston, 1852; New York: Da Capo Press, 1972), p. 523.

98 Lincoln drafted a letter . . . lost his nerve: Joshua F. Speed interview, 1865–1866, in *HI*, pp. 475, 477.
98 "To tell you the truth . . . kissed her": AL, quoted in Herndon and Weik, *Herndon's Life of Lincoln*, p. 169.
98 This second confrontation: Wilson, "Abraham Lincoln and 'That Fatal First of January,' " in Wilson, *Lincoln before Washington*, pp. 103, 112.
98 "ability to keep . . . gem of [his] character": AL to Joshua F. Speed, July 4, 1842, in *CW*, I, p. 289.
98 "not single spies . . . battalions": William Shakespeare, "Hamlet," act 4, scene 5, *William Shakespeare Tragedies, Volume 1. Everyman's Library* (New York and Toronto: Alfred A. Knopf, 1992), p. 105.
98 details of Speed leaving Springfield: Kincaid, *Joshua Fry Speed*, p. 15.
98 Speed's departure would bring: James Conkling to Mercy Ann Levering, January 24, 1841, and Levering to Conkling, February 7, 1841, quoted in Wilson, "Abraham Lincoln and 'That Fatal First of January,' " in Wilson, *Lincoln before Washington*, p. 117; Burlingame, *The Inner World of Abraham Lincoln*, p. 100.
98 "I shall be verry . . . pained by the loss": AL to Joshua F. Speed, February 25, 1842, in *CW*, I, p. 281.
99 worried that he was suicidal: James H. Matheny interview, May 3, 1866, in *HI*, p. 251; Speed, *Reminiscences of Abraham Lincoln*, p. 39.
99 "Lincoln went Crazy . . . it was terrible": Joshua F. Speed interview, [1865–1866], in *HI*, p. 474.
99 "delirious to the extent . . . he was doing": Browning, quoted in Nicolay, *An Oral History of Abraham Lincoln*, p. 2.
99 "Poor L! . . . truly deplorable": James Conkling to Mercy Ann Levering, January 24, 1841, quoted in Wilson, "Abraham Lincoln and 'That Fatal First of January,' " in Wilson, *Lincoln Before Washington*, p. 117.
99 was called hypochondriasis: See J. S. Forsyth, *The New London Medical and Surgical Dictionary* (London: Sherwood, Gilbert & Piper, 1826), p. 379; Robley Dunglison, M.D., *A New Dictionary of Medical Science and Literature, Containing a Concise Account of the Various Subjects and Terms; with the Synonymes in Different Languages; and Formulæ for Various Officinal and Empirical Preparations*, Vol. I (Boston: Charles Bowen, 1833), p. 508; German E. Berrios, "Hypochondriasis: History of the Concept," in Vladan Starcevic and Don R. Lipsitt, eds., *Hypochondriasis: Modern Perspectives on an Ancient Malady* (New York: Oxford University Press, 2001), pp. 3–20.
99 "I have, within . . . to my existence": AL to John T. Stuart, January 20, 1841, in *CW*, I, p. 228. Dr. Henry did not receive the postmastership of Springfield.
99 "I am now the most . . . it appears to me: AL to John T. Stuart, January 23, 1841, in ibid., p. 229.
99 Hoping medical treatment . . . "without a personal interview": Joshua F. Speed to WHH, November 30, 1866, in *HI*, p. 431.
99 the nadir of Lincoln's depression . . . most certainly die: Speed, *Reminiscences of Abraham Lincoln*, p. 39.
99 "done nothing . . . desired to live for": Joshua F. Speed to WHH, February 7, 1866, in *HI*, p. 197.
100 "ideas of a person's . . . perceive him": William G. Thalmann, *The Odyssey: An Epic of Return. Twayne's Masterwork Studies*, No. 100 (New York: Twayne Publishers, 1992), p. 39.
100 "To see memory . . . thought with others": Bruce, "The Riddle of Death," in *The Lincoln Enigma*, p. 141.
100 "thou midway world . . . and paradise": AL to Andrew Johnston, April 18, 1846, in *CW*, I, p. 378.
100 critical to "avoid being *idle*": AL to Joshua F. Speed, February 13, 1842, in ibid., p. 269.
100 *"business and conversation* . . . bitterness of death": AL to Joshua F. Speed, [January 3?, 1842], in ibid., p. 265.
100 he delivered an eloquent address . . . "than a gallon of gall": AL, "Temperance Address. An Address, Delivered before the Springfield Washington Temperance Society," February 22, 1842, in ibid., p. 273.
100 "An outstanding . . . future growth": George E. Vaillant, *Adaptation to Life* (Boston: Little, Brown, 1977), p. 27.
101 "quite clear of the hypo . . . in the fall": AL to Joshua F. Speed, February 3, 1842, in *CW*, I, p. 268.
101 "much alone of late . . . *countenances* me": MTL to Mercy Ann Levering, June 1841, in Turner and Turner, *Mary Todd Lincoln*, pp. 25, 27.
101 mutual friends conspired: Baker, *Mary Todd Lincoln*, p. 93.
101 "worse sort . . . can realize": AL to Joshua F. Speed, February 25, 1842, in *CW*, I, p. 280. For correspondence between Lincoln and Speed discussing Speed's doubts during courtship of Fanny Henning, see AL to Speed, [January 3?], February 3, and February 13, 1842, in ibid., pp. 265–70.
101 "sailed through clear": AL to Joshua F. Speed, July 4, 1842, in ibid., p. 289.
101 " 'Are you now' . . . impatient to know": AL to Joshua F. Speed, October 5, 1842, in ibid., p. 303.
101 and was, in fact, very happy: AL to Joshua F. Speed, March 27, 1842, in ibid., p. 282.
101 description of the wedding: Baker, *Mary Todd Lincoln*, pp. 97–98; Helm, *The True Story of Mary*, pp. 93–95.
101 "Nothing new here . . . of profound wonder": AL to Samuel D. Marshall, November 11, 1842, in *CW*, I, p. 305.
102 "Full many a flower": Thomas Gray, "Elegy Written in a Country Churchyard," in *The Norton Anthology of Poetry*, 3rd edn., ed. Alexander W. Allison, et al. (New York: W. W. Norton, 1983), pp. 249–50.
102 "His melancholy . . . as he walked": Herndon, "Analysis of the Character," *ALQ* (1941), p. 359.
102 "No element . . . profound melancholy": Whitney, *Life on the Circuit with Lincoln*, p. 146.
102 "This melancholy . . . with his brains": Henry C. Whitney to WHH, June 23, 1887, in *HI*, p. 616.
103 "his face was . . . ever looked upon": Joseph Wilson Fifer, quoted in Rufus Rockwell Wilson, *Intimate Memories of Lincoln* (Elmira, N.Y.: Primavera Press, 1945), p. 155.
103 "slightly wrinkled . . . the wrinkles there": William Calkins, "The First of the Lincoln and Douglas Debates," quoted in ibid., pp. 169–70.
103 melancholy does not have: See Jerome Kagan, *Galen's Prophecy: Temperament in Human Nature*, with the collaboration of Nancy Snidman, Doreen Arcus, and J. Steven Reznick (New York: Basic Books, 1994), pp. 7–8.
103 "a tendency to . . . not a fault": AL to Mary Speed, September 27, 1841, in *CW*, I, p. 261.
103 "Melancholy . . . a sense of humor": Thomas Pynchon, introduction to *The Teachings of Don B.: Satires, Parodies, Fables, Illustrated Stories, and Plays of Donald Barthelme*, ed. Kim Herzinger (New York: Turtle Bay Books, Random House, 1992), p. xviii.

103 "When he first came . . . boiled over": James H. Matheny interview, November 1866, in *HI*, p. 432.
103 "he emerged . . . he lived, again": Whitney, *Life on the Circuit with Lincoln*, p. 147.
103 "necessary to his . . . relaxation in anecdotes": Joshua F. Speed to WHH, December 6, 1866, in *HI*, p. 499.
103 He laughed, he explained: Whitney, *Life on the Circuit with Lincoln*, p. 148.
103 "joyous, universal evergreen of life": AL, quoted in Nicolay, *Personal Traits of Abraham Lincoln*, p. 16.
103 "to whistle off sadness": David Davis interview, September 20, 1866, in *HI*, pp. 348, 350.
103 "Humor, like hope . . . to be borne": George E. Vaillant, *The Wisdom of the Ego*, p. 73.
103 "Humor can be marvelously . . . corrosive": Unnamed source, quoted in ibid., p. 73.
103 to rescue a pig . . . "his own mind": AL, quoted in Nicolay, *Personal Traits of Abraham Lincoln*, p. 81.
104 tortured turtles . . . "it was wrong": Nathaniel Grigsby interview, September 12, 1865, in *HI*, p. 112.
104 He refused to hunt animals: Miller, *Lincoln's Virtues*, pp. 26–27.
104 "the never-absent idea": AL to Joshua F. Speed, March 27, 1842, in *CW*, I, p. 282.
104 "By the imagination . . . what he feels": Adam Smith, *The Theory of Moral Sentiments* (London: A. Millar, 1759; facsimile, New York: Garland Publishing, 1971), pp. 2–3.
104 "With his wealth . . . that way themselves": Nicolay, *Personal Traits of Abraham Lincoln*, pp. 213, 77, 78.
104 "marriage was tumultuous . . . was harder for Mary: *With Malice Toward None*, pp. 69–70; Strozier, *Lincoln's Quest for Union*, p. 119; Baker, *Mary Todd Lincoln*, pp. 105–10.
105 Lincoln helped with the marketing and the dishes: Burlingame, *The Inner World of Abraham Lincoln*, p. 279.
105 Julia Bates's early marriage: Darby, "Mrs. Julia Bates" in Bates, *Bates, et al., of Virginia and Missouri*, n.p.; EB to Frederick Bates, June 15 and July 19, 1818, quoted in ibid.
105 Frances Seward spared household chores: Seward, *An Autobiography*, pp. 62, 382, 466; Patricia C. Johnson, " 'I Could Not be Well or Happy at Home . . . When Called to the Councils of My Country': Politics and the Seward Family," *University of Rochester Library Bulletin* 31 [hereafter *URLB*] (Autumn 1978), pp. 42, 47, 49.
105 Lincolns detached from respective families: Baker, *Mary Todd Lincoln*, pp. 105–07, 111–12.
105 When Lincoln was away: Ibid., pp. 108–09.
105 Frances's family surrounded her: Johnson, "I Could Not be Well or Happy at Home," *URLB*, p. 42.
106 Julia Bates's family in St. Louis: Bates, *Bates, et al., of Virginia and Missouri*, n.p.
106 "the kindest . . . was necessary": MTL interview, September 1866, in *HI*, p. 357.
106 a gentle and indulgent father: Herndon and Weik, *Herndon's Life of Lincoln*, p. 344. See also " 'Unrestrained by Parental Tyranny': Lincoln and His Sons," chapter 3 in Burlingame, *The Inner World of Abraham Lincoln*, pp. 57–72.
106 "litterally ran over . . . their importunities": Joseph Gillespie to WHH, January 31, 1866, in *HI*, p. 181.
106 "It is my pleasure . . . child to its parent": AL, quoted in MTL interview, September 1866, in ibid., p. 357.
106 "Now if you should . . . he is mistaken": AL to Richard S. Thomas, February 14, 1843, in *CW*, I, p. 307.
106 "That 'union is strength' . . . 'cannot stand' ": "Campaign Circular from Whig Committee," March 4, 1843, in ibid., p. 315.
107 "We had a meeting . . . own dear 'gal' ": AL to Joshua F. Speed, March 24, 1843, in ibid., p. 319.
107 his defeat in Sangamon . . . "family distinction": AL to Martin S. Morris, March 26, 1843, in ibid., p. 320.
107 in Pekin . . . idea of rotating terms: AL, "Resolution Adopted at Whig Convention at Pekin, Illinois," May 1, 1843, in ibid., p. 322.
107 Lincoln left nothing to chance: Thomas, *Abraham Lincoln*, p. 105.
107 He asked friends to share . . . every precinct: Beveridge, *Abraham Lincoln, 1809–1858*, Vol. II, pp. 74–75.
107 "a quiet trip . . . vigilance": AL to Benjamin F. James, January 14, 1846, in *CW*, I, p. 354.
107 "That Hardin is talented . . . 'is fair play' ": AL to Robert Boal, January 7, 1846, in ibid., p. 353.
108 "not . . . all other grounds": AL to John J. Hardin, February 7, 1846, in ibid., p. 364.
108 "I am not a politician . . . their ends": SPC to Charles D. Cleveland, August 29, 1840, reel 5, Chase Papers.
108 James G. Birney: See Betty Fladeland, *James Gillespie Birney: Slaveholder to Abolitionist* (Ithaca, N.Y.: Cornell University Press, 1955), esp. pp. 129–36.
108 a group of white community leaders: Niven, *Salmon P. Chase*, p. 47.
108 On a hot summer night . . . continued to publish: Fladeland, *James Gillespie Birney*, pp. 136–37; Blue, *Salmon P. Chase*, p. 29.
108 the mob returned . . . tarred and feathered: Fladeland, *James Gillespie Birney*, pp. 140–41.
108 he raced to the hotel . . . "at any time": SPC, quoted in Niven, *Salmon P. Chase*, p. 48.
109 "His voice and commanding . . . right time": Ibid.
109 "No man . . . courage and resolution": Hart, *Salmon P. Chase*, p. 435.
109 "By dedicating himself . . . in its pursuit": Maizlish, "Salmon P. Chase," *JER* (1998), p. 62.
109 background of the *Matilda* case: Niven, *Salmon P. Chase*, pp. 50–51; Hart, *Salmon P. Chase*, pp. 73–74; Schuckers, *The Life and Public Services of Salmon Portland Chase*, pp. 41–44.
110 "Every settler . . . interdicts slavery": SPC, *Speech of Salmon P. Chase in the Case of the Colored Woman, Matilda: Who was Brought Before the Court of Common Pleas of Hamilton County, Ohio, by Writ of Habeas Corpus, March 11, 1837* (Cincinnati: Pugh & Dodd, 1837), pp. 29, 30, 8.
110 they were printed in pamphlet form: SPC, *Speech of Salmon P. Chase in the Case of the Colored Woman, Matilda*.
110 Chase versus the Garrisonians: Hart, *Salmon P. Chase*, pp. 50, 55–56, 65.
110 "a covenant with . . . agreement with hell": Quoted in James Brewer Stewart, *William Lloyd Garrison and the Challenge of Emancipation*. American Biographical History Series (Arlington Heights, Ill.: Harlan Davidson, 1992), p. 164.
110 Chase decided, to try for public office . . . city establishments: Niven, *Salmon P. Chase*, pp. 57–59.
111 the "*vital* question of slavery": SPC to Charles D. Cleveland, August 29, 1840, reel 5, Chase Papers.
111 Chase and the Liberty Party: Niven, *Salmon P. Chase*, pp. 67–70; Eric Foner, *Free Soil, Free Labor, Free Men:*

The Ideology of the Republican Party before the Civil War (New York: Oxford University Press, 1970), pp. 78–81. See also "Liberty Party," in *The Reader's Companion to American History*, ed. Foner and Garraty, p. 657.

111 "to interfere . . . where it exists": "Proceedings and Resolutions of the Ohio Liberty Convention," *Philanthropist*, December 29, 1841, quoted in Niven, *Salmon P. Chase*, p. 68.

111 "without constitutional warrant": SPC to Gerrit Smith, May 14, 1842, reel 5, Chase Papers.

111 "has seen so little . . . the very first": SPC to Joshua R. Giddings, January 21, 1842, reel 5, Chase Papers.

111 "there can be only . . . criminal than unwise": WHS to SPC, August 4, 1845, reel 6, Chase Papers.

112 *"educated in the Whig school"* . . . defining characteristics: SPC to Lyman Hall, August 6, 1849, quoted in Warden, *Private Life and Public Services*, p. 331.

112 decision to leave . . . for Seward: Gienapp, *The Origins of the Republican Party*, p. 7.

112 "one idea" . . . than with the Whigs: Niven, *Salmon P. Chase*, pp. 62 (quote), 67, 88, 90–91.

112 Chase shifted his positions: Hendrick, *Lincoln's War Cabinet*, p. 40.

112 Cincinnati was a natural destination: de Tocqueville, *Democracy in America*, p. 345.

112 "Attorney General for the Negro": Donnal V. Smith, "Salmon P. Chase and the Election of 1860," *OAHQ* 39 (July 1930), p. 515.

112 represented John Van Zandt: See Hart, *Salmon P. Chase*, pp. 75–78; Schuckers, *The Life and Public Services of Salmon Portland Chase*, pp. 53–66; Niven, *Salmon P. Chase*, pp. 76–83.

112 "Moved by sympathy . . . very willingly": SPC to Trowbridge, March 18, 1864, reel 32, Chase Papers.

113 "Under the constitution . . . which made him a slave": SPC, *Reclamation of Fugitives from Service: An Argument for the Defendant, Submitted to the Supreme Court of the United States, at the December Term, 1846, in the Case of Wharton Jones vs. John Vanzandt* (Cincinnati: R. P. Donogh & Co., 1847), pp. 82–84.

113 "a creature of state law": Chase, *Reclamation of Fugitives from Service*, p. 81.

113 "There goes . . . himself to-day": Unnamed judge in Van Zandt trial quoted in *Life and Letters of Harriet Beecher Stowe*, ed. Annie Fields (Boston: Houghton Mifflin, 1897; Detroit: Gale Research Co., 1970), p. 145.

113 Chase enlisted Seward's help as co-counsel: WHS, *In the Supreme Court of the United States: John Van Zandt, ad sectum Wharton Jones: Argument for the Defendant* (Albany, N.Y.: Weed & Parsons, 1847); Seward, *Seward at Washington . . . 1846–1861*, pp. 39–40; Niven, *Salmon P. Chase*, p. 83.

113 "poor old Van Zandt . . . be a gainer": SPC to CS, April 24, 1847, reel 6, Chase Papers (quote); SPC to Trowbridge, March 18, 1864, reel 32, Chase Papers.

113 argument reprinted in pamphlet form: See SPC, *Reclamation of Fugitives from Service*.

113 "the question . . . a *political* movement": CS to SPC, March 12, 1847, reel 6, Chase Papers.

114 Adams and Hale: Charles Francis Adams to SPC, March 4, 1847, reel 6, Chase Papers; SPC to John P. Hale, May 12, 1847, reel 6, Chase Papers.

114 "chaste and beautiful . . . own fame": WHS to SPC, February 18, 1847, reel 6, Chase Papers.

114 "one of the gratifications . . . greatest too": SPC to Lewis Tappan, March 18, 1847, reel 6, Chase Papers.

114 In gratitude . . . sterling silver pitcher: For a description of the event, see *The Address and Reply on the Presentation of a Testimonial to S. P. Chase, by the Colored People of Cincinnati* (Cincinnati, Ohio: Henry W. Derby & Co., 1845); Niven, *Salmon P. Chase*, pp. 85–86.

114 "whenever the friendless . . . unto me!": "Mr. Gordon's Address," in *The Address and Reply on the Presentation of a Testimonial to S. P. Chase*, pp. 12–13, 18.

114 Chase's reply: "Reply of Mr. Chase," in ibid., pp. 19–35.

115 did not make friends easily: Niven, *Salmon P. Chase*, p. 130.

115 "little of human nature": Lloyd, "Home-Life of Salmon Portland Chase," *Atlantic Monthly*, p. 534.

115 "profoundly versed . . . of men": Whitelaw Reid, *Ohio in the War*, paraphrased in Warden, *Private Life and Public Services*, p. 244.

115 Edwin M. Stanton: Frank Abial Flower, *Edwin McMasters Stanton: The Autocrat of Rebellion, Emancipation, and Reconstruction* (Akron, Ohio: Saalfield Publishing Co., 1905), p. 24; Belden and Belden, *So Fell the Angels*, p. 77; Henry Wilson, "Jeremiah S. Black and Edwin M. Stanton," *Atlantic Monthly* 26 (October 1870), pp. 469–70.

115 "when he was a boy . . . to slavery": William Thaw, quoted in Flower, *Edwin McMasters Stanton*, p. 25.

115 death had pursued Stanton: Pamphila Stanton Wolcott, "Edwin M. Stanton: A Biographical Sketch," Ohio Historical Society, Columbus, Ohio; EMS, "Mary Lamson, Wife of Edwin M. Stanton, and their infant daughter Lucy," Edwin M. Stanton Manuscript, Mss. 1648, Louisiana and Lower Mississippi Valley Collections, Louisiana State University Libraries, Baton Rouge, La.

116 "Since our pleasant . . . face to face": EMS to SPC, November 30, 1846, reel 6, Chase Papers.

116 "Taxation . . . sincere love for you": EMS to SPC, August 1846, reel 6, Chase Papers.

116 Stanton felt free . . . "careless of the future": EMS to SPC, November 30, 1846, reel 6, Chase Papers.

116 "Many weeks . . . post office each day": EMS to SPC, January 5, 1847, reel 6, Chase Papers.

116 "Rejoicing, as I do . . . upon your mercy": EMS to SPC, March 11, 1847, reel 6, Chase Papers.

117 "filled my heart . . . bid you farewell": EMS to SPC, December 2, 1847, reel 6, Chase Papers.

117 "How much I regret . . . not have left home": SPC to EMS, January 9, 1848, reel 1, Papers of Edwin M. Stanton, Manuscript Division, Library of Congress [hereafter Stanton Papers, DLC].

117 "The practice of law . . . of the camp": EMS to SPC, May 27, 1849, reel 7, Chase Papers.

117 "While public honors . . . inestimable value": EMS to SPC, May 27, 1849, reel 7, Chase Papers.

117 "well aware . . . among men": EMS to SPC, June 28, 1850, reel 8, Chase Papers.

CHAPTER 4: "PLUNDER & CONQUEST"

Page

119 Washington was a city in progress: Beveridge, *Abraham Lincoln, 1809–1858*, Vol. II, pp. 101–03.

119 "a full view . . . and Virginia": William Q. Force, "Picture of Washington and its Vicinity for 1850," Washington, D.C., p. 49.

119 "stood pig-styes . . . over the fields": Samuel C. Busey, M.D., *Personal Reminiscences and Recollections of Forty-Six Years' Membership in the Medical Society of the District of Columbia, and Residence in this City, with Biographical Sketches of Many of the Deceased Members* (Washington, D.C.: [Philadelphia: Dornan, Printer], 1895), pp. 64–65.

119 population of Washington: Beveridge, *Abraham Lincoln, 1809–1858*, Vol. II, p. 102.

119 Webster . . . would outlive the age: "12 October 1861, Saturday," in John Hay, *Inside Lincoln's White House: The Complete Civil War Diary of John Hay*, ed. Michael Burlingame and John R. Turner Ettlinger (Carbondale and Edwardsville: Southern Illinois University Press, 1997), p. 26.

119 Jefferson Davis . . . Rhett, agitator of rebellion: Robert C. Byrd, *The Senate, 1789–1989*, Vol. I: *Addresses on the History of the United States Senate*, Bicentennial Edition, ed. Mary Sharon Hall (Washington, D.C.: Government Printing Office, 1988), p. 182.

120 "he would lay down . . . merriment": Busey, *Personal Reminiscences*, pp. 25, 27.

120 Mary in Washington: Randall, *Mary Lincoln*, pp. 107–08; Baker, *Mary Todd Lincoln*, pp. 136–40.

120 background of the Mexican War: Robert W. Johannsen, "Mexican War," in *The Reader's Companion to American History*, ed. Foner and Garraty, pp. 722–24; McPherson, *Battle Cry of Freedom*, pp. 47, 49–50.

120 "a romantic . . . exotic land": Johannsen, "Mexican War," in *The Reader's Companion to American History*, ed. Foner and Garraty, p. 723.

121 John Hardin, was . . . "God-speeds of men": Beveridge, *Abraham Lincoln, 1809–1858*, Vol. II, pp. 79–80.

121 "It is a fact . . . growing crops": AL to John M. Peck, May 21, 1848, in *CW*, I, p. 473.

121 combat ended, peace treaty: Johannsen, "Mexican War," in *The Reader's Companion to American History*, ed. Foner and Garraty, p. 723.

121 "not let the whigs be *silent*": AL to Usher F. Linder, March 22, 1848, in *CW*, I, p. 457.

121 "the original justice . . . of the President": AL, "Speech in United States House of Representatives: The War with Mexico," January 12, 1848, in ibid., p. 432.

121 "As you are . . . before long": AL to WHH, December 13, 1847, in ibid., p. 420.

121 "whether the particular . . . hostile array": AL, " 'Spot' Resolutions in the United States House of Representatives," December 22, 1847, in ibid., p. 421.

121 "spotty Lincoln": Beveridge, *Abraham Lincoln, 1809–1858*, Vol. II, p. 135.

121 "unnecessarily . . . be at ease": AL, "Speech in United States House of Representatives: The War with Mexico," January 12, 1848, in *CW*, I, pp. 432, 433, 439–41.

122 "treasonable assault" . . . only a single term: *Illinois State Register*, March 10, 1848, quoted in Beveridge, *Abraham Lincoln, 1809–1858*, Vol. II, p. 135.

122 to "allow the President . . . deems it necessary": AL to WHH, February 15, 1848, in *CW*, I, p. 451.

122 "I saw that Lincoln . . . and again": WHH to JWW, February 11, 1887, reel 10, Herndon-Weik Collection, DLC.

122 only to infuriate the Democrats . . . fainthearted Whigs: Donald, *Lincoln*, pp. 124–25.

122 "no . . . pestilence and famine": AL, quoting Justin Butterfield in entry for August 13, 1863, in Hay, *Inside Lincoln's White House*, p. 73.

122 "Our population . . . shores of the Pacific": WHS, 1846, quoted in Seward, *An Autobiography*, p. 791.

123 "not expect . . . national adversaries": WHS to unknown recipient, May 28, 1846, in ibid., p. 809.

123 "would not have engaged in": SPC to Gerrit Smith, September 1, 1846, reel 6, Chase Papers.

123 "gross . . . plunder & conquest": Bates diary, March 13, 1848.

123 ashamed of his Whig . . . "Presidential election": Bates diary, March 14, 1848.

123 a war of conquest . . . to catch votes": *Delaware State Journal*, June 13, 1848, quoted as "Speech at Wilmington, Delaware, June 10, 1848," in *CW*, I, p. 476.

123 David Wilmot . . . Senate: "Wilmot Proviso," in *The Reader's Companion to American History*, ed. Foner and Garraty, p. 1155; David M. Potter, *The Impending Crisis, 1848–1861*, completed and ed. Don E. Fehrenbacher. New American Nation Series (New York: Harper & Row, 1976), pp. 21–23 (quote p. 21).

123 Lincoln positioned himself . . . "exist in the old": AL to Williamson Durley, October 3, 1845, in *CW*, I, p. 348.

124 Bates considered the problem . . . pull the country apart: Cain, *Lincoln's Attorney General*, pp. 59–60, 66.

124 John Calhoun led the . . . American territory: John C. Calhoun, February 19, 1847, *Congressional Globe*, 29th Cong., 2nd sess., pp. 453–55 (quote p. 455).

124 "The madmen of the North . . . glorious Union": *Richmond [Va.] Enquirer*, February 18, 1847.

124 "When you were . . . marry again": AL to MTL, April 16, 1848, in *CW*, I, pp. 465–66.

124 "My dear Husband . . . love to all": MTL to AL, May 1848, in Turner and Turner, *Mary Todd Lincoln*, pp. 36–38.

125 "The leading matter . . . till I see you": AL to MTL, June 12, 1848, in *CW*, I, p. 477.

125 "I am in favor . . . elect any other whig": AL to Thomas S. Flournoy, February 17, 1848, in ibid., p. 452.

125 "on the blind side . . . hanged themselves": AL to WHH, June 12, 1848, in ibid., p. 477.

125 "very willingly . . . Universal Freedom": WHS to SPC, June 12, 1848, reel 6, Chase Papers.

125 a "doughface": Anonymous, *A Bake-Pan for Dough-Faces* (Burlington, Vt.: Chauncey Goodrich, 1854), p. 1; Byrd, *The Senate, 1789–1989*, Vol. I, pp. 206–07.

126 the Free Soil Convention in Buffalo, 1848: See Foner, *Free Soil. Free Labor, Free Men*, p. 125; Blue, *Salmon P. Chase*, pp. 61–66.
126 asking if his name . . . vice presidency: Bates diary, August 5, 1848.
126 remained a slaveowner: Entry for Edward Bates, Dardenne, St. Charles County, Missouri, Sixth Census of the United States, 1840 (National Archives Microfilm Publication M704, reel 230), RG 29, DNA. According to Bates's entry in the 1840s federal census, there were nine slaves in the Bates household. By 1860, the servants and farmhands employed by Bates seem to have been exclusively Irish. Entry for Edward Bates, Carondelet, St. Louis Township, St. Louis County, Missouri, Eighth Census of the United States, 1860 (National Archives Microfilm Publication M653, reel 656), RG 29, DNA.
126 his belief in the inferiority of the black race: Hendrick, *Lincoln's War Cabinet*, p. 46.
126 one of his female slaves escaped . . . "plagued with them": Bates diary, April 15, 1848.
126 Bates declined . . . "geographical party": Bates diary, August 5, 1848.
126 "Free Soil, Free Speech": SPC to Thomas Bolton, December 1, 1848, reel 7, Chase Papers.
126 to "prohibit slavery extension": Smith, *The Liberty and Free Soil Parties in the Old Northwest*, p. 140.
126 Arriving uninvited . . . without a speaker: Beveridge, *Abraham Lincoln, 1809–1858*, Vol. II, pp. 171–72.
127 "an intellectual face . . . from that State": Boston *Daily Advertiser*, September 14, 1848, reprinted as "Speech at Worcester, Massachusetts," September 12, 1848, in *CW*, II, pp. 1–2, 5.
127 Whig rally at the Tremont Temple; Seward and Lincoln meet: James Schouler, "Abraham Lincoln at Tremont Temple in 1848," *Massachusetts Historical Society Proceedings, October, 1908–June, 1909* XLII (1909), pp. 70–83.
127 "had probably . . . Governor Seward's": AL, quoted in Seward, *Seward at Washington . . . 1846–1861*, p. 80.
127 "the time will come . . . institution of slavery": WHS, "Whig Mass Meeting, Boston, October 15, 1848," *Works of William H. Seward*, Vol. III, pp. 289, 288.
127 "a most forcible . . . applause": *Boston Courier*, September 23, 1848.
127 "rambling, story-telling . . . boldness of utterance": F. B. Carpenter, "A Day with Governor Seward at Auburn," July 1870, reel 196, Seward Papers.
127 "a thoughtful air": Seward, *Seward at Washington . . . 1846–1861*, p. 80.
127 "I reckon . . . have been doing": AL, quoted in ibid., p. 80.
127 voted for the Wilmot Proviso . . . single speech on the issue: Thomas, *Abraham Lincoln*, pp. 126–27.
128 "I went with . . . State in the Union": Edward L. Pierce to JWW, February 12, 1890, in *HI*, p. 697.
128 "a superb dinner . . . arranged at table": Governor Henry J. Gardner statement, [February–May 1890], enclosure in Edward L. Pierce to WHH, May 27, 1890, in *HI*, p. 699.
128 election results, 1848: Congressional Quarterly, *Presidential Elections Since 1789* (Washington, D.C.: Congressional Quarterly, 1991), p. 106.
128 who, four years later . . . only four states: Allan Nevins, *Ordeal of the Union*. Vol. II: *A House Dividing, 1852–1857* (New York and London: Charles Scribner's Sons, 1947), p. 36.
128 he drafted a proposal: AL, "Remarks and Resolution Introduced in United States House of Representatives Concerning Abolition of Slavery in the District of Columbia," January 10, 1849, in *CW*, II, pp. 20–22 (quote p. 21).
128 "that slave hound from Illinois": Wendell Phillips, quoted in Beveridge, *Abraham Lincoln, 1809–1858*, Vol. II, p. 185.
128 once the proposal was distributed . . . never introduced his bill: Donald, *Lincoln*, pp. 136–37.
129 "Finding that I was . . . at that time": AL, quoted in James Q. Howard, Biographical Notes, May 1860, Lincoln Papers.
129 campaigned vigorously . . . Commissioner of the Land Office: Thomas, *Abraham Lincoln*, p. 129. See also Lincoln's correspondence from May to July 1849 in *CW*, II, pp. 51–55, 57–58.
129 "If I have one vice . . . tempted me": AL, quoted in Egbert L. Viele, "A Trip with Lincoln, Chase, and Stanton," *Scribners Monthly* 16 (October 1878), p. 818.
129 applied to patent . . . "buoyant chambers": AL, "Application for Patent on an Improved Method of Lifting Vessels over Shoals," March 10, 1849, in *CW*, II, p. 32.
129 "added practically . . . his reputation": John G. Nicolay, *A Short Life of Abraham Lincoln. Condensed from Nicolay & Hay's Abraham Lincoln: A History* (New York: Century Co., 1902), p. 77.
129 Caleb Smith of Indiana: John P. Usher, *President Lincoln's Cabinet, with a Foreword and a Sketch of the Life of the Author by Nelson H. Loomis* (Omaha, Nebr.: n.p., 1925); Louis J. Bailey, "Caleb Blood Smith," *Indiana Magazine of History* 29 (September 1933), pp. 213–39; *Indianapolis Daily Journal*, January 9, 1864.
129 "handsome, trimly-built man": C. P. Ferguson, quoted in Bailey, "Caleb Blood Smith," *Indiana Magazine of History* (1933), p. 237.
129 "smooth oval face": John Coburn, quoted in ibid., p. 236.
129 "feel the blood . . . up your spine": Usher, *President Lincoln's Cabinet*, p. 17.
129 Smith a more compelling public speaker: Macartney, *Lincoln and His Cabinet*, p. 49; Bailey, "Caleb Blood Smith," *Indiana Magazine of History* (1933), pp. 237–39.
129 Joshua Giddings: James Brewer Stewart, *Joshua R. Giddings and the Tactics of Radical Politics* (Cleveland: Case Western Reserve University Press, 1970); George W. Julian, *The Life of Joshua R. Giddings* (Chicago: A. C. McClurg & Co., 1892).
130 "He had lived . . . with their lot": Julian, *The Life of Joshua R. Giddings*, p. 21.
130 "would walk clear to Illinois": Elihu B. Wasburne to AL, December 26, 1854, Lincoln Papers.
130 "a little slim . . . full of tears yet": AL to WHH, February 2, 1848, in *CW*, I, p. 448.
130 "Mr. Lincoln was careful . . . roar of laughter": Alexander Stephens recollection, in Osborn H. Oldroyd, comp., *The Lincoln Memorial: Album-Immortelles* (New York: G. W. Carleton & Co., 1882), p. 241.

130 "was losing interest in politics": AL, "Autobiography Written for Jesse W. Fell," December 20, 1859, in *CW*, III, p. 512.

131 "the one *great* question of the day": AL, "Eulogy on Zachary Taylor," July 25, 1850, in *CW*, II, p. 89.

131 with "greater earnestness": AL, "Scripps autobiography," in *CW*, IV, p. 67.

131 deaths of Mary's father, grandmother, and Eddie: Randall, *Mary Lincoln*, pp. 139–41; Baker, *Mary Todd Lincoln*, pp. 125–28; Donald, *Lincoln*, p. 153.

131 That destiny had branded her: Baker, *Mary Todd Lincoln*, p. 128.

131 Mary's inconsolable weeping: Ibid., p. 126.

131 "Eat, Mary . . . for we must live": AL, quoted in Randall, *Mary Lincoln*, p. 141.

131 found some solace . . . rented a family pew: Ibid., pp. 143–44.

131 Eddie's death left an indelible scar: See Baker, *Mary Todd Lincoln*, pp. 125–29.

131 "hysterical outbursts": Burlingame, *The Inner World of Abraham Lincoln*, p. 296.

131 chased him through the yard: Stephen Whitehurst interview, 1885–1889, in *HI*, p. 722; WHH to JWW, January 23, 1886, reel 9, Herndon-Weik Collection, DLC.

132 drove him from the house: Mrs. Hillary Gobin to Alfred J. Beveridge, May 17, 1923, container 288, Papers of Alfred J. Beveridge, Manuscript Division, Library of Congress [hereafter Beveridge Papers, DLC].

132 smashed his head with a chunk of wood: Margaret Ryan interview, October 27, 1886, in *HI*, p. 597; WHH to JWW, January 23, 1886, reel 9, Herndon-Weik Collection, DLC.

132 "a protective deafness": J. P. McEvoy, quoted in Randall, *Mary Lincoln*, p. 121.

132 quietly leave the room . . . for a walk: James Gourley interview, 1865–1866, in *HI*, p. 453.

132 If the discord continued . . . storm had ceased: Thomas, *Abraham Lincoln*, p. 91.

132 "a woman of more angelic . . . people outside": Milton Hay interview, c. 1883–1888, in *HI*, p. 729.

132 "rendering [himself] worthy": AL, "Communication to the People of Sangamo County," March 9, 1832, in *CW*, I, p. 8.

132 Weed's campaign for Senate seat for Seward: Van Deusen, *William Henry Seward*, pp. 110–11; Van Deusen, *Thurlow Weed*, pp. 165–66.

133 "There are two . . . and odious": WHS, "The Election of 1848, Cleveland, Ohio, October 26, 1848," *Works of William H. Seward*, Vol. III, pp. 291–302.

133 "of making voters . . . to intermarry": AL's speech, "Fourth Debate with Stephen A. Douglas at Charleston, Illinois," September 18, 1858, in *CW*, III, p. 145.

133 radicalism of the Western Reserve: Smith, *The Liberty and Free Soil Parties in the Old Northwest*, pp. 13–14, 31–32, 128.

133 the *Cleveland Plain Dealer* charged: *Cleveland Plain Dealer*, October 27, 1848.

133 " 'Can nothing' . . . can and must do it": WHS, "The Election of 1848," *Works of William H. Seward*, Vol. III, p. 301.

134 "a political crime . . . political evil": TW, quoted in Van Deusen, *Thurlow Weed*, p. 90.

134 "this question of slavery . . . partisan conflicts": TW, *Albany Evening Journal*, 1836, in Seward, *An Autobiography*, p. 319.

134 his provocative language: WHS to TW, March 31, 1850, Weed Papers; Holman Hamilton, *Zachary Taylor: Soldier in the White House*, Vol. II (New York: Bobbs-Merrill, 1951), pp. 321–22.

134 not fully "ripened": WHS to unknown recipient, May 28, 1846, in Seward, *An Autobiography*, p. 809.

134 "wanted to level society up, not down": Van Deusen, *Thurlow Weed*, p. 166.

134 "Probably no man . . . warmly appreciated": *NYTrib*, quoted in Van Deusen, *William Henry Seward*, p. 113.

134 a Southern senator . . . "a shudder": Seward, *Seward at Washington . . . 1846–1861*, p. 119.

134 "If we ever find . . . your odious neck": "Georgia Savannah" to WHS, January 22, 1850, in ibid., p. 130.

134 balance of power in the Ohio legislature: [Albert G. Riddle], "The Election of Salmon P. Chase to the Senate, February 22, 1849," *The Republic* 4 (March 1875), p. 180; Schuckers, *The Life and Public Services of Salmon Portland Chase*, p. 91.

135 Dr. Norton Townshend and John F. Morse: See Niven, *Salmon P. Chase*, p. 118; Schuckers, *The Life and Public Services of Salmon Portland Chase*, pp. 91–92.

135 drafted a deal . . . extensive patronage: SPC to Sarah Bella D. L. Chase, December 20, 1848, reel 7, Chase Papers; Hart, *Salmon P. Chase*, pp. 104–09, 112.

135 Chase journeyed to Columbus . . . money to more than one paper: Niven, *Salmon P. Chase*, pp. 117–19, 121.

135 "After the Senatorial Election . . . rely on me": SPC to Edward S. Hamlin, January 17, 1849 (erroneously dated 1848), reel 7, Chase Papers.

135 advanced money to . . . "mortgage to myself": SPC to Stanley Matthews (copybook version), February 26, 1849, reel 7, Chase Papers.

135 "It is really important . . . Morse especially": SPC to Edward S. Hamlin, January 17, 1849 (erroneously dated 1848), reel 7, Chase Papers.

135 "Every thing . . . of the Cause": SPC to John F. Morse, January 19, [1849], reel 7, Chase Papers. The recipient's name does not appear on the letter itself, but he has been identified as John F. Morse. See Vol. II of Niven, ed., the *Salmon P. Chase papers*, pp. 216–19.

136 "Every act . . . *meant* His Own": *Ohio State Journal*, quoted in Blue, *Salmon P. Chase*, p. 72.

136 voted to repeal the hated Black Laws: Noah Brooks, *Statesmen* (New York: Charles Scribner's Sons, 1904), p. 158.

136 "not see how . . . or profit by it": Horace Greeley to SPC, April 16, 1852, reel 9, Chase Papers.

136 "It lost to him . . . his political after life": Riddle, "The Election of Salmon P. Chase," *Republic* (1875), p. 183.

136 Certainly, his willingness to sever . . . custom of the times: Ibid., p. 183; Blue, *Salmon P. Chase*, p. 90; Niven, *Salmon P. Chase*, pp. 146–47.

136 "I can hardly . . . of our cause": CS to SPC, February 27, 1849, reel 7, Chase Papers.

136 "to be first wherever I may be": SPC to Charles D. Cleveland, February 8, 1830, reel 4, Chase Papers.

CHAPTER 5: THE TURBULENT FIFTIES

Page

140 population: "Area and Population of the United States: 1790–1970," series A 1–5, in U.S. Bureau of the Census, *Historical Statistics of the United States, Colonial Times to 1970*, Bicentennial Edition, Part 1 (Washington, D.C.: Government Printing Office, 1975), p. 8.

140 Nearly three fourths . . . participated: "Voter Participation in Presidential Elections, 1824–1928," available at infoplease website, www.infoplease.com/ipa/A0877659.html (accessed July 2005).

140 "were the daily fare . . . are undervalued": Charles Ingersoll, quoted in Appleby, *Inheriting the Revolution*, p. 102.

140 "Look into the morning . . . second breakfast": Ralph Waldo Emerson, "The Fugitive Slave Law," reprinted in *The Portable Emerson*, new ed., ed. Carl Bode, with Malcolm Cowley (New York: Penguin Books, 1981), p. 542.

141 "You meet . . . ale- and oyster-houses": Ludwig Gall, quoted in Appleby, *Inheriting the Revolution*, pp. 102–3.

141 "The nullifiers . . . Potomac river": Andrew Jackson, quoted in Marquis James, *Andrew Jackson: Portrait of a President* (New York: Grosset & Dunlap, 1937), p. 324.

141 three fifths of a person . . . lawful masters: U.S. Constitution, Section I, Article II, and Section IV, Article II.

141 "written in the bond . . . its obligations": John Quincy Adams, quoted in Potter, *The Impending Crisis, 1848–1861*, p. 47.

141 "If by your legislation . . . *for disunion*": Robert Toombs, debate in the House of Representatives, December 13, 1849, *Congressional Globe*, 31st Cong., 1st sess., p. 28.

141 Mississippi called for a convention: Potter, *The Impending Crisis, 1848–1861*, pp. 88, 94, 104.

141 "We read . . . nuptial couch, everywhere!": Thomas Hart Benton, May 31, 1848, *Appendix to the Congressional Globe*, 30th Cong., 1st sess., p. 686.

142 "We must concern . . . of life and death": John Randolph, quoted in Margaret L. Coit, *John C. Calhoun: American Portrait* (Atlanta, Ga.: Cherokee Publishing Co., 1990), p. 166.

142 "antagonistical elements": WHS, "The Election of 1848, Cleveland, Ohio, October 26, 1848," *Works of William H. Seward*, Vol. III, p. 295.

142 "It is a great mistake . . . except force": John C. Calhoun, "The Compromise," March 4, 1850, *Congressional Globe*, 31st Cong., 1st sess., p. 453.

143 All eyes turned to . . . Henry Clay: Robert V. Remini, *Henry Clay: Statesman for the Union* (New York and London: W. W. Norton & Co., 1991), pp. 730–38.

143 "regarded by all . . . man for a crisis": AL, "Eulogy on Henry Clay," July 6, 1852, in *CW*, II, p. 129.

143 "the spirit and the fire of youth": James S. Pike, "Mr. Clay's Speech," May 20, 1850, from the *NYTrib*, reprinted in James S. Pike, *First Blows of the Civil War: The Ten Years of Preliminary Conflict in the United States* (New York: American News Company, 1879), p. 72.

143 Henry Clay speech, resolutions: "Compromise Resolutions. Speech of Mr. Clay, of Kentucky, in the Senate of the United States, February 5 and 6, 1850," *Appendix to the Congressional Globe*, 31st Cong., 1st sess., pp. 115–27 (quotes pp. 115, 127).

143 denied a jury trial . . . hunt down escapees: Potter, *The Impending Crisis, 1848–1861*, pp. 130–31.

144 "if the direful . . . heart-rending spectacle": "Compromise Resolutions. Speech of Mr. Clay," *Appendix to the Congressional Globe*, p. 127.

144 Frances Seward in the gallery: FAS to LW, February 10, 1850, reel 119, Seward Papers.

144 F Street house in Washington: Van Deusen, *William Henry Seward*, p. 118; Seward, *Seward at Washington . . . 1846–1861*, p. 111. The house was located on the north side of F Street, NW, between Sixth and Seventh Streets.

144 "He *is* a charming . . . I supposed": FAS to LW, February 10, 1850, reel 119, Seward Papers.

144 John Calhoun in the Senate: Pike, "Speeches of Webster and Calhoun," from the *Portland Advertiser*, March 9, 1850, in Pike, *First Blows of the Civil War*, p. 15; Ben: Perley Poore, *Perley's Reminiscences of Sixty Years in the National Metropolis*, Vol. I (Philadelphia, 1886; New York: AMS Press, 1971), p. 365.

144 Calhoun's speech read by Mason: John C. Calhoun, "The Compromise," March 4, 1850, *Congressional Globe*, 31st Cong., 1st sess., pp. 451–55.

145 the "great triumvirate": Richard N. Current, "Webster, Daniel," in *The Reader's Companion to American History*, ed. Foner and Garraty, p. 1139.

145 "crammed" . . . previous occasion: *National Intelligencer*, Washington, D.C., March 8, 1850.

145 the rumor that Webster . . . was watching: FAS to LW, March 10, 1850, reel 119, Seward Papers.

145 "I wish to speak": "Compromise Resolutions. Speech of Mr. Webster, of Massachusetts, in the Senate, March 7, 1850," *Appendix to the Congressional Globe*, 31st Cong., 1st sess., pp. 269–76 (quote p. 269).

145 "Mr Webster has deliberately . . . years in doing": Journal BO, p. 217, in *The Journals and Miscellaneous Notebooks of Ralph Waldo Emerson*, Vol. XI: *1848–1851*, ed. A. W. Plumstead and William H. Gilman (Cambridge, Mass., and London: Belknap Press of Harvard University Press, 1975), pp. 347–48.

145 Frances Seward on Webster's speech: FAS to LW, March 10, 1850, reel 119, Seward Papers.

145 speech won nationwide approval from moderates: Robert V. Remini, *Daniel Webster: The Man and His Time* (New York and London: W. W. Norton & Co., 1997), pp. 674–75.
145 "How little they know . . . he thinks just": FAS to LW, March 10, 1850, reel 119, Seward Papers.
145 Antislavery advocates had no need: Hendrick, *Lincoln's War Cabinet*, p. 23.
145 He had talked at length . . . before Frances: FAS to WHS, July 8, 1850, reel 114, Seward Papers; Seward, *An Autobiography*, p. 703; Van Deusen, *Thurlow Weed*, p. 175.
145 description of Seward's speaking style: Van Deusen, *William Henry Seward*, p. 122; Bancroft, *The Life of William H. Seward*, Vol. I, pp. 190–91.
145 he quoted Machiavelli: Pike, "Governor Seward's Speech," March 12, 1850, from the *Boston Courier*, in Pike, *First Blows of the Civil War*, p. 18.
146 Webster was riveted . . . "sat still": Holman Hamilton, *Zachary Taylor: Soldier in the White House*, Vol. II (Indianapolis: Bobbs-Merrill, 1951; Norwalk, Conn.: Easton Press, 1989), p. 316.
146 content of Seward's speech: WHS, "California, Union, and Freedom. Speech of William H. Seward, of New York, in the Senate, March 11, 1850," *Appendix to the Congressional Globe*, 31st Cong., 1st sess., pp. 260–69 (quotes pp. 262, 263, and 265).
146 With this single speech: Van Deusen, *William Henry Seward*, p. 128.
146 Tens of thousands of copies: WHS to TW, March 22 and 31, 1850, in Seward, *Seward at Washington . . . 1846–1861*, p. 129.
146 "live longer . . . of the Session": *NYTrib*, March 19, 1850.
146 Chase prepares with Sumner: CS to SPC, February 19, March 22 and 23, 1850, reel 8, Chase Papers.
146 "I find no man . . . yourself": SPC to CS, September 15, 1849, reel 8, Chase Papers.
146 "a tower of strength": CS to SPC, February 7, 1849, reel 7, Chase Papers.
146 "confirm the irresolute . . . confound the trimmers": CS to SPC, February 7, 1849, reel 7, Chase Papers.
146 "I cannot disguise . . . throughout the country": CS to SPC, March 22, 1850, reel 8, Chase Papers.
147 Chase's speech: SPC, "Union and Freedom, Without Compromise. Speech of Mr. Chase, of Ohio, in the Senate, March 26–27, 1850," *Appendix to the Congressional Globe*, 31st Cong., 1st sess., pp. 468–80.
147 Chase's speaking style: Blue, *Salmon P. Chase*, p. 102; Warden, *Private Life and Public Services*, p. 340.
147 "infinitely below . . . who expected much": SPC to Sarah Bella Chase, March 27, 1850, reel 8, Chase Papers.
147 "You know . . . received not much": SPC to Stanley Matthews, May 6, 1850, reel 8, Chase Papers.
147 Benton-Foote argument: William Nisbet Chambers, *Old Bullion Benton, Senator from the New West: Thomas Hart Benton, 1782–1858* (Boston: Little, Brown, 1956), pp. 360–62; Henry S. Foote, *Casket of Reminiscences* (Washington, D.C.: Chronicle Publishing, 1874), pp. 338–39; March 26–27, April 2, and April 17, 1850, in *Congressional Globe*, 31st Cong., 1st sess., pp. 602–04, 609–10, 762–63.
147 "I disdain to carry . . . the assassin fire!": Thomas Hart Benton, quoted in *Congressional Globe*, 31st Cong., 1st sess., p. 762.
147 Sumner's praise . . . "Seward is with us": CS to SPC, April 10, 1850, reel 8, Chase Papers.
147 "You mistake . . . Anti Slavery opinions": SPC to CS, April 13, 1850, reel 8, Chase Papers.
147 "I have never been . . . a politician for me": SPC to CS, December 14, 1850, reel 9, Chase Papers.
148 relationship between Chase and Seward: WHS to SPC, October 2 and 22, 1843; August 4, 1845; reels 5, 6, Chase Papers.
148 "I made this resolution . . . me to keep it": Entry for April 29, 1831, *Chase Papers*, Vol. I, pp. 57–58.
148 reaction to Seward's "Higher Law" speech: Seward, *Seward at Washington . . . 1846–1861*, pp. 128, 130; FAS to LW, March 19 and March 21, 1850, reel 119, Seward Papers; Van Deusen, *William Henry Seward*, pp. 124–27.
148 "Senator Seward is against . . . the South": *NYH*, March 13, 1850.
148 Seward was initially untroubled: Seward, *Seward at Washington . . . 1846–1861*, pp. 120–21.
148 "spoken words . . . when I am dead": WHS to TW, March 31, 1850, in ibid., p. 129.
148 When she looked at him: FAS to LW, undated letter, in ibid., p. 120.
148 "Your speech . . . relieved my apprehensions": TW to WHS, March 14, 1850, reel 36, Seward Papers.
148 "despondency . . . shame": WHS to TW, March 31, 1850, Weed Papers.
148 death of Taylor, succession of Fillmore: Hamilton, *Zachary Taylor*, Vol. II (1951 ed.), pp. 388–94.
149 Under the skillful leadership . . . omnibus bill was broken up: Potter, *The Impending Crisis, 1848–1861*, pp. 109–12; Johannsen, *Stephen A. Douglas*, pp. 294–96.
149 Douglas regarded . . . "drop the subject": Stephen Douglas, quoted in Potter, *The Impending Crisis, 1848–1861*, p. 121.
149 Upon its passage: *NYH*, September 8, 9, and 10, 1850.
149 "The joy of everyone seemed unbounded": *NYTrib*, September 10, 1850.
149 "The crisis is passed—the cloud is gone": Lewis Cass quoted in *NYH*, September 10, 1850.
149 "The elements . . . but never overcome": *Columbus [Ga.] Sentinel*, reprinted in *Charleston [S.C.] Mercury*, January 23, 1851.
149 "devotion to . . . inclined them": AL, "Speech at Peoria, Illinois," October 16, 1854, in *CW*, II, p. 253.
149 Rejecting Seward's concept . . .: AL, "Endorsement on the Margin of the *Missouri Democrat*," [May 17, 1860], in *CW*, IV, p. 50.
149 He relished the convivial life: Strozier, *Lincoln's Quest for Union*, p. 144.
149 "The local belles . . . and eloquence": Whitney, *Life on the Circuit with Lincoln*, p. 63.
150 "plenty of bedbugs": David Davis to Sarah Davis, May 1, 1851, quoted in King, *Lincoln's Manager*, p. 77.
150 "half an inch thick": David Davis to Sarah Davis, April 24, 1851, David Davis Papers, Abraham Lincoln Presidential Library and Museum, Springfield, Ill. [hereafter Davis Papers, ALPLM].
150 slept two to a bed . . . in a room: Whitney, *Life on the Circuit with Lincoln*, p. 62.
150 David Davis: See King, *Lincoln's Manager*, esp. pp. 9–13, 17, 61.

150 "warm-hearted" nature: David Davis to Sarah Davis, November 3, 1851, Davis Papers, ALPLM.
150 "exceeding honesty & fairness": David Davis to Sarah Davis, March 23, 1851, Davis Papers, ALPLM.
   150   "too well to thwart her views": David Davis, quoted in King, *Lincoln's Manager*, p. 42.
150 the judge's letters about Lincoln: David Davis to Sarah Davis, May 3 and October 20, 1851, Davis Papers, ALPLM.
150 "He arrogated . . . personal affection": Unidentified lawyer, quoted in Tarbell, *The Life of Abraham Lincoln*, Vol. I, p. 247.
150 At mealtimes . . . prisoners out on bail: Whitney, *Life on the Circuit with Lincoln*, pp. 63, 72.
150 "such of us . . . those who have": AL, "Temperance Address delivered before the Springfield Washington Temperance Society," February 22, 1842, in *CW*, I, p. 278.
151 "in full laugh till near daylight": WHH to "Mr. N.," February 4, 1874, *Grandview [Ind.] Monitor*, March 15, 1934, quoted in Burlingame, *The Inner World of Abraham Lincoln*, p. 18 n67.
151 "eyes would sparkle . . . than his": Jonathan Birch, "A Student Who Was Aided by Mr. Lincoln," in Wilson, *Intimate Memories of Lincoln*, p. 105.
151 Ethan Allen/George Washington story: Abner Y. Ellis statement, January 23, 1866, in *HI*, p. 174.
151 "who had a great . . . 'than that dress' ": John Usher interview with George Alfred Townsend, December 25, 1878, scrapbook, Papers of George Alfred Townsend, Manuscript Division, Library of Congress.
151 "is the nature . . . is cradled": Walter Benjamin, "The Storyteller," in *Illuminations*, ed. Hannah Arendt, trans. Harry Zohn (New York: Harcourt, Brace & World, 1968; New York: Schocken Books, 1969), p. 91.
151 "Would we do . . . thought and experience": Whitney, *Life on the Circuit with Lincoln*, p. 66.
152 "It makes human nature . . . is possible": AL on George Washington, quoted in ibid., p. 67.
152 When the court closed . . . throughout the weekend: Jesse W. Weik, *The Real Lincoln: A Portrait* (Boston and New York: Houghton Mifflin, 1923), p. 90.
152 "wondered at it . . . pleasant, inviting homes": David Davis, quoted in Herndon and Weik, *Herndon's Life of Lincoln*, p. 249.
152 "as happy as . . . no other place": David Davis interview, September 20, 1866, in *HI*, p. 349.
152 "his home was *Hell* . . . *Heaven*": WHH, *A Letter from William H. Herndon to Isaac N. Arnold*, n.p.
152 "Lincoln speaks very . . . children": David Davis to Sarah Davis, November 3, 1851, quoted in King, *Lincoln's Manager*, p. 85.
152 Davis described a letter . . . Tad was born: David Davis to Sarah Davis, May 17, 1852, and September 18, 1853, Davis Papers, ALPLM; King, *Lincoln's Manager*, pp. 74, 84.
152 remedy the "want of education": Donald, *Lincoln Reconsidered*, p. 71.
152 "nearly mastered . . . Euclid": AL, "Scripps autobiography," in *CW*, IV, p. 62.
152 "he read hard works . . . read generally": John T. Stuart interview, December 20, 1866, in *HI*, p. 519.
152 "so deeply absorbed . . . point of exhaustion": WHH, in Weik, *The Real Lincoln*, p. 240.
153 "Life was to him . . . came before him": Swett, "Lincoln's Story of His Own Life," in *Reminiscences of Abraham Lincoln*, ed. Rice, p. 79.
153 "one of the greatest hardships": Randall, *Mary Lincoln*, p. 79.
153 circuit life was invaluable: Thomas, *Abraham Lincoln*, p. 94; White, *Abraham Lincoln in 1854*, p. 20; Strozier, *Lincoln's Quest for Union*, p. 144.
153 "If I muzzle not . . . the Whig party": WHS to FAS, July 21, 1850, in Seward, *Seward at Washington . . . 1846–1861*, p. 148.
153 Seward's eulogies to Clay and Webster: WHS, "Henry Clay" and "Daniel Webster," in *Works of William H. Seward*, Vol. III, pp. 104–16.
153 "They cannot see . . . of wrath!": WHS to unidentified recipient [FAS?], 1852, in Seward, *Seward at Washington . . . 1846–1861*, p. 194.
153 "I do not wish you . . . true to liberty": FAS to WHS, June 13, [1852], reel 114, Seward Papers.
154 "worldly wisdom . . . current if necessary": FAS to WHS, July 20, 1856, reel 114, Seward Papers.
154 "This fearless defense . . . righteous cause": FAS to CS, September 18, 1852, reel 9, The Papers of Charles Sumner, Chadwyck-Healey microfilm edition [hereafter Sumner Papers].
154 "a Waterloo defeat": Seward, *Seward at Washington . . . 1846–1861*, p. 196.
154 she was tempted . . . "more harm than good": FAS to LW, January 15, 1854, reel 119, Seward Papers.
154 "Would that I were . . . obligation and duty": WHS to FAS, May 16, 1855, quoted in Seward, *Seward at Washington . . . 1846–1861*, p. 251.
154 everywhere Seward went . . . join him: Johnson, "I Could Not be Well or Happy at Home," *URLB* (1978), p. 48.
155 Frances's health problems: FAS to LW, January 2, February 7, 1832; August 31, 1833, reel 118, Seward Papers; FAS, "Diary of Trip through Pennsylvania, Virginia, and Maryland, 1835," reel 197, and FAS, MSS Fragment on Illness, 1865, Seward Papers; entries for December 28, 1858, and March 16, 1859, FS diary, reel 198, Seward Papers; Johnson, "Sensitivity and Civil War," pp. 23–27.
155 her "sanctuary": WHS to FAS, February 12, 1837, in Seward, *An Autobiography*, p. 325.
155 Doctors could not pinpoint: Johnson, "I Could Not be Well or Happy at Home," URLB (1978), pp. 46–47.
155 the "various . . . purpose in their life": FAS, "Womans Mission, Westminster, 1850," reel 197, Seward Papers.
155 "There you are . . . pleasures, except at intervals": WHS to [FAS], June 13, 1847, in Seward, *Seward at Washington . . . 1846–1861*, p. 51.
155 The Sewards' relationship was sustained: Seward, *An Autobiography*, p. 162; Johnson, "I Could Not be Well or Happy at Home," *URLB* (1978), p. 53.
155 "above every other thing in the world": WHS to FAS, August 22, 1834, reel 112, Seward Papers.
155 whose "silver rays" . . . in the mail: WHS to FAS, January 27, 1831, in Seward, *An Autobiography*, p. 173.

155 played in the smoke from his cigar: WHS to FAS, January 15, 1831, in ibid., p. 168.
156 "Clouds and darkness . . . twelve months ago": SPC to CS, September 8, 1850, reel 7, Sumner Papers.
156 isolated in the Senate . . . achieve his position: Niven, *Salmon P. Chase*, pp. 142, 146–47.
156 routine at Miss Haines's School: Julia Newberry, *Julia Newberry's Diary*, intro. Margaret Ayer Barnes and Janet Ayer Fairbank (New York: W. W. Norton & Co., 1933), pp. 35–36: Phelps, *Kate Chase, Dominant Daughter*, pp. 74–75; Alice Hunt Sokoloff, *Kate Chase for the Defense* (New York: Dodd, Mead, 1971), pp. 28–29.
156 "without . . . we could hardly breathe": Newberry, *Julia Newberry's Diary*, p. 36.
156 correspondence between Chase and Kate: Niven, *Salmon P. Chase*, p. 201. Examples of loving but critical letters to KCS: July 22, August 23, September 5, 1850; January 15, March 2, April 19, August 30, September 10, 1851; January 23, 1853; May 27, 1855; April 30, 1859.
156 "Your last letter . . . use your eyes, reflect": SPC to KCS, January 15, 1851, reel 9, Chase Papers.
157 "I wish . . . into your letters": SPC to KCS, January 22, 1851, reel 9, Chase Papers.
157 "Your nice letter . . . drowsy God": SPC to KCS, June 21, 1855, reel 10, Chase Papers.
157 "It will be a . . . pleasurable sensation": SPC to KCS, February 8, 1855, reel 10, Chase Papers.
157 "Remember . . . preparation for another!": SPC to KCS, December 5, 1851, reel 9, Chase Papers.
157 "strong, robust . . . give you grace": SPC to KCS, June 15, 1852, reel 9, Chase Papers.
157 "I am sorry . . . to you the reasons why": SPC to KCS, August 10, 1852, reel 9, Chase Papers.
157 "you have it . . . by ill conduct": SPC to KCS, January 23, 1853, reel 9, Chase Papers.
157 "To an affectionate father . . . delightful future": SPC to KCS, March 27, 1855, reel 10, Chase Papers.
158 "be made President": SPC to KCS, February 21, 1852, reel 9, Chase Papers.
158 "I knew Clay . . . and was a brilliant talker": "Kate Chase in 1893," undated newspaper clipping from the *Star*, "Sprague, Kate Chase" vertical file, Washingtoniana Division, Martin Luther King, Jr. Memorial Library, Washington, D.C. [hereafter KCS vertical file, DWP].
158 "You cannot think . . . hear you praised": SPC to KCS, January 8, 1855, reel 10, Chase Papers.
158 "have visited . . . as they should be": SPC to KCS, August 27, 1852, reel 9, Chase Papers.
158 "The sun shines . . . the chirp of insects": SPC to KCS, June 15, 1852, reel 9, Chase Papers.
158 "I should like . . . a ramble together": SPC to KCS, April 3, 1852, reel 9, Chase Papers.
158 Chase understood her desire: Hart, *Salmon P. Chase*, p. 419.
158 "Miss Lizzie . . . among gentlemen": SPC to KCS, August 4, 1853, reel 9, Chase Papers.
159 the "African mania": Bates diary, January 1, 1850.
159 "lovers of free . . . in the South": Bates diary, January 1, 1850.
159 "a struggle among . . . sectional supremacy": Bates diary, May 31, 1851.
159 radicals . . . personal ambition: Hendrick, *Lincoln's War Cabinet*, p. 46.
159 "in Civil government . . . arbitrary designing knave": Bates diary, July 4, 1851.
159 "the world's best hope . . . so black": Bates diary, March 6, 1850.
159 "if we stood aloof . . . insignificance": Bates diary, November 27, 1850.
159 "A human being . . . crippling effect": Thomas Mann, *The Magic Mountain*, trans. John E. Woods (New York: Alfred A. Knopf, 1999), p. 31.
159 speech at Young Men's Lyceum: AL, "Address Before the Young Men's Lyceum of Springfield, Illinois," January 27, 1838, in *CW*, I, pp. 108–15, esp. 108, 113–14.
160 A train of events . . . grant them territorial status: Henry V. Jaffa, *Crisis of the House Divided: An Interpretation of the Issues in the Lincoln-Douglas Debates* (Chicago: University of Chicago Press, 1982), pp. 104–05; Fehrenbacher, *The South and Three Sectional Crises*, pp. 49, 56–57.
160 Kansas-Nebraska Act: See "Kansas-Nebraska Act," in *The Reader's Companion to American History*, ed. Foner and Garraty, p. 609.
160 Enforcement . . . in Boston and New York: Allan Nevins, *Ordeal of the Union*. Vol. I: *Fruits of Manifest Destiny, 1847–1852* (New York and London: Charles Scribner's Sons, 1947), pp. 387–88.
160 "I had never . . . aggressive and dangerous": Ralph Waldo Emerson, "The Fugitive Slave Law," reprinted in *The Portable Emerson*, pp. 547–48.
161 *Uncle Tom's Cabin*: See Thomas F. Gossett, *Uncle Tom's Cabin and American Culture* (Dallas: Southern Methodist University Press, 1985), pp. 164, 183–84.
161 "a flash . . . hosts of slavery": Frederick Douglass, quoted in ibid., p. 172.
161 "in greater numbers . . . against invasion": Fehrenbacher, *Prelude to Greatness*, p. 23.
161 "blood and treasure": Fehrenbacher, "The Wilmot Proviso and the Mid-Century Crisis" in Fehrenbacher, *The South and Three Sectional Crises*, p. 35.
161 "The day may come . . . out of it!": Thomas Bragg, quoted in Avery O. Craven, *The Growth of Southern Nationalism, 1848–1861*. Vol. VI: *A History of the South* (Baton Rouge: Louisiana State University Press, 1953; 1984), p. 204.
161 "a mighty subject . . . every five minutes": WHS to [FAS?], February 12, 1854, in Seward, *Seward at Washington . . . 1846–1861*, p. 219.
161 "essays against slavery . . . was the leader": Stephen Douglas, quoted in Hart, *Salmon P. Chase*, p. 134.
162 "one of the most effective . . . ever produced": Blue, *Salmon P. Chase*, p. 93 (quote); Gienapp, *The Origins of the Republican Party*, p. 72.
162 "We arraign . . . cause of God": SPC, et al., *Appeal of the Independent Democrats in Congress, to the People of the United States. Shall Slavery be Permitted in Nebraska?* (Washington, D.C.: Towers' Printers, 1854).
162 "Chase's greatest . . . experience of his life": Hart, *Salmon P. Chase*, p. 134.
162 "By far the most . . . of the Senate": *NYT*, February 6, 1854.
162 "high pitch of wrath . . . a corrupt bargain": Pike, "Night Scenes in the Passage of the Nebraska Bill," March 4, 1854, from *NYTrib*, in Pike, *First Blows of the Civil War*, pp. 217–18 (quote p. 217).

162 "I said the man . . . I mean you": *NYTrib*, March 6, 1854.
162 "this discussion . . . man, as man": SPC, "Maintain Plighted Faith. Speech of Hon. S. P. Chase, of Ohio, in the Senate, February 3, 1854," *Appendix to the Congressional Globe*, 33rd Cong., 1st sess., p. 140.
163 "Ah . . . 'negro' with two gs": *NYTrib*, March 7, 1854 (first quote); Carl Sandburg, *Abraham Lincoln: The War Years*, Vol. I (4 vols., New York: Harcourt, Brace & Co., 1939), p. 144 (second quote).
163 "Midnight passed . . . was taken": Pike, "Night Scenes in the Passage of the Nebraska Bill," March 4, 1854, from *NYTrib*, in Pike, *First Blows of the Civil War*, p. 216.
163 The all-night session: Johannsen, *Stephen A. Douglas*, p. 432.
163 by "great confusion . . . galleries participated": *NYTrib*, March 4, 1854.
163 "beastly drunk . . . the Senate room": Ibid.
163 "The Senate is emasculated": Thomas Hart Benton, quoted by Pike, "Night Scenes in the Passage of the Nebraska Bill," March 4, 1854, from *NYTrib*, in Pike, *First Blows of the Civil War*, p. 220.
163 a distant cannonade: Niven, *Salmon P. Chase*, p. 152.
163 "They celebrate . . . itself shall die": Schuckers, *The Life and Public Services of Salmon Portland Chase*, p. 156.
163 "Be assured . . . forces of slavery and freedom": Pike, "A Warning," April 1854, from *NYTrib*, in Pike, *First Blows of the Civil War*, pp. 222–23.
163 "The tremendous storm . . . every week": Nevins, *Ordeal of the Union*. Vol. II: *A House Dividing*, p. 125.
163 Resolutions: *NYTrib*, March 6 and 10, 1854.
163 "led by a band . . . torches and banners": *NYTrib*, March 6, 1854.
163 "he sat on the edge . . . half-slave and half-free": T. Lyle Dickey, paraphrased in Frederick Trevor Hill, *Lincoln the Lawyer* (New York: Century Co, 1906), p. 264.
164 "as he had never been before": AL, "Scripps autobiography," in *CW*, IV, p. 67 (quote); Miller, *Lincoln's Virtues*, pp. 232–34, 238–39.
164 "took us by . . . and stunned": AL, "Speech at Peoria, Illinois," October 16, 1854, in *CW*, II, p. 282.
164 spent many hours in the State Library: *Illinois State Register*, quoted in Donald, *Lincoln*, p. 173.
164 "inside and . . . downside": Herndon and Weik, *Herndon's Life of Lincoln*, p. 478.
164 "I am slow . . . to rub it out": Joshua F. Speed to WHH, December 6, 1866, in *HI*, p. 499.
164 at the annual State Fair: *Illinois State Journal*, October 5, 1854; *Peoria Daily Press*, October 9, 1854; *Illinois State Register*, October 6, 1854.
164 a "world-renowned" plow: *Peoria Daily Press*, October 9, 1854.
164 "a jolly good time ensued": Ibid.
164 Douglas at the State Fair: Thomas, *Abraham Lincoln*, pp. 147–48; Oates, *With Malice Toward None*, p. 124.
164 "He had a large . . . crush his prey": Horace White, *The Lincoln and Douglas Debates: An Address Before the Chicago Historical Society, February 17, 1914* (Chicago: University of Chicago Press, 1914), pp. 7–8.
165 "cast away . . . a half-naked pugilist": John Quincy Adams diary, quoted in William Gardner, *Life of Stephen A. Douglas* (Boston: Roxburgh Press, 1905), p. 20.
165 "He was frequently . . . with him": *Peoria Daily Press*, October 7, 1854.
165 Lincoln announced rebuttal the following day: Thomas, *Abraham Lincoln*, p. 148.
165 Douglas seated in the front row: White, *Abraham Lincoln in 1854*, p. 12.
165 largest audience: Donald, *Lincoln*, p. 174.
165 "awkward . . . knew he was right": White, *Abraham Lincoln in 1854*, p. 10.
165 "one of the world's . . . lapse of time": White, *The Lincoln and Douglas Debates*, p. 12.
165 "thin, high-pitched . . . of the speaker himself": White, *Abraham Lincoln in 1854*, p. 10.
165 Lincoln embedded his argument: AL, "Speech at Peoria Illinois," October 16, 1854, in *CW*, II, pp. 247–83.
165 so "clear and logical . . . most effective": *Illinois Daily Journal*, October 5, 1854.
166 "connected view . . . reclaiming of their fugitives": AL, "Speech at Peoria Illinois," October 16, 1854, in *CW*, II, pp. 248–75. The text of Lincoln's speech in Springfield on October 4, 1854, is no longer extant, but as the editors of *The Collected Works of Abraham Lincoln* have noted, the speech Lincoln delivered in Peoria on October 16, 1854, "is much the same speech." In the absence of a verbatim transcription of the Springfield speech, Lincoln's words from the October 16, 1854, Peoria one have been substituted. See footnote 1 to "Speech at Springfield, Illinois," *CW*, II, p. 240.
168 "thundering tones . . . drunkard on the earth": AL, "Temperance Address. An Address, Delivered before the Springfield Washington Temperance Society," February 22, 1842, in *CW*, I, pp. 273, 279.
168 "joined the north . . . to the latest generations": AL, "Speech at Peoria Illinois," October 16, 1854, in *CW*, II, pp. 264–76.
169 "deafening applause . . . anti-Nebraska speech": *Peoria Daily Press*, October 7, 1854.
169 Once he committed . . . authenticity of feeling: Miller, *Lincoln's Virtues*, p. 14; Donald, *Lincoln*, p. 270.
169 "as my two eyes make one in sight": Robert Frost, "Two Tramps in Mudtime," *The Poetry of Robert Frost: The Collected Poems*, ed. Edward Connery Lathem (New York: Henry Holt & Co., 1969; 1979), p. 277.

CHAPTER 6: THE GATHERING STORM

Page

170 "mainly attributed . . . the first choice": Joseph Gillespie to WHH, January 31, 1866, in *HI*, p. 182.
171 the worst blizzard in more than two decades: Entries for January 20–28, 1855, in *Lincoln Day by Day: A Chronology, 1809–1865*. Vol. II: *1848–1860*, ed. Earl Schenck Miers (Washington, D.C.: Lincoln Sesquicen-

tennial Commission, 1960; Dayton, Ohio: Morningside, 1991), pp. 136–37 [hereafter *Lincoln Day by Day*, Vol. II]; articles in the *Illinois Daily Journal*, Springfield, Ill., January 23–February 8, 1855.

171 "the merry sleigh bells . . . nearly extinct": *Illinois Daily Journal*, January 24, 27, and 30, 1855.

171 "a beehive of activity": *Daily Alton Telegraph*, February 12, 1855, quoted in Mark M. Krug, *Lyman Trumbull, Conservative Radical* (New York and London: A. S. Barnes & Co., and Thomas Yoseloff, 1965), p. 98.

171 "lobby and the galleries . . . and their guests": Krug, *Lyman Trumbull*, p. 98.

171 ladies in the gallery: Ibid.; White, *Abraham Lincoln in 1854*, p. 17.

171 bought a stack of small notebooks: Entry for January 1, 1855, *Lincoln Day by Day*, Vol. II, p. 136; "List of Members of the Illinois Legislature in 1855," [January 1, 1855?], in *CW*, II, pp. 296–98.

171 To reach a majority . . . fragile coalition: Miller, *Lincoln's Virtues*, p. 303.

171 On the first ballot: AL to Elihu B. Washburne, February 9, 1855, in *CW*, II, p. 304.

171 five anti-Nebraska . . . "at home": Joseph Gillespie to WHH, September 19, 1866, in *HI*, p. 344.

172 Trumbull story: AL to Elihu B. Washburne, February 9, 1855, in *CW*, II, pp. 304–06; Joseph Gillespie to WHH, January 31, 1866, and September 19, 1866, in *HI*, pp. 182–83, 344–45.

172 "you will lose both . . . to men": Joseph Gillespie to WHH, January 31, 1866, in *HI*, p. 183.

172 "spectators scarcely . . . the contest": John G. Nicolay and John Hay, *Abraham Lincoln: A History*, Vol. I (New York: Century Co., 1917), p. 390.

172 "perhaps his last . . . high position": Joseph Gillespie to WHH, January 31, 1866, in *HI*, p. 182.

172 Logan put his hands: Oates, *With Malice Toward None*, p. 130.

172 "he never would . . . by the 5": David Davis, quoted in AL to Elihu B. Washburne, February 9, 1855, *CW*, II, p. 306.

172 at Trumbull's victory party: Albert J. Beveridge, *Abraham Lincoln, 1809–1858*, Vol. III (Boston and New York: Houghton Mifflin, The Riverside Press, 1928), p. 287; White, *Abraham Lincoln in 1854*, p. 19.

172 "worse whipped . . . Trumbull is elected": AL to Elihu B. Washburne, February 9, 1855, Lincoln Papers.

172 Lincoln, in defeat, gained friends: Donald, *Lincoln*, p. 185.

172 "cold, selfish, treachery": MTL to Leonard Swett, January 12, 1867, in Turner and Turner, *Mary Todd Lincoln*, p. 406.

172 never spoke another word: Beveridge, *Abraham Lincoln, 1809–1858*, Vol. III, p. 286; Miller, *Lincoln's Virtues*, p. 312.

172 intermediaries tried . . . never healed: Burlingame, *The Inner World of Abraham Lincoln*, p. 310; Strozier, *Lincoln's Quest for Union*, p. 76.

173 to blackball him: MTL to David Davis, January 17, 1861, in Turner and Turner, *Mary Todd Lincoln*, p. 71; entry for December 3, 1865, *Diary of Gideon Welles: Secretary of the Navy Under Lincoln and Johnson*. Vol. II: *April 1, 1864–December 31, 1866*, ed. Howard K. Beale (New York: W.W. Norton & Company, Inc., 1960), p. 390 [hereafter Welles diary, Vol. II].

173 an "agony": AL to Elihu B. Washburne, February 9, 1855, in *CW*, II, p. 304.

173 "He could bear . . . his friends": Joseph Gillespie, quoted in Donald, *Lincoln*, p. 184.

173 celebrated law case: Unless otherwise noted, information and quotations related to the Reaper case have been derived from Robert H. Parkinson to Albert J. Beveridge, May 28, 1923, container 292, Beveridge Papers, DLC.

173 Peter Watson: Beveridge, *Abraham Lincoln, 1809–1858*, Vol. II, p. 280.

174 "At our interview . . . Manny's machine": AL to Peter H. Watson, July 23, 1855, in *CW*, II, pp. 314–15.

174 "Why did you bring . . . no good": WHH to JWW, January 6, 1887, reel 10, Herndon-Weik Collection, DLC.

175 "rapt attention": Ralph and Adaline Emerson, *Mr. & Mrs. Ralph Emerson's Personal Recollections of Abraham Lincoln* (Rockford, Ill.: Wilson Brothers Co., 1909), p. 7.

175 "drinking in his words": Flower, *Edwin McMasters Stanton*, p. 63.

175 "to study law": Emerson, *Emerson's Personal Recollections*, p. 7.

175 "For any rough- . . . will be ready": Flower, *Edwin McMasters Stanton*, p. 63.

175 "You have made . . . to return here": AL, quoted in W. M. Dickson, "Abraham Lincoln in Cincinnati," *Harper's New Monthly Magazine* 69 (June 1884), p. 62.

175 "the most powerful . . . his gift": Miller, *Lincoln's Virtues*, p. 425.

175 despite his initial contempt . . . respect and love Lincoln: Lewis Hutchison Stanton to unknown correspondent, January 4, 1930, quoted in the appendix to Gideon Townsend Stanton, ed., "Edwin M. Stanton: A Personal Portrait as revealed in letters addressed to his wife Ellen Hutchison during his voyage to and sojourn in San Francisco . . . and including letters covering the period 1854 to 1869," undated, typed manuscript, Edwin M. Stanton Manuscript, Mss. 1648, Louisiana and Lower Mississippi Valley Collections, LSU Libraries, Baton Rouge, La. [hereafter Gideon Stanton, ed., "Edwin M. Stanton"]; Thomas, *Abraham Lincoln*, p. 382.

175 the "long armed Ape": WHH to JWW, January 6, 1887, reel 10, Herndon-Weik Collection, DLC.

175 Stanton's comfortable childhood . . . and other works of history: Wolcott, "Edwin M. Stanton," esp. pp. 20–21, 24, 28, 30, 38, 39, 40, 66–67.

176 the "happiest hours of his life": Flower, *Edwin McMasters Stanton*, p. 37.

176 "regenerate the world": Mary Lamson Stanton to EMS, December 13, 1843, quoted in Wolcott, "Edwin M. Stanton," p. 108.

176 Mary Lamson and children: EMS, "Mary Lamson, Wife of Edwin M. Stanton"; Flower, *Edwin McMasters Stanton*, pp. 30, 32, 36–37, 38.

176 "bright and cheery": Wolcott, "Edwin M. Stanton," p. 63.

176 Stanton looked upon . . . and Byron: EMS to Edwin L. Stanton, quoted in Wolcott, "Edwin M. Stanton," p. 113.

176 "We years ago . . . cannot express": EMS to Mary Lamson Stanton, December 16, 1842, EMS, "Mary Lamson, Wife of Edwin M. Stanton."

177 deaths of Lucy and Mary: EMS, "Mary Lamson, Wife of Edwin M. Stanton"; Wolcott, "Edwin M. Stanton," pp. 72, 99; Flower, *Edwin McMasters Stanton*, pp. 38, 44.

177 "verged on insanity": Benjamin P. Thomas and Harold M. Hyman, *Stanton: The Life and Times of Lincoln's Secretary of War* (New York: Alfred A. Knopf, 1962), p. 35.

177 "She is my bride" . . . held that spring: Flower, *Edwin McMasters Stanton*, p. 39.

177 "with lamp in hand . . . Where is Mary?": Wolcott, "Edwin M. Stanton," p. 100.

177 Stanton's responsibilities . . . go of his sorrow: Thomas and Hyman, *Stanton*, pp. 35–36.

177 a letter of over a hundred pages: EMS, "Mary Lamson, Wife of Edwin M. Stanton."

177 "tears obscuring his vision": Gideon Stanton, ed., "Edwin M. Stanton."

177 "anguish of heart": EMS, "Mary Lamson, Wife of Edwin M. Stanton."

177 "but time, care . . . for each other": Ibid.

177 developed a high fever: Thomas and Hyman, *Stanton*, p. 40.

177 "He bled . . . few moments": Alfred Taylor, quoted in Flower, *Edwin McMasters Stanton*, p. 45.

177 His mother watched: Ibid.

177 "the blood spouted . . . ceiling": Thomas and Hyman, *Stanton*, p. 41.

177 Neighbors were sent . . . watching over him: Alfred Taylor, quoted in Flower, *Edwin McMasters Stanton*, p. 45.

178 "Where formerly . . . clasped behind": Mrs. Davison Filson, quoted in ibid., p. 40.

178 Stanton's change of personality in court: Ibid., p. 34.

178 "the most important" . . . He was greatly relieved: EMS to Ellen Hutchison, September 25, 1855, Stanton Papers, Donated Historical Materials, formerly Record Group 200, National Archives and Records Administration, Washington, D.C. [hereafter Stanton Papers, DNA] (quote); Dickson, "Abraham Lincoln in Cincinnati," *Harper's* (1884), p. 62.

178 Ellen Hutchison: See Flower, *Edwin McMasters Stanton*, p. 66.

178 "radiant with beauty and intellect": EMS to Ellen Hutchison, October 10, 1854, Stanton Papers, DNA.

178 in "agony": EMS to Ellen Hutchison, October 28, 1854, Stanton Papers, DNA.

178 "the trouble . . . fresh blossoms": EMS to Ellen Hutchison, October 10, 1854, Stanton Papers, DNA.

178 Ellen was vexed: EMS to Ellen Hutchison, May 21, 1855, and undated letter, Stanton Papers, DNA.

178 "his careless[ness] . . . feelings of all": EMS to Ellen Hutchison, undated, Stanton Papers, DNA.

179 "there is so much . . . overlook": EMS to Ellen Hutchison, May 21, 1855, Stanton Papers, DNA.

179 "blessed with . . . you condemn": EMS to Ellen Hutchison, undated, Stanton Papers, DNA.

179 to marry Edwin on June 25, 1856: EMS to Ellen Hutchison, June 25, 1856, Stanton Papers, DNA.

179 Happier years followed: Gideon Stanton, ed., "Edwin M. Stanton."

179 to Washington . . . a brick mansion: Flower, *Edwin McMasters Stanton*, p. 79.

179 "Twenty-two . . . a monarch's brow": AL, "Fragment on Stephen A. Douglas," [December 1856?], in *CW*, II, pp. 382–83.

179 "She had . . . ambition": John T. Stuart interview, late June 1865, in *HI*, p. 63.

179 "I would rather . . . in the world": MTL, quoted in Elizabeth Todd Edwards interview, 1865–1866, in *HI*, p. 444.

179 "a very little . . . does physically": Helm, *The True Story of Mary*, p. 140.

179 "no equal in the United States": MTL, quoted in ibid., p. 144.

180 "unladylike": MTL to Mercy Ann Levering, December [15?], 1840, in Turner and Turner, *Mary Todd Lincoln*, p. 21.

180 "the first bugle call . . . a new party": Schurz, *Reminiscences*, Vol. II, p. 34.

180 upheaval complicated by the emergence of the Know Nothings: McPherson, *Battle Cry of Freedom*, pp. 142–43; Eugene H. Roseboom, "Salmon P. Chase and the Know Nothings," *Mississippi Valley Historical Review* 25 (December 1938), pp. 335–50.

180 the Know Nothing Party . . . "popery": Potter, *The Impending Crisis, 1848–1861*, pp. 240–52 (quote p. 242); McPherson, *Battle Cry of Freedom*, p. 32.

180 "How can any one . . . Russia, for instance": AL to Joshua F. Speed, August 24, 1855, in *CW*, II, p. 323.

181 Republican Party, comprised of . . . over three decades: Gienapp, *The Origins of the Republican Party*, pp. 114–17, 123–24, 224–25; Potter, *The Impending Crisis, 1848–1861*, pp. 247, 249; McPherson, *Battle Cry of Freedom*, p. 127.

181 Chase . . . unhindered by past loyalties: Riddle, "The Election of Salmon P. Chase," *Republic* (1875), p. 183; Hendrick, *Lincoln's War Cabinet*, p. 33.

181 Chase accomplished . . . statewide ticket: Niven, *Salmon P. Chase*, pp. 157–58, 171: Gienapp, *The Origins of the Republican Party*, pp. 192–203.

181 Chase's campaign for governor: SPC to James S. Pike, October 18, 1855, and SPC to CS, October 15, 1855, reel 10, Chase Papers; Gienapp, *The Origins of the Republican Party*, pp. 200–01.

182 "on a hand car . . . another hand car": SPC to KCS, September 30, 1855, reel 10, Chase Papers.

182 "The anxiety . . . breathe freely!": CS to SPC, October 11, 1855, reel 10, Chase Papers.

182 Seward faced a more difficult challenge: Gienapp, *The Origins of the Republican Party*, pp. 223–25.

182 lavish dinners . . . bishop John Hughes: Hugh Hastings letter, reprinted in Barnes, *Memoir of Thurlow Weed*, pp. 232–33.

182 Working without rest . . . in the Senate: Taylor, *William Henry Seward*, p. 96.

182 "I snatch . . . shattered bark": WHS to TW, February 7, 1855, quoted in Seward, *Seward at Washington . . . 1846–1861*, p. 245.

182 "I have never . . . was made known": FAS to Augustus Seward, February 7, 1855, reel 115, Seward Papers.

183 liberated to join . . . in the state of New York: Gienapp, *The Origins of the Republican Party*, pp. 224–27.

183 "I am so happy. . . . political pew": CS to WHS, October 15, 1855, reel 49, Seward Papers.

183 Seward's October speech: WHS, "The Advent of the Republican Party, Albany, October 12, 1855," in *The Works of William H. Seward*, Vol. IV, ed. George E. Baker (Boston: Houghton Mifflin, 1884; New York: AMS Press, 1972), pp. 225–40 (quote p. 237).

183 organizing the various . . . Republican Party: Donald, *Lincoln*, pp. 189–91.

183 guerrilla war had broken out: Potter, *The Impending Crisis, 1848–1861*, pp. 199–215.

183 "engage in competition . . . in right": WHS, remarks in "The Nebraska and Kansas Bill," May 25, 1854, *Appendix to the Congressional Globe*, 33rd Cong., 1st sess., p. 769.

183 "When the North . . . eager foe": *Charleston Mercury*, June 21, 1854, quoted in Craven, *The Growth of Southern Nationalism*, p. 204.

184 assault on Sumner by Preston Brooks: David Donald, *Charles Sumner and the Coming of the Civil War*, collector's edition (New York: Alfred A. Knopf, 1960; Norwalk, Conn.: Easton Press, 1987), pp. 294–95; William E. Gienapp, "The Crime Against Sumner: The Caning of Charles Sumner and the Rise of the Republican Party," *Civil War History* 25 (September 1979), pp. 218–45.

184 Sumner's speech: CS, "Kansas Affairs. Speech of Hon. C. Sumner, of Massachusetts, in the Senate, May 19–20, 1856," *Appendix to the Congressional Globe*, 34th Cong., 1st sess., pp. 529–44.

184 laced with literary and historical references: Donald, *Charles Sumner and the Coming of the Civil War*, pp. 281–82.

184 "a chivalrous knight . . . humiliating offices": CS, "Kansas Affairs," *Appendix to the Congressional Globe*, 34th Cong., 1st sess., pp. 530–31.

184 advised him to remove the personal attacks: William H. Seward, Jr., "Youthful Recollections," p. 13, folder 36, Box 120, William Henry Seward Papers, Department of Rare Books & Special Collections, University of Rochester Library [hereafter Seward Papers, NRU], Rochester, N.Y.

184 "the most un-American . . . or elsewhere": Response by Lewis Cass to CS's speech, May 20, 1856, *Appendix to the Congressional Globe*, 34th Cong., 1st sess., p. 544.

184 Preston Brooks's attack on Sumner: See *Boston Pilot*, May 31, 1856; *NYT*, May 23, 1856; Donald, *Charles Sumner and the Coming of the Civil War*, pp. 294–97.

184 "You have libelled . . . come to punish you": *Boston Pilot*, May 31, 1856.

184 "Knots of men . . . by the slave power": *Boston Daily Evening Transcript*, May 29, 1856.

184 Mass public meetings: Donald, *Charles Sumner and the Coming of the Civil War*, pp. 300–01.

184 "*see* the slave aggression . . . in Congress": F. A. Sumner to CS, June 24, 1856, quoted in Gienapp, "The Crime Against Sumner," *CWH* (1979), p. 230.

185 "but the knocking-down . . . Southern spirit": *NYTrib*, May 24, 1856.

185 "proved a . . . Republican party": Gienapp, "The Crime Against Sumner," *CWH* (1979), p. 239.

185 Sumner hero in North, Brooks in South: Ibid., pp. 221, 222–23; Donald, *Charles Sumner and the Coming of the Civil War*, pp. 297–99, 304–07.

185 "good in conception . . . in consequence": *Richmond Enquirer*, June 3, 1856, quoted in Gienapp, "The Crime Against Sumner," *CWH* (1979), p. 222.

185 presented Brooks . . . and walking stick: *Columbia [S.C.] Carolinian*, reprinted in *Charleston Daily Courier*, May 28, 1856.

185 "*We are rejoiced . . . catch it next*": *Richmond Whig*, quoted in *NYT*, May 26, 1856.

185 "If thrashing is . . . wretch, Sumner": *Petersburg [Va.] Intelligencer*, quoted in *NYT*, May 29, 1856.

185 "apparent that . . . Brooks-Sumner affair": Donald, *Charles Sumner and the Coming of the Civil War*, p. 309.

185 "all shades . . . and abolitionists": Thomas, *Abraham Lincoln*, p. 165.

185 "fire and energy and force": Herndon and Weik, *Herndon's Life of Lincoln*, p. 313.

185 "That is the greatest . . . the presidency": Jesse K. Dubois, quoted in Weik, *The Real Lincoln*, p. 257.

186 "Lost Speech": Speech at Bloomington, Illinois, May 29, 1856, report in the Alton *Weekly Courier*, June 5, 1856, in *CW*, II, p. 341; Oates, *With Malice Toward None*, pp. 136–37.

186 By the late spring of 1856: Republican National Convention, *One Hundred Years Ago: Proceedings of the First Republican Nominating Convention, Philadelphia, 1856* (n.p.: n.p., 1956); Gienapp, *The Origins of the Republican Party*, pp. 334–45.

186 both Seward and Chase . . . the nomination: Van Deusen, *William Henry Seward*, pp. 174, 176; SPC to Hiram Barney, June 6, 1856, reel 11, Chase Papers.

186 gubernatorial election . . . nomination in 1856: Reinhard H. Luthin, "Salmon P. Chase's Political Career Before the Civil War," *Mississippi Valley Historical Review* 29 (March 1943), p. 525; SPC to Kinsley S. Bingham, October 19, 1855, reel 10, Chase Papers.

186 meeting at Blair home: Smith, *The Francis Preston Blair Family in Politics*, Vol. I, pp. 323–24; Niven, *Salmon P. Chase*, p. 178; Gienapp, *The Origins of the Republican Party*, pp. 250–51.

186 "approving . . . invitation": WHS to TW, December 31, 1855, quoted in Seward, *Seward at Washington . . . 1846–1861*, p. 264.

186 turned to potential candidates: Niven, *Salmon P. Chase*, pp. 178–79.

187 "if the unvarnished . . . people": SPC to Edward Hamlin, June 12, 1856, reel 11, Chase Papers.

187 neglected to appoint a manager . . . failed to unite: Hiram Barney to SPC, June 21, 1856, reel 11, Chase Papers; entry for June 1856, SPC diary, 1845–1859, reel 1, Chase Papers, DLC; Luthin, "Salmon P. Chase's Political Career Before the Civil War," *MVHR* (1943), p. 526.

187 "I know that if . . . been accomplished": Hiram Barney to SPC, June 21, 1856, reel 11, Chase Papers.

187 Seward had greater reason . . . Weed kept him from running: WHS to FAS, June 14 and 17, 1856, quoted in Seward, *Seward at Washington . . . 1846–1861*, pp. 277–78; Van Deusen, *William Henry Seward*, pp. 174, 176–77; Macartney, *Lincoln and His Cabinet*, p. 95; Gienapp, *The Origins of the Republican Party*, pp. 310, 339.

187 Lincoln was staying . . . "two steps at a time": Whitney, *Life on the Circuit with Lincoln*, pp. 94–95 (quote p. 95).

187 110 votes for vice president: Republican National Convention, *One Hundred Years Ago*, p. 67.

187 "Davis and I . . . reckon it's him": Whitney, *Life on the Circuit with Lincoln*, p. 96.

187 Bates refused . . . Whig National Convention: Cain, *Lincoln's Attorney General*, pp. 85, 86–88.

188 American Party . . . preserving the Union: Ibid., p. 82.

188 "I am neither . . . disordered territory": EB before the Whig National Convention in Baltimore, July 1856, quoted in ibid., p. 88.

188 results of 1856 presidential election: Congressional Quarterly, *Presidential Elections Since 1789*, p. 181.

188 *Dred Scott* case: Paul Finkelman, *Dred Scott v. Sandford: A Brief History with Documents. The Bedford Series in History and Culture* (Boston and New York: Bedford Books, 1997); Don E. Fehrenbacher, *The Dred Scott Case: Its Significance in American Law and Politics* (New York: Oxford University Press, 1978).

188 "an uncompromising . . . antislavery movement": Finkelman, *Dred Scott v. Sandford*, p. 29.

189 "Bright skies . . . bland atmosphere": *Star*, March 4, 1857.

189 Buchanan inaugural address: James Buchanan, "Inaugural Address, March 4, 1857," in *The Works of James Buchanan, Comprising His Speeches, State Papers, and Private Correspondence*. Vol. X: *1856–1860*, ed. John Bassett Moore (Philadelphia and London: J. B. Lippincott Co., 1910), p. 106.

189 "are not included . . . bound to respect": Roger B. Taney, opinion quoted in Finkelman, *Dred Scott v. Sandford*, pp. 35–36.

189 did not stop even there . . . was not before it: Potter, *The Impending Crisis, 1848–1861*, pp. 276–79.

189 "become convinced . . . its introduction": Justice Benjamin R. Curtis, quoted in ibid., p. 279 n24.

189 "one of the Court's . . . wounds": Opinion of Felix Frankfurter, in conversation with law clerk Richard N. Goodwin, as told to the author.

190 "often wrestled in the halls . . . justly won it": *Richmond Enquirer*, March 10, 1857.

190 "the accredited interpreter . . . and confused": *Richmond Enquirer*, March 13, 1857.

190 "Sheer blasphemy": Congressman John F. Potter, quoted in Kenneth M. Stampp, *America in 1857: A Nation on the Brink* (New York and Oxford: Oxford University Press, 1990), p. 104.

190 "entitled to just . . . Washington bar-room": *NYTrib*, March 7, 1857.

190 "an impartial judicial body" . . . would fail: Pike, "Decision of the Supreme Court," March 8, 1857, from the *NYTrib*, reprinted in Pike, *First Blows of the Civil War*, pp. 368–69 (quote p. 368).

190 "Judge Taney . . . good, evil": Frederick Douglass, "The *Dred Scott* Decision: Speech at New York, on the Occasion of the Anniversary of the American Abolition Society, May 11, 1857," reprinted in Finkelman, *Dred Scott v. Sandford*, p. 174.

190 "has aroused" . . . reported to Sumner: FAS to CS, April 23, 1857, reel 15, Sumner Papers.

190 Dred Scott was sold . . . to slavery: Potter, *The Impending Crisis, 1848–1861*, p. 290.

190 Speaking in Springfield . . . "circumstances should permit": AL, "Speech at Springfield, Illinois," June 16, 1857, in *CW*, II, pp. 398–410 (quotes pp. 403, 405, 406).

191 "The day of inauguration . . . English liberty": WHS, "Kansas-Lecompton Constitution," March 3, 1858, Senate, *Congressional Globe*, 35th Cong., 1st sess., p. 941.

191 reaction to Seward speech . . . access to the White House: Van Deusen, *William Henry Seward*, p. 190.

191 "have refused . . . to such a man": Samuel Tyler, *Memoir of Roger Brooke Taney* (Baltimore, 1872; New York: Da Capo Press, 1970), p. 391.

191 Seward's Rochester, New York, speech: WHS, "The Irrepressible Conflict, Rochester, October 25, 1858," in *Works of William H. Seward*, Vol. IV, pp. 289–302 (quotes pp. 291, 292; italics added).

191 Frances Seward . . . stance of the South: FAS to CS, January 4, 1859, reel 17, Sumner Papers.

192 "that troubled . . . *irrepressible*?": Kenneth M. Stampp, "The Irrepressible Conflict," in Stampp, *The Imperiled Union: Essays on the Background of the Civil War* (New York: Oxford University Press, 1980; 1981), p. 191.

192 uproar in opposition papers: *Atlas and Argus*, Albany, N.Y., October 28, 1858.

192 "more repulsive . . . Rev. Dr. Parker": *NYH*, October 28, 1858.

192 "never comprehended . . . words": Gienapp, *The Origins of the Republican Party*, p. 191.

192 "if heaven . . . do it again": WHS, quoted in Van Deusen, *William Henry Seward*, p. 194.

192 conciliatory . . . with his adversaries: David M. Potter, *Lincoln and His Party in the Secession Crisis* (New Haven, Conn.: Yale University Press, 1942), pp. 25–26.

192 "alarm and apprehension": WHS to FAS, February 9, 1849, quoted in Seward, *Seward at Washington . . . 1846–1861*, p. 98.

192 "This general impression . . . 'Night's Dream' ": WHS to FAS, February 9, 1849, quoted in ibid., p. 98.

193 "Those who assailed . . . pinch of snuff": *Albany Evening Journal*, May 19, 1890.

193 Seward's extravagant dinner parties: *Columbus [Ohio] Gazette*, April 6, 1860 (quotes); Van Deusen, *William Henry Seward*, pp. 257–58.

193 a trip through Canada: Seward, *Seward at Washington . . . 1846–1861*, pp. 301–22; Van Deusen, *William Henry Seward*, p. 183.

194 "voyage of discovery": FPB to WHS, October 5, 1857, quoted in Seward, *Seward at Washington . . . 1846–1861*, p. 324.

194 "very best traveling" . . . elegant meals: FPB to WHS, November 1, 1857, quoted in ibid., p. 326.

194 "At an age . . . of the nation": *Cincinnati Enquirer*, August 6, 1899.

194 "a scientific knowledge . . . surpassed": Peacock, *Famous American Belles of the Nineteenth Century*, p. 214.

194 "Her complexion . . . of her head": Sara A. Pryor, *Reminiscences of Peace and War.* Revised and enlarged ed. (New York: The Macmillan Company, 1905), pp. 75–76.

195 Gothic mansion on Sixth Street: Niven, *Salmon P. Chase*, pp. 200, 201, 204; SPC to KCS, December 3, 4, 5, and 6, 1857, reel 11, Chase Papers.

195 "I feel I am . . . trust yours": SPC to KCS, December 5, 1857, reel 11, Chase Papers.

195 "you have capacity and will do very well": SPC to KCS, December 4, 1857, reel 11, Chase Papers.

195 role of Ohio's first lady: Ross, *Proud Kate*, pp. 32–33, 36–37.

195 "I knew all . . . very early age": "Kate Chase in 1893," undated newspaper clipping from the *Star*, KCS vertical file, DCPL.

195 first dinner "in society . . . very beautiful": Howells, *Years of My Youth*, pp. 154–55.

195 led to a tryst . . . end to the relationship: *Columbus Special* to the *Chicago Times*, reprinted in *Cincinnati Enquirer*, August 13, 1879.

196 "I find that . . . any other man": SPC to Charles D. Cleveland, November 3, 1857, reel 11, Chase Papers.

196 met in Lecompton . . . applied for statehood: Potter, *The Impending Crisis, 1848–1861*, pp. 300, 306–07, 313–15, 318–20, 322–25.

196 now siding with the Republicans: Potter, *The Impending Crisis, 1848–1861*, pp. 316, 318, 320–21.

196 "My objection . . . a slave State": Stephen A. Douglas's speech, "Third Debate with Stephen A. Douglas at Jonesboro, Illinois," September 15, 1858, in *CW*, III, p. 115.

196 He cared not . . . voted up or down: AL on Stephen Douglas, in "A House Divided": Speech at Springfield, Illinois, June 16, 1858, in *CW*, II, p. 463.

196 "was not the act . . . embody their will": Stephen A. Douglas's speech, "Third Debate with Stephen A. Douglas at Jonesboro, Illinois," September 15, 1858, in *CW*, III, p. 115.

197 "What can . . . freedom and justice": WHS to [FAS?], December 10, 1857, quoted in Seward, *Seward at Washington . . . 1846–1861*, p. 330.

197 Greeley called on Illinois Republicans: Fehrenbacher, *Prelude to Greatness*, p. 61.

197 Lincoln at once . . . destroyed the Republican Party: AL to Elihu B. Washburne, May 27, 1858, in *CW*, II, p. 455; AL to SPC, April 30, 1859, in *CW*, III, p. 378; Donald, *Lincoln*, pp. 204, 208.

197 "accosted by friends . . . to go under": AL, "Fragment of a Speech," [c. May 18, 1858], in *CW*, II, p. 448.

197 "What does . . . here in Illinois?": AL to Lyman Trumbull, December 28, 1857, in ibid., p. 430.

197 "incapable of . . . pure republican position": AL to Charles L. Wilson, June 1, 1858, in ibid., p. 457.

197 interference of the Eastern Republicans: *Illinois Daily Journal*, Springfield, Ill., June 16, 1858; Fehrenbacher, *Prelude to Greatness*, pp. 62–63.

197 "Abraham Lincoln . . . United States Senate": Thomas, *Abraham Lincoln*, p. 179.

198 a statewide Republican convention . . . "Stephen A. Douglas": Fehrenbacher, *Prelude to Greatness*, pp. 63, 48 (quote p. 48).

198 "A house divided . . . another Supreme Court decision": AL, "A House Divided": Speech at Springfield, Illinois, June 16, 1858, in *CW*, II, pp. 461, 465–67. "A House Divided" appears in the Bible in Matthew 12:25; Mark 3:24.

199 If "the point . . . talking about": James M. McPherson, "How Lincoln Won the War with Metaphors," Eighth Annual R. Gerald McMurtry Lecture, 1985, reprinted in James M. McPherson, *Abraham Lincoln and the Second American Revolution* (New York and Oxford: Oxford University Press, 1991), p. 104.

199 *"weight* and *authority* . . . not *promise* to *ever* be": AL, "A House Divided": Speech at Springfield, Illinois, June 16, 1858, in *CW*, II, pp. 462–63, 467–68.

200 "What if Judge" . . . to extend slavery: AL's reply, "First Debate with Stephen A. Douglas at Ottawa, Illinois," August 21, 1858, in *CW*, III, pp. 22, 20 (quote p. 22).

200 "planned to seize . . . nationalize slavery": Cain, *Lincoln's Attorney General*, p. 77.

200 Lincoln, the challenger, asked Douglas: *The Lincoln-Douglas Debates: The First Complete, Unexpurgated Text*, ed. Harold Holzer (New York: HarperCollins, 1993), pp. 2–6.

200 both men covered over 4,000 miles: Ibid., p. 20.

200 marching bands . . . picnics: Baringer, *Lincoln's Rise to Power*, pp. 21–22, 24–25, 28, 30–31, 33–34, 37.

200 "all the devoted . . . for athletic contests": Fehrenbacher, *Prelude to Greatness*, p. 15.

200 "the country people . . . lines in single combat": Schurz, *Reminiscences*, Vol. II, pp. 92, 88.

201 "were the successive . . . of the nation": AL's speech, "Sixth Debate with Stephen A. Douglas, at Quincy, Illinois," October 13, 1858, in *CW*, III, pp. 252–53.

201 "On the whole . . . extreme modest simplicity": Schurz, *Reminiscences*, Vol. II, p. 92.

201 followed the same rules . . . Newspaper stenographers: *The Lincoln-Douglas Debates*, ed. Holzer, pp. 4, 9.

201 "No more striking . . . and staying power": Schurz, *Reminiscences*, Vol. II, p. 94.

201 The highly partisan papers: See *The Lincoln-Douglas Debates*, ed. Holzer, pp. 7–8.

201 "when Mr. Lincoln . . . music in front": *Press and Tribune*, Chicago, following Ottawa debate, quoted in *The Lincoln-Douglas Debates*, ed. Holzer, p. 85.

201 "excoriation of Lincoln . . . in shame": *Chicago Times*, in ibid.

201 "both comparatively . . . Hit him again": Stephen Douglas's speech, "First Debate with Stephen A. Douglas at Ottawa, Illinois," August 21, 1858, in *CW*, III, pp. 5–6.

202 conceded that Douglas . . . "upon principle, alone": AL, "Speech at Springfield, Illinois," July 17, 1858, in *CW*, II, p. 506.

202 "The very notice . . . political physicians": Stephen Douglas, quoted in *NYTrib*, included in AL's reply, "Third Joint Debate at Jonesboro," September 15, 1858, in *The Lincoln-Douglas Debates*, ed. Holzer, p. 173.

202 "Well, I know . . . if he can": AL's reply, "Third Joint Debate at Jonesboro," September 15, 1858, in ibid., pp. 173, 175.

203 a small notebook . . . "pursuit of Happiness": Ibid., p. 17. Quotation from paragraph two of the Declaration of Independence (1776).

203 "majestic interpretation . . . in other ages": AL, "Speech at Lewistown, Illinois," August 17, 1858, quoted in *Press and Tribune*, Chicago, August 21, 1858, in *CW*, II, p. 546.

203 "I care more . . . in Christendom": Stephen Douglas's reply, "Seventh and Last Debate with Stephen A. Douglas at Alton, Illinois," October 15, 1858, in *CW*, III, p. 322.

203 "the doctrine . . . a slave of another": AL, "Speech at Peoria, Illinois," October 16, 1854, in *CW*, II, pp. 265–66.

203 "The difference between . . . these views": AL, "Speech at Edwardsville, Illinois," September 11, 1858, in *CW*, III, p. 92.

204 set of Black Laws . . . on juries: Leon F. Litwack, *North of Slavery: The Negro in the Free States, 1790–1860* (Chicago and London: University of Chicago Press, 1961), pp. 93, 278.

204 "If you desire . . . Never, never": Stephen Douglas's speech, "First Debate with Stephen A. Douglas at Ottawa, Illinois," August 21, 1858, in *CW*, III, p. 9.

204 "the signers . . . that's the truth": Stephen A. Douglas's speech, "Seventh and Last Debate with Stephen A. Douglas at Alton, Illinois," October 15, 1858, in ibid., p. 296.

204 "no purpose . . . the black races": AL's reply, "First Debate with Stephen A. Douglas at Ottawa, Illinois," August 21, 1858, in ibid., p. 16.

204 "of making voters . . . nor to intermarry": AL's speech, "Fourth Debate with Stephen A. Douglas at Charleston, Illinois," September 18, 1858, in ibid., p. 145.

204 "a physical difference . . . of every living man": AL's reply, "First Debate with Stephen A. Douglas at Ottawa, Illinois," August 21, 1858, in ibid., p. 16.

205 only unequivocal statement: Harry Jaffa, *Crisis of the House Divided*, pp. 382–84.

205 passing a special law . . . "whether free or slave": Koerner, *Memoirs of Gustave Koerner*, Vol. II, p. 30.

205 "Seward did not . . . of the whites": Van Deusen, *William Henry Seward*, p. 94.

205 "the two races . . . in other lands": Blue, *Salmon P. Chase*, pp. 83, 84; SPC, quoted in ibid.

205 "The most dreadful . . . prejudice of the white": de Tocqueville, *Democracy in America*, ed. Mansfield and Winthrop, pp. 326, 329, 328.

206 "in the name of . . . to go?": Henry Clay, quoted in Nevins, *Ordeal of the Union*. Vol. I: *Fruits of Manifest Destiny*, p. 515.

206 "My first impulse . . . native land": AL, "Speech at Peoria, Illinois," October 16, 1854, in *CW*, II, p. 255.

206 More than 3 million: Craven, *The Growth of Southern Nationalism*, p. 12.

206 "What then? . . . safely disregarded": AL, quoting his 1854 Peoria speech in his reply, "First Debate with Stephen A. Douglas at Ottawa, Illinois," August 21, 1858, in *CW*, III, p. 15.

206 "With public sentiment . . . this American people": AL's reply, "First Debate with Stephen A. Douglas at Ottawa, Illinois," August 21, 1858, in ibid., pp. 27, 29.

207 "they did not mean . . . all colors everywhere": AL, "Speech at Springfield, Illinois," June 26, 1857, in *CW*, II, p. 406.

207 "penetrate the human soul": AL's reply, "First Debate with Stephen A. Douglas at Ottawa, Illinois," August 21, 1858, in *CW*, III, p. 29.

207 "all this quibbling . . . men are created equal": AL, "Speech at Chicago, Illinois," July 10, 1858, quoted by Stephen Douglas in his reply, "Sixth Debate with Stephen A. Douglas at Quincy, Illinois," October 13, 1858, in ibid., p. 263.

207 "practical recognition of our Equality": Frederick Douglass, quoted in David W. Blight, *Frederick Douglass' Civil War: Keeping Faith in Jubilee* (Baton Rouge and London: Louisiana State University Press, 1989), p. 16.

207 "the first great man . . . the colored race": Frederick Douglass, "Lincoln and the Colored Troops," in *Reminiscences of Abraham Lincoln*, ed. Rice, p. 323.

208 "having strong sympathies . . . and so on": AL's reply, "Seventh and Last Debate with Stephen A. Douglas at Alton, Illinois," October 15, 1858, in *CW*, III, p. 300.

208 "whole town . . . human beings": Eyewitness at Alton debate, quoted in *The Lincoln-Douglas Debates*, ed. Holzer, p. 322.

208 "More than a thousand . . . he ever made": Koerner, *Memoirs of Gustave Koerner*, Vol. II, pp. 66–68.

208 The "real issue . . . same tyrannical principle": AL's reply, "Seventh and Last Debate with Stephen A. Douglas at Alton, Illinois," October 15, 1858, in *CW*, III, p. 315.

208 He drew up . . . "to be struggled for": AL, "1858 Campaign Strategy," [July? 1858], in *CW*, II, pp. 476–81 (quote p. 479).

209 "We are in . . . must be left undone": AL to Gustave P. Koerner, July 25, 1858, in ibid., p. 524.

209 Chase came to Illinois: Niven, *Salmon P. Chase*, p. 210; Blue, *Salmon P. Chase*, pp. 118–19.

209 a gesture Lincoln would not forget: AL to SPC, April 30, 1859, in *CW*, III, p. 378; AL to Samuel Galloway, March 24, 1860, in *CW*, IV, p. 34.

209 a dreary day, November 2, 1858: *Illinois State Journal*, Springfield, Ill., November 3, 1858.

209 Lincoln anxiously awaited the returns: Baringer, *Lincoln's Rise to Power*, p. 43; Oates, *With Malice Toward None*, p. 173.

209 "by the gerrymandering . . . Republican votes": Koerner, *Memoirs of Gustave Koerner*, Vol. II, p. 68.

209 John Crittenden: Fehrenbacher, *Prelude to Greatness*, p. 118.

209 "Thousands of Whigs . . . influence of Crittenden": WHH to Theodore Parker, November 8, 1858, quoted in Baringer, *Lincoln's Rise to Power*, p. 49.

209 "The emotions of defeat . . . anything dishonorable": AL to John J. Crittenden, November 4, 1858, in *CW*, III, pp. 335–36.
210 "I am glad . . . after I am gone": AL to Anson G. Henry, November 19, 1858, in ibid., p. 339.
210 "must not be surrendered . . . *hundred* defeats": AL to Henry Asbury, November 19, 1858, in ibid., p. 339.
210 "You will soon . . . have fun again": AL to Charles H. Ray, November 20, 1858, in ibid., p. 342.

CHAPTER 7: COUNTDOWN TO THE NOMINATION

Page
211 "decided impression . . . candidate for the presidency": Jesse W. Fell, quoted in Oldroyd, comp., *The Lincoln Memorial*, p. 474.
211 "so much better known . . . you or anybody else": AL, quoted by Jesse W. Fell, quoted in ibid., pp. 474, 476.
212 when the Republican editor . . . "for the Presidency": Thomas J. Pickett to AL, April 13, 1859, Lincoln Papers.
212 "I certainly am . . . fit for the Presidency": AL to Thomas J. Pickett, April 16, 1859, in *CW*, III, p. 377.
212 Certain that Seward . . . overseas for eight months: Luthin, *First Lincoln Campaign*, p. 31.
212 "All our discreet friends . . . recess of Congress": WHS to George W. Patterson, April 6, 1859, quoted in Van Deusen, *William Henry Seward*, p. 196.
212 Fanny Seward desolate . . . approaching departure: April 1859 entries, Frances (Fanny) Adeline Seward diary, reel 198, Seward Papers [hereafter Fanny Seward diary, Seward Papers].
212 description of Fanny Seward, literary pursuits: Johnson, "Sensitivity and Civil War," pp. 27, 76–78, 83–84.
212 " 'my affinity' . . . instead of speak": Fanny Seward, quoted in ibid., p. 55.
213 Seward in Europe: Seward, *Seward at Washington . . . 1846–1861*, pp. 362–436.
213 prepared a major address: Taylor, *William Henry Seward*, pp. 115–16.
213 Henry Stanton later . . . "posterity together": Stanton, *Random Recollections*, pp. 212–13.
213 "I wish it were over": FAS to William H. Seward, Jr., February 29, 1860, reel 115, Seward Papers.
213 Fanny . . . seated in the gallery: Entry for February 29, 1860, Fanny Seward diary, Seward Papers.
213 "The whole house . . . was very still": Entry for February 29, 1860, Fanny Seward diary, Seward Papers.
213 Seward took as his theme: WHS, February 29, 1860, *Congressional Globe*, 36th Cong., 1st sess., pp. 910–14.
213 " 'the irrepressible conflict' . . . the political aspirants": Bancroft, *The Life of William H. Seward*, Vol. I, p. 519.
214 "differences of opinion . . . always of their wants": WHS, February 29, 1860, *Congressional Globe*, 36th Cong., 1st sess., pp. 912–14.
214 produced deafening applause: Entry for February 29, 1860, Fanny Seward diary, Seward Papers; Baringer, *Lincoln's Rise to Power*, pp. 197, 198; Van Deusen, *William Henry Seward*, p. 220.
214 half a million copies were circulated: Van Deusen, *William Henry Seward*, p. 219.
214 *"killed Seward with me forever"*: Cassius Marcellus Clay, *The Life of Cassius Marcellus Clay. Memoirs, Writings, and Speeches, Showing His Conduct in the Overthrow of American Slavery, the Salvation of the Union, and the Restoration of the Autonomy of the United States* (n.p.: J. Fletcher Brennan & Co., 1886; New York: Negro Universities Press/Greenwood Publishing Corp., 1969), pp. 242–43.
214 "as an intellectual . . . agrees with me": CS to Duchess Elizabeth Argyll, March 2, 1860, reel 74, Sumner Papers.
214 "From the stand-point . . . matter of party justice": Frederick Douglass, "Mr. Seward's Great Speech," *Douglass' Monthly* (April 1860).
215 "I hear of ultra . . . equally satisfactory": Samuel Bowles to TW, March 5, 1860, quoted in Barnes, *Memoir of Thurlow Weed*, p. 260.
215 "seems to be . . . set toward Seward": Bancroft, *The Life of William H. Seward*, Vol. I, p. 519.
215 Weed assured him that everything was in readiness: TW to WHS, May 2, 6, and 8, 1860, reel 59, Seward Papers.
215 "oceans of money": Halstead, *Three Against Lincoln*, p. 162.
215 a longing for political office: Glyndon G. Van Deusen, *Horace Greeley: Nineteenth-Century Crusader*, (Philadelphia: University of Pennsylvania Press, 1953), pp. 116–17, 185–86; Thurlow Weed, "Recollections of Horace Greeley," *Galaxy* 15 (March 1873), pp. 379–80.
215 Greeley's plaintive letter to Seward: Horace Greeley to WHS, November 11, 1854, reel 48, Seward Papers.
216 "full of sharp, pricking thorns": WHS to TW, November 12, 1854, quoted in Seward, *Seward at Washington . . . 1846–1861*, p. 239.
216 mistakenly assumed . . . "mortal offense": Carpenter, "A Day with Governor Seward," Seward Papers.
216 "insinuated . . . to the nomination": Henry Raymond, quoted in Barnes, *Memoir of Thurlow Weed*, p. 274.
216 Weed had a long talk with Greeley . . . "all right": WHS to home, Seward, *Seward at Washington . . . 1846–1861*, p. 395.
216 Weed's failure to meet . . . Seward relayed the message: WHS to TW, March 15, 1860, quoted in Barnes, *Memoir of Thurlow Weed*, p. 261.
216 Seward's visit to Lochiel: WHS to TW, April 11, 1859, Weed Papers; Lee F. Crippen, *Simon Cameron, Antebellum*, The American Scene: Comments and Commentators series (Oxford, Ohio, 1942; New York: Da Capo Press, 1972), p. 209.
216 "He took me . . . to embarrass me": WHS to TW, April 11, 1859, Weed Papers.

217 "an honest politician . . . stays bought": Simon Cameron, quoted in Macartney, *Lincoln and His Cabinet*, p. 46.

217 "so much money . . . man in Pennsylvania": *NYT,* June 3, 1878.

217 Cameron's political offices: Macartney, *Lincoln and His Cabinet*, p. 26.

217 his "legislative child": Hendrick, *Lincoln's War Cabinet*, p. 53.

217 People's Party state convention: Crippen, *Simon Cameron, Ante-bellum Years*, pp. 201, 205.

217 Andrew Curtin . . . challenging Cameron: Hendrick, *Lincoln's War Cabinet*, pp. 55–56.

218 Chase and the Baileys . . . "in European tradition": Niven, *Salmon P. Chase*, pp. 61, 123, 140–41 (quote p. 140).

218 "detestable" Know Nothings: Gamaliel Bailey to SPC, November 27, 1855, reel 10, Chase Papers.

218 "in the presidential . . . other man": Gamaliel Bailey to SPC, June 26, 1855, reel 10, Chase Papers.

218 "observing the signs . . . integrity or my friendship": Gamaliel Bailey to SPC, January 16, 1859, reel 12, Chase Papers.

218 "I do not doubt . . . spontaneous growth": SPC to Gamaliel Bailey, January 24, 1859, reel 12, Chase Papers.

219 "a slip of your pen . . . as a friend": Gamaliel Bailey to SPC, January 30, 1859, reel 12, Chase Papers.

219 preferred the unrealistic . . . on the first ballot: Hiram Barney to SPC, November 10, 1859, reel 13, Chase Papers.

219 Failing once again to appoint: Donnal V. Smith, "Salmon P. Chase and the Election of 1860," *OAHQ* 39 (July 1930), p. 520.

219 He rejected an appeal from a New Hampshire supporter: Amos Tuck to SPC, March 14, 1860, reel 13, Chase Papers.

219 He never capitalized . . . a series of letters: Reinhard H. Luthin, "Pennsylvania and Lincoln's Rise to the Presidency," *Pennsylvania Magazine of History and Biography* 67 (January 1943), p. 66; SPC to Hiram Barney, September 22, 1860, reel 13, Chase Papers; Smith, "Salmon P. Chase and the Election of 1860," *OAHQ* (1930), pp. 520–21; Luthin, "Salmon P. Chase's Political Career Before the Civil War," *MVHR* (1943), p. 531.

219 "I now begin . . . but *he works*": James M. Ashley to SPC, April 5, 1860, reel 13, Chase Papers.

220 "I shall have nobody . . . of the State": SPC to Benjamin Eggleston, May 10, 1860, reel 13, Chase Papers.

220 "The Ohio delegation . . . as yet": Erastus Hopkins to SPC, May 17, 1860, reel 13, Chase Papers.

220 "in a position . . . to occupy": SPC to Benjamin R. Cowen, May 14, 1860, reel 13, Chase Papers.

220 Kate convinced her father: Ross, *Proud Kate*, p. 42.

220 Seward was very kind . . . "good deal of joking": SPC to James A. Briggs, April 27, 1860, reel 13, Chase Papers (quote); WHS to FAS, April 27, 1860, quoted in Seward, *Seward at Washington . . . 1846–1861*, p. 447.

220 organized a party . . . "two rivals within": WHS to FAS, April 28, 1860, quoted in Seward, *Seward at Washington . . . 1846–1861*, p. 447.

220 the Blairs threw . . . "well-cultivated": WHS to FAS, April 29, 1860, quoted in ibid., p. 448.

220 "attention to Katie . . . kind to me": SPC to Janet Chase Hoyt, May 4, 1860, reel 13, Chase Papers.

220 "Everybody seems . . . confidence in me": SPC to James A. Briggs, April 27, 1860, reel 13, Chase Papers.

220 "a great change . . . I was in Washington": SPC to James A. Briggs, May 8, 1860, reel 13, Chase Papers.

221 But he never left his home state . . . to visit him: See entries from January to May 1860 in *The Diary of Edward Bates, 1859–1866*; Cain, *Lincoln's Attorney General*, p. 95.

221 "the first . . . two years": Entry for February 22, 1860, in *The Diary of Edward Bates, 1859–1866*, p. 101.

221 his distance from the fierce arguments of the fifties: Introduction, ibid., p. xii.

221 his "views and opinions . . . of the country": Entry for April 20, 1859, in ibid., p. 1.

221 The New York Whigs . . . "sectional prejudice": EB to Whig Committee of New York, February 24, 1859, reprinted in entry for April 20, 1859, in ibid., pp. 1–9 (quotes pp. 1–2).

222 "denouncing . . . the Republican party": Entry for April 27, 1859, in ibid., p. 12.

222 confirmed Bates's . . . "well enough alone": Entry for December 17, 1859, in ibid., pp. 78–79.

222 "brighter every day": Note of February 2, 1860, added to entry for January 28, 1860, in ibid., p. 94.

222 "made up of 'Bates men' ": Entries for February 25 and March 1, 1860, in ibid., pp. 102 (quote), 107.

222 "good feeling . . . support Lincoln": Entry for April 26, 1860, in ibid., p. 122.

222 "would be the best . . . the South of it": AL to Richard M. Corwine, April 6, 1860, in *CW,* IV, p. 36.

222 endorsements by conventions: Entries for March 1 and March 13, 1860, in *The Diary of Edward Bates, 1859–1866*, pp. 106, 108 (quote p. 106).

222 the German-American contingent . . . party in 1856: Reinhard H. Luthin, "Organizing the Republican Party in the 'Border-Slave' Regions: Edward Bates's Presidential Candidacy in 1860," *Missouri Historical Review* 38 (January 1944), pp. 149–50.

222 Blair suggested a questionnaire: Parrish, *Frank Blair*, p. 82.

222 "beaten with . . . into the quicksands": Joseph Medill, quoted in O. J. Hollister, *Life of Schuyler Colfax* (New York and London: Funk & Wagnalls, 1886), p. 147.

223 Bates's response to questionnaire: EB to Committee of the Missouri Republican Convention, March 17, 1860, reprinted in *The Diary of Edward Bates, 1859–1866*, pp. 111–14.

223 responses to Bates's statement: See Cain, *Lincoln's Attorney General*, pp. 104–05.

223 "as a clap . . . a clear sky": *Lexington [Mo.] Express*, reprinted in *Daily Missouri Republican*, St. Louis, Mo., April 5, 1860.

223 "just as good . . . the Southern Conservatives": *Louisville [Ky.] Journal*, extracted in the *[Indianapolis] Daily Journal*, quoted in Luthin, "Organizing the Republican Party in the 'Border-Slave' Regions," *MHR* (1944), p. 151.

223 "agitators . . . peace of our Union": *Memphis Bulletin*, reprinted in *Missouri Republican*, St. Louis, Mo., March 31, 1860.

223 Bates himself . . . "a good many papers": Entry of April 7, 1860, in *The Diary of Edward Bates, 1859–1866*, p. 118.

223 "knowing the fickleness . . . a failure": Entry of February 28, 1860, in ibid., pp. 105–06.

224 "neither on the left . . . dead center": Fehrenbacher, *Prelude to Greatness*, p. 147.

224 "fairly headed off . . . of ultimate extinction": AL to John L. Scripps, June 23, 1858, in *CW*, II, p. 471.

224 He arranged to publish: Baringer, *Lincoln's Rise to Power*, pp. 128, 137, 171; Donald, *Lincoln*, p. 237.

224 nearly two dozen speeches: Fehrenbacher, *Prelude to Greatness*, pp. 143–44; Baringer, *Lincoln's Rise to Power*, chapter 3.

224 "I think it is . . . into Liberty": James A. Briggs to AL, November 1, 1859, Lincoln Papers.

224 The crowds that greeted . . . "many a day": *Janesville Gazette*, quoted in Baringer, *Lincoln's Rise to Power*, pp. 110–11 (quote p. 110).

224 "Douglasism . . . of Republicanism": AL to SPC, September 21, 1859, in *CW*, III, p. 471.

225 stop was Cincinnati: Baringer, *Lincoln's Rise to Power*, pp. 103–07.

225 "greeted with . . . rising star": Dickson, "Abraham Lincoln in Cincinnati," *Harper's New Monthly* (1884), p. 65.

225 Lincoln's speech in Cincinnati: AL, "Speech at Cincinnati, Ohio," September 17, 1859, in *CW*, III, p. 454.

225 "as an effort . . . had ever heard": *Cincinnati Gazette*, reprinted in *Illinois State Journal*, Springfield, Ill., October 7, 1859.

225 Lincoln's crowded schedule . . . "the women come": Joshua F. Speed to AL, September 22, 1859, Lincoln Papers.

225 "Your visit to Ohio . . . in your favor": Samuel Galloway to AL, October 13, 1859, Lincoln Papers.

225 "We must take . . . are my choice": Samuel Galloway to AL, July 23, 1859, Lincoln Papers.

225 "to hedge against . . . we shall disagree": AL to Schuyler Colfax, July 6, 1859, in *CW*, III, pp. 390–91.

226 Colfax appreciated . . . "throughout the Union": Schuyler Colfax to AL, July 14, 1859, Lincoln Papers.

226 "with foolish pikes": Stephen Vincent Benét, *John Brown's Body* (New York: Henry Holt & Co., 1927; 1955), p. 52.

226 John Brown at Harpers Ferry: See chapter 19 of Stephen B. Oates, *To Purge This Land with Blood: A Biography of John Brown* (New York: Harper & Row, 1970), pp. 290–306.

226 "I am waiting . . . & of humanity": John Brown to his family, November 30, 1859, quoted in Oswald Garrison Villard, *John Brown, 1800–1859: A Biography Fifty Years After* (Boston and New York: Houghton Mifflin, 1910), p. 551.

226 the dignity . . . eloquence of his statements: Villard, *John Brown, 1800–1859*, pp. 538–39.

226 His death . . . "resolutions were adopted": Potter, *The Impending Crisis, 1848–1861*, p. 378.

226 "sent a shiver of fear . . . woman, and child": *Press and Tribune*, Chicago, October 22, 1859.

227 "Harper's Ferry . . . dissolution must ensue": *Richmond Enquirer*, November 25, 1859.

227 "like a great . . . that abyss": Craven, *The Growth of Southern Nationalism*, p. 309.

227 "Weird John Brown": Herman Melville, "The Portent," in *Battle-Pieces and Aspects of the War*, reprinted in *The Poems of Herman Melville*, rev. edn., ed. Douglas Robillard (Kent, Ohio, and London: Kent State University Press, 2000), p. 53.

227 "I do not exaggerate . . . in great numbers": Robert Bunch, December 9, 1859, quoted in Laura A. White, "The South in the 1850's as Seen by British Consuls," *Journal of Southern History* I (February 1935), p. 44.

227 "for seditious . . . in a good cause": Editor's description of *St. Louis News* article of November 23, 1859, pasted in entry of November 23, 1859, in *The Diary of Edward Bates, 1859–1866*, p. 65.

227 "the natural fruits . . . his subordinates": *Charleston [S.C.] Mercury*, December 16, 1859.

227 "one hundred gentlemen" . . . and Colfax: Advertisement by "Richmond," quoted in Seward, *Seward at Washington . . . 1846–1861*, p. 440.

227 "The first overt act . . . the Shenandoah": *NYH*, October 19, 1859.

228 "necessary and just": WHS, "The State of the Country," February 29, 1860, in *Works of William H. Seward*, Vol. IV, p. 637.

228 "seeking to plunge . . . universal condemnation": *Albany Evening Journal*, October 19, 1859.

228 "the wild extravagance . . . a madman": Entry of October 25, 1859, in *The Diary of Edward Bates, 1859–1866*, pp. 50–51.

228 He discussed the incident . . . "his [dagger]": Entry of November 21, 1859, in ibid., p. 63.

228 "for a household . . . attempted to do": Janet Chase Hoyt, "A Woman's Memories. Salmon P. Chase's Home Life," *NYTrib*, February 15, 1891.

228 Lincoln was back on the campaign trail: Baringer, *Lincoln's Rise to Power*, p. 124; entry for December 2, 1859, *Lincoln Day by Day*, Vol. II, pp. 266–67.

228 "the attempt . . . electioneering dodge": "Second Speech at Leavenworth, Kansas," December 5, 1859, synopsis of speech printed in the *Leavenworth Times*, December 6, 1859, in *CW*, III, p. 503.

228 "make the gallows . . . the cross": Ralph Waldo Emerson, "Courage," November 7, 1859, lecture in Boston, as reported by the *NYTrib*, quoted in John McAleer, *Ralph Waldo Emerson: Days of Encounter* (Boston and Toronto: Little, Brown, 1984), p. 532.

228 "great courage" . . . "rare unselfishness": Elwood *Free Press* on AL, "Speech at Elwood, Kansas," December 1 [November 30?], 1859, in *CW*, III, p. 496.

228 "that cannot . . . think himself right": AL, "Speech at Leavenworth, Kansas," December 3, 1859, in ibid., p. 502.

228 Republican National Committee at Astor House: Luthin, *The First Lincoln Campaign*, pp. 20–21.

229 "attach more consequence": AL to Norman B. Judd, December 14, 1859, in *CW*, III, p. 509.

229 "good neutral ground . . . an even chance": Archie Jones, "The 1860 Republican Convention," transcript of Chicago station WAAF radio broadcast, May 16, 1960, Chicago Historical Society, Chicago, Ill.

229 "carefully kept . . . on the nomination": Whitney, *Lincoln the Citizen*, Vol. I, p. 285.

229 "promised that . . . furnished free": *Press and Tribune*, Chicago, December 27, 1859.

229 Chicago beat St. Louis by a single vote: Luthin, *The First Lincoln Campaign*, p. 21.

229 "a cheap excursion . . . of the State": Whitney, *Lincoln the Citizen*, Vol. I, p. 285.
229 "I like the place . . . take exception to it": John Bigelow to WHS, January 18, 1860, reel 59, Seward Papers.
229 "Had the convention . . . been the nominee": Charles Gibson, "Edward Bates," *Missouri Historical Society Collections* II (January 1900), p. 55.
229 "there is not . . . not much of me": AL to Jesse W. Fell, December 20, 1859, in *CW*, III, p. 511.
229 "a wild region . . . in the woods": AL, "Autobiography by Abraham Lincoln, enclosed with Lincoln to Jesse W. Fell," December 20, 1859, in ibid., p. 511.
229 "If any thing . . . written by myself": AL to Jesse W. Fell, December 20, 1859, in ibid., p. 511.
230 he received an invitation: James A. Briggs to AL, October 12, 1859, Lincoln Papers; Harold Holzer, *Lincoln at Cooper Union: The Speech That Made Abraham Lincoln President* (New York: Simon & Schuster, 2004), p. 10.
230 "His clothes were travel-stained . . . for Monday night": Henry C. Bowen, paraphrased in Henry B. Rankin, *Intimate Character Sketches of Abraham Lincoln* (Philadelphia and London: J. B. Lippincott Co., 1924), pp. 179–80.
230 "Well, B. . . . as a man ought to want": "Recollections of Mr. McCormick," in Wilson, *Intimate Memories of Lincoln*, p. 251 (quote); Holzer, *Lincoln at Cooper Union*, p. 86. Holzer identifies "B." as Mayson Brayman.
230 Lincoln paid a visit . . . "shorten [his] neck": AL, quoted in James D. Horan, *Mathew Brady: Historian with a Camera* (New York: Crown Publishers, 1955), p. 31. For portrait, see plate 93 in Horan.
230 weather and attendance: Thomas, *Abraham Lincoln*, p. 202; Holzer, *Lincoln at Cooper Union*, pp. 103, 303 n55.
230 "this western man": Rankin, *Intimate Character Sketches of Abraham Lincoln*, p. 173.
231 Lincoln's appearance: Herndon and Weik, *Herndon's Life of Lincoln*, p. 369.
231 "one of the legs . . . longer than his sleeves": Russell H. Conwell, "Personal Glimpses of Celebrated Men and Women," quoted in Wayne Whipple, *The Story-Life of Lincoln. A Biography Composed of Five Hundred True Stories Told by Abraham Lincoln and His Friends* (Philadelphia: J. C. Winston Co., 1908), p. 308.
231 had labored to craft his address: Rankin, *Intimate Character Sketches of Abraham Lincoln*, pp. 174–75; Holzer, *Lincoln at Cooper Union*, pp. 50–53.
231 *"Our fathers . . . protection a necessity"*: AL, "Address at Cooper Institute, New York City," February 27, 1860, in *CW*, III, pp. 522, 535.
231 a "hue and cry . . . never can be reversed": AL, "Temperance Address delivered before the Springfield Washington Temperance Society," February 22, 1842, in *CW*, I, p. 273.
231 Cooper Union speech: AL, "Address at Cooper Institute, New York City," February 27, 1860, in *CW*, III, pp. 522–50, esp. 537, 538, 547, 550.
232 erupted in thunderous applause: Baringer, *Lincoln's Rise to Power*, pp. 158–59.
232 Briggs predicted . . . "have heard tonight": James Briggs, quoted in Holzer, *Lincoln at Cooper Union*, p. 147.
232 "When I came out . . . 'since St. Paul' ": Unknown observer, quoted in ibid., p. 146.
232 undertaking an exhausting tour: See copies of Lincoln's speeches in Rhode Island and New Hampshire, in *CW*, III, pp. 550–54, and speeches in Connecticut, *CW*, IV, pp. 2–30; Holzer, *Lincoln at Cooper Union*, pp. 176–77.
232 He was forced to decline . . . "before the fall elections": AL to Isaac Pomeroy, March 3, 1860, in *CW*, III, p. 554.
232 "being within my calculation . . . ideas in print": AL to MTL, March 4, 1860, in ibid., p. 555.
232 Lincoln first met Gideon Welles: J. Doyle DeWitt, *Lincoln in Hartford* (privately printed: n.d.), p. 5; John Niven, *Gideon Welles: Lincoln's Secretary of the Navy* (New York: Oxford University Press, 1973), pp. 287, 289.
232 Gideon Welles's appearance and career: John T. Morse, Introduction, *Diary of Gideon Welles: Secretary of the Navy Under Lincoln and Johnson*, Vol. I: *1861–March 30, 1864* (Boston and New York: Houghton Mifflin/The Riverside Press, 1911), pp. xvii–xxi; Richard S. West, Jr., *Gideon Welles: Lincoln's Navy Department* (Indianapolis and New York: Bobbs-Merrill, 1943).
232 "the party of the Southern slaveocracy": Morse, Introduction, *Diary of Gideon Welles* (1911 edn.), p. xix.
233 had settled on Chase . . . "very expensive rulers": West, *Gideon Welles*, pp. 78–79, 81 (quote p. 78).
233 Lincoln and Welles spent several hours: DeWitt, *Lincoln in Hartford*, p. 5; Niven, *Gideon Welles*, p. 289.
233 the Hartford speech: AL, "Speech at New Haven, Connecticut," March 6, 1860, in *CW*, IV, p. 18.
233 "as if the people . . . out loud": James Russell Lowell, "Abraham Lincoln," in *The Writings of James Russell Lowell*, Vol. V, *Political Essays* (Boston: Houghton Mifflin, 1892), p. 208.
234 "introduced the Trojan horse": WHS, "Admission of Kansas. Speech of Hon. W. H. Seward, of New York, In the Senate, April 9, 1856," *Appendix to the Congressional Globe*, 34th Cong., 1st sess., p. 405.
234 Lincoln met with Welles again: "The Career of Gideon Welles," typescript manuscript draft, Henry B. Learned Papers, reel 36, Welles Papers; Hendrick, *Lincoln's War Cabinet*, p. 78.
234 "This orator . . . in his logic": GW's editorial in *Hartford Evening Press*, quoted in West, *Gideon Welles*, p. 81.
234 "I have been sufficiently . . . and learned men": Rev. J. P. Gulliver article in *New York Independent*, September 1, 1864, quoted in Carpenter, *Six Months at the White House*, p. 311.
234 "I think your chance . . . man in the country": James A. Briggs, "Narrative of James A. Briggs, Esq.," *New York Evening Post*, August 16, 1867, reprinted in *An Authentic Account of Hon. Abraham Lincoln, Being Invited to give an Address in Cooper Institute, N.Y., February 27, 1860* (Putnam, Conn.: privately printed, 1915), n.p.
234 "When I was East . . . to the best": AL, quoted in Briggs, "Narrative of James A. Briggs, Esq."
234 At the end of January 1859: Lyman Trumbull to AL, January 29, 1859, Lincoln Papers.
234 "Any effort . . . a rival of yours": AL to Lyman Trumbull, February 3, 1859, in *CW*, III, pp. 355–56.
235 "A word now . . . suggestions of this sort": AL to Lyman Trumbull, April 29, 1860, in *CW*, IV, p. 46.
235 Lincoln's effort to defuse . . . Judd and Wentworth: Don E. Fehrenbacher, *Chicago Giant: A Biography of "Long John" Wentworth* (Madison, Wisc.: American History Research Center, 1957), pp. 163, 169–74.
235 Wentworth would drag out . . . "at Lincoln's expense": Note 1, accompanying transcript of AL to Norman B. Judd, December 9, 1859, Lincoln Papers (quote); Fehrenbacher, *Chicago Giant*, pp. 169–70.

235 Lincoln hastened to reassure . . . "go uncontradicted": AL to Norman B. Judd, December 9, 1859, in *CW*, III, p. 505.

235 Judd brought a libel suit . . . tried to retain Lincoln: See note 1 provided with John Wentworth to AL, November 28, 1859, Lincoln Papers; Fehrenbacher, *Chicago Giant*, pp. 170–72.

235 "very reason . . . keeping up a quarrel": John Wentworth to AL, December 21, 1859, Lincoln Papers.

235 he did help to mediate: Don E. Fehrenbacher, "The Judd-Wentworth Feud," *Journal of the Illinois State Historical Society* XLV (Autumn 1952), pp. 203, 204.

235 "I am not . . . end of the vineyard?": AL to Norman B. Judd, February 9, 1860, in *CW*, III, p. 517.

236 a resounding editorial: See Baringer, *Lincoln's Rise to Power*, pp. 148–50.

236 "You saw what . . . Was it satisfactory?": Norman B. Judd to AL, February 21, 1860, Lincoln Papers.

236 "That Abraham Lincoln . . . a unit for him": Baringer, *Lincoln's Rise to Power*, p. 186.

236 "what is to be . . . reverse the decree": MTL interview, September 1866, in *HI*, p. 360 n4.

CHAPTER 8: SHOWDOWN IN CHICAGO

Page

237 Forty thousand visitors: Tarbell, *The Life of Abraham Lincoln*, Vol. I, p. 344: *Buffalo Morning Express*, May 16, 1860, David Davis Papers, Chicago Historical Society, Chicago, Ill. [hereafter Davis Papers, ICHi].

237 trains . . . carried the delegates: Baringer, *Lincoln's Rise to Power*, p. 212.

237 youngest political party . . . fastest-growing city: Jones, "The 1860 Republican Convention."

237 crowds gathered . . . "swung their hats": *Press and Tribune*, Chicago, May 15, 1860.

237 the one that began its journey: *Press and Tribune*, Chicago, May 12, 1860.

237 "when 'a mile a minute' . . . in their boots": *Press and Tribune*, Chicago, May 16, 1860.

237 prizefighters hired "to keep the peace . . . broken heads": Clark, "Lincoln's Nomination As Seen By a Young Girl," *Putnam's*, p. 537.

237 "such refreshments . . . among the opponents": *Buffalo Morning Express*, May 15, 1860, Davis Papers, ICHi.

237 "almost ridiculous": Anonymous writer, quoted in *As Others See Chicago: Impressions of Visitors, 1673–1933*, ed. Bessie Louise Pierce (Chicago: University of Chicago Press, 1933), p. 151.

237 "growth is . . . a word": James Stirling, quoted in ibid., p. 123.

238 "a military post and fur station": *A Guide to the City of Chicago* (Chicago: Zell & Co., 1868), pp. 32–33.

238 population of more than a hundred thousand: Thomas, *Abraham Lincoln*, p. 207.

238 "the first grain . . . all of Europe": *A Strangers' and Tourists' Guide to the City of Chicago* (Chicago: Relig. Philo. Pub. Assoc., 1866), p. 24.

238 "the first lumber-market in the world": Anonymous writer, quoted in *As Others See Chicago*, p. 151.

238 "miles of wharves . . . pursuit of trade": *A Strangers' and Tourists' Guide to the City of Chicago*, p. 19.

238 a bold decision to elevate every building: Anonymous writer, quoted in *As Others See Chicago*, pp. 157–58.

238 "Our city has been chosen" . . . Lavish preparations: *Press and Tribune*, Chicago, May 12, 1860.

238 "A most magically . . . the eager crowd": *Press and Tribune*, Chicago, May 15, 1860.

238 Accommodations, restaurants: Baringer, *Lincoln's Rise to Power*, pp. 212–13; *Press and Tribune*, Chicago, May 9, 14, and 17, 1860.

238 The most popular luncheon: *Chicago Daily Evening Journal*, May 15, 1860, Davis Papers, ICHi.

238 As packed trains continued . . . to forty thousand: *Buffalo Morning Express*, May 15, 1860, Davis Papers, ALPLM; Baringer, *Lincoln's Rise to Power*, p. 222.

238 "I thought . . . some popular eruption": *Daily [Ind.] Journal*, May 17, 1860, Davis Papers, ICHi.

239 "with a zest . . . unfeeling bosom": *Press and Tribune*, Chicago, May 17, 1860.

239 "The city is thronged . . . shunned and condemned": *Chicago Daily Evening Journal*, May 15, 1860.

239 If this new party . . . the presidency: Luthin, *The First Lincoln Campaign*, p. 140.

239 "who crowded . . . standing room": *Chicago Daily Evening Journal*, May 16, 1860, Davis Papers, ICHi.

239 When the big doors . . . date for the afternoon: Halstead, *Three Against Lincoln*, pp. 147–48; Baringer, *Lincoln's Rise to Power*, pp. 246–47; Jones, "The 1860 Republican Convention"; Clark, "Lincoln's Nomination As Seen By a Young Girl," *Putnam's*, p. 537 (quote).

239 Exactly at noon . . . officially began: *Press and Tribune*, Chicago, May 17, 1860.

240 "no body of men . . . in [their] faith": Governor Morgan, quoted in Oldroyd, *Lincoln's Campaign*, pp. 27–28; *Press and Tribune*, Chicago, May 17, 1860.

240 an inclusive platform . . . a two-thirds vote: Halstead, *Three Against Lincoln*, pp. 156–58, 159.

240 "The great body . . . cardinal doctrines": Pike, "Mr. Seward's Defeat," May 20, 1860, from *NYTrib*, reprinted in Pike, *First Blows of the Civil War*, p. 517.

240 a move was made to proceed: Halstead, *Three Against Lincoln*, pp. 158, 159, 161; *Press and Tribune*, Chicago, May 18, 1860.

240 A Committee of Twelve . . . "consumed in talking": Charles P. Smith, "The Nomination of Lincoln," undated pamphlet from the Collections of the New Jersey State Library, Archives & History Division, Trenton, N.J., copy in Davis Papers, ICHi.

240 Greeley at convention: Van Deusen, *Horace Greeley*, pp. 245–48; Smith, "The Nomination of Lincoln."

241 "cannot concentrate . . . will be nominated": May 17 telegram from Horace Greeley, reprinted in *NYTrib*, May 18, 1860.

241 "every one of the . . . freely as water": Halstead, *Three Against Lincoln*, pp. 160–61.

241 "Four years ago . . . courage and confidence": TW, quoted in Addison G. Procter, *Lincoln and the Convention of*

1860: An Address Before the Chicago Historical Society, April 4, 1918 (Chicago: Chicago Historical Society, 1918), pp. 6–7.

241 "I suppose . . . confirm what I say": Horace Greeley, quoted in Procter, *Lincoln and the Convention of 1860*, p. 8.

242 "each of whom . . . Greeley had said": Ibid.

242 "I know my people well . . . slavery where it is": Henry Lane, quoted in ibid., pp. 12–13.

242 few were aware of his estrangement: Henry J. Raymond, quoted in Barnes, *Memoir of Thurlow Weed*, p. 274.

242 "While professing so high . . . had his revenge": *Auburn [N.Y.] Daily Advertiser*, May 31, 1860.

242 "In all candor . . . to the same effect": Koerner, *Memoirs of Gustave Koerner*, Vol. II, pp. 88–89.

242 He was much too conservative . . . officially enlisted: *Missouri Republican*, St. Louis, Mo., May 19, 1860; Potter, *The Impending Crisis, 1848–1861*, p. 427.

243 "If united . . . and the West": Halstead, *Three Against Lincoln*, p. 148.

243 Any hope of persuading . . . "promote his interest": John McLean, quoted in Luthin, *The First Lincoln Campaign*, p. 146.

243 "There was no unity . . . pitiable to behold": Statement of Willard Warner, paraphrased in *Columbus [Ohio] Gazette*, May 25, 1860.

243 "If the Ohio delegation . . . [been] relied upon": Francis M. Wright to SPC, May 21, 1860, reel 13, Chase Papers.

243 "There are lots . . . lukewarm friends": Erastus Hopkins to SPC, May 17, 1860, reel 13, Chase Papers.

243 "Men gather . . . the big bell rings": Halstead, *Three Against Lincoln*, pp. 143, 163, 149–50.

244 "You know how . . . no positive objection": AL to Richard M. Corwine, May 2, 1860, in *CW*, IV, p. 47.

244 "to antagonize no one": King, *Lincoln's Manager*, p. 136.

244 "relative ability . . . man who could win": Stampp, "The Republican National Convention of 1860," in Stampp, *The Imperiled Union*, p. 160.

244 "No men ever worked . . . two hours a night": Leonard Swett to Josiah Drummond, May 27, 1860, Davis Papers, ALPLM.

245 "Most of them . . . political morality": Whitney, *Lincoln the Citizen*, Vol. 1, p. 266.

245 "typically methodical way": King, *Lincoln's Manager*, p. 135 (quote); see also p. 136, and chapter 11 generally.

245 "a drawback . . . Gov. Seward": AL, quoted in Luthin, *The First Lincoln Campaign*, p. 145.

245 "It all worked . . . was Indiana": Leonard Swett to Josiah H. Drummond, May 27, 1860, quoted in Oldroyd, *Lincoln's Campaign*, p. 71.

245 "the whole of Indiana . . . to get": AL to Richard M. Corwine, May 2, 1860, in *CW*, IV, p. 47 (quote); AL to Cyrus M. Allen, May 1, 1860, in ibid., p. 46.

245 Claims have been made . . . Caleb Smith: Baringer, *Lincoln's Rise to Power*, pp. 214–15.

245 No deal was needed: Donald, *Lincoln*, p. 249.

245 Indiana . . . to back Lincoln: John D. Defrees to Schuyler Colfax, quoted in Hollister, *Life of Schuyler Colfax*, p. 148.

245 Committee of Twelve . . . "general good of the party": Smith, "The Nomination of Lincoln," Davis Papers, ICHi.

246 Davis had previously . . . might be procured: Whitney, *Lincoln the Citizen*, Vol. I, p. 289.

246 *"Make no . . . bind me"*: AL, Endorsement on the Margin of the *Missouri Democrat*, May 17, 1860, in *CW*, IV, p. 50.

246 "Everybody was mad . . . 'he must ratify it' ": Whitney, *Lincoln the Citizen*, Vol. I, p. 289.

246 The Blairs had supposedly promised: Clay, *The Life of Cassius Marcellus Clay*, pp. 244–46; Luthin, *The First Lincoln Campaign*, p. 68.

246 "oceans of money": Halstead, *Three Against Lincoln*, p. 162.

246 "get every member . . . appointment": King, *Lincoln's Manager*, p. 140.

246 "My assurance to them . . . as much as possible": Leonard Swett to AL, May 20, 1860, Davis Papers, ALPLM.

247 for a celebratory march . . . "a little too far": Halstead, *Three Against Lincoln*, p. 164.

247 had manufactured duplicate tickets: Luthin, *The First Lincoln Campaign*, pp. 160–61.

247 "it was part of . . . the Convention": Swett to Drummond, May 27, 1860, quoted in Oldroyd, *Lincoln's Campaign*, p. 72.

247 friends and supporters from all over the state: Luthin, *The First Lincoln Campaign*, pp. 160–61.

247 "by a deafening shout": Swett to Drummond, May 27, 1860, quoted in Oldroyd, *Lincoln's Campaign*, p. 72.

247 "loud and long": *Albany Evening Journal*, May 18, 1860.

247 "appalled us a little": Swett to Drummond, May 27, 1860, quoted in Oldroyd, *Lincoln's Campaign*, p. 72.

247 "If Mr. Seward's name . . . far and wide": *NYT*, May 21, 1860.

247 "tremendous applause . . . Lincoln's favor": Henry Raymond article, quoted in Barnes, *Memoir of Thurlow Weed*, p. 276.

247 "cold when compared": *NYT*, May 21, 1860.

247 "trial of lungs": *Albany Evening Journal*, May 18, 1860; *NYH*, May 19, 1860; *NYT*, May 19, 1860.

247 "The shouting was . . . infernal intensity": Halstead, *Three Against Lincoln*, p. 165.

247 "five thousand . . . the scene unnoticed": Swett to Drummond, May 27, 1860, quoted in Oldroyd, *Lincoln's Campaign*, p. 72.

247 "Abe Lincoln . . . let us ballot!": *NYH*, May 19, 1860; *Buffalo Commercial Advertiser*, May 19, 1860, Davis Papers, ICHi.

248 "This was not . . . it had its weight": Swett to Drummond, May 27, 1860, quoted in Oldroyd, *Lincoln's Campaign*, pp. 72–73.

248 results of the first ballot: Halstead, *Three Against Lincoln*, p. 167.

248 "This solid vote . . . it was given": Ibid., p. 166.

248 "no pivotal state . . . been delivered": Cain, *Lincoln's Attorney General*, p. 112.

248 results of the second ballot: Halstead, *Three Against Lincoln*, p. 169.

248 "startling . . . of thunder": Barnes, *Memoir of Thurlow Weed*, p. 264.

248 results of the third ballot: Halstead, *Three Against Lincoln*, p. 170.

249 "There was a pause . . . ticks of a watch": Ibid., p. 171.

249 "A profound stillness fell upon the Wigwam": Unidentified spectator, quoted in Allan Nevins, *Ordeal of the Union*. Vol. II: *The Emergence of Lincoln, part II, Prologue to Civil War, 1857–1861*, new introduction by James M. McPherson (New York: Collier Books, Macmillan Publishing Co., 1992), p. 260.

249 "rose to their feet . . . and again": *Press and Tribune*, Chicago, May 19, 1860.

249 "Great men . . . night of struggle": Clark, "Lincoln's Nomination As Seen By a Young Girl," *Putnam's*, p. 538.

249 he, too, could not restrain his tears: Taylor, *William Henry Seward*, p. 9.

249 "the great disappointment of his life": *Chicago Tribune*, July 14, 1878.

249 "her first . . . are themselves forgotten": Austin Blair, quoted in *Albany Evening Journal*, May 23, 1860, in Halstead, *Three Against Lincoln*, p. 173; Baringer, *Lincoln's Rise to Power*, p. 292; Carl Schurz "Speeches at the Chicago Convention," quoted in *Works of William H. Seward*, Vol. IV, p. 682.

249 "with the success . . . highest honor": Carl Schurz, "Speeches at the Chicago Convention," quoted in *Works of William H. Seward*, Vol. IV, p. 682.

249 "Mounting a table . . . clenched nervously": *NYT*, May 21, 1860.

249 "Gentlemen . . . Republican party: *Buffalo Commercial Advertiser*, May 19, 1860, Davis Papers, ICHi.

249 "the spectator . . . noble man indeed": *NYT*, May 21, 1860.

249 A man stationed on the roof . . . Cannons were fired: Halstead, *Three Against Lincoln*, pp. 171–72.

249 "between 20,000 . . . shouting at once": *Buffalo Commercial Advertiser*, May 19, 1860, Davis Papers, ICHi.

250 "The Press and Tribune . . . windows and doors": *Press and Tribune*, Chicago, May 19, 1860.

250 Seward received the news . . . "on the next ballot": Stanton, *Random Recollections*, pp. 215–16 (quote p. 216).

250 "rightly [judged] that . . . to bring": Seward, *Seward at Washington . . . 1846–1861*, p. 452.

250 turned "as pale as ashes": Stanton, *Random Recollections*, p. 216.

250 "that it was no ordinary . . . and irrevocable": Seward, *Seward at Washington . . . 1846–1861*, p. 452.

250 "The sad tidings . . . clouded brow": Stanton, *Random Recollections*, p. 216.

250 "of his sanguine . . . Few men can": Entry for May 19, 1860, Charles Francis Adams diary, reel 75.

250 "he took the blow . . . family and the world": Van Deusen, *William Henry Seward*, pp. 228, 229.

250 "Father told Mother . . . unselfish coolness": Entry for May 18, 1860, Fanny Seward diary, Seward Papers.

251 "No truer . . . nomination have fallen": WHS for the *Auburn Daily Advertiser*, in "Biographical Memoir of William H. Seward," *Works of William H. Seward*, Vol. IV, p. 79.

251 "You have my . . . light as my own": WHS to TW, May 18, 1860, quoted in Barnes, *Memoir of Thurlow Weed*, p. 270; WHS to TW, May 18, 1860, quoted in Seward, *Seward at Washington . . . 1846–1861*, p. 453.

251 in a public letter . . . "progress of that cause": WHS to the New York Republican Central Committee, quoted in Seward, *Seward at Washington . . . 1846–1861*, p. 454.

251 "It was only some months . . . cursing and swearing": Van Deusen, *William Henry Seward*, p. 229.

251 "When I remember . . . competition with his": SPC to Robert Hosea, June 5, 1860, reel 13, Chase Papers.

251 For years, Chase was racked: Blue, *Salmon P. Chase*, p. 126.

251 "adhesion of the . . . own State Convention": SPC to AL, misdated as May 17, 1860, Lincoln Papers.

251 Lincoln responded graciously: AL to SPC, May 26, 1860, in *CW*, IV, p. 53.

252 "While the victory . . . most profoundly": Schurz, *Reminiscences*, Vol. II, pp. 186–87.

252 "melancholy ceremony": *Daily Ohio Statesman*, Columbus, Ohio, May 19, 1860.

252 "As for me . . . I have ever known": EB to Horace Greeley, quoted in Hollister, *Life of Schuyler Colfax*, p. 148.

252 "Some of my friends . . . border slave states": Entry of May 19, 1860, in *The Diary of Edward Bates, 1859–1866*, pp. 129, 130–31.

253 Some claim . . . Others maintain: See Conkling, "How Mr. Lincoln Received the News," *Transactions* (1909), p. 65; Tarbell, *The Life of Abraham Lincoln*, Vol. I, p. 358; *Illinois State Register*, February 13, 1903.

253 "Mr. Lincoln . . . you are nominated": quoted in Tarbell, *The Life of Abraham Lincoln*, Vol. I, p. 358

253 office of the *Illinois State Journal*: Charles S. Zane interview, 1865–1866, in *HI*, p. 492; *Press and Tribune*, Chicago, May 22, 1860.

253 he "looked at it . . . all around": *Chicago Journal* correspondent, quoted in *Cincinnati Daily Commercial*, May 25, 1860.

253 "I knew . . . second ballot": AL, quoted in Donald, *Lincoln*, p. 250.

253 "My friends . . . at last had come": quoted in Tarbell, *The Life of Abraham Lincoln*, Vol. I, p. 358.

253 "the hearty western" . . . rotunda of the Capitol: "Ecarte" [John Hay], *Providence [R.I.] Journal*, May 26, 1860, reprinted in *Lincoln's Journalist: John Hay's Anonymous Writings for the Press, 1860–1864*, ed. Michael Burlingame (Carbondale and Edwardsville: Southern Illinois University Press, 1998), p. 1.

253 "the signal for immense . . . a great party": *Missouri Republican*, May 20, 1860.

253 "the fact of . . . of Lincoln": Halstead, *Three Against Lincoln*, p. 176.

253 "The leader of . . . against a leader": T. S. Verdi, "The Assassination of the Sewards," *The Republic* 1 (July 1873), pp. 289–90.

254 Some have pointed to luck . . . held in Chicago: See Fehrenbacher, *Prelude to Greatness*, p. 5; Alexander McClure, quoted in Taylor, *William Henry Seward*, p. 10.

254 "Had the Convention . . . nominated": Koerner, *Memoirs of Gustave Koerner*, Vol. II, p. 80.

254 Lincoln's team in Chicago played the game: Potter, *The Impending Crisis, 1848–1861*, pp. 427–28; Stampp, "The Republican National Convention of 1860," in Stampp, *The Imperiled Union*, pp. 155, 157–58.

254 Lincoln was the best prepared: Fehrenbacher, *Prelude to Greatness*, p. 2.
255 speeches possessed unmatched . . . moral strength: Miller, *Lincoln's Virtues*, pp. 397–401.
255 "his avoidance of extremes . . . off its balance": *Press and Tribune*, Chicago, May 16, 1860.
255 "comparatively unknown": Verdi, "The Assassination of the Sewards," *The Republic* (1873), p. 290.
255 "give no offence . . . their first love": AL to Samuel Galloway, March 24, 1860, in *CW*, IV, p. 34.
255 he had not made enemies: *Illinois State Journal*, Springfield, Ill., March 23, 1860.
256 "an ambition . . . overindulgence": Fehrenbacher, *Prelude to Greatness*, p. 161.

CHAPTER 9: "A MAN KNOWS HIS OWN NAME"

Page

257 "was received . . . so we adjourned": Entry for May 18, 1860, Charles Francis Adams diary, reel 75.
257 journals . . . "Abraham": *NYT*, May 21, 1860.
257 "it is but fair . . . his own name": *NYH*, June 5, 1860.
257 "It seems as if . . . 'Abraham' ": AL to George Ashmun, June 4, 1860, in *CW*, IV, p. 68.
257 "a third rate Western . . . clumsy jokes": *NYH*, May 19, 1860.
258 "Lincoln is the leanest . . . being ugly": *Houston Telegraph*, quoted in *NYTrib*, June 12, 1860.
258 "After him . . . be President?": *Charleston [S.C.] Mercury*, June 9, 1860, quoted in Emerson David Fite, *The First Presidential Campaign*, (New York: The Macmillan Company, 1911), p. 210.
258 "thrust aside . . . freesoil border-ruffian": *Charleston Mercury*, October 15, 1860.
258 "an illiterate partizan . . . negro equality": *Richmond Enquirer*, May 22, 1860.
258 Democratic National Convention in Charleston: See "The Charleston Convention," chapter 1 in Halstead, *Three Against Lincoln*, pp. 3–10.
258 "in less than sixty . . . of the seceders": Ibid., pp. 84, 87.
258 Baltimore convention: For a full discussion of the Democratic Convention that nominated Douglas, see "The National Democratic Convention at Baltimore," chapter 6 in ibid., pp. 185–264.
259 Breckinridge/Lane; Bell/Everett: For a discussion of the conventions that nominated Breckinridge and Bell, see "Institute Hall ('Seceders') Convention" and "The Constitutional Democratic Convention," respectively, chapters 7 and 2, in ibid., pp. 265–77, 111–17.
259 "The great democratic . . . of their own": Entry for June 23, 1860, Charles Francis Adams diary, reel 75.
259 "the chances were . . . fortunes a turn": AL to Anson G. Henry, July 4, 1860, in *CW*, IV, p. 82.
259 "Mr. Lincoln received . . . the great world": Schurz, *Reminiscences*, Vol. II, pp. 187–88.
260 "the prospects of . . . work with a will": *Autobiography of Thurlow Weed*, ed. Weed, p. 603.
260 apparent to both . . . Lincoln against Douglas: In Pennsylvania, the sole exception, Douglas would finish third to Lincoln and Breckinridge.
260 "Now what difference . . . between them": *Montgomery [Ala.] Daily Mail*, July 6, 1860, quoted in Craven, *The Growth of Southern Nationalism*, p. 342.
260 A Lincoln victory . . . such diverse constituencies: For an analysis of the multifaceted campaign in the North, see Luthin, *The First Lincoln Campaign*, passim; Miller, *Lincoln's Virtues*, pp. 465–67.
261 "*a mere printed circular . . . not to reply at all*": SPC to Lyman Trumbull, November 12, 1860, reel 14, Chase Papers.
261 "much chagrined . . . Mr. Abe Lincoln": *Journal of Commerce*, reprinted in *NYTrib*, June 27, 1860.
261 "Holding myself . . . stand ready": AL to SPC, May 26, 1860, in *CW*, IV, p. 53.
261 "first, that . . . of the people": *NYTrib*, October 25, 1860.
261 Browning called on Bates: Entry for May 31, 1860, in *The Diary of Edward Bates, 1859–1866*, p. 132; Cain, *Lincoln's Attorney General*, p. 115.
261 "declined to take the stump": Entry for May 31, 1860, in *The Diary of Edward Bates, 1859–1866*, p. 132.
261 "probably give offense . . . *Union party*": Entry for September 20, 1860, in ibid., p. 145.
261 "I give my opinion . . . in early life": EB, *Letter of Hon. Edward Bates, of Missouri, Indorsing Mr. Lincoln, and Giving His Reasons for Supporting the Chicago Nominees* (Washington, D.C.: Congressional Globe Office, 1860); EB to O. H. Browning, June 11, 1860, reprinted in "Political: Letter of Judge Bates, pledging his support to the Republican ticket," *NYT*, supplement, June 23, 1860.
262 "His character is . . . firm as Jackson": EB to Wyndham Robertson, November 3, 1860, quoted in Cain, *Lincoln's Attorney General*, p. 120.
262 "The campaign started . . . preside or attend": Procter, *Lincoln and the Convention of 1860*, p. 16.
262 "My personal feelings . . . a public act": CS to WHS, May 20, 1860, reel 59, Seward Papers.
262 "one & only one . . . nomination in '64": George Pomeroy to WHS, May 21, 1860, reel 59, Seward Papers.
262 "the suitable man . . . for mere expediency": William Mellen to FAS, May 21, 1860, reel 59, Seward Papers.
262 considered resigning immediately from the Senate: Van Deusen, *William Henry Seward*, p. 229.
262 "When I went out . . . at every corner": Seward, *Seward at Washington . . . 1846–1861*, pp. 453–54.
263 "give the malignants": Israel Washburn to WHS, May 19, 1860, reel 59, Seward Papers.
263 "in the character . . . response in my heart": WHS to FAS, May 30, 1860, quoted in Seward, *Seward at Washington . . . 1846–1861*, pp. 454–56.
263 "responsibility . . . shorter every day": WHS to home, June 13, 1860, quoted in ibid., p. 458.
263 "You have earned . . . reasonably claim": FAS to WHS, May 30, 1860, reel 114, Seward Papers.
263 "Your services . . . highest success": Charles Francis Adams to WHS, May 22, 1860, reel 59, Seward Papers.

263 "I am content . . . the public interest": WHS to TW, June 26, 1860, quoted in Seward, *Seward at Washington . . . 1846–1861*, p. 459.
264 "was about to take . . . depths of discouragement": Procter, *Lincoln and the Convention of 1860*, p. 16.
264 John Nicolay . . . "life ran down": Helen Nicolay, *Lincoln's Secretary: A Biography of John G. Nicolay* (New York: Longmans, Green & Co., 1949; Westport, Conn.: Greenwood Press, 1971), pp. vii (quote), 27, 34, 36.
264 "He sat down . . . could have desired": *Utica Morning Herald*, reprinted in *NYTrib*, July 9, 1860.
264 "can not only discuss . . . dress a deer-skin": *Missouri Democrat*, reprinted in *NYTrib*, September 29, 1860.
265 "an air of quiet . . . unflinchingly": *Utica Morning Herald*, reprinted in *NYTrib*, July 9, 1860.
265 "Ten thousand inquiries . . . create the necessity": *Press and Tribune*, Chicago, May 23, 1860.
265 "Whatever of awkwardness . . . of society": *New York Evening Post*, reprinted in *Albany Evening Journal*, May 24, 1860.
266 "a very handsome . . . sparkling talker": *Ohio State Journal*, Columbus, Ohio, May 29, 1860.
266 "a Man of the People": *NYTrib*, May 26, 1860, quoted in Nevins, *Ordeal of the Union*. Vol. II: *The Emergence of Lincoln, part II, Prologue to Civil War, 1857–1861*, p. 274.
266 "log-cabin, hard-cider": Samuel Eliot Morison and Henry Steele Commager, *The Growth of the American Republic*, 4th edn. (New York: Oxford University Press, 1930; 1950), p. 556.
266 "It has also afforded . . . be inspired": Ryland Fletcher, quoted in Luthin, *The First Lincoln Campaign*, p. 169.
266 a "nullity . . . a nullity anywhere": Quoted in Tarbell, *The Life of Abraham Lincoln*, Vol. I, p. 365.
266 "here is a stick . . . in 1825": *NYH*, October 20, 1860.
266 "it would be both . . . willingly say": AL to T. Apolion Cheney, August 14, 1860, in *CW*, IV, p. 93.
267 "Your letter . . . I write at all": AL to Leonard Swett, May 30, 1860, in *CW*, IV, p. 57.
267 "he would like . . . of being lynched": Luthin, *The First Lincoln Campaign*, p. 170.
267 the cohesion of the new Republican Party: Ibid., pp. 21–22.
267 "our adversaries . . . to the charge": AL to Abraham Jonas, July 21, 1860, in *CW*, IV, p. 86.
267 this election would not be determined . . . carefully addressed in the Republican Party platform: Luthin, *The First Lincoln Campaign*, pp. 13 (quote), 148–53.
268 an entourage: Seward, *Seward at Washington . . . 1846–1861*, p. 461; Van Deusen, *William Henry Seward*, pp. 232–33.
268 "cannons . . . 'Wide Awakes' ": Seward, *Seward at Washington . . . 1846–1861*, p. 461; Oldroyd, *Lincoln's Campaign*, pp. 104–07.
268 "Viewed from . . . in wild cheerings": "Springfield Correspondence, 9 August 1860," in Hay, *Lincoln's Journalist*, p. 6.
268 the "Chloroformers": Luthin, *The First Lincoln Campaign*, p. 174.
268 "procession of young men . . . carts and wagons": Entry for September 8, 1860, Charles Francis Adams diary, reel 75.
268 "All of this reminded . . . a gaping crowd": Ibid.
268 In St. Paul, Minnesota . . . steps of the Capitol: *Press and Tribune*, Chicago, September 24, 1860.
269 "without repetition . . . of the auditors": Fite, *The First Presidential Campaign*, p. 213.
269 "the whole population . . . Well, I ought to": Supplement to *NYT*, September 29, 1860.
269 "where, when . . . 'this tobacco question' ": Charles Francis Adams, Jr., *Charles Francis Adams, 1835–1915: An Autobiography, with a Memorial Address Delivered November 17, 1915, by Henry Cabot Lodge* (Boston and New York: Houghton Mifflin, 1916), pp. 61–62.
269 "integrity . . . grandest & highest": Israel Washburn, Jr., to WHS, November 14, 1860, reel 60, Seward Papers.
269 "I am sure . . . taken a-back by": Richard Blatchford to FAS, October 3, 1860, reel 60, Seward Papers.
270 "marveled more & more . . . by any American": CS to FAS, October 10, 1860, reel 60, Seward Papers.
270 "Yes Henry is . . . Is that the word": FAS to CS, September 5, 1860, reel 20, Sumner Papers.
270 "There was a rush . . . Seward was seated": *NYH*, October 2, 1860.
270 "was a revelation . . . out of place": Adams, Jr., *Charles Francis Adams, 1835–1915*, pp. 61, 64 (quote).
270 "Twelve years ago . . . believed that it would be": *NYH*, October 2, 1860.
270 Lincoln asked . . . "it already existed": King, *Lincoln's Manager*, p. 157.
270 Seward readily agreed . . . intercourse with the South: *NYT*, September 27, 1860; Van Deusen, *William Henry Seward*, p. 233.
270 "noisy throng . . . approaching greatness": Adams, Jr., *Charles Francis Adams, 1835–1915*, pp. 67–68.
271 "Remembering that Peter . . . I will not": AL to Lyman Trumbull, June 5, 1860, in *CW*, IV, p. 71.
271 a humorous fictional dialogue: AL, "Dialogue between Stephen A. Douglas and John C. Breckinridge," September 29, 1860, in ibid., pp. 123–24.
271 "I give the leave . . . in any respect": AL to William D. Kelley, October 13, 1860, in ibid., p. 127.
271 "for your face . . . like whiskers": Grace Bedell to AL, October 15, 1860, in ibid., p. 130.
271 "As to the whiskers . . . begin it now?": AL to Grace Bedell, October 19, 1860, in ibid., p. 129.
271 "Election news . . . heir apparent": "Springfield Correspondence, 7 January 1861," in Hay, *Lincoln's Journalist*, p. 17.
271 biased . . . prospects in each state: AL to John Pettit, September 14, 1860, in *CW*, IV, p. 115.
271 "the dry, and irksome . . . monster meetings": AL to Henry Wilson, September 1, 1860, in ibid., p. 109.
271 Schurz's "excellent plan . . . than yourself": AL to Carl Schurz, June 18, 1860, in ibid., p. 78.
272 He urged Caleb Smith . . . an Indiana victory: AL to Caleb Smith, [July 23], 1860, in ibid., pp. 87–88.
272 "Ascertain . . . commit me to nothing": AL, "Instructions for John G. Nicolay," [c. July 16, 1860], in ibid., p. 83.

272 "Before this reaches . . . into the news-papers": AL to Simon Cameron, August 6, 1860, in ibid., p. 91.

272 Cameron replied . . . writings: Simon Cameron to AL, August 1, 1860, Lincoln Papers.

272 "I am slow . . . present & future only": AL to John M. Pomeroy, August 31, 1860, in *CW*, IV, p. 103.

272 "Write Mr. Casey . . . in that matter": AL to Leonard Swett, July 16, 1860, in ibid., p. 84.

272 "After all . . . Sebastopol we must take": John Z. Goodrich, quoted in Luthin, *The First Lincoln Campaign*, p. 205.

273 "such a result . . . must not allow it": AL to Hannibal Hamlin, September 4, 1860, in *CW*, IV, p. 110.

273 "intimating that Douglas . . . Please write me": AL to James F. Simmons, August 17, 1860, in ibid., p. 97.

273 "tomorrow is . . . of the Country": David Davis, quoted in King, *Lincoln's Manager*, p. 158.

273 "he was trying . . . the presidential Election": Ward Hill Lamon to AL, October 10, 1860, Lincoln Papers.

273 "We are all in . . . be the next Pres't": David Davis to Sarah Davis, October 12, 1860, Davis Papers, ALPLM.

273 "I never was better . . . any trouble": David Davis to Sarah Davis, October 15, 1860, Davis Papers, ALPLM.

273 With pride . . . "have the trial": MTL to Hannah Shearer, October 20, 1860, in Turner and Turner, *Mary Todd Lincoln*, p. 66.

274 Douglas had been barnstorming . . . to the South: Johannsen, *Stephen A. Douglas*, pp. 778–81, 786–97 (quote p. 781).

274 "the first presidential . . . in person": Paul F. Boller, Jr., *Presidential Campaigns* (New York and Oxford: Oxford University Press, 1984), p. 101.

274 "Mr. Lincoln is the next . . . I will go South": Stephen A. Douglas, quoted in Johannsen, *Stephen A. Douglas*, pp. 797–98.

274 "finest hour": Nevins, *Ordeal of the Union*. Vol. II: *The Emergence of Lincoln, part II, Prologue to Civil War, 1857–1861*, p. 290.

274 "I believe there is . . . must be inaugurated": Stephen A. Douglas, quoted in Johannsen, *Stephen A. Douglas*, p. 800.

274 "The cardinal error . . . danger of secession": Nevins, *Ordeal of the Union*. Vol. II: *The Emergence of Lincoln, part II, Prologue to Civil War, 1857–1861*, p. 305.

274 "we all dwelt in a fool's Paradise": Adams, Jr., *Charles Francis Adams, 1835–1915*, p. 69.

274 "a sort of political . . . frighten the North": Donn Piatt, *Memories of the Men Who Saved the Union* (New York and Chicago: Belford, Clarke & Co., 1887), p. 30.

274 "people of the South . . . of the government": AL to John B. Fry, August 15, 1860, in *CW*, IV, p. 95.

274 "the cry of disunion . . . 'sway Northern sentiment' ": Nashville *Union and American*, November 11, 1860, quoted and paraphrased in Craven, *The Growth of Southern Nationalism*, pp. 352–53.

275 shrugged . . . belligerent politicians: *Press and Tribune*, Chicago, October 3, 1860.

275 "they cry out . . . Nobody!": WHS, "Political Equality the National Idea, Saint Paul, September 18, 1860," in *Works of William H. Seward*, Vol. IV, p. 344.

275 "misrepresentations . . . triumph of our party": FB, et al., to AL, October 31, 1860, Lincoln Papers.

275 Even John Breckinridge . . . splitting up the Union: Craven, *The Growth of Southern Nationalism*, p. 341.

275 "I have a good deal of news . . . it *may* be delusive": AL to John Pettit, September 14, 1860, in *CW*, IV, p. 115.

275 "there will be the most . . . great adroitness": AL to TW, August 17, 1860, in ibid., pp. 97–98.

276 "Can you afford . . . finish the work": TW to WHS, October 25, 1860, reel 60, Seward Papers.

276 "the whole audience . . . tumultuous cheering": *NYTrib*, November 3, 1860.

276 "to stir whatever . . . the populace": *NYTrib*, November 10, 1860.

276 "was chatting . . . than the Presidency": Samuel R. Weed, "Hearing the Returns with Mr. Lincoln," *New York Times Magazine*, February 14, 1932, p. 8.

276 "the candidate . . . for his own electors": William H. Herndon and Jesse W. Weik, *Herndon's Lincoln: The True Story of a Great Life*, Vol. III (Springfield, Ill.: Herndon's Lincoln Publishing Co., 1888), p. 467.

276 "who welcomed him . . . the Court room": [JGN to TB?], November 6, 1860, container 2, Nicolay Papers.

276 wild "burst of enthusiasm": *NYTrib*, November 10, 1860.

276 "He said he had . . . read to the crowd": *Missouri Democrat*, reprinted in *Cincinnati Daily Commercial*, November 9, 1860.

277 "seemed to understand . . . with previous elections": Weed, "Hearing the Returns with Mr. Lincoln," *NYT Magazine*, p. 8.

277 gathered at the telegraph office: *Missouri Democrat*, reprinted in *Cincinnati Daily Commercial*, November 9, 1860.

277 "The news would come . . . any hurry to hear it": Weed, "Hearing the Returns with Mr. Lincoln," *NYT Magazine*, p. 9.

277 "We have made steady . . . victory has been won": Simeon Draper, quoted in ibid.

277 "Uncle Abe . . . I know it": Lyman Trumbull, quoted in ibid.

277 "Not too fast . . . may not be over yet": Ibid.

277 a "victory" supper: Oates, *With Malice Toward None*, p. 206.

277 "Don't wait . . . before 10 o'clock": TW, quoted in Luthin, *The First Lincoln Campaign*, p. 218.

278 "a very happy man . . . such circumstances?": AL, quoted by Henry C. Bowen, *Recollections*, p. 31, reprinted in Whipple, *The Story-Life of Lincoln*, p. 345.

278 "Mary . . . *we are elected!*": Henry C. Bowen, "Recollections of Abraham Lincoln," *The Independent*, April 4, 1895, p. 4.

CHAPTER 10: "AN INTENSIFIED CROSSWORD PUZZLE"

Page

279 "The excitement . . . was upon him": GW to Isaac N. Arnold, November 27, 1872, folder 1, Isaac Newton Arnold Papers, Chicago Historical Society.

279 the citizens of Springfield . . . to their homes: William E. Baringer, *A House Dividing: Lincoln as President Elect* (Springfield, Ill.: Abraham Lincoln Association, 1945), p. 6.

280 "I began at once . . . the burden": Entry for August 15, 1862, *Diary of Gideon Welles: Secretary of the Navy Under Lincoln and Johnson*. Vol. I: *1861–March 30, 1864*, ed. Howard K. Beale (New York: W. W. Norton, 1960), p. 82.

280 "into its usual quietness": JGN to TB, November 11, 1860, container 2, Nicolay Papers.

280 "This was on . . . finally selected": Entry for August 15, 1862, *Welles diary*, Vol. I (1960 edn.), p. 82.

280 On a blank card . . . a former Whig: Enclosure in Kinsley S. Bingham, Solomon Foot, and Zachariah Chandler to AL, January 21, 1861, Lincoln Papers; Donald, *Lincoln*, pp. 261–62.

280 "the mad scramble": Harry J. Carman and Reinhard H. Luthin, *Lincoln and the Patronage* (New York: Columbia University Press, 1943; Gloucester, Mass.: Peter Smith, 1964), p. 3.

280 "muddy boots . . . often ringing laughter": Henry Villard, *Lincoln on the Eve of '61: A Journalist's Story*, ed. Harold G. and Oswald Garrison Villard (New York: A. A. Knopf, 1941; Westport, Conn.: Greenwood Press, 1974), pp. 15, 13.

280 "showed remarkable tact . . . always perfect": Henry Villard, *Memoirs of Henry Villard, Journalist and Financier, 1835–1900*. Vol. I: *1835–1862* (Boston and New York: Houghton Mifflin, 1904; New York: Da Capo Press, 1969), pp. 142, 143.

281 Lincoln's penchant for telling stories: *New York Daily News*, reprinted in *Daily Ohio Statesman*, Columbus, Ohio, November 20, 1860.

281 "helped many times . . . disappointments": Villard, *Memoirs of Henry Villard*, Vol. I, p. 147.

281 "he is the very . . . general disposition": Villard, *Lincoln on the Eve of '61*, pp. 39–40.

281 John Hay: William Roscoe Thayer, *The Life and Letters of John Hay*, Vol. I (Boston and New York: Houghton Mifflin, 1915), pp. 19, 48–49, 52–53, 68–69, 74, 82, 87; Villard, *Memoirs of Henry Villard*, Vol. I, p. 141.

281 For Mary . . . exciting time: Baker, *Mary Todd Lincoln*, p. 165.

281 "Is that the old woman": Villard, *Lincoln on the Eve of '61*, p. 20.

281 he asked Hannibal Hamlin . . . to meet him in Chicago: AL to Hannibal Hamlin, November 8, 1860, in *CW*, IV, p. 136.

281 he invited his old friend: AL to Joshua F. Speed, November 19, 1860, in ibid., p. 141.

282 "was so full of good humor . . . with laughter": Charles Eugene Hamlin, *The Life and Times of Hannibal Hamlin*. Vol. II. American History and Culture in the Nineteenth Century series (Cambridge, Mass.: Riverside Press, 1899; Port Washington, N.Y., and London: Kennikat Press, 1971), p. 367.

282 biographical information on Hamlin: See William A. Robinson, "Hamlin, Hannibal," in *Dictionary of American Biography*, Vol. IV, ed. Allen Johnson and Dumas Malone (New York: Charles Scribner's Sons, 1931; 1960), pp. 196–99; H. Draper Hunt, *Hannibal Hamlin of Maine: Lincoln's First Vice-President* (Syracuse, N.Y.: Syracuse University Press, 1969).

282 two men began . . . of both Adams and Welles: Hamlin, *The Life and Times of Hannibal Hamlin*, Vol. II, pp. 368–70 (quotes p. 368).

282 "threw himself . . . can afford to take": Joshua F. Speed interview, [1865–1866], in *HI*, p. 475.

282 Mary had a splendid time: *NYH*, November 23 and 24, 1860.

283 "an intensified crossword . . . to harmonize": Helen Nicolay, "Lincoln's Cabinet," *Abraham Lincoln Quarterly* 5 (March 1949), p. 258.

283 "in view of . . . influence": JGN memorandum, December 15, 1860, container 2, Nicolay Papers.

283 Seward never questioned: Miller, *Lincoln's Virtues*, p. 12.

283 "Of course . . . any other person": Charles Francis Adams to WHS, November 11, 1860, reel 60, Seward Papers.

283 "You will be offered . . . in the Presidency": Simon Cameron to WHS, November 13, 1860, reel 60, Seward Papers.

283 The Whig Party had provided: Hendrick, *Lincoln's War Cabinet*, p. 79.

283 Thurlow Weed invited Lincoln . . . Lincoln wisely declined: Entry of December 3, 1865, *Welles diary*, Vol. II, pp. 388–89; Hendrick, *Lincoln's War Cabinet*, pp. 93–94.

284 "if obnoxious men . . . otherwise have": JGN to [TB?], November 16, 1860, container 2, Nicolay Papers.

284 he directed Hamlin . . . Lincoln's instructions: Hannibal Hamlin to AL, December 4, 1860, Lincoln Papers.

284 In reply to Hamlin . . . "at once": AL to Hannibal Hamlin, December 8, 1860, in *CW*, IV, p. 147.

284 Hamlin caught up . . . contained the formal invitation: Hamlin, *The Life and Times of Hannibal Hamlin*, Vol. II, p. 372 (quote); "Alphabetical List of Senators and Representatives, with Their Residences in Washington," in William H. Boyd, *Boyd's Washington and Georgetown Directory* (Washington, D.C.: Taylor & Maury, 1860), p. 230.

284 "trembled . . . nervous": Entry for December 3, 1865, *Welles diary*, Vol. II, p. 389.

284 "With your permission . . . fit to be made": AL to WHS, December 8, 1860, in *CW*, IV, p. 148.

285 "pale with excitement . . . practicable moment": Hamlin, *The Life and Times of Hannibal Hamlin*, Vol. II, pp. 372–73.

285 "a little time . . . under existing circumstances": WHS to AL, December 13, 1860, Lincoln Papers.

285 Bates in Springfield: Entry for December 15, 1860, in *Lincoln Day by Day*, Vol. II, p. 301; Cain, *Lincoln's Attorney General*, p. 122.

285 he encountered John Nicolay . . . "genial and easy": JGN memorandum, December 15, 1860, container 2, Nicolay Papers.

285 Bates walked over . . . the afternoon together: Entry for December 16, 1860, in *The Diary of Edward Bates, 1859–1866*, p. 164 (quote); JGN memorandum, December 15, 1860, container 2, Nicolay Papers.

285 "from the time . . . its complete success": Entry for December 16, 1860, in *The Diary of Edward Bates, 1859–1866*, p. 164.

286 "should offer . . . the Attorney Generalship": JGN memorandum, December 15, 1860, container 2, Nicolay Papers.

286 "peace and order" . . . under President Fillmore: Entry for December 16, 1860, in *The Diary of Edward Bates, 1859–1866*, p. 165.

286 "everybody expects . . . family to ridicule": Entry for October 13, 1860, in ibid., p. 153.

286 "in trouble and danger . . . of his country": JGN memorandum, December 15, 1860, container 2, Nicolay Papers.

286 "a good effect . . . border slave States": EB to AL, December 18, 1860, Lincoln Papers.

286 "Let a little . . . which Department": AL to EB, December 18, 1860, in *CW*, IV, p. 154.

287 "we all feel . . . way in our power": Leonard Swett to TW, November 26, 1860, reprinted in Barnes, *Memoir of Thurlow Weed*, p. 301.

287 "Mr. Lincoln . . . his administration": Swett to TW, December 10, 1860, reprinted in ibid., pp. 301–02.

287 "present unsettled . . . a few days ago": WHS to AL, December 16, 1860, Lincoln Papers.

287 Weed arrived in Springfield: Entry for December 20, 1860, *Lincoln Day by Day*, Vol. II, p. 302.

287 uncovered . . . "the rising sun!": Newspaper clipping, Rochester, N.Y., Weed Papers.

287 "took to each other . . . of a nation": Swett to TW, reprinted in Barnes, *Memoir of Thurlow Weed*, pp. 294–95.

287 conversation between Weed and Lincoln: *Autobiography of Thurlow Weed*, ed. Weed, pp. 606–11; Swett, quoted in Barnes, *Memoir of Thurlow Weed*, pp. 293–94; see also *Chicago Tribune*, July 14, 1878.

287 "made strong opposition": Swett to TW, reprinted in Barnes, *Memoir of Thurlow Weed*, p. 294.

287 "more than any one . . . to Mr. Seward": GW to Isaac N. Arnold, November 27, 1872, folder 1, Isaac Newton Arnold Papers, Chicago Historical Society, Chicago, Ill.

288 Far better than Welles: Entry for December 27, 1860, Charles Francis Adams diary, reel 76; *NYTrib*, June 25, 1877.

288 disingenuously claimed . . . "unfit personally": Swett to TW, reprinted in Barnes, *Memoir of Thurlow Weed*, p. 294.

288 Hamlin preferred: Hamlin, *The Life and Times of Hannibal Hamlin*, Vol. II, p. 375.

288 Lincoln claimed . . . "and not theirs": Entry for August 15, 1862, *Welles diary*, Vol. I (1960 edn.), p. 82.

288 "an attractive figure-head . . . secretary of the navy": *Autobiography of Thurlow Weed*, ed. Weed, p. 611.

288 "Has he been . . . Blair, Sr.?": Ibid., p. 607.

288 regret his selection . . . "he would appoint him": Swett to TW, reprinted in Barnes, *Memoir of Thurlow Weed*, p. 294.

288 "You seem to forget . . . and ballasted": *Autobiography of Thurlow Weed*, ed. Weed, p. 610.

289 "capable in the . . . for himself": TW in *Albany Evening Journal*, quoted in Van Deusen, *Thurlow Weed*, p. 261.

289 "In one aspect . . . in the other": TW to WHS, December 25, 1860, reel 60, Seward Papers.

289 he had imagined . . . "for him but acceptance": Entry for December 27, 1860, Charles Francis Adams diary, reel 76.

289 "after due reflection . . . to accept": WHS to AL, December 28, 1860, Lincoln Papers.

289 "I have advised . . . freedom and my country": WHS to FAS, December 1860, quoted in Seward, *Seward at Washington . . . 1846–1861*, p. 487.

290 "In these troublous . . . here at once": AL to SPC, December 31, 1860, in *CW*, IV, p. 168.

290 "they should be placed . . . been your friends": Swett to AL, May 20, 1860, Davis Papers, ALPLM.

290 "from very strong and unexpected quarters": AL to Hannibal Hamlin, November 27, 1860, in *CW*, IV, p. 145.

290 Cameron to Springfield: Carman and Luthin, *Lincoln and the Patronage*, p. 25.

290 "The unexpected arrival" . . . unsavory reputation: Villard, *Lincoln on the Eve of '61*, pp. 45–46 (quotes p. 45).

290 reached the Chenery House: Entry for December 30, 1860, *Lincoln Day by Day*, Vol. II, p. 304.

290 "Shall I have the honor . . . to call here?": Simon Cameron to AL, December 30, 1860, Lincoln Papers.

290 conversation between Lincoln and Cameron: Carman and Luthin, *Lincoln and the Patronage*, pp. 25–26.

291 "an exuberant school boy": Erwin Stanley Bradley, *Simon Cameron, Lincoln's Secretary of War: A Political Biography* (Philadelphia: University of Pennsylvania Press, 1966), p. 168.

291 "There is an odor . . . such an appointment": Lyman Trumbull to AL, December 31, 1860, Lincoln Papers.

291 "Since seeing you . . . tendered you": AL to Simon Cameron, January 3, 1861, in *CW*, IV, pp. 169–70.

291 "travel-stained . . . from Columbus": Niven, *Salmon P. Chase*, p. 222 (quote); entry for January 4, 1861, *Lincoln Day by Day*, Vol. II, p. 3.

291 meeting between Lincoln and Chase . . . "offer it to you": Schuckers, *The Life and Public Services of Salmon Portland Chase*, p. 201.

291 "I frankly said . . . could give": SPC to George Opdyke, January 9, 1861, reel 14, Chase Papers.

292 "without hesitation . . . the advice of friends": SPC to George Opdyke, January 9, 1861, reel 14, Chase Papers.

292 Chase attended Sunday church: Entry for January 6, 1861, *Lincoln Day by Day: A Chronology, 1809–1865*. Vol. III: *1861–1865*, ed. Earl Schenck Miers (Washington, D.C.: Lincoln Sesquicentennial Commission, 1960; Dayton, Ohio: Morningside, 1991), p. 4.

292 Lincoln meets with Koerner and Judd: Entry for January 6, 1861, ibid., pp. 3–4.

292 "I am in a quandary . . . at the convention": Koerner, *Memoirs of Gustave Koerner*, Vol. II, p. 114.

292 "It seems to me . . . brought to co-operate": AL to Lyman Trumbull, January 7, 1861, in *CW*, IV, p. 171.

292 "under great anxiety . . . I consistently can": AL to Simon Cameron, January 13, 1861, in ibid., p. 174.
292 "were entirely free & unreserved": SPC to James S. Pike, January 10, 1861, reel 14, Chase Papers.
293 "What is done . . . to Springfield": SPC to Hiram Barney, January 8, 1861, reel 14, Chase Papers.
293 had convinced Lincoln . . . official offers: Oates, *With Malice Toward None*, p. 220.
293 "I think that in allowing . . . and accept it": SPC to Elizabeth Ellicott Pike, January 27, 1861, reel 14, Chase Papers.
293 "a snowballing process": Elbert B. Smith, *The Presidency of James Buchanan* (Lawrence: University Press of Kansas, 1975), p. 138.
293 "desired by all . . . of the multitude": *Charleston Courier*, quoted in *Richmond Enquirer*, November 16, 1860.
293 the election of a . . . the John Brown raid: Smith, *The Presidency of James Buchanan*, pp. 129–32.
294 The bachelor president . . . "let out from school": Sara Pryor, *Reminiscences of Peace and War*, rev. and enlarged edn. (New York: The Macmillan Company, 1904; New York: Grosset & Dunlap, 1905; 1908), pp. 110–11 (quotes p. 111).
294 "looked stunned . . . of his chair": Entry for December 20, 1860, in E. B. Long, *The Civil War Day by Day: An Almanac, 1861–1865* (Garden City, N.Y.: Doubleday, 1971), p. 13.
294 "both the authority . . . integrity": [JGN to TB?], November 15, 1860, container 2, Nicolay Papers.
294 "indefatigable . . . authorities, etc.": Villard, *Lincoln on the Eve of '61*, p. 37.
294 willing to reduce . . . "a period of years": AL, quoted in Helm, *The True Story of Mary*, p. 161.
294 "a position towards . . . for his election": Koerner, *Memoirs of Gustave Koerner*, Vol. II, p. 105.
294 He was determined to stand . . . impact on the South: Donald, *Lincoln*, p. 260.
294 "I could say nothing . . . clamor all the louder": AL to Nathaniel P. Paschall, November 16, 1860, in *CW*, IV, pp. 139–40.
295 "each and all of the States . . . any administration": AL, "Passage Written for Lyman Trumbull's Speech at Springfield, Illinois," November 20, 1860, in ibid., p. 141.
295 "On the contrary . . . war against them": AL to Henry J. Raymond, November 28, 1860, in ibid., p. 146.
295 "has eyes . . . does not hear": AL, quoted in Oates, *With Malice Toward None*, p. 213.
295 "blaze of passion . . . offended deity": William Smedes to Henry J. Raymond, December 8, 1860, enclosed in Raymond to AL, December 14, 1860, Lincoln Papers.
295 "What a very mad-man . . . forgery out and out": AL to Henry J. Raymond, December 18, 1860, in *CW*, IV, p. 156.
296 the "Great Secession Winter": See Henry Adams, *The Great Secession Winter of 1860–61 and Other Essays*, ed. George Hochfield (New York: Sagamore Press, 1958).
296 "no compromise . . . any time hereafter": AL to Lyman Trumbull, December 10, 1860, in *CW*, IV, pp. 149–50.
296 "fugitive slaves . . . amongst us": AL to WHS, February 1, 1861, in ibid., p. 183.
296 "the Constitution should" . . . Fugitive Slave Law be repealed: Footnote to AL, "Resolutions Drawn up for Republican Members of Senate Committee of Thirteen," [December 20, 1860], in ibid., p. 157n.
296 Seward agreed . . . John Crittenden: WHS to AL, December 26, 1860, Lincoln Papers.
297 The Crittenden Compromise: Potter, *The Impending Crisis, 1848–1861*, pp. 531–32.
297 "the slightest . . . Loyalty stronger": WHS to AL, December 26, 1860, Lincoln Papers.
297 three federal forts . . . all three were in its domain: Entry for December 22, 1860, in Long, *The Civil War Day by Day*, p. 14.
297 three commissioners . . . Buchanan administration: Thomas and Hyman, *Stanton*, p. 95.
297 "From the first . . . the federal government": JGN to TB, December 30, 1860, container 2, Nicolay Papers.
297 "to surrender . . . hang him!": JGN to [TB?], December 22, 1860, container 2, Nicolay Papers.
297 "to either *hold* . . . may require": AL to Elihu B. Washburne, December 21, 1860, in *CW*, IV, p. 159.
297 "vying" . . . bolster Buchanan's will: Thomas and Hyman, *Stanton*, pp. 91, 93 (quote).
297 Anderson preempted . . . Castle Pinckney: Entries for December 26 and 27, 1860, in Long, *The Civil War Day by Day*, pp. 15–16.
298 Buchanan agreed . . . and headed north: Entries for January 2, 5, 8, and 9, 1861, in Long, *The Civil War Day by Day*, pp. 21–24; entries for January 4 and 5, 1860, *Lincoln Day by Day*, Vol. III, p. 3.
298 "a feverish excitement": WHS to AL, December 28, 1860, Lincoln Papers.
298 Edwin Stanton . . . "traitors and spies": Edwin L. Stanton, quoted in George C. Gorham, *Life and Public Services of Edwin M. Stanton*, Vol. I (2 vols., Boston and New York: Houghton Mifflin and The Riverside Press, 1899), p. 168.
298 If Maryland and Virginia . . . "& the navy": Stephen H. Phillips to Horace Gray, January 31, 1861, Papers of Horace Gray, Manuscript Division, Library of Congress.
298 *"be made to believe* . . . this danger": EMS to SPC, January 23, 1861, reel 14, Chase Papers.
298 "came to a momentous . . . for him to turn": Thomas and Hyman, *Stanton*, pp. 98 (first quote), 99 (second quote), 100.
298 Watson would call . . . "discussed and settled": Henry Wilson, "Jeremiah S. Black and Edwin M. Stanton," *Atlantic Monthly* 26 (October 1870), p. 465.
299 "At length I have gotten . . . prudence is omitted": WHS to AL, December 29, 1860, Lincoln Papers.
299 "treason is all around and amongst us": WHS to FAS, December 29, 1860, quoted in Seward, *Seward at Washington . . . 1846–1861*, p. 488.
299 "abettors near the President": WHS to TW, December 29, 1860, quoted in ibid., p. 487.
299 Stanton secretly spread word: Thomas and Hyman, *Stanton*, pp. 108, 110, 111; Henry Wilson, "Edwin M. Stanton," *Atlantic Monthly* 25 (February 1870), p. 237.
299 "By early disclosure . . . enemies of their country": Henry L. Dawes, "Washington the Winter Before the War," *Atlantic Monthly* 72 (August 1893), p. 163.

299 Stanton invited Sumner to his office: Thomas and Hyman, *Stanton*, p. 111; Wilson, "Jeremiah S. Black and Edwin M. Stanton," *Atlantic Monthly* (1870), p. 466.
299 "found and read . . . place of deposit": Dawes, "Washington the Winter Before the War," *Atlantic Monthly* (1893), p. 163.
299 "held the key to all discontent": "Two Manuscripts of Gideon Welles," ed. Muriel Bernitt, *New England Quarterly* XI (September 1938), p. 589.
299 "came to be regarded . . . Republican party": Wilson, "Jeremiah S. Black and Edwin M. Stanton," *Atlantic Monthly* (1870), p. 465.
299 "By common consent . . . ruler of the country": Adams, *The Great Secession Winter*, p. 22.
300 "Never in the history . . . from Lincoln himself": *Chicago Tribune*, January 17, 1861.
300 "The families of nearly" . . . Jefferson Davis: *NYTrib*, January 19, 1861.
300 "No man was . . . his every word": *Boston Atlas and Bee*, reprinted *Cincinnati Commercial*, January 20, 1861.
300 "to set forth . . . destruction would involve": *NYT*, January 14, 1861.
300 of "perpetual civil war . . . everything is lost": WHS, January 12, 1861, *Congressional Globe*, 36th Cong., 2nd sess., p. 342.
300 "difficult to restrain . . . his handkerchief": *Boston Atlas and Bee*, reprinted *Cincinnati Commercial*, January 20, 1861.
300 "to meet prejudice . . . shall have ended": WHS, January 12, 1861, *Congressional Globe*, 36th Cong., 2nd sess., pp. 343–44.
301 five Southern senators: See farewell remarks of Senators Yulee, Mallory, Clay, Fitzpatrick, and Davis, January 21, 1861, *Congressional Globe*, 36th Cong., 2nd sess., pp. 484–87; entry for January 21, 1861, in Long, *The Civil War Day by Day*, pp. 28–29.
301 "inexpressibly sad": William C. Davis, *Jefferson Davis: The Man and His Hour* (New York: HarperCollins, 1991), pp. 295–96 (quote p. 296).
301 "in a state . . . on despair": *NYT*, January 23, 1861.
301 "I am sure . . . wish you well": Farewell remarks of Jefferson Davis, January 21, 1861, *Congressional Globe*, 36th Cong., 2nd sess., p. 487.
301 Seward himself had visited . . . Democrats and Republicans: Davis, *Jefferson Davis*, p. 261.
301 "Your man outtalked . . . but I didn't": Ishbel Ross, *First Lady of the South: The Life of Mrs. Jefferson Davis* (New York: Harper & Bros., 1958), p. 85.
301 "Mrs Jef asked me . . . *bonds* between us": EBL to SPL, December 17, 1860, in ed. Laas, *Wartime Washington*, p. 18.
301 packed up their belongings . . . "ended in Washington": Margaret Leech, *Reveille in Washington, 1860–1865* (New York: Harper & Row, 1941; New York: Carroll & Graf, 1991), p. 31.
301 His "great wish . . . of the disunionists": Adams, *The Great Secession Winter*, pp. 13, 14.
301 "As an indication . . . of every section": *NYT*, January 14, 1861.
301 "many are sanguine . . . tide of secession": *NYT*, January 16, 1861.
302 "fought . . . took new courage": Adams, *The Great Secession Winter*, p. 23.
302 "Secession has run its course": Entry for February 20, 1861, *Diary of George Templeton Strong. Vol. III: The Civil War, 1860–1865*, ed. Allan Nevins and Milton Halsey Thomas (New York: Macmillan Publishing Co., 1952), p. 100.
302 "for the new Administration . . . to subside": WHS to FAS, January 23, 1861, quoted in Seward, *Seward at Washington . . . 1846–1861*, p. 497.
302 "I deplore S[eward]'s speech": CS to John Jay, January 17, 1861, reel 74, Sumner Papers.
302 "read me his speech . . . no such thing": CS to Samuel Gridley Howe, January 17, 1861, reel 64, Sumner Papers.
302 "seeks to purchase peace . . . years war": Thaddeus Stevens to SPC, February 3, 1861, reel 14, Chase Papers.
302 "What do you think . . . be found wanting": Carl Schurz to his wife, February 4, 1861, in Carl Schurz, *Intimate Letters of Carl Schurz, 1841–1869*, trans. and ed. Joseph Schafer, orig. published as Vol. XXX of the *Collections* of the State Historical Society of Wisconsin, 1928 (New York: Da Capo Press, 1970), pp. 242–43.
303 "There he was . . . left him at Auburn": Adams, Jr., *Charles Francis Adams, 1835–1915*, p. 79.
303 "Eloquent as your speech . . . of your dangers": FAS to WHS, January 19, 1861, reel 14, Seward Papers.
303 "I am not surprised . . . most effective weapons": WHS to FAS, quoted in Seward, *Seward at Washington . . . 1846–1861*, pp. 496–97.
303 "It will do . . . by and with": TW to WHS, January 19, 1861, reel 61, Seward Papers.
303 "In the cars . . . jealousies and hatreds": TW to WHS, February 14, 1861, reel 61, Seward Papers.
304 "Your recent speech . . . over the country": AL to WHS, January 19, 1861, in *CW*, IV, p. 176.
304 "he had heard from . . . on it at present": Entry of February 5, 1861, Charles Francis Adams diary, reel 76.
304 "Seward made all . . . says so openly": Carl Schurz to his wife, February 9, 1861, in Schurz, *Intimate Letters of Carl Schurz, 1841–1869*, p. 247.

CHAPTER 11: "I AM NOW PUBLIC PROPERTY"

Page

305 Mary journeyed to New York: Turner and Turner, *Mary Todd Lincoln*, p. 69; Randall, *Mary Lincoln*, pp. 192–94.
305 *"wild* to see": MTL to Adeline Judd, June 13, 1860, in Turner and Turner, *Mary Todd Lincoln*, p. 64.

305 fêted by merchants . . . "an obsession": Randall, *Mary Lincoln*, p. 192.
305 "Could he . . . disgrace the Nation?": Elizabeth Todd Grimsley, "Six Months in the White House," *Journal of the Illinois State Historical Society* XIX (October 1926–January 1927), p. 44.
305 "outward appearance . . . Presidential father": Entries for January 23–25, 1861, *Lincoln Day by Day*, Vol. III, p. 7; Villard, *Lincoln on the Eve of '61*, p. 55 (quote).
306 decided to rent out their house: Turner and Turner, *Mary Todd Lincoln*, p. 72.
306 "the most brilliant . . . in many years": Entry for February 6, 1861, *Lincoln Day by Day*, Vol. III, p. 9; Villard, *Lincoln on the Eve of '61*, p. 63 (quote).
306 "with a rope around . . . tar and feathers": Villard, *Lincoln on the Eve of '61*, pp. 52–53.
306 he sought places to isolate himself: WHH, quoted in Miller, *Lincoln's Virtues*, p. 442; Villard, *Lincoln on the Eve of '61*, pp. 57–58.
306 "unusually grave . . . old and faithful friends": Villard, *Lincoln on the Eve of '61*, p. 64.
306 farewell to his beloved stepmother . . . father's grave: Ibid., pp. 55–56.
306 "If I live . . . nothing had ever happened": AL, quoted in Donald, *Lincoln*, p. 272.
306 packed his own trunk . . . "Washington, D.C.": Weik, *The Real Lincoln*, p. 307.
307 "His face was pale . . . a single word": Villard, *Lincoln on the Eve of '61*, p. 71.
307 "My friends . . . an affectionate farewell": AL, "Farewell Address at Springfield, Illinois [A. Version]," February 11, 1861, in *CW*, IV, p. 190.
307 "As he turned . . . the silent gathering": *NYH*, February 12, 1861.
307 the luxurious presidential car . . . president-elect: Randall, *Mary Lincoln*, p. 202.
307 "sat alone and depressed": Villard, *Lincoln on the Eve of '61*, p. 73.
307 "forsaken . . . hilarious good spirits": "Indianapolis Correspondence, 11 February 1861," in Hay, *Lincoln's Journalist*, p. 24.
307 Jefferson Davis was beginning: Entries for February 11 and 18, 1861, in Long, *The Civil War Day by Day*, pp. 35–36, 38–39; Davis, *Jefferson Davis*, pp. 304–07; *The Papers of Jefferson Davis*. Vol. VII: *1861*, ed. Lynda Lasswell Crist and Mary Seaton Dix (Baton Rouge and London: Louisiana State University Press, 1992), p. 46.
307 Lincoln's spirits began to revive . . . thirty-four guns: Villard, *Lincoln on the Eve of '61*, pp. 76, 77.
307 "the cheers" . . . before leaving Springfield: "Indianapolis Correspondence, 11 February 1861," in Hay, *Lincoln's Journalist*, pp. 25 (quote), 27.
307 a direct, powerful talk . . . "free-love arrangement": AL, "Speech from the Balcony of the Bates House at Indianapolis, Indiana," February 11, 1861, in *CW*, IV, p. 195.
308 "shaken off . . . tragedy would have been": "Cincinnati Correspondence, 12 February 1861," in Hay, *Lincoln's Journalist*, p. 28.
308 fêted in the state Capitol . . . his election official: Entry for February 13, 1861, *Lincoln Day by Day*, Vol. III, p. 13.
308 "The votes have been . . . was no enemy": FWS to Anna (Wharton) Seward, February 14, 1861, reel 116, Seward Papers.
308 "have passed the 13th . . . people have chosen": WHS to home, quoted in Seward, *Seward at Washington . . . 1846–1861*, p. 505.
308 "full evening dress" . . . lavish military ball: Entry for February 13, 1861, *Lincoln Day by Day*, Vol. III, p. 13.
308 he danced with Chase's lovely daughter: This story was told to the author by a tour guide at the Ohio State House during a visit to Columbus, Ohio, in 1998.
309 "Mrs. Lincoln was piqued . . . at Washington": "Kate Chase in 1893," *Star* clipping, KCS vertical file, DWP.
309 Never comfortable with extemporaneous speech: Harold Holzer, "Avoid Saying 'Foolish Things': The Legacy of Lincoln's Impromptu Oratory," in *"We Cannot Escape History": Lincoln and the Last Best Hope of Earth*, ed. James M. McPherson (Urbana: University of Illinois Press, 1995), pp. 105–21.
309 "there is really . . . will come to an end": AL, "Speech at Pittsburgh, Pennsylvania," February 15, 1861, in *CW*, IV, p. 211.
309 "he should hardly . . . did not want to": AL, "Remarks at Ashtabula, Ohio," February 16, 1861, in ibid., p. 218.
309 he kissed Grace Bedell: Entry for February 16, 1861, *Lincoln Day by Day*, Vol. III, p. 14.
309 "a continuous carnival . . . grand popular ovation": "Indianapolis Correspondence, 11 February 1861," in Hay, *Lincoln's Journalist*, p. 23.
309 Every glimpse of Mary: Entry for February 19, 1861, *Lincoln Day by Day*, Vol. III, p. 18.
310 "are rapidly reducing . . . frivolous and uncertain": Entries for February 16 and 20, 1861, Charles Francis Adams diary, reel 76.
310 "observed the utmost . . . his administration": Nicolay, *A Short Life of Abraham Lincoln*, p. 170.
310 "the man does not . . . the foot down firmly": AL, "Address to the New Jersey General Assembly at Trenton, New Jersey," February 21, 1861, in *CW*, IV, p. 237.
310 "lifted his foot" . . . continue his remarks: "Philadelphia Correspondence, 21 February 1861," in Hay, *Lincoln's Journalist*, p. 40.
310 "consent to . . . Union itself was made": AL, "Reply to Mayor Fernando Wood at New York City," February 20, 1861, in *CW*, IV, p. 233.
310 "never had a feeling . . . to surrender it": AL, "Speech in Independence Hall, Philadelphia, Pennsylvania," February 22, 1861, in ibid., p. 240.
310 the Baltimore plot: See Isaac H. [*sic*] Arnold, "Plot to Assassinate Abraham Lincoln," *Harper's New Monthly Magazine* 37 (June 1868), pp. 123–28.
310 "This . . . in the afternoon": Ward Hill Lamon, *Recollections of Abraham Lincoln, 1847–1865*, ed. Dorothy Lamon Teillard (n.p.: A. C. McClurg & Co., 1895; 1911; Lincoln, Nebr., and London: University of Nebraska Press, 1994), p. 39.

311 Fred was in the Senate gallery . . . " 'let you know in the morning' ": Seward, *Seward at Washington . . . 1846–1861*, pp. 509–10.

311 Pinkerton insisted . . . in the afternoon as scheduled: Turner and Turner, *Mary Todd Lincoln*, p. 78.

311 "side-tracked . . . Capitol came in sight": Lamon, *Recollections of Abraham Lincoln*, pp. 40, 45.

311 had "crept into Washington": EMS, quoted in Helen Nicolay, *Our Capital on the Potomac* (New York and London: Century Co., 1924), p. 358.

311 A scurrilous rumor spread . . . a long military cloak: Thomas, *Abraham Lincoln*, p. 244.

312 "It's to be hoped . . . on his Administration": Entry for February 23, 1861, *Diary of George Templeton Strong*, Vol. III, p. 102.

312 "Genl Jackson . . . where he left": MB to AL, December 8, 1860, Lincoln Papers.

312 had rented a private house: Lamon, *Recollections of Abraham Lincoln*, p. 34; Leech, *Reveille in Washington*, p. 36.

312 "now public property . . . he is inaugurated": TW, quoted in Lamon, *Recollections of Abraham Lincoln*, p. 34.

312 "The truth is . . . have access to me": Ibid., p. 35.

312 "the President-elect . . . met him at the depot": Seward, *Seward at Washington . . . 1846–1861*, p. 511.

312 "much out of breath . . . arrival of the train": "Seward and Lincoln: The Washington Depot Episode," *University of Rochester Library Bulletin* (Spring 1965), p. 33.

312 "a virtuoso performance": Daniel W. Crofts, "Secession Winter: William Henry Seward and the Decision for War," *New York History* 65 (July 1984), p. 248.

313 breakfasted together . . . "*pâté de foie gras*": Leech, *Reveille in Washington*, p. 8.

313 "tall awkward Irishman . . . loud & unrefined": Harriet Lane to unknown recipient, February 24, 1861, reel 3, Papers of James Buchanan and Harriet Lane Johnston, Manuscript Division, Library of Congress.

313 Seward shepherded Lincoln . . . conversation with Scott: *Star*, February 23 and 25, 1861.

313 Lincoln had promised Weed and Seward: Crofts, "Secession Winter," *New York History* (1984), p. 248.

313 "*living* position in the South": AL to WHS, January 12, 1861, in *CW*, IV, p. 173.

313 "to grieve . . . in hostility": WHS to AL, January 15, 1861, Lincoln Papers.

313 he had met with a delegation . . . he reached Washington: Baringer, *A House Dividing*, pp. 289–90 (quote p. 289); James Millikin to Simon Cameron, February 22, 1861, in *Concerning Mr. Lincoln: In Which Abraham Lincoln is Pictured as he Appeared to Letter Writers of His Time*, comp. Harry E. Pratt (Springfield, Ill.: Abraham Lincoln Association, 1944), pp. 57–60; Titian J. Coffey to Simon Cameron, February 22, 1861, in ibid., pp. 60–63.

314 Lincoln rested . . . his old adversary: Entry for February 23, 1861, *Lincoln Day by Day*, Vol. III, p. 21; Sandburg, *Abraham Lincoln: The War Years*, Vol. I, p. 90; *Star*, February 25, 1861.

314 "The Blairs . . . they undertake": AL, quoted in "[9 December 1863, Wednesday]," in Hay, *Inside Lincoln's White House*, p. 123.

314 Blairs had been appalled . . . aggression from the South: FPB to AL, January 14, 1861, Lincoln Papers.

314 "that one Southern man . . . to despise": MB to Gustavus V. Fox, January 31, 1861, reprinted in *Confidential Correspondence of Gustavus Vasa Fox, Assistant Secretary of the Navy, 1861–1865*, Vol. I, ed. Robert Means Thompson and Richard Wainwright, orig. published as Vols. IX–X of the *Publications* of the Naval History Society, 1920 (Freeport, N.Y.: Books for Libraries Press, 1972), pp. 4–5.

314 "In your cabinet . . . for the succession": FPB to AL, January 14, 1861, Lincoln Papers.

314 "four carriages . . . considerable swearing": *Star*, Washington, D.C., February 25, 1861.

315 Seward's home for a dinner: Entry for February 23, 1861, *Lincoln Day by Day*, Vol. III, p. 21; Van Deusen, *William Henry Seward*, pp. 265–68.

315 members of the Peace Convention: Entry for February 23, 1861, *Lincoln Day by Day*, Vol. III, p. 21.

315 "to scoff . . . facility of expression": Lucius E. Chittenden, *Recollections of Lincoln and His Administration* (New York: Harper & Bros., 1891), pp. 71, 72.

315 Chase stiffly assumed: Niven, *Salmon P. Chase*, p. 236.

315 "had some apt . . . his name": Chittenden, *Recollections of Lincoln*, p. 72.

315 "He has been both . . . misfortune": William Rives and Thomas Ruffin, both quoted in ibid., p. 77.

316 "clear and blustering . . . with mighty power": Entry for February 24, 1861, Charles Francis Adams diary, reel 76.

316 "Governor Seward . . . you are familiar": Seward, *Reminiscences of a War-Time Statesman and Diplomat*, p. 147.

316 Seward and Lincoln made an informal visit: Entry for February 25, 1861, *Lincoln Day by Day*, Vol. III, p. 22.

316 "affected *nonchalance* . . . plain English": *NYT*, February 27, 1861.

316 "face has not yet . . . of the multitude": *Star*, February 26, 1861.

316 "without a precedent . . . proprieties of his position": *NYT*, February 27, 1861.

316 "I had partly . . . against you in malice": AL to Schuyler Colfax, March 8, 1861, in *CW*, IV, p. 278.

316 opposition to Norman Judd; offered ministry post in Berlin: See King, *Lincoln's Manager*, pp. 170–72.

317 "*Judd* . . . borne inspection": MTL to David Davis, January 17, 1861, in Turner and Turner, *Mary Todd Lincoln*, p. 71.

317 "in an agony . . . in February": Niven, *Gideon Welles*, p. 321.

317 "It is by no means . . . not go at all": GW to Edgar T. Welles, February 27, 1861, reel 18, Welles Papers.

317 "I desire to see you here forthwith": Hannibal Hamlin to GW, February 28, 1861, quoted in Niven, *Gideon Welles*, p. 321.

317 In his hurry to catch the train . . . the navy portfolio: Niven, *Gideon Welles*, pp. 321–22.

317 "The struggle for Cabinet . . . hourly": *Star*, March 1, 1861.

317 conflict over Chase and Seward: Niven, *Salmon P. Chase*, p. 237.

317 Seward sent a note to Lincoln: Entry for March 2, 1861, *Lincoln Day by Day*, Vol. III, p. 23.

317 "I can't afford . . . the first trick": John G. Nicolay and John Hay, *Abraham Lincoln: A History*, Vol. III (New York: Century Co., 1917), p. 371.

317 "It is the subject . . . the same direction": AL to WHS, March 4, 1861, in *CW*, IV, p. 273.

318 "The President . . . the country to chance": WHS to FAS, March 8, 1861, quoted in Seward, *Seward at Washington . . . 1846–1861*, p. 518.

318 Lincoln sent Chase's nomination . . . to the Senate: Entries for March 3, 5, and 6, 1861, *Lincoln Day by Day*, Vol. III, pp. 24, 26; Niven, *Salmon P. Chase*, p. 234.

318 "Ever conscious . . . of protocol": Niven, *Salmon P. Chase*, p. 238.

318 "referred to the . . . finally yielded": SPC to Trowbridge, quoted in Schuckers, *The Life and Public Services of Salmon Portland Chase*, p. 207.

318 "The construction of . . . only by experience": *The States and Union*, Washington, D.C., February 26, 1861.

318 Lincoln's "first decision . . . been nominated": "Campaign of 1860 & Journey to Washington," container 9, Nicolay Papers.

319 James Buchanan . . . "deepened party divisions": Allan Nevins, *Ordeal of the Union. Vol. II: The Emergence of Lincoln, part I: Douglas, Buchanan, and Party Chaos, 1857–1859*, new introduction by James M. McPherson (New York: 1978; New York: Collier Books, Macmillan Publishing Co., 1992), p. 67.

319 "he must risk . . . dangers of rebellion": "Campaign of 1860 & Journey to Washington," container 9, Nicolay Papers.

319 asked Lincoln why . . . "of their services": Joseph Medill, quoted in H. I. Cleveland, "Booming the First American President: A Talk with Abraham Lincoln's Friend, the Late Joseph Medill," *Saturday Evening Post* 172, August 5, 1899, p. 85.

319 For further analysis of the making of the cabinet, see Phillip Shaw Paludan, *The Presidency of Abraham Lincoln* (n.p.: University Press of Kansas, 1994), pp. 21–45.

CHAPTER 12: "MYSTIC CHORDS OF MEMORY"

Page

323 Mary the night before the inaugural: Helm, *The True Story of Mary*, p. 168.

323 strangers swarming . . . streets below: *Star*, March 4, 1861.

323 "Lincoln often resorted . . . or argument": JGN, "Some Incidents in Lincoln's Journey from Springfield to Washington," in Nicolay, *An Oral History of Abraham Lincoln*, p. 107.

324 out of four documents: Herndon and Weik, *Herndon's Life of Lincoln*, p. 386.

324 "such a crowd . . . about him": Orville H. Browning, quoted in Nicolay, *An Oral History of Abraham Lincoln*, p. 6.

324 Browning focused on one imprudent passage: WHS to AL, February 24, 1861, quoted in Nicolay and Hay, *Abraham Lincoln*, Vol. III, p. 322.

324 "threat, or menace . . . palpably in the wrong": Orville H. Browning to AL, February 17, 1861, Lincoln Papers.

324 "strong and conclusive": WHS to AL, February 24, 1861, quoted in Nicolay and Hay, *Abraham Lincoln*, Vol. III, p. 321.

325 "bound by duty . . . shift his position": AL, "First Inaugural Address—First Edition and Revisions," January 1861, in *CW*, IV, p. 250.

325 "exclusive and defiant . . . negro equality": Entry for May 19, 1860, in *The Diary of Edward Bates, 1859–1866*, p. 129.

325 "give such advantages . . . exercise of power": WHS to AL, February 24, 1861, quoted in Nicolay and Hay, *Abraham Lincoln*, Vol. III, pp. 320, 321.

325 "treasonable" . . . would only "aggravate the dispute": AL, "First Inaugural Address—First Edition and Revisions," January 1861, in *CW*, IV, pp. 253 n32, 257 n67, 260, 260 n85.

326 "to the effect . . . and irrevocable": AL, "First Inaugural Address—Final Text," March 4, 1861, in ibid., p. 270.

326 "With *you* . . . 'or a sword?' ": AL, "First Inaugural Address—First Edition and Revisions," January 1861, in ibid., p. 261.

326 "to meet . . . cheerful confidence": WHS to AL, February 24, 1861, quoted in Nicolay and Hay, *Abraham Lincoln*, Vol. III, p. 321.

326 "I close . . . angel of the nation": WHS revision, in AL, "First Inaugural Address—First Edition and Revisions," January 1861, in *CW*, IV, pp. 261–62 n99.

326 "I am loth . . . angels of our nature": AL, "First Inaugural Address—Final Text," March 4, 1861, in ibid., p. 271.

326 Lincoln read the speech . . . left alone: Randall, *Mary Lincoln*, p. 208.

326 the morning newspapers . . . of his house: Seward, *Seward at Washington . . . 1846–1861*, p. 515.

327 "I have been . . . and the free": L. A. Gobright, *Recollection of Men and Things at Washington, During the Third of a Century* (Philadelphia: Claxton, Remsen & Haffelfinger, 1869), p. 291.

327 "Disappointment! . . . little Illinois lawyer!": Schurz, *Reminiscences*, Vol. II, pp. 221–22.

327 As the clock . . . "Hail to the Chief": Stanley Kimmel, *Mr. Lincoln's Washington* (New York: Coward-McCann, 1957), p. 23; Browne, *The Every-Day Life of Abraham Lincoln*, pp. 402–03.

327 cheering crowds . . . throughout the entire route: Julia Taft Bayne, *Tad Lincoln's Father* (Boston: Little, Brown, 1931), pp. 17–18; "The Diary of a Public Man, part III," *North American Review* 129 (October 1879), p. 382.

327 "A sharp, cracking . . . in the aggregate": *Star*, March 4, 1861.

327 "assume[d] an almost idyllic . . . large rural village": Edna M. Colman, *Seventy-five Years of White House Gossip: From Washington to Lincoln* (Garden City, N.Y.: Doubleday, Page & Co., 1926), pp. 279–81 (first and third quotes attributed by Colman to foreign observer J. G. Kohl).

327 platform seating; Baker . . . introduced the president-elect: *NYT*, March 5, 1861; Grimsley, "Six Months in the White House," *JISHS*, pp. 45–46.

328 Douglas reached over . . . his own lap: "The Diary of a Public Man, part III," *NAR* (1879), p. 383; Grimsley, "Six Months in the White House," *JISHS*, p. 46.

328 outdoor venues of the Western states: *NYT*, March 5, 1861; Leech, *Reveille in Washington*, p. 44.

328 "no purpose . . . better angels of our nature": AL, "First Inaugural Address—Final Text," March 4, 1861, in *CW*, IV, pp. 263–66, 269, 271.

329 "The Mansion . . . dinner prepared": Grimsley, "Six Months in the White House," *JISHS*, p. 46.

329 "If you are as happy . . . this country": James Buchanan, quoted in Sandburg, *Abraham Lincoln: The War Years*, Vol. I, pp. 137–38.

329 hasty unpacking . . . dressed for the Inaugural Ball: Randall, *Mary Lincoln*, p. 209.

329 Inaugural Ball: *NYH*, March 6, 1861; *NYT*, March 6, 1861; Colman, *Seventy-five Years of White House Gossip*, p. 268.

329 "because of . . . in its decoration": Colman, *Seventy-five Years of White House Gossip*, p. 268.

329 Brightened by . . . good deal of space: *NYH*, March 6, 1861.

329 "Dressed all in blue . . . and pearls": Leech, *Reveille in Washington*, p. 46.

329 she danced the quadrille . . . her exhausted husband: *Star*, March 5, 1861; Leech, *Reveille in Washington*, p. 46.

329 "What an inappreciable . . . 5th of March": Entry for March 4, 1861, Fanny Seward diary, Seward Papers.

329 "seven days and seventeen hours": Sandburg, *Abraham Lincoln: The War Years*, Vol. I, p. 140.

330 "grand . . . in every respect": *NYTrib*, March 7, 1861.

330 "convincing . . . manner": *New York Evening Post*, reprinted in *NYTrib*, March 7, 1861.

330 "eminently . . . under the Constitution": *Philadelphia Bulletin*, reprinted in *NYTrib*, March 7, 1861.

330 "the work . . . its contents": *Commercial Advertiser*, N.Y., reprinted in *NYTrib*, March 7, 1861.

330 "wretchedly . . . unstatesmanlike paper": *Hartford Times*, reprinted in *NYTrib*, March 7, 1861.

330 "It is he . . . Civil War": *Atlas and Argus*, Albany, N.Y., quoted in *Albany Evening Journal*, March 5, 1861.

330 "couched in the cool . . . civil war": *Richmond Enquirer*, reprinted in *NYTrib*, March 7, 1861.

330 "might as well . . . inevitable": *Herald*, Wilmington, N.C., quoted in *Star*, March 7, 1861.

330 "won some favorable . . . slave states": Thomas, *Abraham Lincoln*, p. 248.

330 "without getting . . . can stand": WHS to FAS, March 8, 1861, quoted in Seward, *Seward at Washington . . . 1846–1861*, p. 518.

330 "been fully justified . . . my country": Entry for March 4, 1861, Charles Francis Adams diary, reel 76.

330 Radicals . . . considered an appeasing tone: T. Harry Williams, *Lincoln and the Radicals* (Madison: University of Wisconsin Press, 1941), p. 22.

331 Frederick Douglass . . . cruel slaveholders: Frederick Douglass, *Narrative of the Life of Frederick Douglass, an American Slave*, introduction by Houston A. Baker, Jr. (The Anti-Slavery Office, 1845; New York: Penguin Books, 1986), chapters I–X.

331 "it was unlawful . . . rid of thinking!": Ibid., pp. 78 (first quote), 84 (second and third quotes).

331 "no more pervasive . . . in America": Blight, *Frederick Douglass' Civil War*, p. 3.

331 "It has taught . . . the Presidency": *Douglass' Monthly* (December 1860).

331 "no lawful power . . . Pierces and Buchanans": *Douglass' Monthly* (April 1861).

332 White House family quarters: William Seale, *The President's House: A History*, Vol. I (Washington, D.C.: White House Historical Association/National Geographic Society, 1986) pp. 366, 368, 377, 379–80, illustration 41.

332 "the grounds . . . closets": WHS to home, March 16, 1861, quoted in Seward, *Seward at Washington . . . 1846–1861*, p. 530.

332 hundreds of people . . . securing a job: Seward, *Reminiscences of a War-Time Statesman and Diplomat*, p. 147; William O. Stoddard, *Inside the White House in War Times: Memoirs and Reports of Lincoln's Secretary*, ed. Michael Burlingame (Lincoln and London: University of Nebraska Press, 2000), p. 5.

332 "from Edward . . . that he was handsome": Grimsley, "Six Months in the White House," *JISHS*, pp. 47, 48.

332 memorizing railroad timetables . . . "perfect precision": John Hay, "Life in the White House in the Time of Lincoln," *Century* 41 (November 1890), p. 35.

332 Tad . . . "worry of the household": Grimsley, "Six Months in the White House," *JISHS*, pp. 48–49.

332 A speech impediment: Bayne, *Tad Lincoln's Father*, p. 8; Hay, "Life in the White House in the Time of Lincoln," *Century* (1890), p. 35.

332 "a very bad . . . discipline": *NYTrib*, July 17, 1871.

332 The boys harried the staff: Stoddard, *Inside the White House in War Times*, pp. 26–27; *NYTrib*, July 17, 1871; Bayne, *Tad Lincoln's Father*, pp. 102–06.

333 "If there was . . . a good time": Bayne, *Tad Lincoln's Father*, p. 107.

333 Seward had proposed: Grimsley, "Six Months in the White House," *JISHS*, p. 49.

333 "For over two hours . . . at the windows": JGN to TB, March 10, 1861, container 2, Nicolay Papers.

333 "well dressed . . . social courtesy": Entry for March 8, 1861, reel 76, Charles Francis Adams diary.

333 "was voted by . . . ever known here": JGN to TB, March 10, 1861, container 2, Nicolay Papers.

333 "This is certainly . . . she has been here": MTL to Hannah Shearer, March [28, 1861], in Turner and Turner, *Mary Todd Lincoln*, p. 82.

333 "light and capricious" . . . morning schedule: Hay, "Life in the White House in the Time of Lincoln," *Century* (1890), p. 34.

333 white marble fireplace . . . a panorama: Browne, *The Every-Day Life of Abraham Lincoln*, p. 416.
333 description of the Cabinet Room: Seale, *The President's House*, Vol. I, pp. 364, 367; Isaac Arnold, quoted in Browne, *The Every-Day Life of Abraham Lincoln*, p. 416.
334 "the very first . . . in his hands": Entry for July 3, 1861, in Browning, *The Diary of Orville Hickman Browning*, Vol. I, p. 476.
334 "that their provisions . . . their relief": Memorandum, July 3, 1861, quoted in John G. Nicolay, *With Lincoln in the White House: Letters, Memoranda, and Other Writings of John G. Nicolay, 1860–1865*, ed. Michael Burlingame (Carbondale and Edwardsville: Southern Illinois University Press, 2000), p. 47.
334 "I now see . . . surrender": Joseph Holt and Winfield Scott to AL, March 5, 1861, Lincoln Papers.
334 to "reclaim . . . yourselves the aggressors": AL, "First Inaugural Address—First Edition and Revisions," January 1861, in *CW*, IV, p. 254 (first and second quotes); AL, "First Inaugural Address—Final Text," March 4, 1861, in ibid., p. 271 (third and fourth quotes).
334 "to eat or sleep": AL, quoted in Villard, *Memoirs of Henry Villard*, Vol. I, p. 156.
334 "he had literally . . . I must see them": Hay, "Life in the White House in the Time of Lincoln," *Century* (1890), pp. 34, 33.
335 "has no conception . . . security now": Entry for March 10, 1861, Charles Francis Adams diary, reel 76.
335 "owes a higher . . . office-hunters": *NYT*, April 4, 1861.
335 "The President proposes . . . upon him most": WHS to home, March 16, 1861, quoted in Seward, *Seward at Washington . . . 1846–1861*, p. 530.
335 "long-skirted . . . around his waist": Browne, *The Every-Day Life of Abraham Lincoln*, p. 418.
335 his large leather Bible . . . "inaudible music": Bayne, *Tad Lincoln's Father*, pp. 32–33.
335 Lincoln penned a note: AL to Winfield Scott, March 9, 1861, in *CW*, IV, p. 279.
335 Scott's reply . . . "20,000 volunteers": Winfield Scott to AL, March 11, 1861, Lincoln Papers.
335 "was disinclined . . . to be understood": *Welles diary*, Vol. I (1960 edn.), p. 6.
335 "was virtually . . . irresistible force": FPB to MB, March 12, 1861, Lincoln Papers.
335 Fox's ingenious plan: "Result of G.V. Fox's Plan for Reinforcing Fort Sumter; In His Own Writing," in *Confidential Correspondence of Gustavus Vasa Fox*, pp. 38–39; West, *Gideon Welles*, p. 98.
335 pacing up and down as he spoke: Helen Nicolay, "Lincoln's Cabinet," *Abraham Lincoln Quarterly* 5 (March 1949), p. 274.
336 "Assuming it to be . . . to attempt it?": AL to WHS, March 15, 1861, in *CW*, IV, p. 284.
336 description of the State Department: Charles Lanman, *Bohn's Hand-Book of Washington* (Washington, D.C.: Casimir Bohn, 1856), p. 35; Robert Mills, *Guide to the National Executive Offices and the Capitol of the United States* (Washington, D.C.: Peter Force Printer, 1841), published work 5007, reel 14, *The Papers of Robert Mills, 1781–1855*, ed. Pamela Scott, Scholarly Resources, microfilm edn.
336 Frederick . . . assistant secretary of state: WHS to FAS, March 8, 1861, in Seward, *Seward at Washington . . . 1846–1861*, p. 518.
336 Seward reiterated . . . emphatic negative reply: WHS to AL, March 15, 1861, Lincoln Papers.
336 "If the attempt . . . cannot advise it": SPC to AL, March 16, 1861, Lincoln Papers.
336 "the organization of . . . its experiment": SPC to Alphonso Taft, April 28, 1861, reel 15, Chase Papers.
336 "it seems to me . . . affirmative answer": SPC to AL, March 16, 1861, Lincoln Papers.
336 "to do any act . . . a civil war": Entry for March 16, 1861, in *The Diary of Edward Bates, 1859–1866*, p. 179.
336 "an inevitable . . . the better": Simon Cameron to AL, March 16, 1861, Lincoln Papers.
337 "impression has gone . . . untold disaster": GW to AL, March 15, 1861, Lincoln Papers.
337 "it would not . . . circumstances": Caleb B. Smith to AL, March 16, 1861, Lincoln Papers.
337 "every new conquest . . . those who administer it": MB to AL, March 15, 1861, Lincoln Papers.
337 if he could keep Virginia . . . give up Sumter: Thomas, *Abraham Lincoln*, pp. 251–52; Van Deusen, *William Henry Seward*, p. 278.
337 "utterly ruinous . . . recognition abroad": AL, "Message to Congress in Special Session," July 4, 1861, in *CW*, IV, p. 424.
337 Lincoln sent Fox to talk directly: Nicolay and Hay, *Abraham Lincoln*, Vol. III, p. 389.
337 half-rations . . . until April 15: Ari Hoogenboom, "Gustavus Fox and the Relief of Fort Sumter," *Civil War History* 9 (December 1963), p. 386.
337 Lincoln sent Stephen Hurlbut . . . "a fixed fact": Nicolay and Hay, *Abraham Lincoln*, Vol. III, pp. 390–91 (quote p. 391).
338 "a cypher . . . a humdrum lawyer": Niven, *Salmon P. Chase*, p. 244.
338 "humiliating . . . their respective states": WHS to AL, March 28, 1861, Lincoln Papers.
338 "certainly have . . . show me": SPC to AL, March 28, 1861, Lincoln Papers.
338 "I believe . . . Whig & Democratic element": FPB to SPC, March 26, 1861, reel 14, Chase Papers.
338 cabinet meetings set for Tuesdays and Fridays: Niven, *Salmon P. Chase*, p. 247 (quote); *Welles diary*, Vol. I, (1960 edn.), pp. 7–8.
338 William Russell: Leech, *Reveille in Washington*, p. 51.
338 "a subtle, quick . . . state mysteries": Entry for March 26, 1861, in William Howard Russell, *My Diary North and South* (Boston: T. O. H. P. Burnham, 1863), p. 34.
338 "put out his hand . . . 'the Mississippi' ": Entry for March 27, 1861, in ibid., p. 39.
338 "was already seated . . . agreeable, and sprightly": Ibid., pp. 41–42.
339 "easily . . . or Reynolds": Belden and Belden, *So Fell the Angels*, pp. 5–6.
339 "In reality . . . charm and magnetism": Mrs. Charles Walker, quoted in *Cincinnati Enquirer*, August 1, 1899.
339 "I shall be glad . . . *me* at any time": *Cincinnati Enquirer*, August 1, 1899; Belden and Belden, *So Fell the Angels*, p. 4 (italics from Belden and Belden).

339 "there was a Babel . . . he is famous": Entry for March 28, 1861, in Russell, *My Diary North and South*, pp. 43, 44.
339 "according to recent . . . slave-holding States": Nicolay and Hay, *Abraham Lincoln*, Vol. III, p. 394.
339 "A very oppressive silence . . . not General": MB to GW, May 17, 1873, reel 25, Welles Papers.
340 "timid temporizing . . . you are lost": FPB, Sr., to Martin Van Buren, May 1, 1861, reel 34, Papers of Martin Van Buren, Manuscript Division, Library of Congress.
340 Lincoln was unable to sleep: Nicolay and Hay, *Abraham Lincoln*, Vol. III, p. 395.
340 "of all the trials . . . to survive them": Memorandum, July 3, 1861, quoted in Nicolay, *With Lincoln in the White House*, p. 46.
340 Lincoln presented . . . "for his expedition": Nicolay and Hay, *Abraham Lincoln*, Vol. III, pp. 429–33 (quote p. 433).
340 "would be impossible . . . of time": JGN to TB, March 31, 1861, container 2, Nicolay Papers.
340 "it was finally . . . to go to war": George Harrington, "President Lincoln and His Cabinet: Inside Glimpses," undated, unpublished manuscript, George R. Harrington Papers, Missouri Historical Society, St. Louis, Mo.
341 "a peaceful . . . of the whole north": Frederick L. Roberts to WHS, March 18, 1861, reel 62, Seward Papers.
341 "Unionists . . . *save the country*": Benjamin Ogle Tayloe to WHS, April 3, 1861, reel 63, Seward Papers.
341 "no conception . . . equal to the hour": Entries for March 28 (first quote) and March 31, 1861, Charles Francis Adams diary, reel 76.
341 "two supreme illusions": Frederic Bancroft, "Seward's Proposition of April 1, 1861, For a Foreign War and a Dictatorship," *Harper's New Monthly Magazine* 99 (October 1899), p. 791.
341 Three commissioners . . . resorted to an indirect link: Thomas, *Abraham Lincoln*, pp. 250–51.
341 "would be evacuated . . . next five days": Ellsworth D. Draper and Joshua L. Rosenbloom, "Secession C: Fort Sumter: The Near Fiasco," p. 9, Case Study, Lincoln and Fort Sumter, Kennedy School of Government, Harvard University, 1983, author's collection.
341 "Some thoughts for the President's consideration": WHS to AL, April 1, 1861, Lincoln Papers.
341 "handwriting . . . hands of any clerk": Seward, *Reminiscences of a War-Time Statesman and Diplomat*, p. 149.
342 "We are . . . domestic or foreign": WHS to AL, "Some thoughts for the President's consideration," April 1, 1861, Lincoln Papers.
342 "the symbolism of Federal authority": Draper and Rosenbloom, "Secession C: Fort Sumter," p. 11.
342 under the heading of "For Foreign Nations": Norman B. Ferris, "Lincoln and Seward in Civil War Diplomacy: Their Relationship at the Outset Reexamined," *Journal of the Abraham Lincoln Association* 12 (1991), pp. 25–26.
342 "that there was no . . . the ruling party": WHS, quoted by Rudolf Schleiden, quoted in Richard N. Current, "Comment," *JALA* (1991), p. 45.
342 "whatever policy . . . assume responsibility": WHS to AL, "Some thoughts for the President's consideration," April 1, 1861, Lincoln Papers.
342 "had Mr. Lincoln . . . the whole affair": Nicolay, *A Short Life of Abraham Lincoln*, pp. 186, 187.
342 dashed off a reply . . . to respond in person: Donald, *Lincoln*, p. 290.
342 "without a policy . . . *I* must do it": AL to WHS, April 1, 1861, in *CW*, IV, pp. 316–17.
343 "to put down . . . this thing through": Entry for March 31, 1861, private journal of Montgomery Meigs (copy), container 13, Nicolay Papers.
343 "fit out the *Powhatan* . . . she is fitting out": AL to Andrew H. Foote, April 1, 1861, in *CW*, IV, p. 314.
343 three hundred sailors: Fox to MB, April 17, 1861, in *Confidential Correspondence of Gustavus Vasa Fox*, p. 33; "Result of G.V. Fox's Plan for Reinforcing Fort Sumpter; In His Own Writing," reprinted in ibid., p. 39.
343 assigned the *Powhatan* simultaneously to both Pickens and Sumpter: "Result of G.V. Fox's Plan for Reinforcing Fort Sumpter" p. 40; Fox to his wife [Virginia Woodbury Fox], May 2, 1861, ibid., pp. 42–43.
344 "Your father says . . . put my name?": Seward, *Reminiscences of a War-Time Statesman and Diplomat*, p. 148.
344 "leave New York . . . disposing of your force": *Welles diary*, Vol. I (1960 edn.), pp. 22–23.
344 "I am directed . . . without further notice": Simon Cameron to Robert S. Chew, April 6, 1861, in *CW*, IV, p. 323.
344 Lincoln had devised a means: Don E. Fehrenbacher, "Lincoln's Wartime Leadership: The First Hundred Days," *Journal of the Abraham Lincoln Association* 9 (1987), esp. p. 7.
344 "embarrassed by . . . errors imputed to them": *Welles diary*, Vol. I (1960 edn.), pp. 23–25.
345 Porter had already set sail . . . had priority: Hoogenboom, "Gustavus Fox and the Relief of Fort Sumter," *CWH* (1963), p. 392.
345 Fox reached Charleston . . . futilely searching: Fox to MB, April 17, 1861, in *Confidential Correspondence of Gustavus Vasa Fox*, p. 32.
345 At 3:30 a.m. . . . in one hour: James Chesnut, Jr., and Stephen D. Lee to Robert Anderson, April 12, 1861, enclosure 5 of Robert Anderson to Lorenzo Thomas, April 19, 1861, *OR*, Ser. 1, Vol. I, p. 14.
345 Anderson's small garrison . . . "fighting launches": Fox to MB, April 17, 1861, in *Confidential Correspondence of Gustavus Vasa Fox*, pp. 32–34 (quote p. 33).
345 "the conflagration . . . taken refuge": Abner Doubleday, *Reminiscences of Forts Sumter and Moultrie in 1860–'61* (New York: Harper & Bros., 1876), p. 157.
345 Thirty-four hours after . . . surrendered: Robert Anderson to Simon Cameron, April 18, 1860, *OR*, Ser. 1, Vol. I, p. 12.
345 a dignified fifty-round salute: Entry of April 14, 1861, *Diary of Edmund Ruffin*, Vol. I, ed. William Kauffmann Scarborough (Baton Rouge: Louisiana State University Press, 1972), p. 599; Robert Anderson to Simon Cameron, April 18, 1860, *OR*, Ser. 1, Vol. I, p. 12.

345 only one Union soldier: David S. Heidler and Jeanne T. Heidler, "Fort Sumter, Bombardment of 12–14 April 1861," in *Encyclopedia of the American Civil War: A Political, Social, and Military History*, ed. David S. Heidler and Jeanne T. Heidler (New York and London: W. W. Norton, 2000), p. 760. Another soldier was mortally wounded in the explosion.
345 "it would be . . . of his friend": Hamilton Basso, *Beauregard: The Great Creole* (New York and London: Charles Scribner's Sons, 1933), p. 84.
345 Convinced that . . . "the general public": "Result of G.V. Fox's Plan for Reinforcing Fort Sumpter," in *Confidential Correspondence of Gustavus Vasa Fox*, p. 41.
345 "by an accident . . . justified by the result": AL to Gustavus V. Fox, in *CW*, IV, pp. 350–51.
346 "but beyond . . . no using of force": AL, "First Inaugural Address—Final Text," March 4, 1861, in ibid., p. 266.
346 fatalities: "The Price in Blood: Casualties in the Civil War," www.civilwarhome/casualties.htm., accessed July 2005.

CHAPTER 13: "THE BALL HAS OPENED"

Page
347 "where the great lamps . . . question of disunion": Walt Whitman, *Specimen Days, The Complete Prose Works of Walt Whitman*, Vol. I (New York: G. P. Putnam's Sons, 1902), pp. 28–30.
347 "Our people now . . . is dead": *Daily National Intelligencer*, Washington, D.C., April 15, 1861.
348 "The ball has opened . . . their glasses": *NYT*, April 13, 1861.
348 cabinet session . . . "to invite disaster": Seward, *Reminiscences of a War-Time Statesman and Diplomat*, p. 152.
348 "history tells us . . . lose their heads": WHS, quoted in entry for March 26, 1861, in Russell, *My Diary North and South*, p. 35.
348 set the Fourth of July . . . "by the Executive": Seward, *Reminiscences of a War-Time Statesman and Diplomat*, p. 152.
348 Nicolay made a copy: JGN to TB, April 14, 1861, container 2, Nicolay Papers.
348 stamped the great seal . . . following day: Seward, *Reminiscences of a War-Time Statesman and Diplomat*, p. 152.
348 Lincoln took a carriage ride: JGN to TB, April 14, 1861, container 2, Nicolay Papers.
348 he welcomed his old rival . . . would be dead: Sandburg, *Abraham Lincoln: The War Years*, Vol. I, p. 213; entry for June 3, 1861, in Long, *The Civil War Day by Day*, p. 82.
348 his solid support . . . "maintain the Government": *Daily Morning Chronicle*, Washington, D.C., October 16, 1864.
348 "In this hour . . . treason and traitors": *New York Leader* (first quote) and *Boston Herald* (second quote), reprinted in *NYTrib*, April 15, 1861.
348 "The response . . . by telegraph": Seward, *Reminiscences of a War-Time Statesman and Diplomat*, p. 153.
349 "We begin to look . . . a week ago": Entry for April 15, 1861, *Diary of George Templeton Strong*, Vol. III, pp. 120–21.
349 Seward predicted . . . in sixty days: Carpenter, "A Day with Governor Seward," Seward Papers.
349 "be bloody . . . and ruin": "Washington Correspondence, 16 April 1861," in Hay, *Lincoln's Journalist*, p. 58.
349 "for the wicked . . . Southern States": Governor of Kentucky (Beriah Magoffin), quoted in Seward, *Reminiscences of a War-Time Statesman and Diplomat*, p. 154.
349 Virginia seceded from the Union: Long, *The Civil War Day by Day*, p. 60.
349 "one of the most . . . history": J. G. Randall, *Lincoln the President*. Vol. I: *Springfield to Gettysburg, part I* (New York: Dodd, Mead & Co., 1946–55; New York: Da Capo Press, 1997), p. 357.
349 "We never saw" . . . soon be fifteen: *Daily Picayune*, New Orleans, April 19, 1861, morning edition (first and second quote), afternoon edition (third quote).
350 "the very best . . . in the field": General Winfield Scott, quoted in *The Wartime Papers of R. E. Lee*, ed. Clifford Dowdey and Louis H. Manarin (Boston: Little, Brown, for the Virginia Civil War Commission, 1961), p. 3.
350 Lincoln had designated Blair: Robert E. Lee to Reverdy Johnson, February 25, 1868, in *Wartime Papers of R. E. Lee*, p. 4.
350 "I come to you . . . the Union army?": FPB, quoted in William Ernest Smith, *The Francis Preston Blair Family in Politics*, Vol. II (New York: The Macmillan Company, 1933), p. 17.
350 "as candidly and as courteously": Lee to Johnson, February 25, 1868, in *Wartime Papers of R. E. Lee*, p. 4.
350 "Mr. Blair . . . my native state?": R. E. Lee, quoted in *National Intelligencer*, Washington, D.C., August 9, 1866.
350 Lee called upon old General Scott: Lee to Johnson, February 25, 1868, in *Wartime Papers of R. E. Lee*, p. 4
350 he contacted Scott . . . "be dear to me": Lee to Scott, April 20, 1861, in ibid., pp. 8–9 (quotes p. 9).
350 "Now we are in . . . draw my sword": Lee to Anne Marshall, April 20, 1861, in ibid., pp. 9–10.
350 Lee was designated . . . Virginia state forces: Ibid., pp. 3, 4, 5.
350 Benjamin Hardin Helm: "Helm, Benjamin Hardin (1831–1863)," in Stewart Sifakis, *Who Was Who in the Confederacy* (New York: Facts on File, 1988), p. 125.
350 While conducting business . . . "liking of men": Helm, *The True Story of Mary*, p. 127.
350 "Southern-rights Democrat": Ibid., pp. 128, 183.
350 "Ben, here is . . . your honor bid": *Daily Picayune*, New Orleans, March 14, 1897 (quotes); AL to Simon Cameron, April 16, 1861, in *CW*, IV, p. 335.
351 Helm unable to sleep . . . "hour of his life": *Daily Picayune*, New Orleans, March 14, 1897.
351 a Commission in the Confederate Army: "Helm, Benjamin Hardin," in Sifakis, *Who Was Who in the Confederacy*, p. 125.

351 Seward argued . . . seize vessels: Ivan Musicant, *Divided Waters: The Naval History of the Civil War* (New York: HarperCollins, 1995), pp. 51–52.
351 Welles countered . . . exiting ships: Niven, *Gideon Welles*, p. 356; Musicant, *Divided Waters*, p. 51.
351 The cabinet split down the middle: Niven, *Gideon Welles*, p. 356.
351 formal blockade proclamation: AL, "Proclamation of a Blockade," April 19, 1861, in *CW*, IV, pp. 338–39.
351 Welles and the Navy Department: Robert V. Bruce, *Lincoln and the Tools of War* (Indianapolis and New York: Bobbs-Merrill, 1956), pp. 6, 16; Musicant, *Divided Waters*, pp. 41–43.
352 a wedding celebration: Grimsley, "Six Months in the White House," *JISHS*, p. 51; Bruce, *Lincoln and the Tools of War*, p. 9.
352 "would soon secede . . . Confederacy": Craig L. Symonds, "Buchanan, Franklin," in *Encyclopedia of the American Civil War*, ed. Heidler and Heidler, p. 303.
352 Buchanan resigned . . . "from this date": Bruce, *Lincoln and the Tools of War*, p. 16 (quote); "Buchanan, Franklin (1800–1874)," in Sifakis, *Who Was Who in the Confederacy*, p. 40.
352 the Norfolk Navy Yard: Musicant, *Divided Waters*, pp. 28–29.
352 "extreme uneasiness . . . made by the first": Entry for April 18, 1861, Charles Francis Adams diary, reel 76.
352 "The scene . . . indescribably fearful": *Sun*, Baltimore, Md., April 20, 1861.
352 The enraged crowd . . . knives and revolvers: John G. Nicolay and John Hay, *Abraham Lincoln: A History*, Vol. IV (New York: Century Co., 1917), p. 115 (quote); *Sun*, Baltimore, Md., April 20, 1861.
352 "It's a notable . . . the anniversary": Entry for April 19, 1861, *Diary of George Templeton Strong*, Vol. III, p. 126.
352 "make no point . . . *around* Baltimore": AL to Thomas H. Hicks and George W. Brown, April 20, 1861, in *CW*, IV, p. 340.
352 an angry committee of delegates: Entry for April 22, 1861, in *Lincoln Day by Day*, Vol. III, p. 37.
352 "I must have troops . . . that they must do": AL, "Reply to Baltimore Committee," April 22, 1861, in *CW*, IV, pp. 341–42.
353 "the censorship" . . . bridges surrounding the city: Ben: Perley Poore, *Perley's Reminiscences of Sixty Years in the National Metropolis*, Vol. II (Philadelphia, 1886; New York, AMS Press, 1971), pp. 78–79.
353 "Literally . . . entire isolation": Villard, *Memoirs of Henry Villard*, Vol. I, p. 167.
353 Cameron slept in his office: Leech, *Reveille in Washington*, p. 61.
353 "Here we were . . . to defend it": JGN to TB, April 26, 1861, container 2, Nicolay Papers.
353 "No despatches . . . are prisoners": Entry for April 20, 1861, *Diary of George Templeton Strong*, Vol. III, p. 127.
353 "rebels are at . . . calm & conceal it": Hiram Barney to SPC, April 21, 1861, reel 15, Chase Papers.
354 to accompany Major Robert Anderson . . . with their relieved father: Janet Chase Hoyt, "A Woman's Memories," *NYTrib*, April 5, 1891.
354 These "were terrible days of suspense" . . . let her join him: Entry for May 19, 1861, Fanny Seward diary, Seward Papers.
354 "It is hard . . . life is in danger": FAS to WHS, April [27? 1861], reel 114, Seward Papers.
354 "a day of gloom and doubt": "24 April 1861, Wednesday," in Hay, *Inside Lincoln's White House*, p. 11.
354 staring out the window . . . "Why don't they come!": Nicolay and Hay, *Abraham Lincoln*, Vol. IV, p. 152.
354 "I don't believe . . . Northern realities": "24 April 1861, Wednesday," in Hay, *Inside Lincoln's White House*, p. 11.
354 "to arrest . . . *not* be justifiable": AL to Winfield Scott, April 25, 1861, in *CW*, IV, p. 344.
354 "the first of the redeemed": "1 May 1861, Wednesday," in Hay, *Inside Lincoln's White House*, p. 16.
355 If resistance along . . . "for the public safety": AL to Winfield Scott, April 27, 1861, in *CW*, IV, p. 347.
355 "arrest, and detain . . . to the public safety": AL, "Message to Congress in Special Session," July 4, 1861, in ibid., p. 429.
355 Seward later claimed . . . "further hesitation": Carpenter, "A Day with Governor Seward," Seward Papers.
355 Taney blasted Lincoln: Hon. Sherrill Halbert, "The Suspension of the Writ of Habeas Corpus by President Lincoln," *American Journal of Legal History* 2 (April 1958), pp. 97–100.
355 Bates, though reluctant to oppose Taney: Cain, *Lincoln's Attorney General*, pp. 145, 147.
355 "in a time . . . the insurgents": EB to AL, July 5, 1861, Lincoln Papers.
355 As chief executive . . . "one be violated?": AL, "Message to Congress in Special Session," July 4, 1861, in *CW*, IV, p. 430.
355 "grave threats . . . extravagant to endure": Justice Thurgood Marshall, dissenting opinion in *Skinner v. Railway Labor Executives' Association*, 489 U.S. 602 (1989), text available through Legal Information Institute website, Cornell Law School, www.law.cornell.edu (accessed June 2003).
355 "government will . . . be less liberty": GW to Mary Jane Welles, May 5, 1861 (transcript), reel 19, Welles Papers.
355 "steps and balconies" . . . Mary and her friends watched: *NYT*, May 1, 1861.
355 "go down to Charleston . . . an Illinois yell": "25 April 1861, Thursday," in Hay, *Inside Lincoln's White House*, p. 11.
356 more than eight thousand troops were in Washington: WHS to FAS, April 26, 1861, quoted in Seward, *Seward at Washington . . . 1846–1861*, p. 559.
356 He did not, however, grant her request: FAS to WHS, April [27? 1861], reel 114, Seward Papers.
356 almost completed . . . "at all hours": Anna Wharton Seward to FAS, April 28, 1861, reel 116, Seward Papers.
356 "immense sacrifice . . . awaits the oppressors": FAS to WHS, April [28? 1861], reel 114, Seward Papers.
356 "there would be . . . serenely adjusted": Conversation between WHS and Charles King, reported in entry of May 20, 1861, *Diary of George Templeton Strong*, Vol. III, p. 144.
356 "to disturb as little . . . of the people": Entry of April 15, 1861, in *The Diary of Edward Bates, 1859–1866*, p. 183.
356 a "fatal error . . . of the North": MB to AL, May 16, 1861, Lincoln Papers.
356 "I consider . . . to govern themselves": "7 May, Tuesday," in Hay, *Inside Lincoln's White House*, p. 20.

356 John Stuart Mill . . . "the civilized world": John Stuart Mill, quoted in McPherson, *Battle Cry of Freedom*, p. 550.
357 "the dissolution . . . established in America": The Earl of Shrewsbury, quoted in ibid., p. 551.
357 "It is of infinite . . . the various parts": George Washington, "Farewell Address," September 17, 1796, in *A Compilation of the Messages and Papers of the Presidents*, Vol. I (New York: Bureau of National Literature, Inc., 1897), p. 207.
357 "a mortar battery . . . assassination suspicion": "19 April 1861, Friday," in Hay, *Inside Lincoln's White House*, pp. 2–3.
357 "Thousands of soldiers . . . to feel secure": MTL to Mrs. Samuel H. Melvin, April 27, 1861, in Turner and Turner, *Mary Todd Lincoln*, p. 86.
357 "The intense . . . around the city": Elizabeth Grimsley to Mrs. John T. Stuart, April 29, 1861, quoted in *Concerning Mr. Lincoln*, comp. Pratt, p. 77.
357 Tad boasted . . . from the roof: Bayne, *Tad Lincoln's Father*, pp. 68–69 (quotes p. 68).
358 "between the grey haired . . . plough hardened hands": "20 April 1861, Saturday," in Hay, *Inside Lincoln's White House*, p. 4.
358 "rather pale . . . all 'go ahead' ": Entry for January 13, 1862, *The Diary of Horatio Nelson Taft, 1861–1865*, available through "Washington During the Civil War: The Diary of Horatio Nelson Taft, 1861–1865," American Memory, Library of Congress, http://memory.loc.gov [hereafter Taft diary].
358 "More than once . . . arm of the chair": Bayne, *Tad Lincoln's Father*, pp. 35, 108.
358 Julia was appalled: Ibid., pp. 101, 102–06, 109–10.
358 "the most lovable . . . gentle-mannered": Ibid., p. 8.
358 retreat to his mother's room . . . write verses: Turner and Turner, *Mary Todd Lincoln*, p. 120.
358 "what she wanted when she wanted it": Bayne, *Tad Lincoln's Father*, p. 49.
358 A curious example . . . purple strings!: Ibid., pp. 43–48 (quotes p. 45).
359 brothers and brothers-in-law: Randall, *Mary Lincoln*, p. 294; Ishbel Ross, *The President's Wife: Mary Todd Lincoln, A Biography* (New York: G. P. Putnam's Sons, 1973), p. 144.
359 the White House . . . "unsuccessful hotel": Stoddard, *Inside the White House in War Times*, p. 26.
359 "the family apartments . . . (first President)": Grimsley, "Six Months in the White House," *JISHS*, p. 47.
359 went on a shopping trip: See entries for May 10–22, 1861, in *Lincoln Day by Day*, Vol. III, pp. 41–43.
359 $20,000 allowance to maintain the White House: Seale, *The President's House*, Vol. I, p. 382.
359 state guest room . . . "clusters of grapes": Betty C. Monkman, *The White House: Its Historic Furnishings and First Families* (New York: Abbeville Press, 2000), p. 125.
359 The press exaggerated . . . never even visited: Grimsley, "Six Months in the White House," *JISHS*, pp. 58–59.
359 the bills added up: Entries for May 13, 21, 24, and 29, 1861, in *Lincoln Day by Day*, Vol. III, pp. 41, 43–45.
360 Kate Chase was hard at work . . . to borrow $10,000: Ross, *Proud Kate*, p. 62; SPC to Henry Carrington, April 16, 1861, reel 15, Chase Papers.
360 Chase later complained . . . with the president: Belden and Belden, *So Fell the Angels*, p. 94.
360 "in a single season" . . . William Sprague: William Perrine, "The Dashing Kate Chase and Her Great Ambition," *Ladies' Home Journal* XVIII (June 1901), p. 11.
360 Kate had first met . . . "see the other": Richard Parsons, quoted in *Ohio State Journal*, Columbus, Ohio, August 4, 1899.
361 Sprague would never forget . . . "it was yesterday": William Sprague to KCS, May 27, 1866, William and Catherine Chase Sprague Papers, 1850–1900, MS 79.17, Manuscript Division, Special Collections Department, Brown University Library, Providence, Rhode Island [hereafter Sprague Papers].
361 William Sprague: Peg A. Lamphier, *Kate Chase and William Sprague: Politics and Gender in a Civil War Marriage* (Lincoln: University of Nebraska Press, 2003), pp. 27–28.
361 "I was thrust . . . highest positions": William Sprague, quoted in Lamphier, *Kate Chase and William Sprague*, p. 32.
361 As the largest employer . . . of his own money: "The Rhode Island Spragues," unknown newspaper clipping, December 5, 1883, in KCS vertical file, DWP.
361 "a loan . . . the troops": Belden and Belden, *So Fell the Angels*, p. 42; ninety-six horses, Lamphier, *Kate Chase and William Sprague*, p. 39.
361 On April 29 . . . "movements of the regiment": *Star*, April 29, 1861.
361 physical description of Sprague: Belden and Belden, *So Fell the Angels*, p. 42.
361 "a small . . . wealth and social standing": "26 April 1861, Friday," in Hay, *Inside Lincoln's White House*, p. 12.
362 "When men like . . . such an army": "30 April 1861, Tuesday," in ibid., p. 14.
362 "the first, the only . . . lodgment there": Entry for November 11, 1868, KCS diary, Sprague Papers.
362 "Do you remember . . . such in life": William Sprague to KCS, May 27, 1866, Sprague Papers.
362 "accustomed to . . . be anticipated": Entry for November 11, 1868, KCS diary, Sprague Papers.
362 Nettie Chase told Kate . . . would marry: KCS to Janet Chase Hoyt, September 29, 1861, reel 17, Chase Papers.
362 Elmer Ellsworth: Brian D. McKnight, "Ellsworth, Elmer Ephraim," in *Encyclopedia of the American Civil War*, ed. Heidler and Heidler, p. 647: Turner and Turner, *Mary Todd Lincoln*, p. 92.
362 wrote a personal note of condolence: AL to Ephrain D. and Phoebe Ellsworth, May 25, 1861, in *CW*, IV, pp. 385–86.
363 "quite unable . . . out of my eyes": JGN to TB, May 25, 1861, container 2, Nicolay Papers.
363 Mary was presented . . . packed away: Bayne, *Tad Lincoln's Father*, p. 39.
363 a resolution . . . belligerent status: Entry for May 6, 1861, in Long, *The Civil War Day by Day*, pp. 70–71; Norman A. Graebner, "Northern Diplomacy and European Neutrality," in *Why the North Won the Civil War*, ed.

David Donald (Baton Rouge: Louisiana State University Press, 1960; New York and London: Collier Books, Macmillan Publishing Co., 1962), p. 60.

363 "younger branch . . . is too late": WHS to FAS, May 17, 1861, quoted in Seward, *Seward at Washington . . . 1846–1861*, pp. 575–76.

363 "God damn 'em, I'll give 'em hell": Van Deusen, *William Henry Seward*, p. 298.

363 On May 21 . . . two wars at once: Jay Monaghan, *Diplomat in Carpet Slippers: Abraham Lincoln Deals with Foreign Affairs* (Indianapolis and New York: Bobbs-Merrill, 1945), p. 114; Allen Thorndike Rice, "A Famous Diplomatic Dispatch," *North American Review* 142 (April 1886), pp. 402–11.

363 "surprised and grieved . . . she has a natural claim": AL, "Revision of William H. Seward to Charles Francis Adams," May 21, 1861, in *CW,* IV, pp. 377–78, 379 n14, 380.

364 the basis for a hard-line policy: Todd Anthony Rosa, "Diplomacy, U.S.A." in *Encyclopedia of the American Civil War,* ed. Heidler and Heidler, p. 602.

364 "currency to Southern bonds": WHS to TW, May 23, 1861, quoted in Seward, *Seward at Washington . . . 1846–1861*, p. 576.

364 "the ablest American" . . . his country's position: Rice, "A Famous Diplomatic Dispatch," *NAR* 142 (1886), pp. 402–3, 404 (quote).

364 "It is due to . . . every day": WHS to FAS, May 17, 1861, quoted in Seward, *Seward at Washington . . . 1846–1861*, p. 575.

364 "Executive skill . . . assiduous cooperation": WHS to FAS, June 5, 1861, quoted in ibid., p. 590.

365 "to his chief . . . personal attachment": Nicolay and Hay, *Abraham Lincoln*, Vol. IV, p. 449.

365 "a brilliant assemblage . . . twenty years more": *NYT,* May 22, 1861.

365 forced to rely on government loans: Blue, *Salmon P. Chase*, pp. 143–46.

365 functions . . . belonged to the War Department: Niven, *Salmon P. Chase*, pp. 253–54; Bradley, *Simon Cameron*, pp. 177–78.

365 "the principal charge . . . regiments in Tennessee": SPC to Trowbridge, March 21, 1864, reel 32, Chase Papers.

365 "The President . . . half-consciousness": *NYT,* April 23, 1861, enclosed with SPC to AL, April 25, 1861, Lincoln Papers.

366 "has too much truth in it": SPC to AL, April 25, 1861, Lincoln Papers.

366 "Oh, it was a terrible time . . . no anything": *NYT,* June 3, 1878.

366 weapons in short supply . . . messengers, and watchmen: A. Howard Meneely, *The War Department, 1861: A Study in Mobilization and Administration* (New York: Columbia University Press, 1928), pp. 25–26, 106–11.

366 "I was . . . to be envied": *NYT,* June 3, 1878.

366 "so large . . . without compensation": AL, "To the Senate and House of Representatives," May 26, 1862, in *CW,* V, p. 242.

366 Alexander Cummings: Bradley, *Simon Cameron*, pp. 196–97.

366 "embargo" on . . . "so strict": *NYT,* June 22, 1861.

366 congressmen and senators . . . "President's message": *NYT,* July 4, 1861.

367 Senator Orville Browning . . . "of the Country": Entry for July 3, 1861, in Browning, *The Diary of Orville Hickman Browning*, Vol. I, p. 475.

367 Jefferson had denounced: "From Time to Time: History of the State of the Union," The White House, www.whitehouse.gov/stateoftheunion/history.html (accessed July 2003); "History of the State of the Union," National Archives and Records Administration, http://clinton4.nara.gov/WH/SOTU00/history /address.html (accessed July 2003).

367 had submitted their written messages: Entry for July 5, 1861, in Russell, *My Diary North and South*, p. 388.

367 "give the legal means . . . the government itself": AL, "Message to Congress in Special Session," July 4, 1861, in *CW,* IV, pp. 426, 431–32, 437, 438.

368 "In spite of . . . masses of the people": *NYT,* July 7, 1861.

368 Congress responded . . . patriotic fervor: Nicolay and Hay, *Abraham Lincoln*, Vol. IV, pp. 370, 375–76, 382–83.

368 "No mention is . . . of the rebellion": *Douglass' Monthly* (August 1861).

368 "We have an honest . . . to Seward": *NYT,* July 7, 1861.

368 Benjamin Butler . . . therefore contraband of war: Benjamin F. Butler to Winfield Scott, May 24, 1861, *OR,* Ser. 1, Vol. II, pp. 649–50; Edward L. Pierce, "The Contrabands at Fortress Monroe," *Atlantic Monthly* 8 (November 1861), pp. 627–28.

369 "I will accept . . . resign your commission": Benjamin F. Butler, *Butler's Book: Autobiography and Personal Reminiscences of Major-General Benjamin F. Butler* (Boston: A. M. Thayer & Co., 1892), p. 242.

369 Butler's order . . . a confiscation law: Endorsements by Winfield Scott and Simon Cameron, in Benjamin F. Butler to Winfield Scott, May 24, 1861, *OR,* Ser. 1, Vol. II, p. 652; Simon Cameron to Benjamin F. Butler, May 30, 1861, container 5, Papers of Benjamin F. Butler, Manuscript Division, Library of Congress [hereafter Butler Papers]; John Syrett, "Confiscation Acts (6 August 1861 and 17 July 1862)," in *Encyclopedia of the American Civil War,* ed. Heidler and Heidler, pp. 477–79.

369 "You were right . . . this new doctrine": MB to Benjamin F. Butler, May 29, 1861, container 5, Butler Papers.

369 hundreds of courageous slaves: Pierce, "The Contrabands at Fortress Monroe," *Atlantic Monthly* (1861), pp. 628, 630.

370 Two weeks into . . . not to eliminate slavery: Entry for July 22, 1861, in Long, *The Civil War Day by Day,* p. 100.

370 "sword . . . slavery *must die*": John Lothrop Motley to his wife, June 23, 1861, in *The Correspondence of John Lothrop Motley*, Vol. I, ed. George William Curtis (New York: Harper & Bros., 1889), p. 390.

370 "Forward to Richmond!": *NYTrib,* June 26, 1861.

370 "the immediate movement . . . 20th July": Entry for July 11, 1861, in Browning, *The Diary of Orville Hickman Browning*, Vol. I, p. 479.

370 General Scott hesitated . . . public would diminish: James A. Rawley, *Turning Points of the Civil War* (Lincoln: University of Nebraska Press, 1966), pp. 52–53.

370 McDowell's plan: John G. Nicolay, *The Outbreak of Rebellion. Campaigns of the Civil War*, new introduction by Mark E. Neeley, Jr. (New York: Charles Scribner's Sons, 1881; New York: Da Capo Press, 1995), p. 173.

370 "a terrible . . . ferocious warriors": Entry for August 1861, in Adam Gurowski, *Diary from March 4, 1861 to November 12, 1862*. Burt Franklin: Research & Source Works #229 (Boston, 1862; New York: Burt Franklin, 1968), pp. 78–79.

370 "Foreigners . . . drive them off": EB to James O. Broadhead, July 13, 1861, James Overton Broadhead Papers, Missouri Historical Society, St. Louis, Mo. [hereafter Broadhead Papers, MoSHi].

370 troop strengths: Rawley, *Turning Points of the Civil War*, p. 54.

371 On June 29 . . . approved McDowell's plan: Nicolay, *Outbreak of Rebellion*, p. 173.

371 The Battle of Bull Run: Many battles of the Civil War came to be known by different names within the Union and the Confederacy. The first battle at Manassas Junction, for example, would be known as the Battle of Bull Run in the North and the Battle of Manassas in the South. As James M. McPherson explains, "In each case but one (Shiloh) the Confederates named the battle after the town that served as their base, while the Union forces chose the landmark nearest to the fighting or to their own lines, usually a river or stream." In the case of Shiloh, the Confederates named the battle for a nearby church, McPherson, *Battle Cry of Freedom*, p. 346 n7.

371 "roar of the artillery . . . grew intense": Grimsley, "Six Months in the White House," *JISHS*, p. 65.

371 "stop the *roar* in [her] ears": EBL to SPL, July 21, 1861, in *Wartime Washington*, ed. Laas, p. 65.

371 "an unusually heavy . . . this time to-morrow": Entry for July 21, 1861, in Russell, *My Diary North and South*, p. 449.

371 In the crowded space . . . responsibilities: David Homer Bates, *Lincoln in the Telegraph Office: Recollections of the United States Military Telegraph Corps during the Civil War*, introduction by James A. Rawley (New York: Century Co., 1907; Lincoln and London: University of Nebraska Press, 1995), p. 87.

371 and read aloud . . . "with joy": *NYT*, July 22, 1861 (quote); *NYT*, July 26, 1861.

371 "There is Jackson . . . like a stone wall": Poore, *Perley's Reminiscences*, Vol. II, p. 85.

371 At 3 p.m. . . . fifteen-minute intervals: Entry for July 21, 1861, in *Lincoln Day by Day*, Vol. III, p. 55.

371 The telegraph line . . . Telegraph Corps: Bates, *Lincoln in the Telegraph Office*, p. 88.

371 "a small three-storied" . . . description of headquarters: Entry for July 19, 1861, in Russell, *My Diary North and South*, p. 431.

372 "his confidence . . . President left": JGN to TB, July 21, 1861, container 2, Nicolay Papers.

372 "the Union Army . . . victory": Seward, *Seward at Washington . . . 1846–1861*, p. 598.

372 Bates confided his anxiety: Cain, *Lincoln's Attorney General*, p. 153; entry for July 21, 1861, in *Lincoln Day by Day*, Vol. III, p. 55.

372 "the first time he ever left home": Entry for July 5, 1861, in *The Diary of Edward Bates, 1859–1866*, p. 188.

372 a new intimacy with his president: Cain, *Lincoln's Attorney General*, p. 153.

372 "A sudden swoop . . . behind them": Edmund C. Stedman, *The Battle of Bull Run* (New York: Rudd & Carleton, 1861), p. 32.

372 "never stopped . . . New-York": Janet Chase Hoyt, "A Woman's Memories," *NYTrib*, June 7, 1891.

372 "Army wagons . . . sights and sounds": Stedman, *The Battle of Bull Run*, p. 35.

372 "General McDowell's . . . of the Army": Seward, *Seward at Washington . . . 1846–1861*, p. 598.

372 "a terribly frightened . . . to Gen. Scott's": JGN to TB, July 21, 1861, container 2, Nicolay Papers.

373 "He listened in silence . . . army headquarters": Nicolay and Hay, *Abraham Lincoln*, Vol. IV, pp. 353–54.

373 "Oh what a sad . . . sabbath been": EBL to SPL, July 21, 1861, in *Wartime Washington*, ed. Laas, p. 65.

373 death of James Cameron: "Cameron, James (?–1861)," in Stewart Sifakis, *Who Was Who in the Union* (New York: Facts on File, 1988), p. 63; Nicolay, *Outbreak of Rebellion*, p. 214.

373 "I loved my brother . . . of his duty": Simon Cameron to SPC, July 21, 1861, reel 16, Chase Papers.

373 "Every thing . . . to the field": WHS to family, July 1861, quoted in Seward, *Seward at Washington . . . 1846–1861*, pp. 598–99.

373 the returning soldiers . . . "at this juncture": Grimsley, "Six Months in the White House," *JISHS*, pp. 66–67 (quotes p. 67).

373 Lincoln did not sleep . . . future military policy: Nicolay and Hay, *Abraham Lincoln*, Vol. IV, p. 368.

373 "be constantly drilled" . . . the blockade operative: AL, "Memoranda of Military Policy Suggested by the Bull Run Defeat," July 23, 1861, in *CW*, IV, p. 457.

373 a telegram was also sent: Lorenzo Thomas to George B. McClellan, July 22, 1861, *OR*, Ser. 1, Vol. II, p. 753; entry for July 22, 1861, in *Lincoln Day by Day*, Vol. III, p. 56.

374 devised a strategy . . . East Tennessee: AL, "Memoranda of Military Policy Suggested by the Bull Run Defeat," July 27, 1861, in *CW*, IV, pp. 457–58.

374 "If there were . . . Union out of it": Walt Whitman, *Specimen Days* (Philadelphia: Rees Welch Co., 1882; Philadelphia: David McKay, 1892; Boston: D. R. Godine, 1971), p. 13.

374 "a weak . . . inefficient Cabinet": *NYH*, July 27, 1861.

374 "Two weeks ago . . . a great victory": SPC to William P. Mellen, July 23, 1861, reel 16, Chase Papers.

374 "public censure . . . on Lincoln": Rawley, *Turning Points of the Civil War*, p. 56.

374 "The sun rises, but shines not": Whitman, *Specimen Days* (1971 edn.), p. 12.

374 "Some had neither . . . blankets": Entry for July 22, 1861, in Russell, *My Diary North and South*, p. 467.

374 "awakened in the . . . stand the hurting": Janet Chase Hoyt, "A Woman's Memories," *NYTrib*, June 7, 1891.

374 "The dreadful disaster . . . could be offered": EMS to James Buchanan, July 26, 1861, reprinted in "A Page of

Political Correspondence. Unpublished Letters of Mr. Stanton to Mr. Buchanan," *North American Review* 129 (November 1879), pp. 482–83.

375 "an overweening confidence": Jefferson Davis, *The Rise and Fall of the Confederate Government*, Vol. I (1881; Richmond, Va.: Garrett & Massie, 1938; New York: Da Capo Press, 1990), p. 330.

375 General Johnston observed . . . faraway hospitals: Joseph E. Johnson, quoted in Nicolay, *Outbreak of Rebellion*, p. 211.

375 "Well we fought . . . our men": Nancy Bates to Hester Bates, July 25, 1861, Bates Papers, MoSHi.

375 "very melancholy": Entry of July 28, 1861, in Browning, *The Diary of Orville Hickman Browning*, Vol. I, p. 489.

375 "black despair . . . to [his] country": Horace Greeley to AL, July 29, 1861, Lincoln Papers.

375 He told humorous stories: Browne, *The Every-Day Life of Abraham Lincoln*, pp. 448–49.

375 "discourage all . . . I believe he would do it": William Tecumseh Sherman, *Memoirs of General W. T. Sherman*, (New York: D. Appleton and Company, 1875; New York: Penguin Books, 2000), pp. 175–76.

376 a "renewed patriotism": *NYT,* July 23, 1861.

376 "Let no loyal . . . greater efforts": *Chicago Tribune,* July 23, 1861.

376 Several papers compared: *Chicago Tribune,* July 23, 1861; *NYTrib,* reprinted in *Star,* July 27, 1861.

376 "The spirit of . . . facilities for defence": *NYT,* July 26, 1861.

376 could "take comfort": *Philadelphia Inquirer,* July 25, 1861.

CHAPTER 14: "I DO NOT INTEND TO BE SACRIFICED"

Page

377 "Nothing but a patent . . . at last": James Russell Lowell, "General McClellan's Report (1864)," in *The Writings of James Russell Lowell.* Vol. V: *Political Essays* (Cambridge, Mass.: The Riverside Press, 1871; 1890), pp. 94, 99.

377 when he arrived . . . Army of the Potomac: Entry for July 27, 1861, in Long, *The Civil War Day by Day,* p. 101.

377 Among the Union's . . . the Mexican War: See chapter 1 of Stephen W. Sears, *George B. McClellan: The Young Napoleon* (New York: Ticknor & Fields, 1988).

378 defeated a guerrilla band: Sears, *George B. McClellan,* p. 80.

378 "the man on horseback": Entry for July 27, 1861, in Russell, *My Diary North and South,* p. 480.

378 "a more martial look": Entry for July 1861, in Gurowski, *Diary from March 4, 1861 to November 12, 1862,* p. 76.

378 drunken soldiers . . . troops wander the city: Entry for July 27, 1861, in Russell, *My Diary North and South,* p. 479; *Star,* July 31, 1861.

378 "You have no idea . . . such yelling": GBM to MEM, [September 11, 1861], in *The Civil War Papers of George B. McClellan, Selected Correspondence, 1861–1865,* ed. Stephen W. Sears (New York: Ticknor & Fields, 1989), p. 98.

378 "the great obstacle": GBM to MEM, August 9, 1861, in ibid., 81.

378 "entirely insufficient . . . in our front": GBM to Winfield Scott, August 8, 1861, in ibid., p. 80.

378 Scott was furious . . . opposition forces: Winfield Scott to Simon Cameron, August 9, 1861, Lincoln Papers.

378 It would not be . . . miscalculations: Sears, *George B. McClellan,* pp. 103, 109.

378 discord . . . continued to escalate: GBM to AL, August 10, 1861, in *Civil War Papers of George B. McClellan,* p. 82; GBM to MEM, September 27, 1861, in ibid., pp. 103–04.

378 "concentric pressure": Sears, *George B. McClellan,* p. 98.

378 "crush . . . in one campaign": GBM to MEM, August 2, 1861, in *Civil War Papers of George B. McClellan,* p. 74.

378 "result . . . in my hands": GBM to MEM, August 9, 1861, in ibid., pp. 81–82.

378 "by some strange . . . of the land": GBM to MEM, July 27, 1861, in ibid., p. 70.

378 "the people call . . . country is saved": GBM to MEM, August 9, 1861, in ibid., pp. 81–82.

379 Scott was "a perfect imbecile . . . a *traitor*": GBM to MEM, August 8, 1861, in ibid., p. 81.

379 "eternal jealousy . . . distinction": GBM to MEM, October 6, 1861, in ibid., p. 106.

379 "The remedy . . . small of the back": Winfield Scott to Simon Cameron (copy), October 4, 1861, reel 1, Stanton Papers, DLC.

379 McClellan's headquarters: Entry for September 2, 1861, in Russell, *My Diary North and South,* pp. 520–21; Sears, *George B. McClellan,* p. 100.

379 "smoking . . . writing": Entry for September 2, 1861, in Russell, *My Diary North and South,* p. 520.

379 "I have just been . . . stories to tell": GBM to MEM, October 16, 1861, in *Civil War Papers of George B. McClellan,* p. 107.

379 "together . . . mortals": Entry for November 1861, in Gurowski, *Diary from March 4, 1861 to November 12, 1862,* p. 123.

379 "lying down, very much fatigued": Brigadier Van Vliet, quoted in entry for October 9, 1861, in Russell, *My Diary North and South,* p. 552.

380 magnificent reviews of more than fifty thousand troops: *Frank Leslie's Illustrated Newspaper,* October 5, 1861; JGN to TB, November 21, 1861, container 2, Nicolay Papers.

380 "not a mistake . . . a hitch": GBM to MEM, November 20, 1861, in *Civil War Papers of George B. McClellan,* p. 137.

380 "A long time . . . not mind that": GBM to MEM, October 6, 1861, in ibid., p. 106.

380 "a slave-catching order" . . . their masters: Entry for September 1861, in Gurowski, *Diary from March 4, 1861 to November 12, 1862,* p. 95.

380 "fighting to preserve . . . to do with him": GBM to Samuel L. M. Barlow, November 8, 1861, in *Civil War Papers of George B. McClellan*, p. 128.

380 "some of the greatest . . . of Job": GBM to MEM, October 10, 1861, in ibid., p. 106.

380 "a meddling . . . old woman": GBM to MEM, October 11, 1861, in ibid., pp. 106–07.

380 "an old fool . . . altogether fancy him!": GBM to MEM, October 31, 1861, in ibid., p. 114.

380 a flattering letter . . . promotion to major general: SPC to GBM, July 7, 1861, quoted in Schuckers, *The Life and Public Services of Salmon Portland Chase*, p. 427.

380 engagement at Ball's Bluff: Entry for October 21, 1861, in Long, *The Civil War Day by Day*, p. 129.

380 "a slight demonstration . . . move them": GMB to Charles P. Stone, October 20, 1861, quoted in note 2 of GBM to Stone, October 21, 1861, in *Civil War Papers of George B. McClellan*, p. 109.

380 casualties at Ball's Bluff: "Return of casualties in the Union forces in the engagement at Ball's Bluff, Virginia, October 21, 1861," *OR*, Ser. 1, Vol. V, p. 308.

380 Oliver Wendell Holmes, Jr. . . . home to recover: SPC to KCS, July 28, 1865, reel 35, Chase Papers.

381 "the death . . . a desert": Noah Brooks, "Recollections of Abraham Lincoln," *Harper's New Monthly Magazine* 31 (July 1865), p. 228.

381 "Mr. Lincoln sat" . . . and kissed him: Benjamin Rush Cowen, *Abraham Lincoln: An Appreciation by One Who Knew Him* (Cincinnati, Ohio: Robert Clarke Co., 1909), pp. 29–30.

381 Eckert . . . received word: Bates, *Lincoln in the Telegraph Office*, pp. 95–96.

381 "with bowed head . . . into the street": Charles Carleton Coffin, "Lincoln's First Nomination and His Visit to Richmond in 1865," in *Reminiscences of Abraham Lincoln*, ed. Rice (1909 edn.), p. 176.

381 Mary was similarly distraught: Entry for October 22, 1861, in Russell, *My Diary North and South*, p. 558.

381 Willie and Tad . . . were heartbroken: Helm, *The True Story of Mary*, p. 191.

381 "On the Death of Colonel Edward Baker": *NR*, November 4, 1861.

382 "to care for him . . . his orphan": AL, "Second Inaugural Address," March 4, 1865, in *CW*, VIII, p. 333.

382 "disaster . . . committed": GBM to Division Commanders, Army of the Potomac, October 24, 1861, in *Civil War Papers of George B. McClellan*, p. 111.

382 "The whole thing . . . *directly* to blame": GBM to MEM, October 25, 1861, in ibid., p. 111.

382 the president defended McClellan: Entry for October 26, 1861, in Hay, *Inside Lincoln's White House*, p. 28.

382 unleashed a diatribe . . . to remove Scott: GBM to MEM, October 26, 1861, in *Civil War Papers of George B. McClellan*, p. 112; Sears, *George B. McClellan*, p. 123.

382 "You may have . . . heads to call me": GBM to MEM, October 30, 1861, in *Civil War Papers of George B. McClellan*, p. 112.

382 "long and brilliant . . . deep emotion": AL, "Order Retiring Winfield Scott from Command," November 1, 1861, in *CW*, V, p. 10.

382 Lincoln designated McClellan: AL to GBM, November 1, 1861, in ibid., pp. 9–10.

382 "I saw there . . . his successor": GBM to MEM, November 3, 1861, in *Civil War Papers of George B. McClellan*, pp. 123–24.

382 All the members . . . on his journey: *Star*, November 2, 1861; Charles Winslow Elliott, *Winfield Scott: The Soldier and the Man*. American Military Experience Series (New York: Arno Press, 1979), p. 743.

383 "quite a number of citizens": *NYH*, November 4, 1861.

383 the young Napoleon: Sears, *George B. McClellan*, p. xi.

383 "I do not intend to be sacrificed": GBM to MEM, October 31, 1861, in *Civil War Papers of George B. McClellan*, p. 113.

383 to confront the rebel forces: GBM to Simon Cameron, October 31, 1861, in ibid., pp. 114–19; GBM to MEM, August 16, 1861, in ibid., p. 85.

383 "to dodge . . . Presdt etc.": GBM to MEM, October 31, 1861, in ibid., p. 113.

383 "the *original* . . . his high position": GBM to MEM, November 17, 1861, in ibid., pp. 135–36.

383 "I wish here to record . . . personal dignity": Entry for November 13, 1861, in Hay, *Inside Lincoln's White House*, p. 32.

383 He would hold . . . could be achieved: Henry Ketcham, *The Life of Abraham Lincoln* (New York: A. L. Burt, 1901), p. 291.

383 "A minute passes . . . rebellious consciousness": Stoddard, *Inside the White House in War Times*, p. 63.

384 His "mouth would relax . . . sea of laughter": Grimsley, "Six Months in the White House," *JISHS*, p. 55.

384 "daily drive . . . so much needed": Ibid.

384 soirées in the Blue Room: Turner and Turner, *Mary Todd Lincoln*, pp. 96–97, 98; MTL to Hannah Shearer, October 6, 1861, ibid., p. 108; Baker, *Mary Todd Lincoln*, p. 231.

384 Daniel Sickles . . . "temporary insanity": Thomas and Hyman, *Stanton*, pp. 83–85.

384 Henry Wikoff . . . "and Thackeray": John W. Forney, *Anecdotes of Public Men*, Vol. I (New York: Harper & Bros., 1873; New York: Da Capo Press, 1970), pp. 366–71 (quote p. 367).

384 "My wife . . . never fallen out": AL, quoted in Baker, *Mary Todd Lincoln*, p. 196.

384 When Prince Napoleon . . . visited: Entry for August 3, 1861, in *Lincoln Day by Day*, Vol. III, p. 58.

385 "We only have . . . proper season": MTL to Hannah Shearer, August 1, 1861, in Turner and Turner, *Mary Todd Lincoln*, p. 96.

385 "beautiful dinner . . . predominated": Grimsley, "Six Months in the White House," *JISHS*, p. 70.

385 Mary requested Volume 9: Entry for August 5, 1861, in *Lincoln Day by Day*, Vol. III, p. 59.

385 William Scott: Court-martial of Private William Scott, Co. K, 3rd Vermont Infantry, case file OO-209, Court-Martial Case Files, 1809–1894, entry 15, Records of the Office of the Judge Advocate General (Army), RG 153, DNA; *NYT*, September 10, 1861.

385 As the story was told: See L. E. Chittenden, *Recollections of President Lincoln and His Administration* (New York and London: Harper & Bros., 1901), p. 267.

385 "Think . . . much as he tried to": Grimsley, "Six Months in the White House," *JISHS*, p. 71.

385 Lincoln walked over . . . " 'Lady President' ": George B. McClellan, *McClellan's Own Story* (New York: Charles L. Webster & Co., 1887), p. 91 (quote); entry for September 8, 1861, in *Lincoln Day by Day*, Vol. III, p. 65.

385 "that it was asking . . . 'only one he had' ": Chittenden, *Recollections of President Lincoln* (1901 edn.), p. 273.

385 "the most beautiful . . . my own": MTL to Hannah Shearer, July 11, 1861, Turner and Turner, *Mary Todd Lincoln*, p. 94.

385 drives with the Sewards: See entries for September 1, 3, and 6, 1861, Fanny Seward diary, Seward Papers, for examples of afternoons spent driving with Sewards; FAS to LW, [August 1861], reel 119, Seward Papers.

386 "a plain . . . & the crops": FAS to LW, [July 1861?], reel 119, Seward Papers.

386 "I liked him . . . all over him": Entry for September 1, 1861, Fanny Seward diary, Seward Papers.

386 "*abandon* of . . . climb a rope": *NYT*, June 17, 1861.

386 "With one impulse . . . mouth to mouth": Entry for September 6, 1861, Fanny Seward diary, Seward Papers.

386 "I love . . . and does": Entry for September 9, 1861, Fanny Seward diary, Seward Papers.

386 "palatial . . . tasteful & attractive": FAS to LW, [July 1861?], reel 119, Seward Papers.

386 confined to her bed by migraines: See FAS to LW, [August 1861], reel 119, Seward Papers; " 'I have supped full on horrors,' from Fanny Seward's Diary," ed. Patricia Carley Johnson, *American Heritage* X (October 1959), p. 62.

386 vacation in upstate New York and Long Branch: Entry for August 14, 1861, in *Lincoln Day by Day*, Vol. III, p. 60.

386 "especially as . . . her husband": FAS to LW, [July 1861?], reel 119, Seward Papers.

386 word came . . . "company in the evening": Entry for September 9, 1861, Fanny Seward diary, Seward Papers.

387 "If things . . . my husband": MTL, quoted in George B. Lincoln to GW, April 25, 1874, quoted in "New Light on the Seward-Welles-Lincoln Controversy," *Lincoln Lore* 1718 (April 1981), p. 3.

387 "It makes me . . . skein of thread": MTL, quoted in Elizabeth Keckley, *Behind the Scenes. Or, Thirty Years a Slave, and Four Years in the White House*. The Schomburg Library of Nineteenth-Century Black Women Writers Series (New York: G. W. Carleton & Co., 1868; New York: Oxford University Press, 1988), p. 131.

387 the long evenings Lincoln spent at Seward's: Hendrick, *Lincoln's War Cabinet*, p. 186.

387 "My friend . . . churchwarden!": Wilson, *Intimate Memories of Lincoln*, p. 422.

387 "a tithe . . . read for ever": Entry for October 12, 1861, in Hay, *Inside Lincoln's White House*, p. 26.

387 "personal courage . . . the enemy is": Entry for October 10, 1861, in ibid., p. 25.

388 brought up the Chicago convention . . . "his life in his hand": Entry for October 17, 1861, in ibid., pp. 26, 27.

388 probably rekindled memories . . . on the circuit: Taylor, *William Henry Seward*, p. 188.

388 the fighting . . . in Missouri: See Nicolay and Hay, *Abraham Lincoln*, Vol. IV, chapter 11, esp. pp. 206–11; Thomas L. Snead, "The First Year of the War in Missouri," in *Battles and Leaders of the Civil War*, Grant-Lee edition (New York: Century Co., 1887–88; Harrisburg, Penn.: Archive Society, 1991), pp. 262–65.

389 Frank Blair . . . General Nathaniel Lyon: Snead, "The First Year of the War in Missouri," *Battles and Leaders of the Civil War*, Vol. I, Pt. 1, pp. 264–68; Williams, *Lincoln and the Radicals*, p. 39; "Missouri for the Union," in Parrish, *Frank Blair*.

389 "thickly veiled" . . . revolvers: Snead, "The First Year of the War in Missouri," *Battles and Leaders of the Civil War*, Vol. I, Pt. 1, p. 265 (quote); see also Franklin A. Dick, "Memorandum of Matters in Missouri," Papers of F. A. Dick, Miscellaneous Manuscripts Collection, Manuscript Division, Library of Congress.

389 the "earnest solicitation": Entry for December 9, 1863, in Hay, *Inside Lincoln's White House*, p. 123.

389 "He is just . . . eminently practical": "Editorial, 3 August 1861," in Hay, *Lincoln's Journalist*, p. 84.

389 "There was . . . magical influence": Koerner, *Memoirs of Gustave Koerner*, Vol. II, p. 162.

389 "recklessness in expenditures": JGN, memorandum of September 17, 1861, container 2, Nicolay Papers.

389 Tales circulated . . . unwanted visitors: Ibid.; FB to Governor Dennison, September 19, 1861, quoted in Smith, *The Francis Preston Blair Family in Politics*, Vol. II, pp. 79–80.

389 Frémont . . . had chosen to stay: Lorenzo Thomas to Simon Cameron, October 21, 1861, in *OR*, Ser. 1, Vol. III, p. 543; Parrish, *Frank Blair*, p. 116.

389 General Lyon's death . . . devastating defeat: Entries for August 10 and September 20, 1861, in Long, *The Civil War Day by Day*, pp. 107, 120.

390 Frémont issued a bold proclamation . . . "declared freemen": Proclamation of John C. Frémont, August 30, 1861, in *OR*, Ser. 1, Vol. III, pp. 466–67 (quotes p. 467).

390 far exceeded . . . their future status: Joseph Holt to AL, September 12, 1861, Lincoln Papers.

390 Lincoln learned of . . . a private letter to Frémont: Nicolay and Hay, *Abraham Lincoln*, Vol. IV, pp. 416, 417–18.

390 unilaterally recast . . . war against slavery: Benjamin Quarles, *Lincoln and the Negro* (New York: Oxford University Press, 1962; repr. New York: Da Capo Press, 1990), p. 71.

390 has "anxiety . . . so as to conform": AL to John C. Frémont, September 2, 1861, in *CW*, IV, p. 506.

390 "Frémont's proclamation . . . future condition": AL to Orville H. Browning, September 22, 1861, in ibid., p. 531.

390 "The trouble . . . only to himself": Carpenter, "A Day with Governor Seward," Seward Papers.

390 "unable to eat . . . on such a principle": Joshua Speed to AL, September 3, 1861, Lincoln Papers.

391 "I know that you . . . to the very foundations": FB to MB, September 1, 1861, Lincoln Papers.

391 he himself had reluctantly concluded: Williams, *Lincoln and the Radicals*, pp. 48–49.

391 "but being . . . public interests": MB to AL, September 4, 1861, Lincoln Papers.

392 General Meigs and Montgomery Blair . . . "look into the affair": JGN, memorandum of September 17, 1861, container 2, Nicolay Papers; entry for September 10 to September 18, 1861, extracts from diary of Montgomery C. Meigs, container 13, Nicolay Papers.
392 Jessie . . . arrived in Washington: "The Lincoln Interview: Excerpt from 'Great Events,' " in *The Letters of Jessie Benton Frémont*, ed. Pamela Herr and Mary Lee Spence (Urbana and Chicago: University of Illinois Press, 1993), pp. 264–65.
392 "If I were . . . I did not do so": John C. Frémont to AL, September 8, 1861, Lincoln Papers.
392 "You are quite a female politician": "The Lincoln Interview," *Letters of Jessie Benton Frémont*, p. 266.
392 "taxed me . . . for himself": Entry for December 9, 1863, in Hay, *Inside Lincoln's White House*, p. 123.
392 she asked Lincoln . . . when he was ready: "The Lincoln Interview," *Letters of Jessie Benton Frémont*, p. 266.
392 Lincoln wrote . . . "an open order": AL to John C. Frémont, September 11, 1861, in *CW*, IV, pp. 517–18.
392 he sent it to be mailed: Jessie Benton Frémont to AL, September 12, 1861, in *Letters of Jessie Benton Frémont*, p. 271 n1.
392 "He had always . . . now very angry": "The Lincoln Interview," *Letters of Jessie Benton Frémont*, p. 267.
392 the elder Blair revealed: Jessie B. Frémont to AL, September 12, 1861, Lincoln Papers.
393 "examine into that Department": AL to Jessie B. Frémont, September 12, 1861, draft copy, Lincoln Papers.
393 "threatened the old man . . . from responsibility": MB to W. O. Barlett, September 26, 1861, copy, reel 21, Blair Family Papers, Manuscript Division, Library of Congress [hereafter Blair Family Papers, DLC].
393 "most incautious": EBL to SPL, October 7, 1861, in *Wartime Washington*, ed. Laas, p. 83.
393 "The rebels . . . for defence": Entry for September 10 to September 18, 1861, extracts from diary of Montgomery C. Meigs, container 13, Nicolay Papers.
393 "a full & plain . . . should be consulted": MB to AL, September 14, 1861, Lincoln Papers.
393 Rumors circulated: Entry for December 28, 1861, in *The Diary of Edward Bates, 1859–1866*, p. 217; EBL to SPL, October 19, 1861, in *Wartime Washington*, ed. Laas, pp. 88, 90 n2.
393 "with a view . . . removal": *NYT*, September 17, 1861.
393 "unbecoming . . . gentleman": Smith, *The Francis Preston Blair Family in Politics*, Vol. II, p. 78.
393 Monty interceded: MB to John C. Frémont, September 20, 1861, copy, reel 21, Blair Family Papers, DLC.
393 the trial, which would never take place: MB to FPB, October 1, 1861, box 7, folder 6, Blair-Lee Papers, Dept. of Rare Books and Special Collections, Princeton University Library [hereafter Blair-Lee Papers, NjP-SC].
393 "Were you not . . . proclamation?": FAS to LW, [c. September 4, 1861], quoted in Seward, *Seward at Washington . . . 1846–1861*, p. 612.
394 "has cast . . . *step backwards*": Joseph Medill to SPC, September 15, 1861, reel 17, Chase Papers.
394 "poor white trash": Benjamin F. Wade to Zachariah Chandler, September 23, 1861, reel 1, Papers of Zachariah Chandler, Manuscript Division, Library of Congress.
394 "Many blunders . . . them all": *Douglass' Monthly* (October 1861), pp. 530–31.
394 Blair and Meigs delivered: Entry for September 18, 1861, in *Lincoln Day by Day*, Vol. III, p. 67.
394 "is determined . . . Missouri": MB to FPB, October 1, 1861, box 7, folder 6, Blair-Lee Papers, NjP-SC.
394 "more damage . . . can do": EB to SPC, September 11, 1861, reel 17, Chase Papers.
394 "distressed & mortified": EB to James O. Broadhead, September 28, 1861, Broadhead Papers, MoSHi.
394 "Immense mischief . . . place of action": EB to Hamilton Gamble, October 3, 1861, Hamilton Rowan Gamble Papers, Missouri Historical Society, St. Louis, Mo. [hereafter Gamble Papers, MoSHi].
394 "I think God . . . in his Cabinet": FB to MB, October 7, 1861, quoted in Smith, *The Francis Preston Blair Family in Politics*, Vol. II, pp. 83–84.
394 "a letter directing . . . and conduct": Simon Cameron to AL, October 12, 1861, Lincoln Papers.
395 "was very much mortified" . . . talked with the president: Simon Cameron to AL, October 14, 1861, Lincoln Papers.
395 "constitution . . . with its management": *NYT*, October 31, 1861. For the report, see Lorenzo Thomas to Simon Cameron, October 21, 1861, in *OR*, Ser. 1, Vol. III, pp. 540–49.
395 "yielded to delay . . . *deserve it*": Entry of October 22, 1861, in *The Diary of Edward Bates, 1859–1866*, pp. 198–99.
395 Lincoln dispatched . . . Swett: Entry for October 24, 1861, in *Lincoln Day by Day*, Vol. III, p. 73.
395 "the most remarkable" . . . publication: *NYT*, October 31, 1861.
395 When Swett reached Missouri: Leonard Swett to AL, November 9, 1861, Lincoln Papers.
396 "frown came over . . . 'my lines?' ": General T. I. McKenny, quoted in Ida M. Tarbell, *The Life of Abraham Lincoln*, Vol. III, Sangamon Edition (4 vols., n.p.: S. S. McClure Co., 1895; New York: Lincoln History Society, 1924), pp. 122–25 (quote p. 124).
396 "justified . . . is possible": *NYT*, November 7, 1861.
396 "Slowly . . . our judgment": *Philadelphia Inquirer*, October 31, 1861.
396 "Lincoln . . . the whole story": *NYH*, November 7, 1861.
396 "I am . . . publ[ic] duty": SPC to Richard Smith, November 11, 1861, reel 18, Chase Papers.
396 the Confederacy had dispatched . . . Mason and Slidell: Van Deusen, *William Henry Seward*, p. 308.
396 Charles Wilkes . . . Fort Warren in Boston: *NYT*, November 17 and 19, 1861.
396 "We do not believe . . . been found": *NYT*, November 17, 1861.
397 Wilkes was fêted . . . a great banquet: *NYT*, November 26 and 27, 1861.
397 "three cheers . . . Wilkes": Smith, *Francis Preston Blair*, p. 315.
397 "great and general satisfaction": Entry for November 16, 1861, in *The Diary of Edward Bates, 1859–1866*, p. 202.
397 Chase reportedly . . . seized the British ship: *NYT*, November 19, 1861.
397 "the items . . . Mason & Slidell!": AL to Edward Everett, November 18, 1861, in *CW*, V, p. 26.

397 "intelligence . . . Mail Steamer": *The Times* (London), quoted in the *NYT*, December 13, 1861.

397 "reparation and apology": *Morning Post* (London), quoted in the *NYT*, December 14, 1861.

397 Fabricated details: Charles Francis Adams to Henry Adams, December 19, 1861, *A Cycle of Adams Letters, 1861–1865*, Vol. I, ed. Worthington Chauncey Ford (Boston and New York: Houghton Mifflin, 1920), p. 86.

397 "acted without . . . directed by us": WHS to Charles Francis Adams, undated, quoted in Frederick W. Seward, *Seward at Washington, as Senator and Secretary of State. A Memoir of His Life, with Selections from His Letters, 1861–1872* (New York: Derby & Miller, 1891), p. 21.

397 The first public response should come from the British government: WHS to Charles Francis Adams, undated, quoted in ibid., p. 24.

397 "if the taking . . . *it means war*": TW to WHS, December 2, 1861, quoted in ibid., pp. 27, 28 (quote).

397 "fanning the popular flame . . . manufactures": *NYT*, December 16, 1861.

397 "certainly jubilant": TW to WHS, December 5, 1861, quoted in Seward, *Seward at Washington . . . 1861–1872*, p. 28.

397 in "high places": TW to WHS, December 6, 1861, quoted in ibid., p. 29.

398 "to provoke . . . getting Canada": TW to WHS, December 2, 1861, quoted in ibid., p. 27.

398 "how created . . . your dismissal": TW to WHS, December 6, 1861, quoted in ibid., p. 29.

398 Seward burst . . . "so foolish a thing": Entry for December 15, 1861, in Browning, *The Diary of Orville Hickman Browning*, Vol. I, p. 515.

398 "I know . . . will not bite?": AL, quoted in Monaghan, *Diplomat in Carpet Slippers*, p. 187.

398 both he and Lord Lyons . . . remained silent: Seward, *Seward at Washington . . . 1861–1872*, p. 187; Lord Thomas Newton, *Lord Lyons: A Record of British Diplomacy*, Vol. I (New York: Longmans, Green, & Co., 1913), p. 55.

398 "Her Majesty's . . . for the aggression": Earl Russell to Lord Lyons, November 30, 1861, quoted in John G. Nicolay and John Hay, *Abraham Lincoln: A History*, Vol. V (New York: Century Co., 1917), pp. 29–30. While the letter was dated November 30, it did not arrive in Washington until December 19, 1861.

398 If the United States . . . return to Britain: Ibid., p. 30; Newton, *Lord Lyons*, p. 62.

398 Lyons carried the document . . . consider their response: Seward, *Seward at Washington . . . 1861–1872*, p. 24.

398 "You will perhaps . . . side of peace": Newton, *Lord Lyons*, p. 69.

398 "devoted one entire day": Seward, *Seward at Washington . . . 1861–1872*, p. 24.

398 "With England . . . 'crushed out' ": TW to WHS, December 10, 1861, quoted in ibid., p. 30.

398 "They can never . . . such a surrender": Quoted in ibid., p. 24.

398 Lincoln himself . . . considered humiliating: Hendrick, *Lincoln's War Cabinet*, p. 205.

399 "the British side . . . cheerfully": WHS to Lord Lyons, December 26, 1861, in *The Works of William H. Seward*, Vol. V, ed. George E. Baker (Boston: Houghton Mifflin, 1884; New York: AMS Press, 1972), pp. 295–309 (quotes pp. 307–09).

399 "There was great . . . power of England": Entry for December 25, 1861, in *The Diary of Edward Bates, 1859–1866*, p. 216.

399 "gall and wormwood . . . I possess": Entry for December 25, 1861, in *Chase Papers*, Vol. I, p. 320.

399 Only Monty Blair . . . with Seward: Hendrick, *Lincoln's War Cabinet*, p. 206.

399 Charles Sumner . . . "the North's problems": Monaghan, *Diplomat in Carpet Slippers*, p. 191.

399 "Governor Seward . . . on each side": Seward, *Seward at Washington . . . 1861–1872*, p. 25.

399 Seward finished . . . read it to Chase: Monaghan, *Diplomat in Carpet Slippers*, p. 191; entry for December 26, 1861, Fanny Seward diary, Seward Papers.

400 "I am consoled . . . simply doing right": Entry for December 25, 1861, in *Chase Papers*, Vol. I, p. 320.

400 "a great point . . . Government": Carpenter, "A Day with Governor Seward," Seward Papers.

400 "an argument . . . the right one": Seward, *Seward at Washington . . . 1861–1872*, p. 26.

400 Seward hosted a dinner party: Entry for December 27, 1861, in Browning, *The Diary of Orville Hickman Browning*, Vol. I, p. 519; entry for December 27, 1861, Fanny Seward diary, Seward Papers.

400 "a great homely . . . iron grey": Entry for December 27, 1861, Fanny Seward diary, Seward Papers.

400 The conversation at dinner . . . "on the floor cloth": Ibid.

400 "swore vehemently": Entry for December 27, 1861, in Browning, *The Diary of Orville Hickman Browning*, Vol. I, p. 519.

400 "doom [Seward] to unpopularity": Seward, *Seward at Washington . . . 1861–1872*, p. 26.

400 "The general . . . domestic treason": Entry for December 29, 1861, *Diary of George Templeton Strong*, Vol. III, p. 198.

400 "Presidents and Kings . . . unselfish heart": Seward, *Seward at Washington . . . 1861–1872*, p. 26.

401 "Houses are being . . . life in the Capital": "Miriam," *Iowa State Register*, Des Moines, November 13, 1861.

401 a mansion transformed: Randall, *Mary Lincoln*, pp. 258–63, 266; Monkman, *The White House*, pp. 123–33.

401 the new rugs . . . "roses at your feet": Mary Clemmer Ames, *Ten Years in Washington. Life and Scenes in the National Capital, as a Woman Sees Them* (Hartford, Conn.: A. D. Worthington & Co., 1871), p. 171.

401 "The President's . . . comparative beauty": *Daily Alta California*, May 12, 1862, quoted in Monkman, *The White House*, p. 132.

401 "elegant fitting up . . . in the least arrogant": George Bancroft to his wife, December 12 and 14, 1862, in M. A. DeWolfe Howe, *The Life and Letters of George Bancroft*, Vol. II (New York: Charles Scribner's Sons, 1908), pp. 144–45.

401 she had overspent . . . extra money over to her: Baker, *Mary Todd Lincoln*, pp. 187, 191.

401 She had replaced . . . the manure account: Entry for November 3, 1861, in *William Howard Russell's Civil War: Private Diary and Letters, 1861–1862*, ed. Martin Crawford (Athens, Ga., and London: University of Georgia Press, 1992), p. 162.

401 She exchanged her patronage . . . wealthy donors: For a general discussion of MTL's financial finagling, see Michael Burlingame, "Mary Todd Lincoln's Unethical Conduct as First Lady," appendix 2 in *At Lincoln's Side: John Hay's Civil War Correspondence and Selected Writings*, ed. Michael Burlingame (Carbondale and Edwardsville: Southern Illinois University Press, 2000).

401 she asked John Hay . . . "the Steward's salary": JH to JGN, April 4 and 5, 1862, in ibid., pp. 19–20.

402 She had no recourse . . . to speak with her husband: Entry for December 16, 1861, in Benjamin Brown French, *Witness to the Young Republic: A Yankee's Journal, 1828–1870*, ed. Donald B. Cole and John J. McDonough (Hanover, N.H., and London: University Press of New England, 1989), p. 382.

402 after he returned home . . . Edward Baker: *NR*, December 14, 1861.

402 "inexorable . . . his own pocket!": Entry for December 16, 1861, in French, *Witness to the Young Republic*, p. 382.

402 "better and better . . . will defend her": Entry for December 22, 1861, in ibid., p. 383.

402 hide a deficiency appropriation: Baker, *Mary Todd Lincoln*, p. 190.

402 "I need hardly . . . his own expences": SPC to KCS, October 25, 1861, reel 17, Chase Papers.

402 a questionable relationship . . . investment account for Chase: Belden and Belden, *So Fell the Angels*, pp. 36–37.

403 "I will take . . . working as you do": Jay Cooke to SPC, quoted in ibid., p. 37.

403 growth in size of the Union army: Simon Cameron to AL, December 1, 1861, *OR*, Ser. 3, Vol. I pp. 669, 700.

403 "incapable . . . general plans": "A Private Paper. Conversation with the President, October 2d, 1861," memorandum, container 2, Nicolay Papers.

403 "he would look . . . in the other": Albert Gallatin Riddle, *Recollection of War Times: Reminiscences of Men and Events in Washington, 1860–1865* (New York and London: G. P. Putnam's Sons, 1895), p. 180.

403 accusations of corruption . . . in the War Department: *NYT*, July 3 and 9, and August 28, 1861.

403 Congress appointed . . . Cameron was not charged: Thomas, *Abraham Lincoln*, p. 293; Macartney, *Lincoln and His Cabinet*, pp. 35–36; Hendrick, *Lincoln's War Cabinet*, pp. 222–23.

404 "It is better . . . with dissolution": *NYT*, July 7, 1861.

404 Cameron sought . . . Republicans: Williams, *Lincoln and the Radicals*, p. 59.

404 "*We* agreed . . . in that opinion": SPC to Trowbridge, March 31, 1844, quoted in Schuckers, *The Life and Public Services of Salmon Portland Chase*, p. 420.

404 "extremist measures . . . absolute ruin": *National Intelligencer*, Washington, D.C., November 14, 1861.

404 heated arguments with Bates, Blair, and Smith: Entry for November 20, 1862, in *The Diary of Edward Bates, 1859–1866*, p. 203; Niven, *Gideon Welles*, p. 392.

404 Cameron maintained . . . "nigger hobby": MB, paraphrased in entry of September 12, 1862, *Welles diary*, Vol. I (1960 edn.), p. 127 (quote); Bradley, *Simon Cameron*, p. 203.

404 Each department customarily presented: Nicolay and Hay, *Abraham Lincoln*, Vol. V, p. 125.

404 Cameron read his draft: Henry Wilson, "Edwin M. Stanton," *Atlantic Monthly* 25 (February 1870), p. 238; Bradley, *Simon Cameron*, p. 203.

404 "I sought out . . . Edwin Stanton": Simon Cameron, quoted in Henry Wilson, "Jeremiah S. Black and Edwin M. Stanton," *Atlantic Monthly* 26 (October 1870), p. 470.

404 "read the report . . . hearty support": Ibid.

404 he suggested his own provocative logic: Bradley, *Simon Cameron*, p. 203; Thomas and Hyman, *Stanton*, p. 134 n7.

405 "It is clearly a right . . . from the enemy": "From the Report of the Secretary of War, Dec. 1, 1861," in Edward McPherson, *The Political History of the United States of America, During the Great Rebellion, 1861–1865*, 2nd edn. (Washington, D.C.: Philp & Solomons, 1865; New York: Da Capo Press, 1972), p. 249 (quote). For the official version of the annual report of the secretary of war sent to Congress, see *OR*, Ser. 3, Vol. I, pp. 698–708 (esp. p. 708).

405 It remains unclear: See Thomas and Hyman, *Stanton*, pp. 134–35; Hendrick, *Lincoln's War Cabinet*, pp. 236–37, 260.

405 "an abolitionist at heart": Jeremiah S. Black, "Senator Wilson and Edwin M. Stanton," *Galaxy* 9 (June 1870), p. 822.

405 his boyhood pledge to his father: Flower, *Edwin McMasters Stanton*, p. 25.

405 "my *personal* friend . . . war against Slavery": CS to Francis Lieber, December 19, 1861, reel 64, Summer Papers.

405 when Stanton talked with fellow Democrats: Thomas and Hyman, *Stanton*, p. 135.

405 his approval emboldened Cameron . . . to the president: Flower, *Edwin McMasters Stanton*, p. 116.

405 "This will never do!" . . . copy already sent: AL, quoted in Carpenter, *Six Months at the White House*, p. 136.

405 "must be provided for in some way": AL, "Annual Message to Congress," December 3, 1861, in *CW*, V, p. 48.

405 "otherwise unconstitutional . . . necessity": AL to Albert G. Hodges, April 4, 1864, in *CW*, VII, pp. 281–82.

405 Lincoln informed Cameron . . . the vetoed language: Nicolay and Hay, *Abraham Lincoln*, Vol. V, p. 127.

405 he complained . . . "dreaded most": Niven, *Gideon Welles*, pp. 394–95 (quote p. 395).

406 "have sought our ships . . . a livelihood": *NYT*, December 4, 1861, p. 3.

406 Welles resolved that . . . into the Confederacy: Niven, *Gideon Welles*, p. 395.

406 he outlined his ideas . . . "new beginner to help him": AL, "Annual Message to Congress," December 3, 1861, in *CW*, V, pp. 48, 49, 52.

407 "Away with . . . free as the white man": Worthington G. Snethen to SPC, December 10, 1861, reel 18, Chase Papers.

407 "his attachment . . . than iron": "The Claims of the Negro Ethnologically Considered: An Address Delivered in Hudson, Ohio, on 12 July 1854," *The Frederick Douglass Papers, Series One: Speeches, Debates, and Interviews*. Vol. II: *1847–54*, ed. John W. Blassingame (New Haven and London: Yale University Press, 1982), p. 524.

407 "Give him wages . . . by hard work": *Douglass' Monthly* (January 1862), p. 579.

407 "One black regiment . . . free colored people": *Douglass' Monthly* (May 1861), p. 451.
407 "We are striking . . . the loyal North": Frederick Douglass, "The Reasons for Our Troubles," ed. Philip S. Foner, *The Life and Writings of Frederick Douglass*. Vol. III: *The Civil War, 1861–1865* (New York: International Publishers, 1952), p. 204.
407 "It appeals to the judgment . . . aspirations": *NYT Supplement*, December 4, 1861.
407 "the moderate men . . . with popularity": Ibid.
408 "country and the world . . . railing accusations": *NYTrib*, December 4, 1861.

CHAPTER 15: "MY BOY IS GONE"

Page
409 "unusually beautiful . . . than January": *NYT Supplement*, January 3, 1862.
409 "For the first time . . . in old times": FAS to LW, January 1, 1862, reel 119, Seward Papers.
409 "All the world" . . . opened at noon: Entry for January 1, 1862, in *The Diary of Edward Bates, 1859–1866*, p. 221.
409 The Marine Band . . . cabinet officials: Poore, *Perley's Reminiscences*, Vol. II, pp. 105–06; *NYT Supplement*, January 3, 1862.
410 "a compact little . . . head arrangement": Entry for January 1, 1862, Fanny Seward diary, Seward Papers.
410 Lincoln cordially greeted every guest: Leech, *Reveille in Washington*, pp. 122–23.
410 "the bottom . . . out of the tub": AL, quoted in Montgomery C. Meigs, "General M. C. Meigs on the Conduct of the Civil War," *American Historical Review* 26 (January 1921), p. 292.
410 "If the new year . . . to be expected": Entry for January 1862, in Gurowski, *Diary from March 4, 1861 to November 12, 1862*, p. 137.
410 Seward questioned whether . . . "to Mr. Cameron": Maunsell B. Field, *Memories of Many Men and of Some Women: Being Personal Recollections of Emperors, Kings, Queens, Princes, Presidents, Statesmen, Authors, and Artists, at Home and Abroad, During the Last Thirty Years* (New York: Harper & Bros., 1874), pp. 266–67.
410 Lincoln's initial preferences . . . Joseph Holt: Flower, *Edwin McMasters Stanton*, p. 116.
410 West Point graduate Montgomery Blair . . . "sound judgment": Gideon Welles, "Narrative of Events," in "Three Manuscripts of Gideon Welles," comp. A. Howard Meneely, *American Historical Review* 31 (April 1926), p. 491.
410 Seward would never forget: Wilson, "Jeremiah S. Black and Edwin M. Stanton," *Atlantic Monthly* (1870), p. 465.
411 "to be loved . . . power to express": EMS to SPC, December 2, 1847, reel 6, Chase Papers.
411 "He puts his whole . . . upon the issue": *Philadelphia Press*, January 20, 1862.
411 an uncharacteristically brusque letter: Memorandum of conversation between SPC and J. W. Schuckers, January 22, 1871, Papers of Jacob William Schuckers, Manuscript Division, Library of Congress.
411 "expressed a desire . . . minister to Russia": AL to Simon Cameron, January 11, 1862, reel 8, Papers of Simon Cameron, Manuscript Division, Library of Congress [hereafter Cameron Papers, DLC].
411 to have wept . . . "personal degradation": Recollection of Alexander McClure, in Hendrick, *Lincoln's War Cabinet*, p. 234.
411 Chase drove Cameron . . . "to all concerned": Entry for January 12, 1862, *Chase Papers*, Vol. I, pp. 325–26.
411 Lincoln agreed to withdraw his terse letter: A. K. McClure, *Abraham Lincoln and Men of War-Times: Some Personal Recollections of War and Politics During the Lincoln Administration*, 4th edn. (Philadelphia: Times Publishing Co., 1892; Lincoln and London: University of Nebraska Press, 1996), p. 165.
411 "gratify . . . could render at home": AL to Simon Cameron, January 11, 1862, reel 8, Cameron Papers, DLC. For Cameron's resignation letter, see Simon Cameron to AL, January 11, 1862, Lincoln Papers.
412 Cameron expressed his fervent opinion: Simon Cameron to Frank A. Flower, March 6, 1887, reel 16, Cameron Papers, DLC.
412 Lincoln asked George Harding . . . "of the three": Charles F. Benjamin, quoted in Thomas and Hyman, *Stanton*, p. 136.
412 Ellen . . . "objected to his acceptance": Wolcott, "Edwin M. Stanton," p. 153.
412 diminish the lifestyle of the Stanton family: Thomas and Hyman, *Stanton*, p. 137.
412 "long by noble deeds": SPC to EMS, January 9, 1848, reel 6, Chase Papers.
412 He accepted the post . . . "swamped at once": Wolcott, "Edwin M. Stanton," p. 154.
412 "Strange" . . . no one but Seward: Entry for January 13, 1862, in *The Diary of Edward Bates, 1859–1866*, p. 226.
412 Welles heard . . . "Lincoln's confidence": Welles, "Narrative of Events," *AHR* (1926), p. 488; Hendrick, *Lincoln's War Cabinet*, p. 234 (quote).
412 Welles had never even met Stanton: *Welles diary*, Vol. I (1960 edn.), p. 54.
412 Stanton's nomination . . . he would arrange a meeting: Francis Fessenden, *Life and Public Services of William Pitt Fessenden*, Vol. I (Boston and New York: Houghton Mifflin, 1907), p. 230.
413 After a lengthy . . . "the negro question": William Pitt Fessenden, quoted in ibid., p. 231.
413 "Not only was . . . the real cause": WHS to home, January 15, 1862, in Seward, *Seward at Washington . . . 1861–1872*, p. 46.
413 the House Committee . . . rotten food: *NYT*, February 6, 1862.
413 "resolved to advise . . . unsound provisions": *Frank Leslie's Illustrated Newspaper*, February 1, 1862.

413 "highly injurious to the public service": House resolution of April 30, 1862, quoted in AL, "To the Senate and House of Representatives," May 26, 1862, in *CW*, V, p. 243.
413 He wrote a long public letter . . . "was committed": AL, "To the Senate and House of Representatives," May 26, 1862, in ibid., p. 243.
413 "one of the most intimate . . . personal friends": Nicolay and Hay, *Abraham Lincoln*, Vol. V, p. 130.
413 Most other men . . . "incur responsibility": Simon Cameron to AL, June 26, 1862, Lincoln Papers.
414 "an entirely new *régime*" . . . removed many of Cameron's people: *NYT*, January 23, 1862.
414 The day after . . . "she never did": EMS, quoted in *Boston Daily Evening Transcript*, January 7, 1870.
414 "As his carriage . . . to their stations": Charles F. Benjamin, "Recollections of Secretary Edwin M. Stanton," *Century* 33 (March 1887), p. 761.
414 "fluent without . . . and large-hearted": Entry for January 29, 1862, *Diary of George Templeton Strong*, Vol. III, p. 203.
415 "Persons at a distance . . . Congress speak it": *NYT*, January 25, 1862.
415 Instead of the traditional . . . an evening ball: Keckley, *Behind the Scenes*, pp. 95–96; *Frank Leslie's Illustrated Newspaper*, February 22, 1862.
415 some five hundred invitations: *Frank Leslie's Illustrated Newspaper*, February 22, 1862.
415 "sought . . . their invitations": JGN to TB, February 6, 1862, container 2, Nicolay Papers.
415 Marine Band . . . midnight supper: Poore, *Perley's Reminiscences*, Vol. II, pp. 116, 119.
415 white satin gown . . . "in better style": Keckley, *Behind the Scenes*, p. 101.
415 "much attached . . . ever known": Entry for February 20, 1862, Taft diary.
415 built a cabin . . . troops on the shore: Entry for January 11, 1862, Taft diary (quote); Bayne, *Tad Lincoln's Father*, p. 177.
415 performances in the attic: Bayne, *Tad Lincoln's Father*, pp. 102, 106.
415 the pony . . . favorite pastime: Keckley, *Behind the Scenes*, p. 98; entries for January 26 and 27, 1862, Taft diary.
415 weather conditions in January: See January 1862 entries in Taft diary.
416 "There is a good deal . . . in the City": Entry for January 8, 1862, Taft diary.
416 "a dreadful eruption . . . expected to live": EMS to Oella Wright, March 24, 1862, in Wolcott, "Edwin M. Stanton," p. 155.
416 "burning fever . . . ulcerated" throat: FAS to LW, February 2, 1862, reel 119, Seward Papers.
416 Seward left Washington: WHS to AL, February 6, 1862, Lincoln Papers.
416 Nettie Chase . . . contracted scarlet fever: SPC to KCS, January 10, 1862, reel 18, Chase Papers.
416 Mary thought it best . . . been sent out: Keckley, *Behind the Scenes*, p. 100.
416 "the dean . . . medical community": Baker, *Mary Todd Lincoln*, p. 209.
416 "in no immediate . . . an early recovery": Keckley, *Behind the Scenes*, p. 100.
416 The carriages . . . received their guests: Poore, *Perley's Reminiscences*, Vol. II, pp. 115–18; *Frank Leslie's Illustrated Newspaper*, February 22, 1862.
416 "exquisite taste . . . a Grecian knot behind": *Frank Leslie's Illustrated Newspaper*, February 22, 1862.
416 At midnight . . . including General McClellan: "Lincoln's First Levee," *Journal of the Illinois State Historical Society* 11 (October 1918), p. 389; Poore, *Perley's Reminiscences*, Vol. II, pp. 119–20 (quote).
417 "The brilliance . . . the suffering boy": Keckley, *Behind the Scenes*, p. 102.
417 "Those who were here . . . others have not": JGN to TB, February 6, 1862, container 2, Nicolay Papers.
417 "frivolity, hilarity . . . within plain sight": *Jeffersonian Democrat*, reprinted in *The Liberator*, February 28, 1862.
417 "a brilliant spectacle": *Star*, February 6, 1862.
417 "our fair 'Republican Queen' . . . of beauty": *Frank Leslie's Illustrated Newspaper*, February 22, 1862.
417 General Ulysses S. Grant: On Ulysses S. Grant's careers prior to the Civil War, see chapters 2–5 of William S. McFeely, *Grant: A Biography* (New York and London: W. W. Norton, 1982).
417 Grant understood . . . an important mission: Ibid., pp. 96–97.
417 "to take and hold Fort Henry": H. W. Halleck to USG, January 30, 1862, *OR*, Ser. 1, Vol. VII, p. 121.
417 Grant and Foote . . . Fort Donelson: McPherson, *Battle Cry of Freedom*, p. 396; Nicolay and Hay, *Abraham Lincoln*, Vol. V, pp. 120–22.
417 "Fort Henry is ours . . . on the 8th": USG to H. W. Halleck, February 6, 1862, *OR*, Ser. 1, Vol. VII, p. 124.
417 Though a severe rainstorm: Ulysses S. Grant, *Personal Memoirs of U.S. Grant* (New York: C. L. Webster, 1885; New York: Modern Library, 1999), p. 152.
417 "plain brother . . . a presentiment": USG to Mary Grant, February 9, 1862, *The Papers of Ulysses S. Grant*. Vol. IV: *January 8–March 31, 1862*, ed. John Y. Simon (Carbondale and Edwardsville: Southern Illinois University Press, 1972), p. 180.
418 Buckner, proposed a cease-fire . . . "can be accepted": USG to Simon B. Buckner, February 16, 1862, enclosure 3 of USG to G. W. Cullum, February 16, 1862, in *OR*, Ser. 1, Vol. VII, p. 161.
418 Buckner . . . taken prisoner: USG to General G. W. Cullum, February 16, 1862, *OR*, Ser. 1, Vol. VII, p. 159.
418 More than a thousand troops: McPherson, *Battle Cry of Freedom*, p. 401.
418 "a most bloody . . . brought through": Captain L. D. Waddell to William Coventry H. Wadell, quoted in *NYT*, February 26, 1862.
418 Hundred-gun salutes: *NYT*, February 18, 1862.
418 "quite wild with Excitement": Entry for February 15, 1862, Taft diary.
418 "the gallery rose . . . enthusiastic cheers": *NYT*, February 18, 1862.
418 to illuminate the capital's public buildings . . . Washington's birthday: *NYH*, February 21, 1862.
418 promoting him to major general: Entry for February 17, 1862, in *Lincoln Day by Day*, Vol. III, p. 95.

418 Lincoln had been following: Sandburg, *Abraham Lincoln: The War Years*, Vol. I, p. 462.
418 "I have come among you . . . fellow-citizen": USG, "Proclamation, to the Citizens of Paducah!" September 6, 1861, *The Papers of Ulysses S. Grant*. Vol. II: *April–September 1861*, ed. John Y. Simon (Carbondale and Edwardsville: Southern Illinois University Press, 1969), p. 194.
418 "Grant had taken the field" . . . items to the front: Isaac N. Arnold, *The Life of Abraham Lincoln* (Chicago: Jansen, McClurg, & Co., 1885), p. 281.
418 Fort Donelson's capture . . . capture of New Orleans: For more on events from the surrender of Fort Donelson to the capture of New Orleans, see McPherson, *Battle Cry of Freedom*, pp. 402–20.
418 It is believed that both boys . . . typhoid fever: Baker, *Mary Todd Lincoln*, p. 208: Seale, *The President's House*, Vol. I, p. 379.
419 Willie was affected . . . more severely: MTL to Julia Ann Sprigg, May 29, 1862, in Turner and Turner, *Mary Todd Lincoln*, p. 128; Milton H. Shutes, "Mortality of the Five Lincoln Boys," *Lincoln Herald* 57 (Spring–Summer 1955), p. 4.
419 "grew weaker . . . shadow-like": Keckley, *Behind the Scenes*, p. 98.
419 symptoms of his illness: "Typhus, Typhoid, and Relapsing Fevers," *Encyclopaedia Britannica*, Vol. XXIII, ed. Day Otis Kellogg (30 vols., New York and Chicago: The Werner Company, 1898), pp. 678–79.
419 "almost wore . . . with watching": Benjamin B. French to Henry F. French, February 27, 1862, reel 5, Papers of Benjamin B. French Family, Manuscript Division, Library of Congress [hereafter French Family Papers, DLC].
419 She canceled the customary: Unknown Washington newspaper, quoted in Helm, *The True Story of Mary*, p. 197.
419 "pretty much all his attention": JGN to TB, February 11, 1862, container 2, Nicolay Papers.
419 Willie would call for . . . "tenderly to bed": Bayne, *Tad Lincoln's Father*, pp. 199–200.
419 celebratory illuminations were canceled: Entry for February 23, 1862, in French, *Witness to the Young Republic*, p. 388; Benjamin B. French to Henry F. French, February 27, 1862, reel 5, French Family Papers, DLC.
419 "the President . . . of their affliction": *Star*, February 18, 1862.
419 "as if they did . . . So the doctors say": Stoddard, *Inside the White House in War Times*, p. 66.
419 on Thursday, February 20, Willie died: Entry for February 20, 1862, in *Lincoln Day by Day*, Vol. III, p. 96.
419 "Well, Nicolay . . . actually gone!": Entry for February 20, 1862, notebook, February–March 1862, container 1, Nicolay Papers.
419 "buried his head . . . of her old age": Keckley, *Behind the Scenes*, pp. 103, 104.
419 She took to her bed . . . ease her grief: Rebecca R. Pomroy to "Mary," March 27, 1862, Rebecca R. Pomroy Letters, Schlesinger Library, Radcliffe College [hereafter Pomroy Letters].
420 He sent his carriage to the Brownings . . . Tad's bedside: Entries for February 20 and 21, 1862, in Browning, *The Diary of Orville Hickman Browning*, Vol. I, p. 530.
420 He asked . . . Mary Jane, to sit with the boy: Niven, *Gideon Welles*, pp. 442–43.
420 Julia Bates . . . also watched over him: Entry for February 22, 1862, in *The Diary of Edward Bates, 1859–1866*, p. 236.
420 Lincoln turned to Dorothea Dix: Anna L. Boyden, *Echoes from Hospital and White House: A Record of Mrs. Rebecca R. Pomroy's Experience in War-times* (Boston: D. Lothrop & Co., 1884), p. 52.
420 a powerful woman . . . "out of fashion": Dorothy Clarke Wilson, *Stranger and Traveler: The Story of Dorothea Dix, American Reformer* (Boston: Little, Brown, 1975), p. 256.
420 Dix chose Rebecca Pomroy . . . "turn right in": Pomroy to "Mary," March 27, 1862, Pomroy Letters.
420 Willie's body lay . . . "Oh, why is it?": AL, quoted in Boyden, *Echoes from Hospital and White House*, pp. 54–56 (quotes pp. 54, 56).
420 Tad would awaken . . . gown and slippers: Pomroy to "Mary," March 27, 1862, Pomroy Letters.
420 Lincoln drove with Browning to Oak Hill Cemetery: Entry for February 23, 1862, in Browning, *The Diary of Orville Hickman Browning*, Vol. I, p. 531.
420 The funeral service . . . in the East Room: *National Intelligencer*, Washington, D.C., February 25, 1862; *Star*, February 24, 1862.
420 "keep the boys . . . in the casket": Bayne, *Tad Lincoln's Father*, p. 200.
420 "He lay with his eyes . . . for the evening": Nathaniel Parker Willis, quoted in Keckley, *Behind the Scenes*, p. 108.
421 "no spectator" . . . the East Room service: Entry for March 2, 1862, in French, *Witness to the Young Republic*, p. 389.
421 Congress had adjourned: *Star*, February 24, 1862; *National Intelligencer*, Washington, D.C., February 25, 1862; entry for February 24, 1862, in Browning, *The Diary of Orville Hickman Browning*, Vol. I, p. 531.
421 a frightful storm arose: Benjamin B. French to Henry F. French, February 27, 1862, reel 5, French Family Papers, DLC; *Star*, February 25, 1862.
421 stormy weather . . . the grave: William G. Greene interview, May 30, 1865, in *HI*, p. 21.
421 Mary found it difficult to endure: Elizabeth Todd Edwards to Julia Edwards Baker, quoted in Randall, *Mary Lincoln*, p. 287.
421 She never invited them back to the White House: Bayne, *Tad Lincoln's Father*, p. 200.
421 In her talks with Mrs. Pomroy . . . her own family: Boyden, *Echoes from Hospital and White House*, pp. 58–59.
421 she should surrender to God's will: Baker, *Mary Todd Lincoln*, p. 214.
421 "to try us . . . is not with us": MTL to Julia Ann Sprigg, May 29, 1862, in Turner and Turner, *Mary Todd Lincoln*, p. 128.
421 speculating that God . . . "of little else": MTL to Hannah Shearer, November 20, 1864, in ibid., p. 189.
422 "foresaken . . . so lovely a child": MTL to Mrs. Charles Eames, July 26, 1862, in ibid., p. 131.

422 "far happier . . . when on earth": MTL to Mary Jane Welles, February 21, 1863, in ibid., p. 147.

422 *"Death* . . . blessed transition": MTL to CS, July 4, 1865, in ibid., p. 256.

422 "where there are . . . *no more* tears shed": MTL to Mary Jane Welles, July 11, 1865, in ibid., p. 257.

422 Through Elizabeth Keckley . . . celebrated medium: Baker, *Mary Todd Lincoln*, p. 219.

422 the "veil . . . the 'loved & lost' ": MTL to CS, July 4, 1865, in Turner and Turner, *Mary Todd Lincoln*, p. 256.

422 "the spirits of the dead . . . have become alive": Princess Felix Salm-Salm, *Ten Years of My Life* (Detroit: Belford Bros., 1877), pp. 59, 60.

422 "offered tangible . . . power of sympathy": Robert S. Cox, *Body and Soul: A Sympathetic History of American Spiritualism* (Charlottesville and London: University of Virginia Press, 2003), p. 85.

422 "an altered woman" . . . look at his picture: Keckley, *Behind the Scenes*, p. 116.

422 She sent all his toys . . . was laid out: Ibid., pp. 116–17; Baker, *Mary Todd Lincoln*, pp. 210, 213.

422 On the Thursday . . . his terrible grief: Stoddard, *Inside the White House in War Times*, p. 67.

422 "That blow . . . never felt it before": AL, quoted by Rev. Willets, in Carpenter, *Six Months at the White House*, pp. 187–88.

423 Three months after . . . "my lost boy Willie": AL, quoted in Le Grand B. Cannon, *Personal Reminiscences of the Rebellion, 1861–1866*. Black Heritage Library Collection (1895; Freeport, N.Y.: Books For Libraries Press, 1971), p. 174; the quotation from *King John* is in Act III, scene IV.

423 Lincoln cherished mementos . . . and tell stories: Randall, *Mary Lincoln*, pp. 291–92.

423 he invited Browning . . . important events: Entry for June 22, 1862, in Browning, *The Diary of Orville Hickman Browning*, Vol. I, p. 553.

423 "the memory . . . you have known before": AL to Fanny McCullough, December 23, 1862, in *CW*, VI, p. 17.

CHAPTER 16: "HE WAS SIMPLY OUT-GENERALED"

Page

425 the "sad calamity . . . be left undone": GBM to AL, February 22, 1862, Lincoln Papers.

425 McClellan's assurances . . . contentious meeting: Williams, *Lincoln and the Radicals*, pp. 77–84; Bruce Tap, "Joint Committee on the Conduct of the War (1861–1865)," in *Encyclopedia of the American Civil War*, ed. Heidler and Heidler, p. 1086.

425 "that neither . . . defer to General McClellan": George W. Julian, *Political Recollections, 1840 to 1872* (Chicago: Jansen, McClurg & Co., 1884), p. 201.

425 Bates strenuously objected . . . "commanders": Entry for January 10, 1862, in *The Diary of Edward Bates, 1859–1866*, pp. 223–24.

426 He borrowed General Halleck's book: Entry for January 8, 1862, in *Lincoln Day by Day*, Vol. III, p. 88.

426 "he was thinking . . . himself": Entry for January 12, 1862, in Browning, *The Diary of Orville Hickman Browning*, Vol. I, p. 523.

426 "The bottom is out of the tub": AL, quoted in Meigs, "General M. C. Meigs on the Conduct of the Civil War," *AHR* 26 (1921), p. 292.

426 The nearly bankrupt Treasury . . . meeting on the following day: Ibid.

426 "can't keep a . . . to Tadd": GBM, quoted in ibid., p. 293.

426 General War Order No. 1: AL, "President's General War Order No. 1," January 27, 1862, in *CW*, V, p. 111.

426 Lincoln correctly believed . . . at the same time: Entry for January 12, 1862, in Browning, *The Diary of Orville Hickman Browning*, Vol. I, p. 523.

426 the Peninsula Campaign: See Stephen W. Sears, *To the Gates of Richmond: The Peninsula Campaign* (New York: Ticknor & Fields, 1992).

426 proposed a different strategy . . . "superior force": EMS to Heman Dyer, May 18, 1862, reel 3, Stanton Papers, DLC.

426 it was feared that the Confederates: AL to GBM, February 3, 1862, Lincoln Papers. On McClellan's plans see GBM to EMS, January 31, 1862, Lincoln Papers.

426 Lincoln reluctantly . . . safe from attack: AL, "President's General War Order No. 3," March 8, 1862, in *CW*, V, p. 151.

427 "there was no more" . . . grown disenchanted: EMS to Heman Dyer, May 18, 1862, reel 3, Stanton Papers, DLC.

427 "while men are striving . . . must be stopped": EMS to Charles A. Dana, January 24, 1862, quoted in Charles A. Dana, *Recollections of the Civil War: With the Leaders at Washington and in the Field in the Sixties* (New York: D. Appleton & Co., 1898), p. 5.

427 Stanton's remark . . . society: Flower, *Edwin McMasters Stanton*, pp. 125–26.

427 "That will be . . . the waiting snub": EMS, quoted in Albert E. H. Johnson, "Reminiscences of the Hon. Edwin M. Stanton, Secretary of War," *Records of the Columbia Historical Society* 13 (1910), p. 73.

427 delivered orders to transfer . . . "his humiliation": Flower, *Edwin McMasters Stanton*, p. 216 (quote); Johnson, "Reminiscences of the Hon. Edwin M. Stanton," *RCHS* (1910), pp. 73–74.

427 The Democratic press . . . "worthy of *Punch*": EMS to Charles A. Dana, February 23, 1862, quoted in Flower, *Edwin McMasters Stanton*, p. 131.

428 on the weekend of March 8 . . . supplies, and weapons: Sears, *George B. McClellan*, pp. 163–64; Sears, *To the Gates of Richmond*, pp. 14, 16–17.

428 "We shall be the . . . we have got one": William P. Fessenden to family, March 15, 1862, quoted in Fessenden, *Life and Public Services of William Pitt Fessenden*, Vol. I, p. 261.

428 *"Anybody . . . must have somebody"*: "Conversation with Vice President Wilson, Nov. 16, 1875," container 10, Nicolay Papers.

428 On March 11 . . . Mountain Department: AL, "President's War Order No. 3," March 11, 1862, in *CW*, V, p. 155.

428 "learned through the" . . . the result of the war: McClellan, *McClellan's Own Story*, pp. 224–26.

429 "not to let . . . doing anything": EBL to SPL, April 12, 1862, *Wartime Washington*, ed. Laas, p. 127 (quote); FPB to GBM, April 12, 1862, reel 20, Papers of George B. McClellan, Sr., Manuscript Division, Library of Congress [hereafter McClellan Papers, DLC].

429 Washington gossip . . . to support McClellan: CS to John Andrew, April 27, 1862, in *The Selected Letters of Charles Sumner*, Vol. II, ed. Beverly Wilson Palmer (Boston: Northeastern University Press, 1990), p. 112.

429 "preservers of slavery": Entry for February 1862, in Gurowski, *Diary from March 4, 1861 to November 12, 1862*, p. 157.

429 Monty Blair privately . . . "mortifying to Frank": MB to FPB, March 12, 1862, box 7, folder 6, Blair-Lee Papers, NjP-SC.

429 "urged by Chase" . . . felt it intensely: EBL to SPL, March 11, [1862], in *Wartime Washington*, ed. Laas, p. 109.

429 Frank Blair had delivered . . . of Blair's address: Smith, *The Francis Preston Blair Family in Politics*, Vol. II, pp. 87–89; Williams, *Lincoln and the Radicals*, pp. 105–09.

429 The *New York Tribune* . . . "of the President": MB to John C. Frémont, August 24, 1861, quoted in *NYTrib*, March 4, 1862.

429 "Brother just took . . . think of it again": EBL to SPL, March 6, 1862, in *Wartime Washington*, ed. Laas, pp. 105–06.

430 A grateful Monty Blair . . . "very well of it": MB to FPB, March 12, 1862, box 7, folder 6, Blair-Lee Papers, NjP-SC.

430 approving Frémont's appointment . . . "opinion and action": *NYT*, March 13, 1862.

430 Seward appreciated . . . at large: Seward, *Seward at Washington . . . 1861–1872*, pp. 50–51.

430 "Somebody must be . . . the S. of S.": WHS to TW, April 25, 1862, quoted in ibid., p. 88.

430 "The President . . . and practical": WHS to TW, April 1, 1862, quoted in ibid., p. 81.

430 Count Gurowski despaired . . . *"strategy?"*: Entry for February 1862, in Gurowski, *Diary from March 4, 1861 to November 12, 1862*, pp. 156, 226–27, 171 (quote).

430 by the middle of March . . . him of command: Allan Nevins, *The War for the Union*. Vol. II: *War Becomes Revolution, 1862–1863* (1960; New York: Konecky & Konecky, undated reprint), p. 44.

430 Seward scorned . . . northern Virginia!: WHS, paraphrased in letter from Sam Ward to S. L. M. Barlow, March 27, 1862, in ibid.

431 While acknowledging . . . " *'stationary'* engine": Carpenter, *Six Months at the White House*, p. 255.

431 he confided to Browning . . . "orders to move": Entry for April 2, 1862, in Browning, *The Diary of Orville Hickman Browning*, Vol. I, pp. 537–38.

431 twenty-four hours before . . . to Fort Monroe: Sears, *To the Gates of Richmond*, p. xi; Sears, *George B. McClellan*, p. 168.

431 presented a sight . . . "seldom seen": Entry for March 16, 1862, in French, *Witness to the Young Republic*, p. 391.

431 "I will bring you . . . of his heart": GBM to the Soldiers of the Army of the Potomac, March 14, 1862, quoted in *NYT*, March 16, 1862.

431 "information . . . defend the Capital": EMS to Heman Dyer, May 18, 1862, reel 3, Stanton Papers, DLC.

431 "explicit order . . . entirely secure": AL to GBM, April 9, 1862, in *CW*, V, p. 184.

431 Stanton referred . . . "wrath of his friends": EMS to Heman Dyer, May 18, 1862, reel 3, Stanton Papers, DLC.

431 McClellan advanced . . . constructing earthworks: Sears, *To the Gates of Richmond*, pp. 36–62; Todd Anthony Rosa, "Peninsula Campaign," in *Encyclopedia of the American Civil War*, ed. Heidler and Heidler, p. 1483.

432 "You now have . . . as you can": AL to GBM, April 6, 1862, in *CW*, V, p. 182.

432 "he had better come & do it himself": GBM to MEM, April 8, [1862], in *Civil War Papers of George B. McClellan*, p. 234.

432 "the enemy . . . strong batteries": GBM and EMS paraphrased in entry of April 9, 1862, in *The Diary of Edward Bates, 1859–1866*, p. 249.

432 "It is indispensable . . . *But you must act*": AL to GBM, April 9, 1862, in *CW*, V, p. 185.

432 "Do not misunderstand . . . batteries built": GBM to AL, April 23, 1862, Lincoln Papers.

432 "the more decisive the results will be": GBM to MEM, April 19, [1862], in *Civil War Papers of George B. McClellan*, p. 243.

432 "compelled to change . . . delay of victory": GBM to EMS, [c. April 27, 1862], in ibid., pp. 248–49.

432 Joe Johnston . . . damage to the rebel army: Sears, *To the Gates of Richmond*, pp. 68, 62; GBM to EMS, May 4, 1862, in *Civil War Papers of George B. McClellan*, p. 254.

433 the long delay . . . a counteroffensive: McPherson, *Battle Cry of Freedom*, p. 455.

433 the spring social season . . . "over the ground": *NR*, April 4, 1862.

433 Mary remained in mourning . . . on the lawn: Commissioner B. B. French to Colonel John Harris, Commandant U.S. Marine Corps, June 12, 1862, p. 134, Vol. 14, Letters Sent by the Commissioner of Public Buildings, Vols. 12, 14 (July 2, 1855–June 9, 1865), reel 7, Records of the District of Columbia Commissioners and of the Offices Concerned with Public Buildings, 1791–1867 (National Archives Microfilm Publication M371), Records of the Office of Public Buildings and Public Parks of the National Capital, RG 42, DNA.

433 "more of a . . . in order to watch her": Mrs. Daniel Chester (Mary) French, *Memories of a Sculptor's Wife* (Boston and New York: Houghton Mifflin, 1928), pp. 147–48.

433 "I a simple . . . her perfection": Fanny Garrison Villard, quoted in Phelps, *Kate Chase, Dominant Daughter*, p. 279.

434 Kate's daily schedule, breakfasts and parties: Ross, *Proud Kate*, p. 78; Phelps, *Kate Chase, Dominant Daughter*, p. 112.
434 "stop at Van Zant's . . . and agreeable occasion": KCS to Jay Cooke, quoted in Ross, *Proud Kate*, p. 94.
434 "Cabinet calling . . . and Mrs. Stanton": "Miriam," February 19, 1862, *Iowa State Register*, Des Moines, quoted in Mrs. John A. Kasson, "An Iowa Woman in Washington, D.C., 1861–1865," *Iowa Journal of History* 52 (January 1954), pp. 66–67.
434 While Kate hosted . . . lively, entertaining conversation: Phelps, *Kate Chase, Dominant Daughter*, pp. 111–12.
434 "Diplomats and statesmen . . . the Bourbons": *Washington Post*, August 1, 1899.
435 the Chase home . . . a forum: Ross, *Proud Kate*, pp. 78, 93.
435 "parlor politics": For more on Washington women using entertaining for political purposes see Catherine Allgor, *Parlor Politics: In Which the Ladies of Washington Help Build a City and a Government* (Charlottesville and London: University Press of Virginia, 2000).
435 a "rival court": Belden and Belden, *So Fell the Angels*, p. 33.
435 the proclamation of General David Hunter: General Orders No. 11, May 9, 1862, quoted in AL, "Proclamation Revoking General Hunter's Order of Military Emancipation of May 9, 1862," May 19, 1862, in *CW*, V, p. 222.
435 "It seems to me . . . your Administration": SPC to AL, May 16, 1862, Lincoln Papers.
435 "No commanding general . . . consulting me": AL to SPC, [May 17, 1862], in *CW*, V, p. 219.
435 "dissatisfaction . . . believe would follow": AL, "Appeal to Border State Representatives to Favor Compensated Emancipation," July 12, 1862, in ibid., p. 318.
435 "among the more advanced . . . pusillanimity": Carl Schurz to AL, May 19, 1862, Lincoln Papers.
435 "all the more warmly . . . of Hunter's proclamation": SPC to Horace Greeley, May 21, 1862, reel 20, Chase Papers.
436 Rumors began to surface: *NYT*, May 20, 1862.
436 "The cabin" . . . his "inexhaustible stock": Viele, "A Trip with Lincoln, Chase, and Stanton," *Scribners Monthly* (1878), pp. 813–14.
436 "called up by . . . behind his back": Entry for April 19, 1862, in Madeline Vinton Dahlgren, *Memoir of John A. Dahlgren, Rear-Admiral United States Navy* (Boston: James R. Osgood & Co., 1882), p. 364 n2.
437 "muscular power . . . in vain to imitate him": Viele, "A Trip with Lincoln, Chase, and Stanton," *Scribners Monthly* (1878), pp. 815–16.
437 pored over maps . . . around Virginia: Ibid., p. 815; William E. Baringer, "On Enemy Soil: President Lincoln's Norfolk Campaign," *Abraham Lincoln Quarterly* 7 (March 1952), p. 6.
437 Union forces at Fort Monroe: "Map of Hampton Roads and Adjacent Shore," in John Taylor Wood, "The First Fight of Iron-Clads," in *Battles and Leaders of the Civil War*, Vol. I, Part 2, p. 699. The mouths of the James, Nansemond, and Elizabeth rivers all converge at Hampton Roads.
437 *Merrimac* . . . devastating engagements: Gene A. Smith, "*Monitor* versus *Virginia* (8 March 1862)," in *Encyclopedia of the American Civil War*, ed. Heidler and Heidler, p. 1348. Although the Confederates had rechristened the ironclad the CSS *Virginia*, the vessel continued to be known by its previous name, the *Merrimac*.
437 "It is a disgrace . . . cannot cope": Montgomery C. Meigs, quoted in Gorham, *Life and Public Services of Edwin M. Stanton*, Vol. I, p. 371.
437 An emergency cabinet meeting . . . "presence": Niven, *Gideon Welles*, p. 403.
437 *Monitor* . . . "cheese box on a raft": Entry for October 10, 1862, in French, *Witness to the Young Republic*, p. 412.
437 "a pigmy to a giant": *NYT*, March 14, 1862 (quote); *NYT*, March 11, 1862.
437 When Stanton learned . . . "with diamonds": *NYT*, March 16, 1862.
437 "The ringing of those plates": Herman Melville, "A Utilitarian View of the *Monitor's* Fight," in *The Works of Herman Melville*, Vol. XVI (London: Constable & Co., 1924), pp. 44, 45.
437 huddled over maps . . . Navy Yard vulnerable: Baringer, "On Enemy Soil," *ALQ* 7 (1952), p. 8; Shelby Foote, *The Civil War: A Narrative*. Vol. I: *Fort Sumter to Perryville* (New York: Random House, 1958; New York: Vintage Books, 1986), p. 414.
438 Lincoln and his little group . . . "Treasury to follow": SPC to Janet Chase Hoyt, May 7, 1862, reel 20, Chase Papers.
438 one leg permanently damaged: Wolcott, "Edwin M. Stanton," p. 131.
438 Goldsborough approved . . . across the water: Foote, *The Civil War*, Vol. I, p. 414.
438 "a smoke curled . . . turned back": SPC to Janet Chase Hoyt, May 8, 1862, quoted in Warden, *Private Life and Public Services*, p. 428.
438 each personally surveyed . . . delay the attack: SPC to Janet Chase Hoyt, May 11, 1862, reel 20, Chase Papers; Baringer, "On Enemy Soil," *ALQ* (1952), pp. 15–18.
438 Chase, accompanying . . . of the region: SPC to Janet Chase Hoyt, May 11, 1862, reel 20, Chase Papers.
439 "The night was very . . . of mere appearances": Carpenter, *Six Months at the White House*, pp. 104–05.
439 reporters noted . . . bouts of vertigo: *Philadelphia Inquirer*, May 13, 1862.
439 "one of the strangest . . . military history": Foote, *The Civil War*, Vol. I, p. 413.
439 "So has ended . . . now virtually ours": SPC to Janet Chase Hoyt, May 11, 1862, reel 20, Chase Papers.
439 "Norfolk . . . my movements": GBM to MEM, May 10, [1862], in *Civil War Papers of George B. McClellan*, p. 262.
439 Welles invited . . . "field glasses and maps": FWS to FAS, undated letter, quoted in Seward, *Seward at Washington . . . 1861–1872*, p. 89.
440 enjoyed an easy camaraderie . . . with one another: Mary Jane Welles to Edgar T. Welles, May 19, 1862, typescript, reel 34, Welles Papers.
440 Seward . . . composed a humorous poem: Entry for May 19, 1862, in Dahlgren, *Memoir of John A. Dahlgren*, p. 368.

440 "Virginia is sad . . . everywhere": WHS to FAS, May 19, 1862, quoted in Seward, *Seward at Washington . . . 1861–1872*, p. 94.

440 "We saw war . . . precedes its march": WHS to FAS, undated letter, quoted in ibid., p. 93.

440 The steamer reached McClellan's camp . . . "its supporting fleet": FWS to FAS, undated letter, quoted in ibid., p. 89.

440 "a nuisance": GBM to MEM, May 15, [1862], in *Civil War Papers of George B. McClellan*, p. 267.

440 he convinced . . . "this side of Richmond": WHS to AL, May 14, 1862, Lincoln Papers.

440 "one of the great . . . of the world": GBM to MEM, May 22, [1862], in *Civil War Papers of George B. McClellan*, p. 274.

440 "At night . . . or New York": FWS to FAS, undated letter, quoted in Seward, *Seward at Washington . . . 1861–1872*, p. 89.

440 Seward advised Lincoln . . . "as soon as possible": WHS to AL, May 14, 1862, Lincoln Papers.

440 McDowell was ordered: AL to Irvin McDowell, [May 17, 1862], in *CW*, V, pp. 219–20.

441 McClellan stood . . . "animal": GBM to MEM, [June 9, 1862], in *Civil War Papers of George B. McClellan*, p. 293.

441 an impromptu visit . . . *Marco Bozzaris*: Entry for May 22, [1862], in Dahlgren, *Memoir of John A. Dahlgren*, pp. 368, 368 n1; John W. M. Hallock, *The American Byron: Homosexuality and the Fall of Fitz-Greene Halleck* (Madison: University of Wisconsin Press, 2000), pp. 96–98; Fitz-Greene Halleck, "Marco Bozzaris," in *Yale Book of American Verse*, ed. Thomas R. Lounsbury (New Haven, Conn.: Yale University Press, 1912), pp. 12–13.

441 "a common baggage . . . think much of McDowell!": Entry for May 23, 1862, in Dahlgren, *Memoir of John A. Dahlgren*, pp. 369–70.

442 General Stonewall Jackson had been sent: McPherson, *Battle Cry of Freedom*, pp. 455–57.

442 "I have been compelled . . . to join you": AL to GBM, May 24, 1862, in *CW*, V, p. 232.

442 "Stripped bare . . . from you instantly": AL to GBM, May 25, 1862, in ibid., pp. 236–37.

442 "Independently . . . shall attack Richmond": GBM to AL, May 25, 1862, Lincoln Papers.

442 "just finished . . . knavery & folly": GBM to MEM, May 25, [1862], in *Civil War Papers of George B. McClellan*, p. 275.

442 "Lincoln's diversion . . . to capture Richmond": McPherson, *Battle Cry of Freedom*, p. 460.

443 Confederate attack at Fair Oaks: Sears, *To the Gates of Richmond*, pp. 111–45, 147, 149; Sears, *George B. McClellan*, p. 196.

443 "McClellan keeps sending . . . has not stirred": Christopher Wolcott to Pamphila Stanton Wolcott, June 11, 1862, in Wolcott, "Edwin M. Stanton," p. 156 (first quote); Wolcott to Wolcott, June 22, 1862, ibid., p. 157a (second quote).

443 bridges to be built: Sears, *To the Gates of Richmond*, p. 158.

443 "if I cannot fully . . . for the results": GBM to EMS, June 16, 1862, reel 3, Stanton Papers, DLC.

443 "utmost prudence . . . all know it": GBM to MEM, June 22, [1862], in *Civil War Papers of George B. McClellan*, p. 305.

443 allowed General Lee to take the initiative: Sears, *To the Gates of Richmond*, p. 151.

443 the Seven Days Battles: For a detailed description of the Seven Days Battles, see Sears, *To the Gates of Richmond*, pp. 181–336.

443 Federals dead, wounded, and missing: Ibid., pp. 344–45.

443 "vastly superior . . . where it belongs": GBM to EMS, June 25, [1862], in *Civil War Papers of George B. McClellan*, pp. 309–10.

443 "pains me . . . if I would": AL to GBM, June 26, 1862, in *CW*, V, p. 286.

443 neither McClellan nor Lincoln was able to sleep: Entry for July 5, 1862, in Dahlgren, *Memoir of John A. Dahlgren*, p. 375; Sears, *George B. McClellan*, p. 209.

443 Gaines' Mill . . . McClellan to retreat: Sears, *To the Gates of Richmond*, pp. 213–50; Sears, *George B. McClellan*, p. 212.

443 "I now know . . . sacrifice this army": GBM to EMS, June 28, 1862, *OR*, Ser. 1, Vol. XI, p. 61.

444 When the supervisor of telegrams . . . it to Stanton: Bates, *Lincoln in the Telegraph Office*, pp. 109–10.

444 McClellan's troops remained a strong: McPherson, *Battle Cry of Freedom*, p. 468.

444 Malvern Hill: Sears, *To the Gates of Richmond*, pp. 308–36.

444 "He was simply out-generaled": Christopher Wolcott to Pamphila Stanton Wolcott, July 2, 1862, in Wolcott, "Edwin M. Stanton," p. 157a.

444 he continued to retreat: McPherson, *Battle Cry of Freedom*, p. 470; Sears, *To the Gates of Richmond*, p. 338.

CHAPTER 17: "WE ARE IN THE DEPTHS"

Page

445 "We are in the . . . gloomy thinking": Entry for July 14, 1862, *Diary of George Templeton Strong*, Vol. III, p. 241.

445 manifesting an anxiety . . . "more momentous": *Iowa State Register*, Des Moines, July 16, 1862.

445 "the gloomiest . . . so low": Entry for July 4, 1862, in Gurowski, *Diary from March 4, 1861 to November 12, 1862*, p. 235.

445 "the past has been . . . the war began": JGN to TB, July 13, 1862, container 2, Nicolay Papers.

446 "It is a startling . . . sustain a spirit": WHS to FS, August 2, 1862, in Seward, *Seward at Washington . . . 1861–1872*, pp. 120–21.

446 "Since the rebellion . . . taken Richmond": SPC to Richard C. Parsons, July 20, 1862, reel 21, Chase Papers.

446 "The house seemed . . . you were gone": SPC to KCS, June 24, 1862, reel 21, Chase Papers.

446 many long letters: SPC to KCS, June 24, 25, 29, and 30, July 1, 2 and 4, 1862, reel 21, Chase Papers.

446 "a mark of love and . . . on many points": SPC to KCS, July 6, 1862, reel 21, Chase Papers.

446 "All your letters . . . very good": SPC to KCS, July 4, 1862, reel 21, Chase Papers.

446 concealed her unhappiness . . . "So with us it came": William Sprague to KCS, May 27, 1866, Sprague Papers.

447 "My confidence . . . and so will I": SPC to KCS, July 6, 1862, reel 21, Chase Papers.

447 to visit the McDowells' . . . "will alarm you": Mrs. McDowell, quoted in Phelps, *Kate Chase, Dominant Daughter*, p. 121.

447 "The first necessity . . . of no more": *NYT*, July 7, 1862.

447 "Journals of all . . . instant removal": *NYT*, July 10, 1862.

447 "So you want . . . unaffected wonder": GBM to MEM, [July] 13, [1862], in *Civil War Papers of George B. McClellan*, pp. 354–55.

447 "*the proof . . .* hypocrite & villain": GBM to MEM, July 22, [1862], in ibid., p. 368.

448 "there had been . . . opposition to McClellan": SPL to EBL, July 6, 1862, box 230, folder 7, Blair-Lee Papers, NjP-SC.

448 John Astor . . . "by a signal victory": Entry for July 11, 1862, *Diary of George Templeton Strong*, Vol. III, p. 239.

448 "If we could help . . . any other way": Frederick Law Olmsted to "My Dear Doctor," July 13, 1862, reel 2, Papers of Frederick Law Olmsted, Manuscript Division, Library of Congress.

448 "very fierce crusade . . . the art of war": *NYT*, July 10, 1862.

448 Mary Ellet Cabell . . . "tears to his eyes": Mary Ellet Cabell, quoted in Flower, *Edwin McMasters Stanton*, p. 164.

449 "the baby was dying" . . . on July 10: Christopher Wolcott to Pamphila Stanton Wolcott, July 6, 1862, in Wolcott, "Edwin M. Stanton," p. 157b (quote); Gideon Welles, "The History of Emancipation," *Galaxy* 14 (December 1872), p. 842.

449 his own health began to suffer: Benjamin, "Recollections of Secretary Edwin M. Stanton," *Century* (1887), p. 759.

449 "He unflinchingly . . . out of it": Whitman, *Specimen Days* (1902 edn.), p. 36.

449 "Allow me to assure . . . all your life": AL to Quintin Campbell, June 28, 1862, in *CW*, V, p. 288.

449 Stanton . . . shutting down recruiting offices: Thomas and Hyman, *Stanton*, p. 201; Sears, *George B. McClellan*, p. 180.

449 "a general panic": AL to WHS, June 28, 1862, in *CW*, V, p. 292.

449 Seward devised an excellent solution: AL, "Call for Troops," June 30, 1862, in ibid., p. 294 n1.

450 Seward telegraphed . . . "We fail without it": WHS to EMS, July 1, 1862, *OR*, Ser. 3, Vol. II, p. 186.

450 "The existing law" . . . his own responsibility: EMS to WHS, July 1, 1862, *OR*, Ser. 3, Vol. II, pp. 186–87 (quote p. 186).

450 He set a precedent . . . answered Seward's call: *NR*, August 14, 1862.

450 William Junior . . . "line of march": William H. Seward, Jr., speech before members of the 9th New York Artillery, 1912, box 121, Seward Papers, NRU.

450 Will's enlistment . . . his mother's fragile health: William H. Seward, Jr., to WHS, July 17, 1862, reel 117, Seward Papers.

450 "As it is obvious . . . no objection": FAS to FWS, August 10, 1862, reel 115, Seward Papers.

450 to make a personal visit . . . at Harrison's Landing: *Sun*, Baltimore, Md., July 11, 1862.

451 "The day had" . . . to over 100 degrees: *NYT*, July 12, 1862 (quote); *NYH*, July 11, 1862.

451 the "almost overpowering" heat: GBM to MEM, July 8, [1862], in *Civil War Papers of George B. McClellan*, p. 346.

451 at Harrison's Landing . . . moonlit evening: *NYT*, July 12, 1862; *NYH*, July 11, 1862.

451 great cheers . . . "deck of the vessel": *NYT*, July 11, 1862.

451 "strong frank . . . will be saved": GBM to MEM, July 8, [1862], in *Civil War Papers of George B. McClellan*, p. 346.

451 the "Harrison's Landing" letter: GBM to AL, July 7, 1862, *OR*, Ser. 1, Vol. XI, pp. 73–74.

451 Lincoln "made no comments . . . to me for it": McClellan, *McClellan's Own Story*, p. 487.

452 the president reviewed . . . wounded: Sears, *To the Gates of Richmond*, pp. 344–45; *NYH*, July 11, 1862.

452 "Mr. Lincoln rode . . . stove-pipe hat": *NYT*, July 11, 1862.

452 "entangled . . . has been universal": Rev. Joseph H. Twichell, "Army Memories of Lincoln. A Chaplain's Reminiscences," *The Congregationalist and Christian World*, January 30, 1913, p. 154.

452 "successive booming . . . Saul of old": *NYH*, July 11, 1862.

452 "thinned ranks . . . with their struggle": *NYT*, July 12, 1862.

452 "On the way . . . swim in the river": *NYH*, July 11, 1862.

452 "Frank was . . . greatly cheered": EBL to SPL, July 18, 1862, in *Wartime Washington*, ed. Laas, p. 165 n8.

452 summoned General Henry Halleck . . . general in chief: AL, "Order Making Henry W. Halleck General-in-Chief," July 11, 1862, in *CW*, V, pp. 312–13.

452 Halleck's victories . . . widely respected: "Halleck, Henry Wager (1815–1872)," in Sifakis, *Who Was Who in the Union*, p. 172.

453 "I do not know . . . I am a General": GBM to MEM, [July] 10, [1862], in *Civil War Papers of George B. McClellan*, p. 348.

453 Senator Chandler of Michigan . . . "the coward": Entry for June 4, 1862, in *The Diary of Edward Bates, 1859–1866*, p. 260.

453 Lincoln was determined . . . "cajoled out of them": Entry for July 24, 1862, in Browning, *The Diary of Orville Hickman Browning*, Vol. I, p. 563.

453 "much of his . . . crushing the rebellion": Benjamin, "Recollections of Secretary Edwin M. Stanton," *Century* (1887), p. 765.

453 "that all that Stanton . . . the President": Entry for July 14, 1862, in Browning, *The Diary of Orville Hickman Browning*, Vol. I, p. 559.

453 All the government departments had closed down: *NR*, August 7, 1862.

453 "never seen more persons . . . resembled": Entry for August 10, 1862, in French, *Witness to the Young Republic*, p. 405.

453 "the ringing of bells . . . Marine Band": *NYT*, August 7, 1862.

454 " 'Well! Hadn't I' . . . once to the stand": Entry for August 6, 1862, *Chase Papers*, Vol. I, p. 360.

454 "I believe there . . . *the Secretary of War*": AL, "Address to Union Meeting at Washington," August 6, 1862, in *CW*, V, pp. 358–59.

454 "He is one of . . . ever created": Entry for August 10, 1862, in French, *Witness to the Young Republic*, p. 405.

454 "originality . . . took all hearts": Entry for August 6, 1862, *Chase Papers*, Vol. I, p. 360.

454 The great rally concluded . . . in the Union: *NR*, August 7, 1862.

454 she had begun riding: *NYT*, April 5, 1862.

454 "she was so hid . . . she was there": Mary Hay to Milton Hay, April 13, 1862, in *Concerning Mr. Lincoln*, comp. Pratt, p. 94.

454 "she seemed to be" . . . Soldiers' Home: Entry for June 16, 1862, in French, *Witness to the Young Republic*, p. 400.

454 Soldiers' Home: Matthew Pinsker, *Lincoln's Sanctuary: Abraham Lincoln and the Soldiers' Home* (Oxford and New York: Oxford University Press, 2003); National Park Service, U.S. Department of the Interior, *President Lincoln and Soldiers' Home National Monument*, Special Resource Draft Study (August 2002).

455 "an earthly paradise": Julia Wheelock Freeman, *The Boys in White; The Experience of a Hospital Agent in and Around Washington* (New York: Lange & Hillman, 1870), p. 171.

455 a choice destination for Washingtonians: Pinsker, *Lincoln's Sanctuary*, p. 12.

455 "this quiet and beautiful . . . along the hills": *Iowa State Register*, Des Moines, July 2, 1862.

455 At Mary's urging: Pinsker, *Lincoln's Sanctuary*, pp. 4–5.

455 "We are truly . . . to Cambridge": MTL to Mrs. Charles Eames, July 26, [1862], in Turner and Turner, *Mary Todd Lincoln*, p. 131.

455 For Tad . . . campfire at night: Pinsker, *Lincoln's Sanctuary*, p. 78.

455 the Lincolns could entertain . . . among family and friends: Ibid., pp. 9–10.

455 "helped him . . . attorney in Illinois": Ibid., pp. 15 (quote), 81–82.

456 "daily habit . . . in the District": *Saturday Evening Post*, June 21, 1862.

456 "But for these humane . . . lost her child": Mrs. E. F. Ellet, *The Court Circles of the Republic* (Hartford, Conn.: Hartford Publishing Co., 1869; New York: Arno Press, 1975), p. 526.

456 "little cares . . . into nothing": Walt Whitman to Louisa Whitman, December 29, 1862, in Walt Whitman, *The Wound Dresser: A Series of Letters Written from the Hospitals in Washington During the War of the Rebellion*, ed. Richard Maurice Bucke (Boston: Small, Maynard & Co., 1898; Folcroft, Penn.: Folcroft Library Editions, 1975), p. 48.

456 "nothing of ordinary . . . it used to": Walt Whitman to Louisa Whitman, August 25, 1863, in ibid., p. 104.

456 "to form an immense army": *NYTrib*, July 9, 1862.

456 steamers arrived . . . Ambulances stood by: *NR*, June 30, 1862.

456 a massive project of . . . military hospitals: see *NR*, June 17–23, 1862; *Iowa State Register*, Des Moines, July 9, 1862.

456 Union Hotel Hospital . . . "sup their wine": *NR*, January 9, 1862.

456 "many of the doors . . . could christen it": Louisa May Alcott, *Hospital Sketches* (New York: Sagamore Press, 1957), p. 59.

456 The Braddock House . . . old chairs and desks: Freeman, *The Boys in White*, p. 37.

456 the Patent Office . . . transformed into a hospital ward: *NR*, June 27 and September 2, 1862.

456 "a curious scene . . . pavement under foot": Walt Whitman, quoted in *NYT*, February 26, 1863.

457 the Methodist Episcopal Church on 20th Street: *NR*, June 18, 1862.

457 covering pews . . . laboratory and kitchen: *NR*, June 23, 1862.

457 more than three thousand patients: *NR*, April 11, 1862.

457 baskets of fruit . . . pillows of wounded men: *NYTrib*, August 13, 1862 (quote); Ellet, *The Court Circles of the Republic*, p. 526; AL to Hiram P. Barney, August 16, 1862, in *CW*, V, pp. 377–78.

457 One wounded soldier . . . signature: MTL to "Mrs. Agen," August 10, 1864, in Turner and Turner, *Mary Todd Lincoln*, p. 179.

457 of "commanding stature . . . for it so eagerly": Alcott, *Hospital Sketches*, pp. 89–92, 99–100, 103, 104.

458 "singularly cool . . . (full of maggots)": Walt Whitman to Louisa Whitman, October 6, 1863, in Whitman, *The Wound Dresser*, pp. 123–24.

458 "heap of feet" . . . hospital grounds: Walt Whitman to Louisa Whitman, December 29, 1862, in ibid., p. 48.

458 she found it difficult . . . "wounded occupant": Alcott, *Hospital Sketches*, p. 59.

458 "Death itself . . . such a relief": Walt Whitman to Louisa Whitman, August 25, 1863, in Whitman, *The Wound Dresser*, p. 104.

458 "was so blackened" . . . eventually recovered: Amanda Stearns to her sister, May 14, 1863, reprinted in Amanda Akin Stearns, *The Lady Nurse of Ward E* (New York: Baker & Taylor Co., 1909), pp. 25–26 (quote p. 25).

458 Another youth . . . "on the Judgment Day": Alcott, *Hospital Sketches*, pp. 62–63 (quote p. 63).

458 "If she were worldly wise . . . many journals": Stoddard, *Inside the White House in War Times*, p. 48.
458 "While her sister-women . . . the White House": Ames, *Ten Years in Washington*, p. 237.
458 Mary continued . . . work discreetly: *Chicago Tribune*, July 4, 1872; Mary Elizabeth Massey, *Bonnet Brigades* (New York: Alfred A. Knopf, 1966), p. 44.
459 "our ever-bountiful benefactress & friend": *NR*, December 27, 1861.
459 "an angel of mercy": *NR*, June 27, 1862.
459 Lincoln had asked the legislature: AL, "Message to Congress," March 6, 1862, in *CW*, V, pp. 144–46.
459 "less than one half-day's" . . . border states combined: AL to James A. McDougall, March 14, 1862, in *CW*, V, p. 160.
459 "to surrender . . . the Union dissolved": *NYT*, July 13, 1862.
459 If the rebels . . . lose heart: AL, "Message to Congress," March 6, 1862, in *CW*, V, p. 145.
459 "emancipation in any form . . . the Border States": Editors' note on majority reply to AL, "Appeal to Border State Representatives to Favor Compensated Emancipation," July 12, 1862, in ibid., p. 319 n1.
460 "never doubted . . . to abolish slavery": AL, "Message to Congress," April 16, 1862, in ibid., p. 192.
460 "I trust I am not . . . seem like a dream": Frederick Douglass to CS, April 8, 1862, reel 25, Sumner Papers.
460 As slaves in the District . . . "when they wished": Smith, *Francis Preston Blair*, p. 354.
460 "all but one . . . quarters": EBL to SPL, April 19, 1862, in *Wartime Washington*, ed. Laas, p. 130.
460 Henry . . . the rest of his life: Henry, quoted in Smith, *Francis Preston Blair*, p. 354.
460 Nanny . . . "children are free": EBL to SPL, April 19, 1862, in *Wartime Washington*, ed. Laas, p. 130.
460 a new confiscation bill: "An Act to suppress Insurrection, to punish Treason and Rebellion, to seize and confiscate the Property of Rebels, and for other Purposes," July 17, 1862, in *Statutes at Large, Treaties, and Proclamations of the United States of America*, Vol. 12 (Boston, 1863), pp. 589–92, available through "Chronology of Emancipation During the Civil War," *Freedmen and Southern Society Project*, University of Maryland, College Park, www.history.umd.edu/Freedmen/conact2.htm (accessed April 2004).
460 "It was . . . a dead letter from the start": "Confiscation Act of July 17, 1862," in Mark E. Neely, Jr., *The Abraham Lincoln Encyclopedia* (New York: McGraw-Hill, 1982), p. 68.
460 a "disturbing influence . . . to break anew": CS, quoted in James G. Blaine, *Twenty Years of Congress: From Lincoln to Garfield*, Vol. I (Norwich, Conn.: Henry Bill Publishing Co., 1884), p. 374.
461 "our friends . . . take it at its flood": Entry for July 14, 1862, in Browning, *The Diary of Orville Hickman Browning*, Vol. I, p. 558.
461 "will be an end . . . errors of policy": Henry Cooke to Jay Cooke, July 16, 1862, in Ellis Paxson Oberholtzer, *Jay Cooke: Financier of the Civil War* (Philadelphia: George W. Jacobs & Co., 1907), p. 199.
461 "looked weary . . . in his voice": Entry for July 15, 1862, in Browning, *The Diary of Orville Hickman Browning*, Vol. I, p. 560.
461 the president traveled . . . final days of the term: JGN to TB, July 18, 1862, container 2, Nicolay Papers.
461 an extraordinarily productive session: See Leonard P. Curry, *Blueprint for Modern America: Nonmilitary Legislation of the First Civil War Congress* (Nashville, Tenn.: Vanderbilt University Press, 1968), pp. 101–36, 147–48, 179–97, 244–52.
462 "he had lately begun . . . d'etat for our Congress": Entry for July 21, 1862, *Chase Papers*, Vol. I, p. 348.
462 "I ask Congress . . . lost one advocate": WHS to FAS, July 12, 1862, quoted in Seward, *Seward at Washington . . . 1861–1872*, pp. 115–16.
462 The debates had grown . . . "part in them": Field, *Memories of Many Men*, pp. 264–65.
462 "a moral . . . political wrong": AL, "Sixth Debate with Stephen A. Douglas, at Quincy, Illinois," October 13, 1858, in *CW*, III, p. 254.
462 uses to which slaves were put by the Confederacy: Welles, "History of Emancipation," *Galaxy* (1872), pp. 843, 844; Hendrick, *Lincoln's War Cabinet*, p. 355.
462 emancipation could be considered a military necessity: Welles, "History of Emancipation," *Galaxy* (1872), p. 850.
463 the funeral of Stanton's infant son: *Star*, July 11, 1862.
463 "emancipating the slaves . . . justifiable": Entry for c. July 1862, *Welles diary*, Vol. I (1960 edn.), pp. 70–71.
463 when messengers . . . by the diplomats in attendance: Entry for July 21, 1862, *Chase Papers*, Vol. I, p. 348.
463 all members save the postmaster: Welles, "History of Emancipation," *Galaxy* (1872), p. 844.
464 books in the library: MTL to Benjamin B. French, July 26, [1862], in Turner and Turner, *Mary Todd Lincoln*, pp. 129–30; Seale, *The President's House*, Vol. I, pp. 291–92, 380.
464 "profoundly concerned . . . and slavery": Entry for July 21, 1862, *Chase Papers*, Vol. I, p. 348.
464 Lincoln read several orders . . . "decide the question": Entry for July 21, 1862, ibid., pp. 348–49.
464 another cabinet session; Carpenter painting: Stoddard, *Inside the White House in War Times*, p. 11; entry for July 22, 1862, *Chase Papers*, Vol. I, p. 351.
464 Lincoln took the floor . . . "on the slavery question": Welles, "History of Emancipation," *Galaxy* (1872), p. 844.
464 "had resolved upon . . . their advice": Carpenter, *Six Months at the White House*, p. 21.
464 His draft proclamation . . . "and forever": AL, "Emancipation Proclamation—First Draft," [July 22, 1862], in *CW*, V, p. 337.
464 statistics on slaves in border states and Confederacy: These statistics are based on 1860 census data for the numbers of slaves living in the border slave states that remained in the Union, and the eleven slave states that formed the Confederacy.
465 "fraught with consequences . . . could not penetrate": Welles, "History of Emancipation," *Galaxy* (1872), p. 841.

465 the members were startled . . . "immediate promulgation": EMS memorandum, July 22, 1862, reel 3, Stanton Papers, DLC.
465 Bates's approval . . . cadet at West Point: Introduction, and entries for April 14, 1862, and November 30, 1863, in *The Diary of Edward Bates, 1859–1866*, pp. xv–xvi, 250, 319.
465 his "very decided . . . the white race": Welles, "History of Emancipation," *Galaxy* (1872), pp. 844–45.
466 "among our colored . . . 'which they profess' ": Entry for September 25, 1862, in *The Diary of Edward Bates, 1859–1866*, pp. 263–64.
466 Welles remained silent . . . "intensify the struggle": Memorandum from September 22, 1862, quoted in Welles, "History of Emancipation," *Galaxy* (1872), p. 848.
466 "extreme exercise of war powers": Entry for October 1, 1862, *Welles diary*, Vol. I (1960 edn.), p. 159.
466 Caleb Smith . . . "attack the administration": Usher, *President Lincoln's Cabinet*, p. 17.
466 Blair spoke up . . . "were in vain": Welles, "History of Emancipation," *Galaxy* (1872), p. 847.
467 "beyond anything . . . universal emancipation": EMS memorandum, July 22, 1862, reel 3, Stanton Papers, DLC.
467 "depredation and massacre . . . soon as practicable": Entry for July 22, 1862, *Chase Papers*, Vol. I, p. 351.
467 The bold proclamation . . . "was his specialty": Entry for August 22, 1863, *Welles diary*, Vol. I (1960 edn.), p. 415.
467 "golden moment . . . four thousand years": Christopher Wolcott to Pamphila Stanton Wolcott, July 27, 1862, in Wolcott, "Edwin M. Stanton," p. 158a.
467 Lincoln later maintained . . . "Seward spoke": Carpenter, *Six Months at the White House*, p. 21.
467 a racial war in the South . . . their economic interests: EMS memorandum, July 22, 1862, reel 3, Stanton Papers, DLC.
468 "The public mind . . . to give them effect": WHS to FAS, August 7, 1862, in Seward, *Seward at Washington . . . 1861–1872*, p. 121.
468 "would have been . . . territory was conquered": Carpenter, "A Day with Governor Seward," Seward Papers.
468 "Mr. President . . . *shriek*, on the retreat": WHS, quoted in Carpenter, *Six Months at the White House*, pp. 21–22.
468 "until the eagle . . . about his neck": Carpenter, "A Day with Governor Seward," Seward Papers.
468 Seward's argument . . . met with Lincoln: Francis B. Cutting to EMS, February 20, 1867, reel 11, Stanton Papers, DLC.
468 "The wisdom of . . . the progress of events": AL, quoted in Carpenter, *Six Months at the White House*, p. 22.
469 "with public sentiment . . . nothing can succeed": AL, "First Debate with Stephen A. Douglas at Ottawa, Illinois," August 21, 1858, in *CW*, III, p. 27.
469 On August 14 . . . opportunity among their own people: "Address on Colonization to a Deputation of Negroes," August 14, 1862, in *CW*, V, pp. 371–75.
469 "We were entirely hostile" . . . to the proposal: Edward M. Thomas to AL, August 16, 1862, Lincoln Papers.
469 "are as much the natives . . . to a distant shore": *Liberator*, August 22, 1862.
470 provoked Frederick Douglass: Christopher N. Breiseth, "Lincoln and Frederick Douglass: Another Debate," *Journal of the Illinois State Historical Society* 68, no. 1 (February 1975), pp. 14–15.
470 "ridiculous . . . and bitter persecution": *Douglass' Monthly* (September 1862).
470 the "drop of honey": AL, "Temperance Address," February 22, 1842, in *CW*, I, p. 273.
470 "How much better . . . homes in America!": Entry for August 15, 1862, *Chase Papers*, Vol. I, p. 362.
470 cheap "clap-trap . . . perhaps of both": Entry for August, 1862, in Gurowski, *Diary from March 4, 1861 to November 12, 1862*, pp. 251–52.
470 "The Prayer of Twenty Millions": *NYTrib*, August 20, 1862.
471 seizing the opportunity to begin instructing the public: *NYT*, August 24, 1862.
471 "As to the policy . . . will help the cause": AL to Horace Greeley, August 22, 1862, in *CW*, V, pp. 388–89.
471 "I am sorry . . . than human freedom": FAS to WHS, August 24, 1862, reel 114, Seward Papers.
471 "killed years ago . . . destruction of slavery": WHS, quoted in Carpenter, *Six Months at the White House*, pp. 72–73.
472 no "truly republican . . . a great moral evil": FAS, miscellaneous fragment, reel 197, Seward Papers.

CHAPTER 18: "MY WORD IS OUT"

Page
473 Halleck ordered McClellan . . . Alexandria: Henry W. Halleck to EMS, August 30, 1862, in *OR*, Ser. 1, Vol. XII, Part III, p. 739; John J. Hennessy, *Return to Bull Run: The Campaign and Battle of Second Manassas* (New York: Simon & Schuster, 1993), p. 10.
474 He argued ferociously . . . "disastrous in the extreme": GBM to Henry W. Halleck, August 4, 1862, in *Civil War Papers of George B. McClellan*, pp. 383–84 (quote p. 383).
474 His only hope . . . of his command: GBM to MEM, August 8, [1862], in ibid., p. 388.
474 After delaying . . . until August 24: GBM to Henry W. Halleck, August 12, [1862], in ibid., pp. 390–93; Henry W. Halleck to EMS, August 30, 1862, in *OR*, Ser. 1, Vol. XII, Part III, p. 739.
474 General Lee moved north . . . the combined forces of Lee, Longstreet, and Jackson: Hennessy, *Return to Bull Run*, pp. 50–51, 55, 92–93, 122–23, 136.

474 "What is the stake? . . . *cause also*": WHS to FAS[?], August 21, 1862, quoted in Seward, *Seward at Washington . . . 1861–1872*, p. 124.

474 a comet appeared in the northern sky: *NR*, August 27, 1862.

474 "When beggars die": William Shakespeare, *The Tragedy of Julius Caesar*, Act II, sc. 2.

474 Although McClellan agreed . . . "leave of absence!": Sears, *George B. McClellan*, pp. 252–56; GBM to MEM, August 24, [1862], in *Civil War Papers of George B. McClellan*, p. 404 (quote).

474 "Pope is beaten . . . Washn again": GBM to MEM, August 23, [1862], in *Civil War Papers of George B. McClellan*, p. 400.

474 "the smell of the gunpowder . . . perceptible": *Star*, August 30, 1862.

474 "distant thunder": *NR*, September 1, 1862.

474 gathered on street corners . . . rumors flew: Leech, *Reveille in Washington*, p. 188; entry for September 3, 1862, *Welles diary*, Vol. I (1960 edn.), p. 106.

475 "Stonewall Jackson . . . about equal proportions": *NR*, September 1, 1862.

475 "prepared to stay all night, if necessary": Bates, *Lincoln in the Telegraph Office*, p. 118.

475 He wired various generals . . . news from Manassas: AL to Ambrose Burnside, August 29, 1862, in *CW*, V, p. 398; Lincoln to Herman Haupt, August 29, 1862, in ibid., p. 399; Lincoln to GBM, August 29, 1862 in ibid.; Bates, *Lincoln in the Telegraph Office*, pp. 119–21.

475 The president now had . . . "perfectly safe": GBM to AL, August 29, 1862, Lincoln Papers.

475 John Hay met the president . . . "his own scrape": "[1 September 1862, Monday]," in Hay, *Inside Lincoln's White House*, pp. 36–37.

475 McClellan's delay . . . "my opinion, required": EMS to Henry W. Halleck, August 28, 1862, in *OR*, Ser. 1, Vol. XII, Part III, p. 706; Henry W. Halleck to EMS, August 30, 1862, in ibid., p. 739 (quote).

475 "like throwing water . . . that in writing": SPC, paraphrased in entry for September 1, 1862, *Welles diary*, Vol. I (1960 edn.), p. 102.

475 Stanton volunteered . . . agreement regarding McClellan: Entries for August 29–30, 1862, in *Chase Papers*, Vol. I, pp. 366–67.

476 "Never before . . . sink into contempt": EB to Hamilton Gamble, September 1, 1862, Bates Papers, MoSHi.

476 written in Stanton's distinctive back-sloping script: Entry for September 1, 1862, *Welles diary*, Vol. I (1960 edn.), p. 100.

476 "unwilling to be . . . commanded by General Pope": Flower, *Edwin McMasters Stanton*, pp. 176–77.

476 Smith was persuaded . . . to Blair or anyone else: Entry for August 31, 1862, *Welles diary*, Vol. I (1960 edn.), pp. 93–95. Howard Beale has identified some of the language included in the 1911 edition of Welles's published diary as having been added later to the original manuscript diary. See Beale's emendations in individual diary entries for subsequent changes made in Welles's diary.

476 Stanton had invited Lincoln . . . "glad tidings at sunrise": "[1 September 1862, Monday]," in Hay, *Inside Lincoln's White House*, p. 37.

477 When Welles stopped by . . . "disrespectful to the President": Entry for August 31, 1862, *Welles diary*, Vol. I (1960 edn.), pp. 95–98 (quotes pp. 97–98).

477 "had called us . . . against him": Entry for September 1, 1862, ibid., pp. 101–02.

477 "he knew of no particular" . . . cabal against the president: Entry for August 31, 1862, ibid., p. 98.

477 "about Eight oclock . . . 'I am afraid' ": "[1 September 1862, Monday]," in Hay, *Inside Lincoln's White House*, pp. 37–38.

477 As rumors spread . . . 16,000 casualties: "5 September 1862, Friday," in ibid., p. 38; FWS to WHS, September 1, 1862, quoted in Seward, *Seward at Washington . . . 1861–1872*, p. 126; McPherson, *Battle Cry of Freedom*, p. 532.

478 "Jeff. Davis . . . before the National Capital": *NYT*, August 31, 1862.

478 put the president in an untenable . . . angrier he became: "1 September 1862, Monday," in Hay, *Inside Lincoln's White House*, p. 37.

478 "There is no . . . now to sacrifice": AL, quoted in "5 September 1862, Friday," in ibid., pp. 38–39.

478 When Halleck recommended . . . Lincoln agreed: Entry for September 12, 1862, *Welles diary*, Vol. I (1960 edn.), p. 124; Sears, *George B. McClellan*, p. 260.

478 Bates rewrote the protest . . . he agreed McClellan should go: Entry for September 1, 1862, ibid., pp. 100–03 (quotes); entry for September 1, 1863, in *Chase Papers*, Vol. I, pp. 367–68.

478 gathered at noon . . . messy controversy over McClellan: Entry for September 2, 1862, in *Lincoln Day by Day*, Vol. III, p. 137; entry for September 2, 1862, *Welles diary*, Vol. I (1960 edn.), p. 104 (quote).

479 Jenny was expecting . . . Clara, was dying: Janet W. Seward, "Personal Experiences of the Civil War," box 132, Seward Papers, NRU; FAS to WHS, August 24, September 7, 1862, reel 114, Seward Papers; FAS to WHS, September 10, 1862, reel 116, Seward Papers.

479 When he heard . . . cut his vacation short: Seward, *Seward at Washington . . . 1861–1872*, p. 127.

479 the president was called out: Entry for September 2, 1862, *Welles diary*, Vol. I (1960 edn.), p. 104.

479 "in a suppressed voice . . . prove a national calamity": Ibid., pp. 104–05 (quotes); entry for September 2, 1862, in *Lincoln Day by Day*, Vol. III, p. 137.

479 Stanton, recognizing . . . "a drooping leaf": *Evening Post*, New York, July 13, 1891 (quote); Flower, *Edwin McMasters Stanton*, p. 179.

479 "seemed wrung . . . to hang himself": EB, quoted in footnote to AL, "Meditation on the Divine Will," [September 2, 1862?], in *CW*, V, p. 404 n1.

479 "In great contests . . . it shall not end yet": AL, "Meditation on the Divine Will," [September 2, 1862?], in ibid., pp. 403–04.

479 Seward drove immediately . . . "during his absence": Seward, *Seward at Washington . . . 1861–1872*, p. 127.

480 "What is the use . . . should have known it": WHS, quoted in "[Mid-September 1862?]," in Hay, *Inside Lincoln's White House*, p. 40.

480 Seward turned to history . . . "preserve hopefulness": WHS to FS, c. November 1862, quoted in Seward, *Seward at Washington . . . 1861–1872*, p. 144.

480 Seward did not question . . . "sea of revolution": WHS to FAS, September 20, 1862, quoted in ibid., p. 132.

480 a president had to work: "5 September 1862, Friday," in Hay, *Inside Lincoln's White House*, p. 38.

480 McClellan smugly returned to his old headquarters: FWS to WHS, September 3, 1862, quoted in Seward, *Seward at Washington . . . 1861–1872*, p. 127.

480 "Again I have . . . 'away from us again' ": GBM to MEM, September 5, [1862], in *Civil War Papers of George B. McClellan*, p. 435.

480 crossed the Potomac . . . three cigars: James M. McPherson, *Crossroads of Freedom: Antietam*. Pivotal Moments in American History Series (New York: Oxford University Press, 2002), pp. 98, 104–05, 107–08. For actual "Lost Orders," see "Special Orders, No. 191, Hd Qrs Army of Northern Va, Sept 9th 1862," reel 31, McClellan Papers, DLC.

480 the Marylanders greeted . . . their countryside: GBM to MEM, September 12 and 14, [1862], and GBM to AL, September 13, [1862], in *Civil War Papers of George B. McClellan*, pp. 450, 458, 453.

481 "We are in . . . battle of the age": GBM to MEM, [September] 17, [1862], in ibid., p. 468.

481 casualties higher than D-Day: McPherson, *Battle Cry of Freedom*, p. 544.

481 "Our victory was . . . so completely": GBM to MEM, September 20, [1862], in *Civil War Papers of George B. McClellan*, p. 473.

481 Lincoln was thrilled . . . and allowed Lee to cross: AL to GBM, September 15, 1862, *CW*, V, p. 426; GBM to Henry W. Halleck, September 19 and 20, 1862, in *Civil War Papers of George B. McClellan*, pp. 470, 475.

481 "At last our Generals . . . National crisis": *NYT*, September 18, 1862.

481 "Sept. 17 . . . of its downfall": *NYT*, September 20, 1862.

481 On September 22 . . . "a graver tone": Carpenter, *Six Months at the White House*, p. 24; entry for September 22, 1862, in *Chase Papers*, Vol. I, p. 393 (quote); EMS, quoted by Judge Hamilton Ward in interview in the *Lockport Journal*, May 21, 1893, reprinted in Whipple, *The Story-Life of Lincoln*, p. 421.

481 reminding his colleagues . . . "to my Maker": AL, quoted in entry for September 22, 1862, in *Chase Papers*, Vol. I, pp. 393–94.

482 "there were occasions . . . the Supreme Will": Welles, "History of Emancipation," *Galaxy* (1872), p. 847.

482 not seeking "advice" . . . suggestions on language: AL, paraphrased in entry for September 22, 1862, in *Chase Papers*, Vol. I, p. 394.

482 "made a very emphatic . . . the measure": Welles, "History of Emancipation," *Galaxy* (1872), p. 846.

482 Blair reiterated . . . the fall elections: Entry for September 22, 1862, in *Chase Papers*, Vol. I, p. 395.

482 "maintain . . . present President"?: WHS, quoted in entry for September 22, 1862, in ibid., p. 394.

482 "it was not my way . . . take this ground": AL, quoted in Carpenter, *Six Months at the White House*, pp. 23–24.

482 "I can only trust . . . never forget them": AL, "Reply to Serenade in Honor of Emancipation Proclamation," September 24, 1862, in *CW*, V, p. 438.

482 proceeded to Chase's house . . . "that horrible name": "[24 September 1862, Wednesday]," in Hay, *Inside Lincoln's White House*, p. 41 (quote); entry for September 24, 1862, in *Chase Papers*, Vol. I, p. 399; *NYT*, September 25, 1862.

483 "in the meanest . . . evoke a generous thrill": Entry for September 23, 1862, in Gurowski, *Diary from March 4, 1861 to November 12, 1862*, p. 278.

483 "did not . . . of a single negro": Fessenden, paraphrased in entry for November 28, 1862, in Browning, *The Diary of Orville Hickman Browning*, Vol. I, p. 587.

483 "We shout for joy . . . confide in his word": *Douglass' Monthly* (October 1862).

483 "My word is out . . . take it back": AL, quoted in George S. Boutwell, *Speeches and Papers Relating to the Rebellion and the Overthrow of Slavery* (Boston: Little, Brown, 1867), p. 362.

483 "render eternal . . . the two sections": *The Times* (London), quoted in *NYT*, September 30, 1862.

483 *Richmond Enquirer* charged . . . "plots their death": *Richmond Enquirer*, October 1, 1862, quoted in *Philadelphia Inquirer*, October 6, 1862.

483 "said he had studied . . . than they did": "[24 September 1862, Wednesday]," in Hay, *Inside Lincoln's White House*, p. 41.

483 "be enthusiastically . . . great act of the age": Hannibal Hamlin to AL, September 25, 1862, Lincoln Papers.

483 "while commendation . . . not very satisfactory": AL to Hannibal Hamlin, September 28, 1862, in *CW*, V, p. 444.

483 "Stanton must leave . . . old place to me": GBM to MEM, September 20, [1862], in *Civil War Papers of George B. McClellan*, p. 476.

483 he would resign . . . "a servile insurrection": GBM to MEM, September 25, [1862], in ibid., p. 481.

484 McClellan drafted a letter . . . not to send the letter: Sears, *George B. McClellan*, pp. 326–27.

484 Though Stanton and Chase . . . considered resigning: Entries for September 25 and October 3, 1862, *Welles diary*, Vol. I (1960 edn.), pp. 148–49, 160–61.

484 Lincoln had made . . . relieved from duty: AL, quoted in "25 September 1863, Sunday," in Hay, *Inside Lincoln's White House*, p. 232.

484 Lincoln journeyed . . . early in October: Entry for October 1, 1862, in *Lincoln Day by Day*, Vol. III, p. 143; John G. Nicolay and John Hay, *Abraham Lincoln: A History*, Vol. VI (New York: Century Co., 1917), p. 174.

484 Halleck, fearing . . . "see my soldiers": AL, quoted in "Lincoln Visits the Army of the Potomac," *Lincoln Lore*, no. 1277, September 28, 1953.

484 As the regiments . . . "greatly amused the company": *NYH*, October 5, 1862.

484 accommodations at Antietam: "Lincoln Visits the Army of the Potomac," *Lincoln Lore*, no. 1277, September 28, 1953.

484 his "over-cautiousness": AL to GBM, October 13, 1862, Lincoln Papers.

484 "was very affable . . . very kind personally": GBM to MEM, October 5, [1862], in *Civil War Papers of George B. McClellan*, p. 490.

484 "real purpose . . . advance into Virginia": GBM to MEM, October 2, [1862], in ibid., p. 488.

484 "if I were . . . trivial": AL, "Speech at Frederick, Maryland," October 4, 1862, in *CW*, V, p. 450.

484 "May our children . . . and his compeers": AL, "Second Speech at Frederick, Maryland," October 4, 1862, in ibid., p. 450.

485 Lincoln had Halleck telegraph . . . "roads are good": Henry W. Halleck to GBM, October 6, 1862, in *OR*, Ser. 1, Vol. XIX, Part II, p. 10.

485 found all manner of excuses: GBM to Henry W. Halleck, October 7, 9, 11, and 18, 1862, and GBM to AL, October 17 and 30, 1862, in *Civil War Papers of George B. McClellan*, pp. 493, 495, 499, 502, 516.

485 "Will you pardon me . . . fatigue anything?": AL to GBM, October [25], 1862, in *CW*, V, p. 474.

485 "Our war on rebellion . . . specimen after all": Entry for October 23, 1862, *Diary of George Templeton Strong*, Vol. III, p. 267.

485 an "ill wind" of discontent: WHS to FS, October 1862, quoted in Seward, *Seward at Washington . . . 1861–1872*, pp. 141, 142 (quote p. 141).

485 the midterm November elections . . . "hurt to laugh": Sears, *George B. McClellan*, p. 335; Hendrick, *Lincoln's War Cabinet*, p. 325; AL, quoted in Sandburg, *Abraham Lincoln: The War Years*, Vol. I, p. 611 (quote).

485 "I began . . . I relieved him": AL, quoted in "25 September 1863, Sunday," in Hay, *Inside Lincoln's White House*, p. 232.

485 McClellan received . . . "visible on my face": GBM to MEM, November 7, [1862], in *Civil War Papers of George B. McClellan*, p. 520.

485 "More than a hundred . . . shed in profusion": *National Intelligencer*, Washington, D.C., November 14, 1862.

486 "In parting . . . an indissoluble tie": GBM to the Army of the Potomac, November 7, 1862, in *Civil War Papers of George B. McClellan*, p. 521.

486 choice of Burnside proved unfortunate: Darius N. Couch, "Sumner's 'Right Grand Division,' " in *Battles and Leaders of the Civil War*, Vol. III, Pt. 1, p. 106; Schurz, *Reminiscences*, Vol. II, pp. 397–98.

486 "ten times . . . as he has *head*": Entry for January 1, 1863, Fanny Seward diary, Seward Papers.

486 Fredericksburg Campaign: McPherson, *Battle Cry of Freedom*, pp. 571–72; Spencer C. Tucker, "Fredericksburg, First Battle of," in *Encyclopedia of the American Civil War*, ed. Heidler and Heidler, pp. 774–79.

486 "The courage . . . popular government": AL, "Congratulations to the Army of the Potomac," December 22, 1862, in *CW*, VI, p. 13.

486 "awful arithmetic . . . Confederacy gone": AL, paraphrased in Stoddard, *Inside the White House in War Times*, p. 101.

486 "more depressed . . . [his] life": Entry for December 18, 1862, in Browning, *The Diary of Orville Hickman Browning*, Vol. I, p. 601.

487 Tuesday, December 16 . . . "cause was lost": Fessenden, *Life and Public Services of William Pitt Fessenden*, Vol. I, pp. 231–32 (quote p. 232).

487 Chase had claimed . . . "of the cabinet": Benjamin Wade, paraphrased in entry for December 16, 1862, in Browning, *The Diary of Orville Hickman Browning*, Vol. I, p. 597.

487 had repeatedly griped . . . "salvation of the country": SPC to John Sherman, September 20, 1862, reel 22, Chase Papers (quote); SPC to Zachariah Chandler, September 20, 1862, reel 1, Chandler Papers, DLC.

487 "paralizing influence . . . the President": Boston *Commonwealth*, December 6, 1862, quoted in David Donald, *Charles Sumner and the Rights of Man* (New York: Alfred A. Knopf, 1970), p. 87.

487 "President *de facto* . . . to Uncle Abe's nose": *Chicago Tribune*, quoted in Thomas, *Abraham Lincoln*, p. 352.

487 "controlling influence . . . of the President": Fessenden, *Life and Public Services of William Pitt Fessenden*, Vol. I, p. 232.

487 "should go in . . . dismissal of Mr Seward": Benjamin Wade, paraphrased in entry for December 16, 1862, in Browning, *The Diary of Orville Hickman Browning*, Vol. I, p. 597.

487 "that measures should . . . to the war": Fessenden, *Life and Public Services of William Pitt Fessenden*, Vol. I, p. 234.

487 "a want of confidence . . . from the Cabinet": Senator Grimes, paraphrased in ibid., p. 233.

487 Fessenden asked . . . "on mere rumors": Ibid., p. 235.

487 "had no evidence . . . our cause greatly": Entry for December 16, 1862, in Browning, *The Diary of Orville Hickman Browning*, Vol. I, pp. 597–98.

488 "without entire . . . productive of evil": Fessenden, *Life and Public Services of William Pitt Fessenden*, Vol. I, p. 236.

488 "give time for reflection": Entry for December 16, 1862, in Browning, *The Diary of Orville Hickman Browning*, Vol. I, p. 598.

488 Preston King felt . . . " 'I can't get out' ": Seward, *Seward at Washington . . . 1861–1872*, pp. 146–47 (quotes); entry for December 19, 1862, *Welles diary*, Vol. I (1960 edn.), p. 194.

488 "They wish to . . . impose upon a child": Entry for December 18, 1862, in Browning, *The Diary of Orville Hickman Browning*, Vol. I, p. 600.

488 "disappointed . . . and chagrined": Entry for December 20, 1862, *Welles diary*, Vol. I (1960 edn.), p. 201.

488 Frances had journeyed . . . family for Christmas: Entry for December 22, 1862, Fanny Seward diary, Seward Papers.

489 "Do not come . . . & uncomfortable night": Entry for c. December 18 and 20, 1862, Fanny Seward diary, Seward Papers.

489 Charles Sumner was particularly . . . of the Confederates: Fessenden, *Life and Public Services of William Pitt Fessenden*, Vol. I, p. 242.

489 Republican senators convened . . . December 18: Ibid., pp. 236–38.

489 "I saw in a moment . . . ray of hope": Entry for December 18, 1862, in Browning, *The Diary of Orville Hickman Browning*, Vol. I, p. 600.

490 during a three-hour session: Fessenden, *Life and Public Services of William Pitt Fessenden*, Vol. I, p. 242.

490 Jacob Collamer . . . "purpose and action": Committee of Nine paper, quoted in ibid., p. 239.

490 "in the hands . . . malignant Democrats: Benjamin Wade, paraphrased in ibid., p. 240.

490 "had been disgraced": Ibid., p. 241.

490 "lukewarmness . . . *of him unperceived*": Entry for December 19, 1862, in *The Diary of Edward Bates, 1859–1866*, p. 269.

490 "shocked and grieved . . . confidence and zeal": Entry for December 19, 1862, *Welles diary*, Vol. I (1960 edn.), p. 195.

490 "earnest and sad . . . nor passionate": Entry for December 19, 1862, in *The Diary of Edward Bates, 1859–1866*, p. 269.

490 "expressed his satisfaction . . . interview": Fessenden, *Life and Public Services of William Pitt Fessenden*, Vol. I, pp. 242–43.

490 "he must work it out . . . on the matter": "30 October 1863, Friday," in Hay, *Inside Lincoln's White House*, p. 104.

490 He sent notices . . . and "good feeling": Entry for December 19, 1862, *Welles diary*, Vol. I (1960 edn.), pp. 194–95.

491 "could not afford to lose": Entry for December 19, 1862, in *The Diary of Edward Bates, 1859–1866*, p. 269.

491 "possible for him" . . . was forced to acquiesce: Entry for December 19, 1862, *Welles diary*, Vol. I (1960 edn.), pp. 195–96 (quote p. 195).

491 Lincoln began . . . "a reasonable consideration": Entry for December 20, 1862, ibid., p. 196; Fessenden, *Life and Public Services of William Pitt Fessenden*, Vol. I, p. 243 (quote).

491 "all had acquiesced . . . once decided": Entry for December 20, 1862, *Welles diary*, Vol. I (1960 edn.), p. 196.

491 He went on to defend Seward . . . Emancipation Proclamation: Fessenden, *Life and Public Services of William Pitt Fessenden*, Vol. I, pp. 243–44, 245–46.

491 "the whole Cabinet . . . and energetic action": Entry for December 20, 1862, *Welles diary*, Vol. I (1960 edn.), pp. 196–97.

491 Blair followed . . . "plural Executive": Ibid., p. 197.

491 "had differed much . . . matters of that kind": MB, paraphrased in Fessenden, *Life and Public Services of William Pitt Fessenden*, Vol. I, p. 245.

491 Bates expressed . . . as did Welles: Entry for December 19, 1862, in *The Diary of Edward Bates, 1859–1866*, p. 270.

491 As he contemplated . . . "regard to his Cabinet": Entry for December 20, 1862, *Welles diary*, Vol. I (1960 edn.), p. 199.

492 "he should not have come" . . . that substantially strengthened it: SPC, paraphrased in Fessenden, *Life and Public Services of William Pitt Fessenden*, Vol. I, pp. 244, 246.

492 Neither Stanton nor Smith: Ibid., p. 249.

492 Lincoln asked each . . . would be made: Ibid., pp. 246–49; Nicolay and Hay, *Abraham Lincoln*, Vol. VI, p. 266.

492 When Collamer . . . "He lied": Jacob Collamer, quoted in entry for December 22, 1862, in Browning, *The Diary of Orville Hickman Browning*, Vol. I, p. 603.

492 Lincoln agreed . . . tell the truth!: AL, paraphrased by Robert Todd Lincoln, in Nicolay, *Personal Traits of Abraham Lincoln*, pp. 159–60.

492 Welles paid an early call . . . where he found Stanton: Entry for December 20, 1862, *Welles diary*, Vol. I (1960 edn.), pp. 199–200.

493 "Suppose you . . . be left in it?": EMS, quoted in Seward, *Seward at Washington . . . 1861–1872*, p. 147.

493 Welles told Seward . . . "greatly pleased": Entry for December 20, 1862, *Welles diary*, Vol. I (1960 edn.), p. 200.

493 Monty Blair entered . . . Seward's resignation: Seward, *Seward at Washington . . . 1861–1872*, p. 147.

493 When Welles returned . . . hand in his own resignation: Entry for December 20, 1862, *Welles diary*, Vol. I (1960 edn.), p. 201.

493 Word had already leaked . . . "course of difficulties": Henry Cooke to Jay Cooke, December 20, 1862, in Oberholtzer, *Jay Cooke*, pp. 224, 226 (quotes p. 226).

493 "had been painfully . . . neither of you longer": Entry for December 20, 1862, *Welles diary*, Vol. I (1960 edn.), pp. 201–02.

494 Lincoln wrote a letter . . . "your Departments respectively": AL to WHS and SPC, December 20, 1862, in *CW*, VI, p. 12.

494 "Seward comforts . . . deems a necessity": Entry for December 23, 1862, *Welles diary*, Vol. I (1960 edn.), p. 205.

494 "Yes, Judge . . . end of my bag!": AL, quoted in Seward, *Seward at Washington . . . 1861–1872*, p. 148.

494 "I have cheerfully . . . to your command": WHS to AL, December 21, 1862, Lincoln Papers.

494 "come as soon as possible": Entry for December 22, 1862, Fanny Seward diary, Seward Papers.

494 "Will you allow me . . . than in your cabinet": SPC to AL, December 20, 1862, Lincoln Papers.

494 When Chase received . . . return to the Treasury: SPC to AL, December 22, 1862, Lincoln Papers.

494 "Seward was feeling . . . had been for weeks": Entry for December 23, 1862, *Welles diary*, Vol. I (1960 edn.), p. 205.

494 Seward magnanimously invited . . . Christmas Eve: SPC to FWS, December 24, 1862, reel 24, Chase Papers.
495 "a triumph over . . . drive him out": JGN to TB, December 23, 1862, container 2, Nicolay Papers.
495 Chase declined . . . "his hospitality": SPC to FWS, December 24, 1862, reel 24, Chase Papers.
495 "she regretted" . . . exception of Monty Blair: EBL to SPL, January 14, [1863], in *Wartime Washington*, ed. Laas, p. 231.
495 a visit to a Georgetown spiritualist . . . "had success": Entry for January 1, 1863, in Browning, *The Diary of Orville Hickman Browning*, Vol. I, pp. 608–09.
495 "I do not now see . . . I put it through": "30 October 1863, Friday," in Hay, *Inside Lincoln's White House*, p. 104.

CHAPTER 19: "FIRE IN THE REAR"

Page
497 a "general air of doubt": *NYT*, December 27, 1862.
497 "Will Lincoln's . . . Nobody knows": Entry for December 30, 1862, *Diary of George Templeton Strong*, Vol. III, p. 284.
497 As Frederick Douglass . . . give up ground: *Douglass' Monthly* (October 1862).
497 The final proclamation . . . "upon this act": Allen C. Guelzo, *Lincoln's Emancipation Proclamation: The End of Slavery in America* (New York: Simon & Schuster, 2004), pp. 178–81, 254–60 (quotes p. 260); entry for December 31, 1862, *Welles diary*, Vol. I (1960 edn.), pp. 210–11.
497 On the morning . . . fitful sleep: Quarles, *Lincoln and the Negro*, p. 140; Guelzo, *Lincoln's Emancipation Proclamation*, p. 181.
497 He then met with General Burnside . . . offered to resign: *Conversations with Lincoln*, ed. Charles M. Segal (1961; New Brunswick, N.J., and London: Transaction Publishers, 2002), pp. 232–34 (quote p. 232); Donald, *Lincoln*, pp. 409–11.
498 he would replace Burnside with "Fighting Joe" Hooker: Entry for January 25, 1863, in *Lincoln Day by Day*, Vol. III, p. 165.
498 A West Point graduate . . . at Antietam: "Hooker, Joseph (1814–1879)," in Sifakis, *Who Was Who in the Union*, pp. 199–200.
498 Seward returned . . . for correction: Guelzo, *Lincoln's Emancipation Proclamation*, p. 181.
498 New Year's reception . . . "trimming on the waist": Entry for January 1, 1863, Fanny Seward diary, Seward Papers.
498 "looking like a fairy queen": EBL to SPL, January 1, 1863, in *Wartime Washington*, ed. Laas, p. 224.
498 "Oh how pretty she is": Entry for January 1, 1863, Fanny Seward diary, Seward Papers.
498 the gates to the White House . . . shake the president's hand: Noah Brooks, *Mr. Lincoln's Washington: Selections from the Writings of Noah Brooks, Civil War Correspondent*, ed. P. J. Staudenraus (South Brunswick, N.J.: Thomas Yoseloff, 1967), pp. 58–60.
498 "grievously altered . . . cavernous eyes": Ibid., p. 29.
498 "his blessed . . . People's Levee": Ibid., p. 60.
498 "Oh Mr. French . . . remain until it ended": Benjamin B. French, quoted in Randall, *Mary Lincoln*, p. 320.
499 At Chase's mansion . . . "china, glass, and silver": Brooks, *Mr. Lincoln's Washington*, pp. 61–62.
499 "little, aristocratic" . . . years as a lawyer: Ibid., p. 176.
499 Stanton's salary . . . Ellen's dreams: Thomas and Hyman, *Stanton*, p. 392.
499 At 2 p.m. . . . soon joined him: Guelzo, *Lincoln's Emancipation Proclamation*, p. 182.
499 he "took a pen" . . . put the pen down: Carpenter, *Six Months at the White House*, p. 269.
499 "I never . . . signing this paper": AL quoted in Seward, *Seward at Washington . . . 1861–1872*, p. 151.
499 "If my name . . . soul is in it": Carpenter, *Six Months at the White House*, p. 269.
499 "stiff and numb": Seward, *Seward at Washington . . . 1861–1872*, p. 151.
499 "If my hand trembles . . . 'He hesitated' ": Carpenter, *Six Months at the White House*, p. 269.
499 "slowly and carefully" . . . sent out to the press: Seward, *Seward at Washington . . . 1861–1872*, p. 151.
500 "Has Lincoln played false to humanity?": Entry for January 1, 1863, in Adam Gurowski, *Diary from November 18, 1862 to October 18, 1863*. Vol. II. Burt Franklin: Research & Source Works #229 (New York, 1864; New York: Burt Franklin, 1968), p. 61.
500 At Tremont Temple . . . Anna Dickinson: Frederick Douglass, *Life and Times of Frederick Douglass, Written by Himself* (1893 edn.), reprinted in *Frederick Douglass, Autobiographies*. Library of America Series (New York: Literary Classics of the United States, 1994) p. 790 (quote); *Boston Journal*, January 2, 1863; *Boston Transcript*, January 2, 1863.
500 At the nearby Music Hall . . . Oliver Wendell Holmes: *Boston Journal*, January 2, 1863; *Boston Post*, January 2, 1863; Quarles, *Lincoln and the Negro*, p. 143.
500 "Every moment . . . one other chance": Douglass, *Life and Times of Frederick Douglass*, p. 791.
500 "had absolutely no foundation . . . to the quick": Helm, *The True Story of Mary*, pp. 208–09.
500 Mary had rushed . . . the joyous occasion: MTL to CS, December 30, 1862, in Turner and Turner, *Mary Todd Lincoln*, p. 144.
500 "was becoming agony . . . joy and gladness": Douglass, *Life and Times of Frederick Douglass*, p. 791.
500 "It was a sublime . . . with us, here": Eliza S. Quincy to MTL, January 2, 1863, Lincoln Papers.
500 a crowd of serenaders . . . in securing their freedom: Guelzo, *Lincoln's Emancipation Proclamation*, p. 186; *NYT*, January 3, 1863 (quote).
501 "Whatever partial . . . goes backward": *Boston Daily Evening Transcript*, January 2, 1863.

501 "Strange phenomenon . . . in all future ages": James A. Garfield to Burke Hinsdale, January 6, 1863, quoted in Theodore Clarke Smith, *The Life and Letters of James Abram Garfield*. Vol. I: *1831–1877* (New Haven: Yale University Press, 1925), p. 266.

501 "Fellow-citizens . . . the latest generation": AL, "Annual Message to Congress," December 1, 1862, in *CW*, V, p. 537.

501 "had done nothing . . . will be realized": AL, paraphrased in Joshua F. Speed to WHH, February 7, 1866, in *HI*, p. 197.

501 "discord in the North . . . spirit of the nation": *Louisville Journal*, quoted in *Boston Post*, January 2, 1863.

501 "union and harmony . . . destruction": WHS to FS, September 1862, quoted in Seward, *Seward at Washington . . . 1861–1872*, p. 135.

501 "It is my conviction . . . sustained it": AL, quoted in Carpenter, *Six Months at the White House*, p. 77.

502 "*slavery and quiet . . . by tremendous majorities*": Walt Whitman, "Origins of Attempted Secession," *The Complete Prose Works of Walt Whitman*, Vol. II (New York: G. P. Putnam's Sons/The Knickerbocker Press, 1902), p. 155.

502 "A man watches . . . strong enough to defeat the purpose": AL, quoted in Carpenter, *Six Months at the White House*, p. 77.

502 Horatio Seymour denounced . . . inaugural message: Guelzo, *Lincoln's Emancipation Proclamation*, p. 187.

502 James Robinson recommended: *NYT*, January 10, 1863.

502 Democratic legislatures . . . "crusade against Slavery": Oliver P. Morton to EMS, February 9, 1863, reel 3, Stanton Papers, DLC.

502 "under the subterfuge . . . oppose the War": JGN to TB, January 11, 1863, container 2, Nicolay Papers.

502 The "fire in the rear": AL, quoted in CS to Francis Lieber, January 17, 1863, quoted in Edward L. Pierce, *Memoir and Letters of Charles Sumner*. Vol. IV: *1860–1874* (Boston: Roberts Brothers, 1893), p. 114.

502 Army of the Potomac into winter quarters . . . "Valley Forge of the war": McPherson, *Battle Cry of Freedom*, pp. 586–88, 590 (quote).

503 Copperheads: McPherson, *Battle Cry of Freedom*, pp. 493, 591, 593, 600; John C. Waugh, *Reelecting Lincoln: The Battle for the 1864 Presidency* (New York: Crown Publishers, 1997), p. 91.

503 "fearfully changed" . . . a piercing shriek: Brooks, *Mr. Lincoln's Washington*, pp. 105–06.

503 "Ought this war" . . . then let her go: Clement L. Vallandigham, "The Constitution—Peace—Reunion," January 14, 1863, *Appendix to the Congressional Globe*, 37th Cong., 3rd sess. pp. 55, 57–59 (quotes on p. 55).

503 The time had come . . . let her go: Brooks, *Mr. Lincoln's Washington*, p. 70.

503 Saulsbury . . . removed from the Senate floor: Ibid., pp. 87–88.

504 "baneful . . . only for the negro": Andrew H. Foote, paraphrased in entry for January 9, 1863, in Browning, *The Diary of Orville Hickman Browning*, Vol. I, p. 611.

504 Orville Browning, who considered . . . "the government": Entry for January 26, 1863, in ibid., p. 620.

504 "conversed with . . . will re enlist": Entry for January 29, 1863, in ibid., pp. 620–21 (quotes p. 621).

504 "the alarming condition . . . a fixed thing": Entry for January 19, 1863, in ibid., p. 616.

504 "the democrats would soon . . . leave them": Entry for January 26, 1863, in ibid., p. 620.

504 "The resources . . . can be maintained": AL, "To the Workingmen of London," February 2, 1863, in *CW*, VI, pp. 88–89.

504 the people's representatives had passed: See Curry, *Blueprint for Modern America*.

504 "the grandest pledge . . . means to prevail": *NYT*, February 20, 1863.

504 "largest popular gathering . . . home of the brave": *NYT*, April 21, 1863.

505 "the greatest popular . . . in Washington": *Daily Morning Chronicle*, Washington, D.C., April 1, 1863.

505 Lincoln was dressed . . . of his father's embrace: Jane Grey Swisshelm, quoted in *St. Cloud [Minn.] Democrat*, April 9, 1863, in Frank Klement, "Jane Grey Swisshelm and Lincoln: A Feminist Fusses and Frets," *Abraham Lincoln Quarterly* 6 (December 1950), pp. 235–36.

505 Lincoln sent a telegram to Thurlow Weed . . . "and so I sent for you": AL, quoted in Barnes, *Memoir of Thurlow Weed*, pp. 434–35.

505 The amount needed was $15,000: Ibid., p. 435; AL to TW, February 19, 1862, in *CW*, VI, pp. 112–13.

505 "to influence . . . Connecticut elections": Entry for February 10, 1863, *Welles diary*, Vol. I (1960 edn.), p. 235.

505 "a stunning blow to the Copperheads": *NYT*, April 8, 1863.

505 "puts the Administration . . . seas to the end": *NYT*, April 9, 1863.

505 "frightened" . . . depress voter sentiment: JH to Mrs. Charles Hay, April 23, 1863, in Hay, *At Lincoln's Side*, p. 38.

505 "I rejoiced . . . the War commenced": EMS to Isabella Beecher Hooker, May 6, 1863, in Wolcott, "Edwin M. Stanton," p. 160.

505 "The feeling of . . . everywhere manifest": JGN to TB, March 22, 1863, container 2, Nicolay Papers.

505 "The glamour . . . the denunciations": Brooks, *Mr. Lincoln's Washington*, p. 138.

506 when Lincoln engaged . . . "*be crippled*": Entry for January 17, 1863, Fanny Seward diary, Seward Papers.

506 "Well . . . not one has got there yet": AL, quoted in "Personal," *Daily Morning Chronicle*, Washington, D.C., May 2, 1863.

506 "smoking cigars . . . 'good victuals' ": Brooks, *Mr. Lincoln's Washington*, p. 175.

506 At one dinner party . . . "[had] ever known": Entry for January 28, 1863, *Diary of George Templeton Strong*, Vol. III, p. 292.

507 welcome diversion in the telegraph office: Bates, *Lincoln in the Telegraph Office*, pp. 41–42, 143, 190.

507 "Abe was in . . . 'none anywhere else' ": AL, quoted in entry for April 21, 1863, in Dahlgren, *Memoir of John A. Dahlgren*, p. 390.

507 "a little after midnight . . . queer little conceits": Entry for April 30, 1864, in Hay, *Inside Lincoln's White House*, p. 194.

507 "Only those . . . heart bleeds": MTL to Mary Janes Welles, February 21, 1863, reel 35, Welles Papers.

507 "Mary had gamely resumed . . . "to bear up": MTL to Benjamin B. French, March 10, 1863, in Thomas F. Schwartz and Kim M. Bauer, "Unpublished Mary Todd Lincoln," *Journal of the Abraham Lincoln Association* 17 (Summer 1996), p. 5.

507 "affable and pleasant . . . out of sight": Entry for February 22, 1863, in French, *Witness to the Young Republic*, p. 417.

507 "much shorter . . . his composition": Entry for February 12, 1863, Fanny Seward diary, Seward Papers.

508 In gratitude to Rebecca Pomroy . . . "look their best": Boyden, *Echoes from Hospital and White House*, pp. 131–32.

508 "brilliantly lighted . . . children's children": Pomroy, quoted in ibid., pp. 132–33.

508 Swisshelm had initially . . . "and its cause": Jane Grey Swisshelm, *Half a Century* (Chicago: J. G. Swisshelm, 1880), pp. 236–37 (quotes p. 237).

508 Mary was delighted . . . Nettie Colburn: Nettie Colburn Maynard, *Was Abraham Lincoln a Spiritualist?, or Curious Revelations from the Life of a Trance Medium* (Philadelphia: Rufus C. Hartranft, 1891), p. 83.

508 "very choice spirits . . . agreeable ladies": Joshua F. Speed to AL, October 26, 1863, Lincoln Papers.

508 "Welcome, Mr. Lincoln . . . *I was coming*": Mr. Laurie and AL, quoted in Maynard, *Was Abraham Lincoln a Spiritualist?*, p. 83.

508 The guests settled into . . . "easy chairs of the day": S. P. Kase, quoted in J. J. Fitzgerrell, *Lincoln Was a Spiritualist* (Los Angeles: Austin Publishing Co., 1924), pp. 18–19.

509 "Well, Miss Nettie . . . say to me to-night?": Maynard, *Was Abraham Lincoln a Spiritualist?*, p. 85.

509 There is no evidence that Lincoln . . . "learn the secret": "Lord Colchester—Spirit Medium," *Lincoln Lore*, no. 1497 (November 1962), p. 4.

509 She spoke for an hour . . . "not this wonderful?": S. P. Kase, quoted in Fitzgerrell, *Lincoln Was a Spiritualist*, pp. 20–21.

509 "I have neither . . . I must resume it": SPC to Horace Greeley, January 28, 1863, reel 24, Chase Papers.

509 Chase became physically ill . . . make it through: SPC to Richard C. Parsons, February 16, 1863, reel 25, Chase Papers.

510 his own handsome face . . . every dollar bill: SPC, *"Going Home to Vote." Authentic Speeches of S. P. Chase, Secretary of the Treasury, During His Visit to Ohio, with His Speeches at Indianapolis, and at the Mass Meeting in Baltimore, October, 1863* (Washington, D.C.: W. H. Moore, 1863), p. 25; Brooks, *Mr. Lincoln's Washington*, p. 176.

510 his own strained finances . . . bonds to the public: SPC to Jay Cooke, June 2, 1863, reel 27, Chase Papers.

510 Charles Benjamin . . . quickly make amends: Benjamin, "Recollections of Secretary Edwin M. Stanton," *Century* (1887), p. 759.

510 asked why he disliked . . . "detested it": Entry for April 25, 1863, *Diary of George Templeton Strong*, Vol. III, p. 314.

510 "nervous irritability": E. D. Townsend, *Anecdotes of the Civil War in the United States* (New York: D. Appleton & Co., 1884), p. 136.

510 his asthma . . . consent to seek rest: Benjamin, "Recollections of Secretary Edwin M. Stanton," *Century* (1887), pp. 759–60.

510 he enjoyed reading . . . attitude to the war: Ibid., p. 766; Johnson, "Reminiscences of the Hon. Edwin M. Stanton," *RCHS* (1910), p. 80 (quote).

511 Stanton refused to bring . . . remained at his post: Wolcott, "Edwin M. Stanton," p. 161; Thomas and Hyman, *Stanton*, pp. 165–66.

511 "would rather make" . . . ask Stanton for a favor: JH to JGN, November 25, 1863, quoted in Hay, *At Lincoln's Side*, p. 69.

511 Even when Stanton's own son . . . an official appointment: Johnson, "Reminiscences of the Hon. Edwin M. Stanton," *RCHS* (1910), p. 92.

511 rarely returned to Steubenville . . . for the funeral in Ohio: *NYT*, April 14, 1863; Wolcott, "Edwin M. Stanton," p. 130a.

511 Pamphila's conviction . . . died from overwork: Wolcott, "Edwin M. Stanton," p. 159.

511 the War Department utilize the services . . . "to Mr. Capen": AL, "Memorandum Concerning Francis L. Capen's Weather Forecasts," April 28, 1863, in *CW*, VI, pp. 190–91.

511 warring factions in Missouri . . . "hold of the case": AL to Henry T. Blow, Charles D. Drake and Others, May 15, 1863, in ibid., p. 218.

512 hastily written note to General Franz Sigel . . . "keep it up": AL to Franz Sigel, February 5, 1863, in ibid., p. 93.

512 The story is told: AL, quoted in Pinsker, *Lincoln's Sanctuary*, pp. 52–53.

512 Carl Schurz laid the blame . . . "We parted as better friends than ever": Schurz, *Reminiscences*, Vol. II, pp. 393–96.

513 excursion to Falmouth: Noah Brooks, "A Boy in the White House," *St. Nicholas: An Illustrated Magazine for Young Folks* 10 (November 1882), p. 62; Brooks, *Mr. Lincoln's Washington*, pp. 147–64.

513 "one of the purest . . . in the world": Anson G. Henry to his wife, April 12, 1863, transcribed in "Another Hooker Letter," *Abraham Lincoln Quarterly* 2 (March 1942), pp. 10–11.

513 Bates agreed . . . spring battles began: Entry for April 4, 1863, in *The Diary of Edward Bates, 1859–1866*, p. 288.

513   weather conditions: *Sun*, Baltimore, Md., April 6, 1863; entry for April 4, 1863, in *The Diary of Edward Bates, 1859–1866*, p. 287; Brooks, *Mr. Lincoln's Washington*, p. 51.

513   the steamer *Carrie Martin* . . . of George Washington: Seward, *Reminiscences of a War-Time Statesman and Diplomat*, p. 185; Noah Brooks, *Washington, D.C., in Lincoln's Time*, ed. Herbert Mitgang (Chicago: Quadrangle Books, 1971; Athens, Ga., and London: University of Georgia Press, 1989), p. 51.

513   the escalating storm . . . to the dinner menu: Brooks, "A Boy in the White House," *St. Nicholas* (1882), p. 62.

513   "the chief magistrate . . . firing a shot": Brooks, *Mr. Lincoln's Washington*, pp. 148–49.

513   "at its height" . . . a special train: *Sun*, Baltimore, Md., April 7, 1863 (quote); Brooks, *Mr. Lincoln's Washington*, p. 149.

513   "snow piled in huge . . . over the hills": *NYH*, April 10, 1863 (quotes); Brooks, *Washington, D.C. in Lincoln's Time*, p. 52.

514   Hooker's headquarters . . . 133,000 soldiers: Brooks, *Mr. Lincoln's Washington*, pp. 150–51; Shelby Foote, *The Civil War: A Narrative. Vol. II: Fredericksburg to Meridian* (New York: Random House, 1963: New York: Vintage Books, 1986), p. 235.

514   General Hooker and his accommodations: Entry for April 27, 1863, Fanny Seward diary, Seward Papers; *NYH*, April 10, 1863; Brooks, *Mr. Lincoln's Washington*, p. 150.

514   "I believe you to be . . . give us victories": AL to Joseph Hooker, January 26, 1863, in *CW*, VI, pp. 78–79.

514   was so moved by . . . printed in gold letters: Anson G. Henry to his wife, April 12, 1863, transcribed in "Another Hooker Letter," *ALQ* 2 (1942), p. 11.

514   "That is just such . . . man who wrote it": Joseph Hooker, quoted in Brooks, *Washington, D.C. in Lincoln's Time*, p. 57.

514   Mary's curiosity . . . "pleasant to her": *NYH*, April 10, 1863 (quote); *Star*, April 7, 1863; Brooks, *Mr. Lincoln's Washington*, p. 150.

515   reported badinage between . . . " 'sort of rebel' ": Brooks, *Washington, D.C. in Lincoln's Time*, p. 59.

515   Stormy weather . . . "shafts of wit": Brooks, *Mr. Lincoln's Washington*, p. 150; *NYH*, April 10, 1863 (quote).

515   The roar of artillery . . . "among them": Brooks, *Washington, D.C., in Lincoln's Time*, p. 53; *NYH*, April 11, 1863; Brooks, *Mr. Lincoln's Washington*, p. 153 (quote).

515   his gray cloak . . . faithfully by his side: Brooks, "A Boy in the White House," *St. Nicholas* (1882), p. 62.

515   "And thereby hangs . . . folds of the banners": *NYH*, April 11, 1863.

516   At the review of the infantry . . . "far away": Brooks, *Mr. Lincoln's Washington*, pp. 154, 158–59 (quote).

516   he extended his visit: Ibid., p. 161.

516   "the former stood . . . turn their backs": *NYH*, April 10, 1863.

516   rebel camps across the river . . . stars and bars: Brooks, *Mr. Lincoln's Washington*, pp. 155–56.

516   Union pickets . . . "belonging to friendly armies": Seward, *Seward at Washington . . . 1861–1872*, p. 162 (first quote); *NYH*, April 10, 1863 (last quote).

516   a Confederate officer . . . "politely and retired": Brooks, *Mr. Lincoln's Washington*, p. 156.

516   "It was a saddening . . . should arrive": Ibid., pp. 153–54.

517   issued one final directive . . . *all your men*": AL, quoted in Couch, "Sumner's 'Right Grand Division,' " in *Battles and Leaders of the Civil War*, Vol. III, Pt. I, p. 120.

517   boarded the *Carrie Martin* . . . "flags displayed": *NYH*, April 12, 1863.

517   were defending James S. Pleasants . . . "very bitter": EBL to SPL, April 16, 1863, in *Wartime Washington*, ed. Laas, p. 259 (quotes); Court-martial file of James Snowden Pleasants, file MM-15, entry 15, RG 153, DNA; *Sun*, Baltimore, Md., April 9, 1863.

517   sent the *Peterhoff* . . . to the Navy Department: Van Deusen, *William Henry Seward*, pp. 350–51; Monaghan, *Diplomat in Carpet Slippers*, pp. 303–04.

517   led to rumors of . . . "from the real question": Entries for April 23–28, 1863, *Welles diary*, Vol. I (1960 edn.), pp. 285–87 (quotes p. 287).

518   Montgomery Blair also sided . . . "in the Cabinet": Entry for April 17, 1863, ibid., pp. 274–75 (quote p. 275).

518   "I feel that . . . my present position": SPC to AL, March 2, 1863, Lincoln Papers.

518   This squabble was provoked . . . "my resignation": SPC to AL, May 11, 1863, Lincoln Papers.

518   "Chase's feelings were hurt": AL to Anson G. Henry, May 13, 1863, in *CW*, VI, p. 215.

518   he called at Chase's . . . "I finally succeeded": Field, *Memories of Many Men*, p. 303.

518   $45 million in bonds . . . "as do ours": *NYT*, May 3, 1863.

519   he placed his prickly secretary's third resignation: Riddle, *Recollections of War Times*, p. 273.

519   Blair, meanwhile, resented Chase . . . "private counsellor": Entry for May 10, 1863, in *The Diary of Edward Bates, 1859–1866*, pp. 290–91.

519   the Battle of Chancellorsville: See Stephen W. Sears, *Chancellorsville* (Boston and New York: Houghton Mifflin, 1996); Stanley S. McGowen, "Chancellorsville, Battle of," in *Encyclopedia of the American Civil War*, ed. Heidler and Heidler, pp. 394–98; Foote, *The Civil War*, Vol. II, p. 263.

519   "We have been . . . definite information": JGN to TB, May 4, 1863, container 2, Nicolay Papers.

519   Welles joined Lincoln: Entry of May 4, 1863, *Welles diary*, Vol. I (1960 edn.), p. 291.

519   Bates was particularly tense . . . "dangerous service": Entry for May 5, 1863, in *The Diary of Edward Bates, 1859–1866*, p. 289.

519   Lincoln admitted . . . what was going on: EBL to SPL, May 4, 1863, in *Wartime Washington*, ed. Laas, p. 264.

519   "no reliable . . . does not express them": Entry for May 5, 1863, *Welles diary*, Vol. I (1960 edn.), pp. 292–93.

519   "While I am anxious . . . or discomfort": AL to Joseph Hooker, April 28, 1863, in *CW*, VI, pp. 189–90.

519   "God bless you . . . with despatches": AL to Joseph Hooker, 9:40 a.m. telegram, May 6, 1863, in ibid., p. 199.

520   an unwelcome telegram . . . the order to retreat: Joseph Hooker to AL, May 6, 1863, Lincoln Papers; Sears,

Chancellorsville, p. 492; Darius N. Couch, "The Chancellorsville Campaign," in *Battles and Leaders of the Civil War*, Vol. III, Pt. I, pp. 164 (first quote), 167, 169–71 (second and third quotes p. 171).

520 "I shall never forget . . . of despair": Brooks, *Washington, D.C., in Lincoln's Time*, p. 60.

520 "Had a thunderbolt . . . would again commence": Brooks, *Mr. Lincoln's Washington*, p. 179.

520 "ashen" face . . . " 'will the country say!' ": Brooks, *Washington, D.C., in Lincoln's Time*, p. 61.

520 The president informed Senator Sumner . . . "I know not where": Entry for May 6, 1863, *Welles diary*, Vol. I (1960 edn.), pp. 293–94.

520 "This is the darkest day of the war": JH paraphrasing EMS, quoted in *Lincoln's Third Secretary: The Memoirs of William O. Stoddard*, ed. William O. Stoddard, Jr. (New York: Exposition Press, 1955), p. 173.

520 At the Willard . . . bound for Hooker's headquarters: Brooks, *Mr. Lincoln's Washington*, p. 180.

521 "All accounts agree . . . back into the fray": *NYT*, May 12, 1863.

521 casualties at Chancellorsville: McPherson, *Battle Cry of Freedom*, p. 645; Sears, *Chancellorsville*, pp. 492, 501.

521 death of Stonewall Jackson: James I. Robertson, Jr., "Jackson, Thomas Jonathan," in *Encyclopedia of the American Civil War*, ed. Heidler and Heidler, p. 1065.

521 "Since the death . . . death of Jackson": *Richmond Whig*, May 12, 1863.

521 "If possible" . . . ready to assist Hooker: AL to Joseph Hooker, May 7, 1863, in *CW*, VI, p. 201.

CHAPTER 20: "THE TYCOON IS IN FINE WHACK"

Page

522 General Orders No. 38 . . . tried by a military court: "General Orders, No. 38," Department of the Ohio, April 13, 1863, in *OR*, Ser. 1, Vol. XXIII, Part II, p. 237.

522 "hurl King Lincoln from his throne": Clement L. Vallandigham speech, May 1, 1863, quoted in Fletcher Pratt, *Stanton: Lincoln's Secretary of War* (New York: W. W. Norton & Co., 1953), p. 289.

522 "The door resisted" . . . a side entrance: *Cincinnati Commercial*, quoted in *Star*, May 9, 1863.

522 found him guilty . . . habeas corpus was denied: Trial of Clement L. Vallandigham, enclosure in Ambrose E. Burnside to Henry W. Halleck, May 18, 1863, and General Orders, No. 68, Headquarters, Department of the Ohio, May 16, 1863, *OR*, Ser. 2, Vol. V, pp. 633–46; McPherson, *Battle Cry of Freedom*, p. 597.

522 the *Chicago Times* . . . the paper down: Entry for June 3, 1863, in Browning, *The Diary of Orville Hickman Browning*, Vol. I, p. 632.

522 While he later admitted . . . uphold Burnside: McPherson, *Battle Cry of Freedom*, p. 597; entry for June 3, 1863, *Welles diary*, Vol. I (1960 edn.), p. 321.

523 Thurlow Weed deplored the arrest: TW to John Bigelow, June 27, 1863, in John Bigelow, *Retrospective of an Active Life*, Vol. II: *1863–1865* (New York: Baker & Taylor Co., 1909), p. 23.

523 Senator Trumbull . . . "government overthrown": Entry for May 17, 1863, in Browning, *The Diary of Orville Hickman Browning*, Vol. I, p. 630.

523 "by a large and honest" . . . the loyal states: Nathaniel P. Tallmadge to WHS, May 24, 1863, Lincoln Papers.

523 Lincoln, searching . . . Confederate lines: Charles F. Howlett, "Vallandigham, Clement Laird," in *Encyclopedia of the American Civil War*, ed. Heidler and Heidler, p. 2012.

523 his Copperhead body . . . "where his heart already was": Schuyler Colfax to AL, June 13, 1863, Lincoln Papers.

523 "general satisfaction . . . power for evil": *NYT*, May 21, 1863.

523 Vallandigham was removed . . . escaped to Canada: McPherson, *Battle Cry of Freedom*, p. 597.

523 Stanton revoked . . . to suppress newspapers: EMS to Ambrose E. Burnside, June 1, 1863, in *OR*, Ser. 2, Vol. V, p. 724; General Orders, No. 91, Headquarters, Department of the Ohio, June 4, 1863, *OR*, Ser. 1, Vol. XXIII, Part II, p. 386.

523 "suppress the . . . of its citizens": Carpenter, *Six Months at the White House*, pp. 156–57.

523 Upon hearing . . . opposed his action: Ambrose E. Burnside to AL, May 29, 1863, Lincoln Papers.

523 Lincoln not only refused . . . "through with it": AL to Ambrose E. Burnside, May 29, 1863, in *CW*, VI, p. 237.

523 "Often an idea . . . from every side": James F. Wilson recollections, quoted in Carl Sandburg, *Abraham Lincoln: The War Years*, Vol. II (New York: Harcourt, Brace & Co., 1936; 1939), p. 308.

524 "It has vigor and ability": Entry for June 5, 1863, *Welles diary*, Vol. I (1960 edn.), p. 323.

524 "we are Struggling . . . in Rhetoric": MB to AL, June 6, 1863, Lincoln Papers.

524 The finished letter . . . "if he shall desert": AL to Erastus Corning and Others, [June 12,] 1863, in *CW*, VI, pp. 260–69 (quotes pp. 264, 266–67).

524 "It is full . . . and conclusive": *NYT*, June 15, 1863.

524 Edward Everett . . . "the step complete": Edward Everett to AL, June 16, 1863, Lincoln Papers.

524 "It is a grand document . . . every citizen": "The President's Letter," June 15, 1863, in William O. Stoddard, *Dispatches from Lincoln's White House: The Anonymous Civil War Journalism of Presidential Secretary William O. Stoddard*, ed. Michael Burlingame (Lincoln and London: University of Nebraska Press, 2002), p. 160.

525 Printed in a great variety . . . 10 million people: Donald, *Lincoln*, pp. 443–44.

525 Welles noted . . . "assistant is present": Entry for June 2, 1863, *Welles diary*, Vol. I (1960 edn.), pp. 319–20 (quote p. 320).

525 Blair, frustrated . . . word with Lincoln: Hendrick, *Lincoln's War Cabinet*, p. 387; entry for May 12, 1863, in *The Diary of Edward Bates, 1859–1866*, p. 292.

525 "At such a time . . . interchange of views": Entry for June 30, 1863, *Welles diary*, Vol. I (1960 edn.), p. 351.

525 "There is now . . . consent of the members": Entry for May 16, 1863, in *The Diary of Edward Bates, 1859–1866*, pp. 292–93.

525 "But how idle . . . furnish the means": SPC to David Dudley Field, June 30, 1863, reel 27, Chase Papers.

525 If he were president . . . "of importance": SPC to James A. Garfield, May 31, 1863, reel 12, Papers of James A. Garfield, Manuscript Division, Library of Congress [hereafter Garfield Papers, DLC].

525 Blair decried . . . of Seward and Stanton: Entry for June 23, 1863, *Welles diary*, Vol. I (1960 edn.), p. 340.

525 Lincoln's unwillingness . . . restore McClellan: Entry for June 26, 1863, ibid., p. 345.

525 In Blair's mind . . . "throat if he could": "19 July 1863, Sunday," in Hay, *Inside Lincoln's White House*, p. 65.

526 Blair's hatred for Stanton . . . military information: Entry for June 30, 1863, *Welles diary*, Vol. I (1960 edn.), p. 352.

526 "Strange, strange . . . Stanton and Seward": Entry for June 15, 1863, ibid., p. 329.

526 Recognizing Blair's desire . . . to get through: For a description of Blair's innovations with the postal service, see chapter 31 of Smith, *The Francis Preston Blair Family in Politics*, Vol. II, pp. 90–111.

526 catch up with his "Neptune" . . . telegraph office: Entry for July 14, 1863, *Welles diary*, Vol. I (1960 edn.), p. 370.

526 When he felt compelled . . . "admirable success": AL to GW, July 25, 1863, in *CW*, VI, p. 349.

526 A particularly bitter . . . "be very mad": AL, quoted in entry for May 26, 1863, *Welles diary*, Vol. I (1960 edn.), p. 313.

527 the humorist Orpheus Kerr . . . "as regards myself": Entry for June 17, 1863, ibid., p. 333.

527 William Rosecrans . . . "to do hastily": AL to William S. Rosecrans, May 20, 1863, in *CW*, VI, p. 224.

527 felt compelled to remove General Samuel Curtis . . . "faithful, and patriotic": AL to Samuel R. Curtis, June 8, 1863, in ibid., p. 253.

527 a note from Governor Gamble . . . "grossly offensive": Hamilton R. Gamble to AL, July 13, 1863, Lincoln Papers.

527 was told "to put it away": "23 July 1863, Thursday," in Hay, *Inside Lincoln's White House*, p. 66.

527 "trying to preserve . . . should offend you": AL to Hamilton R. Gamble, July 23, 1863, Lincoln Papers.

528 Milroy railed about "the . . . hatred" of Halleck: Robert H. Milroy to AL, June 28, 1863, Lincoln Papers. See also Robert H. Milroy to John P. Usher, June 28, 1863, Lincoln Papers.

528 "I have scarcely seen . . . you have split": AL to Robert H. Milroy, June 29, 1863, in *CW*, VI, p. 308.

528 "Truth to speak . . . so, ranks you": AL to William S. Rosecrans, March 17, 1863, in ibid., p. 139.

528 Grant had advanced . . . settled into a siege: Stanley S. McGowen, "Vicksburg Campaign (May–July 1863)," in *Encyclopedia of the American Civil War*, ed. Heidler and Heidler, pp. 2021–25.

528 "Whether Gen. Grant . . . brilliant in the world": AL to Isaac N. Arnold, May 26, 1863, in *CW*, VI, p. 230.

528 Stanton had sent Charles Dana . . . long, detailed dispatches: Bruce Catton, *Grant Moves South*. Vol. I: *1861–1863* (Boston: Little, Brown, 1960; 1988), pp. 388–89; Thomas and Hyman, *Stanton*, p. 267.

528 Requesting that General Banks . . . "should prefer that course": Charles A. Dana to EMS, May 26, 1863, reel 5, Stanton Papers, DLC.

528 In a misguided effort . . . other valuables behind: "General Orders, No. 11," Department of the Tennessee, December 17, 1862, in *OR*, Ser. 1, Vol. XVII, Part II, p. 424. See also USG to Christopher P. Wolcott, December 17, 1862, in ibid., pp. 421–22; D. Wolff & Bros, C. F. Kaskell, and J. W. Kaswell to AL, December 29, 1862, in ibid., p. 506; Bertram Wallace Korn, *American Jewry and the Civil War* (Philadelphia: Jewish Publication Society of America, 1951), pp. 122–23.

529 a delegation of Jewish leaders . . . "have at once": Leaders quoted in Korn, *American Jewry and the Civil War*, pp. 124–25.

529 wrote a note to Halleck: Ibid., p. 125.

529 after assuring Grant . . . "necessary to revoke it": Henry W. Halleck to USG, January 21, 1863, in *OR*, Ser. 1, Vol. XXIV, Part I, p. 9 (quote); Henry W. Halleck to USG, January 4, 1863, in *OR*, Ser. 1, Vol. XVII, Part II, p. 530; Circular, 13th Army Corps, Department of the Tennessee, January 7, 1863, in ibid., p. 544.

529 Elizabeth Blair heard . . . "all the time": EBL to SPL, May 8, 1863, in *Wartime Washington*, ed. Laas, p. 266.

529 Bates was told . . . "bloated" appearance: Entry for May 23, 1863, in *The Diary of Edward Bates, 1859–1866*, p. 293.

529 In Grant's case . . . "idiotically drunk": Murat Halstead to SPC, April 1, 1863, Lincoln Papers.

529 After dispatching investigators to look into: Catton, *Grant Moves South*, Vol. I, pp. 388–89; Jean Edward Smith, *Grant* (New York: Simon & Schuster, 2001), p. 231.

529 A memorable story . . . rest of his generals!: John Eaton, *Grant, Lincoln and the Freedmen: Reminiscences of the Civil War* (New York: Longmans, Green & Co., 1907; New York: Negro Universities Press, 1969), p. 90.

529 Wade and Chandler told Lincoln . . . "in reply": JGN to TB, May 17, 1863, container 2, Nicolay Papers.

530 Seward accompanied . . . his garden: See entries for May 1863, in Fanny Seward diary, Seward House, Auburn, New York.

530 favorite old poplar . . . "stroke of the axe": FAS to WHS, June 5, 1863, reel 114, Seward Papers.

530 Fanny wrote that . . . "very lonely": FS to WHS, June 7, 1863, reel 116, Seward Papers.

530 troubling rumors . . . "when I am there": FAS to WHS, June 5, 1863, reel 114, Seward Papers; FS to WHS, June 7, 1863, reel 116, Seward Papers (quote).

530 Seward noted . . . "an invasion of Washington": WHS to [FAS], June 11, 1863, in Seward, *Seward at Washington . . . 1861–1872*, p. 169.

530 Mary and Tad left . . . Continental Hotel: Entry for June 8, 1863, in *Lincoln Day by Day*, Vol. III, p. 188; MTL to John Meredith Read, June 16, [1863], in Turner and Turner, *Mary Todd Lincoln*, p. 152 n2.

530 Welles spoke with Lincoln . . . "thought best": Entry for June 8, 1863, *Welles diary*, Vol. I (1960 edn.), p. 325.

530 "Think you better . . . ugly dream about him": AL to MTL, June 9, 1863, in *CW*, VI, p. 256.
530 Seward sent a telegram . . . "pic-nic to the Lake": Entry for June 15, 1863, in Johnson, "Sensitivity and Civil War," p. 813.
531 Lee had crossed . . . "adds to our strength": WHS to [FAS], June 15, 1863, in Seward, *Seward at Washington . . . 1861–1872*, pp. 169–70.
531 *"Invasion! . . . in Maryland and Pennsylvania"*: *NYT* headline, June 16, 1863.
531 "It is a matter of choice . . . anything at all": AL to MTL, June 16, 1863, in *CW*, VI, p. 283.
531 "The country, now . . . is wide awake": Entry for June 18, 1863, in French, *Witness to the Young Republic*, p. 423.
531 "something of a panic pervades the city": Entry for June 15, 1863, *Welles diary*, Vol. I (1960 edn.), p. 329.
531 he called out a hundred thousand troops: AL, "Proclamation Calling for 100,000 Militia," June 15, 1863, in *CW*, VI, p. 277.
531 "I should think . . . kindness & Patriotism": Entry for June 18, 1863, in French, *Witness to the Young Republic*, p. 424.
531 the committee charged with . . . "all he could ask for": Stoddard, *Inside the White House in War Times*, p. 117.
531 Lincoln's primary concern . . . "outgeneraled": Brooks, *Mr. Lincoln's Washington*, p. 196.
531 "observed in Hooker . . . taken from other points": Entry for June 28, 1863, *Welles diary*, Vol. I (1960 edn.), p. 348.
531 When Hooker delivered a prickly telegram: Joseph Hooker to Henry W. Halleck, June 27, 1863 (9:00 a.m.), in *OR*, Ser. 1, Vol. XXVII, Part I, p. 59; Hooker to Halleck, June 27, 1863 (3:00 p.m.), in ibid., p. 60; Halleck to Hooker, June 27, 1863 (8:00 p.m.), in ibid., p. 60.
531 Lincoln and Stanton replaced him: Henry W. Halleck to George G. Meade, June 27, 1863, in *OR*, Ser. 1, Vol. XXVII, Part I, p. 61; Meade to Halleck, June 28, 1863, in ibid., pp. 61–62; "Meade, George Gordon (1815–1872)," in Sifakis, *Who Was Who in the Union*, p. 266.
532 "Chase was disturbed . . . cared should appear": SPC to Joseph Hooker, June 20, 1863, quoted in Schuckers, *The Life and Public Services of Salmon Portland Chase*, p. 468; entry of June 28, 1863, *Welles diary*, Vol. I (1960 edn.), p. 348 (quote).
532 "You must have been . . . exceeded mine": SPC to KCS, June 29, 1863, reel 27, Chase Papers.
532 "The turning point . . . such a suspense": JGN to TB, July 5, 1863, container 3, Nicolay Papers.
532 "poor and desultory" . . . in the telegraph office: Bates, *Lincoln in the Telegraph Office*, p. 155.
532 Chandler would "never forget . . . on the wall": Zachariah Chandler, quoted in Browne, *The Every-Day Life of Abraham Lincoln*, pp. 597–98.
532 a dispatch from Meade . . . "at all points": George G. Meade to Henry W. Halleck, July 2, 1863 (8:00 p.m.), in *OR*, Ser. 1, Vol. XXVII, Part I, p. 72.
532 "no reliable advices . . . anxiety prevails": *NYT*, July 3, 1863.
532 a messenger handed . . . "reliable": Entry for July 4, 1863, *Welles diary*, Vol. I (1960 edn.), p. 357.
532 a telegram from Meade . . . after severe losses: George G. Meade to Henry W. Halleck, July 3, 1863, *OR*, Ser. 1, Vol. XXVII, Part I, pp. 74–75.
533 Casualties were later calculated: Richard A. Sauers, "Gettysburg, Battle of," in *Encyclopedia of the American Civil War*, ed. Heidler and Heidler, p. 836.
533 "as being the most . . . covered with the dead": McPherson, *Battle Cry of Freedom*, p. 664; Brooks, *Mr. Lincoln's Washington*, pp. 202, 203 (quotes).
533 a celebratory press release: AL, "Announcement of News From Gettysburg," July 4, 1863, in *CW*, VI, p. 314.
533 "the gloomiest Fourth" . . . Fireworks were set off: Entry for July 4, 1863, Fanny Seward diary, Seward Papers.
533 "The results . . . for the moment at least": Entry for July 6, 1863, *Diary of George Templeton Strong*, Vol. III, p. 330.
533 Grant's forty-six-day siege: McGowen, "Vicksburg Campaign (May–July 1863)," in *Encyclopedia of the American Civil War*, ed. Heidler and Heidler, p. 2026; Foote, *The Civil War*, Vol. II, p. 607.
533 Welles had received . . . dispatch in hand: Entry for July 7, 1863, *Welles diary*, Vol. I (1960 edn.), p. 364; Brooks, *Mr. Lincoln's Washington*, pp. 177 (quote), 201.
533 "executed a double . . . excited as he was then": Brooks, *Washington, D.C., in Lincoln's Time*, p. 82.
533 "caught my hand . . . 'it is great!' ": Entry for July 7, 1863, *Welles diary*, Vol. I (1960 edn.), p. 364.
533 "The Father . . . to the sea": AL to James C. Conkling, August 26, 1863, *CW*, VI, p. 409.
533 "The rebel troops" . . . about thirty thousand: Charles A. Dana to EMS, July 5, 1863, reel 5, Stanton Papers, DLC.
534 "I write this now . . . and I was wrong": AL to USG, July 13, 1863, in *CW*, VI, p. 326.
534 a large crowd . . . "the beginning of the end": *NYH*, July 8, 1863.
534 the official bulletins were read . . . "beasts at sunrise": Brooks, *Mr. Lincoln's Washington*, p. 201.
535 Mary's carriage accident: *Star*, July 2, 1863; *NYH*, July 11, 1863; Boyden, *Echoes from Hospital and White House*, pp. 143–44; Pinsker, *Lincoln's Sanctuary*, pp. 102–04, 105–06.
535 "never quite recovered . . . of her fall": Robert Todd Lincoln, quoted in Helm, *The True Story of Mary*, p. 250.
535 "complete his work . . . destruction of Lee's army": AL to Henry W. Halleck, [July 7, 1863], in *CW*, VI, p. 319.
535 both Halleck and Lincoln urged Meade: Henry W. Halleck to George G. Meade, July 8, 1863, *OR*, Ser. 1, Vol. XXVII, Part III, p. 605; note 1 of AL to Henry W. Halleck, [July 7, 1863], in *CW*, VI, p. 319.
535 Robert Lincoln later said . . . "his vindication": "[Robert Todd Lincoln's Reminiscences, Given 5 January 1885]," in Nicolay, *An Oral History of Abraham Lincoln*, pp. 88–89.
535 he nonetheless failed to move . . . "anxious and impatient": "13 July 1863, Monday," in Hay, *Inside Lincoln's White House*, p. 62.
535 he received a dispatch from Meade: "14 July 1863, Tuesday," in ibid., p. 62; Circular, Army of the Potomac,

July 14, 1863, in *OR*, Ser. 1, Vol. XXVII, Part III, p. 690; Sauers, "Gettysburg, Battle of," in *Encyclopedia of the American Civil War*, ed. Heidler and Heidler, p. 836.

535 Stanton was reluctant to share . . . president "was not": Entry for July 14, 1863, *Welles diary*, Vol. I (1960 edn.), p. 370.

536 Lincoln caught up . . . "and discouraged": Entry for July 14, 1863, ibid., p. 371.

536 "Our Army held . . . we did not harvest it": AL, quoted in "19 July 1863, Sunday," in Hay, *Inside Lincoln's White House*, pp. 64–65.

536 his profound gratitude . . . "never sent, or signed": AL to George G. Meade, July 14, 1863, Lincoln Papers.

536 Meade's failure to attack . . . "I might run away": Carpenter, *Six Months at the White House*, pp. 219–20.

536 the draft: Samantha Jane Gaul, "Conscription, U.S.A.," in *Encyclopedia of the American Civil War*, ed. Heidler and Heidler, p. 487.

536 Governor Seymour had told . . . the black man: Governor Horatio Seymour, quoted in John G. Nicolay and John Hay, *Abraham Lincoln: A History*, Vol. VII (New York: Century Co., 1917), p. 17.

536 *Daily News* . . . "kill off Democrats": *New York Daily News*, quoted in ibid., p. 18.

536 A provision in the Conscription Act: Gaul, "Conscription, U.S.A.," in *Encyclopedia of the American Civil War*, ed. Heidler and Heidler, p. 488.

537 "a rich man's war and a poor man's fight": Sandburg, *Abraham Lincoln: The War Years*, Vol. II, p. 362.

537 the first day of the draft proceeded: *NYT*, July 14, 1863; Nicolay and Hay, *Abraham Lincoln*, Vol. VII, p. 18.

537 "Scarcely had two dozen" . . . continued unchecked for five days: *NYT*, July 14, 1863 (quotes); *NYT*, July 16, 1863; Sandburg, *Abraham Lincoln: The War Years*, Vol. II, p. 360; Gaul, "Conscription, U.S.A." and "New York City Draft Riots (13–17 July 1863)," in *Encyclopedia of the American Civil War*, ed. Heidler and Heidler, pp. 488, 1414–15.

537 "the all engrossing topic of conversation": Brooks, *Mr. Lincoln's Washington*, p. 219.

537 "have the power for a week": SPC to William Sprague, July 14, 1863, reel 27, Chase Papers.

537 The mob violence finally ended . . . go forward: *NYT*, July 18, 1863.

537 Auburn's draft . . . "apprehension of a riot": FAS to Augustus Seward, July 20, 1863, reel 115, Seward Papers.

537 she reported that Copperheads . . . riots in New York: FAS to WHS, July 18, 1863, reel 114, Seward Papers.

537 several Irishmen fought . . . the Seward home: FAS to WHS, June 28, 1863, reel 114, Seward Papers; FAS to WHS, July 12, 1863, reel 114, Seward Papers; FAS to FWS, July 23, 1863, reel 115, Seward Papers.

537 Frances awoke one morning . . . "I possessed": Janet W. Seward, "Personal Experiences of the Civil War," Seward Papers, NRU.

538 "Do not give yourself . . . not without benefit": WHS to FAS, July 21, 1863, in Seward, *Seward at Washington . . . 1861–1872*, p. 177.

538 "As to personal injury . . . willing to assist them": FAS to WHS, July 18, 1863, reel 114, Seward Papers.

538 everyone was "somewhat" . . . police force: FAS to FWS, July 23, 1863, reel 115, Seward Papers.

538 "The best of order . . . Our recent victories": *NYT*, July 24, 1863.

538 Seward had predicted . . . "up a long time": WHS to [FAS], July 17, 1863, quoted in Seward, *Seward at Washington . . . 1861–1872*, p. 176.

538 "incitement . . . resist the government": FAS to WHS, July 15, 1863, reel 114, Seward Papers.

538 John Hay learned . . . handling of the situation: "25 July 1863, Saturday," in Hay, *Inside Lincoln's White House*, p. 67.

538 "lost ground . . . best men": John A. Dix to EMS, July 25, 1863, reel 5, Stanton Papers, DLC.

538 "The nation is great . . . in 1850 to 1860!": WHS to [FAS], July 25, 1863, quoted in Seward, *Seward at Washington . . . 1861–1872*, p. 177.

538 "President was in . . . sack Phil-del": "19 July 1863, Sunday," in Hay, *Inside Lincoln's White House*, pp. 64, 306 n80.

539 "A few days having passed . . . a true man": AL to Oliver O. Howard, July 21, 1863, in *CW*, VI, p. 341.

539 the six straight hours . . . power to pardon: JH to JGN, [July 19, 1863], in Hay, *At Lincoln's Side*, p. 45.

539 Hay marveled . . . "instead of shooting him": "18 July 1863, Saturday," in Hay, *Inside Lincoln's White House*, p. 64.

539 Lincoln acknowledged . . . "upon him unawares": Eaton, *Grant, Lincoln and the Freedmen*, p. 180.

539 "overcome by a physical . . . the battle begins": "Conversation with Hon. J. Holt, Washington Oct 29 1875," in Nicolay, *An Oral History of Abraham Lincoln*, p. 69.

539 Rather than fearing . . . deserters were executed: Eaton, *Grant, Lincoln and the Freedmen*, p. 180.

539 "where meanness or cruelty were shown": "18 July 1863, Saturday," in Hay, *Inside Lincoln's White House*, p. 64.

539 the case of a captain . . . "Count Peeper": "[July–August 1863]," in ibid., p. 76.

540 "Men and horses . . . every day": JH to JGN, August 13, 1863, in Hay, *At Lincoln's Side*, p. 50.

540 "The garments cling . . . is over everything": Brooks, *Mr. Lincoln's Washington*, p. 223.

540 "hot, dusty weather . . . discomfort of Washington": EMS to Ellen Stanton, August 25, 1863, quoted in Gideon Stanton, ed., "Edwin M. Stanton" (quotes); Pinsker, *Lincoln's Sanctuary*, pp. 116–17.

540 "Nearly everybody . . . skeddadled from the heat": Brooks, *Mr. Lincoln's Washington*, p. 223.

540 Mary fled the capital . . . through most of August: AL to MTL, August 8, 1863, Lincoln Papers; Turner and Turner, *Mary Todd Lincoln*, pp. 153–54.

540 A correspondent . . . "smiling face": *Boston Journal*, August 10, 1863.

540 Lincoln talked about the heat . . . "distress about it": AL to MTL, August 8, 1863, Lincoln Papers.

540 Only in mid-September . . . with her and with Tad: AL to MTL, September 21 and 22, 1863, in *CW*, VI, pp. 471, 474.

540 Mary understood . . . "to letter writing": MTL to AL, November 2, [1862], in Turner and Turner, *Mary Todd Lincoln*, p. 139.

541 "I wish I could gain . . . put to the test": FAS to WHS, June 17, 1863, reel 114, Seward Papers.
541 "Every day . . . gone to the field": WHS to [FAS], July 25, 1863, quoted in Seward, *Seward at Washington . . . 1861–1872*, p. 177.
541 she despaired when . . . "killed & wounded": FAS to WHS, July 5, 1863, reel 114, Seward Papers.
541 Only with Frances . . . exhaustion: WHS to FAS, June 8, 1863, reel 112, Seward Papers.
541 "Thenceforth . . . constant devotion to business": Robert Todd Lincoln to Dr. J. G. Holland, June 6, 1865, box 6, folder 37, William Barton Collection, Special Collections of the Regenstein Library at the University of Chicago.
541 the Equinox House . . . dining facilities: "From The Beginning," historical pamphlet, Equinox House, Manchester, Vt.
541 Mary climbed a mountain . . . Doubleday and his wife: Randall, *Mary Lincoln*, p. 229; *NYH*, September 1, 1863.
541 "We did again . . . fortunes": William Sprague to KCS, May 27, 1866, Sprague Papers.
542 his immense manufacturing company . . . weekly: "The Rhode Island Spragues," December 5, 1883, unidentified newspaper, KCS vertical file, DWP.
542 "I want to show you . . . undone or destroyed": William Sprague to KCS, May 1, 1863, Sprague Papers.
542 "The Gov and Miss Kate . . . into their fold": William Sprague to Hiram Barney, May 18, 1863, Salmon Portland Chase Collection, Historical Society of Pennsylvania, Philadelphia [hereafter Chase Papers, Phi.].
542 "The business . . . lost its identity": William Sprague to KCS, June 16, 1863, Sprague Papers.
542 "a wilderness, a blank": William Sprague to KCS, July 1, 1863, Sprague Papers.
542 He kept her miniature . . . "strong a hold": William Sprague to KCS, June 3, 7 and 8, 1863, Sprague Papers (quotes from June 7 letter).
542 "I am my darling up . . . with the sunshine": William Sprague to KCS, May 21, 1863, Sprague Papers.
542 "I hope my darling . . . morning and adieu": William Sprague to KCS, June 1, 1863, Sprague Papers.
542 Chase opened the discussion . . . "any due to me": SPC to William Sprague, June 6, 1863, reel 27, Chase Papers.
542 "Probably no woman . . . her successes": *Washington Post*, August 1, 1899.
543 "Scarcely a person . . . lent a charm to the whole": FS to LW, February 1, 1863, reel 116, Seward Papers.
543 Kate persuaded William: William Sprague to SPC, May 31, 1863, reel 27, Chase Papers; William Sprague to KCS, June 12, 1863, Sprague Papers; SPC to William Sprague, July 14, 1863, reel 27, Chase Papers.
543 "idea of taking . . . So I yield the point": SPC to William Sprague, July 14, 1863, reel 27, Chase Papers.
543 Chase would continue . . . William would cover: SPC to William Sprague, July 14, 1863, reel 27, Chase Papers; William Sprague to KCS, July 22, 1863, Sprague Papers; Niven, *Salmon P. Chase*, p. 342.
543 "the delicate link . . . united father & daughter": William Sprague to SPC, November 4, 1863, reel 29, Chase Papers.
543 Sprague wisely decided . . . "enduring love": William Sprague to KCS, June 12, 1863, Sprague Papers.
543 "Katie showed me . . . full wealth of her affections": SPC to William Sprague, June 6, 1863, reel 27, Chase Papers.
543 "as much of the pecuniary burden as possible": William Sprague to SPC, May 31, 1863, reel 27, Chase Papers.
543 to divest himself: Belden and Belden, *So Fell the Angels*, pp. 84–85.
543 he informed Jay Cooke . . . "all right-minded men": SPC to Jay Cooke, June 1, 1863, reel 27, Chase Papers.
544 he returned a check . . . "as be right": SPC to Jay Cooke, June 2, 1863, reel 27, Chase Papers.
544 Chase joined Kate . . . returned to Washington: Lamphier, *Kate Chase and William Sprague*, p. 54.
544 his only companion . . . "sympathetic way": SPC to Janet Chase Hoyt, August 19, 1863, reel 28, Chase Papers (quote). See also note 2 to published edition of August 19 letter in *The Salmon P. Chase Papers. Vol. IV: Correspondence, April 1863–1864*, ed. John Niven (Kent, Ohio, and London: Kent State University Press, 1997), p. 106 n2.
544 He chastised Nettie . . . carelessness pained him: SPC to Janet Chase Hoyt, August 19, 1863, reel 28, Chase Papers.
544 he reprimanded Kate . . . vacation expenses: SPC to KCS, August 19, 1863, reel 28, Chase Papers.
544 a warm correspondence . . . "her letters": Belden and Belden, *So Fell the Angels*, pp. 88–89 (quote p. 89).
544 Mrs. Eastman described . . . "of his own idolatry?": Charlotte S. Eastman to SPC, July 19, 1863, reel 27, Chase Papers.
544 "What a sweet letter" . . . attend to the president: SPC to Charlotte S. Eastman, August 22, 1863, reel 28, Chase Papers.
545 "The Tycoon is in fine whack . . . where he is": JH to JGN, August 7, 1863, in Hay, *At Lincoln's Side*, p. 49.
545 Hay had a good sense of humor . . . "peal of fun": Stoddard, *Inside the White House in War Times*, pp. 93–94.
545 Hay accompanied the president: August 9, 1863, photograph of AL, in Philip B. Kunhardt, Jr., Philip B. Kunhardt III, and Peter W. Kunhardt, *Lincoln: An Illustrated Biography* (New York: Alfred A. Knopf, 1992), p. 216.
545 "very good spirits": "9 August 1863, Sunday," in Hay, *Inside Lincoln's White House*, p. 70.
545 Rigidly posed . . . unsmiling portrait: Kunhardt, et al., *Lincoln*, p. 216.
545 required to sit . . . "Don't move a muscle!": George Sullivan, *Mathew Brady: His Life and Photographs* (New York: Cobblehill Books, 1994), pp. 17–18 (quote p. 18).
545 "contrived grinning . . . become obligatory": James Mellon, ed., *The Face of Lincoln* (New York: Viking Press, 1979), pp. 13–14.
546 "the rebel power . . . to disintegrate": "9 August 1863, Sunday," in Hay, *Inside Lincoln's White House*, p. 70.
546 pleasant outings . . . "sent me to bed": "23 August 1863, Sunday," in ibid., pp. 75–76 (quote p. 76); *Washington Post*, August 3, 1924; Pinsker, *Lincoln's Sanctuary*, p. 115.

546 "I see the President . . . on K Street": Whitman, *Specimen Days* (1971 edn.), p. 26.
546 "The President and I . . . the season is over": EMS to Ellen Stanton, August 25, 1863, quoted in Gideon Stanton, ed., "Edwin M. Stanton."
546 Stanton finally joined his wife . . . the Soldiers' Home: Thomas and Hyman, *Stanton*, p. 284.
546 typically wide-ranging . . . "party to oppose a war": "13 August 1863, Thursday," in Hay, *Inside Lincoln's White House*, pp. 72–73 (quote); Pamela Scott and Antoinette J. Lee, *Buildings of the District of Columbia*. Buildings of the United States Series (New York and Oxford: Oxford University Press, 1993), pp. 119, 128; "*Progress of Civilization,*" Architect of the Capitol website, www.aoc.gov/cc/art/pediments/prog_sen_r.htm (accessed November 2004).
546 tour of upstate New York . . . picnic on the lake: Philip Van Doren Stern, *When the Guns Roared: World Aspects of the American Civil War* (Garden City, N.Y.: Doubleday & Co., 1965), p. 230; Seward, *Seward at Washington . . . 1861–1872*, pp. 186–87.
547 "All seemed . . . themselves very much": FAS to Augustus Seward, August 27, 1863, reel 115, Seward Papers.
547 "When one comes really . . . to like in him": Lord Lyons to Lord Russell, quoted in Stern, *When the Guns Roared*, p. 231.
547 "Hundreds of factories . . . and canals": Seward, *Seward at Washington . . . 1861–1872*, p. 186.
547 European shipbuilders . . . not be delivered: Van Deusen, *William Henry Seward*, pp. 352–56, 361; entries for August 12, 29, September 18, 25, 1863, *Welles diary*, Vol. I (1960 edn.), pp. 399, 429, 435–37, 443.
547 "The White House . . . health of the nation": Dispatch of August 31, 1863, in Stoddard, *Dispatches from Lincoln's White House*, p. 166.

CHAPTER 21: "I FEEL TROUBLE IN THE AIR"

Page
548 180,000 soldiers . . . black males: Eric Foner, *Reconstruction: America's Unfinished Revolution, 1863–1877* (New York: Harper & Row, 1988; 1989), p. 8.
548 Emancipation Proclamation flatly declared . . . "United States": AL, "Emancipation Proclamation," January 1, 1863, in *CW*, VI, p. 30.
548 Stanton authorized . . . and other Northern states: Quarles, *Lincoln and the Negro*, p. 156; Dudley Taylor Cornish, *The Sable Arm: Black Troops in the Union Army, 1861–1865* (Lawrence: University Press of Kansas, 1956; 1987), p. 105.
549 the war would not be won . . . "suppressing the rebels": *Douglass' Monthly* (August 1862).
549 He wrote stirring appeals . . . many other cities: Blight, *Frederick Douglass' Civil War*, pp. 157–59.
549 "Why should a colored . . . that claim respected": *Douglass' Monthly* (April 1863).
549 thousands of Bostonians . . . high-ranking military officials: *Boston Daily Evening Transcript*, May 28, 1863.
549 "No single regiment . . . admirable marching": Ibid.
549 He urged Banks . . . the enlisting process: AL to Nathaniel P. Banks, March 29, 1863, in *CW*, VI, p. 154; AL to David Hunter, April 1, 1863, in ibid., p. 158; AL to USG, August 9, 1863, in ibid., p. 374.
549 "The colored population . . . rebellion at once": AL to Andrew Johnson, March 26, 1863, in ibid., pp. 149–50.
549 Chase . . . "nearly two years ago": SPC to James A. Garfield, May 31, 1863, reel 12, Garfield Papers, DLC.
550 a series of obstacles . . . losing their freedom or their lives: Benjamin Quarles, *Frederick Douglass*. Studies in American Negro Life Series (Associated Publishers, 1948; New York: Atheneum, 1970), pp. 209–10; Quarles, *Lincoln and the Negro*, pp. 167, 169, 173–74, 177.
550 "this is no time . . . to embrace it": *Douglass' Monthly* (August 1863).
550 they earned great respect . . . "bravery and steadiness": Cornish, *The Sable Arm*, pp. 142–43 (quote p. 143).
550 "dooming to death . . . negro troops": *NYTrib*, reprinted in *Liberator*, May 15, 1863.
550 As word of the unique . . . swiftly diminishing: James M. McPherson, *The Negro's Civil War: How American Blacks Felt and Acted During the War for Union* (New York: Pantheon Books, 1965; New York: Ballantine Books, 1991), pp. 176, 179.
550 "What has Mr. Lincoln . . . responsible for them": *Douglass' Monthly* (August 1863).
550 "When I plead . . . rulers at Washington": Frederick Douglass to Major G. L. Stearns, August 1, 1863, reprinted in ibid.
550 he asked Halleck . . . "placed at hard labor": AL, "Order of Retaliation," July 30, 1863, in *CW*, VI, p. 357.
551 The order was "well-written . . . became impossible": Entry for August 4, 1863, in Gurowski, *Diary from November 18, 1862 to October 18, 1863*, pp. 292–93.
551 Douglass agreed . . . "required to act": Douglass to Stearns, August 1, 1863, in *Douglass' Monthly* (August 1863).
551 the lack of "fair play" . . . to the president: Douglass, *Life and Times of Frederick Douglass*, pp. 784–85.
551 "tumult of feeling": Frederick Douglass, quoted in the *Washington Post*, February 13, 1888.
551 "I could not know . . . an interview altogether": Douglass, *Life and Times of Frederick Douglass*, p. 785.
551 a large crowd in the hallway . . . into the office: *Liberator*, January 29, 1864; Philip S. Foner, *Frederick Douglass* (New York: Citadel Press, 1950; repr. 1964), p. 216.
551 "I was never more . . . Abraham Lincoln": Douglass, *Life and Times of Frederick Douglass*, p. 785.
551 The president was seated . . . "began to rise": Douglass, "Lincoln and the Colored Troops," in *Reminiscences of Abraham Lincoln*, ed. Rice, p. 316.
551 Douglass hesitantly began . . . "glad to see you": Douglass, *Life and Times of Frederick Douglass*, p. 786.
551 Lincoln's warmth . . . "Abraham Lincoln": Frederick Douglass to George L. Stearns, August 12, 1863 (photo-

copy), container 53, Papers of Frederick Douglass, Manuscript Division, Library of Congress [hereafter Douglass Papers, DLC].

551 Douglass laid before . . . "very apparent sympathy": Douglass, "Lincoln and the Colored Troops," in *Reminiscences of Abraham Lincoln*, ed. Rice, p. 317.

551 "Upon my ceasing . . . not suspected him": Douglass to Stearns, August 12, 1863, Douglass Papers, DLC.

551 it "seemed a necessary . . . at all as soldiers": Douglass, *Life and Times of Frederick Douglass*, p. 787.

552 "in the end they shall . . . as white soldiers": AL quoted in Douglass, "Lincoln and the Colored Troops," in *Reminiscences of Abraham Lincoln*, ed. Rice, p. 318.

552 "he would sign . . . commend to him": Douglass, *Life and Times of Frederick Douglass*, p. 787.

552 Lincoln's justification . . . "killed for negroes": Douglass to Stearns, August 12, 1863, Douglass Papers, DLC.

552 "once begun . . . humane spirit": Douglass, *Life and Times of Frederick Douglass*, p. 787.

552 he had read a recent speech . . . "retreated from it": *Liberator,* January 29, 1864.

552 "as though I could . . . his shoulder": Douglass, "Lincoln and the Colored Troops," in *Reminiscences of Abraham Lincoln*, ed. Rice, p. 325.

552 "The manner of" . . . in the Mississippi Valley: Douglass, *Life and Times of Frederick Douglass*, pp. 787–88 (quote); Quarles, *Lincoln and the Negro*, pp. 168, 172.

552 The War Department followed up . . . commission was not included: Quarles, *Lincoln and the Negro*, p. 169.

552 "I knew too much . . . mark of my rank": Douglass, *Life and Times of Frederick Douglass*, p. 788.

553 "Perhaps you may like . . . I felt big there!": *Liberator,* January 29, 1864.

553 Conkling had invited . . . loyal Unionists: AL to James C. Conkling, August 26, 1863, in *CW,* VI, p. 406.

553 False rumors circulated: *NYT,* August 8 and 13, 1863.

553 "Ah! I'm glad" . . . he bade him good night: Stoddard, *Inside the White House in War Times*, pp. 129–30.

554 "deceptive and groundless . . . they have strove to hinder it": AL to James C. Conkling, August 26, 1863, in *CW,* VI, pp. 407–10.

554 Lincoln continued to refine . . . public duties: "23 August 1863, Sunday," in Hay, *Inside Lincoln's White House*, p. 76.

554 "You are one of the best . . . very slowly": AL to James C. Conkling, August 27, 1863, in *CW,* VI, p. 414.

554 An immense crowd . . . "the country calls": *Illinois State Journal,* Springfield, Ill., September 2, 1863.

554 he was furious to see . . . around the country: John W. Forney to AL, September 3, 1863, Lincoln Papers.

555 "I am mortified . . . How did this happen?": AL to James C. Conkling, September 3, 1863, in *CW,* VI, p. 430.

555 When a petitioner tried . . . "obvious to any one": AL to D. M. Leatherman, September 3, 1863, in ibid., p. 431.

555 a message arrived from Conkling . . . "the next day": James C. Conkling to AL, September 4, 1863, Lincoln Papers.

555 "Disclaiming the arts . . . wants to discuss": *NYTrib,* September 3, 1863.

555 "The most consummate . . . which needs driving": *NYT,* September 7, 1863.

555 The *Philadelphia Inquirer* . . . "continue to write": *Philadelphia Inquirer,* September 5, 1863.

555 "His last letter . . . logicians of all schools": JH to JGN, September 11, 1863, in Hay, *At Lincoln's Side,* p. 54.

555 the *New York Times* also commended . . . "their faith in him": *NYT,* September 7, 1863.

556 "I know the people . . . on the ground": JH to JGN, September 11, 1863, in Hay, *At Lincoln's Side,* p. 54.

556 Seward came back . . . the diplomatic corps: WHS to Charles Francis Adams, August 25, 1863, quoted in Seward, *Seward at Washington . . . 1861–1872*, p. 188.

556 to celebrate his seventieth . . . "good as I deserve": Entry for September 4, 1863, in *The Diary of Edward Bates, 1859–1866*, pp. 305–06.

556 his ten-day visit . . . "perhaps more missed": Entry for September 11, 1863, *Welles diary,* Vol. I (1960 edn.), p. 431.

556 Lincoln and Stanton had hoped . . . "blow to the rebellion": EMS to William S. Rosecrans, July 7, 1863, in *OR,* Ser. 1, Vol. XXIII, Part II, p. 518.

556 Rosecrans delivered . . . "victory at Chattanooga": JH to JGN, September 11, 1863, in Hay, *At Lincoln's Side,* p. 54.

556 "unexpectedly appeared . . . of [the] Chicamauga": Charles A. Dana to EMS, September 12, 1863, reel 5, Stanton Papers, DLC.

556 battle of Chickamauga: See Dave Powell, "Chickamauga, Battle of," in *Encyclopedia of the American Civil War,* ed. Heidler and Heidler, pp. 427–31.

556 "Chicamauga is as fatal . . . as Bull Run": Charles A. Dana to EMS, September 20, 1863, reel 6, Stanton Papers, DLC.

557 Union casualties: Entry for September 20, 1862, in Long, *The Civil War Day by Day,* p. 412.

557 "We have met with . . . scattered troops there": William S. Rosecrans to Henry W. Halleck, September 20, 1863, in *OR,* Ser. 1, Vol. XXX, Part I, pp. 142–43.

557 the dispatches reached him . . . "awake and watchful": Entry for September 21, 1863, *Welles diary,* Vol. I (1960 edn.), p. 438.

557 wandered into Hay's room . . . "air before it comes": "[27 September 1863, Sunday]," in Hay, *Inside Lincoln's White House,* p. 85.

557 Lincoln telegraphed Mary . . . "see you and Tad": AL to MTL, September 21, 1863, in *CW,* VI, p. 471.

557 Mary responded . . . plans to do so: MTL to AL, September 22, 1863, quoted in Helm, *The True Story of Mary,* p. 215.

557 proved "less unfavorable . . . feared": Entry for September 22, 1863, in *Chase Papers,* Vol. I, p. 449 (quote); Charles A. Dana to EMS, September 20, 1863, in *OR,* Ser. 1, Vol. XXX, Part I, p. 193.

557 Thomas's corps had held . . . than the Federals: Powell, "Chickamauga, Battle of," in *Encyclopedia of the American Civil War*, ed. Heidler and Heidler, p. 430.

557 "still remains in . . . to twenty days": Charles A. Dana to EMS, September 23, 1863, reel 6, Stanton Papers, DLC.

557 Stanton came up with . . . dispatched messengers: Flower, *Edwin McMasters Stanton*, p. 203.

557 Chase had just retired . . . and his entire army: Entry for September 23, 1863, in *Chase Papers*, Vol. I, p. 450.

557 John Hay was sent to the Soldiers' Home . . . back to the War Department: "[27 September 1863, Sunday]," in Hay, *Inside Lincoln's White House*, p. 86 (quotes); John G. Nicolay and John Hay, *Abraham Lincoln: A History*, Vol. VIII (New York: Century Co., 1917), p. 112.

557 "I have invited . . . serious for jokes": Entry for September 23, 1863, in *Chase Papers*, Vol. I, pp. 450–52 (quotes); Flower, *Edwin McMasters Stanton*, p. 203.

558 "he had fully considered . . . with excellent arguments": Entry for September 23, 1863, in *Chase Papers*, Vol. I, p. 452.

558 Stanton immediately sent an orderly . . . "make a few figures": W. H. Whiton recollections, quoted in Gorham, *Life and Public Services of Edwin M. Stanton*, Vol. I, pp. 123–24.

558 "I can complete . . . given my consent": McCallum, EMS, and AL, quoted in Flower, *Edwin McMasters Stanton*, p. 204.

558 "Colonel McCallum . . . I will approve them": AL, quoted in W. H. Whiton recollections, quoted in Gorham, *Life and Public Services of Edwin M. Stanton*, Vol. I, pp. 124–25.

558 Stanton worked . . . stop to resupply: EMS to J. T. Boyle, September 23, 1863, in *OR*, Ser. 1, Vol. XXIX, Part I, p. 147; EMS to R. P. Bowler, September 24, 1863, in ibid., p. 153; Daniel Butterfield to Oliver O. Howard, September 26, 1863, in ibid., p. 160; W. P. Smith to EMS, September 26, 1863, in ibid., p. 161; Flower, *Edwin McMasters Stanton*, pp. 204–06. For documentation of Stanton's efforts to move the 11th and 12th Army Corps to the Army of the Cumberland, see *OR*, Ser. 1, Vol. XXIX, Part 1, pp. 146–95.

559 The first train left Washington . . . arrived in Tennessee: W. P. Smith to EMS, September 26, 1863, in *OR*, Ser. 1, Vol. 29, Part I, p. 161; Flower, *Edwin McMasters Stanton*, pp. 205–06.

559 Monitoring reports . . . agree to leave his post: Flower, *Edwin McMasters Stanton*, pp. 205–07; W. P. Smith to EMS, September 26, 1863, in *OR*, Ser. 1, Vol. XXIX, Part I, p. 162.

559 "It was an extraordinary . . . the twentieth century": McPherson, *Battle Cry of Freedom*, p. 675.

559 Dana's reports . . . troops had lost confidence: Charles A. Dana to EMS, September 30, 1863, in *OR*, Ser. 1, Vol. XXX, Part I, p. 204.

559 Stanton telegraphed Grant . . . discussing the overall military situation: Grant, *Personal Memoirs of U.S. Grant*, pp. 315–16.

559 the general departed for Chattanooga . . . Lookout Mountain: Ibid., pp. 320–51; James H. Meredith, "Chattanooga Campaign" and "Lookout Mountain, Battle of," in *Encyclopedia of the American Civil War*, ed. Heidler and Heidler, pp. 411–15, 1216–18.

559 "would have been a terrible disaster": Grant, *Personal Memoirs of U.S. Grant*, p. 318.

559 "The country does . . . nights work": Entry for September 23, 1863, in *Chase Papers*, Vol. I, p. 453.

560 affectionately call his "Mars": Bates, *Lincoln in the Telegraph Office*, p. 400.

560 "esteem and affection . . . French comic opera": Benjamin, "Recollections of Secretary Edwin M. Stanton," *Century* (1887), pp. 768, 760–61.

560 "No two men were . . . a necessity to each other": *New York Evening Post*, July 13, 1891.

560 "in dealing with the public . . . than his heart": A. E. Johnson, opinion cited in Bates, *Lincoln in the Telegraph Office*, p. 389.

560 the story of a congressman . . . "step over and see him": Julian, *Political Recollections, 1840 to 1872*, pp. 211–12.

561 "remarkable passages . . . at Cincinnati": EMS, quoted in Parkinson to Beveridge, May 28, 1923, container 292, Beveridge Papers, DLC.

561 "Few war ministers . . . for Mr. Lincoln": "The Late Secretary Stanton," *Army and Navy Journal*, January 1, 1870, p. 309.

561 When Stanton was eighteen . . . near death from cholera: Wolcott, "Edwin M. Stanton," p. 36.

561 he insisted on including . . . to stand guard: Joseph Buchanan and William Stanton Buchanan, quoted in Flower, *Edwin McMasters Stanton*, pp. 39, 40.

561 *Oh! Why should the spirit* . . . : William Knox, "Mortality," quoted in Bruce, "The Riddle of Death," in *The Lincoln Enigma*, p. 135.

561 He could recite from memory . . . "in the English language": Carpenter, *Six Months at the White House*, p. 59.

561 *The mossy marbles rest*: Oliver Wendell Holmes, "The Last Leaf," in *The Poetical Works of Oliver Wendell Holmes*, Vol. I (Boston and New York: Houghton Mifflin, 1892), p. 4.

562 he had written . . . "he should be honored?": EMS, "Our Admiration of Military Character Unmerited," 1831, reel 1, Stanton Papers, DLC.

562 an army of more than 2 million men: Margaret E. Wagner, Gary W. Gallagher, and Paul Finkelman, eds., *The Library of Congress Civil War Desk Reference* (New York: Grand Central Press/Simon & Schuster, 2002), p. 376.

562 "There could be no greater . . . to eternity": EMS, quoted in Gideon Stanton, ed., "Edwin M. Stanton."

562 "Doesn't it strike you . . . flowing all about me?": AL quoted in Louis A. Warren, *Lincoln's Youth: Indiana Years, Seven to Twenty-one, 1816–1830* (New York: Appleton Century Crofts, 1959), p. 225 n29.

562 an audience to a group of Quakers: AL to Eliza P. Gurney, September 4, 1864, in *CW*, VII, p. 535.

562 "If I had had . . . still governs it": AL, quoted in Eliza P. Gurney, copy of interview with AL, [October 26, 1862], Lincoln Papers.

562 "On principle . . . no mortal could stay": AL to Eliza P. Gurney, September 4, 1864, in *CW*, VII, p. 535.

563 Stanton still wrote . . . " 'our love in two' ": EMS to SPC, March 7, 1863, Chase Papers, Phi.
563 Stanton would ask Chase to stand: EMS to SPC, December 30, 1863, reel 30, Chase Papers.
563 "It is painful . . . after concurrence, action": SPC to George Wilkes, August 27, 1863, reel 28, Chase Papers.
563 Radicals insisted . . . both the Union and emancipation: Foner, *Reconstruction*, pp. 35–50, 60–62.
564 "standard-bearer . . . of the Radicals": Brooks, *Mr. Lincoln's Washington*, p. 236.
564 Chase's desire . . . proclaim his campaign: Ibid., p. 237.
564 he wrote hundreds of letters . . . Lincoln administration: Hendrick, *Lincoln's War Cabinet*, p. 400.
564 "I should fear nothing . . . management of the War": SPC to Edward D. Mansfield, October 18, 1863, reel 29, Chase Papers.
564 "If I were myself . . . man should be had": SPC to William Sprague, November 26, 1863, reel 30, Chase Papers.
564 He was thrilled . . . on another candidate: Horace Greeley to SPC, September 29, 1863, reel 28, Chase Papers.
565 "first choice . . . should receive it": Edward Jordan to SPC, October 27, 1863, reel 29, Chase Papers.
565 Governor Dennison alerted him . . . "like a beaver": "17 October 1863, Saturday, New York," in Hay, *Inside Lincoln's White House*, p. 92.
565 Seward cautioned . . . "for Mr. Chase": TW note, quoted in "28 November 1863, Saturday," in ibid., p. 119.
565 Samuel Cox . . . "New England States": "24 December 1863, Thursday," in ibid., p. 132.
565 A Pennsylvanian politician . . . "out of both eyes": "25 October 1863, Sunday," in ibid., p. 100.
565 John Hay learned . . . *Independent* to his side: "28 November 1863, Saturday," in ibid., p. 120.
565 "Chase's mad hunt after the Presidency": "29 October 1863, Thursday," in ibid., p. 103.
565 "plowing corn . . . make his department go": "[July–August 1863]," in ibid., pp. 78, 313 n143.
565 Lincoln agreed . . . "very bad taste": AL, quoted in "18 October 1863, Sunday," in ibid., p. 93.
565 "was sorry . . . that it ought to": "29 October 1863, Thursday," in ibid., p. 103.
565 Lincoln's friends . . . "President's interests": Eaton, *Grant, Lincoln and the Freedmen*, p. 176.
565 let "Chase have . . . what he asks": "29 October 1863, Thursday," in Hay, *Inside Lincoln's White House*, p. 103.
565 a "frank, guileless . . . for the first one": Leonard Swett to WHH, January 17, 1866, in *HI*, pp. 168, 164.
566 After criticizing . . . "So I still work on": SPC to James Watson Webb, November 7, 1863, reel 29, Chase Papers.
566 "all along clearly . . . from New Orleans": AL, quoted in "18 October 1863, Sunday," in Hay, *Inside Lincoln's White House*, p. 93.
566 "Chase would try . . . spot he can find": "29 October 1863, Thursday," in ibid., p. 103.
566 the people of Missouri . . . extinguish slavery: AL to Charles D. Drake and Others, October 5, 1863, in *CW*, VI, pp. 499–504; Foner, *Reconstruction*, pp. 41–42.
566 Governor Gamble worried . . . a conservative partisan: Hamilton R. Gamble to AL, October 1, 1863, Lincoln Papers.
567 He was accused . . . guise of military necessity: AL to Charles D. Drake and Others, October 5, 1863, in *CW*, VI, p. 500; "Conversation with Hon. M. S. Wilkinson, May 22 1876," in Nicolay, *An Oral History of Abraham Lincoln*, pp. 59–60; Williams, *Lincoln and the Radicals*, p. 299.
567 a delegation of radicals . . . "not to alienate them": "29 September 1863, Tuesday," in Hay, *Inside Lincoln's White House*, pp. 88–89 (quote); Williams, *Lincoln and the Radicals*, p. 299.
567 "these Radical men . . . side with the Radicals": AL, paraphrased in "10 December 1863, Thursday," in Hay, *Inside Lincoln's White House*, p. 125.
567 "they are nearer . . . set Zionwards": AL, quoted in "28 October 1863, Wednesday," in ibid., p. 101.
567 resented the radicals' demand . . . "short statutes of limitations": "10 December 1863, Thursday," in ibid., p. 125.
567 "So intense and fierce . . . saddest features of the times": Entry for September 29, 1863, *Welles diary*, Vol. I (1960 edn.), p. 448.
567 "show that . . . powerful as they may be": AL, quoted in "29 September 1863, Tuesday," in Hay, *Inside Lincoln's White House*, pp. 88–89.
568 an invitation to spend the evening: EB to J. O. Broadhead, October 24, 1863, Broadhead Papers, MoSHi.
568 "surprised and mortified . . . as traitors": EB to Hamilton R. Gamble, October 10, 1863, Bates Papers, MoSHi (quote); entry for September 30, 1863, in *The Diary of Edward Bates, 1859–1866*, p. 308.
568 Bates should hardly be . . . if he were to decide to run against Lincoln: Hamilton R. Gamble to EB, October 17, 1863, Bates Papers, MoSHi.
568 meeting with the Missourians . . . "instead of wind": "30 September 1863, Wednesday," in Hay, *Inside Lincoln's White House*, p. 89.
568 Lincoln listened attentively . . . remove him from command: AL to Charles D. Drake and Others, October 5, 1863, in *CW*, VI, pp. 500 (quotes), 503.
568 "The President never . . . his candid logic": "30 September 1863, Wednesday," in Hay, *Inside Lincoln's White House*, pp. 89–90.
568 Lincoln emerged . . . "as he supposed": Entry for September 30, 1863, in *The Diary of Edward Bates, 1859–1866*, p. 308.
568 "whoever commands . . . or conservatives": AL to Charles D. Drake and Others, October 5, 1863, in *CW*, VI, p. 504.
569 he wrote to remind . . . "injury to the Military": AL to John M. Schofield, October 1, 1863, in ibid., p. 492.
569 leaning toward . . . "conflicting elements": "13 December 1863, Sunday," in Hay, *Inside Lincoln's White House*, p. 127.
569 he decided to replace him with Rosecrans: "Rosecrans, William Starke (1819–1898)," and "Schofield, John McAllister (1831–1906)," in Sifakis, *Who Was Who in the Union*, pp. 342, 355.

569 Before an overflowing crowd . . . Jefferson Davis himself: Speech by Frank Blair, reprinted in *Missouri Republican*, St. Louis, September 27, 1863.
569 The *Liberator* criticized . . . "which he advocates": *Roxbury Journal*, quoted in *Liberator*, October 16, 1863.
570 "not let even . . . share of his resentment": EBL to SPL, [October 24, 1863], in *Wartime Washington*, ed. Laas, p. 316.
570 He wrote a letter to Monty . . . "skill and usefulness": AL to MB, November 2, 1863, in *CW*, VI, p. 555.
570 a gentle letter of reprimand . . . "would not cure the bite": AL to James M. Cutts, Jr., October 26, 1863, in ibid., p. 538, and note.
570 Chase again intervened . . . eligibility to vote: Niven, *Salmon P. Chase*, p. 339.
570 voiced his opposition at Rockville: Speech of Montgomery Blair, reprinted in the *Star*, October 5, 1863.
571 it aroused deep hostility . . . Blair from his cabinet: Smith, *The Francis Preston Blair Family in Politics*, Vol. II, pp. 241–43, 248; Williams, *Lincoln and the Radicals*, pp. 298, 303.
571 Lincoln refused to support . . . "against him": "22 October 1863, Thursday," in Hay, *Inside Lincoln's White House*, p. 97.
571 Noah Brooks attended a mass rally . . . "utterances": Brooks, *Mr. Lincoln's Washington*, pp. 246–48.
571 Chase was a featured . . . his "fossil theories": Ibid., pp. 247–49.
571 Chase was elated . . . "*a Cardinal principle*": SPC to Horace Greeley, October 31, 1863, reel 29, Chase Papers.
571 Worried that Lincoln's . . . "were producing logical results": Leonard Swett to WHH, January 17, 1866, in *HI*, pp. 164–65.
572 "the most truly progressive . . . struggles with them": John W. Forney, quoted in "31 December 1863, Thursday," in Hay, *Inside Lincoln's White House*, p. 135.

CHAPTER 22: "STILL IN WILD WATER"

Page
573 Lincoln was visibly unsettled . . . his presidential race: Entry for October 14, 1863, *Welles diary*, Vol. I (1960 edn.), p. 470.
573 Civil liberties was also . . . instituted conscription: William C. Davis, *Look Away! A History of the Confederate States of America* (New York: Free Press, 2002), pp. 174–76, 226.
573 Toombs accused . . . "tide of despotism": Burton J. Hendrick, *Statesmen of the Lost Cause: Jefferson Davis and His Cabinet* (New York: Literary Guild of America, 1939), p. 417.
573 concerned about Ohio: Waugh, *Reelecting Lincoln*, pp. 14–15.
573 Lincoln was disheartened . . . "to the country": Entry for October 14, 1863, *Welles diary*, Vol. I (1960 edn.), p. 470.
573 In Pennsylvania . . . "of the United States": McPherson, *Battle Cry of Freedom*, p. 685.
574 the Woodward campaign . . . "voice & my vote": GBM to Charles J. Biddle, October 12, 1863, in *Civil War Papers of George B. McClellan*, p. 559.
574 took steps to ensure . . . return home to vote: Waugh, *Reelecting Lincoln*, p. 16.
574 If the president granted . . . Union ticket: SPC, "*Going Home to Vote*," p. 22; Niven, *Salmon P. Chase*, p. 336.
574 the journalist Whitelaw Reid: Niven, *Salmon P. Chase*, p. 336; Hendrick, *Lincoln's War Cabinet*, p. 401.
574 Chase in Columbus . . . "misfortunes averted": SPC, "*Going Home to Vote*," p. 4.
574 "I come not to speak . . . and without exceptions": Ibid., pp. 5, 13.
575 In public squares . . . "turn to Ohio": *Daily Ohio State Journal*, Columbus, Ohio, October 13, 1863; SPC, "*Going Home to Vote*," p. 8 (quote).
575 begged his audiences . . . "sixty-five days in the year": SPC, "*Going Home to Vote*," p. 8.
575 Lincoln took up his usual post: Waugh, *Reelecting Lincoln*, p. 14.
575 a welcome telegram . . . was counted: SPC to AL, October 14, 1863, Lincoln Papers.
575 By 5 a.m. . . . to 100,000: Browne, *The Every-Day Life of Abraham Lincoln*, p. 603; Waugh, *Reelecting Lincoln*, p. 14.
575 "*Glory to God . . . saved the Nation*": Browne, *The Every-Day Life of Abraham Lincoln*, p. 603.
575 "All honor . . . foe at the ballot-box": EMS to John W. Forney, *NYT*, October 15, 1863.
575 found him "in good spirits": Entry for October 14, 1863, *Welles diary*, Vol. I (1960 edn.), p. 470.
575 "No man knows . . . till he has had it": AL, quoted in James B. Fry, in *Reminiscences of Abraham Lincoln by Distinguished Men of His Time*, ed. Allen Thorndike Rice (New York: North American Publishing Co., 1886), p. 390.
575 "all right" . . . a good secretary: AL, quoted in "18 October 1863, Sunday," in Hay, *Inside Lincoln's White House*, p. 93.
576 "I'm afraid . . . of the presidency": Entry for October 17, 1863, in *The Diary of Edward Bates, 1859–1866*, p. 310.
576 "That visit to the west . . . saved my country": Entry for October 20, 1863, in ibid., p. 311.
576 "it is of the nature . . . with its victim": Edward Bates to James O. Broadhead, October 24, 1863, Broadhead Papers, MoSHi.
576 had "warped" . . . party behind him: Entry for August 22, 1863, *Welles diary*, Vol. I (1960 edn.), p. 413.
576 were moderate compared to the scathing indictments: See Smith, *The Francis Preston Blair Family in Politics*, Vol. II, pp. 234–37.

576 "I little imagined . . . me deeply": SPC to Edward D. Mansfield, October 18, 1863, reel 29, Chase Papers.
576 "The late election" . . . unfit for active duty: James H. Baker to SPC, November 7, 1863, reel 29, Chase Papers.
576 "To him, more than . . . system of slavery": *Liberator,* November 13, 1863.
576 *Liberator* maintained . . . "again acting President": *Liberator,* November 13, 1863.
577 the relationship between the two . . . "gave it new light": Seward, *Seward at Washington . . . 1861–1872,* p. 197.
577 "They say, Mr. President . . . as a Governor": WHS and AL, quoted in ibid., pp. 193–94.
577 a proclamation . . . "tranquillity and Union": AL, "Proclamation of Thanksgiving," October 3, 1863, in *CW,* VI, p. 497 (quote); Seward, *Seward at Washington . . . 1861–1872,* p. 194.
577 Lincoln told Nicolay . . . "whole of that letter": December 8, 1863 memorandum, container 3, Nicolay Papers.
578 Seward assured Lincoln . . . "will collapse": Seward, *Seward at Washington . . . 1861–1872,* p. 196.
578 Seward left for Auburn . . . short periods of time: See Seward family correspondence in October 1863 on reels 112, 114, and 115 of Seward Papers, and FAS to Anna (Wharton) Seward, November 17, 1863, reel 115, Seward Papers.
578 The previous spring . . . his intelligence safely: William H. Seward, Jr., "Reminiscences of Lincoln," *Magazine of History* 9 (February 1909), pp. 105–06.
578 he delivered a speech . . . "will perish with it": WHS, quoted in Williams, *Lincoln and the Radicals,* p. 301.
578 "as in religion . . . whole United States": WHS, quoted in Seward, *Seward at Washington . . . 1861–1872,* p. 195.
579 arousing the wrath . . . "always be open to him": WHS, quoted in Williams, *Lincoln and the Radicals,* p. 301.
579 Lincoln telegraphed . . . "How is your son?": AL to WHS, November 3, 1863, in *CW,* VI, p. 562.
579 "Thanks . . . majority in the state": WHS to AL, November 3, 1863, Lincoln Papers.
579 a 30,000 majority: Seward, *Seward at Washington . . . 1861–1872,* p. 195.
579 "the Copperhead . . . and humbled": "8 November 1863, Sunday," in Hay, *Inside Lincoln's White House,* p. 109.
579 invitations to the Chase-Sprague wedding: See Niven, *Salmon P. Chase,* p. 342.
579 a diamond tiara worth $50,000: Ibid., p. 343.
579 "about the bridal *trousseau* . . . Millionaire Wedding": *NYT,* November 18, 1863.
579 "to realize" . . . undivided attention: SPC to William Sprague, October 31, 1863, reel 29, Chase Papers.
579 Sprague reassured Chase . . . "and generation": William Sprague to SPC, November 4, 1863, reel 29, Chase Papers.
580 Hay recounted . . . *The Pearl of Savoy:* "22 October 1863, Thursday," in Hay, *Inside Lincoln's White House,* p. 98.
580 The play revolves . . . Marie goes mad: Gaetano Donizetti, *The Pearl of Savoy: A Domestic Drama in Five Acts. French's Standard Drama.* Acting Edition No. 337 (New York: S. French, [1864?]). *The Pearl of Savoy* was an adaptation of Donizetti's *Linda de Chamounix.*
580 "was a coldly calculated . . . father and politics": See J. P. Cullen, "Kate Chase: Petticoat Politician," *Civil War Times Illustrated* 2 (May 1963), p. 15.
580 "in her eyes . . . upon her affections": Perrine, "The Dashing Kate Chase," *Ladies' Home Journal* (1901), p. 11.
580 "wholly innocent . . . several millions": *Daily Eagle,* Brooklyn, N.Y., November 14, 1863.
580 "Miss Kate has . . . sufficient for both": Entry for May 19, 1863, *Welles diary,* Vol. I (1960 edn.), p. 306.
580 Henry Adams . . . as Jephthah's daughter: Ross, *Proud Kate,* p. 121. The tale of Jephthah's daughter is in Judges 11:30–40.
581 "Memory has been busy . . . found a lodgment there": KCS diary, November 11, 1868, Sprague Papers.
581 In the hours before . . . proceeded inside: *Daily Morning Chronicle,* Washington, D.C., November 13, 1863.
581 Monty Blair, who refused . . . "of the occasion": EBL to SPL, November 12, [1863], in *Wartime Washington,* ed. Laas, p. 319.
581 Lord Lyons . . . and Robert C. Schenck: *Daily Morning Chronicle,* Washington, D.C., November 13, 1863; Perrine, "The Dashing Kate Chase," *Ladies' Home Journal* (1901), pp. 11–12; "12 November 1863, Thursday," in Hay, *Inside Lincoln's White House,* p. 111.
581 "Much anxiety" . . . and without Mrs. Lincoln: *Daily Morning Chronicle,* Washington, D.C., November 13, 1863.
581 "bow in reverence . . . *Chase & daughter*": MTL to Simon Cameron, June 16, [1866], in Turner and Turner, *Mary Todd Lincoln,* p. 370.
581 Mary's absence . . . "presidential party": Brooks, *Mr. Lincoln's Washington,* pp. 260–61.
582 "a gorgeous white velvet" . . . specifically for the occasion: *Daily Morning Chronicle,* Washington, D.C., November 13, 1863 (quote); Brooks, *Mr. Lincoln's Washington,* p. 261; Ross, *Proud Kate,* p. 140.
582 "Chase was . . . newly made wife": Brooks, *Mr. Lincoln's Washington,* p. 261.
582 A lavish meal . . . midnight: *Daily Morning Chronicle,* Washington, D.C., November 13, 1863.
582 "a very brilliant . . . had *arrived*": "12 November 1863, Thursday," in Hay, *Inside Lincoln's White House,* p. 111.
582 The young couple left the next morning: *NYT,* November 18, 1863.
582 "Your letter . . . how welcome it was": SPC to KCS, November 18, 1863, reel 29, Chase Papers.
582 "My heart is full . . . perfect honor & good faith": SPC to William Sprague, November 26, 1863, reel 30, Chase Papers.
583 He had been asked . . . would speak: David Wills to AL, November 2, 1863, Lincoln Papers.
583 Lincoln told his cabinet . . . could not spare the time: Entry for December 1863, *Welles diary,* Vol. I (1960 edn.), p. 480; SPC to KCS, November 18, 1863, reel 29, Chase Papers; entry for November 19, 1863, in *The Diary of Edward Bates, 1859–1866,* p. 316.
583 "extremely busy . . . public expectation": Lamon, *Recollections of Abraham Lincoln,* p. 173.

583 Stanton had arranged . . . "the gauntlet": AL to EMS, [November 17, 1863], in *CW*, VII, p. 16 and note.
583 The day before . . . "half of his speech": James Speed quoted in John G. Nicolay, "Lincoln's Gettysburg Address," *Century* 47 (February 1894), p. 597.
583 Various accounts suggest . . . "a makeshift desk": George D. Gitt, quoted in Wilson, *Intimate Memories of Lincoln*, p. 476.
583 Others swear . . . on an envelope: See Garry Wills, *Lincoln at Gettysburg: The Words That Remade America* (New York: Simon & Schuster, 1992), p. 27.
583 Nicolay . . . and humorous stories: Nicolay, "Lincoln's Gettysburg Address," *Century* (1894), p. 601.
583 he was escorted . . . and Edward Everett: David Wills to AL, November 1, 1863, Lincoln Papers.
583 "All the hotels . . . of Gettysburgh immortal": *NYT*, November 21, 1863.
584 He came to the door . . . "say nothing at all": AL, "Remarks to Citizens of Gettysburg, Pennsylvania," November 18, 1863, in *CW*, VI, pp. 16–17.
584 Lincoln sent a servant: Frank L. Klement, "The Ten Who Sat in the Front Row on the Platform During the Dedication of the Soldiers' Cemetery at Gettysburg," *Lincoln Herald* 88 (Winter 1985), p. 108.
584 A telegram arrived . . . Tad was better: EMS to AL, November 18 and 19, 1863, Lincoln Papers.
584 the crowd surged over . . . "part of the human race": WHS, quoted in Seward, *Seward at Washington . . . 1861–1872*, p. 201 (quote); *NYT*, November 21, 1863.
584 the convivial secretary . . . "men of this generation": Entry for November 22, 1863, in French, *Witness to the Young Republic*, p. 434.
584 He wanted to talk . . . and retiring: Klement, "The Ten Who Sat," *Lincoln Herald* (1985), p. 108; Wills, *Lincoln at Gettysburg*, p. 31; entry for November 22, 1863, in French, *Witness to the Young Republic*, p. 434.
584 The huge, boisterous crowd . . . "thousand more": Entry for November 22, 1863, in French, *Witness to the Young Republic*, p. 434.
584 made his final revisions: Nicolay, "Lincoln's Gettysburg Address," *Century* (1894), pp. 601, 602.
584 a chestnut horse . . . three cabinet officers: Sandburg, *Abraham Lincoln: The War Years*, Vol. II, p. 466.
585 Seward, riding . . . "homemade gray socks": Henry Clay Cochrane, quoted in ibid.
585 An audience . . . between Everett and Seward: Klement, "The Ten Who Sat," *Lincoln Herald* (1985), p. 106.
585 "leaned from one side . . . of his right hand": Gitt, quoted in Wilson, *Intimate Memories of Lincoln*, p. 478.
585 Another member . . . to his pocket: Monaghan, *Diplomat in Carpet Slippers*, p. 341.
585 "could not be surpassed by mortal man": Entry for November 22, 1863, in French, *Witness to the Young Republic*, p. 435.
585 "Seldom has a man . . . not like an orator": Klement, "The Ten Who Sat," *Lincoln Herald* (1985), p. 108.
585 "flutter and motion . . . an empty house": Gitt, quoted in Wilson, *Intimate Memories of Lincoln*, p. 478.
585 steel-rimmed spectacles . . . at his pages: Sandburg, *Abraham Lincoln: The War Years*, Vol. II, p. 468.
585 "He had spent . . . supreme principle": Wills, *Lincoln at Gettysburg*, p. 120.
585 "all this quibbling . . . created equal": AL, "Speech at Chicago, Illinois," July 10, 1858, in *CW*, II, p. 501.
585 "the central idea . . . govern themselves": AL, quoted in "7 May 1861, Tuesday," in Hay, *Inside Lincoln's White House*, p. 20.
586 "Four score and seven . . . shall not perish from the earth": AL, "Address Delivered at the Dedication of the Cemetery at Gettysburg, November 19, 1863; Edward Everett Copy," in *CW*, VII, p. 21.
586 "the assemblage . . . there came applause": Gitt, quoted in Wilson, *Intimate Memories of Lincoln*, p. 479.
586 he turned to Ward Lamon . . . "disappointed": Lamon, *Recollections of Abraham Lincoln*, p. 173.
586 "I should be glad . . . in two minutes": Edward Everett to AL, November 20, 1863, Lincoln Papers.
587 Zachariah Chandler . . . tardiness on emancipation: Bruce Tap, "Chandler, Zachariah," in *Encyclopedia of the American Civil War*, ed. Heidler and Heidler, pp. 398–99.
587 "Your president . . . & hold him": Zachariah Chandler to Lyman Trumbull, quoted in Williams, *Lincoln and the Radicals*, p. 179.
587 Having read in the press . . . "buried three days": Zachariah Chandler to AL, November 15, 1863, Lincoln Papers.
587 "My dear Sir . . . wreck the country's cause": AL to Zachariah Chandler, November 20, 1863, in *CW*, VII, pp. 23–24.
588 a mild case of smallpox: Entry for December 2, 1863, in French, *Witness to the Young Republic*, p. 439; entry for December 1863, *Welles diary*, Vol. I (1960 edn.), p. 480.
588 "Yes, it is a bad . . . that calls": *NYT*, December 18, 1863.
588 "the greatest question . . . practical statesmanship": "31 July 1863, Friday," in Hay, *Inside Lincoln's White House*, p. 69.
588 everyone assumed . . . of his divided party: Brooks, *Mr. Lincoln's Washington*, p. 271.
588 John Hay was present . . . "highly satisfactory": "[9 December 1863, Wednesday]," in Hay, *Inside Lincoln's White House*, pp. 121–22.
588 Radicals were thrilled . . . "acts of Congress": AL, "Annual Message to Congress," December 8, 1863, in *CW*, VII, p. 51.
588 "He makes Emancipation . . . of reconstruction": CS to Orestes A. Brownson, December 27, 1863, in *Selected Letters of Charles Sumner*, Vol. II, p. 216.
588 "God bless Old Abe . . . in the President": "[9 December 1863, Wednesday]," in Hay, *Inside Lincoln's White House*, p. 122.
588 had written a letter to Nathaniel Banks . . . "included in the plan": AL to Nathaniel P. Banks, in *CW*, VI, p. 365.
589 He offered full pardons . . . remain as they were: AL, "Proclamation of Amnesty and Reconstruction," December 8, 1863, in *CW*, VII, pp. 54–56.

589 Conservatives hailed . . . as it wished: EBL to SPL, December 8, 1863, in *Wartime Washington*, ed. Laas, p. 325.
589 "theory is identical . . . different nomenclature": CS to Orestes A. Brownson, December 27, 1863, in *Selected Letters of Charles Sumner*, Vol. II, pp. 216–17.
589 Lincoln assured . . . "otherwise would": AL, "Annual Message to Congress," December 8, 1863, in *CW*, VII, p. 52.
589 would devastate Confederate morale: Foner, *Reconstruction*, pp. 36–37.
589 When the Blairs . . . "of modern times": Brooks, *Mr. Lincoln's Washington*, p. 273.
589 "is the great man . . . clearly than anybody": "[9 December 1863, Wednesday]," in Hay, *Inside Lincoln's White House*, p. 122.
589 Judd called . . . "was Mr. Chase": Norman Judd and AL, quoted in "[9 December 1863, Wednesday]," in Hay, *Inside Lincoln's White House*, p. 124.
590 Chase had obstinately . . . perpetuate emancipation: SPC to AL, November 25, 1863, Lincoln Papers.
590 "more positive . . . is not to be had": SPC to Henry Ward Beecher, December 26, 1863, reel 30, Chase Papers.
590 he detected a more hopeful . . . surprisingly well: AL, "Annual Message to Congress," December 8, 1863, in *CW*, VII, pp. 49–50.
590 invited his sister-in-law . . . "and left him alone": David Davis, quoted in *Daily Picayune*, New Orleans, March 14, 1897.
590 Emilie had been living . . . through Union lines: Helm, *The True Story of Mary*, p. 220.
590 "I am totally at a loss . . . secure a pass?": John L. Helm to Mrs. Robert S. Todd, October 11, 1863, quoted in ibid., p. 219.
591 Lincoln personally issued . . . "to Kentucky": AL to Lyman B. Todd, October 15, 1863, in *CW*, VII, p. 517.
591 When Emilie arrived . . . explaining the dilemma: Helm, *The True Story of Mary*, pp. 220–21.
591 "Send her to me": AL, quoted in ibid., p. 221.
591 was received at the White House . . . Confederate Army: Emilie Todd Helm diary [hereafter Helm diary], quoted in ibid., pp. 221–22.
591 "Often the boundaries . . . chose sides": John W. Shaffer, *Clash of Loyalties: A Border County in the Civil War* (Morgantown: West Virginia University Press, 2003), p. 2.
591 they carefully avoided mention . . . "into other channels": Helm diary, quoted in Helm, *The True Story of Mary*, p. 224.
591 Mary did her utmost: Helm diary, quoted in ibid., pp. 222–23.
591 "He comes to me . . . most of the time": MTL, quoted in Helm diary, in ibid., p. 227.
592 "the scape-goat . . . thrill in her voice": MTL, quoted in Helm diary, in ibid., pp. 225, 227.
592 he confided her presence . . . "it known": Entry for December 14, 1863, in Browning, *The Diary of Orville Hickman Browning*, Vol. I, p. 651.
592 invited Emilie to join them: Helm, *The True Story of Mary*, p. 228.
592 Lincoln had personally . . . restore his spirits: Edgcumb Pinchon, *Dan Sickles: Hero of Gettysburg and "Yankee King of Spain"* (Garden City, N.Y.: Doubleday, Doran & Co., 1945), pp. 203–04.
592 Mary also considered . . . merriment: MTL to Sally Orne, [December 12, 1869], in Turner and Turner, *Mary Todd Lincoln*, pp. 533–34.
592 Senator Harris turned . . . "and Manassas": Helm diary, quoted in Helm, *The True Story of Mary*, p. 229.
592 Mary's face "turned . . . assistance in the matter": Helm diary, quoted in ibid., pp. 227, 229–31.
593 prompted Emilie to leave: Helm diary, quoted in ibid., p. 231.
593 "Oh, Emilie . . . hideous nightmare?": MTL, quoted in Helm diary, ibid., p. 226.
593 he took Nicolay and Hay . . . about the play: "[18 December 1863]," in Hay, *Inside Lincoln's White House*, p. 128; *Daily Morning Chronicle*, Washington, D.C., December 19, 1863.
593 "in fine spirits": Entry for December 15, 1863, *Welles diary*, Vol. I (1960 edn.), p. 485.
593 returned to Ford's . . . Bayard Taylor: "[18 December 1863]," in Hay, *Inside Lincoln's White House*, p. 128; *Daily Morning Chronicle*, Washington, D.C., December 18 and 19, 1863.
593 a peculiarly pleasant dream . . . the next day: "23 December 1863," in Hay, *Inside Lincoln's White House*, p. 132.
593 Seward entertained . . . "cloud of smoke": Seward, *Seward at Washington . . . 1861–1872*, p. 206.
593 Bates's children: See introduction, entries for May 28; June 5 and 20; July 1; November 15, 22, 25, and 30; December 16, 19 and 22, 1863, *The Diary of Edward Bates, 1859–1866*, pp. xv–xvi, 294, 295, 299, 315, 319, 320–21, 323.
594 After forty years . . . word against him: Entry for September 4, 1863, in *The Diary of Edward Bates, 1859–1866*, p. 306.
594 he attended a funeral . . . "and die soon": Entry for December 25, 1863, in ibid., p. 324.
594 Edgar's return . . . "on earth forever": Entry for December 25, 1863, *Welles diary*, Vol. I (1960 edn.), p. 494.
594 "The year closes . . . the future than now": Entry for December 31, 1863, ibid., pp. 499–500.
594 the birth of a new baby girl . . . baptismal celebration: EMS to SPC, December 30, 1863, reel 30, Chase Papers.
594 He shared with the men . . . "guests of the nation": *NYT*, December 29, 1863.
594 Lincoln invited Stanton . . . Point Lookout: AL to EMS, December 26, 1863, in *CW*, VII, p. 95 (quote); *NYTrib*, December 29, 1863.
594 He had heard that . . . Confederate strongholds: Thomas and Hyman, *Stanton*, p. 309; "28 December 1863, Monday," in Hay, *Inside Lincoln's White House*, p. 134.
595 "Oh! dying year! . . . brighter hopes dawn": Entry for December 31, 1863, in Adam Gurowski, *Diary: 1863–'64–'65*, Vol. III. Burt Franklin: Research & Source Works #229 (Washington, D.C., 1866; New York: Burt Franklin, 1968), p. 57.

595 "a tall . . . polish of appearance": Entry for February 24, 1861, Charles Francis Adams diary, reel 76.
595 "sphere of civilization": Entry for March 8, 1861, Charles Francis Adams diary, reel 76.
595 no "heroic qualities": Entry for February 21, 1861, Charles Francis Adams diary, reel 76.
595 "not equal . . . of his position": Entry for August 16, 1861, Charles Francis Adams diary, reel 76.
595 At a festive dinner . . . "to one great purpose": Charles Francis Adams, quoted in *NR*, February 2, 1864.
595 "foremost American . . . in his time": "Lowell, James Russell," in *Dictionary of American Biography*, Vol. VI, ed. Dumas Malone (New York: Charles Scribner's Sons, 1933), p. 458.
595 "Never did a President . . . still in wild water": James Russell Lowell, "The President's Policy," *North American Review* 98 (January 1864), pp. 241–43, 249, 254–55.
596 "very excellent . . . over-much credit": Entry for January 5, 1864, *Welles diary*, Vol. I (1960 edn.), p. 504.

CHAPTER 23: *"THERE'S A MAN IN IT!"*

Page

597 New Year's Day . . . scattered the clouds: Brooks, *Mr. Lincoln's Washington*, pp. 273–74 (quote); *Star*, January 1, 1864; *NR*, January 2, 1864.
597 "Murfreesboro . . . excel these": *NR*, January 1, 1864.
597 "We have a right . . . weathered the gale": *NR*, January 13, 1864.
598 "The instinct of all . . . danger is over": Dispatch of January 18, 1864, in Stoddard, *Dispatches from Lincoln's White House*, p. 203.
598 the traditional New Year's reception: Entry for January 1, 1864, in *Lincoln Day by Day*, Vol. III, p. 231; dispatch of January 4, 1864, in Stoddard, *Dispatches from Lincoln's White House*, p. 199.
598 "a human kaleidescope . . . petitioners": *NR*, January 2, 1864.
598 *"public-opinion baths* . . . and duty": Carpenter, *Six Months at the White House*, pp. 281–82.
598 "European democrats . . . American a custom": Dispatch of January 4, 1864, in Stoddard, *Dispatches from Lincoln's White House*, p. 199.
598 Lincoln "appeared to be . . . word or two": *NR*, January 2, 1864.
598 Mary Lincoln "never looked better" . . . velvet dress: Brooks, *Mr. Lincoln's Washington*, pp. 274–75 (quote p. 275).
598 "We seem to have . . . cared about it": FWS, quoted in Seward, *Seward at Washington . . . 1861–1872*, p. 207.
598 The winter social calendar . . . of cabinet officers: *NR*, January 19, 1864.
599 "grace and elegance": *NR*, January 26, 1864.
599 "who with such . . . once a week": *NR*, January 16, 1864.
599 "observed of all observers": *NR*, January 2, 1864.
599 "one of the most lovable women": Entry for January 3, 1864, in French, *Witness to the Young Republic*, p. 443.
599 "frosty . . . a very close examination": Brooks, *Mr. Lincoln's Washington*, p. 275.
599 Mary found it necessary . . . "human tide": Stoddard, *Inside the White House in War Times*, p. 49; *NR*, January 2, 1864.
599 ill dressed . . . their carpetbags: *NR*, January 13, 1864.
599 "the lace curtains . . . as a man's hand": Brooks, *Mr. Lincoln's Washington*, p. 253 (quote); B. B. French to Charles R. Train, January 5, 1863, p. 181, Vol. 14, reel 7; French to John H. Rice, March 7, 1864, p. 313, Vol. 14, reel 7; French to Rice, June 16, 1864, pp. 375–76, Vol. 14, reel 7, M371, RG 42, DNA.
600 would inaugurate "the fashionable 'season' ": *NR*, January 6, 1864.
600 visiting members . . . "with their families": *NYT*, January 8, 1864.
600 "not so largely attended as usual": *NYH*, January 13, 1864.
600 she was "disappointed": Entry for January 14, 1864, in French, *Witness to the Young Republic*, p. 443.
600 The Sewards hosted . . . "most brilliant": *NR*, January 26, 1864 (first quote); *NR*, January 15, 1864 (second quote); *NYT*, January 26, 1864 (third quote); *Star*, January 26, 1864.
600 a pleasant evening . . . "relief from care": Seward, *Seward at Washington . . . 1861–1872*, p. 208.
600 Mary could not relinquish . . . and supporters: Anson G. Henry to Isaac Newton, April 21, 1864, Lincoln Papers.
600 Mary's anger . . . "a patriot": Keckley, *Behind the Scenes*, pp. 127–29 (quotes pp. 128, 129).
600 and crossed out . . . "Schleswig-Holstein difficulty": JGN to JH, January 18, 1864, in Nicolay, *With Lincoln in the White House*, p. 124.
600 directed her wrath . . . "night or two": JGN to JH, January 29, 1864, in ibid., p. 125.
601 dinner "was pleasant . . . off very well": Entry for January 22, 1864, *Welles diary*, Vol. I (1960 edn.), p. 512.
601 unable to share . . . "merry-making at a funeral": GW to Edgar T. Welles, February 14, 1864, reel 22, Welles Papers.
601 "the old secession" . . . stars of every occasion: Dispatch of February 6, 1864, in Stoddard, *Dispatches from Lincoln's White House*, pp. 206–07 (quote p. 206).
601 Ulric . . . expert waltzer: Stoddard, *Inside the White House in War Times*, p. 128.
601 Fernando Wood . . . "personal intercourse": Dispatch of February 1, 1864, in Stoddard, *Dispatches from Lincoln's White House*, p. 205.
601 Mary Lincoln sent . . . "to believe it": MTL to Daniel E. Sickles, February 6, 1864, in Turner and Turner, *Mary Todd Lincoln*, pp. 167–68; see also note 3 of MTL to Sickles.
601 when Emilie . . . Martha Todd White: See note 1 to JGN to Benjamin F. Butler, April 19, 1864, Lincoln Papers.

602 Lincoln issued a pass: On the subject of Martha Todd White's dealings with the Lincolns, see JGN to Butler, April 19, 1864; Butler to JGN, April 21, 1864, Lincoln Papers.

602 "Here . . . of your master": Undated newspaper article pasted in JGN to Butler, April 19, 1863, container 28, Butler Papers; newspaper reports of Martha Todd White's statements to General Butler, quoted in Butler to JGN, April 21, 1864, Lincoln Papers.

602 he directed Nicolay to ascertain the facts: JGN to Butler, April 19, 1863, container 28, Butler Papers.

602 Butler replied . . . untoward had been found: Butler to JGN, April 21, 1864, Lincoln Papers.

602 Nicolay used Butler's letter: JGN to Butler, April 28, 1864; JGN to Horace Greeley, April 25, 1864; Greeley to JGN, April 26, 1864, Lincoln Papers. For an example of rebuttal issued, see *NYTrib*, April 27, 1864.

602 Butler was surprised . . . so "silly": Butler to JGN, April 21, 1864, Lincoln Papers.

602 Nor did he want . . . sustain the rebel cause: O. Stewart to AL, April 27, 1864, Lincoln Papers.

602 Browning requested a favor . . . "very good humor": Entry for February 6, 1894, in Browning, *The Diary of Orville Hickman Browning*, Vol. I, p. 659.

602 he had visited . . . Owen Lovejoy: Entry for February 6, 1864, in *Lincoln Day by Day*, Vol. III, p. 238.

602 "the best friend [he] had in Congress": AL, quoted in Carpenter, *Six Months at the White House*, p. 18.

602 suffering from a debilitating liver and kidney ailment: *NYT*, March 28, 1864; Edward Magdol, *Owen Lovejoy: Abolitionist in Congress* (New Brunswick, N.J.: Rutgers University Press, 1967), pp. 400, 402–03.

602 "This war is eating . . . live to see the end": AL, quoted in Carpenter, *Six Months at the White House*, p. 17.

603 a fire alarm rang . . . his brother, Willie: Robert W. McBride, *Personal Recollections of Abraham Lincoln* (Indianapolis: Bobbs-Merrill, 1926), pp. 29–30, 44–46 (quotes pp. 44–45); *Star*, February 11, 1864; *Daily Morning Chronicle*, Washington, D.C., February 11, 1864.

603 A coachman . . . setting the fire: *Star*, February 11, 1864; JGN to JH, February 10, 1864, in Nicolay, *With Lincoln in the White House*, p. 126.

603 instructed him to consult . . . "have it rebuilt": Commissioner B. B. French to John H. Rice, February 11, 1863, pp. 295–96, Vol. 14, reel 7, M371, RG 42, DNA (quote); *Star*, February 11, 1864.

603 "carefully veiled . . . a hopeless one": McClure, *Abraham Lincoln and Men of War-Times*, p. 136.

603 Friends of Chase . . . biographical sketch: Niven, *Salmon P. Chase*, p. 358.

603 "no matter how . . . flimsy political trick": William Orton to SPC, January 6, 1864, in *Chase Papers*, Vol. IV, p. 247.

604 "malignant denunciations": SPC to AL, January 13, 1864, reel 30, Chase Papers.

604 twenty-five long letters . . . inspirational book: Chase's series of autobiographical letters to John T. Trowbridge began on December 27, 1863, and ended on March 22, 1864, see Chase Papers; [John T. Trowbridge], *The Ferry-Boy and the Financier, by a Contributor to the "Atlantic"* (Boston: Walker, Wise, & Co., 1864).

604 An excerpt appeared: J. T. Trowbridge, "The First Visit to Washington," *Atlantic Monthly* 13 (April 1864), pp. 448–57.

604 "So far . . . otherwise than I have": SPC to J. W. Hartwell, February 2, 1864, reel 31, Chase Papers.

604 "I think of you . . . you are—where?": SPC to Charlotte S. Eastman, February 1, 1864, reel 31, Chase Papers.

604 Susan Walker . . . "bluestocking": Niven, *Salmon P. Chase*, pp. 97 (quote), 203–04.

604 "*I wish* you could come . . . you enough": SPC to Susan Walker, January 23, 1864, reel 31, Chase Papers.

605 the public announcement . . . held a large interest: Niven, *Salmon P. Chase*, pp. 357, 359–60; Blue, *Salmon P. Chase*, p. 222.

605 "eating a man's bread . . . the same time": David Davis, quoted in King, *Lincoln's Manager*, p. 213.

605 Chase busied himself lining up support: Hart, *Salmon P. Chase*, pp. 309–10.

605 "gratified . . . should he be reelected": SPC to Flamen Ball, February 2, 1864, reel 31, Chase Papers.

605 "lamented the . . . distinct feeler": Entry for February 3, 1864, *Welles diary*, Vol. I (1960 edn.), pp. 520–21.

605 "immeasurably" . . . to any other candidate: Entry for March 22, 1864, in *The Diary of Edward Bates, 1859–1866*, p. 350.

606 "fair plump lady . . . altogether the advantage": Entry for February 19, 1864, *Welles diary*, Vol. I (1960 edn.), p. 528.

606 the Pomeroy Committee . . . "available candidate": "The Pomeroy Circular," quoted in Schuckers, *The Life and Public Services of Salmon Portland Chase*, pp. 499–500.

606 Pomeroy circular was leaked to the press: J. M. Winchell, quoted in *NYT*, September 15, 1874.

606 "No sensible man . . . if it killed me": David Davis, quoted in King, *Lincoln's Manager*, p. 215.

606 "had no knowledge . . . entire confidence": SPC to AL, February 22, 1864, Lincoln Papers.

606 the circular's author . . . "would sustain": J. M. Winchell, quoted in *NYT*, September 15, 1874.

607 He understood the political . . . "*enemies*": Entry for February 13, 1864, in *The Diary of Edward Bates, 1859–1866*, p. 333.

607 acknowledged receipt . . . "time to do so": AL to SPC, February 23, 1864, reel 31, Chase Papers.

607 "Its recoil . . . than Lincoln": Entry for February 22, 1864, *Welles diary*, Vol. I (1960 edn.), p. 529.

607 "It is unworthy . . . of this movement": *NYT*, February 24, 1864.

607 the effect of the circular . . . Chase's prospects: JGN to TB, February 28, 1864, container 3, Nicolay Papers.

607 In state after state . . . Lincoln's renomination: *NYT*, February 24, 1864; Fitz Henry Warren to TW, March 25, 1864, Lincoln Papers.

607 Pomeroy's home state . . . support for Lincoln: W. W. H. Lawrence to Abel C. Wilder and James H. Lane, February 15, 1864, Lincoln Papers.

607 the "long list . . . degree with Abraham Lincoln": *NYT*, February 29, 1864.

607 *Harper's Weekly* . . . "had been blinded": *Harper's Weekly*, March 5, 1864, p. 146.

608 "The masses . . . earnest and honest": Entry for January 3, 1864, in Gurowski, *Diary: 1863–'64–'65*, p. 60.

608 The fatal blow: Niven, *Salmon P. Chase*, p. 361.

608 "brought matters . . . of the gravest character": Richard C. Parsons to SPC, March 2, 1864, reel 32, Chase Papers.

608 to answer Chase's . . . "occasion for a change": AL to SPC, February 29, 1864, reel 31, Chase Papers.

608 In a public letter . . . "given to my name": SPC to James C. Hall, March 5, 1864, reel 32, Chase Papers.

608 Chase told his daughter . . . "welfare of the country": SPC to Janet Chase Hoyt, March 15, 1864, reel 32, Chase Papers.

609 "It proves only . . . openly resisted": Entry for March 9, 1864, in *The Diary of Edward Bates, 1859–1866*, p. 345.

609 Leonard Grover estimated . . . "a hundred times": Leonard Grover, "Lincoln's Interest in the Theater," *Century* 77 (April 1909), p. 944.

609 "It gave him . . . seen by the audience": Noah Brooks, "Personal Reminiscences of Lincoln," *Scribners Monthly* 15 (March 1878), p. 675.

609 "the drama . . . entire relief": Stoddard, *Inside the White House in War Times*, p. 191.

609 At a performance . . . "Hal's time": Ibid., p. 107.

610 developments with gaslight . . . onto the stage: Mary C. Henderson, "Scenography, Stagecraft, and Architecture in the American Theatre: Beginnings to 1870," in Don Wilmeth and Christopher Bigsby, eds., *The Cambridge History of American Theatre*. Vol. I: *Beginnings to 1870* (New York: Cambridge University Press, 1998), p. 415.

610 "To envision nineteenth-century . . . intimate space: Levine, *Highbrow / Lowbrow*, pp. 26, 24–25.

610 Frances Trollope complained . . . "and whiskey": Trollope, *Domestic Manners of the Americans*, p. 102.

610 The years surrounding . . . Charlotte Cushman: Garff B. Wilson, *Three Hundred Years of American Drama and Theatre: From Ye Bear and Ye Cubb to Hair* (Englewood Cliffs, N.J.: Prentice-Hall, 1973), p. 144.

610 "she was not . . . vitality of her presence": *NYTrib*, February 19, 1876.

610 Seward and Miss Cushman . . . at the Seward home: Van Deusen, *William Henry Seward*, p. 338.

611 a close relationship with young Fanny: See Fanny Seward diary, Seward Papers; FAS to CS, June 10, 1858, reel 17, Sumner Papers.

611 "Imagine me . . . use in the world": FS to FAS, February 11, 1864, reel 116, Seward Papers.

611 "the greatest man" . . . outside their family: Charlotte Cushman, quoted in entry for October 14, 1864, Fanny Seward diary, Seward Papers.

611 Lincoln made his way . . . purpose of her visit: Charlotte Cushman to [WHS], July 9, 1861, Lincoln Papers.

611 "Perhaps the best . . . at criticism": AL to James H. Hackett, August 17, 1863, in *CW*, VI, p. 392.

611 Hackett shared . . . "without much malice": On the dissemination of Lincoln's letter to Hackett, see note 1 to AL to James H. Hackett, August 17, 1863, in ibid., p. 393; James H. Hackett to AL, October 22, 1863, Lincoln Papers; AL to James H. Hackett, November 2, 1863, in *CW*, VI, pp. 558–59 (quote p. 558).

612 recalled bringing . . . "pleasant interval" from his work: William Kelley, in *Reminiscences of Abraham Lincoln*, ed. Rice (1886 edn.), pp. 264–67, 270.

612 "Edwin Booth has done . . . any other man": Lucia Gilbert Calhoun, "Edwin Booth," *Galaxy* 7 (January 1869), p. 85.

612 captivated audiences . . . generation: Richard Lockridge, *Darling of Misfortune: Edwin Booth, 1833–1893* (New York: Century Co., 1932; New York: Benjamin Blom, 1971), pp. 14, 24, 38–39, 56, 78–79, 81; *Harper's New Monthly Magazine* 22 (April 1861), p. 702; E. C. Stedman, "Edwin Booth," *Atlantic Monthly* 17 (May 1866), p. 589.

612 Lincoln and Seward attended . . . *Merchant of Venice*: Entries for February 19, 25, 26; March 2, 4, and 10, 1864, in *Lincoln Day by Day*, Vol. III, pp. 241–45; *NR*, March 3, 5, and 10, 1864; Grover, "Lincoln's Interest in the Theater," *Century* (1909), p. 946.

612 Booth came to dinner . . . "want of body in wine": Entry for March 1864, Fanny Seward diary, Seward Papers.

613 anticipating Booth's Hamlet . . . "upon the stage": Carpenter, *Six Months at the White House*, pp. 49–51 (quote p. 51).

613 "laugh . . . ' "Midsummer Night's Dream" ' ": Ibid., p. 150.

613 Chase and Bates considered . . . "Satanic diversion": Hendrick, *Lincoln's War Cabinet*, p. 10.

613 Stanton came only once . . . Tad loved the theater: Grover, "Lincoln's Interest in the Theater," *Century* (1909), pp. 946, 944–45.

614 Tad would laugh . . . "seeing clearly why": "24 April 1864, Sunday," in Hay, *Inside Lincoln's White House*, p. 188.

614 "felt at home" . . . actually appeared in a play: Grover, "Lincoln's Interest in the Theater," *Century* (1909), p. 945.

614 who broke down in tears . . . and the Taft boys: Bayne, *Tad Lincoln's Father*, p. 201.

614 arrived in the nation's capital: Brooks, *Mr. Lincoln's Washington*, p. 290.

614 Congress had revived . . . the Western armies: Smith, *Grant*, pp. 284, 286, 293, 294.

614 He walked into the Willard . . . the accommodations: Smith, *Grant*, p. 289; Brooks D. Simpson, *Ulysses S. Grant: Triumph Over Adversity, 1822–1865* (Boston and New York: Houghton Mifflin, 2000), pp. 258–59.

614 Grant took his son . . . and took a bow: Brooks, *Mr. Lincoln's Washington*, p. 290 (quotes); Smith, *Grant*, p. 289.

614 walked over to the White House . . . "a tone of familiarity": Horace Porter, *Campaigning with Grant* (New York: Century Co., 1897; New York: Konecky & Konecky, 1992), pp. 18–19.

615 "a degree of awkwardness": Entry for March 9, 1864, *Welles diary*, Vol. I (1960 edn.), p. 538.

615 Lincoln referred him to Seward: Smith, *Grant*, pp. 289–90; entry for March 9, 1864, *Welles diary*, Vol. I (1960 edn.), pp. 538–39.

615 "laces were torn . . . much mixed": Brooks, *Mr. Lincoln's Washington*, p. 290.

615 Seward rapidly maneuvered . . . see his face: Carpenter, *Six Months at the White House*, p. 56.

615 "He blushed . . . and over his face": *NYH*, March 12, 1864.

615 "his warmest campaign during the war": Carpenter, *Six Months at the White House*, p. 56.

615 The president . . . "walk it abreast": Porter, *Campaigning with Grant*, p. 20.
615 Grant wanted nothing more . . . "presidential chair": J. Russell Jones recollections, quoted in Tarbell, *Life of Abraham Lincoln*, Vol. II (1917 edn.), pp. 187–88.
615 made their way back . . . Grant wrote out his statement: Smith, *Grant*, p. 290; Memorandum, March 9, 1864, container 3, Nicolay Papers.
616 "quite embarrassed . . . difficult to read": Memorandum, March 9, 1864, container 3, Nicolay Papers.
616 went upstairs to talk . . . assistance was needed: Grant, *Personal Memoirs of U.S. Grant*, p. 370.
616 Grant journeyed . . . " 'show' business!": Carpenter, *Six Months at the White House*, p. 57.
616 "trappings and . . . canopy of heaven": Elihu Washburne, quoted in Blaine, *Twenty Years of Congress*, p. 510.
616 his preference for pork . . . "in spasms": *NYT*, March 31, 1864.
616 "was done exactly . . . into history": McFeely, *Grant*, p. 152.
617 "unusually backward" . . . end of the month: Entry for May 1, 1864, in *The Diary of Edward Bates, 1859–1866*, p. 363.
617 "stormy and inclement . . . of the Old Dominion": Dispatch of April 11, 1864, in Stoddard, *Dispatches from Lincoln's White House*, p. 219.
617 "the toughest snowstorm . . . ever I saw him": Entry for March 23, 1864, in French, *Witness to the Young Republic*, p. 447.
617 "as pleasant and funny" . . . Saturday levee: Benjamin B. French to Pamela Prentiss French, April 10, 1864, transcription, reel 10, French Family Papers, DLC.
617 he strolled into John Hay's room . . ." 'is of me' ": "24 April 1864, Sunday," in Hay, *Inside Lincoln's White House*, p. 188.
617 "a beleaguered nation . . . was never bright": J. G. Randall, *The Civil War and Reconstruction* (1937; Boston: D. C. Heath & Co., 1953), pp. 670, 347.
617 "real suffering . . . in the social scale": *NYT*, July 7, 1864.
617 Food riots had broken out . . . vandalized: Randall, *The Civil War and Reconstruction*, p. 670; Emory M. Thomas, *The Confederate Nation, 1861–1865*. New American Nation Series (New York: Harper & Row, 1979), pp. 199–206.
617 Davis's health gradually . . . isolated himself: Davis, *Jefferson Davis*, pp. 539–40, 551–53.
618 The "tramp" of his feet: Entry for May 8, 1864, in Mary Chesnut, *Mary Chesnut's Civil War*, ed. C. Vann Woodward (New Haven: Yale University Press, 1981), p. 601.
618 Washington was filled . . . were imminent: Dispatch of May 2, 1864, in Stoddard, *Dispatches from Lincoln's White House*, p. 223.
618 "beginning to feel . . . generally been failures": JGN to TB, May 1, 1864, container 3, Nicolay Papers.
618 Lincoln wrote him a letter . . . "dignity at once": "30 April 1864, Saturday," in Hay, *Inside Lincoln's White House*, p. 192.
618 "entire satisfaction . . . power to give": AL to USG, April 30, 1864, in *CW*, VII, p. 324.
618 "been astonished . . . fault is not with you": USG to AL, May 1, 1864, Lincoln Papers.
618 the Army . . . from the James River: Michael Korda, *Ulysses S. Grant: The Unlikely Hero*. Eminent Lives Series (New York: HarperCollins, 2004), p. 97.
618 "This concerted movement . . . in numbers": "30 April 1864, Saturday," in Hay, *Inside Lincoln's White House*, p. 193.
618 great "solicitude . . . great advantages": Entry for May 1, 1864, in Browning, *The Diary of Orville Hickman Browning*, Vol. I, p. 668.
619 the Wilderness: E. M. Law, "From the Wilderness to Cold Harbor," in *Battles and Leaders of the Civil War*, Vol. IV, Pt. I, p. 122; McFeely, *Grant*, p. 167; Gordon C. Rhea, *The Battle of the Wilderness, May 5–6, 1864* (Baton Rouge and London: Louisiana State University Press, 1994), pp. 27, 51, 142, 163, 178, 193.
619 climb over the dead . . . "three and four deep": *NYT*, May 15, 1864.
619 "a nightmare of inhumanity": McFeely, *Grant*, p. 165.
619 86,000 Union and Confederate casualties: Table of casualties, Noah Andre Trudeau, *Bloody Roads South: The Wilderness to Cold Harbor, May–June 1864* (Boston: Little, Brown, 1989), p. 341.
619 "The world has never seen . . . never will again": USG to Julia Dent Grant, May 13, 1864, in *The Papers of Ulysses S. Grant*. Vol. X: *January 1–May 31, 1864*, ed. John Y. Simon (Carbondale and Edwardsville: Southern Illinois University Press, 1982), p. 444.
619 "always regretted . . . was ever made": Grant, *Personal Memoirs of U. S. Grant*, p. 462.
619 as steamers reached the city . . . "torture and pain": Brooks, *Mr. Lincoln's Washington*, pp. 320, 323 (quotes).
619 Judge Taft was present . . . others limping along: Entry for May 11, 1864, Taft diary.
619 As each steamer landed . . . "and manly": Brooks, *Mr. Lincoln's Washington*, p. 323.
619 Elizabeth Blair fled . . . "for my nerves": EBL to SPL, May 30, 1864, in *Wartime Washington*, ed. Laas, p. 386.
619 "The carnage has been unexampled": Entry for May 15, 1864, in *The Diary of Edward Bates, 1859–1866*, p. 366.
619 "it seems to myself . . . battle of the war": WHS, diplomatic circular of May 16, 1864, quoted in Seward, *Seward at Washington . . . 1861–1872*, p. 219.
619 "The intense anxiety . . . for mental activity": Entry for May 17, 1864, *Welles diary*, Vol. II, p. 33.
619 "more nervous and anxious . . . and disaster": JGN to TB, May 15, 1864, container 3, Nicolay Papers.
620 nights when Lincoln did not sleep: Entry for May 7, 1864, *Welles diary*, Vol. II, p. 25.
620 "met him . . . his breast": Carpenter, *Six Months at the White House*, p. 30.
620 made time . . . an opera: Grover, "Lincoln's Interest in the Theater," *Century* (1909), p. 947; entry for May 18, 1864, in *Lincoln Day by Day*, Vol. III, p. 259; Schuyler Colfax, *Life and Principles of Abraham Lincoln* (Philadelphia: Jas. B. Rodgers, 1865), p. 12.

860 NOTES

620 "People may think . . . it will kill me": AL, quoted in Colfax, *Life and Principles of Abraham Lincoln*, p. 12.

620 "I saw [Lincoln] walk . . . and anxious scrutiny": Colfax in *Reminiscences of Abraham Lincoln*, ed. Rice (1886 edn.), pp. 337–38.

620 "any other General . . . that wins": "9 May 1864, Monday," in Hay, *Inside Lincoln's White House*, p. 195.

620 Lincoln hugged and kissed . . . "no turning back": Henry E. Wing, *When Lincoln Kissed Me: A Story of the Wilderness Campaign* (New York: Eaton & Mains, and Cincinnati: Jennings & Graham, 1913), pp. 12–13, 38–39.

620 "I propose to fight it out . . . all summer": USG to EMS, May 11, 1864, in *Papers of Ulysses S. Grant*, Vol. X, p. 422.

620 Lincoln's face lit up . . . "the secret" to the army's fortunes: *NYT*, May 18, 1864.

621 Chase grew restless . . . retained the hope: Niven, *Salmon P. Chase*, p. 364.

621 Weed had repeatedly warned . . . Treasury employees: JGN to AL, March 30, 1864; TW to AL, March 25, 1864; W. W. Williams to TW, March 25, 1864, Lincoln Papers.

621 corrupt Treasury agents . . . "inevitably sink": TW to FWS, June 2, 1864, reel 84, Seward Papers.

621 Frank Blair had resigned . . . Treasury agent: Leonard B. Wurthman, Jr., "Frank Blair: Lincoln's Congressional Spokesman," *Missouri Historical Review* LXIV (April 1970), pp. 278–79, 284–86; "Charges Against a Member," April 23, 1864, *Congressional Globe*, 38th Cong., 1st sess., pp. 1827–29; Parrish, *Frank Blair*, p. 192.

621 he began by calmly . . . for the presidency: FB remarks before the House of Representatives, April 23, 1864, *Congressional Globe*, 38th Cong., 1st sess., pp. 1828–32 (quote p. 1829).

622 Elizabeth Blair . . . "revenge is suicide": EBL to SPL, April 23 and June 13, 1864, in *Wartime Washington*, ed. Laas, pp. 369, 392.

622 "mendacious slanders": Thomas Heaton to SPC, April 29, 1864, reel 33, Chase Papers.

622 "violent and injudicious . . . with discretion": Entry for April 28, 1864, *Welles diary*, Vol. II, p. 20.

622 told about the speech . . . "approval of the President": Riddle, *Recollection of War Times*, pp. 267, 268.

622 He considered Frank Blair . . . "did while here": James A. Garfield to J. Harrison Rhodes, April 28, 1864, quoted in Smith, *The Life and Letters of James Abram Garfield*, Vol. I, p. 376.

622 Chase told Riddle . . . "perfectly satisfied": Riddle, *Recollection of War Times*, pp. 268, 270–76.

623 "in the midst . . . actual din of battle": Brooks, *Mr. Lincoln's Washington*, p. 325.

623 the National Union Convention: Ibid., pp. 332–33. According to Brooks, twenty-three states "were represented without contest," and the contested delegations of Missouri and Tennessee were allowed to vote. Unofficial representatives from Confederate states and the territories attended but were not included on the official roll.

623 David Davis . . . "no one is necessary": David Davis to AL, June 2, 1864, Lincoln Papers.

624 Horace Greeley . . . "so heavy investments": Horace Greeley, quoted in *Conversations with Lincoln*, ed. Segal, pp. 320–21.

624 "popular instinct . . . the popular will": William Dennison, et al., to AL, June 14, 1864, Lincoln Papers.

624 "the country at large . . . but Lincoln's": Brooks, *Washington, D.C., in Lincoln's Time*, p. 140.

624 gathered in Cleveland's: Waugh, *Reelecting Lincoln*, pp. 177–80.

624 with a platform . . . "among the soldiers": Resolutions of the "Radical Democracy" party platform, quoted in *NYT*, June 1, 1864.

624 in the telegraph office . . . "four hundred men": Bates, *Lincoln in the Telegraph Office*, pp. 194–95 (quote p. 195).

624 "renomination . . . the odd bits of gossip": Brooks, *Washington, D.C., in Lincoln's Time*, p. 141.

625 was initially confronted . . . "short-haired women": Clark E. Carr, quoted in Waugh, *Reelecting Lincoln*, p. 192.

625 the radicals had tacitly . . . unanimous: Ibid., pp. 195, 196.

625 the tumultuous applause . . . "defense of their country": "Platform of the Union National Convention," quoted in note 1 of AL, "Reply to the Committee Notifying Lincoln of His Renomination," June 9, 1864, in *CW*, VII, pp. 381–82.

625 "The enthusiasm . . . Lincoln was spoken": Brooks, *Mr. Lincoln's Washington*, p. 335.

625 "a purge of any" . . . platform in full: Sixth plank of Union Convention platform, paraphrased in Waugh, *Reelecting Lincoln*, p. 193.

625 "Harmony was . . . their kerchiefs": *NR*, June 9, 1864.

625 his towering presence . . . allotted to a single state: Waugh, *Reelecting Lincoln*, pp. 199–200; Brooks, *Mr. Lincoln's Washington*, p. 326.

626 Weed had initially supported . . . the victorious Johnson: Thomas, *Abraham Lincoln*, p. 429.

626 "Stanton's theory . . . the United States": Albert E. H. Johnson, quoted in *New York Evening Post*, July 13, 1891.

626 a clerk handed him a dispatch . . . "a President?": AL, quoted in Carpenter, *Six Months at the White House*, p. 163.

626 "the cart before the horse": *NR*, June 9, 1864.

626 The embarrassed operator . . . "on my return": AL, quoted in Carpenter, *Six Months at the White House*, p. 163.

626 a committee appointed . . . of his nomination: Ibid., p. 166; entry for June 9, 1864, in *Lincoln Day by Day*, Vol. III, p. 263.

626 did not assume . . . " 'when crossing streams' ": AL, "Reply to Delegation from the National Union League," June 9, 1864, in *CW*, VII, pp. 383–84 (quote p. 384).

626 the Ohio delegation . . . "under his command": AL, "Response to a Serenade by the Ohio Delegation," June 9, 1864, in ibid., p. 384.

626 "nothing could defeat . . . like to die of": *NYT*, June 13, 1864.

CHAPTER 24: "ATLANTA IS OURS"

Page

627 "Our troops have . . . but little": Entry for June 20, 1864, *Welles diary*, Vol. II, pp. 54–55.

627 "The immense slaughter . . . sickens us all": Entry for June 2, 1864, ibid., p. 44.

627 "steady courage": Dispatch of June 6, 1864, in Stoddard, *Dispatches from Lincoln's White House*, p. 234.

628 nearly lost his life at Cold Harbor: Janet W. Seward, "Personal Experiences of the Civil War," Seward Papers, NRU.

628 "I cannot yet . . . a holy cause": FAS to William H. Seward, Jr., May 20, 1864, reel 115, Seward Papers.

628 a "righteous" conflict . . . Mexican War: FAS to Augustus Seward, May 15, 1864, reel 115, Seward Papers.

628 "so nervous . . . all night with terror": EBL to SPL, June 19, [1864], in *Wartime Washington*, ed. Laas, p. 394.

628 "grave & anxious": EBL to SPL, June 21, 1864, in ibid., p. 395.

628 if Frank were taken . . . "are politically": EBL to SPL, June 22, 1864, in note 2 of EBL to SPL, June 21, 1864, in ibid., p. 396.

628 Welles was pained . . . "unfit for any labor": Entry for July 20, 1864, *Welles diary*, Vol. II, p. 82.

628 the Great Central Fair in Philadelphia: William Thompson, "Sanitary Fairs of the Civil War," *Civil War History* 4 (March 1958), p. 60; *NR*, June 16, 1864.

628 "miracles as many . . . world of magic": Unknown observer, quoted in Thompson, "Sanitary Fairs of the Civil War," *CWH* 4 (1958), p. 60.

628 Lincoln, Mary, and Tad left: Entry for June 16, 1864, in *Lincoln Day by Day*, Vol. III, p. 265.

628 they were escorted . . . "in Philadelphia": *NR*, June 16 and 17, 1864 (quote June 17).

629 "War, at the best . . . until that time": AL, "Speech at Great Central Sanitary Fair, Philadelphia, Pennsylvania," June 16, 1864, in *CW*, VII, pp. 394, 395.

629 his own "intense anxiety . . . his post here": Entry for June 20, 1864, *Welles diary*, Vol. II, p. 55.

629 Accompanied by Tad . . . of June 20: Entry for June 20, 1864, in *Lincoln Day by Day*, Vol. III, p. 266.

629 "came down from . . . all who met him": Porter, *Campaigning with Grant*, pp. 217, 218.

629 "plain and substantial . . . hero of Vicksburg": *NYH*, June 25, 1864.

629 Lincoln conversed . . . "three capital jokes": Sylvanus Cadwallader, *Three Years with Grant: As Recalled by War Correspondent Sylvanus Cadwallader*, ed. Benjamin P. Thomas (New York: Alfred A. Knopf, 1956), p. 232.

629 Grant suggested a ride . . . "met him on all sides": Porter, *Campaigning with Grant*, p. 218 (quote); *NR*, June 24, 1864.

630 "a long and lingering look": *NYH*, June 25, 1864.

630 passed a brigade . . . "spontaneous outburst": Cadwallader, *Three Years with Grant*, p. 233.

630 "and his voice . . . if he had inherited it": Porter, *Campaigning with Grant*, pp. 222–23.

630 General Grant took Lincoln aside . . . "but I will go in": USG, quoted in entry for June 26, 1864, in Browning, *The Diary of Orville Hickman Browning*, Vol. I, p. 673.

630 "sunburnt and . . . position and good spirits": "23 June 1864, Thursday," in Hay, *Inside Lincoln's White House*, p. 210.

630 regular Friday cabinet meeting . . . "the General and army": Entry for June 24, 1864, *Welles diary*, Vol. II, p. 58.

631 project his own renewed hope . . . "as a commander": *NYTrib*, June 25, 1864.

631 "of the condition . . . terms of confidence": *Philadelphia Inquirer*, June 25, 1864.

631 "Having hope . . . your goals": Daniel Goleman, *Emotional Intelligence* (New York: Bantam Books, 1995), p. 87. Goleman quotes C. R. Snyder in the third quote.

631 "We are today . . . within a year": Brooks, *Mr. Lincoln's Washington*, p. 343.

631 John Cisco . . . own presidential hopes: John G. Nicolay and John Hay, *Abraham Lincoln: A History*, Vol. IX (New York: Century Co., 1917), p. 91.

631 Lincoln told Chase . . . for Maunsell Field: SPC to AL, June 27, 1864, Lincoln Papers.

631 Field was serving . . . "executive character": Chittenden, *Recollections of President Lincoln* (1901 edn.), pp. 371, 374.

632 Chase awoke the morning after . . . to the Ephesians: Entry for June 28, 1864, in *Chase Papers*, Vol. I, pp. 465–66.

632 "Stand therefore . . . righteousness": Ephesians 6:14.

632 "I can not" . . . on another nominee: AL to SPC, June 28, 1864, in *CW*, VII, pp. 412–13.

632 Chase wrote an immediate request: SPC to AL, June 28, 1864, Lincoln Papers.

632 He telegraphed Cisco . . . three months: SPC to John J. Cisco, June 28, 1864, reel 34, Chase Papers; entry for June 28, 1864, in *Chase Papers*, Vol. I, p. 467.

632 "The difficulty . . . open revolt": AL to SPC, June 28, 1864, in *CW*, VII, pp. 413–14.

632 He began his letter . . . "my resignation": John J. Cisco to SPC, June 28, 1864; SPC to AL, June 29, 1864, Lincoln Papers.

633 "I opened it . . . I did not long reflect": AL, quoted in Field, *Memories of Many Men*, pp. 301–02.

633 "You have been acting . . . I will go": "30 June 1864, Thursday," in Hay, *Inside Lincoln's White House*, p. 213.

633 "Your resignation . . . with the public service": AL to SPC, June 30, 1864, in *CW*, VII, p. 419.

633 Lincoln called John Hay . . . the opening prayer: "30 June 1864, Thursday," in Hay, *Inside Lincoln's White House*, p. 212.

633 Lincoln's penitent request . . . he was needed: Field, *Memories of Many Men*, p. 303.

633 After breakfast . . . it had been accepted: *Chase Papers*, Vol. I, pp. 469–70 (quotes p. 470).

634 spoke of "mutual embarrassment": AL to SPC, June 30, 1864, in *CW*, VII, p. 419.

634 "I had found . . . fitness of selection": Entry for June 30, 1864, in *Chase Papers*, Vol. I, p. 470.

634 "his full armor of noble sentiments": Nicolay and Hay, *Abraham Lincoln*, Vol. IX, p. 84.
634 "The Senators were struck" . . . vehement protest: Brooks, *Washington, D.C., in Lincoln's Time*, p. 119.
634 "Fessenden was frightened . . . was mad": AL, quoted in "30 June 1864, Thursday," in Hay, *Inside Lincoln's White House*, p. 213.
634 Lincoln listened patiently . . . "meet each other": Brooks, *Washington, D.C., in Lincoln's Time*, pp. 119–120 (quotes p. 120).
634 Chase had declined to attend: Entry for June 24, 1864, *Welles diary*, Vol. II, p. 58.
634 "unendurable . . . the last straw": Brooks, *Washington, D.C., in Lincoln's Time*, pp. 120, 121.
634 "very nervous & cut up": "30 June 1864, Thursday," in Hay, *Inside Lincoln's White House*, p. 214.
634 Chittenden was equally . . . "thoroughly miserable": AL, quoted in Chittenden, *Recollections of President Lincoln* (1901 edn.), pp. 377–79 (quotes pp. 378–79).
635 Lincoln paused . . . "loftier motives than any man": Ibid., pp. 379–80.
635 a similar remark . . . "of good will": Entry for June 30, 1864, in *Chase Papers*, Vol. I, p. 471.
635 "the great magician . . . financier of his century": *Chicago Tribune*, July 3, 1864.
635 "Mr. Chase is . . . Webster and Calhoun": *NYTrib*, July 1, 1864.
635 he received a telegram . . . reasons of health: David Tod to AL, June 30, 1864, Lincoln Papers.
635 "laid awake . . . public men": Carpenter, *Six Months at the White House*, p. 182.
635 By morning . . . William Pitt Fessenden: Chittenden, *Recollections of President Lincoln* (1901 edn.), p. 381.
635 "First . . . of many radicals": "1 July 1864, Friday," in Hay, *Inside Lincoln's White House*, p. 216.
636 Lincoln handed Hay . . . "at once to the Senate": AL, quoted in "1 July 1864, Friday," in ibid., p. 215.
636 Lincoln greeted Fessenden . . . would kill him: William Pitt Fessenden, quoted in Fessenden, *Life and Public Services of William Pitt Fessenden*, Vol. I, pp. 315–16.
636 "If you decline . . . the nomination": AL, quoted in "1 July 1864, Friday," in Hay, *Inside Lincoln's White House*, p. 216.
636 "Telegrams came pouring . . . the most miserable": William Pitt Fessenden to his cousin, quoted in Fessenden, *Life and Public Services of William Pitt Fessenden*, Vol. I, p. 320.
636 "Very well . . . save your country": EMS, quoted in ibid., p. 321.
636 As he was driven . . . "danger to the country": William Pitt Fessenden to Justice Tenney, quoted in ibid., pp. 317–18.
636 "He is a man . . . personal integrity": *Chicago Tribune*, July 2, 1864.
636 "He is honest . . . Republican Senators": EBL to SPL, July 2, 1864, in *Wartime Washington*, ed. Laas, p. 398.
637 "I am the most popular man in my country": William Pitt Fessenden, quoted in Fessenden, *Life and Public Services of William Pitt Fessenden*, Vol. I, p. 326.
637 "So my official life closes": Entry for June 30, 1864, in *Chase Papers*, Vol. I, p. 471.
637 the oppressive heat of Washington . . . "are wilting": Entry for July 31, 1864, in *The Diary of Edward Bates, 1859–1866*, p. 392.
637 "laid broad foundations" . . . was still unfinished: Entry for June 30, 1864, in *Chase Papers*, Vol. I, p. 471.
637 Blair and Bates called . . . "as a blessing": Entry for June 30, 1864, *Welles diary*, Vol. II, pp. 62–63 (quote p. 63).
637 "the courage and candor to admit his errors": Entry for March 23, 1864, ibid., p. 545.
637 "his jokes are . . . destitute of wit": Entry for March 22, 1864, ibid., p. 545.
637 "a vague feeling . . . to be cordial": Entry for June 30, 1864, in *The Diary of Edward Bates, 1859–1866*, p. 381.
637 "dropped off . . . every body else": FPB to FB, July 4, 1864, quoted in Smith, *The Francis Preston Blair Family in Politics*, Vol. II, p. 271.
637 Seward, unlike . . . "first day of the Administration": WHS to FAS, [July] 2, 1864, quoted in Seward, *Seward at Washington . . . 1861–1872*, p. 230.
637 he noted sadly . . . "since my resignation": Entry for July 13, 1864, in *Chase Papers*, Vol. I, p. 479.
637 If Chase believed . . . he was mistaken: SPC to EMS, June 30, 1864, in Warden, *Private Life and Public Services*, p. 618.
637 Chase searched for reasons . . . "hostile to me": Entry for July 4, 1864, in *Chase Papers*, Vol. I, p. 476.
638 "The root . . . a joke out of this war": SPC to Whitelaw Reid, quoted in Albert Bushnell Hart, *Salmon P. Chase*. American Statesmen Series (Boston and New York: Houghton Mifflin, 1899), p. 318.
638 To Kate . . . "cannot finish what I began": SPC to KCS, July 3, 1864, reel 34, Chase Papers.
638 whose marriage to William . . . "the balance of power": Lamphier, *Kate Chase and William Sprague*, p. 78.
638 "Can it be . . . even with far less material wealth": Entry for November 4, 1868, KCS diary, Sprague Papers (quotes); Lamphier, *Kate Chase and William Sprague*, pp. 74, 84–85.
639 occasionally loathing . . . "learned to submit": Entry for November 11, 1868, KCS diary, Sprague Papers.
639 Chase witnessed a fight . . . her first child: Entry for September 9, 1864, in *Chase Papers*, Vol. I, p. 501 (quote); Belden and Belden, *So Fell the Angels*, pp. 135–36, 144.
639 The Wade-Davis bill: H. R. 244, 38th Cong., 1st sess. ("Wade-Davis Bill"), in *The Radical Republicans and Reconstruction, 1861–1870*, ed. Harold Hyman. American Heritage Series (Indianapolis and New York: Bobbs-Merrill, 1967), pp. 128–34.
639 In a written proclamation . . . single, inflexible system: AL, "Proclamation Concerning Reconstruction," July 8, 1864, in *CW*, VII, p. 433.
640 he likened the Wade-Davis . . . "fit the bedstead": Brooks, *Washington, D.C., in Lincoln's Time*, pp. 156–57.
640 Lincoln understood . . . "fixed within myself": "4 July 1864, Monday," in Hay, *Inside Lincoln's White House*, pp. 218–19.
640 Wade and Davis published . . . manifesto against him: "The Wade-Davis Manifesto, August 5, 1864," in *The Radical Republicans and Reconstruction, 1861–1870*, ed. Hyman, pp. 137–47.
640 He was not surprised by . . . "that can befall a man": Brooks, *Washington, D.C. in Lincoln's Time*, p. 156.

640 The rumors alarmed . . . eager to get started: EBL to SPL, July 6, 1864, in *Wartime Washington*, ed. Laas, p. 400.

640 In a letter to Frank . . . "a remote future": FPB to FB, July 4, 1864, quoted in Smith, *The Francis Preston Blair Family in Politics*, Vol. II, p. 272.

640 admonitions concerned Monty . . . the Pennsylvania countryside: EBL to SPL, July 6, 1864, in *Wartime Washington*, ed. Laas, p. 400.

640 tried to convince her mother . . . "pulled to pieces": EBL to SPL, July 14, 1864, in ibid., p. 403.

641 Grant's decision . . . General Lew Wallace: John Henry Cramer, *Lincoln Under Enemy Fire: The Complete Account of His Experiences During Early's Attack on Washington* (Baton Rouge: Louisiana State University Press, 1948), pp. 2–8.

641 Wallace understood . . . prepared itself for attack: Seward, *Seward at Washington . . . 1861–1872*, p. 231.

641 "The battle lasted . . . superior numbers": Seward, 9th N.Y. Artillery speech, 1912, Seward Papers, NRU.

641 Will's horse . . . have been captured: Seward, *Seward at Washington . . . 1861–1872*, pp. 244–45.

641 Seward spent a tense . . . he had not been captured: Letter to FAS, quoted in Seward, *Seward at Washington . . . 1861–1872*, p. 233 (quote); Lew Wallace to Henry W. Halleck, July 9, 1864, *OR*, Ser. 1, Vol. XXXVII, Part II, p. 145.

641 "God be praised for the safety of our boy": FAS to WHS, July 11, 1864, reel 114, Seward Papers.

641 "With the help . . . rejoining the forces": Seward, *Seward at Washington . . . 1861–1872*, pp. 231–32.

641 Falkland mansion . . . "top to bottom": Mr. Turton, quoted in *National Intelligencer*, reprinted from the *Daily Morning Chronicle*, Washington, D.C., July 16, 1864.

642 "blackened ruin": EBL to SPL, August 5, 1864, quoted in note 2 of EBL to SPL, July 16, 1864, in *Wartime Washington*, ed. Laas, p. 405.

642 the soldiers scattered papers . . . "great frolic" on the lawn: EBL to SPL, July 16 and 31, [1864], in ibid., pp. 404, 413 (quotes).

642 "perfect saturnalia": EBL to SPL, July 31, [1864], in ibid., p. 413.

642 Breckinridge made them . . . "side of the Mts.": EBL to SPL, July 16 and 31, [1864], in ibid., pp. 404, 413 (quote).

642 He explained . . . "refuge & of rest": EBL to SPL, July 16, [1864], in ibid., p. 405.

642 "made more fuss . . . came back to us": EBL to SPL, July 16, [1864], in ibid., pp. 404–05.

642 In his initial panic . . . during the crisis: Thomas and Hyman, *Stanton*, pp. 319–20.

642 "all convalescents . . . and rifle-pits": Henry W. Halleck to George Cadwalader, July 9, 1864, *OR*, Ser. 1, Vol. XXXVII, Part II, p. 153.

642 "in a pleasant and confident humor": "12 July 1864, Tuesday," in Hay, *Inside Lincoln's White House*, p. 222.

642 "in the least concerned . . . force in our front": "11 July 1864, Monday," in ibid., p. 221.

643 "exhibits none . . . on former occasions": Entry for July 11, 1864, *Welles diary*, Vol. II, p. 72.

643 drove together . . . "were not *frightened*": Entry for July 11, 1864, Taft diary.

643 allowing the residents of Washington . . . "troops to the south": Seward, *Reminiscences of a War-Time Statesman and Diplomat*, p. 246.

643 "Before even the first . . . direction of Washington": Jubal A. Early, "The Advance on Washington in 1864. Letter from General J. A. Early," *Southern Historical Society Papers*, Vol. IX, January–December 1881 (Richmond, Va.: Southern Historical Society; Wilmington, N.C.: Broadfoot Publishing Co., Morningside Bookshop, 1990), p. 306.

643 "to be exceedingly . . . impregnable": Jubal Anderson Early, *War Memoirs: Autobiographical Sketch and Narrative of the War Between the States*, ed. Frank E. Vandiver. Civil War Centennial Series (Bloomington: Indiana University Press, 1960), p. 390.

643 at Fort Stevens: Benjamin Franklin Cooling, *Jubal Early's Raid on Washington, 1864* (Baltimore: Nautical & Aviation Publishing Co. of America, 1989), pp. 117–55.

643 "The President evinced . . . standing upon it": Cramer, *Lincoln Under Enemy Fire*, p. 30.

643 "Get down" . . . unusual incident: Oliver Wendell Holmes, Jr., quoted in ibid., p. 22.

643 "was exciting and wild . . . to have occurred": Entry for July 12, 1864, *Welles diary*, Vol. II, pp. 75–76.

644 "an egregious blunder": Charles A. Dana, *Recollections of the Civil War* (New York: Collier Books, 1963), p. 205.

644 Welles knew . . . appeared "contemptible": Entry for July 13, 1864, *Welles diary*, Vol. II, p. 76.

644 "Mrs. Lincoln . . . away as they did!": Carpenter, *Six Months at the White House*, pp. 301–02 (quote p. 302).

644 "I am informed . . . dismissed from the cabinet": Henry W. Halleck to EMS, July 13, 1864, Lincoln Papers.

644 "Whether the remarks . . . shall be dismissed": EMS to AL, July 14, 1864, Lincoln Papers; AL to EMS, July 14, 1864, in *CW*, VII, pp. 439–40 (quote).

645 "It would greatly pain . . . now or hereafter": AL, "Memorandum Read to Cabinet," [July 14?], 186[4], in *CW*, VII, p. 439.

645 Learning that Ben Butler . . . "civilians on either side": MB to Benjamin F. Butler, August 10, 1864, in *Private and Official Correspondence of Gen. Benjamin F. Butler During the Period of the Civil War*. Vol. V: *August 1864–March 1868* (Norwood, Mass.: Plimpton Press, 1917), p. 32 (quote); Cooling, *Jubal Early's Raid on Washington, 1864*, pp. 152–53.

645 "The loss is . . . is unrelieved[?]": MB to R. A. Sloane, July 21, 1864, reel 22, Blair Family Papers, DLC.

645 "The month of August" . . . throughout the North: Brooks, *Lincoln Observed, Civil War Dispatches of Noah Brooks*, ed. Michael Burlingame (Baltimore, Md., and London: Johns Hopkins University Press, 1998), p. 129.

645 mid-July call for five hundred thousand additional volunteers: *NYT*, July 19, 1864.

645 "dissatisfaction . . . with the colors flying": Ibid.

645 An ingenious attempt: See Dorothy L. Drinkard, "Crater, Battle of the (30 July 1864)," in *Encyclopedia of the American Civil War*, ed. Heidler and Heidler, p. 517; McPherson, *Battle Cry of Freedom*, pp. 758–60.

646 "Piled on top . . . frightened sheep": Brooks, *Lincoln Observed*, p. 130.

646 "It was the saddest . . . again to have": USG to Henry W. Halleck, August 1, 1864, *OR*, Ser. 1, Vol. XL, Part I, p. 17.

646 "less however from the result . . . of the future": Entry for August 2, 1864, *Welles diary*, Vol. II, p. 92.

646 he admitted feeling . . . "of our generals": Entry for August 1, 1864, in *The Diary of Edward Bates, 1859–1866*, p. 392.

646 he met with Grant at Fort Monroe: *NYH*, August 3, 1864.

646 dispatched General Philip Sheridan . . . "troops go also": USG to Henry W. Halleck, August 1, 1864, *OR*, Ser. 1, Vol. XXXVII, Part II, p. 558.

646 "This, I think, is exactly right": AL to USG, August 3, 1864, in *CW*, VII, p. 476.

646 "a long and very pleasant . . . both in time": Benjamin B. French to Henry F. French, August 9, 1864, typescript copy, reel 10, French Family Papers, DLC.

646 "much wretchedness . . . in the land": Entry for August 4, 1864, *Welles diary*, Vol. II, p. 93.

646 "The People are wild for Peace": TW to WHS, August 22, 1864, Lincoln Papers.

646 *"two Ambassadors . . . for a peace"*: William C. Jewett to Horace Greeley, July 5, 1864, Lincoln Papers.

646 Urging the president . . . "doing great harm": Horace Greeley to AL, July 7, 1864, Lincoln Papers.

647 commissioned Horace Greeley . . . escort them to Washington: AL to Horace Greeley, July 9, 1864, in *CW*, VII, p. 435.

647 dispatched John Hay to join Greeley: "[ca. 21 July 1864]," in Hay, *Inside Lincoln's White House*, pp. 224–25; "[after 22 July 1864]," in ibid., p. 228; entry for July 18, 1864, in *Lincoln Day by Day*, Vol. III, p. 273.

647 "To Whom it may concern . . . collateral points": AL, "To Whom It May Concern," July 18, 1864, in *CW*, VII, p. 451.

647 the two envoys . . . to stop the war: "[after 22 July 1864]," in Hay, *Inside Lincoln's White House*, p. 228.

647 He hoped the failed mission . . . of freeing the slaves: Eaton, *Grant, Lincoln and the Freedmen*, p. 176; Nicolay and Hay, *Abraham Lincoln*, Vol. IX, pp. 193–94.

647 "are told . . . an impossibility": TW to WHS, August 22, 1864, Lincoln Papers.

647 Swett felt compelled . . . situation was hopeless: Leonard Swett to his wife, September 8, 1864, quoted in Tarbell, *The Life of Abraham Lincoln*, Vol. II (—: S. S. McClure Co., 1895; New York Doubleday & McClure Co., 1900), p. 202.

647 were mystified . . . "his Cabinet": Entry of August 17, 1864, *Welles diary*, Vol. II, p. 109.

648 "I am in active . . . *of the Constitution*": Henry J. Raymond to AL, August 22, 1864, Lincoln Papers.

648 "I confess that I . . . prosperity to the country": "The Interview between Thad Stevens & Mr. Lincoln as related by Col R. M. Hoe," compiled by JGN, container 10, Nicolay Papers.

648 asked all cabinet members . . . a successful conclusion: "11 November 1864, Friday," in Hay, *Inside Lincoln's White House*, pp. 247–48.

648 "This morning . . . possibly save it afterwards": AL, "Memorandum Concerning His Probable Failure of Re-election," August 23, 1864, in *CW*, VII, p. 514.

648 "was considering" . . . would lend his hand: Eaton, *Grant, Lincoln and the Freedmen*, pp. 173–75 (quotes pp. 173, 175).

649 Douglass met with . . . "within our boundaries": Douglass, *Life and Times of Frederick Douglass*, pp. 796–97.

649 Douglass promised to confer: Frederick Douglass to AL, August 29, 1864, Lincoln Papers.

649 Randall had hand-delivered . . . "Democrats may stand": Charles D. Robinson to AL, August 7, 1864, Lincoln Papers.

650 Lincoln shared a draft: Frederick Douglass to Theodore Tilton, October 15, 1864, in *The Life and Writings of Frederick Douglass*, Vol. III, ed. Foner, p. 423.

650 "To me it seems . . . matter of policy": AL to Charles D. Robinson, [August] 1864, Lincoln Papers.

650 "as it seems you would . . . made the offer supposed": AL to Charles D. Robinson, August 17, 1864, Lincoln Papers.

650 Douglass saw clearly . . . "do you serious damage": Frederick Douglass to Theodore Tilton, October 15, 1864, in *The Life and Writings of Frederick Douglass*, Vol. III, ed. Foner, p. 423.

650 a messenger informed Lincoln . . . "my friend Douglass": AL, quoted in Douglass, "Lincoln and the Colored Troops," in *Reminiscences of Abraham Lincoln*, ed. Rice, p. 320.

650 "suppress his excitement . . . men in America": Eaton, *Grant, Lincoln and the Freedmen*, pp. 175, 176.

651 "The President was free . . . reminiscences of the past": "Interview with Alexander W. Randall and Joseph T. Mills," August 19, 1864, quoted from the diary of Joseph T. Mills, State Historical Society of Wisconsin, Madison, in *CW*, VII, pp. 506–08 (quotes); Pinsker, *Lincoln's Sanctuary*, p. 158.

651 Lincoln permanently shelved the draft: Note 1 of AL to Charles D. Robinson, August 17, 1864, in *CW*, VII, p. 501.

651 Raymond's suggestion . . . "by peaceful modes": AL to Henry J. Raymond, August 24, 1864, in ibid., p. 517.

652 "slept undisturbed" . . . biography of Lincoln: Nicolay and Hay, *Abraham Lincoln*, Vol. IX, p. 221.

652 "a sort of political Bull Run": JGN to TB, August 28, 1864, container 3, Nicolay Papers.

652 "ever present and companionable": Entry for August 19, 1864, *Welles diary*, Vol. II, p. 112.

652 Mary and Tad . . . Vermont: AL to MTL, August 31, September 8 and September 11, 1864, in *CW*, VII, p. 526, 544, 547.

652 but did not feel he should . . . "than another arises": WHS to FAS, August 27, 1864, quoted in Seward, *Seward at Washington . . . 1861–1872*, p. 241.

652 "the signs of discontent . . . all to disappear": WHS to home, August 16, 1864, quoted in ibid., p. 240.

652 "firm and hopeful": WHS to FAS, August 27, 1864, quoted in ibid., p. 241.

652 Welles observed . . . "an understanding": Entry for August 19, 1864, *Welles diary*, Vol. II, p. 112.
652 the sight of a disabled soldier: Benjamin, "Recollections of Secretary Edwin M. Stanton," *Century* (1887), p. 761.
652 Lincoln invited Raymond . . . "utter ruination": JGN to JH, August 25, 1864, in Nicolay, *With Lincoln in the White House*, p. 152.
652 chairing a meeting . . . mobilize the party: Leonard Swett to his wife, September 8, 1864, quoted in Tarbell, *The Life of Abraham Lincoln*, Vol. II (1900 edn.), pp. 202–03.
652 "the turning-point . . . we are saved": JGN to JH, August 25, 1864, in Nicolay, *With Lincoln in the White House*, p. 152.
653 Nicolay was relieved . . . "encouraged and cheered": JGN memoranda, quoted in Nicolay and Hay, *Abraham Lincoln*, Vol. IX, p. 221.
653 Noting that the members . . . "for the Union party": *NYT*, August 27, 1864.
653 "I happen temporarily . . . an inestimable jewel": AL, "Speech to One Hundred Sixty-sixth Ohio Regiment," August 22, 1864, in *CW*, VII, p. 512.
653 "giants in the . . . of the opposition": JGN to JH, August 25, 1864, in Nicolay, *With Lincoln in the White House*, p. 152.
654 "we have had nothing . . . change all this": Noah Brooks to JGN, August 29, 1864, Lincoln Papers.
654 "They have a peace . . . to rest upon": Waugh, *Reelecting Lincoln*, p. 89.
654 "It was noticeable" . . . virtual silence: Noah Brooks to JGN, August 29, 1864, Lincoln Papers.
654 "His partisans are united . . . their own choice": Brooks, *Mr. Lincoln's Washington*, p. 368.
654 "was expected . . . surrender and abasement": Entry for September 2, 1864, *Diary of George Templeton Strong*, Vol. III, p. 479.
654 the platform declared . . . "cessation of hostilities": "The Democratic National Platform of 1864 (August 29 1864)," in *Encyclopedia of the American Civil War*, ed. Heidler and Heidler, p. 2375.
654 Strong predicted . . . "on such terms": Entry for September 2, 1864, *Diary of George Templeton Strong*, Vol. III, p. 480.
654 "Atlanta is ours, and fairly won": William T. Sherman to Henry W. Halleck, September 3, 1864, *OR*, Ser. 1, Vol. XXXVIII, Part V, p. 777.
655 Lincoln to order that one hundred guns: AL, "Order for Celebration of Victories at Atlanta, Georgia, and Mobile, Alabama," September 3, 1864, in *CW*, VII, p. 532.
655 "Atlanta is ours . . . are ours now": *NYT*, September 5, 1864.
655 the departing Confederates . . . "of military value": McPherson, *Battle Cry of Freedom*, p. 774.
655 "Glorious news . . . event of the war": Entry for September 3, 1864, *Diary of George Templeton Strong*, Vol. III, pp. 480–81.
655 Seward received the news . . . at his house to celebrate: Seward, *Seward at Washington . . . 1861–1872*, p. 242.
655 the crowd swelled . . . "effective speeches": *NYT*, September 6, 1864.
655 the twin victories . . . "perish and leave no root": WHS, quoted in Seward, *Seward at Washington . . . 1861–1872*, pp. 242–44.
655 "For a man of not very" . . . the upcoming campaign: Entry for September 10, 1864, *Welles diary*, Vol. II, p. 140.
656 "This intelligence will . . . on a peace platform": Entry for September 3, 1864, ibid., pp. 135–36.
656 Peace Democrats threatened . . . "their support": Clement L. Vallandigham to GBM, September 4, 1864, reel 36, McClellan Papers, DLC.
656 six drafts . . . midnight on September 8: *Civil War Papers of George B. McClellan*, p. 588; GBM to MEM, [September 9, 1864], ibid., p. 597.
656 He began with a nod . . . "brethren had been in vain": GBM to the Democratic Nomination Committee, September 8, 1864, in *Civil War Papers of George B. McClellan*, pp. 595–96.
656 "We are going to win . . . unite on Mr. Lincoln": Theodore Tilton to JGN, September 6, 1864, Lincoln Papers.
656 believed that God . . . "nearly capsized it": Leonard Swett to his wife, September 8, 1864, quoted in Tarbell, *The Life of Abraham Lincoln*, Vol. II (1900 edn.), p. 203.
656 "conspiracy against Mr. Lincoln collapsed": TW to WHS, September 10, [1864], Lincoln Papers.
657 "to weaken the President . . . now support Lincoln": Entry for September 10, 1864, *Welles diary*, Vol. II, pp. 140–41.
657 Chase stopped en route . . . "judgment of history?": Entry for September 13, 1864, in *Chase Papers*, Vol. I, p. 502.
657 "Mr. Chase had a long . . . at the north": EBL to SPL, September 16, 1864, in *Wartime Washington*, ed. Laas, p. 429.
657 Chase accompanied Stanton . . . with Lincoln: Entry for September 16, 1864, in *Chase Papers*, Vol. I, pp. 503–04.
657 "I have been . . . demonstrative": SPC to KCS, September 17, 1864, reel 35, Chase Papers.
657 "wronged and hurt . . . fidelity to his Administration": Entry for September 17, 1864, in *Inside Lincoln's Cabinet: The Civil War Diaries of Salmon P. Chase*, ed. David Donald (New York: Longmans, Green, 1954), p. 255.
657 "conviction that . . . in securing it": SPC to KCS, September 17, 1864, reel 35, Chase Papers.
657 He traveled . . . before overflowing crowds: Entries for September 24–November 11, 1864, in *Chase Papers*, Vol. I, pp. 507–10.
658 the state elections . . . previous year: JGN to TB, September 11, 1864, container 3, Nicolay Papers; *NYT*, September 13, 1864.
658 "Three weeks ago . . . confident of success": JGN to TB, September 11, 1864, container 3, Nicolay Papers.

658 Philip Sheridan . . . of Early's army: McPherson, *Battle Cry of Freedom*, p. 777.
658 "shouting of Clerks" . . . news became known: Entry for September 20, 1864, in *Chase Papers*, Vol. I, p. 506.
658 "This will do much . . . loving men": Entry for September 20, 1864, *Welles diary*, Vol. II, p. 151.
658 Blair was aware . . . his resignation to Lincoln: MB to Mary Elizabeth Blair, September 23, 1864, quoted in Smith, *The Francis Preston Blair Family in Politics*, Vol. II, p. 288.
658 his father had repeated . . . "an avowed enemy": FPB to FB, quoted in EBL to SPL, September 24, [1864], in *Wartime Washington*, ed. Laas, p. 433.
658 Henry Wilson warned Lincoln . . . "account of the Blairs": Henry Wilson to AL, September 5, 1864, Lincoln Papers.
658 Monty Blair detested Stanton . . . "a thief": "26 September 1864, Monday," in Hay, *Inside Lincoln's White House*, p. 233.
659 "interchanged words for weeks": Entry for August 11, 1864, *Welles diary*, Vol. II, p. 102.
659 when the opportunity arose . . . stayed in the race: William Frank Zornow, *Lincoln & the Party Divided* (Norman: University of Oklahoma Press, 1954), pp. 144–47.
659 Frémont announced his withdrawal: *NYT*, September 23, 1864.
659 "You have generously . . . connection therewith": AL to MB, September 23, 1864, in *CW*, VIII, p. 18. For Blair's resignation letter, see MB to AL, September 23, 1864, Lincoln Papers.
659 Blair was surprised . . . "yielded to that": Entry for September 23, 1864, *Welles diary*, Vol. II, pp. 156–57.
659 Blair had been . . . "irritating bickerings": Addition to entry for September 23, 1864, ibid., p. 158 n1.
659 "In parting with Blair . . . discriminating and correct": Entry for September 23, 1864, ibid., p. 157.
660 "the removal of . . . befallen the Cabinet": Entry for September 27, 1864, ibid., p. 161.
660 did not consider . . . straight-speaking colleague: Entry for August 2, 1864, ibid., p. 93.
660 "I think Mr. Lincoln . . . *malign influences*": Entry for September 23, 1864, in *The Diary of Edward Bates, 1859–1866*, p. 413.
660 "an unnecessary mortification . . . best all around": MB to Mary Elizabeth Blair, September 23, 1864, quoted in Smith, *The Francis Preston Blair Family in Politics*, Vol. II, p. 288.
660 "In my opinion . . . the reelection of Lincoln": FPB to FB, quoted in EBL to SPL, September 24, [1864], in *Wartime Washington*, ed. Laas, p. 433.
660 "somewhat mortifying . . . a penny to make": FB to FPB, September 30, 1864, Lincoln Papers.
660 hearing the noble . . . "fine manly bearing": EBL to SPL, September 24, [1864], in *Wartime Washington*, ed. Laas, p. 434.
660 Monty insisted . . . "father to the President": MB, quoted in *Chicago Tribune*, October 1, 1864.
661 "very handsomely and is doing his utmost": "26 September 1864, Monday," in Hay, *Inside Lincoln's White House*, p. 233.
661 "a grand central rallying point": "11 October 1864, Tuesday," in Hay, *Inside Lincoln's White House*, p. 240.
661 Lincoln made his . . . chief of the telegraph office: Bates, *Lincoln in the Telegraph Office*, pp. 276–77; Charles A. Dana, "Lincoln and the War Department," *Reminiscences of Abraham Lincoln*, ed. Rice, p. 278.
661 Lincoln took from his pocket . . . "a new passage": Dana, "Lincoln and the War Department," in *Reminiscences of Abraham Lincoln*, ed. Rice (1909 edn.), p. 278. "Petroleum Vesuvius Nasby" was the pseudonym of David Ross Locke.
661 "immensely amusing": "11 October 1864, Tuesday," in Hay, *Inside Lincoln's White House*, p. 239.
661 "I shall never forget . . . such frivolous jests": Dana, "Lincoln and the War Department," in *Reminiscences of Abraham Lincoln*, ed. Rice (1909 edn.), pp. 278–79. Dana's recollection is that this episode occurred while Lincoln was waiting for the results of the November presidential election. Other sources, however, suggest that it probably occurred while a larger crowd waited in the telegraph office for results of the state elections in October. Given that Stanton was ill and remained at home during November elections, Dana has probably confused the two dates.
662 the news from Ohio . . . Republican majority: Waugh, *Reelecting Lincoln*, p. 335.
662 In Indiana . . . congressional seats: AL to USG, October 12, 1864, in *CW*, VIII, p. 45.
662 Lincoln sent a telegram . . . "does it stand now?": AL to Simon Cameron, October 11, 1864, in ibid., p. 43.
662 No answer was received . . . "ominous": "11 October 1864, Tuesday," in Hay, *Inside Lincoln's White House*, p. 240.
662 the margin was so close . . . claim a slight margin: Waugh, *Reelecting Lincoln*, p. 336.
662 "Seward was quite exultant . . . has ever known": Entry for October 13, 1864, *Welles diary*, Vol. II, p. 176.
662 Two nights after . . . 117 to 114: Bates, *Lincoln in the Telegraph Office*, pp. 277–79, 282.
662 "the moral effect . . . greatly impaired": McClure, *Abraham Lincoln and Men of War-Times*, p. 202.
662 voters in Maryland . . . making the difference: Waugh, *Reelecting Lincoln*, p. 354.
662 "Most heartily . . . upon the event": AL, "Response to a Serenade," October 19, 1864, in *CW*, VIII, p. 52.
663 "I had rather have . . . cleaned up effectually": AL, quoted in Brooks, *Lincoln Observed*, p. 138.
663 "We are as certain . . . the sun shines": *New York World*, October 14, 1864.
663 "a quarter-million" . . . deposit in their hometowns: William C. Davis, *Lincoln's Men: How President Lincoln became Father to an Army and a Nation* (New York: Free Press, 1999), pp. 214 (quote), 211.
663 had wired General Sherman . . . "no sense, an order": AL to William T. Sherman, September 19, 1864, in *CW*, VIII, p. 11.
663 Stanton followed up . . . "re-election of Mr. Lincoln": Dana, *Recollections of the Civil War* (1963 edn.), p. 227.
664 Weed alerted . . . New Yorkers ready to vote: TW to FWS, October 10, 1864, reel 85, Seward Papers.
664 Lincoln asked Welles . . . "to gather votes": Entry for October 11, 1864, *Welles diary*, Vol. II, p. 175.
664 "I would rather be . . . elected without it": Ida M. Tarbell, *A Reporter for Lincoln: Story of Henry E. Wing, Soldier and Newspaperman* (New York: The Macmillan Company, 1927), p. 70.

664 "before this morning's . . . ceaseless strife": *NYT*, November 8, 1864.
664 "dark and rainy . . . entirely alone": Brooks, *Washington, D.C., in Lincoln's Time*, p. 195.
664 the tenth time . . . beginning of the country: WHS, "Perseverance in War. Auburn, November 7, 1864," in *Works of William H. Seward*, Vol. V, p. 505.
664 Fessenden was in New York . . . with a fever: Brooks, *Washington, D.C., in Lincoln's Time*, p. 195; Brooks, *Mr. Lincoln's Washington*, p. 385.
664 "I am just enough . . . of Tad's quick-wittedness": Brooks, *Washington, D.C., in Lincoln's Time*, p. 196.
665 As the clock struck . . . a supper of fried oysters: "8 November 1864, Tuesday" in *Inside Lincoln's White House*, pp. 243–46.
665 Lincoln's victory was assured . . . separated by about 400,000 votes: Waugh, *Reelecting Lincoln*, p. 354.
666 the results were far better . . . of U.S. senators: Zornow, *Lincoln & the Party Divided*, p. 198.
666 It was after 2 a.m. . . . "tops of their voices": Pratt, *Stanton*, p. 391.
666 "the verdict of the people . . . no dispute": Brooks, *Washington, D.C., in Lincoln's Time*, p. 197.
666 the soldier vote . . . seven out of every ten soldiers: Waugh, *Reelecting Lincoln*, p. 354.
666 the Confederacy was obviously . . . Napoleon would win: Davis, *Lincoln's Men*, p. 210.
666 "The men had come . . . the term implied": Corporal Leander Stillwell, quoted in ibid., p. 226.

CHAPTER 25: "A SACRED EFFORT"

Page

667 immense crowd . . . second-floor window: Brooks, *Washington, D.C., in Lincoln's Time*, p. 200.
667 "undesirable strife . . . a possibility": AL, "Response to a Serenade," November 10, 1864, in *CW*, VIII, p. 101.
667 "in an exceedingly . . . frame of mind": Brooks, *Washington, D.C., in Lincoln's Time*, p. 200.
668 "we will all come . . . United States": WHS, "The Assurance of Victory," November 10, 1864, *Works of William H. Seward*, Vol. V, pp. 513–14.
668 "I advise you . . . my foreign relations": Brooks, *Washington, D.C., in Lincoln's Time*, pp. 200–01.
668 symbolized the animosity . . . the cabinet: William C. Harris, *Lincoln's Last Months* (Cambridge, Mass., and London: Belknap Press of Harvard University Press, 2004), p. 83.
668 Welles even acknowledged . . . "amicable": Entry for November 26, 1864, *Welles diary*, Vol. II, p. 185.
668 Stanton was sounding . . . Reconstruction: Entry for November 25, 1864, ibid., p. 179.
668 asserted that Seward . . . had outlived: *NYT*, November 29, 1864.
668 "His confidence in Seward is great": Entry for September 27, 1864, *Welles diary*, Vol. II, p. 160.
668 "spends more or less . . . the President": Entry for October 1, 1864, ibid., p. 166.
668 "of the gravest . . . and adviser": Entry for July 22, 1864, ibid., p. 84.
669 plan to foster . . . "by contribution": H. P. Livingston to AL, November 14, 1864, Lincoln Papers; AL to WHS, November 17, 1864, endorsement on Livingston to AL, ibid.; WHS to AL, November 17, 1864, endorsement on Livingston to AL, ibid. (quote).
669 Seward had long since . . . "by the President": Seward, *Seward at Washington . . . 1846–1861*, p. 528.
669 "Henceforth . . . of the human race": WHS, quoted in Seward, *Seward at Washington . . . 1861–1872*, p. 250.
669 "looked older . . . long one, perhaps": Benjamin, "Recollections of Secretary Edwin M. Stanton," *Century* (1887), pp. 758, 759–60.
669 letter to Chase . . . "labor and care": EMS to SPC, November 19, 1864, quoted in Thomas and Hyman, *Stanton*, p. 334.
669 unwritten code . . . "felt it necessary": Thomas and Hyman, *Stanton*, p. 390.
669 president's assent . . . "interfere with him": Flower, *Edwin McMasters Stanton*, pp. 369–70.
670 pressed by relatives . . . "circumspection": AL to EMS, March 18, 1864, in *CW*, VII, pp. 254–55.
670 Stanton replied . . . "promptly obeyed": EMS to AL, March 19, 1864, Lincoln Papers.
671 Lincoln looked . . . "his friends": Carpenter, *Six Months at the White House*, p. 172.
671 clerk recalled . . . "wail of anguish": William H. Whiton, quoted in Flower, *Edwin McMasters Stanton*, pp. 418–19.
671 group of Pennsylvania . . . "have to be done": EMS and AL, quoted in Thomas and Hyman, *Stanton*, p. 387.
671 "I send this . . . in this blunder": AL to USG, September 22, 1864, in *CW*, VIII, p. 17.
672 "his firmness . . . into arrogance": Alonzo Rothschild, *Lincoln, Master of Men: A Study in Character* (Boston and New York: Houghton Mifflin, 1906), p. 231.
672 "hard to vote . . . is a ruffian": Entry for September 17, 1864, in *Diary of George Templeton Strong*, Vol. III, p. 489.
672 "Go home . . . be found guilty": Carpenter, *Six Months at the White House*, p. 246.
672 "Folks come up . . . don't know 'em!": AL, quoted in Rothschild, *Lincoln, Master of Men*, p. 285.
672 discreet New Englander . . . "political gossip": Entry for August 31, 1864, *Welles diary*, Vol. II, p. 131.
672 *Times* of London . . . "first class power": *NR*, January 7, 1865.
673 Bates had contemplated . . . "to your age": Barton Bates to EB, May 13, 1864, Bates Papers, MoSHi.
673 prospect of going home . . . "god's blessing": Entry for May 29, 1864, *The Diary of Edward Bates, 1859–1866*, p. 371.
673 Bates believed . . . "as long as I live": EB to AL, November 24, 1864, Lincoln Papers.
673 first months as Attorney General . . . military matters: Entry for December 31, 1861, *The Diary of Edward Bates, 1859–1866*, pp. 218–19; entry for January 10, 1862, ibid., pp. 223–26.

674 deliver a legal opinion . . . "and clothing": EB to AL, July 14, 1864, *OR*, Ser. 3, Vol. IV, pp. 490–93 (quote p. 493).

674 Abolitionists applauded: Entry for May 26, 1864, *The Diary of Edward Bates, 1859–1866*, p. 371.

674 citizenship issue . . . of the United States: Frank J. Williams, "Attorney General Bates and Attorney President Lincoln," R. Gerald McMurtry Lecture, Lincoln Museum, Fort Wayne, Ind., September 23, 2000, author's collection; Cain, *Lincoln's Attorney General*, pp. 222–23.

674 "Though esteemed . . . constitutional interpretation": *Daily Morning Chronicle*, Washington, D.C., December 4, 1864, quoted in *The Diary of Edward Bates, 1859–1866*, p. 430.

674 reveals frustration . . . "no subordination": Entry for October 1, 1861, ibid., p. 196.

674 General Butler . . . arrests in Norfolk: Entry for August 4, 1864, ibid., pp. 393–94.

675 "chief fear . . . easy good nature": Entry for February 13, 1864, ibid., p. 334.

675 troubled at the start . . . "sure to prevail": EB, quoted in Carpenter, *Six Months at the White House*, pp. 68–69.

675 each of his colleagues . . . "affable and kind": Entry for December 2, 1864, *The Diary of Edward Bates, 1859–1866*, p. 429.

675 Bates left . . . "with regret": Entry for November 30, 1864, ibid., p. 428.

675 forever connected . . . "when I am gone": Poem, quoted in entry for October 13, 1864, ibid., p. 419.

675 "My Cabinet . . . would have to be heeded": AL, quoted in Titian J. Coffey, "Lincoln and the Cabinet," in *Reminiscences of Abraham Lincoln*, ed. Rice (1909 edn.), p. 197.

675 Holt declined the offer . . . "personal character": Joseph Holt to AL, December 1, 1864, Lincoln Papers.

676 "I appoint you . . . come on at once": AL to James Speed, in *CW*, VIII, p. 126.

676 "Will leave tomorrow for Washington": James Speed to AL, December 1, 1864, Lincoln Papers.

676 "I am a . . . everywhere forever": James Speed, quoted in Gary Lee Williams, "James and Joshua Speed: Lincoln's Kentucky Friends" (Ph.D. diss., Duke University, 1971), p. 137.

676 "We are less now but true": James Speed to AL, November 25, 1864, quoted in ibid., p. 138.

676 "a man I know . . . ought to know him well": AL, quoted in Coffey, "Lincoln and the Cabinet," in *Reminiscences of Abraham Lincoln*, ed. Rice (1909 edn.), p. 197.

676 Had it been . . . "freely and publicly": David Herbert Donald, *"We Are Lincoln Men": Abraham Lincoln and His Friends* (New York: Simon & Schuster, 2003), p. 38.

676 "You will find . . . by a big office": AL, quoted in Coffey, "Lincoln and the Cabinet," in *Reminiscences of Abraham Lincoln*, ed. Rice (1909 edn.), p. 197.

677 only position . . . "Stanton ever desired": Wolcott, "Edwin M. Stanton," p. 162.

677 "You have been wearing . . . owes it to you": Robert Grier to EMS, October 13, 1864, Stanton Papers, DLC.

677 Ellen Stanton . . . "subject tomorrow": Entry for October 16, 1864, in Browning, *The Diary of Orville Hickman Browning*, Vol. I, p. 687–88.

677 Matthew Simpson . . . "I will do it": AL, quoted in Gideon Stanton, ed., "Edwin M. Stanton."

677 Grant worried . . . stay at his post: Thomas and Hyman, *Stanton*, p. 337.

677 Stanton informed . . . "among candidates": Edwards Pierrepont to AL, November 24, 1864, Lincoln Papers.

677 He "felt that . . . higher ambition": Wolcott, "Edwin M. Stanton," p. 162.

677 "The country cannot . . . fame already": Henry Ward Beecher to EMS, November 30, 1864, quoted in ibid., p. 163.

678 "Often, in dark hours . . . fresh hope": EMS to Henry Ward Beecher, December 4, 1864, quoted in ibid., pp. 163–64.

678 Welles told Lincoln . . . "suppose he would": Entry for November 26, 1864, *Welles diary*, Vol. II, p. 182.

678 taken his son's . . . personal blow: Entry for September 27, 1864, ibid., p. 161.

678 "I beg you to indulge . . . of that Bench": FPB to AL, October 20, 1864, quoted in Smith, *The Francis Preston Blair Family in Politics*, Vol. II, pp. 298–99.

678 "Chase and his friends . . . Chief-Justiceship": MTL, quoted in "If All the Rest Oppose," in *Conversations with Lincoln*, ed. Segal, p. 360.

679 "had been tried . . . stood by him": FPB to John A. Andrew, quoted in ibid., p. 360.

679 "a crowning and retiring honor": Entry for November 22, 1864, *The Diary of Edward Bates, 1859–1866*, p. 428.

679 had "personally solicited": Entry for October 18, 1864, in Browning, *The Diary of Orville Hickman Browning*, Vol. I, p. 688.

679 "If not overborne . . . to private life": Entry for November 22, 1864, *The Diary of Edward Bates, 1859–1866*, pp. 427–28.

679 "Of Mr. Chase's . . . not hesitate a moment": AL, quoted in John G. Nicolay and John Hay, *Abraham Lincoln: A History*, Vol. IX (New York: Century Co., 1890), p. 394.

679 similar comment . . . "life to the Bench": Schuyler Colfax, quoted in Blue, *Salmon P. Chase*, p. 245.

679 "Now, I know . . . men can tell me": Noah Brooks, "Personal Reminiscences of Lincoln," *Scribner's Monthly* 15 (March 1878), p. 677.

679 "we have stood . . . fitness for the office": AL, quoted in Blue, *Salmon P. Chase*, pp. 244–45.

680 Oblivious to Stanton's . . . "life & work": SPC to EMS, October 13, 1864, *Chase Papers*, Vol. IV, p. 434.

680 "I have something . . . will be satisfied": AL and John B. Alley, quoted in John B. Alley, in *Reminiscences of Abraham Lincoln*, ed. Rice (1886 edn.), pp. 581–82.

680 Lincoln later told Senator Chandler . . . "nominated Chase": Entry for December 15, 1864, *Welles diary*, Vol. II, p. 196.

680 "Probably no other . . . of the President": JGN to TB, December 8, 1864, container 3, Nicolay Papers.

680 got the official word . . . "or office": SPC to AL, December 6, 1864, Lincoln Papers.

680 "overflowing with . . . 'So help me God' ": Brooks, *Washington, D.C., in Lincoln's Time*, pp. 175–76.

681 "I hope the President . . . in the court": Entry for December 6, 1864, *Welles diary*, Vol. II, p. 193.

681 Within hours . . . first black barrister: John S. Rock to CS, December 17, 1864, enclosed in CS to SPC, December 21, 1864, in *Selected Letters of Charles Sumner*, Vol. II, ed. Palmer, p. 259 n1 (quote); entry for January 21, 1865, *Chase Papers*, Vol. I, p. 519.

681 Sumner stood before . . . "of this Court": CS, quoted in Quarles, *Lincoln and the Negro*, p. 232.

681 Rock stepped forward . . . "of a great people": *Harper's Weekly*, February 25, 1865.

681 "has been quite . . . with good feeling": MTL to Mercy Levering Conkling, November 19, [1864], in Turner and Turner, *Mary Todd Lincoln*, p. 187.

682 she had been terrified . . . "run in debt": Keckley, *Behind the Scenes*, pp. 147, 149–50 (quotes).

682 exposed her . . . could not curtail: "Mary Todd Lincoln's Unethical Conduct as First Lady," appendix 2, in Hay, *At Lincoln's Side*, pp. 185–205.

682 "Here is the carriage . . . many questions": Entry for December 14, 1864, Taft diary.

682 new dress . . . "kid gloves": Entry for July 3, 1873, Browning diary, quoted in appendix 2, in Hay, *At Lincoln's Side*, p. 187.

682 "I can neither . . . your acting thus": MTL to Ruth Harris, December 28, [1864], in Turner and Turner, *Mary Todd Lincoln*, p. 196.

682 Newspaper reports . . . "tasteful decoration": *NR*, January 10, 1865.

683 "Mrs. Lincoln was . . . throughout": *NR*, February 17, 1865.

683 "Overcoats . . . for safe-keeping": *NR*, January 6, 1865.

683 "a more general . . . and themselves": *NR*, January 10, 1865.

683 "*I* was pleased . . . *two* school boys": MTL to Sally Orne, [December 12, 1869], quoted in Turner and Turner, *Mary Todd Lincoln*, p. 534.

683 lingering grief . . . favorite rooms: Entry for March 31, 1864, Benjamin B. French journal, reel 2, French Family Papers, DLC.

683 "darling Boy! . . . *far* from being": MTL to Hannah Shearer, November 20, 1864, in Turner and Turner, *Mary Todd Lincoln*, p. 189.

683 Lincoln wrote to General Grant . . . "encumbered": AL to USG, January 19, 1865, in *CW*, VIII, p. 223.

684 Grant replied . . . "Military family": USG to AL, January 21, 1865, Lincoln Papers.

684 Stationed at Grant's . . . "of the nation": Porter, *Campaigning with Grant*, pp. 388–89.

684 "passing time and accumulating years": Entry for January 1, 1865, *Welles diary*, Vol. II, p. 218.

684 last surviving . . . buried in Ohio: Entry for January 1, 1865, *Chase Papers*, Vol. I, p. 511.

684 Chase wrote to . . . New Year's reception: SPC to AL, January 2, 1865, Lincoln Papers.

684 "Without your note . . . bereavement": AL to SPC, January 2, 1865, in *CW*, VIII, p. 195.

684 "a great contrast . . . in good spirits": Entry for January 1, 1865, Taft diary.

684 "Our joy . . . Confederacy were numbered": Hugh McCullough, quoted in Thomas and Hyman, *Stanton*, p. 342.

684 "*anxious* . . . than to acquiesce": AL to William T. Sherman, December 26, 1864, in *CW*, VIII, p. 181.

685 "We have destroyed . . . for six months": FB to FPB, December 16, 1864, quoted in Smith, *The Francis Preston Blair Family in Politics*, Vol. II, p. 180.

685 also paid tribute . . . "great light": AL to William T. Sherman, December 26, 1864, in *CW*, VIII, p. 182.

685 telegram announcing . . . "candle in his hand": Bates, *Lincoln in the Telegraph Office*, pp. 316–17 (quotes p. 317).

685 Fort Fisher . . . "rebels from abroad": *NR*, January 17, 1865 (quote); *NR*, January 18, 1865.

685 at the cabinet . . . "President was happy": Entry for January 17, 1865, *Welles diary*, Vol. II, p. 227.

685 Stephens considered . . . "or Atlanta": Alexander H. Stephens, *A Constitutional View of the Late War Between the States*, Vol. II (Philadelphia: National Publishing Company, 1870), p. 619.

685 nearly every other . . . munitions and supplies: Ibid., p. 620.

685 was in Savannah . . . "delivered to [him]": EMS to AL, quoted in *NR*, January 18, 1865.

685 journeyed to North Carolina . . . "the *real* Stanton": Mrs. Rufus Saxton, quoted in Flower, *Edwin McMasters Stanton*, p. 420.

686 confer with Sherman . . . "*criminal* dislike": Sherman, *Memoirs of General W. T. Sherman*, pp. 604–07; Henry W. Halleck to William Sherman, December 30, 1865, *OR*, Ser. 1, Vol. XLIV, p. 836 (quote).

686 Sherman countered . . . "our substance": William T. Sherman to SPC, January 11, 1865, in *The Salmon P. Chase Papers*, Vol. 5: *Correspondence, 1865–1873*, ed. John Niven (Kent, Ohio, and London, England: Kent State University Press, 1998), pp. 6–7.

686 "Special Field Orders . . . tillable ground": Sherman, *Memoirs of General W. T. Sherman*, p. 609; Special Field Orders, No. 15, Headquarters, Military Division of the Mississippi, January 16, 1865, *OR*, Ser. I, Vol. XLVII, Part II, pp. 60–62.

686 Freedmen's Bureau . . . the South: Foner, *Reconstruction*, pp. 68–69.

686 "A question might . . . all the evils": AL, "Response to a Serenade," February 1, 1865, in *CW*, VIII, p. 254.

686 previous spring . . . party lines: "Thirteenth Amendment," in Neely, *The Abraham Lincoln Encyclopedia*, p. 308.

686 annual message . . . bipartisan unity: AL, "Annual Message to Congress," December 6, 1864, in *CW*, VIII, p. 149.

687 "I have sent for you . . . border state vote": AL, quoted by James S. Rollins, "The King's Cure-All for All Evils," in *Conversations with Lincoln*, ed. Segal, pp. 363–64.

687 assigned two . . . "procure those votes": AL, quoted in John B. Alley, in *Reminiscences of Abraham Lincoln*, ed. Rice (1886 edn.), pp. 585–86.

687 powers extended . . . in New York: "Thirteenth Amendment," in Neely, *The Abraham Lincoln Encyclopedia*, p. 308.

687 Elizabeth Blair noted . . . several members: EBL to SPL, January 31, 1865, in *Wartime Washington*, ed. Laas, p. 469.

687 Ashley learned . . . "the more resolute": AL, quoted in JGN memorandum, January 18, 1865, in Nicolay, *With Lincoln in the White House*, pp. 171, 257 n11.

688 leader of the . . . "political associates": Blaine, *Twenty Years of Congress*, p. 537.

688 Democrats who considered changing: Harris, *Lincoln's Last Months*, p. 128.

688 "We are like whalers . . . into eternity": AL, quoted in John G. Nicolay and John Hay, *Abraham Lincoln: A History*, Vol. X (New York: Century Co., 1890), p. 74.

688 Rumors circulated . . . "have failed": AL and James M. Ashley correspondence, quoted in James M. Ashley to WHH, November 23, 1866, in *HI*, pp. 413–14.

688 "never before . . . within hearing": *Address of Hon. J. M. Ashley, before the Ohio Society of New York*, February 19, 1899 (privately published), p. 21.

688 Chief Justice Chase . . . foreign ministries: Brooks, *Washington, D.C., in Lincoln's Time*, pp. 185–86; *Address of Hon. J. M. Ashley*, p. 21.

689 McAllister . . . "Southern Confederacy": Brooks, *Washington, D.C., in Lincoln's Time*, p. 186.

689 brought forth applause . . . "without a murmur": Alexander Coffroth, quoted in Carl Sandburg, *Abraham Lincoln: The War Years*, Vol. IV (New York: Harcourt, Brace & Company, 1939), p. 10.

689 "Hundreds of tally" . . . votes short: *Address of Hon. J. M. Ashley*, pp. 23–24.

689 Colfax stood . . . "Resolution has passed": Brooks, *Washington, D.C., in Lincoln's Time*, pp. 186–87.

689 five Democrats . . . would have lost: Harris, *Lincoln's Last Months*, p. 132.

689 "For a moment . . . ever heard before": Brooks, *Washington, D.C., in Lincoln's Time*, p. 187.

689 "Before the members . . . had passed": Arnold, *The Life of Abraham Lincoln*, p. 365.

689 Ashley brought . . . "great honor": EMS, quoted in Flower, *Edwin McMasters Stanton*, p. 190.

689 "The passage . . . emancipation proclamation": Arnold, *The Life of Abraham Lincoln*, pp. 365–66.

689 "The occasion was . . . They will do it": AL, "Response to a Serenade," February 1, 1865, in *CW*, VIII, p. 254.

689 legislatures in twenty . . . had spoken: "Thirteenth Amendment," in Neely, *The Abraham Lincoln Encyclopedia*, p. 308.

690 "And to whom . . . to Abraham Lincoln!": William Lloyd Garrison, quoted in Nicolay and Hay, *Abraham Lincoln*, Vol. X, p. 79n.

690 remained unconvinced . . . a pass: AL, pass for FPB, December 28, 1864, Lincoln Papers.

690 proceeding on . . . "without reserve": FPB to Jefferson Davis, December 30, 1864, Lincoln Papers.

690 arrived in Richmond . . . "around him": *NR*, January 19, 1865.

690 "Oh you Rascal . . . to see you": EBL to SPL, January 16, 1865, in *Wartime Washington*, ed. Laas, p. 463.

690 "might be the dreams . . . in his prayers": FPB, memorandum of conversation with Jefferson Davis [January 12, 1865], Lincoln Papers.

690 his proposal . . . allied against the French: FPB, address made to Jefferson Davis [January 12, 1865], Lincoln Papers.

691 Davis agreed . . . "a Foreign Power": FPB, memorandum of conversation with Jefferson Davis [January 12, 1865], Lincoln Papers.

691 Davis agreed to send . . . "two Countries": Jefferson Davis to FPB, January 12, 1865, Lincoln Papers.

691 Lincoln consulted . . . immediately agreed: EMS, quoted in Flower, *Edwin McMasters Stanton*, p. 257.

691 "You may say . . . one common country": AL to FPB, January 18, 1865, in *CW*, VIII, pp. 220–21.

691 Davis called a cabinet . . . Campbell: Davis, *Jefferson Davis*, p. 590.

691 flag of truce . . . the commissioners: *Philadelphia Inquirer*, February 3, 1865.

691 "By common consent . . . a gala day": *NYH*, February 4, 1865.

691 "harbingers of peace . . . common sentiment": *NR*, February 3, 1865.

691 "It was night . . . throughout the country": Stephens, *A Constitutional View of the Late War*, pp. 597–98.

692 Seward headed south . . . "sincere liberality": AL to WHS, January 31, 1865, in *CW*, VIII, p. 250.

692 "convinced" . . . meet with them personally: USG to EMS, February 1, 1865, Lincoln Papers.

692 "Induced by a despatch of Gen. Grant": AL to WHS, February 2, 1865, in *CW*, VIII, p. 256.

692 "Say to the gentlemen . . . can get there": AL to USG, February 2, 1865, in ibid.

692 a single valet . . . Annapolis: *NYH*, February 3, 1865.

692 "supposed to be" . . . little past ten: *NYH*, February 5, 1865.

692 Lincoln joined Seward . . . *River Queen*: *NYT*, February 6, 1865.

692 saloon of . . . "streamers and flags": Stephens, *A Constitutional View of the Late War*, p. 599; *NYT*, February 6, 1865 (quote).

693 Stephens opened . . . "Sections of the country?": Stephens, *A Constitutional View of the Late War*, p. 599.

693 "was altogether . . . was written or read": Seward, *Seward at Washington . . . 1861–1872*, p. 260.

693 "steward, who came" . . . agreement on any issue: Stephens, *A Constitutional View of the Late War*, pp. 619, 600–01, 612, 613, 609, 617.

694 radicals had worked . . . excoriated him: Brooks, *Washington, D.C., in Lincoln's Time*, p. 202.

694 "the leading members . . . will dishonor us": *NYT*, February 3, 1865.

694 Both branches . . . on the proceedings: Brooks, *Washington, D.C., in Lincoln's Time*, pp. 203–04.

694 Stanton worried . . . "serve their purpose": Bates, *Lincoln in the Telegraph Office*, p. 338.

694 Lincoln's report . . . "given to Seward": Brooks, *Lincoln Observed*, pp. 162–63.

694 "as the reading . . . President Lincoln": Brooks, *Washington, D.C., in Lincoln's Time*, pp. 207, 208.

694 "Indeed . . . than Abraham Lincoln": *Harper's Weekly*, February 25, 1865.

695 employed the failed . . . slavery intact: *Richmond Dispatch*, February 7, 1865, quoted in Nicolay and Hay, *Abraham Lincoln*, Vol. X, p. 130.

695 "I can have . . . element of my nature!": Jefferson Davis, quoted in *NR*, February 13, 1865.

695 drafted a proposal . . . "executive control": AL, "To the Senate and House of Representatives," February 5, 1865, in *CW*, VIII, pp. 260–61.

695 unanimous disapproval . . . "adverse feeling": Entry for February 6, 1865, *Welles diary*, Vol. II, p. 237.

695 Usher believed . . . "assault on the President": J. P. Usher, quoted in Nicolay, *An Oral History of Abraham Lincoln*, p. 66.

695 Stanton had long maintained . . . "compensation for slaves": Flower, *Edwin McMasters Stanton*, p. 258.

695 Fessenden declared . . . "come from us": William Pitt Fessenden, quoted in Francis Fessenden, *Life and Public Services of William Pitt Fessenden*, Vol. II (Boston and New York: Houghton, Mifflin, 1907), p. 8.

695 sum he proposed . . . "approved the measure": J. P. Usher, quoted in Nicolay, *An Oral History of Abraham Lincoln*, p. 66.

696 Sherman had headed north . . . on February 17: Entry for February 17, 1865, in Long, *The Civil War Day by Day*, pp. 639–40.

696 Stanton ordered . . . "parts of the city": *NR*, February 22, 1865.

696 "cheerful . . . brightest day in four years": Entry for February 22, 1865, *Welles Diary*, Vol. II, p. 245.

696 "more depressed" . . . in the four years: Entry for February 23, 1865, in *The Diary of Orville Hickman Browning*, Vol. II, 1865–1881, ed. Theodore Calvin Pease and James G. Randall; *Collections of the Illinois State Historical Library*, Vol. XXII (Springfield: Illinois State Historical Library, 1933), p. 8.

696 low spirits . . . "brigand, and pirate": Jonathan Truman Dorris, *Pardon and Amnesty Under Lincoln and Johnson: The Restoration of the Confederates to Their Rights and Privileges, 1861–1898* (Chapel Hill: University of North Carolina Press, 1953), pp. 76–78 (quote p. 77).

696 "I had to stand . . . out of my mind yet": Henry P. H. Bromwell, quoted in *Recollected Words of Abraham Lincoln*, ed. Don E. Fehrenbacher and Virginia Fehrenbacher (Stanford, Calif.: Stanford University Press, 1996), p. 41.

697 he would "not receive . . . seven o'clock p.m.": *NR*, March 2, 1865.

697 "The hopeful condition" . . . the capital: *NR*, March 1, 1865.

697 so overcrowded . . . "found for them": *NR*, March 3, 1865.

697 Douglass decided . . . "of other citizens": Douglass, *Life and Times of Frederick Douglass*, p. 803.

697 visited Chase's . . . "a strange thing": Ibid., pp. 799–800.

697 steady rain . . . foreign ministries: Brooks, *Washington, D.C., in Lincoln's Time*, pp. 210–11; Brooks, *Mr. Lincoln's Washington*, pp. 418, 420 (quote).

697 "One ambassador . . . feet on the floor": Brooks, *Mr. Lincoln's Washington*, p. 421.

697 Johnson rose . . . "extraordinarily red": Brooks, *Washington, D.C., in Lincoln's Time*, p. 211.

697 "in a state of manifest . . . a petrified man": Brooks, *Mr. Lincoln's Washington*, pp. 422, 423.

698 "All this is . . . drunk or crazy": Entry for March 4, 1865, *Welles diary*, Vol. II, p. 252.

698 Dennison . . . "serene as summer": Brooks, *Mr. Lincoln's Washington*, pp. 423–24.

698 "emotion on . . . revisiting the Senate": Entry for March 4, 1865, *Welles diary*, Vol. II, p. 252.

698 Lincoln listened . . . harangue to end: Brooks, *Mr. Lincoln's Washington*, p. 423.

698 his eyes shut: Marquis de Chambrun [Charles Adolphe Pineton], "Personal Recollections of Mr. Lincoln," *Scribner's* 13 (January 1893), p. 26.

698 "You need not . . . a drunkard": AL, as quoted by Hugh McCullough in *Recollected Words of Abraham Lincoln*, p. 320.

698 audience proceeded . . . "glory and light": Brooks, *Mr. Lincoln's Washington*, pp. 424, 425 (quote).

698 an auspicious omen . . . Freedom: Brooks, *Washington, D.C., in Lincoln's Time*, pp. 213, 20–21.

698 "Both read the same . . . this terrible war": AL, "Second Inaugural Address," March 4, 1865, in *CW*, VIII, p. 333. For a thorough discussion of Lincoln's Second Inaugural Address, see Ronald C. White, *Lincoln's Greatest Speech: The Second Inaugural* (New York: Simon & Schuster, 2002).

699 "the eloquence of the prophets": Chambrun, "Personal Recollections of Mr. Lincoln," *Scribner's*, p. 27.

699 "Fondly do we hope . . . with all nations": AL, "Second Inaugural Address," March 4, 1865, in *CW*, VIII, pp. 332–33.

699 "as he became . . . Church member": Leonard Swett to WHH, January 17, 1866, in *HI*, pp. 167–68.

699 crowd cheered . . . drew to a close: *Boston Daily Evening Transcript*, March 4, 1865.

699 "the largest crowd . . . been here yet": JGN to TB, March 5, 1865, container 3, Nicolay Papers.

699 president was . . . five thousand people: *Star*, March 6, 1865.

699 "It was a grand . . . every 4 minutes": Entry for March 5, 1865, in French, *Witness to the Young Republic*, p. 466.

700 "On reaching the door . . . you liked it!": Douglass, *Life and Times of Frederick Douglass*, pp. 803–04.

700 his own assessment . . . "Almighty and them": AL to TW, March 15, 1865, *CW*, VIII, p. 356.

700 *New York World* . . . "statesmanship": *New York World*, March 6, 1865, quoted in Harris, *Lincoln's Last Months*, p. 149.

700 *Tribune* charged . . . chance for peace: *NYTrib*, March 6, 1865, quoted in Harris, p. 150.

701 "That rail-splitting . . . keynote of this war": Charles Francis Adams, Jr., to Charles Francis Adams, Sr., quoted in Harris, *Lincoln's Last Months*, p. 148.

701 London *Spectator* . . . "village lawyer": London *Spectator*, March 25, 1865, quoted in *Lincoln As They Saw Him*, ed. Herbert Mitgang (New York and Toronto: Rinehart & Company, Inc., 1956), pp. 447, 446.

701 Arnold overheard . . . Seward himself: Harris, *Lincoln's Last Months*, p. 148.

701 "The President's . . . position in history": Arnold, *The Life of Abraham Lincoln*, pp. 404–05.

701 "He has called . . . sickening to the heart": *Charleston [S.C.] Mercury*, January 10, 1865, reprinted in *Liberator*, March 3, 1865.

701 "it was always plain . . . judicious and appropriate": Charles A. Dana, quoted in Hay, "Life in the White House in the Time of Lincoln," *Century* (1890), p. 36.

CHAPTER 26: THE FINAL WEEKS

Page

702 "he was in mind . . . all-sufficing strength": Hay, "Life in the White House in the Time of Lincoln," *Century* (1890), p. 37.

703 "a tired spot": Brooks, *Mr. Lincoln's Washington*, p. 161.

703 avoid the thousands . . . "Egyptian locusts": JGN to TB, March 5, 1865, in Nicolay, *With Lincoln in the White House*, p. 175.

703 "The bare thought . . . *crush* me": AL, quoted in Carpenter, *Six Months at the White House*, p. 276.

703 "they don't want . . . must see them": AL, quoted in Hay, "Life in the White House in the Time of Lincoln," *Century* (1890), p. 33.

703 "I think now . . . *nineteen* enemies": AL, quoted in Carpenter, *Six Months at the White House*, p. 276.

703 hope that consul . . . wished to help: AL to WHS, March 6, 1865, *CW*, VIII, p. 337.

703 "at all times . . . of public trusts": AL to Winfield Scott and others, March 1, 1865, *CW*, VIII, p. 327.

704 Fessenden had been assured . . . "with regret": Fessenden, *Life and Public Services of William Pitt Fessenden*, Vol. I, pp. 365, 367 (quote).

704 "I desire gratefully . . . this great people": William Pitt Fessenden to AL, quoted in Fessenden, *Life and Public Services of William Pitt Fessenden*, Vol. I, p. 366.

704 he was nervous . . . "never sorry": Hugh McCulloch, *Men and Measures of Half a Century: Sketches and Comments* (New York: Charles Scribner's Sons, 1888; 1900), pp. 193–94.

704 intended to replace Usher: "Usher, John Palmer," in Neely, *The Abraham Lincoln Encyclopedia*, p. 317.

704 Hay was particularly adept . . . "his influence": William Leete Stone, quoted by Michael Burlingame, in introduction to Hay, *Inside Lincoln's White House*, p. xiii.

704 Nicolay functioned . . . and New York: Donald, *"We Are Lincoln Men,"* p. 209.

704 Hay was chosen . . . reconstruction of Florida: "Hay, John Milton," in Neely, *The Abraham Lincoln Encyclopedia*, p. 149.

705 had come to believe . . . "the hand of God": JH to JGN, August 7, 1863, in Hay, *At Lincoln's Side*, p. 49 (quote); "Hay, John Milton," in Neely, *The Abraham Lincoln Encyclopedia*, p. 149.

705 If the "patent . . . blinking eyes": JH to WHH, September 5, 1866, in *HI*, p. 332.

705 contemplating the purchase of a newspaper: Nicolay, *Lincoln's Secretary*, p. 224.

705 Mary had enlisted . . . Noah Brooks: Anson G. Henry to his wife, March 13, 1865, in *Concerning Mr. Lincoln*, comp. Pratt, p. 117.

705 tried to talk . . . any such discussion: JGN to TB, quoted in Nicolay, *Lincoln's Secretary*, p. 223.

705 Seward found . . . dissenting vote: *NR*, quoted in ibid., p. 224.

705 position paid . . . start married life: JGN to TB, March 12, 1865, quoted in ibid., p. 225.

706 Hay had recognized . . . "personal preeminence": "Hay's Reminiscences of the Civil War," in Hay, *At Lincoln's Side*, p. 129.

706 arranged for Hay . . . for another month: JH to Charles Hay, March 31, 1865, in Hay, *At Lincoln's Side*, p. 103.

706 "It will be . . . at the same time": JGN to TB, quoted in Nicolay, *Lincoln's Secretary*, p. 227.

706 "We are having . . . laid aside": MTL to Abram Wakeman, March 20, [1865], in Turner and Turner, *Mary Todd Lincoln*, pp. 205–06.

706 note to Sumner . . . "familiar to me": MTL to CS, March 23, 1865, in ibid., p. 209.

706 "an emotional temperament . . . heart would break": Helm, *The True Story of Mary*, p. 32.

706 an incident . . . "giving me up the key": Carpenter, *Six Months at the White House*, pp. 91–92.

707 "so full of life . . . little sprite": *NYTrib*, July 17, 1871.

707 Grant had issued . . . "to be asked": *The Personal Memoirs of Julia Dent Grant (Mrs. Ulysses S. Grant)*, ed. John Y. Simon (New York: G. P. Putnam's Sons, 1975), p. 141.

707 "Can you not . . . would do you good": USG to AL, March 20, 1865, Lincoln Papers.

707 Fox was not happy . . . "making the journey": John S. Barnes, "With Lincoln from Washington to Richmond in 1865," Part 1, *Appleton's* 9 (June 1907), p. 519.

707 ordered John Barnes . . . "very funny terms": Ibid., pp. 517–20.

708 presidential party . . . Wharf at Sixth Street: Entry for March 23, 1865, in *Lincoln Day by Day*, Vol. III, p. 322.

708 Stanton had been laid up . . . minutes after: Thomas and Hyman, *Stanton*, p. 350.

708 "a hurricane swept over the city": *Star*, February 15, 1896.

708 "terrific squalls . . . and its driver": *NYH*, March 24, 1865.

708 "while down the river . . . great violence": *Star*, February 15, 1896.

708 Stanton went . . . "at Point Lookout": EMS to AL, March 23, 1865, Lincoln Papers.

708 Tad raced around . . . "delicious fish": William H. Crook, "Lincoln as I Knew Him," *Harper's Monthly* 115 (May/June 1907), p. 46.

709 "Feeling *so* . . . loved so well": MTL to Francis B. Carpenter, November 15, [1865], in Turner and Turner, *Mary Todd Lincoln*, p. 284.

709 "it was after . . . headquarters at the top": Crook, "Lincoln as I Knew Him," *Harper's Monthly* (1907), p. 46.

709 Robert Lincoln . . . "was awaiting": *Personal Memoirs of Julia Dent Grant*, p. 142.
709 men went into . . . talked late into the night: Crook, "Lincoln as I Knew Him," *Harper's Monthly* (1907), pp. 46, 47.
709 While the Lincolns . . . original line: Shelby Foote, *The Civil War: A Narrative*. Vol. III: *Red River to Appomattox* (New York: Random House, 1958; New York: Vintage Books, 1986), pp. 838, 840–45.
710 walked up the bluff . . . "ruin of homes": Barnes, "With Lincoln from Washington to Richmond in 1865," Part 1, *Appleton's* (1907), pp. 521–22.
710 "I am here . . . states—1600": AL to EMS, March 25, 1865, *CW*, VIII, p. 374.
710 Stanton replied . . . " 'further off' ": EMS to AL, March 25, 1865, Lincoln Papers.
710 Lincoln's presence . . . "of their triumphs": *NYH*, March 28, 1865.
710 Lincoln seemed . . . "anecdotes": Porter, *Campaigning with Grant*, p. 407.
710 "Mr. President . . . old grudge against England to stand": USG and AL, quoted in Porter, *Campaigning with Grant*, pp. 408–9.
711 Porter's naval flotilla . . . "Come along!": Barnes, "With Lincoln from Washington to Richmond in 1865," Part 1, *Appleton's* (1907), pp. 522–23.
711 ambulance carrying . . . "ark of refuge": Porter, *Campaigning with Grant*, pp. 413–14 (quotes p. 414).
712 saw the attractive . . . "shocked and horrified": Adam Badeau, quoted in Foote, *The Civil War*, Vol. III, p. 847.
712 "was always that . . . impressed by it": John S. Barnes, "With Lincoln from Washington to Richmond in 1865," Part II, *Appleton's* (1907), p. 743.
712 had no desire . . . irrational outburst: Randall, *Mary Lincoln*, pp. 372–74.
712 Sherman was on his way . . . final push: William T. Sherman to Isaac N. Arnold, November 28, 1872, in Arnold, *The Life of Abraham Lincoln*, p. 421.
712 "their hands locked" . . . *River Queen*: Porter, *Campaigning with Grant*, pp. 417–18, 419.
712 greeted Sherman . . . depend upon the actions: William T. Sherman to Isaac N. Arnold, November 28, 1872, in Arnold, *The Life of Abraham Lincoln*, pp. 421–22.
713 long talk with Lincoln . . . "their shops": Sherman, *Memoirs of General W. T. Sherman*, p. 682.
713 "Let them have . . . to the laws": AL, quoted in David D. Porter, *Incidents and Anecdotes of the Civil War* (New York: D. Appleton and Company, 1886), p. 314.
713 privately wished . . . "goodness, than any other": Sherman, *Memoirs of General W. T. Sherman*, pp. 682–83.
713 walked to the railroad . . . "bless you all!": AL, quoted in Porter, *Campaigning with Grant*, pp. 425–26.
714 "I think . . . the wisest course": Entry for March 30, 1865, *Welles diary*, Vol. II, p. 269.
714 "We presume . . . palpable to be doubted": *NYTrib*, March 30, 1865.
714 "change of air & rest": MTL to CS, March 23, 1865, in Turner and Turner, *Mary Todd Lincoln*, p. 209.
714 "to escape the . . . pressure of visitors": *Philadelphia Inquirer*, March 24, 1865.
714 underscore his directive . . . "own hands": EMS to USG, March 3, 1865, *CW*, VIII, pp. 330–31.
714 "I begin to feel . . . little had been done": AL to EMS, March 30, 1865, ibid., p. 377.
714 "I hope you will . . . All well here": EMS to AL, March 31, 1865, ibid., p. 378 n1.
715 accompanied Mary . . . was well: Entry for April 1, 1865, in *Lincoln Day by Day*, Vol. III, p. 324; Randall, *Mary Lincoln*, p. 374.
715 "overwhelmingly charming . . . astounding person": Carl Schurz to his wife, April 2, 1865, in Schurz, *Intimate Letters of Carl Schurz, 1841–1869*, pp. 326–27.
715 "the flash of the cannon . . . in his that night": *Through Five Administrations: Reminiscences of Colonel William H. Crook, Body-Guard to President Lincoln*, ed. Margarita Spalding Gerry (New York and London: Harper & Brothers, 1910), p. 47.
715 broken through Petersburg's . . . and Richmond: Foote, *The Civil War*, Vol. III, pp. 876–80.
715 Lincoln received . . . "12,000 prisoners": AL to MTL, April 2, 1865, *CW*, VIII, p. 384.
715 Lincoln had moved . . . "a foot sideways": AL, quoted in Porter, *Incidents and Anecdotes of the Civil War*, pp. 284–85.
716 "a comfortable . . . yard in front": Porter, *Campaigning with Grant*, p. 449.
716 battlefields, littered . . . "lines of sadness": *Through Five Administrations*, ed. Gerry, p. 48.
716 "dismounted in the street" . . . strolled by: Porter, *Campaigning with Grant*, pp. 450, 451.
716 Grant surmised . . . "and cut him off": Grant, *Personal Memoirs of U. S. Grant*, p. 559.
716 back at City Point . . . "nightmare is gone": AL, quoted in Porter, *Incidents and Anecdotes of the Civil War*, p. 294.
716 in his customary pew . . . "retreating that evening": Davis, *Jefferson Davis*, p. 603; Jefferson Davis to Varina Davis, quoted in Robert McElroy, *Jefferson Davis: The Unreal and the Real* (New York and London: Harper & Brothers, 1937; New York: Smithmark, 1995), p. 454 (quote).
716 "Thereupon . . . all eyes in the house": *NYTrib*, April 8, 1865.
716 Summoning his cabinet . . . west to Danville: Davis, *Jefferson Davis*, p. 604.
716 small fire . . . "three-quarters of a mile": Charles A. Dana to EMS, April 6, 1865, *OR*, Ser. 1, Vol. XLVI, Part III, p. 594.
717 All the public buildings . . . were destroyed: *NYTrib*, April 8, 1865.
717 leaving only . . . the Spotswood Hotel: Charles A. Dana to EMS, April 6, 1865, *OR*, Ser. 1, Vol. XLVI, Part III, p. 594.
717 "Here is . . . Richmond has fallen": Bates, *Lincoln in the Telegraph Office*, pp. 360–61.
717 "spread by a thousand mouths": *Star*, April 3, 1865.
717 "almost by magic . . . fullness of their joy": Brooks, *Washington, D.C., in Lincoln's Time*, p. 219.
717 "wept as children . . . vows of friendship": *NYH*, April 4, 1865.

717 crowd called for Stanton . . . "his emotion": *Star*, February 15, 1896.
717 "gratitude to Almighty . . . with their blood": EMS, quoted in Brooks, *Washington, D.C., in Lincoln's Time*, p. 220.
717 "so overcome by emotion . . . speak continuously": Ibid.
717 Seward . . . "Secretary of War as this": WHS, quoted in ibid., p. 221.
717 crowd erupted . . . "loud and lusty" cheers: *NR*, April 3, 1865.
717 "beaming" Stanton . . . "The Star Spangled Banner": *NYTrib*, April 4, 1865.
717 "The demand seemed . . . press to supply": *Star*, April 3, 1865.
717 One hundred *Herald* . . . section of the city: *NYH*, April 4, 1865.
718 EXTRA! . . . first to enter the city: *NR*, April 3, 1865.
718 eight hundred guns, fired at Stanton's order: Brooks, *Mr. Lincoln's Washington*, p. 431.
718 dinner at Stanton's house: Thomas and Hyman, *Stanton*, p. 353.
718 "if there were to be . . . of the danger": James Speed to Joseph H. Barrett, 1885 September 16, Lincoln Collection, Lincoln Miscellaneous Manuscripts, Box 9, Folder 66, Special Collections, Research Center, University of Chicago Library.
718 tried to keep Lincoln . . . "the same condition": EMS to AL, April 3, 1865, Lincoln Papers.
718 Lincoln was already . . . Richmond the next day: AL to EMS, April 3, 1865, *CW*, VIII, p. 385.
718 At 8 a.m. . . . historic journey to Richmond: Barnes, "With Lincoln from Washington to Richmond in 1865," Part II, *Appleton's* (1907), p. 746.
718 channel approaching . . . "and touched them": *Through Five Administrations*, ed. Gerry, pp. 51–52.
718 "Here we were . . . well to be humble": AL, quoted in Porter, *Incidents and Anecdotes of the Civil War*, pp. 294–95.
719 Lincoln was surrounded . . . "hereafter enjoy": Ibid., p. 295.
719 men stood up . . . "and from the water-side": Ibid., pp. 296–97.
719 crowd trailed Lincoln . . . easily visible: Ibid., p. 299.
719 "walking with his usual . . . in everything": Thomas Thatcher Graves, "The Occupation," Part II of "The Fall of Richmond," in *Battles and Leaders of the Civil War*, Vol. IV, Pt. II, p. 727 (quote); Porter, *Incidents and Anecdotes of the Civil War*, p. 299; *Through Five Administrations*, ed. Gerry, p. 53.
719 Lincoln's bodyguard . . . along the route: *Through Five Administrations*, ed. Gerry, p. 54.
719 occupied the stucco mansion . . . glass of water: Barnes, "With Lincoln from Washington to Richmond in 1865," Part II, *Appleton's* (1907), pp. 748–49.
719 bottle of whiskey . . . "condition for the Yankees": *Through Five Administrations*, ed. Gerry, p. 55.
719 toured the mansion . . . "interested in everything": Graves, "The Occupation," in *Battles and Leaders of the Civil War*, Vol. IV, Pt. II, p. 728.
719 met with the members . . . troops from the war: J. G. Randall and Richard N. Current, *Lincoln the President: The Last Full Measure*, originally published as Vol. 4 of *Lincoln the President* (New York: Dodd, Mead, 1955; Urbana: University of Illinois Press, 1991), pp. 353–56; AL to Godfrey Weitzel, April 6, 1865, *CW*, VIII, p. 389.
720 Confederate statehouse . . . greatly relieved: Porter, *Incidents and Anecdotes of the Civil War*, pp. 302–03.
720 "nothing short of miraculous . . . go in peace": *Through Five Administrations*, ed. Gerry, p. 54.
720 all the public buildings . . . "one blaze of glory": Brooks, *Mr. Lincoln's Washington*, p. 434.
720 "the entire population . . . of lighted candles": *NR*, April 5, 1865.
720 he told Welles . . . "schemes are his apology": Entry for April 5, 1865, *Welles diary*, Vol. II, p. 275.
720 Fanny and her friend . . . horses bolted: Seward, *Seward at Washington . . . 1861–1872*, p. 270 (quote); entry for April 5, 1865, in Johnson, "Sensitivity and Civil War," p. 867; *NR*, April 6, 1865.
720 "swinging the driver . . . a cat by the tail": *NR*, April 6, 1865.
720 Fred and Seward jumped . . . consciousness: Seward, *Seward at Washington . . . 1861–1872*, p. 270 (quote); entry for April 5, 1865, in Johnson, "Sensitivity and Civil War," pp. 867–68; Verdi, "The Assassination of the Sewards," *The Republic* (1873), p. 290.
720 "The horses tore" . . . his broken body: Entry for April 5, 1865, in Johnson, "Sensitivity and Civil War," pp. 867–68.
721 "blood streaming from his mouth": Verdi, "The Assassination of the Sewards," *The Republic* (1873), p. 290.
721 delirious with pain . . . his side for hours: Entry for April 5, 1865, in Johnson, "Sensitivity and Civil War," pp. 868, 869.
721 Stanton sent . . . "presence here is needed": EMS to AL, April 5, 1865, Lincoln Papers.
721 Lincoln advised Grant . . . return to Washington: AL to USG, April 6, 1865, *CW*, VIII, p. 388.
721 Mary and her invited . . . "arrive at City Point": MTL to EMS, April 6, 1865, in Turner and Turner, *Mary Todd Lincoln*, p. 214 (quote); Foote, *The Civil War*, Vol. III, p. 903; Keckley, *Behind the Scenes*, p. 163.
721 Stanton informed . . . "remaining at City Point": EMS to MTL, April 6, 1865, Lincoln Papers.
721 he sent word . . . "clear and spirits good": EMS to AL, April 6, 1865, Lincoln Papers.
721 Mary's party arrived . . . bulletins, all positive: Chambrun, "Personal Recollections of Mr. Lincoln," *Scribner's* (1893), p. 27.
721 "His whole appearance . . . had been attained": James Harlan, quoted in Foote, *The Civil War*, Vol. III, P874p. 903.
721 "it was impossible . . . much less of vanity": Chambrun, "Personal Recollections of Mr. Lincoln," *Scribner's* (1893), p. 28.
722 telegram from Sheridan . . . "Lee will surrender": Phil Sheridan to USG, quoted in AL to EMS, April 7, 1865, *CW*, VIII, p. 389.
722 "Let the *thing* be pressed": AL to USG, April 7, 1865, *CW*, VIII, p. 392.

722 Julia Grant . . . "that we be not judged": *Personal Memoirs of Julia Dent Grant*, p. 149; Chambrun, "Personal Recollections of Mr. Lincoln," *Scribner's* (1893), p. 33 (quote).

722 "he gave orders . . . the great oaks": Chambrun, "Personal Recollections of Mr. Lincoln," *Scribner's* (1893), p. 29 (quote); Keckley, *Behind the Scenes*, p. 169.

722 "an old country . . . quiet place like this": AL, quoted in Arnold, *The Life of Abraham Lincoln*, p. 435.

722 observed a turtle . . . shared "a happy laugh": Keckley, *Behind the Scenes*, p. 170.

722 visited injured soldiers . . . "no more fighting": Chambrun, "Personal Recollections of Mr. Lincoln," *Scribner's* (1893), pp. 30, 33–34.

722 came to say farewell . . . "floating palace": Keckley, *Behind the Scenes*, pp. 171–72.

723 asked them to play . . . "upon literary subjects": Chambrun, "Personal Recollections of Mr. Lincoln," *Scribner's* (1893), pp. 34, 35.

723 "a beautiful quarto . . . in his hands": Edward L. Pierce, *Memoir and Letters of Charles Sumner*, Vol. IV (London: Sampson Low, Marston and Co., 1893), p. 235.

723 passages from *Macbeth* . . . *touch him further*: William Shakespeare, *Macbeth*, Scene II, in *The Riverside Shakespeare*, 2nd edn., Vol. II (Boston and New York: Houghton Mifflin, 1997), p. 1373; Chambrun, "Personal Recollections of Mr. Lincoln," *Scribner's* (1893), p. 35.

723 "how true a description . . . the same scene": Chambrun, "Personal Recollections of Mr. Lincoln," *Scribner's* (1893), p. 35.

723 ominous selection . . . "in continual dread": Speed to Barrett, September 16, 1885, University of Chicago Library.

723 "that the people know . . . without fear": AL, quoted in Thomas and Hyman, *Stanton*, p. 395.

723 passed by Mount Vernon . . . "would again reappear": Chambrun, "Personal Recollections of Mr. Lincoln," *Scribner's* (1893), pp. 35, 32.

724 He had observed . . . "in ruined Richmond": *Through Five Administrations*, ed. Gerry, p. 59.

724 "It was in the evening . . . injuries and the shock": Seward, *Seward at Washington . . . 1861–1872*, pp. 271, 270.

724 his face "so marred . . . patient and uncomplaining": FAS to LW, quoted in ibid., p. 271.

724 "The extreme sensitiveness . . . from the door": Seward, ibid., p. 271.

724 Lincoln entered the room . . . "the end, at last": WHS and AL, quoted in ibid., p. 271.

724 stretched out . . . "satisfied at the labor": Seward, *Seward at Washington . . . 1861–1872*, p. 271; entry for April 9, 1865, in Johnson, "Sensitivity and Civil War," p. 872 (quotes).

725 saw that Seward . . . got up and left the room: Seward, *Seward at Washington . . . 1861–1872*, p. 272.

725 telegram from Grant . . . "proposed by myself": USG to EMS, April 9, 1865, *OR*, Ser. 1, Vol. XLVI, Part III, p. 663.

725 "the President hugged him with joy": *Star*, February 15, 1896.

725 close to 10 p.m. . . . "first time in my life": Entry for April 9, 1865, in Johnson, "Sensitivity and Civil War," p. 871.

725 Both Grant and Lee . . . "dignified in defeat": Jay Winik, *April 1865: The Month That Saved America* (New York: HarperCollins, 2001), p. 193.

725 Grant had sent a note . . . "effusion of blood": USG to Robert E. Lee, April 7, 1865, *OR*, Ser. 1, Vol. XLVI, Part III, p. 619.

725 Lee refused to accept . . . ready to surrender: McPherson, *Battle Cry of Freedom*, p. 848.

725 dressed for the historic . . . "deep, red silk": Douglas Southall Freeman, *R. E. Lee: A Biography*, Vol. IV (New York: Charles Scribner's Sons, 1936), p. 118.

725 imprisoned before . . . "my best appearance": Robert E. Lee, quoted in ibid., p. 118.

725 terms of surrender . . . "properly exchanged": USG to Robert E. Lee, April 9, 1865, quoted in Grant, *Personal Memoirs of U.S. Grant*, p. 581.

725 "the thought occurred to me" . . . twenty-five thousand men: Grant, *Personal Memoirs of U.S. Grant*, pp. 581–83.

726 tried to speak . . . "tears came into his eyes": Freeman, *R. E. Lee*, Vol. IV, p. 144.

726 "Men, we have fought . . . best I could for you": Robert E. Lee, quoted in ibid.

726 "each side of . . . as ever, General Lee!": Charles Blackford, quoted in ibid. pp. 146, 147.

726 "a great boom . . . laid down its arms": Brooks, *Washington, D.C., in Lincoln's Time*, p. 223.

726 "The nation seems . . . terminates the Rebellion": Entry for April 10, 1865, *Welles diary*, Vol. II, p. 278.

726 several thousand gathered . . . "people cheered": *National Intelligencer*, Washington, D.C., April 11, 1865, quoted in *CW*, VIII, p. 393 n1.

726 planning a speech . . . "dribble it all out": AL, "Response to Serenade," *National Intelligencer* version, April 10, 1865, *CW*, VIII, p. 393.

726 If he said something . . . "not to make mistakes": AL, "Response to Serenade," *NR* version, April 10, 1865, *CW*, VIII, p. 394.

726 finally appeared . . . "waving their handkerchiefs": *NR*, April 11, 1865.

727 "I am very greatly . . . with its performance": AL, "Response to Serenade," *National Intelligencer* version, April 10, 1865, *CW*, VIII, p. 393.

727 "it is good to show the rebels . . . hear it again": Chambrun, "Personal Recollections of Mr. Lincoln," *Scribner's* (1893), p. 34.

727 band followed "Dixie" . . . "in high good-humor": *Through Five Administrations*, ed. Gerry, p. 62 (quote); *National Intelligencer*, April 11, 1865, in *CW*, VIII, pp. 393–94 n1.

727 "If possible . . . than last Monday": MTL to CS, April 10, 1865, in Turner and Turner, *Mary Todd Lincoln*, p. 216.

727 exhilaration was evident . . . "qu'en pensez vous?": MTL to CS, April 11, 1865, in ibid., p. 217.
727 Illuminated once again . . . miles around: Brooks, *Washington, D.C., in Lincoln's Time*, p. 225.
727 "Bonfires blazed . . . rockets were fired": *NYTrib*, April 12, 1865.
727 decorating the front . . . "and evergreens": *Star*, February 15, 1896.
727 a second-story window . . . "of a different character": Brooks, *Washington, D.C., in Lincoln's Time*, pp. 226–27.
727 "the greatest question . . . practical statesmanship": "31 July 1863, Friday," in Hay, *Inside Lincoln's White House*, p. 69.
728 acknowledged that in Louisiana . . . "by smashing it?": AL, "Last Public Address," April 11, 1865, *CW*, VIII, pp. 403–04.
728 John Wilkes Booth . . . passion for the rebels' cause: Lockridge, *Darling of Misfortune*, p. 111.
728 evolved a plan to kidnap . . . not ready to yield: Michael W. Kauffman, *American Brutus: John Wilkes Booth and the Lincoln Conspiracies* (New York: Random House, 2004), pp. 134, 211–12.
728 "Our cause being almost . . . great must be done": Text of John Wilkes Booth diary, available through Abraham Lincoln research website, http://members.aol.com/RVSNorton1/Lincoln52.html (accessed May 2005).
728 Two other conspirators . . . "put him through": John Wilkes Booth, quoted in Donald, *Lincoln*, p. 588.
728 Curiously . . . "God knows what is best": Lamon, *Recollections of Abraham Lincoln*, pp. 116–18.
729 Fehrenbacher is persuasive . . . confused: Commentary on Lamon recollection, *Recollected Words of Abraham Lincoln*, ed. Fehrenbacher and Fehrenbacher, p. 293.
729 While radicals . . . control of the seceded states: Pierce, *Memoir and Letters of Charles Sumner*, Vol. IV, p. 236; SPC to AL, April 12, 1865, Lincoln Papers.
729 "a large majority of the people": *NYH*, quoted in Harris, *Lincoln's Last Months*, p. 216.
729 "Reunion . . . in the minds of men": Brooks, *Washington, D.C., in Lincoln's Time*, p. 228.
729 "there must be . . . robber bands and guerillas": Entry for April 13, 1865, *Welles diary*, Vol. II, p. 279.
729 Lincoln had hoped . . . "their own work": Ibid.
729 "that to place . . . bring trouble with Congress": A. E. H. Johnson, quoted in Flower, *Edwin McMasters Stanton*, p. 272.
729 Stanton insisted . . . "absolutely null and void": EMS, quoted in ibid., p. 271.
730 Speed expressed his accord . . . with Lincoln: Williams, "James and Joshua Speed," p. 148.
730 confessed to Welles . . . tremendously: Gideon Welles, "Lincoln and Johnson," *Galaxy* 13 (April 1872), p. 524.
730 "doubted the policy . . . correct it if he had": Entry for April 13, 1865, *Welles diary*, Vol. II, pp. 279–80.
730 telegram from Campbell . . . originally discussed: John A. Campbell to Godfrey Weitzel, April 7, 1865, *CW*, VIII, pp. 407–08 n1.
730 Lincoln walked over . . . "any specific acts": A. E. H. Johnson, quoted in Flower, *Edwin McMasters Stanton*, p. 272.
730 Lincoln stood up . . . "safe-return to their homes": AL to Godfrey Weitzel, April 12, 1865, *CW*, VIII, p. 407 (quote); EMS, in Flower, *Edwin McMasters Stanton*, p. 271.
730 "that . . . was exactly right": Ibid.
730 "As we reached . . . 'candles from my department' ": *Personal Memoirs of Julia Dent Grant*, pp. 153, 154.
731 received a delightful note . . . "drive with me!": MTL to Mary Jane Welles, July 11, 1865, in Turner and Turner, *Mary Todd Lincoln*, p. 257.
731 "We are rejoicing . . . glorious victories": MTL to James Gordon Bennett, [April 13, 1865], in ibid., p. 219.
731 "charming time . . . into a lad of sixteen": MTL to Abram Wakeman, April 13, [1865], in ibid., p. 220.
731 told Sumner . . . a visit with General Grant: MTL to CS, [April] 13, [1865], in ibid., p. 219.
731 "Well, my son . . . for a long while": Keckley, *Behind the Scenes*, pp. 137–38.
731 Grant arrived . . . this event would be favorable: Entry for April 14, 1865, *Welles diary*, Vol. II, pp. 282–83.
732 Stanton had drafted . . . "asked me to read it": EMS, quoted in Flower, *Edwin McMasters Stanton*, p. 301.
732 cabinet concurred . . . two separate states: Entry for April 14, 1865, *Welles diary*, Vol. II, p. 281; Nicolay and Hay, *Abraham Lincoln*, Vol. X (1890 edn.), p. 284.
732 "he thought it providential . . . harmony and union": Gideon Welles, "Lincoln and Johnson," *Galaxy* 13 (April 1872), p. 526.
732 "Didn't our Chief . . . hair and whiskers": Speed to Barrett, September 16, 1885, Lincoln Collection, University of Chicago Library.
732 Lincoln seemed "more cheerful . . . at home and abroad": EMS to Charles Francis Adams, April 15, 1865, Telegrams Sent by the Secretary of War, Vol. 185–186, December 27, 1864–April 20, 1865, Telegrams Collected by the Office of the Secretary of War (Bound) (National Archives Microfilm Publication M-473, reel 88), Records of the Office of the Secretary of War, RG 107, DNA.
732 "spoke very kindly . . . of the Confederacy": EMS to John A. Dix, April 15, 1865, *OR*, Ser. 1, Vol. XLVI, Part III, p. 780.
732 "in marked degree . . . distinguished him": EMS to Charles Francis Adams, April 15, 1865 (M-473, reel 88), RG 107, DNA.
732 "a conspicuous . . . best to let him run": Dana, *Recollection of the Civil War* (1996 edn.), pp. 273–74.
733 She had never seen . . . " 'been very miserable' ": MTL to Francis B. Carpenter, November 15, [1865], in Turner and Turner, *Mary Todd Lincoln*, pp. 284–85.
733 "he spoke of his old . . . riding the circuit": Arnold, *The Life of Abraham Lincoln*, pp. 429–30.
733 hoped to travel . . . back home to Illinois: MTL interview, [September 1866], in *HI*, p. 359; Randall, *Mary Lincoln*, p. 382.
733 group of old friends . . . "to dinner at once": Tarbell, *The Life of Abraham Lincoln*, Vol. II (1900 edn.), p. 235.
734 met with Noah Brooks . . . "its pleasures": AL, quoted in Hollister, *Life of Schuyler Colfax*, p. 252.
734 invited Colfax to join . . . that night: Ibid., p. 253.

734 "more hopeful . . . nearly so with gold": Brooks, *Mr. Lincoln's Washington*, p. 443.

734 *Republican* had announced . . . box that night: *NR*, April 14, 1865.

734 Julia Grant . . . asked to be excused: Grant, *Personal Memoirs of U. S. Grant*, p. 592; *Personal Memoirs of Julia Dent Grant*, p. 155.

734 The Stantons also declined: Thomas and Hyman, *Stanton*, p. 395.

734 "unwilling to encourage . . . poker over his arm": Bates, *Lincoln in the Telegraph Office*, p. 367.

734 "I suppose it's time . . . would rather stay": AL, quoted in Hollister, *Life of Schuyler Colfax*, p. 253.

734 "It has been advertised . . . disappoint the people": AL, quoted in *Through Five Administrations*, p. 67.

735 Booth had devised a plan . . . assassinate the president: Kauffman, *American Brutus*, pp. 212–15.

735 Booth believed he would be . . . "greater tyrant": Text of John Wilkes Booth diary, available through Abraham Lincoln research website, http://members/aol.com/RVSNorton1/Lincoln52.html (accessed May 2005).

735 "Booth knew . . . martyr of Caesar": Kauffman, *American Brutus*, p. 212.

735 slept well the previous . . . "for the first time": Entry for April 14, 1865, in Johnson, "Sensitivity and Civil War," p. 876.

735 "listened with a look . . . the Cabinet meeting": Seward, *Reminiscences of a War-Time Statesman and Diplomat*, p. 258.

735 Fanny's reading . . . how much he enjoyed it: Entry for April 14, 1865, in Johnson, "Sensitivity and Civil War," p. 876.

735 Stanton had stopped by . . . serenading him: Thomas and Hyman, *Stanton*, p. 396.

736 "quiet arrangements" . . . opposite side of the bed: Entry for April 14, 1865, in Johnson, "Sensitivity and Civil War," p. 877.

736 "there seemed nothing unusual . . . presented himself": Seward, *Reminiscences of a War-Time Statesman and Diplomat*, p. 258.

736 Powell told the servant . . . but Fred refused: Verdi, "The Assassination of the Sewards," *The Republic* (1873), p. 293.

736 "stood apparently irresolute . . . pulled the trigger": Seward, *Reminiscences of a War-Time Statesman and Diplomat*, p. 259.

736 last memory Fred would have . . . unconscious: *Cincinnati [Ohio] Commercial*, December 8, 1865.

736 Private Robinson . . . headed toward Seward: Charles F. Cooney, "Seward's Savior: George F. Robinson," *Lincoln Herald* (Fall 1973), p. 93.

736 begging him not to kill . . . "face bending over": Entry for April 14, 1865, in Johnson, "Sensitivity and Civil War," pp. 879–80.

736 large bowie knife . . . "loose on his neck": Verdi, "The Assassination of the Sewards," *The Republic* (1873), p. 291.

736 his only impressions . . . "overcoat is made of": WHS, quoted in *Cincinnati [Ohio] Commercial*, December 8, 1865.

736 Fanny's screams . . . the floor: Entry for April 14, 1865, in Johnson, "Sensitivity and Civil War," p. 880.

737 managed to pull Powell away . . . the right hand: Verdi, "The Assassination of the Sewards," *The Republic* (1873), p. 292.

737 Gus ran for his pistol . . . fled through the city: Seward, *Seward at Washington . . . 1861–1872*, p. 279.

737 lifted Seward onto the bed . . . rooms on the parlor floor: Entry for April 14, 1865, in Johnson, "Sensitivity and Civil War," pp. 882, 884.

737 "He looked like an . . . yes, of one man!": Verdi, "The Assassination of the Sewards," *The Republic* (1873), pp. 291–92.

738 Atzerodt had taken a room . . . "not to kill": Donald, *Lincoln*, p. 596.

738 seated at the bar . . . and never returned: Winik, *April 1865*, p. 226.

738 had attended a dress rehearsal . . . Harry Ford: Kauffman, *American Brutus*, pp. 214, 217.

738 play had started . . . "with a smile and bow": Charles A. Leale, M.D., to Benjamin F. Butler, July 20, 1867, container 43, Butler Papers, DLC.

738 armchair at the center . . . sofa on her left: "Major Rathbone's Affidavit," in J. E. Buckingham, Sr., *Reminiscences and Souvenirs of the Assassination of Abraham Lincoln* (Washington, D.C.: Rufus H. Darby, 1894), pp. 73, 75.

738 "rested her hand . . . situation on the stage": Charles Sabin Taft, "Abraham Lincoln's Last Hours," *Century* 45 (February 1893), p. 634.

738 later recalled . . . "think any thing about it": Randall, *Mary Lincoln*, p. 382.

738 footman delivered a message . . . and fired: Winik, *April 1865*, p. 223; Harris, *Lincoln's Last Months*, p. 224.

739 "As he jumped . . . struck the stage": Taft, "Abraham Lincoln's Last Hours," *Century* 45 (1893), p. 634.

739 "he was suffering . . . he struggled up": Annie F. F. Wright, "The Assassination of Abraham Lincoln," *Magazine of History* 9 (February 9, 1909), p. 114.

739 "his shining dagger . . . it had been a diamond": Leale to Butler, July 20, 1867, container 43, Butler Papers, DLC.

739 shouted . . . "Sic semper tyrannis": Wright, "The Assassination of Abraham Lincoln," *Magazine of History* (1909), p. 114.

739 saw Mary Lincoln . . . "shot the President!": Ibid.

739 Charles Leale . . . pressure on Lincoln's brain: Leale to Butler, July 20, 1867, container 43, Butler Papers, DLC.

739 Charles Sabin Taft . . . boardinghouse: Taft, "Abraham Lincoln's Last Hours," *Century* 45 (1893), p. 635.

739 Joseph Sterling . . . headed for Seward's house: Joseph A. Sterling, quoted in *Star*, April 14, 1918.

740 already gone to bed . . . set forth in the foggy night: Entry for April 14, 1865, *Welles diary*, Vol. II, pp. 283–84.

740 Blood was everywhere . . . floor of the bedroom: Entry for April 14, 1865, in Johnson, "Sensitivity and Civil War," p. 886.

740 "was saturated with blood" . . . he decided to join them: Entry for April 14, 1865, *Welles diary*, Vol. II, pp. 285–86 (quote p. 285).

740 Chase had already retired . . . "a night of horrors": Entries for April 14, 1865, *Chase Papers*, Vol. 1, pp. 528–29.

741 Lincoln had been placed . . . "spare appearance": Entry for April 14, 1865, *Welles diary*, Vol. II, p. 286.

741 "would have killed most men . . . *much vitality*": Entry for April 30, 1865, Taft diary.

741 Mary spent most . . . "overcome by emotion": Entry for April 14, 1865, *Welles diary*, Vol. II, p. 287.

741 "Why didn't he shoot me?" . . . not told, out of fear: Field, *Memories of Many Men*, p. 322.

741 "clean napkins . . . stains on the pillow": Taft, "Abraham Lincoln's Last Hours," *Century* 45 (1893), p. 635.

741 Robert, who had remained . . . "leaving his cheeks": Thomas F. Pendel, *Thirty-Six Years in the White House* (Washington, D.C.: Neale Publishing Company, 1902), pp. 42–43.

741 to summon Tad . . . his father's condition: Leale to Butler, July 20, 1867, container 43, Butler Papers, DLC.

741 Tad and his tutor . . . to see *Aladdin*: M. Helen Palmes Moss, "Lincoln and Wilkes Booth as Seen on the Day of the Assassination," *Century* LXXVII (April 1909), p. 951.

741 decorated with patriotic . . . "shrieking in agony": *NR*, April 15, 1865.

742 "Poor little Tad . . . fell into a sound sleep": Pendel, *Thirty-Six Years in the White House*, p. 44.

742 entire cabinet . . . "heartrending lamentations": *NYH*, April 16, 1865.

742 "there was not a soul . . . love the president": *Star*, February 15, 1896.

742 "While evidently swayed . . . in all things": A. F. Rockwell, quoted in Flower, *Edwin McMasters Stanton*, p. 283.

742 dictated numerous dispatches . . . "wait for the next": *Star*, February 15, 1896.

742 first telegram . . . "in a dangerous condition": Thomas T. Eckert to USG, April 14, 1865, *OR*, Ser. 1, Vol. XLVI, Part III, pp. 744–45.

742 reached Grant . . . "in perfect silence": Porter, *Campaigning with Grant*, p. 499.

742 he had turned "very pale": *Personal Memoirs of Julia Dent Grant*, p. 156.

742 Julia Grant guessed . . . "that could be received": Porter, *Campaigning with Grant*, pp. 499–500.

742 he told Julia . . . "tenderness and magnanimity": *Personal Memoirs of Julia Dent Grant*, p. 156.

743 At 1 a.m., Stanton telegraphed . . . "best detectives": EMS to John H. Kennedy, April 15, 1865, *OR*, Ser. 1, Vol. XLVI, Part III, p. 783.

743 "The wound is mortal . . . is now dying": EMS to John A. Dix, April 15, 1865, 1:30 a.m., *OR*, Ser. 1, Vol. XLVI, Part III, p. 780.

743 "The President continues . . . shot the President": Ibid., 4:10 a.m., p. 781.

743 Shortly after dawn . . . "death-struggle had begun": Entry for April 14, 1865, *Welles diary*, Vol. II, p. 288.

743 "As she entered" . . . sofa in the parlor: Taft, "Abraham Lincoln's Last Hours," *Century* 45 (1893), p. 635.

743 "the town clocks . . . be again resumed": Field, *Memories of Many Men*, p. 325.

743 "Let us pray" . . . everyone present knelt: Leale to Butler, July 20, 1867, container 43, Butler Papers, DLC.

743 At 7:22 a.m. . . . "belongs to the ages": Donald, *Lincoln*, p. 599. As David Donald notes, witnesses thought they heard several variations of Stanton's utterance, including "He belongs to the ages now," "He now belongs to the Ages," and "He is a man for the ages." Donald, *Lincoln*, p. 686, endnote for p. 599 beginning "*to the ages.*"

743 "Oh, why did you not . . . he was dying": *NYH*, April 16, 1865.

743 moans could be heard . . . taken to her carriage: Taft, "Abraham Lincoln's Last Hours," *Century* 45 (1893), p. 636; Field, *Memories of Many Men*, p. 326.

743 Stanton's "coolness" . . . streamed down his cheeks: *NYH*, April 16, 1865.

743 "Stanton's grief . . . break down and weep bitterly": Porter, *Campaigning with Grant*, p. 501.

743 "Not everyone knows . . . his honor and yours": JH to EMS, July 26, 1865, in Hay, *At Lincoln's Side*, p. 106.

744 "Is he dead? . . . entire face was distorted": Field, *Memories of Many Men*, p. 327.

744 walked to Seward's house . . . Blair and his father: Entry for April 15, 1865, *Chase Papers*, Vol. I, pp. 529, 530.

744 "with tearful eyes . . . of our side": EBL to SPL, April 15, 1865, in *Wartime Washington*, ed. Laas, p. 495.

744 *Richmond Whig* . . . "South has descended": *Richmond Whig*, quoted in Robert S. Harper, *Lincoln and the Press* (New York: McGraw-Hill, 1951), p. 360.

744 St. Louis . . . comfortable study: Entry for January 27, 1865, *The Diary of Edward Bates, 1859–1866*, p. 443.

744 "the astounding news . . . country and for myself": Entry for April 15, 1865, in ibid., p. 473.

744 News of Lincoln's death . . . "sinking into his mind": Brooks, *Mr. Lincoln's Washington*, pp. 458–59 (quotes p. 459).

745 "The history of governments . . . confidence and regard": "Hay's Reminiscences of the Civil War," in Hay, *At Lincoln's Side*, pp. 128–29.

745 Flags remained . . . "the farewell march": Brooks, *Washington, D.C., in Lincoln's Time*, pp. 271 (quote), 273.

745 nearly two hundred thousand Union soldiers: Smith, *The Francis Preston Blair Family in Politics*, Vol. II, p. 185.

745 "Never in the history . . . shrill call of bugles": Brooks, *Washington, D.C., in Lincoln's Time*, pp. 272–74.

745 "magnificent and imposing spectacle": Entry for May 19, 1865, *Welles diary*, Vol. II, p. 310.

745 "You see in these . . . half a dozen presidents": EMS, quoted in Flower, *Edwin McMasters Stanton*, p. 288.

746 "more and more dim . . . found in every family": AL, "Address Before the Young Men's Lyceum of Springfield, Illinois," January 27, 1838, in *CW*, I, p. 115.

746 "a new birth of freedom . . . perish from the earth": AL, "Address Delivered at the Dedication of the Cemetery at Gettysburg," final text, November 19, 1863, in *CW*, VII, p. 23.

746 second day belonged . . . "with our swords": Sherman, *Memoirs of General W. T. Sherman*, p. 731.

746 All of Washington . . . "All felt this": Entry for April 19, 1865, *Welles diary*, Vol. II, p. 310.

746 "a Cabinet which should . . . than one counsellor": WHS, "The President and His Cabinet," October 20, 1865, *Works of William H. Seward*, Vol. V, p. 527.

747 "I have no doubt . . . greatest man I ever knew": Tribute by General Grant, in Browne, *The Every-Day Life of Abraham Lincoln*, p. 7.
747 "I have more than once . . . Nineteenth Century": Walt Whitman, "November Boughs," *The Complete Prose Works of Walt Whitman*, Vol. III (New York: G. P. Putnam's Sons, Knickerbocker Press, 1902), pp. 206–07.
747 Leo Tolstoy . . . "light beams directly on us": Leo Tolstoy, quoted in *The World*, New York, February 7, 1908.
748 "Every man is said . . . yet to be developed": AL, "Communication to the People of Sangamo County," March 9, 1832, in *CW*, I, p. 8.
748 "he had done nothing . . . that he had lived": AL, paraphrased in Joshua F. Speed to WHH, February 7, 1866, in *HI*, p. 197.
749 "conceived in Liberty . . . all men are created equal": AL, "Address Delivered at the Dedication of the Cemetery at Gettysburg, November 19, 1863; Edward Everett Copy," in *CW*, VII, p. 21.
749 "With malice toward none; with charity for all": AL, "Second Inaugural Address," March 4, 1865, *CW*, VIII, p. 333.

EPILOGUE

Page
751 "night of horrors": Entries for April 14, 1865, *Chase Papers*, Vol. I, p. 529.
751 "vicarious suffering": FAS, in "Miscellaneous Fragments in Mrs. Seward's Handwriting," reel 197, Seward Papers.
751 "the largest . . . woman in America": *New York Independent*, undated, in Seward family scrapbook, Seward House Foundation Historical Association, Inc., Library, Auburn, N.Y.
751 Fanny remained . . . tuberculosis: Taylor, *William Henry Seward*, p. 266.
751 Seward was inconsolable: Van Deusen, *William Henry Seward*, p. 417.
751 "Truly it may . . . mother and daughter": *Washington Republican*, undated, in Seward family scrapbook, Seward House.
751 attempts to mediate . . . radicals in Congress: Van Deusen, *William Henry Seward*, p. 452.
751 "Seward's Folly": Taylor, *William Henry Seward*, p. 278.
751 spent his last years traveling: Ibid., pp. 290–91, 292–94; *NYT*, October 11, 1872.
751 Jenny asked . . . "Love one another": Taylor, *William Henry Seward*, p. 296; Seward, *Seward at Washington . . . 1861–1872*, p. 508 (quote).
751 Thurlow Weed . . . wept openly: Taylor, *William Henry Seward*, p. 296.
751 Stanton's remaining . . . asked for his resignation: Pratt, *Stanton*, p. 452; Thomas and Hyman, *Stanton*, p. 583.
751 Refusing to honor . . . removal order: George C. Gorham, *Life and Public Services of Edwin M. Stanton*, Vol. II (Boston and New York: Houghton, Mifflin, Riverside Press, 1899), p. 444.
751 "barricaded himself": Pratt, *Stanton*, p. 452.
751 taking his meals in the department: Thomas and Hyman, *Stanton*, p. 595.
751 Tenure of Office Act: "Tenure of Office Act," in *The Reader's Companion to American History*, ed. Foner and Garraty, pp. 1,063–64.
752 impeachment failed . . . submitted his resignation: Thomas and Hyman, *Stanton*, p. 608.
752 Grant nominated him . . . "only office": Wolcott, "Edwin M. Stanton," p. 178.
752 short-lived . . . severe asthma attack: *Dictionary of American Biography*, Vol. IX, ed. Dumas Malone (New York: Charles Scribner's Sons, 1935; 1964), p. 520; Thomas and Hyman, *Stanton*, pp. 637–38; Christopher Bates, "Stanton, Edwin McMasters," in *Encyclopedia of the American Civil War*, ed. Heidler and Heidler, p. 1852.
752 "I know that it is . . . he was then": Robert Todd Lincoln to Edwin L. Stanton, quoted in Thomas and Hyman, *Stanton*, p. 638.
752 close-knit family . . . Confederate Army: Cain, *Lincoln's Attorney General*, p. 330.
752 "it was in his social . . . death cannot sever": Address by Colonel J. C. Broadhead, in "Addresses by the Members of the St. Louis Bar on the Death of Edward Bates," Bates Papers, MoSHi.
752 impeachment trial . . . resting with the Democrats: Blue, *Salmon P. Chase*, p. 285.
752 Kate serving . . . derailed his ambitions: *Dictionary of American Biography*, Vol. II, ed. Allen Johnson and Dumas Malone (New York: Charles Scribner's Sons, 1929; 1958), p. 33.
752 switched his allegiance . . . to Horace Greeley: Niven, *Salmon P. Chase*, pp. 447–48.
752 physical condition weakened . . . depression: Ibid., pp. 444, 448–49.
752 "too much of an invalid . . . I were dead": SPC to Richard C. Parsons, May 5, 1873, *Chase Papers*, Vol. V, p. 370.
752 Kate saw her marriage . . . died in poverty: Belden and Belden, *So Fell the Angels*, pp. 297–98, 306–10, 320, 326–27, 348.
753 Frank Blair . . . intemperate denunciations: *Dictionary of American Biography*, Vol. I, ed. Allen Johnson (New York: Charles Scribner's Sons, 1927; 1964), pp. 333–34.
753 died from a fall: *NYT*, July 10, 1875.
753 "his physical vigor . . . of disposition": *Sun*, Baltimore, Md., October 19, 1876.
753 Montgomery served . . . biography of Andrew Jackson: *Dictionary of American Biography*, Vol. I (1964 edn.), p. 340.
753 wrote a series . . . "herculean tasks": Niven, *Gideon Welles*, pp. 576–77 (quote p. 576).
753 perceptive diary . . . streptococcus infection: Ibid., pp. 578, 580.
753 remained friends . . . abridged version: Nicolay, *Lincoln's Secretary*, pp. 301, 342.

753 Shortly before he died . . . "overpowering melancholy": William Roscoe Thayer, *The Life and Letters of John Hay* (Boston and New York: Houghton Mifflin, 1929), pp. 405, 407.

753 "each morning . . . as an impossibility": MTL to EBL, August 25, 1865, in Turner and Turner, *Mary Todd Lincoln*, p. 268.

753 "precious Tad . . . gladly welcome death": MTL to Alexander Williamson, [May 26, 1867], in ibid., p. 422.

753 Tad journeyed . . . "beyond his years": *NYTrib*, July 17, 1871.

754 "compression of the heart": Turner and Turner, *Mary Todd Lincoln*, p. 585.

754 "The modest and cordial . . . fantastic enterprises": *NYTrib*, July 17, 1871.

754 "It is very hard . . . to the contrary": Robert Todd Lincoln to Mary Harlan, quoted in Helm, *The True Story of Mary*, p. 267.

754 erratic behavior . . . permanently estranged: Randall, *Mary Lincoln*, pp. 430–34.

754 virtual recluse . . . fulfilled at last: Ibid., pp. 442–43.

ILLUSTRATION CREDITS

Numbers in roman type refer to illustrations in the inserts; numbers in *italics* refer to book pages.

Chicago Historical Society: 1, 33, *702*

Abraham Lincoln Presidential Library & Museum: *xx–1*, 2, 3, 4, 5, 13, 19, 22, 23, 26, 29, 31, 32, 35, 36, 39, 44, 46, 47, 48, 49, 51, 55, 62, 63, 72, 73, 74, 76, *170, 321, 409, 445, 667*

Courtesy of the Department of Rare Books and Special Collections, University of Rochester Library: 6, 7, 9

Seward House, Auburn, New York: 8, 10, 34, 50

From the collection of Louise Taper: 11, 12

Ohio Historical Society: 14, 52

The Saint Louis Art Museum: *60*

Library of Congress: 15, 21, 24, 25, 27, 37, 41, 43, 56, 59, 64, 65, 68, 69, *347, 377, 548*

Missouri Historical Society: 16, 17, 18

Picture History: 20, 28, 30, 54, *473*

Western Reserve Historical Society, Cleveland, Ohio: 38

Brown University Library: 40

United States Army Military History Institute: 42

National Archives: 45, 53, 60, 61, 66, 67, 71, 75

Courtesy of J. Wayne Lee: 57, 58

National Portrait Gallery, Smithsonian Institution / Art Resource, New York: 70

Courtesy, American Antiquarian Society: *279*

Civil War Collection, Eastern Kentucky University Archives, Richmond, Kentucky: *323*

White House Historical Association (White House Collection): *597, 627*

INDEX

Doris Kearns Goodwin won the Pulitzer Prize in history for *No Ordinary Time*. She is also the author of the bestselling *Wait Till Next Year, The Fitzgeralds and the Kennedys,* and *Lyndon Johnson and the American Dream*. She lives in Concord, Massachusetts, with her husband, Richard Goodwin.

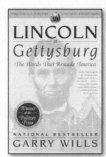
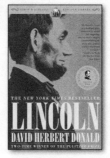
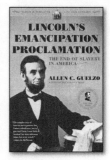
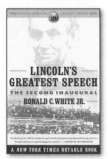
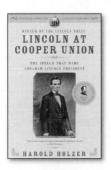
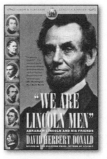